P9-CDG-983

Fodor's

INDIA
5TH EDITION

Where to Stay and Eat
for All Budgets

Must-See Sights
and Local Secrets

Ratings You Can Trust

Fodor's Travel Publications   New York, Toronto, London, Sydney, Auckland
www.fodors.com

FODOR'S INDIA
Editor: Diane Mehta

Editorial Production: David Downing
Editorial Contributors: Soumya Bhattacharya, Christine Cipriani, Vaihayasi Daniel, Candice Gianetti, Shanti Menon, Kavita Watsa
Maps: David Lindroth, Inc.; Ed Jacobus, *cartographers;* Bob Blake and Rebecca Baer, *map editors*
Design: Fabrizio La Rocca, *creative director;* Guido Caroti, *art director;* Moon Sun Kim, *cover designer;* Melanie Marin, *senior photo editor*
Production/Manufacturing: Robert B. Shields
Cover Photo (*Woman at saris factory, Rajasthan*): Bruno Morandi/age fotostock

Fifth Edition

ISBN 1–4000–1312–7

ISSN 1079–6444

SPECIAL SALES
This book is available for special discounts for bulk purchases for sales promotions or premiums. Special editions, including personalized covers, excerpts of existing books, and corporate imprints, can be created in large quantities for special needs. For more information, write to Special Markets/Premium Sales, 1745 Broadway, MD 6-2, New York, New York 10019 or e-mail specialmarkets@randomhouse.com.

AN IMPORTANT TIP & AN INVITATION
Although all prices, opening times, and other details in this book are based on information supplied to us at press time, changes occur all the time in the travel world, and Fodor's cannot accept responsibility for facts that become outdated or for inadvertent errors or omissions. So **always confirm information when it matters,** especially if you're making a detour to visit a specific place. Your experiences—positive and negative—matter to us. If we have missed or misstated something, **please write to us.** We follow up on all suggestions. Contact the India editor at editors@fodors.com or c/o Fodor's at 1745 Broadway, New York, New York 10019.

DESTINATION INDIA

ndia's mysticism and wealth of religion are legendary. Also famous is the rich cultural diversity prevalent from north to south—from the mountains to the jungle, and among the billion-odd citydwellers, villagers, and tribes who live here. For many first-time visitors, India conjures up images of maharajas, palaces, tigers, yoga, cobras, ayurvedic medicine, strange-looking gods, the Taj Mahal, Mahatma Gandhi, the Himalayas, and the era of the British Raj. But once you visit this magnificent and complicated country you'll surely return home with experiences far more exotic than what you came here to seek. India has some of the most stunning scenery in the world—the whitest beaches, the quietest and wildest jungles, towering snow-capped mountains, mysterious backwaters, fields of fluorescent green, and shining deserts. You can slip into any era of world history you prefer while you're here—Hindu temples from the 5th century BC, Portuguese relics from the 16th century AD, Islamic monuments circa AD 1400, or streets lined with Raj-era mansions. Bazaars sell anything you can imagine: from hundreds of types of fabrics, to pearls, crafts, 22-karat gold, and every color of spice. India's passion is entrancing, her indomitable spirit example-setting. But more than anything else, India is a reality check. A few days in India will bring out every emotion you possess—from anger, disgust, and revulsion, to love, compassion, wonder, awe, and astonishment. India shakes you awake and makes you feel alive.

Tim Jarrell, Publisher

CONTENTS

About This Book *F6*
On the Road with Fodor's *F10*
What's Where *F12*
Great Itineraries *F16*
When to Go *F18*
On the Calendar *F20*
Pleasures & Pastimes *F23*
Fodor's Choice *F27*
Smart Travel Tips *F34*

1 The Himalayas *1*

2 Delhi *70*

3 North Central India *121*

4 Rajasthan *189*

5 Bombay (Mumbai) & Maharashtra *261*

6 Goa *345*

7 Karnataka *380*

8 Kerala *427*

9 Tamil Nadu *464*

10 Hyderabad *509*

11 Orissa *522*

12 Calcutta (Kolkatta) *546*

Understanding India *577*

India at a Glance *578*
Cosmic Chaos *580*
Beyond Curry *584*
India's Religions *588*

Books & Movies *596*
Chronology *599*
The Hindi Language *605*

Index 608

Maps

India *F8*
Northwest Indian
  Himalayas *11*
Sikkim *58*
Delhi *76–77*
Where to Stay & Eat
  in Delhi *92–93*
North Central India *130*
Agra *132*
Khajuraho *150*
Varanasi *163*
Rajasthan *194*
Jaipur *198*
Maharashtra *268–269*
Bombay (Mumbai) *270–271*
Where to Stay & Eat in
  Downtown Bombay *282*

Where to Stay & Eat in
  Greater Bombay *283*
Ajanta Caves *337*
Ellora Caves *341*
Goa *352–353*
Karnataka *388*
Bangalore *390*
Mysore *404*
Kerala *434*
Cochin *436*
Tamil Nadu *470*
Madras *472*
Mahabalipuram *488*
Hyderabad *515*
Orissa *528*
Calcutta *552–553*

CloseUps

The Himachal Circuit *13*
Eye-Popping Drive:
  Shimla–Manali *18*
The Garhwal Circuit *37*
The Kumaon Circuit *42*
The Darjeeling–Sikkim
  Circuit *56*
Chat & Chew *109*
Dressing the Part *112*
Holy Inspiration *166*
Palace on Wheels *200*
Rajasthani Fashions *211*
Paintings *242*
Muzzles in the Air *253*
Dawn at the Docks in
  Colaba *273*
Indian Jews & Their
  Synagogues *275*
Song & Dance, Bollywood
  Style *300*

After-Hours Dance Bars *302*
Custom Tailors & Fine
  Fabrics *308*
Sizzling Street Food *311*
Beach Shacks & Rooms for
  Rent *354*
The Flea Market at Anjuna *356*
Take Home the Taste
  of Goa *364*
Inner Peace *375*
Karnataka's Adventure
  Trail *399*
The Rural Theatre of
  Yakshagana *415*
Early-Morning Art *474*
Penance Piercing *502*
A Walk in the Old City *514*
Tribal Village Tours *530*

ABOUT THIS BOOK

There's no doubt that the best source for travel advice is a like-minded friend who's just been where you're headed. But with or without that friend, you'll have a better trip with a Fodor's guide in hand. Once you've learned to find your way around its pages, you'll be in great shape to find your way around your destination.

SELECTION

Our goal is to cover the best properties, sights, and activities in their category, as well as the most interesting communities to visit. We make a point of including local food-lovers' hot spots as well as neighborhood options, and we avoid all that's touristy unless it's really worth your time. You can go on the assumption that everything you read about in this book is recommended wholeheartedly by our writers and editors. Flip to **On the Road with Fodor's** to learn more about who they are. It goes without saying that no property mentioned in the book has paid to be included.

RATINGS

Orange stars ★ denote sights and properties that our editor and writers consider the very best in the area covered by the entire book. These, the best of the best, are listed in the **Fodor's Choice** section in the front of the book. Black stars ★ highlight the sights and properties we deem **Highly Recommended,** the don't-miss sights within any region. Fodor's Choice and Highly Recommended options in each region are usually listed on the title page of the chapter covering that region. Use the index to find complete descriptions. In cities, sights pinpointed with numbered map bullets ❶ in the margins tend to be more important than those without bullets.

SPECIAL SPOTS

Pleasures & Pastimes focuses on types of experiences that reveal the spirit of the destination. Watch for **Off the Beaten Path** sights. Some are out of the way, some are quirky, and all are worth your while. If the munchies hit while you're exploring, look for **Need a Break?** suggestions.

TIME IT RIGHT

Wondering when to go? Check **On the Calendar** up front and chapters' **Timing** sections for weather and crowd overviews and best days and times to visit.

SEE IT ALL

Use Fodor's exclusive **Great Itineraries** as a model for your trip. (For a good overview of the entire destination, follow those that begin the book, or mix regional itineraries from several chapters.) In cities, **Good Walks** guide you to important sights in each neighborhood; ▶ indicates the starting points of walks and itineraries in the text and on the map.

BUDGET WELL

Hotel and restaurant price categories from ¢ to $$$$ are defined in the opening pages of each chapter—expect to find a balanced selection for every budget. For attractions, we always give standard adult admission fees; reductions are usually available for children, students, and senior citizens. Look in **Discounts & Deals** in Smart Travel

Tips for information on destination-wide ticket schemes. Want to pay with plastic? AE, D, DC, MC, V following restaurant and hotel listings indicate whether American Express, Discover, Diner's Club, MasterCard, or Visa are accepted.

BASIC INFO

Smart Travel Tips lists travel essentials for the entire area covered by the book; city- and region-specific basics end each chapter. To find the best way to get around, see the transportation section; see individual modes of travel ("Car & Driver," or "Train Travel") for details. We assume you'll check Web sites or call for particulars.

ON THE MAPS

Maps throughout the book show you what's where and help you find your way around. Black and orange numbered bullets ❶ ❶ in the text correlate to bullets on maps.

BACKGROUND

In general, we give background information within the chapters in the course of explaining sights as well as in CloseUp boxes and in Understanding India at the end of the book. To get in the mood, review the suggestions in Books & Movies. The Hindi Language section can be invaluable.

FIND IT FAST

Within the book, chapters are arranged in a roughly north–south direction starting with the Himalayas, following the west coast down through Bombay (Mumbai) and south to Tamil Nadu state, then going up around the east coast and ending in Calcutta.

SYMBOLS

Many Listings

★ Fodor's Choice
★ Highly recommended
⊠ Physical address
✛ Directions
🕮 Mailing address
☎ Telephone
🖷 Fax
⊕ On the Web
✉ E-mail
💷 Admission fee
☉ Open/closed times
► Start of walk/itinerary
Ⓜ Metro stations
🖃 Credit cards

Outdoors

🏌 Golf
⛺ Camping

Hotels & Restaurants

🏨 Hotel
🛏 Number of rooms
♨ Facilities
🍽 Meal plans
✗ Restaurant
🍽 Reservations
🏛 Dress code
🚬 Smoking
🍷 BYOB
✗🏨 Hotel with restaurant that warrants a visit

Other

☾ Family-friendly
🈯 Contact information
⇨ See also
⊠ Branch address
☞ Take note

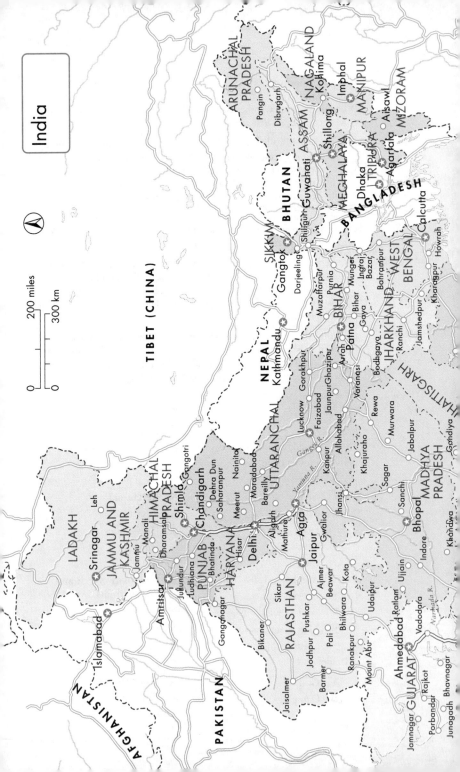

ON THE ROAD WITH FODOR'S

A trip takes you out of yourself. Concerns of life at home completely disappear, driven away by more immediate thoughts—about, say, what marvels will beguile the next day, or where you'll have dinner. That's where Fodor's comes in. We make sure that you know all your options, so that you don't miss something that's around the next bend just because you didn't know it was there. Because the best memories of your trip might well have nothing to do with what you came to India to see, we guide you to sights large and small all over the region. You might set out to laze on the beach at Goa, but back at home you find yourself unable to forget exploring the way the city of Jaisalmer strikingly rises in the Thar Desert of Rajasthan or the backwaters of Kerala.

Our success in showing you every corner of India is a credit to our extraordinary writers. Although there's no substitute for travel advice from a good friend who knows your style, our contributors are the next best thing—the kind of people you would poll for travel advice.

Soumya Bhattacharya is Deputy Editor of *Hindustan Times,* Calcutta. He has lived and worked in London, Sydney, New Delhi, and Calcutta, and has traveled widely in Europe, Australia, and southeast Asia. Calcutta, where he lives with his wife Chandrani and two-year-old daughter Oishi, is the only city in which he can find his way around blindfolded.

A native New Yorker, **Christine Cipriani** recently spent three years in New Delhi as an editor at Penguin Books India, acquiring both fiction and nonfiction. She has traveled widely in India, written on travel for Indian publications, and served as a political and cultural consultant on India for Microsoft.

A granddaughter of Estonian and Indian freedom-fighters, on both sides, **Vaihayasi Pande Daniel** was born in Montréal, grew up in Baltimore, married a Tamil Christian, and has lived in India since 1976. Peri-patetic tendencies draw her (and her two young daughters) all over India and elsewhere, but she prefers Bombay to any other place in the world. A deputy managing editor at www.rediff.com's New York–based publication *India Abroad,* she earlier managed rediff's travel site and now writes on travel and current affairs for this popular Indian news service.

Candice Gianetti is a freelance travel editor and writer based in New York City. Her previous work for Fodor's was *Escape to Tuscany.*

Shanti Menon is a freelance writer in New York City. She has covered travel destinations from China to New Zealand, but has a special relationship with Kerala, where she can claim the privileges of a visitor and the advantages of a local. She looks forward to her frequent visits as a chance to catch up with family, as well as an all-too-rare opportunity to eat some form of coconut with every meal.

Kavita Watsa grew up in Mysore, Bangalore, and Calcutta, and now lives in Madras (Chennai), the sultry capital of Tamil Nadu, where she works for a multilateral development bank. She has just written her first travel book, *Brahmins and Bungalows,* published in spring 2004 by Penguin India. A collection of essays on places from the Konkan to the Coromandel, the book is a journey through the history of South India. For Fodor's, she spent time in Goa and Rajasthan, two of her favorite states, and explored her home territory—the south—yet again.

For their assistance in preparing this edition, we'd also like to thank the Taj Group of Hotels, particularly Jodi Leblanc; the Government of India Tourism Office in New York; Jet Airways; and the staff at Banjara Camps. Thanks also to everyone at the Casino Group of Hotels (CGH Earth); K.P. Francis of Malabar House; Shelley Thayil of Kumarakom Lake Resort; Davina Taylor of Lagoona Davina; M.K. Matthew of Kayaloram; Penny George of

Le Meridien Cochin; Tapan Piplani of Oberoi Hotels, Shimla; Zaffer Ahmed of RBS Travels, New Delhi; Abhijay Verma of Usha Shriram Hotels, Manali; Ajay Kareer and Sanjeev Joshi of Leisure Hotels; Diamond Oberoi of the Elgin, Darjeeling; and Shubhana Rai at Windamere Hotel, Darjeeling. Special gratitude goes to Sarita Hegde Roy, Taj Hotels, Mumbai; Deepraj, Laxmi Vilas Palace, Bharatpur; Ragini Chopra, Oberoi Hotels, New Delhi; Janardan Ranawat, Kankarwa Haveli, Udaipur; Ravindra Jain, Ranthambhore Regency, Sawai Madhopur; Bhupendra Chundawat, Bassi Fort, Bassi; Kulbhushan Bhatt, Neemrana Group, New Delhi; K. N. Patil, KSTDC, Bangalore; Agnes D'-Costa, Radisson White Sands, Goa; Vincent Ramos, Taj Exotica, Goa; and Management and drivers, Le Passage to India, Rajasthan.

India lies in the Northern Hemisphere, bisected laterally by the Tropic of Cancer (which also bisects Mexico). With a total land area of 3,287,000 square km (1,261,000 square mi) and a coastline 6,100 km (3,535 mi) long, it's the world's seventh-largest country. To the north, the Himalayas separate India from Nepal and China. To the east is Bhutan, still closely connected to India by a special treaty. More mountains separate India from Myanmar (formerly Burma) on the eastern border. Also to the east lies Bangladesh, wedged between the Indian states of Assam, Meghalaya, Tripura, and West Bengal. Pakistan borders India's northwest. Just off the subcontinent's southeastern tip lies the island nation of Sri Lanka, separated from the mainland by 50 km (31 mi) of water, the Palk Straits. Conversely, the Lakshadweep Islands in the Arabian Sea and the Andaman and Nicobar islands in the Bay of Bengal, much farther away, are part of the Indian Union.

The Himalayas (*hima* means snow; *laya,* abode), the wall of mountains sweeping 3,200 km (1,984 mi) across north India, are divided into distinct ranges. Among them are the Greater Himalayas, or Trans-Himalayas, a crescendo of peaks that includes some of the world's highest massifs—many above 20,000 feet. In Ladakh, the lunar Karakorams merge into the northwestern edge of the Greater Himalayas. In both ranges, massive glaciers cling to towering peaks; rivers rage through deep gorges, chilled with melting snow and ice; and wild blue sheep traverse craggy cliffs.

Stretching south of the Himalayas is the densely populated Indo-Gangetic Plain. Mountains and hills separate numerous plateaus, and the basins of the Ganga (Ganges) and Brahmaputra rivers make the land rich and productive. This is particularly true in the Punjab, India's breadbasket. The enormous plain also includes the Thar Desert, which extends across western Rajasthan. Except when the vegetation from irrigated fields grows lush after the monsoon, most of its terrain is marked by scrub, cactus, and low rocky hills. The unusual Rann of Kutch, a wide salt flat, is southwest of Rajasthan in the state of Gujarat (which, because of its political instability, we have decided not to include in this edition). Just a few feet above sea level, this strange land mass, which floods during the monsoon, is home to former nomads dependent on camels and what meager income they receive from their exquisite handicrafts.

More mountains cut through India's peninsula and follow its contour. The Eastern Ghats mark off a broad coastal strip on the Bay of Bengal; the Western Ghats define a narrower coast on the Arabian Sea. These low ranges merge in the Nilgiri Hills, near India's southern tip. In the more remote areas of these mountains and plateaus, as in the states of Madhya Pradesh and Orissa, numerous tribes continue to share forested land with wild animals.

South India is tropical, with rice paddies, coffee plantations, and forests that shade spice crops. In the southwestern state of Kerala and part of neighboring Karnataka, exquisite waterways thread inland from the Arabian Sea through a natural network of canals connecting palm-fringed fishing villages.

1 The Himalayas

Inspiring awe like no other mountain range in the world, the snow-capped Himalayas cut a border between India, Nepal, and China, passing through the Indian states of Jammu and Kashmir, Himachal Pradesh, Uttaranchal, and Sikkim. A few hours north of Delhi you can indulge an adventure or spiritual retreat—river rafting, paragliding, yoga by the Ganges in the Garhwal foothills, or tiger spotting from elephant-back at Corbett National Park. Imagine hiking through the surreal landscapes of Ladakh or Spiti, or making a pilgrimage to some of India's most fascinating religious sites.

2 Delhi

India's capital is in every way a sophisticated city. From the old bazaars and hectic, twisting streets of Old Delhi to the avenues lined with British-built bungalows, international hotels, museums, and restaurants in New Delhi, the city is unique among Indian cities. It's one of few places where the West strives alongside a more traditional India. Top sights include Jama Masjid, India's largest mosque, and Qutab Minar, the seventh wonder of Hindustan and the tallest stone tower in India. Other important monuments include the Imperial City, designed by the British architect Sir Edwin Lutyens, and Lal Qila, Emperor Shah Jahan's 17th-century capital.

3 North Central India

Anchored by Agra, Khajuraho, and Varanasi, this section of the traveler's trail heads southeast of Delhi into the state of Uttaranchal, detouring into Madhya Pradesh and Bihar. The history of these lands is ancient and vast, with a religious heritage spanning Hinduism, Islam, Buddhism, and even, in Lucknow, Christianity. The spectacular architecture includes Agra's incomparable Taj Mahal and Khajuraho's exciting Hindu temples. Varanasi is the holiest city in Hinduism, drawing a constant stream of pilgrims to bathe in the Ganges River.

4 Rajasthan

Literally the "Land of Kings," Rajasthan spans a wide, arid stretch of northwestern India. The region is best known for its martial history—the indomitable Rajput warriors who defended themselves against invaders and divided the region into princely states. The region is equally famous for its exuberant festivals and colorful folk-art traditions. Travelers come from all over the world to visit the Pink City of Jaipur, the Jain temples in Ranakpur and Mount Abu, the enchanting lake-city of Udaipur, and Jaisalmer Fort, which rises dramatically out of the barren Thar Desert.

Gujarat

The birthplace of Mahatma Gandhi, Gujarat (despite it's boundary with Pakistan) was—but no longer is—India's most politically stable state. Given the riots and sporadic violence that have taken place here, we feel it isn't the ideal time to visit the region. So we have decided not to include Gujarat in this year's edition. Gujarat is a place where, in pre-colonial India, Hindus and Muslims once lived in harmony. Major cities such as Ahmedabad and Vadodara, although modernized and culturally active, are preserved to the pace and progress of the local population, and are virtually unknown to tourists. The Kathiawar peninsula is best known for its territorial resort island of Diu, where Gujaratis and foreigners alike take refuge from the dry state. Folk life, crafts, and the traditions of Gujarat's nomadic culture are best preserved in the harsh but unfortunately earthquake-ravaged region of Kutch.

5 Bombay (Mumbai)

Once Bombay was a string of seven islands belonging to fisherfolk. Today these precious seven islands, now united into an isthmus, are India's most important and prosperous urban center. Bombay, renamed Mumbai by the state government, embodies India's most modern and contradictory face—the city is home to the most glamorous, upwardly mobile, and wealthy of Indian citizens, as well as to millions who barely eke out a living. Bombay is famously the center of India's bustling film industry, dubbed Bollywood, and embraces both traditional *desi* (Indian) values and keenly hip Western styles.

6 Goa

Goa's remarkably beautiful beaches are India's most famous by far, and this former Portuguese colony is well frequented by Indians and foreigners alike. A bright blue coastline stretches down sparkling, palm-lined beaches along the Arabian Sea. Wide inland rivers meander around small pastel houses and churches, revealing the Portuguese influence—Goa was once a trade center for spices, silk, and pearls. Goan cuisine, of pomfret, prawns, and other seafood preparations heavily doused with coconut meat and milk, is legendary. For some local culture, come at Christmas or in February for Carnival—and plan to take in some spectacular coastline views and to explore small villages and local markets.

7 Karnataka

Karnataka is known for two things: its high-tech, cosmopolitan capital of Bangalore, and the religious monuments scattered in nearby cities and villages. Most famous is Mysore, the City of Palaces, famous for its silks and sandalwood products. There are also Belur and Habelid villages, with meticulously wrought 12th-century temples, and the vast ruins of Hampi, the 14th-century center of the largest Hindu empire in South India. Then there's the coastline to the west, with palm-fringed beaches, and other delights, including watching wild elephants in Nagarhold National Park and visiting the monolithic statue of a Jain saint in Sravanabelagola.

8 Kerala

Natural splendor and a 5,000-year-old health-care system have combined to make Kerala India's hottest destination. The palm-strewn beach resorts of southern Kerala offer pampering ayurvedic massage and wellness packages. The best way to see the central region is to float through backwater villages on a wooden houseboat, anchoring in the fabled port city of Cochin for a dose of colonial history and some spicy seafood. Lush forests swarm the cool hillsides of the inland districts, where elephants, wildlife sanctuaries, and tea, coffee, and spice plantations abound. The astonishing Theyyam dancers of unspoiled north Kerala offer a living glimpse into pre-Hindu society. Today, Kerala society has Hindu, Muslim, Christian, and Jewish communities, and is India's most densely populated, as well as its most literate (more than 90%) state.

9 Tamil Nadu

A state that takes great pride in its age-old religious and cultural traditions, lush, tropical Tamil Nadu stretches between the Eastern Ghats (mountains) and the Bay of Bengal, down to the southernmost tip of the subcontinent. Since the days of the Pallava dynasty, more than 13 centuries ago, the state has welcomed foreign trade and interaction, but has retained a personality distinct from other parts of Asia, and indeed from India itself. There is much of historical interest here: age-old temples endure on coastal sands and paddy fields, and colonial architectural splendor graces the towns and cities. Tamil Nadu is also a center for classical Indian dance, known as Bharatanatyam, and classical Carnatic music; in December, the Carnatic festival in Madras Chennai, the capital, is a magnet for music-lovers.

10 Hyderabad

Known for its dynamic software and telecommunications industries, as well as for its textile, jewelry, and pearl trades, Hyderabad is a young city—only 400 years old. It has its roots in Buddhism and Islam, which are still reflected today, though the majority of people are Hindu. Hyderabadi cuisine is famously fiery—chilies, which grow on the plateaus, figure prominently in the cooking. Shopping is another draw: look for handicrafts, textiles, and, most importantly, pearls. Hyderabad is the center of India's pearl trade, so you'll find a fantastic selection here, especially in the bustling Charminar Market.

11 Orissa

This agrarian state along India's eastern seaboard is often overlooked. But if you come here you'll find a different version of India: tropical countryside, crafts villages famous for their hand-loomed silk or paintings and sculptures, animist tribes still thriving in villages, white tigers, and miles and miles of unpopulated coastline and pearly beaches. Add to all that the capital city of Bhubaneshwar, better known as the city of temples (500) and the ancient kingdom of Kalinga, not to mention the center for Odissi dance. It's less like the typically hectic cities of modern India and more like a slow-paced village. Outside Bhubaneshwar are more delights: the monumental Sun Temple of Konark, the 12th-century Jagannath temple of Puri, the artisans of Ragurajpur and Pipli, and Buddhist Dhauli. There is much to be remembered here in Orissa.

12 Calcutta

About 120 km (75 mi) from the Bay of Bengal and perched on the eastern bank of the river Hooghly, cosmopolitan Calcutta is the gateway to eastern India. It's also the artistic and literary soul of India, with an intellectual heritage that's famous worldwide—it's a city known for its writers, musicians, filmmakers, dancers, and philosophers. Home to more than 12 million people, Calcutta is a place of swank high rises and upscale residential blocks, as well as shanties and tenements. It's India's best city for walkers, with teeming bazaars and crowded narrow streets, colonial mansions, Victorian architecture, temples, mosques, and gardens and parks to get away from it all.

Classic India
17 days

This tour is a broader version of the well-trod Golden Triangle, which concentrates on Delhi, Jaipur, and Agra. For a more comprehensive and exciting experience, start in Bombay and include Khajuraho and Varanasi. You can fly any or all of these legs, but touring with a hired car and driver gives you a better look at the countryside and allows for impromptu stops along the way.

BOMBAY **2 days.** Dive into this heady metropolis for a crash course in all things Indian. Explore the historic Fort district, navigate some bazaars, and stroll around lovely Malabar Hill, saving time to wander from Chowpatty Beach down Marine Drive along the Arabian Sea. ⇨ *Bombay in Chapter 5.*

DELHI TO JAIPUR **3 days.** Fly to Delhi. After touring Delhi, drive from Delhi to Rajasthan's Neemrana Fort Palace, just off the main highway between Delhi and Jaipur. Set high on a bluff, this restored fort has amazing views and invites complete relaxation or scenic afternoon walks. The next day, drive about three hours to Jaipur, where you can stay at a converted palace or Heritage Hotel while you explore Jaipur's unforgettable bazaars and monuments. ⇨ *Delhi in Chapter 2 and Rajasthan in Chapter 4.*

FATEHPUR SIKRI & AGRA **3 days.** En route from Jaipur to Agra, tour the splendid buildings of the ancient and deserted Moghul capital Fatehpur Sikri. In Agra you'll encounter the world-famous Taj Mahal and the much less famous, but almost equally beautiful, tomb of Itmad-ud-Daulah. ⇨ *Rajasthan in Chapter 4 and North Central India in Chapter 3.*

GWALIOR & ORCHHA **2 days.** Drive from Agra to Gwalior to see its spectacular pre-Moghul Hindu fort and palace built into a high escarpment. An optional excursion brings you to Orchha, another seat of Hindu rajas that mixes palaces, temples, and monuments on a small, picturesque river. ⇨ *North Central India in Chapter 3.*

KHAJURAHO **2 days.** Drive on to Khajuraho and spend two days absorbing the exuberantly carved 10th- and 11th-century temples and the surrounding villages. ⇨ *North Central India in Chapter 3.*

VARANASI **2 days.** Fly from Khajuraho to Varanasi. Take a peaceful morning cruise on the Ganges River to witness Hindu rituals on the steps of the sacred waters. Wander among Varanasi's temples and silk or carpet emporiums and drive out to nearby Sarnath, imbued with Buddhist significance. ⇨ *North Central India in Chapter 3.*

DELHI **3 days.** Fly to Delhi to explore the old and new capitals. Old Delhi has Moghul remnants, such as the Red Fort, Jama Masjid, and Chandni Chowk, now a hodgepodge market; New Delhi has the Moghul Humayun's tomb and also the seat of the former British Raj and the lovely Lodi Gardens. Have a look at the Crafts Museum and save time for last-minute shopping. ⇨ *Delhi in Chapter 2.*

Transportation Fly to Delhi, drive from Delhi to Khajuraho, fly to Varanasi, and fly back to Delhi.

Southern Idyll
13 to 14 days

Experience the tropical south beginning in Tamil Nadu with ancient towns and massive temples. Relax at seaside resorts and on small boats as you cruise through the lush backwaters of Kerala. Search for wildlife at Kerala's excellent Lake Periyar Wildlife Sanctuary. Add one more cultural dimension—say, a Kathakali dance performance—and, as a personal indulgence, a soothing ayurvedic massage to chase away any lingering stress.

MADRAS & MAMALLAPURAM **4 days.** Spend two days in Madras, originally developed by the Portuguese and British but now decidedly South Indian, with bazaars, bustling Hindu temples, and a thriving film industry. Take a leisurely two-day excursion to Mamallapuram via Kanchipuram, a silk-weaving center and the site of more than 200 temples. At Mamallapuram, on the Bay of Bengal, see the exquisite cave sculptures and shore temple left behind by the Pallava dynasty (4th–8th centuries). Catch some sun and surf at a relaxing resort, and return to Madras Chennai. ⇨ *Tamil Nadu in Chapter 9.*

MADURAI **2 days.** Fly from Madras to Madurai and spend two days exploring the city and its astonishing Meenakshi Temple, whose marvelous architecture includes soaring *gopurams* (entrance towers) and prominent displays of ritual. Comb through the bazaars surrounding the temple complex. ⇨ *Tamil Nadu in Chapter 9.*

LAKE PERIYAR WILDLIFE SANCTUARY **2 days.** Drive west from Madurai across the Western Ghats to Kerala's Lake Periyar, where boat rides provide the leisurely means for a safari: wild elephants and other animals roam the banks of this lovely preserve. ⇨ *Tamil Nadu in Chapter 9 and Kerala in Chapter 8.*

COCHIN **2 days.** Proceed northwest by car to Cochin, and take two days to see this ancient port city, with its 16th-century synagogue, curio shops, and Portuguese fort. At night, try to attend a Kathakali dance performance, where you can see how the dancers apply their complicated makeup before they mesmerize you with their hard-honed talent. ⇨ *Kerala in Chapter 8.*

BACKWATER CRUISE **1 to 2 days.** Drive to Alleppey early in the morning and cruise through some of Kerala's backwaters, past palm trees, shaded villages, and bright-green paddy fields. If you get hooked, take an overnight houseboat cruise. Back in the car, repair to a special beach resort just south of Kovalam. ⇨ *Kerala in Chapter 8.*

KOVALAM **2 days.** Spend two nights at the Surya Samudra Beach Garden, tucked away in a cove on the Arabian Sea. Swim, have an ayurvedic massage, and loll about; you can even study yoga and meditation here. Fly out from nearby Trivandrum. ⇨ *Kerala in Chapter 8.*

Transportation Hire a car and driver for excursions from Madras, then fly from Madras to Madurai. Hire another car and driver for the trip west to Lake Periyar in Thekkady; continue to Cochin and then pause for a slow cruise on the backwaters near Alleppey. Drive on to Kovalam and wind up at Trivandrum, where you can catch flights to other major cities.

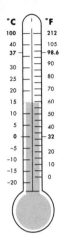

India's peak tourist season for the plains and the south (which encompass most major sights) is fall and winter: mid-September through March. **Make all reservations well in advance**—especially for trips to Rajasthan, Kerala, and Goa. By May and June, only the Himalayas are comfortable; the rest of India is unbearably hot. Himachal Pradesh and Ladakh, where the mountains usually hold back the monsoons, are spared the torrential July and August rains that inundate most of North India; and summer is often the only time to visit these otherwise snowbound places.

India's monsoons disrupt plane schedules, phone and electrical systems, and roads can wash out. That said, the monsoons can be a pleasant time to see most of the South (except Kerala), central Gujarat, and the Deccan Plateau (Madhya Pradesh and parts of Maharashtra). Rajasthan is verdant and Goa's resorts are cheap then, too (but your swimming and sunbathing will be curtailed).

Climate
India's climate is monsoon-tropical, with local variations. Temperate weather, with cool evenings, lasts from October to the end of February. Hot and muggy weather hits South India from April to the beginning of June, when monsoon rains move north, watering nearly every part of India until September. The Himalayas can be extremely cold in winter, with snow clogging mountain passes. Below are average daily maximum and minimum temperatures for key Indian cities.

🎬 Forecasts **Weather Channel** ⊕ www.weather.com.

BOMBAY

Jan.	88F	31C	May	92F	33C	Sept.	86F	30C
	61	16		79	26		76	24
Feb.	90F	32C	June	90F	32C	Oct.	90F	32C
	63	17		79	26		74	23
Mar.	92F	33C	July	86F	30C	Nov.	92F	33C
	68	20		77	25		68	20
Apr.	92F	33C	Aug.	85F	29C	Dec.	90F	32C
	76	24		76	24		65	18

CALCUTTA

Jan.	79F	26C	May	97F	36C	Sept.	90F	32C
	54	12		79	26		79	26
Feb.	85F	29C	June	94F	34C	Oct.	88F	31C
	59	15		79	26		75	24
Mar.	94F	34C	July	90F	32C	Nov.	85F	29C
	68	20		79	26		64	18
Apr.	97F	36C	Aug.	90F	32C	Dec.	81F	27C
	76	24		79	26		55	13

DELHI

Jan.	70F	21C	May	106F	41C	Sept.	93F	34C
	45	7		81	27		77	25
Feb.	93F	34C	June	104F	40C	Oct.	95F	35C
	50	10		84	29		66	19
Mar.	86F	30C	July	95F	35C	Nov.	84F	29C
	59	15		81	27		54	12
Apr.	97F	36C	Aug.	93F	34C	Dec.	73F	23C
	70	21		79	26		46	8

GANGTOK

Jan.	57F	14C	May	72F	22C	Sept.	73F	23C
	39	4		57	14		61	16
Feb.	59F	15C	June	73F	23C	Oct.	72F	22C
	41	5		61	16		54	12
Mar.	66F	19C	July	73F	23C	Nov.	66F	19C
	48	9		63	17		48	9
Apr.	72F	22C	Aug.	73F	23C	Dec.	59F	15C
	54	12		63	17		43	6

MADRAS

Jan.	84C	29C	May	100F	38C	Sept.	93F	34C
	68	20		82	28		77	25
Feb.	88F	31C	June	99F	37C	Oct.	90F	32C
	70	21		82	28		75	24
Mar.	91F	33C	July	95F	35C	Nov.	84F	29C
	73	23		79	26		73	23
Apr.	95F	35C	Aug.	95F	35C	Dec.	82F	28C
	79	26		79	26		70	21

SHIMLA

Jan.	48F	9C	May	73F	23C	Sept.	68F	20C
	36	2		59	15		57	14
Feb.	50F	10C	June	75F	24C	Oct.	64F	18C
	37	3		61	16		50	10
Mar.	57F	14C	July	70F	21C	Nov.	59F	15C
	45	7		61	16		45	7
Apr.	66F	19C	Aug.	68F	20C	Dec.	52F	11C
	52	11		59	15		39	4

TRIVANDRUM

Jan.	88F	31C	May	88F	31C	Sept.	86F	30C
	72	22		77	25		73	23
Feb.	90F	32C	June	84F	29C	Oct.	86F	30C
	73	23		75	24		73	23
Mar.	91F	33C	July	84F	29C	Nov.	86F	30C
	75	24		73	23		73	23
Apr.	90F	32C	Aug.	84F	29C	Dec.	88F	31C
	77	25		72	22		73	23

India holds religious celebrations year-round, along with numerous fairs and cultural festivals. Dates of some celebrations are determined by the lunar calendar, so check with the Government of India Tourist Office for details.

WINTER

Dec.

For the five-day Konark Dance Festival, Odissi (classical Orissan) dances are performed at the Sun Temple and a craft fair is held. The Shekhavati Festival celebrates the frescoes on the local havelis (mansions), as well as other local arts, traditional music and dance, and cuisine from this Rajasthan region. At the Shilp Darshan Mela near Udaipur, master craftsmen show how they create award-winning handicrafts, and dancers and musicians perform.

Jan.

Republic Day, the 26th, commemorates the adoption of India's constitution with a big parade in Delhi and celebrations elsewhere. Kerala's four-day Great Elephant March features caparisoned elephants, snake-boat races, and cultural events in various locales. The two-day Camel Festival in Bikaner (Rajasthan) celebrates the ship of the desert with parades, races, and dancing. Makar Sankranti has people engaging in kite duels from rooftops in Ahmedabad. In Tamil Nadu, Pongal, a colorful three-day festival at the close of the harvest season gives thanks to the rain god, the sun god, and the cow with bonfires, games, dancing, and cows bedecked with garlands.

Jan. and Feb.

During Gangasagar Mela, the festival of the Ganges River, pilgrims from all over India celebrate the most important natural element in their mythology. Nagaur (Rajasthan) holds an enormous cattle fair complete with camel races and cultural programs. The five-day Desert Fair, Jaisalmer's gala, includes traditional Rajasthani music and dance, handicrafts, camel caravans, camel races, and turban-tying events.

Feb.

For the three-day Elephanta Festival of Music and Dance, artists perform nightly on a platform near these Maharashtra caves. The Surajkund Crafts Mela draws crowds to a village near Delhi to watch traditional dances, puppeteers, magicians, and acrobats and to shop for crafts made by artisans from every state. On Losar, the Buddhist New Year, costumed *lamas* (monks) perform dances at monasteries in Sikkim.

Feb. and Mar.

On the eve of Holi, the festival of spring, Hindus nationwide light a bonfire and send an effigy of a female demon up in flames, demonstrating the destruction of evil; the next day, children throw colored water on each other and you. On Id-ul-Fitr, the Muslim holiday that concludes the month-long Ramadan fast, the devout give alms to the poor, offer prayers, and feast and rejoice. The Kumbh Mela, a celebration of immortality, is India's largest religious festival and a stun-

	ning spectacle of bathers in the Ganges. Held every three years in Allahabad, Haridwar, Nasik, or Ujjain, it came to Ujjain in May 2004. The two-week Taj Mahotsav spotlights Agra's heritage through handicrafts and cultural events.
Mar.	India's best dancers present classical works at the Khajuraho Dance Festival, held in part on an outdoor stage against the temples. Pachyderms have their day in Jaipur when the Elephant Festival sets off processions, races, and even elephant polo.
Mar. and Apr.	Carnival—the Mardi Gras held just before Lent—hits Goa as a big party with masked dancers, floats, and good eating. The Gangaur Festival of Jaipur and Udaipur honors the goddess Parvati with processions of young girls and images of the goddess and, in Udaipur, fireworks, dancing, and a procession of boats on Lake Pichola.
SPRING	
Apr.	Honoring Lord Jagannath, Bhubaneswar's 21-day Chandan Yatra features processions in which images of deities are carried to sacred tanks and rowed around in decorated boats.
Apr. and May	At Puram, a major temple festival in Trichur (Kerala), elephants sporting gold-plated mail carry Brahmins with ceremonial umbrellas and the temple deity, Vadakkunathan (Shiva), in a procession to the beat of temple drums. The spectacular 10-day Chitra Festival celebrates the marriage of goddess Meenakshi to Lord Shiva at Madurai's Meenakshi Temple.
May	Buddhists celebrate Buddha Jayanti—the birthday, enlightenment, and death of Sakyamunni (Historic Buddha)—with rituals and chants at monasteries. Special celebrations are held in Sikkim and other major pilgrimage centers, such as Sarnath and Bodhgaya. On Muharram, Shiite Muslims commemorate the martyrdom of the Prophet Mohammed's grandson Hussain, who died in the battle of Karbala. Participants' intense self-flagellation may disturb the squeamish. On Bakrid or Id-ul-Zuha, celebrating the sacrifice of Harrat Ibrahim (Abraham), Muslims solemnly sacrifice one animal per family (or group of families) and conclude with a feast and joyous celebration.
SUMMER	
June and July	Puri's seven-day Rath Yatra, honoring Lord Krishna, is Orissa's most sacred festival and draws big crowds. The two-day Hemis Festival at Ladakh's largest monastery commemorates the birthday of Guru Padmasambhava with masked lamas performing ritual *chaams* (dances) and haunting music.
July and Aug.	In Jaipur, women and girls observe Teej, the arrival of the monsoon, dedicating their festivities to the goddess Parvati.
Aug.	Independence Day, on the 15th, commemorates India's independence from British rule in 1947.

Aug. and Sept.	**Ganesha Chaturthi**, a 10-day festival celebrated in Bombay and Pune, marks the birthday of the Hindus' elephant-head god; clay images of Ganesh are paraded through streets and installed on platforms. **Onam** celebrates Kerala's harvest season with dancing, singing, and exotic snake-boat races in Alleppey, Aranmula, and Kottayam. **Pang Lhabsol** offers thanks to Mt. Kanchenjunga, Sikkim's guardian deity, and honors Yabdu, the great warrior who protects the mountain.
FALL	
Sept. and Oct.	Calcutta turns into one big party for **Durga Puja**, a five-day festival honoring the 10-armed Hindu goddess Durga. Farther south, Mysore hosts concerts and cultural events in Durbar Hall, and the maharaja himself comes out in full regalia, complete with some palace treasures, for the traditional procession.
Oct.	On **Gandhi Jayanti**, Mahatma Gandhi's birthday (Oct. 2nd), pilgrims visit the Raj Ghat, where Gandhi was cremated. Jaipur's **Marwar Festival** brings to life myth and folklore in Marwari culture, music, and dance.
Oct. and Nov.	**Diwali**, the festival of lights, is India's most important Hindu festival, celebrating the day the Hindu God Rama (Vishnu) ended a 14-year exile, as well as the start of the New Year. Hindus worship Lakshmi, the goddess of prosperity; oil lamps flicker in most homes symbolizing the victory of truth (light) over ignorance (darkness); cities crackle with the explosion of fireworks; and Bengalis worship Kali, the black goddess of destruction.
Nov.	Nomads assemble with their camels and gaily festooned cattle for Rajasthan's carnivalesque **Pushkar Festival**.
Nov. and Dec.	India's best performers entertain on a full-moon night, with historic Kailasa Temple as a backdrop, for the three-day **Ellora Festival of Classical Music and Dance**. The **International Seafood Festival** at Miramar Beach, near Panaji (Goa), offers three to five days of good food, music, and Indian, Western, and local folk dances.

PLEASURES & PASTIMES

Beaches Between October and March you can spend a few days or an entire vacation at a deluxe resort, a beach cottage, or even a safari-style tent on a luscious Indian beach. Goa is perennially popular with Westerners; far less trafficked are the picture-perfect Lakshadweep Islands, off Kerala, where you can snorkel around coral reefs. On Kerala's own coast, the sandy beaches at Kovalam are lined with palm-fringed lagoons and rocky coves. At Mamallapuram, south of Madras, the beaches are steps from some of India's finest temple ruins.

Dining Indian cuisine varies widely from region to region. You'll find meat, seafood, vegetables, lentils, and grains in subtle and enticing combinations. The generic term "curry" doesn't really exist in India, but means, more or less, that a dish is cooked in a spicy sauce. Over the centuries, invading forces brought new techniques, ingredients, and dishes to India. The Moghuls revolutionized Indian cooking, especially in the north, introducing *biriyanis* (rice dishes), *kormas* (braised meat or vegetable dishes), kababs, *kofta* (meat or vegetable balls), *dum pukht* (aromatic, slow-cooked dishes), and *tandoori* cooking (which requires a tandoor, or clay oven). The British introduced simple puddings and custards. Tibetan immigrants brought *momos* (steamed dumplings), *kothay* (fried dumplings), and hearty noodle soups called *thukpa*. In the northeast, near the water, the Bengalis and Assamese learned to emphasize fish and seafood. Gujaratis, Rajasthanis, and South Indian Hindus, all of whom tend to avoid meat, developed India's vegetarian cuisine.

Tea, a staple in India, is brewed with milk and sugar. In Buddhist areas you'll find yak-butter tea, made with milk and salt; the butter keeps your lips from cracking in the dry Himalayan air. South Indian filter coffee has a caramel tang, something like café au lait; elsewhere you'll find little but instant coffee. India produces excellent beer, and its Riviera wine is reasonably good. Luxury hotels also import Western spirits, and sell them at luxury prices. Sikkim produces good rum, brandies, and *paan* liqueur. *Chang,* a local brew made from fermented barley, is available in many mountain areas. Goa makes tasty sweet wines and *feni,* a potent liquor made from coconuts or cashew nuts.

Performing Arts India's folk dances derive from various sources, but Indian classical dance originates in the temple. The four main dance forms are Bharatanatyam in the south, particularly in Tamil Nadu; Kathakali in Kerala; Manipur in the northeast; and Kathak in the north.

Bharatanatyam is a dynamic, precise style in which the dancer wears anklets of bells to emphasize the rhythm. Many figures in South Indian temple sculptures strike Bharatanatyam dance poses. Kathakali, developed over the 16th and 17th centuries, was inspired by the heroic myths and legends of Hindu Vedas (sacred writings) and involves phenomenal body control, right down to synchronized movements of the eyeballs. Boys between the ages of 12 and 20 study this dance form for six years. Kathakali makeup is a particularly elaborate process, with characters classified into distinct types according to the colors of their makeup and costumes. Manipur dances revolve around episodes in the life of Vishnu. They are vigorous when performed by men, lyrical when performed by young women. The women's costumes are richly embroidered. Kathak is exciting and entertaining—the most secular of the classical dances. The footwork is fast, clever, expressive, and accentuated by bands of bells around the dancers' ankles. The great masters of each of these dance forms command great respect in India. They have studied for years to perfect their artistry, and their age becomes a factor only when they decide to put away their costumes.

Buddhist dances are as stylized as classical Hindu dance forms, except that the movements of the masked and costumed monks are more ritualized, usually working from a slow pace up to a whirl in which flowing skirts become a blur of color. The accompanying music, usually dominated by long horns and cymbals, adds an eerie counterpoint to the monks' deliberate footwork. The dances are usually enactments of important Buddhist legends, or are performed to ward off demons.

As with classical dance, the beginnings of classical Indian music can be traced to the Hindu Vedas. Over time, this music—an adjunct to worship—developed definite laws of theory and practice. It also evolved into two broadly divided forms, Carnatic in South India and Hindustani in the north. North Indian music uses a wide range of beautiful instruments such as the sitar and the flute; in the south, musical forms are stricter, with less improvisation. In both schools, the fundamental form is a raga, a song based on a 12-tone system unusual, at first, to the Western ear. At a concert of ragas or bhajans (Hindu devotional songs with lyrics), the audience will participate with comments or gestures, expressing enthusiasm for the singer's technical skill and artistic power.

The arrival of the Moghuls in the 12th century led to a new form of northern music incorporating the Persian ghazal, an Urdu rhyming couplet expressing love. In the ghazal, however, the object of devotion can be a woman or the divine or even the singer's home state. Part of the joy in hearing ghazals, at least for those who understand Urdu, comes from deciphering oblique references that give layers of meanings to a single line and are attributed to the skill of the poet and even the singer. Audiences at ghazal performance show appreciation by mirroring a hand motion of the musician or singer, or by praising a turn of phrase.

As with dancers, years of concentrated study lead to revered status for musicians. India's finest singers and instrumentalists are well over the age of 30 and frequently in their 60s.

Shopping

Each part of India specializes in different products. There are still plenty of villages where the majority of residents are weavers, painters, or sculptors, and similar artisan districts are clustered in the old bazaars of large cities.

India has the world's largest rug industry. Exotic silk and wool carpets are crafted in Kashmir and Uttaranchal. Tibetan refugees and the Sikkimese make superb carpets with Buddhist themes. Dhurries, in wool or cotton, have charming folk or tribal motifs; some of the finest dhurries come from Rajasthan and Madhya Pradesh.

Delhi, Rajasthan, and Karnataka have wonderful silver work, including old ethnic and tribal jewelry. (Buyer beware: The silver is not always pure.) Gold jewelry is a smart purchase, and in many cities (Bombay, Calcutta, Delhi, Jaipur, and Madras in particular) you'll find jewelers who can quickly design to order. The price per gram is determined by the world rate, but the cost for the workmanship is a bargain. Precious and semiprecious stones, beautifully cut and highly polished, are another great buy here—Jaipur has wonderful gems that you can buy separately or have fashioned into exquisite jewelry. Jaipur also sells intricately worked enamelware, as does Madhya Pradesh. In Hyderabad, the center of India's pearl trade, pearls of every shape and hue are polished and sold according to sheen, smoothness, and roundness.

Intricate Moghul- and Rajput-style miniature paintings and cloth batik wall hangings are specialties of Rajasthan. Orissa is known for dhokra (animal and human figures in twisted brass wires), pata chitra (finely wrought temple paintings), and tala patra (palm-leaf art). Weavers throughout India work textile designs into cotton or silk, the latter sometimes threaded with real gold or silver. Beautiful brocades and crêpe silk come from Varanasi; the finest heavy silks, many in brilliant jewel tones, are made in Kanchipuram, near Madras. Bangalore and Mysore are also important weaving centers. Himru (cotton and silk brocade) is woven in Aurangabad. Jamdani weaving, a cotton brocade with zari (silver) thread, comes from West Bengal. Orissa is known for ikat, a weave that creates a brush-stroke effect to color borders on silk or cotton. Gujarat and Rajasthan create marvelous tie-dye and embroidered fabrics. To scan a good selection of all these products, stop into one of the fixed-price Central Cottage Industries Emporiums in Bangalore, Bombay, Calcutta, Delhi, Hyderabad, or Madras.

Beautiful brass and copper work are sold everywhere, but Tamil Nadu has especially fine sculptures and temple ornaments. Tribal areas in Orissa and Madhya Pradesh specialize in metal figurines. Hyderabad and Aurangabad produce jet and silver bidriware, especially boxes and bangles. Sculptors chisel delightful stone statues in Orissa, Tamil Nadu, and Rajasthan. Artisans in Agra create exquisite marble inlay work, carrying on a Moghul tradition: jewels are sliced petal-thin and embedded in marble with such precision that the joints are imperceptible even with a magnifying glass.

Wherever people live in wooden dwellings, you find hand-crafted teak, ebony, cedar, sandalwood, or walnut. Rajasthan is known for objects covered with enchanting thematic paintings, from small boxes to furniture and doors. Artisans in Orissa and Andhra Pradesh create charming painted toys. *Lac* turnery is an Indian art form in which layers of color are added to wood and then polished; the best lac products—bangles, toys, boxes—come from Jaipur and Gujarat. Kashmir specializes in carved walnut items: boxes, tables, and gorgeous screens. Kerala and Karnataka are known for finely wrought carvings in sandalwood.

Wildlife Sanctuaries

India has 59 national parks and more than 250 sanctuaries, home to more than 350 different mammals and 1,200 birds. Many of these creatures are unique to the subcontinent, such as the white tiger, royal Bengal tiger, Asian lion, lion-tailed macaque, Andaman teal, great Indian bustard, and monal pheasant.

Before 1947 India did not protect its wildlife. By 1952, 13 species had been declared endangered, and today the list has multiplied to 70 species of mammals, 16 species of reptiles, and 36 species of birds. Tigers, the symbolic mascot of India, were killed so frequently that by 1970, only 1,500 remained. In 1972 the Indian government finally passed the Wildlife Act, which designates natural parks and sanctuaries and provides for the protection of wild animals, particularly endangered species. Three years later, Corbett National Park became India's first tiger reserve, part of Project Tiger—a large-scale enterprise cosponsored by India's Department of Wildlife and the World Wildlife Fund to ban killing and set up 10 reserves. The total number of tigers has risen to more than 4,000, but poachers may yet finish off this rare animal.

India is also attempting to recover a third of its land with forests—a daunting task that requires more than saplings. The rural poor must find viable fuel sources to replace wood, and a humane initiative is needed to control the movement of foraging livestock, including the sacrosanct cow.

Still, many of India's parks and sanctuaries are enchanting. If you have a safari in mind, remember that many of India's animals are elusive, moving in small packs at daybreak and twilight or at night. Count yourself lucky if you spot a tiger, an Asian lion, or a leopard. Come with the proper expectations and you *will* see many animals: numerous species of deer, wild boar, langur of all descriptions, and spectacular birds. Keep your camera and binoculars ready. Shooting is prohibited, but the hunter's loss is the photographer's gain. Wear neutral clothes to better blend into the forest. If you want to stay overnight *inside* a sanctuary, arrange to arrive before it closes at sunset.

FODOR'S CHOICE

Fodor's Choice
★

The sights, restaurants, hotels, and other travel experiences on these pages are top picks. They're the best of their type in the area covered by the book—not to be missed and always worth your time. In the destination chapters that follow, you will find all the details.

LODGING

$$$$	**Ananda in the Himalayas**, Rishikesh. A breathtaking ascent through a forest deposits you into this maharaja's palace turned spa resort. Indulge an ayurvedic oil massage, a trek to nearby temples, or a river rafting trip. The lazy can opt for a spin in the Jacuzzi or lounge in the 100-year-old library.
$$$$	**Brunton Boatyard colonial hotel**, Cochin, Kerala. This elegant Dutch–Portuguese colonial hotel with antiques and whitewashed arcades faces the famous Chinese fishing nets in the harbor.
$$$$	**Green Magic**, Wyanad, Northern Kerala. These two extraordinary tree houses perched 90 feet above the forest floor are constructed mainly with indigenous materials. Lighting is kerosene lamps, meals are served on banana leaves, and a resident elephant is available for treks.
$$$$	**The Imperial**, Delhi. This landmark 1931 hotel with twisting hallways and soaring palms outside expresses a unique mixture of colonial, Victorian, and art deco styles, and is filled with lithographs and engravings.
$$$$	**Kabini River Lodge**, Nagarhole National Park, Karnataka. In the heart of a wildlife sanctuary and among roaming monkeys and colorful trees is Kabini, a blend of rusticity and comfort, and once a royal hunting lodge.
$$$$	**Kumarakom Lake Resort**, Vembanad Lake, Kerala. Experience the lifestyle of Kerala's backwaters at this 25-acre lakefront property with palatial traditional villas, reassembled from old houses and set around a network of canals.
$$$$	**Lake Palace**, Udaipur. This 250-year-old palace floats like a vision of white marble in the middle of Lake Pichola, oozing history and romance. The suites are colorfully opulent, and most rooms have lake views.
$$$$	**The Leela Goa**, Cavelossim, Goa. You'll need the welcome coconut drink and map to get your bearing at this 75-acre resort on a secluded beach. The lobby is designed like an ancient temple and villas are arranged around a lagoon.
$$$$	**Nor-Khill**, Gangtok. Traditional Sikkimese architecture defines this royal guesthouse on a ridge. Religious artwork decorates the rooms and masks, etchings, and paintings are hung throughout the hotel.

$$$$	**Oberoi Amarvilas,** Agra. Live the lifestyle of the opulent Moghul emperors at this Moorish fantasy of sandstone arches and glistening pools. Each richly decorated room has a private terrace overlooking the Taj Mahal.
$$$$	**The Oberoi Bangalore,** Karnataka. It doesn't get much more lavish: spacious rooms with private balconies and brass-and-teak furnishings, green marble floors, and a garden with a waterfall cascading into a fish-filled lotus pond.
$$$$	**Oberoi Udaivilas,** Udaipur, Rajasthan. On the edge of Lake Pichola with a sublime view, this incredibly luxurious, exclusive hotel has numerous domes, a marble lotus pond in the courtyard, and a private wildlife reserve.
$$$$	**Oberoi Vanyavilas,** Ranthambhore, Rajasthan. Elephants welcome you at this fancy jungle resort on the edge of a national park. Luxury tents with teakwood floors, gardens, and decks evoke the magnificence of the former royal lifestyle.
$$$$	**Park Hyatt Goa Resort and Spa,** Cansaulim Beach, Goa. A sleek, modern design, fancy spa, and the largest swimming pool in India, as well as a food village and a tapas bar on-site, define the experience here.
$$$$	**Taj Bengal,** Calcutta. The fusion of contemporary life and ancient traditions blend well here, with modern Indian art, artifacts, and antiques among Eastern accents and Indian prints, and Western-style atriums.
$$$$	**Taj Exotica,** Benaulim Beach, Goa. Rooms at this ultraluxurious, popular resort have shady verandahs and look out over golf courses, a tranquil beach, and extensive grounds. There's even a lobster shack on the beach.
$$$$	**Taj Mahal Palace & Tower,** Bombay. India's most famous hotel, this Victorian–Gothic extravaganza looks past the Gateway of India to the Arabian Sea. Built in 1903, its stunning exterior, with rows of jutting white balconies, has made it a Bombay landmark.
$$$$	**Taj Malabar,** Cochin, Kerala. On Willingdon Island, this hotel has a traditional "Heritage" wing with Kerala-style furnishings and fancy modern section. Shower with a sea view or indulge in a treatment at the ayurvedic spa.
$$$$	**Taj Residency,** Lucknow. Relax outside town in this British colonial-style building on 30 acres filled with fountains, gardens, and palm trees. Rooms are adorned with rich fabrics and artwork depicting the life and architecture of the Moghuls.
$$$$	**Trident Hilton,** Bhubaneswar, Orissa. This Thai-designed hotel is tranquil and sophisticated, set among papaya, mango, banana, and coconut trees.

$$$$ | **Windamere,** Darjeeling. This landmark of British Darjeeling sports verandas with dramatic views of the hills, and rooms with Raj, art deco, and Tibetan touches.

$$$–$$$$ | **Ladakh Sarai,** Ladakh. This green resort outside Leh offers stays in yurts and pretty views of the Indus River and the whitewashed Stok Palace.

$$$–$$$$ | **Oberoi Grand,** Calcutta. This impeccably maintained Victorian landmark in the center of town has a rich marble and dark-wood interior, top-notch service, and excellent restaurants.

$$–$$$$ | **Neemrana Fort Palace,** near Shekhavati, Rajasthan. Rooms in this 15th-century fort are gorgeously decorated with Rajput handicrafts. Latticework screens, terraces, and courtyards with peacocks and parrots abound.

$$$ | **Banjara Camp,** Sangla Valley. Deluxe tents, amazing food, views of the surrounding mountains, and proximity to jaw-dropping scenery in the heart of the Kinnaur district will characterize your stay here.

$$$ | **Ladakl Sarai,,** Leh. Stay here in a yurt (tent) that overlooks the valley to the Indus River and a mountain range.

$$$ | **Taj Garden Retreat,** Madurai, Tamil Nadu. Rooms at this hilltop hotel are either in a period bungalow, with a British-colonial appeal—vintage etchings on the walls, hardwood floors, and airy verandas—or in modern villas.

$$–$$$ | **Ajit Bhawan,** Jaipur, Rajasthan. This enchanting palace and village complex has a garage full of royal vintage cars you can hire. The colorful rooms have traditional Rajasthani fabrics; some even have trees growing inside.

¢–$$$ | **Chonor House,** Dharamshala. Run by the Norbulingka Institute, this hotel is furnished with decorative elements created by resident artists. Each room has a mural depicting a Tibetan theme.

$$ | **The Manor,** Delhi. Next to a country club is Delhi's only boutique hotel, an ultramodern vision of lanterns and soft lighting, wood- or stone-paneled walls, stark rooms, and dark-marble bathrooms.

$$ | **Mayfair Lagoon,** Bhubaneswar, Orissa. At this excellent resort, quiet, spacious, tastefully decorated guest rooms, each with a private balcony, are set around a jungle-landscaped lagoon.

$ | **Mrs. Bhanderi's Guesthouse,,** Amritzar. These family-run cantonment bungalows bring you back to an earlier age of travel in India.

| **Houseboat Cruise,** Central Kerala. Float along the labyrinthine inland waterways on a *ketuvellam*, a boat fashioned out of cane and the wood of the jackfruit tree, for a distinctly unique form of accommodation. Between 200 and 250 houseboats operate in Kerala.

RESTAURANTS	
$$$$	**Alegria,** Goa. Designed like an old drawing room, this place serves excellent Goan cuisine, from classic pork to crabmeat, curries, and coconut chicken. For dessert, there's mousse infused with *feni* (hooch).
$$$$	**Chinoiserie,** Calcutta. One of India's best Chinese restaurants serves the famous Peking duck and a highly unusual selection of corn dishes.
$$$$	**The History,** Cochin, Kerala. The intensively researched menu draws on the myriad influences on Cochin's history: foods from the Middle East, Portugal, the local Jewish community, and the British Raj.
$$$$	**Kewpies,** Calcutta. Extremely fine Bengali *thalis* (combination platters) are served on banana leaves at this exclusive and very in-demand restaurant.
$$$–$$$$	**Bukhara,** Delhi. Blood-red rugs and copper urns set the tone for the mind-blowingly delicious marinated meats and black lentils from the Northwest Frontier, between Pakistan and Afghanistan.
$$$–$$$$	**Spice Route,** Delhi. As its name implies, this popular, unusual place serves cuisines from the ancient spice route through Asia, and decorates the walls with scenes from the ancient epics.
$$$	**Masala Art,** Delhi. Come here to taste the flawless convergence of ethnic authenticity and international style.
$$	**Fernando's Nostalgia,** Madgaon, Goa. One of the best restaurants in the state is unpretentious and serves wonderful Goan food: salted ox tongue, fried and spiced fish cutlets, and Portuguese dishes generally not found elsewhere in the state.
$$	**Khyber,** Bombay. Named for the Himalayan mountain pass, Khyber is decorated in Northwest Frontier style. The kitchen serves pungent, delectable Muhglai and tandoori food that you'll have a hard time forgetting.
$$	**Sea Lounge,** Bombay. Innumerable marriages have been fixed and business deals struck over the years at the Taj Mahal hotel's most attractive restaurant. The backdrop is a Technicolor view of the magnificent Gateway of India and the blue ocean.
$–$$	**Tangerine,** Calcutta. The best multicuisine spot in Calcutta is cozy, with a minimalist design, and overlooks a lake; the seafood is dynamite.
$	**Chokhi Dhani,** Jaipur, Rajasthan. Come hungry to this village complex where you eat vegetarian food Indian-style (without silverware) and get entertained by folk songs, puppet shows, and jugglers.
$	**Mahesh Lunch Home,** Bombay. Owner Mr. Karkera personally selects the freshest seafood from the Fort fish market every morning, which is why locals—office workers and film stars—all come here for succulent seafood seasoned with tangy tandoori or Mangalorean spices.

$ Park Balluchi, Delhi. This kabab house in Hauz Khas serves some of the most sumptuous barbecue dishes in India: marinated chicken wrapped around mutton and flambéed, and cheese stuffed with nuts and currents, then grilled.

FORTS, PALACES & MONUMENTS

Fort, Jaisalmer. Five thousand people still live inside this spectacular sand-color 12th-century citadel that rises strikingly out of Rajasthan's Thar Desert. Inside is a network of temples, palaces, mansions, and tiny winding lanes.

Fort Aguada, Goa. Spectacularly perched on a hill overlooking the Arabian Sea, this beautiful 17th-century fort once housed a jail and working lighthouse.

Marble Palace, Calcutta. Everything about this 1855 palace is baroque: sculptures of animals and religious figures, strutting peacocks, and an interior filled with urns, chandeliers, strange lamps, and famous paintings.

Mehrangarh Fort, Jodhpur. Climb up the steep walkway to this 15th-century fort filled with palaces decorated with mirror work, murals, and gilt. From the ramparts, the city's blue houses look ethereal at sunset.

Victoria Memorial, Calcutta. The British took 20 years to finish this monument, leaving behind the single greatest symbol of the Raj. Inside is a collection of Indian miniature paintings, Raj-related exhibits, and a museum of the history of Calcutta.

TEMPLES, TOMBS & MOSQUES

Ajanta and Ellora cave temples, Maharashtra. Dating back more than 2,000 years, these monolithic temples rank among the wonders of the ancient world. Monks and artisans carved them out of solid rock, decorating them with lavish frescoes and profusely carved statues.

Brihadiswara Temple, Thanjavur, Tamil Nadu. Sculptures on this carefully executed temple, a UNESCO World Heritage Site, depict the Hindu god Vishnu, while those inside are Buddhist. Also here are frescoes and paintings from various dynasties, a giant bull, and a 190-foot tower.

Hampi, Karnataka. This ruined city was the center of the largest Hindu empire in South India prior to the 16th century. A jumble of vast stone temples, elephant stables, barracks, and palaces, it's an awesome spectacle.

Humayun's Tomb, Delhi. This 16th-century Persian tomb of red sandstone and white marble exemplifies the Moghul love of design in its perfectly square gardens, its fountains, and its precedent-setting dome-within-a-dome mausoleum.

Jama Masjid, Delhi. This exquisite Islamic statement in red sandstone and marble, with an onion dome and tapering minarets, is India's largest mosque, completed in 1656 after six years of work by 5,000 laborers.

Kandariya Mahadev, Khajuraho. Carved on Khajuraho's most evolved, five-shrine Shiva temple are some of the most voluptuous sculptures in India: Hindu gods and goddesses, mithunas, celestial handmaidens, and lions.

Meenakshi Temple, Madurai, Madurai, Tamil Nadu. Both people and elephants crowd the sanctuaries of this temple complex, and the air is thick with incense and the sound of chanting. Glimpse the elaborate carvings in the Hall of the Thousand Pillars and take in the feeling of passionate worship.

Old Goa churches, Goa. The famous 16th- and 17th-century churches of this Portuguese colony contain some curiosities: the body of St. Francis Xavier, patron saint of Goa; a huge belfry with the largest bell in Goa; and beautiful chapels and carvings.

Sanchi, northeast of Bhopal. A World Heritage site and major Buddhist pilgrimage destination, serene Sanchi includes a group of stupas and monastery and temple ruins on a remote hilltop. Gates are elaborately carved with scenes from the life of Buddha.

Sun Temple, Konark, Orissa. Built in the form of the sun god Surya's chariot, the temple has 24 giant wheels pulled by seven horses; every inch is carved with mythical animals, erotic pairings, and whimsical scenes from daily life.

Taj Mahal, Agra. Resplendent in soft-white marble and resonant with a bittersweet love story, the Taj lives up to its reputation. Both the photogenic exterior and the quiet, exquisitely decorated interior leave a lingering sense of peace and wonder.

UNFORGETTABLE SCENES

Bird-watching at dawn at Keoladeo Ghana National Park, Bharatpur. Between Agra and Jaipur, in Rajasthan, is a sanctuary for 400 species of waterbirds. Some waterbirds migrate annually here from Siberia, the Himalayas, and Europe.

Chandni Chowk, Delhi. Along this former imperial avenue, now a bazaar, you'll find every conceivable form of commerce, from taxis and auto-rickshaws to street astrologers and sidewalk doctors.

Charminar Old City markets, Hyderabad. Browse the phenomenal pearl and bangle markets beside this 1591 granite edifice.

Chowpatty Beach and Marine Drive, Bombay. Bombay's setting is part of what makes it so intoxicating. Chowpatty Beach is a taste of the Bombay carnival, with vendors, food stalls, and rides. Walk east along the perfectly curved Marine Drive for an encounter with the incredible geography and with locals of every stripe.

Durga Puja, Calcutta. Calcutta's biggest annual festival spans the better part of a week every September or October. Durga, a Hindu goddess, is worshipped during this period in marquees that spring up in every other street all over town. There are complex arrangements of lights, musical soirees, and thousands of people in the streets day and night, visiting marquee after marquee to see the idol and its decoration. The ebullience and magic captures the pulse of the city.

Dashashvamedh Ghat at dawn, Varanasi. Come to this main ghat on the Ganges at sunrise, when pilgrims and devotees perform ablutions on the riverbank, lit by the sun's darkly golden first rays.

Flea market at Anjuna Beach, Goa. Getting here by motorcycle or boat for the Wednesday market is half the fun. In a clearing above a rocky beach, tribal nomads and craftspeople sell jewelry, mirror-work tops, sarongs, and more.

The Penance of Arjuna mural, Mahabalipuram, Tamil Nadu. The world's largest bas-relief, carved on two adjacent boulders during the 7th century, depicts a scene from the epic poem, the *Bhagavad Gita*; cave temples are cut into the rock hill behind the boulders.

Sound-and-light show at Golconda Fort, Hyderabad. Don't miss the stunning nightly show at the ruins of what was once an imposing fort, which, at its prime, had a water supply system that sheltered entire communities under siege for months.

Tiger safari at Ranthambhore National Park, south of Jaipur. Come in summer, before the monsoon, to see wild tigers up close (in official government Jeeps) at this 1,334 square km park in Rajasthan's rugged Aravalli and Vidhya hills.

SMART TRAVEL TIPS

Addresses
Air Travel
Airports
Beggers & Hawkers
Bus Travel
Business Hours
Cameras & Photography
Car Rental
Car Travel
Children in India
Computers on the Road
Consumer Protection
Customs & Duties
Disabilities & Accessibility
Discounts & Deals
Eating & Drinking
Electricity
Embassies
Emergencies
Etiquette & Behavior
Gay & Lesbian Travel
Food & Drink
Gifts
Holidays
Insurance
Language
Lodging
Mail & Shipping
Money Matters
Packing
Passports & Visas
Rest Rooms
Safety
Senior-Citizen Travel
Shopping
Students in India
Taxes
Telephones & Cell Phones
Time
Tipping
Tours & Packages
Train Travel
Travel Agencies
Visitor Information
Web Sites

Finding out about your destination before you leave home means you won't squander time organizing everyday minutiae once you've arrived. You'll be more street-wise when you hit the ground and better prepared to explore the aspects of India that drew you here in the first place. The organizations in this section can provide information to supplement this guide; contact them for up-to-the-minute details, and consult the A to Z sections that end each chapter for facts on the various topics as they relate to India's many regions. Happy landings!

ADDRESSES

Indian addresses are often haphazard. Building numbers may appear in postal addresses, but they aren't very useful as they rarely appear on the buildings themselves. And in some towns and some residential areas, numbers do not even have a chronological order—house number 45/234 could be next to house 32/342. This makes neighborhood names, which are often included in urban addresses, very important. Addresses for places in small villages may include the name of the nearest large town or big city. In India, postal codes play a big part in ensuring that a letter reaches its destination.

Common terms for the word "road" in local languages (India has many) include *marg, galli, rasta, salai, peth,* and *sarani.* Like many Indian cities, streets and roads have an older, British name and a newer, post-Independence name. Residents often refer to roads by their old names or use abbreviated versions of cumbersome names. In Bombay, for instance, Netaji Subhash Chandra Marg is still called by its old, easy-to-remember name of Marine Drive and Jay Prakash Road is referred to as J. P. Road. Bombay and its post-Independence name, Mumbai, are used interchangeably, too, which make it doubly confusing.

AIR TRAVEL
BOOKING

When you book, look for nonstop flights and remember that "direct" flights stop at least once. Try to avoid connecting flights, which require a change of plane. Two airlines may operate a connecting flight jointly, so ask whether your airline operates every segment of the trip; you may find that the carrier you prefer flies you only part of the way. To find more booking tips and to check prices and make online flight reservations, log on to www.fodors.com.

CARRIERS

Many international companies are constantly re-evaluating their service to southern Asia. Call the air carriers listed below to confirm their flights and schedules, or work with a travel agent who's knowledgeable about the region.

Although some domestic carriers don't sell their tickets outside of India, try to **buy tickets for flights within India when you buy tickets to the subcontinent.** Within India, flights can be delayed, so **don't schedule back-to-back domestic flights.** Competition has forced Indian Airlines, the national domestic carrier, to improve its service and become more timely—with some success. (You can book tickets and buy air passes for Indian Airlines at Air-India offices abroad, even if you're not flying to the subcontinent on Air-India.) More service-oriented than Indian Airlines are the private carriers, Jet Airways and Sahara Airlines. Domestic flights cost about 50% more than train trips in first-class, air-conditioned cars—if a tight budget is a bigger concern than a tight itinerary, consider taking the train. Know that visitors are charged higher dollar fares, whereas Indian residents pay less.

🛪 **From North America** Air France ☎ 800/237-2747. Air-India ☎ 212/751-6200. Delta ☎ 800/241-4141. Luftansa ☎ 800/399-5838. Northwest ☎ 800/447-4747. United ☎ 800/328-6877.
🛪 **From the U.K.** Air-India ☎ 208/495-7950. British Airways ☎ 0345/222-111. United ☎ 0800/888-555.
🛪 **From Australia** Qantas ☎ 13-1313.
🛪 **Within India** Indian Airlines ☎ 11/2569-6327, 11/2567-5301 in India ⊕ indian-airlines.nic.in. Jet Airways ☎ 925/866-1205 toll-free, 866/835-9538 in North America, 208/970-1525 in U.K., 612/9244-2132 in Australia, 11/516-41414 in India

⊕ www.jetairways.com. Sahara Airlines ☎ 818/990-9733, 212/685-5456 in North America, 208/897-1164, 870/127-1000 in U.K., 2/9299-1818 in Australia, 11/2332-6851 in India ⊕ www.airsahara.net.

CHECK-IN & BOARDING

Always **find out your carrier's check-in policy.** Plan to arrive at the airport about two hours before your scheduled departure time for domestic flights and 2½ to 3 hours before international flights. You may need to arrive earlier if you're flying from one of the busier airports or during peak air-traffic times. To avoid delays at airport-security checkpoints, try not to wear any metal. Jewelry, belt and other buckles, steel-toe shoes, barrettes, and underwire bras are among the items that can set off detectors.

Security in Indian airports is tight, and procedures (searches and scans, equipment checks, having you identify your luggage on the tarmac before you board) require considerable time. You'll spend less time standing if you show up early. **Check in at least two hours before a flight within India.** Golf clubs aren't allowed in the cabin; neither are pocket knives or other sharp implements. Be sure that batteries are charged and installed in flashlights, cameras, tape and CD players, and computers; you may be asked to turn such equipment on to prove it's what it appears to be. Note that on some flights, you may be asked to dispose of extra batteries or those in such equipment (computers aside) for safety reasons.

CUTTING COSTS

The least expensive airfares to India are priced for round-trip travel and must usually be purchased in advance. Airlines generally allow you to change your return date for a fee; most low-fare tickets, however, are nonrefundable. It's smart to call a number of airlines and check the Internet; when you are quoted a good price, book it on the spot—the same fare may not be available the next day, or even the next hour. Always check different routings and look into using alternate airports. Also, price off-peak flights, which may be significantly less expensive than others. Travel agents, especially low-fare specialists (⇨ Discounts & Deals), are helpful.

Consolidators are another good source. They buy tickets for scheduled flights at reduced rates from the airlines, then sell them at prices that beat the best fare available directly from the airlines. Sometimes you can even get your money back if you need to return the ticket. Carefully read the fine print detailing penalties for changes and cancellations, purchase the ticket with a credit card, and confirm your consolidator reservation with the airline.

When you fly as a courier, you trade your checked-luggage space for a ticket deeply subsidized by a courier service. There are restrictions on when you can book and how long you can stay. Some courier companies list with membership organizations, such as the Air Courier Association and the International Association of Air Travel Couriers; these require you to become a member before you can book a flight.

Many airlines, singly or in collaboration, offer discount air passes that allow foreigners to travel economically in a particular country or region. These visitor passes usually must be reserved and purchased before you leave home. Information about passes often can be found on most airlines' international Web pages, which tend to be aimed at travelers from outside the carrier's home country. Also, try typing the name of the pass into a search engine, or search for "pass" within the carrier's Web site.

Children under 12 and students ages 12 to 26 (with a valid I.D.) qualify for discounts on most domestic airlines. Groups are eligible for discounts, too. Indian Airlines' Discover India pass gives you 15 days of unlimited travel within the country for US$500; a 21-day package costs US$750. These passes allow unlimited economy travel as long as you travel in one continuous geographic direction and do not back-track.

Indian Airlines' India Wonder Fare pass gives you a week of unlimited travel within the north, south, east, or west of India for US$300 (plus a US$5 tax). If you buy your pass at a travel agent representing Indian Airlines abroad, be sure to have

it endorsed upon arrival in India. It's easier if you pay for the pass in foreign currency, but you can pay in rupees upon arrival if you furnish an exchange receipt.

Jet Airways offers 7-day (US$300), 14-day (US$500), and 21-day (US$750) Visit India passes. The 7-day pass is regional only. These also require you to pay a tax of US$10 per flight. You can buy the passes on arrival in India or at Jet Airways agents abroad.

🖅 Consolidators **AirlineConsolidator.com** ☎ 888/ 468-5385 ⊕ www.airlineconsolidator.com, for international tickets. **Best Fares** ☎ 800/576-8255 or 800/576-1600 ⊕ www.bestfares.com; $59.90 annual membership. **Cheap Tickets** ☎ 800/377-1000 or 888/922-8849 ⊕ www.cheaptickets.com. **Expedia** ☎ 800/397-3342 or 404/728-8787 ⊕ www.expedia. com. **Hotwire** ☎ 866/468-9473 or 920/330-9418 ⊕ www.hotwire.com. **Now Voyager Travel** ✉ 45 W. 21st St., 5th fl., New York, NY 10010 ☎ 212/459-1616 🖷 212/243-2711 ⊕ www.nowvoyagertravel. com. **Onetravel.com** ⊕ www.onetravel.com. **Orbitz** ☎ 888/656-4546 ⊕ www.orbitz.com. **Priceline. com** ⊕ www.priceline.com. **Travelocity** ☎ 888/ 709-5983, 877/282-2925 in Canada, 0870/111-7060 in U.K. ⊕ www.travelocity.com.

🖅 Courier Resources **International Association of Air Travel Couriers** ☎ 308/632-3273 ⊕ www. courier.org; $45 annual membership.

🖅 Airline Discounts in India **Indian Airlines** ☎ 11/ 2569-6327 or 11/2567-5301 in India, 1-866-4359-422 toll-free in U.S., 0-8000-34-4000 toll-free in U.K., 1-866-770-7799 toll-free in Canada ⊕ http://indian-airlines.nic.in/fares. **Jet Airways** ☎ 925/866-1205 toll-free, 866/835-9538 in North America, 208/970-1525 in U.K., 612/9244-2132 in Australia, 11/516-41414 in India ⊕ www.jetairways.com.

ENJOYING THE FLIGHT

Ask the airline whether a snack or meal is served on the flight. If you have dietary concerns, request special meals when booking. These can be vegetarian, low-cholesterol, or kosher, for example. It's a good idea to pack some healthful snacks and a small (plastic) bottle of water in your carry-on bag. On long flights, try to maintain a normal routine, to help fight jet lag. At night, get some sleep. By day, eat light meals, drink water (not alcohol), and **move around the cabin** to stretch your legs. For additional jet-lag tips consult

Fodor's FYI: Travel Fit & Healthy (available at bookstores everywhere).

Smoking policies vary from carrier to carrier. Many airlines prohibit smoking on all of their flights; others allow smoking only on certain routes or certain departures. Ask your carrier about its policy.

FLYING TIMES

Flying time to either Delhi or Bombay is 16 hours from New York, 18 hours from Chicago, 20 hours from Los Angeles, 8 hours from London or Amsterdam, and 14 hours from Sydney.

HOW TO COMPLAIN

If your baggage goes astray or your flight goes awry, complain right away. Most carriers require that you **file a claim immediately.** The Aviation Consumer Protection Division of the Department of Transportation publishes *Fly-Rights,* which discusses airlines and consumer issues and is available on-line. You can also find articles and information on mytravelrights.com, the Web site of the nonprofit Consumer Travel Rights Center.

Airline Complaints Aviation Consumer Protection Division ✉ U.S. Department of Transportation, C-75, Room 4107, 400 7th St. SW, Washington, DC 20590 ☎ 202/366-2220 ⊕ airconsumer.ost.dot.gov. **Federal Aviation Administration Consumer Hotline** ✉ For inquiries: FAA, 800 Independence Ave. SW, Washington, DC 20591 ☎ 800/322-7873 ⊕ www.faa.gov.

RECONFIRMING

Check the status of your flight before you leave for the airport. You can do this on your carrier's Web site, by linking to a flight-status checker (many Web booking services offer these), or by calling your carrier or travel agent. Always confirm international flights at least 72 hours ahead of the scheduled departure time.

AIRPORTS

India's major international gateways are Indira Gandhi International Airport in Delhi (DEL) and Mumbai International Airport in Bombay (BOM).

Airport Information Indira Gandhi International Airport ☎ 11/2565-2011. **Mumbai International Airport** ☎ 22/2682-9112.

BEGGARS & HAWKERS

Try not to get upset by the number of beggars who beseech you for spare rupees, motioning from hand to mouth to indicate they have nothing to eat. If you give a beggar money, a dozen more will immediately spring up, and you'll be forced to provide for all; it can also be difficult to get the first beggar, or the entire group, off your tail. Know, too, that beggars aren't always as destitute as they look. Be firm and do not allow a beggar to tail you—a raised voice or mild threats usually work. If you're not firm, expect to be followed by a pack of beggars—they do not give up easily. If all else fails, duck into a hotel and remain there for a while.

If you want to contribute, donate to a legal charity or pass out candy to the child beggars you encounter. It's very rare for a tourist to come to India and not encounter two dozen beggar kids. It's not a bad idea to plan for this—interesting hairclips and ball-point pens are wonderful handouts. The smiles you'll be rewarded with are unforgettable. But be discreet when you're handing out trinkets or candy as you'll be hounded. Consider gift-gifting from a moving taxi as the light changes or before you re-enter your hotel.

Hawkers and touts can also be a tremendous nuisance. If you're not interested in what a hawker is offering give him a firm, polite no and ignore him after that. If he persists, tell him to clear off and employ some mock anger or else he will follow you for blocks. Do not encourage touts at all.

BUS TRAVEL

Bus travel isn't the most safe or comfortable way to travel in India, especially at night. If you do take buses, try to travel on the most luxurious privately run air-conditioned coaches, like the Volvo buses, and stick to popular routes where buses are recommended as the best option. Also know that rest-room arrangements for long-distance bus rides are pretty poor.

BUSINESS HOURS
BANKS & OFFICES
Most banks are open weekdays 10 to 2 and Saturday 10 to noon, but ATMs are open around the clock in larger cities. International airports and some top hotels have 24-hour currency-exchange facilities, and the major American Express branches have extended hours for check-cashing. Post offices are generally open Monday through Saturday 10 to 5.

GAS STATIONS
Gas stations are usually open daily from 6 AM to 10 PM. In larger cities, some stay open 24 hours.

MUSEUMS & SIGHTS
Most museums are closed on Monday. Site museums (adjoining archaeological monuments) are normally closed on Friday.

PHARMACIES
Pharmacies are usually open daily from 9:30 to 8, though in cities there are some 24-hour establishments. In some places you can also buy medicine from the 24-hour pharmacies at large hospitals. (Note that in India pharmacies are called "chemists.")

SHOPS
Outside the four major metropolitan areas (Bombay, Delhi, Calcutta, and Madras), many shopkeepers close their establishments for an afternoon siesta. Many stores are closed Sunday.

CAMERAS & PHOTOGRAPHY
Ask before you snap. Photography isn't permitted in airports, on airplanes, at some government buildings, at military sites (including some bridges), and at certain religious sites and events. Some women and tribal peoples may also object to having their pictures taken. Other people may ask for money before allowing you a snapshot; carry a bit of change for such moments. If someone asks you to send a copy of the photo, don't say yes unless you intend to keep the promise. By and large, however, Indians love being photographed—just be polite about it.

It's best to pack special high speed film (above 800 ASA) with you before coming, or special types of film, such as Adventix. If you arrive in Bombay or Delhi, it's fine to buy films and batteries there, since it will be much cheaper. Developing film in India is significantly cheaper, too.

The *Kodak Guide to Shooting Great Travel Pictures* (available at bookstores everywhere) is loaded with tips.
🗗 Photo Help **Kodak Information Center** ☎ 800/ 242-2424.

EQUIPMENT PRECAUTIONS
Don't pack film or equipment in checked luggage, where it is much more susceptible to damage. X-ray machines used to view checked luggage are extremely powerful and therefore are likely to ruin your film. Try to ask for hand inspection of film, which becomes clouded after repeated exposure to airport X-ray machines, and keep videotapes and computer disks away from metal detectors. Always keep film, tape, and computer disks out of the sun. Carry an extra supply of batteries, and be prepared to turn on your camera, camcorder, or laptop to prove to airport security personnel that the device is real. Dust can be troublesome in India, so keep gear under wraps when it's not in use and keep a good eye on it at all times. Note that India uses the PAL video standard; don't expect to find video easily, however; do bring enough of your own.

CAR RENTAL
Renting a car and driving yourself around India isn't recommended. The rules and road conditions are probably like nothing you've ever experienced, so taking taxis or hiring a car and driver are better choices. If you must get behind the wheel yourself, there are just a few reliable rental agencies in India's major cities. Rates in Bombay begin at $42 a day and $280 a week for an economy car with unlimited mileage.
🗗 Major Agencies **Avis** ☎ 800/331-1084, 800/ 879-2847 in Canada, 0870/606-0100 in the U.K., 02/ 9353-9000 in Australia, 09/526-2847 in New Zealand ⊕ www.avis.com. **Budget** ☎ 800/527- 0700, 0870/156-5656 in the U.K. ⊕ www.budget. com. **Hertz** ☎ 800/654-3001, 800/263-0600 in

Canada, 0870/844-8844 in the U.K., 02/9669-2444 in Australia, 09/256-8690 in New Zealand ⊕ www. hertz.com.

INSURANCE

When driving a rented car you are generally responsible for any damage to or loss of the vehicle as well as for any property damage or personal injury that you may cause. Before you rent, see what coverage your personal auto-insurance policy and credit cards provide.

REQUIREMENTS & RESTRICTIONS

Your own driver's license is not acceptable in India—you need an International Driver's Permit. In North America you can get one of these from the American or Canadian automobile associations; in the United Kingdom, contact the Automobile Association or Royal Automobile Club.

SURCHARGES

Before you pick up a car in one city and leave it in another, **ask about drop-off charges or one-way service fees,** which can be substantial. Note, too, that some rental agencies charge extra if you return the car before the time specified in your contract. To avoid a hefty refueling fee, **fill the tank just before you turn in the car,** but be aware that gas stations near the rental outlet may overcharge.

CAR TRAVEL

Driving in India isn't for the faint of heart. Traffic is multifarious: slow-moving cyclists, bullock carts, cows, and even camels or elephants share the road with speeding, honking, quick-to-pass, ready-to-brake-for-animals vehicles of all shapes and sizes. Barring a few principal routes, Indian roads are a mess, especially during monsoon. Speed limits, set according to road conditions, are often ignored. Road signs, when they exist, are usually in Hindi or the local language. In larger cities traffic can get badly backed up during rush hour, when a VIP is racing through, or for some unexpected strike or a festival procession.

In rural areas, two-way roads are often only one-lane wide, so vehicles frequently dodge oncoming traffic for hours on end. Some roads also serve as innovative exten-sions to farms, with grain laid out to dry on the pavement or sisal rope strung over the route so that vehicles tramp the grain down. British-style left-side driving creates one more challenge to many motorists. Bottom line: **hire a car and driver or a taxi rather than take to the road yourself.**

EMERGENCY SERVICES

Outside of some places where traffic police patrol the highways, there aren't any emergency services to speak of. If your car breaks down, you have few options aside from flagging down a ride to the nearest service station.

GASOLINE

Gas stations are full service, but the only people who expect tips are the attendant who wipes your windshield and the man who provides "free" air. At this writing, 1 liter of gas costs Rs. 31. Plan to pay with cash, as few stations—or petrol pumps, as they're called—accept credit cards.

Leaded fuel and diesel are readily available. Unleaded fuel or petrol is harder to find, particularly on secondary highways. When tanking up for a long journey, choose a busy pump along a major highway. Smaller stations often sell adulterated gas.

HIRED CARS WITH DRIVERS

Hiring a car and driver is affordable by Western standards; just be sure to **establish terms, rates, and surcharges in advance.** Shorter trips are generally priced by kilometer. Figure Rs. 6 to Rs. 10 per kilometer for a non–air-conditioned Ambassador—a hefty, roomy car designed by the British in the 1950s. Ambassadors are not as universal as they used to be, and now the most economic rates often gets you a Maruti van or Uno. Neither is as comfortable as the Ambassador, as these are lighter cars that get bounced about on pot-holed roads. In some locations, a higher rate gets you a diesel Sumo jeep or an air-conditioned Cielo, Contessa, or Audi; yet more cash gets you a Toyota, a minivan, or a Mercedes-Benz. On longer trips one price usually covers a certain number of hours and kilometers; beyond that you pay extra. Add to this a halt charge of Rs. 100

to Rs. 200 per night for overnight trips. Some companies also charge a driver's fee for an eight-hour day.

Arrange a car and driver only through a licensed, government-approved operator or, for quite a bit more money, through your hotel. Be sure to discuss your itinerary up front. Roads in some areas—wildlife sanctuaries for example—require a jeep; better to iron out all the details than miss sights because you don't have the appropriate vehicle. On long journeys, decide in advance where and when you'll stop for tea or meal breaks. The dare-devil road maneuvers that are the norm in India can be unsettling. Ask the driver to travel slowly, or have the operator inform the driver of this request.

CHILDREN IN INDIA

Bringing your kids to India may seem daunting, but children love it here. India is like a giant circus, with color, chaos, and a side show every minute. Kids are warmly welcomed everywhere except, perhaps, in the stuffiest of restaurants, and most Indians will bend over backward to help you with a child-related need. In fact, so much affection is lavished on children here—everyone wants to pick them up, pinch their cheeks, talk to them—that your little ones may even get perturbed.

However, there are many diseases prevalent in India that no longer exist elsewhere. Check with your pediatrician first before bringing your kids. It's easiest to bring an infant (who cannot yet crawl, and who is still dependent on breast-feeding or formula) or a child who is a bit older and who can walk on his or her own.

If you're renting a car, don't expect to get a car seat—bring your own (don't expect, either, that seat belts will always work). For general advice about traveling with children, consult *Fodor's FYI: Travel with Your Baby* (available in bookstores everywhere).

FLYING

If your children are two or older, ask about children's airfares. As a general rule, infants under two not occupying a seat fly at greatly reduced fares or even for free. But if you want to guarantee a seat for an infant, you have to pay full fare. Consider flying during off-peak days and times; most airlines will grant an infant a seat without a ticket if there are available seats. When booking, confirm carry-on allowances if you're traveling with infants. In general, for babies charged 10% to 50% of the adult fare you are allowed one carry-on bag and a collapsible stroller; if the flight is full, the stroller may have to be checked or you may be limited to less.

Experts agree that it's a good idea to use safety seats aloft for children weighing less than 40 pounds. Airlines set their own policies: if you use a safety seat, U.S. carriers usually require that the child be ticketed, even if he or she is young enough to ride free, because the seats must be strapped into regular seats. And even if you pay the full adult fare for the seat, it may be worth it, especially on longer trips. Do **check your airline's policy about using safety seats during takeoff and landing.** Safety seats are not allowed everywhere in the plane, so get your seat assignments as early as possible.

When reserving, request children's meals or a freestanding bassinet (not available at all airlines) if you need them. But note that bulkhead seats, where you must sit to use the bassinet, may lack an overhead bin or storage space on the floor.

LODGING

Most hotels in India allow children under a certain age to stay in their parents' room at no extra charge or for a nominal charge, but others charge for them as extra adults. Confirm the cutoff age for children's discounts.

SIGHTS & ATTRACTIONS

Places that are especially appealing to children are indicated by a rubber-duckie icon (🐤) in the margin.

SUPPLIES & EQUIPMENT

Indian cities don't have much sidewalk space for strollers, but such a conveyance is a clean, safe, comfortable place to park your toddler. **Pack all necessary medicines as well as rash creams, zinc oxide, sunscreen, diapers, and diaper wipes.** Clean bathrooms are also hard to come by in both cities and the countryside, so **carry toilet paper and moist towelettes with you at all times.** Even more useful are the alcohol-based hand sanitizers available in tiny purse-size bottles marketed by Purell and other companies. Your curious child may end up getting his hands dirty every so often and it's a good idea to clean up to avoid bacteria.

Although major brands of disposable diapers, as well as Nestlé instant baby cereals, are available in most cities, they can be hard to find. Powdered milk produced by such companies as Amul and Nestlé is readily available and better idea to carry around rather than looking for fresh milk that needs to be boiled properly. Baby formula, called Lactogen, is available in a pinch, but it's best not to switch over from the formula you currently use, so bring enough of your own. Bottled mineral water and packaged snacks—potato chips, cookies, chocolate bars, fruit juices, and soft drinks—are sold throughout India. Though not nutritious, such snacks are often preferable to food that may be spicy or not entirely hygienic. If you're heading out for a day of sightseeing, ask your hotel staff if they can pack a lunch for your child. A small hot pot or kettle can be useful for making instant soup or noodles; you may want to bring a few packages of these with you.

Pack cool, loose, easy-to-wash clothes. If you'll be taking any air-conditioned trains, bring a few pieces of warm clothing, as the cars get cold. Leggings help protect against mosquitoes in the evening, hats shade youthful faces from the sun, and rubber slippers or sandals are always practical. A few pairs of socks can come in handy. If you plan to travel by car **bring a portable car seat.** Choose accommodations that are air-conditioned or have rooms equipped with mosquito netting to protect your child from mosquito bites. **Pack plenty of insect repellent as well as a 3-square-foot piece of soft cloth netting** (available in fabric stores), which you can drape over a carriage or car seat to shield your child from insects. Pellet repellants that plug into the wall and release

a mosquito-repelling scent are available in stores across India, and are effective in keeping a room mosquito-free. It's a good idea to purchase such a gizmo on arrival. (Try Good Night or All Out.) **Consult you pediatrician about having your child take antimalaria pills,** as malaria is common even in the big cities.

COMPUTERS ON THE ROAD

If you plan to bring a laptop to India, **carry a spare battery and spare adapter.** New batteries and replacement adapters are expensive and hard to find. Never plug your computer into a socket before asking about surge protection—some hotels don't have built-in current stabilizers, and extreme electrical fluctuations can short your adapter or even destroy your computer. IBM sells a pen-size modem tester that plugs into a phone jack and tells you whether or not the line is safe to use; this gadget is invaluable in India, where phone lines aren't always reliable and can harm your modem. In larger cities rooms have in-room data ports, but it is essential to check the charges for telephone usage or use of the port beforehand. Internet cafés are now located in towns large and very small, and rates are extremely cheap—so consider not bringing a laptop altogether.

CONSUMER PROTECTION

Whether you're shopping for gifts or purchasing travel services, **pay with a major credit card** whenever possible, so you can cancel payment or get reimbursed if there's a problem (and you can provide documentation). If you're doing business with a particular company for the first time, contact your local Better Business Bureau and the attorney general's offices in your state and (for U.S. businesses) the company's home state as well. Have any complaints been filed? Finally, if you're buying a package or tour, always consider travel insurance that includes default coverage (⇨ Insurance).

🗗 **BBBs Council of Better Business Bureaus** ✉ 4200 Wilson Blvd., Suite 800, Arlington, VA 22203 ☎ 703/276-0100 🖷 703/525-8277 ⊕ www.bbb.org.

CUSTOMS & DUTIES

When shopping abroad, keep receipts for all purchases. Upon reentering the country, **be ready to show customs officials what you've bought.** Pack purchases together in an easily accessible place. If you think a duty is incorrect, appeal the assessment. If you object to the way your clearance was handled, note the inspector's badge number. In either case, first ask to see a supervisor. If the problem isn't resolved, write to the appropriate authorities, beginning with the port director at your point of entry.

IN AUSTRALIA

Australian residents who are 18 or older may bring home A$400 worth of souvenirs and gifts (including jewelry), 250 cigarettes or 250 grams of cigars or other tobacco products, and 1,125 ml of alcohol (including wine, beer, and spirits). Residents under 18 may bring back A$200 worth of goods. Members of the same family traveling together may pool their allowances. Prohibited items include meat products. Seeds, plants, and fruits need to be declared upon arrival.

🇦🇺 **Australian Customs Service** ✑ Regional Director, Box 8, Sydney, NSW 2001 ☎ 02/9213–2000 or 1300/363263, 02/9364–7222 or 1800/803–006 quarantine-inquiry line ☎ 02/9213–4043 ⊕ www.customs.gov.au.

IN CANADA

Canadian residents who have been out of Canada for at least seven days may bring in C$750 worth of goods duty-free. If you've been away fewer than seven days but more than 48 hours, the duty-free allowance drops to C$200. If your trip lasts 24 to 48 hours, the allowance is C$50. You may not pool allowances with family members. Goods claimed under the C$750 exemption may follow you by mail; those claimed under the lesser exemptions must accompany you. Alcohol and tobacco products may be included in the 7-day and 48-hour exemptions but not in the 24-hour exemption. If you meet the age requirements of the province or territory through which you reenter Canada, you may bring in, duty-free, 1.5 liters of wine or 1.14 liters (40 imperial ounces) of liquor or 24 12-ounce cans or bottles of beer or ale. Also, if you meet the local age requirement for tobacco products, you may bring in, duty-free, 200 cigarettes and 50 cigars. Check ahead of time with the Canada Customs and Revenue Agency or the Department of Agriculture for policies regarding meat products, seeds, plants, and fruits.

You may send an unlimited number of gifts (only one gift per recipient, however) worth up to C$60 each duty-free to Canada. Label the package UNSOLICITED GIFT—VALUE UNDER $60. Alcohol and tobacco are excluded.

🇨🇦 **Canada Customs and Revenue Agency** ✉ 2265 St. Laurent Blvd., Ottawa, Ontario K1G 4K3 ☎ 800/461-9999, 204/983-3500, or 506/636-5064 ⊕ www.ccra.gc.ca.

IN NEW ZEALAND

All homeward-bound residents may bring back NZ$700 worth of souvenirs and gifts; passengers may not pool their allowances, and children can claim only the concession on goods intended for their own use. For those 17 or older, the duty-free allowance also includes 4.5 liters of wine or beer; one 1,125-ml bottle of spirits; and either 200 cigarettes, 250 grams of tobacco, 50 cigars, or a combination of the three up to 250 grams. Meat products, seeds, plants, and fruits must be declared upon arrival to the Agricultural Services Department.

🇳🇿 **New Zealand Customs** ✉ Head office: The Customhouse, 17–21 Whitmore St., Box 2218, Wellington ☎ 09/300–5399 or 0800/428–786 ⊕ www.customs.govt.nz.

IN THE U.K.

From countries outside the European Union, including India, you may bring home, duty-free, 200 cigarettes or 50 cigars; 1 liter of spirits or 2 liters of fortified or sparkling wine or liqueurs; 2 liters of still table wine; 60 ml of perfume; 250 ml of toilet water; plus £145 worth of other goods, including gifts and souvenirs. Prohibited items include meat products, seeds, plants, and fruits.

🇬🇧 **HM Customs and Excise** ✉ Portcullis House, 21 Cowbridge Rd. E, Cardiff CF11 9SS ☎ 0845/010–

9000 or 0208/929-0152, 0208/929-6731 or 0208/910-3602 complaints ⊕ www.hmce.gov.uk.

IN THE U.S.

U.S. residents who have been out of the country for at least 48 hours may bring home, for personal use, $800 worth of foreign goods duty-free, as long as they haven't used the $800 allowance or any part of it in the past 30 days. This exemption may include 1 liter of alcohol (for travelers 21 and older), 200 cigarettes, and 100 non-Cuban cigars. Family members from the same household who are traveling together may pool their $800 personal exemptions. For fewer than 48 hours, the duty-free allowance drops to $200, which may include 50 cigarettes, 10 non-Cuban cigars, and 150 ml of alcohol (or 150 ml of perfume containing alcohol). The $200 allowance cannot be combined with other individuals' exemptions, and if you exceed it, the full value of all the goods will be taxed. Antiques, which the U.S. Bureau of Customs and Border Protection defines as objects more than 100 years old, enter duty-free, as do original works of art done entirely by hand, including paintings, drawings, and sculptures. This doesn't apply to folk art or handicrafts, which are in general dutiable.

You may also send packages home duty-free, with a limit of one parcel per addressee per day (except alcohol or tobacco products or perfume worth more than $5). You can mail up to $200 worth of goods for personal use; label the package PERSONAL USE and attach a list of its contents and their retail value. If the package contains your used personal belongings, mark it AMERICAN GOODS RETURNED to avoid paying duties. You may send up to $100 worth of goods as a gift; mark the package UNSOLICITED GIFT. Mailed items do not affect your duty-free allowance on your return.

To avoid paying duty on foreign-made high-ticket items you already own and will take on your trip, register them with Customs before you leave the country. Consider filing a Certificate of Registration for laptops, cameras, watches, and other digital devices identified with serial numbers or other permanent markings; you can keep the certificate for other trips. Otherwise, bring a sales receipt or insurance form to show that you owned the item before you left the United States.

🖪 **U.S. Bureau of Customs and Border Protection** ✉ For inquiries and equipment registration, 1300 Pennsylvania Ave. NW, Washington, DC 20229 ⊕ www.customs.gov ☎ 877/287-8667 or 202/354-1000 ✉ For complaints, Customer Satisfaction Unit, 1300 Pennsylvania Ave. NW, Room 5.5D, Washington, DC 20229.

DISABILITIES & ACCESSIBILITY

India has a large population of people with disabilities, but in a country with so many fundamental problems, the needs of these people aren't a high priority. Similarly, if you're a traveler with a disability, getting around will be significantly more difficult for you in India. Luxury hotels sometimes have ramps for those using wheelchairs or walkers, but few bathrooms are designed for use by people with disabilities. Also, except for a few international airports, disembarkation from planes is via staircase. There are very few sidewalks in India, and no such thing as the pedestrian right of way.

🖪 **Complaints** Aviation Consumer Protection Division (⇨ Air Travel) for airline-related problems. **Departmental Office of Civil Rights** ✉ For general inquiries, U.S. Department of Transportation, S-30, 400 7th St. SW, Room 10215, Washington, DC 20590 ☎ 202/366-4648 📠 202/366-9371 ⊕ www.dot.gov/ost/docr/index.htm. **Disability Rights Section** ✉ NYAV, U.S. Department of Justice, Civil Rights Division, 950 Pennsylvania Ave. NW, Washington, DC 20530 ☎ 202/514-0301 ADA information line, 800/514-0301, 202/514-0383 TTY, 800/514-0383 TTY ⊕ www.ada.gov. **U.S. Department of Transportation Hotline** ☎ 800/778-4838 for disability-related air-travel problems, 800/455-9880 TTY.

TRAVEL AGENCIES

In the United States, the Americans with Disabilities Act requires that travel firms serve the needs of all travelers. Some agencies specialize in working with people with disabilities.

🖪 **Travelers with Mobility Problems** Access Adventures/B. Roberts Travel ✉ 206 Chestnut Ridge Rd., Scottsville, NY 14624 ☎ 585/889-9096

⊕ www.brobertstravel.com ✎ dltravel@prodigy.
net, run by a former physical-rehabilitation coun-
selor. **Flying Wheels Travel** ✉ 143 W. Bridge St.,
Box 382, Owatonna, MN 55060 ☎ 507/451–5005
🖷 507/451–1685 ⊕ www.flyingwheelstravel.com.

DISCOUNTS & DEALS

Be a smart shopper and compare all your
options before making decisions. A plane
ticket bought with a promotional coupon
from travel clubs, coupon books, and di-
rect-mail offers or purchased on the Internet may not be cheaper than the least
expensive fare from a discount ticket
agency. And always keep in mind that
what you get is just as important as what
you save.

DISCOUNT RESERVATIONS

To save money, look into discount reservations services with Web sites and toll-
free numbers, which use their buying
power to get a better price on hotels, airline tickets (⇨ Air Travel), even car
rentals. When booking a room, always
call the hotel's local toll-free number (if
one is available) rather than the central
reservations number—you'll often get a
better price. Always ask about special
packages or corporate rates.

When shopping for the best deal on hotels
and car rentals, look for guaranteed exchange rates, which protect you against a
falling dollar. With your rate locked in,
you won't pay more, even if the price goes
up in the local currency.

🚩 Airline Tickets **Air 4 Less** ☎ 800/2474–5377;
low-fare specialist.

🚩 Hotel Rooms **Accommodations Express**
☎ 800/444–7666 or 800/277–1064 ⊕ www.
accommodationsexpress.com. **Steigenberger
Reservation Service** ☎ 800/223–5652 ⊕ www.srs-
worldhotels.com. **Turbotrip.com** ☎ 800/473–7829
⊕ www.turbotrip.com.

EATING & DRINKING

The restaurants we list are the cream of
the crop in each price category. Properties
indicated by an ✕🏠 are lodging establishments whose restaurant warrants a special
trip. Delhi and Bombay are in a financial
league of their own, so chapters for those
cities are assigned higher pricing categories for meals. For the rest of India, cat-

egories are divided as follows. Major
cities, including Agra, Bangalore, Calcutta, Jaipur, Madras, Pune, and Varanasi,
are in a second-tier. Dining categories in
other areas of India reflect substantially
less expensive prices.

MEALS & SPECIALITIES

The Indian cuisine you may have been exposed to in Indian restaurants abroad is
probably one percent of the cuisine available in India. It's essential to travel across
India cautiously but bravely, to eat. Indians love to feed guests and a food adventure is inevitable. The cuisine of India
varies vastly. In the north you have Punjab's heavy, charcoal-roasted food and the
Kashmiri meat dishes; in central India the
food is lighter, and you also have the mus-
tard-flavor fish of Bengal in the East and
Tibetan and Chinese-influenced food in
the Northeast. In the west, there's the extravagant vegetarian cuisine of Gujarat
and Rajasthan. Along the coast in the
south—from the Konkan coast to Mangalore and down to Kerala—you'll find delicious fish and prawn curries. *Biryanis* and
kababs are native to Hyderbad in
south–central India. And, of course, you
have a zillion varieties of *dosas* (giant
semolina or lentil-flour crêpe filled with
spicy potatoes), meat curries, fried fish,
and light vegetarian dishes in Tamil Nadu,
all the way south.

India does its own brand of Chinese very
well. Don't miss out sampling the spicy,
cilantro-flavored Indo-Chinese that has a
huge variety of vegetarian food incorporated in it—Manchurian cottage cheese
or *paneer*, or Chinese spring onion dosas.
The British, too, had its own brand of
Anglo-Indian cooking. Do experience the
mince cutlets, curry puffs, steak and kid-
ney pie, Waldorf salad, and mulligatawny
soup available in old-style clubs and
older hotels.

A regular Indian meal consists of a portion
of rice or bread, served up with a portion
of spiced vegetables, meat, and lentils. In
some parts of India rice is eaten first and
in other parts the bread comes first and
the rice later. Accessories to the meal can
be *chaas* (a digestive drink), *lassi* (a sweet

or salty yogurt drink), pickle, *papad* (a deep-fried or dry roasted wafer-like savory made from lentil or rice), chutney, *farsan* (a snack), and *raita* (spiced yogurt). A sweet, usually very sugary and milk-based, is the last course. At the end of the meal, as a digestive, *paan* (betel nut and other flavors wrapped in a leaf), *supari* (plain betel nut), cracked rock candy, or anise seed may be served.

Indian breakfasts are none too light and not that early. They can consist of any of the following: *idlis* (steamed rice and lentil cakes) with chutney, *rasam wada* (deep-fried lentil fritters served with a hot, spicy watery lentil curry), *dosas, jalebis* (deep-fried bright yellow flour fritters soaked in sugar syrup) served with milk, *upma* (light semolina with vegetables served up like hominy or couscous), or *aloo poha* (spicy potatoes mixed with rice flakes).

A good portion of India is vegetarian for economic and religious reasons—meat is not part of a daily meal. Indians rarely eat beef and pork, except in certain regions or communities. Many Hindus consider the cow sacred and do not eat beef. Muslims do not touch pork as they consider it unclean. And many Hindus choose to eat only chicken and seafood and stay way from red meat. Jains are not only vegetarian but do not eat any vegetable grown under the ground—because plucking up the root destroys life. As you travel through India, expect to encounter folks who don't eat meat on Tuesday or eat only fruits on Friday; much of India's religious and ethical life, indeed, revolves around food.

MEALTIMES

Lunches are early—not later than 1 PM. Restaurants in cities normally stay open until 11 PM or midnight. In other areas, expect an earlier dinner (finished by 9) unless you're staying in a luxury hotel. Coffee shops in urban luxury hotels are often open 24 hours. Unless otherwise noted, the restaurants listed in this guide are open daily for lunch and dinner, and may offer snacks between mealtimes.

Four o'clock is considered snack time, which means another round of elaborate savories and sweets served with tea. India is a major tea-drinking nation: *masala chai* (spiced tea) and ginger tea are extremely popular and are often consumed four to five times a day. But as you go south, coffee becomes equally important and is served boiling hot, creamy, and foamy (sort of like a triple expresso with cream and sugar).

RESERVATIONS & DRESS

Reservations are always a good idea; we mention them only when they're essential or not accepted. Book as far ahead as you can, and reconfirm as soon as you arrive. (Large parties should always call ahead to check the reservations policy.) We mention dress only when men are required to wear a jacket or a jacket and tie. Very few restaurants require formal attire. By and large India is very casual about dress codes. However, certain clubs do not allow guests visiting—even in daylight hours—to wear shorts or men to wear sandals unless with Indian-style clothes.

WINE, BEER & SPIRITS

India sells a range of liquor. Its locally produced rums, vodka, and gin are very good quality. Beer is a tad stronger but generally enjoyed by most foreigners. You won't find a wide variety of wine, champagne, or liquor available, but you will find that most are decent quality—though Indian–brand Scotch is a bit substandard. Imported Scotch is now easily available but expensive, about Rs. 1,000–Rs. 3,500 for 750 ml.

Alcohol at luxury hotels is expensive. Consider purchasing your own liquor and having it in your room—you can always call for a glass, bottled water, and soda. If you're a woman traveling alone, drinking in your room is a better option.

India customs may appear prudish toward drinking—but open a bottle and you may find you're quite popular. According to proper Indian etiquette, alcohol is often excluded from many occasions. When you visit someone's house you may not be offered a drink even in the evening, and the strongest beverage you may get is tea. At many weddings and at festival time alcohol may not be served. Women are infrequent drinkers. However, don't be surprised if you encounter quite a few male teetotalers.

Dry days—when alcohol isn't available anywhere in the country—are observed on January 26, August 15, October 2, and on certain festival dates. Some states observe additional dry days; others prohibit everything but beer. Gujarat is always dry. As a foreigner you may apply to the Gujarat Tourism Development Corporation for a permit that allows you to buy alcohol in the state; Cama Hotel (Khanpur Rd., Ahmedabad ☎ 79/560–1234), has a liquor shop and can organize a liquor permit if you bring your passport. The Government of India Tourist Office in Bombay or Delhi (or even abroad) can also issue a three to six month liquor permit on your passport allowing you to carry liquor into Gujarat.

ELECTRICITY

Blackouts—lasting anywhere from 30 minutes to 12 hours—are a part of everyday Indian life, particularly in summer when the load is high. Storms also play havoc with electricity. In addition, low-voltage electricity and surges are problems. Carry a flashlight at all times, and consider packing a small hand-held fan.

To use electric-powered equipment purchased in the United States or Canada, **bring a converter and adapter.** The electrical current in India is 220 volts, 50 cycles alternating current (AC); wall outlets take plugs with two round prongs.

If your appliances are dual-voltage (as are most laptop computers) or British in origin, you'll need only an adapter. Don't use 110-volt outlets marked FOR SHAVERS ONLY for high-wattage appliances such as hair dryers.

EMBASSIES

🏠 Australia ✉ No. 1/50 G Shantipath, Chanakyapuri, New Delhi ☎ 11/2688-8223.
🏠 Canada ✉ 7/8 Shantipath, Chanakyapuri, New Delhi ☎ 11/5178-2000.
🏠 New Zealand ✉ 50, Edmund Hillary Marg, Chanakyapuri, New Delhi ☎ 11/2688-3170.
🏠 United Kingdom ✉ Shantipath, Chanakyapuri, New Delhi ☎ 11/2687-2161.

🏠 United States ✉ Shantipath, Chanakyapuri, New Delhi ☎ 11/419-8000.
🏠 Indian Embassies Abroad **Australia** ✉ 3-5 Moonah Pl., Yarralumla, Canberra ☎ 26/273-3999 or 26/627-33774 ⊕ www.highcommissionofindiaaustralia.org. **Canada** ✉ 10 Springfield Rd., Ottawa ☎ 613/744-3751 or 613/744-3752 ⊕ www.hciottawa.ca. **New Zealand** ✉ 180 Molesworth St., Wellington ☎ 4/473-6390 or 4/473-6391. **United Kingdom** ✉ India House, Aldwych, London ☎ 71/836-8484 ⊕ www.hcilondon.org. **United States** ✉ 2107 Massachusetts Ave. NW, Washington, DC ☎ 202/939-7000 ⊕ www.indianembassy.org.

EMERGENCIES

Delhi's 24-hour East-West Medical Center has a referral list of doctors, dentists, pharmacists, and lawyers throughout India. Its staffers can arrange treatment wherever you are in the country, and it's the only clinic in India recognized by *most* international insurance companies. Note: you must pay the center when you receive assistance—credit cards are accepted—and then apply for reimbursement by your insurance company later. It's necessary to get in touch with East-West first so that they can verify your policy details. This can take anywhere from a few hours to a day, depending on the day of the week and whether the details are in order; at that point East-West will organize payment.

For life-threatening conditions go to Indraprastha Apollo Hospital, Delhi's premier private hospital, southeast of town. From there, you can call Meera Rescue, based in Delhi with branches in Bombay and Goa, if international evacuation is necessary. (Whatever happens, *do not* go to a government hospital. In a grave emergency, contact your embassy.) Meera Rescue is an extremely professional evacuation service recognized by international insurance companies; the company evacuates from anywhere in the country to hospitals in major cities, as well as overseas if necessary; it's open 24 hours. Like East-West, you must pay Meera and be reimbursed by your insurance company later.

🏠 **Indraprastha Apollo Hospital**
✉ Delhi-Mathura Rd., Sarita Vihar ☎ 11/2692-5801 or 11/2692-5858 ⊕ www.apollohospdelhi.com.

East-West Medical Center ✉ 38 Golf Links, New Delhi 110003 ☎ 11/2462-3738, 11/2469-9229, 11/2469-0429, or 11/2469-8865 🖷 11/469-0428 or 11/463-2382 🌐 www.eastwestrescue.com. **Meera Rescue** ✉ 112 Jor Bagh, New Delhi 110003 ☎ 11/2469-3508 or 11/2465-3170 🖷 11/2461-8286 🌐 www.meera-rescue.com or www.meeraassistance.com.

ETIQUETTE & BEHAVIOR

In India food and food-related hospitality is very important. Indians believe in showing their warmth by feeding a guest endless cups of tea, snacks, and meals. If you refuse to eat a meal or have a cup of tea you may offend your host. Indians also believe in offering food over and over again, and overstuffing the guest. Hospitality always means plying a guest with limitless food and not taking no for an answer. So if you have had enough of something, be firm but polite in your refusals.

If you're invited to a traditional Indian home, observe the prevailing seating rules. Men often sit separate from women. Sometimes, when the men entertain a foreign visitor (even a woman), the women of the house shy away or don't emerge; they may not speak English, or may be mildly xenophobic. Don't be surprised if the woman of the house serves you but doesn't join the gathering. **Don't protest, and don't follow her into the kitchen**—in orthodox Hindu homes the kitchen is frequently off-limits—just accept her behavior as the tradition of this particular home. In some homes, shoes are taken off before entering; here, too, inquire, or watch what the family does.

Numerous customs govern food and the partaking of meals. In many households, you arrive, sit and talk, and then have your meal; after you eat the evening is over. When you eat in remote areas, you may not be given utensils, **eat only with your right hand,** as the left is considered unclean. (Left-handers can use utensils, though left-handedness in general is considered curious.) If you want a second helping or are buying openly displayed food, don't help yourself with your hands; this act pollutes the food. Let your host or vendor serve you.

Indians have an entire set of rules on *jhuta* food, or food that has been touched to your plate, your hand, or your mouth. You do not touch your "food-contaminated" hand to a serving spoon or a pile of rotis or papads. At that time **you must use your clean left hand** to take a fresh serving. You do not touch the serving spoon to your plate. And take care to not mix serving spoons for vegetarian and nonvegetarian food. Do not take a spoon out from a meat dish and use it to serve yourself some rice, for instance. There may be others in the room who do not eat meat or food "contaminated" by meat.

BUSINESS ETIQUETTE

Indians aren't a very formal people, and this carries over into the world of business. Rarely do Indians wear suits to meetings, though ties are now popular. Executives greet each other by shaking hands; occasionally, a woman executive may prefer not to do this. Business cards are de rigueur.

Indians are gracious hosts and will often foot the bill for business lunches or dinners. Unless he or she is invited, do not bring your spouse to a business dinner, but if you were to mention that you are traveling with a spouse your host will most likely suggest that she attend a meal.

SACRED SITES

Religious monuments demand respect. With all of India's faiths, you must **remove your shoes before entering a shrine,** even if it appears to be in ruins. All religions require that you **don't smoke, drink alcohol, or raise your voice** on the premises. Some temples and mosques are off-limits to travelers who don't practice the faith; **don't try to bribe your way inside.** Women visiting sacred places should dress modestly—no shorts and tank tops—and cover their heads before entering a Sikh temple or a mosque. Cameras and video cameras are sometimes prohibited inside houses of worship. On rare occasions, a Hindu or Muslim festival involves animal sacrifice, which may upset you or your child; do a little research on the festival rituals ahead of time.

Some Hindu and Jain temples don't allow any leather products inside their shrines, including wallets, purses, shoes, belts, and camera cases. Many temples also expect you to **purify yourself by washing your hands and feet in a nearby tap or tank before you enter.** In Sikh temples, don't point your feet toward the Holy Book or step over anyone sitting in prayer or meditation. Play it safe in both Hindu and Sikh temples: if you sit on the floor, **sit cross-legged or with your feet tucked beneath you.** In some shrines, the sexes are separated; look around (or follow instructions) and let the situation govern what you do. **Step into the courtyards of mosques with your right foot first.**

Many well-meaning travelers commit an unforgivable sacrilege when they visit a Buddhist monastery. You're welcome to spin any prayer wheel, but just as you must circumambulate the interior and exterior of a monastery, *stupa,* or *mani* wall in a clockwise direction, you must **spin prayer wheels clockwise only.** Inside the monastery, cushions and chairs are reserved for *lamas* (monks), so sit on the steps outside or on the floor. If you meet a *rimpoche* (head lama) or a respected monk, it's polite not to turn your back on him when you leave. Also **remove your hat and lower your umbrella** in the confines of a monastery and in the presence of a lama.

GAY & LESBIAN TRAVEL

Although India is a sexually conservative society, there's a growing awareness and acceptance of homosexuality in major cities. Still, gay and lesbian travelers should keep their sexual preference to themselves. Legally India does not accept homosexuality. No hotel will object to two people of the same sex sharing a room, but **don't display your affection in public.** Note that Indian men and boys commonly walk hand in hand as a sign of friendship. Bombay now has a strong gay community and a few pubs and bars have gay nights.

🏳 Gay- & Lesbian-Friendly Travel Agencies Different Roads Travel ⊠ 8383 Wilshire Blvd., Suite 520, Beverly Hills, CA 90211 ☎ 323/651-5557 or 800/429-8747 (Ext. 14 for both) 🖷 323/651-3678 ✑ lgernert@tzell.com. **Kennedy Travel** ⊠ 130 W. 42nd St., Suite 401, New York, NY 10036 ☎ 212/840-8659 or 800/237-7433 🖷 212/730-2269 ⊕ www.kennedytravel.com. **Now, Voyager** ⊠ 4406 18th St., San Francisco, CA 94114 ☎ 415/626-1169 or 800/255-6951 🖷 415/626-8626 ⊕ www.nowvoyager.com. **Skylink Travel and Tour** ⊠ 1455 N. Dutton Ave., Suite A, Santa Rosa, CA 95401 ☎ 707/546-9888 or 800/225-5759 🖷 707/636-0951, serving lesbian travelers.

FOOD & DRINK

The major health risk in India is traveler's diarrhea, caused by eating contaminated fruit or vegetables or drinking contaminated water. So watch what you eat. Avoid ice, uncooked food, and unpasteurized milk and milk products, and **drink only bottled water or water that has been boiled for 20 minutes.** Avoid tap water, ice, fruit juices, or drinks to which water has been added. **Turn down offers of "filtered" or "aquaguard" water;** it may have been filtered to take out particles but not purified to kill parasites. **Buy bottled water from a reputable shop;** Bisleri, Kinley (a Coca-Cola product), or Aquafina (a Pepsi product) are widely available, reputable brands. **Check that the cap hasn't been tampered with.** Bottles are sometimes refilled with tap water. Soft drinks, in bottles or cans, and packaged fruit juices are safe, readily available options. Always **keep at least one bottle of water in your hotel room** for brushing your teeth as well as for drinking.

Mild cases of intestinal distress may respond to Imodium (known generically as loperamide) or Pepto-Bismol (a little weaker), both of which can be purchased over the counter. Drink plenty of purified water or tea—ginger (*adrak*) tea is a good folk remedy. In severe cases, rehydrate yourself with a salt-sugar solution—½ teaspoon salt (*namak*) and 4 tablespoons sugar (*shakar*) per quart of water. To find out if the water has been boiled for several minutes, ask in Hindi: *Kya aap ne paani ko kafi der se ubala hai?* To ask for a drink without ice: *In usme barf mat daliye bi.* Although it is available, you can not always find Imodium in India, so bring your own.

Avoid raw vegetables and fruit, even those that have been peeled unless it was cut and peeled by you. Stay away from pork products outside luxury hotels; make sure that all meats are thoroughly cooked. It's not necessary to go vegetarian, and to do so would mean missing out on some delicious dishes, just choose restaurants with care, and eat hot foods while they're hot. A little bit of personal hygiene can also go a long way in preventing stomach upsets. Wash your hands before you eat anything, and carry moist towelettes. These are readily available in large cities; Fresh Ones is a common brand.

Know that locally popular, worn-looking restaurants often serve the safest food. Such restaurants often can't afford refrigeration, so the cooks prepare food acquired that day—not always the case with the upscale places. Some hotel chefs buy in bulk and, thanks to temperamental electricity, a refrigerator may preserve more than just foodstuffs. Stomach upsets often are due as much to the richness and spice of Indian cuisine as to the lack of hygiene. Many hotel restaurants cook Indian dishes with quite a bit of oil, which can trigger Delhi Belly. If you have a sensitive stomach, ask the chef to use less oil. Fried foods from street vendors often look delicious, but inspect the oil: if it looks as old as the pot, it could be rancid.

MEDICAL PLANS

No one plans to get sick while traveling, but it happens, so consider signing up with a medical-assistance company. Members get doctor referrals, emergency evacuation or repatriation, hot lines for medical consultation, cash for emergencies, and other assistance.

🔢 Medical-Assistance Companies **International SOS Assistance** ⊕ www.internationalsos.com ✉ New Delhi ☎ 11/2335-2702 ✉ 8 Neshaminy Interplex, Suite 207, Trevose, PA 19053 ☎ 215/245-4707 or 800/523-6586 🖷 215/244-9617 ✉ Landmark House, Hammersmith Bridge Rd., 6th fl., London, W6 9DP ☎ 20/8762-8008 🖷 20/8748-7744 ✉ 12 Chemin Riantbosson, 1217 Meyrin 1, Geneva, Switzerland ☎ 22/785-6464 🖷 22/785-6424 ✉ 331 N. Bridge Rd., 17-00, Odeon Towers, Singapore 188720 ☎ 6338-7800 🖷 6338-7611.

PESTS & OTHER HAZARDS

All Indian cities are heavily polluted, though serious efforts are now in progress to reduce vehicle pollution. Regulations and devices were introduced in 1995, but quite a few vehicles still use leaded gas or diesel fuel. Bombay and Delhi require their taxis to run on compressed natural gas, which has considerably reduced the smog. People with breathing problems, especially asthma, should **carry the appropriate respiratory remedies.** India's heat can dehydrate you, and dust can irritate your throat, so **drink plenty of liquids.** Dehydration will make you weak and more susceptible to other health problems. Seek air-conditioned areas, which are not hard to find; it's not difficult to make certain you are moving from air-conditioned vehicles (train/plane/bus/taxi) to air-conditioned hotels to air-conditioned restaurants or shops. Plan your day so you're visiting tourist sites in the early morning when the sun is less strong.

If you travel into forested areas during or right after monsoon, **protect yourself against leeches** by covering your legs and carrying salt. Don't wear sandals. If a leech clings to your clothing or skin, dab it with a pinch of salt and it will fall off. If itching persists, apply an antiseptic; infection is rare.

For bedbugs, buy a bar of Dettol soap (available throughout India) and use it when you bathe to relieve itching and discomfort. If you're staying in a dubious hotel, **check under the mattress** for bedbugs, cockroaches, and other unwanted critters. Use Flit, Finit, or one of the other readily available spray repellents on suspicious-looking furniture and in mosquito-infested rooms. Tortoise coils, or *kachua,* and Good Knight pellets are fairly effective at "smoking" mosquitoes away; these are either plugged into the wall or lit with a match and placed under a bed or table. On the road, **treat scratches, cuts, or blisters at once.** If you're trekking, save the bottle and cap from your first bottled water so you can refill it with water that you purify yourself.

Send your clothes to be laundered only through decent hotels. *Dhobi,* or washerman's itch—that is, scabies—can be picked up from poorly washed clothes. It's better to **wash your clothes yourself** and send them out for ironing, or give them directly to a reliable dry-cleaner. Definitely wash all underwear and lingerie yourself.

Beware of overexposure even on overcast days. To avoid sunburn, **use a sunscreen** with a sun-protection factor of at least 24. To play it safe, **wear a wide-brimmed hat.** If you plan to travel above 10,000 feet, use zinc oxide, lip balm with sunblock, and sunglasses that block ultraviolet rays. When you're on snowy terrain, remember that UV rays reflect from below.

If you're up in the mountains, watch out for signs of altitude sickness, an adverse reaction to low oxygen pressure—it can be deadly. If your urine turns bright yellow, you're not drinking enough water. To minimize high-altitude misery, **drink lots of water, eat foods high in carbohydrates, and cut back on salt.** Stop and rest immediately if you develop any of the following symptoms: nausea, loss of appetite, extreme headache or lightheadedness, unsteady feet, sleeplessness. If resting doesn't help, head for lower ground immediately.

SHOTS & MEDICATIONS

No vaccination certificate or inoculations are required to enter India from the United States, Canada, or the United Kingdom unless you're coming via Africa, in which case, you'll need proof of inoculation against yellow fever. If you're coming from Africa it's crucial to have proof of inoculation against yellow fever or you will be quarantined on arrival in dismal government facilities. **Talk to your doctor about vaccinations three months before departure.** The Centers for Disease Control and Prevention post a list of recommended vaccinations for the Indian subcontinent on its Web site; these include hepatitis and typhoid fever.

In areas where malaria and dengue—both carried by mosquitoes—are prevalent, use mosquito nets, wear clothing that covers the body, apply repellent containing DEET, and use spray for flying insects in living and sleeping areas. On arrival in India, you'd be wise to purchase repellants that plug into the wall and release a mosquito-repelling scent. These are effec-

tive in keeping a room mosquito-free. (Try Good Knight or All Out.) **Consider taking antimalaria pills,** as malaria is common even in the big cities. There's no vaccine to combat dengue.

Bring a medical kit containing aspirin or its equivalent, diarrhea medication, moist towelettes, antibacterial skin ointment and skin cleanser, antacids, antihistamines, dandruff shampoo, adhesive bandages, antibiotics, a water-purification kit, and plastic strip thermometers.

⑦ Health Warnings National Centers for Disease Control and Prevention (CDC) ✉ National Center for Infectious Diseases, Division of Quarantine, Travelers' Health, 1600 Clifton Rd. NE, Atlanta, GA 30333 ☎ 877/394-8747 international travelers' health line, 404/498-1600 Division of Quarantine, 800/311-3435 other inquiries 🖷 888/232-3299 ⊕ www.cdc.gov/travel.

GIFTS

If you visit someone's home for dinner or you're staying with an Indian family be sure to bring a gift from abroad. If there are youngsters in the home, bring something for them. Liquor, toys, cosmetics, perfume, and aftershaves are all excellent options.

HOLIDAYS

India's fixed national holidays are January 26 (Republic Day), August 15 (Independence Day), October 2 (Gandhi's birthday), and December 25 (Christmas). Endless festivals enliven—and shut down—different parts of the country throughout the year. Festivals often affect availability of travel connections or the time taken to reach the airport so do inquire about holidays coming up before you plan your itinerary.

INSURANCE

The most useful travel-insurance plan is a comprehensive policy that includes coverage for trip cancellation and interruption, default, trip delay, and medical expenses (with a waiver for preexisting conditions).

Without insurance you'll lose all or most of your money if you cancel your trip, regardless of the reason. Default insurance covers you if your tour operator, airline, or cruise line goes out of business. Trip-delay covers expenses that arise because of bad weather or mechanical delays. Study the fine print when comparing policies.

If you're traveling internationally, a key component of travel insurance is coverage for medical bills incurred if you get sick on the road. Such expenses aren't generally covered by Medicare or private policies. U.K. residents can buy a travel-insurance policy valid for most vacations taken during the year in which it's purchased (but check preexisting-condition coverage). British and Australian citizens need extra medical coverage when traveling overseas.

Always **buy travel policies directly from the insurance company**; if you buy them from a cruise line, airline, or tour operator that goes out of business you probably won't be covered for the agency or operator's default, a major risk. Before making any purchase, review your existing health and home-owner's policies to find what they cover away from home.

🚩 Travel Insurers In the U.S.: **Access America** ✉ 6600 W. Broad St., Richmond, VA 23230 ☎ 800/284-8300 🖷 804/673-1491 or 800/346-9265 ⊕ www.accessamerica.com. **Travel Guard International** ✉ 1145 Clark St., Stevens Point, WI 54481 ☎ 715/345-0505 or 800/826-1300 🖷 800/955-8785 ⊕ www.travelguard.com.

🚩 In the U.K.: **Association of British Insurers** ✉ 51 Gresham St., London EC2V 7HQ ☎ 020/7600-3333 🖷 020/7696-8999 ⊕ www.abi.org.uk. In Canada: **RBC Insurance** ✉ 6880 Financial Dr., Mississauga, Ontario L5N 7Y5 ☎ 800/565-3129 🖷 905/813-4704 ⊕ www.rbcinsurance.com. In Australia: **Insurance Council of Australia** ✉ Insurance Enquiries and Complaints, Level 3, 56 Pitt St., Sydney, NSW 2000 ☎ 1300/363683 or 02/9251-4456 🖷 02/9251-4453 ⊕ www.iecltd.com.au. In New Zealand: **Insurance Council of New Zealand** ✉ Level 7, 111–115 Customhouse Quay, Box 474, Wellington ☎ 04/472-5230 🖷 04/473-3011 ⊕ www.icnz.org.nz.

LANGUAGE

A good portion of India is bilingual, and you'll find many people who speak English and their native language with equal fluency. Hindi is the national language, but India isn't truly unified linguistically—most states and countless smaller areas have their own tongues. The country functions in English alongside Hindi, however, so barring rural areas you aren't likely to experience too much of a language barrier.

LODGING

The lodgings we list are the cream of the crop in each price category. We always list the facilities that are available, but we don't specify whether they cost extra; when pricing accommodations, always ask what's included and what costs extra. Properties are assigned price categories based on the range between their least and most expensive standard double rooms at high season, which in India is approximately November through February, excluding Christmas and New Year's. Properties marked ✕🖾 are lodging establishments whose restaurants warrant a special trip. Assume that hotels operate on the European Plan (EP, with no meals) unless we specify that they use the Continental Plan (CP, with a Continental breakfast), Breakfast Plan (BP, with a full breakfast), Modified American Plan (MAP, with breakfast and dinner), Full American Plan (FAP, with all meals), or are all-inclusive (including all meals and most activities). When you book a room at a hotel, however (especially an expensive hotel), ask for their best rate and push them to include breakfast and a station or airport pick-up. Be a hard bargainer; consider asking them to knock the rate down further, even after they have given you a discount. You can always shop around and come back.

Secure all room reservations before arrival, especially during peak season (September to March) and in the major cities and popular tourist destinations, such as Bombay, Delhi, Agra, Kerala, and Goa. Indians vacation during school holidays in April, May, and early June; for a few days in October or November (for Diwali, or, in eastern India, Durga Puja); and for 10 days between Christmas and the New Year. Reservations are extra-difficult during these times.

Room rates are skyrocketing in business-oriented cities, such as Bangalore, Bombay, Calcutta, Delhi, and Madras. Urban hotels rarely have off-season discounts, though some international chains have incentive programs for frequent guests. In other areas, hotels may be seeking guests, so you may be able to negotiate your price. When you reserve, **ask about additional taxes** and service charges, which increase the quoted room price. Do not agree to an airport pick-up or breakfast without asking if these services involve extra costs. Airport pick-ups organized by luxury hotels are expensive.

Delhi and Bombay are in a financial league of their own, so chapters in this book for those cities are assigned higher pricing categories for lodging. For the rest of India, categories are divided as follows: major cities, including Agra, Bangalore, Calcutta, Jaipur, Madras, Pune, and Varanasi, are in a second-tier. Lodging categories in other areas of India reflect substantially less expensive prices.

GOVERNMENT LODGING

The national and state governments, the public works department, and the forestry department manage inexpensive accommodations throughout India. Most of these facilities are poorly maintained, and government employees and officials receive priority booking. Some states, however—particularly Madhya Pradesh, Maharashtra, and Kerala—run fairly competent hotels and often provide the best lodgings in remote destinations. For more information contact the tourist office in the capital of the state you plan to visit.

HERITAGE HOTELS

The Indian government has an excellent incentive program that encourages owners of traditional *havelis* (mansions), forts, and palaces to convert their properties into hotels or bring existing historic hotels up to government standards. (But do be careful where you stay, because government standards aren't always ideal for Westerners.) Many of these official Heritage Hotels—noted in reviews throughout this guide—are well outside large cities. Their architecture and style are authentically Indian, not Western. If this type of lodging appeals to you, contact the Government of India Tourist Office for a list of Heritage Hotels. There are more than 60 such establishments in Ra-

jasthan; about 15 in Gujarat; and 1 or 2 in Madhya Pradesh, Himachal Pradesh, Kerala, and other states.

HOSTELS

No matter what your age, you can save on lodging costs by staying at hostels. In some 4,500 locations in more than 70 countries around the world, Hostelling International (HI), the umbrella group for a number of national youth-hostel associations, offers single-sex, dorm-style beds and, at many hostels, rooms for couples and family accommodations. Membership in any HI national hostel association, open to travelers of all ages, allows you to stay in HI-affiliated hostels at member rates; one-year membership is about $28 for adults (C$35 for a two-year minimum membership in Canada, £13.50 in the U.K., A$52 in Australia, and NZ$40 in New Zealand); hostels charge about $10–$30 per night. Members have priority if the hostel is full; they're also eligible for discounts around the world, even on rail and bus travel in some countries.

▣ Organizations Hostelling International–USA ✉ 8401 Colesville Rd., Suite 600, Silver Spring, MD 20910 ☎ 301/495-1240 🖷 301/495-6697 ⊕ www.hiayh.org. **Hostelling International–Canada** ✉ 205 Catherine St., Suite 400, Ottawa, Ontario K2P 1C3 ☎ 613/237-7884 or 800/663-5777 🖷 613/237-7868 ⊕ www.hihostels.ca. **YHA England and Wales** ✉ Trevelyan House, Dimple Rd., Matlock, Derbyshire DE4 3YH, U.K. ☎ 0870/870-8808, 0870/770-8868, or 0162/959-2700 🖷 0870/770-6127 ⊕ www.yha.org.uk. **YHA Australia** ✉ 422 Kent St., Sydney, NSW 2001 ☎ 02/9261-1111 🖷 02/9261-1969 ⊕ www.yha.com.au. **YHA New Zealand** ✉ Level 4, Torrens House, 195 Hereford St., Box 436, Christchurch ☎ 03/379-9970 or 0800/278-299 🖷 03/365-4476 ⊕ www.yha.org.nz.

HOTELS

India's tourism department approves and classifies hotels based on a rating system of five stars (the fanciest) to no stars (no frills). The ratings are based on the number of facilities and on hotel and bedroom size. Hotels without pools or those that serve only vegetarian food—including some historic, charming, comfortable properties—don't qualify for five-star status but are often just as luxurious as those that do. The rating system also fails to take service and other important intangibles into account. Although these ratings can be misleading, tour operators often use them, so ask what a star-rating means when booking.

In small towns, opt for the best room in the best hotel. If the room or bathroom still looks doubtful, tip the bellboy to have it re-cleaned in front of you. Regardless of where you stay, **inspect your room before checking in,** even if you have a prior reservation. Examine the door lock, the air-conditioner, the curtains, and the bathroom and its plumbing (hot water, toilet flush). Be sure the room has candles, matches, a telephone for room service, and sufficient bed linen. Confirm that renovations aren't taking place nearby.

If you opt for room service in your hotel, instead of dining elsewhere, here are a few tips to remember if you're not staying in a luxury hotel. Tea or coffee, unless specified comes premixed. Ask to have a pot of tea or coffee with the milk, sugar, and tea bags or coffee powder brought separately. Ask that your food be cooked with less oil and specify your spice preferences. Ask for fruit juice without ice or sugar. Make sure the mineral water is sealed and do not use water from flasks in the room.

🚩 **Toll-Free Numbers Best Western** ☎ 800/528-1234 ⊕ www.bestwestern.com. **Choice** ☎ 800/221-2222 ⊕ www.choicehotels.com. **Comfort Inn** ☎ 800/424-6423 ⊕ www.choicehotels.com. **Days Inn** ☎ 800/325-2525 ⊕ www.daysinn.com. **Hilton** ☎ 800/445-8667 ⊕ www.hilton.com. **Holiday Inn** ☎ 800/465-4329 ⊕ www.sixcontinentshotels.com. **Howard Johnson** ☎ 800/446-4656 ⊕ www.hojo.com. **Hyatt Hotels & Resorts** ☎ 800/233-1234 ⊕ www.hyatt.com. **Inter-Continental** ☎ 800/327-0000 ⊕ www.intercontinental.com. **Marriott** ☎ 800/228-9290 ⊕ www.marriott.com. **Le Meridien** ☎ 800/543-4300 ⊕ www.lemeridien-hotels.com. **Nikko Hotels International** ☎ 800/645-5687 ⊕ www.nikkohotels.com. **Oberoi Hotels** ☎ 800/562-3764 in U.S. and Canada, 800/1234-0101 in U.K. and western Europe ⊕ www.oberoihotels.com. **Quality Inn** ☎ 800/424-6423 ⊕ www.choicehotels.com. **Radisson** ☎ 800/333-3333 ⊕ www.radisson.com. **Ramada** ☎ 800/228-2828, 800/854-7854 international reservations ⊕ www.ramada.com or

www.ramadahotels.com. **Renaissance Hotels & Resorts** ☎ 800/468-3571 ⊕ www.renaissancehotels.com. **Sheraton** ☎ 800/325-3535 ⊕ www.starwood.com/sheraton.

🚩 **Indian Hotel Chains Ashok Hotels** Reserve through a travel agent or Ashok Sales Office ⊠ Jeevan Vihar, 3rd fl., 3 Sansad Marg, New Delhi 110001 ☎ 11/2336-0607 ⊕ www.theashokgroup.com. **Clarks** ⊠ U.P. Hotels, 1101 Surya Kiran, 19 Kasturba Gandhi Marg, New Delhi 110001 ☎ 11/2331-2367 or 11/2331-2515 ⊕ www.hotelclarks.com. **Indian Heritage Hotels Association** ⊠ 306 Anukampa Tower, Church Rd., Jaipur 302001 ☎ 141/371-194, 141/374-112, or 141/374-130 ⊕ www.heritagehotels.com. **Oberoi Hotels** ⊠ New Delhi ☎ 11/2389-0606 ⊕ www.oberoihotels.com. **Taj Group** ☎ 800/458-8825, 212/515-5889 in U.S., 800/282-699 in U.K. ⊕ www.tajhotels.com. **Welcomgroup** ⊠ A-9 U. S. O. Rd., Qutab Institutional Area, New Delhi ☎ 11/2685-0242 ⊕ www.welcomgroup.com.

MAIL & SHIPPING

Airmail letters and postcards take a week to 10 days to reach most destinations from India. Postal delays are caused by holiday rushes (during Diwali and the Christmas season) and strikes.

EXPRESS-MAIL SERVICES

Express mail is known as "speed post" in India. There are speed-post centers all over the country; they're generally open daily from 9 to 5. It costs Rs. 425 to send a letter or parcel of 250 grams or less to Australia, Canada, New Zealand, or the United States, and Rs. 675 to the United Kingdom. Every additional 250 gram will cost Rs. 100 for U.S. and Canadian destinations and Rs. 75 for destinations in Australia, New Zealand, or the United Kingdom. You can send a package that weighs as much as 20 kg by speed post.

Private couriers and parcel companies—Airborne Express, Blue Dart, DHL, UPS—operate in India as well. A letter sent through such a service takes about three working days to reach Australia, Canada, New Zealand, the United Kingdom, or the United States. Rates are higher than speed-post rates.

POSTAL RATES

Airmail letters (weighing 10 grams) to the Australia, New Zealand, United States,

Canada, South Africa, or Europe cost Rs. 15; airmail postcards cost Rs. 15. Aerograms to anywhere in the world are Rs. 8.50.

RECEIVING MAIL

To receive mail in India, **have letters or packages sent to an American Express office.** Mail is held at these offices for 30 days before it's returned to the sender; it can also be forwarded for a nominal charge. To retrieve your mail, show your American Express card or American Express Travelers Checks plus one piece of identification, preferably a passport. This service is free to AmEx cardmembers and traveler's-check holders; others pay a fee.

SHIPPING PARCELS

You can send parcels home "surface air lifted," a special service provided by the Indian postal department that's cheaper than airmail. A letter or parcel of 250 grams or less costs Rs. 395 to Australia, Canada or New Zealand, Rs. 470 to the United Kingdom and the United States.

MONEY MATTERS

India is cheaper than most destinations when it comes to shopping, eating, and staying in comfortable hotels. Domestic travel is on the rise and room rates at fancy urban hotels are comparable to those in New York, London, or Paris. All top hotels and some airlines charge foreigners US-dollar prices that are substantially higher than the rupee prices paid by Indians.

A cup of tea from a stall costs about Rs. 2 (US$5–10¢), but in top hotels it can cost more than Rs. 45 (US$1). A 650-ml bottle of beer costs about Rs. 45 (US$1) in a shop, Rs. 200 (US$4) without taxes in a top hotel. A 5-km (3-mi) taxi ride in Delhi is supposed to cost about Rs. 65 (US$1.50), though it rarely does. Throughout this book, we quote admission fees for adults, which in India are usually the same as those for children.

ATMS

There are only a few cash machines in smaller towns in India. Larger cities are dotted with ATMs. Look for ICICI, HDFC, or HSBC ATMs. If you think you'll need cash from your bank account

or cash advances through your credit card, **make sure that your bank and credit cards are programmed for ATM use in India** before you leave home and make sure you have (or obtain) a four-digit PIN, because the ATM will require it.

CREDIT CARDS

American Express is not widely accepted in India; neither is Diner's Club, and Discover isn't accepted at all. In this book we use the following abbreviations: **AE,** American Express; **DC,** Diner's Club; **MC,** MasterCard; **V,** Visa. Make sure you check with your credit card company to find out the number (or Web site) for reporting lost or stolen cards abroad.

CURRENCY

The units of Indian currency are the *rupee* and the *paisa*—100 paise equal one rupee. Paper money comes in denominations of 2, 5, 10, 20, 50, 100, 500, and 1,000 rupees. Coins are worth 5, 10, 20, 25, and 50 paise, 1 rupee, 2 rupees, and 5 rupees. At this writing, the rate of exchange was approximately US$1 = Rs. 48; £1 = Rs. 69; C$1 = Rs. 30; AUS$1 = Rs. 25; NZ$1 = Rs. 20.

CURRENCY EXCHANGE

India has strict rules against importing or exporting its currency. The currency-exchange booths at the international airports are always open for arriving and departing overseas flights. When you change money, remember to get a certain amount in small denominations to pay taxi drivers and such. **Reject torn, frayed, taped, or soiled bills,** as many merchants, hotels, and restaurants won't accept them, and it's a hassle to find a bank to get them exchanged.

Always **change money from an authorized money-changer and insist on receiving an encashment slip.** Some banks now charge a nominal fee for this slip, which you'll need if you want to pay hotel bills or travel expenses in rupees, and again if you want to reconvert rupees into your own currency on departure from India. Don't be lured by illegal street hawkers who offer you a higher exchange rate.

For the most favorable rates, **change money at banks.** Although ATM transaction fees may be higher abroad than at home, ATM rates are excellent because they're based on wholesale rates offered only by major banks. India's state-run banks can take forever to cash traveler's checks; if possible, save time and use an American Express office or the foreign-exchange service at your hotel. Rates will be slightly lower, but you'll save irritation and time. Rates are also unfavorable in airports, at train and bus stations, in restaurants, and in stores.

Exchange Services International Currency Express ✉ 427 N. Camden Dr., Suite F, Beverly Hills, CA 90210 ☎ 888/278-6628 orders 🖷 310/278-6410 ⊕ www.foreignmoney.com. **Thomas Cook International Money Services** ☎ 800/287-7362 orders and retail locations ⊕ www.us.thomascook.com.

TRAVELER'S CHECKS

Traveler's checks are best exchanged in major cities as soon as you need more cash. Most merchants, whether urban or rural, don't accept them. Lost or stolen checks can usually be replaced within 24 hours. To ensure a speedy refund, buy your own traveler's checks—don't let someone else pay for them. The person who bought the checks should also make the call to request a refund. **Don't leave traveler's checks in your hotel room, and keep the counterfoil with the check numbers separate from the checks.**

NEWSPAPERS & MAGAZINES

Several English-language newspapers are read in India—*Hindustan Times,* the *Hindu,* the *Indian Express,* the *Telegraph,* the *Times of India,* and the *Deccan Herald*—and are readily available. These papers will keep you up-to-date with world affairs, too. Just about any international magazine or newspaper is available in luxury hotel bookshops and large bookstores in larger cities. *India Today, Business India,* the *Week,* and the *Outlook* are magazines that may give you some insight into India. Consider buying a few issues beforehand, at an Indian grocer abroad, to familiarize yourself with India. Or read *India Abroad* or *India West,* also available at Indian grocers, but only in the United States and Canada; these are papers marketed to the Indian-American–Canadian

community. Or log onto www.rediff.com or www.thehindu.com.

PACKING

Delicate fabrics don't stand up well to Indian laundering facilities except at deluxe hotels. Although dry-cleaning is available at all top hotels in major cities, the cleaning fluid can be harsh. Plain cottons and cotton–synthetic blends are coolest in summer and easiest to wash; in general, **avoid synthetic fabrics that don't breathe.** Pack a hat; the sun is strong. Sensible footwear is necessary—a pair of rubber sandals and comfortable walking shoes. Hiking boots, though comfortable, are inappropriate for Indian travel; they're hot and are difficult to unlace when you want to remove your shoes to enter religious spots.

Most importantly, **dress modestly.** Only children can get away with short shorts. Men should wear comfortable jeans or longer shorts. T-shirts are fine, but the male topless look should be left to wandering *sadhus* (Hindu ascetics). To deter undesired attention and command more respect, women should **most definitely avoid tight tank tops or sheer tops, and those with plunging necklines—or see-through dresses. Stick to long skirts or lightweight slacks regardless of the weather.** It's not that Indian girls never wear shorts or miniskirts but foreigners wearing shorts attract more attention. Bring a pair of shorts along and depending on where you're going, and after judging the milieu, wear them; wearing respectable-looking shorts in Goa is usually not a problem. Also avoid doing odd things like wearing a kurta as a dress or a sari blouse as a top.

To visit sacred sites, women *must* wear a below-the-knee skirt or dress or neat pants. Travel in a Muslim community calls for even more discretion: women should consider wearing a *salwar kameez,* the popular Indian outfit of a long tunic over loose pants gathered at the ankle. (A cotton one is inexpensive, comfortable, and flattering.) Bathing suits should be conservative. All that said, India is not a dressy society. If you attend an upscale function (barring weddings), men can wear a standard business suit or even just a formal shirt and pants; women can wear a dress or skirt and blouse with flats or low heels. But do pack that dress, skirt, blouse, or formal shirt, because as hospitable as India is, you may very well be invited to dinner or need it for an evening at a nightclub or upscale restaurant.

A money pouch or belt is especially useful for Indian travel, as are medical and hygienic supplies (including towelettes and a hand-sanitizing liquid); a sewing kit; a lock and key for each piece of luggage; a high-power, impact-resistant flashlight; and spare batteries (unless they're a popular size). Good sanitary napkins are sold in India, but tampons are substandard; plan accordingly. For bird-watching or wildlife-spotting, bring binoculars. Sports enthusiasts should bring their own tennis or golf balls, which are expensive in India. Smokers should carry their own cigarettes, cigars, and pipe tobacco; low-nicotine cigarettes aren't readily available. You might also consider carrying packaged snack or granola bars.

If you visit in monsoon season, bring a collapsible umbrella. In winter, bring a sweater or a light jacket for cool evenings, and **if you plan to spend time in the Himalayas, bring a warm wardrobe.** Plan to triple layer: the first layer (long johns) should be made of synthetic fabrics or silk that carry moisture away from the skin (cotton soaks up perspiration and keeps you wet). Wool, fleece, or a synthetic fabric knitted into thick pile make a good second layer. Bring a down vest if you anticipate extremely cold weather. For the third layer, opt for a well-made, oversize windbreaker or lightweight parka insulated with a small amount of down and made of Gore-Tex (or an equivalent fiber like Zepel or VersaTech); such material not only allows moisture to escape but is waterproof—not merely water-repellent. Bulky down parkas are advisable only for winter excursions or a climb into higher altitudes. A pair of lined Gore-Tex over-pants is indispensable when you're thrashing through wet underbrush.

Most adventure-travel firms supply sleeping bags for their clients. If you're roughing it on your own, choose a lightweight sleeping bag with an outer shell. You don't need a bag designed for an assault on a mountain peak unless that's the trip you've planned. A down bag guaranteed to keep you warm at 15°F (a fairly low temperature in the Himalayan trekking season) is adequate. If you plan to take overnight trains, consider a sleeping-bag liner. On any outdoor adventure, long or short, **assemble a day pack for your sweater, camera, moist towelettes, and plastic water bottle.** Trekkers should also pack out their nonbiodegradable garbage and bury biodegradable refuse away from water sources. Use a trekking agency that carries kerosene for cooking.

In your carry-on luggage, pack an extra pair of eyeglasses or contact lenses and enough of any medication you take to last a few days longer than the entire trip. You may also ask your doctor to write a spare prescription using the drug's generic name, as brand names may vary from country to country. In luggage to be checked, **never pack prescription drugs, valuables, or undeveloped film.** And don't forget to carry with you the addresses of offices that handle refunds of lost traveler's checks. Check *Fodor's How to Pack* (available at online retailers and bookstores everywhere) for more tips.

To avoid customs and security delays, carry medications in their original packaging. Don't pack any sharp objects in your carry-on luggage, including knives of any size or material, scissors, and corkscrews, or anything else that might arouse suspicion.

To avoid having your checked luggage chosen for hand inspection, don't cram bags full. The U.S. Transportation Security Adminstration (TSA) suggests packing shoes on top and placing personal items you don't want touched in clear plastic bags.

CHECKING LUGGAGE

You're allowed to carry aboard one bag and one personal article, such as a purse or a laptop computer. Make sure what you carry on fits under your seat or in the overhead bin. Get to the gate early, so you can board as soon as possible, before the overhead bins fill up.

Baggage allowances vary by carrier, destination, and ticket class. On international flights, you're usually allowed to check two bags weighing up to 70 pounds (32 kilograms) each, although a few airlines allow checked bags of up to 88 pounds (40 kilograms) in first class. Some international carriers don't allow more than 66 pounds (30 kilograms) per bag in business class and 44 pounds (20 kilograms) in economy. On domestic flights, the limit is usually 50 to 70 pounds (23 to 32 kilograms) per bag. In general, carry-on bags shouldn't exceed 40 pounds (18 kilograms). Most airlines won't accept bags that weigh more than 100 pounds (45 kilograms) on domestic or international flights. Check baggage restrictions with your carrier before you pack.

Airline liability for baggage is limited to $2,500 per person on flights within the United States. On international flights it amounts to $9.07 per pound or $20 per kilogram for checked baggage (roughly $640 per 70-pound bag), with a maximum of $634.90 per piece, and $400 per passenger for unchecked baggage. You can buy additional coverage at check-in for about $10 per $1,000 of coverage, but it often excludes a rather extensive list of items, shown on your airline ticket.

Before departure, itemize your bags' contents and their worth, and label the bags with your name, address, and phone number. (If you use your home address, cover it so potential thieves can't see it readily.) Include a label inside each bag and **pack a copy of your itinerary.** At check-in, make sure each bag is correctly tagged with the destination airport's three-letter code. Because some checked bags will be opened for hand inspection, the TSA recommends that you leave luggage unlocked or use the plastic locks offered at check-in. TSA screeners place an inspection notice inside searched bags, which are resealed with a special lock.

If your bag has been searched and contents are missing or damaged, file a claim with the TSA Consumer Response Center as soon as possible. If your bags arrive damaged or fail to arrive at all, file a written report with the airline before leaving the airport.

🚩 Complaints **U.S. Transportation Security Administration Consumer Response Center** ☎ 866/ 289-9673 ⊕ www.tsa.gov.

PASSPORTS & VISAS

When traveling internationally, carry your passport even if you don't need one (it's always the best form of I.D.) and **make two photocopies of the data page** (one for someone at home and another for you, carried separately from your passport). If you lose your passport, promptly call the nearest embassy or consulate and the local police.

U.S. passport applications for children under age 14 require consent from both parents or legal guardians; both parents must appear together to sign the application. If only one parent appears, he or she must submit a written statement from the other parent authorizing passport issuance for the child. A parent with sole authority must present evidence of it when applying; acceptable documentation includes the child's certified birth certificate listing only the applying parent, a court order specifically permitting this parent's travel with the child, or a death certificate for the nonapplying parent. Application forms and instructions are available on the Web site of the U.S. State Department's Bureau of Consular Affairs (⊕ www.travel.state.gov).

ENTERING INDIA

Unless you hold an Indian passport or are a citizen of Nepal or Bhutan, you need a visa to enter India. This applies to children and infants as well. A standard, multiple-entry six-month tourist visa costs US$60 for Americans. If you are not American, or if you're not a foreigner in America, check with your government or the Indian consulate for fees. **Make sure you follow all directions exactly, and do not wait until the last minute to get your visa.** You must arrive in India within six months of the date your visa is issued. If you need to extend your visa, go to the Foreigners' Regional Registration Office in one of the major cities or any of the Offices of the Superintendent of Police in the District Headquarters. (Note that travelers to certain parts of the Himalayas need special permits. Bring extra passport photographs; you may need them for these permits.)

You can obtain a visa through the mail by paying additional postal costs, but this takes up to a month. To prevent delays get your Indian visa in your home country through the Indian embassy or a consulate or through your travel agent or tour operator. If you're traveling on business or as a student, or you work in journalism or publishing, you require a different (and costlier) three-month visa; be sure to check. The Indian government operates a Web site that provides visa information and the appropriate forms.

If you're entering India with dutiable or valuable articles, you must stop at customs and mention this; officials may ask you to fill in a Tourist Baggage Re-Export Form (TBRE), as such articles must be re-exported when you depart. You'll have to pay a duty on anything listed on the TBRE that is not being re-exported. Depending on the attitude of the customs official, you may have to list your laptop computer, camera or video equipment, and mobile phone on a TBRE form. However, it's not a good idea to go searching out a form or a customs officer if you are not queried.

You may bring the following into India duty-free: personal effects (clothing and jewelry); cameras and up to 20 rolls of film; a camcorder with accessories and not more than 12 cassettes; binoculars; a portable television; a laptop computer; a cell phone; an electronic diary; professional audio or video equipment; a stroller; a portable typewriter; a portable musical instrument; a radio or portable tape recorder; a tent and camping equipment; sports equipment (a sporting firearm with 50 cartridges, a canoe, a bicycle, a golf set and a dozen balls, a fishing rod, a pair of skis, two tennis rackets); 200 cigarettes or 50 cigars or 250 grams of tobacco; 1 liter of liquor each; and gifts not exceeding a value of Rs. 4,000 (about US$80). You may *not* bring in dangerous or addictive drugs, firearms, gold coins, gold and silver bullion or silver coins not in use, Indian currency, or plants.

Visa Information ⊕ www.indiacgny.org/visainst.htm.

LEAVING INDIA

Rupees aren't allowed out of India; you must exchange them before you depart. Foreign-exchange facilities are usually in the same airport halls as the check-in counters—note that you'll have no access to these facilities once you pass through immigration. Tourists cannot take out more foreign currency then they brought in. There is no limit on gold jewelry.

All animal products, souvenirs, and trophies are subject to the Wildlife Protection Act of 1972. The export of ivory (unless you can prove it's antique) and skins made from protected species aren't allowed, and such items aren't allowed *into* many other countries, including the United States, anyway. Export of exotic birds, wildlife, orchids, and other flora and fauna is forbidden as well. You may make queries with the regional deputy director for wildlife preservation or the chief wildlife wardens of the state government at Bombay, Calcutta, Delhi, and Madras.

In general items more than 100 years old cannot be exported without a permit from the Archaeological Survey, which has offices in many cities, including Delhi, Bombay, Calcutta, Bhubaneswar, Madras, and Bangalore. Reputable shops will provide you with the necessary permit or help you procure it.

PASSPORT OFFICES

Australian Citizens Passports Australia ☎ 131-232 ⊕ www.passports.gov.au.

Canadian Citizens Passport Office ✉ To mail in applications: 200 Promenade du Portage, Hull, Québec J8X 4B7 ☎ 819/994-3500 or 800/567-6868 ⊕ www.ppt.gc.ca.

New Zealand Citizens New Zealand Passports Office ☎ 0800/22-5050 or 04/474-8100 ⊕ www.passports.govt.nz.

U.K. Citizens U.K. Passport Service ☎ 0870/521-0410 ⊕ www.passport.gov.uk.

F U.S. Citizens **National Passport Information Center** ☎ 900/225-5674, 900/225-7778 TTY, calls are 55¢ per minute for automated service or $1.50 per minute for operator service, 888/362-8668, 888/498-3648 TTY, calls are $5.50 each ⊕ www.travel.state.gov.

REST ROOMS

When you need a rest room, ask for the "loo" or the toilet. Two types of toilets are available wherever you go in India. Traditional Indian toilets are holes in the ground—a squat variety with two steps to put your feet. Western-style toilets are also easily available, but the toilet seat, except in luxury hotels and better restaurants, may be messy—so it's not a good idea to sit on it, and you'll probably find the traditional toilet more hygienic. In many bathrooms you'll see a faucet, a small hand-held shower head, and/or a bucket with a beaker or other small vessel; Indians use these to rinse, bidet-style, after using the toilet. Hands are always washed elsewhere. Keep toilet paper handy (toilet paper, paper towels, and clean soap are often not available), and bring towelettes. Outside of hotels and some restaurants, clean public rest rooms are hard to find, and are best avoided. On long road journeys finding any public rest room—let alone a clean one—is difficult. Always use the rest room before you set out and ration your fluid intake during a long journey. Be on the look out for a decent hotel or opt for the outdoors. Luxury hotels and fancier restaurants usually have clean bathrooms.

Nicer hotels and restaurants provide toilet paper, but you can't depend on this, as most Indians don't use the stuff (they use their left hand, which is why this hand is considered unclean). And often soap and paper towels are not available for washing up afterwards. **Keep toilet paper and towelettes with you at all times;** it's readily available in pharmacies and grocery stores in large cities. **Never throw anything in a toilet;** India's septic systems can't handle it. In many bathrooms you'll find sanitary bags, which you can use, close, and place in the trash bin.

SAFETY

Avoid leaving unlocked suitcases in your hotel room, and unless your room has a safe, **never leave money, traveler's checks, passports, or jewelry in a hotel room.** Even when you are in your hotel room or showering do not leave your passports, tickets and purse in view; tuck them away. Don't even leave other personal items—cosmetics, perfume, aftershave—strewn about; you don't want them to get pinched either. Avoid wandering around late at night, especially in smaller towns where shutters close early, and avoid road journeys after dark. As anywhere, never leave suitcases unattended in airports or train stations.

India has no tourist police, except in Bombay, and they patrol infrequently in orange jeeps. The most visible policemen are traffic cops, clad in white and khaki; they can usually help out, even with a nontraffic problem (though taxis are in their jurisdiction). Otherwise, look for a regular policeman, clad in khaki.

LOCAL SCAMS

Avoid strangers who offer their services as guides or money changers and do not agree to be taken anywhere with anyone. In crowds, **be alert for pickpockets**—wear a money belt, and/or keep your purse close to your body and securely closed. Be careful, too, when you use credit cards; when dining out, you can ask that the machine be brought to your table to make sure the card isn't used to make an impression on more than one form. If you travel by train, **don't accept food or beverages from a fellow passenger.** Foreigners who accept such generosity sometimes ingest drug-laced refreshment and are robbed once the drug takes effect. It's very likely that you will be offered food on a train; Indians feel uncomfortable eating meals in front of another without sharing, but politely offer an excuse and refuse. In train stations, **ignore touts who tell you that your hotel of choice is full or has closed;** they hope to settle you into a place where they get a kickback for bringing in business. **Do not agree to carry a parcel for anyone.**

WOMEN IN INDIA

It doesn't take much imagination to figure out the people, places, and things a lone woman should avoid: traveling late at night in town or out of town (or even earlier in the evening in smaller places and Delhi); avoiding seedy areas, hotels, touts volunteering their services, or over-friendly strangers; and jostling crowds of men. Also, **never get into a taxi or auto-rickshaw if a second man accompanies the driver.** If you find yourself in a tricky situation—a taxi driver demanding a king's ransom, a hawker plaguing you, a stranger following you—head straight for a policeman or at least threaten to do so, which often works just as well. Don't hesitate to **protest loudly if you're harassed.** It's also important to learn how to negotiate a crowd so you don't get pinched-fingered—don't walk into a dense crowd. Skirt the edge and make sure you have plenty of room around you while you walk. One previous Miss India usefully suggested to swing your arms and walk so no one approaches too closely for fear of bumping into your moving hands.

India is a conservative culture, and women here have fairly conservative manners. There are certain things Indian women, young or old, are careful not to do, even urban sophisticated Indian women. These are best avoided by women tourists, too—don't shake hands unless you are at a business meeting or with friends; you are not expected to. Wear appropriate clothes. Don't touch a man by way of a friendly gesture or vice-versa. Do not continuously look a man in the eye as you talk, and do not smile excessively. Do not sit next to the taxi driver–chauffeur in the front seat; sit at the rear. Avoid smoking publicly or drinking alcohol alone in public unless you are at a luxury hotel. Don't allow a man to buy you a meal or a drink or give a gift to you if you are alone. Definitely do not share your table or taxi with anyone. Do not invite anyone you do not know well enough to your hotel or your hotel room or let anyone even know the name of the hotel where you are staying if you are traveling alone (avoid having anything delivered to your hotel). And don't let on that you are traveling alone. (Most definitely shun crummy hotels if you are.)

If you're traveling alone, consider wearing a wedding ring to avoid harassment, and tell people you're meeting your husband later that day; Indians seldom understand why women would not be married in their twenties (unless they are widows). Do avoid long personal conversations on trains and in public places or with shop-keepers–hawkers or with unknown, excessively curious men; you may find it difficult to get rid of the person later. On trains and buses if you are suspicious of a fellow passenger's behavior or are being bothered, even in the middle of the night, make it public, raise a commotion, and attempt to call the conductor. If you're being bothered by someone, anywhere, make your displeasure known publicly and loudly and even complain to a passerby if a policeman is not nearby; create a ruckus.

Chain-lock the door to your hotel room, as staffers often knock quickly and then come right in. If your train companions seem suspicious, attempt to switch your seat for one near other women. Better yet, when reserving your ticket, **request a berth in one of the "ladies compartments" that exist on some long-distance trains.**

SENIOR-CITIZEN TRAVEL

To qualify for age-related discounts from Western chain hotels, **mention your senior-citizen status when you reserve,** not when you check out.

🖪 **Educational Programs Elderhostel** ✉ 11 Ave. de Lafayette, Boston, MA 02111-1746 ☎ 877/426–8056, 978/323-4141 international callers, 877/426–2167 TTY 🖶 877/426-2166 ⊕ www.elderhostel.org. **Interhostel** ✉ University of New Hampshire, 6 Garrison Ave., Durham, NH 03824 ☎ 603/862-1147 or 800/733-9753 🖶 603/862-1113 ⊕ www.learn.unh. edu. **Folkways Institute** ✉ 14600 S.E. Aldridge Rd., Portland, OR 97236-6518 ☎ 503/658-6600 🖶 503/658-8672 ⊕ www.folkwaysinstitute.org.

SHOPPING

India is a fantasyland for shopping. Goods are very cheap and often unusually beautiful. Handicrafts, cotton clothes, silks, home linen, leather, furniture, herbal lotions, beauty aids, jewelry, and furnishings are all great buys. It's very easy, with a little bit of patience, to have something custom-made—be it a statue, shoes, clothes, a piece of furniture, silk curtains, embroidered bedspreads, stationery items, jewelry, especially in larger cities like Delhi and Bombay.

India's natural resources are rich and varied: an excellent variety of fabrics, a wide range of stone, marble, wood, and gems—and first-rate craftsmen who are absolutely wonderful with their hands. A few inquiries with a local shopkeeper or a resident may lead you to a craftsman. If you have something in mind beforehand, bring a picture or pattern or measurements, or better still, a sample with you.

Many items are much cheaper in India than Europe, North America, or Australia and it's good to know this beforehand—electronics, cell phones, framing, branded sportswear, clothes, or shoes (Levis, Reebok, Nike, Wrangler), film, clothes, medicines, eyeglasses (spectacles), haircuts, manicures, oil massages, some types of furniture, art, fabrics, and jewelry.

Some Indian goods are flimsy, however, so it's important to have a keen eye when you're out shopping. Shoes with cardboard soles will not last. A lot of Indian fabric, especially cotton, is delicate; and if you choose to purchase it, remember that it needs to be washed delicately (hand-washed, separately as colors run, drip-dry). And buy larger sizes to combat shrinkage.

Shop around; prices vary tremendously. Learn the going price of an item or class of goods at a fixed-price government emporium, then hit the rest of the retail trail. Note that government-approved shops aren't the same as government-run shops; the quality of goods is usually assured in government-approved shops, but prices aren't fixed. Bargaining is expected in bazaars. **Offer one-third the stated price,** then settle for about 60%.

Check wares for damage, defects, or tears before making a purchase. Carefully count—in front of the shop owner—the money being paid for a purchase and any change you receive. Also be sure to verify your bill before signing a credit-card slip.

Don't buy items made of wild-animal skins or ivory; technically such goods are illegal, and poaching is decimating India's wildlife. The same goes for sandalwood. (You may not be allowed to bring these items into your own country anyway.)

WATCH OUT

Be careful when buying jewelry, leather goods, and silk items. Fakes abound: a string of pearls might be made of plastic, a silver necklace of white metal. In popular shopping areas such Rajasthan, **beware of drivers or touts who want to take you to a certain store,** particularly an alleged friend's or relative's store. These hucksters get a commission. You'll feel pressure to buy from the moment you arrive at the shop, and you'll pay a higher price (to cover the commission) if you do.

Before you purchase any item that a shopkeeper claims is 100 years old, **ask for an export permit.** A reputable shopkeeper will have the permit or help you procure it. If he refuses, the item is a fake or hasn't been approved by the government for export.

STUDENTS IN INDIA

▨ I.D.s & Services STA Travel ⊠ 10 Downing St., New York, NY 10014 ☎ 212/627-3111, 800/777-0112 24-hr service center 🖷 212/627-3387 ⊕ www.sta.com. **Travel Cuts** ⊠ 187 College St., Toronto, Ontario M5T 1P7, Canada ☎ 800/592-2887 in U.S., 416/979-2406, 866/246-9762 in Canada 🖷 416/979-8167 ⊕ www.travelcuts.com.

TAXES

AIRPORT

You may have to pay an airport departure tax when you leave India (increasingly, this tax is included in the price of airline tickets). If you're moving on to Bhutan, Nepal, Pakistan, Sri Lanka, Bangladesh, Myanmar (Burma), or the Maldives, the tax is Rs. 500; otherwise, it's Rs. 700.

HOTEL

India levies a 6% expenditure tax on any room costing more than Rs. 1,200 (about US$32). The hotel industry is lobbying to reduce these taxes, as they can increase the cost of a hotel room by 30%. You should also expect an additional sales tax on food and beverages; the percentage varies from state to state. However, be prepared to be taxed up to approximately 20% at your hotel.

TAXIS & AUTO-RICKSHAW

One of the best ways to get around an Indian city, and even from one town to another, is by taxi. It's unwise to drive yourself around—depending on where you go Indian roads may lack signs and directions, and if you get stuck in the countryside you're really up the creek unless you speak the local language. Hiring a car-and-driver or a taxi is a much better bet. Within towns and cities (except Bombay) you can also hire an auto-rickshaw three-wheeler, which is fast and cheap, if not as comfortable as a taxi with air-conditioning. But you must follow some basic rules or you may get ripped off.

First, find out in advance the approximate fare for the distance you will be going—ask the hotel clerk or a shopkeeper before using a taxi or auto-rickshaw. Second, find out if taxis go by the meter, a rate card, or a meter plus rate card; that way you'll know in advance if you are going to have to negotiate fares. Third, if you think you're going to a place that may not have vehicles for the return journey (you discover that when you reach there, unfortunately), then, when you arrive, negotiate a waiting fare and a return fare with the driver.

Remember that prepaid taxi and auto-rickshaw counters exist at airports and railway stations in major cities. This means you go up to a counter called the pre-paid counter, tell the clerk your destination, and pay for it it advance. Make sure you tell him how much luggage you have—Rs. 5 is the norm for each large bag or suitcase. The clerk will give you a receipt and the number of the taxi or auto-rickshaw (waiting outside) you should take. Once you're in the car, give him the exact and correct destination, and make sure you collect your change. Do not get waylaid by auto-rickshaw and taxi drivers who try to persuade you to come to them instead of going to the counter. They can be quite aggressive in places like New Delhi, so you must be firm about telling

them to clear off. Once you have your receipt, locate the taxi or auto-rickshaw and set off to your destination; do not pay him anything extra, even if he claims you gave the wrong the destination to the counter clerk or tries to feed you other excuses. Taxis outside luxury hotels are notorious for swindling customers who hire them outside the hotel. Ascertain beforehand, with the help of the doorman, that the taxi driver will follow his meter or rate card, or negotiate the fare beforehand in presence of the doorman.

TELEPHONES & CELL PHONES

Many Indian businesses have a series of phone numbers instead of just one, as networks can get congested. If a number reads 562/331701 through 562/331708, for example, you can reach the establishment using any number between 331701 and 331708. Some of the numbers could be telefax numbers, so if you're trying to send a fax and someone answers, ask them to put the fax machine on. Homes may also have two phones. The number of digits in Indian phone numbers varies, even within one city.

Many of the cities in India are going through a phase where a "2" needs to be added to the front of a number after the area code. Not all cities have changed over to the extra 2, but they are, nonetheless, scheduled to do so. So if you're not getting through on a number, try adding that extra 2 after the area code.

AREA & COUNTRY CODES

The country code for India is 91. **In India, when dialing a long-distance number listed in this book, add 0 before the area code.** The country code is 1 for the United States and Canada, 61 for Australia, 64 for New Zealand, and 44 for the United Kingdom.

CELL PHONES & PHONE CARDS

If you're based in Europe or Australia and you have a cell phone, definitely bring it along. Network coverage is rather good in India and you will be able to use your phone even in small towns. Hotel phones are expensive and public phones often awkwardly located, so cell phones are extremely useful. You can also buy a local calling card and you're in business. Outlets hawking cell phone cards have mush-roomed; ask a local shopkeeper and he will direct you to the nearest retailer. The retailer will require your passport details and a few other details to issue a card. Cell phones in America, unfortunately, run on another system, so unless you have an international instrument it will not work. Indian cell phones work on the GSM standard, so those designed for the American standard are not suited for use in India. But a number of newer phone models are compatible to systems all over the world. Cell service is available in more and more parts of the country, and in many cities you can rent a cell phone for a day or a week from a luxury hotel or the airport. Luxury hotels can also, at a cost, can provide you with a pager or cell.

DIRECTORY & OPERATOR ASSISTANCE

For local phone numbers, dial 197. In big cities 197 operators speak English; in small towns and rural areas ask a local to help with the verification. For long-distance numbers within India, dial 183. Speak slowly, but don't be surprised if the operator just hangs up on you; India is modernizing its phone system, and the operator may not even have the latest number. If you're not calling from an International Subscriber Dialing (ISD) facility, dial 186 to reach an international operator.

The Internet is a good source for telephone numbers; most of India's city directories are now on the Internet: www.bsnl.co.in/onlinedirectory.htm.

INTERNATIONAL CALLS

International calls can be subject to long delays, but most hotels, airports, and post offices are connected to the computerized International Subscriber Dialing (ISD) system, which eliminates the need for an operator. You just dial 00, followed by the country code, the area code, and the number. Remember that hotels add an enormous surcharge to international calls and faxes; in addition, they sometimes charge a fee per call made on your calling card. Find out what the charges are before you

dial. To avoid the surcharge, make your calls at an ISD offices (even then, the price will be around US$3 a minute to most places). There are no reduced-rate calling hours for international calls.

LOCAL CALLS

A local call normally costs between Rs. 1 and Rs. 5. Some deluxe hotels have coin-operated public phones that take Rs. 1 coins or special tokens available at the reception desk.

LONG-DISTANCE CALLS

Domestic long-distance calls are expensive. You can make them quickly through a computer system called Subscriber Trunk Dialing (STD), which is available in most hotels, at specially designated public phones, and at private ISD/STD offices, easily spotted by their bright-yellow signs. The system carries no surcharge, though most hotels will add their own.

LONG-DISTANCE SERVICES

AT&T, MCI, and Sprint access codes make calling long distance relatively convenient, but you may find the local access number blocked in many hotel rooms. First ask the hotel operator to connect you. If the hotel operator balks, ask for an international operator, or dial the international operator yourself. One way to improve your odds of getting connected to your long-distance carrier is to travel with more than one company's calling card (a hotel may block Sprint, for example, but not MCI). If all else fails, call from a pay phone.

🛂 **Access Codes AT&T USADirect** ☎ 000117. **MCI Call USA** ☎ 000126 or 000127. **Sprint Express** ☎ 000136 or 000137.

PUBLIC PHONES

To use a public phone, dial the number, then deposit the required coin once the connection is made. (Public phone cards are not prevalent in India, though cell phone cards are.) The time limit is three minutes, and can be extended to six. The dial tone sounds, but often after you dial the number you'll hear a pulsing tone for a few seconds before the ring cuts in. If you use an ISD/STD facility, there's no time limit—a meter records the duration of your chat, and you pay the the required amount.

When using an STD booth, **check the meter reading before you pay** to see that the time on the slip matches the actual time used on the phone, and that the number recorded on the slip matches the number you dialed. Rates for domestic calls decrease by 50% after 7 PM and 75% after 10:30 PM.

TIME
India is 5½ hours ahead of Greenwich Mean Time, 10½ hours ahead of Eastern Standard Time, 13½ hours ahead of Pacific Standard Time, 4½ hours behind Sydney time, and 7½ hours behind Auckland time.

TIPPING
India runs on tips, and waiters, room-service attendants, housekeepers, porters, and doormen all expect to receive one. Some hotels include in their bills a service charge of 10%, which is also an appropriate amount to leave the waiter in any restaurant. But even if a service charge is built into your bill you should still leave a tip. You won't go wrong if you tip your room valet Rs. 20 per night. Bellboys and bell captains should be paid Rs. 10 per bag. For room service, tip 10% of the bill. Tip the concierge about Rs. 5 if he gets you a taxi. Train-station and airport porters should be paid Rs. 5–Rs. 10 per bag, depending on the weight; set the rate before you let him take your bags. Taxi drivers don't expect tips unless they go through a great deal of trouble to reach your destination; in such a case Rs. 10–Rs. 15 is fair. They expect Rs. 5 per piece of luggage over and above the meter charge. If you hire a car and driver, tip the driver about Rs. 50–Rs. 100 per day, depending on the distance traveled and about Rs. 25 for each lunch or dinner; also give him a larger amount at the end of the journey if you have been using him for many days. Tip local guides Rs. 40 for four hours, Rs. 80 for a full day.

TOURS & PACKAGES
Because everything is prearranged on a prepackaged tour or independent vacation, you spend less time planning—and often

get it all at a good price.

BOOKING WITH AN AGENT
Travel agents are excellent resources. But it's a good idea to collect brochures from several agencies, as some agents' suggestions may be influenced by relationships with tour and package firms that reward them for volume sales. If you have a special interest, find an agent with expertise in that area; the American Society of Travel Agents (ASTA; ➪ Travel Agencies) has a database of specialists worldwide. You can log on to the group's Web site to find an ASTA travel agent in your neighborhood.

Make sure your travel agent knows the accommodations and other services of the place being recommended. Ask about the hotel's location, room size, beds, and whether it has a pool, room service, or programs for children, if you care about these. Has your agent been there in person or sent others whom you can contact?

Do some homework on your own, too: local tourism boards can provide information about lesser-known and small-niche operators, some of which may sell only direct.

BUYER BEWARE
Each year consumers are stranded or lose their money when tour operators—even large ones with excellent reputations—go out of business. So check out the operator. Ask several travel agents about its reputation, and try to **book with a company that has a consumer-protection program.** (Look for information in the company's brochure.) In the United States, members of the National Tour Association and the United States Tour Operators Association are required to set aside funds to cover payments and travel arrangements in the event that the company defaults. It's also a good idea to choose a company that participates in the American Society of Travel Agents' Tour Operator Program; ASTA will act as mediator in any disputes between you and your tour operator.

Remember that the more your package or tour includes, the better you can predict the ultimate cost of your vacation. Make sure you know exactly what is covered, and beware of hidden costs. Are taxes, tips, and transfers included? Entertainment and excursions? These can add up.

Tour-Operator Recommendations American Society of Travel Agents (⇨ Travel Agencies). **National Tour Association** (NTA) ⊠ 546 E. Main St., Lexington, KY 40508 ☎ 859/226–4444 or 800/682–8886 ⧉ 859/226–4404 ⊕ www.ntaonline.com. **United States Tour Operators Association** (USTOA) ⊠ 275 Madison Ave., Suite 2014, New York, NY 10016 ☎ 212/599–6599 ⧉ 212/599–6744 ⊕ www. ustoa.com.

TRAIN TRAVEL

Traveling by train in India can be a fine experience if you plan it well. Trains connect the tiniest places across India, and train journeys are a terrific way to see the real, off-the-beaten-track India. Traveling on second-class non–air-conditioned trains can be tough, but you'll get better views of the countryside, since the windows are wide open, not sealed, and don't have a smoky film on them (as in air-conditioned cars). On the other hand, air-conditioned trips are much more comfortable. Trains, especially on smaller routes, can often be late, so be prepared to cope with delays. Make an attempt to get off at stations when the train halts, and have a walk around to observe station life. Certain train routes are famous for their views and are historical routes established by the British—the narrow gauge toy trains, for example, up to Darjeeling, Matheran, Ooty, and Shimla.

Like its international airports, India's railway stations are rather chaotic—though highly entertaining to observe. Hawkers sell everything from hot *puris* (deep-fried whole wheat bread) to boiled eggs and squeaky toys to hot coffee on a crude portable stove. Porters, also known as coolies, balancing unimaginable configurations of trunks and bags on their heads weave in and out. Invariably, in India, when one person sets out on a journey, five come to see him off. The platforms swirl with crowds and luggage. You need to be careful to hang on to your possessions and your bearings so you don't get bumped or swept away. Plan to be early and keep your tickets safe. If the train is

delayed in departing or has not yet arrived, find the first class or air-conditioned class, or, if you're a single woman traveler, the ladies' waiting room, and wait there. These places are safe, though usually drab and not very comfortable, but they have bathrooms attached. Many large railway stations have restaurants where you take a break, too.

India's two luxury trains—Rajasthan's *Palace on Wheels* and Gujarat's *Royal Orient,* which travel in parts of Rajasthan and Gujarat—are destinations in themselves, offering sumptuous meals and quarters as well as fine itineraries. Packages, which are very expensive, include food, coach tours in stations (after you disembark you're loaded onto a luxury bus for sightseeing), rail travel, and more—but you'll pay between US$350 and US$285 per person per day for the *Palace on Wheels* and between US$170 and US$350 per person per day for the *Royal Orient,* depending on whether you opt for single occupancy, double occupancy, or triple occupancy for a coupe. They are well worth it, and offer a peek into an ancient and Raj-era India. The entire seven-night tour is priced at US$4,900 per couple on *Palace on Wheels.* A seven-night tour for a couple on the *Royal Orient* costs US$2,800. Off-season—from March to October—is less expensive. *The Deccan Odyssey,* another luxury train that started running in January 2004 from Bombay along the coast to Karnataka, takes you to Ganapatiphule, Sindhudurg, Goa, Pune, Aurangabad, Ajanta, and Ellora. The seven-day journey costs between US$240 and US$700 per person per day depending on the type of accommodation you choose and the season. Coaches are state-of-the-art and embellished with Raj-era style, but are also equipped with CD and MP3 players, a gym, an ayruvedic massage room, plasma televisions, and access for the handicapped.

The *Shatabdi* and *Rajdhani* expresses, are fast and have air-conditioned cars and reclining seats but only offer services between major cities. The next-fastest trains are called "mail" trains. "Passenger" trains, which usually offer only second-class accommodations, make numerous stops, and are crowded. Even on the best trains in this group, lavatories are less than pleasant and seats can be well worn. But traveling by first class air-conditioned makes for a leisurely and grand journey and is well worth experiencing; the bathrooms are considerably better and the prices are roughly one-fourth less than an air journey.

The *Shatabdi Express* and *Taj Express* travel between Delhi and Agra. Both leave early in the morning from Delhi; the *Shatabdi* takes about two hours, the *Taj* 2½. Each allows for a full day of sightseeing before returning to Delhi. The *Pink Express,* which links Delhi and Jaipur, takes six hours and gives you five hours of sightseeing before returning to Delhi. Another convenient *Shatabdi Express* runs overnight between Bombay and Delhi; and the overnight *Rajdhani Express* connects Delhi and Calcutta.

For long train rides, **buy a yard-long chain with loops and a padlock to secure your luggage.** (You might find a vendor on the platform at a large train station.) After you've *locked* your bag and stowed it in its place, loop the chain through its handle and attach it to a bar or post below the seat. Lock it once more and you won't have to mind your luggage. You can even step off the train to stretch your legs at interim stations, knowing your possessions are safe. Be sure to chain your luggage as soon as possible; a lot of small bag thefts take place during journey embarkation and disembarkation. (And keep your shoes safe.) Your journey will be more pleasant if you bring along packaged snacks, sandwiches from a fast-food chain, juice, bottled water, plastic glasses, and a tea cup. Alternatively, **ask the staff at your hotel to prepare sandwiches or a traditional Indian train meal.** Bigger trains provide sumptuous meals as part of the ticket/tariff, and you can expect a number of the items on a food tray to be packaged.

CLASSES

Trains have numerous classes: first-class air-conditioned (private compartments with two or four sleeping berths), ordinary first-class (non–air-conditioned private compartments with two or four sleeping berths), second-class air-conditioned sleeper (only available on some trains), second-class two-tier sleeper (padded berths), and ordinary second-class (always crowded and never comfortable). Whatever the class, remember to request an inside berth and not a "side" one along the corridor. Berths are located in configurations of 4 or 6 in an open coupe arrangement on one side of a train carriage. On the other (corridor) side, berths are against the wall, in pairs of two; corridors run parallel past these "side" berths and bring in noise and traffic.

You'll find two kinds of lavatories, the Western-style commode lavatory and the Indian-style toilet (essentially a hole over which you squat). Although it can be hard to get used to Indian-style facilities, they're actually safer in the sense that there's no contact.

RAIL PASSES

A rail pass may cost more than individual tickets. If you plan to cover considerable ground **look into Indian Railways Indrail Pass,** which is available for second-class to first-class air-conditioned trains. The costs are: 1-day pass, US$19–US$95; 7-day pass, US$80–US$270; 15-day pass, US$90–$370; 21-day pass, US$100–$440; 30-day pass, US$125–US$550; 60-day pass, US$185–US$800; 90-day pass, US$235–US$1,060. Children between 5 and 11 pay half. The Indian Railways International Tourist Bureau, on the first floor of the New Delhi Railway Station, may very helpful if you're planning on traveling a lot by train. They're efficient, and can help you with plans, reservations, and ticketing.

Try to **buy rail passes at least two months before your trip.** Provide your agent with a complete itinerary to ensure seat confirmation. Every Government of India Tourist Office overseas has copies of the Tourist Railway Timetable, or you can consult Thomas Cook's International Railway Timetable. At any railway station you can find *Travel Links, Trains at a Glance,* and

Travel Hour, all of which list plane and some train schedules.

To buy the Indrail Pass outside India, contact your travel agent, the Government of India Tourist Office, or one of the designated sales agents listed below. In India, you can buy the pass at railway offices in major cities; international airports; and government-recognized travel agents in Bombay, Calcutta, Delhi, and Madras. You must pay in U.S. dollars, U.S.-dollar traveler's checks, or pounds sterling.

🔢 Indrail Pass Agents Abroad **Australia** Adventure World 🏷 Box 480, North Sydney, NSW 2059 ☎ 02/9958-7766 🖷 02/9956-7707. **Canada** Hari World Travel Inc. ✉ 1 Financial Pl., 1 Adelaide St. E, Concourse Level, Toronto MSC 2V8 ☎ 416/366-2000 🖷 416/366-6020. **United Kingdom** SD Enterprise ✉ 103 Wembley Park Dr., Middlesex, London ☎ 0208/903-3411 🖷 0208/903-0392. **United States** Hari World Travel Inc. ✉ 30 Rockefeller Plaza, North Mezzanine, Shop 21, New York, NY 10112 ☎ 212/957-3000 🖷 212/997-3320.

🔢 Luxury Train Contacts **Deccan Odyssey** ✉ Travelers Hub Pvt. Ltd., New Delhi, 110058 ☎ 11/2554-2045 or 11/5545-3565 🖷 11/2562-1464 🌐 www.deccan-odyssey-india.com. *Palace on Wheels* Rajasthan Tourism Development Corp., Palace on Wheels Division ✉ Bikaner House, Pandara Rd., near India Gate, New Delhi 110011 ☎ Delhi 11/2338-1884, 888/463-4299 or 609/683-5018 U.S. and international 🌐 www.palaceonwheels.com. *Royal Orient* Gujarat State Tourism Development Corp. ✉ A/6 State Emporia, Baba Kharak Singh Marg, New Delhi 110008 ☎ 11/2334-0305 🌐 www.gujarattourism.com.

🔢 Train Information **Indian Railways** 🌐 www.indianrail.gov.in. **Indian Railways International Tourist Bureau** ✉ New Delhi Railway Station ☎ 11/2340-5156 or 11/2334-6804 🕐 Mon.-Sat. 8-8, Sun. 8-2.

PAYING

In large cities, you can buy tickets with major credit cards. Elsewhere, expect to pay cash.

RESERVATIONS

You must **reserve seats and sleeping berths in advance,** even with a rail pass. If your plans are flexible, you can make reservations once you arrive in India. To save time, **use a local travel agent** (who

may need to borrow your passport); otherwise, head to the train station and prepare for long lines and waits. Large urban stations have a special counter for foreigners, where you can buy "tourist quota" tickets. (Every train reserves a few seats for tourists who haven't made reservations.) If you arrive early in the morning—around 8—getting a ticket shouldn't take you more than half an hour; however, in peak season, tourist quotas fill quickly, and you may have to change your dates altogether. When it's time to travel, **arrive at the station at least half an hour before departure** so you have enough time to find your seat. Sleeper and seat numbers are displayed on the platform and on each carriage, along with a list of passengers' names and seat assignments.

If you are not buying from the tourist quota and are booking during nonpeak season, booking through the Internet is a wonderful option if you have the local address of a friend, which you can give for delivery. Log onto www.irctc.co.in to make a reservation.

TRAVEL AGENCIES

A good travel agent puts your needs first. Look for an agency that has been in business at least five years, emphasizes customer service, and has someone on staff who specializes in your destination. In addition, **make sure the agency belongs to a professional trade organization.** The American Society of Travel Agents (ASTA)—the largest and most influential in the field with more than 20,000 members in some 140 countries—maintains and enforces a strict code of ethics and will step in to help mediate any agent-client disputes involving ASTA members if necessary. ASTA (whose motto is "Without a travel agent, you're on your own") also maintains a Web site that includes a directory of agents. (If a travel agency is also acting as your tour operator, *see* Buyer Beware *in* Tours & Packages.)

🔢 Local Agent Referrals **American Society of Travel Agents** (ASTA) ✉ 1101 King St., Suite 200, Alexandria, VA 22314 ☎ 703/739-2782, 800/965-2782 24-hr hot line 🖷 703/739-3268 🌐 www.astanet.com. **Association of British Travel Agents**

✉ 68–71 Newman St., London W1T 3AH ☎ 020/7637-2444 🖷 020/7637-0713 🌐 www.abta.com. **Association of Canadian Travel Agencies** ✉ 130 Albert St., Suite 1705, Ottawa, Ontario K1P 5G4 ☎ 613/237-3657 🖷 613/237-7052 🌐 www.acta.ca. **Australian Federation of Travel Agents** ✉ Level 3, 309 Pitt St., Sydney, NSW 2000 ☎ 02/9264-3299 🖷 02/9264-1085 🌐 www.afta.com.au. **Travel Agents' Association of New Zealand** ✉ Level 5, Tourism and Travel House, 79 Boulcott St., Box 1888, Wellington 6001 ☎ 04/499-0104 🖷 04/499-0786 🌐 www.taanz.org.nz.

VISITOR INFORMATION

🖪 Government of India Tourist Offices Abroad **Australia** ✉ Level 2 Piccadilly, 210 Pitt St., Sydney, NSW 2000 ☎ 02/9264-4855. **Canada** ✉ 60 Bloor St. W, Suite 1003, Toronto, Ontario M4W 3B8 ☎ 416/962-3787. **United Kingdom** ✉ 7 Cork St., London W1X 2AB ☎ 020/7437-3677. **United States** ✉ 30 Rockefeller Plaza, Room 15, North Mezzanine, New York, NY 10112 ☎ 800/953-9399 ✉ 3550 Wilshire Blvd., Suite 204, Los Angeles, CA 90010 ☎ 213/380-8855.

🖪 Government Advisories **U.S. Department of State** ✉ Overseas Citizens Services Office, Room 4811, 2201 C St. NW, Washington, DC 20520 ☎ 202/647-5225 interactive hot line, 888/407-4747 🌐 www.travel.state.gov; enclose a cover letter with your request and a business-size SASE. **Consular Affairs Bureau of Canada** ☎ 800/267-6788 or 613/944-6788 🌐 www.voyage.gc.ca. **U.K. Foreign and Commonwealth Office** ✉ Travel Advice Unit, Consular Division, Old Admiralty Bldg., London SW1A 2PA ☎ 020/7008-0232 or 020/7008-0233 🌐 www.fco.gov.uk/travel. **Australian Department of Foreign Affairs and Trade** ☎ 02/6261-1299 Consular Travel Advice Faxback Service 🌐 www.dfat.gov.au. **New Zealand Ministry of Foreign Affairs and Trade** ☎ 04/439-8000 🌐 www.mft.govt.nz.

WEB SITES

Do check out the World Wide Web when planning your trip. You'll find everything from weather forecasts to virtual tours of famous cities. Be sure to visit Fodors.com (🌐 www.fodors.com), a complete travel-planning site. You can research prices and book plane tickets, hotel rooms, rental cars, vacation packages, and more. In addition, you can post your pressing questions in the Travel Talk section. Other planning tools include a currency converter and weather reports, and there are loads of links to travel resources.

India is extraordinarily well represented on the World Wide Web, so use the Web to help plan your trip. You'll find everything from splendid photos of Heritage Hotels to close-ups of temple carvings to testimonials from former travelers. Visit the official Indian tourism ministry site, www.tourindia.com, or email the New York Indian tourist office at ny@itonyc.com. Another good Web site frequented by Indians is www.rediff.com.

THE HIMALAYAS

1

RIDE AN ELEPHANT
through Corbett National Park ⇨*p.41*

DRINK IN LOCAL HISTORY
at High Tea at the Windamere
in Darjeeling ⇨*p.53*

ESCAPE FROM CIVILIZATION
in a yurt at Ladakh Sarai ⇨*p.33*

REFLECT ON SIKH SPIRITUALISM
at the Golden Temple in Amritsar ⇨*p.5*

PAMPER YOURSELF
amid breathtaking natural scenery
at Ananda in the Himalayas ⇨*p.38*

By Andy
McCord,
Michael
Bollom,
Kathleen Cox,
and Gaye
Facer

LIKE THE TEETH OF A GIANT RIPSAW, the snowcapped Himalayas cut a border between India and China, passing through four Indian states: Jammu and Kashmir, Himachal Pradesh, Uttaranchal, and Sikkim. They strike awe like no other mountain range in the world. A few hours north of Delhi you can escape the heat of the plains in a Raj-era hill station, hike through terraced fields and alpine passes on exhilarating treks, or absorb religious teachings in a Hindu temple or Buddhist monastery. The regions of the Indian Himalayas are united only by their proximity to the same mountain range. Culturally, and even physically, they're quite different. The people of Sikkim look more East Asian and practice Tibetan Buddhism, whereas Kumaonis from Uttaranchal are Hindus with distinctly Aryan features and darker skin. The people of Leh speak Ladakhi and eat *papa*, a gruel made from barley and vegetables, and even some Tibetan-style foods such as *momos* (stuffed dumplings), whereas just several hundred miles away Kashmiris converse in Urdu over meals of kababs. Geographically, the moonscapes of Ladakh stand in sharp contrast to the lush tea gardens of the Kangra Valley, and Manali's pine forests are a world apart from the rhododendron jungles around Gangtok. Because transportation between these regions is limited, few travelers have the time and energy to experience more than one or two, so choose your destination carefully.

If you're headed for the mountains of Himachal Pradesh, you may find Amritsar a worthwhile cultural detour. The largest city in the affluent, predominantly Sikh state of Punjab, Amritsar is the holiest city to the Sikh religion, its massive Golden Temple is an inspiring destination in its own right. History buffs may also want to visit the site of the infamous Amritsar Massacre, a turning point in the fight for Indian Independence. Farther east—on the other side of Nepal—if you're Sikkim-bound, or just want a pastoral break from Calcutta, the historic hill station of Darjeeling invites exploration and easy alpine walks.

Exploring the Himalayas

Whatever your interest in the Himalayas, contact the recommended tour operators for details. Most will design a special trip just for you, whatever your budget or age. Try to make arrangements at least two months in advance. If you're planning a trek, contact a tour operator who is familiar with the specific area you have in mind. Play it safe: don't embark on any route without a guide. Travelers in high-altitude areas should heed all warnings about sun exposure and high-altitude sickness: even if you'll be ensconced in a jeep, bring powerful UVA/UVB sunblock, a wide-brim hat, and sunglasses that block ultraviolet rays. Allow three days for full acclimatization. For travel to remote areas, bring a means of water purification, a quart-size canteen, and energy-producing snacks.

Foreigners must obtain an Inner Line Permit and travel with at least three other foreigners *and* a government-recognized tour operator to visit the Spiti Valley in Himachal Pradesh and the Nubra, Khaltse (Drokhpa area), and Nyoma subdivisions in Ladakh. Trekking in Sikkim requires a Re-

stricted-Area Permit. Most tour operators can help you secure a permit
(*see* ⇨ Permits *in* The Himalayas A to Z).

*Numbers in the margin correspond to points of interest on the North-
west Indian Himalayas and Sikkim maps.*

About the Restaurants
Most of the best restaurants in Chandigarh are in Sector 17, where you'll
also find staple fast-food and coffee outlets. Fast-food restaurants and
coffee houses in Shimla abound on the Mall—Devicos, Indian Coffee
House, and Barista—are good for quick fixes—but ambience is not a priority; for that you're better off driving outside town for lunch at a hotel.

All of Leh's restaurants are small and informal. Try the standards:
momos and the noodle soup called *thukpa.* You may also have a chance
to try *chang* (a local brew made from fermented barley) or, more likely,
some *gur-gur cha,* yak-butter tea mixed with milk and salt.

Most of Darjeeling's best restaurants are in the hotels, notably the Windamere and New Elgin, but there are a few stand-alone classics within
walking distance of the Mall. All are open throughout the day. Take a
flashlight if you plan to walk back to your hotel after dark, as the
town's power supply is erratic.

Try Sikkimese sautéed ferns in season, sautéed bamboo shoots, nettle
soup, and roast pork. If you like momos, order beef or vegetable—pork
is risky if undercooked. Sikkim also makes good libations: cherry and
musk brandy, wine, Teesta River white rum, juniper gin, *paan* liquor
(made from a mixture of leaves and betel nuts), and, best of all, *chang*
(Tibetan barley beer) and *tomba,* a tipple concocted from millets and
served in a giant wooden or bamboo mug. Note that new-moon days
and the first day of the full moon are dry. For traditional Sikkimese meals,
restaurants require advance notice and usually ask for parties of four
or more; if you're solo, try to make some friends.

About the Hotels
Chandigarh lacks an international-standard hotel, though a few are under
construction. Facilities in Lahaul and Spiti are generally open between
April and October. Banjara Camps runs the best accommodation: an
11-room lodge on a high, arid plateau in Tabo, Spiti. Ladakh has no
particularly exciting hotels; standards are lower than they are in the rest
of the Indian Himalayas.

Hotels in Darjeeling are not centrally heated, and space heaters are not
always adequate, nor is the hot-water supply. If you come in winter, you'll
pay about half the usual price, but ask for a room with a fireplace and
carry lots of warm clothing. Many hotels in Sikkim do not have generators, so be prepared for power cuts.

WHAT IT COSTS In Rupees				
$$$$	$$$	$$	$	¢
RESTAURANTS				
over 350	250–350	150–250	100–150	under 100
HOTELS				
over 4,000	3,000–4,000	2,000–3,000	1,000–2,000	under 1,000

Restaurant prices are for an entrée plus dal, rice, and a veg/non-veg dish. Hotel prices are for two people in a standard double room in high season.

Timing

May through August is the ideal window for a comfortable Himalayas visit, particulalry during May and June, when the rest of the country is broiling. And when torrential rains inundate most of North India in July and August, Himachal Pradesh and Ladakh make great escapes, as the mountains usually hold back the monsoons. The Himalayas can be extremely cold in winter, and deep snow renders many mountain passes and valleys impassable, so summer is often the best bet. If you do head for the hills in summer, reserve lodging well in advance.

AMRITSAR

❶ Because of its proximity to the Pakistani border—Lahore is only 64 km (40 mi) away—Amritsar has not seen the development and attendant sprawl of other North Indian towns. The city is an important commercial hub: much of the aromatic Basmati rice that's now an international staple is exported by Amritsar dealers, and dried fruits and woolens from hill regions are handled by wholesalers here. The robust rural culture of Punjab's farmlands permeates the city, with tractors plying the roads and peasants making their way through the market centers and the famous Sikh temple.

The Golden Temple of the Sikhs is reason enough to come to Amritsar, and even if you think you've had enough of India's overwhelming religious pageantry you should not miss it. It resembles more a Moghul palace than a typical Indian temple, and its layout and ambience are a living lesson in the teachings of the Sikh faith, a syncretic movement that was formed to combine Hinduism's *bhakti* (devotion to a personalized god) with Islam's monotheism and egalitarianism. Sikhism was founded by Guru Nanak around the turn of the 16th century, and developed into a distinct new religion under the gurus who succeeded him. Amritsar ("Pool of Nectar" in Punjabi and Sanskrit) takes its name from an ancient sacred pool that Nanak is said to have preferred for his meditation and teaching. The site was granted to the fourth guru, Ramdas, in 1577 by the great Moghul emperor Akbar, and gradually developed as a pilgrimage center. As the 1500s came to a close, songs by the Sikh gurus and selections from Hindu and Muslim poet-saints were canonized as the *Adi Granth* ("First Book") at the same time as the great *gurdwara* (temple; "door to the guru") was being constructed here. In succeeding years, the temple and the sacred book together gained increasing importance, and in 1699 the tenth guru, Gobind Singh, consolidated the faith by establishing a distinctive appearance for his followers—most notably long hair kept in a turban for men, and braids for women. Upon his death in 1708, Singh's disciples announced his instruction that the Sikh faith would henceforth be centered on the teachings of the sacred book (now called the *Guru Granth Sahib*) rather than a human guru. To this day, life in the Golden Temple and all gurdwaras revolves around the *Guru Granth Sahib*, starting before dawn, when the book is taken out of a building called the Akal Takht and carried processionally across the huge, white marble compound—including a causeway over a square artificial pond—to Harmandir Sahib, the central temple whose gilded copper plating gives the complex its popular name. The temple's day ends late in the evening, when the book is brought back to its resting place.

During the time of the gurus, the Sikhs' development as a community often brought them into conflict with other forces in Moghul India. In 1761, as the Moghul empire declined, the temple was sacked by the Afghan raider Ahmad Shah Durrani. (It was rebuilt three years later.) In 1802 the temple was covered in gilt copper by Maharaja Ranjit Singh (1780–1839), whose rule marked the height of Sikh power, extending as far as Kashmir and Kabul. In 1984 the Indian Army's "Operation Bluestar" brought tanks into the complex in a disastrous four-day firefight with heavily armed Sikh separatists who had virtually taken over the complex. India's Prime Minister Indira Gandhi was assassinated about five months later by two of her Sikh bodyguards, in what was widely believed to be retribution for the Army attack on the temple. Amazingly, the temple now shows few signs of this tragic event, or of the decade of separatist violence and state repression that plagued Punjab afterward.

All day long, while a select group of singers, or *ragis*, broadcast hymns from the *Guru Granth Sahib* throughout the complex, pilgrims from rustic Punjabi towns and villages—India's hugely productive breadbasket—make their way around it, some performing *seva* (voluntary service) by cleaning the marble or completing other tasks. The dignity that pilgrims invest in the site, the grandeur of its design, and the hospitality extended to visitors transcend the turmoil of the past.

★ Most hotels and the train station are near the British-built cantonment, about 15 minutes from the **Golden Temple.** You approach the temple through the Hall Bazaar, which leads to the **clock-tower** gate. (To symbolize their egalitarian welcome to all castes, all Sikh gurdwaras have four entrances, but this is the main one.) To the left of the stairway is a counter where visitors leave their shoes—many of the attendants here are volunteers, and their handling of others' shoes is another illustration of the Sikh doctrine of caste equality. If you smoke, leave all tobacco products behind, as they're forbidden here. Pilgrims wash their feet at a spigot by the gate before entering the temple complex. Sikhs will already have their heads covered, with turbans for males and *chunnis* (large scarves) for women; if you haven't brought a head covering, make use of the bin of scarves by the stairs.

From the top of the gateway stairs, you look across a wide pool of water—known as the *sarovar* (sea)—at the golden roof of Harmandir Sahib. Go down the steps on the other side and you'll reach the white marble 24-foot wide walkway, known as the *parikrama* (circumambulatory path), that surrounds the pool. Each side of the pool is 510 feet long, and pilgrims normally make a complete circuit before approaching the Harmandir Sahib. Doing so gives a good sense of the scale of the place, as well as providing a series of views of the temple itself. You can take pictures from a distance, but you must put your camera away before you leave the causeway. Various points around the parikrama are considered auspicious places to bathe; the bathing steps along the east length of the walkway are said to mark a spot that equals the purifying power of Hinduism's 68 most holy *tirthas* (holy places). Just behind this is the entrance to a small garden that adjoins an assembly hall on the right and two pilgrims' hostels to the rear. On the left, under two tall minarets that have yet to be fully restored from the damage they suffered in the 1980s, is the **Guru Ram Das Langar**—the temple's communal dining hall, named after the fourth Sikh guru. All gurdwaras have such a *langar* (the name of the place as well as the free meal served here), as eating together and serving a meal to others is perhaps the most fondly practiced of all Sikh rituals. Don't hesitate to join in; meals are served daily from 11 to 3 and 7 to 11, and the food, usually a few thick *chapatis* and some *dal,* is simple and robust. In another kitchen at the southwest corner of the parikrama, pilgrims make a donation in return for a packet of *halvah,* a sweet, sticky pudding usually made from cream of wheat, which they then take to Harmandir Sahib and present as an offering. A portion is given back to worshippers as *prasad,* which some translate as the "edible form of God's grace."

Halfway across the east side of the parikrama, the causeway out to Harmandir Sahib is on your right, and to the left is the five-story **Akal Takht,** topped by a gilt dome. This building, whose name means "Timeless Throne," represents Sikh temporal authority—day-to-day administration—as opposed to the spiritual authority of Harmandir Sahib. It was here that much of the heavy fire that met the Indian Army during Operation Bluestar originated; the first building was largely destroyed during the fighting, but has now been fully restored.

To reach **Harmandir Sahib** you go under an archway known as the **Darshani Deorhi** ("Gateway of Vision") and cross a 204-foot long causeway, which has brass guide rails to separate arriving pilgrims from departing ones, as well as a central passageway for temple functionaries. Take the left passageway. (Note that pilgrims sometimes arrive in large numbers for ceremonies, particularly at dusk. Access to the Harmandir Sahib is controlled at such times and pilgrims can back up the causeway, making a visit to the sanctum a lengthy undertaking.) Pilgrims typically bow down at the doorway after crossing the causeway, then circumambulate the central temple around a small parikrama. Some stop to bathe on the east side. The exterior walls are decorated in beautiful *pietra dura* (marble inlaid with semiprecious stones) said to have been brought by Maharaja Ranjit Singh from Moghul monuments in Lahore.

On the temple's ground level, the *Guru Granth Sahib* sits on a special throne. Attendants wave whisks over it to keep flies away, and a *granthi* (lay specialist) sits reciting the text with harmonium players and other musicians off to one side. Feel free to enter the temple and listen to the recitation of the holy book, or witness the continuous recitation (*akhand path*) of the second and third stories; just remember to keep your head covered and refrain from taking pictures. As you go back through the Darshani Deorhi, a temple priest or volunteer will usually be stationed under a small tree handing out servings of the halvah that previous pilgrims have offered. The ritual of receiving prasad is one that Sikhs share with Hindus. Just around the northwest corner of the parikrama stands an old jujube tree that is said to have healing powers.

The **Central Sikh Museum,** upstairs in the clock-tower entrance, contains graphic paintings depicting the tumultuous history of the Sikh gurus and their followers. Included are scenes from the British period and Operation Bluestar. ⊙ *Daily, usually 5 AM–10 PM; museum daily 10–6* ☜ *Free.*

Outside the temple's clock-tower entrance, about 500 yards north, a small plaque and narrow gateway mark the entrance to **Jallianwala Bagh.** Here, on April 13, 1919, occurred one of the defining moments in India's struggle for independence. The day was Baisakhi, celebrated by Sikhs as both the first day of the new year and the day that Guru Gobind Singh consolidated the faith under the leadership of the Khalsa ("God's own"; a fraternity of the pious) in 1699. The city was under curfew after reported attacks on some British residents, yet some 20,000 people had gathered here to protest the arrest of Indian nationalist leaders under the Rowlatt Act, a British legislation that allowed for detention without trial. Seeing this crowd, British Brigadier General Reginald E. H. Dyer positioned his troops just inside the narrow entrance to the small garden (which is surrounded on all sides by residential buildings) and ordered them to open fire. Some 1,200 people were wounded, and several hundred died. This massacre, chillingly reenacted in Richard Attenborough's film *Gandhi,* caused widespread outrage and contributed to the launch of Mahatma Gandhi's noncooperation movement. The British attempted to suppress news of the incident, and when an inquiry was finally held, such comments as "It was no longer a question of merely dispersing the crowd, but one of producing a sufficient moral effect" (Dyer) did nothing to assuage the worldwide response. Nobel Laureate poet Rabindranath Tagore renounced his English knighthood, and even Winston Churchill, himself no enemy of the empire, raised an uproar in Parliament (though a majority in the House of Lords approved of Dyer's actions). Jallianwala Bagh was subsequently purchased by Indian nationalists to prevent its being turned into a covered market, and it remains one of the most moving monuments to India's 20th-century history. Queen Elizabeth visited in 1997, after much negotiation over whether or not she should make a formal apology (she didn't, but she and Prince Philip removed their shoes before entering the grounds). Today the garden is planted with a few rosebushes, but the bullet holes from the British fusillade remain. The well, into which some dove in a vain attempt to save themselves, is on the north side. A modern memorial occupies the east end, and a small display to the left as you enter the garden features contemporary newspaper accounts of the incident. ▣ *Free* ☉ *Dawn–dusk.*

Other sights in Amritsar include the 16th-century **Durgiana Temple** (opposite Gole Bagh, south of the train station), a Hindu shrine to the goddess Durga, which in its design replicates its more famous Sikh neighbor. The **Ram Bagh** gardens, northeast of the train station (enter on Mall Road), date from the period of Maharaja Ranjit Singh (1780–1839). At the center of the garden, the **Punjab Government Museum** displays weapons and portraits from the maharaja's era in a period building; it's open Tuesday through Sunday 10 to 7.

The **Wagah–Attari border crossing** about 30 km (19 mi) west of Amritsar is a well-known checkpost on the India–Pakistan border. The daily flag-lowering ceremony is the draw here—with great pomp, Pakistani and Indian soldiers in full-dress uniform go through a sort of competitive ritual of winding up the day, and even shake hands at the end.

Where to Stay & Eat

$$ ✕ **Bharawan Dhaba.** Amritsar is famous for its cheap *dhabas*, restaurants where the Punjabi love of good country cooking is emphasized over decor. Try this one or Surjit's Chicken House on Lawrence Road. River fish are a special attraction, as is chicken, cooked dry in a tandoor (oven) or with a spicy sauce. In winter ask for *sarson ka saag*—mustard greens stewed in ginger with a dollop of *ghee* (clarified butter) and served with *makki ki roti* (delicious cornmeal chapatis). ⊠ *Opposite Town Hall on way to Golden Temple* ▤ *No credit cards.*

$$ ⌂ **Mohan International.** Though several new ones are going up, this remains Amritsar's best-run modern hotel. The rooms are spacious, clean, and air-conditioned, and the restaurant is a popular place for Amritsar families to enjoy a fancy night out. ⊠ *Albert Rd., 143001 Punjab* ☎ *183/222–7801 to 03* 🖷 *183/222–6520* ✉ *hotel@gla.vsnl.net.in* ⤶ *76 rooms* △ *Restaurant, coffee shop, pool, bar, laundry service, travel services* ▤ *AE, MC, V.*

$ ⌂ **Mrs. Bhandari's Guesthouse.** Run by the same family for more than 50 years, this sprawling set of cantonment bungalows harkens back to an earlier age of travel in India. If you like character in your lodgings, look no further. The rooms, some of which have air-conditioners, are huge and well maintained, with high ceilings and polished-wood furnishings. Every room has a fireplace (a fee is charged for lighting it), and most rooms open onto a well-maintained lawn. Mildly spiced Indian, Punjabi, and Anglo-Indian meals are served in your room or in the dining room. ⊠ *10 Cantonment Rd., 143001 Punjab* ☎ *183/222–8509 or 183/222–5714* 🖷 *183/222–2390* ⊕ *bhandari_guesthouse.tripod.com* ⤶ *12 rooms* △ *Restaurant, pool, playground, laundry service, travel services; no a/c in some rooms, no room phones, no room TVs* ▤ *AE, MC, V.*

FodorśChoice
★

CHANDIGARH

② Most of India's major cities emerged gradually, around ancient or colonial monuments. Chandigarh, in starkly modernist contrast, was designed in the 1950s—in the pink of India's new-found independence—by the French architect Le Corbusier. The capital of two bordering states, Haryana and Punjab, it's a refreshing stop on the long day's drive from Delhi to Shimla or other Himachal Pradesh destinations. Blessed with spacious avenues and plenty of green, including bright bougainvillea, the city has a downtown devoid of the usual scruffy chaos—no sidewalk stalls, *paan* (betel leaf) shops, slums, trash, or hawkers. Over time, admittedly, Chandigarh's neglected areas, replete with barbed wire and garbage, have made Corbusier's trademark concrete buildings somewhat less attractive.

It's easy to get around, as Chandigarh is organized on a grid, and you can see the main sights in a day. Hire an auto-rickshaw or cycle-rickshaw (Rs. 40 and Rs. 20, respectively, from one sector to the next) for short distances. Sector 17 is the hub of the city, where all the restaurants, banks, theaters, and shops are; much of this sector is pedestrian-only and easy to negotiate. Adjoining and surrounding 17, forming the rest of the city center, are Sectors 1, 8, 9, 10, 16, 18, 21, 22, and 23.

The innovative **Rock Garden,** three sectors from 17, near Sector 1, was designed by Nek Chand, an Indian artist who, despite his acclaim, still calls himself "an untutored former road inspector." This 6-acre fantasy is a maze of waterfalls and walkways through sculptures made from a mixture of oddly shaped stones from the Shivalik foothills, industrial waste, and discarded materials collected by the artist on his bicycle. There's also an open-air pavilion and a theater with giant swings. The artist is available to meet visitors; ask at the main reception area. The modernist **Art and Picture Gallery** in Sector 10 is worth a look, especially for its outdoor sculpture gallery, open Tuesday to Sunday 10 to 4:30. The 2 km (1 mi) walk around the well-kept, man-made **Sukhna Lake,** near Sector 1, is pleasant in early evening, when all of Chandigarh comes out to stroll; during the day you can rent pedal-boats.

In Pinjore, 20 km (12 mi) northeast of Chandigarh, the 17th-century Moghul-style **Yadvindra Gardens** are laid out on a gentle slope, with seven terraces of pools and fountains.

Where to Stay & Eat

$$ ✕ **Kwality.** With its abundance of rich wooden furniture, this cozy, warmly lit restaurant is a nice place to tuck into North Indian favorites—butter chicken (otherwise known as chicken *makhni,* cooked in a mildly spiced tomato sauce), *paneer tikka* (grilled cubes of soft cottage cheese), butter *naan,* and Indian-style Chinese food. ☒ *Sector 17E* ☏ *172/501–9613* ▤ *MC, V.*

$$ ✕ **Mehfil.** Named for the gatherings once enjoyed by the Urdu-language poets, this restaurant-pub is popular for its Mughlai food, though it also serves sizzlers (steaming metal platters of meat and vegetables), kababs, and Chinese dishes. Located in a shiny food mall with a variety of other restaurants, it's fairly happening, a good place to sample Chandigarh's nightlife. ⊠ *Sector 17C, near Titan showroom* ☎ *172/270–3539 or 172/270–4224* ➦ *MC, V.*

$$$ 🏨 **Mount View.** Transcending its inherent limitations as a government-run operation, the Mount View is actually the best hotel in Chandigarh. The plush, tastefully decorated rooms overlook a manicured lawn and garishly lit silhouettes of palm trees. You're walking distance from the Art and Picture Gallery and a rose-garden park. The hotel's delightful Chinese restaurant, the Wok, serves huge portions laced with fresh garlic and ginger, plus Indian and Western food. Room rates include breakfast. ⊠ *Sector 10, 160011* ☎ *172/274–0544 or 172/274–3126* 🖷 *172/274–2220* ✉ *citco10@sanchar.net.in* ➦ *156 rooms* △ *2 restaurants, coffee shop, pool, health club, hair salon, bar, laundry service, Internet, business services, travel services* ➦ *AE, MC, V* ⊘ *CP.*

$$ 🏨 **Shivalikview.** If you're stopping in Chandigarh because you're a modernist at heart, you're likely to enjoy this place, which has all the modern conveniences at a push of a button, plus large picture windows in all the common areas. The café serves a range of delicious South Indian snacks, and the bar, Indian restaurant, and rooftop Chinese restaurant are popular and lively. Rates include breakfast and dinner, a great value all around. ⊠ *Sector 17E, 160017* ☎ *172/270–3521 or 172/270–0001* 🖷 *172/270–1094* ✉ *shivalik17@satyam.net.in* ➦ *104 rooms, 4 suites* △ *2 restaurants, coffee shop, pool, hair salon, bar, laundry service, business services, travel services* ➦ *AE, MC, V* ⊘ *MAP.*

$ 🏨 **Maya Palace.** Standard rooms in this modern hotel are quite small, but they're clean, comfortable, and have tidy bathrooms. Tiled floors are surrounded by wood-panel walls and simple modern furniture. Because of the building's odd design, the cheaper rooms look out on the stairwell; all you can do is draw the curtain across. Breakfast is included. ⊠ *Sector 35B, 160022* ☎ *172/260–0547* 🖷 *172/266–0555* ⊕ *www.mayahotels.com* ➦ *26 rooms* △ *Restaurant, laundry service, business services, travel services* ➦ *AE, DC MC, V* ⊘ *CP.*

HIMACHAL PRADESH

Threaded with rivers and dotted with lakes, the lovely state of Himachal Pradesh spans five Himalayan mountain ranges—the Shivalik, Dhauladhar, Pir Panjal, Great Himalayas, and Zanskar. Except for the capital, Shimla, and the overpopulated towns of Dharamshala and Manali, Himachal is a land of alpine villages, speckled with thousands of Hindu and Buddhist temples and monasteries.

Various cultures inhabit this region, and each has its own customs, clothing, religion, food, and lifestyles. Most Himachalis are Hindu, but the people of Lahauli and Spiti are Buddhist, and Kinnauris follow both Hindu and Buddhist traditions. Two seminomadic tribes, the Gaddi and Gujjar, also maintain many of their ancient customs here. The Gaddi, who travel with sheep, goats, and cattle, are Hindu, and generally believe in evil spirits that are appeased by animal sacrifices and animist rituals. Gaddi men traditionally wear a *chola* (white thigh-length woolen

coat) over *sutthan* (tight woolen trousers) held in place by a *dora* (a black rope of sheep's wool) coiled around the waist. Women wear a *luanchari* (a long, colorful dress) with a woven dora tied around the waist and lots of jewelry, both for good luck and to indicate wealth. The Muslim Gujjar travel with buffalo, and make their living selling fresh milk and ghee. Gujjar men, usually bearded, wear turbans and long robes. Women wear the traditional Indian Muslim *salwar-kameez*, a long tunic over loose pants tapered at the ankle. Often somber in color, this outfit is accentuated by paisley scarves and chunky silver necklaces, bracelets, and dangling earrings.

Trekking, driving, fishing, and biking in Himachal can take you through flowering alpine meadows, forests of pine, oak, fir, and ash, Buddhist monasteries, mountain wildlife, and generally unforgettable panoramas. Inquire with a tour company (⇨ The Himalayas A to Z) about the routes covering Lahaul–Spiti–Kinnaur, McLeod Ganj–Machhetar (through the Dhauladhar range, from the Kangra Valley to the Ravi Valley), and Manali–Bir (from the Kullu Valley to the Kangra Valley). Jeep safaris are an easy option on the three-day stretch from Manali to Leh, or the longer, quieter stretch from Shimla into Kinnaur and on to Spiti. Mountain biking from Manali to Leh is another way to cover this popular route; avid bikers can complete the ride in eight days. There's plenty to see along the way, including spectacular views from towering passes including the impressive Rohtang Pass (13,130 feet), gateway to Lahaul and Spiti.

Fish for trout in the Pabar River near Rohru, a two-day trip from Shimla, or in the Larji River, at its confluence with the Tirthan River over the Jalori Pass. You can also catch trout in the Uhl River, near Barot, and in the Sangla. Try for *mahaseer,* a Himalayan river fish, in the Beas near Dharamshala. Between July and September you can also go whitewater rafting on the Beas.

The peak tourist season in Himachal Pradesh runs from May though September. June and September are dry and warm; July and August have monsoon rains and are not the best months to visit, as roads can deteriorate and landslides occur. In April and November, the days can be sunny enough for short sleeves, and hotel prices drop. In winter, temperatures hover around freezing and some hotels close from December through February; the others discount their rates up to 50% (except Christmas and the New Year). Only a few hotels have central heating; in the others you may end up worshipping your wee electric heater, for which the cheaper hotels charge Rs. 50–Rs. 100 extra per night.

Shimla

❸ *360 km (225 mi) north of Delhi, about 117 km (73 mi) northeast of Chandigarh.*

The capital of Himachal Pradesh, Shimla is perhaps best perceived as a gateway to the district of Kinnaur. If it's fresh mountain air and serenity you seek, use Shimla only as a base. The charms of Rudyard Kipling's city have faded: paint peels on Victorian structures, and mortar is left to crumble. Garish new developments now dot the surrounding hills,

THE HIMACHAL CIRCUIT

To see Himachal Pradesh thoroughly—a life-changing experience—allow both time and money for a series of long, winding road trips in a car handled by a local driver (⇨ *Travel Agents & Tours* in *The Himalayas A to Z*). Most trips between any two destinations take a full day, as daylight hours are short, and you don't want to drive in the dark. Even a basic tour covering **Shimla** ❸ (two days), **Manali** ❹ (two days), and **Dharamshala** ❺ (three days) requires 7½ days including travel to and from Delhi. A longer itinerary—covering **Shimla/Mashobra** (four days), **Kinnaur** (three days), **Spiti/ Lahaul** (six days), **Manali** ❹ (three days), **Dharamshala** (three days), **Dalhousie** ❻ (one day), and Pragpur, for **Judge's Court** (one day)—takes three weeks including travel to and from Delhi. Save money and energy on the first leg out of Delhi by taking a train to Shimla or to Pathankot, near Dharamshala.

and traffic lines the road in high season, sometimes causing delays on miles of switchbacks en route. The town is often packed with Indian families on holiday, and also attracts British travelers whose antecedents made an annual trip to this summer capital during the Raj.

The crowds that swarm Shimla's main plaza and thoroughfare, the pedestrian-only **Mall,** sweep you along at their pace, providing a gracious break from motor traffic. The Mall is well preserved, its old buildings pleasantly lighted at night. Chattering, yelping monkeys are about as common as tourists, so you'll see them vaulting off electricity polls and swinging from eave to eave chewing plants, potato chips and whatever else they find in their path. **Scandal Point,** where the Mall meets the Ridge, offers an endlessly fascinating view not just of the town but of families shopping, strolling, buying treats from vendors, and riding ponies. It's a good place to rest and meet fellow travelers. **Christchurch,** the **Gaiety Theatre,** the **Town Hall,** and the **General Post Office** present a lively facade of architectural reminders of the Raj in the Gothic, Arts and Crafts, and timbered Tudor styles. Sadly, many of the less famous buildings are worn, and their facades obscured with modern shop fronts and advertising.

The **Oberoi Cecil** hotel makes a good stop for high tea or, better still, a superb Himachali dinner of vegetables or meat cooked in a yogurt-based curry, chickpeas sautéed with spinach and burnt walnuts, or lentils, potatoes, and other specialties spiked with aniseed. Beyond the Cecil is the gigantic **Viceregal Lodge,** which houses the Indian Institute of Advanced Study and is well worth a visit just for its teak-panel library or the view from its well-tended gardens. Easily one of the grandest and haughtiest buildings in North India, it reeks of the days when the British ruled all they surveyed.

Take in the architectural and historical highlights with a walk through town and up to **Jakhoo Hill** (2 km [1 mi] uphill from the center of town)—at 8,054 feet, it's the highest peak around, crowned with a temple dedicated to the monkey god Hanuman. The monkeys en route are notoriously mischievous, so don't walk around with food. If you're nervous about encountering monkeys, take a local guide along—the creatures all recognize **Sanjay Sood** (☎ 177/280–5806 or 98170–16580), who lives in Rothney Castle near the base of the hill, on Jakhoo Road, and visits the temple daily. Sood also leads walks to local heritage sites and temples. The **Temple of Kamna Devi,** 5 km (3 mi) from Shimla on the way to Jutogh, perches on the top of Prospect Hill—accessible partly on foot and partly by car—and offers glorious views of the surrounding hills and the Toy Train from Taradevi to Jotogh. The **Sankat Mochan Temple,** dedicated to Hanuman, is about 7 km (4 mi) outside town at 6,073 feet.

The town of **Chail** is built on three forested hills 45 km (28 mi) southeast of Shimla, just over an hour by car. Once the summer capital of the maharaja of Patiala, it's best known for having the highest cricket pitch in the world, and makes an excellent spot for picnics.

Shimla is not a shopping destination, but the lack of car traffic in the Mall area makes it easy to wander and browse. There are bargains to be had on woolens (blankets, shawls, sweaters) and handwoven items from Kashmir and Tibet. The **Dewandchand Atmaram** (⊠ The Mall ☎ 177/265–4455) is rated the best in town for woolen clothing and shawls. **Shezadi** (⊠ The Mall ☎ 177/213333) sells designer salwar-kameez, shawls, and bathrobes. Fixed-price crafts are available at the state-run **Himachal Emporium** (⊠ The Mall ☎ 177/280–1234). **Lakkar Bazaar,** beyond the Ridge, sells a wide range of interesting and inexpensive wooden handicrafts. There are several bookshops on the Mall, stacked with a mixture of best sellers and unexpected titles; **Maria Brothers** is recommended for rare books, old prints, and lithographs.

Where to Stay & Eat

$ ✕ **Alfa.** One of the Mall's more upscale restaurants has blond-wood furniture, bright green and red trimmings, and a cheerful ambience. Hop in for an Indian meal—naan, black dal, your choice of meat or vegetable—or sample the Chinese dishes. There are also Western dishes and fried Indian snacks. They make a good cup of piping-hot Bournvita, the classic British malted milk. ⊠ *The Mall* ☎ *177/265–7151* ⊟ *No credit cards.*

$ ✕ **Baljees.** Owned by the hotel of the same name, but located on the Mall, Baljees is one of Shimla's toniest places to dine, though admittedly this is not saying much. The second-floor air-conditioned dining room offers a wide range of Indian, Chinese, and Western food in simple, comfortable surroundings. ⊠ *The Mall* ☎ *177/265–2313* ⊟ *No credit cards.*

$$$$ ▦ **Chapslee.** Faded opulence surrounds you in this ivy-covered old manor house, built in 1835 and once home to the maharaja of Kapurthala: Gobelin tapestries, European wallpaper, Persian carpets, Indian pottery, and rare furnishings from the Doge's Palace in Venice. Each suite is uniquely decorated. Expect a hot-water bottle slipped into your bed at night, an antique walking stick for your stroll, afternoon tea, and sumptuous fixed-menu Indian and Western meals. Nonguests may dine by

reservation only. ⊠ *Lakkar Bazar, 171001* ☎ *177/280–2542* 🖷 *177/ 265–8663* ⊕ *www.chapslee.com* 🔊 *6 rooms* ⚵ *Restaurant, tennis court, croquet, library, playground, travel services; no a/c, no room TVs* ☰ *MC, V* ⊚ *FAP.*

★ **$$$$** ▦ **Oberoi Cecil.** The towering Oberoi rises on a ridge overlooking the valley, a 25-minute walk from Shimla's town center. Guest rooms have hardwood floors, Kashmiri carpets, Victorian Raj–style furnishings, and luxurious bathrooms. As the only hotel in Shimla with modern creature comforts and a high level of quality and efficiency, it's a magnificent retreat. The heated indoor pool looks out on the hills, and you can follow your walks with an ayurvedic massage in the spa. Afternoon tea (5–6 PM), pastries, and cocktails are served in the atrium lounge. The children's activity center is well equipped with computers and a life-size dollhouse. Nonguests are welcome for dinner—try the Himachali thali (sampler platter) even if you can't stay here. ⊠ *Chaura Maidan, 171004* ☎ *177/280–4848* 🖷 *177/281–1024* ⊕ *www.oberoihotels.com* 🔊 *79 rooms, 8 suites* ⚵ *Restaurant, pool, spa, billiards, bar, library, laundry service, Internet, business services, meeting room, travel services* ☰ *AE, DC, MC, V.*

★ **$$$$** ▦ **Wildflower Hall.** Once the home of Lord Kitchener, who famously demanded nothing but the best for himself, this majestic "destination spa" run by the Oberoi group is a 45-minute drive from Shimla in the forested hills. At 8,250 feet above sea level, it's an ideal base for exploration. Facilities are state of the art: the greenhouse-style indoor pool is full of sunlight, and the Jacuzzi feels like it's floating in the snow-capped panorama. Service is incredibly attentive; during a short walk to the lookout point, you might be interrupted by a limo bearing a fancy picnic lunch. At mealtimes, try the Raj cuisine or a regional thali. The staff can organize rafting at Tatapani or Chabha and picnics at any number of scenic spots. ⊠ *Mashobra, Chharabra, 171012* ☎ *177/264–8585* 🖷 *177/264–8686* ⊕ *www.oberoihotels.com* 🔊 *87 rooms* ⚵ *2 restaurants, in-room VCRs, golf privileges, tennis court, pool, gym, hot tub, spa, mountain bikes, billiards, croquet, horseback riding, ice-skating, bar, laundry service, business services, meeting room, travel services* ☰*AE, DC, MC, V.*

$$$ ▦ **Springfields.** The former summer retreat of the royal family of Shekhupura offers 11 Victorian rooms in a large period bungalow, set in a garden about 5 km (3 mi) from the center of town in Chhotta Shimla. The spacious rooms have a 1920s air, with antique pieces, wood floors, fireplaces, and balconies. Located well away from the madness of the Mall, Springfields has lovely views of the valley. A one-way taxi ride to the Mall costs Rs. 100. ⊠ *Chotta Shimla, 171002* ☎ *177/262–1297 or 177/262–1298* 🖷🖷 *177/262–1289* ⊕ *www.ushashriramhotels.com* 🔊 *11 rooms, 4 suites* ⚵ *Restaurant, billiards, laundry service, meeting room, travel services; no a/c* ☰ *MC, V.*

$$ ▦ **Woodville Palace.** Indian movie producers use this hotel as a backdrop for their fanciful productions. Topped with a jumble of towers and red-roof turrets, the rambling palace is captivating, perched on top of a hill in the midst of Indian cedars. Dating back to 1866 and still owned by local royalty, Woodville is a heritage hotel with the appropriate quota of antiques, faded portraits, deer heads, and history throughout its public spaces. Rooms are simple and comfortable, with white furniture and blue carpets. ⊠ *Raj Bhavan, 171002* ☎ *177/262–3919* 🖨 *177/ 262–3098* ⊕ *www.chapslee.com* ⤵ *25 rooms* ⚬ *Room service, restaurant, tennis court, badminton, billiards, Ping-Pong, travel services; no a/c* ⊟ *AE, MC, V.*

$ 🏨 **Baljees Residency.** Just a few minutes from the Mall, Baljees probably offers the best value for money in Shimla. Although not terribly imaginative, the rooms are neat and comfortable—with green carpets, simple furnishings, and small sitting areas—and have decent views. You may want to opt for a deluxe room, as they're somewhat more pleasant for just Rs. 200 extra. The bathrooms, done in red granite, are reasonably clean. ⊠ *Circular Rd., 171003* ☎ *177/281–4054* 🖨 *177/265–2202* ⊕ *www.hotelbaljeesregency.com* ⤵ *30 rooms* ⚬ *Restaurant, bar, laundry service, travel services* ⊟ *AE, MC, V.*

en route | To access the Kinnaur region, which holds the wonderful Sangla Valley, head northeast of Shimla. Sangla is eight hours (227 km [140 mi]) from Shimla on a road that gets more precarious in the second half of the trip. You'll be on NH-22 until Karcham; at Karcham, turn right and drive the remaining 18 km (12 mi) south to Sangla. If you're approaching Kinnaur from Lahaul or Spiti, consider accessing Sangla from Tabo, a large Spiti town 47 km (29 mi) south of Kaza. This 185-km (115-mi) journey takes six to seven hours, and you can stay at the friendly Banjara Camps at both ends.

Kinnaur

Sangla is 227 km (141 mi) northeast of Shimla.

The Sutlej River runs through the eminently green district of Kinnaur, which comprises the Baspa and Sangla valleys in the towering Kinnaur Kailash Range. Like Spiti, Kinnaur hides wonderful old Buddhist monasteries; yet, despite the proximity to Tibet, only the far eastern and northern, cold-desert parts of Kinnaur are Buddhist. The curved roofs of gompas (Tibetan monasteries) reflect the transition of the landscape from Hinduism to Buddhism. Kinnauris are decked in green jackets, cummerbunds, hats teamed with shawls, and elaborate silver jewelry.

The Sangla valley is magnificently green and dramatic, with orchards, burbling streams, and stupendous alpine landscapes. Day hikes, overnight treks, and jeep excursions are well worth the effort it takes to drive here from Shimla. Kinnaur was opened to travelers in 1992, and you still need an Inner Line permit to travel beyond Rekong Peo to Puh en route to Spiti.

Where to Stay

$$$ 🏨 **Banjara Camp.** The Sangla Valley's best lodging is a group of deluxe tents with full-size beds and attached cement-floor bathrooms (bucket bath only). At 8,850 feet the camp is smack on the banks of the Baspa River just 30 km (19 mi) shy of Chitkul, the last village on the Old Hindustan–Tibet Road (some 50 km from the China border). Relax in a clearing overlooking the water after a rousing day hike, and listen to

the river rush by as you drift off to sleep. The price includes excellent vegetarian meals, served three times a day in a mess tent. The friendly, attentive staff can take you on day hikes or drives, complete with a home-cooked Indian lunch. ⊠ *Reserve through 1A Hauz Khas Village, New Delhi 110016* ☎ *11/2685–5153* 📠 *11/2685–5152* ⊕ *www. banjaracamps.com* ➪ *18 tents* ⚭ *Dining room; no a/c, no room phones, no room TVs* ⊟ *No credit cards* |◎| *FAP.*

$ 🖼 **Kinner Villa.** This simple hotel in the town of Kalpa has a splendid location amid forests, alpine pastures, apple orchards, and glaciers, overlooking the dramatic Kinnaur Kailash—the winter abode of Lord Shiva. The staff can organize treks and jeep safaris. Kalpa is 290 km (180 mi) northeast of Shimla, not too far from Sangla; take NH-22 from Shimla via Rampur, Karcham, and Rekong Peo. ⌂ *Reserve through Travel Circuit, New Delhi 110062* ☎ *1786/226006 in Delhi, 11/2905–4037, 11/2905–2049* 📠 *11/2905–4746* ⊕ *www.himalayaindia.com/kinnervilla. htm* ➪ *10 rooms* ⚭ *Restaurant; no a/c, no room phones, no room TVs.*

Manali

❹ *280 km (174 mi) north of Shimla.*

Until about 15 years ago, Manali was a small, relaxed place. On one side of town was a settlement of Tibetan refugees; on the other side, near the bus stop, Western backpackers smoked dope and swapped trekking stories. Then, in 1989, Kashmir descended into chaos following the kidnapping of the Indian Home Minister's daughter by separatist militants. Most of the Indian honeymooners and foreign travelers who would otherwise have vacationed in Kashmir detoured to the village of Manali. The subsequent explosion of development has ruined Manali's tranquillity—concrete hotels have risen cheek-by-jowl, and today Manali is a resort town. The new Manali overshadows the original settlement, Old Manali, whose popularity with hippie Israeli backpackers is reflected in the many Hebrew shop signs. Unfortunately, many of the old homes are now gone, and the area is associated mainly with dope deals. Avoid it after dark.

That said, Manali is deep in the culturally rich Kullu Valley, in the shadow of some magnificent Himalayan peaks. The neighboring hillsides are cloaked in forests of towering deodhars. The friendly Kullu Valley people are known for their unique traditional dress, including men's pillbox caps with colorful geometric embroidery. Most of the town revolves around its main strip, the **Mall,** and you can negotiate small distances to and from the Mall with auto-rickshaws (Rs. 20 for a few kilometers). In the heart of town is a Tibetan monastery, the brightly colored **Gadhan Thekchhokling Gompa,** worth a visit if you don't plan to visit any Buddhist areas. The stalls outside sell Tibetan trinkets.

The Mall, Manali's main commercial strip, is lined with shops selling shawls, Kashmiri crafts, and woolens. **Sultaan Kashmir** (⊠ Shop 1, City Heart Shopping Complex ☎ 1902/251610) has lovely embroidered shawls and jackets—but bargain hard. The **Bhutti Weaver Cooperative Society showroom** (⊠ Manu Market, off Mall) sells pretty Kullu shawls, Himachali vests, and pashmina shawls and scarves.

CloseUp
EYE-POPPING DRIVE: SHIMLA–MANALI

AFTER SPENDING TWO TO FOUR DAYS IN THE SHIMLA AREA, consider driving on to Manali via Mandi and Kullu—this trip (260 km [160 mi]) takes about six hours and is one of the most enjoyable drives in the region. The route curves a fair bit for the first two hours, past bright-green terraced fields, but once it reaches the banks of the Beas River, near Mandi (156 km [100 mi]), the road straightens out and the scenery grows steadily more spectacular. As the road, NH-21, approaches the Kullu Valley it wanders beside the emerald-green Beas between impossibly steep mountains and gorges dotted with traditional mud-and-brick Himachali homes with slate roofs. The regions on the opposite side of the river, bordering Spiti, are incredibly remote—their only form of transport is the basket, a sort of manual cable car that runs from mountaintop villages down to the road. During the monsoon season (July and August), waterfalls drop from the peaks high above. This road was built largely with the labor of Tibetan refugees after their exodus in 1959; they were employed by the Indian government to pave the way north for army convoys.

As you approach Kullu, snow-covered peaks pop up on the horizon, and you start to pass apple orchards and traditional wooden dwellings. After March, the apple trees flower—apples are a major cash crop in this area, and apple-flavor liquor is popular with locals. You might see some Angora rabbit farms, too, as their hair is used to weave shawls. Locals are colorfully dressed in traditional pattus (robes) and Himachali topis (hats). Stop in Kullu, a thriving market town, to take in a bit of local color. Kullu shawls, in solid colors with distinctive borders, are cheap here. On the outskirts of town is the **Bhuttico** showroom for the work of the Bhutti Weavers Cooperative Society

(✉ Bhutti Colony, Bhuntar ☎ 1902/ 260049). **Gagan Shawl Industries** (✉ Bhutti Colony, Bhuntar ☎ 1902/ 265325), which sells shawls and more.

Manali is 42 km (26 mi) beyond Kullu. After 21 km (11 mi), turn right off the highway at Patlikuhl, toward Nagar. As the road ascends, the slopes are forested with pines and deodar, and herds of sheep graze on the mountains. A tea stop at the medieval **Hotel Castle** (☎ 1902/ 47816) in Nagar, on the eastern side of the Beas (5 km [3 mi] beyond Patlikuhl), gives you a spectacular view of the Kullu Valley. Built by Raja Sidh Singh in 1460, the castle has a small museum and some rooms for overnight stays; nearby there's a gallery featuring the Russian artist Nicholas Roerich.

Ten kilometers (6 mi) before Manali, you'll reach the hamlet of Jagat Sukh, a cluster of typical Kullu Valley homes that gives you an idea of what Manali was like before tourists. In these two-story dark-wood houses, livestock is kept on the ground floor while the family lives upstairs. Handlooms whir in many homes, weaving colorful pattus. Have a look at the ancient-looking Shiva temple, with its age-old deity, in the heart of the village—according to a local, "It must be 500 years old, but don't ask the priest. He'll tell you it's over 1,000 years old."

Manali's main bazaar, **Manu Market,** occupies a network of lanes near the bus stand on the Beas side of the road. Vendors of wool, fresh local fruit and vegetables (the Kullu Valley is famous for its produce), and colorful Kullu lace, woolens, and caps do brisk business. Noodle kitchens and snack counters beckon with snacks. There are several shops selling Tibetan artifacts; try **Samten,** near the taxi stand in one of the market's first lanes.

Make time for a walk to the Hadimba Temple (also called Dunghri Temple), nestled in the woods 20 minutes from the Mall. A cross between temple and pagoda, this ancient shrine has a wooden exterior decorated with deer antlers. Dedicated to Hadimba Devi, a demoness who turned respectable when she married one of the noble Pandava brothers, Bhima. Animal sacrifices, usually chickens, take place here, as they do in many Himachali temples; as local Hindus have a tradition of appeasing the *devi,* or fearsome goddesses. Yaks from Ladakh are parked outside for those who want joy rides on these giant beasts. Summer sees a carnival open up in the park behind the temple.

Fall—when the valley's many apple trees bear fruit—brings the famous Perahera Festival: a local variation of the Hindu festival of Dussehra, celebrated all over North India in October. Ten days after the new moon, villagers bring their local deities—more than 200—from their temples down to Kullu, at the head of the valley. Dragged by hand on palanquins or wheeled on carts known as *raths,* the idols are brought to pay respect to Raghunathji, Kullu's patron god. For three nights, people from all over the valley, including the descendants of local royalty, mill around a temporary market on the dusty fairgrounds next to the Beas River.

At the high end of the Kullu Valley, farther up toward the Rohtang Pass, 20,000-foot peaks loom on three sides. Day hikers will find endless exhilarating paths, often alongside Gujjar shepherds with flocks of goats. Manali is also the origin and endpoint for more serious adventures into the Himalayan wilderness—from here you can launch trekking, driving, and rafting trips into Lahaul, Spiti or, to the west, the Kangra and Chamba valleys. Moreover, the road north from Manali over the Rohtang Pass is currently the only open road to Ladakh.

In winter Indian tourists head out from Manali to Snow Point for sledding, tobogganing, skiing, and snowmobiling.

Where to Stay & Eat

$ ✕ **Chopsticks.** Almost identical in appearance to its neighbor, Mountain View, this little eatery is a me-too restaurant offering Japanese dishes as well as Tibetan and Chinese cuisine. Some of Manali's best Chinese food is available here. ✉ *The Mall, opposite taxi stand* ☎ *1902/252639* ▭ *No credit cards.*

$ ✕ **Il Forno.** An Italian couple returns to Manali every summer to open up this restaurant, set in a traditional wooden Manali home, and cook up a storm. Their homemade pastas and other Italian specialities are famous for miles around. Quantities are limited, so it's best to show up by about 8 PM for dinner. ✉ *Beyond the Log Huts next to Hadimba temple, 15 min steep walk uphill* ☎ *No phone* ▭ *No credit cards.*

$ ✕ **Mount View.** Booths and tables are crammed into this narrow space, and the walls hold photos of the Dalai Lama and Lhasa. The Tibetan chef creates Tibetan, Chinese, and Japanese dishes (mizutaki, sukiyaki, om rice, yakigyoza, tempura). Try the momos, soups with homemade noodles, or spicy Szechuan fare. ✉ *The Mall, opposite taxi stand* ☎ *1902/253617* ▭ *No credit cards.*

$ ✕ **Sagar.** This cubbyhole offers vegetarian food in an upstairs room with a view of Manali's main thoroughfare. The eclectic menu mixes Indian food, Chinese dishes, pizzas, pastas, and sizzlers in a cozy, wood-panel atmosphere, with green carpeting and white furniture. ✉ *The Mall, at taxi stand* ☎ *1902/251172* ▭ *No credit cards.*

¢–$$ ✕⌂ **Johnson's Lodge.** Perfect for families or groups of four, these apartments are spacious, clean, and cozy. Across the garden is a new wing of double rooms and a popular restaurant (closed in winter) serving Indian and Western dishes to guests and nonguests. Fresh local trout, when available, is a house specialty—locals rave about it. Ask about the family's apple-orchard lodge 13 km (8 mi) south of Manali, in Raison, where the rooms are large but sparsely furnished. ✉ *Circuit House Rd., The Mall, Manali, at top of Mall Rd., turn left at Nehru Park and look for sign to Johnson's Restaurant* ☎ *1902/253023* 🖷 *1902/245123* ⇄ *12 rooms, 2 cottage rooms* ♢ *Restaurant, travel services; no a/c, no TV in some rooms* ▭ *No credit cards.*

$–$$$$ ⌂ **Retreat Cottages.** Run by a local Himachali–Tibetan couple, this little lodge in the woods is easily one of Manali's most attractive places to stay. The large Swiss-style chalet has self-contained sections on different levels, each with a sitting area and kitchenette with dining area, as well as a little porch and a loft. Airy and well lighted, the units are sparsely but attractively furnished with Tibetan artifacts and carpets and simple wooden furniture. The restaurant serves homestyle meals. Call in advance in winter, as the hotel sometimes closes. ✉ *Log Huts Area, Manali 175131* ☎ *1902/252042 or 1902/252673* ✉ *chuki_mahant@hotmail.com* ⇄ *8 rooms* ♢ *Restaurant, travel services; no a/c, no TV in some rooms* ▭ *AE, DC, MC, V.*

$$$ ⌂ **Ambassador Resorts.** Instead of turning left, crossing the Beas and entering "downtown" Manali, continue northward to find Ambassador Resorts. Built on several levels, the red-roof hotel has interesting little nooks and lounges, with an accent on wood. Rooms are large and cheerful, with wood floors, wood paneling and special low sitting areas, and the command pretty views of the valley and the snow-capped peaks. The area is quiet and secluded, but at this writing the hotel was under renovation, so ask for a room away from the construction. Rates include breakfast and dinner. ✉ *Sunny Side, Chadiyari, Manali 175131* ☎ *1902/252235* 🖷 *1901/252173* ⊕ *www.ambassadorresorts.com* ⇄ *50 rooms, 4 suites, 1 cottage* ♢ *2 restaurants, gym, hot tub, billiards, Ping-Pong, roller skating, bar, dance club, laundry service, business services, meeting room, travel services* ▭ *AE, MC, V* ⎮◎⎮ *MAP.*

$$ ⌂ **Usha Sriram Snowcrest Manor.** High on a hill above Manali town, this large modern-style hotel with hospitable staff has spectacular views of the Beas River, the Kullu Valley, and the Rohtang Pass on clear days. The deck is especially nice for meals on a sunny day. In summer and during fall fes-

tivals you'll meet with crowds of Indian families and honeymooners. Rooms are rather shabby, but reasonably clean and comfortable. Hiking, river rafting, fishing, paragliding, and skiing can be arranged through the travel desk, and the restaurant serves reasonably tasty Indian and Western meals. Traveler's checks are not accepted. ⊠ *Beyond Log Huts, 175131* ☎*1902/253351 to 2* 🖷*1902/253188* ⊕*www.ushashriramhotels. com* ➹*32 rooms* 🕭 *Restaurant, health club, billiards, dance club, Internet, meeting room, travel services; no a/c* ▤ *AE, DC, MC, V.*

$ 🖻 **Mayflower.** Situated at the edge of the woods, Mayflower is a relatively new two-story hotel. The large yet snug guest rooms have fireplaces, wooden floors and paneling, and some bathrooms have tubs. About a 10-minute walk uphill from the Mall, it offers good value for money. ⊠ *Club House Rd., Manali 175131* ☎ *1902/252104* 🖷 *1901/253923* ➹ *16 rooms* 🕭 *Restaurant, travel services; no a/c* ▤ *No credit cards.*

---

en route | The districts of Lahaul and Spiti are best accessed from Manali. The Manali–Leh road, open in summer only, sweeps north into Lahaul across the Rohtang Pass, taking about five hours (114 km [70 mi]) to reach the town of Keylong, district headquarters of Lahaul.

Kaza, the district headquarters of Spiti, is 201 km (125 mi) northeast of Manali, a seven- or eight-hour drive. Follow the Manali–Leh highway north up to Gramphoo (62 km [38 mi]), then turn right and head east toward Kaza via Batal.

Lahaul & Spiti

Keylong, Lahaul, is 114 km (70 mi) north of Manali; Kaza, Spiti, is 201 km (124 mi) southwest of Manali.

The district comprising Lahaul and Spiti (pronounced "piti") is the largest in the state of Himachal Pradesh. The pretty town of Kibber, in Spiti, is one of the highest settlements in the world, at 4,205 meters (13,688 feet) above sea level.

Beginning 51 km (32 mi) north of Manali on the far side of the Rohtang Pass, **Lahaul** is a heady place for treks and jeep safaris. It's much smaller than Ladakh and has fewer and simpler *gompas* (monasteries), but the two share a general mingling of religion and landscape. Tibetan influences are all over this district. From Tabo, Spiti—famous in the Tibetan world for its gompa, which has some spectacular murals—Tibet is hardly 25 km (16 mi) away. Mountains bear in from all directions, and windswept passes overlook stunningly harsh, remote landscapes of stark mountains, boundless sky, and deserted spaces. Expect extremes of weather: mornings and evenings are freezing, whereas afternoons blaze. The glaciers look icy and somber, and an occasional lake sparkles under the hot sun. Prayer flags and the rare green valley pulse with color. As word gets out, Lahaul is experiencing an influx of trekkers, so work with your tour operator to choose a route that avoids crowds.

You can raft, day-hike, trek, and tool around by jeep in the **Spiti Valley,** a sensitive border area southeast of Lahaul, on the other side of the Kunzum Pass (15,055 feet). Spiti's landscape is more arid than Lahaul's; its mountains, split by the raging Spiti River, are steeper; and the culture is more thoroughly Buddhist. Here you'll find the 11th-century **Tabo Gompa** (46 km [29 mi] east of Kaza), one of the holiest monasteries for Tibetan Buddhists. Foreigners need an Inner Line Permit to visit Spiti, though formalities are getting looser over time.

en route | Two routes, both snowbound in winter, connect Lahaul and Spiti with the rest of the state. To reach southern Himachal Pradesh from Spiti, you can drive via Kaza and Tabo to Kinnaur; to access western Himachal Pradesh from Lahaul, you must go through Manali.

The drive from Manali to **Dharamshala** (253 km [146 mi]) takes six hours. The route is not as picturesque as the drive through the Kullu Valley, but once you enter the **Kangra Valley** (beyond Mandi) on the NH-20, you pass through an endless patchwork of vividly green fields sown with wheat, corn, rice, and bright-yellow mustard. At Baijnath, you'll see the ancient stone Vaidyanath Temple. Closer to Palampur, as the land begins to roll, is a large belt of tea plantations stretching out to the snowy Dhauladhar range—Kangra tea is a specialty here. Consider stopping at the Taragarh Palace Hotel (⇨ *below*) for a meal or an overnight stay. An hour beyond Palampur, the road climbs sharply to Dharamshala.

Kangra Valley

References to the Kangra Valley date back 3,500 years to the age of the Hindu *Vedas*. Now densely populated, the valley climbs gently into Himachal Pradesh from the plains of Punjab, with the pine-covered Dhauladhar Range jutting out to the west like a Himalayan spur on the northern horizon. The upper part of the valley gave birth to the famous Kangra style of painting, featuring scenes from the life of Lord Krishna, often highly romantic, in a style heavily influenced by Moghul miniatures.

Aside from the Vaidyanath Temple in Baijnath, the Kangra Valley has no sights per se; it's just a pleasant place to wander around, and it has two lovely Heritage Hotels. With a heady mixture of tropical and alpine terrain backed by snow-topped mountains and intersected by rivers, the valley is a popular destination for trekking, fishing, and horseback riding. Experienced riders can take in lovely Himalayan views from spirited polo ponies. Wandering through meadows and forests, you can visit Kangra villages and a Tibetan monastery, spending each night in a tent at a different idyllic campsite. Given the relatively low elevation and lack of air-conditioning, try to come to Kangra before mid-April or after mid-September.

Much of the land here is cultivated. Although local farmers grow mostly "winter" crops such as wheat and fruit, the plantations in **Palampur** contain the only tea gardens in this part of India. Take home a box of "Kangra Green Gold" to sip while remembering this gentle valley. Up the road from Palampur is Baijnath, home of the **Vaidyanath Temple.** Dedicated to Lord Shiva, this 9th-century temple is well worth a visit for the intricate stone carvings of Surya (the sun god) and the Garuda (a birdlike creature) on its interior and exterior walls.

Where to Stay

$$$$ 🏨 **Judge's Court.** In a 12-acre orchard of mango, lychee, plum, persimmon, clove, and cardamom trees and fields of vegetables, this beautifully restored 300-year-old ancestral home of the Kuthiala Sood family includes the family's historic cottage and a country manor. In spring and fall you can sit on a shady veranda, smell the trees in the garden, and look out to the Dhauladhar range; in winter a fire can be arranged in the sitting room. The staff can organize angling, water sports, treks, and picnics. ✉ *Jai Bhawan, Pragpur 177107* ☎ *1970/245035 or 245335 or in Delhi 11/2467–4135 or 11/2410–2223* 🖂 *3/44 Shanti Niketan, New Delhi 110021* 🖷 *1970/245823 or 11/2688–5970* ⊕ *www.judgescourt.com* 🛏 *10 rooms, 2 suites* ♨ *Restaurant, travel services; no room TVs* ▱ *AE, MC, V.*

$–$$ 🏨 **Taragarh Palace Hotel.** This 1930s summer resort and its 15-acre forested estate now comprise a Heritage Hotel owned by a member of Kashmir's Hindu royalty. The art deco lounge is a lovely place to relax after a dip in the pool, and the teak-panel dining room has an exquisite fireplace and smoked-glass windows. Guest rooms are not opulent, but they have eclectic furnishings from the family's estate. Rooms in the back are larger; the cheapest rooms require you to share a bathroom with one other party. The hotel is 45 km (27 mi) southeast of Dharamshala on the NH-20, between Palampur and Baijnath, but the drive takes just over an hour. 🖂 *Taragarh, Kangra Valley 176081* ☎ *1894/242034 or 1894/243077, 11/2464–3046 in Delhi* 🖷 *11/2469–2317* ⊕ *www.taragarh.com* 🛏 *16 rooms, 4 suites* ♨ *Restaurant, tennis court, pool, badminton, horseback riding, travel services; no a/c in some rooms* ▱ *AE.*

Dharamshala

❺ *253 km (157 mi) west of Manali, 248 km (154 mi) north of Chandigarh.*

Perched high above the floor of the Kangra Valley, Dharamshala is an old British hill station, but its main attraction is the cloistered upper part of town, McLeod Ganj. Here, 9 km (6 mi) uphill through the Indian Army cantonment, is the Tibetan Government in Exile and the home of the Dalai Lama, Tenzin Gyatso, and an entire Tibetan community.

On March 31, 1959, as the Chinese army took over Lhasa, the 24-year-old Dalai Lama, dressed as a soldier, crossed from Tibet into the safety of India via the Khenzimana Pass. After a 15-day, 800-mi trek, across the wide Brahmaputra river, from Lhasa with six cabinet ministers in tow, he reached the Tawang Monastery in the northeastern Indian state of Arunachal Pradesh. Some 80,000 Tibetans followed him into exile in the days that followed. Looking for a mountain home for his displaced people, His Holiness arrived in Dharamshala in 1960, and finally settled here.

Visiting Dharamshala is the best way to see Tibet without actually going there. A population of 15,000 Tibetans has turned McLeod Ganj into a miniature Tibet to the point where it feels anachronistic, like a phony Shangri-La (they call it "Dhasa"). The town attracts a strange mix of soul-seekers and dope-seekers, not to mention down-at-the-heel back-packers looking for a cheap extended holiday. Simply put, McLeod Ganj is a tourist zoo, with crowds of yuppies, hippies, American Bud-dhists, honeymooners, mooners . . . and occasionally Richard Gere.

Thousands of Buddhists live here, as well as in the remote, high-alti-tude districts of Lahaul, Spiti, and Kinnaur. Most practice a Tibetan form of tantric Buddhism. Tibetan women twist their hair into numerous long pigtails held in place by a silver ornament, and wear a long robe outfit called a *chuba* with a colorful apron; many men wear long maroon or brown overcoats. As in most Buddhist communities, men and women share all tasks, from raising a family to working in the fields where they grow crops of barley, buckwheat, and potatoes.

Devastated by an earthquake in 1905, Dharamshala now suffers from a profusion of travelers and ugly hotels, which disturb the tranquillity that should ideally surround His Holiness. The tourist office and many hotels are in lower Dharamshala, but there's no real reason to linger here. Just before you reach the bus and taxi stands on your way up from Dharamshala, you'll see one of the few remaining structures from the British days, **St. John's Church in the Wilderness,** built in 1852 (☉ Daily 10–5, Sun. service 11:30). The headstones in the churchyard attest to the difficulties and diseases the British suffered; among them are the graves of David McLeod, lieutenant governor of Punjab, who founded Dharamshala in the mid-19th century, and Lord Elgin, Viceroy of India, who died in 1862 and asked to be buried here (his grave lies just be-hind the church, marked by a large monument). So fond was Lord Elgin of Dharamshala that, had he lived, it might have become the sum-mer capital of the British Raj.

McLeod Ganj is at the center of Tibetan efforts to preserve and main-tain their culture during their exile. Several sites devoted to this effort are worth checking out. The **Tibetan Institute of Performing Arts (TIPA),** on the road to Dharamkot, hosts wonderful evenings of music and dance, and an International Himalayan Festival every December. The **Norbul-ingka Institute for Tibetan Culture,** 40 minutes (15 km [9 mi]) below McLeod Ganj in Sidhpur, and registered as a trust under the Dalai Lama, is committed to preserving Tibetan arts and crafts skills. Master artists train young apprentices in *thangka* (intricate Tibetan scroll paint-ing depicting meditational deities), metalwork, appliqué, embroidery, and woodcarving. You can visit the artists in their studios, pick up a sample in the gift shop, and pop into the **Losel Doll Museum** to see a wonderful collection of traditional Tibetan costumes.

The **Dalai Lama's private residence** and the Thekchen Choling temple (some-times called the Central Cathedral) are on the east end of Temple Road, joined to each other by a footpath. The view across the valley from the temple balcony is magnificent, and the complex, run by 200 monks who assist the Dalai Lama, includes a bookstore and restaurant. Buddhist pil-grims come here from near and far, so you might see crowds of monks, urbanites, and devotees from Lahaul and Spiti arriving with packets of biscuits and chocolates to pay homage. The **Tibet Museum** (☉ Tues.–Sun. 10–6 ☜ Rs. 5) highlights the struggle for a Free Tibet and many Tibetans' escapes from the Chinese regime, including the blood-stained prison clothes of one victim. The Dalai Lama gives **public audiences** several times a year, so inquire at your hotel and apply for clearance at the security office (✉ Bhangsu Rd., next to Hotel Tibet ☎ 1892/221560)—bring your passport. The Dalai Lama's birthday, July 6, is a festive occasion, with performances by students from the Tibetan Children's Village school. For more information on the Tibetan Government in Exile and the history of their struggle, see the Web site of the Department of Information and International Relations (www.tibet.com).

For educators and students, a trip to the **Tibetan Children's Village** (TCV), on the road north to Naddi, is a memorable experience. Try to arrange a visit in advance (☎ 1892/221053 ⊕ www.tibchild.com). Established in 1960, the TCV boarding school is home to 2,400 Tibetan orphans and refugees supported by individual and agency donors from all over the world, primarily the SOS Kinderdorf International in Vienna. In all, the organization has more than 14,000 children under its care in branches extending from Ladakh down to Bylakuppe, near Mysore. The pleasant 30-minute walk to the school takes you through deodar cedars (follow the water pipe). The **Handicraft Centre** (☎ 1892/221592) below the school has good crafts and carpets at reasonable prices.

Tibetan crafts, antiques, jewelry, and clothing are available in McLeod Ganj. **Tibetan Gallery** (☎ 1892/221398), near the bus stand, stocks a wide ranges of Tibetan-style blouses, skirts, shirts, kurtas, and T-shirts for adults and children. The **Tibetan Handicraft Center** at the McLeod Ganj post office (✉ Jogibara Rd.) sells thick, reasonably priced Tibetan carpets. **Norling Designs** (✉ Temple Rd., next to Little Lhasa bookshop) has expensive but very fine crafts and clothing from the Norbulingka Institute. The local **wine shops** sell apple beer and apple wine.

A drive or trek into the countryside makes for a nice change. *Do not* linger after dark—incidents have been reported on Bhagsu Road—and do take an umbrella or raincoat, as Dharamshala's weather is variable. There's a **Shiva temple** below a waterfall at Bhagsunag, 2 km (1 mi) northwest of the McLeod Ganj bus stand. Venture about 3 km (2 mi) north to **Dal Lake,** a muddy apology to the real Dal Lake in Kashmir. About 3 km (2 mi) north of Dal Lake is **Talnoo,** where you can take in a pretty view that might include Gaddi shepherds and their flocks. Gaddis are a distinctive group of nomadic Himachalis, with fair skin and hazel eyes, who cover their heads with scarves. Some still move from place to place with their livestock. Near Talnoo is the large Gaddi village of Naddi.

On the spiritual and physical levels, there's lots to do at McLeod Ganj. You can enroll in yoga classes, have your long-term ailments considered by a doctor of Tibetan medicine, learn Buddhist philosophy, or study Tibetan art. Pick up a copy of *Contact,* which lists current courses of study, in any popular Tibetan restaurant.

Where to Stay & Eat

★ $$$ ✕ **Snow Lion.** McLeod Ganj's one fine-dining venue is attached to a low-end hotel. Run by the Tibetan Administration Welfare Society, the restaurant has a parquet floor and basic decor. Unfortunately, its windows overlook garbage and slum dwellings; concentrate on the distant Himalayas, the black-and-white Tibetan photos on the walls, or the food: Japanese, Chinese, Western (including grilled meats), and authentic Tibetan. ⊠ *Hotel Tibet, Bagsunagh Rd., McLeod Ganj* ☎ *1892/221587* ▭ *MC, V.*

$ ✕ **McLlo.** The hub of tourist life in Dharamshala, the dimly lit McLlo is the place to nurse a beer and watch the crowd. The restaurant has no particular decor; rather, its diverse clientele provides the atmosphere. The menu is fairly diverse, swinging from Indian and Tibetan to Chinese, South Indian, Israeli, and Western—including Baskin-Robbins ice cream. Doors are open until 10:30 PM. ⊠ *Next to bus stand* ☎ *1892/221280* ▭ *No credit cards.*

★ $ ✕ **Nick's Italian Kitchen.** If you need a break from tandoori chicken, try this excellent vegetarian restaurant in the Kunga Guest House. Quiches, pizzas, lasagna, and other pastas are cooked by a Tibetan family whose skills were inspired by a benefit organized by a traveling Italian-American from New York. Richard Gere has been known to drop by occasionally for the vegetarian pastas, and he apparently loves the lemon curd pie. ⊠ *Kunga Guest House, Bhagsunag Rd.* ☎ *1892/221180 or 1892/221569* ▭ *No credit cards.*

$ ✕ **Yak.** Stop in for a snack and watch the cook at work: these are the best (cheesy) momos and (hearty) Tibetan noodle soups in town. Don't be put off by the dark doorway, the tiny seating area, or the grease-stained walls—Yak is full of local Tibetans for a reason. ⊠ *Jogibara Rd., opposite Aroma and Ashoka restaurants* ☎ *No phone* ▭ *No credit cards.*

¢–$ ✕🖳 **India House.** One of McLeod Ganj's more modern hotels, India House has an excellent restaurant with an eclectic menu offering Indian, Chinese, Western, and Tibetan food. Beer is served. The well-lighted rooms have wood paneling and small balconies with pleasant views; bathrooms are clean and user-friendly. The furnishings are a bit heavy on velour, but service is attentive and the rates are reasonable. ⊠ *Bhagsunag Rd., just beyond Tibet House* ☎ *1892/221457* 🖶 *1892/221–144* ⊕ *www. hotelindiahouse.com* ◿ *18 rooms* ⚲ *Restaurant, laundry service, travel services; no a/c* ▭ *MC, V.*

★ ¢–$$$ 🖳 **Glenmoor Cottages.** The Indian owners of this secluded hideaway, a 20-minute (½-km) walk from McLeod Ganj, live in a Scottish bungalow that's been in their family since the 1940s. The five cottages have spectacular mountain and valley views, and their modest concrete-and-wood facades conceal charming interiors: crisp white walls contrast with modern spruce and pine furnishings. Bathrooms are modern, with showers only, and some cottages have kitchenettes. Two simple rooms with a shared bathroom are available in the bungalow. ⊠ *First right turn (no sign) uphill after you exit Dharamshala on road to Dal Lake, also called Mall Rd., McLeod Ganj 176219* ☎ *1892/221010* 🖶 *1892/221021* ⊕ *www.glenmoorcottages.com* ◿ *2 rooms, 5 cottages* ⚲ *Restaurant, travel services; no a/c* ▭ *MC, V.*

$–$$ ⛱ **Chonor House.** Built and run by the Norbulingka Institute, this is the
Fodor'sChoice   best place to stay in McLeod Ganj. The pretty lounge and guest rooms
★   are furnished with handmade furniture, carpets, and linens made by institute artists, and most rooms have balconies. But the special touch is the murals, painted in each guest room on the Tibetan themes of myth, religion, and ecology. The restaurant serves excellent Tibetan cuisine, and you can take meals outdoors on a large balcony in season. The local Lhasa Apso dogs, which often set up a chain reaction of midnight yelping, are unfortunately beyond the staff's control. ⊠ *Temple Rd.* 🕾 *1892/ 221468, 1892/221006, or 1892/221077* 🖷 *1892/221468* ⊕ *www. norbulingka.org* 🗩 *11 rooms* ⚭ *Restaurant, Internet, meeting room, travel services; no a/c, no room TVs* ⊟ *AE, MC, V.*

★ ¢   ⛱ **Pema Thang Guest House.** The selling point of this Tibetan-run hotel is its simplicity—clean, unfussy rooms with wood floors, large glass windows, wood trimmings, and valley views. The bathrooms have showers only. The cozy restaurant serves Tibetan meals. You can't miss the building—look for the long, red-and-green strip along the eaves. ⊠ *Opposite Hotel Bhagsu, a few minutes away from Chinar Lodge, McLeod Ganj 176219* 🕾 *1892/221871* ⊕ *www.pemathang.com* 🗩 *12 rooms* ⚭ *Restaurant, travel services; no a/c, no TV in some rooms* ⊟ *No credit cards.*

⬭ **en route**   Allow two days for a trip from Dharamshala to Dalhousie, plus another two for a trip to Chamba. The drive to Dalhousie takes 4½ hours on a bumpy road. The landscape is unforgiving, with the road slicing through stark brown mountains. The quiet town of **Chamba**—which has a small art museum featuring Kangra miniature paintings and local embroidered pictures called *rumals*—is 2½ hours (50 km [31 mi]) beyond Dalhousie, accessed by a treacherous road that weaves past the Ravi River. Aim to see Chamba if you have a great deal of time and can follow a relaxed pace.

Dalhousie

❻   *130 km (81 mi) northwest of Dharamshala.*

The hill station of Dalhousie was fashionable with British administrators based in Lahore (now in Pakistan) in the mid-19th century. It was established by the Lord Dalhousie, who, as India's governor-general, founded the Indian rail system. Today Dalhousie draws crowds of Indian tourists in the summer, so try to see it between March and May or September and November. The setting that drew the British is still spectacular, with forested slopes, green valleys, and the snow-capped Pir Panjal peaks on the town's doorstep; here you really get a sense of being close to the great Himalayas.

There's not much to occupy you in this sleepy, two-rickshaw settlement. The main town is actually the nondescript Banikhot (6 km [4 mi] downhill), which you climb through on the way up. The best way to soak in the atmosphere is to take walks, and perhaps watch some migratory birds. Evidence of the colonial days is mostly gone, barring the two churches at each *chowk* (crossroads or marketplace)—one of the prettiest, **St. Francis Church** on Subhash Chowk, was built in 1894. The town has pedestrian-only walkways between Gandhi Chowk and Subhash Chowk, and along Potryn Road. At Gandhi Chowk, in the Garam Sarak area, a few shops sell Himachal Pradesh handicrafts: walnut and oak-wood boxes and trays, and colorful jute Chamba slippers.

Before Tibetan exiles were directed to Dharamshala, Dalhousie housed them for a short time. A visit to the **Tibetan Handicraft Center** in Upper Bakrota, nearly 2 km (1 mi) from the Dalhousie's main square on the Khajjiar Road, is a must if you like hand-knotted Tibetan carpets.

Where to Stay & Eat

$–$$ ✕ **Davat.** For a quick bite, try this restaurant in the Hotel Mount View. The noise from the nearby bus stand detracts somewhat from the experience, but the food—Mughlai, tandoori, and Chinese cuisine—is reliable. ⊠ *Dalhousie St., Dalhousie* ☎ *1899/242120.*

$–$$ ✕ **Kwality.** Owned by the Grand View hotel, this branch of the Kwality chain is one of Dalhousie's fanciest restaurants. The menu centers on classic tandoori and North Indian food, with a few Chinese, South Indian, and Western options. The restaurant has a strongly woodsy look, with wooden tables, chairs, walls, and ceilings. ⊠ *Gandhi Chowk, Dalhousie* ☎ *No phone.*

$ 🏨 **Alps Resorts.** Located 2½ km from the center of town on the crest of a hill, this pretty, red-roof white resort commands a view of the valley. The two buildings are set in a pretty garden with a tree house, a swing, and wrought-iron garden furniture surrounded by a picket fence. Guest rooms are plain, with slightly moth-eaten carpets, but they're comfortable. Taxis charge Rs. 80 to reach the hotel from the market. ⊠ *Thandi Sarak (Mall walkway)* ☎☎ *1899/240721 or 1899/240781* ⊕ *www.alpsresortdalhousie.com* ⇨ *19 rooms, 2 suites* ♨ *2 restaurants, badminton, billiards, travel services; no a/c* ☐ *MC, V.*

$ 🏨 **Guncha Siddhartha.** Each room in this new building has a terrace overlooking the affable owner, J. B. Singh's apple orchard and residence, with a 180-degree panorama of the valley and mountains beyond. The rooms, tiered down the hillside, are comfortable, but rather chilly in winter. Each room has carpeting, heavy velour decor, and a sitting area; bathrooms have showers only. Take your meals on the terrace to soak in the best views in town. Rates drop 50% in winter, and holders of this book get breakfast on the house. The restaurant serves only vegetarian food. ⊠ *Church Baloon Rd.* ☎ *1899/242709 or 1899/240620* 🖷 *1899/240818* ✉ *hotel gunchasiddhartha@hotmail.com* ⇨ *20 rooms, 11 suites* ♨ *Restaurant, laundry service, travel services; no a/c* ☐ *AE, MC, V.*

$ 🏨 **Silverton Estate Guest House.** Built in 1939, this small and gracious home has both charm and location—a hilltop in a forest where troops of langurs live. The estate, which includes a terraced garden, is run by the genial Vickram Singh, who will tailor your entire stay to your preferences in both food and activities. The cuisine is Indian and Western vegetarian. ⊠ *Top of Moti Tibba, above Circuit House, off Mall Rd.* ☎ *1899/240674, 94180–10674 off-season* ☎☎ *1899/240674* ⊕ *www. heritagehotels.com/list.htm* ⇨ *5 rooms* ♨ *Restaurant, putting green,* *badminton, croquet, travel services; no a/c, no room TVs* 🖳 *No credit cards* ⊙ *Closed Jan.–Mar.*

¢–$ 🏨 **Grand View.** Enter this charming hotel and you're in another age, full of Raj grace and character. The long wooden building has a suitably vast dining room. The hotel has seen better days, and although its suites are still grand, the standard rooms are a bit shabby. Furnishings are modern except for the heavy wood furniture and red or blue carpets. Each room has an indoor sitting area and a small garden with valley views. ⊠ *Thandi Sarak (Mall walkway)* ☎ *1899/240760 or 1899/242823* 🖷 *1899/240609* ⊕ *www.grandviewdalhousie.com* ⟿ *27 rooms, 5 suites* ⚄ *Restaurant, billiards, squash privileges, laundry service, travel services; no a/c* 🖳 *No credit cards.*

en route | The road from Dalhousie to Chamba has two delightful stops for nature lovers. The first is **Kalatope Wildlife Sanctuary,** a forest preserve with beautiful mountain views. Leave your car at the entrance (unless you have a permit from the Forest Officer in Chamba) and stroll to the end of the 3 km (2 mi) paved road, which continues through mature deodar cedars and yews. Halfway to Chamba is **Khajjiar,** a spacious glade encircled by virgin forest and centered on a pond with a grassy island that seems to float. Some literature says there's a golf course here, but all that seems to remain are eight wire circles guarding the greens against grazing sheep and cattle.

LADAKH

Tucked between the two highest mountain ranges in the world—the Karakoram to the north and Greater Himalayas to the south—Ladakh beckons you into the world of Mahayana Buddhism. The region is actually part of the disputed state of Jammu and Kashmir, but bears little cultural resemblance to either; sometimes called Little Tibet, Ladakh is now more culturally pure than its namesake. Tourists in Leh, the capital, are diluting the Buddhist culture, but Ladakh's gompas (Tibetan monasteries) are still splendid, with beautiful interior frescoes and statues as breathtaking as the landscape. With gray barren crags, an occasional green valley, jewel-like waterways, and mountains of different hues, this high-altitude desert is punctuated by colorful prayer flags and scattered *chortens*—memorial stupas or shrines for relics. Initiate Ladakhi greetings of "*Ju-le*" (ju-*lay*) and you'll be pleased with the smiles and kindness you receive in return.

Outside Leh it's still possible to travel up and down Ladakh's windswept terrain without encountering many people. The region's 150,000 residents occasionally appear near the remnants of Buddhist culture scattered around the countryside. On even the most deserted stretch of road, you'll find stones stacked into little chortenlike piles and *mani* (walls of beautifully engraved stones) that Ladakhis have erected to protect the land from demons and evil spirits. The walls are enticing, but don't touch the stones—they're sacred to the people who put them there.

Ladakh offers world-famous trekking opportunities, such as Manali–Leh, Spiti–Tso Moriri, Lamayuru–Chilling, and the Nubra Valley. You can also raft on the challenging Zanskar and Indus rivers. Runs are best in July and August; just make sure your outfitter has all the right equipment and expertise. The Government of India oversees specified tour circuits here—foreign tourists in groups of four, sponsored by recognized tour operators, are allowed to visit the Nubra, Khaltse (Drokhpa area), and Nyoma subdivisions after obtaining a permit from the District Directorate in Leh. Ladakh's trekking season lasts from late May, after most of the snow has melted, until mid-October, with the biggest crowds appearing in July and August. Rafting is best from July to mid-September. June and September are the best months to come—if you come in early to mid-June, before the plows have opened the road from Manali, you'll have your pick of lodgings in Leh, and by September the crowds will thin out again. When you come, take all precautions against high-altitude sickness and bring a flashlight to see the paintings in poorly lit gompas.

Winter is an opportunity to see a tourist-free Ladakh, albeit in searingly cold conditions: temperatures can drop to -36°F. Since Ladakh is a cold desert, only the higher mountain roads get snowbound, and even some of those are cleared quickly. Many hotels are closed, and those that stay open are fairly chilly (despite heaters) and have no running water because the pipes freeze. Even electricity is in short supply, since the frozen rivers affect local hydroelectric projects, so you must choose a hotel that has its own generator. Food is slightly more expensive, as fresh vegetables and chicken are hard to come by.

Leh

❼ *473 km (295 mi) north of Manali, 434 km (271 mi) east of Srinagar, 230 km (143 mi) east of Kargil.*

Ladakh's capital city is built into the base of the snow-covered Karakoram Range, at just over 11,500 feet. The two-day drive from Manali to Leh is a legendary ordeal, with rough, narrow, mountain-hugging roads prone to traffic jams and landslides; but this mode of arrival is incredibly scenic, and a good way to acclimatize yourself to the altitude. The army convoys on the road increase the danger *and* the time involved, as they have immediate right-of-way over all traffic. The prudent and the humble simply fly from Delhi: flights leave early in the morning, with the sun beginning to rise as you leave the plains and enter the Shivalik Hills. As the first snow-capped mountains appear, the plane seems to skim over the summits, and the ice fields stretch to the horizon before you reach the barren moonscape of the high Tibetan plateau. The flight attendant may instruct you to lower your window blind as you approach Leh, your first hint of military security: you must take no photos from the plane. The 20th century turned Leh into an important Indian military base thanks to its proximity to Kashmir.

Take strong sunblock, aspirin, and a thick novel to Ladakh: the altitude change and intense sunshine will require you to spend a few days relaxing and taking slow walks. Drink water and avoid alcohol. An af-

ternoon in Leh's **Ecology Centre** (☎ 1982/252–5814 or 1982/253221
☉ fall–spring, 10–4:30, winter 10:30–4) will distract you while you acclimatize; in addition to various exhibits, its excellent video, *Ancient Fu-*
tures (not shown in winter), illustrates how Ladakhi culture is threatened
by a rapidly changing world.

An important Buddhist center since the 3rd century BC, Leh was also a
hub on the ancient Silk Road of central Asia. Sadly, the city's 16th-cen-
tury, nine-story **palace** with a grandeur reminiscent of Lhasa'a Potala
Palace, and, above it, the **Temple of the Guardian Deities** are both in
disrepair, but they're worth the steep walk uphill if you're a history buff
or want to take in the view from the palace roof. Handicraft shops and
pavement stalls around Leh's **market** sell Tibetan antiques, Chinese silk,
Buddhist ornaments, turquoise stones, woolens, and silver jewelry.

For a magnificent view of the valley, taxi to the **Shanti Stupa,** in the village of Changspa—then walk down the 500-plus steps leading up to it.
On your way south out of town, stop at the **Tibetan Refugee Handicraft**
Center in the village of Choglamsar, open weekdays from 9 to 5. The
beautiful crafts here include handwoven rugs and thick woolens.

Before you leave Leh, arrange trips to area monasteries and get a festival
schedule from the tourist office (or check ⊕ www.jktourism.org/cities/
ladakh/festivals/cal.htm); dates vary according to the Tibetan lunar calendar. Periodic dance-drama festivals called *chaams,* which bejeweled locals attend in droves in their finest costumes, are not to be missed; those
held at the Hemis and Thiksay gompas are particularly colorful. **Gompas**
are the center of Ladakhi religion and culture—drive south to explore the
Shey, Thiksay, Matho, and Hemis gompas—northwest are Spituk, Phyang,
Likir, and Alchi Choskor—the jewel of Ladakh's religious sites. It's possible to get gompa-ed out, so choose one or two depending on your interests and schedule. Seventeenth-century **Hemis** (45 km [28 mi] south of
Leh) is Ladakh's most popular gompa, but it's often swamped with
tourists. The imposing **Thiksay** (19 km [12 mi] south of Leh), built around
the 15th century, is tiered down the side of a barren hillside like an ancient apartment building, with a 14-foot golden statue of Buddha within.
The pretty 15th-century **Spituk,** with 600-year-old paintings inside, sits
on a hillside overlooking the Indus River and gives you a bird's-eye view
of this expanding town. The 16th-century **Phyang** gompa is famous for
its collection of thangkas and bronzes and its stunning location, overlooking
the countryside 24 km (15 mi) northwest of Leh.

A tour of **Alchi Choskor** (70 km [43 mi], or 2½–3 hours west of Leh),
can be done in a day and about Rs. 2,000 if you don't combine it with
anything else. The drive takes you through stark mountains, past the
confluence of the serene, blue Indus and Zanskar rivers, postcard-per-
fect villages, willow groves, farms, and lonely monasteries. Your journey will be enlivened by the numerous road signs entreating you to be
ALERT TODAY, ALIVE TOMORROW or MILD ON MY CURVES, because FAST
WON'T LAST. The road goes via tiny **Nimmo**—the largest settlement
you'll pass—and ancient **Basgo**, once a capital of Ladakh and an invincible
fortress against Mughal and Tibetan invasion. The monastery here is a

UNESCO World Heritage Site. Stop before Nimmo at the army-maintained **Pathar Sahib** *gurdwara* (25 km [16 mi] northwest of Leh), built in 1964 to provide a place of worship for Sikh soldiers. If you happen to be traveling on a Sunday, stop here for lunch, known as *langar,* served free of charge from noon to 2. In summer as many as 600 come here to fortify themselves. *See* ⇨ Amritsar, *above,* for more on Sikhism.

Alchi is one of the oldest monasteries in Ladakh, dating back to 1020 AD. This small, low-slung cluster of mud buildings on the banks of the Indus River shelters some of the oldest and finest Buddhist murals and wood carvings in the world. The murals are said to have been created by a specially hired group of Tibetan and Kashmiri artisans; do bring a flashlight so you can see them properly.

To visit Alchi Choskor, you might want to plan an overnight stay thereabouts. One of the better options is the **Uley Tokpo Camp** (☎1982/253640 📠1982/252735). From here you can also access the gompa at **Lamayuru** (130 km [80 mi] northwest of Leh), one of Ladakh's most strikingly situated gompas—on top of an impossibly steep mountain. The monastery's age is uncertain, but it might date back to the 10th century.

On your return to Leh, turn left just beyond Saspol and drive 6 km (4 mi) to **Likir.** As you approach this 18th-century monastery, its giant golden Buddha rises out of the horizon against the craggy hills, overlooking green fields and sleepy hamlets. It's an unforgettable sight.

Leh's taxi union has reasonable fixed fares, but the roads are bumpy, so request a Sumo or a Qualis (*not* a Maruti van) for a safe, reasonably smooth trip. For a knowledgeable, English-speaking guide, who does trekking and cultural tours contact Tundup Rahul (☎ 1982/253476). Respect religious customs when visiting gompas: wear appropriate clothing, remove your shoes, don't smoke, circle all chortens and spin prayer wheels clockwise, leave a small donation, and never take a mani stone. Most monasteries do not allow flash photography.

Where to Stay & Eat

$–$$$ ✕ **Tibetan Kitchen.** Many locals feel that this summer-only joint serves the most authentic Tibetan food in Leh. ⊠ *Hotel Tsokar, Fort Rd.* ☎ *No phone* ▭ *No credit cards.*

$ ✕ **Himalayan Cafe.** A large painting of Lhasa's Potala Palace and other Tibetan artifacts, dim lights shaded with dark-red lampshades, and wooden tables give an intimate feel to this Tibetan-run café, which commands a good view of Leh's main thoroughfare from its upstairs perch. The menu is vast, with Indian, Chinese, Tibetan, and Western options. ⊠ *32 (6) A, Upstar, Main Market* ☎ *1982/250144* ▭ *No credit cards.*

$ ✕ **Summer Harvest.** Sample both Tibetan and Kashmiri food in this tiny shack, fitted with decor of the plastic-tablecloth-and-flowers variety. The combination of steamy, tasty Tibetan thukpas, momos, and noodles with Kashmiri mutton *yakhni* (simmered in a fragrant sauce of yogurt, cardamom, and aniseed) and *rogan josh* (lamb) attracts plenty of locals, attesting to the quality of the cooking. ⊠ *Down Fort Rd. from taxi stand* ☎ *1982/253226* ▭ *No credit cards.*

$$$ ✕🏨 **Ladakh Sarai.** Not only are you far from civilization here, but you
Fodor'sChoice stay in a *yurt* (large circular tent) in a willow grove, with a view west
★ across the valley to the Indus River and the majestic Stok Kangi Range.
Each yurt has twin beds and a sitting area, with a bathroom attached
in the rear (bucket bath only). You dine in a hexagonal hall tastefully
decorated with Ladakhi artifacts. The camp is in the village of Sabu, 6
km (4 mi) south of Leh. Rates include all meals, airport pickup, and sight-
seeing. ✉ *Reserve through Mountain Travel India: 33 Rani Jhansi Rd.,
New Delhi 110055* 📞*11/2367–1055 or 11/2363–3483* 📠*11/2367–7483*
⊕ *www.tigermountainindia.com* 🛏 *14 tents* ⚐ *Restaurant, travel ser-
vices; no a/c, no room phones, no room TVs* 🖃 *AE, DC, MC, V*
☉ *Closed Nov.–Apr.* 🍴 *FAP.*

$$ 🏨 **Omasila.** Since 1980 a hospitable Ladakhi family has run this hotel
below the Shanti Stupa. It's popular for its views, cleanliness, colorful
Ladakhi decor, privacy, and food. The spacious terrace looks south to
a stunning vista, the grounds are planted with flowers, and a stream runs
along the edge of the property. Each room has a selection of Buddhist
reading material. Bathrooms have only showers and there are no room
phones, but the front desk has a cordless phone. Only six rooms are heated
in winter: ask for a room number in the 40s. Dinner is a buffet.
✉ *Changspa, Leh 194101 Ladakh* 📞📠 *1982/252119 or 1982/251178*
✉ *hotelomasila@yahoo.com* 🛏 *35 rooms, 5 suites* ⚐ *Restaurant,
travel services; no a/c, no room phones* 🖃 *No credit cards.*

$ 🏨 **Khangri.** Like all hotels in Leh, the Khangri has great views, but it
goes one step further—it's open year-round. The rooms have a certain
Ladakhi elegance, with red carpets, Tibetan rugs on the furniture, and
wooden sofas, and they're sunny and bright, with rows of windows on
two walls. Alas, the plumbing is not ideal, so bathrooms (showers only)
are a bit smelly; and aside from the courtyard, the public spaces are dark
or unattractive. Note that credit cards are not always accepted in winter due to electricity problems. ✉ *Near Nehru Park, Leh 194101 Jammu
and Kashmir* 📞 *1982/252311 or 1982/252762* 📠 *1982/252051* 🛏 *35
rooms, 15 in winter* ⚐ *Restaurant, laundry service, travel services; no
a/c* 🖃 *AE, MC, V.*

$ 🏨 **Lasermo.** One of Leh's older hotels, the modern Lasermo is centrally
located and stays open year-round, aided by central heating. You can bask
in the sun in a central courtyard. Rooms are large and reasonably comfortable, with sun-drenched sitting areas, but the shabby bathrooms
(showers only) need improvement. The newest rooms are the best, and
from these you can access the rooftop terrace, with wonderful views of
the countryside. ✉ *Chulung Old Rd., Leh 194101 Jammu and Kashmir*
📞*1982/252313 or 1982/250778* 📠*1982/252313* ✉*ashraflamkhan@vsnl.
net* 🛏 *19 rooms* ⚐ *Restaurant, billiards, laundry service, travel services;
no a/c* 🖃 *AE.*

★ **$** 🏨 **Lha-Ri-Mo.** A short walk from the market, behind an attractive gar-
den, Lha-Ri-Mo is one of the loveliest hotels in Leh. The hotel's three
buildings, white with black-and-red trim, surround a courtyard garden,
so the rooms are secluded and quiet. The Ladakhi look continues in the
lobby and the restaurant, which also has intricately hand-painted beams.
Guest rooms are simple but comfortable. ✉ *Old Fort Rd., Leh 194101
Ladakh* 📞 *1982/252101 or 1982/252177* 📠 *1982/253345* ✉ *lhari-*

mohotel@hotmail.com ↻ *30 rooms* ⌂ *Restaurant, travel services; no a/c* ☰ *AE* ⊘ *Closed Nov.–Apr.*

$ ⛺ **Shambha-La.** This charming, family-owned, Ladakhi-style two-tier motel sits in a shaded courtyard in an apple orchard, a little way outside town. Comforts include a rooftop deck, a public VCR and video library, and—in half the rooms—stove heaters in May and October. The better rooms are pretty and plush, with colorful rugs and elegant Ladakhi trimming; bathrooms have showers only. Adjust to the altitude by relaxing in a hammock strung between poplar trees in the garden, or taking a walk through the surrounding meadows or to the nearby village. The manager will recommend local treks—his jeep drops you at one location and picks you up in another in time for the next meal—and organize camping at Nubra Valley. The motel is just south of Leh, off the airport road. ⊠ *Reserve through K-40 Hauz Khas, 1st fl., New Delhi 110016* ☎ *1982/252607 or 1982/253500, 11/2652–0970 in Delhi* ☎☎ *1982/251100, 11/2686–7785 in Delhi* ⊕ *www.hotelshambhala. com* ↻ *27 rooms* ⌂ *Restaurant, laundry service, travel services; no a/c* ☰ *AE* ⊘ *Closed Nov.–Apr.*

Padam

270 km (169 mi) southwest of Leh.

Once capital of the Kingdom of Zanskar, Padam sits in the vast, high-altitude Zanskar Valley, ringed by mountains, with the Karsha Gompa perched on a nearby cliff. The valley's sweeping panoramas are framed by mountains, and the bases of the barren slopes are barricaded by sand and shaped by the wind and the water into oversize ramparts. Parts of the district consist of rocky desert punctuated by bits of green, with the Zanskar River racing along a deep gorge. Zanskar men in robes gallop by on handsome ponies.

In this sparsely populated district, the dominant sounds come from chattering birds or the wind, which grows intense by late afternoon, rustling the wheat, barley, and countless prayer flags. The arrival of tourists, especially trekkers, has begun to alter Zanskar's lifestyle; the men, who traditionally worked alongside the women in the fields and helped with the household chores and child-rearing, now look for jobs as porters while the women sell crafts. A growing attraction to money and Western goods is changing a society accustomed to bartering, and is threatening Buddhist traditions here.

Pangong & Moriri Lakes, Nubra Valley & Drogpa Villages

Foreigners need an Inner Line Permit to visit any of these areas.

The brackish Pangong Tso and Tso Moriri (*tso* means "lake") in the eastern district of Changthang are astonishing alpine bodies of water. Both lakes are accessible by road from Leh between late May and October. **Pangong Tso,** at 14,018 feet, is more than 150 km (90 mi) long—and two-thirds of it lie in China. **Tso Moriri,** 240 km (150 mi) southeast of Leh at 15,000 feet, is a pearl-shape lake rich in mineral deposits, giving it a mysterious range of colors against the barren mountains.

North of Leh, Ladakh's "Valley of Flowers," the **Nubra Valley,** is sublime: a heady mixture of cultivated fields set in an arid desert surrounded by the Karakoram Range and sliced by rivers. (*Nubra* means "garden.") Getting to this richly vegetated area around the Shayok and Siachen rivers requires a journey over Khardungla Pass—the world's highest navigable road, at 18,383 feet. From here you descend through the towering peaks to the villages of Nubra, which were important stops for rations along the Silk Road to Central Asia. Today's population is a mixture of Buddhists, Muslims, and the double-humped Bactrian camels once used for transport on the Silk Road. Local trekking routes go through virtually untouched territory, and you can explore by camel as well as on foot or by jeep. River rafting is also available, and hot springs warm weary travelers at Panamik village.

In the **Drogpa villages** west of Leh, the Buddhist Dard people still inhabit the shimmering Indus Valley. Isolated from the modern world, they subsist on farming, eking a living from the rugged mountainsides. You can arrange an overnight stay in Khaltse, where the main road forks off toward Kargil, and in new tourist bungalows in the Dard village of Biama.

UTTARANCHAL

The lower-Himalayan state of Uttaranchal is locked in by Himachal Pradesh, Uttar Pradesh, Tibet, and Nepal. Figuring prominently in the Hindu epics, where it's known as Uttarakhand, this area is the mythological abode of the Hindu pantheon. Every year thousands of pilgrims make *yatras* (Hindu pilgrimages) to the Garhwal mountains and the sacred Char Dhams (Four Temples)—Yamunotri, Gangotri, Kedarnath, and Badrinath—the homes of the Hindu gods Vishnu and Shiva and source of the holy Yamuna and Ganges rivers.

With more than 100 peaks towering above 20,000 feet, Uttaranchal's Garhwal mountains (especially Mt. Nanda Devi, at 26,056 feet) inspire climbers from all over the world. Trekkers are drawn to its natural sanctuaries, such as Nanda Devi (surrounding the peak of the same name) and the Valley of Flowers, strewn with blossoms and surrounded by glaciers and white-capped mountains. Few foreigners, however, are aware of other good treks through equally sublime Himalayan scenery to mountain villages and the revered Char Dhams and other hallowed shrines. Serious white-water rafters will find that Uttaranchal's runs, ranked with Asia's best, are swift, long, and away from the mainstream.

In the Garhwal foothills, next to the Nepali border, is Uttaranchal's second major region, the Kumaon (pronounced "koom-ow," to rhyme with "cow"). A relatively peaceful, underdeveloped corner of the country, the Kumaon is a wonderful place to begin a love affair with India. Ceded by Nepal to British India in 1815, it remains a place of forests, mountains, farmland, temples, and tigers. The Kumaon has ancient culture, but it's not such an epicenter of Indian civilization as Varanasi, and its cities don't feel like onslaughts. Like the Garhwal, this is a place of temples and mountain walks, but on a smaller scale—the topography is gentler, the forests thicker, and you can enjoy it all without the effort of a full-blown trek. Far from the frenzy of Garhwal's Hindu pilgrims and Mussoorie's honeymooners, the Kumaon has a relaxed vibe, and the animal-rich Corbett National Park makes it a must-see destination.

Coming to Uttaranchal in summer lets you avoid the crowds of foreigners that descend on Himachal Pradesh and Ladakh. Aside from a few routes frequented by Hindu and Sikh pilgrims (the road to Rishikesh can get very busy), you'll be alone with the villagers and shepherds. Given the great rafting on the headwaters of the Ganges and its tributaries, tour companies recommend combination trips, which include trekking and rafting in addition to, say, fishing and mountain biking. Trekking from Gangotri–Gaumukhis moderate, whereas routes in the Bhilangana Valley are for more experienced trekkers.

White-water rafting has become a major industry in Uttaranchal. At this writing there were close to 45 rafting camps between Rishikesh and Kudiala, set up by tour companies to provide Delhi's smart set with relaxing adventure vacations. People now drive up for weekends of rafting and horseplay on a sandy beach by the upper Ganges. This is a great time, highly recommended if you want to escape the city and do some rafting without committing to a long, strenuous adventure trip. The season runs from October to June, and you choose from several swift rivers—the Alakananda, Bhagirathi, Tons, Kali, and Ganges. Contact Aquaterra Adventures, Himalayan River Runners, Snow Leopard, or Outdoor Adventures India (⇨ Travel Agents & Tours *in* The Himalayas A to Z, *below*). Outdoor Adventures India—run by a charming couple, Ajay Maira and Pavanne Mann—stands out, with a focus is on safety, ecology, and good food. Aquaterra, led by Vaibhav Kala and his team of experienced, enthusiastic, fun-loving river guides, is recommended for its hearty spirit and campfire barbecues.

Rishikesh & Haridwar

★ ❽–❾ *Rishikesh is 238 km (148 mi) northeast of Delhi and 67 km (42 mi) southeast of Mussoorie; Haridwar is 214 km (137 mi) northeast of Delhi and 91 km (56 mi) south of Mussoorie.*

Yoga, ayurvedic healing, spiritual retreats . . . the resurgence of Western interest in the mind-body-spirit connection has put the ancient holy city of **Rishikesh** on the map in recent years, revitalizing its appeal for the first time since the Beatles visited in the 1960s. The town's location on the Ganges is sacred, but its streets are anything but tranquil: you'll find them crowded with *sadhus* (holy men), Hindu pilgrims, con men, peddlers, monkeys, and hippies. Whether you come to check into an ashram or just to check out the scene, to "find" yourself or watch herds of others doing so, you'll find that Rishikesh has a slightly bizarre, sometimes irresistible energy.

Only one side of Rishikesh is accessible by road. You have to cross one of the two suspension bridges or by boat to see the other half. The Ram Jhula bridge area is the most vigorous part of town, packed with shops, tiny eateries, and yoga ashrams. Sandalwood bead necklaces, complete with authentic fragrance, make nice souvenirs. Shivananda Ashram

THE GARHWAL CIRCUIT

It takes about six days to connect the Garhwali dots: **Mussoorie** ⑩, **Rishikesh** and **Haridwar.** You can drive the entire way, or go partially by train. By road the trip is more expensive and tiring, but you can set your own pace and enjoy slightly better views—just don't drive at night. There are trains from Delhi and Dehra Dun (for Mussoorie) and Delhi and Haridwar. (Jagson Airlines sometimes flies between Delhi and Dehra Dun, but service is intermittent.) Catch the early-morning Shatabdi from Delhi to Dehra Dun, where your hotel can pick you up or you can hire a taxi for the 50-minute ride to Mussoorie. After two nights, hire another car to take you to Rishikesh, a journey of no more than three hours. Spend two or three days around Rishikesh and Haridwar, perhaps including some rafting and hiking, then catch the six-hour evening train from Haridwar to Delhi.

(135/243–0040 or 135/243–1190 ⊕ www.divinelifesociety.com) is the hub of ashram life in Rishikesh and organizes everything from yoga and meditation classes to overnight stays in spartan rooms. The visitor center is right next to Ram Jhula. A boat ride on the Ganges from Ram Jhula just after dawn will set you back Rs. 75–Rs. 400 depending on your bargaining skills and the length of time you want to spend on the river. About a kilometer from Ram Jhula, in a more peaceful part of town, is Rishikesh's older, more famous suspension bridge, the Lakshman Jhula. Stop into one of the nearby cafés to watch the world go by, or cross the bridge to find a relatively quiet spot along the bathing ghats (steps going down to the river, where people perform their ablutions or do laundry). This neighborhood is packed with craft emporiums and shops selling jewelry, shoes, spiritual music, and pipes.

About a half-hour's drive (24 km [16 mi]) from Rishikesh is **Haridwar,** which many feel is the holier town—the real thing. Visit Haridwar around sunset. Head to the heart of town to see the activity on one of the most sacred bathing ghats, Har-ki-Pairi (you may not be allowed to walk on the ghat itself), then visit some of the temples in this neighborhood. At sunset the Ganga Maha Aarti begins, a simple ceremony that beautifully distills the essence of Hinduism. Pilgrims from all over India gather on the riverbank holding little leaf baskets of flowers and *diyas* (oil candle lamps). At nightfall, all the temples along the Ganges begin their evening *puja* (worship) and *bhajans* (hymns) at once, and the baskets holding lighted diyas are floated down the river to accompaniment of rousing music.

Where to Stay & Eat

$ ╳ **German Bakery.** German bakeries invariably spring up in places hot with budget European travelers. The Rishikesh version, like all the rest, is run by a Nepali, and serves a variety of cakes, beverages (juices, lassis, and hot drinks) and simple Western meals. Located at a bit of a height off the road overlooking the Ganges at Lakshman Jhula, it's an ideal place for a break. ⊠ *Lakshman Jhula* ☎ *135/244–2089* ▭ *No credit cards.*

$ ✕▥ **The Great Ganga.** The best hotel in the town sits on a hill a few minutes from Ram Jhula, overlooking the Ganges at some distance from the chaos. Ask for a room with a river view. Rooms are nondescript and modern, slightly overbearing in color and texture, but they're comfortable. The restaurant serves Indian, Chinese, and a few Western dishes, and on request in summer they offer Garhwali food, much of which is made with black lentils. ⊠ *Muni-ki-reti, near Ram Jhula, 249201* ☎ *135/244–2243* ☒ *135/244–2119* ⊕ *www.thegreatganga.com* ⇩ *21 rooms, 2 suites* ⌂ *Restaurant, a/c, tennis court, billiards, bar, lobby lounge, business services, travel services* ▭ *MC, V.*

$$$$ ▥ **Ananda in the Himalayas.** In the heart of the Tehri Garwhal region,
Fodor'sChoice at Narendra Nagar—a breathtaking 17-km (11-mi) ascent from Rishikesh
★ through *sal* trees—is this magnificent spa resort, a converted maharaja's palace that glows by night like a jewel on the mountain. Each room has a balcony that looks into the forest and down the Ganges and Rishikesh—and better still, you get the same view from your glass-pane bathroom. Furnishings are understated, with ivory-color hand-sewn quilts. In the restaurant, rich tandoori kababs are artfully balanced with tasty organic spa food and freshly baked bread and cakes. The 14-room spa offers massage, yoga, and sybaritic health treatments; if you're feeling vigorous, day-trek to the Kunjapuri Temple, visit the Rajaji National Park, or go river rafting. ⊠ *The Palace Estate, Narendra Nagar 249175* ☎ *1378/227500* ☒ *137/227550* ⊕ *www.anandaspa.com* ⇩ *75 rooms, 5 suites* ⌂ *2 restaurants, pool, gym, hot tub, spa, steam room, bicycles, billiards, hiking, bar, concert hall, library, business services, travel services* ▭ *AE, MC, V.*

★ $$ ▥ **The Glass House.** The crystal-clear Ganges flows auspiciously past the verandas in front of this charming, secluded Heritage Hotel, once a garden retreat of the maharajas of Tehri Garhwal. Spend the day at a nearby rafting camp, walk into the jungle or down to a river beach, visit a nearby ashram, or just read in the tropical garden packed with fruit trees. In the evening, you can stretch out by a log fire and fill up on plain but tasty Indian and Western buffet meals before retiring. The rooms and gracious suites are in the main building and several quiet cottages, each one simply but uniquely decorated with hand-dyed fabrics and paintings. ⊠ *23rd Milestone, Rishikesh-Badrinath Rd., Village Gular Dogi, 23½ km (15 mi) or 45 min north of Rishikesh just before village of Byasi, 249303* ☎ *01378/269224 or 1378/269218, 11/435–8962 in Delhi* ☒ *11/2435–1112* ⊕ *www.neemranahotels.com* ⇩ *16 rooms, 12 suites* ⌂ *Restaurant, laundry service, travel services; no room phones, no room TVs* ▭ *AE, MC, V* ⦿ *FAP.*

$ ▥ **Haveli Hari Ganga.** A few minutes' walk from the famous Har-ki-Pauri ghat is a *haveli* (royal home) built 90 years ago by the maharaja of Jaipur and owned by the maharaja of Pilibhit. Now restored into a Heritage Hotel, the haveli is perched on a ghat on the shores of the Ganges. Rooms are done in the old-fashioned stately style, and the entire building feels like a royal lodge. One terrace serves as a river-view sitting area, and guest rooms open onto an atrium. ⊠ *Pilibhit House, 21 Ramghat,*

Haridwar 249401 ☎ *1334/226443* 🖷 *11/2641–3303* ⊕ *www. leisurehotels.co.in* ⇆ *20 rooms* ♨ *Restaurant, spa, travel services* ▭ *No credit cards* ¶⊙¶ *CP.*

Mussoorie

⑩ *278 km (172 mi) northeast of Delhi, 110 km (68 mi) northwest of Rishikesh.*

As you approach Mussoorie, you'll encounter billboards advertising hotels, and fleets of cars carrying young, middle-class Indians. Both are tip-offs: Mussoorie is no longer a peaceful mountain getaway. Still, this former British hill station at about 6,500 feet is a good place to escape Delhi's brutal summer heat, and makes an interesting break from the plains if you're on a short trip to India. The main part of town looks down on the plains, but the northern side of its hill has wonderful views of the Himalayas. Founded in 1823 by a British Army captain, Mussoorie has a few remnants of the Raj—churches, an old British library, the "Gun Hill" from which the noon cannon was fired, and a dilapidated grand hotel—but they're less extensive than those in Shimla or Nainital. The best way to experience the town, besides strutting your stuff on the main thoroughfare, is to take a long walk up the hill to its quieter sections.

Mussoorie has grown around its **Mall,** which extends 5 km (3 mi) from the Library (Kithab Ghar, or Gandhi Chowk) to Landour Bazaar, so almost everything is a short walk off it. There are four 19th-century churches on or near the Mall—Christ Church, Union Church, Central Methodist Church, and St. Paul's—all of which hold Sunday services at 10 or 11 AM.

The peaceful, 5-km (3-mi) **Camel Back Road** grants wonderful views of the Himalayas and valleys below while it winds past the British Cemetery (ask permission at Christ Church to enter; it's usually locked), the oddly shaped Gun Hill, and groups of mischievous black-faced langurs. A rickshaw can take you from end to end for Rs. 50 if you don't want to walk.

The **Savoy Hotel,** a five-minute walk from the Library end of the Mall, is a must-see (though not a must-stay). Built in 1890, the hotel has gone to seed and is manned by an ancient watchman, who presides over cinematic Edwardian ballrooms and dining rooms opening onto verandas, lounges, and a billiards room (where a sign notes that a leopard was once spotted under the table). A total of 121 rooms sprawl across an area as large as two football fields. You can technically still stay here, but it's not recommended. Visit after dark for an amazingly creepy experience—the hotel stays open but feels haunted, not least by the festive crowds who must have filled the place with laughter less than 100 years ago.

On the other side of the Library, a road leads up to the majestic abode of the maharaja of Kapurthala's. You won't be allowed in, but you can have a look from the gates.

For the best impression of Mussoorie, set aside a full afternoon and walk up through Landour Bazaar, with its imperial clock tower, toward Sisters Bazaar and the exceedingly tranquil **Landour** area. This was the original settlement, and it's pleasantly dotted with old cottages and bungalows. Landour Bazaar has a few interesting shops selling antiques, probably from Raj-era homes. It's a long, uphill 7 km (4 mi) walk from Gandhi Chowk, in the Mall, to Char Dukhan, in the heart of Landour, so you may want to hire a taxi (Rs. 300) and consider walking down.

There isn't much to shop for in Mussoorie; wooden crafts and simplistic, gaudy Garhwali tapestries rule the bazaar. But several Mall emporiums sell artifacts from other states, especially Kashmir and, for some reason, Karnataka.

You only need two nights and one full day here, unless you want to spend more time walking in the wilderness. The most pleasant way to arrive is to take the 5½-hour *Shatabdi Express* train (departing Delhi 7:30 AM) to Dehra Dun, then take a 50-minute taxi ride (34 km [21 mi]) from the station to Mussoorie. Alternately, the road trip from Delhi to Mussoorie via Dehra Dun takes seven hours; leave early in the morning to reach Mussoorie by late afternoon. Make arrangements through a Delhi travel agency.

Where to Stay & Eat

$ ✕ **Atul.** The tiny, no-frills, second-floor eatery serves good wholesome vegetarian food. The hot butter rotis with your choice of vegetable are a good bet. Decor is nonexistent, apart from the view of the Gandhi Chowk. ✉ *Gandhi Chowk, The Mall* ☎ *135/263–2398* ▭ *No credit cards.*

$ ✕ **Cafe Coffee Day/Le Chef.** A branch of the modern all-India chain, this is Mussoorie's sleekest coffee house. A giant picture window looks out on the street. Dig into the well-made cakes and sandwiches or just take a chai or coffee break. Alternately, climb up to the second-floor restaurant, Le Chef, and have a hot Indian meal—they serve curries and vegetables with rice and tandoori breads. ✉ *Nirmal Ashram Estate, The Mall, Kulri* ☎ *135/263–0880* ▭ *No credit cards.*

$ ✕ **The Rice Bowl.** Mussoorie's most popular Chinese restaurant is also famous for its Thai cuisine and Tibetan momos. ✉ *Amitash hotel, next to Kwality, Kulri* ☎ *135/362–1684* ▭ *No credit cards.*

$ ✕ **Suruchi.** This Gujarati restaurant has a twist—before you arrive, you phone to order your food, and you can suggest just about anything Indian. A sumptuous *thali* (sampler platter), served noon to 3 and 8 to 10, costs just Rs. 150, but they're only available in season. You can also try Punjabi and South Indian specialties. ✉ *Library, The Mall, 2-min walk down from Vasu Cinema* ☎ *135/263–1093* ▭ *No credit cards.*

★ $$$ ▥ **Claridges Nabha.** Once the property of the maharaja of Nabha, this summer bungalow consciously maintains the aura of an old-fashioned hill station. Away from the crowded Mall, it lets you unwind in peaceful surroundings. The 1845 main bungalow has a typical red-tin roof and an enormous foyer. Guest rooms, created in the 1940s, have understated elegance; the best rooms open onto a veranda facing a courtyard. You can sit under a huge cypress on the front lawn and watch langurs jump through the trees; stroll through the terraced gardens; or walk in the nearby woods. At this writing the hotel was under renovation, so opt for a finished room away from the noise. The staff can drop you off at the Mall and pick you up free of charge. ⊠ *Airfield, Barlowganj Rd., 4 km (2½ mi) from Mall, toward Dehra Dun, 248179* ☎ *135/263–1426 or 135/263–1427* 🖨 *135/263–1425* ✐ *claridges.hotel@gems.vsnl.net.in* ⌿ *22 rooms* ⌂ *Restaurant, tennis court, gym, badminton, billiards, Ping-Pong, bar, business services, travel services* ⊟ *AE, DC, MC, V.*

$–$$ 🏨 **Padmini Nivas.** Built in the mid-19th century, Rushbrooke Estate, a cluster of rambling cream-color buildings with green roofs, was later acquired by the maharaja of Rajpipla. Now a hotel, it has numerous nooks and crannies converted into sitting and eating areas. Each room has its own interesting character and furniture. The staff can organize river rafting and trips to Rajaji National Park. All meals are vegetarian. ⊠ *Library, The Mall, 2-min walk down from Vasu Cinema, 248179* ☎ *135/263–1093* 🖨🖨 *135/263–2793* ⊕ *www.hotelpadmininivas.com* ⌿ *27 rooms, 5 suites* ⌂ *2 restaurants, library, playground, travel services* ⊟ *MC, V.*

$ 🏨 **Kasmanda Palace.** High above the Mall, past Christ Church, is this snow-white lodge with red-roofed turrets. Built in 1836 by the Bengal Engineers, it later became the summer home of the local royalty. The genial proprietor, Dinraj Pratap Singh of the erstwhile principality of Kasmanda, has a fund of stories on Mussoorie. Rooms vary widely, so inspect a few; the largest rooms upstairs have chunky antique furniture, mementos, and valley views. The public areas are decorated with old photographs, tiger and leopard skins, and stuffed trophies from yesteryear hunts. Garhwali meals are prepared on request. The down side is that service is lax, rooms can be chilly in winter, and the walk from town is very steep. ⊠ *Above Mall next to Christ Church, a steep 5-min climb from Vasu Cinema, 248179* ☎ *135/263–2424* 🖨 *135/263–0007* ⊕ *www.indianheritagehotels.com* ⌿ *14 rooms* ⌂ *Dining room, croquet, bar, playground, travel services* ⊟ *AE, MC, V.*

$ 🏨 **Roselynn Estate.** Rooms in this pretty white building, complete with Raj-era green roof, open onto a courtyard lawn. The modern decor— checked carpets and curtains—is not terribly charming, but the rooms are clean and comfortable, with neat, tiled bathrooms. The price makes it a great value, and prices fall further off-season. ⊠ *Library, The Mall, 2-min walk uphill from near Vasu Cinema, 248179* ☎ *135/263–2201 or 135/263–0201* 🖨 *135/263–0426* ⌿ *40 rooms, 6 suites* ⌂ *Restaurant, travel services* ⊟ *No credit cards.*

Corbett National Park

★ ⑪ *Ramnagar is 250 km (155 mi) northeast of Delhi.*

India's oldest wildlife sanctuary, founded in 1936, Corbett National Park is named after Jim Corbett, the fearless hunter and author of *Man-Eaters of Kumaon* who later became a conservationist and photographer. Corbett grew up in these hills, and the local people—a number of whom he saved from tigers at the risk of his own life—revered him. Corbett hunted tigers, but later came to regret the sport as he saw the turn-of-

CloseUp

THE KUMAON CIRCUIT

THIS ROUTE WILL GIVE YOU A GENTLE but colorful introduction to the region. Hire a car or jeep through a Delhi travel agency. Start by driving northeast from Delhi to Ramnagar, site of **Corbett National Park** ⓫. The drive takes six hours if you leave Delhi at about 5 AM; after that, traffic near Delhi will extend the trip by several hours. When you've had your fill of Corbett, drive east to **Nainital** ⓬ for a taste of modern Indian culture with a Raj flavor. From Nainital, go north to **Ranikhet** ⓭ for golf or peaceful walks through the pine forests; from here you can make side trips to some important **Hindu temples**. Finish by looping back at the north end of Corbett, and perhaps by fishing on the Ramganga River. The entire trip takes anywhere from seven days to two weeks, depending on how long you want to linger over such diversions as searching for tigers.

The drive back to Delhi takes about seven hours if you leave the Corbett area before noon. If you don't, rush-hour traffic outside Delhi will again add an hour or four, and it's not a great idea to be on country roads after dusk. The appeal of the Kumaon region fluctuates with the weather, but March and December are the best times to make this trip. Corbett National Park is generally closed from mid-June to mid-November for the monsoon; Nainital and Ranikhet get snow in January; and Indians throng the hills during their school holidays, which begin April 15.

the-20th-century population of up to 40,000 tigers drastically reduced. Upon his death in 1956, India honored Corbett by renaming Hailey National Park after this beloved man.

The park, with elephant grass, forests, and the Ramganga River slicing through its entire length, covers 1,318 square km (527 square mi) and its well-preserved ecological diversity makes it one of the finest parks in the world. You can explore the park on the back of an elephant as it sways quietly through the jungle brush; sit in an open jeep as it rolls along miles of tracks; or just take in the sights and sounds from the top of a watchtower. The park is extraordinarily peaceful and unspoiled, worthy of Corbett's memory: you'll see several species of deer, monkeys, and migratory birds (over 500 species), and, if you're lucky, wild elephants, leopards, foxes, jackals, jungle cats, black bears, wild boars, snakes (including pythons), and crocodiles. If you're so inclined, spend three or four days here and make eight or nine different safaris through the park's various gates. Fishing for the giant mahaseer river fish in the rivers of this area is another absorbing pastime.

Many people, however, come to Corbett to see a tiger, so you'll pass jeeploads of visitors wearing woebegone "Where's the tiger?" looks. Remember that there are about 123 tigers roaming through more than 1,300 square km, so this quest is like searching for a needle in a haystack. (Your chances improve radically in summer, especially May, since there are fewer watering holes to track.) Still, trying to track a tiger down generates plenty of excitement and adrenaline even if you fail, and it's fun to listen to tiger tales from the naturalists and guides.

The park can be accessed by several different gates, including Amdanda, Jhirna, Dhangari, Durga Devi, and Dhikala. The most popular entrance is Amdanda Gate, just 2 km (1 mi) from Ramnagar and about 10 km (6 mi) from Dhikhuli, where most hotels are located. Only 100 day-trippers are allowed into the park for six hours each day—from three hours after sunrise to three hours before sunset, and all gates except one (Jhirna) are closed from June 15 to November 15. To enter by Amdanda Gate for a day trip, you must get an entry permit from either the gate or the tourist office in Ramnagar—this allows you into the park's Bijrani area for morning and evening safaris. If you stay at a private lodge, the staff there will make your daily arrangements. Each vehicle must be accompanied by a guide, available at the park or through your hotel. A few advisories for cruising: You cannot get out of your vehicle in the park; matches, lighters, and firearms are not allowed; it is important to keep silent; and eating is not encouraged. A three-hour safari with a guide, organized by your hotel, costs about Rs. 700 by jeep, Rs. 800 by elephant. Don't forget to bring binoculars and, if you're coming in winter, warm clothes and a jacket.

Before leaving Corbett, you might want to stop at the small **museum** at Dhangarhi Gate, which houses some stuffed wildcats, or purchase a bottle of Corbett honey at one of the shops outside the park entrance.

Ramnagar is roughly six hours from Delhi via Moradabad, and the drive is pleasant—past fields of sugarcane or rice and quaint mud hut villages—though at times the road deteriorates into a bumpy pathway or grows severely narrow, squeezing the traffic. You can also take an overnight train from Delhi to Kathgodam and drive the last 63 km (39 mi) to Ramnagar, a 90-minute drive—hire a taxi at Kathgodam, or ask your hotel to pick you up (about Rs. 800). You can also access Corbett from Ranikhet, and this three-hour drive (85 km [51 mi]) southwest into the park is breathtaking, both for its Himalayan views and for the sometimes frightening way the narrow road hugs the mountainsides. If you're prone to motion sickness, you might want to take medication before setting off; the road is almost deserted, so at least the drive is peaceful. After passing through a small town, the route meanders through hillsides and farmlands, then sinks into sal forests. (The Corbett Ramganga Resort is off this road, 34 km [22 mi] from Ramnagar.) Just before you reach Corbett, turn right at the town of Mohan, and climb over the heavily forested ridge that separates the Kosi from the Ramganga river valleys—this brings you to the north side of the park, which offers anglers a unique fishing experience and all travelers a rest stop en route back to Delhi. ⊠ *Ramnagar* ✆ *Reserve through Kumaon Mandal Vikas Nigam Ltd., Indra Prakash, 21 Barakhamba Rd., 1st fl., New Delhi*

110001 ☎ 11/2371–2246 or 11/2851–9366 ⊕ www.kmvn.org ☞ Rs.
200, video camera Rs. 500, car Rs. 200, guide Rs. 200.

Where to Stay & Eat

Most hotels are grouped around Dhikhuli, 10 km (6 mi) from Amdanda
Gate. The staff at each hotel can organize transport to the park, a guide
or naturalist, and park-fee payment. Room prices are on the high side,
but they often include all meals. To bring costs down, ask about room-
basis tariffs and have some meals at other hotels, such as the glass-fronted
restaurant at **Corbett Riverside Resort** (✉ Next to Claridges Corbett Hideaway ☎ 5947/284125) on the Kosi River. On request, most hotels will
cook you some local Kumaoni food.

No trip to Corbett is complete without at least one night in the park itself. At the government-owned Forest Rest Houses—most of which
were originally built as stopping points for British forest officers on their
way to and from inspections deep in the jungle—you can beat the convoys of tourists entering the park in the morning to watch game until
sunset, then fall to sleep amid a deep silence pierced only by the occasional cry of a wild animal. There are a total of 24 Forest Rest Houses
in the park. Some, such as Dhikala, are quite large, with electricity and
food service, but most are very basic, with four to six beds in two to
three rooms, no electricity, bucket baths, and only seasonal access.
Bring your own sleeping bags and sheets.

Although you can make personal arrangements to stay in a rest house,
it's not advisable; their bureaucratic management is not attuned to customer service. Instead, stay at one of the lodges listed below, inform them
of your wish in advance, and for a fee they'll make the necessary arrangements, including conveyance, bedding, meals, and housekeeping pro-
visions. These resorts are very close to Amdanda Gate, and their package
stays ("Jungle Plans") include full board and jeep and elephant safaris
with knowledgeable naturalists. One independent guide recommended
for wildlife tours is **Manoj Sharma,** who lives near the park—contact his
agent in New Delhi, Manoj Mehta (☎ 11/2557–1489, 11/2557–3489,
or 98101–11124) several weeks in advance to book his services.

$$$ ✕▣ **Infinity Resorts Corbett Lodge.** Still widely known by its old name,
Tiger Tops, this popular resort sits on a high bank of the Kosi River, so
you can listen to rushing water while looking across the foothills. Each
spacious room has a large picture window, a wall of rough stone, a bam-
boo-and-tile ceiling, a modern bathroom with shower, and a large bal-
cony overlooking the pool. The circular central lodge, with its vaulted
timber dome, is where you can eat, drink, and relax in front of the fire
in winter. The deck outside overhangs the river, with lush jungle on the
opposite bank. The price includes all meals (delicious homestyle Indian
food, plus Western options) *and* activities, such as safaris, hiking, raft-
ing, and pony treks. ✉ Dhikuli, Ramnagar 244715 ☎ 5947/251279,
5947/251280, or 5947/284157 🖷 5947/2251880 ✆ In Delhi, contact
Khatau International, A-3 Geetanjali Enclave, New Delhi 110017
☎ 11/2669–1189 or 11/2669–1209 🖷 11/2669–1219 ⊕ www.
tigercorbettindia.com ⇝ 24 rooms ⚿ Restaurant, fishing, Ping-Pong,

bar, playground, meeting room, travel services; no room TVs ⊟ *AE, DC, MC, V* ⍾❶ *FAP.*

★ **$$$$** 🏨 **Claridges Corbett Hideaway.** This rustic resort is on the banks of the Kosi River, but its rooms do not overlook the water. Fortunately the old-fashioned ambience, professional management, and lush mango-or-chard setting more than compensate. Pebble walkways lead to the ocher cottages, which have baked-tile roofs, stone-tile floors, bamboo-mat ceilings, and fireplaces. Rattan and jute furniture lend a rustic feel. Each cottage has a porch, indoor sitting area, and modern bathroom with shower. Tea and snacks are served poolside. Fixed-menu meals are served in the new lodge on the riverbank, or you can tuck into grilled meals at Jim's; these are followed by bonfires on the lawn. With advance notice, the staff can arrange mountain-biking trips and horseback safaris to Nainital. Five minutes away is a sister concern, the more economical—but still charming **River View Retreat.** ✉ *Zero Garjia, Dhikuli, Ramnagar 224715* ☎ *5947/284132 or 5947/284134, 11/2641–3304, 11/2629–3905, or 11/2629–3906 in Delhi* 📠 *5947/284133, 11/ 2641–3303 in Delhi* ✏ *corbett@ndf.vsnl.net.in* ➥ *38 cottage rooms* ⌂ *2 restaurants, pool, gym, massage, archery, Ping-Pong, bar, meeting room, travel services; no room TVs* ⊟ *AE, DC, MC, V.*

$$$$ 🏨 **Quality Inn Corbett Jungle Resort.** Isolation is the strong suit here: the Quality Inn lies on the Kosi River 10 km (6 mi) ahead of the main cluster of hotels, 21 km (13 mi) from Ramnagar just beyond the village of Mohan. A good vantage point for bird-watching, it attracts bird lovers from all over. The cool, stone cottages are furnished simply, with jute carpets and furniture; each room has wood paneling, wood floors, and a small porch. You can also stay in a larger building near the main lodge overlooking the river. The lodge, where meals are served, is plain but charming, with a large central fireplace and wooden balconies over immaculate lawns sweeping down to the river. The staff can organize fishing and swimming at its riverside beach. ✉ *Mohan, Almora district, 244715* ☎ *5947/287820 or 5947/287850* 📠 *5947/287851* ⊕ *www. corbettjungleresort.net* ➥ *24 rooms* ⌂ *2 restaurants, lawn tennis, badminton, Ping-Pong, volleyball, bar, library, meeting room, travel services; no room TVs* ⊟ *AE, DC, MC, V* ⍾❶ *FAP.*

$$$ 🏨 **Corbett Ramganga Resort.** Other Corbett resorts allude to fishing opportunities but this extraordinarily peaceful facility, smack on the clear Ramganga River in the absolute wilderness, specializes in helping the angler. The collection of casting rods is well maintained, and the successes of the fishing guide are documented with photos in the reception room. From September to December, you can also go rafting. Stay in a small, clean, yellow-brick cottage, an airy suite, or, best of all, a cozy "safari tent" with attached brick bathroom. The grounds are dotted with flower beds. The staff plans safaris to the park's less popular gates, not least since Amdanda Gate is an hour away. Ramganga is off the beaten path, so tell your driver: Drive from Ramnagar to Dhikhuli 11 km (7 mi), then on to Mohan 10 km (6 mi). Turn left and drive 13 km (8 mi) to Marchula, over the forested ridge that separates the Kosi from the Ramganga river valleys. ✉ *Village Jhumaria, Marchula, near Corbett National Park; reserve through Surbhi Adventures P. Ltd., New Delhi*

☎ *05962/281592 or 05962/281692, 11/2652-2955, 11/26523722, or 11/26523744 in Delhi* 🖷 *11/2685-5428* ⊕ *www.ramganga.com* ⮐ *10 cottages, 10 tents, 6 suites* ⚲ *Restaurant, pool, travel services; no a/c, no room phones, no room TVs* ⊟ *AE, DC, MC, V* ⦿ *FAP.*

Nainital

🕐 *63 km (39 mi) east of Corbett National Park, 277 km (172 mi) northeast of Delhi.*

The drive from Corbett to Nainital takes less than two hours, but is memorable for its solitude and scenery. East of Ramnagar the road leads you on a tour of unspoiled agrarian India: mud dwellings with grass roofs stand next to fields of sugarcane, wheat, and lentils. Interspersed with the fields are small stands of teak and *sal* (tall trees that resemble black oak), with the occasional banana plantation thrown in. In the distance glimpses of the Himalayan foothills that await you. Just before you turn up into the hills at Kaladungi, you'll pass Jim Corbett's old winter home, a small colonial bungalow with a museum. The road uphill begins in a sal forest, which occasionally gives way to terraced fields. As the trees thin out, the road gets steep and starts to wind. Toward the top you might be held up by troops of langurs sunning themselves on the road or children on their way home from school in the city. Suddenly the road turns downhill, and the congestion of Nainital begins.

Nainital is one of India's most popular hill stations. "Discovered" by the British in the 1840s, this one was later made the official summer capital of Uttaranchal (then known as the United Provinces). The town clutches steep slopes around a lake of the same name, and is one of India's few hill stations with this distinction to add to its beauty. It's easy to see why the British fell in love with this idyllic spot, yet development is beginning to take its toll in the form of congestion, pollution, and noise. Indian tourists, especially honeymooners, come to Nainital year-round to enjoy the cool air and mountain views. The school holidays, April 15–June 15, bring the largest crowds and should be avoided if possible.

Nainital is best known for its pretty woodlands and boating opportunities, but as a former colonial capital, it packs quite a bit of history. Those interested in colonial architecture are in for a treat—there's another British building, generally with a high-gable tin roof, around every corner, including the clock tower, the Boat Club, the Masonic Hall, the High Court, the library, and the Church of St. John of the Wilderness. Most of these buildings are, unfortunately, slowly tumbling down. The northern end of town is built around the **Flats,** a large open field created by a landslide in the late 19th century. Facing the Municipal Office, this area has an air of perpetual carnival, with magicians and acrobats performing while tourists munch away on snacks purchased from the many vendors. Sit and watch a cricket game, or take in a Hindi movie at the old Capital Cinema Hall on the Flats.

Elusive to the eye but unavoidable to the ear is the busy **Sri Ma Naini Temple** on the Flats. Open sunrise to sunset, this lakeside shrine is dedicated to many gods, including Shiva, but Naina Devi (an incarnation of Parvati, the wife of Shiva) is its focus. Take off your shoes, wander around, and watch devotees make offerings to the large black Shiva lingam by the lake. For a classic Indian experience of the coexistence of faiths, you can also visit the gurdwara (Sikh temple) that faces the Flats, or the mosque across from the flats.

A fabulous place to take in Nainital's famous Himalayan views is **Cheena Peak** (Chinese Peak). The highest point near Nainital, at 2,611 meters (8,566 feet), it was technically renamed Naini Peak after India's 1962 war with China. You can reach the peak on foot or rent a horse and ride over. The outlook called **Snow View** can be reached on foot or horseback, and there's a Tibetan monastery on the way. Tourists commonly take a gondola ride (the "Ropeway") to Snow View from town, which runs roughly, not reliably, 9:30 to 1 and 2 to 5 daily. At some point, do take a boat ride into the middle of this serene *tal,* or crater lake. Boatmen will approach you on the Mall; rates vary from Rs. 50 to Rs. 200 an hour, depending on the season, and you must bargain hard. A large number of boats are moored at Nainital Boat Club, next to the Flats, and you can organize a sailboat through the club.

The **Mall** is dotted with shops selling wooden items—bowls, boxes, pencil holders, furniture—but none are of outstanding quality. For quality Almora tweeds and woolens such as shawls and scarves, head out to **Ram Lal and Brothers** (✉ Bara Bazaar ☎ 5942/235484) at the Capitol Cinema end of the Mall.

Where to Stay & Eat

$ ✕ **Ritz.** This simple eatery offers a variety of cuisines. The best dishes are made Punjabi-style: chicken curry, butter naan, biriani (rice with meat or vegetables mixed it). You can also try Indian-style Chinese, which tends to be spicy and oily; ask them to hold both for a more subtle experience. ✉ *The Mall, ½ km from Flats* ☎ *5942/223–5824* ▭ *No credit cards.*

¢ ✕ **Ahar Vihar.** Located on the second floor above the Mall, looking over the lake, this simple, reasonably clean joint offers wholesome Gujarati vegetarian thalis (sampler platters). Even meat eaters will appreciate this light, home-style, sweet-and-sour cuisine. ✉ *The Mall* ☎ *5942/223–5446* ▭ *No credit cards.*

$$ ✕▢ **Classic.** For those who like to be in the thick of things, this hotel on the Mall is walking distance from most shops and sights. For a few dollars extra, you can book a room that peeps out on the misty lake. The comfortable, no-frills rooms, with simple wooden furniture and reasonably tasteful furnishings, have clean modern bathrooms with showers. The restaurant serves good Indian and Chinese food. In winter opt for the *sarson ka saag* (hot mustard greens) with butter *roti* or the tandoori meat dishes; in summer try some Kumaoni food. ✉ *The Mall, Nainital 263001* ☎ *5942/223–5173 or 5942/223–5174* ✉ *newagehotel@now-india.net.in* ➥ *23 rooms, 16 suites* ⌕ *Restaurant, meeting room, travel services* ▭ *AE, DC, MC, V.*

$$$ ▢ **Claridges Naini Retreat.** In this elegant retreat with a splendid view of the Mall, the new combines almost seamlessly with the old. The old is Hari Bhavan, built as a summer residence of the maharaja of Pilibhit in 1926; the new is a hotel run by Claridges of Delhi. Set around a red-tile garden patio, the bluestone buildings have classic Kumaoni red-tin roofs with latticework windows and high gables. Rooms are simple, with hardwood floors and furniture; some look down past wrought-iron railings to Nainital and the lake. Part of the building was under renovation at press time, so opt for a finished room away from the noise. ⊠ *Ayarpatta Slopes, Nainital 263001* ☎ *05942/223–5105 or 05942/ 223–5108* 🖷 *05942/223–5103* ⊕ *www.leisurehotels.co.in* ⏎ *32 rooms, 1 suite, 6 duplex rooms, 3 cottages* ⚭ *Restaurant, golf privileges, massage, billiards, Ping-Pong, bar, laundry service, travel services* ⊟ *AE, DC, MC, V.*

$$$ 🏨 **Manu Maharani.** One of Nainital's top hotels is a charming, rambling, bright-white building with a red roof, overlooking the Mall. The inviting rooms are stylishly furnished, almost plush, and each has a sitting area looking out onto the garden. The bathrooms, with showers only, are neat and modern. Common areas are spacious and attractive. Pickup and drop-off at the Mall is complimentary. ⊠ *Grassmere Estate, Mallital, Nainital 263001* ☎ *5942/223–7341 or 5942/223–7342* 🖷 *05942/ 223–7350* ✉ *manumaharani@vsnl.com* ⏎ *66 rooms* ⚭ *Restaurant, tea shop, health club, bar, laundry service, meeting room, travel services* ⊟ *AE, DC, MC, V.*

$$$ 🏨 **Mountain Quail Camp.** To avoid the congestion of Nainital, try this "camp" more than a half-hour's drive away, pretty much cut off from civilization. The deluxe tents have attached bathrooms (bucket baths only) and comfortable beds, and the cottages are cozy. At night you can sit around a communal fire and enjoy the peaceful, woodsy surroundings. The proprietor, "Sid" (Siddharth), is a true outdoorsman and naturalist, so allow him to arrange your hikes if you're so inclined. Fishing, pony-trekking, bird-watching, mountain biking, and rock climbing are other distractions. The hotel is closed in winter. ⊠ *Pangot, 17 km (11 mi) out of Nainital, accessible by narrow Kilbury Rd., 263001* ☎ *5942/ 224–2126 in Kaladhungi* 🖷 *5942/223–5493* ⊕ *www.birdtours.co.uk/ campcorbett/MQC.htm* ⚭ *Restaurant, travel services; no a/c, no room phones, no room TVs* ⊟ *No credit cards* ⏇ *FAP.*

Ranikhet

⑬ *55 km (34 mi) north of Nainital.*

As with Nainital, the drive here takes less than two hours but is an event in itself. After leaving the crowded confines of Nainital on a road that hugs the mountain, you'll quickly enter the town of Bhiwali—a grubby little place, with small shops and tea stalls that serve as the center of the local fruit industry. In season the roadside is crowded with men selling crates of apples, peaches, and plums to travelers and dealers, and for the next hour of your drive the bottom of the river valley is filled with small orchards. After crossing another small river, you'll head back up to Ranikhet, at which point the forests give way to some spectacular sections of terraced farmland.

Ranikhet itself is ensconced in evergreen confines on a Himalayan hilltop. Of all the British hill stations in India, only Ranikhet retains some of its original sylvan tranquillity. This may be because it's an army town, home of the Kumaon Regiment ever since the Raj, so development has been controlled. The spacious army cantonment stretches along the Mall, which winds along the top of hill, and many of the regiment's stone buildings, erected well before Independence, are still smartly maintained specimens of colonial architecture. Walk on the **Upper Mall Road** to see the Parade Ground or Regimental Headquarters.

Ranikhet has at least six old colonial churches that are usually open to visitors. Although each is unique, all are made of stone and have the high tin roofs typical of this area. Two of these churches, facing each other across a small athletic field in the center of the cantonment, have been deconsecrated and converted into the **Ranikhet Tweed and Shawl Factory,** a hand-loom production center of woolens. This operation is run by the Kumaon Regiment for soldiers injured in the line of duty and for army widows. Let the clattering draw you inside for a look at how hand looms work, or visit the little store down by the field, housed in the regiment's old bank. The factory and store are open Monday through Saturday from 9 to 5.

Heading uphill (south) from the Westview Hotel, take the **Lower Mall Road**, almost completely abandoned now, for a peaceful stroll through a forest of pine and oak. About 2 km (1 mi) up the road, it merges once again with Upper Mall Road and you come upon the small, relatively new **Jhula Devi Temple**, open sunrise to sunset. The temple is bursting with brass bells, as Hindu temple bells are traditionally rung to alert the god to the devotee's need. If you keep walking, in a few more miles you'll reach the **Chaubatia Orchards**, a 260-acre fruit orchard run by the state government. Feel free to stroll among the trees.

Where to Stay & Eat

$ ✕▦ **Westview.** Perched on a small hill, the Westview's yellow-flagstone main building was designed as a home in the mid-19th century. It's now a Heritage Hotel, but renovations have not altered the unique design of each room; the Westview Suite and Suite 28 are large, bright, and quiet. In winter you can drift off in front of your own fireplace or wood-burning exceptional. The Western food is superior to the Indian: try the roast leg of lamb with mint sauce or fish munière. Order meals an hour in advance. ✉ *Mahatma Gandhi Rd., 263645* ✆ *Reserve through C-16 Greater Kailash 1, New Delhi 110048* ☎ *5966/220261, 11/5163–3692, 11/2648–5981 in Delhi* ✍ *westviewhotel@hotmail.com* ➥ *18 rooms, 7 suites* ⚐ *Restaurant, coffee shop, badminton, horseback riding, Ping-Pong, playground, travel services; no a/c* ⊟ *No credit cards* ⦿ *CP.*

Hindu Temples

If you have an extra few days, take a side trip from Ranikhet to see several important temples dedicated to Lord Shiva. Many are old, dating from the Katyuri (8th–14th centuries) and Chand (15th–18th centuries) dynasties. The most significant temples northeast of Ranikhet are at **Baijanth, Bhageshwar,** and **Jageshwar.** Unlike temples on the North Indian plains, these are built from rough-hewn stone, and their alpine locations—

such as the cedar forest in Jageshwar—give these temples a totally different feel. The hill at **Binsar** has both a nature sanctuary and some ruins of the Chand dynasty's capital. Views from the top are fabulous.

Where to Stay

$$$ ⌂ **Binsar Valley Resort.** This small resort is both a pleasant rest stop after a temple tour and a base for Himalayan adventures. Ideally situated at the edge of the Binsar Sanctuary (with exemplary bird-watching), it was built in 1934 as the summer home of Indian Army major B. P. Pande. Rooms are in separate cottages; all have wood stoves and the public sitting room has an open fireplace, so winter stays are as enjoyable as summer visits. The staff can arrange adventures, including trekking, rafting, and camping, but the crown offering here is a stable full of trained Austrian mountain horses (Haflingers) for experienced riders and sturdy Tibetan ponies for beginners and children. ⌂ *Village Basoli, Bhainsori, Almora-Bageshwar district, 263684* ☎ *5962/253028* ⊠ *5962/253035* ⊕ *www.mhril.com* ⟲ *35 rooms* ⌂ *Dining room, horseback riding, travel services no a/c* ⊟ *MC, V.*

DARJEELING

⑭ Anyone with a yen for hill stations must see the "Queen of the Hills" in the far northwestern corner of West Bengal. Built during the British Raj as a center for the tea trade, Darjeeling quickly earned a reputation as a superb Himalayan spa resort. Most of the graceful old colonial buildings are a bit scruffy, but some still bear their regal stamp. Outside the pedestrianized town center, high-season traffic can impede an exploratory stroll; yet the town's old-world charm enchants even jaded travelers. In a few days here you can soak up the alpine scenery—dominated, in good weather, by far-off Mt. Kanchenjunga (28,208 feet)—bargain in a local market, and trek on a nearby hillside. Fog engulfs the town from below at unpredictable intervals, but when it clears and the sun sparkles on snowy Kanchenjunga, third-highest mountain in the world (the name means "House of Five Treasures," in honor of its five summits), the effect dazzles.

Long before you reach Darjeeling, as you ascend a winding road from the plains, you'll smell an invigorating blend of tea, wood smoke, verdant undergrowth, cedar, and wildflowers. The largely Nepali population, some of whose ancestors migrated centuries ago, has made its imprint more subtly than the Raj—even the simplest homes are embellished with brightly painted trim, small gardens, or flower pots. Nepali youths on every street corner play *chungi*—a kind of kickball with a ball made from a bunch of rubber bands.

The pride of Darj, as it's affectionately called, is its main promenade, the **Mall.** Stroll around, or hop on a pony, mall-watch, and drink in the general air of well-being. If you're hungry after a long train journey, stop in a roadside café for a plate of steamed Tibetan momos or opt for roasted corn-on-the-cob (for yourself or the ponies) or popcorn masala. From the Mall you can wander off into some of the town's hilly cobble lanes.

Nature lovers have plenty to see right in town. Just be aware that many streets are one-way, so it can be confusing to get around.

Most of Darjeeling's indoor sights are closed on Thursday. The **Bengal Natural History Museum** (⊠ Meadowbank Rd. ⊙ Fri.–Wed. 10–4 ▭ Rs. 5) has an exhaustive collection of alpine fauna and a curiously eccentric display of big-game trophies and pickled snakes. Just north of the museum en route to the zoo, but not generally open to the public, is **Raj Bhavan,** former home of the maharaja of Burdwan, crowned by a shining blue dome. The clean, neatly laid out **Padmaja Naidu Zoo** (⊠ off Jawahar Rd. W ⊙ Fri.–Wed. 8:30–3:30 ▭ Rs. 5) is justly famous for its rare snow leopards, gorgeous clouded leopards, shy red pandas, and other alpine animals. On the walk to or from the zoo, take a picnic or just a detour up the hill—follow the sign for "River Hill District Magistrate's Office"—to **Shrubbery Park,** a quiet garden behind the Raj Bhavan, with great views. Two minutes past the zoo (enter via zoo gates) is the **Himalayan Mountaineering Institute** (⊙ Fri.–Wed. 8:30–3:30 ▭ Rs. 5), a training center with some public exhibits. The institute was long directed by none other than Sherpa Tenzing Norgay, who accompanied Sir Edmund Hillary up Mt. Everest in 1953. Norgay's samadhi, or grave, is a few minutes from the Institute.

Sacred sites also abound here. South of the town center, below the train station, the **Dhirdham Temple** was built along the lines of the Pashupatinath Temple in Kathmandu. Both Buddhists and Hindus revere **Observatory Hill,** above the Windamere Hotel—the hill is topped by an unusual shrine blending Hindu and Buddhist styles, the **Mahakal Temple.** The monkeys at the top can be quite aggressive, so walk with a group and don't carry food; but the monkeys antics at the temple can be interesting to watch, especially if you're traveling with children. There are several gompas, or Tibetan monasteries, nearby, including **Aloobari** on Tenzing Norgay Road. The monastery **Bhutia Busti** houses the original *Bhardo Thudol* (Tibetan *Book of The Dead*). Darjeeling's most celebrated house of worship, 8 km (5 mi) south of town in Ghoom, is the **Yiga-Choling** monastery, built in 1875, which houses the extremely sacred Maitreya Buddha ("Coming Buddha") image.

★ A ride on the **Darjeeling Toy Train** is a must, a rare trip into the past. The engines run on coal, and the carriages are narrow and tiny. Spraying its passengers with particles of coal, the little train moves ahead in a cloud of smoke and steam, edging closely past homes and shops, fields and forests. A journey to New Jalpaiguri is dramatic, but it takes about eight hours—the train is so slow that you can safely hop off and on as it moves along, and it stops to refuel almost every half hour. Consider going only to Ghoom, perhaps to see the Yiga-Choling monastery—the toy train leaves Darjeeling every day at 9 and 3, stopping at Ghoom after one hour and continuing to New Jalpaiguri. Be at the station 15 minutes before departure to buy a ticket and grab a window seat on the right side, facing the engine. There are several unscheduled shuttles each day, so you can return by train or by taxi.

Ghoom is a regular stop on the return journey from the **Tiger Hill** lookout point, where views of Kanchenjunga, the Eastern Himalayas, and even Mt. Everest make it worth getting up well before sunrise. The fit and adventurous can walk back to Darjeeling on a quiet side road. If you're catching a flight from Bagdogra to Delhi or Calcutta and will be leaving Darjeeling early in the morning, consider leaving a little earlier to stop at Tiger Hill on your way down. On the way back from Tiger Hill, you can also ask your driver to stop at the **Japanese Peace Pagoda** for a lovely view of both the town and the mountains. Overlooking the Mall on Birch Hill, **St. Andrew's Church,** built in 1843, still takes pride of place. You're welcome to attend the Sunday service, and the Christmas carol service is a highlight of Darjeeling's holiday season.

India is the world's largest producer of tea, producing about 850 million kilograms annually. Tea cultivation in Darjeeling began in 1841, when Chinese tea was introduced here by the British and Nepali labor was hired to pick leaves and maintain the estates. By the early 20th century, the Darjeeling area had some 117 tea gardens over some 42,000 acres. Today, Darjeeling black tea is one of the world's most prized varieties, and around 80,000 people are employed in these gardens. Some are temporary, earning about Rs. 45 per day during the plucking season. To see how Darjeeling tea is processed, visit the **Happy Valley Tea Estate,** 3 km (2 mi) outside town. It's an easy walk downhill through tea bushes, but fairly strenuous on the way back up. In this dilapidated factory, tea is still made the orthodox way, and some 1,000 kilograms are processed daily. Between Tuesday and Saturday, an obliging employee can be an impromptu but effective guide (tip about Rs. 100) to the production process. Tea production stops between December and March, but you can still pop into the factory and hear the process explained. If you won't be going on to Sikkim, consider driving 27 km (17 mi) to the Sikkim border at Jorethang to see the heart of the tea country. At the **Goomtee Tea Estate** at Mahanadi, near Kurseong, 30 km (19 mi) and about 90 minutes from Darjeeling, you can stay overnight in a century-old bungalow at the heart of the tranquil estate. Contact the Mahanadi Tea Company in Calcutta (☎ 33/2247–1036 ⊕ www.darjeelingteas.com/visit.htm).

Darjeeling taxis charge the earth for even small distances; Rs. 100 seems to be the starting point for any fare. Decide in advance the sights you want to see, and plan taxi trips accordingly. The tea estate and Tibetan Refugee Self-Help Center are in the general direction of the zoo and the Himalayan Mountaineering Institute, so you can visit the tea estate on the way to the zoo and the HMI, and the Tibetan center on the way back to town.

The weather in Darjeeling is delightful year-round, barring only the monsoon season, when rain and fog can make driving treacherous. You'll get the best views of Kanchenjunga between November and March. The town sometimes gets snow in December; bring heavy woolens in winter, light woolens in summer.

Where to Stay & Eat

★ **$–$$** ✕ **Dekeva's.** This tiny corner café has crumpled old menus—endearing evidence that the prices have not changed in years—and a friendly, happy buzz. It's a hot destination for pizza, momos, stir-fried noodles, excellent Chinese meals, and big, slurpy, garlicky soups, not to mention North Indian lassis. There are plenty of vegetarian options, and the laid-back atmosphere allows you to meet new people or just hang out with a book. ⊠ *51 Gandhi Rd., just east of Mall, below Dekeling Hotel* ☎ *354/225–4159.*

$–$$ ✕ **Glenary's.** Darjeeling's best independent restaurant is a popular meeting place for locals and travelers alike. All three floors have great views, and the top floor is particularly atmospheric in the evening (reserve a booth near the window). The kitchen serves tandoori, Chinese, and Western food with Indian beers and wines, and the downstairs pub has a range of cocktails. Most revered of all is the ground-floor tea service, established in 1938, with its classic desserts and alpine backdrop. ⊠ *Nehru Rd.* ☎ *354/225–4122* 🖃 *V.*

$ ✕ **Frank Ross Cafe.** This vegetarian café has a typically ambitious international menu: have a South Indian *dosa,* a Mexican or Lebanese bite, or just a glass of fresh orange juice. A few minutes from the Mall, the homey room has wood floors, cane furniture, and marble tables. ⊠ *14 Nehru Rd.* ☎ *354/225–8194.*

$ ✕ **The Park.** Come here for hearty Mughlai food, such as mutton curry, butter naan, and *palak paneer* (cubes of soft cottage cheese in creamed spinach). Decor is simple: black leather chairs and glass-top tables with little in the way of a view. The place fills up at lunchtime, a testament to its popularity, and a few Chinese dishes are available for those tired of North Indian food. ⊠ *41, Laden La Rd.* ☎ *354/225–5270* 🖃 *No credit cards.*

$$$$ ✕🏨 **Windamere.** Set in the heart of Darjeeling, this grande dame of the
Fodor'sChoice Raj is a justly famous landmark. The drawing rooms and bar are packed
★ with artifacts of British Darjeeling, and the verandas have magnificent views of the hills. High tea, served from 4 to 6, is an institution in itself, worth a trip if you aren't staying here. The rooms, which combine Raj, art deco, and Tibetan furnishings, have fireplaces, heaters, hot-water bottles, and Victorian claw-foot bathtubs (though hot water is limited). The staff, skilled at serving royals and film stars, works under the exacting eye of owner Mrs. Tenduf-La. Breakfasts are sumptuous, and all meals are cooked on wood-burning stoves. Prices include all meals. ⊠ *Observatory Hill* ☎ *354/225–4041* 🖷 *354/225–4043* ⊕ *www. windamerehotel.com* 🛏 *37 rooms, 6 suites* ⚬ *Restaurant, bar, babysitting, playground, laundry service, business services, travel services; no a/c, no TV in some rooms* 🖃 *AE, MC, V* ⍩ *FAP.*

★ $$$$ 🏨 **New Elgin.** Rooms are decorative and elegant in this classic, welcoming, centrally located Heritage Hotel with a pretty white-and-green Raj exterior and manicured gardens. The delightfully regal lounges and public spaces take you back 60 years or more. Antique furniture, Tibetan carpets, thick drapes, and working fireplaces add to the coziness. Bathrooms have modern conveniences and are in green marble. Prices include all meals. ⊠ *18 H. D. Lama Rd.* ☎ *354/225–7227, 354/2257226, or 354/2257501* 🖷 *354/225–4267* ⊕ *www.elginhotels.com* 🛏 *22 rooms, 2 suites* ⚬ *Restaurant, bar, laundry service, travel services* 🖃 *AE, DC, MC, V* ⍩ *FAP.*

$$$ 🏨 **Cedar Inn.** Nestled in majestic cedars high above the town center, this renovated Victorian Gothic resort is a serene retreat from the bustle, with free shuttle buses to take you to and fro. Wood, glass, and light predominate, and the rooms are bright, cozy, and elegant, with handcrafted woodwork, stripped-wood floors, and fabrics in soft neutral colors. Each room is built on two levels, with a small sitting area, and some have fireplaces and bathtubs. ⊠ *Jalapahar Rd., 734101* ☎ *354/225–4446* 🖶 *354/225–6764* ⊕ *www.cedar-inn.com* 🛏 *22 rooms* ⚒ *Restaurant, gym, billiards, bar, library, laundry service, business services, travel services; no a/c* ⊟ *MC, V* 🍴 *CP.*

$ 🏨 **Sailung.** This charming lodging is minutes from a spot called Viewpoint, near Observatory Hill, where people come to catch sunset *dekhos* (views) of Mt. Kanchenjunga. Occupying different levels in a pretty bungalow on the side of the hill, the rooms are simple but attractive, with red jute floor mats, wood paneling, cane furniture, and neat bathrooms. Inspect a few rooms for the best mountain view. ⊠ *Oakdane, East Mall, 22/1 B B Sarani, 734101* ☎ *354/225–6289* 🛏 *10 rooms* ⚒ *Restaurant, travel services; no a/c* ⊟ *No credit cards.*

¢–$ 🏨 **Dekeling.** You're welcomed as part of the family in this friendly, bustling Tibetan hotel. The slightly shabby rooms have cedar paneling and simple furnishings, including Tibetan wall hangings and, in some cases, stained-glass windows. Ask for an attic room with a view, an exceptional value. Solo travelers might enjoy the communal sitting room, and the "library" (a bookcase made up of guest donations) has a great selection of paperbacks. For twice the money, you can also rent one of four lovely Tibetan suites at the owners' Dekeling Resort at Hawk's Nest, perched on a steep hill 2 km (1 mi) away. ⊠ *Above Dekeva's restaurant, 51 Gandhi Rd., 734101* ☎ *354/225–4159* 🖶 *354/225–3298* ⊕ *www.dekeling.com* 🛏 *22 rooms* ⚒ *Restaurant, travel services; no a/c, no TV in some rooms* ⊟ *MC, V.*

¢–$ 🏨 **Mall Guest House.** This tiny, family-run guesthouse hugging the edge of the Mall offers excellent value for the money. It's cozy but simple, with a tiny café where the owner rustles up just about anything you ask for. The rooms—with wood paneling, Tibetan carpets, and plain furnishings—are comfortable and clean, with nice views. Rooms with mountain views cost more. ⊠ *6/A Hermitage Mall Rd., 734101* ☎ *354/225–9154* ⊕ *www.geocities.com/mallguesthouse* 🛏 *8 rooms* ⚒ *Restaurant, travel services; no a/c, no room phones* ⊟ *No credit cards.*

Shopping

For such a small town, Darjeeling is a serious shopping center, with top-quality tea, Tibetan artifacts, jewelry, thangka silk-scroll paintings, antiques, statues, woolens, shawls, hats, carpets, and brass jewelry and hand-loom items from the northeastern states of Mizoram and Manipur available in abundance. Most of the best shops, open every day but Sunday, are in the pedestrian-only area near Chowrasta. Some take half-hour lunch breaks. Prices are generally better, and service friendlier, than in large cities, but you still have to bargain.

Established in 1890, **Habeeb Mullick and Son** (☎ 354/225–4109) is a local landmark specializing in fine gifts: handicrafts and curios, jewelry (particularly amber, turquoise, and moonstone), Kashmiri pashmina shawls, carpets, hand-carved wooden bowls from the northeastern state of Nagaland, and exquisite silver Buddhas. The shop gets crowded after dinner, so go early for personal attention, as the proprietor has plenty on offer beyond the packed displays. Across the square from Habeeb Mullick, **Jolly Arts** (☎ 354/225–4059) offers silk thangka paintings, soft Tibetan shawls, and ritual silver, copper, gold-painted, and bronze puja objects. **Arts Crafts and Curios** (☎ 354/225–2872) has a good selection of Tibetan artifacts. At the corner of Chowrasta and Nehru Road, Latif Badami at **Eastern Arts** (☎ 354/52917) lets you take your time browsing through ornate silver jewelry and lapis lazuli. Clothing, bags, and other items crafted from Kashmiri leather and fur are the specialty at **Kashmir Arts** on Nehru Road.

For traditional hand-knotted Tibetan carpets, try **Third Eye** (⊠ Laden La Rd., opposite State Bank of India ☎ 354/225–2920), a women-only enterprise with experience in export shipping. The **Tibetan Refugee Self-Help Center** (⊠ 65 Gandhi Rd. ☎ 354/225–2346) is worth a taxi ride out of town to see the artisans (mostly elderly women) at work, dyeing, weaving, and spinning wool on old bicycle wheels. Cuddly Lhaso Apso puppies (for sale if you're not going abroad) scamper around in the yard. In addition to brightly colored handwoven textiles (made into shirts, jackets, wallets, and backpacks), the store has a limited selection of beautiful carpet samples. You can even bring your own design to be custom-made and shipped. The center is is open from 9 to 4 every day but Sunday; a good time to visit is around 11, when the workshop is humming.

Nathmull's (⊠ Laden La Rd. ☎ 354/225–6437 or 354/225–2327) has a vast selection of Darjeeling tea and an unusual variety of tea cozies and silver-plated tea services, but it's in a busy traffic area. To avoid the bustle, try the **Chowrasta Tea Store** (⊠ The Mall ☎ 354/225–4059) for a good selection of high-quality teas. No picnic is complete without a visit to **Chowrasta Stores** (⊠ The Mall ☎ 354/225–4153), an old-fashioned general store with everything from soup to nuts—wine, whiskey, chocolates, ice cream, cheese, biscuits, toiletries, and so on. Just don't go around 3 PM or you'll have to fight the local schoolchildren for penny candy. Next door to Chowrasta Stores, with the same glass-cabinet displays and friendly service, **S. Lekhraj and Co.** (⊠ The Mall ☎ 354/225–4275) has all manner of "suitings and hosiery," from fun cotton T-shirts with Darjeeling designs to socks, underwear, and towels to fabrics for on-site tailoring.

SIKKIM

It's not surprising that Lepchas, or Rongkup (Children of Rong), the first known inhabitants of Sikkim, gave their mountain home a name meaning "land of happiness." Sikkim is probably the least explored and most unspoiled part of India–far off the tourist beat. Palden Thondup Namgyal, the last *chogyal* (king) to rule over Sikkim until it became India's

CloseUp

THE DARJEELING–SIKKIM CIRCUIT

I F YOU WANT TO VISIT BOTH DARJEELING AND SIKKIM, consider a clockwise tour of this region. The closest railhead for both is New Jalpaiguri–Siliguri (sister stations; most trains terminate at one of the two) and the closest airport is at Bagdogra. From airport at Bagdogra or the railway stations at Siliguri–New Jalpaiguri the drive to Darjeeling takes about three hours; to Gangtok about five.

Start with Darjeeling. At the airport or train station, hire a sturdy vehicle such as a Sumo jeep (not a Maruti van); the standard rates are listed at the taxi counters. You'll pay about Rs 1,200 from Bagdogra to Darjeeling, possibly less from Siliguri. Better, but a little more expensive, is to have your hotel pick you up. Alternately, the brave can buy a spot in a shared jeep, which fits 10 passengers and takes mountain curves at breakneck speed.

A half hour outside Siliguri, you'll find yourself deep in tea country. Miles of rich green bushes unfold before you, starting in the lowlands and continuing as you ascend. The most famous tea gardens are at higher altitudes, such as the Makaibari Estate and Castleton Estate, which makes the most expensive tea in the world. The road makes hairpin bends as it climbs, and about 30 km (19 mi) before Darjeeling is the town of Kurseong, known for its orchids and other rich flora. As you approach Darjeeling, the track for Darjeeling's historic Toy Train weaves in and out of view, and you might pass one chugging feistily along in a cloud of smoke. Just 8 km (5 mi) short of Darjeeling is Ghoom, site of the Yiga-Choling Tibetan monastery. Five km (3 mi) east of Ghoom, off the highway, is the region's highest point, Tiger Hill, at 2,520 meters (8,268 feet). Tourists flock here before dawn for spectacular views of the Kanchejunga and, on lucky days, Mt. Everest. Back on

the road, you enter an amphitheater of towering snowy mountains and sweeping valleys, with Darjeeling perched precariously along the tops of the hills.

After about three days in Darjeeling, press on for Sikkim, ideally via Pelling 74 km (45 mi), about four hours northeast of Darjeeling. One pretty route descends through Darjeeling's densest tea gardens and tea villages to Jorethang, on the border of West Bengal and Sikkim. The road is narrow and bumpy, but this route is a rare glimpse at the underbelly of one of the world's wealthiest industries. Some villages have brightly painted wooden homes decked out with pots of flowers; others are miserably poor, as many tea gardens around here have closed due to falling tea prices or labor issues. Lush Sikkim and the soaring Himalayas are constantly in view beyond the Rangeet River.

Jorethang is a bustling border town in a gorge on the banks of the Rangeet. Beyond it, you'll be in the heart of Sikkim's mountainous countryside, traveling through hills and vales of forest, bamboo jungles, immaculate terraced fields, high waterfalls, groves of oranges, and thickets of cardamom and khicho grass, used to make brooms. You'll also pass flourishing villages, busy market towns, and fertile fields in the high mountains or at the bottom of steep valleys along riverbeds.

Two days is about all you need in Pelling, unless you have time to detour to Yoksum. Gangtok is 117 km (73 mi) from Pelling via Singtam, a six-hour drive. If you head directly to Gangtok (64 km [40 mi]) from Jorethang, skipping Pelling, the trip will take a little more than three hours.

22nd state in 1975, was an avid conservationist who protected his Buddhist kingdom from development. And not that much has changed. As you cross the border into Sikkim, there's a sense of having entered another country; the state has a culture and lifestyle all its own.

Three distinct ethnic groups live in Sikkim. The Lepchas originally lived in seclusion in north Sikkim, where they developed a harmonious relationship with the environment to ensure their survival. Although most Lepchas converted to Buddhism, many still worship aspects of their physical surroundings: rainbows, clouds, rivers, and trees. Village priests preside over elaborate rituals, including animal sacrifices, to appease their animist deities.

Bhutias from Tibet came into Sikkim with the first chogyal in the 17th century. Buddhism governs Bhutia life, with the monastery and the lama exerting tremendous influence over daily activities. Every village has its prayer flags and chortens (memorial stupas or shrines for relics), every home has an altar room, and most families have one relative in a monastery or convent. Buddhism works its way into weavings, hand-woven rugs, *thangka* (scroll) paintings, statues, and delicately carved *choktses* (low, colorfully carved wooden tables). In turn, the Bhutias' culture dominates Sikkim, right down to the women's national dress: the traditional *kho* or *bhoku*, the epitome of elegance, worn over a *wanju* (blouse), with the *pangden* (apron), the final colorful touch, restricted to married women and formal occasions. Today's best-known Bhutias are Bhaichung Bhutia, captain of the Indian soccer team.

Also sharing Sikkim are the Nepalese, who introduced terrace farming to the region. Although most Nepalese are Hindu, you'll see few Hindu temples in Sikkim, and their faith often incorporates Buddhist beliefs and practices (as it does in Nepal). The Nepalese are dominant in business, and theirs is the language most often heard in Sikkim. In addition to these three groups, Sikkim has a small Tibetan community who tend to run restaurants and hotels.

Much of Sikkim is a continuous flow of hills and valleys, that are excellent for trekking and rafting. The state is famous for its wildflowers, particularly orchids and rhododendrons in spring. Trekking in Sikkim (March–May and September–December) means warm days and frigid nights. From Yuksom, in western Sikkim, you can trek closer to Mt. Kanchenjunga. Rafting on the Teesta and Rangeet rivers is best from October to December.

Because of Sikkim's sensitive border location, foreigners need a Restricted-Area Permit (RAP) to visit. Acquiring one takes about a half hour, and can even be done at the border at Rongpo as well as in Darjeeling or Calcutta. The best times to visit Sikkim are March through May and September through mid-November. June, July, and August bring monsoon rains, and December and January have cold snows. The peak period, when tourist services are taxed to the limit, is late September–early October, during the Hindu festival Durga Puja.

Gangtok

⑮ *94 km (56 mi) northeast of Darjeeling, 117 km (73 mi) northeast of Pelling, 114 km (68 mi) north of Siliguri.*

Sikkim's capital is expanding fast across several valleys and ridges. With its pagoda-style roofs and tall buildings, not to mention its relative wealth, it has a different feel from other Indian hill stations. If you're not planning to trip to Rumtek, visit the **Enchey Monastery,** in a grove of pines, and the pretty, whitewashed Do-Drul Chorten to get a taste of the Sikkimese Buddhist monastery—more colorful and modern than a Ladakhi gompa, but less cozy, with a metal roof and a stone, rather than wooden, floor. Indian tourists swamp **Ganesh Tok,** a look-out point on the outskirts of town, for photo ops. The new **Himalayan Zoological Park** next door, in the Bulbulay area (✉ Rs. 10) houses snow leopards and other Himalayan creatures in a park setting.

The main thoroughfare, M. G. Road, has a few shops selling Buddhist items—statues, prayer wheels, *dorjes* (ornaments signifying lightning), and prayer bells. You might want to try Sikkim's famous *paan* liqueur, sold for Rs. 60 a bottle in several shops on this road. For shawls, carpets, and choktse tables, try the sales emporium at the **Directorate of Handicrafts and Handloom** (✉ Zero Point near Raj Bhavan ☎ 3592/223126 or 3592/222926), open 9:30 to 12:30 and 1 to 3 every day but Sunday.

Once you escape city boundaries, you're surrounded by tropical forests rich with 600 species of orchids and 46 varieties of rhododendron. Waterfalls splash down mountains, powering prayer wheels. Tidy hamlets with cultivated terrace fields and prayer flags flapping in the breeze populate idyllic valleys. Sikkim's guardian deity, Mt. Kanchenjunga—the world's third-highest peak, at 28,208 feet also spelled Khangchendzonga—is still revered by all who live in its shadow.

The Tibetan border is a short 55 km (34 mi), or three hours, from Gangtok at Nathu La pass, one of the highest motorable roads in the world. Two-thirds of the way along this road—the former Silk Route—is the gorgeous **Tsomgo Lake,** also called Changu Lake, a calm high-altitude (12,400 feet) lake with snowy mountainsides tapering right down to its shores. The color of the water varies with the season, and it's said that lamas once forecast the future by studying its colors. Nearby are a tiny Shiva temple and the peaceful **Kyongnosla Alpine Sanctuary,** with its red panda bear and an abundance of wildflowers from May to August. Non-Indians need special permission to visit this border area, but your hotel or travel agent can arrange this for you.

Where to Stay & Eat

$–$$ ✗ **Baker's Cafe.** Gangtok's trendiest café is sleek and modern, furnished in wood and green granite with wrought-iron tables and chairs. It serves burgers, pizza, and excellent cakes and pastries. ✉ *M. G. Marg, 737101* ☎ *3592/220195* ▭ *No credit cards.*

$–$$ ✗ **Tibet Kitchen.** This upstairs eatery near Hotel Tashi Delek is simple, clean, authentic, friendly, cheap, and open for breakfast. Highlights are the *then-tuk* (flat-noodle soup) and delicious Tibetan bread with honey;

they serve tasty Chinese food. You can sample home-brewed chang at the small bar. ⊠ *M. G. Marg* ☎ *3592/221153* ⊟ *No credit cards.*

$$$$ ✕⊞ **Nor-Khill.** Built in 1932 as a royal guesthouse, Nor-Khill (House of Jewels) has a stately elegance, lovely landscaped gardens, and excellent views from its quiet ridge below the city. Traditional Sikkimese architecture is emphasized throughout, with colorful masks, etchings, and local paintings. The rooms are decorated with Sikkimese details, such as traditional carpets and religious artwork; request a room with a view. Service is excellent. The small Shangrila Restaurant serves good Sikkimese, North Indian, Chinese, and Western food. ⊠ *Paljor Stadium Rd., 737101* ☎ *3592/225637* 🖷 *3592/225639* ⊕ *www.elginhotels. com* ⇨ *32 rooms, 2 suites* ♻ *Restaurant, hair salon, bar, laundry service, travel services; no a/c* ⊟ *AE, MC, V* ⼁◎⼁ *FAP.*

Fodor'sChoice
★

$$$ ✕⊞ **Netuk House.** Staying at this traditional small Sikkimese hotel is like living in a pleasant Gangtok home. Rooms are simple but attractive, with wood floors and tasteful Sikkimese furnishings. The building, which has a view of the valley, is in a quiet garden next to the owner's home. Prices include all meals, and Sikkimese food is served. The hotel has no generator. ⊠ *Paljor Stadium Rd., 737101* ☎ *3592/222374* 🖷 *3592/224802* ⌂ *slg_netuk@sancharnet.in* ⇨ *10 rooms* ♻ *Restaurant, travel services; no a/c, no room TVs* ⊟ *AE, DC, MC, V* ⼁◎⼁ *FAP.*

★ $$ ✕⊞ **Tashi Delek.** Don't be fooled by the drab facade: public areas in this modern hotel are wonderfully bright, and decorated in a sort of baroque Sikkimese style. The guest rooms are simple in comparison, but they're pleasant and well maintained, with carpets and solid wooden furniture. The suites have sitting rooms with Sikkimese decor. Ask for a mountain view, as many rooms lack it. The menu at Dragon Hall's includes exotic seasonal greens such as ferns and stinging nettles and serves excellent Sikkimese, Indian, Chinese, and Western food. In season the rooftop garden is the nicest place in town to enjoy an afternoon meal or drink. ⊠ *M. G. Marg, 737101* ☎ *3592/222991 or 3592/222038* 🖷 *3592/ 222362* ⊕ *www.hoteltashidelek.com* ⇨ *40 rooms, 6 suites* ♻ *2 restaurants, laundry service, travel services; no a/c* ⊟ *AE, MC, V.*

$–$$ ✕⊞ **Chumbi Residency.** Built against a hillside, this modern, multistory hotel (with no elevator) is airy and bright, with oodles of white marble. The rooms, which look out over a ridge, are furnished in a pleasing Sikkimese style, with rich green carpets, royal red bedspreads, and wood furniture. Opt for the Jade rooms, which are spacious, very plush, and comfortable. The spacious and elegant suite is a good value. ⊠ *Tibet Rd., 737101* ☎ *3592/226618 to 19* 🖷 *3592/222709* ⌂ *chumbi@dte.vsnl. net.in* ⇨ *26 rooms, 1 suite* ♻ *Restaurant, travel services; no a/c* ⊟ *AE.*

$ ⊞ **Dho Tapu Guest House.** Located in the Deorali area, a few kilometers from the city center, this homey guesthouse in a modern block offers good value for money, especially for longer stays. The rooms are basic but comfortable—carpets, dressing table, and clean, well-fitted bathrooms with showers. ⊠ *1st fl., SNOD Shopping arcade, Deorali, 737102* ☎ *3592/281501 or 3592/280734* 🖷 *3592/280124* ⌂ *dhotapu@homail. com* ⇨ *5 rooms, 3 suites* ♻ *Restaurant, Internet, travel services; no a/c* ⊟ *No credit cards.*

Rumtek

The great **Rumtek Monastery,** a large, low-lying, multitier building an hour's drive (24 km [15 mi]) south of Gangtok, is one of the most revered Tibetan Buddhist pilgrimage sites and Sikkim's most important monastery. It's the seat of the Karma Kagyu lineage or the Black Hat order of Tibetan Buddhist monks. Bring your passport, as police check your permit at the entrance. There has been a shrine at Rumtek since the 16th century, but the monastery is actually new and mildly gaudy, if impressive for its size and atmosphere. The drive here takes you past terraced fields, woods, and Himlayan peaks. A few minutes from Rumtek are two pleasant rural places to stay.

Where to Stay & Eat

$$ Bamboo Resort. This ecofriendly mountain hideaway is tucked away in paddy fields about 1 km (½ mi) short of Rumtek in the village of Sajong. A road is planned, but right now the only access path is a 100-step climb along a slippery path, strictly for the energetic. Run by a Sikkimese–Swiss couple, Topgay and Helen Takapa, the resort has a spartan Sikkimese style; each room has a different bright-color scheme and is furnished with crisp linens, wood furniture, and cane items. The restaurant has a wood-burning oven and an organic vegetable patch, and serves Italian, Swiss, Sikkimese, and North Indian food. There's no generator. ⊠ *Sajong, 1 km (½ mi) from Rumtek, 737101 Sikkim* ☎ *98320–61986 or 353/ 220–2049* ⊕ *www.sikkim.ch* ⟿ *10 rooms* ⌂ *Restaurant, fitness center, spa, mountain bikes, library, laundry service, travel services; no a/c, no room phones no room TVs* ▭ *No credit cards* ⦿ *FAP.*

$$ Shambhala Mountain Resort. A few kilometers before Rumtek on the Gangtok–Rumtek Road, Shambhala is a spacious lodge, whose lobby has a high ceiling, a flagstone floor, and blond-wood trimmings. The rooms are immaculate, airy, and pleasing to the eye, with a continuing accent on wood; even the bathroom is lined with wood. Each room has a little balcony. The hotel can organize transport to Gangtok. There's no generator. ⊠ *Rumtek, 737135 Sikkim* ☎ *3592/252240 or 3592/ 252243* ⊞ *3592/222707* ⊕ *www.hotelshambhala.com* ⟿ *25 rooms* ⌂ *Restaurant, bar, laundry service, travel services; no a/c, no room phones, no room TVs* ▭ *No credit cards.*

Pelling

117 km (73 mi) west of Gangtok.

After two or three days in and around Gangtok, you may want to travel toward Kanchenjunga by making a five-hour trip to Pelling. As you head west, the scenery is stunning nearly every kilometer of the way—traditional Sikkim farms, orchards, terraced fields and breathtaking mountain vistas. Pelling is a tiny provincial town with just one sight—**Mt. Kanchenjunga.** People flock here to view the grand peak by dawn. Perched at a height, the town looks down on lakes, gorges, glaciers, forests, farmland, and the flat valley where the town of Yoksum marks the start of the Dzongri Trail. On a lonely hilltop nearby, peering down at Darjeeling and the swift Rangeet river, is the unforgettable 18th-century **Pe-**

mayangtse Monastery, an important religious seat. The monastery is a site of exquisite woodwork, statues and sculpture, lovely thangkas and murals, and Buddhist texts.

Where to Stay

$$ ☒ **Norbu Ghang Resort.** This is really the only comfortable, cheery place to stay in Pelling. The hotel is built around a garden at the edge of a flat hilltop, with an envious view of Kanchenjunga. Rise at dawn, order a cup of coffee, and watch the revered peak turn an awesome array of hues until finally it glows pink. The rooms are simple, with red carpets, cheery bedspreads and furnishings, and basic furniture; the cottages, with their own little porches, are cozier. There's no generator. Norbu Ghang also runs a nearby lodge with rooms for Rs. 800. ☒ *Pelling, Sikkim, 737113* ☎ *3595/250566 or 3595/258245* ⊕ *www.sikkiminfo.net/ norbughang* ↻ *30 rooms, 3 suites, 11 cottages* ⚑ *Restaurant, bar, travel services; no a/c* ▤ *MC, V.*

THE HIMALAYAS A TO Z

To research prices, get advice from other travelers, and book travel arrangements, visit www.fodors.com.

AIR TRAVEL

Flying is the quickest way to reach the hills, but flight schedules can be thrown off, especially in winter, by variable weather in the mountains and stubborn winter fog in Delhi. Prepare for long delays on either end. It's crucial to double-check the flight schedule with the airline a few hours before departure. If a flight gets canceled overnight because of weather, the airline is liable to put you up for the night.

Jagson Airlines flies Tuesday, Thursday, and Saturday from Delhi to **Shimla**'s airstrip, Jubbarhatti Airport, a plateau created on top of a mountain 23 km (14 mi) south of Shimla. The flight costs US$125 one-way (for non-Indians), and taxis into Shimla cost Rs. 500. For US$170. Jagson Airlines flies daily from Delhi to Kullu, whose airport is at Bhuntar, 9 km (5½ mi) from Kullu town and 50 km (30 mi) from **Manali.**

Indian Airlines and Jet Airways fly daily from Delhi to Jammu (US$110–US$115 one-way), from which it's a roughly four-hour drive to **Dharamshala.**

Ladakh is *only* accessible by air in winter (October–May), as the roads are blocked by snow. Indian Airlines and Jet Airways fly daily from Delhi to **Leh.** Summer flights are more frequent but also more popular, so reserve well in advance and remember to confirm your seats with the airline (your travel agent can help) 72 hours in advance. The fare is US$115 one-way. Check in early on your return from Leh, as security is strict— make sure your hand luggage is free of scissors, pen knives, lighters, matches, batteries, and anything else sharp.

In Uttaranchal, Jagson Airlines now flies three times a week to Jolly Grant Airport in **Dehra Dun.** The fare is US$125 one-way.

The airport at Bagdogra, West Bengal, is about 90 km (56 mi) southeast of **Darjeeling** and 124 km (77 mi) south of **Gangtok.** Jet Airways and Indian Airlines fly daily from Calcutta (US$90 one-way) and Delhi (US$195 one-way). Hire a car from Bagdogra to Darjeeling, a three-hour drive, or taxi the 15 km (9 mi) to New Jalpaiguri to catch the Toy Train (⇨ Train Travel). For Sikkim, hop on one of the jeeps that make the five-hour run from Bagdogra to Gangtok. Sikkim Tourism also runs a five-passenger helicopter between Bagdogra and Gangtok; it times its departure with the flights arriving in Bagdogra from Delhi and Calcutta, departing at 2 PM for Gangtok. The journey takes a half hour and costs Rs. 1,500 per head.

CARRIERS **⚆ Indian Airlines** ☎ 141 or 11/2569–4070 in Delhi, 183/213392 or 183/213393 in Amritsar, 172/270–4539 or 172/270–5062 in Chandigarh, 191/243–0449 or 191/254–6086 in Jammu, 1982/252255 or 1982/252076 in Leh, 33/2211–6869, 33/ 2211–3135, or 33/2511–9433 in Calcutta, 3592/223354 in Gangtok, 354/ 225–4230 or 354/225231 in Darjeeling, 353/251–1495 or 353/255–1666 in Bagdogra, 353/251–1495 in Siliguri ⊕ indian-airlines.nic.in.

Jagson Airlines ☎ 11/372–1593 or 11/372–1594 in Delhi, 177/262–3405 or 177/262–5177 in Shimla, 1902/265222 or 1902/266187 in Kullu, and 1902/252843 in Manali ⊕ www.jagsonairline.com.

Jet Airways ☎ 11/5164–1414 or 11/2567–5404 in Delhi, 172/274–1465 or 172/274–0550 in Chandigarh, 191/257–4312, 191/257–4315, or 191/ 245–3888 in Jammu, 1982/250–999, 1982/250444, 1982/250324 in Leh, 33/2229–2227 or 33/2511–9894 in Calcutta, 353/243–5876, 353/243– 5877, or 353/255–1588 in Bagdogra ⊕ www.jetairways.com.

Sikkim Tourism Development Corporation ☎ 3592/222634 or 3592/225277 in Gangtok, 353/255–1036 in Bagdogra ⊕ www.sikkiminfo.net/travel guide.htm.

AIRPORTS

Local airports can be useful for travel information after hours or on holidays, when airline offices have closed.

⚆ Airport Information **Bagdogra** ☎ 353/255–1431. **Kullu** ☎ 1902/265037. **Jammu** ☎ 191/243–9030. **Leh** ☎ 1982/252255. **Shimla** ☎ 177/273–6800.

BUS TRAVEL

Bus fares are a tiny fraction of what it costs to travel by hired car, but non-air-conditioned (ordinary class, state-run) buses are not recommended. The handiwork of their drivers produces severe motion sickness, not to mention serious accidents, and they tend to make frequent stops and take unnecessary breaks. Air-conditioned deluxe buses are safer—opt for the most expensive category, such as a Volvo or picture-window coach with good suspension; check out the bus before buying a ticket, and travel only by day. (In Uttaranchal, so-called "luxury" buses sometimes turn out to be rattle traps with taped TV entertainment blaring up front.) Deluxe coaches usually depart from roughly the same stands as state buses, and seat reservations are usually not required; a travel agent or hotel can help you make arrangements.

CAR TRAVEL

Most Himalayan drives involve endlessly winding, often bumpy, some-times precarious roads on the edges of steep slopes. If you're prone to motion sickness, carry medication and eat light meals before and during your journey. Even more important, hire a heavy and powerful car. Ambassadors and jeeps (the Sumo or Qualis models) are sturdy but not that speedy; a solid sedan car such as a Cielo or Esteem moves faster. Do *not* take a Maruti van, as it's not heavy enough to be safe. Expect to pay as much as Rs. 16–17 per kilometer for a non-air-conditioned Ambassador or a diesel Toyota jeep, a bit more for a better car. The cost is highest if the vehicle starts in Delhi or takes you from one state into another, which involves road taxes; if you hire the car in the Himalayas for use only in that state, the rate will be slightly cheaper. If your driver will be staying with you the entire time, ask your hotels whether they have have food and accommodation for drivers. If not, the daily tip you give the driver (over and above the initially agreed-upon charge) should cover these costs for him. If you're starting from Delhi, plan to leave the city early—before 6 AM—to avoid wasting hours in traffic.

Night driving in the hills is extremely dangerous and must be avoided at all costs.

RBS Travels maintains a large fleet of cars and offers reasonable rates and, more importantly, experienced and safety-conscious mountain drivers. Their Delhi office is open 24 hours; ⇨ Travel Agents & Tours.

CELL PHONES & INTERNET CAFÉS

Internet cafés are common in Himalayan towns, though connection speeds can be slow. One hour on the Internet will set you back around Rs. 50; just inquire before you sit down. There are no Internet facilities at Corbett Park, and very few in Dalhousie.

If you have a cell phone, purchase a calling card with roaming facilities in Delhi before you go—just pop into an STD phone shop in the nearest market. Connectivity is decent in most places, except Corbett Park and Dalhousie.

EMERGENCIES

In remote areas, the best emergency measures are your own caution—followed by an experienced and knowledgeable tour company, hotel manager, guide, and/or driver, who can get you quickly to the most appropriate doctor or emergency facility (*not* necessarily the nearest government-run hospital). Carry a good first-aid kit, including plenty of bandages for blisters if you're trekking. Take altitude precautions seriously—the waiting list for flights out of Leh is often filled with those who did not.

East-West Rescue, based in New Delhi, has an air ambulance for urgent evacuations from the remotest parts of India, Pakistan, Nepal, and Bhutan.

The experienced staff in the 24-hour alarm center can recommend a network of medical centers, hospitals, and doctors throughout India.

📌 **East–West Medical Centre** ✉ B-28 Greater Kailash I, New Delhi ☎ 11/2629-3701, 11/2629-3702, 11/2462-3738, 11/2464-1494, 11/2469-9229, 11/2469-0429, or 11/2469-8865 ⊕ www.eastwestrescue.com.

MONEY MATTERS

ATMS

Carry enough cash and traveler's checks to cover your entire trip in the Himalayas, as you simply can't depend on withdrawing cash here. Most ATMs are for local account-holders only. Only at ICICI and UTI banks can you withdraw cash against your Visa or MasterCard—check the banks' Web sites for a list of ATM locations. In tourist towns, currency-exchange agents and banks might advance you cash against your Visa or MasterCard, but they usually charge a 10% commission.

📌 **Cash Machines Amritsar** ✉ ICICI, Hotel City Heart, Jallianwala Bagh ✉ UTI, 50 Court Rd. **Chandigarh** ✉ ICICI, Accountant General Office, Sector 17 ✉ UTI, Booth 1, Sector 10D. **Darjeeling** ✉ ICICI, Laden La Rd., opposite SBI Bank. **Dehra Dun** ✉ ICICI, Rajpur Rd. ✉ UTI, 56 Rajpur Rd. **Gangtok** ✉ UTI, New Market, M. G. Rd., near Star Cinema. **Mussoorie** ✉ UTI, library, The Mall. **Rishikesh** ✉ UTI, Bharat Bazaar, 16 Adarsh Gram, Dehra Dun Rd. **Shimla** ✉ ICICI, Scandal Point, The Mall ✉ UTI, Trishool Tours and Travels, 53 The Mall.

📌 **Web Sites ICICI Bank** ⊕ infinity.icicibank.co.in/web/services/jsp/Locateus.jsp. **UTI Bank** ⊕ www.utibank.com/atm/atmlocate.asp.

CURRENCY
EXCHANGE

Try to carry American Express traveler's checks, as you might have a problem cashing Thomas Cook checks in smaller towns. Checks can be cashed at your hotel or a local bank; just note that most banks keep short hours, from 10 to 2 weekdays and 10 to noon on Saturday. There's a State Bank of India in just about every town—count on branches in Dalhousie, Darjeeling, Dharamshala–McLeod Ganj, Leh, Manali, Mussoorie, Nainital, Rishikesh, Gangtok, Shimla. If you're curious about smaller towns, check the full list of branches on the bank's Web site.

📌 **Exchange Services State Bank of India** ⊕ www.statebankofindia.com/branchlocator/branchlocator.asp.

PERMITS

Because of diplomatic tensions with Pakistan and China, which have occasionally esclated into war, India's northern borders have been sensitive for decades and remain heavily guarded. Movement is restricted in these regions, which means foreigners need permits to enter some parts of Ladakh, Himachal Pradesh, and Sikkim. It's generally easiest to apply for a permit in advance through a travel agent or tour operator. Have two or three passport photographs and photocopies of your passport and your Indian visa handy. Once you have the permit, keep several photocopies of it with you, and make sure you have it stamped at checkposts. Remember not to take pictures of bridges, airports, or military installations in restricted areas.

In Himachal Pradesh, permits are required for sections of the Spiti and Lahaul Valleys and upper Kinnaur. Groups of four foreigners can get permits from the Himachal Pradesh Tourism Development Corporation in New Delhi, which supposedly offers next-day service—but given the nature of Indian bureaucracy, we don't recommended this route. Whether you're traveling with a group or not, let your tour operator handle your permit in advance; just bring extra passport photos.

You need an Inner Line Permit to enter the state of Sikkim, and additional permits (Restricted Area or Protected Area Permits) to move closer to the China border. The Sikkim permit is good for 15 days, and you can get it within 24 hours at any Indian embassy or consulate overseas, the Sikkim Tourist Information Centres in Delhi and Calcutta, the district magistrate's office in Siliguri, or—if you don't mind waiting a half hour—at the border post at Rongpo (the easiest method). If you apply in advance, you must specify your date of entry into Sikkim. A 15-day extension is available in Gangtok from the Tashiling Secretariat (Home Department); one more 15-day extension brings you to the permitted total of 45 days. After that, you may not re-enter Sikkim within three months. No special permit is needed for Khecheopari Lake, Yuksom, Pelling (Pemayangtse), or Tashiling in western Sikkim, but for points beyond these, you need to travel with a government-recognized tour operator, and often in a group of at least four people. The tour company will take care of the paperwork.

You do not need a permit to enter Ladakh, but you need a Restricted Area Permit to visit parts of Ladakh that border on China, such as the Nubra Valley, Pangong Tso, and Tso Moriri. Again, have a tour operator process the application. For official information on Ladakh before you arrive, contact the Jammu and Kashmir Tourism office in New Delhi. 🔢 **District Magistrate, Siliguri** ⊠ SNT Bus Compound, Tenzing Norgay Rd., Siliguri ☎ 353/251-2646.

TRAIN TRAVEL

Shatabdi Express trains—India's fastest and most comfortable trains, with air-conditioned cars and minimal stops—can drop you at several gateways to the Himalayas. If you'll be in one place long enough to receive a delivery, you can order tickets online at ⊕ www.indianrailways. com. Reserve as far in advance as possible, as trains fill up early.

One *Shatabdi* departs New Delhi Railway Station at 7:20 AM for the nearly six-hour trip to Amritsar.

A *Shatabdi Express* departs at 7:40 AM for the 3½-hour trip to **Chandigarh**, from which buses go to Dharamshala, Kullu, and Manali. Spend the night in Chandigarh and start by car or bus the next day for the 12-hour trip to Kullu or the 14-hour trip to Manali. If you hire a driver to tour Himachal Pradesh, consider sending him ahead to Chandigarh and arranging for him to meet you as you arrive on the train from Delhi at 11 AM—this will save you three hours of a potentially tiring road trip.

The train is also the best way to get to **Shimla.** A 95-km (62-mi) narrow-gauge track built in 1903 climbs the final leg from Kalka (2,131 feet) to Shimla (7,170 feet). You're best off with the *Himalayan Queen,* which leaves Delhi at 5:25 AM to reach Kalka at 11:20 AM. The line continues to Shimla under the same name, but you must change in Kalka to the narrow-gauge train. The overnight *Howrah–Kalka Mail* leaves Delhi at 10:50 PM to reach Kalka at 5 AM, where you can catch the 6 AM *Shivalik Express* to Shimla, but the night train is often delayed. Both connect with the Toy Train up to Shimla—a tiny train that travels at 9–15 mph, passing through 102 tunnels and over 845 bridges to make the journey in five hours. First class on the Toy Train is extremely comfortable, with upholstered chairs to sink into as you marvel at the scenery and take refreshments; second class is crowded, with people pushing and shoving to sit on the wooden seats. It's a stiff uphill walk from the train station to the center. A taxi will take you to the pedestrian-only Mall for about Rs. 100. If you hire a porter, he'll expect at least Rs. 50, depending on the amount of luggage; just beware that porters double as hotel touts, so don't let them steer you away from your lodging of choice.

The trip to **Dharamshala** and the **Kangra Valley** is also more pleasant by train than by car. The *Delhi–Jammu–Tawi Jammu Mail,* which leaves Delhi at 9:10 PM to reach Pathankot at 8:15 AM, has first- and second-class air-conditioned compartments; after a good night's sleep you can hop in a car and enjoy the remaining three hours to Dharamshala. You can also ride the Kangra Toy Train between Pathankot and Dharamshala to Pathankot, but this is rather slow.

A *Shatabdi Express* departs New Delhi at 6:55 AM for the 4½-hour trip to **Haridwar** and the roughly six-hour trip to **Dehra Dun.** From there you can hire a taxi to **Rishikesh** or **Mussoorie** respectively.

The best train from Delhi to **Corbett National Park** or **Nainital** drops you in Kathgodam—the Delhi–Kathgodam *Ranikhet Express* leaves New Delhi at 10:45 PM to reach Kathgodam at 6:15 AM. From here, you must still drive 90 minutes to Ramnagar (for Corbett) or an hour to Nainital. The night train from Delhi to Ramnagar is only for the adventurous, as it has no upper-class bogies.

Overnight trains go from Calcutta's Sealdah Station to New Jalpaiguri, where you can grab a taxi for the three- to four-hour drive to **Darjeeling.** Serious rail enthusiasts should board the famous Toy Train for a stunning but very slow eight-hour journey up a series of hairpin turns through terraced fields. If you prefer not to spend eight hours covering 90 km (56 mi), you can always experience the Toy Train as an excursion from Darjeeling.

Most people headed for **Sikkim** use the train station at Siliguri, West Bengal. From here, shared jeeps and buses can take you on to Gangtok, 114 km (71 mi) away, in four hours. In Gangtok, reserve your return trip at the Sikkim Nationalized Transport Petrol Pump on Paljor Namgyal Stadium Road.

TRAVEL AGENTS & TOURS

Most of the outfits listed here offer treks and jeep safaris; some also lead rafting and angling expeditions. The Delhi-based firms Aquaterra Adventures India, Himalayan River Runners, Ibex Expeditions, and Outdoor Adventures India are highly recommended for trips anywhere in the Himalayas, as is Snow Leopard Adventures for rafting on the Ganges. If you're planning your own itinerary, call Delhi's reliable RBS Travels to make driving arrangements and Outbound Travels for airline bookings.

Modern Tours and Travels offers treks in western Sikkim, with excellent food and service. Tashila Tours and Travels leads the way in rafting on the beautiful Teesta and Rangeet rivers. Tenzing Norgay Adventures is run by the sons of Norgay Tenzing, who climbed Mt. Everest with Sir Edmund Hillary. In addition to physical and cultural adventures in Sikkim, they lead expeditions to Nepal, Bhutan, and Tibet.

HIMALAYAS–GENERAL ⊠ **Aquaterra Adventures India** ⊠ S-507 Greater Kailash II, New Delhi ☎ 11/2921–2641 or 11/ 2921–2760 ⊕ www.treknraft.com. **Great Himalayan Adventures** ⊠ N-95 Sham Nagar, New Delhi ☎ 11/2546–5783 ⊕ www.wildquestindia.com. **Himalayan River Runners** ⊠ N-8 Green Park Main, upper floor, New Delhi ☎ 11/2685–2602 or 11/2696–8169 ⊕ www.hrrindia.com. **Ibex Expeditions** ⊠ G-66 East of Kailash, New Delhi ☎ 11/2691–2641 or 11/2682–8479 ⊕ www.ibexpeditions.com. **RBS Travels** ⊠ Shop A1, Connaught Palace Hotel, 37 Shaheed Bhagat Singh Marg, New Delhi ☎ 11/2336–4603 or 11/2336–4952.

HIMACHAL PRADESH ⊠ **Band Box Heights and Valleys** ⊠ 9, The Mall, Shimla ☎ 177/265–8157 or 98160–61160. **Himalayan Journeys** ⊠ The Mall, Box 15, Manali ☎ 1902/252365 or 1902/253355 ⊕ www.himalayanjourneysindia.com. **Naresh Tours and Travels** ⊠ 3 Chaura Maidan, Shimla ☎ 177/265–6692, 177/265–7445, or 98170–16692. **Yeti Travels** ⊠ The Mall, Manali ☎ 1902/253135 or 1902/252655.

LADAKH ⊠ **Adventure North Tours and Travels** ⊠ C/o Dragon Hotel, Old Leh Rd., Leh ☎ 1982/252720 or 1982/252139.

UTTARANCHAL ⊠ **Outbound Travels** ⊠ 216A/11 Gautam Nagar, 3rd fl., New Delhi ☎ 11/2652–6316. **Outdoor Adventures India** ⊠ S-234 Panchsheel Park, 2nd fl., New Delhi ☎ 11/2601–7485 ⊕ www.outdooradventuresindia.com. **Skylark Travels** ⊠ Alka Hotel Annexe, The Mall, Nainital ☎ 5942/235165 or 5942/236096. **Snow Leopard Adventures** ⊠ Sector C-9, Vasant Kunj, New Delhi ☎ 11/2689–8654 ⊕ www.snowleopardadventures.com.

DARJEELING–SIKKIM ⊠ **Bayul Tours** ⊠ Below C.P.W.D office, Bajra Cinema Hall Rd., Gangtok ☎ 3592/228341. **Blue Sky Tours and Travels** ⊠ Lachung Khangsar, Tibet Rd., Gangtok ☎ 3592/225113 or 3592/223330. **Modern Tours and Travels** ⊠ Opposite Sikkim Tourist Information Centre, Traffic Point, M. G. Marg, Gangtok ☎ 3592/227319. **Sikkim Taxi Owner Association** ⊠ Near head post office, Gangtok ☎ 3592/232391 or 98320–97331, ask for Pemba Bhutia. **Tashila Tours and Travels** ⊠ 31-A National Hwy., P.B. No. 70, Gangtok ☎ 3592/222979. **Vinayak Travels** ⊠ L M Moulik Complex, Hill Cart Rd., Siliguri ☎ 3593/253–1067. **Yak and Yeti Travels** ⊠ Hotel Super View, Zero Point, Gangtok ☎ 3592/224643. **Tenzing Norgay Adventures** ⊠ 1 D. B. Giri Rd., Darjeeling, West Bengal ☎ 354/225–3718 ⊕ www.tenzing-norgay.com.

VISITOR INFORMATION

⊠ **Tourist Offices Amritsar** ⊠ Palace Hotel, opposite railway station ☎ 183/240–2452. **Chandigarh** ⊠ 1st fl., Interstate Bus Terminus, Sector 17 ☎ 172/270–4614. **Himachal Pradesh** ⊠ Chandralok Bldg., 36 Janpath, New Delhi ☎ 11/2332–5320 ⊠ Kotwali Bazaar, Dharamshala ☎ 1892/224928 ⊠ Dolma Chowk, McCleod Ganj ☎ 1892/221205

✉ Hotel Kunjum, near taxi stand, The Mall, Manali ☎ 1902/253531 ✉ The Mall, Shimla ☎ 177/265-2561. **Jammu and Kashmir** ✉ 201-203 Kanishka Shopping Plaza, 19 Ashok Rd., New Delhi ☎ 11/2334-5373 ⊕ www.jktourism.org. **Ladakh** ✉ Tourist Reception Center, 3 km (2 mi) outside town, Leh ☎ 1982/252297. **Sikkim** ✉ 14 Panchsheel Marg, Chanakyapuri, New Delhi ☎ 11/2611-5346 ✉ 4/1 Middleton St., Calcutta ☎ 33/2281-5328 ✉ SNT Bus Compound, Tenzing Norgay Rd., Siliguri ☎ 353/251-2646, 353/255-1036 Bagdogra Airport ✉ M. G. Marg, Gangtok ☎ 3592/221634 or 3592/227720. **Uttaranchal** ✉ 102 Indra Prakash Bldg., 21 Barakhamba Rd., New Delhi ☎ 11/2332-6620 or 11/2335-0481. **West Bengal** ✉ Silver Fir Bldg., The Mall, Darjeeling ☎ 354/254214.

DELHI

2

SAMPLE THE SUMPTUOUS CUISINE
of the Northern Frontier
at Bukhara in Chanakyapuri ⇨*p.94*

SLEEP LIKE A KING
at the Imperial hotel ⇨*p.99*

IMMERSE YOURSELF
in the hustle and bustle of the bazaar
at Chandni Chowk in Old Delhi ⇨*p.78*

SINK YOUR TEETH
into a kabab at Park Balluchi
in Hauz Khas Village ⇨*p.95*

NIBBLE ON INDIAN SNACK FOODS
from neighborhood markets ⇨*p.109*

By Christine
Cipriani

OF ALL OF INDIA'S major cities, only Delhi was already ancient when the British arrived. Smack in the middle of the northern plains, the city has always been prized by South Asia's rulers—their dwellings and forts still stand in clusters and layers, testaments to a long imperial cycle of sacking and rebuilding. The Moghuls, with their exalted Persian aesthetic, left the most striking legacy, but now, in modern-day India, even they compete for attention with bustling cafés and gleaming DVD shops.

The ancient epic *Mahabharata* places the great town of Indraprastha on the banks of the Yamuna River, perhaps in what is now Delhi's Old Fort. Late in the first millennium A.D., Delhi became an outpost of the Hindu Rajput rulers (warrior kings of what is now Rajasthan)—but it was after 1191, when Mohammad Ghori of Central Asia invaded and conquered, that the city acquired its Islamic flavor. Other Afghan and Uzbek sultanates handed Delhi back and forth over the next 300 years, until the mighty Moghuls settled in. Beginning with the invasion of Babur in 1526, the Moghuls shifted their capital between Delhi and Agra until 1858, leaving stunning architecture at both sites, including Shahjahanabad, now known as Old Delhi.

The fall of the Moghul empire coincided with the rise of the British East India Company, first in Madras and Calcutta and eventually throughout the country. When several of Delhi's Indian garrisons mutinied against their Company employers in 1857, the British suppressed them, moved into the Red Fort, and ousted the aging Moghul emperor. In 1911, with anti-British sentiment growing in Calcutta, they moved their capital from Calcutta to Delhi—the ultimate prize, a place where they could build a truly imperial city that would dwarf the older ones around it. Architect Sir Edwin Lutyens was hired to create New Delhi, a majestic sandstone government complex surrounded by wide, leafy avenues and roundabouts, in contrast to Old Delhi's hectic lanes.

When India gained independence on August 15, 1947, with Jawaharlal Nehru the first prime minister, the subcontinent was partitioned into the secular republic of India and the Muslim nation of Pakistan, divided into West Pakistan (now Pakistan) and East Pakistan (now Bangladesh). Trapped in potentially hostile new countries, thousands of Muslims left Delhi for Pakistan while millions of Hindu and Sikh refugees streamed in—changing Delhi's cultural overtone almost overnight from Persian to Punjabi.

Since Prime Minister Rajiv Gandhi (grandson of Nehru) and his successor, Narasimha Rao, began to liberalize India's planned economy in the late 1980s and early '90s, Delhi has experienced tremendous change. Foreign companies have arrived and hired locals for white-collar jobs, residential enclaves and shopping strips have sprouted in every crevice, and land prices have skyrocketed. Professionals seeking affordable living space now move to the suburbs and drive into town, aggravating the already substantial pollution problem. At the same time, North Indian villagers still come here in search of work and build shanties wherever they can, sometimes in the shadows of forgotten monuments. It is they—Rajasthani women in colorful saris digging holes with pickaxes, men climbing rickety scaffolds in sarong-like lungis—who build new homes for the affluent. Many Delhiites say, with a sigh, that their city is in a perpetual state of flux.

Precisely because of its cheek-by-jowl mixture of Old Delhi's Moghul glory, Central Delhi's European grandeur, and South Delhi's boutiques and lounge bars, Delhi is a profoundly Indian place. In the Delhi Golf Course, Islamic monuments share the fairways with peacocks; in Lodi Garden, they're interspersed with young lovers. Hindu temples, Sikh *gurdwaras* (temples), and secular discos are packed with their respective devotees. Young men push ice-cream carts by hand while managers cruise past in air-conditioned Mitsubishis, punching e-mails into their cell phones. Yet, even as private enterprise transforms its business climate and social life, the capital remains a bureaucracy, with political bigshots the talk of the town. Delhi is not the most beautiful city in India, but it is in many ways the grandest.

EXPLORING DELHI

Delhi's commercial and geographic hub used to be Connaught Place, a fact reflected in the area's hub-and-spokes layout. Connaught Place remains popular with tourists, particularly backpackers—hence its abundance of beggars, money changers both legitimate and illegitimate, and drug dealers—but it's no longer the capital's nerve center. As development sprawls south, now spilling over into suburbs, South Delhi has become the center of social and, to a large extent, commercial life.

Central Delhi, between Connaught Place and South Delhi, is also known as Lutyens' Delhi. Designed by the British architect Sir Edwin Lutyens (1869–1944) for the ruling British government of the early 20th century, Lutyens' Delhi remains the home of the Indian government, including Rashtrapati Bhavan (the Presidential Palace), the North and South Secretariats, Sansad Bhavan (Parliament House), and India Gate, a massive monument to British Indian Army soldiers killed in World War I and the Afghan wars. Most of Delhi's museums are nearby, and the surrounding area is filled with tree-lined boulevards, lovely old bungalows, and affluent residential neighborhoods.

Sprawling New Delhi is best navigated on wheels—hire a car, taxi, or auto-rickshaw to get around. In contrast, the narrow lanes of Old Delhi are a walker's delight.

Note that brochures, maps, floor plans and annotation are nonexistent at most sights; you must be guided by your own inclination. Be prepared to remove your shoes when visiting religious institutions, including the Charity Birds Hospital; women should bring a scarf to cover their heads. Shorts are not appropriate attire for any adult.

About the Restaurants & Hotels

Restaurants are generally open daily 12:30 to 3 for lunch and 7:30 to 11 for dinner. Strict liquor laws prevent many restaurants from serving alcohol, but this is changing fast; all the restaurants below serve alcohol unless we indicate otherwise. Just note that imported liquor is ex-

Avoid tackling Old Delhi on your first day, especially if you've never been to India before—its chaos can be overwhelming. Starting with New Delhi will also give you a better idea of the aesthetic and cultural dichotomy between the two cities.

If you have
3 days

Begin with New Delhi, where a drive through the graceful avenues of Lutyens' imperial city will ease you gently into the capital. Depending on your interests, visit some Independence sites (the Nehru Museum or Gandhi Smriti), a museum, or a temple or gurdwara. The next day, plunge into Old Delhi—explore the Lal Qila (Red Fort) and the stunning Jama Masjid, then venture into Chandni Chowk. After a breather, visit Humayun's Tomb and the Hazrat Nizamuddin Darga, two little "pockets" of Old Delhi in New Delhi. Return to New Delhi on Day 3: drive south to the Qutub Minar in the morning, then check out some museums or galleries, do some shopping, and, before sunset, stroll through the Lodi Garden.

2

If you have
5 days

Follow the three-day itinerary above, and on day four make an overnight excursion to the Neemrana Fort Palace outside the Shekhavati region of Rajasthan and unwind in Rajput splendor. On day five, make a leisurely return to Delhi to see another museum or do some more shopping.

If you have
8 days

Follow the five-day itinerary above. On Day 6, drive six hours northwest to Corbett National Park in Uttaranchal, one of India's most famous and enjoyable wildlife parks, and devote Day 7 to a Jeep safari. *Alternately,* if Corbett is closed for the rainy season, head north to Mussoorie (via the train to Dehra Dun) for an eyeful of the Himalayan foothills in an old-fashioned British-style resort town.

tremely expensive—inquire before you imbibe. Expect a 20% tax on your food and beverage bill.

Unless we note otherwise, all the hotels we list have air-conditioning, bathrooms with tubs, currency exchange, and room service. Most have a doctor on call. In addition, all deluxe hotels have wireless or broadband Internet access and executive floors with special lounges and services for business travelers. You *must* reserve in advance for stays between October and February, as even the largest hotels fill up.

WHAT IT COSTS In Rupees				
	$$$$	**$$$**	**$$**	**$**	**¢**
RESTAURANTS	over 1,000	850–1,000	500–850	200–500	under 200
HOTELS	over 11,500	8,500–11,500	5,500–8,500	2,500–5,500	under 2,500

Restaurant prices are for an entrée plus dal, rice, and a veg/non-veg dish. Hotel prices are for a standard double room in high season, excluding a tax of up to 20%.

Timing

It's best to visit Delhi between mid-October and March. The heat is intense from April until the monsoon arrives in July, after which rain and intense humidity add to the misery. If you'll only be in Delhi a few days, note that the Red Fort and most museums are closed on Monday, and the Jama Masjid is closed to non-Muslims on Friday.

Old Delhi

Old Delhi (6 km [4 mi] north of Connaught Place)—once known as Shahjahanabad for the emperor who built it—lies in a perpetual state of decay. The grand old homes, or *havelis,* that line the *galis* (lanes; origin of the word "gully") are architecturally stunning but irreversibly crumbling. Old Delhi's monuments—the Jama Masjid and Red Fort—are magnificent, and the main artery, Chandni Chowk, is great fun to explore.

Old Delhi is crowded and hectic, and the roads and footways are poorly maintained. Fast-moving carts and overloaded laborers plow through whatever comes in their way. If you find the throng too daunting, or just need a break after a few hours, try a cycle-rickshaw tour: For about Rs. 100, you can be carted around in a cycle-rickshaw (which seats two slim people) for about an hour. The rickshaw-wallahs in front of the Red Fort are serious bargainers, but they know the city well, and many can show you places you wouldn't discover on your own.

Numbers in the text correspond to numbers in the margin and on the Delhi map.

a good walk

Start in Old Delhi with a morning tour of the **Lal Qila** ❶ ▶, or Red Fort, Emperor Shah Jahan's sprawling 17th-century capital. When you emerge, set your sights on the red Jain temple across the boulevard, and walk around to its left side. Inside the gate, remove your shoes and proceed into the **Charity Birds Hospital** ❷, a one-of-a-kind institution.

After leaving the hospital, return to the main road and walk back around the temple (keeping it on your left) to enter the famous strip known as **Chandni Chowk** ❸. Chaos reigns supreme here, so gather your wits and watch your feet lest they be flattened by a cart or cycle-rickshaw. You'll pass a short but fragrant row of flower-sellers. About four blocks down the street on the left, identifiable by its small gold dome, is the marble **Sisganj Gurdwara** ❹, a Sikh shrine. After seeing it, continue down Chandni Chowk and cross three more lanes (galis); then, at Kanwarji's sweet shop (across the street from the Central Bank of India), turn left on **Gali Paranthe Wali** ❺. Stop for a snack if you need fortification; then continue down the lane, following its jogs to the right, until the road hits a T at the Sant Lal Sanskriti sari shop. Turn left into Kinari Bazaar, a sparkling bridal-trimming market where Hindu families can buy every item required, and then some, for their wedding festivities. Scooters and rickshaws can mess things up in this narrow thoroughfare, so don't be in a hurry.

At 2130 Kinari Bazaar (a bric-a-brac shop called Krishna & Co.), turn right into one of Chandni Chowk's most beautiful lanes, Naughara Gali,

2

Dining

Stylized restaurants are relatively new to India, as tradition favors the warm, informal hospitality of inviting friends to one's home; but the burgeoning middle class, with its hunger for new foods and experiences, is fueling an exciting trend. Various Indian cuisines, such as Kashmiri and Mangalorean, now have their own restaurants, and cheap, authentic non-Indian food is finally available to Delhi's increasingly well-traveled diners.

Serious food lovers should seek out *Flavours of Delhi,* by Charmaine O'Brien (Penguin India, 2003), which mixes Delhi's culinary history with detailed recommendations and a few recipes.

From Five-Star to Flophouse

Charming, affordable lodging is not one of Delhi's strong points. Hotels tend to be either posh or flophouse, with the middle ground largely lacking. If you're not sure where to turn, consider staying at a guest house—a small, fairly spartan hotel with room service and a small dining room—as prices are about a fifth of those at the big hotels. Backpackers traditionally head for the lodgings in Paharganj, some of which are adequate but none of which stands out in its own right.

Indian law requires all upscale hotels (not guest houses) to charge foreigners a dollar rate that's higher than the rupee rate paid by Indians—and to top it off with luxury and service taxes amounting to around 20% on both room and food.

Arts & Culture

Delhi has the richest arts scene in the country. If you love dance, music, theater, or painting you'll have plenty of opportunities to experience the Indian versions: the dazzling footwork of Kathak dance, the otherworldly sounds of Hindustani music, the freshness of contemporary Hindi plays, cleverly curated group art shows, and much more. You just have to be on your toes, as the arts are ill-publicized and performances tend to start at 6:30 PM. Pick up the monthly magazine *First City* for citywide listings and profiles of featured artists.

Shopping

Delhi's shopping options are virtually inexhaustible. Handmade crafts and fabrics from all over the country are sold in a pleasant outdoor setting at Dilli Haat, and in a plethora of government-run emporiums featuring typical items from India's many states. Various neighborhood markets invite you to join Delhiites in their quest for the latest fashions and sportswear (Greater Kailash I, South Extension, Hauz Khas Village, Connaught Place), jewelry, curios, and antiques (Sundar Nagar), books (Khan Market), and cheap apparel of every kind (Sarojini Nagar). The INA Market is a true Eastern experience, bursting with fresh produce, spices, salty snacks, and squawking chickens. In Old Delhi, endless holes-in-the-wall sell brassware, curios, and silver jewelry.

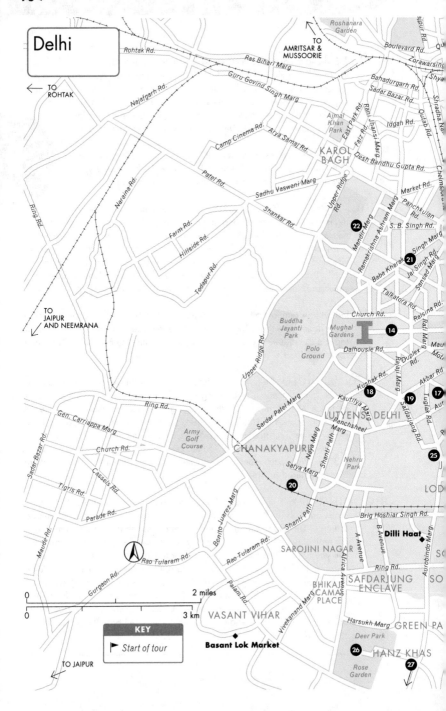

Delhi

← TO
ROHTAK

TO JAIPUR
AND NEEMRANA

TO JAIPUR

Rohtak Rd.

Najafgarh Rd.

Guru Govind Singh Marg

Ras Bihari Marg

TO
AMRITSAR &
MUSSOORIE

Roshanara
Garden

Boulevard Rd.

Zorawarsing

Bahadurgarh Rd.

Sadar Bazar Rd.

Idgah Rd.

Qutab Rd.

Shradha

Camp Cinema Rd.

Arya Samaj Rd.

Ajmal
Khan
Park

East Park Rd.

Rani Jhansi Marg

Faiz Rd.

KAROL
BAGH

Desh Bandhu Gupta Rd.

Market Rd.

Panchkulan
Rd.

S. B. Singh Rd.

Chelmsfo

Patel Rd.

Sadhu Vaswani Marg

Shankar Rd.

Upper Ridge Rd.

22

Mandir Marg

Ramakrishna Ashram Marg

Baba Kharak Singh Marg

Jai Singh Rd.

Sansad Marg

21

Naraina Rd.

Farm Rd.

Hillside Rd.

Todapur Rd.

Buddha
Jayanti
Park

Polo
Ground

Church Rd.

Mughal
Gardens

Dalhousie Rd.

Talkatora Rd.

Raisina Rd.

14

Ring Rd.

Upper Ridge Rd.

Kushak Rd.

Kautilya Marg

Sardar Patel Marg

18

Hailey Rd.

Duplex
Rd.

Akbar Rd.

Tuglak Rd.

19

17

Mau

Moti

Aur

Gen. Carriappa Marg

Ring Rd.

Army
Golf
Course

CHANAKYAPUR

LUTYENS DELHI

Panchsheel
Marg

Safdarjang Rd.

Sadar Bazar Rd.

Church Rd.

Cassels Rd.

Naya Marg

Shanti Path

Nehru
Park

25

LOD

Tigris Rd.

Parade Rd.

Satya Marg

20

Maude Rd.

Rao Tularam Rd.

Bento Juarez Marg

Rao Tularam Rd.

Shanti Path

Brig Hoshiar Singh Rd.

A Avenue

B. Avenue

Dilli Haat ◆

Aurobindo Marg

So

Gurgaon Rd.

Palam Rd.

Vivekanand Marg

Africa Avenue

SAROJINI NAGAR

Ring Rd.

SAFDARJUNG
ENCLAVE

SO

0 _____ 2 miles
0 _____ 3 km

BHIKAJ
CAMA
PLACE

VASANT VIHAR

Basant Lok Market ◆

Harsukh Marg

GREEN PA

Deer
Park

26

Rose
Garden

HANZ KHAS

27

KEY

► *Start of tour*

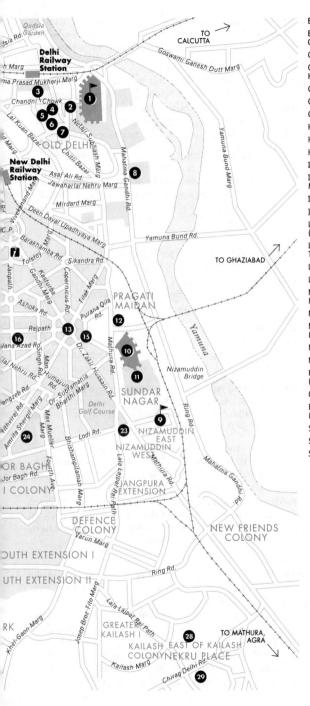

Bahai House of Worship **29**

Bangla Sahib
Gurdwara **21**

Chandni Chowk **3**

Charity Birds
Hospital **2**

Crafts Museum **12**

Gali Paranthe Wali **5**

Gandhi Smriti **17**

Hauz Khas Village **26**

Hazrat Nizamuddin Darga **23**

Humayun's Tomb **9**

India Gate **13**

Indira Gandhi
Memorial Museum **19**

ISCON Temple **28**

Jama Masjid **7**

Lal Qila
(Red Fort) **1**

Laxmi Naryan
Temple **22**

Lodi Garden **24**

Lutyens' Delhi **14**

National Gallery of
Modern Art **15**

National Museum **16**

National Rail
Museum **20**

National Zoological Park **11**

Nehru Memorial Museum **18**

Purana Qila
(Old Fort) **10**

Qutub Minar **27**

Raj Ghat and National Gandhi
Museum **8**

Safdarjung's Tomb **25**

Sisganj Gurdwara **4**

Svetamber Jain Temple **6**

where a community of Jains lives in some old havelis painted in aquas, pinks, and yellows. At the end of this peaceful alley is the **Svetamber Jain Temple** ❻. Even if the temple is closed, Naughara Gali is a temporary escape from the bustle of the bazaar.

Return to Kinari Bazaar and turn right. If it suits your fancy, stop in a glitzy wedding shop called **Shivam Zari Palace** (2178 Kinari Bazaar) and spend half an hour dressing a tiny brass statue of Gopal (baby Krishna) in an outfit of your choice, including a headpiece, necklace, and bangles. The cost of your finished memento is Rs. 750, more for a larger statue.

Continue down Kinari Bazaar until it intersects with **Dariba Kalan,** or "Silver Street." If you're in the market for jewelry or curios, check out the shops to the left; if not, turn right and head down Dariba Kalan to its end. Turn right again and you'll find yourself on a broad street in the brass and copper district. Take the next right, then an immediate left under a stone arch. Now head up Chah Rahat, a typical narrow lane with old wooden balconies and verandas.

When Chah Rahat opens into a courtyard, take the hairpin turn to the left and follow the arrow on the sign for "Singh Copper and Brass Palace." After about 30 feet, a second sign directs you down an alley on the right. Singh's emporium is filthy, but every floor has an interesting collection of miscellany.

From Singh's, return to the courtyard on Chah Rahat and take the short, narrow lane to the left. You'll emerge to see the splendid **Jama Masjid** ❼, preceded by a somewhat incongruous tool bazaar. To reach the mosque's entrance, head right, then follow the bazaar to the left.

At the end of this long tour, you'll probably be ready for a proper Muslim meal. Walk out of the Jama Masjid to Karim's, conveniently located on the colorful lane heading away from the mosque's entrance, or take a cycle-rickshaw to Chor Bizarre.

TIMING   Allow a full day for this tour, and don't attempt it on a hot day. Avoid Friday, when entrance to the mosque is tricky for non-Muslims; Sunday, when most shops in Old Delhi are closed; and Monday, when the Red Fort is closed. (If you have to choose between Sunday and Monday, go for Monday. The bazaars are crucial to Old Delhi's flavor.) Note, too, that the Jain temple—near the end of the walk—is closed between 12:30 and 6:30 each afternoon, so if art and architecture make your heart sing, try to start very early *or* right after lunch.

What to See

❸ **Chandni Chowk.** This was Delhi's former imperial avenue, where the Moghul emperor Shah Jahan rode at the head of his lavish cavalcade. That scene is hard to picture today, as bullock carts, bicycles, taxis, freight carts, cows, auto-rickshaws, horse-drawn tongas (two-wheeled cart taxis) and pedestrians create a constant, breathtaking bazaar. As in the days of the Moghuls, astrologers set up their charts on the pavement; shoemakers squat and repair sandals; sidewalk photographers with old box cameras take pictures for a small fee; medicine booths conceal doctors attending to patients; and oversize teeth grin from the windows of dentists' offices. Peer through a portico and you might see men getting shaved, silver being hammered into paper-thin edible sheets, or any other conceivable form of commerce, while outside a goat blithely chews vegetables from a merchant's cart. ⊠ *East–west artery from Red Fort 1.5 km (1 mi) west to Fatehpuri Masjid, Old Delhi* ☉ *Most shops closed Sun.*

②   Charity Birds Hospital. Across from the Red Fort is a delightful and unusual attraction: a hospital for birds and rabbits. Founded by Jains in 1956, the hospital is modest, but it shows how tender loving care can stretch limited funds. Go all the way upstairs to see the "general ward," a feeding frenzy; there's even an intensive-care ward and a research laboratory. Bathed, fed, and given vitamins, the healthy birds refuse to leave, and that's how you can spot the building—flocks of birds swirl around its roof. ⊠ *Netaji Subhash Marg, opposite Red Fort, Old Delhi* ☒ *Free, donations welcome* ☉ *Daily 8–8.*

⑤   Gali Paranthe Wali. This narrow, festive lane is filled with shopkeepers selling fabric and saris, including the well-known Ram Chandra Krishan Chandra's, where young brides choose their red-and-gold finery. The lane is named for its other industry: the fabulous *paranthas* (fried flatbreads) that are sold here in no-frills open-air eateries. Stuffed or served with a variety of fixings, such as radishes, soft cheese, and seasonal vegetables, parathas are a decadent treat. A few kitchens have seating, making them excellent places to refuel, even if the staff doesn't speak English. ⊠ *South off Chandni Chowk, Old Delhi.*

⑦   Jama Masjid. An exquisite Islamic statement in red sandstone and marble, India's largest mosque was the last monument commissioned by Shah Jahan. Completed in 1656 after six years of work by 5,000 laborers, it's arguably one of the loveliest houses of worship in the world. Three sets of broad steps lead to two-story gateways and a magnificent courtyard with a square ablution tank in the center. The entire space is enclosed by pillared corridors, with domed pavilions in each corner. Thousands gather to pray here, especially on Friday.

FodorśChoice
★

With its onion-shape dome and tapering minarets, the mosque is characteristically Moghul, but Shah Jahan added an innovation: the stripes running smartly up and down the marble domes and minarets. The whole structure exudes peace and harmony—climb the south minaret to see the domes up close, complete with swarms of pigeons, and to see how finely the mosque contrasts with the commercial streets around it. (Women cannot enter the minaret without a man; if you're a woman traveling solo, enlist a man to help you, as the beauty of the architecture is best appreciated from above.) Look into the prayer hall (you can only enter after a ritual purification at the ablution tank) for the pulpit carved from a single slab of marble. In one corner is a room where Shah Jahan installed the marble footprints of the Prophet Mohammed. ⊠ *6 km (4 mi) north of Connaught Pl., across from Red Fort, Old Delhi* ☏ *11/ 2326–8344* ☒ *Free, Rs. 10 to climb minaret, Rs. 100 for camera or camcorder* ☉ *Non-Muslims: winter, 8:30 AM–12:15 PM and 1:45–½ hr before sunset; summer, 7 AM–12:15 and 1:45–½ hr before sunset. Closed for prayer ½ hr each afternoon. Muslims, daily 5 AM–8 PM.*

★ ⌐ ❶ **Lal Qila** (Red Fort). Named for its red-sandstone walls, the Red Fort, near the Yamuna River in Old Delhi, is the greatest of Delhi's Moghul palace-cities, outdoing even Lutyens' Delhi in majesty. Built by Shah Jahan in the 17th century, Lal Qila recalls the era of Moghul power and magnif-icence—imperial elephants swaying by with their *mahouts* (elephant drivers), a royal army of eunuchs, court ladies carried in palanquins, and other vestiges of Shah Jahan's pomp. At its peak, the fort housed about 3,000 people. After the Indian Mutiny of 1857, the British moved into the fort, built barracks, and ended the grand Moghul era; eventually the Yamuna River changed course, so the view from the eastern ramparts is now a busy road. Still, if you use your imagination, a visit to the Red Fort gives an excellent idea of what a fantastic city Shahjahanabad was.

The view of the main entrance, called **Lahore Gate,** flanked with tow-ers facing Chandni Chowk, is unfortunately blocked by a barbican (gatehouse), which the paranoid Aurangzeb added for his personal se-curity—much to the grief of Shah Jahan, his father. From his prison, where he was held captive by his power-hungry son, Shah Jahan wrote, "You have made a bride of the palace and thrown a veil over her face."

Once you pass through Lahore Gate, continue down the **Chhatta Chowk** (Vaulted Arcade), originally the shopping district for the royal harem and now a bazaar selling rather less regal goods. (Tula Ram, on the right side near the end, is an exception, with excellent miniature paintings.) From the end of the arcade, you'll see the **Naubat Khana** (Welcome Room), a red-sandstone gateway where music was played five times daily. Be-yond this point, everyone but the emperor and princes had to proceed on foot. Upstairs, literally inside the gateway, is the Indian War Memo-rial Museum (Tues.–Sun. 10–5; free), with arms and military regalia from several periods.

An expansive lawn leads to the great **Diwan-i-Am** (Hall of Public Au-dience)—you have now entered the Delhi of Shah Jahan. Raised on a platform and open on three sides, the hall is studded with some of the most emblematic arches in the Moghul world. In the center is Shah Jahan's royal throne, once surrounded by decorative panels that sparkled with inlaid gems. (Stolen by British soldiers after the Indian Mutiny, some of the panels were restored 50 years later by Lord Curzon.) Watched by throngs of people from the courtyard below, the emperor heard the pleas of his subjects; the rest of the hall was reserved for rajas and foreign en-voys, all standing with "their eyes bent downwards and their hands crossed." High above them, wrote the 17th-century French traveler François Bernier, under a pearl-fringe canopy resting on golden shafts, "glittered the dazzling figure of the Grand Moghul, a figure to strike terror, for a frown meant death."

Behind the Diwan-i-Am, a row of palaces overlooks the now-distant river. To the extreme right is the **Mumtaz Mahal,** now the Red Fort Museum (Tues.–Sun. 10–5; free), with numerous paintings and relics from the Moghul period, some in better lighting than others. Heading back north, you'll come next to the **Rang Mahal** (Painted Palace), once richly dec-orated with a mirrored ceiling that was dismantled to pay the bills when the treasury ran low. Home of the royal ladies, the Rang Mahal contains a cooling water channel—called the Canal of Paradise—that runs from the marble basin in the center of the floor to the rest of the palace and to several of the others. Alas, you can't enter this or any of the palaces ahead, so you must peer creatively from the side.

The emperor's private **Khas Mahal** has three sections: the sitting room, the "dream chamber" (for sleeping), and the prayer chamber, all with lavishly carved walls and painted ceilings still intact. The lovely marble screen is carved with the Scale of Justice—two swords and a scale that symbolize punishment and justice. From the attached octagonal tower the emperor Muthamman Burj would appear before his subjects each morning or watch elephant fights in the nearby fields.

The **Diwan-i-Khas** (Hall of Private Audience) was the most exclusive pavilion of all. Here Shah Jahan would sit on his Peacock Throne, made of solid gold and inlaid with hundreds of precious and semiprecious stones. (When Nadir Shah sacked Delhi in 1739, he hauled the famous throne back to Persia.) A Persian couplet written in gold above a corner arch sums up Shah Jahan's sentiments about his city: IF THERE BE A PARADISE ON EARTH—IT IS THIS! IT IS THIS! IT IS THIS!

The **Royal Hammam** was a luxurious three-chamber Moghul bath with inlaid-marble floors. The fountain in the center supposedly had rose-scented water. Sometimes called a Turkish bath, the *hammam* is still used in many Muslim cultures. Peek through the windows for a look.

Next door to the hammam is the **Moti Masjid** (Pearl Mosque), designed by Aurangzeb for his personal use and that of his harem. The building is now closed, but the prayer hall is inlaid with *musalla* (prayer rugs) outlined in black marble. Though the mosque has the purity of white marble, some critics say its excessively ornate style reflects the decadence that set in late in Shah Jahan's reign.

Beyond the mosque is a typical Moghul *charbagh*, or four-section garden. Stroll through this quieter part of the fort to see some small pleasure palaces including the Zafar Mahal, decked out with carved sandstone *jalis* (screens) and once surrounded by water. ⊠ *Eastern end of Chandni Chowk, Old Delhi* 🎫 *Rs. 100* ⊙ *Tues.–Sun. sunrise–sunset. Sound-and-light show, weather permitting: Rs. 50. Purchase tickets 30 min in advance. Show times: Nov.–Jan., 7:30 PM–8:30 PM; Feb.–Apr., Sept. and Oct., 8:30 PM–9:30 PM; May–Aug., 9 PM–10 PM.*

❹ Sisganj Gurdwara. Old Delhi's most famous Sikh shrine is a restful place to see one of North India's emblematic faiths in practice. Built at various times between 1784 (when the Sikhs conquered Delhi) and the 20th century, it marks the site where the Moghul emperor Aurangzeb beheaded Guru Teg Bahadur in 1675, when the guru refused to convert to Islam. As in any gurdwara (Sikh temple), sections of the *Guru Granth Sahib* scripture are chanted continuously; depending on the season, you might also find decorations of tinsel, colored foil, and blinking lights. Leave your shoes at the opening about 30 feet to the right of the entrance, then cover your head before entering. Women: if you don't have a head covering, climb the stairs and ask the man on the left to lend you one (it's free). If you have any questions about Sikhism or the shrine after your visit, stop into the friendly information office to the left of the entrance to hear legends and symbols unfold. ☒ *Chandni Chowk, Old Delhi* ☉ *Daily 24 hrs.*

★ ❻ **Svetamber Jain Temple.** Properly called the Indraprastha Tirth Sumatinatha Jain Svetamber Temple, this splendid house of worship is painted head-to-toe with finely rendered murals and decorations covering the walls, arches, and ceilings. Reflecting the building's surroundings, some of the artwork shows Moghul influence. Look inside the silver doors of the shrine to Sumatinatha—the 5th of Jainism's 24 *tirthankaras* (perfect souls)—to see some incredible original painting finished with gold leaf. ☒ *End of Naughara Gali, Old Delhi* ☎ *11/2327–0489* ☉ *Daily 5:30 AM–12:30 PM and 6:30 PM–8 PM.*

New Delhi

New Delhi, which begins in Connaught Place and extends about 6 km (4 mi) south, is the city the British built when they moved their capital from Calcutta to Delhi in 1911. South Delhi, the southern part of New Delhi, ironically has even older monuments, such as the Qutub Minar, Hauz Khas, and numerous Muslim tombs that lie abandoned in the midst of contemporary houses and apartments.

Numbers in the text correspond to numbers in the margin and on the Delhi map.

a good tour

Hire a car or taxi and head to **Humayun's Tomb** ❾ ➤ in the early morning. Created by the wife of the Moghul emperor, the 16th-century tomb is relatively peaceful at this time of day. Proceed north to see where Humayun actually died—in the **Purana Qila** ❿, or Old Fort—and check out the white tigers in the adjacent **National Zoological Park** ⓫. Go north one more block to the **Crafts Museum** ⓬ for a taste of India's artisanal heritage. From here, head west to Dilli Haat and the INA Market, two wonderful shopping-and-eating bazaars

After lunch, proceed to **India Gate** ⓭ and drive along Raj Path to see the grandeur of **Lutyens' Delhi** ⓮. If you're interested in art, visit the **National Gallery of Modern Art** ⓯.

Choose one or two of the following sights—all within a few kilometers of one another—to occupy the rest of your afternoon. If you're an ancient-history buff, drive east, back down Raj Path, to see the Hindu sculptures and artifacts at the **National Museum** ⓰. If you're interested in politics and the Independence movement, visit **Gandhi Smriti** ⓱, the **Nehru Memorial Museum** ⓲, and the **Indira Gandhi Memorial Museum** ⓳. A good alternative, especially for railroad enthusiasts and children, is to continue south and visit the **National Rail Museum** ⓴ near Nehru Park. Drive northwest to the Sikh temple **Bangla Sahib Gurdwara** ㉑ to listen to hymns; then drive a few streets west to check out the nearby colorful and ornate **Laxmi Naryan Temple** ㉒.

Around 5 PM, drive to the Old World Muslim bazaar in Nizamuddin West, about 3 km (2 mi) east of Lodi Garden, and walk down the winding lanes to **Hazrat Nizamuddin Darga** ㉓, the tomb of a Sufi saint. It's a lovely place to linger at dusk, and if you're lucky, qawwali singers will perform as the sun sets.

If you have an extra afternoon, chill out in **Lodi Garden** ㉔ amidst the tombs of the 15th- and 16th-century Lodi rulers. Walk a few blocks west of the garden to see **Safdarjung's Tomb** ㉕. Drive south and wander through **Hauz Khas** ㉖ and head farther south to see the towering **Qutub Minar** ㉗. Another option, especially in the early evening, is to visit the **ISKCON Temple** ㉘ of the Hare Krishna sect or the lotus-shape **Bahai House of Worship** ㉙, both in southeastern New Delhi.

TIMING Divide this itinerary into two or three days. Choose a monument and museum (or the zoo) for morning and midday, then punctuate it with a visit to a temple at sunset. Traffic and heat will slow you down considerably—especially between April and October, when the sun is intense. Lodi Garden is a good place to take a break. Note that museums are closed on Monday, and that Sunday is the traditional family day out in India, so many sights, particularly outdoor sights such as the Bahai House of Worship and the zoo, are more crowded then.

What to See

㉙ **Bahai House of Worship.** The lotus flower is a symbol of purity throughout India, and Delhi's Bahai Temple celebrates this in a unique architectural way. Designed by Fariburz Sahba, an Iranian-born Canadian architect, and completed in 1986, the building incorporates the number nine—the highest digit and, in the Bahai faith, a symbol of unity. The sleek structure has two layers: nine white marble-covered petals that point to heaven, and nine petals that conceal the portals. From a short distance, it looks like a fantastic work of origami. The nine pools outside signify the green leaves of the lotus and cool the starkly elegant, usually silent marble interior. The interior conforms to that of all Bahai houses of worship: there are no religious icons, just copies of the Holy Scriptures and wooden pews. The road to the temple passes through a colorful temple bazaar connected to the nearby Kalkaji Mandir. ⊠ *Bahapur, Kalkaji, near Nehru Place* 🎫 *Free* ⊙ *Apr.–Sept., Tues.–Sun. 9–7; Oct.–Mar., Tues.–Sun. 9:30–5:30.*

㉑ **Bangla Sahib Gurdwara.** This massive *gurdwara* (Sikh temple) is always full of activity—no surprise given Delhi's huge Sikh population, most of whom came here as refugees from Pakistan in 1947. If you can't make it to Amritsar to see the Golden Temple, by all means come here to admire the distinctively ostentatious style of their temples. Like Sikhism itself, gurdwaras reflect both the symmetry of Moghul mosques and the chaos of Hindu temples. Bangla Sahib is built of white marble and topped with a shiny, gold onion dome.

The gurdwara stands on the site where Guru Hari Krishan, the 8th of 10 Sikh gurus who lived between 1469 and 1708, performed a small miracle. Before entering, remove your shoes and socks (check them at the counter on the left), get rid of cigarettes, and cover your head with a piece of cloth. As you walk up the stairs and enter the sanctum, you'll see people filling jugs of water from enclosed cisterns. Guru Hari Krishan used to distribute sanctified water to the sick, believing it had a miraculous healing effect on their mind, body, and soul, and people still treat the contents of these pools as holy water. Inside, devotees sit facing a small pavilion in the center that holds the *Granth Sahib* (Sikh scriptures). Hymns from the holy book are sung continuously from well before sunrise until approximately 9 PM, and you're welcome to sit and listen; if you fancy something cultural in the evening, come at about 9 to see the ceremony by which the book is stored away for the night. As you walk around inside, be careful to proceed in a clockwise direction, and exit on the right side in back. Out the door to the right a priest distributes *prasad,* a ritual resembling the Christian sacrament of communion: take a lump of this sugar, flour, and oil concoction with both hands, pop it into your mouth with your right hand, then rub the remaining oil into your hands. ⊠ *Baba Bangla Sahib Marg, across from Gole Post Office, Connaught Place* 🖃 *Free* ☉ 4 AM–9 PM.

off the
beaten
path

CHATTARPUR TEMPLES – If you're on your way south to Agra or Jaipur, drive a few miles beyond the Qutub Minar on Mehrauli Road and check out this massive Hindu temple complex. It's an untamed mishmash of architectural styles, but the unifying factor—from the huge dome over the Shiva lingam to the 92-foot statue of the monkey god Hanuman—is the ostentatious Punjabi Baroque architecture. Enter through the sanctum with the devotees, stop at the idols to pay respects, and take some prasad on the way out. Many gods and goddesses are represented, but the inner sanctum is dedicated to Adhya Ma Katyan, a mother goddess. Hymns are sung all night during full moons. ⊠ *Chattarpur* 🖃 *Free* ☉ *Daily sunrise–sunset.*

⑫ Crafts Museum. Designed by the Indian architect Charles Correa, this charming complex near the Purana Qila houses thousands of artifacts and handicrafts. You're greeted outside by playful terra-cotta sculptures from Tamil Nadu. Inside, the annotations are sketchy, but the collection is fascinating. Items in the Folk and Tribal Art Gallery, including some charming toys, illustrate village life throughout India. In one courtyard you'll see a giant wooden temple cart, built to carry deities in festive processions; one of the adjacent buildings contains a lavishly decorated Gujarati haveli (upper-class house). The Courtly Crafts section suggests the luxurious lives of India's erstwhile royalty, and the entire upper floor is a spectacular showcase of saris and textiles. In the village complex out back, craftspeople demonstrate their skills and sell their creations in replicas of village homes. The museum shop is the best in Delhi, with high-quality art books and crafts, and there's a small snack bar. ⊠ *Pragati Bhavan, just off Mathura Rd., Pragati Maidan* ☎ 11/2337–1817 🖃 *Free* ☉ *Tues.–Sun.* 10–5.

⑰ Gandhi Smriti. Mohandas K. Gandhi, better known as Mahatma (Great Soul), lived a life of voluntary poverty, but he did it in some attractive places. It was in this huge colonial bungalow, designed by a French architect for Indian industrialist G. D. R. Birla, that Gandhi was staying as a guest when he was assassinated on his way to a prayer meeting in the back garden. Gandhi's bedroom is just as he left it, with his "worldly remains" (only 11 items, including his glasses and a walking stick) mounted on the wall. Pictures and text tell the story of Gandhi's life and the Independence movement; there's also a collection of dioramas depicting events in Gandhi's life. In the theater, 10 different documentaries are available for viewing, on request. Take off your shoes before entering the somber prayer ground in back; an eternal flame marks the very spot where Gandhi expired. This, not the National Gandhi Museum at Raj Ghat, is the government's official museum dedicated to the Mahatma. ⊠ *5 Tees January Marg, Central Delhi* ☎ *11/2301–2843* ⊡ *Free* ⊙ *Tues.–Sun. 10–5.*

㉖ Hauz Khas Village. The road south to the urban village of Hauz Khas is lined on both sides by ancient stone monuments, and the entire village is dotted with domed structures—the tombs of minor Muslim royalty from the 14th to the 16th centuries. At the end of the road is the tomb of Firoz Shah Tughluq, who ruled Delhi in the 14th century. Hauz Khas means "Royal Tank," referring to the now-meager artificial lake visible from Firoz Shah's pillared tomb. The tank was actually built a century earlier by Allauddin Khilji as a water source for his nearby fort, then called Siri (the second city of Delhi). Back in the village, wander through the narrow lanes to experience a medley of old and new structures—expensive shops and art galleries in a medieval warren. In the 1980s Hauz Khas was designated an upscale tourist destination, but (fortunately) the process of redevelopment was never completed, so some of the village character persists. After exploring, stop for a meal at one of the village's restaurants, particularly Park Balluchi (in the Deer Park), Naivedyam, or the Village Bistro.

★ ㉓ Hazrat Nizamuddin Darga. One of Delhi's greatest treats is hearing devout Sufis sing *qawwalis,* ecstatic devotional Muslim songs with a decidedly toe-tapping quality. To get here, follow the twisting lanes in the bazaar section of Nizamuddin West—you'll pass open-air restaurants serving simple meat-based meals, tiny shops selling Urdu-language books and cassettes (some by famous qawwali singers), and probably a number of beggars appealing to the Muslim tradition of alms for the poor. When you see vendors selling flowers and garlands, you're getting close to the *darga* (tomb) of Hazrat Nizamuddin Aulia, who was born in Bukhara (now in Uzbekistan) in 1238 and later fled with his family to Delhi, where he became an important Sufi mystic and attracted a dedicated following. He died in 1325.

The saint's tomb, built in 1562 in the center of a courtyard, is covered with intricate painting and inlay work—best viewed on the carved parapet above the verandas—and topped with an onion-shape dome. Men can enter the shrine to pay their respects; women must peer in from outside. The tomb is flanked by a mosque and the graves of other important Muslims, including the great Sufi poet Amir Khusro and Jahanara, a daughter of the Moghul emperor Shah Jahan. Evenings from around 5 to 7, especially Thursday, the saint's male followers often sing in front of the darga. ⊠ *Old Nizamuddin Bazaar, Nizamuddin West; enter bazaar from Mathura Rd.* ⊡ *Free, donations to shrine and musicians accepted* ⊙ *Daily 24 hrs.*

9 Humayun's Tomb. Built in the middle of the 16th century by the widow
Fodor'sChoice of the Moghul emperor Humayun, this tomb launched a new architec-
★ tural era that reflected its Persian influence, culminating in the Taj
Mahal and Fatehpur Sikri. The Moghuls brought to India their love of
gardens and fountains and left a legacy of harmonious structures, such
as this mausoleum, that fuse symmetry with decorative splendor.

Resting on an immense two-story platform, the tomb structure of red sandstone and white marble is surrounded by gardens intersected by water channels in the Moghuls' beloved *charbagh* design: perfectly square gardens
divided into four (*char*) square parts. The marble dome covering the actual tomb is another first: a dome within a dome (the interior dome is set
inside the soaring dome seen from outside), a style later used in the Taj
Mahal. As you enter or leave the tomb area, stand a moment before the
beveled gateway to enjoy the view of the monument framed in the arch.

Besides Humayun, several other important Moghuls are buried here, along
with Isa Khan Niyazi, a noble in the court of Sher Shah—who lies in
the fetching octagonal shrine that precedes the tomb itself. The site's
serenity belies the fact that many of the dead buried inside were murdered princes, victims of foul play. To see where Humayun actually died,
combine this visit with a trip to the Purana Qila. ⊠ *Off Mathura Rd.,
Nizamuddin East* ⌫ *Rs. 250* ⊘ *Daily sunrise–sunset.*

13 India Gate. Anchoring a traffic circle near the far end of Rajpath from
the Indian government, this massive sandstone arch was designed by Lutyens in 1931, in memory of the 90,000 soldiers of the British Indian
Army who fell in World War I and the third Afghan War of the late 19th
century. In the 1970s, the government of India added a memorial to India's
unknown soldier, the Amar Jawan Jyoti, beneath the arch. While traffic speeds neatly around the outer circle, vendors occupy the inner circle, and people amble and socialize on the lawns. Come in early evening
and you'll find all sorts of activity, from men offering to make monkeys
"dance" for a fee to impromptu cricket matches to youngsters splash-
ing in the decorative stream nearby. ⊠ *East end of Rajpath, Central Delhi.*

19 Indira Gandhi Memorial Museum. On October 31, 1984, Prime Minister
Indira Gandhi was shot outside her home by two of her Sikh bodyguards,
in retaliation for her violent suppression of a violent Sikh independence
movement in Punjab. The murder sparked gruesome anti-Sikh riots in
Delhi and political turmoil ensued. The simple white bungalow in which
Mrs. Gandhi lived from the 1960s to 1980s is now a small museum with
endless photographs, quotations, and newspaper articles, plus a few
rooms preserved as they were used. The photos get more interesting as
you progress, and the museum ends with displays on Indira's son, Rajiv,
himself prime minister for a brief spell before he, too, was assassinated.
Displays include the sari, handbag, and shoes Mrs. Gandhi was wearing when she was killed, and the sneakers Rajiv was wearing during his
even more grisly demise at the hands of a female suicide bomber involved
in Sri Lanka's civil war. Outside, the spot where Indira fell is marked and
preserved. Popular with Indian tourists, the museum can get very crowded;
allow extra time if you want to peruse things carefully. ⊠ *1 Safdarjung
Rd., Central Delhi* ☎ *11/2301–0094* ⌫ *Free* ⊘ *Tues.–Sun. 9:30–4:45.*

28 ISKCON Temple. The International Society for Krishna Consciousness is better known to some as the Hare Krishna sect, and despite the 1960s association they are very much alive and kicking. In the 1990s ISKCON erected enormous, gleaming Krishna temples in several Indian cities, and these offer a unique glimpse into the remaining pockets of international Hinduism, with shaven-headed foreigners in saffron robes mingling with Indian colleagues, devotees, and tourists. Built impressively on a rock outcropping near a residential market, Delhi's temple is an amalgam of architectural styles: Moghul, Gupta, and the flashy Delhi style jokingly called Punjabi Baroque. The sanctum contains three idols—Balram Krishna, Radha-Krishna, and Laksman (along with Ram and Sita)—each representing a different incarnation of Lord Krishna. The art gallery behind the idols must be viewed in a clockwise direction, as this *parikrama* (revolution) is the only appropriate way to move around the gods. To learn more about Krishna, pop into the "Vedic Expo," where an upstairs collection of dioramas illustrate his life in the incarnation of Lord Chaitanya, and various sound-and-light shows (even a robotics display) enact the *Bhagavad Gita* scriptures and the ancient epic, the *Mahabharata*, from which the scriptures come. It's all a bit Southern California, but ISKCON's temples are by far the cleanest in India, and very welcoming to visitors. Finish with a meal at Govinda's, the on-site restaurant, where a vegetarian buffet goes for the low price of Rs. 150. ⊠ *Hare Krishna Hill, Sant Nagar Main Rd., East of Kailash* ☎ *11/2623–5133 or 11/2623–3400* ⊡ *Free* ⊙ *Daily 4:30 AM–1 PM and 4 PM–9 PM.*

22 Laxmi Naryan Temple. This large, red-and-yellow temple (known as Birla Mandir) west of Connaught Place is an excellent example of a reformist Hindu temple—both architecturally and in terms of temple practices. It was built in 1938 by Indian industrialist G. D. R. Birla—the same man whose house is now the Gandhi Smriti—as a nondenominational temple. (The sign outside welcomes all "Hindus," including Jains and Sikhs.) The temple is colorful and ornate: note the lotus patterns at the top of each phallic steeple and the inlaid lotus pattern on the floor in front of the main *murti* (idol) of Laxmi Narayan. Although the temple exhibits many of the gaudier elements of Hindu design, overall it's relatively subdued. This is a common feature of reformist, 20th-century Hindu architecture, which was influenced by European architecture. ⊠ *Mandir Marg, Connaught Place.*

★ **24 Lodi Garden.** After Timur ransacked Delhi at the end of the 14th century, he ordered the massacre of the entire population—acceptable retribution, he thought, for the murder of some of his soldiers. As if in unconscious response to this horrific act, the subsequent Lodi and Sayyid dynasties built no city, only a few mosques and some mausoleums and tombs, the latter of which stand in what is now a delightful urban park. Winding walks cut through landscaped lawns with trees and small flowers, past schoolboys playing cricket, politicians taking some air, and friends and lovers relaxing in the greenery. Near the southern entrance on Lodi Road is the dignified mausoleum of Mohammed Shah, third ruler of the Sayyid dynasty, and some members of his family. This octagon, with a central chamber surrounded by verandas carved with arches, is a good example of the architecture of this period. The smaller, equally lovely, octagonal tomb of Sikandar Lodi, surrounded by a garden in the park's northwestern corner, has an unusual double dome. ✉ *Lodi Rd., across from Jor Bagh,* 🎟 *Free* ⊙ *Daily sunrise–sunset.*

★ ⑭ **Lutyens' Delhi.** Raj Path—the broadest avenue in Delhi—leads to Delhi's eighth capital: Sir Edwin Lutyens' imperial city, built between 1914 and 1931 in a symbolically imperialistic design after the British moved their capital from Calcutta to Delhi in 1911. (While the British were building, they hit marshy land prone to floods, so they reversed direction and put the bulk of their capital, the imperial city, a few miles to the south.) Starting from India Gate at the lowest and eastern end of Raj Path, nearby land was allocated to numerous princely states, which built small palaces, such as the **Bikaner House** (now the Rajasthan tourism office) and **Jaipur House** (now the National Gallery of Modern Art). It might be said that this placement mirrored the British sentiments toward the princes, who lost much of their former power and status during the British Raj. Moving up the slowly inclining hill at the western end of the avenue, you also move up the British ladder of power, a concept inherent in the original design. First you come to the enormous **North and South Secretariats,** facing each other on Raj Path and reflecting the importance of the bureaucracy, a fixture of Indian society since the time of British rule. Identical in design, the two buildings have 1,000 rooms and miles of corridors.

Directly behind the North Secretariat is the Indian parliament house, **Sansad Bhavan,** a circular building in red and gray sandstone, with an open colonnade that extends around its circumference. Architecturally, the Indian design is meant to mirror the spinning wheel that was the symbol of Mahatma Gandhi, but the building's secondary placement, off the main avenue, may suggest the attitude of the British toward the Indian legislative assembly.

At the top of the hill is the former Viceroy's House, now called **Rashtrapati Bhavan,** where the President of India (not the prime minister) resides. It was built in the 20th century, but the building's daunting proportions seem to reflect an earlier, more lavish time. Its scale was meant to express British supremacy. The Bhavan contains 340 rooms and its grounds cover 330 acres, including a Moghul-style garden that opens to the public for several weeks in February. The shape of the central brass dome, the palace's main architectural feature, reflects that of a Buddhist *stupa* (shrine).

The execution of Lutyens' design has a flaw: the entire palace was supposed to fill the vista as you approach the top of the hill, but the gradient is too steep, so only the dome dominates the horizon. And in a nicely ironic twist, a few years after the imperial city was completed, the British packed up and went home, and this lavish architectural complex became the grand capital of newly independent India. Permission to enter Rashtrapati and Sansad Bhavan is almost impossible to obtain; unless you have contacts in high places, satisfy yourself with a glimpse from outside. ✉ *Central Delhi.*

⑮ **National Gallery of Modern Art.** Facing India Gate, this neoclassical building was built by the British in the early 20th century as a palace for the maharaja of Jaipur. With its small dome and large, open rooms, the structure makes a fine space for this art museum, established in 1954 to preserve Indian art forms (mainly painting) that developed after 1850. The displays are attractive by local standards but distinctly uneven, unexplained, and, alas, partial—thousands of works are hidden away due to lack of gallery space. Highlights are the colorful paintings of Amrita Sher-Gil (the Frida Kahlo of India) and, upstairs, the myth-inspired works of Raja Ravi Varma and the Bengali Renaissance oils and watercolors of the Tagore family, Jamini Roy, and Nandalal Bose. There are a few representative works by contemporary masters such as M. F. Husain and Ganesh Pyne. Documentaries, shown daily at 11 and 3, explain Indian art. ⊠ *Jaipur House, India Gate, Central Delhi* ☎ *11/ 2338–2835* 💷 *Rs. 150* ⊙ *Tues.–Sun. 10–5.*

⓰ National Museum. The facade of this grand building imitates Lutyens' Presidential Palace: a sandstone dome is supported by classical columns of brown sandstone on a red-sandstone base. When you enter, you'll see a 13th-century idol—from the Konark Sun Temple in Bhubaneswar— of Surya, the sun god, standing beneath the dome. Such a statue is emblematic of the National Museum's strength—it showcases ancient, mainly Hindu, sculptures. An entire room is dedicated to artifacts from the Indus Valley Civilization, circa 2,700 BC; others display works from the Gandharan, Chandela, and Chola periods. Besides sculpture, also on exhibit are jewelry, painting, musical instruments, coins, carpets, and weapons. However, the museum is not very well maintained, and there's no brochure to help you navigate. ⊠ *Corner of Janpath and Rajpath, Central Delhi* ☎ *11/2301–9272* 💷 *Rs. 150* ⊙ *Tues.–Sun. 10–5.*

☾ ⓴ National Rail Museum. This large, mostly outdoor, museum offers a glimpse into the largest railway system in the world. The 10-acre grounds are home to 75 authentic engines, bogies (railway cars), and even a working roundabout (a device that spins rail cars). Parked behind glass is the Fairy Queen; built in 1855, it's the oldest running steam engine in the world. It still takes nine trips a year to Sariska National Park and back for a weekend trip (contact the Director of the Museum if you're interested, but it's not worth the outrageous price). Inside the museum are displays that discuss the history of the India rail system. The museum will intrigue not only history buffs but also children, who love riding the tiny train that circumambulates the grounds. ⊠ *Near Nehru Park; from Ring Rd., turn left onto Nyaya Marg, then left again, Chanakyapuri* ☎ *11/2688–1816 or 11/2688–0939* 💷 *Rs. 10* ⊙ *Oct.–Mar., Tues.–Sun. 9:30–5, Apr.–Sept., Tues.–Sun. 9:30–7.*

☾ ⓫ National Zoological Park. White tigers are the draw at Delhi's zoo, which was designed in the late 1950s by noted German designer Carl Hagenbeck. There are many noteworthy animals roaming about, such as emu, gazelle, Indian rhino, and a great many deer, not to mention some smart-looking water birds. Animals in cages, including the famous white tigers and Asiatic lions, are part of the national collection. The zoo is spacious and leafy, a virtual botanical garden for peaceful walks, and the central lake hosts numerous Central Asian migratory aquatic birds (pelicans, storks, and cranes) pausing on their way to Keoladeo National

Park in Bharatpur, Rajasthan, for the winter. If you don't have time to make it to Bharatpur or a tiger reserve, this is a pretty good alternative. ⊠ *Mathura Rd., behind Sundar Nagar* 🖾 *Foreigners Rs. 50* ⊘ *Mid-Oct.–Mar., Sat.–Thurs. 9:30–4; Apr.–mid-Oct., Sat.–Thurs. 9–4:30.*

★ ⑱ **Nehru Memorial Museum.** This colonial mansion, also known as Teen Murti Bhavan, was originally built for the commander of the British Indian Army. When the Viceroy's residence, Rashtrapati Bhavan (at the other end of South Avenue), became the home of India's president, India's first prime minister, Jawaharlal Nehru, took up residence here. Those interested in the Independence movement should not miss this landmark or the nearby Gandhi Smriti. Nehru's yellow mansion is fronted by a long, oval-shape lawn; out back, there's a tranquil flower garden. Inside, several rooms remain as Nehru left them, and extensive displays chronicle Nehru's life and the Independence movement. Move through the rooms in order: one by one, photographs, newspaper clippings, and personal letters tell the breathtaking story of the birth of the world's largest democracy. On your way out, stop and see the 14th-century hunting lodge next to the Nehru Planetarium. (The latter, good for children, has shows in English at 11:30 AM and 3 PM.) ⊠ *Teen Murti Marg, Central Delhi* 🖀 *11/2301–3765* 🖾 *Free* ⊘ *Tues.–Sun. 9–5:30.*

⑩ **Purana Qila** (Old Fort). India's sixth capital was the scene of a fierce power struggle between the Afghan Sher Shah and Humayun, son of the first Moghul emperor, Babur, in the 16th century. When Humayun started to build his own capital, Dinpanah, on these grounds in the 1530s, Sher Shah forced the emperor to flee for his life to Persia. Sher Shah destroyed what existed of Dinpanah to create his own capital, Shergarh. Fifteen years later, in 1555, Humayun returned and seized control, but he died the following year, leaving Sher Shah's city for others to destroy.

Unfortunately, once you enter the massive Bara Darwaza (Main Gate), only two buildings are intact. The **Qila-i-Kuhna Masjid,** Sher Shah's private mosque, is an excellent example of Indo-Afghan architecture in red sandstone with decorative marble touches—walk around to the "back" to see the beautiful front of the building. The nearby **Sher Mandal,** a two-story octagonal tower of red sandstone and white marble, became Humayun's library and ultimately his death trap: hearing the call to prayer, Humayun started down the steep steps, slipped, and fell to his death. On pleasant afternoons, every bush on these grounds hides a pair of young lovers in search of a little privacy. ⊠ *Off Mathura Rd., near Delhi Zoo and Pragati Maidan* 🖾 *Rs. 100* ⊘ *Daily sunrise–sunset.*

★ ㉗ **Qutub Minar.** Named for the Muslim sultan Qutub-ud-din Aibak, this striking tower is known as the seventh wonder of Hindustan. The 234-foot-high tower, with 376 steps, is the tallest stone tower in India. The Muslim campaigner Qutub-ud-din-Aibak began construction in 1193; his son-in-law and successor, Iltutmish, added the top four stories. The result is a handsome sandstone example of Indo-Islamic architecture, with terra-cotta frills and balconies. At its foot lies the **Quwwat-ul-Islam Masjid,** the first Muslim mosque in India. The Muslims erected the mosque in the 12th century after they defeated the Hindu Chauhan dynasty—

they built it on the site of a Hindu temple and used materials from 27 demolished Hindu and Jain shrines. (Which explains why you see Hindu and Jain sculptures in the mosque.) The mosque is also famous for a 24-foot-high, 5th-century iron pillar, inscribed with six lines of Sanskrit. According to legend, if you stand with your back to the pillar and can reach around and touch your fingers, any wish you make will come true. (Unfortunately, it's now fenced off.) ⊠ *Aurobindo Marg, near Mehrauli* 🖼 *Rs. 250* ☉ *Daily sunrise–sunset.*

⑧ Raj Ghat and National Gandhi Museum. After Mohandas K. Gandhi was shot and killed by a Hindu fanatic on January 30, 1948, his body was cremated on the banks of the Yamuna River. His *samadhi,* or cremation site, is now a national shrine, where Indian tourists and pilgrims stream across the peaceful lawn to pay their respects to the saintlike Father of the Nation. At the center of a large courtyard is a raised slab of black marble adorned with flowers and inscribed with Gandhi's final words, HAI RAM! (Oh, God!). An eternal flame burns at its head. The sandstone walls enclosing the shrine are inscribed with passages written by Gandhi, translated into several tongues including Tamil, Malayalam, Nepali, Urdu, Spanish, Arabic, and Chinese. Near Raj Ghat are the cremation sites of two other assassinated heads of state, Indira Gandhi and her son Rajiv. Back across the boulevard is the **National Gandhi Museum,** run by a private foundation, which houses a great many photographs, a display of spinning wheels with some information on Gandhi's *khadi* (handmade cotton) crusade, and some of the Mahatma's personal effects, including the blood-stained *dhoti* he was wearing at the time of his murder. The tiny art gallery has a poignant wooden sculpture, made by a South African, of Gandhi in a pose suggesting Jesus's Crucifixion. A film on Gandhi's life is shown on weekends at 4. ⊠ *Mahatma Gandhi Marg (Ring Rd.), near Old Delhi* 🖼 *Free* ☉ *Raj Ghat, daily sunrise–sunset; museum, Tues.–Sun. 9:30–5:30.*

㉕ Safdarjang's Tomb. Delhi's last great garden tomb, built in 1754 for the prime minister of the emperor Mohammad Shah, is pleasantly located in the center of town. With its oversize dome and minarets, it can't compete with Humayun's resting place, but the finials and other details have a distinctly Moghul fineness, and the *charbagh* (four-section garden) is a peaceful place to listen to the birds chirp. The site would be lovelier if water still ran through the four large channels in the gardens, but you have to imagine that part to complete the 18th-century scene. ⊠ *Aurobindo Marg at Lodi Rd., near Jor Bagh* 🖼 *Rs. 100* ☉ *Daily sunrise–sunset.*

WHERE TO EAT

North Indian

$$$$ ✕ **Dum Pukht.** Like the *nawabi* (princely) culture from which it's drawn, the food and style at this restaurant are subtle and refined. Chef Imtiaz Qureshi, descended from court cooks in Avadh (Lucknow), creates delicately spiced meals packed with flavor: *dum ki khumb* (button mushrooms in gravy, fennel, and dried ginger), *kakori kabab* (finely minced

Where to Stay & Eat in Delhi

Restaurants ▼

Baan Thai **15**
Basil and Thyme **16**
The Big Chill **28**
Bukhara **20**
Chillie Seasson **18**
China Fare **12**
Chor Bizarre **2**
Coconut Grove **8**
Daniell's Tavern **7**
Dum Pukht **20**
House of Ming **9**
Karim's **1**
Masala Art **19**
Moti Mahal Delux **27**
Naivedyam **25**
Park Balluchi **26**
Punjabi by Nature **24**
Rampur Kitchen **12**
Sagar **22**
San Gimignano **7**
Spice Route **7**
Swagath **22**
Taipan **15**
Yellow Brick Road **13**

Hotels ▼

Ahuja Residency **14**
Ambassador **13**
Claridges **11**
The Connaught **5**
Hans Plaza **6**
Hyatt Regency **21**
The Imperial **7**
InterContinental ParkRoyal **29**
ITC Maurya Sheraton
Hotel and Towers **20**
Jor Bagh 27 . . . .**17**
Jukaso Inn Downtown **4**
Maharani Guest House **10**
Maidens **3**
The Manor **23**
Nirula's Hotel **4**
The Oberoi **15**
Taj Mahal **9**
Taj Palace **19**

mutton, cloves, and cinnamon, drizzled with saffron), and the special *raan-e-dumpukht,* a leg of mutton marinated in dark rum and stuffed with onions, cheese, and mint. The formal room is white, blue, and hushed. ✉ *ITC Maurya Sheraton Hotel, Chanakyapuri* ☎ *11/2611–2233* ⊟ *AE, DC, MC, V.*

$$$–$$$$ ✕ **Bukhara.** Served amid stone walls, rough-hewn dark-wood beams, cop-
Fodor'sChoice per urns, and blood-red rugs, this food is so mind-blowingly delicious
★ that it hasn't changed in years. The cuisine of the Northwest Frontier—now the border between Pakistan and Afghanistan—is heavy on meats, marinated and grilled in a *tandoor* (clay oven). The *murgh malai kebab* (boneless chicken marinated with cream cheese, malt vinegar and green coriander) is unforgettable; red-meat lovers find the tender *sikandari raan* (leg of lamb marinated in herbs) equally heavenly. Bukhara's *dal* (black lentils simmered overnight with tomatoes, ginger, and garlic) is so famous it's now sold in cans. Vegetarians can opt for a tandoori salad of vegetables, pineapple, and paneer (soft cheese). ✉ *ITC Maurya Shera-ton Hotel, Chanakyapuri* ☎ *11/2611–2233* ⊟ *AE, DC, MC, V.*

$$$ ✕ **Daniell's Tavern.** One of Delhi's more creative menus is "cuisine of the Raj" as discovered by Thomas and William Daniell, two English painters who spent seven years exploring East India Company territories in the late 18th century. The selection reflects cuisines the brothers encoun-tered, such as Lucknawi, Mughal, Bengali, Mangalorean, and Tamil-ian, including a few recipes from their own diaries. Try some of the harder-to-find dishes, such as *phaldhari kabab* (fried spiced patties of banana, potato, and soft cheese, served with fruit salsa), Bengali fish curry (a classic in yogurt-based mustard-flavored gravy), or *murgh Be-misal* (grilled chicken flavored with saffron, cooked in tomato gravy, and garnished with hard-boiled egg). ✉ *Imperial Hotel, Janpath, Con-naught Place, New Delhi* ☎ *11/5111–6634* ⊟ *AE, D, MC, V.*

$$$ ✕ **Masala Art.** Ten years from now, restaurant dining in India might look
Fodor'sChoice more like this: a flawless convergence of ethnic authenticity and inter-
★ national style. Service is the best in the country, hip and articulate. If you opt for a taster's menu instead of à la carte, you're installed at a counter overlooking an open kitchen, where charming chefs and servers talk you through the meal. The food is superb either way, but a taster's menu—seafood, meat, or vegetarian—gives you greater variety and usually costs less. *Lasooni palak* (spinach with garlic) is out of this world, as are *achari jheenga* (jumbo shrimp brushed with mango pickle and grilled in a tandoor), *paneer makai bhurjee* (soft cheese scrambled with corn and spices), and *nakti kabab* (tender lamb chunks in a mildly sweet sauce). The room is smartly pan-Asian contemporary, but you won't even notice. ✉ *Taj Palace Hotel, 2 Sardar Patel Marg, Chanakyapuri* ☎ *11/2611–0202* ⊟ *AE, DC, MC, V.*

★ $–$$ ✕ **Punjabi by Nature.** Marked by the exuberance for which Punjabis are famous, this lovable restaurant burst onto the scene in 2001 with a gim-mick: *golgappas* (fried dough) filled with vodka instead of traditional spicy water. The food, however, is classic: *murgh Punjabi masala* is the house chicken curry, *raan-e-Punjab* is a whole leg of lamb grilled just so, and the baby-vegetable platter with masala (spiced) okra is an un-forgettable feast. *Besan di missi roti,* rarely seen in restaurants, is a flat, crunchy corn bread that's relished in winter. It's all extremely rich, so come hungry. The rooms are a mixture of rustic and modern, with dark tones, amber lighting, and portraits of turbaned Punjabis. ✉ *11 Basant Lok, Vasant Vihar* ☎ *11/5151–6669* 🖃 *AE, DC, MC, V.*

$ ✕ **Chor Bizarre.** Delhi's only Kashmiri restaurant is also one of its most beautiful, an art deco enclave with a tile floor, a spiral staircase leading nowhere, lamps in pinks and yellows, and a mixture of antique furniture and mirrors from various chor (thieves') bazaars. The bar is all dark wood and stained glass, and the salad bar is a 1927 Fiat roadster. Kashmiri food uses milder spices than many Indian cuisines, exemplified by mutton *yakhni* (simmered in a sauce of yogurt, cardamom, and aniseed), mutton *mirchi korma* (in a gravy of cardamom and cloves), and *haaq*, Kashmiri spinach cooked in its own juice. Try a *tarami* platter to sample several dishes, and punctuate your meal with *kahwah*, fragrant Kashmiri tea. ✉ *Hotel Broadway, 4/15A Asaf Ali Rd., just outside Old Delhi, near Delhi Gate* ☎ *11/2327–3821* 🖃 *AE, DC, MC, V.*

$ ✕ **Moti Mahal Delux.** This old-fashioned family restaurant serves North Indian comfort food. It's a knock-off of an Old Delhi classic, Moti Mahal, but some say the food here is even better. The meal of choice is butter chicken, otherwise known as chicken *makhni*, a tomato-based Punjabi classic that sticks to your ribs. (It's a bit like chicken cacciatore.) The basic chicken curry is also good. There's no plain rice here; the so-called "plain pulao" is made with cumin and has a kick of its own. All meals are served with zesty little pickled onions. ✉ *M-30 Greater Kailash I* ☎ *11/2628–0480* 🖃 *No credit cards* ☉ *Closed Tues.*

$ ✕ **Park Balluchi.** No, the name isn't Italian; it refers to Baluchistan, part **Fodor's**Choice of present-day Pakistan. Tucked away in Hauz Khas Deer Park, this ★ kabab house serves some of the most sumptuous barbecue dishes in India. The building is glass on three sides, the better to enjoy the greenery; stone floors, cast-iron furniture, and traditional dress complete the lush environment. The amazing victuals include *nawabi kesri kabab* (chicken marinated in a saffron mixture, stuffed with chopped chicken, and grilled), *murg potli* (marinated chicken breast wrapped around minced mutton and served flambéed), and *mewa paneer tukra* (soft cheese stuffed with nuts, currants, and mushrooms, marinated in cream and grilled). Kababs are served all day; other dishes are not served between 3:30 and 6. ✉ *Deer Park, Hauz Khas Village* ☎ *11/2685–9369* 🖃 *AE, DC, MC, V.*

¢ ✕ **Karim's.** A popular addition to the Jama Masjid tour, Karim's is an Old Delhi institution. Mutton (goat) is king here, especially in thick, rich gravies; try *mutton Mughlai* or *badaam pasanda* ("almond delight," mutton in a slightly sweet gravy) for the full experience. To get here, walk down the street that runs out from the mosque's main entrance, Gate 1, and about four shops down on the left, walk through the passageway into a small courtyard—you'll see smoking kababs on spits and several indoor seating areas. The newer Karim's, **Dastar Khwan-e-Karim**, near Hazrat Nizamuddin Darga, is more of a restaurant proper. Alcohol is not served. ✉ *Matiya Mahal, opposite Hotel Bombay Orient, Old Delhi* ☎ *11/2326–9800* ✉ *168/2 Jha House Basti, Nizamuddin West* ☎ *11/2469–8300* ☉ *Daily 7 AM–midnight; closed during daylight hrs of Ramadan* 🖃 *No credit cards.*

¢ ✕ **Rampur Kitchen.** This cheerful little restaurant serves traditional Muslim cuisine from the old nawabi city of Rampur. The house specialty is *haleem,* a thick, scrumptious paste made from ground mutton and ideally eaten with warm Mughlai roti. Rampuri Chicken Ishtew (that's "stew" with tongue in cheek), a mild, bone-colored curry, is also recommended, and the kababs make good starters. Nimbupani Rampuri is a variation on classic lime juice, made here with a bit of cumin. Try to have dessert here: *gullathi* is a fancy rice pudding, *shahi tukra* is a slice of bread fried in a sweet, sticky saffron-flavor sauce, and *Rampur ki sewian* is pudding made with sweetened vermicelli. Alcohol is not served. ⊠ *8A Khan Market* ☎ *11/2463–1222* ⊟ *AE, MC, V.*

South Indian

$ ✕ **Coconut Grove.** Malayali cuisine (from Kerala) is inspired by the coconut and the sea, as exemplified by the delicious *konju theng*—prawn curry in a mild, turmeric-colored coconut sauce—and the coconut-based mutton stew. Coconut Grove also features spicy Chettinad cuisine from Tamil Nadu, which you can sample in a mixed platter served on a banana leaf. Order any other main course with *appams,* Kerala's inimitable fluffy rice-based flatbreads, and use the bread to scoop up the morsels. The restaurant is cavernous and plain, with green tablecloths the only real nod to South India. ⊠ *Hotel Janpath, Janpath, Connaught Place* ☎ *11/2336–8553* ⊟ *AE, DC, MC, V.*

★ $ ✕ **Swagath.** Delhi's only Mangalorean restaurant—specializing in fish and seafood preparations from the western coast between Goa and Kerala—is one of the best things to happen to the city in years. Choose your sauce, then decide whether you want fish, prawns, or crab. Anything served *sawantwadi* (in a spicy mint-and-coriander sauce) is unforgettable, as is *gassi,* a mild coconut-flavored gravy, and the butter-pepper-garlic sauce. Another specialty is Chettinad food from Tamil Nadu, cooked in a very spicy black-pepper sauce. Mop up your food with an *appam* or *neer dosa,* soft South Indian rice breads. The prim dining rooms, stacked vertically, are softly lit, and service is excellent. Doors are open all day. ⊠ *14 Defence Colony Market* ☎ *11/2433–0930* ⊟ *AE, DC, MC, V.*

¢ ✕ **Naivedyam.** This dark, soothing restaurant with gold-embossed paintings was designed by artisans from the Tamil town of Thanjavur. The food is Udupi, a vegetarian cuisine from a temple town near Mangalore. All meals begin with a *rasam* (peppery soup) that must be the best in Delhi, and the rice dishes, served with coconut chutney and *sambar* (tomato-based dal), are great introductions to South Indian home cooking. To plunge into a dosa—a giant semolina or lentil-flour crêpe filled with spicy potatoes—consider the *maharaja sajjige masala dosa,* which includes vegetables. At night, look for the stained-glass entrance; by day, follow signs for the "South Indian Eating Panorama." Alcohol is not served. ⊠ *1 Hauz Khas Village* ☎ *11/2696–0426* ⊟ *AE, DC, MC, V.*

¢ ✕ **Sagar.** This no-frills, three-story vegetarian family joint bustles nonstop from 8 AM to 11 PM. The *dosa* is king, and you can choose from 20 varieties, including some made with *rava* (semolina) rather than lentil flour. The vegetable *uttapam* (rice-flour pancake) is also good, and there's a North Indian menu with delicious *bhindi masala* (spicy okra). The wonderful *thalis,* or combination platters, are served from 11 to 3 and 7 to 11. ⊠ *18 Defence Colony Market* ☎ *11/2433–3110* ▤ *No credit cards.*

Chinese

$$$–$$$$ ✕ **Taipan.** Formal yet friendly, Taipan is the finest Chinese restaurant in Delhi. The food is authentic, luscious, and artfully presented, and the view from the top of the Oberoi—over the Delhi Golf Course toward the high-rise buildings of Connaught Place—is grand. The menu highlights Cantonese and Szechuan cooking, including salt-and-pepper prawns, minced prawns with asparagus, Calcutta bekti fish in a *nonya* (spicy lemon) chili sauce, and various forms of duck. The best-loved house specialty is dim sum, available in a Rs. 825 daily fixed-price lunch—reserve in advance for this feast. ⊠ *The Oberoi, Dr. Zakir Hussain Rd., next to Delhi Golf Club* ☎ *11/2436–3030* ▤ *AE, DC, MC, V.*

$$ ✕ **House of Ming.** This popular upscale Chinese restaurant is inspired by the Ming Dynasty, which introduced Cantonese cuisine to the West. Pale teak latticework, pagoda-style ceilings, and the dynasty's favorite colors—pale blues and greens—are illuminated by soft lighting from brass lanterns. The menu changes every few months, but the Beijing-bred chef incorporates four major cuisines: Cantonese, Szechuan, Shanghai, and Jiangshu. Highlights include fried Kenyan beans with *chachoy,* a chili-and-tomato seasoning; steamed bekti (a local fish) or chicken in *tausa,* a dried-green-bean sauce; *zhang cha* duck, smoked with tea leaves; and the incredible crispy spinach. Dim sum are served at lunchtime. ⊠ *Taj Mahal Hotel, 1 Mansingh Rd., Central Delhi* ☎ *11/2302–6162* ▤ *AE, DC, MC, V.*

¢–$ ✕ **China Fare.** Chinese food in Delhi tends to be five-star or takeout, with little in-between. China Fare is an exception, with delicious meals at modest prices in attractive (if cramped) faux-Tuscan surroundings. The menu is basic, with strengths in poultry and noodles: options include crispy honey chicken, chicken with mushrooms and baby corn, the devilishly spicy Chicken Singapore, and "chilly garlic" noodles. The crispy lamb dishes are also good, and you don't have to be vegetarian to make a meal of the mixed vegetables in hot garlic sauce. Alcohol is not served. ⊠ *27-A Khan Market* ☎ *11/2461–8602* ▤ *AE, DC, MC, V.*

Contemporary

$ ✕ **Basil and Thyme.** Celebrity chef Bhicoo Manekshaw is now in her eighties, but that doesn't stop her from creating daily specials and seasonal menus. There's no telling what she'll come up with, but you can bank on fresh flavors, such as carrot-and-orange soup, pita triangles with garlic butter, roast chicken stuffed with black mushrooms, or a "filo parcel" stuffed with vegetables and glazed with a coriander hollandaise. The room is minimalistic warm white, with stone floors and large windows onto the greenery of Santushti market. Alcohol is not served, but this lunch spot is beloved of Delhi's upper crust and the embassy crowd. ⊠ *Santushti Shopping Complex, Chanakyapuri* ☎ *11/*

2467–3322 ✍ *Reservations essential* ☰ *AE, DC, MC, V* ☾ *Closed Sun. No dinner.*

$ ✕ **Yellow Brick Road.** This tiny 24-hour coffee shop is so bright you have to wear shades, and Delhiites love it. The blinding-yellow striped wallpaper, vintage French-colonial posters, and distressed-yellow tables are a perfect cure for jet lag. The menu wears several hats, mainly North Indian and European, and everything is cheerfully presented. Vegetarian options are many, including tasty paneer (cubed soft cheese) dishes, ravioli calabrese (with spinach and basil), mushroom crêpes, and sweet corn soup. The *chote miya biryani* (lamb in seasoned rice) is rich and filling. ⊠ *Ambassador Hotel, Cornwallis Rd., Sujan Singh Park* ☎ *11/ 2463–2600* ☰ *AE, DC, MC, V.*

¢ ✕ **The Big Chill.** Should you crave casual Western food, make tracks for this bistro, which takes its name from the Lawrence Kasdan film and is decorated with old film posters. The pastas are outstandingly hearty, especially those with chicken, and the Lebanese and Greek salads, however inauthentic, are good light meals. The real draw for the hip young crowd is the promise of hefty desserts: Mississippi mud pie, Irish-cream cheesecake, and ice-cream flavors like Vanilla Kit-Kat and Banana Walnut Chocolate Chip. The East of Kailash branch is larger, but both are open all day, making them ideal for an afternoon snack or early dinner. Alcohol is not served. ⊠ *F-38 East of Kailash* ☎ *11/2648–1020 or 11/ 2648–1030* ✉ *68 Khan Market, Sujan Singh Park New Delhi* ☎ *11/ 5175–7588* ☰ *MC, V.*

Italian

$$$$ ✕ **San Gimignano.** Chef Ravi Saxena uses his Tuscan training to create playful, sensuous dishes in Delhi's most rarefied Italian restaurant. The three-course regional menu changes periodically, but you might find such fancies as a "flan" of spinach, black olives, and risotto with fresh basil and tomato sauce; tagliatelle with a fresh herb sauce of minced duck and Parmesan cheese; sliced grilled tenderloin with grilled polenta and marsala sauce; or grilled milk-fed baby lamb chop with grilled balsamic vegetables. The wood-panel rooms are small and inviting, accented by ceramics and large sepia photos of the town of San Gimignano. In winter you can dine in the fabulous garden, complete with terra-cotta tile floor. Service is excellent. ⊠ *Imperial Hotel, Janpath, Connaught Place* ☎ *11/5111–6634* ✍ *Reservations essential* ☰ *AE, DC, MC, V.*

Pan-Asian

$$$–$$$$ ✕ **Spice Route.** Designed by Delhi's flamboyant Rajeev Sethi and seven
FodorsChoice years in the making, Spice Route is known internationally as an aesthetic
★ experience. Each section focuses on a different stage in life (relationships, wealth, etc.), and every inch of the walls and ceiling is hand painted with corresponding scenes from ancient epics. Antique rosewood and teak columns add to the enchantment. The clever menu gathers cuisines from the lands of the ancient spice route—Kerala, Sri Lanka, Myanmar (Burma), Malaysia, Indonesia, Thailand, and Vietnam. The Sri Lankan curries are surprising and delicious; you might also find Kerala-style

prawns stir-fried with coconut, curry leaves and black tamarind and flavored with mustard seeds, or Thai-style lobster stir-fried with ginger and black Thai mushrooms. ✉ *Imperial Hotel, Janpath, Connaught Place* ☎ *11/5111–6634* ▤ *AE, DC, MC, V.*

Thai

$$$–$$$$ ✕ **Baan Thai.** Thai food has taken off in Delhi, but the city's first Thai restaurant, modeled on a traditional Thai *baan* (house), remains arguably the best. The entrance corridor is an Asian art gallery, and the formal dining room is partitioned by Burmese-teak latticework. Sit at a regular table, adorned with an orchid, or on a traditional Thai *khantok* (floor cushion) on the raised platform. The husband-and-wife chefs create traditional cuisine, from *thod man koong* (crisp golden cake of Thai-spiced prawns, served with plum sauce) to *kai phad med mamuang* (diced chicken stir-fried with cashews, mushrooms and sun-dried chilis), all served on sage-green crockery. The lunch buffet is popular. ✉ *The Oberoi, Dr. Zakir Hussain Rd., next to Delhi Golf Club* ☎ *11/2436–3030* ▤ *AE, DC, MC, V.*

★ **$**   ✕ **Chilli Seasson.** Don't be fooled by the name—this chic Southeast Asian place gets everything else right. The rooms are airy and cheerful, with cream-color walls and blond-wood furniture, and the contemporary artwork is often for sale. The tangy papaya salad is a stunner, and it looks fantastic on the restaurant's contemporary yellow and coral-color crockery. The Thai curries are equally divine, and best of all, the vegetable dishes are intriguing and delicious, from phak choy to stir-fried Tibetan zucchini to eggplant with white mushrooms. There are plenty of salads and noodles to distract you as well. It's hard to have a bad meal here, especially at these prices. ✉ *18 Lodi Colony Market* ☎ *11/2461–8358 or 11/2464–3362* ▤ *AE, DC, MC, V.*

WHERE TO STAY

$$$$ ▦ **The Imperial.** This landmark luxury hotel was designed by Edward
Fodor'sChoice   Lutyens' associate D. J. Bromfield in a unique mixture of colonial, Vic-
★   torian, and art deco styles. Opened in 1931, it was restored in the '90s and is easily the most appealing hotel in Delhi, with twisting hallways and small-pane windows. The driveway is lined with 24 soaring king palms, and the terrace of the Royal Imperial Suite peeks out from above the entrance. Inside, the entire building is lit and decorated in warm creams and taupes, and hung with original lithographs and engravings from the hotel's enormous collection. Guest rooms continue the Raj look with quilted bedspreads, wardrobes, and marble or parquet floors; "Heritage" rooms have sitting areas and are significantly more sumptuous than the cheapest rooms. Restaurants are top-notch, especially the other-worldly Spice Route and the garden section of 1911, with its tile floor and cane furniture. A spa, with ayurvedic treatments and squash and tennis courts, will open in late 2004. ✉ *Janpath, south of Tolstoy Marg, Connaught Place, 110001* ☎ *11/2334–1234* 🖷 *11/2334–2255* ⊕ *www.theimperialindia.com* ⤴ *185 rooms, 45 suites* ⚐ *3 restaurants, coffee shop, pool, health club, hair salon, 3 bars, baby-sitting, laundry service, Internet, business services, travel services* ▤ *AE, DC, MC, V.*

$$$$ ☷ **The Oberoi.** Delhi's first modern deluxe hotel, built in 1965, is distinguished by its calm—even when the hotel is packed, the sleek, black-marble lobby is peaceful. You're welcomed by a small, marble lotus fountain strewn with rose petals, and the windows opposite reception look down on the zig-zag pool. Rooms have Western furnishings with pleasant sitting areas and Indian accents; deluxe rooms have more amenities, such as DVD players. All rooms have 24-hour butler service. Pool-facing rooms take in the greenery of the Delhi Golf Club; those on the other side face Humayun's Tomb. The Thai and Chinese restaurants, Baan Thai and Taipan, are some of the finest in Delhi. ⊠ *Dr. Zakir Hussain Rd., next to Delhi Golf Club, 110003* ☎ *11/2436–3030* 🖷 *11/ 2436–0484* ⊕ *www.oberoihotels.com* 📞 *258 rooms, 31 suites* ♤ *5 restaurants, golf privileges, pool, health club, hair salon, bar, baby-sitting, laundry service, business services, convention center, travel services* ▤ *AE, DC, MC, V.*

$$$$ ☷ **Taj Mahal.** The Taj Mansingh, as it's locally known, is Delhi's premier social hotel, with nightly cocktail affairs, cultural events, and the occasional society weddings drawing the glitterati. The lobby has Mughal-inspired decorative domes, a giant Oriental rug, and a general feeling of bustle, so you won't feel like you're off in a tourist enclave. Rooms are smallish, with simple Western furnishings; those on the pool side overlook plenty of greenery. The coffee shop, Machan, is popular with Delhiites and throws frequent food festivals. Centrally located in prestigious Lutyens' Delhi, the Taj is popular with business travelers and celebrities, and the service is correspondingly slick. ⊠ *1 Mansingh Rd., Central Delhi, 110011* ☎ *11/2302–6162* 🖷 *11/2301–7299* ⊕ *www. tajhotels.com* 📞 *275 rooms, 19 suites* ♤ *3 restaurants, coffee shop, health club, hair salon, bar, baby-sitting, laundry service, Internet, business services, convention center, travel services* ▤ *AE, DC, MC, V.*

$$$ ☷ **InterContinental ParkRoyal.** Primarily for business travelers, this is one of the few luxury hotels in South Delhi. The lobby is sedate, with wood paneling, a lampshaded chandelier, and a tea lounge with slow service. Business amenities are top-notch, including wireless and broadband Internet connections, an outdoor rooftop lounge, and a newspaper machine that prints same-day papers from all over the world. Guest rooms have separate dressing areas, a nice touch if you're tired of staring at your suitcase. Rooms on one side face the Bahai and ISKCON temples; the rest have city views. The Singh Sahib restaurant has a creative menu featuring the food of undivided Punjab (before it was split between India and Pakistan). ⊠ *Nehru Place, 110019* ☎ *11/2622–3344* 🖷 *11/ 2622–4288* ⊕ *www.newdelhi.intercontinental.com* 📞 *218 rooms, 15 suites* ♤ *2 restaurants, coffee shop, tea shop, in-room data ports, pool, health club, hair salon, bar, dance club, baby-sitting, laundry service, Internet, business services, convention center, travel services* ▤ *AE, DC, MC, V.*

$$$ ☷ **ITC Maurya Sheraton Hotel and Towers.** A favorite with executives and dignitaries, the Maurya works hard to style itself as the swankest hotel in Delhi. The lobby soars, yet somehow creates intimacy in reds, browns, and a three-tiered, wood-beamed dome painted with a fantastic technicolor mural. Fountains outside the picture windows add a natural touch.

Rooms are essentially Western, in masculine color schemes, but they take many forms; the more money you spend, the more wood paneling, plush carpeting, and pampering you receive. The restaurants draw as many locals as travelers, especially the famous Bukhara, and the whole place has a buzz of importance. ⊠ *Diplomatic Enclave, Chanakyapuri, 110021* ☎ *11/2611–2233* 🖷 *11/2611–3333* ⊕ *www.welcomgroup.com* 🗗 *515 rooms, 44 suites* ⚭ *4 restaurants, coffee shop, patisserie, tennis courts, pool, health club, hair salon, bar, nightclub, baby-sitting, laundry service, Internet, business services, travel services* 🚍 *AE, DC, MC, V.*

$$$ 🏨 **Taj Palace.** Facilities are top-notch in this giant, boomerang-shape business hotel. The teak-panel business center provides the online Knight-Ridder service and laptops for hire, the health club is amply outfitted, the beauty salon has a range of treatments, and the outdoor pool overlooks manicured lawns. There's even a putting green. Giant traditional lanterns serve as chandeliers in the sprawling marble lobby, but the rest of the building is Western, designed for corporate convenience and tour groups. Half the rooms face the pool and a swath of greenery; the rest have city views. The romantic Orient Express is one of India's finest European restaurants, with dishes from the fabled old train route. ⊠ *2 Sardar Patel Marg, Chanakyapuri, 110021* ☎ *11/2611–0202* 🖷 *11/2611–0808* ⊕ *www.tajhotels.com* 🗗 *421 rooms, 40 suites* ⚭ *3 restaurants, coffee shop, 9-hole putting green, pool, health club, hair salon, hot tub, massage, steam room, bar, baby-sitting, laundry service, Internet, business services, convention center, travel services* 🚍 *AE, DC, MC, V.*

★ **$$** 🏨 **Ambassador.** Service is heart-warmingly friendly in this quiet hotel, which is run by the Taj Group but costs half the price of its glamorous siblings. The building is a converted section of Sujan Singh Park, an exclusive 1930s neighborhood dripping with late-Raj charm. You're next door to Khan Market and close to Lodi Garden. The small marble lobby has comfortable banquette seating; upstairs, the hallways are windowed and bright. Most rooms have carpeting, basic teak furniture, and a modern bathroom with window; a few have tile floors, area rugs, and old-style bath fixtures. Try to get a room in front, with a balcony overlooking the garden, as rooms in back can be noisy. ⊠ *Cornwallis Rd., Sujan Singh Park, 110003* ☎ *11/2463–2600* 🖷 *11/2463–2252* ⊕ *www.tajhotels.com* 🗗 *76 rooms, 12 suites* ⚭ *2 restaurants, hair salon, bar, baby-sitting, laundry service, Internet, business services, travel services* 🚍 *AE, DC, MC, V.*

★ **$$** 🏨 **Claridges.** In 1950, three years after Independence, an Indian family was talked into building a hotel with a British aesthetic, and the result was a winner: tasteful yet unpretentious, in a central yet quiet location. The old-fashioned charm reveals itself on the front lawn—unusual in Delhi—where cane chairs invite you to take a breather, and in the lobby, where two swing staircases suggest a way up. Long, marble-floor hallways lead to Delhi's most stylish guest rooms, with designer bedding, down duvets, high moulded wainscoting, crystal sconces, and lightly painted bathroom tiles. Standard rooms are medium-size, but all rooms facing the pool have either window seat, terrace, or balcony. ⊠ *12 Aurangzeb Rd., Central Delhi, 110011* ☎ *11/2301–0211* 🖷 *11/2301–0625* ⊕ *www.claridges.com* 🗗 *112 rooms, 26 suites* ⚭ *3 restaurants, cof-*

fee shop, pool, health club, hair salon, bar, laundry service, Internet, business services, travel services $\equiv$ *AE, DC, MC, V.*

$$ ⌧ **The Connaught.** About 1 km (½ mi) from Connaught Place, this spiffy mid-size hotel is close to the center of things yet far enough away from the hubbub. The cream-and-rust lobby is large yet cozy, with a few wooden beams overhead, and filled with sunlight in late afternoon. Guest rooms are small, but they're attractively decorated with jewel-tone bedspreads and watercolors of Delhi monuments. Rooms on the east side directly overlook a field-hockey stadium, which is more appealing than it sounds. The bar is a soothing sea green, and dinner is accompanied by live *ghazals* (Urdu-language love songs) every night but Tuesday. Discounts of up to 30% can be negotiated between April and August. ⊠ *37 Shaheed Bhagat Singh Marg, Connaught Place, 110001* ☎ *11/2336–4225* ⌂ *11/2334–0757* ⌐ *72 rooms, 9 suites* ⌂ *Restaurant, coffee shop, room service, bar, laundry service, Internet, business services, travel services* $\equiv$ *AE, D, MC, V* ⍥ *CP.*

★ $$ ⌧ **Hyatt Regency.** The Hyatt has a surprisingly homey feel, with the mirror-spangled cream-color lobby suffused with light from the pool-facing pastry shop at the back—where you can relax at a marble-top window table with one of the best European desserts in town. A clay waterfall spills past this aerie to the ground-level coffee shop. Guest rooms have cream-color walls and parquet floors, a rarity in India; views on the pool side are superior. Rates are very reasonable considering the deluxe facilities. The shopping arcade is easily the best in Delhi, with dozens of shops selling jewelry, handicrafts, and Kashmiri carpets and shawls. ⊠ *Ring Rd., Bhikaji Cama Place, 110066* ☎ *11/2679–1234* ⌂ *11/2679–1212* ⊕ *www.delhi.hyatt.com* ⌐ *508 rooms, 29 suites* ⌂ *3 restaurants, coffee shop, patisserie, 2 tennis courts, pool, health club, hair salon, 2 bars, baby-sitting, laundry service, Internet, business services, travel services* $\equiv$ *AE, DC, MC, V* ⍥ *BP.*

$$ ⌧ **The Manor.** Nestled next door to a country club in one of Delhi's
Fodor's Choice wealthiest residential neighborhoods is Delhi's only boutique hotel.
★ It's the perfect place to come home to at dusk, with lanterns highlighting the greenery and softening the building's sharp lines. The interior is ultramodern but in soft tone—taupes and creams as well as white. Some walls are paneled in wood or stone; otherwise the guest rooms are fairly stark, accented by a fresh flower or two. Bathrooms are in dark marble, and most have separate shower stalls. The restaurant, which serves Indian and Mediterranean food, is beautifully candlelit at night. ⊠ *77 Friends Colony W, 110065* ☎ *11/2692–5151* ⌂ *11/2692–2299* ⊕ *www.themanordelhi.com* ⌐ *12 rooms* ⌂ *Restaurant, massage, bar, laundry service, Internet, meeting room, travel services* $\equiv$ *AE, DC, MC, V* ⍥ *CP.*

$–$$ ⌧ **Hans Plaza.** This pleasant hotel has a twist: it occupies six upper floors of a hideous office building just off Connaught Place. The cream-color lobby is warm and welcoming, with plush sitting areas and contemporary paintings. The larger rooms overlook Barakhamba Road; look to the right and you'll see Delhi's prestigious redbrick Modern School. All rooms have earth-tone Western furnishings, including teak wardrobes. Deluxe rooms have polished marble floors, Oriental rugs, and bathtubs;

standard ("executive") rooms have wall-to-wall carpeting and showers. The 21st-floor art deco restaurant and bar have fabulous views, a rarity in Delhi; try to dine on the terrace in winter. ⊠ *15 Barakhamba Rd., Connaught Place, 110001* ☎ *11/2331–6861* 🖷 *11/2331–4830* ⊕ *www. hanshotels.com* ⟿ *67 rooms, 3 suites* ⌂ *Restaurant, coffee shop, room service, bar, laundry service, Internet, business services, travel services* ⊟ *AE, DC, MC, V.*

$$ 🏨 **Maidens.** It opened in 1907, before New Delhi even existed, and it's the oldest hotel in the city. Now run by the Oberoi group, the hotel remains a classic Raj building, with high-arched windows, deep verandas, grand old trees, pleasant lawns, and a quirky interior. Thanks to the building's age, the rooms and bathrooms are huge, but they're dark and have 1970s carpeting. The Maidens' problem is location—it's north of Old Delhi, in the middle of a Metro-train construction zone, making it ideal for Old Delhi excursions but not for much else. The coffee shop has a nice patio and an English feel, enhanced by the British tour groups that often stay here. ⊠ *7 Sham Nath Marg, Civil Lines, 110054* ☎ *11/2389–0505* 🖷 *11/2389–0582* ⊕ *www.oberoihotels.com* ⟿ *53 rooms, 3 suites* ⌂ *1 restaurant, coffee shop, 2 tennis courts, pool, bar, laundry service, travel services* ⊟ *AE, DC, MC, V.*

$ 🏨 **Nirula's Hotel.** The name "Nirula" is close to the hearts of Delhiites for the fast food and ice cream served at its chain of cheap restaurants. Less well known is this hotel, which occupies a historic building on top of several bustling Nirula's eateries. The walls are hung with old photos, sketches, and paintings of Delhi and elsewhere, and the sitting areas have cane furniture; the British Raj look seems to justify the slightly dated bedspreads. The gleaming bathrooms have showers only. A few rooms have large balconies, but most are quite dark, and bed arrangements vary; specify all preferences up front. ⊠ *L-Block, Connaught Place, 110001* ☎ *11/2341–7419* 🖷 *11/2341–8957* ✍ *delhihotel@nirulas. com* ⟿ *31 rooms* ⌂ *2 restaurants, ice-cream parlor, room service, bar, laundry service, Internet, travel services* ⊟ *DC, MC, V.*

¢–$ 🏨 **Jukaso Inn Downtown.** This little inn might be the best deal in Connaught Place. Rooms are small but welcoming, with a wool bedspread, marble-top table, and either plush carpet or marble floor with rug. Bathrooms have showers only; and rooms on the road side are noisy, so request an inside room when you reserve. The halls are adorned with photos and paintings of random sights around the world, and the first-floor sitting area has faux-medieval stone walls. Management is flexible; the restaurant can open very early to accommodate those leaving on day trips to Agra. Don't confuse this Jukaso Inn with its cousin in Sundar Nagar, which is inferior. ⊠ *L-Block, Connaught Place, 110001* ☎ *11/2341–5450 or 11/2341–5450* 🖷 *11/2341–4448* ⟿ *37 rooms, 2 suites* ⌂ *Restaurant, laundry service, Internet, business services, travel services* ⊟ *AE, DC, MC, V.*

★ ¢ 🏨 **Ahuja Residency.** This little-known guest house is a jewel, Delhi's only combination of style and affordability. It's in a converted house in a quiet, leafy, upper-class neighborhood, so it's a great way to get a feel for residential life. Rooms are simple but cozy, with bright-color fabrics, blond-wood furniture, gleaming floors, and large windows. Bathrooms have showers only. The restaurant is delightful, with terra-cotta floors and yellow-and-orange plaid fabrics and crockery; and the rooftop terrace, with flowering plants and wrought-iron furniture, is unbeatable on a winter day. Reserve early, and if all rooms are booked, ask about the sister facility in Defence Colony. ⊠ *193 Golf Links, 110003* ☎ *11/2462–2255* 🖷 *11/2464–9008* 🌐 *www.ahujaresidency.com* ⇌ *12 rooms* ⚭ *Dining room, laundry service, Internet, travel services* ▤ *AE, MC, V.*

¢ 🖾 **Jor Bagh 27.** Peace, proximity, and price are the benefits at this whitewashed guest house. With plenty of greenery and excellent markets, not to mention Lodi Garden and Safdarjung's Tomb a short hop away, Jor Bagh is one of Delhi's most desirable residential neighborhoods. Rooms are very simple, and some are shabby; look at what's available before you settle in. Bathrooms have showers only. Breakfast is served in the dining room, but other meals must be ordered in (deluxe rooms have refrigerators). Alas, the generator cannot run all the air-conditioners for very long, so this isn't your best bet in summer. ⊠ *27 Jor Bagh, 110003* 📧 *guesthouse27@hotmail.com* ☎ *11/2469–8647* 🖷 *11/2469–8475* ⇌ *18 rooms* ⚭ *Dining room, laundry service* ▤ *MC, V* ⚬ *CP.*

¢ 🖾 **Maharani Guest House.** Friendly service redeems this simple Sundar Nagar guest house; the staff are eager to please their international guests. Rooms are slightly shabby, and some of the various decorating schemes are dated to the point of hilarious kitsch, but everything is clean. Twenty-four-hour room service tries to compensate for the lack of a restaurant, and the garden is pleasant in winter. You're close enough to walk to Sundar Nagar Market and a short drive from Khan Market and the sights of Central Delhi. ⊠ *3 Sundar Nagar, 110003* ☎ *11/2435–9521* 🖷 *11/2435–4562* ⇌ *24 rooms* ⚭ *Laundry service, travel services* ▤ *AE, DC, MC, V.*

NIGHTLIFE & THE ARTS

The Arts

Delhi is India's cultural hub, if only because performers from all over the country come to the capital at least once a year to cultivate their national audience. Painting, music, dance, theater, and, of course, film are all well represented. The India Habitat Centre, a large, modern cultural center, has the best combination of all of the above; on any given evening, it hosts several good programs. The only problem is that hype is nonexistent, so you must be persistent to find out what's happening—pick up the monthly magazine *First City* for details. Failing that, the daily newspapers, especially the *Indian Express* and the *Hindustan Times,* are also good sources. The staff at your hotel may be able to help, too.

Art Galleries

Delhi's art scene is extremely dynamic. Contemporary Indian painting—which often blends traditional Indian motifs with Western techniques—is blossoming, and private galleries are following suit. Much of the work is very affordable, and almost completely devoid of the pretension that can dog its Western counterparts. Most galleries are quite small, so if you want a broad view of what's happening, hire a car or taxi for an afternoon of gallery-hopping. Pick up the latest *First City* for exhibit details and profiles of featured artists. Galleries are closed on Sunday.

Art Heritage (⊠ Triveni Kala Sangam, 205 Tansen Marg, Connaught Place ☎ 11/2371–9470), part of a government-run cultural institute with several galleries, has some of the finest exhibits in town. **Dhoomimal Art Centre** (⊠ A-8 Connaught Place ☎ 11/2332–4492) is a bit chaotic but often has good shows. **Gallery Espace** (⊠ 16 Community Centre, New Friends Colony ☎ 11/2632–6267) is a tiny but remarkable space featuring both new and canonical artists, sometimes mixed together in interesting theme shows. The various exhibition spaces at **Habitat World** in the India Habitat Centre (⊠ Lodi Rd., Lodi Institutional Area ☎ 11/2468–2222) showcase painting, sculpture, Indian craft, and creativity of every kind. The main Visual Arts Gallery is just inside Gate 2. The government-run **Lalit Kala Akademi** (⊠ Rabindra Bhavan, Copernicus Marg, Connaught Place ☎ 11/2338–7243) is a large 1950s building showing several exhibits at once, usually of varying quality. **Vadehra Art Gallery** (⊠ 40 Defence Colony ☎ 11/2461–5368) is respected for its permanent collection of 20th-century masters.

Hauz Khas Village has a cluster of galleries. **Art & Deal** (⊠ 23 Hauz Khas Village ☎ 11/2652–3382) has a large contemporary collection. **Art Konsult** (⊠ 12 Hauz Khas Village ☎ 11/2652–3382) hangs some accomplished contemporary work. **Delhi Art Gallery** (⊠ 11 Hauz Khas Village ☎ 11/2656–8166) has a substantial collection of paintings by old masters and contemporary artists; for major purchases, try to verify authenticity. **Navratana** (⊠ 2A Hauz Khas Village ☎ 11/3101–0846) is a tiny but spirited hoard of old paintings, photographs, and movie posters, with a few contemporary works thrown in. The **Village Gallery** (⊠ 14 Hauz Khas Village ☎ 11/2685–3860) has tasteful, relatively small-scale contemporary work.

Film

India's Bombay-based film industry, known as Bollywood, produces more films annually than any other country in the world. Most Bollywood films are in Hindi, but anyone can understand them—most are romantic musicals, with dollops of family drama and occasionally a violent villain. Delhi cinemas show all the latest Hindi movies plus a few current Hollywood films, the latter tending toward action and young romantic comedy. To find out what's playing, check listings in the magazine section of any daily newspaper. If your movie of choice is a hot new release, consider buying tickets a day in advance; your hotel can help. **Chanakya** (⊠ Yashwant Pl., off Vinay Marg, Chanakyapuri). **Priya** (⊠ Basant Lok, Vasant Vihar). **PVR Anupam** (⊠ Community Centre, Saket).

Art films from all over the world are shown at various cultural institutes; the monthly magazine *First City* has listings.

Music & Dance

Great musicians and dancers are always passing through Delhi. Incredibly, most performances are free, but tickets ("passes") are sometimes required for high-demand performers. The **India Habitat Centre** (⊠ Lodi Rd., Lodi Institutional Area ☎ 11/2468–2222) has several events every evening. **India International Centre** (✉ 40 Lodi Estate, ☎ 11/2461–9431) is an established performance space near the Habitat Centre. **Kamani Auditorium** (✉ Copernicus Marg, Connaught Place ☎ 11/2338–8084) is a long-standing venue for Indian classical music and dance. The Chamber Theatre at **Triveni Kala Sangam** (✉ 205 Tansen Marg, Connaught Place ☎ 11/2371–8833) is long-established.

Theater

India has an ancient dramatic tradition, and *nautanki* plays, which combine drama, comedy, and song, are still held in many villages. Delhi has an active theater scene in both English and Hindi, with many shows locally written, produced, and acted. Most run only for one weekend and don't travel afterward, so they can seem a bit unpolished even when they're fundamentally good. For all the options, pick up *First City* magazine. The **India Habitat Cenre** (✉ Lodi Rd., Lodi Institutional Area ☎ 11/2468–2222) is Delhi's biggest and best theater venue, with several different shows each week. **LTG Auditorium** (✉ Copernicus Marg, Connaught Place ☎ 11/2338–9713) is a veteran theater. **Shri Ram Centre** (✉ Mandi House, Safdar Hashmi Marg, Connaught Place ☎ 11/2371–4307) stages a constant stream of plays, some for one day only.

Nightlife

Delhi is traditionally the boring old uncle of lively Bombay and Bangalore, with Delhiites preferring to socialize at home and turn in at a decent hour. With wallets and local liquor laws loosening, however, Delhi's bar and club culture is exploding. Happy hour is still not a ritual, but the crowd comes out in force late at night. Quiet pubs are thin on the ground—most of the popular bars are aggressively loud.

Bars & Pubs

Among the growing set of youngsters who can afford it, Delhi's nightlife is intense. Various forms of the watering hole are now on offer, with the lounge bar and the British pub emerging as the most successful formulas. **Blues** (✉ N-18 Outer Circle, Connaught Place ☎ 11/2331–0957) is vaguely Chicagoesque. The music is live on Thursday. **Djinns** (✉ Hyatt Regency, Ring Rd., Bhikaji Cama Place ☎ 11/2679–1234) looks like the set for a *Cheers* episode, complete with hardwood floors and brass fittings. A band usually plays in the evening, and the crowd, an odd mixture of young Indians and Western businessmen, hits the floor. Brick-walled **DV8** (✉ 13 Regal Bldg., Connaught Place ☎ 2336–3358) is a casual place to kick back. The ultra-cool **F Bar & Lounge** (✉ Tavern on the Greens, beyond Saket Community Centre, near Lado Sarai Golf Course ☎ no phone) is currently ablaze with Delhi's most fashionable, for whom it is actually named. The Victorian **Pegasus Bar** (✉ Nirula's Hotel, L-Block, Connaught Place ☎ 11/2341–7419) is a smart but relaxed little pub. Slick **Rick's** (✉ Taj Mahal Hotel, 1 Mansingh Rd., Central Delhi ☎ 11/2302–6162) is a magnet for Delhi's beautiful people, with as many voices yelling into their cell phones as talking to each other. The booze selection is hard to beat, and the snacks are Southeast Asian. Go before 9 PM if you want a seat. Loungelike **Senso** (✉ 33 Basant Lok, Vasant Vihar ☎ 11/2615–5533) is currently hot and likely to remain that way, with its clean, white Miami look, nightly house music, and cool crowd. **Ssteel** (⊠ Ashok Hotel, 50-B Chanakyapuri ☎ 11/2611–0101) is one of the latest nocturnal sizzles, with an urban-industrial look that would transport you out of India were it not for the crowd of Delhiites enjoying it. **Suede** (⊠ 27 Community Centre, Saket ☎ 11/2651–1261 or 11/2652–2518), near the popular PVR Anupam cinema, is a hot South Delhi hangout.

Discos

Now that Delhi has a bar scene, clubs have faded from prominence, but there are still a few places to shake a leg. **Floats** (⊠ ParkRoyal Inter-Continental Hotel, Nehru Place ☎ 11/2622–3344) is a bit of a Djinn's rip-off, but it's still a great place to hang out. **My Kind of Place** (⊠ Taj Palace Hotel, 2 Sardar Patel Marg, Chanakyapuri ☎ 11/2611–0202) gets a modest crowd, but the dance floor is correspondingly comfortable.

Hotel Bars & Lounges

All the major hotels have bars, but most are better suited for a collective nap with a few tired foreigners than a night of Indian camaraderie. Richly decorated, often aiming for a British Raj look, these bars attract an older, quieter crowd than those listed above, and drink prices match those in London and New York. The large bar in **1911** (⊠ Imperial Hotel, Janpath, Connaught Place ☎ 11/2334–1234) is a classic watering hole decked out the way it looked during the Independence movement in the 1940s. The drink menu is massive, and lounge music keeps the vibe contemporary. Casual little **H2O+** (⊠ Ambassador Hotel, Sujan Singh Park ☎ 11/2463–2000) is ideal for quiet conversation; the whimsical underwater theme, complete with soft blue lighting and Western pop music, is oddly soothing. There's a small menu featuring fish, meat, and a few vegetable dishes. The **Patiala Peg** (⊠ Imperial Hotel, Janpath, Connaught Place ☎ 11/2334–1234) is an intimate, masculine old-world bar with an extensive cocktail menu. The **Polo Lounge** (⊠ Hyatt Regency, Ring Rd., Bhikaji Cama Place ☎ 11/2679–1234), while very much a hotel bar, can be very lively. The wood-panel room has a curved bar, a leather sofa, a library with newspapers, an oddball collection of books, and sports channels on cable TV.

SPORTS & THE OUTDOORS

Participant Sports

Golf

Call well in advance if you want to play on a weekend in winter. The **Army Golf Club** (⊠ Delhi Cantonment ☎ 11/2569–1972) is close to Delhi. To play against a backdrop of ancient monuments, try the 27-hole **Delhi Golf Club** (⊠ Dr. Zakir Hussain Rd. ☎ 11/2436–0002 Ext. 227 or 98100–03064) in the center of town.

Swimming

The top hotels have excellent pools, but most are open only to guests, or to nonguests at prohibitively high cost (Rs. 800–Rs. 1,000). City pools should be avoided, as there's no way to judge the water quality.

Tennis
If your hotel doesn't have a tennis court, reserve one at the **Delhi Lawn Tennis Association** (✉ Africa Ave., next to Safdarjung Enclave ☎ 11/2617–6140).

Yoga
The international **Sivananda Yoga Vedanta Nataraja Centre** (✉ A-41 Kailash Colony, ☎ 11/2648–0869) holds several classes daily.

Spectator Sports

Check any newspaper or ask your hotel about **cricket** and **football** (soccer) matches. Rivalries are intense, so these games are popular; see if your hotel can get you tickets. Delhi's polo games (Oct.–Feb.) are another crowd-pleaser—contact the **Delhi Polo Club** (✉ 61st Cavalry, Cariappa Marg, Delhi Cantonment ☎ 11/2569–9777), maintained by the Army Polo and Riding Club.

SHOPPING

Delhi is a shopping center for goods from all over India, making it the best place to stock up on gifts and souvenirs. Bargaining is often appropriate. A good rule of thumb: When the price is written down, it's probably fixed. When you have to inquire about the price, it's negotiable.

In shops where foreign customers are uncommon, the staff is likely to follow your every move with great interest. If this bothers you, simply state your objective or emphasize that you're just looking; they'll cooperate if you indicate nicely that you don't need to be followed around.

Most shops are open six days a week, as each neighborhood's market area closes one day a week, usually Sunday, Monday, or Tuesday. Most shops in Old Delhi are closed on Sunday.

Bazaars & Markets

Connaught Place, open every day but Sunday from about 10 to 7:30, is the former commercial district of the British Raj. Pillared arcades and a wheel-shape layout make it a pleasant place to stroll, especially the inner circle, though you have to get used to the intermittent entreaties of hawkers and beggars. Shops run the gamut from scruffy to upscale. Beneath the green park at the center of Connaught Place is Palika Bazaar, a cheap underground market with all the charm of a Times Square subway station. Avoid it: it's a favorite haunt of pickpockets and many shopkeepers are dishonest.

☾ **Dilli Haat** (✉ Aurobindo Marg ☎ 11/2611–9055) is a government-run food and crafts bazaar that invites artisans from all over the country to sell their wares directly. More than 60 do so at any given time; the vendors rotate every two weeks according to changing themes such as handicrafts, textiles, or Rajasthani goods. Constants include Kashmiri shawls, Lucknavi *chikan* (white embroidery on pastel cotton), woodwork, pottery, and cotton dhurries. At the back of the bazaar, 25 stalls

CHAAT & CHEW

NO TRIP TO INDIA IS COMPLETE without some Indian snack food. The most popular street foods are papri chaat (fried wafers piled high with potatoes, chick peas, yogurt, and chili powder), chole bhatura (also known as chana bhatura—spicy chick peas with fried, airy puri bread), and golgappas (fried dough in a hollow golf-ball shape, which you fill with a spicy mixture of potatoes, chick peas, tamarind, and coriander sauce), pakoras (fried-dough with various fillings), and the Bombay delicacy known as bhel puri (spicy rice with bits of onion). The best places to nosh on these snacks are in neighborhood markets. Near Connaught Place, the **Bengali Sweet House** (⊠ 27–37 Bengali Market, Connaught Pl.) is a classic spot for evening golgappa outings. **Evergreen Sweet House** (⊠ S-30 Green Park Market) has a charming tin ceiling under which a large crowd stuffs itself with chole bhatura and vegetarian thalis. **Nathu's** (⊠ 2 Sundar Nagar Market) is the perfect place to kick back after shopping for high-end souvenirs, with its robust Indian sweets and pleasant seating area. The nearby Sweets Corner supplies the fried stuff outdoors. **Prince Paan Box** (⊠ M-Block Market, eastern corner, Greater Kailash I) has one of Delhi's most popular chaat-wallahs (snack vendors), with a crowd at all hours. They're also known, of course, for their paan (betel nut leaves that include various ingredients). There's no place to sit. At the **Bikanerwala** (⊠ Hauz Khas Market) you can sample Gujarati snacks—ask for khandvi (a delicious cold, pan-fried snack made from a seasoned batter of chick-pea flour and buttermilk, then cut into rolls and sprinkled with coconut and coriander) or dhokla, a savory, fluffy, steamed cake made with chick-pea flour, mustard seeds, and a pinch of sugar and topped with coriander leaves.

serve regional food from around the country, a rare opportunity to sample Goan fish curry, Bengali fish in mustard sauce, and Kerala chicken stew outside their states of origin. Best of all, doors are open daily from 10 to 9 (10 to 10 in summer). Admission is Rs. 10.

In the narrow medieval alleys of South Delhi's **Hauz Khas Village**, boutiques and shops in converted old homes sell crafts, curios, jewelry, artisanal furniture, and clothing (mostly glitzy Indian wear). Most stores are open every day but Sunday from 10:30 to 6 or 7.

INA Market (⊠ Aurobindo Marg), across the street from Dilli Haat, is a colorful stop open every day but Monday. This is one of Delhi's most exciting food bazaars, with shops full of imported packaged foods giving way to a covered fruit-and-vegetable market complete with coolies (porters) ready to carry your choices in a basket while you shop. Dry-goods merchants sell spices, nuts, and Indian salty snacks, and meat is prepared and sold on a slushy lane in back.

Khan Market is one of the capital's most pleasant and popular markets, with dozens of fine shops selling books, CDs, cameras and film processing, drugs, ayurvedic cosmetics, clothing, home decorations, imported magazines, and imported foods. The shops are open roughly 10 to 7 every day but Sunday; some of the cafés and restaurants stay open for dinner. The crowd is thick with Delhi intelligentsia and expats.

Lajpat Nagar Market is a lively market where middle-class locals stock their households. Several Western brand names have outlets here, but Lajpat is best known for cheap kitchenware, curtains, Indian clothing, raw fabric, and shoes. A good place to take in the chaos and sample some street food, it's open every day but Monday from about 10:30 to 8.

Old Delhi is an endlessly interesting place to shop, admittedly more for the experience than for what you'll take away. The sidewalks of Chandni Chowk are lined with everything from clocks to baby clothes to tacky toys and blankets, and the shops on Dariba Kalan are filled with silver and gold jewelry. Stalls behind the Jama Masjid sell metalware and utensils, and one street specializes in stationery, especially Indian wedding invitations. Kinari Bazaar glistens with Hindu wedding paraphernalia. Khari Baoli, west of Chandni Chowk toward Lahori Gate, is renowned for its wholesale nuts, spices, and Indian pickles and chutneys. Shops are closed on Sunday.

The **Santushti Shopping Complex** in Chanakyapuri, open every day but Sunday from 10 to 6 or 7, is a collection of posh and arty boutiques scattered around a small, quiet garden across from the Ashok Hotel in the Diplomatic Enclave. Prices match those in the West, but this is a relaxing place to stroll and browse. Clothing is the main draw, followed by home furnishings, jewelry, leather, and ayurvedic beauty products. The restaurant Basil and Thyme serves excellent contemporary Euro-American food.

Sarojini Nagar Market is popular with locals for its endless array of cheap clothing, from Indian nightgowns and flashy kurtas to rejected Western export apparel. Note how much is charged for brand-name T-shirts and sweats compared with what you pay back home. The fruit and vegetable bazaar is great fun, especially at night. The market is open every day but Monday from about 10:30 to 8.

Specialty Stores

Books
As the center of India's English-language publishing industry, and, arguably, India's intellectual capital, Delhi has something of a literary scene. For those with hard currency, Indian books are great bargains, including lower-price local editions of titles published abroad. If you'll be in Delhi for a while, hunt down the elusive but excellent *Old Delhi: 10 Easy Walks,* by Gaynor Barton and Laurraine Malone (New Delhi: Rupa, 1997)—these painstakingly detailed routes are fascinating and manageable. The top hotels have small bookshops, but Khan Market has several of the capital's best.

A candy store for history lovers is the cramped showroom for **Asian Educational Services** (⊠ 31 Hauz Khas Village ☎ 11/2656–0187 ⊗ closed 2nd Sat. each month). This enterprising publisher reproduces old histories and travelogues on Asia, with hundreds of books on India. **Bahri Sons** (⊠ Opposite main gate, Khan Market ☎ 11/2469–4610) is stuffed to the ceiling with dusty nonfiction, particularly academic history, politics, and Indian heritage. **The Bookshop** (✉ 14A Khan Market ☎ 11/2469–7102) is strong on literary fiction, including hot new titles from abroad. In Connaught Place, **Bookworm** (✉ B-29 Connaught Pl. ☎ 11/2332–2260) has general fiction and Indian nonfiction, including academic social-science books. In South Delhi, **Fact and Fiction** (✉ 39 Basant Lok, Vasant Vihar ☎ 11/2614–6843) caters to the diplomatic community with books on international affairs, history, science, and language study. **Faqir-Chand** (✉ 15A Khan Market ☎ 11/2461–8810) has a fair number of coffee-table books. **Full Circle** (✉ 5B Khan Market ☎ 11/2465–5641) is known for its spirituality, self-help, and coffee-table books. Geared toward travelers, **Mascot's** (✉ 6 Sundar Nagar Market ☎ 11/2435–8808) has sundry books on India.

> **need a break?**
>
> Two flights up, in the Full Circle bookshop, the **Turtle Cafe** (✉ 5B Khan Market ☎ 11/2465–5641 ◷ Mon.–Sat. 10–7:30) serves light bistro food, exotic fruit juices, and excellent Western desserts in a smart contemporary setting, with music from the record shop below. The terrace is very pleasant in winter.

Carpets

India has one of the world's foremost Oriental-rug industries, and there are carpet vendors all over Delhi. Unfortunately, carpet sellers are a notoriously dishonest crowd. In addition to being obnoxiously pushy, they are likely to sell you inauthentic merchandise at colossally inflated prices and then deny it later. There are some exceptions to this rule, but they tend to sell out of their homes rather than upscale showrooms—so call before you go. Jasim Jan, of **Janson's Carpets** (✉ A-14 Nizamuddin East ☎ 11/2435–5615, 98111–29095 cell phone), delivers exactly what he describes—carpets old and new, silk and wool, Persian and tribal—and at fair (not cheap) prices. The family that runs **Novel Exports** (✉ D-23 Jangpura Extension ☎ 11/2431–2226) comes from Kashmir, and they have stunning Kashmiri carpets, shawls, jewelry, and lacquered papier-mâché items.

Clothing

Clothes shopping is one of Delhi's great pleasures. *Khadi,* the hand-spun cotton that Gandhi turned into a nationalist symbol during the Independence movement, has made a roaring comeback and is now worn by many Delhi women during the long, hot summer. You can experience khadi in a salwar-kameez—the classic North Indian ensemble of long tunic and loose pants, also popular in a variation called the kurta-churidar—and in Western-style tops and skirts.

WOMEN'S FABRIC & SALWAR-KAMEEZ SETS Stylish Delhiites, expats, and tourists rub shoulders at **Anokhi** (✉ 32 Khan Market ☎ 11/2460–3423 ✉ Santushti Shopping Complex, Chanakyapuri ☎ 11/2688–3076) for stylish kurtas, dupattas, and Western separates in boldly colored block-printed cottons. **Daman Choli** (✉ V-1 Green Park Main ☎ 11/2656–2265) has bright, tastefully decorated cotton salwar-kameez and a convenient while-you-wait alteration service. The outdoor **Dilli Haat** market (✉ Aurobindo Marg ☎ 11/2611–9055) usually

CloseUp

DRESSING THE PART

MANY TRAVELING WOMEN (and a few traveling men) are inspired to buy an Indian outfit to wear for the duration of their trip. This is recommended, as your willingness to walk the walk can endear you to a great many people and arguably make you less prone to exploitation. It's also very comfortable. Here's a primer:

The traditional North Indian women's ensemble of a long tunic over loose pants is known as a salwar-kameez. Today, it is equally common in a variation called the kurta-churidar. The word kameez is a general term meaning "shirt," whereas kurta specifies a traditional Indian tunic worn by both women and men. The pants worn beneath women's kurtas take two forms: the salwar, which is very loose, with only a slight gather at the ankle, and the churidar, which is loose in the thigh but tight along the calf, bunched up near the ankle like leggings. Presently the churidar is in greater vogue than the salwar, and true fashionistas now wear very short (above the knee) kurtas over thigh-tight churidars, a look with a Western element: it favors skinny women. Most women opt for knee- or calf-length kurtas.

The outfit is usually finished with a matching dupatta or chunni, a long scarf draped over the chest with the ends dangling in back, traditionally two meters long and one meter wide. These days you're free to drape the dupatta however you like; slinging it back from the neck, or even forward from the neck (Western-style), gives the outfit a modern twist. Just beware of dupattas made of stiff or starchy fabric—no matter how beautiful they look, you will probably find them unwieldy. A dupatta is particularly useful in places like Old Delhi and Nizamuddin, where you can pull it over your head as a kerchief if you feel too conspicuous.

You won't have to invest much in any of these items; at FabIndia or Dilli Haat you can buy an smart trio of kurta, churidar–salwar, and dupatta for US$15. Another option at Dilli Haat and some fabric stores is to buy uncut "suit fabric," a smartly matched set of three pieces of fabric meant to be sewn into the full regalia. If you buy suit fabric, simply take it all to a tailor (ask any market merchant to suggest one; most are holes-in-the-wall), allow him to measure you, tell him what kind of neckline you fancy and whether you want a churidar or salwar, and come back for your custom-made "suit." This can take a few days, but the tailoring costs only US$5–10 and these ensembles are very attractive.

Men's kurtas are traditionally paired with a churidar or with loose, straight-legged "pyjamas." Most urban Indian men wear Western shirts and trousers, but Delhi's politicians keep the white cotton kurta-pyjama and the more formal dhoti (a loose, bunchy men's skirt) alive and kicking. Formal silk kurta-churidars are trotted out only for weddings, but men sometimes wear a cotton kurta with jeans for a hip East-West look.

Many Western women who buy salwar-kameez choose muted colors, perhaps on the premise that light skin tones need light fabric tones. Unfortunately, muted colors often make Westerners look washed-out and even more "foreign." Be bold! Women of all complexions are flattered by the jewel tones of Indian vegetable dyes.

has the capital's largest selection of cheap, distinctive cotton kurtas and raw salwar-kameez fabric. Designs vary widely, from Rajasthani mirror work to gossamer Maheshwari cotton to *ikat* weaves from Orissa. **FabIndia** (⊠ N-14 Greater Kailash I ☎ 11/2646–5497 ⊘ closed Sun.) is a Delhi institution—an emporium stuffed with block-printed kurtas, salwars, churidars, dupattas, Western tops, and skirts in subtle colors for trendy Delhiites, their mothers, expats, and tourists. Quality can vary. Avoid Saturday, when the place is a madhouse and it's difficult to get your hands on the stock. **Kanika** (⊠ M-53 Connaught Pl. ☎ 11/2341–4731) has beautiful, if somewhat pricey, salwar-kameez in contemporary cuts of traditional fabrics. **Khanna Creations** (⊠ D-6 Connaught Pl. ☎ 11/2341–1929) sells handsome salwar-kameez, some hand-embroidered, and raw fabric sets in great colors and patterns at good prices. Their in-house tailor can create a salwar-kameez in as little as four hours for Rs. 200. **Kilol** (⊠ 31 Hauz Khas Village, upstairs ☎ 11/2653–1974) has some of the most stunning salwar-kameez fabric sets in India, with color-drenched crêpe dupattas topping off soft, block-printed cottons. They're stacked on shelves in the back. **Tulsi** (⊠ Santushti Shopping Complex, Chanakyapuri ☎ 11/2687–0339) sells supple garments and home furnishings of handwoven silk, linen, and cotton.

need a break? Upstairs from Anokhi's boutique, the **FabCafe** (⊠ 32 Khan Market ⊘ Mon.–Sat. 10–7:30) serves light Western salads, pastas, and desserts and refreshing cold drinks in an airy contemporary setting.

SARIS If you find yourself shopping for a sari, savor the experience of learning about this amazing handicraft. Silks and attractive cotton saris are sometimes sold at Dilli Haat market, depending on which vendors have set up shop that week. Silks are sold en masse at upmarket stores in South Extension, Greater Kailash I, and Connaught Place, but the highest thumbs-up go to Kalpana and Padakkam. **Banaras House** (⊠ N-13 Connaught Pl. ☎ 11/2331–4751) sells the rich brocaded silks of Varanasi. **Kalpana** (⊠ F-5 Connaught Pl. ☎ 11/2331–5368) is like an upscale version of Dilli Haat, with exquisite traditional saris from all over India plus gorgeous Kashmiri shawls. **L'Affaire** (⊠ M-59 Greater Kailash I ☎ 11/2641–9977) has flamboyant party wear at prices to match. **Nalli** (⊠ F-44 South Extension I ☎ 11/2462–9926 ⊠ P-7/90 Connaught Pl. ☎ 11/2336–7334) is a Madras-based chain specializing in gold-trimmed silks from the Tamil town of Kanchipuram. The South Extension store is larger. **Padakkam** (⊠ Santushti Shopping Complex, Chanakyapuri ☎ 11/2465–4695) has incredible one-of-a-kind saris—mostly South Indian silks, but also interesting cottons—and Kashmiri shawls. In Old Delhi, the venerable **Ram Chandra Krishan Chandra** (⊠ Gali Parante Wali ☎ 11/2327–7869) has several rooms full of traditional silks.

MEN'S FABRIC & TAILORS The oldest and finest men's tailors are in Connaught Place. The venerable **D. Vaish & Sons** (⊠ 17 Regal Bldg., Connaught Place ☎ 11/2336–1806) has a huge selection of fabric and can tailor both men's and women's Western suits, not to mention Indian outfits, for about US$60 plus fabric. **Mohanlal & Sons** (⊠ B-21 Connaught Pl. ☎ 11/2332–2797) whips up men's Western and Indian suits at very low prices. **Vedi Tailors** (✉ M-60 Connaught Pl. ☎ 11/2341–6901) has a good reputation.

Crafts & Curios

Delhi's fixed-price government emporiums, near Connaught Place, offer good values to travelers with limited time. They're also conveniently open seven days a week. The best market for fine curios and antiques is in the exclusive leafy neighborhood of Sundar Nagar. In addition to the shops listed here, a few shops on the southern (right-hand) side of the market have collections of old optical instruments.

Art Bunker (✉ 24/2 Hauz Khas Village ☎ 98103–88804 mobile) has lovely picture frames and other gifts in wood, cane, and jute. **Bharany's** (✉ 14 Sundar Nagar Market ☎ 11/2435–8528) sells rare old shawls and wall hangings from all over India. The **Central Cottage Industries Emporium** (✉ Jawahar Vyapar Bhavan, Janpath, opposite Imperial Hotel, Connaught Place ☎ 11/2332–6790) has crafts from all over the country. The subterranean **Cottage of Arts & Jewels** (✉ 50 Hauz Khas Village ☎ 11/2696–7418) is a musty jumble of old prints, photos, maps, curios, and junk. **Curio Palace** (✉ 17 Sundar Nagar Market ☎ 11/2435–8929) has an overwhelming array of silver and brass curios, with much of the brass oxidized for an antique look. Among the bizarre, kitschy miscellany at **Friends Oriental Arts** (✉ 15 Sundar Nagar Market ☎ 11/2435–8841) are Kashmiri lacquerware, antique glassware, and old optical instruments. **India Arts Palace** (✉ 33 Sundar Nagar Market ☎ 11/2435–7501) is an absolute hurricane of Indian ephemera, with dangling colored lanterns, Hindu icons, cute animal curios, drawer pulls, and so forth. **La Boutique** (✉ 20 Sundar Nagar Market ☎ 11/2435–0066) pleases the eye with painted wooden items from Rajasthan, plus Hindu and Buddhist icons and other curiosities. **Ladakh Art Gallery** (✉ 10 Sundar Nagar Market ☎ 11/2435–8679) has distinctive silver items and small, tasteful Hindu icons. Exclusive **Natesan's** (✉ 13 Sundar Nagar Market ☎ 11/2435–9320) has elaborate Hindu sculptures in bronze and teak. In Old Delhi, **Shivam Zari Palace** (✉ 2178 Kinari Bazaar ☎ 11/2327–1464) and its neighbors sell inexpensive Hindu wedding paraphernalia such as turbans, fabric-covered boxes, *torans* (auspicious door hangings), tiny brass gods, and shiny bric-a-brac. **Singh Copper & Brass Palace** (✉ 1167 Chah Rahat Gali, near Jama Masjid, Old Delhi ☎ 11/2326–6717) has several dusty floors filled with brass, copper, and wood artifacts. The many **state emporiums** (✉ Baba Kharak Singh Marg, Connaught Place) strung out over three blocks, can keep you busy for hours: the Kashmir store specializes in carpets, Karnataka in sandalwood, Tripura in bamboo, and so on. **Tula Ram** (✉ Shop 36, Red Fort, Old Delhi ☎ 11/2326–9937 or 98111–04930), in business for five generations, has Delhi's best selection of miniature paintings, plus brass and wooden curios. The future of the Red Fort bazaar currently hangs in the balance, so if you don't find the shop, call the owners to see if they've moved.

Home Furnishings

Anokhi (✉ 9 Khan Market ☎ 11/2462–8029 ✉ Santushti Shopping Complex, Chanakyapuri ☎ 11/2688–3076) is loved for its block-print cotton home furnishings and gifts, including tablecloths, bedcovers, makeup bags, bathrobes, and cloth-bound journals. **FabIndia** (⌗ N-5, 7, and 9 Greater Kailash I ☎ 11/2646–5497) has cheap, attractive cotton table-cloths, placemats, bedcovers, curtains, and rugs. The upscale **Neemrana Shop–Kotwara Studios** (⌗ 12 Khan Market, middle lane, upper fl. ☎ 11/2462–0262) has some beautiful India-inspired women's clothing, men's kurtas, and household gifts at Western prices. **Noor Jehan** (⌗ Santushti Shopping Complex, Chanakyapuri ☎ 11/2611–2971) is all about color, with blinding combinations of jewel tones on silk pillow covers, bed-spreads, handbags, and dupattas.

Jewelry

India consumes more gold annually than any other country in the world, mainly because gold is an essential part of a bride's trousseau. With Delhi's upper middle class spending ever more money, and now chasing such Western fancies as diamonds and platinum, jewelry is big business here. The flashiest jewelry stores are clustered in South Ex-tension, Greater Kailash I, and Connaught Place, offset by a handful of older shops in Sundar Nagar. Indian gold is 22-karat, and some West-erners tend to find its bright-yellow tone a bit garish. For a gold In-dian piece in a subtler antique style, stroll through the market in Sundar Nagar. Hit the glitzier stores for the princess look. Indian jewelers as a group have been accused of adulterating their gold, but alas, you as a consumer will have no way to determine the content of each piece. Old Delhi is packed with jewelry and curio shops, though you have to search harder for fine designs. Stroll Dariba Kalan for the best selec-tion of silver and gold.

Aakaar (⌗ 5-L Shahpur Jat ☎ 11/2649–7632) is hard to find—enter from Khel Gaon Marg and park near the electricity plant behind Siri Fort—but its arty silver baubles are hard to resist. **Bharany's** (⌗ 14 Sun-dar Nagar Market ☎ 11/2435–8528) has traditional gold earrings and beaded necklaces in muted colors and styles. **Cottage Gallery** (⌗ Claridges Hotel, 12 Aurangzeb Rd. ☎ 11/2301–4658), in business for more than 30 years, has necklaces, bracelets, and earrings, includ-ing some antiques. **Ethnic Silver** (⌗ 9A Hauz Khas Village ☎ 11/2696–9637) has supremely elegant pieces, especially earrings, and is open daily till 9 PM. **Hazoorilal** (⌗ M-44 Greater Kailash I ☎ 11/2646–0567) has relatively modern designs. **Ivory Mart** (⌗ F-22 Con-naught Pl. ☎ 11/2331–0197) has a huge selection of smashing neck-laces in updated traditional styles. Reproductions of antique *kundan* jewelry, in which several gems are set in a gold-outlined design, are a specialty. **Lotus Eaters** (⌗ Santushti Shopping Complex ☎ 11/2688–2264) has interesting chunky silver and a few gold pieces, all very expensive. **Mehrasons** (⌗ E-1 South Ext. II ☎ 11/2625–3138) is a bit of a factory—service is surly, but the selection is immense. **Multan Enamel Mart** (⌗ No. 246–247 Dariba Kalan, Old Delhi ☎ 11/2325–5877) sells old and new silver jewelry and curios by weight. **Roopchand** (⌗ C-13 Connaught Pl. ☎ 11/2341–1709) has some eye-popping regal pieces in antique styles. **The Studio** (⌗ 4 Sundar Nagar Market ☎ 11/2435–9360) has beauti-ful silver and gold jewelry, especially necklaces, in tasteful traditional styles, including gemstone wedding sets.

Music

South Delhi is best for discriminating music lovers. **Dua** (✉ F-27/2 Connaught Pl. ☎ 11/2335–4283) is a hole-in-the-wall with a small but representative selection of Indian music. **Mercury** (✉ 20 Khan Market) looks ordinary but is strong on Indian classical music and ghazals (Urdu-language love songs). **The Music Shop** (✉ 18AB Khan Market ☎ 11/2461–8464) has a good selection of Bollywood, Bombay lounge, Indian classical, and Western rock music and a helpful staff. **Music Street** (✉ B-29 Connaught Pl. ☎ 11/2332–1171) has mostly Hindi-film pop and DVDs. Delhi's largest music store is **Music World** (✉ Ansal Plaza, Khel Gaon Marg, near South Extension II ☎ 11/2625–0411), where uniformed youngsters help you find your heart's desire in any category, Indian or international.

Tea & Coffee

Scruffy but friendly **Mittal** (✉ 12 Sundar Nagar Market ☎ 11/2435–8588 ✉ 8A Lodi Colony Market ☎ 11/2461–5709) is stuffed to the ceiling with Indian teas, herbs, and spices. **Regalia** (✉ 12 Sundar Nagar Market ☎ 11/2435–0115), next door to Mittal, sells fine teas and tea paraphernalia.

DELHI A TO Z

To research prices, get advice from other travelers, and book travel arrangements, visit www.fodors.com.

AIR TRAVEL

CARRIERS   International airlines fly into Indira Gandhi International Airport (⇨ Air Travel *in* Smart Travel Tips). Most flights from the West arrive close to midnight.

On domestic routes, the top private carriers are Jet Airways and Sahara Airlines. Indian Airlines is the national carrier.

🔢 **Domestic Airlines Indian Airlines** ☎ 11/2462–0566 or 11/2331–0517. **Jet Airways** ✉ N-40 Connaught Pl. ☎ 11/5164–1414. **Sahara Airlines** ✉ N-41 Connaught Pl. ☎ 11/2331–0860 or 11/2332–3695.

AIRPORTS & TRANSFERS

Delhi's two airports are close together, about 23 km (14 mi) southwest of Connaught Place. International flights use Indira Gandhi International Airport, whereas domestic flights use Palam Airport. (Just tell your taxi driver you're going to the "international" or "domestic" airport.) Palam has two terminals, but they're far apart and your driver isn't likely to know which one you need—so when you buy or reconfirm a domestic ticket, *find out which terminal to use.*

The trip between either airport and Delhi itself should take about 30 minutes if you arrive before 9 AM or after 8 PM. During the day, traffic can increase the time to an hour. Every major hotel provides airport transfers for Rs. 500–Rs. 1,000, depending on the hotel's location.

Taking a cab is the easiest way to reach your hotel. A taxi from the international airport to the city center should cost Rs. 250–Rs. 300; from the domestic airport, Rs. 200–Rs. 250. To avoid being overcharged, use the prepaid taxi service in either airport, run by the Delhi Traffic Police from a counter near the exit. Unfortunately, hucksters have set up similar services, so ignore the men shouting at you and press on toward the door. In the domestic airport, the counter is just inside the exit; at the international airport, leave the building altogether and use the outdoor counter with the yellow sign. Your destination determines the fare, to which a small fee for each piece of luggage is added. Pay in advance at the counter, then take the receipt and exit. When you get outside, people might try to help you with your luggage; ignore them, and make sure they do not touch your things. Wheel your luggage down the ramp toward the black taxis with yellow tops, at which point the drivers will appear. If your receipt contains a taxi number, use that cab; if not, the drivers will decide among themselves who should take you. Tell the driver where you're going, and hold on to the receipt until you arrive. Tips are not expected.

Be aware that people at the airports, and even at hotel-reservation counters, may try to trick you into booking a hotel room by claiming that your prior reservation is invalid. Ignore them. If you do need a room, go to the Government of India Tourist Office counter.

BUS TRAVEL WITHIN DELHI
Avoid public buses, which are filthy, crowded, unpleasant for women, and notoriously dangerous to pedestrians—stay far away from them generally.

CARS & DRIVERS
Driving is not recommended for newcomers to India, as traffic takes highly unfamiliar forms here. If you're not on a tight budget, let an experienced driver take you around Delhi and outside town. Cars and drivers are available for half a day (four hours, 40 km [24 mi]) at about Rs. 350 or a full day (eight hours, 80 km [50 mi]) at about Rs. 700. Ask about different prices for different cars. The cheapest car is usually an Ambassador without air-conditioning; newer, more comfortable cars cost more.

For out-of-town journeys, you'll pay upward of Rs. 3,000 per day for an air-conditioned car with an English-speaking driver, based on mileage and hours. If you're staying in a deluxe hotel, note that arranging a car through the travel desk costs significantly more than arranging one yourself through a travel agent, which is easy to do.

EMBASSIES
The consular-service branch of each embassy is open weekdays from roughly 8:30 to 1 and 2 to 5. Call to confirm hours before you go.

🚩 Australia **Australian High Commission** ✉ 1/50G Shanti Path, Chanakyapuri ☎ 11/2688-8223.

🚩 Canada **Canadian High Commission** ✉ 7/8 Shanti Path, Chanakyapuri ☎ 11/5178-2000.

🚩 New Zealand **New Zealand High Commission** ✉ 50N Nyaya Marg, Chanakyapuri ☎ 11/2688-3170.

🔖 United Kingdom **British High Commission** ⊠ Shanti Path, Chanakyapuri ☎ 11/2687–2161.
🔖 United States **United States Embassy** ⊠ Shanti Path, Chanakyapuri ☎ 11/2419–8000.

EMERGENCIES

For life-threatening conditions go to Indraprastha Apollo Hospital, Delhi's premier private hospital, southeast of town. From there, you can call Meera Rescue if international evacuation is necessary. Whatever happens, *do not* go to a government hospital. In a grave emergency, contact your embassy.

Although not equipped for trauma, the Max Medcentre—in conjunction with Harvard Medical International, one of India's major pharmaceutical companies—runs a first-rate 24-hour clinic. Many of the physicians are American-trained; the equipment, including such high-tech items as CAT scans, is imported; and there's a 24-hour pharmacy on-site. The East–West Medical Centre is also a great resource for travelers, with ambulance service and regional evacuation, though it has no pharmacy. Most hotels have physicians on call.

For dental problems contact Dr. Siddhartha Mehta or Dr. Poonam Batra, who look after many in Delhi's expatriate community.
🔖 Medical Care **East-West Medical Centre** ⊠ B-28 Greater Kailash I ☎ 11/2629–3701, 11/2629–3702, 11/2462–3738, 11/2464–1494, 11/2469–9229, 11/2469–0429, or 11/2469–8865 ⊕ www.eastwestrescue.com. **Indraprastha Apollo Hospital** ⊠ Sarita Vihar, Delhi-Mathura Rd. ☎ 11/2692–5801 or 11/2692–5858 ⊕ www.apollohospdelhi.com. **Max Medcentre** ⊠ N-110 Panchsheel Park ☎ 11/2649–9870. **Meera Rescue** ⊠ 112 Jor Bagh ☎ 11/2469–3508 or 11/2465–3170.
🔖 Dentists **Siddhartha Mehta** ⊠ 41 Khan Market ☎ 11/2461–5914. **Poonam Batra** ⊠ B4/54 Safdarjung Enclave ☎ 11/2616–5173.
🔖 24-Hour Pharmacies **New Delhi Medicos** ⊠ RML Hospital, back side, Connaught Pl. ☎ 11/2334–7151. **Max Medcentre** ⊠ N-110 Panchsheel Park ☎ 11/2649–9870.

MAIL & SHIPPING

One centrally located post office is on the roundabout just southwest of Connaught Place; another is the Eastern Court Post Office on Janpath. Hotels have mailing facilities, but if you really want your postcards to reach their destinations, go to a post office and have them postmarked in front of you.
🔖 Post Offices **Main Post Office** ⊠ Baba Kharak Singh Marg at Ashoka Rd., Connaught Pl. **Eastern Court Post Office** ⊠ 11 Eastern Court, Janpath, Connaught Place.

MONEY

ATMS ATMs are sprouting like mushrooms in India. Machines on the Cirrus and NYCE networks can now be found in every major market in Delhi, including Connaught Place, Khan Market, Defence Colony, Greater Kailash, Basant Lok, and so forth. Your hotel can point you to the closest one. The AmEx machine is for cardholders only.
🔖 Cash Machines **American Express** ⊠ A-Block, Connaught Place. **ANZ Grindlays Bank** ⊠ E-Block, Connaught Place. **Bank of America** ⊠ 16 DCM Bldg., Barakhamba Rd., Connaught Place. **Citibank** ⊠ Jeevan Bharati Bldg., Outer Circle, Connaught Place;

✉ Archana Shopping Centre, W-Block, Greater Kailash I ✉ New Delhi Railway Station, back side, near Platform 12. **HSBC** ✉ Khan Market.

CURRENCY EXCHANGE Most hotels have foreign-exchange facilities for their guests and will cash traveler's checks with twice the speed and half the hassle of banks, albeit at inferior rates. The Central Bank of India in the Ashok Hotel is open 24 hours (except national holidays), but hours for the other banks vary; the Bank of America cashes traveler's checks only weekdays 10 to 2 and Saturday 10 to noon. Note that American Express and Thomas Cook cash only their own traveler's checks.

If you want to change money at the international airport, be sure to do it at the Bank of India counter—on the left as you exit Immigration, *before* you go through Customs. Thomas Cook runs a 24-hour exchange booth at the back side of New Delhi Railway Station, near Platform 12. 📋 **Exchange Services American Express** ✉ Wenger House, A-Block, Connaught Place ☎ 11/2371-2513 or 11/2332-4119. **Thomas Cook** ✉ Imperial Hotel, Janpath, Connaught Place ☎ 11/5111-6328 ✉ International Trade Tower, 717-718 Nehru Pl., 7th fl. ☎ 11/2646-7484 ✉ New Delhi Railway Station, back side, near Platform 12 ☎ No phone. 📋 **Banks Central Bank of India** ✉ Ashok Hotel, Chanakyapuri ☎ 11/2611-0101 Ext. 2584. **Bank of America** ✉ 16 DCM Bldg., Barakhamba Rd., Connaught Place ☎ 11/2372-2332. **Citibank** ✉ Jeevan Bharati Bldg., Connaught Place ☎ 11/2371-4211.

TAXIS & RICKSHAWS
Apart from a hired car, the best way to get around New Delhi is by taxi. Black-and-yellow metered taxis are available at every major hotel and at taxi stands in every shopping area and residential neighborhood and shopping area, and most drivers speak a little English. Tell the driver where you want to go and *make sure he turns on the meter* before you set off. If he insists the meter is broken, get out of the car and find another cab. Most taxi drivers are honest, so it's not worth dealing with one who isn't.

Three-wheeled auto-rickshaws, known locally as "autos," are half the price of taxis and roughly half as comfortable—except in summer, when the open-air breeze keeps you cool while taxis trap the heat horrendously. The problem is that auto drivers refuse to use their meters (here they really are broken, as the drivers deliberately break them), and if you look even remotely new to Delhi they will quote absurdly high fares. A trip around the corner costs Rs. 15; most trips cost Rs. 30–Rs. 60. A very long trip from one end of Delhi to the other might cost Rs. 90; under no circumstances pay more than that. Try to have exact change, as many drivers will claim to have none, and discussion is difficult as most do not speak English.

In Old Delhi, you can still hire a cycle-rickshaw to cruise Chandni Chowk, explore the maze of narrow lanes, and get from one sight to the next. A short one-way trip costs Rs. 15; work out a higher fare, perhaps Rs. 100, if you want to ride around for an hour. Don't bargain too aggressively—these guys pedal hard for a living, and many are kindly old gentlemen.

TRAIN TRAVEL
Delhi's main train stations are New Delhi Railway Station, Delhi Railway Station (usually called Old Delhi Railway Station), and Hazrat Niza-

muddin. The name of the station you need is printed on your ticket; if you can't find it or read it, check with someone in your hotel to be absolutely sure. New Delhi station can be particularly chaotic and consumer-unfriendly, so keep your wits about you.

For information and tickets, try to save time and energy by using your hotel's travel desk or a travel agent. Otherwise, you must present yourself at the International Tourist Bureau on the upper floor of New Delhi station, open Monday through Saturday from 8 to 8 and Sunday from 8 to 2 for the use of foreigners with tourist visas only. Unless you've saved the encashment slip from a recent currency exchange, you must purchase tickets in U.S. dollars or pounds sterling. If you don't have an encashment slip *or* dollars or pounds, you can purchase a ticket in rupees at the general ticket counter, open daily 9:30 to 8 on the ground floor, but this can be a long and complicated process. Before you board any train, you must have a confirmed ticket and a reservation, including a reservation for your sleeping berth if you're traveling overnight (⇨ Rail Travel *in* Smart Travel Tips). When you arrive at the train for your journey, find your car—the coach number is printed on the ticket—and then find your name on the printout posted on that car.

Upon arrival in Delhi, if hotel touts approach you at the station to offer you a room or claim that your hotel is closed or full, ignore them.

Train Information International Tourist Bureau ⊠ New Delhi Railway Station, 1st fl.

TRAVEL AGENTS & TOURS
Travel agencies offer varying rates for cars and drivers, tours, excursions, and even hotel rooms, so shop around, and use only government-recognized agents (ask to see a license if necessary). RBS Travels offers extremely competitive rates, has a huge fleet of cars, and is open 24 hours. Ashok Travel and Tours is open every evening until 9 in all Ashok hotels. American Express has travel services for card members only.

Travel Agencies American Express ⊠ A-1 Hamilton House, inner circle, Connaught Place ☎ 11/2331-1763. **Ashok Travel and Tours** ⊠ L-1 Connaught Pl. ☎ 11/2341-2336 or-5331. **Cox and Kings** ⊠ Indira Palace, H-16 Connaught Pl. ☎ 11/2373-6031. **RBS Travels** ⊠ Shop A-1, Connaught Palace Hotel, 37 Shaheed Bhagat Singh Marg, Connaught Place ☎ 11/2336-4603 or-4952. **Sita Travels** ⊠ F-12 Connaught Pl. ☎ 11/2331-1122 or-1133. **Thomas Cook** ⊠ Imperial Hotel, Janpath, Connaught Place ☎ 11/5111-6328.

VISITOR INFORMATION
The Government of India Tourist Office south of Connaught Place is open weekdays 9 to 6 and Saturday 9 to 2, but it doesn't have anything a decent hotel can't offer. Its airport counters are open for major flight arrivals, and its train-station counters are open 24 hours.

New Delhi Government of India Tourist Office ⊠ 88 Janpath, Connaught Place ☎ 11/2332-0005.

NORTH CENTRAL INDIA

3

TAKE A RITUAL BATH AT DAWN
at Dashashvamedh Ghat in Varanasi ⇨*p.166*

RELAX IN MOGHUL OPULENCE
at Agra's Oberoi Amarvilas resort ⇨*p.135*

SEE THE SUN RISE OVER THE TAJ MAHAL
then return at sunset
for a different perspective ⇨*p.131*

DINE UNDER THE (FAUX) STARS
at the Mughal Room in Agra ⇨*p.134*

FIND YOUR INNER PEACE
at Sanchi, a Buddhist site near Bhopal ⇨*p.160*

By Candice
Gianetti, Gaye
Facer, Andy
McCord, Smita
Patel, and
Vikram Singh

ANCHORED BY AGRA, KHAJURAHO, AND VARANASI, this section of the traveler's trail heads southeast of Delhi into the state of Uttar Pradesh, detouring into Madhya Pradesh and Bihar. This Hindi heartland has long held the balance of power in North India, from the ancient Gupta kingdoms through the Moghuls and the British Raj to the present day. Sometimes disparaged as the Cow Belt, North Central India has often been slow to advance economically, but it remains a vital part of India's heritage and contemporary culture.

Agra was a seat of Moghul power. Dominated by Muslim influences in culture, art, architecture, and cuisine—the city is a testament to the beauty and grandeur of Moghul aesthetics, most notably in the form of the Taj Mahal, but also some exquisite smaller Muslim tombs and monuments. Today Agra, in Uttar Pradesh, is dirty and crowded, and the spectacular Taj Mahal is being damaged by air pollution, and the nearby Moghul ghost town of Fatehpur Sikri is being choked by commercial encroachments. Still, the courts have stepped in with far-reaching orders that should go a long way toward cleaning up the urban environment, and in Agra, at least, efforts have been in place since the late 1990s to protect India's most enduring symbol.

Southeast of Agra, in the northern part of Madhya Pradesh, the sleepy village of Khajuraho predates the Moghuls. Khajuraho was founded at the end of the classical age of Hindu civilization—its stunning temples celebrate an eroticized Hinduism that flourished when Hindu kings adopted the Tantric religion. Excavations here have also uncovered a previously unknown complex of Buddhist temples.

In many ways, Varanasi, in southwestern Uttar Pradesh, is the antithesis of Khajuraho. The holiest city in Hinduism and one of the oldest continuously inhabited cities in the world, Varanasi teems with pilgrims, hospice patients, ascetics, priests, Hindu pundits, and worldly citizens of many religions. Unlike those of Khajuraho, Varanasi's temples are squeezed into the city itself, and the *ghats* (wide stone stairways leading down to the Ganges) are both key religious sites and secular promenades.

The popular Agra–Khajuraho–Varanasi route has plenty of worthwhile arteries. From Agra, it's an hour's drive southwest to Fatehpur Sikri and 30 minutes more to Keoladeo Ghana National Park—a bird sanctuary in Bharatpur, across the Rajasthan border. A separate day trip takes you from Agra to the Moghul-influenced Hindu provincial capital at Gwalior. The magical town of Orchha, a two-hour drive southeast of Gwalior toward Khajuraho, is riddled with 16th- and 17th-century ruins built by the Hindu Bundela rulers, including underground chambers and passageways. Buddha preached his first sermon in Sarnath, just outside Varanasi; superb sculpture and the peaceful resonance of stupas and monastery ruins at Sanchi draw Buddhists from all over Asia; and the international Buddhist center of Bodhgaya is east of Varanasi in the state of Bihar. Lucknow, capital of Uttar Pradesh, was once the seat of an elegant Muslim province on a northern route between Varanasi and Delhi.

Exploring North Central India

Agra and Varanasi are at opposite ends of India's largest state, Uttar Pradesh. Both lie on the Gangetic plain, and the countryside around each is similar: a dry landscape planted with sugarcane, mustard, and wheat in winter and inhabited by poor peasants and well-off landowners. The monsoon hits harder to the east, around Varanasi, so the terrain there is a little more lush. The Yamuna River—backdrop to the Taj Mahal—joins the Ganges at Allahabad, about 161 km (100 mi) west of Varanasi. Khajuraho has a more dramatic setting, at the edge of the hills and ravines that separate the northern plains south of the Vindhya hills from the Deccan plateau. This area, called the Bundelkhand, has been notorious since British times for harboring *dacoits* (highway robbers), including Phoolan Devi, the "Bandit Queen," who held a seat in Parliament until she was assassinated in 2001; yet the area is pacific from day to day.

Numbers in the text correspond to numbers in the margin and on the North Central India map.

About the Restaurants

Restaurants on this route generally serve kababs and other grilled meats, *birianis* (rice casseroles), and the rich almond- and-saffron-scented concoctions of Mughlai cuisine. Most hotels offer a menu of Indian (with choices from various regions), Continental, Chinese (sort of), and sometimes Thai or Japanese dishes; Khajuraho has several Italian restaurants. Small places in villages along the way have simple local vegetarian dishes that are often delicious and cheap. When watching pennies, look for a South Indian joint, where a delicious spiced-potato-filled *dosa* (crisp rice crêpe) will fill you up for a dollar or less and is tremendously satisfying. Most restaurants are open from 7 to 10 for breakfast, noon to 3 for lunch, and 7:30 to 11 for dinner; hotels often have a 24-hour or all-day coffee shop.

Hotels in Agra serve particularly good Mughlai dishes. Varanasi, with its abundant food for the soul, is extremely light on restaurants—orthodox Hindus do not eat meat and prefer to keep food preparation a family affair. Out of respect, any spot near the holy river will be "pure vegetarian," meaning no onion, garlic, or spices. However, the city is known for its sweets, mostly based on such distillations of milk and cream, such as *lavan lata,* a kind of supercharged baklava. Lucknow, too, is known for excellent sweets (and without the swarms of flies that swirl around the wares in Varanasi's famous shops), as well as for Avadhi cuisine, a very refined style of cooking, characterized by subtle blending of flavors and aromas, which was developed under the luxury-loving nawabs of Avadh.

WHAT IT COSTS In Rupees				
$$$$	**$$$**	**$$**	**$**	**¢**
IN AGRA AND VARANASI				
AT DINNER over 500	400–500	300–400	150–300	under 150
OUTSIDE AGRA AND VARANASI				
over 350	250–350	150–250	100–150	under 150

Restaurant prices are for an entrée plus dal, rice, and a veg/non-veg dish.

About the Hotels

India's main hotel groups are represented in this region, providing increased amenities and efficiency at increasing prices. More and more good, air-conditioned hotels cater to India's upper-middle class, but they're often quite generic. Outside the old British cantonment areas, where most top hotels are clustered, and often closer to the center of town, you'll find clean, well-run guest houses and small Heritage Hotels. Unless otherwise noted, all hotels listed have air-conditioning and private baths.

WHAT IT COSTS In Rupees				
$$$$	**$$$**	**$$**	**$**	**¢**
IN AGRA AND VARANASI				
FOR 2 PEOPLE over 8,000	6,000–8,000	4,000–6,000	2,000–4,000	under 2,000
OUTSIDE AGRA AND VARANASI				
over 4,000	3,000–4,000	2,000–3,000	1,000–2,000	under 1,000

Prices are for a standard double room in high season, excluding up to 20% tax.

Timing

Nowhere in India is the common advice to come between October and March more crucial. This region is hot, and the sights in Agra and Khajuraho involve hours in the sun. Early October in Bhopal is warm but still pleasant, and because there are fewer tourists you'll be better able to enjoy the peaceful surroundings. December and January are ideal, if crowded, but it can get chilly in the evening in late December and January. The weather from early February to mid-March is wonderfully temperate. The mid-monsoon period (late July through early August) is not an unreasonable alternative: temperatures are usually in the 70s and 80s, downpours are intermittent, and hotel rates are significantly lower. Orchha, in fact, is at its best during the monsoon, when the river is in full flow and the surrounding scrubland is green.

AGRA & ENVIRONS

The journey from Delhi to Agra follows the Grand Trunk Road—a royal route established by India's Moghul emperors in the 16th and 17th centuries, when their capital alternated between Delhi, Agra, and Lahore (now in Pakistan). If you get an early start, you can see Agra's sights in

Agra, Khajuraho, and Varanasi are well connected by air. Hire a car if you're supremely adventuresome, but know that traffic is heavy between Agra and Delhi. Avoid driving at night. Train service is reliable and comfortable among Delhi, Agra, Gwalior, and Bhopal, and between Delhi and Varanasi. Between Agra and Khajuraho, a morning train runs as far as Jhansi, with Orchha just a few miles away and a pleasant overnight stop. The scenic drive on to Khajuraho takes about four hours. From Khajuraho to Varanasi the rail and road connection is more complicated; you may prefer the afternoon plane. Agra makes a convenient starting point for this region: from there you can fly to Khajuraho (35 minutes), then Varanasi (40 minutes), then back to Delhi. If you fly from point to point, aim for at least five days in this region; if you stick to land travel, allow at least a week.

3

If you have
4 days

If time is limited and you're returning to Delhi, skip either Khajuraho or Varanasi, since plane schedules make it necessary to stay overnight in each place. From Delhi, you can take a morning flight or a train to ⊞ **Agra** and proceed immediately to the Taj Mahal (note: it's closed on Friday) while the morning light lasts. Allow at least an hour to wander the grounds and inspect the fine marblework inside the tomb. After lunch you can visit Agra Fort and Itmad-ud-Daulah's Tomb, a stunning but little-visited gem of Moghul architecture, *or* take a half-day road trip to **Fatehpur Sikri** ⑤. The next morning, fly to ⊞ **Khajuraho** and explore the Western Group of Temples; on your third day you can briefly visit some other temples or the museum before flying to ⊞ **Varanasi** for a late-afternoon boat ride on the Ganges. If you're a serious art lover, consider spending an afternoon at the Bharat Kala Bhavan, on the campus of Banaras Hindu University; returning to town, you can stop at the Durga and Sankat Mochan temples. The Buddhist center of **Sarnath** ㊹ is an easy day trip from Varanasi. The next morning, take a sunrise boat ride to see the ritual bathing and Varanasi's lovely skyline; then visit the main temple area around Kashi Vishvanath, the Golden Temple.

If you have
6 days

Spend two days and nights in ⊞ **Agra,** visiting Agra Fort, **Fatehpur Sikri** ⑤, and Itmad-ud-Daulah's or Akbar's Tomb. If you've had enough urban bustle, head to Keoladeo Ghana National Park at **Bharatpur,** Rajasthan, a half hour from Fatehpur Sikri or a two-hour train ride or drive (55 km [31 mi]) from Agra. Two days in ⊞ **Khajuraho** will allow leisurely exploration of the temples and a trip to the wildlife park at Panna. With two days in ⊞ **Varanasi** you can take at least one boat ride on the Ganges, visit the main temples, tour Ramnagar palace, admire the art in the Bharat Kala Bhavan, and detour to **Sarnath** ㊹.

If you have
8–10 days

If you're coming from Delhi, consider hiring a car for the potentially nerve-wracking three-hour trip to Agra, as driving will allow you to stop at Mathura, with its excellent archaeological museum; the tiny temple town of Vrindavan, where the god Krishna grew up as a cowherd; and Sikandra, site of Akbar's Tomb. Spend two days in ⊞ **Agra.** Then, either take a 40-minute plane ride to ⊞ **Khajuraho,** where you should also spend two days, or opt instead for a two-day road trip, which involves a total of about 10 hours' driving and includes stops at ▣ **Gwalior** ⑥, with its spectacular Hindu fort, and ▣ **Orchha,** ⑦ another seat of Hindu rajas. (From Khajuraho straight to Orchha is about 175 km [109 mi] and takes about 4–5 hours.) To minimize your time on the road, you might arrange through a travel agent for a car to meet your train at Mathura, and perhaps travel from Agra to Gwalior or Orchha by train. Finally, fly from Khajuraho to ▣ **Varanasi** and spend the better part of two days here. The morning of your eighth day, head west toward **Lucknow** ㊺ or east to **Bodhgaya** ㊺ (The latter will lengthen your stay in the region to nine days—to fly out of Bodhgaya, unless you're headed to Calcutta, you'll need to stay the night and drive early the next morning to Patna.) Alternately, you can add two or three days in **Bhopal** ㉚ and **Sanchi** by extending your train journey from Orchha (returning to Jhansi and continuing on the *Shatabdi Express* to Bhopal, or flying direct from Delhi).

one day: turn off the Grand Trunk Road 10 km (6 mi) north of Agra to visit Akbar's Tomb, then move on to Itmad-ud-Daulah's Tomb, the Taj Mahal, and Agra Fort.

Excursions make the trip to Agra more interesting. Many find Akbar's deserted dream city at Fatehpur Sikri as rewarding as the Taj Mahal; a short drive farther, toward Jaipur, brings you to Rajasthan's Keoladeo Ghana National Park, winter home of the Siberian crane. Another day trip takes you to the Moghul-influenced Hindu provincial capital at Gwalior. If you drive on to Khajuraho, Orchha makes an excellent place to spend the night amid temple and palace ruins.

Agra

200 km (124 mi) southeast of Delhi.

Under the Moghul emperor Akbar (1542–1605) and his successors Jahangir (1605–1627) and Shah Jahan (1628–1658), Agra flourished. However, after the reign of Shah Jahan's son Aurangzeb (1658–1707), and the gradual disintegration of the empire, the city passed from one invader to another before the British took charge early in the 19th century. The British, particularly Governor General Lord Curzon (in office 1898–1905), did much to halt and repair the damage inflicted on Agra's forts and palaces by raiders and vandals.

Agra today is crowded and dirty. Although some of the Moghul buildings are irrevocably scarred, the government has taken steps to protect the city's most important site from pollution, closing the streets around the Taj Mahal to gas-fueled vehicles (visitors are ferried from a remote parking lot by battery-powered buses) and relocating small factories and fire-burning shops away from the area. Still, Agra's monuments remain strewn like pearls in ashes, evoking that glorious period in Indian history when Agra was the center of the Moghul empire, and the empire itself was the focus of political, cultural, and artistic evolution.

Opening hours change constantly; inquire in advance at your hotel or the Uttar Pradesh State Tourist Office.

Numbers in the text correspond to numbers in the margin and on the Agra map.

a good tour

If you arrive in Agra late in the day, set out early the next day. Hire a car and driver, and stop first to see the morning light on the **Taj Mahal ❶** ☞. Drive 5 km (3 mi) north—about a 20-minute drive on a congested road—from there to **Itmad-ud-Daulah's Tomb ❷** and then 8 km (5 mi) northwest—about a half-hour drive, with traffic—to **Akbar's Tomb ❸**. From here it's a 12 km (7 mi), or 45-minute, drive northeast to **Agra Fort ❹**, where you'll want to spend an hour or more. If you have time and energy, drive southwest for an hour, for 37 km (23 mi), to **Fatehpur Sikri ❺**. Return to the Taj Mahal to see it at sunset.

Alternately, if you leave Delhi at 5 AM by car, you should reach Sikandra (10 km [6 mi] north of Agra on Grand Trunk Rd.) at 7:30 and can see Akbar's Tomb in less than an hour. From there it's a half-hour drive to Itmad-ud-Daulah's Tomb, another short but delightful visit. A 20-minute drive south will bring you to the Taj Mahal. You can then visit Agra Fort or Fatehpur Sikri in the afternoon and relax by the Taj Mahal at twilight.

TIMING If you try to pack all of Agra's sights into a day that starts in Delhi, you'll have quite a long, tiring day; starting fresh in the morning from Agra will make for a full, but fairly easy day.

What to See

★ ❹ **Agra Fort.** The architecture of this fort—one of the area's 3 World Heritage Sites (and India's 16), along with the Taj Mahal and Fatehpur Sikri, reflects the collective creative brilliance of Akbar, and his son Jahangir and grandson Shah Jahan. The structure was built by Akbar on the site of an earlier fort. As with similar Moghul facilities in Delhi and Lahore, the word "fort" is misleading; the complex, really a fortified palace, contains royal apartments, mosques, assembly halls, and a dungeon—indeed the entire cityscape of an imperial capital. A massive wall 2½km (1½mi) long and 69 feet high surrounds the fort's roughly triangular shape. With the Yamuna River running at its base, the fort was also protected by a moat and another wall, presenting a daunting barrier to anyone hoping to access the treasures within.

The fort's entrance is easily accessible through the Amar Singh Gate. North of this entrance sits the fort's largest private residence, the **Jahangiri Mahal,** built as a harem for Jahangir. (Akbar's own palace, closer to the entrance, is in ruins.) Measuring 250 feet by 300 feet, the Jahangiri Mahal juxtaposes *jarokhas* (balconies) and other elements of Hindu architecture with pointed arches and other Central Asian influences imported by the Moghuls—a mixture foreshadowing the stylistic synthesis that would follow at Fatehpur Sikri. The palace's central court is lined with two-story facades bearing remnants of the rich, gilded decoration that once covered much of the structure. Next to architecture and the arts, Jahangir's greatest loves were wine and his Persian-born wife Nur Jahan, who, failing to persuade him to pay some attention to managing his empire, did it for him, making short work of all rivals. However, this strong-willed woman was unable to consolidate her power after her husband died, and lived out her days in virtual seclusion in Lahore.

After Jahangir's death in 1628, Shah Jahan (whose mother was one of Jahangir's other wives) assumed the throne and started his own buildings inside the fort, often tearing down those built by his father and grandfather in the process. The **Anguri Bagh** (Grape Arbor) shows the outlines of a geometric garden built around delicate water courses and chutes by Shah Jahan. The 1637 **Khas Mahal** (Private Palace) is an early masterpiece of Shah Jahan's craftsmen. The central pavilion, made of white marble, follows the classic Moghul pattern: three arches on each side, five in front, and two turrets rising out of the roof. Of the two flanking pavilions, quarters of Shah Jahan's two daughters, one is of white marble and was supposedly decorated with gold leaf while the other is made of red stone. The arched roofs of all three pavilions are stone translations of the bamboo architecture of Bengal. In one part of the Khas Mahal, a staircase leads down to the palace's "air-conditioned" quarters—cool underground rooms that were used in summer.

The octagonal tower of the **Mussaman Burj** has fine inlay work and a splendid view down the river to the Taj Mahal. This is where Shah Jahan is said to have spent the last seven years of his life, imprisoned by his son Aurangzeb for massive overspending but still able to look out on his greatest monument, the Taj Mahal. On the northeastern end of the Khas Mahal courtyard stands the **Sheesh Mahal** (Palace of Mirrors), built in 1637 as a bath for the private palace and dressing room for the harem. Each of the two chambers contained a bathing tank fed by marble channels.

The emperor received foreign ambassadors and other dignitaries in the **Diwan-i-Khas** (Hall of Private Audience), built by Shah Jahan in 1636–37. Outside, the marble throne terrace holds a pair of black and white thrones. The black throne, carved from a single block of marble, overlooks the Yamuna. The white throne is made of several marble blocks; the inscription indicates that it was used by Shah Jahan, whereas the black throne was his father's seat of power. Both thrones face the **Machhi Bhavan,** an enclosure of fountains and shallow pools, and a number of imperial offices.

To the empire's citizens and to the European emissaries who came to see these powerful monarchs, the most impressive part of the fort was the **Diwan-i-Am** (Hall of Public Audience), set within a large quadrangle. This huge, low structure rests on a 4-foot platform, its nine cusped Moghul arches held aloft by rows of slender supporting pillars. Here the emperor sat and dispensed justice to his subjects.

Northeast of the Diwan-i-Khas is the **Nagina Masjid**, a private mosque raised by Shah Jahan for the women of his harem. Made of white marble and walled in on three sides, it has typical cusped arches, a marble courtyard, and three graceful domes. Nearby is the lovely **Moti Masjid,** a perfectly proportioned pearl mosque built in white marble by Shah Jahan. ⊠ *Yamuna Kinara Rd.* 🖃 *Rs. 300* ☽ *Daily sunrise–sunset.*

3

Dance, Drums, & Art

This region provides ample opportunity to experience Indian classical music and dance. Agra, Khajuraho, Gwalior, and Lucknow host annual festivals that gather the best talents; Khajuraho's includes performances in front of the Western Group of temples. Varanasi, home of Ravi Shankar, also maintains a vibrant local tradition of music and dance and is noted particularly for its *tabla* (drum) players. Many hotels throughout the area offer live classical music in the evening.

The visual arts are strong as well. Khajuraho's archaeological museum displays sculptures that once graced the niches of the town's temples, and its tribal-arts museum has superb folk pieces from all over Madhya Pradesh and Chhattisgarh's Bastar region. The Bharat Kala Bhavan at Banaras Hindu University has superb collections of miniature paintings and locally discovered classical sculpture. The archaeological museum in Mathura, some 56 km (35 mi) northwest of Agra on the road from Delhi, has one of the country's best collections of classical sculpture. Bhopal's Bharat Bhawan has a thoughtfully displayed collection of contemporary and tribal arts.

Festivals

Agra's cultural festival, Taj Mahotsav (10 days in February), and the Khajuraho Festival of Dance (a week between late February and March) are geared primarily to visitors. During Gwalior's Tansen Music Festival (5 nights in November or December), renowned singers come to perform classical ragas near the tomb of the greatest classical singer of them all, Tansen. While the wares at the endless crafts booths from all over India are less than magnificent at the Lucknow Mahotsav (December 1–5; some events begin on November 25), the evening music and dance performances are excellent.

In Varanasi there's a major religious festival practically every week; because the Hindu calendar is based on lunar months, festival dates shift every year, catching up to the solar calendar when a leap month is added every third year. Varanasi's great bathing days, when thousands stream down the ghats into the Ganges, include Makar Sankranti (January), the full moon of the Hindu month Kartik (October or November), and Ganga Dussehra (May or June). Durga Puja (September or October) ends with the city's large Bengali community marching to the river at sunset to immerse large mud-daubed images of the goddess Durga. The month leading up to Dussehra, also in September or October, features nightly reenactments of the epic of Rama in the Ramnagar palace, across the river from Varanasi (some episodes also take place in the city itself).

Buddhists from Tibet and all over Asia celebrate their festivals in Sarnath, Bodhgaya, and Sanchi. Muslim holidays are observed in Bhopal and by Varanasi's large Muslim minority as well as in the more predominantly Muslim cities of Agra and Lucknow.

Shopping

Agra is known for marble inlay, jewelry, and leather; Varanasi, for exquisite silk (particularly brocade) and rug weaving. Lucknow is known for a traditionally white-on-white straight-stitch embroidery style called *chikan*. Everywhere you'll find shops selling Kashmiri pashminas, embroidered shawls, and other attractive goods.

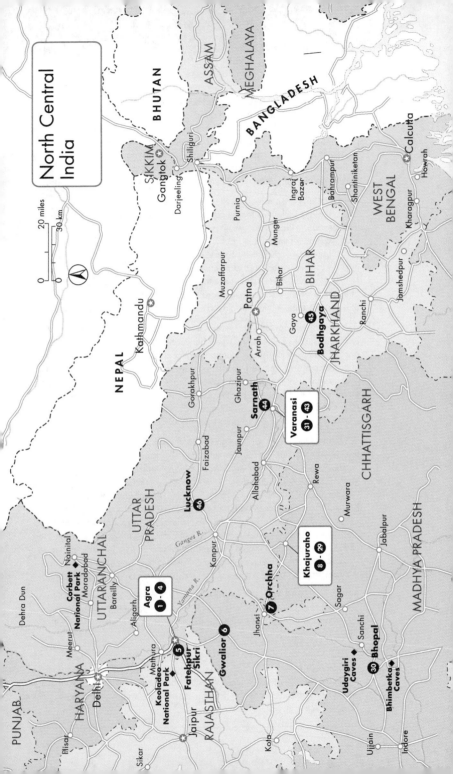

❸ **Akbar's Tomb.** Akbar's resting place was begun by the emperor himself in 1602 and completed after his death by Jahangir. Topped with white marble and flanked by graceful minarets, this mausoleum of rough red sandstone sits in a typical Moghul garden—four quadrants separated by waterways. The garden, unfortunately, is not well tended, and Jat raiders (who invaded Agra after the fall of the Moghul empire) destroyed much of the gold work that once adorned the tomb, though the British partially restored it. In a domed chamber three stories high, the crypt is inscribed with the 99 names of Allah, plus the phrases *Allah-o-Akbar* (God is great) at the head and *Jalla Jalalahu* (Great is His glory) at the foot. You can actually see the tomb's enormous gateway, topped with bright tilework, from the train from Delhi—look out the left window 10 or 15 minutes before the train is due to reach Agra. ⊠ *Sikandra, 10 km (6 mi) north of Agra on Grand Trunk Rd. to Delhi* 🎟 *Rs. 110* ⏱ *Daily 6–5:30.*

★ ❷ **Itmad-ud-Daulah's Tomb.** The empress Nur Jahan (Jahangir's favorite wife) built this small but gorgeous tomb for her father, a Persian nobleman who became Jahangir's chief minister. The monument, one of Agra's loveliest, was supposedly built by workers from Persia. The tomb incorporates a great deal of brown and yellow Persian marble and marks the first use of Persian-style marble inlay in India—both features that would later characterize the style of Shah Jahan. Particularly in its use of intricate marble inlay (known in Italy as *pietra dura*), this building was a precursor of, and very likely an inspiration for, the Taj Mahal. The roof is arched in the style of Bengali terra-cotta temples, and the minarets are octagonal, much broader than the slender cylinders of the Taj Mahal; yet in its fine proportions this mausoleum almost equals that masterpiece. Inside, where the elegant decoration continues, the central chamber holds the tombs of Itmad-ud-Daulah and his wife; other relations are buried in adjacent rooms. Most travelers to Agra never see this place, yet its beauty and tranquillity are extraordinary, and its well-maintained gardens make it a wonderful place to pause and reflect. ⊠ *5 km (3 mi) north of Taj Mahal on left bank of Yamuna River* 🎟 *Rs. 110* ⏱ *Daily sunrise–sunset.*

❶ **Taj Mahal.** The architecture alone has inspired reams of rapture over the

Fodor'sChoice years, but what really makes this marble monument so endearing is its

★ haunting tale of love and loss. Arjuman Banu, the niece of Jahangir's wife Nur Jahan, supposedly captured the heart of the young Shah Jahan the minute he saw her. In 1612, at the age of 21, she married him and became his favorite wife, his Mumtaz Mahal (the Exalted of the Palace) and Mumtazul-Zamani (the Distinguished of the Age). Numerous stories recall this woman's generosity and wisdom, both as a household manager and as an adviser to her beloved husband. She bore 14 children, and it was in childbirth that she died in 1630 while accompanying Shah Jahan on a military campaign. On her deathbed, it is said, she begged the king to build a monument so beautiful that the world would never forget their love. Shattered by her death, legend claims, Shah Jahan locked himself in his private chambers for a month; when he finally emerged, his hair was white. Five months later, a huge procession

Agra Fort **4**

Akbar's
Tomb **3**

Itmad-ud-Daulah's
Tomb **2**

Taj Mahal **1**

brought Mumtaz Mahal's body to Agra, where Shah Jahan began the process of honoring her request.

The shah's chief architect, Ustad Ahmad Lahori, oversaw the construction, which began in 1632. Shah Jahan put an army of 20,000 laborers to work, even building a new village (Taj Ganj, which still stands) to house them as they spent 17 years creating a vast tomb of white marble on the banks of the Yamuna River, visible from Agra Fort. The Taj Mahal was completed on the exact anniversary of Mumtaz Mahal's death. The great emperor spent his last years locked in one of his own creations, gazing, according to the popular story, across the Yamuna at his wife's final resting place.

It's easy to focus on the legend behind this building—as well as the equally undocumented story of Shah Jahan's plan to build a black marble tomb for himself across the Yamuna—yet the Taj Mahal, one of the world's great treasures, speaks for itself. It is both the culmination of and the best introduction to the elaborate aesthetic world that the Moghuls created in India, sometimes at the expense of their political power.

The Taj Mahal stands at the end of a large, four-quartered garden, or *charbagh,* symbolizing paradise, extending about 1,000 feet in each direction from a small central pool. You enter the grounds through a huge sandstone gateway boldly emblazoned with an inlaid Koranic inscription. Ahead, facing the long reflecting pool, the Taj Mahal stands on two bases, one of sandstone and, above it, a marble platform measuring 313 square feet and worked into a chessboard design. A slender marble minaret stands at each corner of the platform, blending so well into the general composition that it's hard to believe each one is 137 feet tall. The minarets are built at a slight tilt away from the tomb so that, in case of an earthquake, they'd fall away from the building. Facing the Taj Mahal from beneath its platform are two majestic sandstone buildings, a mosque on the left and its mirror image (built purely for symmetry) on the right. Behind the tomb, the Yamuna winds along its broad, sandy bed.

The tomb's central archway is deeply recessed, as are the smaller pairs of companion archways along the sides and the beveled corners of the 190-square-foot structure. The Taj Mahal's most extraordinary feature is its onion dome, crowned by a brass finial mounted in a scalloped ornament, which is an inverted Hindu motif of the lotus. The dome uses the Central Asian technique of placing a central inner dome, in this case 81 feet high, inside an outer shell to attain the extraordinary exterior height of 200 feet; between the two is an area nearly the size of the interior hall itself. Raising the dome above the minarets was the builders' great stroke of genius. Large *chattras* (umbrellas), another feature borrowed from Hindu design, balance the dome.

Inside the mausoleum, the changing light creeps softly in through marble screens that have been chiseled like silver filigree. Look closely at the tiny flowers drawn in inlaid semiprecious stones—at the detailed stonework on each petal and leaf. The work is so fine that not even a magnifying glass reveals the tiny breaks between stones, yet a single one-inch flower on the queen's tomb comprises 60 pieces. Shine a flashlight to see the delicate stones' translucence. Directly under the marble dome lie the tombs of Mumtaz Mahal and Shah Jahan, surrounded by a jali screen carved from a single block of marble, with latticework as intricate as lace. In the center of the enclosure, diminishing rectangles lead up to what looks like a coffin; in fact, both Mumtaz Mahal and Shah Jahan are buried in a crypt below these tombs in deference to the Islamic tradition that no one should walk upon their graves. After his death, Shah Jahan was buried next to his wife by his son Aurangzeb, upsetting the perfect symmetry, most likely a cost-cutting measure that forms an ironic postscript to the munificence of Shah Jahan. But it's fitting that the emperor lies in perpetuity next to his favorite wife. Mumtaz Mahal's tomb bears a Persian inscription: "The illustrious sepulcher of Arjuman Banu Begum, called Mumtaz Mahal. God is everlasting, God is sufficient. He knoweth what is concealed and what is manifest. He is merciful and compassionate. Nearer unto him are those who say: Our Lord is God." The emperor's epitaph reads: "The illustrious sepulcher of His Exalted Majesty Shah Jahan, the Valiant King, whose dwelling is in the starry Heaven. He traveled from this transient world to the World of Eternity on the 28th night of the month of Rajab in the year of 1076 of the Hegira [February 1, 1666]."

It's worth making more than one trip to see the Taj Mahal in varying lights (you'll have to bite the bullet and pay the exorbitant fee each time, but it may help to know most of the money goes to the Archaeological Survey of India, which beautifully maintains all of its many sites and museums). In early morning, the pale rays of the sun give the marble a soft pink luster, whereas at sunset the west side of the monument turns lemon yellow, then pumpkin orange. Once the sun goes down, the marble is pure white against a black sky.

The **Taj Mahal Museum** stands near the mosque to the left of the Taj. Though small, it holds Moghul memorabilia and provides some historical background to the Taj, as well as paintings of the famous couple, manuscripts, letters, and a display of precious stones used in the construction of the Taj. ⊠ *Taj Ganj, Taj Rd.* ☎ *562/233–0498* ⌑ *Taj Mahal Rs. 750; museum Rs. 150* ☉ *Taj Mahal Sat.–Thurs. sunrise–sunset; museum Sat.–Thurs. 8–5.*

Where to Stay & Eat

$$$$ ✕ **Esphahan.** Through the Amarvilas' Moghul courtyard with illuminated pools and 64 fountains, then the grand marble lobby, is this intimate den whose decoration celebrates local craftsmanship—from square pillars of alternating red sandstone and white marble to carved wooden screens. Through the glass wall of the display kitchen, watch the chefs prepare breads and meats in the tandoori ovens, then make your selections from the Indian menu with an emphasis on Avadhi cuisine (from the Lucknow area). Specialties include *Esphahani raan,* leg of lamb marinated for 24 hours, roasted for 6 to 8 more, deboned, then cooked in the tandoor until it's crisp. Another good choice: tiger prawns marinated in citrus yogurt. Live instrumental music adds to the mood. ⊠ *Oberoi Amarvilas, Taj East Gate Rd.* ☎ *562/223–1515* ⊟ *AE, DC, MC, V.*

★ **$$$$** ✕ **Mughal Room.** A ceiling of faux twinkling stars floats over this top-floor restaurant, done in rich reds, with brass trays hanging on walls and tables set with silver goblets. During daylight hours, the panoramic view from a wall of windows takes in both the Taj Mahal and the fort—the cream of Agra in one fell swoop. At night live *ghazals* (Urdu-language love songs) set the mood for Mughlai cuisine. At a display window, a chef at a tandoori oven makes delicious *bajari tikka,* boneless chicken cubes marinated with cream and yogurt, coated with spices, and topped with cashews; and *kabuli naan,* bread stuffed with dried fruits and cheese and sprinkled with black cumin seeds. ⊠ *Clarks Shiraz, 54 Taj Rd.* ☎ *562/222–6121 to 32* ⊟ *AE, DC, MC, V.*

★ **$$$–$$$$** ✕ **Jhankar.** Rajeev Bansal, chef at this restaurant at the Taj Mahal, which occupies an elegant, airy space open to the lobby, cooks up excellent dishes such as the house specialty, *aloo dum chutneywale* potatoes with dried fruits and herbs simmered in a mint and coriander sauce. Also terrific is the Agra delicacy *magazi murgh korma,* chicken in yogurt, cashews, and poppy seeds, garnished with rose petals and melon seeds. Flavors are subtle and distinct; many herbs and vegetables come from the kitchen garden. ⊠ *Taj-View, Taj Ganj, Fatehabad Rd.* ☎ *562/223–2400 to 18* ⊟ *AE, DC, MC, V.*

$$$–$$$$ ✕ **Nauratna.** Named for the Nine Jewels (ministers) of Akbar's court, this intimate restaurant serves Mughlai cuisine, similar to what Akbar himself ate. Try a biriani, the quintessential Mughlai rice-and-meat dish, or one of the excellent kababs. In the evening there's live ghazal-singing. ☒ *WelcomHotel Mughal Sheraton, Taj Ganj, Fatehabad Rd.* ☎ *562/233–1701* ▭ *AE, DC, MC, V.*

★ ¢ ✕ **Dasaprakash.** The light and spicy South Indian vegetarian dishes served here are a nice change from Agra's usual rich Mughlai fare. Though the Formica tables and fake Tiffany lamps evoke an American pizza joint, the food is excellent and service is fast. The *thali* (a sampler combination plate) may include crisp *aplam* (fried wafers) and *rasam* (thin, spicy lentil soup), as well as fluffy *idlis* (steamed rice cakes) and crisp *dosas* (rice crêpes). Also available are an unusual selection of fresh juices and a great dessert menu with ice creams and floats. (There's another, unaffiliated Dasaprakash in the city, but locals prefer this one.) ☒ *1 Meher Cinema Complex, Gwalior Rd., 5 min from Taj Mahal, near Hotel Agra Ashok* ☎ *562/226–0269 or 562/236–3368* ▭ *No credit cards.*

$$$$ 🏨 **Oberoi Amarvilas.** One of India's best resorts brings to life the opu-
Fodor'sChoice lent lifestyle of the Moghul emperors. At this Moorish fantasy of sand-
★ stone arches and glistening pools, each spacious room—understatedly elegant, with teak floors and rich fabrics—has a breathtaking view of the Taj Mahal over a seaof green treetops. Agra's culture and heritage are celebrated in details taken from the Taj Mahal, from the colonnade with its floral frescoes to the guest rooms' marble-inlay tables. Standards of service from staff, including your own butler, are high. If you don't stay here, come to dine, or stop at the bar for a drink and a terrace view of the Taj Mahal and, in the evening, the Rajasthani dancers performing on the roof of the pool pavilion. ☒ *Taj East Gate Rd., 282001* ☎ *562/ 223–1515 or 800/562–3764* 🖷 *562/223–1516* ⊕ *www.oberoihotels.com* ⟿ *106 rooms, 7 suites* ᕦ *2 restaurants, room service, IDD phones, in-room data ports, in-room safes, minibars, DVD players, cable TV, pool, health club, hair salon, spa, bar, lounge, shops, baby-sitting, dry cleaning, laundry service, concierge, business services, meeting rooms, travel services* ▭ *AE, DC, MC, V* ¶⊙¶ *EP.*

$$ 🏨 **Clarks Shiraz.** Extensive renovations on this 1961 property, set on 8 acres with extensive gardens, took place in 2003 and 2004, and include an all-deluxe-room 1992 Tower Wing. The comfortable rooms have subdued contemporary furnishings. There are many Taj Mahal–facing rooms; the best are from the Taj Mahal end of the tower's top floors. There's an excellent restaurant, and a post office and five travel agencies, from Lufthansa to Indian Airlines, are on site; an astrologer visits daily. ☒ *54 Taj Rd., 282001* ☎ *562/222–6121 to 32* 🖷 *562/222–6128* ⊕ *www.hotelclarksshiraz.com* ⟿ *235 rooms, 2 suites* ᕦ *Restaurant, coffee shop, dining room, room service, IDD phones, minibars, cable TV, VCRs, miniature golf, pool, health club, hair salon, croquet, bar, recreation room, shops, baby-sitting, Internet, business services, conference center, travel services, no-smoking rooms* ▭ *AE, DC, MC, V* ¶⊙¶ *EP.*

★ **$$**   🏨 **Trident Hilton Agra.** Built around a lovely garden courtyard with fountains, water spilling over rocks, a soothing expanse of green lawn, and a pool, this place is a real oasis in Agra. The spacious rooms are tastefully done in soft greens and browns, with terra-cotta-like tile floors, large desk areas, and coffeemakers; rooms facing the courtyard have the best views. A thoughtful feature—rare in India—is two handicap-accessible rooms. Live Indian classical music accompanies dinner at the poolside barbecue. There's an Avis counter on-site. ⊠ *Tajnagri Scheme, Fatehabad Rd., 282001* ☎ *562/233–1818 or 800/774–1500* 🖷 *562/233–1812* ⊕ *www.hilton.com* ➳ *136 rooms, 2 suites* ♨ *Restaurant, room service, in-room data ports, in-room safes, cable TV, pool, hair salon, badminton, volleyball, bar, shops, baby-sitting, playground, dry cleaning, laundry service, travel services, no-smoking rooms* ▤ *AE, DC, MC, V* ◎ *EP.*

★ **$–$$** 🏠 **WelcomHotel Mughal Sheraton.** This complex of brick and marble is one of Agra's class acts, though its size can be overwhelming—there's a lot of walking between one section and another. Within the 36 acres of lush gardens there's even a miniature lake. Most of the big, bright rooms have modern furnishings, with marble-top desks and headboards upholstered in a light floral-print fabric—but you can request an Indian-style room. Chamber of Emperors deluxe rooms have lots of green and cream-color marble, light woods, and silky deep-green and gold spreads. Forgetting nothing, the hotel has a full activities program, including Saturday-night dancing to a DJ, and its own astrologer. There's also a jogging track. ⊠ *Taj Ganj, Fatehabad Rd., 282001* ☎ *562/233–1701* 🖷 *562/233–1730* ⊕ *www.welcomgroup.com* ➳ *274 rooms, 5 suites* ♨ *3 restaurants, coffee shop, room service, minibars, cable TV, miniature golf, 2 tennis courts, pool, boating, croquet, lounge, shops, baby-sitting, playground, dry cleaning, laundry service, business services, convention center, travel services, no-smoking rooms* ▤ *AE, DC, MC, V* ◎ *EP.*

$ 🏠 **Taj-View.** Many rooms at this fine Taj-group hotel do, in fact, have good views of the Taj Mahal, a kilometer away. The best are from suites 522, 422, and 322, where, as part of a top-to-toe renovation from 2002 to 2004, daybeds are placed so you can sit before the huge windows and savor a dead-on frontal view of the palace (albeit across a bit of unsightly Agra). The lobby is now an elegant expanse of marble opening onto an excellent restaurant. The new room furnishings include headboards in red sandstone with marble inlay and dressing alcoves set off by screens of inlaid white marble. A blue-tile pool is fringed with palm trees and surrounded by acres of landscaped lawn. All in all, this is one of the city's best values. ⊠ *Taj Ganj, Fatehabad Rd., 282001* ☎ *562/ 223–2400 to 18* 🖷 *562/223–2420* ⊕ *www.tajhotels.com* ➳ *95 rooms, 5 suites* ♨ *Restaurant, coffee shop, cable TV, pool, health club, badminton, bar, baby-sitting, dry cleaning, laundry service, business services, meeting rooms, travel services* ▤ *AE, DC, MC, V* ◎ *EP.*

$ 🏠 **Agra Ashok.** Big changes have begun at this formerly government-owned hotel 3 km (1.9 mi) from the Taj Mahal and a short hop from the train station. As part of a propertywide upgrading, to be completed in early 2005, down-at-heels bathrooms are being sheathed in black granite; a floor of deluxe rooms is being created; and the restaurant Mandarin's will have an appealing new room with Chinese-style woodwork and a fountain. At this writing, rooms are spacious and modern; their makeovers—including the addition of 25-inch TVs—began in spring 2004.

A 5,000-square-foot health club is also planned for early 2005. Another new addition will be packages for day-trippers from Delhi,which include lunch, dinner, and day use of a guest room. ⊠ *6B The Mall, 282001* ☎*562/2361223 to 42* ☒*562/236–1620* ⤳*56 rooms, 2 suites* ☼*2 restaurants, room service, some in-room data ports, minibars, cable TV, pool, bar, shops, baby-sitting, laundry service, business services, meeting rooms, travel services, no-smoking floor* ☰ *AE, MC, V.*

Shopping

Tourist shops are generally open daily 10 until 7:30. Many Agra shops sell hand-knotted dhurries and other carpets, jewelry made from precious and semiprecious stones, brass statues, and marble inlays that continue the form and motifs seen in the city's great monuments. Resist drivers and touts who want to take you to places offering special "bargains"; they receive big commissions from shopkeepers, which you pay in the inflated price of the merchandise. Beware, too, of soapstone masquerading as marble: this softer, cheaper stone is a convincing substitute, but you can test it by scraping the item with your fingernail—Indian marble won't scrape. Finally, for what it's worth, local lore has it that miniature replicas of the Taj Mahal bring bad luck.

Cottage Industry (⊠ 18 Munro Rd. ☎ 562/222–6019) sells good dhurries and other carpets. **Cottage Industries Exposition** (⊠ 39 Fatehabad Rd. ☎ 562/222–6813) carries a good selection of high-quality rugs (mostly Kashmiri), silks, gemstones, and, like everyplace else in Agra, marble inlay. **Ganeshi Lall and Son** (⊠ WelcomHotel Mughal Sheraton, Fatehabad Rd. ☎ 562/233–0181 ☒ 13 Mahatma Gandhi Rd. ☎ 562/236–4567), a reliable, family-owned jeweler since 1845, specializes in older pieces and also creates new ones; the Mahatma Gandhi Road location, adjacent to the owner's home and open only by appointment, is a museumlike gallery of very fine old textiles, paintings, wood carvings, and some jewelry. Past clients have included major museums and Jackie Onassis. **Kohinoor** (⊠ 41 Mahatma Gandhi Rd. ☎ 562/236–4156 or 562/236–8855) has been designing jewelry in cut and uncut emeralds and other precious stones since 1862; a special connoisseur's room is open by appointment. Don't miss the little museum of fantastic 3-D *zardoji* (embroidered paintings). Some paintings know as Shams, have been encrusted with gems by the master of the technique, Shamsuddin (some are for sale). **Oswal Exports** (⊠ 30-B Munro Rd. ☎ 562/222–5710 or 562/222–5712 ⊕ www.oswalonline.com) has excellent examples of inlaid white, pink, green, and black marble; you can watch them being made and learn the technique. **Sanjay Cottage Industry** (⊠ 1A Jasoria Enclave, Fatehabad Rd. ☎ 562/309–0828 or 562/233–4209), near the Taj-View hotel, is the larger showroom of Cottage Industry, with workmen at looms demonstrating weaving technique. It has a great collection of tribal, Mughal-design, Kashmiri silk, and Agra rugs. **Subhash Emporium** (⊠ 18/1 Gwalior Rd. ☎ 562/222–5828 to 30 ⊕ www.subhashemporium.com) was the first store to revive Agra marble work in the 1960s; today you'll find perhaps the finest, best-priced examples of it here. Ask to see some of the incredible pieces in the private gallery to give you a better perspective on quality.

Fatehpur Sikri

★ ❺ *37 km (23 mi) southwest of Agra.*

In 1569, so the story goes, the mystic Salim Chisti blessed the Moghul emperor Akbar with a much-wanted male heir. Two years later, Akbar began building a new capital in Chisti's village of Sikri, later renaming it Fatehpur Sikri (City of Victory) after a great triumph in Gujarat. Standing on a rocky ridge overlooking the village, Fatehpur Sikri, in the state of Uttar Pradesh, originally had a circumference of about 11 km (7 mi). Massive walls enclosed three sides, and a lake (now dried up) protected the fourth. When the British came to Fatehpur Sikri in 1583 to meet Akbar, they were amazed to see a city that (by 16th century standards) exceeded London in both population and grandeur—with more rubies, diamonds, and silks than they could count. What remains is a beautiful cluster of royal dwellings on the top of the ridge, landscaped with lawns and flowering borders. The remarkably preserved buildings, mostly of local red sandstone, elegantly blend architectural styles from Persia as well as Akbar's various Indian holdings, a reflection of the synthesizing impulse that characterized the third and greatest of the Moghul emperors. Akbar ruled here for only 14 years before moving his capital—perhaps in pursuit of water, but more likely for political reasons—to Lahore and then eventually back to Agra. Because it was abandoned and never resettled, the city was not modified by later rulers and thus is the best reflection of Akbar's aesthetic and design philosophies. Fatehpur Sikri now stands as an intriguing ghost town, reflecting a high point in India's cultural history.

The usual starting point for exploring is the **Buland Darwaza** (Great Gate, built to celebrate the Gujarat victory) at the city's southwestern end. Unfortunately, the hawkers and guides who crowd the parking lot can be unrelenting. If you arrive by car, you can avoid this minor annoyance by asking to be dropped at the subsidiary entrance at the northeastern end of the city, where the following tour begins. Coming from Agra, bear right just after passing through Agra Gate, the main one in Akbar's day.

Approaching the complex, you'll walk through the **Naubat Khana,** a gate that was manned by drummers and musicians during imperial processions. Just ahead on the right is the **Mint,** a workshop that may have minted coins. Across the road is the **Archaeological Survey of India (ASI) museum** (☎ 562/ 228–2248, ☏ free, ☉ Sat.–Thurs. 9–6), which opened in mid-2004 in the reconstructed old Treasury building. One section has dioramas replicating the area's painting-decorated prehistoric rock shelters. Another section is devoted to 11th-century Jain sculptures that were excavated nearby. The third section is devoted to the history of Akbar, with exhibits on the material culture of his time, such as coins, miniature paintings, tiles, and costumes, as well as near life-size models of Akbar and his ministers— the Nine Jewels. The museum also has an interpretive center.

A few steps from the museum is the **Diwan-i-Am** (Hall of Public Audience), a large courtyard 366 feet long and 181 feet wide, with colonnades on three sides. Ahead is the balcony where the emperor sat on his throne to meet subjects or observe celebrations and other spectacles. Through chiseled marble jali screens, the women of the court would watch discreetly as Akbar, the empire's chief justice, handed down his decisions: those condemned to die were reportedly impaled, hanged, or trampled under the feet of an elephant. What looks like a square two-story building with domed cupolas at each corner is the **Diwan-i-Khas** (Hall of Private Audience). Inside it's actually one tall room where Akbar sat on a remarkably elaborate elevated platform and, it's thought, conducted meetings with his ministers. Supported by a stone column topped with a giant lotus flower intricately carved in stone, it's connected by causeways to four balconies with window seats on which the ministers sat. The throne's position is thought to have symbolized the center of the world or, alternatively, the one god sought by several major religions; it also may have shielded the emperor from would-be assassins. Across from the hall is the **Ankh Michauli** (Hide and Seek), named for Akbar's reported habit of playing the game with his harem inside the broad rooms and narrow passageways. As with many structures here, the building's function is a matter of legend and educated guesswork. Adjacent is the **Astrologer's Seat,** a platform where Akbar's royal astrologer sat. Surrounding it is a whimsical structure whose stone *chattri* (umbrella) roof is supported by pillars joined by brackets intricately carved as stylized elephant trunks.

Pass through the courtyard paved with a board on which Akbar played *pachisi* (an early form of Parcheesi using slave girls as life-size pieces), into the pavilion centered by the **Anup Talao** (Peerless Pool), a square pool with a central platform, connected by four bridges, where the famous court musician Tansen would sing for the emperor. (The sound of water from a nearby fountain softened the echo.) Below the basement of the pavilion is a recently excavated underground palace whose entrances cleverly concealed it until archaeologists, led by reports from Akbar's day, discovered it. The emperor would come to these rooms, constructed at the center of a water-filled tank, to escape the summer heat. Unearthed within them was the 12-foot-high stone bowl (now displayed on the pavilion) used to store water transported from the Ganges—the only water Akbar would drink. At the edge of the pool is the **Turkish Sultana's Pavilion,** a charming structure covered with elaborate Persian carvings in floral and zigzag patterns and once enclosed by sandalwood doors plated with silver. It is said to have been the home of the emperor's Turkish wife, but was more likely a place to relax by the pool—the ultimate cabana. Separated from the sultana's pavilion as well as from the official buildings of the palace by the Anup Talao are **Akbar's private chambers,** where he would have his favorites read to him or converse with courtiers, philosophers, and close advisers.

The Imperial Harem, for the women of Akbar's household, consists of several buildings connected by covered passages and screened from view of the more public areas. The **Panch Mahal** is a breeze-catching structure with five arcaded stories, each smaller than the one below. Its 176 columns are carved with tiny flowers or other motifs (no two of the first floor's 56 columns have the same design). Fatehpur Sikri's tallest building, it affords grand views of the city and the surrounding landscape from its upper stories. When the women wished to pray, they did so behind the screened arches of the **Nagina Mosque,** behind the Panch Mahal across a small garden. The largest residence in the complex is the Gujarati-influenced **Jodh Bai's Palace,** more properly called Principal Haram Sara, says the Archaeological Survey, because behind its eunuch-guarded entrance lived a number of the emperor's wives rather than just that of his Hindu wife Jodh Bai. The **Hawa Mahal** (Palace of the Winds) is a cool vantage point from which women could peek out at the court unseen from beautifully carved stone screens. The **House of Maryam** (on a diagonal between Jodh Bai's Palace and the Panch Mahal), the home of either Akbar's Christian wife or, more likely, his mother, is said to suggest the wooden architecture of the Punjab at that time. Look for the faded paintings of horses and elephants on the exterior walls and in an apselike area inside; some of the brackets supporting the eaves are carved with scenes from mythology. **Birbal's Palace,** which sits a few yards northwest of Jodh Bai's Palace and the Hawa Mahal, was named for the emperor's playfully irreverent Hindu prime minister. Because it's unlikely that he would have lived inside the harem, the ASI ascribes it more probably to Akbar's two senior wives. The palace's ornamentation makes use of both Hindu and Islamic motifs.

The big open colonnade behind the harem is known as the **Royal Stables,** with stalls once thought to have housed elephants and horses. Again, however, the modern verdict differs: "It is doubtful that a structure which required a crowd of men passing in and out could have been placed so close to the Haram Sara." It is more likely, according to ASI, that it was the quarters of the serving women, and that the open stalls were enclosed by curtains tied to the stone rings once thought to have tethered the animals. Follow the path down to the east gate of the **Jama Masjid** (Imperial Mosque); built around 1571 and designed to hold 10,000 worshipers, it's still in active use. Note the deliberate incorporation of Hindu elements in the design, especially the pillar decorations.

In the courtyard of the Jama Masjid (opposite the Buland Darwaza) lies **Salim Chisti's tomb,** surrounded by walls of marble lace, each with a different design. Begun upon the saint's death in 1571 and finished nine years later, the tomb was originally faced with red sandstone but was refinished in marble by Jahangir, the heir Akbar received after the saint's blessing. Women of all faiths come here to cover the tomb with cloth and tie a string on the marble latticework in hopes of giving birth to a son. From here you can cross the courtyard and exit through the imposing Buland Darwaza. With its beveled walls and inset archways, the southern gate rises 134 feet over a base of steps that raise it another 34 feet, dwarfing everything else in sight. Akbar built it after conquering Gujarat, and it set the style for later gateways, which the Moghuls built habitually as symbols of their power. Directly ahead is the parking lot, where you can prearrange to have your driver meet you.

To reach Fatehpur Sikri from Agra, hire a car and driver or join a tour. Plan to spend two or three hours wandering the grounds. ⌦ *Rs. 10* ⊙ *Daily sunrise–sunset.*

need a break? The simple Indian restaurant at the **Gulistan Tourist Complex** (☎ 5613/288–2490), just down the road (toward Agra) from Fatehpur Sikri, is a convenient lunch stop.

Gwalior

⑥ *120 km (75 mi) south of Agra.*

Now a busy commercial city in Madhya Pradesh, Gwalior traces its history back to a legend: The hermit saint Gwalipa cured a chieftain named Suraj Sen of leprosy. On the hermit's advice, Suraj Sen founded his city here and named it for his benefactor. The city changed hands numerous times, and each dynasty left its mark. Gwalior was also the home of the classical singer Tansen, one of the Nine Jewels of Akbar's court, whom many regard as the founder of North Indian classical music. The annual Tansen Music Festival, held here in late November or early December, is one of the best in India.

The huge **Gwalior Fort** sits on a high, rocky plateau, and its 2-mi-long, 35-foot-high wall dominates the skyline. (Take a taxi up and have the driver wait for you—auto-rickshaws can't make it up the steep hill.) The first Moghul emperor, Babur, admired the structure, which may explain why it's the only pre-Moghul Hindu–palace complex to survive in this region. The fort was often captured and achieved its greatest glory under the Tomar rulers in the 15th century. At **Man Mandir,** or Mansingh Palace, bands of gilded and enameled blue, green, and yellow mosaic tiles wrap the vast structure, giving a glimpse of its former splendor. Bring a flashlight to explore the underground dungeons where the Moghuls kept their prisoners after finally capturing the fort in Akbar's time in the late 16th century. Don't miss the beautifully carved 11th-century **Sas-Bahu** or the 9th-century **Teli ka Mandir** temple. The state museum in the **Gujari Mahal,** at the base of the fort, displays an excellent collection of sculptures and archaeological treasures dating as far back as the 2nd century BC. Ask to see the statue of the goddess Shalbhanjika, an exquisite miniature kept in the curator's custody. An English version of the sound-and-light show on the history of Gwalior fort runs for 45 minutes in the evening (plan a separate trip for that as everything else will be closed or dark by 5 or 6). ⊠ *Gwalior Rd.* ☎ *751/248–0011* ⌨ *Fort Rs. 100, museum Rs. 2, sound-and-light show Rs. 100* ⊙ *Fort: daily sunrise–sunset; museum: Sat.–Thurs. 10–5; sound-and-light show: Oct.–Feb., daily 7 PM, Mar.–Sept., daily 8 PM.*

An opulent structure with Tuscan and Corinthian architecture, the **Jai Vilas Palace** belonged to the *Scindias,* Gwalior's rulers up through Indian Independence (the current maharaja now has a palace adjacent to this one). Lots of photographs throughout depict the maharajas' past glories, including many of shooting parties where Brits and Indian royals stand proudly over tiger carcases. Jai Vilas is quite down-at-heels these days, but there's a gallery of miniature paintings, a few tatty royal costumes, furniture galleries, an arms room, a pretty marble courtyard centered by an unusual marble-and-cut-glass fountain, and a large pull-no-punches sculpture of Leda and the swan. Enormous chandeliers hang from the coffered and gilded ceiling of the massive **Durbar Hall** (look for the photo with Bill Clinton). In a case in the dining room below is a crystal train that carried liqueurs along the maharaja's banquet table. ⊠ *Jayandra Gang* ☎ *751/232–1101* ⬛ *Rs. 175* ☉ *Thurs.–Tues. 10–5.*

Sarod Ghar is an elegantly designed museum with a collection of musical instruments and photographs from the family of the late Amjad Ali Khan (d. 1979), the greatest sarod player of his day. Cases are arranged in rooms off the leafy interior courtyard of a pretty house. ⊠ *Jiwaji Ganj, Ustad Hafiz Ali Khan Marg, Lashkar* ☎ *751/242–5607* ⬛ *Free* ☉ *Tues.–Sun. 10–4.*

Where to Stay

★ **$$** ⊞ **Usha Kiran Palace.** Since it was built just down the drive from the Jai Vilas, this white palace trimmed with filigree sandstone has served as a royal guest house, a royal residence, and the grandest hotel in town. In 2003 the Taj group took it over and closed it for a total, much-needed renovation. By late 2004 it should reopen, done with Taj's typical good taste and luxurious appointments befitting the regal structure. To see the view granted to the women of the royal family, look out through the stone jali screen over the beautifully landscaped lawns. ⊠ *Jayendraganj, Lashkar 474009* ☎ *751/232–3213* ⊕ *www.tajhotels.com* ⏎ *20 rooms, 10 suites* ⚭ *Restaurant, cable TV, indoor pool, badminton, billiards, croquet, horseback riding, bar* ⊟ *AE, DC, MC, V* ¶◯¶ *EP.*

$ ⊞ **Central Park.** Despite its name, this hotel, with renovations done in 2004, is not on a park but on a busy road, and it is central (2 km [1.2 mi]) from both the railway station and Jai Vilas. Everything here is new, modern, and comfortable, yet uninspired. Hallways and stairways are long sweeps of marble with cheerful art on the walls. A concierge on each floor, a big bright gym with lots of equipment, evening barbecue by the pool bar, and a bake shop make this a nice place to stay. ⊠ *2-A City Centre, Side No. 1, 474009* ☎ *751/223–2440 to 43 or 751/501–1140 to 43* 🖷 *751/234–6502* ⊕ *www.thecentralpark.net* ⏎ *72 rooms, 6 suites* ⚭ *Restaurant, patisserie, room service, IDD phones, in-room data ports, refrigerators, cable TV, pool, gym, sauna, steam room, ayurvedic massage, baby-sitting, dry cleaning, laundry services, Internet, business services, meeting rooms* ⊟ *AE, MC, V* ¶◯¶ *EP.*

¢ ⊞ **Hotel Tansen.** This very basic accommodation, run by the Madhya Pradesh State Tourism Development Corporation and just down the street from the Central Park, is worn but nonetheless clean, &and the staff are friendly. All rooms have private baths; two-thirds have full amenities; suites have dining tables and minirefrigerators. The non-air-conditioned rooms are for die-hard budgeteers only; they're priced very low (Rs. 450). There's a state tourism office on-site. ⊠ *6-A Gandhi Rd., 474009* ☎ *751/234–0370 or 751/234–2606* 🖷 *751/234–0371* ⊕ *www.mptourism.com* ⏎ *24 rooms, 12 suites* ⚭ *Restaurant, room service, some refrigerators, bar, dry cleaning, laundry service, meeting room, pets allowed; no a/c, no room phones, no TV in some rooms* ⊟ *AE, MC, V* ¶◯¶ *EP.*

Orchha

❼ *119 km (74 mi) southeast of Gwalior, 16 km (10 mi) east of Jhansi, 170 km (105 mi) northwest of Khajuraho.*

In the 16th and 17th centuries the Hindu Bundela rulers, allies of the Moghuls, built up Orchha as a provincial capital on the banks of the winding Betwa River. They were great patrons of the arts, and the palace became a magnet for artists and craftsmen, who left their mark on it in beautiful stonework and murals. Orchha also attracted poets, including the Hindi poet Keshav Das. In 1783 the Bundela capital was moved from this isolated location, and today Orchha is little more than a sleepy village crowded with palaces, temples, and *chattras*—funerary monuments that resemble Muslim tombs but contain no remains of the Hindu rulers, who were cremated on the riverbanks. Orchha's isolation proved useful to nationalist leader Chandrashekhar Azad, who hid from the British here in the 1920s, and even today you may feel you've entered a sort of benignly protected corner of the world.

Orchha, in the state of Madhya Pradesh, is a great place to explore in peace, without the crowds you'll find at other sites. Take a flashlight so you can explore the rooms and passageways constructed under the town's buildings as escapes from the hot summer. Most of the sites are accessible around the clock, but some are open only daily from 10 to 5; inquire at the Sheesh Mahal Hotel, where, with luck, the excellent self-guided audio tour of the complex will be back in stock. Unless otherwise indicated, all sites are free. It's worth hiring the very good Madhya Pradesh Directorate of Archaeology, Archives and Museums guide to make sure you don't miss a thing.

Fifteen sandstone **cenotaphs** (also known as chattras), built in honor of the former rulers sit serenely on the bank of the rock-strewn Betwa River—an especially fine place to catch the sunset. The arches of these chattras and their placement in a garden setting evoke Islamic architecture; the spires, or *shikharas,* recall North Indian Hindu temples. ✉ *5-min walk south of the Ram Raja Temple.*

The four-story, many-arched **Chaturbhuj Temple,** next to the Ram Raja Temple on a rise facing the Raja Mahal, towers over Orchha. It was built in the 16th century to house an image of the Hindu god Rama that would be brought back from Ayodhya, capital of Rama's mythic kingdom, by Kunwari, wife of Madhukar Shah (1554–92), the third and greatest of Orchha's kings. According to local lore, however, the temple was incomplete when she returned, so she installed the icon in her own nearby palace, the Rani Mahal—now the Ram Raja—from which it refused to move. The temple was rededicated to Krishna and Radha. 🎟 *Free with ticket from fort-palace complex* ☯ *Daily 9–5.*

Perched on a slight rise on a small seasonal island where the river splits ★ as it passes through town, Orchha's **fort-palace** complex is approached by a multiarch granite bridge leading to a broad courtyard with historic buildings on three sides. To your left as you arrive is the 16th-century **Raja Mahal** (Royal Palace), which has beautiful murals in 15 rooms, including the bedrooms of the king's seven wives (find a watchman or a guide to unlock the rooms for you). The paintings, all done with natural pigments on walls prepared with a wash of lime and shell powder, include scenes from Hindu mythology (such as the 10 incarnations of Vishnu and the life of Rama), hunting, wrestling, and geometric and floral designs. The Diwan-i-Khas, a spacious hall with 12-sided pillars, has paintings of the royal procession. From the upper stories there are good views of the rest of the complex. In one courtyard is a platform where dancers would perform for the royals and their guests. Adjacent is the **Sheesh Mahal,** built in 1763 as a raja's country house and today a government-run hotel; stray remaining bits of blue tilework on the west facade hint at the original grandeur, now almost gone except in the views and proportions of the rooms to the right side of the courtyard, is the jewel in this crown: the 17th-century **Jahangir Mahal** palace, constructed around a large, fountain-centered courtyard in five terraced stories, and with wide-open views of the countryside and the river below. Built for a visit from the Moghul emperor Jahangir—who married the sister of an Orchha king—the palace elegantly blends Hindu and Moghul themes, as in the courtyard's colonnade, where rows of ornamentation alternate between the Moghul geometric style (no figural representations allowed) and a Hindu frieze of elephants, which rests on 112 elephant brackets supported on lotus-bud pendentives. According to legend, Jahangir stayed only one night, and no one ever lived in the palace's 136 rooms, many of them graced with lovely wall paintings or intricately carved stone jali screens. Two great stone elephants holding bells and garlands of welcome flank the main entrance; on this east wall traces of the original green and blue coloring remain. At the entrance is a small museum whose collection includes pillars built to commemorate kings' wives who committed *sati* (self-immolation) upon their husbands' death. 🖼 *Jahangir Mahal Foreigners Rs. 30, Indians Rs. 5; museum free ☉ Jahangir Mahal and Raja Mahal, daily sunrise–sunset; Jahangir Mahal museum Tues.–Sun. 10–5.*

★ The **Laxminarayan Temple,** on a hilltop about 1 km (½ mi) west of town, is a 17th-century mix of temple and fort architecture (with renovations from 1793). Vibrant, well-preserved murals on the walls and ceilings depict mythological and historical subjects. The drawings etched in a red wash are from the 19th century—watch for the wall depicting the First War of Independence (otherwise known as the 1857 Mutiny, or Sepoy War), Bundela armies on one half and British armies, with generals in tents drinking wine, on the other. The upper terrace provides lovely views of the countryside. 🖼 *Rs. 30 ☉ Daily 9–5.*

Scattered among agricultural fields on the floodplain below the fort-palace complex are a number of other buildings, including a hammam, stables, and several royal chattras, all within walking distance. Nearest to the complex, at the base of the hill, is the **Rai Praveen Mahal,** a two-story brick palace named for the dancer-poet consort of King Indramani (1672–76); her praises were sung in many of Keshav Das's poems. On the upper floor are paintings of *nayikas* (mortal women) and a warrior on horseback. The underground rooms, where the lovers took refuge from the hot summer sun, can be explored. A short walk leads to the **Panchmukhi Mahadeva** (Shiva with Five Faces Temple), a group of three temples accompanied by three cenotaphs. One of Panchmukhi's four sides has nicely preserved paintings, and the sanctum sanctorum holds an appealing carving of the elephant-headed god Ganesh.

Facing the bridge to the fort-palace complex is the **Ram Raja Temple,** a large low-rise palace building fronted by a tidy, pleasant plaza that is the center of community life as well as the center of town. It is especially vibrant in the early evening, when the sellers of snacks and religious items in the illuminated plaza peddle their wares to the locals who've come to worship and the few tourists who've discovered there's nothing else to do in town. In late November, a reenactment of Rama's marriage, complete with elephants and big crowds, takes place here. ⊠ *Free* ☉ *Daily 8–12:30 and 7–9:30.*

Where to Stay

$$ 🏨 **Amar Mahal.** Orchha's newest hotel, opened in late 2003, is just up the hill from the river and the cenotaphs (as well as the Orchha Resort), so most rooms have good views of water and/or monuments. Built in the style of the Bundela monuments, with rooms off a colonnade around a garden courtyard, the hotel has such accents as floral-painted arches echoing those in the palaces dividing the large, marble-floor guest rooms, and elaborately carved Rajasthani beds. The restaurant, with a coffered ceiling painted with enamel and gilt flowers, serves a creditable version of the standard veg/nonveg Indian/Chinese/Continental hotel menu— plus good old sandwiches at lunch. Plans call for a health club by fall 2004. ⌂ *Reserve through Unwind Inc., 37A Shapurjad, New Delhi 110049* ☎ *11/2649–9195 or 11/2649–6745* ⊠ *Bypass Rd., Tikamgarh District, Orchha 472246* ☎ *7680/252–102 or 7680/252–202* 🖷 *7680/252–203* ⊕ *www.amarmahal.com* ⟳ *21 rooms, 3 suites* ⌂ *Restaurant, room service, refrigerators, cable TV, pool, health club, meeting rooms, travel services* ☰ *AE, MC, V* ⏀ *EP.*

$$ 🏨 **Orchha Resort.** On the riverbank, literally butting up against one of the cenotaphs, this resort built in 1996 is pointedly Indian, from the lobby's brightly colored wall panels of scenes from the Hindu epics to the rooms' marble-inlay floors and tables (the owner is noted Agra inlay maker Oswal). The ex-Taj general manager has added polish, from a beautiful lotus-shape pool to new mattresses and stylish bathroom accessories in the comfortable rooms. A less expensive option ($; Rs. 1,600 for a double) is available October through March: a tent with private bath, phone, TV, and air-conditioning. The buffet restaurant ($$$; Rs. 425 for dinner) serves good vegetarian food. ⊠ *Kanchana Ghat, Tikamgarh District, Orchha 472246* ☎ *7680/252–222 to 24* 🖷 *7680/252–677* ⊕ *www.orchharesort. com* ⌂ *Reserve through Oswal Motels and Resorts, 30 Munro Rd., Agra 282001* ☎ *562/222–5710 to 12* ⟳ *34 rooms, 11 tents* ⌂ *Restaurant, room service, refrigerators, cable TV, tennis court, pool, gym, massage, badminton, shop, dry cleaning, laundry service, business services, no-smoking rooms* ☰ *AE, MC, V* ⏀ *EP.*

¢ 🏨 **Betwa Cottages.** These cute, clean cottages for two, each on its own lawn near the river and the cenotaphs, have simple wood furnishings with small paintings, plus phones and TVs. Cottage No. 5, on slightly higher ground, has a view of the well-maintained gardens and a bit of the river. The restaurant serves good kababs and Chinese food; the tables on the lawn are a convenient place to stop for a drink or snack while visiting the cenotaphs. ⌂ *Reserve through MPSTDC, Gangotri Bldg., 4th fl., T. T. Nagar, Bhopal 462003* ☎ *755/277–8383 or 755/277–4340* 🖷 *755/277–4289* 🖅 *mail@mptourism.com.* ✉ *Tikamgarh District, Orchha, 472246* ☎ *7680/252–618* 🖷 *7680/252–624* 🖅 *bcorcha@rediffmail.com* 🛏 *10 cottages* ᐃ *Restaurant, room service, cable TV, dry cleaning, laundry service, Internet, pets allowed; no a/c in some rooms* ▤ *MC, V* ⍦ *EP.*

¢ 🏨 **Sheesh Mahal.** This government-run hotel—part of the fort-palace complex—was built in 1763 as a royal guest house. It's no longer quite as regal these days, but it can't be beat for the location. Many of the rooms, especially the huge Royal Suite, offer a view of a field full of monuments (though the best views are sometimes from the bathroom). Furnishings are simple, but rooms (if not rugs) are clean. The Royal and Deluxe rooms ($$ and $, or Rs. 2,990 and Rs. 1,990, respectively) have the original huge marble-slab tubs. There's no air-conditioning, but you won't need it before March or April. Staff are friendly and helpful. Some evenings a candlelit dinner is served on the roof as musicians entertain. ⌂ *Reserve through MPSTDC, Gangotri Bldg., 4th fl., T. T. Nagar, Bhopal 462003* ☎ *755/277–8383 or 755/277–4340* 🖷 *755/277–4289* 🖅 *mail@mptourism.com.* ✉ *Tikamgarh District, Orchha 472246* ☎ *7680/252–624* 🖷 *755/252–624* 🖅 *hsmorcha@sancharnet.in* 🛏 *8 rooms* ᐃ *Restaurant, room service, Internet; no phones in some rooms, no TV in some rooms, no a/c* ▤ *V* ⍦ *EP.*

Shopping

Taragram (✉ 1077 Civil Lines, Jhansi ☎ 7680/52821), 8 km (5 mi) outside Orchha, is an innovative development program that focuses on the revival of traditional papermaking methods. A little shop sells handmade notebooks and other items; walk around back and you can observe the papermaking process in its various stages. The small local **market** has less hard-sell pressure than more touristy areas and sells an abundance of inexpensive mixed-metal objects, from votive *diyas* (prayer lamps) to *kum-kum* boxes with tiny compartments to separate color powders. For inexpensive, beautifully crafted plaster sculptures of Hindu and Jain gods, stop at the small, nameless **shop** just inside the entrance gate to the Raja Mahal.

KHAJURAHO

This small Madhya Pradesh village, with the Vidhya hills as a backdrop, is so rural that it's hard to imagine it as the 10th- to 12th-century religious capital of the Chandelas—one of the most powerful Rajput dynasties of Central India. The only significant river is some distance away, and Khajuraho—395 km (245 mi) southeast of Agra—seems far removed from any substantial economic activity. Yet this is where the Chandelas built 85 temples, 25 of which remain to give a glimpse of a time when Hindu art and devotion reached its apex.

During the Chandelas' rule, the temples' royal patrons were rich, the land was fertile, and everyone lived the good life, trooping off to hunts, feasts, and theater, music, and dance performances. This abundance was the perfect climate for creativity, and temple-building emerged as the major form of expression. There were no strict boundaries between the sacred and the profane, no dictates on acceptable deities: Shiva, Vishnu, Brahma, and the Jain saints were all lavishly honored here. Excavations have also uncovered a complex of Buddhist temples. Despite the interest in heaven, the real focus was Earth, particularly the facts of human life. Here, immortalized in stone, virile men and voluptuous women cavort and copulate in the most intimate, erotic, and sometimes bewildering postures. Khajuraho represents the best of Hindu temple sculpture: sinuous, twisting forms, human and divine, pulsing with life, tension, and conflict.

The dynasty reigned for five centuries, succumbing eventually to invaders. In 1100 Mahmud the Turk began a holy war against the "idolaters" of India, and by 1200 the sultans of Delhi ruled over the once-glorious Chandela domain. Khajuraho's temples lapsed into obscurity until their rediscovery by the British explorer Captain T. S. Burt in 1838.

The temples—designated a World Heritage Site—have more to offer than erotic sculpture. Their soaring *shikharas* (spires) are meant to resemble the peaks of the Himalayas, abode of Lord Shiva: starting with the smallest, over the entrance, each spire rises higher than the one before it, as in a range of mountains that seems to draw near the heavens. Designed to inspire the viewer toward the highest human potential, these were also the builders' attempts to reach upward, out of the material world, to *moksha,* the final release from the cycle of rebirth. One scholar has suggested that Khajuraho's temples were in effect chariots of the kings, carrying them off to a heavenly world resembling an idealized view of courtly life. Their combination of lofty structure and delicate sculpture gives them a unique sense of completeness and exuberance.

Of the extant temples, all but two were made from sandstone mined from the banks of the River Ken, 30 km (19 mi) away. The stone blocks were carved separately, then assembled as interlocking pieces. Though each temple is different, all observe precise architectural principles of shape, form, and orientation and contain certain essential elements: a high raised platform, an *ardh mandapam* (entrance porch), a *mandapam* (portico), an *antrala* (vestibule), and a *garbha griha* (inner sanctum). Some of the larger temples also have a walkway around the inner sanctum, a *mahamandapam* (hall), and subsidiary shrines at each corner of the platform, making a complete *panchayatana* (five-shrine complex).

A number of sculptural motifs run through the temples. Certain gods, for instance, have directional positions: elephant-headed Ganesh faces north; Yama, the god of death, and his mount, a male buffalo, face south. The two goddesses guarding the entrance to the sanctum are the rivers Ganges and Yamuna. Other sculptures include the *apsaras* (heavenly maidens), found mainly inside, and the Atlas-like *kichakas,* who support the ceilings on their shoulders. Many sculptures reflect everyday activities, such as a dance class, and there are sultry *nayikas* (mortal women) and plenty of *mithunas* (amorous couples). The scorpion appears as an intriguing theme, running up and down the thighs of many female sculptures as a kind of erotic thermometer. It appears, too, on the breastbone of the terrible, emaciated goddess Chamundi on the corners of several temple platforms, suggesting a complex and imaginative view of sexuality on the part of the sculptors and their patrons.

No one knows why erotic sculptures are so important here, though many explanations have been suggested. The female form is often used as an auspicious marker on Hindu gateways and doors, in the form of temple sculptures as well as domestic wall paintings. In the late classical and early medieval periods, this symbol expanded into full-blown erotic art in many places, including the roughly contemporary sun temple at Modhera, in Gujarat, and the slightly later one at Konark, in Orissa. Khajuraho legend has it that the founder of the Chandela dynasty, Chandravarman, was born of an illicit union between his mother and the moon god, which resulted in her ostracism. When he grew up to become a mighty king, his mother begged him to show the world the beauty and divinity of lovemaking. A common folk explanation is that the erotic sculptures protect the temples from lightning; and art historians have pointed out that many of the erotic panels are placed at junctures where some protection or strengthening agent might be structurally necessary. Others say the sculptures reflect the influence of a Tantric cult that believed in reversals of ordinary morality as a religious practice. Still others argue that sex has been used as a metaphor: the carnal and bestial sex generally shown near the bases of the temples represent uncontrolled human appetites, whereas the couples deeply engrossed in each other, oblivious to all else, represent a divine bliss, the closest humans can approach to God. The mystery lives on, but it's clear that the sculptors drew on a sophisticated and sensual worldly heritage, including the *Kama Sutra*. Some of the far-out positions recommended in that classical Hindu love manual are in fact illustrated here.

The best way to see Khajuraho is to hire a guide (especially for the Western Group of temples) and to visit the Western Group in the first rays of the morning sun, follow them with the Eastern Group, see the museum in the afternoon, and make it to the Chaturbhuj Temple in the Southern Group in time for sunset. Alternately, an audio guide is available at the entrance to the Western Group for Rs. 50 (with a Rs. 500 security deposit). The nearbly India Tourism office has a helpful map locating all the temples. And if you want even more information, an Archaeological Survey of India book—authoritative, unlike the tourist books you'll come across—is available for Rs. 99; entering the Western Group gate, go all the way left and then right to the office building for a copy.

Khajuraho holds an annual, weeklong **dance festival**, set in part against the backdrop of the temples. If you'll be in India in late February or early March, try to catch this superb event, which attracts some of the country's best performers. Contact Madhya Pradesh Tourism's head office (☎ 755/255–3006 ⊕ www.mptourism.com). From August through mid-April, for Rs. 250 you can see folk dances from all over India performed nightly at 7 and 8:30 PM at **Kandariya,** a theater attached to the shop **Shilpgram** (⊠ Bamitha Rd. near Jhankar hotel).

For Rs. 20 to Rs. 30 you can **rent a bicycle** for the day from one of the many stands near the town center; it's a great way to get around this relatively traffic-free town and to explore the small streets of Khajuraho village, the old residential area near the Eastern Group of temples, teems with shops, animals, and children. Entrepreneurial boys will gladly guide you around for Rs. 50.

The popular 50-minute **sound-and-light show,** which runs in Hindi and English every evening (except during monsoon season) at the Western Group, traces the story of the Chandela kings and the temples from the 10th century to the present. Showtime varies based on sunset, so confirm it with your hotel or the tourist office. There are no shows in summer. ▨ *Rs. 200* ✆ *English-language show: Oct.–Mar. 6:30; Apr.–June and Sept. 7:30.*

Western Group of Temples

Numbers in the text correspond to numbers in the margin and on the Khajuraho map.

Most of the Western Group temples are inside a formal enclosure whose entrance is on Main Road, opposite the State Bank of India. Although the rest of the town's temples are always accessible and free, these are open daily from sunrise to sunset and have an admission charge of Rs. 250.

⑱ The first three temples, though considered part of the Western Group, are at a slight distance from the enclosure. The **Chausath Yogini Temple,** on a granite outcrop southwest of the Shivsagar Tank, a small artificial lake, is the oldest temple at Khajuraho, possibly built as early as AD 820. It's dedicated to Kali (a form of the Goddess Durga, Slayer of Demons), and its name refers to the 64 (*chausath*) female ascetics who serve this fierce goddess in the Hindu pantheon. Unlike its counterparts of pale, warm-hue sandstone, this temple is made of granite. Scholarly supposition holds that this and a handful of other open-air temples, usually circular, in remote parts of India were focal points for an esoteric cult.

⑲ Though **Lalguan Mahadeva**—600 meters west of Chausath Yogini—lies in ruins and the original portico is missing, this Shiva temple is historically significant because it was built of both granite and sandstone, marking the transition from Chausath Yogini to the later temples.

⑳ Just outside the boundary of the Western Group (there's a separate gate to the left of the entrance) stands the **Matangesvara Temple,** the only one still in use here; worship takes place in the morning and afternoon. The lack of ornamentation, the square construction, and the simple floor plan date this temple to the early 10th century. It has oriel windows, a projecting portico, and a ceiling of overlapping concentric circles. An enormous lingam, nearly 8½ feet tall, is enshrined in the sanctum.

Temples ▼

Adinath **12**

Bijamandala ..**16**

Brahma **10**

Chaturbhuj **17**

Chausath
Yogini **18**

Chitragupta ...**26**

Devi
Jagdamba **24**

Duladeo **15**

Ghantai **11**

Javari **9**

Kandariya
Mahadev **23**

Lakshmana ...**22**

Lalguan
Mahadeva **19**

Mahadeva **25**

Matangesvara .**20**

Nandi **28**

Parsvanath **13**

Parvati **29**

Shantinath **14**

Vamana **8**

Varaha **21**

Vishvanath **27**

Khajuraho

WESTERN GROUP OF TEMPLES

State Museum
of Tribal and
Folk Arts ◆

Madhya
Pradesh
Tourism
Office

Link Rd. No. 1

Bypass Rd.

Prem
Sagar

See Detail

WESTERN GROUP
OF TEMPLES

India
Tourism

Ninora
Tank

Entrance

Archaeological
Museum

Shivsagar
Tank

Lan. Temple Rd.

Basti Rd.

EASTERN GROUP
OF TEMPLES

Link Rd. No. 2

Bus Stand ◆

◆ Post
Office

Bypass Rd.

Main Rd.

SOUTHERN GROUP
OF TEMPLES

Khodar River

TO
AIRPORT

| 0 | 400 yards |
| 0 | 400 meters |

The **Archaeological Museum,** across the street from Matangesvara Temple, displays exquisite carvings and sculptures that archaeologists have recovered from the temple sites. The three galleries attempt to put the works into context according to the deities they represent. ⊠ *Main Rd.,* ☎ *7686/272–320* ⊯ *Rs. 5* ⊙ *Sat.–Thurs. 10–5.*

Just inside the main entrance gate, to your left, next to a small Laxmi temple, is the **Varaha Temple** (circa 900–925). It's dedicated to Vishnu's Varaha avatar, or Boar Incarnation, which Vishnu assumed in order to rescue the earth after a demon had hidden it in the slush at the bottom of the sea. In the inner sanctum, all of creation is depicted on the massive and beautifully polished sides of a stone boar, who in turn stands on the serpent Shesha. The ceiling is carved with a lotus relief.

★ Across from the Varaha Temple is the **Lakshmana Temple,** dedicated to Vishnu and the only complete temple remaining. Along with Kandariya Mahadeva and Vishvanath, this edifice represents the peak of achievement in North Indian temple architecture. All three temples were built in the early to mid-10th century, face east, and follow an elaborate plan resembling a double cross, with three tiers of exterior sculpture above the friezes on their high platforms. The ceiling of the mandapam is charmingly carved with shell and floral motifs. The lintel over the entrance to the main shrine shows Lakshmi, goddess of wealth and consort of Vishnu, with Brahma, Lord of Creation, on her left and Shiva, Lord of Destruction, on her right. A frieze above the lintel depicts the planets. The relief on the doorway portrays the gods and demons churning the ocean to obtain a pitcher of miraculous nectar from the bottom. The wall of the sanctum is carved with scenes from the legend of Krishna (one of Vishnu's incarnations). An icon in the sanctum with two pairs of arms and three heads represents Vishnu as Vaikuntha, or the supreme god, and is surrounded by images of his 10 incarnations (9 past and 1 future). Around the exterior base are some of Khajuraho's most famous sculptures, with gods and goddesses on the protruding corners, erotic couples or groups in the recesses, and apsaras and *sura-sundaris* (apsaras performing everyday activities) in between. Along the sides of the tall platform beneath the temple, friezes depict social life, including battle scenes, festivals, and amorous sport.

❷❸ The **Kandariya Mahadev,** west of the Lakshmana, is the tallest and most
Fodor'sChoice evolved temple in Khajuraho in terms of the blending of architecture
★ and sculpture, and one of the finest in India. Probably built around 1025–50, it follows the five-shrine design. Its central shikhara, which towers 102 feet above the platform, is actually made up of 84 subsidiary towers built up in increments. The feeling of ascent is repeated inside, where each succeeding mandapam rises a step above the previous one, and the garbha griha is higher still; dedicated to Shiva, this inner sanctum houses a marble lingam with a 4-foot circumference. Even the figures on this temple are taller and slimmer than those elsewhere. The rich interior carving includes two beautiful *toranas* (arched doorways). Outside, three bands of sculpture around the sanctum and transept bring to life a whole galaxy of Hindu gods and goddesses, mithunas, celestial handmaidens, and lions.

❷❹ The **Devi Jagdamba Temple** was originally dedicated to Vishnu, as indicated by a prominent sculpture over the sanctum's doorway. It now honors Parvati, Shiva's consort, but because her image is black—a color associated with Kali—it's also known as the Kali Temple. From the inside, its three-shrine design makes the temple appear to be shaped like a cross. The third band of sculpture has a series of erotic mithunas. The ceilings are similar to those in the Kandariya Mahadev, and the three-headed, eight-armed statue of Shiva is one of the best cult images in Khajuraho.

Sharing the platform with the Kandariya Mahadev and the Devi Jagdamba is the small, mostly ruined **Mahadeva Temple.** Now dedicated to
❷❺ Shiva, it may originally have been a subsidiary temple to the Kandariya, probably dedicated to Shiva's consort. In the portico stands a remarkable statue of a man caressing a mythical horned lion.

❷❻ The **Chitragupta Temple** lies just north of the Devi Jagdamba and resembles it in construction. In honor of the presiding deity, Surya—the sun god—the temple faces east, and its cell contains a 5-foot-tall image of Surya complete with the chariot and seven horses that carry him across the sky. Surya also appears above the doorway. In the central niche south of the sanctum is an image of Vishnu with 11 heads; his own face is in the center, and the other heads represent his 10 incarnations. Sculptural scenes of animal combat, royal processions, masons at work, and joyous dances depict the lavish country life of the Chandelas.

㉗ Two staircases lead up to **Vishvanath Temple,** the northern flanked by a pair of lions and the southern by a pair of elephants. The Vishvanath probably preceded the Kandariya, but here only two of the original corner shrines remain. On the outer wall of the corridor surrounding the cells is an impressive image of Brahma, the three-headed Lord of Creation, and his consort, Saraswati. On every wall the female form predominates, portraying women's daily 10th-century occupations: writing a letter, holding a baby, applying makeup, or playing music. The nymphs of paradise are voluptuous and provocative, the erotic scenes robust. An inscription states that the temple was built by Chandela King Dhanga in 1002. The temple sits on a terrace to the east of the Chitragupta and

㉘ Devi Jagdamba temples. The simple **Nandi Temple,** which faces Vishvanath, houses a monolithic statue of Shiva's mount, the massive and richly harnessed sacred bull Nandi.

㉙ The small and heavily rebuilt **Parvati Temple,** near Vishvanath, was originally dedicated to Vishnu. The present icon is that of the goddess Ganga standing on her mount, the crocodile.

need a break? Exit the gate, and smack across the street from Vishvanath and Nandi temples is **Blue Sky** (☎ 7686/274–647), a café on the main road, open for all meals. It has a great view of the entire Western Group from its second-floor and rooftop terraces. The view's the thing, but the food's not bad. You can just stop by for a *lassi* (a yogurt-based drink; they serve five flavors) or tea, or try the breakfast menu of omelets, porridge, and Indian items; at lunch, there are soups and salads, plus Indian, Chinese, Italian, and Japanese choices. At dinner you can watch the sound-and-light show from your table.

★ The **State Museum of Tribal and Folk Arts** has an excellent collection of more than 500 artifacts of terra-cotta, metal, and wood crafts, paintings, jewelry, and masks from all over Madhya Pradesh and the Bastar region (known for tribal crafts) in the neighboring state of Chhattisgarh. ⊠ *Chandela Cultural Complex, Rajnagar Rd.* ☎ 7686/274–051 ☜ *Rs. 50* ☉ *Tues.–Sun. 10–5.*

Eastern Group of Temples

Scattered around the edges of the old village of Khajuraho, the Eastern Group of temples includes three Brahmanical and four Jain temples, whose proximity attests to the religious tolerance of the times in general and the Chandela rulers in particular.

❽ Northernmost is the late-11th-century **Vamana Temple,** dedicated to Vishnu's dwarf incarnation (though the image in the sanctum looks more like a tall, sly child). The sanctum walls show unusual theological openness, depicting most of the major gods and goddesses; Vishnu appears in many of his forms, including the Buddha, his ninth incarnation. Outside, two tiers of sculpture are concerned mainly with the nymphs of paradise, who strike charming poses under their private awnings. The small, well-proportioned **Javari Temple,** just south of the Vamana and roughly contemporary, has a simplified three-shrine design. The two main exterior bands of sculpture bear hosts of heavenly maidens.

⑩ The granite-and-sandstone **Brahma Temple,** one of the earliest here (circa 900), is probably misnamed. Brahma, a titular member of the triad of Hinduism's great gods, along with Shiva and Vishnu, rarely gets a temple to himself, and this one has a *lingam,* the abstract, phallus-shape icon of Shiva. It differs in design from most of the other temples, particularly in the combination of materials and the shape of its shikhara.

⑪ All that's left of the **Ghantai Temple** are its pillars, festooned with carvings of pearls and bells. Adorning the entrance of this little gem are an eight-arm Jain goddess, Chakreshvari, riding the mythical bird Garuda and a relief illustrating the 16 dreams of the mother of Mahavira, the greatest religious figure in Jainism and a counterpart to the Buddha. The temple sits south of the Vamana, Javari, and Brahma temples, toward the Jain complex.

⑫ The late-11th-century **Adinath Temple,** a minor shrine, is set in a small walled compound southeast of the Ghantai temple. Its porch and the statue of the Tirthankara (literally, Ford-Maker, a figure who leads others to liberation) Adinatha are modern additions. Built at the beginning of the Chandelas' decline, this temple is relatively small, but the shikhara and base are richly carved.

⑬ The **Parsvanath Temple,** built in the mid-10th century, is the largest and finest in the Eastern Group's Jain complex and holds some of the best sculpture in Khajuraho, including images of Vishnu. In contrast to the intricate calculations behind the layout of the Western Group, the plan for this temple is a simple rectangle, with a separate spire in the rear. Statues of flying angels and sloe-eyed beauties occupied with children, cosmetics, and flowers adorn the outer walls. The stone also conveys even the texture of the women's thin garments. The early-11th-century **Shantinath Temple** has been remodeled extensively but does contain some old Jain sculpture.

Southern Group of Temples

⑮ Though built in the customary five-shrine style, the 12th-century **Duladeo Temple** (about 900 yards south of the Eastern Group's Ghantai) looks flatter and more massive than most Khajuraho shrines. Probably the last temple built in Khajuraho, the Duladeo lacks the usual ambulatory passage and crowning lotus-shape finials. Here, too, in this temple dedicated to Shiva, eroticism works its way in, though the amorous figures are discreetly placed.

As part of continuing explorations, the largest temple yet—4 meters longer than the Kandariya Mahadeva—has been partially unearthed since 1999 between the Duladeo and the Chaturbhuj. At the **Bijamandala Tem-**

ple, the plinth, multiple tiers of beautifully carved moldings, and a Shiva lingam placed on a marble pedestal at the top can be seen. Archaeologists surmise that the temple, begun in the late 10th or early 11th century, may never have been completed, judging by the remains and unfinished statues found on the site, but further excavation may resolve the question.

⑰ The small, 12th-century **Chaturbhuj Temple,** nearly 3 km (2 mi) south of Duladeo, has an attractive colonnade entrance and a feeling of verticality thanks to its single spire. It enshrines an impressive four-hand image of Vishnu that may be the single most striking piece of sculpture in Khajuraho. With few exceptions, the temple's exterior sculpture falls short of the local mark (a sign of the declining fortunes of the empire), but this temple is definitely the best place in Khajuraho to watch the sun set.

Where to Stay & Eat

$$$$ ✕ **Apsara.** This pleasant restaurant, with lattice screens of teak and bird paintings on silk, offers good Indian and Continental fare. Try the tandoori kababs or the *sarsonwala machli tikka,* fish cubes marinated in yogurt flavored with mustard and cooked in a clay oven. If you're homesick, you can even get a tenderloin steak here. ⊠ *Jass Radisson, Bypass Rd.* ☎ *7686/272–344* ▭ *AE, DC, MC, V.*

$$–$$$ ✕ **Mediterraneo.** Eat on the rooftop or in a small dining room at this Italian restaurant near the Western Group. It has not a single frill, but the pizzas, one of the many pasta dishes (the carbonara has actual bacon), or standbys like eggplant Parmigiana or lamb cacciatore may just do the trick when you're tired of the Indian-Continental-Chinese menu popular throughout India. At breakfast, you can order crêpes and omelets. (Note: The TRAINED IN ROME chef, as the sign proclaims, seems to have moved on to Jaipur.) ⊠ *Jain Temple Rd., opposite Surya Hotel* ☎ *7686/272–246* ▭ *No credit cards.*

★ $$$ ▥ **Chandela.** Though without the usual sparkle of Taj-group hotels, the Chandela is a fine property with every amenity, and each comfortable room has a balcony or patio facing the pool or the gardens (if you come in summer, request one of the rooms with the extra air conditioner). The junior suites have a small room with a TV so you can watch without disturbing your sleeping spouse. Worriers will be glad to know that all rooms have sprinklers and smoke detectors, more the exception than the rule in India. A camel and a bullock cart are on standby for rides around the property; there's also a jogging track. ⊠ *Batmitha Rd., Khajuraho 471606* ☎ *7686/272–355–364* ▤ *7686/272–365 or 7686/272–366* ⊕ *www.tajhotels.com* ⇆ *89 rooms, 5 suites* ♧ *Restaurant, coffee shop, room service, in-room data ports, minibars, cable TV, tennis court, pool, gym, hair salon, massage, badminton, croquet, bar, library, shops, baby-sitting, laundry services, Internet, business services, meeting rooms, travel services, some pets allowed, no-smoking rooms* ▭ *AE, DC, MC, V* ▯◯▮ *EP.*

★ $$$ ▥ **Holiday Inn Khajuraho.** You're not in Kansas anymore at this Holiday Inn. The Indian version is all cool white-marble elegance, complete with chandeliers, curving white staircases, and well-chosen Indian antiques throughout. The rooms (some with king beds) are decorated in soft cream shades and rich fabrics and have large bay windows, some with temple views. New rooms added in late 2003 are more spacious and luxurious, with 18-carat-gold fittings and deco lights in the marble baths, lamp-lit oil paintings, and great carved-teak headboards from Rajasthan. There's a poolside puppet show and classical music in the lobby every evening; on weekends, the bar turns into the only disco in town. ⊠ *Airport Rd., Khajuraho 471606* ☎ *7686/272–301 to 03 or 800/465–4329* 📠 *7686/272–304* ⊕ *www.ichotelsgroup.com* ⇨ *76 rooms, 6 suites* ⌂ *Restaurant, room service, IDD phones, in-room data ports, some minibars, cable TV, tennis court, pool, hair salon, hot tub, massage, sauna, steam room, bar, dance club, shop, baby-sitting, library, dry cleaning, laundry service, Internet, business services, meeting room, travel services, no-smoking rooms* ⊟ *AE, DC, MC, V* ⍥ *EP.*

$$$ 🏨 **Ken River Lodge.** Near Panna National Park, about a half hour from Khajuraho, this lodge has rock-bottom-basic mud huts and spacious tents with hot water and private baths (no phones, TVs, or air-conditioning). You'll feel like Robinson Crusoe eating at the restaurant, a platform built in a tree on a bank of the picturesque Ken River, or barbecuing over a campfire. If you plan to see Panna, you may want the Rs. 4,000-per-person-daily package, which includes all home-style Indian meals and two jeep trips into the park with an experienced guide and the lodge's own naturalist (it's Rs. 3,400 without the jeep trips). For accommodations and meals only, it's Rs. 1,700 per person. The owner has two other properties in the area: a new night-safari camp and a jungle wildlife camp reached by boat. ⊠ *Reserve through Delhi office* ☎ *09810024711 mobile* ⊠ *Near Madla Village, Panna District 488001* ☎ *7686/275–235* ⊕ *www.kenriverlodge.com* ⇨ *8 cottages, 8 tents* ⌂ *Restaurant, beach, boating, fishing; no room phones, no room TV, no a/c* ⊟ *No credit cards* ☉ *Closed June–Sept.* ⍥ *FAP.*

$$–$$$ 🏨 **Jass Radisson.** Formerly an Oberoi Trident hotel, the Jass became a Radisson in late 2003. Rooms are modern and have balconies overlooking either the pool or the hills. A total renovation of the interior was completed in September 2004, including minibars and data ports in all rooms and a new coffee shop. ⊠ *Bypass Rd., Khajuraho 471606* ☎ *7686/272–344 or 7686/274–461 to 64* 📠 *7686/272–345* ⊕ *www.radisson.com* ⇨ *91 rooms, 3 suites* ⌂ *Restaurant, cable TV, tennis court, pool, health club, bar, meeting room, travel services* ⊟ *AE, DC, MC, V* ⍥ *EP.*

$$–$$$ 🏨 **Usha Bundela.** This two-story white hotel has abundant marble, which gives it a generally cool feel. The rooms are very comfortable, with French doors and balconies overlooking the gardens. Puppet shows are held on the lawn in the evenings, and yoga and meditation classes can be arranged. There's also a jogging track. ⊠ *Temple Rd., Khajuraho 471606* ☎ *7686/272–386 or 7686/272–387* 📠 *7686/272–385* ⊕ *www.ushashriramhotels.com* ⇨ *68 rooms, 2 suites* ⌂ *Restaurant, coffee shop, room service, cable TV, pool, massage, badminton, bar, shop, baby-sitting, dry cleaning, laundry service, Internet, meeting room, travel services* ⊟ *AE, DC, MC, V* ⍥ *EP.*

¢ ⊡ **Jhankar.** This one-story government-owned hotel has spacious, clean rooms with worn modern furnishings and either air-conditioning or fans. ⬩ *Reserve through MPSTDC, Gangotri Bldg., 4th fl., T. T. Nagar, Bhopal 462003* ⊠ *Airport Rd., Khajuraho 471606* ☎ *7686/274–063 or 7686/274–194* 🖶 *755/774–289* ⬩⚲ *19 rooms* ⌂ *Restaurant, room service, cable TV, bar, laundry service, dry cleaning, Internet; no a/c in some rooms* ▤ *MC, V* ⍥❘ *EP.*

Shopping

Numerous shops around the Western Group of temples sell curios, including humorous knockoffs of Khajuraho's erotic sculptures, as well as tribal metalwork. **Shilpgram** (⊠ Bamitha Rd., near Jhankar hotel ☎ 7686/272–243 or 7686/274–031 ⊕ www.oswalonline.com) is a large crafts shop owned by Agra marble-inlay makers Oswal. It's associated with a government project that hosts craftspeople from all over India for residences during peak travel season (⊙ shop and residency : Oct.–Feb., daily 11–9); you can watch the artisans at work as you shop. **Tijori** (⊠ Holiday Inn Khajuraho, Airport Rd. ☎ 7686/272–305) is a two-story shop with fine, beautifully displayed crafts, such as new and antique silver and gold jewelry, diamonds from a local mine, silver boxes and vases, enameled silver elephants, sandalwood carvings, small and very large brass statues, Varanasi and Kashmiri carpets, papier-maché, and silk and paper paintings.

Side Trips

If you have time, take an extra day to explore and picnic in the beautiful countryside around Khajuraho. Backed by the distant mountains, **Khajuraho Village**—the old residential part of town near the Eastern Group of temples—is a typical Indian village. Drive or bike to the **Gharial Sanctuary** on the Ken River, 28 km (17 mi) away; the park was set up to protect the slender-snouted crocodile and has some lovely waterfalls. October through June, hire a jeep and driver to take you to **Panna National Park**, 31 km (19 mi) from Khajuraho, to see wildlife including various antelope, deer, and a lot of monkeys; if you're lucky (and arrive very early in the morning *and* hire a guide at the park or come with Ken River Lodge), you'll see one of the 35 elusive tigers. Sign on for the elephant safari for Rs. 300. The best viewing season is January through March. (Sightings are said to be better at Bandhavgarh Park, a five-hour, 237-km [147 mi] drive from Khajuraho: it has more tigers, and the tigers have had since 1968 to get used to visitors.)

BHOPAL & ENVIRONS

Bhopal, the capital of Madhya Pradesh, blends natural beauty—it's known as the City of Lakes—ancient history, and modern comforts. Fine mosques, palaces, and markets take you back to the city's 18th- and 19th-century roots (little remains of the original 11th-century settlement), yet much of the city is new and modern. With two superb hotels, Bhopal is an ideal base for day trips to such places as Sanchi.

Bhopal

 744 km (461 mi) south of Delhi, 383 km (237 mi) southwest of Khajuraho.

Bhopal is best known for the 1984 toxic-gas leak at a Union Carbide chemical plant, which killed somewhere between 4,000 and tens of thousands of people and injured thousands more. Perhaps for this reason, the city has been slow to develop as a tourist destination, meaning its charms have thus far been preserved from the excesses of the tourism industry. It's a pretty city centered by two tree-fringed lakes—as evening approaches, a string of little sunken fountains around the edges of the lakes spout flumes into the air, adding whimsy to the scene while aerating the water. Bhopal is also a nurturing ground for the study, composition, and performance of Urdu poetry; readings draw the kind of crowds you'd expect at a pop concert. One urban legend tells of a taxi driver who kidnapped his favorite poet and forced him to recite.

Indian architect Charles Correa designed Bhopal's center for visual and performing arts, **Bharat Bhawan,** to harmonize with its surroundings as it spills down the hillside toward the lake. Various gallery spaces house excellent collections of modern and tribal arts (which you can appreciate but not learn anything about, since it's all labeled only in Hindi—here's where a guide will come in handy), a theater, indoor and outdoor auditoriums, libraries of Indian poetry and music, and a café. ⊠ *Shamla Hills* ☎ *755/266–0239 or 755/266–0353* 🖃 *Rs. 10* 𖤐 *Feb.–Oct., Tues.–Sun. 2–8; Nov.–Jan., Tues.–Sun. 1–7.*

The small **Birla Museum,** attached to the Lakshmi Narayan Temple, houses a good collection of ancient sculpture from various districts of Madhya Pradesh. ⊠ *Arera Hill* ☎ *755/255–1388* 🖃 *Rs. 3* 𖤐 *Tues.–Sun. 9:30–1 and 1:30–5.*

The **Government Archaeological Museum** has 10th- to 12th-century temple sculptures—from all over Madhya Pradesh—nicely displayed indoors and out in the garden. Among the other exhibits are 87 Jain lost-wax bronzes found in a single hoard and copies of paintings from the Bagh Caves near Mandu. ⊠ *2 Banganga Rd., opposite Ravindra Bhavan* ☎ *755/255–3542* 🖃 *Rs. 30* 𖤐 *Tues.–Sun. 10–5.*

The only way into the 1837 **Jama Masjid,** with its gold-crown minarets, is on foot through the bustling narrow lanes of the Chowk (central market). Consider combining a visit to the mosque with a shopping excursion; after an hour of negotiating prices, you may appreciate the spiritual respite.

Madhya Pradesh tourism's **Boat Club,** on the road to the zoo, rents motor-, paddle-, sail-, and rowboats as well as kayaks, canoes, and windsurfers for exploration of the Upper Lake. Fees are nominal; with notice, the club staff can arrange for a guide to go with you. ⊠ *Lake View Rd.* ☎ *755/313–0405* 𖤐 *Daily sunrise–sunset.*

Manav Sangrahalaya (the National Museum of Mankind) celebrates the many cultures of India past and present. One part of the 200-acre campus is the open-air Tribal Heritage Park, which exhibits some 40 tribal houses and other structures transported from their original locations. The houses are grouped together—sometimes with such additions as farm implements or surrounded by typical grass fences—to give a picture of life in villages from Gujarat's Kutch area, with its whitewashed, mirror-studded sculpted-mud furnishings, to coastal Kerala, with its beautiful wood houses that elegantly screen out the hot southern sun. Avoid venturing off the path into the long grass, the authentic natural habitat of snakes. Aside all this tradition is a very modern-looking new building that houses a museum, which was built in 2004, with a permanent collection of 12,000 objects, from costumes and arts and crafts to agricultural and household implements. ⊠ *Shamla Hills* ☎ *755/254–5458* 🖼 *Rs. 10* ⊙ *Tues.–Sun. 10–6.*

The **Taj-ul-Masajid** (Crown of Mosques), one of India's largest mosques, is a striking red sandstone building with white marble onion-shaped domes, octagonal minarets, and a vast main prayer hall noted for its massive pillars. Construction began during the reign of Shah Jehan Begum (1868–1901), third in a line of powerful woman rulers of Bhopal, but wasn't completed until 1971. Come just before dusk, when the sun sets over the nearby lake and small boys play cricket in the spacious courtyard. Note that this place is closed to non-Muslims during worship hours: 6:30 to 7:30 AM, 1 to 2 PM, 4 to 5 PM. ⊠ *Airport Rd.* ⊙ *Daily 6:30 AM–8 PM.*

☾ **Van Vihar** (Bhopal National Park), on the Upper Lake, is really a glorified zoo, but makes for a pleasant walk. Park stations allow you to observe tigers, leopards, lions, bears, and crocodiles from the safe side of a fenced ravine. The best time to view wildlife is just before feeding times (usually 7 AM and 4:30 PM). ⊠ *Lake View Rd.* 🖼 *Rs. 100, cars Rs. 30* ⊙ *Sat.–Thurs. 7–11 and 3–5:30.*

Where to Stay & Eat

$$ ✗ **At Home in Bhopal.** Tour guide Rekha Chopra of Radiant Travels shares her home and family with you as she serves her delicious, eggless vegetarian cooking—generally dal, rice, roti, and cheese and vegetable dishes. After eating, you're welcome to try your hand at rolling and making fresh roti. Before you leave, she'll wrap you in wedding garb (male or female) so you can have a picture of yourself decked out in regal Indian fashion. ⊠ *24 Ahmedabad Rd.* ☎ *755/254–0560* 🕭 *Reservations essential* 🖃 *No credit cards.*

★ **$$$** ✗🖽 **Jehan Numa Palace.** At this graceful onetime royal guest house convenient to the New Market area, most of the pleasant rooms, simply decorated in Indian fabrics, open off a garden courtyard filled with flowers. Rooms in a brand-new wing are a third larger, face the huge, palm-fringed pool, and have Internet access. There's lots to do here, thanks to a good health club with ayurvedic massage (a spa is planned for late 2004), a pub with dancing on weekends, a new bakery/café for when you need a cappuccino fix, and a backyard area where children can ride horses. Shahnama ($$$$; Rs. 450–Rs. 500) serves excellent Indian and Continental food; an evening outdoor dining area is built around an open-fire kitchen. ⊠ *157 Shamla Hills, 462013* ☎ *755/266–1100 to 04*

☎ *755/266–1720* ⊕ *www.hoteljehanumapalace.com* ☁ *69 rooms, 6 suites* ⟁ *Restaurant, coffee shop, in-room data ports, café, minibars, cable TV, tennis court, pool, hair salon, gym, fitness classes, yoga, 2 bars, shop, Internet, business services, convention center, travel services* ▭ *AE, DC, MC, V* |◎| *EP.*

★ **$$–$$$** ▦ **Noor-Us-Sabah Palace.** Built in the 1920s for the daughter of a nawab, the "Light of Dawn" palace is an elegant Heritage Hotel near the old city's mosques and market. It sits high up on a hill, with a wonderful view of the Upper Lake from the lawn (where you can take your meals) and from the balconies of all guest rooms. Reception areas are resplendent with Italian white marble, crystal chandeliers, and such antiquities as a silver-clad royal wedding palanquin. Guest rooms are beautifully done with carved-wood furniture, gilt-frame art, and marble baths; rooms on the first floor (especially the Nazir ud-Daulah Suite) have the best views and furnishings. A previously unused wing is being converted into guest rooms, to be open by the end of 2004. ✉ *VIP Rd., Koh-e-Fiza 462001* ☎ *755/522–3333* ⌨ *755/522–7777* ⊕ *www. noorussabahpalace.com or www.welcomheritage.com* ☁ *36 rooms, 3 suites* ⟁ *2 restaurants, room service, IDD phones, in-room data ports, some minibars, cable TV, pool, croquet, bar, library, baby-sitting, dry cleaning, laundry service, Internet, business services, travel services* ▭ *AE, DC, MC, V* |◎| *EP.*

$$ ▦ **Hotel Lake View Ashok.** At this government-run hotel right on the lake, each room has a tiny private balcony overlooking the water. The style is simple and functional, with no frills, but it's all very clean. Suites have minirefrigerators; third-floor rooms have tubs. The pleasant multicuisine restaurant, with wraparound windows, takes full advantage of the lake view. ✉ *Shamla Hills, 462013* ☎ *755/266–0090 to 93 or 755/523– 0090 to 93* ⌨ *755/266–0096* ✎ *hlvashok@sancharnet.in* ☁ *39 rooms, 4 suites* ⟁ *Restaurant, room service, IDD phones, in-room data ports, cable TV, bar, shops, baby-sitting, dry cleaning, laundry services, business services, meeting rooms* ▭ *AE, DC, MC, V* |◎| *EP.*

Shopping

Shops are generally open from 10:30 to 8; those in the New Market close on Monday, and those in the old town around Jama Masjid close on Sunday. At the **Chowk,** the market in the heart of the old city, you can spend hours wandering or bargaining for all manner of Bhopali crafts and specialties, including silver jewelry, saris, and ornately beaded and embroidered purses and pillows. **Mrignayani** (✉ 23 Shopping Centre ☎ 755/255–4162), in the shop-filled New Market area, carries gold- and silver-embroidered saris, ready-to-wear clothing, silk and other yardgoods, and lots of kitschy crafts.

Side Trips from Bhopal

The 11th-century **Bhojeshwar Temple** is a simple square in which a huge Shiva lingam—a cylinder of stone 7½ feet tall with an 18-foot circumference—rises from a stone pedestal. An apparatus of ropes and pulleys "feed" the lingam with offerings of fresh milk, and devotees dress it with fresh flowers. The temple was never completed, and the earthen ramp used to raise it still stands. There are carvings on the dome, doorway, and pillar brackets. This isn't essential viewing unless you're already going to visit the nearby Bhimbetka Caves. ⊠ *28 km (17 mi) southeast of Bhopal, in Bhojpur* ☜ *Rs. 10* ☉ *Daily sunrise–sunset.*

Fifteen of the **Bhimbetka Caves,** actually naturally formed open rock shelters with well-preserved prehistoric paintings, are accessible to visitors along a marked path. (About 500 others are scattered throughout this World Heritage Site, but you're advised to stick to the paths—there are animals, including a boar, that you might not want to meet up with.) The paintings, in white, red, green, or yellow, date from the Paleolithic era (huge bison, tigers, and rhinos) to the Mesolithic (small, stylized figures hunting with weapons or dancing with hands joined) to the cruder efforts of medieval times. Among the paintings you'll also spy musical instruments, monkeys, hunters on horseback, and a big, yellow vase of flowers. You can combine a visit here with a trip to Bhojeshwar Temple, about 1 km away, for a half-day excursion. ⊠ *46 km (29 mi) southeast of Bhopal on rural rd.* ☜ *Rs. 10* ☉ *Daily sunrise–sunset.*

Fodor'sChoice
★
One of India's most important Buddhist sites as well as a World Heritage Site, serene **Sanchi** consists of a group of stupas, and monastery and temple ruins on a hilltop chosen for its isolation, and is conducive to contemplation. The famous domed Stupa 1, 36.6 meters in diameter, was built in the 2nd century BC over a damaged brick stupa built a century earlier by the Mauryan emperor Ashoka. Its four amazing gates, or *toranas,* opening into a ground-level path by which devotees may circumambulate the stupa, were added in the 1st century BC. Once painted, as traces reveal, the toranas are elaborately and beautifully carved with stories from the life of Buddha, scenes from the *Jatakas,* royal processions, glimpses of heaven, monkeys and elephants, musicians and dancers, and even erotic scenes (at odds with Buddhism). An inscription on the west gateway identifies the sculptors as ivory workers, an explanation for the carvings' precision. The north gate is the best preserved and fully displays the carvers' artistry in its natural, supple forms and movement. Against the walls facing the gates are four images of a haloed Buddha seated under a pillared canopy; these images date to Gupta rule in the 5th century AD. Twin staircases lead to a second processional path along a gallery. The Archaeological Survey of India Museum, just before the entrance to Sanchi, displays some of India's earliest known artworks, found during excavation of the site, including the superb capital from the Ashoka Pillar by the south gate. Restoration and excavation are ongoing. ⊠ *46 km (29 mi) northeast of Bhopal on rural rd.* ☜ *Sanchi Rs. 250; museum Rs. 5* ☉ *Site: Sat.–Thurs. sunrise–sunset; museum: Sat.–Thurs. 10–5.*

★
A 13-km (8-mi) detour from Sanchi takes you to the remarkable **Udaygiri Caves,** a group of sanctuaries carved into caves and rock faces on a sandstone hill. Some of the sculptures—distinctive examples of Gupta art—date to the 4th and 5th centuries AD. A few not to miss: in cave 5, by the road, a beautifully carved giant Vishnu in his boar incarnation stands, victorious, dangling the goddess Prithvi from his tusk as rows and rows of sadhus thank him for saving the earth (Prithvi), who had

been held captive under the sea. In cave 12, another giant image of Vishnu reclines on a bed of snakes, having given birth from his navel to the god Brahma (now missing) to again save the earth. In cave 3, the face of Shiva appears on a lingam, his third eye prominent on his forehead. ⊠ *60 km (37 mi) northeast of Bhopal* 🎫 *Free* ⊙ *Daily sunrise–sunset.*

VARANASI, LUCKNOW, & BODHGAYA

Spread out along the Ganges, Varanasi's interior lanes and ghats (staircases leading down to the river) throb with religious and commercial energy like no other place in India. Sarnath, just north of Varanasi, is the historic center of the Buddhist world, and Bodhgaya, east of Varanasi in the state of Bihar, is an international center of Buddhist worship. European-flavored Lucknow, the capital of Uttar Pradesh, is an easy diversion between Varanasi and Delhi.

Varanasi

676 km (419 mi) northeast of Bhopal, 406 km (252 mi) east of Khajuraho, 765 km (474 mi) southeast of Delhi, 677 km (420 mi) northwest of Calcutta.

Varanasi, in Uttar Pradesh, has been the religious capital of Hinduism through all recorded time. No one knows the date of the city's founding, but when Siddhartha Gautama, the historic Buddha, came here around 550 BC to deliver his first teaching he found an ancient and developed settlement. Contemporary with Babylon, Nineveh, and Thebes, Varanasi has been called the oldest continuously inhabited city on earth.

Every devout Hindu wants to visit Varanasi to purify body and soul in the Ganges, to shed all sin, and, if possible, to die here in old age and achieve *moksha,* release from the cycle of rebirth. Descending from the Himalayas on its long course to the Bay of Bengal, the Ganges is believed by Hindus to hold the power of salvation in each drop. Pilgrims seek that salvation along the length of the river, but their holiest site is Varanasi. Every year, the city welcomes millions of pilgrims for whom these waters—fouled by the pollution of humans both living and dead—remain pristine enough to cleanse the soul.

Commonly called Banaras or Benares—or, by devout Hindus, Kashi ("resplendent with light")—Varanasi has about 1 million inhabitants. About 70 ghats line a 6-km (4-mi) stretch of the Ganges, effortlessly wedding the great Hindu metropolis to the river. At the heart of the city is a maze of streets and alleys, hiding a disorderly array of at least 2,000 temples and shrines. Domes, minarets, pinnacles, towers, and derelict 18th-century palaces dominate the river's sacred left bank. The streets are noisy and rife with color, and the air hangs heavy, as if in collaboration with the clang of temple gongs and bells. Some houses have simply decorated entrances; other buildings are ornate with lacy, Indian-style gingerbread (filigreed ornamentation) on balconies and verandas. You're likely to encounter funeral processions, cows munching on garlands destined for the gods, and, especially near the Golden Temple (Kashi Vishvanath) and centrally located Dashashvamedh Ghat, assertive hawkers and phony guides.

Its variety of shrines notwithstanding, Varanasi is essentially a temple city dedicated to Shiva, Lord of Destruction. Shiva is typically said to live in the Himalayas, but myths say he was unable to leave Kashi after manifesting himself here. Exiling the earthly maharaja to Ramnagar, across the river, Shiva took up permanent residence here. (As a popular song has it, in Varanasi "every pebble is a Shiva linga.") The city itself is said to rest on a prong of Shiva's trident, above the cycles of creation, decay, and destruction that prevail in the rest of the world.

The maze of lanes may seem daunting, but you're never far from the river, where you can hire a boat for a quiet ride. Banarasis, as the locals call themselves, typically hire boats at sundown for twilight excursions, sometimes with tiny candlelit lamps made of leaves and marigolds, which they leave on the water as offerings. The Ganges turns sharply at Varanasi to flow south to north past the city, giving the riverbank a perfect alignment with the rising sun. In sacred geography the city is demarcated by the Ganges to the east and two small rivers—the Varana, to the north, which winds by the cantonment area and joins the Ganges near Raj Ghat, and the Asi, a small stream in the south.

Traditionally, Varanasi is seen as a field divided into three sections named after important temples to Shiva. Omkareshvara is the namesake temple in the northern section, which is probably the oldest area but is now impoverished and seldom visited by pilgrims. The central section is named after Kashi Vishvanath, the famous "Golden Temple." Vishvanath itself means "Lord of the Universe," one of Shiva's names, and there are many Vishvanath temples. The southern area, the Kedar Khand, is named for Kedareshvara, a temple easily picked out from the river thanks to the vertical red and white stripes painted on its walls, a custom of the South Indian worshipers who are among the temple's devotees. The ghats stretch along the river from Raj Ghat in the north to Asi Ghat in the south; beyond Asi is the university, across the river from Ramnagar Fort and Palace. The city itself spreads out behind the ghats, with the hotels in the cantonment area about 20 minutes from the river by auto-rickshaw.

It's wise to hire a guide in Varanasi. For one to four people, India Tourism's licensed guides cost Rs. 280 for one to four hours, Rs. 400 for up to eight hours (if your block of time starts before 7:30 AM or finishes after 8:30 PM, add Rs. 30); cars and boats can be hired from the office as well—a way to avoid haggling on the streets or the ghats. Also, many temples and mosques are open only to their own sects, so a government guide may help get you in.

a good walk

Numbers in the text correspond to numbers in the margin and on the Varanasi map.

To get a sense of the pilgrim's experience, walk from Dashashvamedh Road down the relatively broad, shop-lined lane (Vishvanath Gali, the main sari bazaar) to Vishvanath Temple. The lane turns sharply right

Alamgir
Mosque **34**

Bharat Kala
Bhavan
Museum **42**

Chausath Yogini
Temple **37**

Dashashvamedh
Ghat **35**

Dhobi Ghat ...**38**

Durga Temple .**40**

Gyanvapi
Mosque **32**

Kashi Vishvanath
Temple **31**

Kedareshvara
Temple **39**

Manikarnika
Ghat **33**

Ramnagar Fort
and Palace **43**

Sankat Mochan
Temple **41**

Shitala Temple .**36**

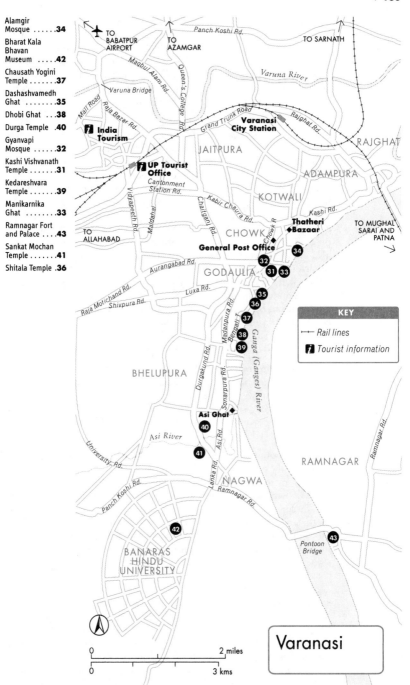

Varanasi

at a large image of the elephant-head god Ganesh, then passes the brightly painted wooden entrance to the 1725 temple of Vishvanath's consort, Annapurna, on the right, and **Kashi Vishvanath Temple** ㉛ itself, on the left, with the silver doorway and the policeman ready to pat you down before you enter. Step across the street to get a peek at Kashi's gold stupa. Just past the temple complex the Vishvanath lane intersects with Kachauri Gali, a lane (*gali*) named for the small, deep-fried puris cooked here for pilgrims.

Turn left; the entrance to the **Gyanvapi Mosque** ㉜ compound (closed to non-Muslims) is on your left. The short, stepped lane passes under a room in a house that spans both sides of the lane. On the left are the Gyanvapi well and a cluster of tree-shaded Hindu shrines. Here many Hindus begin their pilgrimage to Kashi, declaring their purpose with the help of a Brahmin *panda* (temple priest) in a rite known as *sankalp,* or declaration of intention. Here a young tout will probably offer to escort you to a rooftop from which you can see into the Vishvanath Temple compound. The view is fascinating; just know that this process will also involve offers of tea and the display of various wares. Farther up Kachauri Gali, a lane on the right is marked by a sign pointing toward Lalita Ghat; take this lane to a junction beside a small temple dedicated to Neelkanth Mahadev. On the right, a lane marked Bishwanath Singh Lane leads to the main cremation ground at **Manikarnika Ghat** ㉝. You can often find your way just by following the processions of funeral biers that pass with startling regularity toward Manikarnika, their bearers moving swiftly and chanting, "Ram nam satya hai" ("God's name is truth").

Walk north (upstream) past the broad, gradual steps of Scindia Ghat to Panchganga Ghat, the mythic confluence of five invisible rivers. The **Alamgir Mosque** ㉞ towers above Panchganga, and from its relatively short minaret you get a sweeping view of Varanasi and the Ganges. You can walk along the river back to **Dashashvamedh Ghat** ㉟, where a rickshaw-wallah can pedal you onward or you can take a boat.

Down the right fork of Dashashvamedh Road is Prayag Ghat. Here, at the top of the ghats on the right, is the white **Shitala Temple** ㊱. Continue south along the ghats fronting the somewhat quieter Kedar Khand section of town, which in ancient times was heavily forested and dotted with hermitages. After about 10 minutes you'll see steep steps leading up toward a house at the top of Chausath Yogini Ghat; a few yards up the lane on the right is the **Chausath Yogini Temple** ㊲. Farther south is the **Dhobi Ghat** ㊳, where washer men and women beat clothes against stone slabs on the water's edge. A little farther south is the **Kedareshvara Temple** ㊴, recognizable from the river by its South Indian–style red-and-white stripes. Anywhere along this section you can climb up the ghats and enter the city; you'll soon reach a broader gali that runs parallel to the river through Bengali Tola, home to a large community from Bengal as well as South India. You can pick up transport a little farther south, where a broad road reaches the river by the small burning ground at Harish Chandra Ghat, preferred cremation site of the *panditas,* or learned Brahmins. If you'd like to break for lunch, head to the nearby restaurant Kerala Cafe at Bhelupura Crossing.

Another half-hour's walk south brings you to Asi Ghat. Tulsi Ghat, just north of Asi, is where Tulsi Das, a medieval saint, is said to have composed his hugely popular Hindi version of the *Ramayana* epic (translated and revised from Sanskrit). The ghat is now home to the offices of the Swachha Ganga Campaign, a movement aimed at cleaning up the Ganges. From the top of Tulsi Ghat, the lane to the right leads to Lolark Kund, a deep step well surrounded by several small but important shrines. This is an extraordinary place to visit just after sunrise, when people from the neighborhood offer devotions. Asi Ghat itself is an important bathing point and the only ghat in Varanasi where bathers access the river from a plain mud bank rather than stone steps. From here, walk or hire a cycle-rickshaw to take you to the **Durga Temple** 40, or Monkey Temple, a few hundred yards west of the river. From here you can walk or drive to **Sankat Mochan Temple** 41, whose *mahant,* or head priest, leads the Swachha Ganga Campaign. A 20-minute cycle-rickshaw ride or shorter cab ride takes you to the **Bharat Kala Bhavan Museum** 42 at Banaras Hindu University. Have your driver wait for you, and if you have time (and if, in the case of a cycle-rickshaw, your driver has the energy), proceed from the university across the Ganges to **Ramnagar Fort and Palace** 43. If the pontoon bridge is closed, which it is each year from July through October and into November, after the monsoon washes it out and until it is rebuilt, you'll have to get to Ramnagar the long way—so save it for another day.

TIMING The first part of this tour, starting and ending at Dashashvamedh Road, takes about two hours. The walk from Dashashvamedh to Kedareshvara takes 45 minutes if you stop to see the temples, plus 30 minutes more from Kedar Ghat to Asi Ghat. From Asi Ghat to Bharat Kala Bhavan takes two more hours. A trip to Ramnagar by car adds about two hours more (more if the pontoon bridge is out). Varanasi is a labyrinth, however, so by all means allow time to get lost. A boat ride will also stretch your sightseeing time. Note that ghats are always open—they're essentially just steps.

What to See

34 **Alamgir Mosque.** From a dramatic high point, the Alamgir Mosque overlooks the Ganges River. Destroying the 17th-century temple Beni Madhav ka Dharehara, which had been dedicated to Vishnu, the Moghul emperor Aurangzeb built this mosque with an odd fusion of Hindu (lower portions and wall) and Muslim (upper portion) designs. Panchganga Ghat, down below, is an important bathing point, particularly on Makar Sankranti (January 14), when the sun crosses the tropic of Capricorn as the earth shifts on its axis following the winter solstice. The mosque is closed to non-Muslims. ✉ *From Dashashvamedh or Manikarnika Ghat, head north along the river; the mosque towers above Panchganga Ghat* ⏲ *Daily sunrise–sunset.*

42 **Bharat Kala Bhavan Museum.** No one interested in Indian art should miss this museum on the campus of Banaras Hindu University. The permanent collection includes brocade textiles, excellent Hindu and Buddhist sculptures, and miniature paintings from the courts of the Moghuls and the Hindu princes of the Punjab hills. One sculpture with particu-

CloseUp

HOLY INSPIRATION

Varanasi is a magnet for people with mystical leanings of any kind. Some come to Shiva's city seeking inspiration from masters of classical music or of yoga, including kundalini master (and Madonna's Sanskrit coach) Dr. Vagish Shastri of the Kundalini Meditation Center at Shivala Ghat, one of 75 yoga centers in the city. Some find temporary bliss through shared weed on the ghats. Others come simply to absorb the holiness of the site and the focused spiritual energy from so many centuries of fervent belief.

In the months before he died of cancer in November 2001, ex-Beatle and Hare Krishna devotee George Harrison, who discovered both mysticism and the sitar music of Varanasi native Ravi Shankar here during the 1960s, is said to have come to bathe in the waters. For days after his death fans poured into the city and kept vigil by the river on the rumor—which turned out to be false—that his wife and son would be arriving to scatter his ashes.

lar power is a 4th-century Gupta-dynasty frieze depicting Krishna (an incarnation of Vishnu) holding up Mt. Govardhan to protect his pastoral comrades from the rain. Have your car or rickshaw wait for you, as transport can be hard to find on the university's sprawling campus. ⊠ *Banaras Hindu University, Lanka* ☎ *542/230–7621* 🖃 *Rs. 40* ⊗ *Mon.–Sat. 11–4.*

③⑦ Chausath Yogini Temple. The interesting temples between Prayag and Asi ghats include this one, at the top of a particularly steep set of steps by the ghat of the same name. Originally devoted to a Tantric cult that is also associated with an important ruined temple at Khajuraho, it's now dedicated to Kali (the goddess most popular with Bengalis), known here simply as "Ma"—Mother. The worshippers are mainly widows from Varanasi's Bengali quarter; in the early morning you'll see them coming for the *darshan* (vision) of Kali after bathing in the Ganges. The temple is closed to non-Hindus. ⊗ *Daily sunrise–sunset.*

③⑤ Dashashvamedh Ghat. If you decide to hire a boat, an essential Varanasi experience, come to this unofficial "main" ghat for most purposes. The best time to see the ghats is at sunrise, when a solemn group of people and even animals—lit by the sun's darkly golden first rays—hover on the water's edge, bent on immersion in the holy stream. As you float on the river, you'll see young bodybuilders, members of the city's many wrestling clubs, exercising. Older men sit cross-legged in meditation or prayer. A carcass may even float by. ⊠ *Head east to the water from Godaulia Crossing, the central traffic circle in the Chowk area.*

FodorsChoice ★

③⑧ Dhobi Ghat. At this ghat south of Dashashvamedh, washer men and women do early morning laundry by beating it against stones in the river while their donkeys bray disconsolately on the bank. This may be the sight that moved Mark Twain to declare that "a Hindu is someone who spends his life trying to break stones with wet clothes."

40 Durga Temple. This 18th-century shrine, dedicated to the goddess Durga, Shiva's consort, stands beside a large, square pool of water due west about a kilometer from Asi Ghat. The shikhara is formed on top of five lower spires, a convergence symbolizing the belief that all five elements of the world (earth, air, water, fire, and ether) merge with the supreme. This shrine is also called the Monkey Temple, for good reason: the pests are everywhere, and they'll steal anything. The temple is closed to non-Hindus. ✉ *Durgakund Rd.* ☉ *Daily sunrise–noon and 2–sunset.*

need a break?

The **Vaatika Café,** an easygoing, inexpensive second-floor outdoor eatery with tables looking out on Asi Ghat, serves excellent thin-crust pizza made in an Italian oven with real mozzarella, as well as pasta dishes, bona fide espresso, and other unlikely delicacies.

32 Gyanvapi Mosque. Moghul emperor Aurangzeb pulled down Vishveswara Temple to erect this mosque, and the building's foundation and rear still show parts of the original temple. The tallest of the mosque's minarets, which dominated the skyline of the holy city, collapsed during a flood in 1948. The surrounding area—next to Kashi Vishvanath—has been the focus of Hindu revivalist attempts to reconsecrate the site of the former temple, and is staffed with police and fenced with barbed wire. It's normally very sedate, however, and is an important starting point for Hindu pilgrims. The mosque is closed to non-Muslims. ☉ *Daily sunrise–sunset.*

31 Kashi Vishvanath Temple. Dedicated to Shiva, whose pillar of light is said to have appeared on this spot, this temple in the old city is the most sacred shrine in Varanasi. Known as the Golden Temple for the gold plate on its spire—a gift from the Sikh maharaja Ranjit Singh in 1835—the temple is set back from the Ganges between Dashashvamedh and Manikarnika ghats. Vishvanath is technically off-limits to non-Hindus, so your best bet is to glimpse it from the top floor of the house opposite (pay the owner a few rupees). You'll see men and women making offerings to the lingam in the inner shrine. The present temple was built by Rani Ahalyabai of Indore in 1776, near the site of the original shrine, which had been destroyed by Aurangzeb. Various forms of the *arti* prayer ceremony are performed outside at 3:30 AM, noon, and 7:30 and 11 PM. The temple is closed to non-Hindus. ✉ *Vishvanath Gali* ☉ *Daily 4 AM–11 PM.*

39 Kedareshvara Temple. You can recognize this temple, the most important Shiva temple in this part of town, by its red-and-white candy-stripe walls. Take off your shoes at the small rear door at the top of the ghats before entering. The lingam here is an unsculpted stone and is said to have emerged spontaneously when a pure-hearted yet feeble devotee of Shiva prayed for a chance to visit Kedareshvara Shiva temple in the Himalayas. Shiva is the god of destruction and fierce in aspect, but, paradoxically, he is famously kind to his devotees, or *bhaktas.* In this myth, Shiva was touched by his bhakta's piety, so instead of bringing him to the mountain, Shiva brought his own image to the bhakta. The lingam emerged out of a plate of rice and lentils, called *kichiri,* which believers see in the rough surface of the lingam's natural stone. ✉ *Bengali Tola at Kedar Ghat* ☉ *Daily 5 AM–11 PM.*

★ ㉝ **Manikarnika Ghat.** Thin blue smoke twists up to the sky from fires at Varanasi's main burning ghat. Day and night, bodies wrapped in silk or linen—traditionally white for men, red or orange for women—are carried through the streets on bamboo stretchers to the smoking pyres. After a brief immersion in the Ganges and a short wait, the body is placed on the pyre for the ritual that precedes the cremation. Funeral parties dressed in white, the color of mourning, hover with their deceased. Photographing funeral ghats is strictly forbidden, but you are allowed to watch. At the top of Manikarnika's steps is a small, deep pool, or *kund,* said to have been dug by Vishnu at the dawn of creation and thus to be the first *tirtha*—literally, "ford," and figuratively a place of sacred bathing. Shiva is said to have lost an earring (*manikarnika*) as he trembled in awe before this place, one of the holiest sites in Varanasi.

㊸ **Ramnagar Fort and Palace.** Across the Ganges is the 17th-century palace of the Maharaja of Varanasi, who still lives here (if the flag is up, he's in residence)—thus the coterie of guards sleeping in open rooms off the entranceway—and performs important ceremonial and charitable functions. The Durbar Hall (Public Audience Chamber) and Royal Museum have good collections, but the place is sadly run-down and the objects are not well maintained. A case full of beautiful black musical instruments, for example, is so completely white with dust and the case so covered with grime that it's almost impossible to see anything, and the royal costumes are plain ratty. Still, there are palanquins and howdahs in ivory, goldplate, or silver (completely tarnished); old carriages and cars; furniture; portraits of maharajas; and arms from Africa, Burma, and Japan. The palace was built to resist the floods of the monsoon, which play havoc with the city side of the river. (Official taxi rate for four hours from the Cantonment area to here: Rs. 400.) Note that the site is closed some days during monsoon season. ⊠ *End of Pontoon Bridge, off Ramnagar Rd.* ☎ *542/233–9322* 🎟 *Rs. 7* ☉ *Daily 10–5.*

㊶ **Sankat Mochan Temple.** Sankat Mochan (Deliverer from Troubles) is one of Varanasi's most beloved temples, as well as one of its oldest—it was built in the late 16th century. Though the city has encroached all around it, the building still stands in a good-size, tree-shaded enclosure, like temples elsewhere in India. (Most temples in Varanasi are squeezed between other buildings.) Although most of the city's major shrines are dedicated to Shiva or various aspects of the mother goddess, Sankat Mochan belongs to Hanuman, the monkey god, revered for his dedicated service to Rama, an incarnation of Vishnu whose story is told in the *Ramayana*. The best time to see Sankat Mochan is early evening, when dozens of locals stop for a brief visit at the end of the workday, and on Tuesday and Saturday—sacred days for Hanuman—when worshippers come in large numbers to pay their respects. The temple is closed to non-Hindus. ⊠ *Durgakund Rd.* ☉ *Daily 5 AM–11 PM.*

㊱ **Shitala Temple.** This unassuming but very popular white temple near Dashashvamedh Ghat is dedicated to Shitala, the smallpox goddess. Despite the eradication of smallpox, Shitala is still an important folk goddess in North India. Here, as in many Shitala temples, a shrine has been added in honor of Santoshi Mata, the "Mother of Contentment"—a goddess who gained popularity in the 1970s when a Hindi movie was made about her. The temple is closed to non-Hindus. ⊠ *Shitala Ghat* ⊙ *Daily 5 AM–11 PM.*

Where to Stay & Eat

$$$ ✗ **Amrapali.** At this big wood-paneled restaurant lit by crystal domes and overlooking a garden full of palm trees, the lunch and dinner buffets—including several soups, steamed vegetables, and a great dessert section—are excellent. Or you can choose from four separate menus, including kababs, tandoori dishes, and thalis (served with superbly soft, warm naan), plus Chinese dishes, Continental choices, and snacks. ⊠ *Clarks Varanasi, The Mall* ☎ *542/250–1011* ▭ *AE, DC, MC, V.*

¢ ✗ **Anandaram Jaipuriya Bhavan.** Most Hindu pilgrims in Varanasi dine in a sort of cafeteria called a *bhojanalaya*, where they can eat reliable, affordable meals cooked in the style of their native region. Housed in the third story of a building that's also a guest house for affluent Rajasthani pilgrims, this one is considered the best in the city. Large vegetarian meals of dal, rice, chapatis, vegetables, and yogurt are served on thalis to patrons seated in rows on planks on the floor. The food is delicious. ⊠ *About 100 yards north of Godaulia Crossing, on west side of rd. to Chowk* ☎ *542/235–2674, 542/235–2709, or 542/235–2766* ▭ *No credit cards.*

¢ ✗ **Bread of Life Bakery.** This pleasant café and haven for homesick Western palates is about 10 minutes' walk northwest from Asi Ghat. It makes a great place for breakfast after a morning boat ride. Or stop in anytime to write postcards over coffee and sweets, from chocolate-chip cookies and apple strudel to eclairs and Black Forest cake. Simple lunches and dinners include omelets, quiches, sandwiches, soups and stews, pastas, and some Chinese dishes. All profits of the café and the art gallery upstairs go to charities or are used for employees' education. ⊠ *B 3/ 322 Shivala* ☎ *542/227–5012* ⊕ *www.bolbar.com* ▭ *No credit cards.*

¢ ✗ **Kerala Cafe.** As the name might tip you off, South Indian food is on the short menu at this unprepossessing, but popular little diner. The specialty is dosas—specifically masala dosas—and they're terrific, full of juicy chunks of potatoes, onion, and peas. In addition to choices like plain, tomato, or coconut *uttapams* (Indian-style pancakes), *idlis* (roasted rice pancakes), and *vadas* (fermented dal), they do a great lemon rice, with peanuts and a sprinkling of coriander leaves, and beautiful puffy pooris as big as your head. It's open for breakfast. ⊠ *Bhelupura Crossing* ☎ *No phone* ▭ *No credit cards.*

$$ ▦ **Clarks Varanasi.** Guest rooms at this fine hotel in the relatively quiet Cantonment area, where the upscale properties are located, have attractive light and cheery modern furnishings. The best rooms overlook the palm-fringed pool or lawn. The best thing about staying here—besides the great shopping arcade—may be the restaurant, Amrapali. For this property and Clarks Tower down the street, Clarks maintains a *haveli*, a traditional Rajput mansion, at Raja Ghat for evening cultural programs and morning demonstrations of Hindu rituals; trips are arranged for groups, but you can sign on individually if space is available. ⊠ *The Mall, 221002* ☎ *542/250–1011 to 20* ▤ *542/250–2736* ⊕ *www. hotelclarks.com* ⤴ *111 rooms, 2 suites* ⌂ *Restaurant, coffee shop,* *room service, IDD phones, in-room data ports, minibars, cable TV, pool, bar, shops, Internet, business services, travel services, meeting rooms* ▭ *AE, DC, MC, V* ⑩ *EP.*

★ **$$** ⌨ **Taj Ganges.** This is Varanasi's quietest hotel, particularly if you get an upper-story room facing the adjacent Nadesar Palace, once the maharaja's palace but long abandoned. (Taj recently acquired the palace and is turning it into an eight-suite boutique hotel, set to open sometime in 2005.) Rooms are spacious and modern, done in soft colors with brass-accent furniture, and service is superior. Hop a horse-drawn carriage to tour Taj's 40 acres of grounds, complete with rose and peacock gardens. There's also a jogging track. Weekend nights there's an hour of dancing on the lawn. ✉ *Raja Bazaar Rd., 221002* ☎ *542/250–3001 to 19* 📠 *542/250–1343 or 542/250–2724* ⊕ *www.tajhotels.com* ⇨ *120 rooms, 10 suites* ♨ *2 restaurants, coffee shop, room service, in-room data ports, in-room safes, minibars, cable TV, tennis court, pool, gym, hair salon, massage, sauna, spa, steam room, croquet, badminton, recreation room, bar, baby-sitting, dry cleaning, laundry service, concierge, Internet, business services, meeting rooms, travel services, no-smoking rooms* ▭ *AE, DC, MC, V* ⑩ *EP.*

$ ⌨ **Palace on Ganges.** At this comfortable new heritage hotel created from a century-old building on Asi Ghat, rooms recall Gujarat (with brightly colored quilted drapes studded with mirrorwork), Rajasthan (elaborately carved doors and furnishings), Assam (lots of bamboo), or other states while delivering all the modern comforts of home. Rooms at the front have a great view of the ghat, but others are quieter. Meals are "pure" vegetarian, meaning no plant parts that grew underground, such as onion, garlic, etc. ✉ *B-1/158 Asi Ghat, 221001* ☎ *542/231–5050 or 542/231–4304 to 05* 📠 *542/231–4306* ⊕ *www.palaceonganges.com* ⇨ *42 rooms* ♨ *Dining room, room service, minibars, cable TV, laundry service* ▭ *MC, V* ⑩ *EP.*

★ **¢–$** ⌨ **Ganga View.** This guest house has small, basic rooms with quirky charm—for example, there's a jungle painting and stone shrine (with goddess) you sleep under in Room 13—and a great veranda with tables overlooking the river and Asi Ghat. (The Rs. 1,200 rooms without air-conditioning are closest to the ghat's noises and are best avoided unless you're a heavy sleeper.) Converted from the owner's family home, the hotel still has a homey feeling; dinners are served under a galaxy of lamps and chandeliers that light the classical Indian concerts or lectures often held here. The meals are pure vegetarian, but so delicious you won't miss a thing that's been left out. Book months ahead for peak season. ✉ *Asi Ghat, 221006* ☎ *542/231–3218* 📠 *542/236–9695* ⇨ *11 rooms* ♨ *Dining room; no room phones, no TVs, no a/c in some rooms* ▭ *No credit cards* ⑩ *EP.*

¢ ⌨ **Hotel India.** For a less expensive option in the Cantonment area, try this hotel, renovated in May 2003. There are five restaurants in all, including a multicuisine and Chinese–Thai restaurant, a rooftop Punjabi spot with a stone fountain, and a bar–restaurant on a lower rooftop that's good for a drink and a kabab. Attractive standard rooms are done in browns and golds with twin beds, which can be joined, and carpets. Executive rooms have king beds, marble floors and big marble baths, armchairs with silky red-and-gold upholstery, and drapes that look like tapestries. ⊠ *59 Patel Nagar, 221001* ☎ *542/250–7593 to 97* 🖷 *542/ 250–7598* ⊕ *www.hotelindiavns.com* ⇨ *68 rooms, 2 suites* ⌂ *5 restaurants, gym, bar* ⊟ *AE, MC, V* ▮⊙▮ *EP.*

★ ¢ 🔲 **Pradeep.** This shining example for inexpensive lodgings in India is clean without feeling institutional. It's in the Lahurabir area, a 20-minute walk northwest of the Chowk and the river. Hallways are cheerful, and rooms attractively furnished in browns and golds against cream walls (ask for one away from the road). For the price, consider springing for the bigger and nicer executive rooms, with twin or king beds. The rooftop restaurant, Eden—with white wrought-iron garden furniture set amid tidy plots of green lawn, flowers, and fountains—serves barbecue and the usual multicuisine mix, as does the popular Poonam. The owners also run Palace on Ganges. ⊠ *Jagatganj 221002* ☎ *542/220–4963, 542/220–4594, or 542/220–7231* 🖷 *542/220–4898* ⊕ *www.hotelpradeep.com* ⇨ *45 rooms* ⌂ *2 restaurants, room service, refrigerators, cable TV, bar, dry cleaning, laundry service, business services, meeting room, travel services; no a/c in some rooms* ⊟ *AE, DC, MC, V* ▮⊙▮ *EP.*

Shopping

The city's shops are open generally from 10 to 8; the larger shops close on Sunday, but the street sellers and smaller shops are open daily. One of India's chief weaving centers, Varanasi is famous for its silk-brocade saris. Some saris are still woven with real gold and silver threads, though in most noncustom work the real thing has been replaced by artificial fibers. (You can see the fabric being woven by entire families in Muslim neighborhoods like Qazi Sadullahpura.) Most hotels sell silk-brocade saris in their shops, but the main bazaars for saris are in **Vishvanath Gali**—the lane leading from Dashashvamedh Road to the Kashi Vishvanath Temple, where the customers are mainly pilgrims and tourists. Among the brass vendors in **Thatheri Bazaar** (Brass Market), on a small lane just 50 meters north of the Chowk, some shops sell silks and woolens to a local crowd. **Banaras Art Culture** (⊠ Shri Krishna Kunj, B–2/114 Bhadhaini, near Bread of Life Bakery ☎ 542/231–3615 or 542/231–1715) displays regional and other Indian art, folk art, and crafts—bronzes, terra-cottas, marble sculptures, wood carvings, paintings—in many rooms of an old home. **Cottage Industries Exposition** (⊠ Mint House, Nadesar, across from the Taj ☎ 542/250–0814) has excellent Varanasi weaves in silk and cotton, a vast rug room, plus brass wares and Kashmiri embroidered shawls. **Dharam Kumar Jain & Sons** (⊠ K 37/12 Sona Kuan ☎ 542/233–3354), operating out of their home near Thatheri Bazaar, have an extraordinary private collection of old brocade saris, pashmina shawls, and other textiles. **Mehta International** (⊠ S 20/51 Varuna Bridge ☎ 542/234–4489 or 542/250–7364), in the Cantonment-area around the corner from the Radisson, is a large showroom with a wide selection of fine saris, scarves, bed covers, fabric, and some elaborately worked tapestries.

Nightlife & the Arts

Ganga Arti is a new *arti* (prayer ceremony) performed at Dashashvamedh Ghat every night at sunset. The steps fill with people singing Vedic hymns, lighting lamps, and praying along with the priests, but it's perhaps best appreciated from a boat so you can take in the whole scene without the crush on the ghat. **Gyanpravaha Institute for Indological Learning** (⊠ east side of Pontoon Bridge ☎ 542/236–6326) holds seminars and cultural shows, and has a **museum and library** (☉ Tues.–Sun. 10–5). **Nagari Natak Mandal** (⊠ Kabir Chowra) presents infrequent concerts of some of Varanasi's—and India's—best musicians. There are also numerous music festivals. Ask your hotel to check the local Hindi newspaper, *Aj,* for events while you're in town.

Sarnath

④ *11 km (7 mi) north of Varanasi.*

In 528 BC Siddhartha Gautama, having attained enlightenment at Bodhgaya, preached his first sermon (now called Dharma Chakra Pravartan, or Set in Motion the Wheel of Law) in what is today Sarnath's Deer Park. Here he revealed his Eightfold Path leading to the end of sorrow and the attainment of enlightenment. Three hundred years later, in the 3rd century BC, the Mauryan emperor Ashoka arrived. A zealous convert to Buddhism, he built in Sarnath several stupas (large, mound-shape reliquary shrines) and a pillar with a lion capital that was adopted by 20th-century India as the national emblem. The wheel motif under the lions' feet represents the *dharma chakra,* the wheel (*chakra*) of Buddhist teaching (*dharma*), which began in Sarnath. The chakra is replicated at the center of the national flag. Sarnath reached its zenith by the 4th century AD, under the Gupta dynasty, and was occupied into the 9th century, when Buddhist influence in India began to wane. By the 12th century, Sarnath had more or less fallen to Muslim invaders and begun a long decay. In 1836 Sir Alexander Cunningham started extensive excavations here, uncovering first a stone slab with an inscription of the Buddhist creed, then numerous other relics. It was then that the Western world realized the Buddha had been an actual person, not a mythical figure. Most of the sites are in a well-manicured park behind a gate (admission is Rs. 100). Any taxi or auto rickshaw will take you to Sarnath from Varanasi; India Tourism also arranges a three-hour trip (giving you two hours to explore) from Cantonment area hotels or its office for Rs. 300.

In the 16th century, the Moghul emperor Akbar built a terraced brick tower on top of the 5th-century **Chaukhandi Stupa** to commemorate his father's visit some years earlier. It's the first monument you come to in Sarnath, on the left-hand side of Ashoka Marg on the way to the park.

Legend has it that the Buddha was incarnated as King of the Deer in the **Deer Park,** north of Dhamekh Stupa. Before you leave Sarnath, take a short walk here, pay a few rupees for some carrots, and feed the current denizens.

Dappled with geometric and floral ornamentation, the stone-and-brick **Dhamekh Stupa** is, at 43.6 meters in height and 228 meters in diameter (at the base), the largest surviving monument in Sarnath. Built around AD 500, Dhamekh is thought to mark the place where the Buddha delivered his sermon, though excavations have unearthed the remains of an even earlier stupa of Mauryan bricks of the Gupta period (200 BC).

The **Mulagandha Kuti Vihari Temple,** built in 1931, joins the old foundations of seven monasteries. The walls bear frescoes by a Japanese artist, Kosetsu Nosu, depicting scenes from the Buddha's life, and relics of Sakyamuni Buddha are enshrined here. On the anniversary of the temple's foundation—the first full moon in November—monks and devotees from all parts of Asia assemble here. The temple is behind a separate gate just outside the park.

★ At the entrance to the excellent **Sarnath Archaeological Museum** is Ashoka's Lion Capital, moved here from its original location in the park. Other beautiful sculpture is here as well, including lots of Buddhas; still more of Sarnath's masterpieces are in the National Museum, Delhi, and the Indian Museum, Calcutta. ✉ *Ashoka Marg at Dharmapal Marg* ☎ *542/ 585–002* 🎟 *Rs. 2* ⊘ *Sat.–Thurs. 10–5.*

Bodhgaya

④⑤ *266 km (165 mi) east of Varanasi.*

In central Bihar, one of the poorest states in India, is one of the four main pilgrimage centers of Buddhism: Bodhgaya. Here, sometime around 520 BC (or later—the commonly accepted dates are in dispute), Prince Siddhartha Gautama meditated under a pipal tree and achieved enlightenment. A descendant of that tree, grown from a cutting, still stands, and in recent decades Buddhists from around the world have built monasteries and temples nearby, each in the style of their own country. Today the so-called Buddhist Circuit (including Lumbini, his birthplace, in Nepal; and in Uttar Pradesh, Sarnath, where he preached his first sermon, and Kushinagar, where he died) brings the faithful by the busload—and a new airport just outside town brings them by the planeload from Thailand, Singapore, and elsewhere, particularly when the Dalai Lama comes to lecture, usually in late December. In the temples and while wandering the village—which can be seen by foot or bicycle rickshaw—you'll encounter lay Buddhists from Maharashtra (center of a 20th-century Buddhist revival); Tibetan monks in maroon robes, some prostrating themselves repeatedly as they approach the temple; Sri Lankan and Thai *bhikkus* (monks) in yellow robes; and a small number of Westerners, believers as well as the merely curious.

Many of India's other Buddhist centers are primarily archaeological monuments, whereas Bodhgaya gives you an idea of how Buddhism thrives as a contemporary faith. The monasteries have tried to be good neighbors: most run a school, clinic, or other project for the benefit of the local people. And other Buddhist institutions here provide charitable assistance as well. The Mahabodhi Society, a Sri Lankan organization that played a key role in reviving the practice of pilgrimage to Buddhist centers in India, runs a clinic and ambulance service from its complex on the main road. The Maitreya Project (⊕ www.maitreyaproject.org)— whose grander mission includes building a 500-foot-tall bronze Buddha in Kushinagar as an enduring symbol of "loving kindness"—has a free school for more than 200 children. The Root Institute for Wisdom Culture (☎ 631/220–0714 ⊕ www.rootinstitute.com), which runs residential workshops on Buddhism and meditation, also has a clinic with a polio-rehabilitation center. (Less structured classes are available through the International Meditation Center; ☎ 631/220–0707.)

It's a pleasure to wander among the town's temples and monasteries (most close for an hour or two at lunchtime). Many have ornately decorated interiors, including beautiful, wildly colorful wall frescoes that usually depict scenes from the life of the Buddha. The tourist office has a hard-to-read map of town; the Mahayana Guest House, on the one main road, has a better map, which they may give you if you ask nicely.

Bodhgaya's **Archaeological Museum** holds some of the Mahabodhi Temple's original railing—6-foot pillars and cross-bands of granite and sandstone, carved with themes from the *Jatakas*, zodiac signs, folk scenes, and inscriptions—which have been arranged like a Buddhist Stonehenge in a courtyard. Also here is some good classical sculpture, including a beautiful black stone four-sided Buddha pillar. ✉ *On south side of town, off the short road leading to the Lotus Nikko hotel* ☎ *631/220– 0739* 🎟 *Rs. 2* 🕐 *Sat.–Thurs. 10–5.*

The physical and symbolic center of Bodhgaya is the **Mahabodhi Temple,** in a large, tree-shaded compound you enter through a gateway off a tidy but crowded pedestrian plaza. Here, as on each of the village's few streets, stalls, shops, and vendors with wares laid out on cloths sell pilgrims sandalwood beads, prayer bells, and Buddha statues, cassette tapes, Tibetan blankets, and snacks. Built before the 7th century, possibly as early as the 2nd century, and remodeled several times, the Mahabodhi is one of the earliest examples of the North Indian *nagara* style, which emphasizes the shikhara; rising some 160 feet, the spire can be seen far and wide from the surrounding flat country. At the top is a stone stupa, a representation of the reliquary mounds the first Buddhists built all over the subcontinent, topped by a series of stone chattras, symbols of both the Buddha's princely lineage and the shelter provided by the faith he founded. The temple's four flat sides are tiered with niches that hold Buddha images offered by pilgrims (other offerings: the small stone stupas that dot the grounds). The temple is enclosed on three sides by a stone railing, which opens under a high *torana* (archway) on the east side. Much of the original railing has been carted away to museums (including Bodhgaya's) and replaced by less elaborately carved reproductions. Pilgrims typically circumambulate the temple before entering the tall central chamber that houses a large gilt image of the Buddha in meditation. The sanctum is strung with colored lights, and the surrounding space is enlivened by the obvious emotion of pilgrims. The **Bodhi Tree,** in an enclosed courtyard, gives a more visceral feeling of sanctity. Pilgrims place flowers on the stone slab representing the **vajrasan** ("diamond seat") where the Buddha meditated, and tie bits of colored cloth to the tree. Contemporary Buddhists often sit in emulation of his practice along the railing surrounding the tree. The carved-stone path next to the north wall is said to mark the track of the Buddha's walking meditation, and he is thought to have bathed in the lotus pond on the southeast side. 🎟 *Free* 🕐 *Outer gate: daily 4 AM–9 PM; temple: daily 5 AM–9PM.*

Near the Tourist Bungalow on the main road is the **Thai Monastery,** with gilded "sky tassels" curling up from the eaves, two giant guardian *yakshas* keeping evil spirits from entering the temple, and a big gold Buddha in the elegant, chandelier-lit interior. (The largest Buddha of all is found behind the nearby Japanese Daijekyo Temple—it's about three stories high.)

The main **Tibetan Monastery,** representing the Dalai Lama's *gelugpa* (Yellow Hat) tradition, is on the north side of town behind the Mahabodhi Society building; inside are wall paintings and a big gold Buddha surrounded by hundreds of little gold Buddhas. When the Dalai Lama visits, he teaches under a large tent in an adjacent field. On the opposite side of the street from the Tibetan Monastery and next to the Mahayana Guest House is the lovely **Shechen Gompa,** where every surface has been brightly painted with murals, dragons, flowers, and all manner of ornament.

off the beaten path

RAJGIR & NALANDA – These two towns are 85 km (53 mi) and 101 km (63 mi), respectively, northeast of Bodhgaya, a four-hour train ride on the *Budhpumima Express,* which leaves Gaya three afternoons a week, arriving in Nalanda at 5:30 and Rajgir 20 minutes later. (The timing of this requires an overnight stay.) Alternatively, you can take a three-hour taxi ride on rough roads. Rajgir is the capital of the 6th-century BC kingdom of Magadha and the site of the first Buddhist Council in Buddha's time. Today the town, encircled by remnants of a pre-Mauryan cyclopean wall and known for its hot springs, is a winter health resort. A chairlift leads to an impressive contemporary Peace Pagoda erected by Japanese Buddhists on the hilltop where the Buddha preached each year during the rainy season. Treks lead to 26 Jain temples. If you have time, visit the redbrick ruins of the great 5th-century Buddhist university at **NALANDA, –** but don't go on Friday, when the archaeological museum, with Buddhist and Hindu bronzes and statues of the Buddha found in the area, is closed. Middle Way Travels (⇨ Tours, North Central India A to Z) can organize a trip for you. You can also get information at the Bodhgaya tourist office.

Where to Stay & Eat

$$$$ 🏨 **Royal Residency.** Surrounded by farmland and palm trees, about 1.5 km (1 mi) from the Mahabodhi Temple, this hotel has grand aspirations, evidenced in the elegant white-marble lobby. Though it opened in February 2002, at this writing the place still had a bit of a deserted feel and a too-spare look (no wall art or bedspreads). The rooms are large and attractive, with green-and-gold marble floors and marble baths with large showers and separate tubs. Nine Japanese-style rooms have wood floors and mattresses on tatami mats (the owners are Japan-based). None of Bodhgaya's hotels have extras like pools, but the Residency does have big men's and women's marble Japanese-style group baths with blue mosaic-tile ceilings. There's an Indian Airlines office on-site. ⊠ *Domuhan Rd., Gaya District, Bodhgaya 824231* ☎ *631/220–0124, 631/220–1156, and 631/220–1157* 📠 *631/220–0181* 📞 *59 rooms, 5 suites* ⚒ *Restaurant, room service, IDD phones, refrigerators, cable TV, bar, dry cleaning, laundry service, travel services* ▤ *AE, MC, V* ⍾ *EP.*

$$–$$$ 🏨 **Lotus Nikko.** Since taking over the former government-owned Ashok in late 2001, the new owners have been upgrading this ideally located hotel at the center of Bodhgaya. Renovations, including 30 brand-new rooms, were finished in fall 2004, all rooms will be fresh and pleasant, but not fancy: cream walls, blue carpet and fabrics, and woven leather headboards. Suites are simply very large rooms. ⊠ *Gaya District, Bodhgaya 824231* 📞 *631/220–0700 or 631/220–0790 to 92* 🖷 *631/220–0788* ⊕ *www. lotustranstravels.com* ⇋ *60 rooms, 2 suites* ⚲ *Restaurant, room service, IDD phones, refrigerators, cable TV, bar, shops, laundry service, travel services, some pets allowed, no-smoking rooms* ▭ *AE, MC, V* ⦿ *EP.*

$$ 🏨 **Sujata.** In the 2001 wing, which doubled the size of this well-liked hotel, rooms are larger but still simply furnished, with Formica-esque furniture. All the older rooms are scheduled for renovation in 2004. Like the Residency, Sujata has separate marble Japanese group baths for males and females. The restaurant, the best choice in a town of limited reliable dining options, is also a good choice. Try the delicious *kaju kanthi kababs,* boneless chunks of chicken marinated in cashew paste and cream. ⊠ *Gaya District, Bodhgaya 824231* 📞 *631/220–0481 or 631/220– 0761* 🖷 *631/220–0515* ⊕ *www.hotelsujata.com* ⇋ *43 rooms, 2 suites* ⚲ *Restaurant, room service, refrigerators, cable TV, dry cleaning, laundry service, Internet, business services, travel services* ▭ *AE, MC, V* ⦿ *EP.*

$ 🏨 **Mahayana Guest House.** This sprawling guest house is operated by Tibetan monks from the nearby Namgyal monastery. Don't come if you expect snappy service; what you'll find is inexpensive, clean, and pleasantly furnished rooms ranged around an open-air atrium. All but the 10 shared-bath rooms have phones and TVs; suites have mini-refrigerators and bathtubs. The vegetarian restaurant serves Tibetan, Chinese, and Indian food, and the bookshop will fill any gaps in your knowledge of Buddhism or Tibet. ⊠ *Box 04, Gaya District, Bodhgaya 824231* 📞 *631/220–0756 or 631/220–0675* 🖷 *631/220–0676* ✉ *mahayanagt@yahoo.com* ⇋ *67 rooms, 6 suites* ⚲ *Restaurant, some refrigerators, cable TV, dry cleaning, laundry service, some pets allowed; no a/c in some rooms, no phones in some rooms* ▭ *No credit cards* ⦿ *EP.*

¢ 🏨 **Hotel Siddhartha Vihar.** This government-run property in the Bihar Tourist Bungalow complex provides clean, basic private-bath, twin-bed rooms (more pleasant than some at this price) with phones and small TVs. There's a railway counter on the campus, which is shared with the tourist office and two rock-bottom state hotels. ⊡ *For reservations contact B.S.T.D.C., Paryatan Bhawan, Beer Chand Patel Path, Patna* 📞 *612/222–5411* 🖷 *612/223–6218* ⊠ *Gaya District, Bodhgaya 824231* 📞🖷 *631/220–0445* ⊕ *bstdc.bih.nic.in* ⇋ *13 rooms* ⚲ *Restaurant, room service, cable TV, dry cleaning, laundry service, Internet, travel services; no a/c in some rooms* ▭ *No credit cards* ⦿ *EP.*

Lucknow

➍ *300 km (186 mi) northwest of Varanasi, 516 km (320 mi) southeast of Delhi.*

The capital of Uttar Pradesh, Lucknow is—in its lingering self-image, anyway—a city of ornate manners, inherited from the last significant

Muslim court to hold sway in North India. Settled on the banks of the Gomti River in the earliest period of Indian history, it came to prominence in 1775, after Moghul power had declined in Delhi, as capital of the independent kingdom of Avadh. The nawabs of Avadh were members of the Shia sect of Islam, and the city remains an important center for that minority. Shia *imambaras*—gathering places used during Muharram, the month of mourning for Hussain, the martyred third imam of Islam—are Lucknow's most important monuments. Wajid Ali Shah, the last *nawab* and a legendarily impractical aesthete, was deposed by the British, who annexed Avadh in 1856. Resentment over that act, combined with the decades of indirect control that preceded it, contributed to Lucknow's strong support for the rebels during the Sepoy Mutiny of 1857, with members of Avadh's disbanded army manning the barricades against the British. British residents and troops, and an equal number of Indian troops and servants, were besieged for almost five months. After the Mutiny, the British drastically altered the city's plan in the name of safety: many congested, easily defensible (by the locals) older parts of the city were razed, and narrow alleyways became broad avenues where troops could move safely and smoothly.

Today Lucknow is a pleasant city—less crowded, dirty, and hassle-ridden than Agra and Varanasi, though without Agra's killer monuments or Varanasi's fascination. For a few days here you can relax in good hotels, dine extremely well on the elegant cuisine of the nawabs, plunder the shops in markets modern and medieval, visit the few tourist sites at leisure, and just pedal or be pedaled around the back streets past remnants of the town's past as a cultural and royal capital, including 18th- and 19th-century nawabi palaces.

Driving along the Gomti River at the eastern end of the city, just past the Rumi Dawaza, or Turkish Gate, you'll see the **Bara Imambara.** Preceded by a wide plaza and set at an oblique angle to its accompanying mosque, Lucknow's largest imambara is noted for its great vaulted hall with a vast roof unsupported by pillars. Guides will pester you to avail yourself of their services, and you may need them when you climb up to the top floor: here a labyrinth of identical doorways (supposedly 489 of them), passages, and stairways, with hidden routes and many dead ends, makes up the *bhul bhulaiya*—roughly, "place of forgetting"—leading back down to the ground level. You can go through the warren solo, but it takes time and patience, and with dark stairways and broken pavement in some places, it can be slightly hazardous. The imambara's raison d'être is the **tomb of Nawab Asaf-ud-Daulah,** who built his own resting place in 1784. The excellent views from the top floor take in a deep step well on the opposite side of the plaza from the mosque. ⊠ *Husainabad Rd.* ▣ *Rs. 100* ⊙ *Daily sunrise–sunset.*

The **Chota (or Husainabad) Imambara,** built in 1838, is about half a kilometer west of the Bara Imambara. At the end of a courtyard with a large ornamental pool is this elegant white building with calligraphy etched across the facade and a gilded onion dome. Inside is a hanging garden of chandeliers from China, Japan, everywhere; a fantastic pair of German torcheres about 8 feet high, with gold accents and cranberry glass bowls; a huge stepped throne of heavily embossed silver; an intricately inlaid-marble floor; and the tombs of Muhammad Ali Shah, third *nawab* of Avadh, and his mother. ⊠ *Husainabad Rd.* 🎫 *Combined pass for Imambara, Picture Gallery, and Clock Tower is Rs. 100* ☉ *Daily sunrise–sunset.*

Part of the fun of visiting Lucknow is exploring its markets. The oldest is the **Chowk,** dating from the medieval period. You enter via the Akbari or the Gol Gate. Once the street of highly accomplished courtesans patronized by wealthy men and even nawabs, later a red-light district off-limits to British soldiers, it's today a run-down but teeming market with temples, madrasas, and the odd merchant's haveli thrown in here and there for the scooters, people, and cows to wander among. In workshops you'll see men pounding silver into whisper-thin foil that will grace the tops of sweet confections. At night, here and in Aminabad market and in Nakkhas, which meets the Chowk at Akbari Gate, food stalls set up in front of closed shops send good smells wafting through the lanes, and locals mill about, sipping tea and catching up with one another. ☉ *Shops Fri.–Wed. 10:30 AM or 11–8 PM, food stalls daily 10 AM–10:30 PM.*

need a break? There are three prime snacking stops in the Chowk (aside from the yummy nuggets of water-buffalo liver cooked in the evening on skewers, over charcoal made from the wood of tamarind trees). **Prakash Kulfi** (☎ 522/222–6737) is renowned for its version of kulfi, a rich almond-, cardamom-, and saffron-flavor ice cream, served with *faluda* (pudding), or its vermicelli noodles in a sweet cream sauce. **Radhey-Lal Misthan Bhandar** (Gol Gate ☎ 522/225–6087 or 522/238–1868) has a wonderful selection of Indian sweets, such as *barfi*, a dense milk-based wedge topped with edible silver foil; the shredded-carrot treat *gajer halwa*, redolent of cardamom and spiked with cashews and dried fruit; and another milk sweet, the Lucknow specialty *malai gilori*. **Tunday Kebabi** (near the Akbari Gate ☎ no phone)—the city's most famous hole-in-the-wall eatery, in the same family for a century—continues to be thronged with devoted fans of its *gelawat* ("melt in your mouth") kababs, small fried patties made from twice-minced lamb mixed with more than 100 spices. Its street-front stoves make only these, and *parathas* to eat them with; for more choices, try Grandson of Tunday Kebabi, the family's newer spot near Ghari Wali Masjid in Aminabad.

The 221-foot-high gunmetal **Clock Tower,** with components transported from London's Ludgate Hill, is a striking Victorian structure. Reminiscent of that other British clock tower, Big Ben, it was built in 1887 to mark the arrival of the first lieutenant governor of Avadh. ⊠ *Husainabad Rd., between Bara Imambara and Chota Imambara.*

The Saturn-shape **Indira Gandhi Planetarium,** built in 2003, has a 40-minute show in English at 2 PM. Unlike most places in India, the building is accessible to people with disabilities. ⊠ *9 Mabiullah Rd., Suraj Kund Park* ☎ *522/222–9176 or 522/221–1773* 🎫 *Rs. 25* ☉ *Tues.–Sat. 2–6.*

At the eastern edge of the city, on the banks of the Gomti, is **La Martinière,** the most outlandish building in town. Built in the late 18th century as a palace by Major-General Claude Martin, a French adventurer who profited handsomely from his military service to the nawabs and happily spread his epicurean tastes, it's now a school for boys of any religion, as provided by Martin in his will. The lower floors were designed to flood in summer—an innovative, if malarial, cooling system. From the outside you can get a good sense of the place, with its oddly angled wings, four octagonal towers that rise from basement to roof, and four stone lions growling down from the parapet. With advance notice, Uttar Pradesh State Tourism (☎ 522/263–8105) can arrange a tour.

The **Picture Gallery** is a small room with life-size oil paintings of the nawabs of Avadh. ⊠ *Husainabad Rd. near Satkhanda Palace* ☎ *No phone* 🎫 *Combined pass for Chota Imambara, Picture Gallery, and Clock Tower is Rs. 100. Daily sunrise–sunset*

About 1 ½ km (1 mi) toward the city center from the Bara Imambara is the **Residency** compound, where the British garrison was besieged on June 30, 1857. A relief force entered (as you will) through the **Baillie Guard Gate** on September 25, only to end up besieged themselves. On the right is the **Treasury** building, and behind that a large **Banquet Hall** that served as a hospital. (About 2,000 people died in the siege, more from disease than from gunfire.) Up a slight rise is a large open green, with an active shrine to a Muslim *pir* (holy man) under a tree to the left and an obelisk on the right commemorating Henry Lawrence, the chief commissioner who gathered his people here only to fall to gunfire on July 4. The Residency itself lies largely in ruins. Part of the building has been converted into a museum, called the **Model Room**, displaying a model of the compound under siege as well as cannonballs, arms, photographs, and other artifacts. Below ground are the chambers where many of the women and children escaped intermittent fire from the rooftops of surrounding buildings. Down the slope on the far side of the Residency is a **cemetery** for the many who were lost before the siege was finally broken on November 17. The wording of pre- and post-Independence markers and signs indicates the differences in how events here have been viewed. (Until August 15, 1947, a Union Jack flew over the compound.) Other buildings are scattered throughout, and you'll want at least an hour and a half to absorb the Residency's melancholy significance. Come back in the evening for the sound-and-light show, but have your hotel call before you set out to check the time for the English version, which depends on the time of the sunset; also, be aware that shows generally won't run unless there are at least 15 people. 🎫 *Grounds and museum Rs. 100, sound-and-light show Rs. 25* ⊙ *Grounds daily 10–4:30, museum Mon.–Sat. 10–4:30.*

Where to Stay & Eat

★ **$$$$** ✕ **Falaknuma.** At lunchtime at this rooftop restaurant, the city and the river spread out below you beyond a wall of windows. At night the scene is romantic, especially with the musicians singing ghazals. The style is vaguely tropical, with white-lattice planters and green plants, and the Avadhi food (local cuisine, characterized by a subtle blend of flavors) is excellent. The *taron ka haar* meat sampler is a brilliant introduction to the world of kababs, especially the *lasooni kabab,* boneless chicken marinated with garlic, yogurt, mint, and spices; *naushai jaan,* a drumstick marinated with spices and herbs and cooked in a tandoor; the Lucknow specialty *kakori kabab,* a cigar-shape lamb kabab cooked on a skewer; and fish Afghani, chunks of sole cooked with herbs in a tandoor oven. ⊠ *Clarks Avadh, 8 Mahatma Gandhi Marg* ☎ *522/262–0131* ▭ *AE, DC, MC, V.*

★ $$$$ ✕ **Oudhyana.** The Taj's formal restaurant—an elegant, seafoam-green room lit by gorgeous chandeliers, with a floral Persian carpet in deep maroon, green, and gold—was relaunched in 2003 with a new menu featuring specialties of the *nawabs.* A banquet of superb Avadhi dishes, served *nawabi*-style with heavy pounded-brass tableware and goblets, may include *kakori kabab,* here made with finely minced lamb, saffron, rose petals, and cardamom; *gelawat kababs,* pan-fried finely minced spiced lamb; *nahari gosht,* lamb on the bone, cooked in lamb extract with herbs and spices; and *sheermal,* an orange Lucknow flat bread made with milk, fat, and saffron. ⊠ *Taj Residency, Vipin Khand, Gomti Nagar* ☎ *522/239–3939* ▭ *AE, DC, MC, V.*

$$$$ ▦ **Taj Residency.** Though a bit far from the center of town (which al-
Fodor'sChoice lows it to rest on 30 acres), this luxurious hotel is well worth the com-
★ mute. It's a beautiful building in the British colonial style, with an elegant lobby and a pale turquoise pool centered by a fountain and landscaped with big palm trees. The spacious guest rooms (renovated in 2003) have queen or king beds, rich fabrics, artwork depicting the life and architecture of the Moghuls, and a welcome fruit basket. The bar, a classy place for a drink even if you're not staying here, features live ghazals each evening, and there's a large business center with boardrooms, lounges, and Internet facilities. ⊠ *Vipin Khand, Gomti Nagar, 226010* ☎ *522/239–3939 or 522/239–1201 to 03* 🖷 *522/239–2282 or 522/239–2465* ⊕ *www.tajhotels.com* ↩ *106 rooms, 4 suites* ⟨ *Restaurant, coffee shop, room service, in-room data ports, in-r7oom safes, minibars, cable TV with movies, golf privileges, putting green, pool, gym, health club, hair salon, hot tub, massage, steam bath, bar, dry cleaning, laundry service, baby-sitting, business services, convention center, meeting rooms, travel services, no-smoking rooms* ▭ *AE, DC, MC, V* ⑩ *EP.*

$$$–$$$$ ▦ **Clarks Avadh.** With its prime location on the river, Clarks is ideally situated for good views—especially from the rooftop restaurant, Falaknuma—and easy sightseeing. Rooms are spacious, though dimly lit. The Privilege Club floor, with rooms done in rich fabrics, has a lounge with a computer, a TV and VCR, a chess table, and a small chandelier-lit room for private meetings, parties, or lunch. The green-and-gold suites have miles of silk drapes and expansive river views. Plans call for a new indoor pool, a sauna, and a steam room to be completed by the end of 2004. ⊠ *8 Mahatma Gandhi Marg, 226001* ☎ *522/262–0131 to 33 or 522/261–6500 to 09* 🖷 *522/261–6507* ⊕ *www.hotelclarks.com* ↩ *92 rooms, 3 suites* ⟨ *2 restaurants, room service, IDD phones, cable TV, gym, hair salon, bar, dry cleaning, laundry service, Internet, business services, convention center, travel services* ▭ *AE, DC, MC, V* ⑩ *EP.*

$$–$$$ ▦ **La Place Park Inn.** Built in 2000, this Hazratganj area inn targeting business travelers (it even offers mobile phones), has spacious rooms with

green or cream marble floors and marble-top bedside tables; rich fabrics in greens, reds, and golds; hand-colored prints; and large baths. The rooftop restaurant and bar serves tandoori and barbecue dishes; the main restaurant has candlelit dinners on weekends with pop or jazz bands. Discounted rates at a nearby fitness center are available. ⊠ *6 Shahnajaf Rd., 226001* ☎ *522/222–0220 or 522/228–2201 to 04, 800/670–7275 in North America, 800/963–255 in U.K., 800/553–843 in Australia* 🖷 *522/222–0522* ⊕ *www.parkinnlucknow.com* ➲ *49 rooms, 1 suite* ⚏ *2 restaurants, room service, IDD phones, in-room data ports, minibars, cable TV, 2 bars, baby-sitting, dry cleaning, laundry service, Internet, business services, meeting rooms, travel services* ▭ *AE, DC, MC, V* ❙❙❙ *BP.*

$ ▦ **Arif Castles.** Guest rooms—renovated in early 2004—are comfortable, and service is pleasant and efficient. Deluxe (standard) rooms are small and have twin beds; the larger executive rooms have double beds. The location is convenient: about 1½ km (1 mi) each from Clarks, Hazratganj, and the Botanical Gardens (a good place for morning walks). ⊠ *4 Rana Pratap Marg, Hazratganj 226001* ☎ *522/221–1313 to 17* 🖷 *522/ 261–1360* ⊕ *www.arifcastles.com* ➲ *52 rooms* ⚏ *Restaurant, room service, cable TV, dry cleaning, laundry service, business services, meeting rooms, travel services* ▭ *AE, DC, MC, V* ❙❙❙ *EP.*

$ ▦ **Sagar International.** In the Butler Palace area, where visiting bureaucrats stay (about 2½ km [1.6 mi] east of Hazratganj and 5½ km [3.4 mi] from the Residency), Sagar opened in 2000, offering plenty of amenities at a fair price. Rooms on the Executive Floor have better furnishings (such as ornate wooden headboards) and face greenery instead of the city; all rooms, done mostly in shades of red, have desks. The rooftop restaurant has wraparound windows. ⊠ *14A Jopling Rd., 226001* ☎ *522/220–6601 to 05* 🖷 *522/220–6644* ⊕ *www.hotelsagar.com* ➲ *60 rooms, 1 suite* ⚏ *2 restaurants, room service, IDD phones, minibars, cable TV, bar, dry cleaning, laundry service, Internet, business services, convention center, travel services, no-smoking floor* ▭ *MC, V* ❙❙❙ *EP.*

Shopping

Shops in Lucknow are generally open daily from 10 to 7, except those in Hazratganj, which close on Sunday, and in Aminabad and the Chowk, which close on Thursday.

Lucknow is famous for a style of straight-stitch embroidery on fine cotton cloth known as *chikan,* found in great variety and at bargain prices in the old **Chowk** and **Aminabad** markets, as well as at more upmarket shops in the modern **Hazratganj** area. Also in the markets is another characteristic Lucknow product, *attar,* the essential oils used in perfumes, made from aromatic herbs, spices, flowers, and leaves. The attar merchant with the longest pedigree is **Asghar Ali Mohammed Ali and Sons** (⊠ Gol Darwaza La., Chowk, near the Medical College ☎ no phone), begun in 1830 by a perfumier brought to Lucknow to create his fragrances for the nawab. **Chhangamal Ramsaran Garg** (⊠ 88 Hazratganj ☎ 522/222–3252 ⊕ rohia_chikangarment.tripod.com) specializes in chikan work; you'll find both very fine and inexpensive pieces here. **Ram Advani** (⊠ Mayfair Bldg., Mahatma Gandhi Rd., Hazratganj ☎ 522/

222–3511 or 522/222–4057) is a bookshop with a well-edited general selection and works on Lakhnavi history by scholars from around the world. The eponymous gracious owner has run the place since 1948.

Nightlife & the Arts

The courtly cultivation of singing, dance, and poetry that characterized Lucknow in earlier eras has waned, but efforts are on to revive it. Each December 1 through 5, the Lucknow Mahotsav festival hosts excellent musicians and dancers for nightly performances; some events begin on November 25.

NORTH CENTRAL INDIA A TO Z

To research prices, get advice from other travelers, and book travel arrangements, visit www.fodors.com.

AIR TRAVEL

To Agra: Indian Airlines has regular flights from Delhi, Khajuraho, and Varanasi. To Bhopal: Indian Airlines and Jet Airways have daily flights from Delhi, Indore, and Mumbai. To Bodhgaya: Indian Airlines has one evening flight a week to Gaya Airport from Calcutta (and one from Gaya to Bangkok). To Khajuraho: Indian Airlines has regular flights from Agra, Delhi, and Varanasi; Jet Airways has daily flights from Varanasi and (via Varanasi) from Delhi. To Lucknow: Indian Airlines has daily flights from Delhi and Mumbai; Jet Airways has daily flights from Delhi; Air Sahara has daily flights from Delhi and Mumbai and regular flights from Allahabad. To Patna in the state of Bihar (135km [84 mi] from Bodhgaya): Indian Airlines has daily flights from Delhi and Mumbai; Air Sahara has daily flights from Delhi and Calcutta. To Varanasi: Indian Airlines has daily flights from Delhi and Mumbai and regular flights from Agra, Khajuraho, and Kathmandu; Jet Airways has daily flights from Delhi, Khajuraho, and (via Delhi) Mumbai; Air Sahara has daily flights from Delhi.

CARRIERS 🚹 Indian Airlines **Agra** ☎ 562/222-6820 or 562/222-6821, 562/230-2274 at airport. **Bhopal** ☎ 755/778-434 or 755/770-480, 755/646-123 at airport. **Delhi** ☎ 11/2462-0566 or 11/2462-2220, 11/2567-5433 at airport. **Gaya** ☎ 631/241-0506. **Khajuraho** ☎ 7686/274-035, 7686/274-036 at airport. **Lucknow** ☎ 522/222-0927 or 522/222-4618, 522/243-2335 at airport. **Patna** ☎ 612/222-2554 or 612/222-6433, 612/222-3199 at airport. **Varanasi** ☎ 542/250-2527 or 542/250-2529, 542/262-2090 at airport. ⊕ www.indian-airlines.nic.in.

🚹 Jet Airways **Delhi** ☎ 11/5164-1414, 11/2567-5404 at airport. **Khajuraho** ☎ 7686/74406, 7686/74407 at airport. **Lucknow** ☎ 522/223-9612 to 14, 522/243-4009 to 11 at airport. **Varanasi** ☎ 542/250-6444 or 542/250-6555, 542/262-2795 to 97 at airport. ⊕ www.jetairways.com.

🚹 Air Sahara **Mumbai** ☎ 22/2283-6000 24-hr helpline. **Delhi** ☎ 11/2335-9801 24-hr helpline. **Lucknow** ☎ 522/243-6188, 522/243-4949, or 522/243-2425, 522/237-2742 at airport. **Patna** ☎ 612/223-9569, 612/223-2722, or 612/223-2733, 522/222-8308 at airport. **Varanasi** ☎ 542/250-7872 or 542/250-7873, 542/262-2547 at airport. **Web site** ⊕ www.airsahara.net.

AIRPORTS

Agra's Kheria Airport is roughly 7 km (4 mi) from the Taj Mahal. Ask your hotel whether it participates in the local airport shuttle; if not, you can generally have your hotel send an air-conditioned car to pick you up for about Rs. 250. You can also take a fixed-rate taxi or auto-rickshaw from the airport to the city center for less than Rs. 200.

Bhopal's Raja Bhoj airport is 10 km (6 mi) from town. The taxi ride costs Rs. 250.

The brand-new Gaya Airport (the runway's in business, but the terminal won't be complete until 2005) is about 15 minutes from Bodhgaya. It has service from Calcutta and on to Bangkok via Indian Airlines; Thai, Singaporean, Sri Lankan, and Bhutanese carriers also have regular flights. Indian Airlines and Air Sahara fly into Patna Airport, from which it's a bumpy 4-plus-hour, 125-km (78-mi), Rs. 1,000 (Rs. 1,400 for an air-conditioned car) taxi ride to Bodhgaya.

Khajuraho Airport is 5 km (3 mi) from town; the taxi ride costs Rs. 100 to Rs. 125.

Lucknow's Amausi airport is about 22 km (14 mi) or 30 minutes by car from most hotels; a taxi costs around Rs. 200.

The nearest airport to Varanasi, Bhabatpur, is 22 km (14 mi), or a 45-minute drive, from most hotels. A taxi costs about Rs. 350 or Rs. 500 (air-conditioned) to the cantonment area, or from Rs. 400 to Rs. 600 into the city proper. Of the airport's two prepaid-taxi counters, Airport Rent-a-Car Service, inside the terminal, is more reliable. The shuttle bus is convenient only if your hotel is in the cantonment; otherwise, you can be dropped on the far side of the cantonment train station.

AUTO-RICKSHAWS

Be prepared to negotiate on auto-rickshaw rates, especially in Agra, as fares depend on several factors, including how far you want to go, how many times you want to stop, the time of day, and whether it's raining. You can generally expect to pay about Rs. 100 for a half day, Rs. 200 for a full day. If you're not comfortable with the price you're given, look for another auto-rickshaw, and if you don't want to haggle, take a metered taxi or book a car.

Auto-rickshaws are a fast way to scoot through Varanasi's crowded streets, but the fumes from other automobiles can be horrendous at busy times. When traffic is heavy, take an air-conditioned taxi with the windows closed, especially if you're coming from one of the hotels far from the ghats. Ask your hotel or the tourist office for the going rate, and agree on a fare in advance. Note that from 9 AM to 9 PM these and other motor vehicles are not allowed beyond Godaulia Crossing, the traffic circle near the central bathing ghat, Dashashvamedh; they'll drop you off a short walk from the river if that's where you're headed.

BICYCLE & CYCLE-RICKSHAW TRAVEL

Renting a bike in Khajuraho costs about Rs. 30 per day and is one of the most popular ways to get around this tranquil town. You can rent bikes across from the bus stand, behind the museum, and from some hotels.

You can get the latest rate estimates for cycle-rickshaws from the local India Tourism office. Cycle-rickshaws should cost no more than Rs. 30 per hour in Agra or Khajuraho. They're a particularly pleasant way to get around Khajuraho, especially to the outlying temples. Distances are long in Varanasi, so a cycle-rickshaw is better for a leisurely roll through the old city (it frees you from fighting the crowds) than for cross-town transport. A trip from the cantonment to the ghats should cost about Rs. 50. If you hire a cycle-rickshaw for the day, agree on the price in advance and expect to pay about Rs. 150. Though Lucknow has plenty of traffic on the main tourist route, the back streets are pleasant viewed from a cycle-rickshaw, and short hops cost about Rs. 10.

BOAT TRAVEL

Boat rides on the Ganges in Varanasi should cost Rs. 50 for an hour for a small boat; the bigger, sturdier boats fit more people and cost Rs. 75–Rs. 100 per hour. At Dashashvamedh Ghat, however, touts will demand a lot more. If you just show up at sunset, you'll have limited time to shop around; for a reasonable rate, chat with some boatmen the previous evening and arrange to meet one by the river the next morning. A boat from the main ghats to Ramnagar should cost about Rs. 200 round-trip.

CAR & DRIVER

Hire a car and driver only through your hotel or tour operator; UP Tours, the government of Uttar Pradesh's tour arm (⇨ Tours); the Madhya Pradesh State Tourism Development Corporation (⇨ Visitor Information); or a recommended local travel agent.

For trips to Agra from Delhi, contact Dhanoa Tours and Travels. An air-conditioned Ambassador with driver costs Rs. 4,000 (including tax and a guide); a Qualis van for up to seven people costs Rs. 7,000. Expect to pay about Rs. 350 extra for a worthwhile detour to Fatehpur Sikri.

Prices in Agra are generally Rs. 6–Rs. 8 per kilometer. A non-air-conditioned car for four hours or 40 km (25 mi) should cost about Rs. 400—the minimum charge. For overnight excursions, add a halt charge of Rs. 200. The standard charge for a trip to Fatehpur Sikri is Rs. 650, but you may be able to bargain a driver down to Rs. 500. You can hire a taxi at the train station under a fixed-rate system. If you'd prefer not to be taken to the driver's choice of stores, restaurants, or hotels (where he gets a commission), say so firmly up front.

In Bhopal, a car is essential for side trips into the countryside. Rates depend on how much you want to see and the mileage involved. For sightseeing in town, expect to pay Rs. 400 for a half-day, Rs. 650 for a full day, for a non-air-conditioned car; Rs. 500 for a half-day, Rs. 800 for a full day, for an air-conditioned car.

In Khajuraho, a hired car can be convenient if you want to wander outside town or can't walk the 3 km to the most distant temples. A non-air-conditioned car should cost about Rs. 200 for two hours or 30 km. You can hire a taxi for about Rs. 6 per km.

In Lucknow, the officially recommended rates are Rs. 110 for less than 5 km (3 mi), Rs. 160 for 5 to 10 km (3 to 6 mi); Rs. 450 for 40 km (25 mi); and Rs. 800 for 80 km (50 mi). UP Tours charges Rs. 400–Rs. 500 per day; its car-hire number is ☎ 522/261-2659.

To reach Orchha from Jhansi, the railhead 16 km (10 mi) away, you can hire a car from Touraids; the half-hour trip costs Rs. 400.

In Varanasi, a four-hour car excursion should cost Rs. 350 in a non-air-conditioned car, Rs. 450 with air-conditioning. For eight hours (90 km or 56 mi) a car should cost you about Rs. 600. A taxi from Varanasi will drop you in Sarnath and wait about three hours for Rs. 300. (Auto-rickshaws will make the round-trip for about Rs. 200.) The Grand Trunk Road (NH 2) east of Varanasi passes south of Bodhgaya. The local connecting roads, for which you turn off just east of Aurangabad, are in poor condition and sometimes beset by robbers.

⚑ **Ashok Tours and Travel** ⊠ Indian Airlines Building, near India Tourism in the Cantonment area, Varanasi ☎ 542/250-3432. **Dhanoa Tours and Travels** ⊠ Hara Marg, near Malcha Marg Market, Chanakyapuri, New Delhi ☎ 11/2611-4969 or 11/2688-6051. **Touraids Travel Service** ⊠ 46 Gopichand Shivhare Rd., Agra Cantonment, Agra ☎ 562/222-5029 or 562/222-5074 ✎ touraids@sancharnet.in ⊠ Moti Mahal, Moti Palace, Gwalior ☎ 751/232-4354 or 751/232-0758 ✎ touraidsi@yahoo.com ⊠ Jai Complex, Civil Lines, Jhansi ☎ 517/233-1760 ✎ tourjhs@sancharnet.in ⊠ Kandariya Campus, Khajuraho ☎ 7686/274-060 or 7686/274-121.

CAR TRAVEL
For a delightful, scenic five- or six- day trip covering Agra, Gwalior, Orchha, Khajuraho, Bhopal, and Sanchi, hire a car in Delhi or Agra from a tour operator or travel agency.

Agra is 200 km (124 mi) south of Delhi on roads built by the Moghul emperors to connect their two capitals. The roads are good but heavily used—don't expect to travel much above 50 kph (30 mph). The trip should take 3½ to 4 hours. The best route is National Highway 2 (NH 2).

Lucknow is connected to Delhi by National Highway (NH) 2, the Grand Trunk Road, which runs through Agra and the industrial city of Kanpur before NH 25 turns north to Lucknow. This is one of the most heavily used truck routes in India, and is for the most part devoid of lanes. An alternate route is NH 24 through Bareilly and central Uttar Pradesh. NH 56 links Lucknow with the Grand Trunk Road at Varanasi and allows a stop in little-visited Jaunpur, capital of an early Muslim sultanate.

To reach Varanasi by car, take NH 2 or NH 56 from the northwest, NH 29 from Gorakhpur (if you started in Kathmandu), NH 2 from Calcutta, or NH 30 and NH 2 from Patna.

MONEY
ATMS ATMs that accept MasterCard, Visa, and Plus can be found in larger towns; ask at your hotel or your taxi driver for one close to you. In Varanasi foreign ATM cards cannot be used at any of the city's

ATMs, but cash advances on Visa cards can be obtained from all ICICI Bank ATMs.

CURRENCY EXCHANGE Your hotel is the easiest place to change currency, but you can also do so at the State Bank of India in Agra, Bhopal, Bodhgaya, Khajuraho, Lucknow, and Varanasi. Other banks may change money as well, but note that not even all State Bank branches will accept foreign travelers' checks. 🏧 **Allahabad Bank** ⊠ Taksal Bldg., Nadesar, Varanasi ☎ 542/250-4281 or 542/250-7570 telefax. **State Bank of India** ⊠ The Mall, near Surya Hotel, Varanasi ☎ 542/250-3245, 542/250-2763, or 542/250-2764. **Union Bank of India** ⊠ Sri Das Foundation, The Mall ☎ 542/250-2033.

TOURS

UP Tours (Uttar Pradesh's tour agency) has a vast offering of tours, including Buddhist circuit tours and a daily guided bus tour of Fatehpur Sikri, Agra Fort, and the Taj Mahal for Rs. 1,600 per person (this covers transport, guide, and admission fees, including the Rs. 750 admission to the Taj); a half-day tour of Fatehpur Sikri alone is Rs. 500. For a personal guide, ask your hotel or contact the nearest India Tourism office.

Middle Way Travels runs multiday pilgrimage tours and will organize tours of Bodhgaya's temples and other sights as well as day trips to Rajgir and Nalanda. Radiant Travels has one of the region's few female tour guides, who gives a feminine perspective on Bhopal. Tornos specializes in Lucknow's Avadhi culture, crafts, and cuisine, as well as the history of the British in India, and can really make a visit to the city fun and enlightening. Offerings include a visit or a traditional royal meal (*dastarkhwan*) with the *nawab*, who has a wonderful collection of antique chikan garments; a tour of chikan workshops; transport by horse cart; picnics in a traditional village with singing and dancing; and theme events. 🏧 **Middle Way Travels** ⊠ 7/11 Main Rd., near Mahabodhi Temple, Bodhgaya ☎ 631/220-0648 or 631/220-0668. **Radiant Travels** ⊠ 243-B, Mezzanine Fl., Krishna Palace, M.P. Nagar, Zone 1, Bhopal ☎ 755/276-1540 or 755/276-1541 ⊠ 24 Ahmedabad Rd., Bhopal ☎ 755/273-8540. **Tornos** ⊠ Tornos House, C-2016, Indira Nagar, Lucknow ☎ 522/234-9472 or 522/234-6965 ⊕ www.tornosindia.com. **UP Tours** ⊠ Hotel Taj Khema, near Taj Mahal's eastern gate, Agra ☎ 562/233-0140 ✍ hoteltajkema@sify.com ⊠ Tourist Bungalow, Parade Kothi, Varanasi ☎ 542/220-8545 or 542/220-8413, or 542/220-6638 telefax ✍ tbvaranasi@sify.com ⊠ Central Reservations Centre, Hotel Gomti, 6 Sapru Marg, Lucknow ☎ 522/221-5005, 522/221-4708, or 522/261-4284.

TRAIN TRAVEL

The Indian Railways Web site (⊕ www.indianrail.gov.in) provides comprehensive train information and lets you make reservations online. Don't rely on telephone bookings; instead go to the station to collect your ticket in advance. Every main station has a tourist reservation office. If you reserve at least two days before you travel, you should have priority.

Because fog often causes delays of up to several hours on morning flights into Delhi's airport, especially in winter, trains can be more reliable for visiting Agra. To reserve tickets, head to the International Tourist Bureau, on the first floor of the New Delhi Railway Station, near the Paharganj entrance.

The *Shatabdi Express,* India's best train, runs daily on the Delhi–Agra–Gwalior–Jhansi–Bhopal–Mumbai route, offering frequent meals and snacks en route; from Delhi to Agra takes 2 hours, from Agra to Gwalior 1 hour and 15 minutes, from Gwalior to Jhansi (a major rail junction and the nearest to Orchha, 16 km [10 mi] away) 1 hour, and from Jhansi to Bhopal 3½ hours. The slower *Bhopal Express* and *Lakshadweep Express* run the same route daily. The daily *Taj Express* connects Delhi, Agra, and Gwalior.

The *Marudhar Express* travels the Jodhpur–Jaipur–Agra–Lucknow–Varanasi route daily; the Jaipur–Agra leg takes 13 hours, the Agra–Lucknow 6 hours, and the Lucknow–Varanasi 6½ hours.

The *Rajdhani Express,* India's other premier train, passes through Bhopal frequently, including twice a week in each direction on the Delhi–Chennai route and four times a week on the Delhi–Bangalore route. The Delhi–Bhopal leg takes about 8 hours; two routes have late-night departures from Bhopal with arrival in Delhi at 5:30 the next morning, saving a night's hotel fare in Delhi.

Gaya is served by the *Rajdhani,* which connects it daily with Delhi (12 hours) and with Mughal Serai (about 9 hours), an hour's drive from Varanasi. The slower *Poorva Express* connects Gaya with Delhi (16½ hours) and Varanasi (3½ hours) three days a week. The *Budhpumima Express* leaves Gaya three afternoons a week, arriving in Nalanda (4 hours) at 5:30 and Rajgir 20 minutes later (the same train connects Sarnath with Varanasi and Gaya).

Lucknow is connected to Delhi by many trains, including the 7½- to 8-hour *Rajdhani* twice a week in each direction and the 6¼-hour *Shatabdi* on weekdays. The *Lucknow Express* makes the 15½-hour trip between Lucknow and Agra daily, and the 12½- to 14½-hour trip between Lucknow and Bhopal five days a week. The *Jan Shatabdi* makes the 5½-hour trip between Lucknow and Varanasi every day but Sunday; the *Nalanda Express* makes the same trip daily, in 5 hours.

Varanasi is 12½ hours from Delhi on the daily *Shiv Ganga Express,* 5½ hours from Lucknow on the *Jan Shatabdi,* 17 hours from Bhopal on the daily *Varanasi Kamayani Express* and from Gwalior on the daily *Bundelkhand Express,* 4 hours from Gaya on the weekly *Ranchi Express,* and 28 hours from Mumbai on the daily *Mahanagan Express.*

VISITOR INFORMATION

You can pick up maps and information on approved guides at India Tourism offices in Agra, Khajuraho, and Varanasi's cantonment, and at an information desk at Varanasi's airport. If you are planning your trip from New Delhi, India Tourism's offices on Janpath, across from the Imperial Hotel and south of Cottage Industries, are worth a visit. Outbound Travels in Delhi can arrange flights and coordinate flights with train or car travel to help you make the most of limited travel time.

The Madhya Pradesh State Tourism Development Corporation, one of India's better state tourist offices, has friendly staff and information on Khajuraho, Gwalior, Orchha, Bhopal, and Sanchi.

The Uttar Pradesh State Tourism Development Corporation arranges tours and cars in Agra and Lucknow. The New Delhi office (centrally located near the Imperial Hotel) has maps, brochures, and information on approved guides. The best information at Varanasi's Uttar Pradesh State Tourism office is in Hindi, but the staff can still help you, and there's a satellite desk at the train station.

🚩 Tourist Information **Bihar State Tourism Development Corporation** ✉ Tourist Bungalow, Bodhgaya ☎ 631/220-0672 ⊕ bstdc.bih.nic.in. **India Tourism** ✉ 88 Janpath, New Delhi ☎ 11/2332-0005 or 11/2332-0008 ✍ goitodelhi@tourism.nic.in ✉ 191 The Mall, Agra ☎ 562/222-6378 or 562/222-6368 telefax ✍ goitoagr@sancharnet.in ✉ Opposite Western Group of temples, Khajuraho ☎ 7686/272-347 or 7686/272-348 ✉ Sudama Palace, Kankar Bagh Rd., Patna ☎ 612/234-5776 or 612/234-8558 ✉ 15B The Mall, Varanasi ☎ 542/250-1784 ⊕ www.tourismofindia.com. **Madhya Pradesh State Tourism Corporation** ✉ Kanishka Shopping Plaza, 2nd fl., 19 Ashoka Rd., New Delhi ☎ 11/332-1187 or 11/336-6528 ✉ Chandella Cultural Center, Rajnagar Rd., Khajuraho ☎ 7686/274-051 ✉ At airport and bus station ✉ Hotel Palash, T. T. Nagar, Bhopal ☎ 755/277-4343 ✉ Hotel Tansen, 6 Gandhi Rd., Gwalior ☎ 751/234-0370 ✉ Railway station, Jhansi ☎ 517/442-622 ⊕ www.mptourism.com. **Outbound Travels** ✉ New Delhi ☎ 11/5164-0567, 11/2652-2617, mobile 98100-73626 ⊕ www.outboundtravels.com. **Uttar Pradesh State Tourism** ✉ Chandralok Bldg., 36 Janpath, New Delhi ☎ 11/2332-2251 ✉ 64 Taj Rd., Agra ☎ 562/222-6431 ✉ Parade Kothi, opposite train station, Varanasi ☎ 545/220-8413 or 545/220-8545 ✉ Dashashvamedh Ghat ✉ Hotel Mrigdava Campus, Sarnath ☎ 542/259-5965 ✉ 10 Station Rd., Lucknow ☎ 522/263-8105 ✉ At railway station and airport ⊕ www.up-tourism.com.

RAJASTHAN

4

ADORN YOURSELF
with locally-produced jewelry ⇨*p.193*

DINE IN LUXURY ON LAKE PICHOLA
at the Lake Palace hotel in Udaipur ⇨*p.238*

HIRE A ROYAL VINTAGE CAR
during your stay at Ajit Bhawan ⇨*p.227*

EAT WITH YOUR HANDS
at Chokhi Dhani village complex ⇨*p.204*

GO WILD ON A TIGER SAFARI
in Ranthambhore National Park ⇨*p.212*

Updated by
Kavita Watsa
and Scott
Carney

STEEPED IN TALES OF CHIVALRY AND ROMANCE, and famous for its strik-ing desert landscape and colorful festivals, Rajasthan is one of India's best-loved regions. From its legendary cities of Jaipur, Jodhpur, Udaipur, and Jaisalmer, built by the mighty Rajput warriors, to its indigenous tribal and artisan communities, Rajasthan is a unique combination of royal and tribal India. The variety of its landscape is unparalleled: the region is packed with awe-inspiring forts, sparkling palaces, soothing lakes and gardens, and exquisite temples and shrines. The crafts and folk art pro-duced here are world-renowned. Once called Rajputana—"Abode of Kings"—this vast land consisted of more than 22 princely states before they were consolidated into modern Rajasthan in 1956. Each state was ruled by a Rajput, an upper-caste Hindu warrior-prince, and the Ra-jputs were divided into three main clans: the Suryavanshis, descended from the sun, the Chandravanshis, descended from the moon, and the *agnikuls,* who had been purified by ritual fire. When they were not fight-ing among themselves for power, wealth, and women, the Rajputs built the hundreds of forts, palaces, gardens, and temples that make this re-gion so enchanting.

For centuries, many Hindu Rajputs valiantly resisted invasion, includ-ing attempts by the Muslim Moghuls. Their legendary codes of battle emphasized honor and pride, and they went to war prepared to die. When defeat on the battlefield was imminent, the strong Rajput women of Chit-taur would perform the rite of *jauhar,* throwing themselves onto a flam-ing pyre en masse rather than live with the indignity of capture. With the prominent exception of the princes of Mewar, major Rajput states such as Jaipur, Bikaner, Bundi, and Kota eventually stopped fighting and built strong ties with the Moghuls. The Moghul emperor Akbar was par-ticularly skilled at forging alliances with the Rajputs; he offered them high posts in his *darbar,* or court, and sealed the deal with matrimonial ties. (He himself married two Rajput princesses.) Those kingdoms who sided with Akbar quickly rose in importance and prosperity.

Maharaja Man Singh of Jaipur was the first to marry his sister to Akbar. As the emperor's brother-in-law and trusted commander-in-chief, Man Singh led Moghul armies to many a victory. Both rulers benefited im-mensely, as a traditional saying indicates: *"Jeet Akbar ki, loot Man Singh ki"* ("The victory belongs to Akbar, the loot to Man Singh").

In addition to securing wealth, these marriages opened the gates of the royal Rajput households to the Moghuls' distinctive culture. Ironically, the same people who initially sacrificed their lives to resist the Moghuls quickly adapted themselves to Moghul domination and started borrow-ing heavily from Moghul aesthetics. Skilled craftsmen from the Moghul courts were enticed to Rajasthan to start craft schools, fomenting what would become a golden age of Indian art and architecture. The Moghuls' influence in Rajasthan is still visible in everything from food to palace ar-chitecture, from intricate miniature paintings to new musical styles, and from clothing to the tradition of *purdah* (the seclusion of women from males or strangers, or the act of covering the head and face with a veil).

Distances here are long, and transportation is relatively slow. The best way to see Rajasthan is to fly to Jaipur, Jodhpur, and/or Udaipur and make excursions from each.

4

If you have 3 days

Fly into ⊡ **Udaipur** ㉑ and spend the day wandering the narrow, hilly lanes of the old city and visiting the vast City Palace. That evening, take a boat ride on Lake Pichola or a cab up to the Monsoon Palace at sunset. If you can, stay at the Lake Palace Hotel, smack in the middle of the lake—it's a sight in itself. The next day, fly to ⊡ **Jaipur** and explore the pink-hue old city. Take a taxi out of town to the Amer Fort and Palace, then spend the night in one of Jaipur's havelis or palace hotels. On your third day, hire a car and driver to explore **Shekhavati,** stopping in villages such as Jhunjhunu and Mandawa to see the lovely havelis, some with magnificent frescoes. Treat yourself to a meal at one of the Heritage Hotels. From here you can easily drive to Delhi.

If you have 6 days

As on the three-day itinerary, fly into ⊡ **Udaipur** ㉑ and spend a day and a night here. Try to pop outside the city to the crafts village of Shilpgram. The next day, drive northwest to the Jain temple at **Ranakpur** ㉒, and spend a few hours exploring the temple and the surrounding countryside. Continue on to ⊡ **Jodhpur** ⑰ and spend the night in one of the city's splendid hotels. Head up to the fort the next morning, then spend the day exploring Jodhpur itself. Take the overnight train to ⊡ **Jaisalmer** ㉘ and spend Day 4 and the following night here. The morning of Day 5, embark on a half-day camel trek. Return to Jaisalmer in time for dinner and the overnight train back to Jodhpur. On your last day, fly to Jaipur to see the Amer Fort and Palace and the delightfully pink-color old city.

If you have 10 days

Spend your first day exploring ⊡ **Jaipur.** After a night in one of Jaipur's luxurious hotels, hire a car, and leave early for a trip to one of Rajasthan's wildlife parks. ⊡ **Bharatpur** ⑭, on the eastern edge of the state, is one of the finest bird sanctuaries in India; if you prefer tigers, head to ⊡ **Ranthambhore National Park** ⑫. Spend the afternoon in the great outdoors and the night at a park lodge, then venture out early the following morning to watch the animals as they wake. Leave the park on Day 3 for ⊡ **Shekhavati** (it's a long, approximately 300 km (185 mi) drive from Bharatpur or Ranthambhore to the heart of Shekhavati). Spend your third night at one of the Heritage Hotels in this region, and drive back to Jaipur on Day 4.

From Jaipur, fly to ⊡ **Jaisalmer** ㉘ and consider devoting Days 5 and 6 to a camel safari, which means you'll be sleeping in the desert those two nights. Fly or take the overnight train to ⊡ **Jodhpur** ⑰ for Day 7. Fly the next morning to ⊡ **Udaipur** ㉑, and splurge on one of the city's magical hotels for your last two nights here. If you like temple architecture, make a detour to the Jain temples at **Ranakpur** ㉒ and **Mount Abu** ㉓ or the Hindu temples at **Nathdwara** ㉖. Leave Rajasthan on Day 10. This is a crowded schedule, but you'll get to see most of Rajasthan's highlights.

The beginning of the 18th century marked the decline of the Moghul period, and with it came the decline of the Rajputs. The incoming British took advantage of the prevailing chaos. Not only did they introduce significant administrative, legal, and educational changes in Rajasthan, they also exposed the Rajputs to new levels of decadence. The British introduced polo and other equestrian sports, the latest rifles and guns, *shikar* (hunting) camps, Belgian glass, English crockery, French chiffons, Victorian furniture, European architecture, and—eventually—fancy limousines. The influence extended to Rajput children: sons were sent to English universities, and daughters to the best finishing schools in Switzerland.

While the rest of India launched their struggle for independence, many Rajput princes ended up defending the Raj. Unwilling to give up their world of luxury and power, they did their best to suppress rebellion outside their own kingdoms by sending their soldiers to help the British forces. When India won independence, the Rajput princes and kings were forced to merge their kingdoms into one state as part of the new nation, but they were allowed to keep the titles to their palaces, forts, lands, jewels, and other sumptuous possessions. Since then, however, the government has taken over much of their land and many of their palaces and forts. Stripped of feudal power, many of the maharajas became hotel owners, while others have turned their properties over to leading hotel chains. A few have become paupers or recluses.

Rajasthan's heritage goes well beyond the illustrious maharajas, however. The Marwari trading community is known far and wide for its dynamic entrepreneurial spirit and its ornate *havelis* (mansions with interior courtyards). Semi-nomadic indigenous tribes, such as the Bhils, Meenas, Garasias, and Sahrias, create a rich canvas of folk life and folklore, their art, dance, music, and drama contributing much to Rajasthan's vibrant, festive culture. The exquisite craft work of the state's rural artisan communities—leatherwork, textiles, puppetry, and miniature painting—is admired in India and around the world. The presence of saints and spiritual leaders from a variety of religious communities has also, over the years, made Rajasthan a trove of shrines, temple art, and religious architecture.

Cultures within Rajasthan vary in everything from the colors of their sandstone buildings to the languages they speak. Though five principal Rajasthani dialects are spoken here (Marwari, Mewari, Dhundari, Mewati, and Hadauti), a local saying has it that you hear a new language every 4 km. And despite the overwhelming spread of both English and Hindi, villagers continue to maintain the rich literary traditions, both oral and written, of their local tongues. Also regionally significant—and perhaps more noticeable to the traveler—are the brilliant colors of the women's *lehangas* (long skirts with separate veils), designed to stand out against the starkness of the desert. Women also wear elaborate jewelry, and Rajasthani men are famous for their turbans—called *saafas*—which vary in style from region to region and caste to caste; the style of wearing high turbans with a tail is preferred by Rajputs, for instance, whereas *pagris* (compact turbans, often orange) are worn by business-

4

Jewelry & Leather
Rajasthani women adorn themselves with spectacular jewelry: bangles; tinkling anklets; armbands; and finger, nose-, toe-, and earrings. Men are also fond of wearing gold hoops in their ears and amulets around their arms. In Jaipur, look for gold settings of *kundan* (a glasslike white stone) and *mina* (enamel) work. Udaipur, Nathdwara, and Jaisalmer are all known for antique and contemporary silver jewelry. Decorated *lac* (lacquer) bangles are worn for good luck. Rajasthani artisans also specialize in cutting precious and semiprecious stones. Jaipur is a trade center for precious stones, and one of the emerald capitals of the world.

Men and women work together to produce Rajasthan's fantastic leather work. Men do the tanning, cutting, and stitching, and women add embroidery and ornamentation. Look for leather shoes (jootis), sandals, fans, pouches, saddles, and even musical instruments.

Marionnettes
Puppetry (known as *kutputli*) has a proud history here. Most villages have a resident puppeteer, and many hotels and restaurants stage daily puppet shows. The wood-and-string creatures are sold throughout the state. Udaipur and Jaipur are the hubs: Udaipur's folk museum has a well-known puppetry program, and Jaipur's Kalbalia dancers also perform puppetry routines.

Tie-Dye & Embroidery
Rajasthan is famous for its dyed and hand-blocked printed fabric, often further embellished by embroidery. Some hand-blocked patterns are familiar in the West, but the range of colors here is stunning. Of particular note are the *bandhani* (tie-dye), embroidered-mirror, and appliqué (patchwork) styles.

---

men. Even facial hair is unique in these parts: Rajputs, in particular, sport long, Salvador Dali–like handlebar moustaches.

The region's natural variety is also compelling. The Aravalli Hills are a natural divider between northwest and southeast Rajasthan. Arid sand dunes characterize the northwest: the sizzling Thar Desert is referred to in the ancient Hindu epic *Mahabharata* as the Maru-Kantar, "the Region of Death." The landscape of the southeast, however, belies Rajasthan's image as a desert state: craggy hills, lush forests, and shimmering lakes are typical. A rich array of birds, animal life, and insect species makes its home in each environment, and these may be seen in the several wildlife preserves of the state.

With its bright colors and rich folk traditions, and the sheer variety of experiences it has to offer the traveler, Rajasthan is one of India's most popular tourist destinations. Cultural festivals, crafts fairs, and religious gatherings take place throughout the year. In the last decade, Rajasthan's poverty rate has plunged and the literacy rate skyrocketed to almost double what it was. Tensions with Pakistan have, in the past, made some

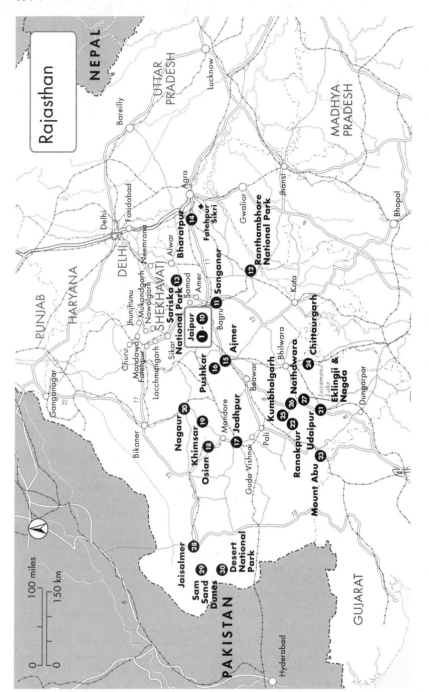

Rajasthan

people wary of coming here, but there is really nothing to fear. The cities and people remain lively and unaffected.

Exploring Rajasthan

You could easily spend a month in Rajasthan alone. The state's south-western corner centers on Udaipur, a hilly town of palaces and artificial lakes. Central Rajasthan is anchored by Jodhpur, home to a glorious fort and the eye-catching blue houses of the Brahmin caste. Jaipur, the state capital, is in the east (toward Delhi). Western Rajasthan, largely given over to the Thar Desert, can best be explored via camel or jeep from the golden city of Jaisalmer. In the northeast, between Jaipur and Delhi, the Shekhavati region is home to lovely painted havelis, the mansions of prosperous merchants. The southern and eastern regions also have a number of first-rate wildlife parks.

Note that Rajasthan is a big state, with long stretches of territory between the most popular destinations. If you have limited time here, it's best to stay in one city and explore the surrounding area rather than try to rush through all the highlights.

Numbers in the text correspond to numbers in the margin and on the Rajasthan and Jaipur maps.

About the Restaurants

Rajasthan's culinary traditions are heavily influenced by its desert setting. Food tends to be highly spiced, for preservation. Instead of the rice and vegetables that are popular in regions with more rainfall, Rajasthani cuisine includes a lot of lentils and corn. Both posh, pricey restaurants and local dives are bound to serve regional food, so do try some local delicacies, such as *dal baati churma* (lentils with wheat-flour dumplings), *gatte ki subzi* (dumplings made out of chick pea flour, also known as gram flour), and *ker sangri* (green beans). Breads include *bajra ki roti* (maize bread), *makki ki roti* (corn bread), and *missi ki roti* (chick pea- and wheat-flour bread). *Mirchi badas* (spicy green pepper fritters) and *kachoris* (fried stuffed pastries) make hearty appetizers. Dessert is a highlight here—in some parts, sweets actually open the meal. Favorites include *ghevar* (funnel cake), *laddoo* (balls of sugar, flour, clarified butter, and spices), *malpuas* (syrupy pancakes), and *diljani* (mini sugar balls).

About the Hotels

The most opulent hotels in India—and perhaps in the world—are in Rajasthan. You can literally live like a king in one of several converted palaces, surrounded by glittering mirrored walls, tiger skins, and stained-glass windows. The best-known of these lush lodgings are Udaipur's Lake Palace and Udaivilas, Jodhpur's Umaid Bhawan Palace, and Jaipur's Taj Rambagh Palace and Rajvilas. Unique to Rajasthan, too, are the Heritage Hotels, a group of castles, forts, and havelis that have been converted to elegant accommodations. Samode Haveli (Jaipur), Castle Mandawa (Shekhavati), Rohet Garh (near Jodhpur), Fateh Prakash Palace (Udaipur), Jagat Niwas and Kankarwa (Udaipur), and Laxmi Niwas Palace (Bharatpur) are among the finest. Ranthambhore has the Vanyavilas, the finest tented hotel in India.

	$$$$	**$$$**	**$$**	**$**	**¢**
	WHAT IT COSTS In Rupees				
	JAIPUR				
RESTAURANTS	over 500	400–Rs. 500	300–400	150–Rs. 300	under 150
HOTELS	over 8,000	6,000–8,000	4,000–6,000	2,000–4,000	under 2,000
	RAJASTHAN BEYOND JAIPUR				
RESTAURANTS	over 350	250–350	150–250	100–150	under 100
HOTELS	over 4,000	3,000–4,000	2,000–3,000	1,000–2,000	under 1,000

Restaurant prices are for a main course, defined as an entrée plus dal, rice, and a veg/non-veg dish. Hotel prices are for two people in a standard double room in high season, excluding tax.

Timing

The best time to visit Rajasthan is from October to March. Unfortunately, everyone knows this, so sights get crowded. If you want to get away from the hordes and can bear the heat of a desert summer, go in April. By May and June, it's brutally hot. The monsoon season (July–September) is fine unless you want to see the wildlife parks, which tend to flood. Alternatively, come for a festival: the Pushkar camel fair in November, the Shekhavati art festival in December, the Jaisalmer desert festival in January, Udaipur's Gangaur festival in April, and Mount Abu's summer festival in June.

JAIPUR & ENVIRONS

Jaipur, the state capital, is worth halting in for a couple of days until you find your bearings; it's a delightful mixture of modernity and folk tradition. Don't be surprised to see camels pulling carts on the main streets, mingling ill-temperedly with vehicular traffic. With its towering forts and impressive city palace, Jaipur is a good indicator of what to expect as you progress to interior Rajasthan. A number of day trips are possible around the countryside from the capital. The craft villages of Sanganer and Bagru, just outside Jaipur, are populated almost entirely by artisans, and you're free to stop in and watch them make fine paper and block-print textiles by hand. You may want to check out the town of Ajmer, a one-time Rajput stronghold that was later conquered by the Muslims, and which houses one of the most important shrines to a Sufi saint (Khwaja Mu'in-ud-din Chisti, 1142–1236) in India. The Hindu pilgrimage town of Pushkar is known for its annual camel festival. To escape civilization altogether, go tiger-spotting at Ranthambhore or bird-watching at Bharatpur's Keoladeo National Park.

Jaipur

261 km (163 mi) southwest of Delhi, 343 km (215 mi) east of Jodhpur, 405 km (251 mi) northeast of Udaipur.

A Rajasthani proverb asks, *"Je na dekhyo Jaipario, To kal men akar kya kario?"* ("What have I accomplished in my life, if I have not seen Jaipur?").

Surrounded on three sides by the rugged Aravalli Hills, and celebrated for the striking, if somewhat run-down pink buildings in the old part of the city, Jaipur is the capital of Rajasthan, and a fine starting point for a trip through the region. Significantly, the city is also known for being one of the few planned cities in the world.

Jaipur takes its name from Maharaja Sawai Jai Singh II, an avid scientist, architect, and astronomer, and is said to epitomize the dreams of the ruler and the creative ideas of his talented designer and builder, Vidhydar. Jaipur was founded in 1727, when Sawai Jai Singh moved down from Amer (commonly misrendered as Amber), the ancient rockbound stronghold of his ancestors. Rectangular in shape, the city is divided into nine blocks based on the principles of the ancient architectural treatise *Shilp Shastra*. Every aspect of Jaipur—streets, sidewalks, building height, and number and division of blocks—was based on geometric harmony, sound environmental and climatic considerations, and the intended use of each zone. Part of the city is still enclosed in 20-foot-high fortified walls, surrounded by eight gates.

Originally colored yellow (a color you can still see on the backs of the buildings), the capital was painted pink when Prince Albert, consort of Queen Victoria, visited India in 1883. This explains why Jaipur is commonly referred to as "the Pink City." The tradition stuck: by law, buildings in the old city must still be painted pink.

Timelessly appealing bazaars full of colorful textiles and trinkets—*lac bangles* (imitation fashion jewelry), steel utensils, copper ornaments—and *mehendi* (henna) artists form an integral part of the city center and its outlying villages. Another cultural highlight of Jaipur is its mouth-watering cuisine, particularly desserts: *ghevar* (lentil paste), *pheeni* (strawlike sweets), *jalebis* (fried, pretzel-shape orange sweets), *malpua* (deep-fried wheat flour rolls), and *churmas* (tasty wheat-flour dumplings). The sensory whirl and jumble of colorful *ghagharas* (skirts), complex turbans, and sturdy *jutis* (pointed shoes), of sidewalk shops overflowing with pottery and dyed or sequinned fabric, and of streets packed with camel carts, cycle-rickshaws, and wandering cows make Jaipur a dazzling, spirited city like no other.

a good tour

Start outside the walled old city, at the **Albert Hall Museum ❶** ▶, then walk north on Chaura Rasta into the old city. Pass through the Atishpol Gate to reach the **Jantar Mantar ❷** observatory and the **City Palace ❸**. A walk "around the block" through Sireh Deorhi Bazaar takes you to the **Hawa Mahal ❹** (you can see the back of the facade from the observatory). After a break for lunch, take a taxi north of town to the **Amer Fort and Palace ❺**. Continue to **Jaigarh ❿** and **Nahargarh ❻** forts, and watch the sun set at the nearby **Kanak Vrindavan Gardens ❼** and admire the Man Sagar with its Jal Mahal, a lake palace not open to the public.

The next day, visit **Sisodia Rani ka Bagh ❽** and, if you'd like to meet some local artists, **Jawahar Kala Kendra ❾**.

TIMING This tour can be done in one very exhausting day, as long as you start early; the Amer Fort closes at 4:30. You're better off saving the Amer

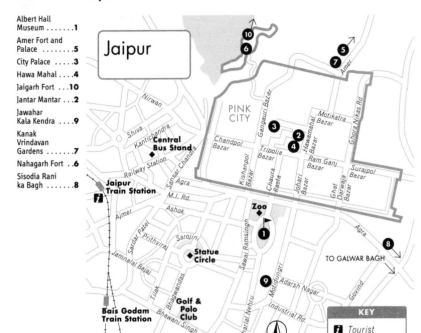

Albert Hall
Museum 1

Amer Fort and
Palace 5

City Palace 3

Hawa Mahal 4

Jaigarh Fort . . .10

Jantar Mantar . . .2

Jawahar
Kala Kendra 9

Kanak
Vrindavan
Gardens 7

Nahagarh Fort . .6

Sisodia Rani
ka Bagh 8

Fort and Palace, Jaigarh, and Nahargarh for day two, however, because these involve a lot of walking.

What to See

▶ ❶ **Albert Hall Museum.** Worth a visit just for its architecture, this sandstone-and-marble building was built in the late 19th century in the Indo-Saracenic style. The collection, which unfortunately is not well-maintained or well-organized, includes folk arts, miniature paintings, traditional costumes, unexpected exhibits of yoga postures, and visual explanations of Indian culture and traditions. Photography is not allowed. ⊠ *In Ram Niwas Gardens* 🎟 *Rs. 30* ☉ *Sat.–Thurs. 10–4:30.*

★ ❺ **Amer Fort and Palace.** Surrounded by ramparts, this marvelous fortress is perched on a hill near Maota Lake. Raja Man Singh began building it in 1592; Mirza Raja Jai Singh and Sawai Jai Singh continued the construction over a period of 125 years. For centuries the fortress was the capital of the Kachhawah Rajputs, but when the capital shifted to Jaipur in the early 18th century, the site was abandoned. Although the fort is in ruins, the interior palaces, gardens, and temples retain much of their pristine beauty. Both the art and the architecture combine Rajput and Moghul influences in felicitous ways.

You approach the palace complex by walking or riding an elephant up a sloping incline to the **Singh Pole** gate and **Jaleb Chowk,** the preliminary courtyard. If you choose to come up on an elephant, know that these animals are not native to Rajasthan and are often in poor health because of the arid climate and overuse by owners. An effort is being made to increase awareness about the condition of the Amer elephants and you could contribute by questioning the *mahout* (driver) and keeping an eye open for sores and abscesses. The more tourists express concern, the greater the chance of something actually being done about the problem.

Two flights of stairs lead up from Jaleb chowk; for now, skip the one leading to the Shila Mata temple and take the one leading to the palace itself. In the next courtyard, the pillared **Diwan-i-Am** (Hall of Public Audience) contains alabaster panels with fine inlay work—the kind of craftsmanship for which Jaipur is famous. Typical of the Moghul period, the rooms are small and intimate, whereas the palace's successive courtyards and narrow passages are characteristically Rajput.

From the latticed corridor over the elaborately carved and painted gate known as **Ganesh Pol,** after the elephant god Ganesh, the queen—always in purdah, or hiding—would await the King's return from battle and sprinkle scented water and flowers down upon him. Each room shows some vestige of its former glory, especially the **Sheesh Mahal** (Palace of Mirrors), with glittering mirror-work on the ceiling. Narrow flights of stairs lead up to the lavish royal apartments, and beyond the corridors and galleries here you'll find the small, elegant **Char Bagh** garden. Drink in the views of the valley, the palace courtyards, the formal gardens abutting the octagonal pool next to the lake, and the vast **Jaigarh Fort,** the ancient fortress on the crest of the hill above you. Also on the upper floor is **Jas Mandir,** a hall with filigreed marble *jalis* (screens) and delicate mirror and stucco work.

On your way out, peek into the 16th century **Shiladevi Temple** to the goddess Kali, with its silver doors and marble carvings. Raja Man Singh installed the image of the goddess after bringing it here from lower Bengal (now Bangladesh). Exit the palace by the gate near the temple, and just a few minutes down the road is the 450-year-old **Jagat Shiromani** temple. Dedicated to Krishna, this exquisitely carved marble-and-sandstone temple was built by Raja Man Singh I in memory of his son. ⊠ *Delhi Rd., 11 km (7 mi) north of Jaipur, Amer* 🖼 *Rs. 50; camera Rs. 75; video camera Rs. 150* ⊗ *Daily 9–4:30.*

★ ❸ **City Palace.** This complex of pavilions, courtyards, chambers, and palace was begun by Jai Singh II in 1727, with additions done by later maharajas. Once you're in the outer courtyard, the marble-and-sandstone building directly in front of you is the **Mubarak Mahal** (Guest Pavilion), built by Maharaja Madho Singh in the late 19th century. Now a museum, it's an ideal place to admire at close range some of the royals' finest brocades, silks, and hand-blocked garments and robes, many made in nearby Sanganer and some dating from as far back as the 17th century. The collection also includes musical instruments. The **armory** in the northwest corner of the courtyard has one of India's best collections of arms and weapons, including an 11-pound sword belonging to Akbar's Ra-

PALACE ON WHEELS

IF YOU ONLY HAVE A WEEK, *the most exciting and convenient way to see Rajasthan is to board the* Palace on Wheels. *This train, which runs September through April, takes you on one of the most luxurious rail journeys in the world, through a region well known for its historical architecture, varied wildlife, and heady culture. Your eight days aboard this locomotive begin at Delhi, from where you travel to Jaipur, the capital of Rajasthan, with its "pink" city, forts, palaces, and caparisoned elephants. From there, you travel across the desert to Jaisalmer, whose fort is a vision in sandstone, and to Jodhpur with its magnificent and well-preserved Meherangarh Fort. Then you continue on to Ranthambhore, where you can spot tigers in the wild, and Chittaurgarh—at the heart of chivalrous Mewar state. At Udaipur, the city of lakes, you have a chance to lunch at the famous Lake Palace hotel (the James Bond movie Octopussy was filmed here). The last leg of the journey takes you to Bharatpur, which you'll appreciate if you're a bird-watcher. You'll also go to Fatehpur Sikri, chosen capital of the Moghul emperor Akbar, and finally Agra, where the stunning, ethereal Taj Mahal is the crowning experience of a breathtaking week.*

The destinations, however, are only half the fun. The train's 14 splendid coaches are replicas of those once owned by the rulers of the erstwhile princely states of Rajputana, Gujarat, and Hyderabad, and

the Viceroy of colonial India. The plush accommodation allows you to sink blissfully into an unforgettable experience of India's sophisticated royal past while watching rural scenery through elegant, wood-framed picture windows. Bedchambers have private baths, whereas shared facilities include two dining cars and a lounge coach with a bar and library. Service is warm and attentive; each coach has a captain and an attendant. Your ticket on board this opulent train—$295 to $350 per person per night for double occupancy—covers all meals, including those taken off-the-train, entrance fees to every monument and national park, and cultural entertainment. Liquor is not included. If your time in India is limited, this train's well-planned route and thoughtful itinerary allows you to take in as much as you can in a week—and this is possibly more than you might have accomplished if you tried to reach the same destinations on your own.

(For reservations, contact TravBuzz, Inc., USA at 609–683–5018, Rajasthan Tourism Development Corporation [RTDC], Bikaner House, New Delhi at 11/ 2338–1884; or RTDC, Swagatam Complex, Jaipur at 141/220–2586.)

jput general. Some of the paints on the beautiful, 18th century ceiling are said to be made of crushed semiprecious stones.

In the inner courtyard, through the gateway guarded by two stone elephants, is the art gallery housed in the cavernous **Diwan-i-Am** (Hall of Public Audience). Built in the late 18th century, the building has rows of gray marble columns, the second-largest chandelier in India, and a magnificent, vintage-1930s painted ceiling. The art includes scores of miniatures from the Moghul and various Rajput schools, rare manuscripts, and 17th-century carpets from the Amer Palace. From the inner courtyard, enter the Zenana courtyard on the left to see the seven-story **Chandra Mahal** (Moon Palace). Built by Jai Singh II, this attractive cream-hue building is still the official residence of the present maharaja, "Bubbles"—Lieutenant Colonel Sawai Bhawani Singh—who lives on the upper floors. The ground floor has sumptuous chandeliers, murals, and a painting of an old maharaja. Photography is not allowed in the gallery area, and there's a Rs. 500 fine for using a video camera without a special ticket, which should be purchased with your admission ticket. ⊠ *Center of the old city, enter the complex at the Virendra Pole gate, Pink City* 🎫 *Adult Rs. 180; camera free; video camera Rs. 200* ⊙ *Daily 9:30–5.*

❹ **Hawa Mahal.** Jaipur's photogenic Palace of Winds was built by Maharaja Sawai Pratap Singh in 1799 so that the women of the court could discreetly take some air and watch the activity on the street below. Every story has semi-octagonal overhanging windows, and each has a perforated screen. This curious five-story structure—mainly a facade, named after the westerly winds that blow cool breezes through the windows— is just one room thick. The wind easily passes through the building and works like a cooler. (Traditionally, servants also threw water on the lattice, so any breeze would be cooled by the water, and would lower the temperature.) The building facade has a delicate honeycomb design with close to 1,000 windows, and is fashioned from pink sandstone. ⊠ *Sireh Deorhi Bazaar, Pink City* 🎫 *Rs. 5; camera Rs. 30; video camera Rs. 70* ⊙ *Sat.–Thurs. 9–4:30.*

<table>
<tr><td>

need a
break?

</td><td>

Known affectionately as LMB, **Laxmi Misthan Bhandar** (⊠ Johari Bazar, Pink City ☎ 141/256–5844 ▭ MC, V) is famous all over Rajasthan for fresh and sumptuous sweets, including *ghevar* (lentil paste), *mave ki kachori* (a milk-base pastry), and other savory snacks and meals. The rest of the food is average, though the *shahi* thali has an impressive 15 items. This is a great place to pick up gifts for Indian families, or sweets to donate at an evening *aarti*. The store sells sweets by the kilogram; prices range from Rs. 95 to Rs. 600 per kilogram, but you'll probably spend about Rs. 200 on sweets here.

</td></tr>
</table>

❿ **Jaigarh Fort.** The middle fort of Jaipur's three, both in position and altitude, Jaigarh Fort—originally the royal treasury—has large watertanks meant to store rainwater channeled down the hill from imposing Nahargarh. There's a fantastic view from the watchtower, and an air of ruin and abandonment. A large monkey population now provides endless entertainment in the center of the fort, while the largest wheeled cannon in the world draws visitors to its periphery. It's possible to drive from Jaigarh to Amer; you might need a driver who knows the way through the narrow lanes. Guides are also available at the entrance, an English-speaking person will charge about Rs. 100. ⊠ *About 7 km (4 mi) from Jaipur, off the Amer Rd.* 🎫 *Adult Rs. 35; camera Rs. 35; video camera Rs. 150; vehicle Rs. 50* ⊙ *Daily 9–4:30.*

★ ❷ **Jantar Mantar.** The Newton of the East, Jai Singh II was well aware of European developments in the field of astronomy, and wanted to create the world's finest observatories. He supervised the design and construction of five remarkable facilities in northern India, of which this is the largest and best preserved. Built in 1726 of masonry, marble, and brass, it's equipped with solar instruments called *yantras,* which look like large, abstract sculptures, and are remarkably precise in measuring celestial data. If you don't have a guide with you, try to recruit one to explain how these devices work, as they're fascinating and, for nonscientists, somewhat complicated. Avoid the observatory at noon, as it can be very hot. ⊠ *Tripoliya Bazaar, near entrance to City Palace, Pink City* 🎫 *Rs. 10; camera Rs. 50; video camera Rs. 100* ☉ *Daily 9–4:30.*

❾ **Jawahar Kala Kendra.** Jaipur's center for arts and crafts was founded by the state government with a specific vision: to create a space for understanding and experiencing culture and folk traditions amid the chaos and traffic of urban life. It's also becoming a venue for theatrical and musical performances. You can drop in to meet some of the locals who exhibit and perform here, or just to collect information on cultural events. ⊠ *Jawaharlal Nehru Marg, opposite Jhalana Institutional Area, Moti Dhungri* ☉ *Daily 10–6; concerts some evenings.*

❼ **Kanak Vrindavan Gardens.** This picturesque set of gardens and temples is just below the majestic Amer and Nahar Garh forts. From here you can take a good look at the Jai Mahal palace in Man Sagar Lake. The gardens also make a great picnic spot, especially if you like to people-watch. If you're lucky you might even catch a glimpse of Bollywood's brightest filming a Hindi movie. ⊠ *Amer Rd., Man Sagar* 🎫 *Rs. 5* ☉ *Daily sunrise–sunset.*

❻ **Nahargarh Fort.** You can get a breathtaking view of Jaipur and its natural defenses from Nahargarh Fort's scenic hilltop location. Initially built by Sawai Jai Singh in 1734, it was enlarged to its sprawling, present-day glory in 1885 by Sawai Madho Singh, who commandeered it as a lookout point. Cannons placed behind the walls recall the days when artillery was positioned against potential attackers below. The Rajasthan tourist board runs a snack bar at the fort, and indeed it's a great place for a picnic. The palace of nine queens—with nine separate apartments for the wives of Maharaja Ram Singh—within the fort is also worth a short visit. Interestingly, massive channels (which can still be seen from the approach road) carried rainwater from Nahargarh to nearby Jaigarh fort, where it was stored in large tanks. ⊠ *10 km (6 mi) north of Jaipur off Amer Rd.* 🎫 *Rs. 5; camera Rs. 30; video camera Rs. 70; vehicle Rs. 5* ☉ *Fort daily sunrise–sunset, palace daily 10–5:30.*

❽ **Sisodia Rani ka Bagh.** On the road to Bharatpur stands one of many palaces built for the *ranis,* or Sisodia Rajput queens, of Sawai Jai Singh II. Built in 1779, the palace still looks lovely against the backdrop of the hills. Its terraced garden is punctuated with fountains, and the palace itself is furnished with murals illustrating hunting scenes and the romantic legend of Krishna and Radha. From the terrace, you can see dancing peacocks and plenty of monkeys. Come during the day, as the site is often reserved for weddings and parties at night. ⊠ *8 km (5 mi) east of Jaipur on road to Bharatpur* ☞ *Rs. 5* ☉ *Daily 8–6.*

off the beaten path

GALWAR BAGH – Known by locals and rickshaw wallahs simply as Monkey Temple, Galwar Bagh is a popular pilgrimage site and temple complex on the outskirts of town. The temple itself is called **Gulta Ji Mandir**; it's a 30-minute walk from the ceremonial gate called Gulta Pol, located at the far eastern edge of the city, off Ajmer Road—about five minutes from the Muslim quarter. The walk leads you over a small mountain pass and past, inevitably, at least a few Hindu *sadhus* (holy men) and small temples. Jaipuri Hindus believe that at the site of the Gulta Ji Mandir, a local saint named Gala Rishi—nicknamed Gulta Ji—brought forth a spring of holy water from the Ganges and filled a water tank 18 feet deep. The waters here are said to be spiritually connected to the Ganges—if you bathe here, you get the same benefits as a pilgrimage to the Ganges. The temple, which venerates Lord Brahma, Creator of the Universe, is in violation of a curse by Brahma's wife Savatri; she confined his temples to Pushkar. ⊠ *Outside Gulta Pol, near Agra Rd. on the east side of town* ☞ *Free.*

Where to Eat

$$$$ ✕ **Suvarna Mahal.** Once the maharaja's royal banquet hall, this room is so grand—with a soaring, painted ceiling, handsome drapes, and tapestry-covered walls—that it's hard to concentrate on the menu, which includes Indian, Chinese, and Continental dishes. Regional specialties include *murgh tikka zaffrani* (chicken marinated in yogurt and saffron and cooked in a tandoor) and *dahi ka mass* (lamb cooked in a yogurt-base curry). Go for the enormous thali, which mixes things up deliciously. The restaurant is only open for dinner. ⊠ *Taj Rambagh Palace, Rambagh* ☎ *141/238–1919* ⌂ *Reservations essential* ☰ *AE, DC, MC, V.*

$$$–$$$$ ✕ **Gulab Mahal.** This many-arched and chandeliered restaurant at the Taj Jai Mahal is one of the few places in the city with a large selection of Rajasthani specialties. Try the *pyaaz aur boondi ki kadhi* (curry of gram flour and yogurt with onions and garlic), the delicate *hara mattar sisua*, a tasty blend of green peas and ginger, or the *papad ki subji*, (thin lentil wafers cooked with spices) for the traditional vegetarian experience. The classic nonvegetarian dishes include a hearty *murg methi ki bhajia* (chicken with fenugreek leaves in a yogurt-based gravy), a pungent *maas ka soyeta* (lamb on the bone with millets and spices), and tender, skewered *maas ka soola* (spiced boneless lamb cooked over charcoal). ⊠ *Taj Jai Mahal Palace, Jacob Rd., Civil Lines* ☎ *141/222–3636* ⌂ *Reservations essential* ☰ *AE, DC, MC, V.*

$–$$ ✕ **Niros.** This Jaipur institution is probably the most popular restaurant with the city's upper middle class. Amid mirrors and marble floors, it serves good Indian and Chinese food, as well as Continental dishes. Specialties include *reshmi* kabab (skewered boned chicken), paneer tikka (Indian cheese with skewered tomatoes, onions, and green peppers), and mutton *tikka masala* (tandoori lamb simmered in a spicy tomato-and-butter sauce). Niros also has the best cold coffee in town, topped with a scoop of ice cream. ⊠ *M. I. Rd., Panch Batti* ☎ *141/237–4943* ⌂ *Reservations essential* ☰ *AE, DC, MC, V.*

$ ✕ **Chokhi Dhani.** Come hungry to this village complex, where you'll sit
Fodor'sChoice on the floor in a lantern-lit hut and enjoy Rajasthani vegetarian dishes
★ Indian-style (with your hands, no silverware). Be prepared to consume
a large quantity of *shuddh desi ghee* (pure clarified butter) as it's poured
on practically every dish. Around the compound, you'll see traditional
dances, including the dramatic fire dance, folksinging, *katputli* (puppet
shows), and juggling. A mehendi-wali may offer to apply intricate designs on your palms while a persistent *rabdi-wala* (a man selling a spicy,
milk-based drink served hot) urges you to keep yourself warm with a
spicy traditional drink. Entertainment is included in the cost of the
meal, and tipping is discouraged. The temples here are real. If you're
here at sunset, you'll see the traditional village *aarti* (prayer ceremony).
Camel and boat rides cost Rs. 5; only rupees are accepted throughout.
⊠ *Tonk Rd., 19 km (12 mi) south of Jaipur via town of Vatika,* ☎ *141/
277–0555 or 141/514–2122* ▭ *AE, MC, V.*

$ ✕ **The Copper Chimney.** Jaipur's jet set needs some place to go for a night
on the town, and this restaurant often is the evening's start. It takes its
name from a copper chimney that's displayed center stage. Diners sit behind beautiful etched glass and look out onto the street below. Although
the menu has Continental, Chinese, and Indian selections, it would probably be best to avoid some of the odd hybrids such as *paneer Manchurian*
(cottage cheese served Chinese style). However, the *palak paneer* (peas
with cheese) and the sweet-and-sour lassis are exceptional. This is also
a good place to try the traditional *lal mas* (mutton gravy) and Rajasthani-
style *kadai* chicken (cooked in a heavy wok, and spicy). ⊠ *Mirza Ismail
Rd., near G.P.O., Panch Batti* ☎ *141/237–2275* ▭ *DC, MC, V.*

$ ✕ **Handi Restaurant.** This no-frills restaurant with bamboo walls and a
thatch roof has some of the best kababs and nonvegetarian Mughlai food
in town. One bite of the *kathi* kabab (garlicky mutton wrapped in
thinly rolled bread with onions and tomatoes) and you'll forget all
about the plastic chairs. Other specialties include a tangy butter chicken
(chicken marinated in yogurt and baked in a tandoor, then cooked in a
tomato curry) and the specialty, *handi* meat (a spicy mutton dish cooked
in a handi, or clay pot). Only rupees are accepted. ⊠ *M. I. Rd., opposite G.P.O., Panch Batti* ☎ *141/236–4839* ▭ *No credit cards.*

$ ✕ **Natraj.** This is a terrific place for coffee and dessert, although the set-
ting is a little rough around the edges. It's one of the few places open
for breakfast—if you're in the mood for stuffed *parathas* (bread). If you
dine upstairs, over the main dining room, you can sit in a fiberglass shell
made to look like a cave. The house specialty is *bundi ki laddu* (sugary,
deep-fried chick-pea-flour balls), and the *rasgulla* (cheese balls in a sugary syrup) and *ras malai* (sweet cheese dumplings smothered in cream)
melt in your mouth. The silver thali has a good assortment of vegetables and breads, and is one of the best on M. I. Road. ⊠ *M. I. Rd., Panch
Batti* ☎ *141/237–5804 or 141/510–2804* ▭ *AE, MC, V.*

¢–$ ✕ **Shivir.** This restaurant at the Man Singh Hotel serves good Punjabi
and Mughlai food. Sadly, it no longer operates from the rooftop of the
hotel. Live *ghazals* (Urdu love songs) set the mood during lunch and dinner. Shivir is known for its tandoori dishes, baked breads, and curries;
try *aloo bhojpuri* (potato stuffed with cheese) and chicken *lajawaab* (boneless chicken served in a spiced gravy). Top things off with a creamy dessert

of rasmalai. ⊠ *Man Singh Hotel, M. I. Rd., Govt. Hostel Junction, Panch Batti* ☎ *141/237–8771* ⊟ *AE, DC, MC, V.*

¢   ✕ **Sharma Dhaba.** A treat for the adventurous, this popular place is an Indian *dhaba* (truck stop); it serves only vegetarian food. The hot, fresh Punjabi food is extraordinary: mouth watering and finger-licking good. It's amazing to watch the tandoori chefs in action here, pounding dough and stir-frying vegetables with grace. Sharma Dhaba may well serve the best *naan* (bread) in all of Rajasthan, and the *aloo jira* (potato with cumin seeds), *palak paneer* (spinach with cheese), and garlic chutney are other choice sides. Ask them to spice to your taste. ⊠ *Sikar Rd., 15 km (9 mi) from Jaipur* ☎ *141/233–1582* ⊟ *No credit cards.*

Where to Stay

★ **$$–$$$**   ▥ **Taj Jai Mahal Palace.** This palace built in 1747 was once the residence of the chief minister of the state. It's away from the city center, and the elegant white structure is extremely romantic. The lavish, Moghul-style garden has a row of fountains and an enormous chessboard with life-size pieces. The interior has been restored with Rajasthani handicrafts and heirlooms: the suites are sumptuous, with priceless antiques and art-work, and the other rooms are comfortable with ornate furnishings. Rooms look out over the lawns or the solar-heated pool. On-site en-tertainment includes puppet shows and folk dances. Soft strains of live Indian classical music waft over the lawn at breakfast time. ⊠ *Jacob Rd., Civil Lines 302006* ☎ *141/222–3636* ☒ *141/222–0707* ⊕ *www.tajhotels.com* ⤶ *96 rooms, 6 suites* ⌂ *Restaurant, coffee shop, cable TV, pool, lawn tennis, hair salon, croquet, yoga, bar, laundry service, travel services* ⊟ *AE, DC, MC, V* ⊙I *EP.*

★ **$$$$**   ▥ **The Oberoi Rajvilas.** Twenty minutes outside Jaipur, Rajvilas is a des-tination unto itself. Marble-and-stone carving and handmade brass doors have created a hotel that's luxurious and blends well with the arid environment. You arrive into a lovely scene: pastel-color buildings, or-chards, and fountains. Rajvilas's standard double rooms are spacious and minimalist in concept, but the real stand-out is the marble and glass bathtubs, which look out over private gardens. The separate villas with private pools have been a favorite with Bill Clinton (price range for these villas is from US$1,500 to US$2,250, several times the price of an or-dinary room). Luxury tents are also available. The ayurvedic spa treat-ments are gaining a worldwide reputation as some of the most comprehensive available. The food at the courtyard restaurant is excellent, with a Continental–Indian menu that changes daily. Service is impec-cable. ⊠ *Reserve through Oberoi Group, New York* ☎ *800/662–3764 or 212/223–8800* ☒ *212/223–8500* ⊠ *Goner Rd., Babaji-ka-Mod, 18 km/11 mi from Jaipur, 303012* ☎ *141/268–0101* ☒ *141/264–0202* ⊕ *www.oberoihotels.com* ⤶ *54 rooms, 3 villas with private pools, 13 luxury tents, 1 tented villa* ⌂ *Restaurant, cable TV, 2 tennis courts, pool, hot tub, health club, spa, horseback riding, elephant safaris, library bar, business services, meeting room, airport shuttle, helipad, travel services* ⊟ *AE, DC, MC, V* ⊙I *EP.*

$$$$ ▥ **Rajputana Palace Sheraton.** This sprawling brick structure designed as a *haveli* (mansion) has four courtyards and numerous fountains, but it's more chic than it is traditional. The Western-style rooms are plush and comfortable. The pool, set in the main courtyard along with an outdoor bar, is beautifully designed, and the nightclub is one of the central meeting points for the city's upper-class youth. This is the place to be if you value comfort over nostalgia. ⊠ *Palace Rd., Bani Park, 302006* ☎ *141/510–0100, 888/625–4988 in U.S.* 🖷 *141/510–2102* ⊕ *www. welcomgroup.com* ✒ *200 rooms, 16 suites* 🖒 *3 restaurants, cable TV, pool, health club, hair salon, billiards, bar, dance club, recreation room, business services, travel services* ▭ *AE, DC, MC, V* ⦿ *CP.*

★ **$$$$** ▦ **Taj Rambagh Palace.** Once home to the Maharaja of Jaipur, this airy, cream-color palace is relaxing and wistfully romantic, down to the peacocks strutting across the lawns and the arcaded back patios. Standard rooms are spacious and largely contemporary; Superior and Luxury rooms have traditional furnishings, and colorful Shekhavati-style frescoes on the walls. Most higher-end rooms have original furnishings. The suites are opulent: the exotic Maharani Suite has a ruby-red cushioned alcove—and the enormous Prince's Suite has its own fountain. The grandest suites are on ground-level, with floor-to-ceiling windows that look out over lush foliage. The hotel is on the edge of Jaipur—not within walking distance of tourist sites. ⊠ *Bhawani Singh Rd., Rambagh, 302005* ☎ *141/238–1919* 🖷 *141/238–1098* ⊕ *www.tajhotels.com* ✒ *71 rooms, 19 suites* 🖒 *Restaurant, coffee shop, cable TV, golf privileges, 3 tennis courts, indoor pool, health club, hair salon, badminton, Ping-Pong, squash, bar, baby-sitting, business services, meeting room, travel services* ▭ *AE, DC, MC, V* ⦿ *EP.*

$$$–$$$$ ▦ **Samode Palace and Samode Bagh.** Nestled in a narrow valley between red-and-green hills 45 km (28 mi) from Jaipur, this 18th-century palace, built in the shadow of a small fort, towers over its little village. The palace has splendidly painted and enameled public rooms. Guest rooms, which have pillars and arches, are furnished with traditional Rajasthani-style chairs and beds with mosquito-net canopies. The rooms are not regal, but they're clean and comfortable. Royal Suites are spacious and even have their own fireplace, courtyard, and Jacuzzis. The staff can arrange horse, camel, and Jeep safaris. Three kilometers (1.9 mi) from the palace is Samode Bagh, a luxurious tented camp, or "garden retreat." 🏠 *Gangapol, Pink City 302002* ⊠ *45 km (28 mi) northwest of Jaipur, off Jaipur-Delhi Hwy.* ☎ *Palace: 1423/240–013 to 14 or 1423/240–023, Bagh 1423/240–235 to 36* 🖷 *141/2632370 Jaipur* ⊕ *www.samode.com* ✒ *Palace: 25 rooms, 18 suites; Bagh: 44 tents* 🖒 *Restaurant, cable TV, pool, hot tub, health club, massage, horseback riding, bar, travel services* ▭ *AE, DC, MC, V* ⦿ *CP.*

$$ ▦ **Trident Hilton.** This rose-color, modern hotel benefits from a superb location between the Pink City and Jaipur's three forts, with wonderful views of Man Sagar and the Jal Mahal as well as of the Aravalli hills. Rooms, furnished in earth tones, have *jharokhas* (balconies) that offer one or the other of these views. The Jal Mahal restaurant serves both Indian and Continental cuisine, and the Man Sagar bar has one of the loveliest views in the city. ⊠ *Opposite Jal Mahal Palace, Amer Rd., Man Sagar, 302002* ☎ *141/267–0101* 🖷 *141/267–0303* ⊕ *www.tridenthotels. com* ✒ *136 rooms, 2 suites* 🖒 *Restaurant, pool, bar, laundry service, travel services* ▭ *AE, DC, MC, V* ⦿ *EP.*

★ $ 🏨 **Alsisar Haveli.** This gorgeous, cheerful yellow haveli—one of the most popular Heritage Hotels in the state—is close to the Pink City, but its large lawn distances you from urban noise. Built in 1892 as the city residence of Shekhavati Rajputs, the bungalow has elegant rooms with carved antique furniture, restored frescoes, bedspreads with traditional Rajasthani prints, rug-covered tile floors, and brass-frame mirrors (in the bathrooms). In the public areas are crystal chandeliers, hunting trophies, and various weapons. Jeep and camel safaris—for hire at an extra charge—take you to a nearby village and fort. ✉ *Sansar Chandra Rd., Chandpol, 302001* ☎ *141/236–4685, 141/510–7167, or 141/510–7157* 🖷 *141/236–4652* ⊕ *www.alsisarhaveli.com* ⏎ *30 rooms, 6 suites* ⚐ *Restaurant, cable TV, pool, billiards, bar, travel services* ⊟ *AE, MC, V* ⊠ *EP.*

$ 🏨 **Chokhi Dhani.** Separated by a wall from the restaurant and ethnic village of the same name, this little hotel south of Jaipur offers a village setting plus modern conveniences. Although its distance from the city is a little inconvenient, the setting is delightful enough to make it worthwhile, plus transportation is arranged to and from town. Opt for a room in one of the mud huts, with wooden doors and carved furniture—unless you prefer to live like a landowner in the large painted haveli, with marble floors and modern bathrooms. The complex mirrors a village right down to the swimming pool—designed to look like a village water tank—and the lobby, with a sunken sitting area and hookahs. The vegetarian restaurant does, however, have Western-style tables and chairs. ✉ *Tonk Rd., 19 km (12 mi) south of Jaipur via Vatika, 303905* ☎ *141/277–0555 to 56* 🖷 *141/277–0558* ⊕ *www.chokhidhani.com* ⏎ *65 rooms, 8 suites* ⚐ *Restaurant, cable TV, tennis court, pool, gym, massage, sauna, spa, bar, laundry service, airport shuttle, meeting room* ⊟ *AE, DC, MC, V* ⊠ *EP.*

$ 🏨 **Holiday Inn.** Although modern and a trifle characterless, this hotel is comfortable and conveniently located—between the Pink City and Jaipur's forts. Some rooms have views of the Aravalli hills. An ethnic outdoor village restaurant has folk dancers, a fortune teller, and a fire-eater. ✉ *Amer Rd., 302002* ☎ *141/267–2000* 🖷 *141/267–2335* ⊕ *www.holiday-inn.com* ⏎ *56 rooms, 16 suites* ⚐ *2 restaurants, coffee shop, bar, laundry service, travel services* ⊟ *AE, DC, MC, V* ⊠ *CP.*

$ 🏨 **Raj Mahal Palace.** Built in 1729 by Sawai Jai Singh II, this small palace has a world-weary air. Now a Heritage Hotel, the palace offers spacious, if modest, rooms with high ceilings and few windows. The Maharaja suite doesn't cost much more than the somewhat lackluster standard rooms. ✉ *Sardar Patel Marg, C-Scheme, Civil Lines, 302001* ☎ *141/510–5665 or 141/510–5666* 🖷 *141/2381887* ⏎ *18 rooms, 5 suites* ⚐ *Restaurant, cable TV, pool, badminton, croquet, bar* ⊟ *AE, DC, MC, V* ⊠ *EP.*

★ $ 🏨 **Samode Haveli.** Tucked away in a corner of the Pink City, this lemon-yellow haveli is now a Heritage Hotel. Built for a prime minister of the royal court in the mid-19th century, and arranged around two courtyards, the haveli still has an air of stately grace and some original frescoes. Rooms are spacious and simply furnished. For opulence, stay in one of the two Sheesh Mahals, the luxurious quarters of the local Rajput himself (the rooms are still moderate in price), which have antique furniture, walls, and pillars inlaid with mirror work. Low arches and mazelike corridors add to its Rajasthani style. The best views are of the elegant palace gardens. The hotel can arrange camel and elephant rides.

The haveli also runs the **Samode Bagh** luxury-tent encampment and **Samode Palace,** a heritage resort, 45 km (28 mi) northwest from Jaipur. You can reserve for both through the Jaipur haveli. ✉ *Gangapol, Pink City, 302002* ☎ *141/263–2407, 141/263–2370, or 141/263–1942* 📠 *141/263–1397* ⊕ *www.samode.com* ⬚ *12 rooms, 9 suites* ♨ *Restaurant, cable TV, pool, hot tub, health club, bar, laundry service, travel services* ▤ *AE, DC, MC, V* ⍥ *CP.*

¢ ⌸ **Bissau Palace.** This two-story 1919 bungalow, now a Heritage Hotel, is on the outskirts of the old city. There's a small Royal Museum with weapons from the 17th century. Guest rooms in the old wing have original furniture, cotton *dhurries* (rugs), and murals; those in the new wing are furnished with four-poster beds, divans, and pieces from the armory. Rooms aren't fancy, but are neat and clean, and have ethnic touches. The family also has a beautiful retreat (visited by British royalty) 27 km (19 mi) outside town, from where you can take a camel ride through the surrounding villages. The retreat charges the same price as the palace. ✉ *Outside Chandpol, near Sarod Cinema, 302016* ☎ *141/230–4371 or 141/230–4391* 📠 *141/230–4628* ⊕ *www.bissaupalace.com* ⬚ *20 rooms, 22 suites* ♨ *Restaurant, tennis court, pool, library, bar, baby-sitting, travel services; no room phones, no room TVs* ▤ *AE, MC, V* ⍥ *EP.*

¢ ⌸ **Jasvilas.** If you stay at this guest house, you'll forego the facilities of a larger hotel for the comfort of a home away from home. Built during colonial times, the residence retains the traditional haveli shape of a mansion built around a courtyard. It also has a private pool in the courtyard. The Western-style rooms have marble floors, two sinks, and bathtubs. The Rajput family who runs it are happy to give tourist advice about Jaipur, and do their best to cater to the needs of foreigners. ✉ *C-9 Sawai Jai Singh Hwy., Bani Park, 302016* ☎ *141/220–4638 or 141/220–4902* ⊕ *www.jasvilas.com* ⬚ *9 rooms* ♨ *Dining room, in-room data ports, cable TV, pool* ▤ No credit cards ⍥ *EP.*

¢ ⌸ **Santha Bagh.** Once a lush garden commissioned by the Maharaja to stem local desertification, this Rajput family-run lodge offers personal service. The rooms contain beautifully carved antique and modern furniture. Only five of the rooms have air-conditioning; similarly, only some have television. The dining room gives you a glimpse into a martial past: elephant armor and photographs from the era of the Raj are on display. For a hotel that's just a few minutes from the center of town, the property is surprisingly peaceful and secluded. ✉ *Kalyan Path, near Police Memorial, Moti Dhungri, 302004* ☎ *141/256–6790 or 141/256–6791* 📠 *141/256–0332* ⬚ *14 rooms* ♨ *Dining hall, laundry services; no a/c, no TV in some rooms* ▤ No credit cards ⍥ *EP.*

Nightlife & the Arts

Your best bet for a night out is one of the hotel bars, which are usually open from about 11 AM to 3 PM and 7 PM to 11:30 PM. Hotel discos kick in from about 7 to 11:30.

Many hotels stage cultural programs for their guests, such as the dance performances with dinner in Panghat, at the Rambagh Palace. In addition, some restaurants, including Apno Gaon and the Chokhi Dhani village complex, combine excellent performances of Rajasthani folk dance with traditional regional meals. **Ravindra Rang Manch** (✉ Ram Niwas

Gardens ☎ 141/2619061), a cultural organization, hosts occasional dinner-and-dance programs.

To experience a contemporary Indian institution, head to the movies. **Rajmandir Movie Theatre** (✉ 16 Bhagwandas Rd., near Panch Batti ☎ 141/2379372) plays song-and-dance Bollywood films only. It has a beautifully ornate interior and is known as the best movie hall in Asia. The theater disperses different blends of incense at occasional points in the film. Widely visited by Indian and foreign tourists, Rajmandir is still constantly flooded with locals, who sing, cheer, and whistle throughout each film. Shows are at 3, 6:15 and 9:30. Book in advance.

Sports & the Outdoors

Polo is a passion in Jaipur. In season (late March and late October), matches are held at the **Rajasthan Polo Club.** (☎ 141/238–3580). You can also call the Taj Rambagh Palace (☎ 141/2381919) for information about polo matches in the city. The **Rajasthan Mounted Sports Association** (☎ 141/221–1276) gives polo lessons. Year-round polo lessons are organized by Pritam Singh of **Anokhi** (☎ 141/275–0861) at Rs. 1,750 per hour.

To play golf, phone the **Taj Rambagh Palace** (☎ 141/2381–919) to reserve access to a driving range.

Shopping

Rajasthan's craftspeople have been famous for centuries for their jewel settings, stonework, blue pottery, enamel, lacquer, filigree work, tie-dye, and block-printed silk and muslin. You'll find all this and more in Jaipur, but watch out: your drivers and/or guides are likely to insist that they know the best shops and bargains in the city. (They get a commission on whatever you purchase.) If you have a specific shop in mind, be firm. Don't rely on the phrase "government-approved." Easily painted over a shop door, it's essentially meaningless. The following shops are reliable, and you're bound to find others in your explorations. Note that many shops are closed on Sunday.

ARTS & CRAFTS If you have limited time and lots of gifts to buy or don't relish bargaining, head to an emporium. The enormous, government-run **Rajasthali** (✉ Government Hostel, M. I. Rd., Panch Batti ☎ 141/237–2974) is always flooded with crafts and textiles, though you might have to sift through a bewildering variety before you find what you want. **Tharyamal Balchand** (✉ M. I. Rd., Panch Batti ☎ 141/237–0376 or 141/236–1019) sells a variety of authentic, good-quality crafts, including jewelry, brasswork, textiles, blue pottery, and woodwork. Here you'll get a good sense of the diversity of crafts and textiles from the different parts of Rajasthan. **Manglam Arts** (✉ Durgapura Station Rd., off the Tonk Rd. ☎ 141/272–1428) is filled with exquisite antique and contemporary fine art, including Hindu *pichwais* (cloth paintings depicting Lord Krishna in various moods), Jain temple art, tantric and folk art, terra-cotta sculptures, silver furniture, handwoven *dhurries,* wood carvings, and wonderful old fabrics.

For specialty shops, wander through the **Kazana Walon ka Rasta** (✉ Pink City) lane in the old city (accessible through Chandpol gate) and watch stone-cutters create artworks in marble. For brass or other metalwork, visit **P. M. Allah Buksh and Son** (✉ M. I. Rd., Panch Batti), established in 1880, which still sells the finest hand-engraved, enameled, or embossed brassware—including oversize old trays and historic armor. The tiny, unpretentious shop **Bhorilal Hanuman Sahar** (✉ Shop 131, Tripoliya Bazaar, Pink City) has burlap bags full of old brass, copper, and bronze pieces that are sold by weight at bargain prices. The **Popular Art Palace** (✉ B/6 Prithviraj Rd., C-Scheme ☎ 141/229–2541 or 141/229–2571) is great for both brass and wooden furniture, as well as miniature crafts and antiques.

For demonstrations of hand-block printing and other craftsmanship, visit **Rajasthan Cottage Industries** (✉ Shilpgram Complex, Golimar Garden, Amer Rd. ☎ 141/267–1853 or 141/267–1184). It offers a fine variety not only of textiles, but also of other handicrafts and gems. Purchases are guaranteed. **Rajasthan Small Scale Cottage Industries** (✉ Jagat Shiromani Temple Rd., Amer ☎ 141/253–0519) sells textiles, gems, and handicrafts, including hand-block printing.

A special treat for lovers of miniature paintings is a trip to the home of award-winning artist **Tilak Gitai** (✉ E-5 Gokhle Marg, C-Scheme ☎ 141/237–2101), who creates exquisite miniatures in classic Moghul, Rajput, Pahari, and other styles. Using antique paper, Gitai applies colors made from semiprecious stones, then real gold and silver leaf, in designs so fine he'll give you a magnifying glass to admire them. This is not a quick visit—it's a great way to spend a few hours with a friendly Rajasthani family and learn about Indian art. **Juneja Art Gallery** (✉ Lakshmi Complex, M. I. Rd., Panch Batti ☎ 141/236–7448) is Jaipur's leading gallery of contemporary art.

need a break? No visit to Jaipur is complete without a stop at **Lassiwallah** (✉ M. I. Rd., across from Niros, Panch Batti), the most famous vendor of its kind in all of India. Located on the periphery of a long chain of imposters, the real thing can only be found under the sign "Kisan lal Govind Narayan Agrawal." Expect a long line. The lassi wallah himself wears a *tilak* (an auspicious dot on the forehead) and *moti mala* (necklace) to demonstrate his devotion to God and good service, and sits elevated above a large bowl of yogurt and cream (*lassi* drinks cost Rs. 10–Rs. 20). Served in disposable red-clay cups with a dash of hard cream on top, drinks come only in medium and large sizes.

JEWELRY **Gem Palace** (✉ M. I. Rd., Panch Batti ☎ 141/237–4175) has Jaipur's best gems and jewelry, a small collection of museum-quality curios, and a royal clientele; prices range from US$2 to US$2 million. **Amprapalli Jewels** (✉ M. I. Rd., Panch Batti ☎ 141/237–7940 or 141/236–2768) has some great silver and ornamental trinkets, as well as semiprecious stone artifacts. For precious jewels, including gold ornaments, find the **Bhuramal-Rajmal Surana Showroom** (✉ 368 J. L. N. Marg, Moti Dhungri ☎ 141/257–0429 or 141/257–0430), known worldwide for its *kundan* (a glasslike white stone) and *mina* (enamel) work. If you want something that's not so expensive and you're willing to bargain, you'll find your niche on **Chameli Valon ka Rasta** (✉ Off M. I. Rd., Panch Batti). Walk among the shops on this lane for silver and semiprecious jeweled ornaments, trinkets, and small toys.

RAJASTHANI FASHIONS

W**HETHER IT'S A BRIGHTLY COLORED SKIRT** *swishing over a sand dune, a mirror-work veil hanging on a clothesline, or a dashing turban standing out in the crowd, you're bound to come away from Rajasthan with unforgettable images of the state's beautiful cotton textiles, and all the accessories that go with them. Life in rural Rajasthan is simple and difficult; it's not been easy to eke out a livelihood from dry desert land. And it seems as if people here have tried to enliven their very existence with brilliant splashes of color—all the more extravagant when seen against the monotonous, arid landscape of their homeland.*

Perhaps this is why the prettiest bandhani lehengas (tie-dyed full-length skirts) are worn by the simplest rural women, the biggest, most attractive pajebs (anklets) seen on the grubbiest bare feet on a railway platform, the most striking gold studs in the ears of the taxi driver who collects you at the airport. Take your cues for assembling your own

Rajasthani outfits from the people you see around you—the more you people-watch, the easier it becomes to distinguish between regional styles and nuances. And, Rajasthan is so tourist-savvy that you'll also find a whole range of Western clothes using Rajasthani fabrics and decorative techniques. Most of these are at throwaway prices—you can buy a simple mirror-work short kurta (ethnic top) for as little as US$2.

It's impossible to ignore the jewelry in Rajasthan—this is the one place in the world where even intricate silver jewelry seems run-of-the-mill. Rubies, emeralds, garnets, lapis lazuli; there's a wide range of stunning precious stones to be bought here. Enameled gold-and-silver bangles are unique—these are made using a traditional technique called minakari. Much cheaper and further down the social scale—but no less attractive—are the ordinary lac (imitation fashion jewelry) and glass bangles to be found in glittering stacks in dozens of bazaar shops.

POTTERY **Jaipur Blue Pottery Art Center** (⊠ Amer Rd., near Jain Mandir ☎ no phone) sells a broad selection of Rajasthan's fetching blue pottery. Clay pots are "thrown," or made, on the premises. Blue pottery from the kiln of Kripal Singh can be bought at **Kripal Kumbh** (⊠ B-18A Shiv Marg, Bani Park ☎ 141/220–1127) The blue pottery at **Neerja Internationals** (⊠ S-19 Bhawani Singh Rd., C-Scheme Extension, Bais Godam ☎ 141/238–0395 or 141/238–3511) is particularly funky—the designer–owner Lela Bordie has exhibited all over the world, and she runs this shop for a discriminating crowd.

TEXTILES For fine hand-block fabrics, go south to the nearby towns of Sanganer (16 km [10 mi] south of Jaipur) and Bagru (35 km [22 mi] southwest of Sanganer). **Channi Carpets and Textiles** (⊠ Mount Rd. opposite Ramgarh Rd. ☎ 141/267–2231 or 141/267–2214) has an excellent selection of handwoven merino wool carpets, cotton dhurries, and hand-block cottons and silks. The staff can also tailor clothes on short notice.

Anokhi (⊠ 2 Tilak Marg, opposite Udhyog Bhawan, C-Scheme, Ashok Nagar ☎ 141/238–1247) is a leading shop for designer and ethnic wear, mostly in cotton. The selection includes beautiful bedspreads, quilts, cloth bags, saris, and other clothing—both Indian and casual Western. It has the prettiest *lehengas* (skirts) in the state. You can also visit the on-site workshop. Run and managed by women, the boutique **Cottons** (⊠ 4 Achrol Estate, Jacob Rd., Civil Lines) carries simple, attractive clothes for men and women, as well as little bags, quilts, and other decorative household items. Catering to the ultra-elegant crowd, **Soma** (⊠ 5 Jacob Rd., Civil Lines ☎ 141/222–2778) is a second-floor shop filled with vibrant colors. Here you'll find everything from clothing to chutneys to decorative fabrics—including fabulous, hand-painted white cloth lamp shades.

off the beaten path

APNO GAON – If you don't have time to visit a small village, here's your chance to get a feel for Rajasthani folk culture. Like the state's half-dozen simulated villages, Apno Gaon offers camel rides, playground swings, traditional music, and puppet shows. The food is so good even locals feast here. You'll get farm-fresh, organically grown vegetables, and *bhajra* (maize) delicacies and milk products. Be prepared to sit on the ground and eat with your hands. Apno Gaon is open from 11 AM to 11 PM, but is better at night. The street signs are in Hindi, so ask your driver for directions. ⊠ *Sikar Rd., past Vishwa Karma Industrial Area* ☎ *141/233–1802* ▭ *No credit cards.*

Sanganer

⓫ *16 km (10 mi) south of Jaipur up Tonk Rd., near the airport.*

Watch artisans in action throughout this well-known craft town, where nearly every family is involved in the production of block- and screen-printed textiles, blue pottery, or handmade paper. Whatever handmade paper you've seen back home may well have come from **Salim's Paper** (⊠ Gramodyog Rd. ☎ 141/273–0222). In this factory you can see each step of the fascinating process. Some of the thick, beautiful papers are made with crushed flower petals; it's fun to see them thrown into the mixture of cotton and resin. **Shri Digamber Jain Temple,** roughly 1,000 years old and covered with amazingly ornate carvings from its piled spires on down, is a highlight of Sanganer. The temple is right in town. The inner shrine has no roof, yet somehow the space seems to achieve total tranquillity. On your way into or out of town, check out the line of blue potters on Tonk Road.

off the beaten path

BAGRU – This small Rajput township, 35 km (22 mi) southwest of Sanganer on Ajmer Road, is famous for its hand-printed cloth industry. Bagru's simple, popular designs feature earthen colors of green, brown, black, and blue.

Ranthambhore National Park

⓬ *161 km (100 mi) south of Jaipur.*

Fodor'sChoice
★

Now incorporating several nearby sanctuaries in its borders, Ranthambhore National Park encompasses 1,334 square km (515 square mi), and is spectacular: the rugged Aravalli and Vindhya hills, highland boulder plateaus, and lakes and rivers provide homes for hundreds of species of birds, mammals, and reptiles. Ranthambhore is noted for its tiger and leopard population, although you still have only a 50% to 75% chance of seeing a large cat on any given expedition. The best time to see tigers is right before the monsoon, in summer, when the tigers emerge to drink from small water holes. (When it's dry and the water table is low, the tigers are forced out of hiding to quench their thirst.) What you will definitely see are numerous peacocks, *sambar* (deer), *chital* (spotted deer), *chinkara* (gazelle), wild pigs, jackals, crocodiles, and often sloth bears.

Sighting a wild tiger in Ranthambhore is an exciting experience: if you're lucky, open jeeps sometimes take you as close as 10 feet away from an animal. Before that, of course, you will hear the jungle sounds that warn of a tiger's presence. Monkeys and peacocks scream loudly and the deer in the area become agitated and nervous. Despite conservation efforts, the tiger population in Ranthambhore is small: there are less than 40 of the great amber-eyed cats in the reserve. Sighting a leopard is much more difficult, as these cats live on high, inaccessible slopes and are extremely shy.

The park is run by the Indian government, and the rules are somewhat inflexible: you can only enter the park in an official government jeep, and the jeeps keep strict hours, daily from 6:30 AM to 9:30 AM and 3:30 PM to 6:30 PM. Book a jeep two months in advance—there's heavy demand for them. (If you make bookings through your hotel, expect a service charge.) In the off-hours, you can explore the surrounding region; the 10th century **Ranthambhore Fort,** perched on a nearby hill, is one of Rajasthan's more spectacular military strongholds. You could also visit Dastkar, a craft-and-textile shop on the Ranthambhore Road, run by a nongovernmental organization.

Within the park is a government-run hotel called **Jhoomar Baori** (12 rooms, Rs. 650 to Rs. 800) offers the chance to spend a night near the animals, but little else. A better option is to stay at one of the hotels along Ranthambhore Road. The neighboring town of Sawai Madhopur has numerous hotels, but most are extremely basic. *For park information call Sawai Madhopur Tourist Information Center* ☎ *7462/220–808* 🖃 *Rs. 1,250 per jeep (5 persons), Rs. 125 per person in a canter and Rs. 155 per person in a deluxe canter* ⊙ *Oct.–June.*

Where to Stay

$$$$ 🏨 **Oberoi Vanyavilas.** A startlingly luxurious new jungle resort is one of
Fodor'sChoice the best resorts in all India. In landscaped gardens on the edge of the na-
★ tional park, its ceremonial gateway (complete with welcoming elephants) leads to a magical lobby with beautiful frescoes and a splendid residential area, where luxury tents evoke all the magnificence of the former royal lifestyle. The air-conditioned tents have teakwood floors, walled gardens, private decks, and incredibly charming bathrooms with standalone bathtubs. The sand-tone resort blends with the hills and the forest. When not at the park, you can take advantage of the excellent spa facilities and swimming pool here, or take an elephant picnic into the countryside. A renowned conservationist, Fateh Singh Rathore, delivers a lecture every evening. Organically grown vegetables from the resort's own garden contribute to the freshness of the flavors at the restaurant. The staff are young, warm, and ever ready to go the extra mile to ensure your comfort. ✉ *Ranthambhore Rd., Sawai Madhopur 322001* ☎ *7462/223–999*

🏠 7462/223–988 ⊕ *www.oberoihotels.com* 📠 *25 tents* ♨ *Restaurant, in-room data ports, pool, spa, bar, billiards, baby-sitting, laundry service, safari bookings, elephant rides* ☰ *AE, DC, MC, V* ❏ *EP.*

$$$$ 🏨 **Sawai Madhopur Lodge.** This Taj-run property is laid-back, if in need of new upholstery, and may give you the impression that you're still in the old hunting-lodge days as you sit on the verandah and look out on the lawn. The colonial building that houses the lobby occupies the site of the royal tented camp, which was once a regular hunting event. A railway line once extended right up to the camp; you can see old photographs of the days when the railway line brought royalty and their guests all the way up to the camp! ⊠ *Ranthambhore Rd., Sawai Madhopur 322001* 🕿 *7462/220–541 to 47* 🏠 *7462/220718* ⊕ *www.tajhotels.com* 📠 *27 rooms, 6 tents, 2 suites* ♨ *Restaurant, cable TV, tennis court, pool, billiards, croquet, bar, laundry service, safari bookings, travel services* ☰ *AE, DC, MC, V* ❏ *FAP.*

$$$ 🏨 **Ranthambhore Regency.** This is definitely the most comfortable mid-price place on the Ranthambhore Road. A long line of rooms is set against a rectangular courtyard with a pool, and a restaurant serves buffet meals (all meals are included). There's also a barbecue outside. The rooms are spotless, with bright Rajasthani furnishings. The helpful owner, Ravinder Jain, is committed to making your Ranthambhore experience pleasant, and is a mine of local information. ⊠ *Ranthambhore Rd., Sawai Madhopur 322001* 🕿 *7462/223456 or 7462/221176* 🏠 *7462/221672 or 7462/222299* ⊕ *www.ranthambhor.com* 📠 *10 cottages, 28 rooms, 1 suite* ♨ *Restaurant, pool, laundry service, trekking, baby-sitting, travel services* ☰ *MC, V* ❏ *FAP.*

Sariska National Park

⑬ *110 km (68 mi) northeast of Jaipur, 110 km (68 mi) southwest of Delhi, 40 km (25 mi) southwest of Alwar.*

Sariska was once the exclusive game preserve of the rulers of the princely state of Alwar. Today, this sanctuary in the hills of the Aravalli Range makes a great weekend escape from Delhi. Traditionally a tiger reserve, Sariska is now better populated with other carnivorous animals, including the leopard, jackal, caracal, and jungle cat (though the cats' nocturnal habits make sightings rare). The terrain—mostly scrub and lush clusters of forest and grasslands—also provides an excellent habitat for herbivores. Peacocks abound here, as do monkeys, blue bulls, spotted deer, and wild boars. You do have a good chance of seeing langurs and other monkeys, porcupines, hyenas, and numerous species of deer (including the *chowsingha,* a four-horned deer unique to India), and all kinds of birds.

Forest officials have created water holes for the animals, which help you catch glimpses of otherwise elusive wildlife. The best times to view animals at Sariska are early morning and evening from November through June (though it starts getting hot by March). Jeeps are available at the hotels. Wear neutral colors to avoid scaring the animals away, and take a jacket in winter.

In Sariska you can also find a number of historic monuments. Within the park is the **Pandupol,** a huge hole in the rock supposedly made by

Bhim, one of the five Pandava brothers who are celebrated in the ancient Hindu epic, the *Mahabharata*.

Outside the sanctuary, but still close by, is the **Neelkanth Mahadev,** an ancient ruin that includes pieces from about 300 Hindu and Jain temples. Among these ruins are some beautiful sculptures and an entire temple devoted to Shiva, as well as the ruins of the Kankwari Fort perched high on a hill (a good picnic spot).

Where to Stay

$$$ ⊞ **Sariska Palace Hotel.** This former palace and royal hunting lodge was built in 1892 by the Maharaja of Alwar for the visit of Queen Victoria's son, the Duke of Connaught. The high-ceiling rooms and suites are gigantic and clean. Animals often find their way in to the flower-speckled grounds, so you may see wildlife while relaxing on the terrace. Horse, camel, and jeep safaris are easily arranged. ✉ *Reserve through 1/1-B Mohammedpur, Bikhaji Cama Pl., New Delhi 110066* ✉ *Alwar district, 301022* ☎ *144/284–1322 to 25, 11/2615–4388 to 89 reservations* 🖷 *11/26154390 or 144/2841323* ⊕ *www.sariska.com* 🛏 *51 rooms, 5 suites* ᗺ *Restaurant, tennis court, pool, horseback riding, bar, travel services; no a/c in some rooms, no room TVs* ▭ *AE, DC, MC, V* ⏽⏺ *EP.*

Bharatpur

⑭ *150 km (93 mi) east of Jaipur, 55 km (34 mi) west of Agra, 18 km (11 mi) west of Fatehpur Sikri.*

Fodor'sChoice Founded by the Jat ruler Suraj Mal in 1733 and named for the brother
★ of Lord Ram, the city of Bharatpur is famous for the **Keoladeo National Park** (also known as the Ghana Bird Sanctuary), once the duck-hunting forest of the local maharajas. The park is home to mammals and reptiles—blue bulls, spotted deer, otters, and Indian rock pythons—but birds are the main attraction. This famous waterbird haven is an ornithologist's dream—29 square km (10 square mi) of forests and wetlands with 400 species, more than 130 of which are resident year-round, such as the Saras crane, gray heron, snake bird, and spoonbill. In winter, birds arrive from the Himalayas, Siberia, and even Europe.

The best way to see the park is on foot or by boat (Rs. 75–Rs. 150 per hour), but there are plenty of other options. The park's main artery is a blacktop road that runs from the entrance gate to the center. Surrounded by marshlands but screened by bushes, this road is the most convenient viewpoint for bird-watching, and is also traveled by cycle-rickshaws (Rs. 50 per hour), a horse and buggy, and the park's electric bus (Rs. 25 per person). The rickshaw drivers, trained by the forest department, are fairly good at finding and pointing out birds. You can also rent a bicycle (about Rs. 20) and head into more remote areas; just remember that most roads are unpaved. The excellent guides at the gate (Rs. 150 per excursion) are familiar with the birds' haunts, and can help you spot and identify them.

Try to bring a bird guidebook: former royal-family member Salim Ali's *The Birds of India* is a good choice. The best time to see the birds is early morning or late evening, November–February; by the end of February, many birds start heading home. Stick around at sunset, when the water takes on a mirrorlike stillness and the air is filled with the calls of day birds settling down and night birds stirring. *For information, contact the Director, Keoladeo National Park* ⊠ *5 km (3 mi) south of city center, Bharatpur 321001* ☎ *5644/222–777* 🖷 *Rs. 200; camera Rs. 10; video camera Rs. 200, professional movie cameras Rs. 5,000* ☉ *Park daily 6 AM–6:30 PM.*

In Bharatpur's Old City is the **Lohagarh Fort,** also known figuratively as the Iron Fort. Built of mud, the structure might seem fragile, but it was tested by a British siege in 1805: armed with 65 pieces of field artillery, 1,800 European soldiers and 6,000 Indian sepoys did manage to win the battle, but they failed to break the invincible fort. 🖷 *Rs. 5* ☉ *Daily 10–5.*

The town of **Deeg,** 34 km (21 mi) north of Bharatpur, is known for its graceful palaces and gardens, complete with swings and ancient fountains. (The latter now serve as musical fountains—their waters dance to the rhythm of taped classical music.) Built in the 1730s, Deeg was the first capital of the Jat state.

Where to Stay

$$ ✕🏨 **Ashok Bharatpur Forest Lodge.** This ivy-covered bungalow inside the sanctuary has clean, comfortable rooms—some with decorative interior swings. All rooms have balconies, from which you may see spotted deer nibbling the grass outside. Indian and Continental buffets are served in the restaurant. ⊠ *Inside Keoladeo National Park, 1 km after the entrance, Bharatpur 321001* ☎ *5644/222–722 or 5644/222–760* 🖷 *5644/222–864* 🖵 *17 rooms* 🛆 *Restaurant, cable TV, bar* 🖃 *AE, MC, V* ⑩ *EP.*

★ **$$** 🏨 **Laxmi Vilas Palace Hotel.** Still home to the descendants of the former maharaja's younger brother, this cozy Heritage Hotel is a two-story haveli built in 1887. With its rural location and old-fashioned feel, it's certainly the best place to stay in Bharatpur. The palace, on a 40-acre estate covered with mustard and wheat fields, blends Moghul and Rajput styles. Each room is different, but many contain old brass beds and antique furniture. Pricier rooms have original tiles and painted walls and fireplaces; the others are smaller and have newer furniture, but they're still pleasant. A variety of cuisines are served in the dining room and there are cultural programs in the evening. Deep Raj, the owner, is happy to organize jeep safaris or excursions to surrounding areas, such as Deeg, Agra, and Fatehpur Sikri, and is a great source of local information. ⊠ *Kakaji Ki Kothi, Bharatpur 321001* ☎ *5644/231–199 or 5644/223–523* 🖷 *5644/225–259* ⊕ *www.laxmivilas.com* 🖵 *14 rooms, 16 suites* 🛆 *Restaurant, cable TV, pool, hot tub, massage, bar, Internet, travel services* 🖃 *AE, MC, V* ⑩ *EP.*

Ajmer

⑮ *131 km (81 mi) southwest of Jaipur.*

Roughly three hours' drive from Jaipur, the town of Ajmer has a typically Indian past—with Hindu, Muslim and colonial influences. Founded by Raja Ajay Pal Chauhan in the 7th century, the town was a center of Chauhan power until 1193, when Prithvi Raj Chauhan lost the kingdom to Mohammed Ghori. From then on, many dynasties contributed to making Ajmer what it is today, a fascinating blend of Hindu and Islamic culture. Demographically, Ajmer is primarily a Muslim town, but its proximity to Pushkar gives it a Hindu feel—it has a famous mosque as well as temples, and all pilgrims to Pushkar pass through Ajmer. It also has remnants of colonial-era architecture.

Accommodation options in Ajmer are somewhat limited; most travelers pass through on their way to Pushkar, where there are comfortable places to stay. Ajmer makes a convenient half-day halt, as it's the nearest rail station to Pushkar. The two places are separated by Nag Pahar mountain, across which an 11-km (7-mi) ghat, or mountain pass, traverses.

In the heart of the city is **Dargah Sharif,** the tomb of the Sufi saint Khwaja Moin-ud din Chisti. This site is comparable to Mecca in significance for South Asian Muslims, and is frequented by Muslims and non-Muslims alike, especially during Urs (a death anniversary celebration that takes place during six days in the Islamic month of Rajab—around September or October). Be prepared to deal with aggressive beggars on the street leading to the dargah.A peaceful place of worship worth visiting is the 19th-century **Nasiyan Temple,** sacred to the Jains. If you have enough time in Ajmer, take a guide with you to the **Dhai din ka Jhonpra,** a ruined 12th-century mosque, which, according to legend, was built in two-and-a-half (*dhai*) days.

Pushkar

★ *11 km (7 mi) northwest of Ajmer.*

With more than 500 temples, Pushkar is one of Hinduism's holiest sites and an interesting place to visit even when the famous camel fair is absent. In its narrow traffic-free main bazaar, sadhus, tribals, hippies, and five-legged cows (many have birth deformities) vie for space, while shops selling implements of the ascetic lifestyle rub shoulders with the Pink Floyd café and other such establishments selling porridge and pancakes to backpackers. Although goods from all over Rajasthan find their way to the bazaar, rules regarding food are very strict: no alcohol or meat can be sold anywhere in Pushkar.

Pushkar's religious significance derives from the Vedic text, *Padma Purana,* which describes how the town was created. Lord Brahma, Creator of the Universe, was looking for a place to perform the *yajna*—a holy ritual that involves placing offerings into a sacrificial fire for Agni, the fire god—that would signify the beginning of the human age. He dropped a lotus from his hand and Pushkar was the place it struck the ground. The most important temple, in the center of town, is **Brahma Temple,** supposedly the only temple dedicated to Brahma in the world. Pilgrims visiting the temple climb a long stairway into the walled area of the temple to take the blessings of the god—in the form of small sweets. There are varying versions of legend concerning the temple, but most have to do with Brahma's wife Savitri, who refused to attend the ceremony. Impatient, Brahma married the goddess Gayatri (some say she was a milkmaid), and when Savitri found out, she put a curse on Brahma, declaring that the earth would forget him completely. She then relented, and said that Brahma could only be worshipped in Pushkar.

Before you visit the Brahma Temple, make an early start to check out the **Saraswati temple** on a hill overlooking Pushkar Lake. It's a short walk: it only takes between a half-hour and an hour, and the view at sunrise is worth it. You could also go up in the evening.

During auspicious pilgrimage times, tens of thousands of people swarm the **holy bathing ghats** (flights of steps) on Pushkar Lake and get blessings from local Brahmins. Make sure you spend some time at these ghats. Many of the marble ghats were constructed for pilgrims by royal families who wanted to ensure power and prosperity in their kingdoms throughout Rajasthan by appeasing the gods. Even the British Raj built a ghat for Queen Elizabeth. When you pass an entrance to a ghat, be prepared for a priest to solicit you—he'll want you to receive a blessing, "The Pushkar Passport." He'll lead you to the water's edge, say a prayer, and will ask you to recite a blessing in Sanskrit (you'll repeat after him). Then he'll paste a *tilak* (rice and colored powder) on your forehead and tie a *raki* (a string bracelet, denoting a blessing) to your wrist. After the ceremony, you're expected to give a donation of about Rs. 100.

If you really want an experience, go to Pushkar during its famous annual **Camel Fair.** Every October or November—depending on the lunar calendar—people flock here to see the finest camels parade around the fairground in colorful costumes. People come to buy, sell, and trade camels, and to race one camel against another. A good male camel goes for about US$250. The town gets packed during festival time, so make sure you reserve a room at least several weeks—if not longer—ahead of time. Several tented camps with modern conveniences also mushroom during the fair. Contact a travel agent for details. You could also directly ask the Pushkar Palace (Pushkar), the Balsamand Palace (Jodhpur), or Rajasthan Tourism Development Corporation (RTDC) in Jaipur (☎ 141/220–2586).

Where to Stay

$$–$$$ ⌂ **Pushkar Palace.** This small palace sits above its own ghat—private stairs leading down to the lake—with fabulous, panoramic views of Pushkar. Built by the Maharaja of Jaisalmer in the 15th century, the Pushkar Palace was later presented to the Maharaja of Kishangarh. In 1998 the hotel served as headquarters for the film *Holy Smoke,* starring Kate Winslet. All the rooms are outfitted with antique furniture from Rajputana's heyday. If you ask for a pickup from Ajmer station, insist on a new car in decent condition. The restaurant is the best in Pushkar and is on a terrace overlooking the lake. Horse, camel, and jeep safaris are available. ⌂ *Chhoti Basti, southeast corner of Pushkar lake, off Pushkar Bazaar (the main st.) 305022* ☎ *145/277–2001 or 145/277–2401* 🖷 *145/277–2226* ⊕ *www.hotelpushkarpalace.com* ⇱ *27 rooms, 25 suites* ⌂ *Restaurant, cable TV, horseback riding, bar, laundry service, travel services* ⊟ *AE, MC, V* ¶◎¶ *EP.*

$$ ⌂ **Pushkar Resorts.** The spirit of the maharajas blends well with the comforts of resort living here. Relax poolside under the shade of a palm tree and escape from Pushkar's chaotic main bazaar, a 15-minute jeep ride away. European-style rooms (in cottages) have views of the Savitri tem-

ple that crowns a mountain near the resort. Famous here are the hotel's regal camel cart rides—you journey through nearby sand dunes while watching the sun set. The restaurant, only for guests, serves nonvegetarian food. ⊠ *Village Ganhera, Motisar Rd., outside Pushkar* ☎ *145/ 277–2944 or 145/277–2945* ⊕ *www.pushkarresorts.com* ↝ *40 rooms* ⚮ *Restaurant, cable TV, golf course, pool, massage, camel rides, yoga, croquet, library, bar, travel services* ⊟ *AE, DC, MC, V* ⎮◎⎮ *EP.*

SHEKHAVATI

This region in northeastern Rajasthan is renowned for its painted havelis and old forts. Shekhavati (literally "Garden of Shekha") takes its name from Rao Shekhaji, a Rajput king of this region, who was born in 1433. He was named after a *fakir* (Muslim holy man) named Sheikh Burhanby, who granted a boon to his parents that they would bear a son. In another unwitting contribution to history, the sheikh had come to India with the Mongol invader Tamerlane in 1398, dressed in a blue robe—hence the color of Shekhavati's flag. The region has had a turbulent history ever since, experiencing the conquests and defeats of Rajput princes, alliances with the Moghuls after Akbar, and finally suzerainty under the British Raj. The region is made up of smaller principalities, including Sikar, Lachhmangarh, Churi Ajitgarh, Mukundgarh, Jhunjhunu, Mandawa, Fatehpur, and Churu.

A regional center of trade between the 18th and 20th centuries, Shekhavati is now known as Rajasthan's open-air art gallery, thanks to the frescoes painted on the walls of ornate havelis throughout the region. Influenced by the Persian, Jaipur, and Moghul schools of painting, Shekhavati's frescoes illustrate subjects ranging from mythological stories and local legends to hunting safaris and scenes of everyday life. You'll even find illustrated experiences with the British and cars or planes. The introduction of photography in 1840 gave Shekhavati's painters still more to work with. The painters themselves were called *chiteras* and belonged to the caste of *kumhars* (potters). Initially, they colored their masterpieces with vegetable pigments; after mixing these with lime water and treating the wall with three layers of a very fine clay, the chiteras painstakingly drew their designs on a last layer of filtered lime dust. Time was short, as the design had to be completed before the plaster dried, but the highly refined technique ensured that the images would not fade.

The havelis that contain these masterpieces are themselves spectacular. These havelis have courtyards, exquisitely latticed windows, intricate mirror work, vaulted ceilings, immense balconies, and ornate gateways and facades. They date from the British Raj, during which traditional overland trading routes to Central Asia, Europe, and China were slowly superseded by rail and sea routes. In the 19th century, Marwari traders (Hindus from the *vaisya*, or trading, caste) who had once profited from the overland trading system, then migrated to Calcutta, Bombay, and Madras to seek new fortunes. The wealthy Marwaris maintained connections with their ancestral homes, sending remittance from their new enterprises. Often this money was used to build lavish havelis, adorned with elaborate frescoes. Many of the havelis, as well as some old Rajput forts, are now open to the public. Some have been converted to Heritage Hotels. Stay in a few if you can, and take a day or two to explore the towns around them.

The golden age of fresco painting came to an end by the 1930s with the mass exodus of the Marwaris, who had left to resettle in the commercial centers. Since then, many of these beautiful mansions and their paintings have fallen into disrepair. Only a handful have survived—some have been restored by their owners, and a few have been converted into hotels. In **Sikar,** formerly the wealthiest trading center, look for the Biyani, Murarka, and Somani havelis. **Lachhmangarh** features the grand Char Chowk Haveli, particularly evocative of the prosperous Marwari lifestyle. A planned city like Jaipur, Lachhmangarh is home to a popular ayurvedic center, **SPG Kaya Kalp and Research Center** (Tara Kung, Salasar Rd., ☎ 1573/64230), which teaches yoga, meditation, and various therapies. In the village of **Churi Ajitgarh,** unusually erotic frescoes are painted behind doors and on bedroom ceilings in the Shiv Narain Nemani, Kothi Shiv Datt, and Rai Jagan Lal Tibrewal havelis. The frescoed temples of **Jhunjhunu** make for interesting comparisons: visit Laxmi Nath, Mertani Baori, Ajeet Sagar, and Qamrudin Shah Ki Dargah Fatehpur. **Mukandgarh** has an excellent craft market, known especially for textiles, brass ware, and iron scissors, in addition to the Kanoria, Ganeriwala, and Bheekraj Nangalia havelis. Warrior-statesman Thakur Nawal Singh founded **Nawalgarh** in 1737, and the town boasts some of the best frescoes in Shekhavati in its Aath, Anandilal Poddar, Jodhraj Patodia, and Chokhani havelis, as well as in the Roop Niwas Palace hotel.

You need at least two days to explore Shekhavati even perfunctorily; it certainly cannot be accomplished en route between Jaipur and Delhi in a single day. Jhunjhunu, for instance, is 180 km (112 mi) northwest from Jaipur and 240 km (150 mi) west from Delhi. You would need to halt two nights in Shekhavati, perhaps one at Jhunjhunu and one at Dundlod/Mukandgarh/Mandawa (55 km [34 mi], 45 km [28 mi], and 30 km [19 mi] southwest, respectively, from Jhunjhunu) or Nawalgarh (35 km [22 mi] southwest from Jhunjhunu). Alternatively, spend one night at Jhunjhunu and one at Neemrana if you're en route to Delhi.

Between Shekhavati and Delhi, just off the main Jaipur-Delhi highway (100 km [60 mi] southwest of Delhi, off National Hwy. 8, in Village Neemrana in the Alwar district) is the beautiful **Neemrana** Fort Palace, now a hotel and an outstanding example of imaginative restoration.

Where to Stay & Eat

$$–$$$ ×▢ **Castle Mandawa.** Towering high above the town of Mandawa, this rugged, amber-color fort has been converted to a luxury Heritage Hotel. Sword-bearing guards welcome you at the gate; inside, the walls display 16th-century portraits of the Mandawa family. The spacious, airy rooms are furnished with period furniture. Check out the panoramic view from the canopied balconies and turreted battlements. Dinner is an enchanting candle-lit affair in an open-air courtyard. Camel, horse, and jeep safaris are available. 🖉 *Reserve through Mandawa Haveli, Sansar Chandra Rd., Jaipur 302001* ✉ *Mandawa 333704, Jhunjhunu district, 168 km (109 mi) northwest of Jaipur* ☎ *159/222–3124, 159/222–3432, or 159/222–3480 to 84, 141/237–1194 Jaipur reservations* 🖷 *159/222–3171,141/237–2084 Jaipur reservations* ⊕ *www.mandawahotels.com* ⇦ *60 rooms, 8 suites* ♨ *Restaurant, horseback riding, bar; no room TVs* ☱ *AE, MC, V* ❢❢ *EP.*

$$–$$$$ 🏨 **Neemrana Fort Palace.** This 15th-century fort, now a Heritage Hotel,
Fodor'sChoice is one of the finest retreats in India. The fort is perched on a plateau in
★ the Aravalli Hills. The rooms, which vary in size and price, are masterpieces. The architecture is characterized by wooden jalis (latticework screens), cusped arches, gleaming pillars, squinches, and niches. Forget about phones and TVs, because there are none. Just relax and watch preening peacocks and swooping parrots from the countless terraces, balconies, and courtyards. The restaurant serves fixed Rajasthani and French menus. A word of caution: the hotel has a reputation for peace and quiet, so don't be surprised at requests for silence—with all the steep drops, narrow stairways, and low parapets here, any noise echoes considerably down the corridors. 🖉 *Reserve through A-58 Nizamuddin E, New Delhi 110013* ✉ *Village Neemrana, Alwar district, 301705, 100 km (60 mi) southwest of Delhi, off National Hwy. 8* ☎ *1494/246–007 to 8, 11/2435–6145, 11/2435–8962, or 11/2435–5214* 🖷 *11/2435–1112* ⊕ *www.neemranahotels.com* ⇦ *18 rooms, 27 suites* ♨ *Restaurant, pool, health club, massage, spa, bar, travel services; no a/c in some rooms, no room phones, no room TVs* ☱ *AE, DC, MC, V* ❢❢ *EP.*

$$–$$$ 🏨 **Desert Resort.** An eco-friendly resort and the subject of many foreign travel features for its authentic village construction, this place is an unusual, but worthwhile, stop. The interiors of its clay-covered "village huts" on a large sand dune sparkled with the inlaid glass embedded in the walls, and glow with the warmth of Rajasthani fabrics and handicrafts. Even the main lounge is made of mud, and the dining room gleams from the bits of glass and shells in *its* walls. Sit by the pool or in the garden, and enjoy the striking desert panorama. 🖉 *Reserve through 309 Anukampa Tower, Church Rd., Jaipur 302001* ✉ *Mandawa 333704, Jhunjhunu district, 250 km (150 mi) southwest of Delhi* ☎ *1592/223–151, 1592/223–245, or 1592/223–515, 141/237–1194 reservations* 🖷 *141/237–2084* ⊕ *www.mandawahotels.com* ⇦ *60 rooms, 9 suites* ♨ *Restaurant, 9-hole golf course, tennis court, pool, croquet, billiards, bar; no a/c in some rooms, no room TVs* ☱ *AE, MC, V* ❢❢ *EP.*

$ 🏨 **Dera Dundlod Kila.** In the heart of the Shekhavati region, Dundlod was built in 1750. Now a Heritage Hotel, the fort is still owned by the descendants of the former *thakur* (landowner). Surrounded by a moat, it has a mix of Moghul and Rajput architecture. Inside, the stunning Diwan-i-Khas (Hall of Private Audience) has original wall frescoes, European-style portraits, Louis XIV furniture, and a well-stocked library. The clean, simple bedrooms have painted walls. Horse safaris (and camel and jeep trips) are available. 🖉 *Reserve through Dundlod House, Hawa Sadak, Civil Lines, Jaipur 302019* 🖉 *Dundlod, Jhunjhunu district, 333702* ✉ *250 km (150 mi) southwest of Delhi, 165 km (103 mi) from Jaipur* ☎ *1594/252–519* 🖷🖷 *141/221–1276 or 141/221–1498*

🏨 *141/221–1276* 💬 *22 rooms, 5 suites* ♨ *Restaurant, horseback riding, bar; no a/c in some rooms, no room TVs* ▭ *AE, DC, MC, V* 🍴 *EP.*

$ 🏰 **Hill Fort Kesroli.** This stone fort overlooking farmland and distant hills has been turned into a Heritage Hotel by the same duo responsible for Neemrana. Kesroli doesn't have the same grandeur or scale as Neemrana, but it's elegant nonetheless, and a good base from which to explore the area. The origin of the seven-turret fort goes back to the 14th century. Built by Yaduvanshi Rajputs, the building was later conquered by the Moghuls and then the Jats before reverting to the Rajputs in 1775. The hotel is decorated with a tasteful mix of Indian antiques and traditional crafts. The evening meal is a sumptuous event. ⌖ *Reserve through A-58 Nizamuddin E, New Delhi 110013* ✉ *Alwar district, Kesroli Village 301030* ☎ *1468/289–352, 11/2435–6145, 11/2435–8962, or 11/2435–5214* 🖶 *11/2435–1112* ⊕ *www.neemranahotels.com* 💬 *8 rooms, 12 suites* ♨ *Restaurant; no a/c in some rooms, no room TVs* ▭ *AE, DC, MC, V* 🍴 *EP.*

$ 🏰 **Mukandgarh Fort.** Founded in the mid-18th century by Raja Mukand Singh, this picturesque fort in the town of Mukandgarh, famous for its artisans, is now a Heritage Hotel. A bar overlooks the courtyard, where at an outdoor barbecue you can get kababs and curry in the evening. Guest rooms have painted walls and ceilings, tie-dye curtains, and patchwork bedspreads. Some of the rooms in the new wing don't have windows, so check your room before you book it. The fort is a five-minute walk from the Babali Baba Mandir, the main temple in town. ✉ *Jhunjhunu district, 250 km (150 mi) southwest of Delhi, Mukandgarh 333705* ☎ *1594/252–398 or 1594/252–397* 💬 *46 rooms, 1 suite* ♨ *Restaurant, pool, bar, travel services; no room TVs* ▭ *No credit cards* 🍴 *EP.*

$ 🏰 **Piramal Haveli.** Among the grandest of the traditional homes, this one in the village of Bagar has three courtyards enclosed by colonial pillared corridors. Originally built as the home of Seth Piramal Chaturbhuj Makharia (1892–1958), who made his fortune trading cotton, opium, and silver in Bombay, the frescoes here allude to Makharia's wealth—they depict flying angels and gods in motorcars. The hotel is run by the Neemrana Group. ⌖ *Reserve through A-58 Nizamuddin E, New Delhi 110013* ✉ *Bagar, Jhunjhunu district 333023, 250 km (150 mi) southwest of Delhi* ☎ *1592/221–220, 11/2435–6145, or 11/2435–8962, 11/2435–5214 reservations* 🖶 *11/2435–1112* 💬 *8 rooms* ♨ *Restaurant; no a/c in some rooms, no room TVs* ▭ *AE, DC, MC, V* 🍴 *EP.*

$ 🏰 **Roop Niwas Palace.** This Heritage Hotel on the outskirts of Shekhavati combines Rajput and European architecture in its beautiful gardens and private cottages. It's far from grand, but the owners, descendants of the former *thakur* (landowner), aim to please. The rooms, with Victorian furniture, are modest but clean. The dining room is quaint and the grounds are lovely. The restaurant contains an eclectic assortment of antiques of both Rajput and British origin, and some firearms, including six-shooters and a blunderbuss. It serves vegetarian and non-vegetarian cuisine and has a bar license. Jeep and camel safaris and bird-watching trips can be arranged. ✉ *Jhunjhunu district, Shekhavati, Nawalgarh 333042, 250 km (150 mi) southwest of Delhi* ☎ *1594/222–008* 🖶 *1594/223–388* 💬 *37 rooms, 1 suite* ♨ *Restaurant, pool, horseback riding, bar; no room TVs* ▭ *AE.*

JODHPUR & ENVIRONS

Jodhpur is rich in fort and palace treasures and a great place from which to take side trips—to Guda Vishnoi, home of the gentle Vishnoi community and a haven for wildlife, or the temple town of Osian in the Thar Desert. Nagaur Fort also entices—you can camp here splendidly, in fine tents, during the town's winter cattle fair.

Jodhpur

17 *343 km (215 mi) west of Jaipur, 266 km (165 mi) northwest of Udaipur.*

Known as the Blue City because of the color the Brahmins paint their houses, and guarded by one of the most imposing fortresses of Rajputana, Jodhpur looks like a sea on the fringe of the Thar Desert. Jodhpur is encircled by a wall 9 km (6 mi) around, which keeps out the desert sands. The city, at the base of a sandstone ridge, was the capital of the Marwar kingdom for five centuries. It was named after its 15th-century founder, Rao Jodha, chief of the Rathore clan of Marwar—which traces its lineage to Lord Rama, hero of the ancient Hindu epic, *The Ramayana.*

Getting around Jodhpur is relatively easy. Walk through the massive and impeccably maintained Meharangarh fort and the Ummaid Bhawan palace, and the markets full of fruit, textile, and handicraft stalls. Take special note of Jodhpuri and *pathar* peach-color stone that makes Jodhpur's houses and buildings stand apart from others in Rajasthan. If you have extra time, take a desert safari on camelback.

Jodhpur is also famous for its food and hospitality, especially its *mithai* (sweets) and the *manuhar* ritual that accompanies its food. When you're offered a *mave ki kachori* (milk-base pastry) or *besan ki barfi* (a fudge-like sweet made of gram, or chick pea, flour), along with mirchi bada (fried, breaded green peppers) and *kofta* (deep-fried balls of potatoes or vegetables), don't resist: the offer will be repeated until you take some.

a good tour

Start your day early, and spend a few hours at the majestic **Meharangarth Fort.** Take one of the waiting rickshaws down the mountain and north to the **Jaswant Thada** memorial. After a break for lunch, hire a car and driver for the short drive 9 km (6 mi) north of Jodhpur to the **Mandore Gardens.** From there, it's just a short drive to **Balsamand Lake and Garden.** If you have a little extra time, visit **Mahamandir.** End your day at the **Umaid Bhawan Palace Museum**—walk through the museum before it closes at 5, then linger for a drink and dinner and enjoy the fabulous sunset views.

TIMING With this plan you can tour Jodhpur in a day, covering the essentials first. If you have three days here, drive 25 km (16 mi) south of Jodhpur once again to see the wildlife-loving town of **Guda Vishnoi,** where deer and birds feed at water holes early in the morning. If you're very lucky, you might spot the elusive barasingha or blackbuck. Return to Jodhpur for lunch and a bit of shopping. The next day, make a pilgrimage 58 km (36 mi) north to the temple town of **Osian.**

What to See

Balsamand Lake and Garden. At this public park (really a wildlife sanctuary) you can enjoy the view of the park's 12th-century artificial lake and the royal family's beautiful 19th-century summer palace, now a hotel. The lake is surrounded by a thick jungle of fruit trees called *badis*. It's the perfect place for a tranquil stroll—just beware the mischievous monkeys, who are always on the watch for good pranks (and good vegetable *pakoras*, or fritters). Don't try to pluck the fruit from the trees, as the monkeys will fight you for it. ✉ *5 km (3 mi) northeast of Jodhpur.*

Jaswant Thada. The royal marble crematorium was built in 1899 for Maharaja Jaswant Singh II. Capping the enormous white structure are marble canopies under which individual members of the royal family are buried. You may see people bowing before the image of the king, who is considered to have joined the ranks of the deities. ✉ *½ kmnortheast of Mehrangarh Fort* 🎫 *Rs. 19* ⊘ *Daily 8–6.*

Mahamandir. Built in 1812 just outside Jodhpur, this old, walled monastery complex ("Mahamandir" means great temple) still contains a few hundred houses. The monastery belongs to the Nath community, warrior-priests who worked closely with the royal family to arrange support in times of war. Mahamandir is best known for the 84 beautifully carved pillars that surround it. ✉ *4 km (2.5 mi) northeast of Jodhpur.*

Mandore Gardens. Within the old Marwar capital at Mandore, these gardens house the exquisitely sculpted red-sandstone *davals* (memorials) to former rulers. The Hall of Heroes depicts 16 colorfully painted heroes and deities carved from a single piece of stone. The small **museum** on the grounds has sculptures from the 5th to the 9th centuries and ivory and lacquer work. There's even a **cactus nursery.** Unfortunately, due to the large number of picnics and *dal baati churma* (lentils with wheat-flour dumplings) feasts held here, the gardens have grown dirty and are not terribly well-maintained. ✉ *Mandore, 8 km (5 mi) north of Jodhpur* 🎫 *Free* ⊘ *Gardens daily sunrise–sunset, museum Sat.–Thurs. 10–4.*

Fodor'sChoice **Mehrangarh Fort.** Perched on the top of a hill, this enormous fort was built
★ by Rao Jodha in 1459, when he shifted his capital from Mandore to Jodhpur. Looking straight down a perpendicular cliff, the famously impregnable fort is an imposing landmark, especially at night, when it's bathed in yellow light. Approach the fort by climbing a steep walkway (the 40-minute hike is much more enjoyable than the rickshaw alternative), passing under no fewer than eight huge gates. The first, the Victory Gate, was built by Maharaja Ajit Singh to commemorate his military success against the Moghuls at the beginning of the 18th century; the other seven commemorate victories over other Rajput states. The last gate, as in many Rajput forts, displays the haunting handprints of women who immolated themselves after their husbands were defeated in battle.

Inside the rugged fort, delicate latticed windows and pierced sandstone screens are the surprising motifs. The palaces—**Moti Mahal** (Pearl Palace), **Phool Mahal** (Flower Palace), **Sheesh Mahal** (Glass Palace), and the other apartments—are exquisitely decorated; their ceilings, walls, and even floors are covered with murals, mirror work, and gilt. The palace museum has exquisite rooms filled with lavish royal elephant carriages (howdahs), palanquins, thrones, paintings, and even a giant tent. It also has an interesting weapons gallery. From the ramparts you can get an excellent city view; the blue houses at sunset look magical. The fort is possibly the best maintained historic property in all Rajasthan, and offers headphones (included in the admission price, for foreigners) with recorded commentary in English. ⊠ *Fort Rd.* ☎ *291/254–9790 or 291/254–8790* ✉ *Foreigners Rs. 250, including camera and audio tour; video cameras Rs. 200* ☉ *Daily 9–5.*

need a break? In the highly competitive world of lassi wallahs, only the strong survive. Standing in the shadow of Jodhpur's famous clocktower in Sadar Market, **Shri Misrilal Hotel**, a lassi shop misleadingly called a hotel, is an age-old favorite among locals and foreigners. Look past the simple interior and neon lighting, and settle down on one of the long wooden benches. Then sit back and take in the rose water flavors; lassis here are consumed with a spoon.

Umaid Bhawan Palace Museum. Built between 1929 and 1942 at the behest of Maharaja Umaid Singh during a long famine—the public-works project employed 3,000 workers—this palace is part museum, part royal residence, and part Heritage Hotel. Its art deco design makes it unique in the state. Amazingly, no cement was used in construction; the palace is made of interlocking blocks of sandstone, a fact to bear in mind when you stand under the imposing 183-foot-high central dome. The collection includes royal finery, local arts and crafts, miniature paintings, stuffed big cats, and a large number of clocks. You may catch a glimpse of the Maharaja of Jodhpur, who still lives in one large wing of the palace, but in any case you won't miss the magnificent peacocks that strut around the palace's marble *chattris* (canopies) and lush lawns. Photography is allowed on the lawns but not in the museum. ⊠ *Airport Rd., Umaid Bhawan Palace* ☎ *291/251–0101* ✉ *Rs. 50* ☉ *Daily 9–5.*

Where to Stay & Eat

Watch the hearty consumption of local grub at the local eating area **Rawat Mishtan Bhandar**, next to the train station. Your system might find the street food problematic, but the sight of crowds tucking into hot and spicy *kachoris* (fried stuffed pastries), *koftas* (deep-fried balls of potatoes or vegetables), and *mave ki kachori* (milk-base pastry) can be enough of an appeal to indulge.

All the hotels listed below can arrange camel and jeep safaris and usually other excursions, on request.

$$$–$$$$ ✕ **Marwar.** Clearly one of the better attempts at upscale cuisine in Jodhpur, this restaurant serves both Continental and Indian food, and a few Rajasthani specialties. Try Jodhpuri *gatta* curry (steamed chick-pea flour dumplings in yogurt-base gravy); the Jodhpuri *maas* (lamb) curry is also typical of this region. You can choose from a buffet or order à la carte. The restaurant is built in a neo-Moghul architectural style. Every night, live classical Indian music plays in the background. ⊠ *Taj Hari*

Mahal, 5 Residency Rd. ☎ *291/243–9700* ⊛ *Reservations essential* ▭ *AE, DC, MC, V.*

$$$-$$$$ ✕ **Marwar Hall.** Huge chandeliers hang from the high vaulted ceilings of this gorgeous palace dining room, which was once the primary banquet hall of the Maharaja of Jodhpur. The chef prepares impeccable Continental and Indian food, including tasty Mughlai and regional Marwari dishes. Meals are served buffet-style. The restaurant is only open to group (up to 25 people) bookings; reserve in advance. ⊠ *Umaid Bhawan Palace* ☎ *291/251–0101* ▭ *AE, DC, MC, V.*

$ ✕ **Midtown Vegetarian Restaurant.** This unpretentious but spotlessly clean joint has Rajasthani wall hangings and specializes in Rajasthani and South Indian cuisine. Midtown specials include a *dosa* (Indian-style crêpe) filled with potato and cashews and *kabuli* (rice layered with vegetables, bread, and dried fruits and nuts). A salad bar rounds out the vegetarian menu. ⊠ *Hotel Shanti Bhawan, Station Rd.* ☎ *291/262–1689* ▭ *No credit cards.*

$ ✕ **On the Rocks.** This outdoor jungle-theme restaurant is aptly named, not because it has a well-stocked bar, but because the ground inside the restaurant (which is entirely outside) is primarily gravel. The recorded sounds of birds chirping might take it all a little too far over the top, but it's all done to match the style of Ajit Bhawan, the hotel next door to which the restaurant is housed. The standard Indian fare is famous all around Jodhpur with the local upwardly mobile. After the meal try one of the milk shakes or relax with a drink by the fountain. ⊠ *Ajit Bhawan Hotel* ☎ *291/251–0410* ▭ *MC, V.*

¢ ✕ **Sukh Sagar.** This place specializes in South Indian food, but also serves North Indian and Chinese dishes. Try the *rava idli* (steamed semolina and rice cakes) and *vada sambar* (deep-fried lentil doughnuts served with spicy lentil stew), and take care to specify how hot you like your food. Down some South Indian filter coffee for an extra kick. ⊠ *Ratanada Bazaar* ☎ *291/251–1450 or 291/262–1450* ▭ *No credit cards.*

¢ ✕ **Tulsi Ram ki Dhani.** Come for lunch in the home of Tulsi Ram, under the sanctity of a thatch roof. It's the only restaurant in the area. For the duration of the lunch, expect to feel as if you're part of his family. This absolutely authentic meal is a must for anyone interested in Rajasthani cuisine and culture. As with all places in the area, this restaurant is very difficult to find unless you have a guide. ⊠ *South of Jodhpur, near town of Salwas* ☎ *No phone.*

$$$$ ▦ **Shree Ram International.** This hotel has taken over a large part of the Ratanada Polo Palace and has renovated it completely. The restaurant serves only multicuisine vegetarian food and has a slightly institutional feel. The low-rise modern building hotel, which is popular with Indian tourists, is set back from the dusty road and surrounded by lush, quiet gardens. Rooms are spotless and comfortable, with marble flooring and bronze drapes, and ethnic Rajasthani furnishings. ⊠ *Near Panch Batti Chauraha, Residency Rd., 342001* ☎ *291/243–1913, 291/243–8100, or 291/243–8568* 🖷 *291/243–1914* ⊕ *www.shreeraminternational. com* ⬲ *50 rooms, 4 suites* ⟁ *Restaurant, cable TV, pool, bar, business services, travel services* ⦿ *EP.*

$$$$ ▦ **Taj Hari Mahal.** The Taj's motif of running water is a cooling change from the often harsh climate of Jodhpur. The rooms have original modern artwork from Rajasthan and other parts of the world, and the bath-rooms are spacious and modern. This magnificent hotel is a respite from the hustle-bustle of Jodhpur—it has a grand and elegant amber-color lobby, and is, without a doubt, the place to stay if you're looking for leisure and friendly service. The Chinese restaurant opens only for dinner, but a good multicuisine restaurant is open all day. For special occasions, ask for a demonstration of the elaborate chess dance, during which women in Rajasthani dress swirl across a life-size chess board. ⊠ *5 Residency Rd., Jodhpur 342001,* ☎ *291/243–9700* 🖷 *291/261–4451* ⊕ *www.tajhotels.com* ⟳ *2 restaurants, cable TV, pool, gym, spa, bar, shops, meeting rooms, travel services* ▤ *AE, DC, MC, V* ⋅⃝⃝ *EP.*

★ **$$$$** ▥ **Umaid Bhawan Palace.** Built in the 1930s of pink sandstone—in the art deco style particular to colonial India—this magnificent fort palace is one of the grandest of Rajasthan's many such hotels. Still home to the Maharaja of Jodhpur, it has served as a backdrop for many Indian and foreign films. The public rooms are lavish, and filled with objects d'art; many of the rooms, though not opulent, are designed in period style. The newer rooms tend to be small and ordinary. There's a beautiful, blue indoor pool. The hotel is now run by Aman Resorts, and is very exclusive. ⊠ *Airport Rd., Jodhpur 342006* ☎ *291/251–0101* 🖷 *291/251–0100* ↘ *24 rooms, 18 suites* ⟳ *3 restaurants, cable TV, golf privileges, 2 tennis courts, indoor pool, health club, sauna, billiards, horseback riding, squash, bar, travel services* ▤ *AE, DC, MC, V* ⋅⃝⃝ *EP.*

$$$–$$$$ ▥ **Fortune Ummed.** This luxurious modern hotel is outside the city on the Jodhpur–Jaipur Highway. However, once you're here it's a pleasant retreat, among peaceful, landscaped gardens. Rooms are uncarpeted, with gleaming marble floors and cream-color drapes, and have traditional Rajsthani paintings on the walls. You can choose between garden, courtyard, or pool views. ⊠ *Jodhpur–Jaipur Hwy., Jodhpur 342027* ☎ *291/226–3430 to 39* 🖷 *291/226–3244* ⊕ *www.welcomgroup.com* ↘ *80 rooms, 8 suites* ⟳ *Restaurant, minibars, cable TV, tennis court, pool, health club, ayurvedic massage, sauna, volleyball, cricket pitch, bar, library, children's programs (all ages), Internet, travel services* ▤ *AE, DC, MC, V* ⋅⃝⃝ *EP.*

$$–$$$ ▥ **Ajit Bhawan.** This small but enchanting palace and village complex
Fodor'sChoice has a garage full of royal vintage cars (which you can hire). The color-
★ ful rooms have painted tables and doors, and traditional Rajasthani fabrics; some even have trees growing inside. The garden areas are ample; between the garden and the restaurant On the Rocks, next door, the complex effectively creates its own retreat. ⊠ *Near Circuit House, 342006* ☎ *291/251–0410 or 291/251–1410* 🖷 *291/251–0674* ⊕ *www. ajitbhawan.com* ↘ *54 rooms* ⟳ *Restaurant, cable TV, pool, health club, horseback riding, bar* ▤ *AE, MC, V* ⋅⃝⃝ *EP.*

$$–$$$ ▥ **Balsamand Lake Palace.** A fine example of Rajput architecture, this red sandstone Heritage Hotel is surrounded by lush, expansive green gardens on the outskirts of Jodhpur. On the banks of Balsamand Lake, an artificial lake built in the 12th century, the palace has long been a dreamy setting for royal R&R. The park around the lake contains a small bird sanctuary; just watch out for aggressive monkeys. Meals are prepared for guests only. ⊠ *Mandore Rd., 9 km (5.6 mi) northeast of Jodhpur, 342006* ☎ *291/2571991* 🖷 *291/2571240* ↘ *36 rooms* ⟳ *Restaurant, cable TV, tennis court, pool, horseback riding, bar* ▤ *MC, V* ⋅⃝⃝ *EP.*

$$–$$$ 🏨 **Rohet Garh.** This 17th-century desert fortress 40 km (25 mi) south of Jodhpur is both a Heritage Hotel and the home of its Rajput family, whose members are your hosts. It's a great place to experience the lifestyle of Rajput nobility. The public rooms are decked out in original paintings and weapons. Guest rooms have traditional carved furniture and colorful hand-blocked prints, and some even have swings. Horseback safaris are a specialty, as there are plenty of bird species and other animals nearby. Trips can be organized to Bishnoi (tribal villages). ✎ *Reserve through Rohet House, P. W. D. Rd., 342001* ✉ *Pali district, Rohet Garh Village* ☎ *2936/268–231, 291/243–1161 reservations* 📠 *291/264–9368* ⊕ *www.rohetgarh.com* 🛏 *28 rooms, 2 suites* ⚒ *Restaurant, pool, health club, massage, horseback riding, laundry service, travel services; no room phones, no room TVs* ▭ *MC, V* �𝍐 *EP.*

$$–$$$ 🏨 **Sardarsamand Lake Resort.** The hunting lodge of Jodhpur's former Maharaja Umaid Singh is now a resort. Built in 1933, the verandas of this pink sandstone-and-granite building have fabulous views of an artificial lake that attracts birds migrating between October and March. Just beyond the lake are the expansive sands of the Thar Desert. Rooms are decorated in their original fittings, though they also have some art deco furnishings. Reserve through Ummaid Bhawan Palace (the phone line is more likely to be working there). ✉ *66 km (41 mi) southeast of Jodhpur, 20 km (12 mi) from Pali District, Sardarsamand 306103* ☎ *291/251–0101 Ummaid Bhawan Palace, 2960/245–001 to 3 Sardarsamand* 📠 *291/257–1240* 🛏 *18 rooms* ⚒ *Restaurant, cable TV, tennis court, pool, squash, horseback riding, bar; no a/c in some rooms, no TV in some rooms* ▭ *MC, V* ⟨⟩ *EP.*

$$ 🏨 **Fort Chanwa.** This century-old, somber red fort in the dusty village of Luni is now a Heritage Hotel with spacious courtyards and delightful rooms that have small, arched windows called *jharokhas,* Rajasthani-style furniture and fabrics, and old photographs. Many of the small rooms have stairways leading to an alcove or to the bathroom. The water wheel—now a fountain in the bar—was originally used to channel water around the fort. The restaurant has a fixed-price Indian menu. ✎ *Reserve through Dilip Bhawan House 1, P. W. D. Rd., 342001* ✉ *Luni, 58 km (36 mi) south of Jodhpur* ☎ *2931/284–216, 291/243–2460 reservations* 🛏 *28 rooms, 3 suites* ⚒ *Restaurant, pool, health club, hot tub, horseback riding; no room TVs* ▭ *MC, V* ⟨⟩ *EP.*

$ 🏨 **Jhalamand Garh.** Run and managed by the extremely hospitable Jhalamand family, this small Heritage Hotel is an ideal setting for a peaceful holiday. In addition to making sure you're comfortable, the Jhalamands will help you plan your stay. By the end of your time here, you'll feel like a member of the family. Rooms have ethnic furnishings and the terrace has stunning views of Jodhpur. ✉ *Village and Post Jhalamand, 342005, 10 km (6 mi) outside town* ☎ *291/272–0481* 🛏 *12 rooms, 6 suites* ⚒ *Restaurant, horseback riding, jeep safari, laundry service, bar; no a/c in some rooms, no room TVs* ▭ *AE, DC, MC, V* ⟨⟩ *EP.*

$ 🏨 **Karni Bhavan.** This colonial-style bungalow, built of red sandstone in 1947, is now a Heritage Hotel. The hotel is famous for its personalized service. It also has great views of Mehrangarh Fort and Umaid Bhawan Palace. The rooftop restaurant serves Indian and Continental cuisine (the Rajasthani food is exquisite). ⊠ *Palace Rd., 342006* ☎ *291/ 251–2101 to 02* 🖷 *291/251–2105* ⊕ *www.karnihotels.com* 🖘 *25 rooms, 5 suites* ঙ *Restaurant, pool; no a/c in some rooms, no room TVs* ⊟ *AE, MC, V* ⏚⏄ *EP.*

¢ 🏨 **Devi Bhawan.** One of the most moderately priced hotels in Jodhpur, and an excellent value for your money, is run by a friendly young couple, Prithviraj and Rambha Singh. The hotel is in a pleasant garden, and the homey rooms here are spotless and tastefully furnished. A small restaurant serves *thalis* to guests only. ⊠ *1 Ratanada Circle, Defence Lab. Rd., 342001* ☎ *291/251–1067* 🖷 *291/251–2215* ⊕ *www.devibhawan.com* 🖘 *10 rooms* ঙ *Restaurant, cable TV, pool, Internet; no a/c in some rooms* ⊟ *MC, V* ⏚⏄ *EP.*

¢ 🏨 **Haveli Guesthouse.** The old city has only one or two places to stay—despite the fact that it's clearly best to lodge in Jodhpur, with easy access to its important sites. The rooftop restaurant, which serves vegetarian food, has excellent views of the city, and you'll be close enough to hear evening *arthi* (a Hindu prayer service) at the temples near the clocktower. The rooms are basic and unpretentious, and lack phones and bathtubs—but what the hotel lacks in facilities it more than makes up for in convenience by being so close to the sights. ⊠ *Makrana Mohalla, behind clocktower and opposite Tuvarji-ka-Jhalra (a stepped well)* ☎ *291/ 261–4615* 🖉 *havelighj@sify.com* 🖘 *25 rooms* ঙ *Restaurant; no a/c in some rooms, no TV in some rooms* ⊟ No credit cards ⏚⏄ *EP.*

Nightlife & the Arts

Your best bet for Jodhpur nightlife is one of the hotel bars, which are usually open from 11 AM to 2:30 PM and 6 PM to 11 PM. The **Trophy Bar** (⊠ Umaid Bhawan Palace ☎ 291/251–0101), with richly paneled walls and carpeted floors, is regal, but still feels intimate.

Mehrangarh Fort stages festivals and exhibits throughout the year; inquire at the **Tourist Information Center** (☎ 291/254–5083) or your hotel to see if anything is going on.

Sports & the Outdoors

Many hotels offer excursions to outlying villages. If yours doesn't, try one of the horse or camel trips offered by **Rohet Safaris** (☎ 291/2431161).

Shopping

Jodhpur's vibrant bazaars are among the city's key sights, particularly **Sardar Bazaar** and the **Girdikot Bazaar,** near the clocktower. Wandering among the tiny shops dotting narrow lanes in the heart of town, you'll get a real feel for the life and color of Marwar. Everything from jewelry to underclothes, steel utensils to leather shoes, and trinkets to wedding clothes is sold here. Local spice merchants deal in saffron and other spices from all over India. Beware of tourist markups and young men guiding to their "uncle's store." There are plenty of stores to shop in, too, if you don't like haggling in bazaars (such as emporiums). **M. V. Spices** (⊠ Shop 209B, near Clocktower, Sadar Market) has a wide selection of spices clearly marked and packed in plastic for travelers with a passion for cooking Indian food. There's also an outlet (really a tent pitched on the sidewalk) at the entrance to Mehrangarh Fort.

Lalji Handicrafts Emporium (⊠ opposite Umaid Bhawan Palace ☎ 291/
251–1378) has woodwork, antiques, leatherwork, and brass furniture.
The collection includes unique painted boxes and *jharokhas* (carved doorways or windows) made of dark wood with brass decoration. This
place is a joy if you love antiques. **Bhandari Handicrafts** (⊠ Old Police
Line, Raika Bagh ☎ 291/251–0621) sells wood items and antiques. For
textiles, including cotton dress fabric, and other handicrafts, check out
the four-story emporium **National Handloom Corporation** (⊠ Nayi Sadak
☎ 291/506–1103 or 291/503–1198). For a vast selection of cushion covers, bedspreads, handicrafts, and authentic handstitched jodhpurs (these
riding trousers are priced at Rs. 1,800 and can be tailored to order), visit
Shree Govindam and don't forget to look at the range of wholesale textiles in the basement (⊠ opposite Circuit House, A163 Ajit Colony Rd.
☎ 291/251–0519 or 291/251–6333).

Roopraj Dhurry Udyog. Local artisan Roopraj learned the art of weaving dhurries (carpets) from his father, who learned it from *his* father—
the tradition goes back to the early 19th century. His cotton carpets were
originally reserved for the village thakur, or landowner, but once Indira
Gandhi enacted the Integrated Rural Development Project (IRDP), his
carpets were finally able to reach a wider market. The Roopraj Dhurry
Udyog co-op cottage industry employs weavers from the village and keeps
the tradition alive. It's as rewarding to watch the weaving process as it
is to come with a purchase in mind, or just to shop for souvenirs. You'll
definitely need a guide to help you get here. ⊠ *Salawas, 4 km (2½ mi)
from the village, on the way to the town of Kakani; Salawas is near the
railway crossing* ☎ 291/289–6658.

off the
beaten
path

GUDA VISHNOI – This is one of several immaculately kept villages of
the Vishnoi community, a Hindu caste that takes its name from the 29
edicts its members agree to follow. In 1520, during a 20-year drought,
the saint Jamboji came to the Vishnoi to ease their troubles by finding
new water sources for them, and creating natural springs. Jamboji
made a pact with the Vishnoi that if they accepted his commandments,
they would never experience a water shortage again. The next year,
the drought ended. The Vishnoi, who have faithfully kept to the
teachings of Jamboji for almost 500 years, are one of Jodhpur's most
distinct scheduled castes. Part of their pact was to respect the land and
treat animals like their family—they are staunch believers in plant and
animal life. The Vishnoi are very protective of their environment, and
look harshly on anyone who appears to hurt their sacred deer and
antelope populations, which they look on as members of their family.
Notable are the rare migratory birds, such as the godavan and sara
cranes, that pass through here. The Vishnoi are extremely outgoing
and hospitable—they will invite you into their home for a cup of chai
or *amala*, a mixture of opium and water traditionally reserved for
special occasions and lazy days. Remember to bring your camera—
you might just see a barasingha, or blackbuck, at dusk. One word of
advice: this area is difficult to navigate, as there are no real landmarks.
Ask at your hotel for transport arrangements and make sure you come
with a tour guide. ⊠ *25 km (16 mi) south of Jodhpur.*

Osian

18 *58 km (36 mi) north of Jodhpur.*

The ancestral home of the Oswal Jains, Osian was one of the strongholds of Jainism in India. Many invasions and several hundred years later, Osian is now a popular Hindu pilgrimage site—though it has no significant Jain community remaining. It's worthwhile coming here just to see the temples, or to take a camel safari. Perched on a hill in the center of town is the **Sachiya Mata Mandir** temple, where the (Jain) Naga Snake god reliefs and etchings of Jain saints are readily apparent. Built around 1177 AD, some of the older statues were damaged during the reign of Aurangzeb (1658–1707). An older, and arguably more important, 7th century temple—said to be the first Jain temple in the world—is hidden in the twisting alleys of the city. This temple, the **Mahavira Jain Temple,** is venerated from all over India. The feet of one particular statue of Bharu on the outside of the temple are often covered with bright paper, oil, coconuts, and even human hair. Hindus (not just Jains) believe that if they make offerings here before they get married, their union will be blessed, and they'll be able to produce a child. To invoke the powers of the god Bharu, devotees must make two pilgrimages to the temple. During the first pilgrimage they leave traditional offerings of coconuts and oil to ask the god for fertility, they must also promise to return after the child's birth to offer the newborn's hair to the god.

Just outside town is the home of **Chuna Ram**—he carves new statues to help temple renovations, does all sorts of restoration work using old techniques, and encourages people to watch him work. He's lives in Osian, but right on the outskirts; call to make sure he's home. ✉ *Near Kushi Mundi, toward Jodhpur* ☎ *2922/274–577.*

Where to Stay

$$$$ 🏕 **Reggie's Camel Camp.** Perched on top of a sand dune is Camel Camp, run by Reggie Singh as a base for operations for camel safaris in the Thar Desert. This is a great alternative to the more touristy camps that operate around Jaisalmer. All costs are included in the price of camp. Every route takes you through several different types of terrain and into the homes of local craftsmen. Make sure you watch the sunset from the dunes—it's truly breathtaking. Accommodation throughout the trip is in deluxe tents, and you are well taken care of. The outfit even has its own musicians. Camel races and camel polo begin in the winter of 2004. 🖂 *The Safari Club, High Court Colony, Jodhpur 342001* ✉ *Near Railway Station* ☎ *2922/274–333 in Jodhpur, 291/243–7023, 291/ 261–0192 reservations* ⊕ *www.camelcamposian.com* 🛏 *80 tents* 🍽 *FAP.*

Khimsar

19 *90 km (56 mi) northeast of Jodhpur.*

The 16th-century fort at Khimsar, a three-hour drive from Jodhpur, was once the province of one of Rao Jodha's sons. His descendants still live in the palace. Surrounded by a small village, green fields, and sand dunes, it's now a Heritage Hotel, and a delightful place to relax. The building is gorgeously floodlit at night.

Where to Stay

$$$ 🏨 **Welcomgroup Khimsar Fort.** You'll find the best rooms in this graceful palace-and-fort in the original structure; some have furniture from the 1920s. Dinner is served by candlelight in the crumbling ruins of one of the original fort towers. Relax and enjoy the fine service, as well as the peace and quiet—none of the rooms has a phone or TV. If you feel like exploring, you can take a horse, camel, or jeep safari or tea on the nearby sand dunes. ✉ *Reserve through Welcomgroup Khimsar Fort, 27 Shivaji Nagar, Civil Lines, Jaipur 302006* ⌖ *Khimsar, Nagaur district, 341025* 🕾 *1585/262–345 to 49 Jaipur, 141/222–9700 to 04 reservations* 🖷 *1585/262–228 Jaipur, 141/222–9705 reservations* 🛏 *15 rooms, 35 suites* ♨ *Restaurant, tennis court, pool, health club, horseback riding, bar; no room TVs* ▤ *AE, MC, V* ⏻ *EP.*

Nagaur

⑳ *150 km (94 mi) northeast of Jodhpur.*

Try to visit Nagaur during its colorful cattle fair, in late January or early February, as only then can you can camp out royally at the historic Nagaur Fort. Make sure you check out the remnants of beautiful frescoes on the fort's crumbling walls. Also note that the complex has an amazing engineering system, which supplied enough water for the fountains and royal baths. The system also functions as a kind of air-conditioning in this otherwise arid land. Nagaur and its surrounding area are famous for making clay toys.

Where to Stay

🏨 **Nagaur Fort.** Built between the 4th and 16th centuries, this enormous fort serves as backdrop to a royal camp of spacious tents, decorated inside with hand-blocked designs. Conveniently, the tents also have electric lanterns, and attached bathrooms with flush toilets (hot water is hand-carried in; it arrives via bucket). To signal for service, you hang a little red flag outside the door of your tent. Meals are served in a marble pavilion, in what was once a Moghul garden; in the evening, you can sip cocktails and sit back on cushions, in front of a bonfire, to watch a performance of traditional folk dances. Note: the camp is open only during the cattle fair or by special arrangement. Reserve at least 60 days in advance. ✉ *Ahhichatragarh Fort, Gandhi Chowk, Nagaur 341001* 🕾 *1582/242–082* 🛏 *35 tents* ♨ *Restaurant; no a/c or room TVs* ▤ *AE, MC, V* ☯ *Closed Mar.–Dec.* ⏻ *FAP.*

UDAIPUR & ENVIRONS

Expect to see marble palaces, elaborate gardens, serene temples, lush forests, and sparkling lakes as you explore Mewar, Rajasthan's southern region, in the marvelously green Aravalli Hills. Mewar also has several famous temples and religious sites attended yearly by thousands of pilgrims.

The region is perhaps most famous for having a rich military history—the chivalry and courage of its Rajput warriors are legendary. The Sisodia rulers of Mewar, who claim descent from the divine Lord Rama, are considered the most senior and respected members of all Rajput clans. The Mewar rulers were among the most determined foes of the Moghuls: long after other Rajput rulers conceded defeat, they alone resisted. The name Maharana Pratap still inspires pride in Mewar—Pratap resisted Emperor Akbar's reign through several guerilla wars. His struggle against Akbar is celebrated in murals and ballads all over Rajasthan, and it has been said that "As a great warrior of liberty, his name is, to millions of men even today, a cloud of hope by day and a pillar of fire by night." Udaipur's airport is named after him.

Also famous for the vibrant festivals that take place in its cities and villages, Mewar's motto—"*Saat vaar, aur nau tyauhaar,*" which means "Seven days, nine festivals"—is apt. The biggest festival of the year is Gangaur, held in April in honor of the goddess Parvati, and observed primarily by girls of marriageable age. In the villages, the ancient tradition of *raati jagga*—all-night singing of mainly devotional songs by saint-poets, such as Kabir and Mirabai—takes place after weddings, childbirth, and sometimes even mourning, as a form of thanksgiving to a particular deity.

Mewar has two major indigenous tribal groups, the Bhils (also called *van putras,* or sons of the forest) and the Garasiyas. The lively songs, music, art exhibits, and dances of the tribes' festivals are a compelling reason to visit the region. Particularly memorable is the Ghoomer dance, in which hundreds of women dance in a giant circle. If you're here during a festival, try to see the *terahtal* dance, in which women dance—from a seated position—with *manjiras* (little brass discs) tied to their wrists, elbows, waists, arms, and hands. For added effect, the women may hold a sword between their teeth or balance pots or even lighted lamps on their heads.

To get a real feel for the spirit of the Mewar region, plan at least two or three days here, if not an entire week. Mewar is best seen at a somewhat leisurely pace: whether you see the area by taking quiet walks, long treks, or bike rides, you'll find lots of cultural variety, and you'll see some stunning sights. Romantic Udaipur, the major city here, warrants at least several days. From Udaipur, you can explore the ornately carved Jain temples of Ranakpur and Mount Abu, or see the medieval citadel of Chittaurgarh. West from Chittaurgarh, it's worth a stop to see the remarkable fort at Kumbalgarh. You can also take a wildlife safari or learn more about pichwai paintings at Nathdwara's Krishna temple.

Udaipur

21 *335 km (207 mi) southeast of Jodhpur.*

The jewel of Mewar is Udaipur, the City of Lakes. Some have dubbed it the Venice of the East. In his *Annals and Antiquities of Rajasthan,* Colonel James Tod described the valley of Udaipur as "the most diversified and most romantic spot on the sub-continent of India." The city of Udaipur was founded in 1567, when, having grown weary of repeated attacks on the old Mewar capital of Chittaur—Chittaur is the historic name of the area, and Chittaurgarh literally means "the fort of Chit-taur"—Maharana Udai Singh asked a holy sage to suggest a safe place for his new capital. The man assured Udai Singh that his new base would never be conquered if he established it on the banks of Lake Pichola, and thus was born Singh's namesake, Udaipur.

Despite being one of Rajasthan's largest cities, with a population of about a half-million people, modern Udaipur retains a small-town vibe; its weather is balmy year-round, and the locals are friendly. Udaipur's city center is the old city, a labyrinth of winding streets, which borders Lake Pichola's eastern side. Five main gates lead into Udaipur's old city: Hathi Pol (Elephant Gate) to the north; Kishan Gate to the south; Delhi Gate to the northeast, Chand Pol (Moon Gate) to the west; and Suraj Pol (Sun Gate) to the east.

Anchoring Udaipur's old city are the famed City Palace and Lake Palace—right in the middle of Lake Pichola, and now a hotel. The old city itself is built on tiny hillocks and raised areas, so its lanes are full of twists and turns, leaving plenty of shady little niches to be discovered. Many lanes converge on the Jagdish Temple area, near the northeastern corner of Lake Pichola. The major landmarks in the new section are Chetak Circle, Sukhadia Circle, and Sahelion Ki Bari gardens.

The Mewar region is famous for its silver jewelry, wooden folk toys, miniature paintings, tribal arts, *molela* (terra-cotta work), appliqué, and embroidery. The landscape around Udaipur is dotted with crafts villages; the unique creations of the villages are sold in the city itself. Udaipur is also one of Rajasthan's great centers of contemporary art, as well as of miniature paintings. Mewar gastronomy features *diljani* (mini sugar balls) and *imarti* (pretzel-shape pastries dipped in sugary syrup) sweets, *dal baati churma* (lentils with balls of baked wheat dough), *chaach* (buttermilk with masala), various *makhi* (corn) products, and the guava. In or around Udaipur, make sure you travel with cash: most smaller shops and restaurants here accept rupees only.

Udaipur is also known for its spirit of voluntarism: it has one of the largest numbers of non-government organizations (NGOs) in India. Many of these groups are grappling with crucial environmental issues, such as drought and deforestation, and social issues, including the displacement of tribes and bride dowries.

a good tour

Start by wandering through the **Sahelion Ki Bari** gardens, north of the old city. Then head south: walk or hire a car (it's a short walk, about 1½ km [1 mi]) to **Bharatiya Lok Kala Mandal,** the folk museum. **MLV Tribal Research Institute** near the university (near the City Palace) also offers an in-depth look into rural Rajasthani culture. Continue to the **City Palace** and Jagdish Temple area, where you can have some lunch and explore; from here you can take a boat ride to see the two palaces on **Lake Pichola.** (Nonguests must pay a fee of Rs. 200.) Finish your day with dinner at the legendary Lake Palace Hotel (make reservations).

TIMING   You can cram these activities into one very full day, but you should really spend at least two days in this glorious city, especially if you want to also fit in a trip to the arts-and-crafts village of Shilpgram, see some of Udaipur's art galleries, or check out the views from the **Sajjan Garh** fort or the **Neemach Mata** temple.

What to See

Bagore ki Haveli. This elegant 18th-century haveli on Gangaur Ghat was built by a prime minister of Mewar. It takes a while to explore the many rooms and terraces of this roomy old mansion. Folk dance performances are organized every evening at 7. ⊠ *Gangaur Ghat* ☎ *294/252–3858* ✆ *Rs. 25, dance performance Rs. 60; camera Rs. 10; video camera Rs. 50* ⊙ *Daily 10–7, performance 7–8.*

Bharatiya Lok Kala Mandal. This folk-art museum displays a collection of puppets, dolls, masks, folk dresses, ornaments, musical instruments, and paintings. The museum is known for its cultural performances—this is the reason to come here, because the museum itself is not well maintained. The nightly puppet shows, which run about 15 minutes, are cute. ⊠ *½ km north of Chetak Circle, Panch Batti, near Mohta Park* ☎ *294/252–9296* ✆ *Rs. 25, evening program Rs. 50* ⊙ *Daily 9–6, evening program 6–7.*

City Palace. The sprawling maharana's palace—the largest in Rajasthan—stands on a ridge overlooking the lake. Begun by Udai Singh and extended by subsequent maharanas, the sand-color City Palace has a harmonious design: it rises five stories, with a series of balconies. Cupolas crown its octagonal towers, which are connected by a maze of narrow passageways. The City Palace is one of a complex of palaces—two have been converted to hotels and one houses the current maharana, Arvind Singh of Mewar. Part of the palace is also a museum; the museum's entrance is near the Jagdish Mandir and the entrance to the City Palace Hotel is at the bottom of the hill, to the south. The rooms inside the City Palace Museum contain decorative art: beautiful paintings, colorful enamel, inlay glasswork, and antique furniture. This is one place to have a full-fledged site publication (buy one in the book shop) or a guide (hire one at the gate). ⊠ *City Palace Complex* ☎ *294/252–8016* ✆ *Rs. 75, or Rs. 50 for guests of at Shiv Niwas, Fateh Prakash, and Lake Palace; camera Rs. 100; video camera Rs. 300* ⊙ *Daily 9:30–4:30.*

need a break? Overlooking Lake Pichola from a gallery adjoining the magnificent Durbar Hall in Fateh Prakash Palace, **Gallery** (⊠ Fateh Prakash Palace, City Palace Complex ☎ 294/252–8016 to 19) serves high tea only between 3 PM and 7 PM. There's a full–cream tea (cakes and scones with jam and cream, tea or coffee) as well as sandwiches. If you're visiting the crystal gallery above the restaurant, your Rs. 300 ticket also includes a soft drink, plain tea, or coffee at the restaurant. (The crystal gallery houses the palace's early-19th–century collection of Birmingham crystal, including everything from wine decanters to beds.)

Lake Pichola. You can't leave Udaipur without seeing the stunningly romantic **Lake Palace** (Jag Niwas), which seems to float serenely on the waters of Lake Pichola. A vast, white-marble fantasy, the palace has been featured in many Indian and foreign films, including the James Bond film,

Octopussy. Unfortunately, the palace's apartments, courts, fountains, and gardens are off-limits unless you're a guest at the Lake Palace Hotel or you have reservations at the restaurant (well-worth it). The equally isolated, three-story **Jag Mandir** palace occupies another island at the southern end of the lake. You can take a boat there during daylight hours. Built and embellished over a 50-year period beginning in the 17th century, Jag Mandir is made of yellow sandstone, lined with marble, and crowned by a dome. The interior is decorated with arabesques of colored stones. Shah Jahan, son of the Moghul emperor Jahangir, took refuge in Jag Mandir after leading an unsuccessful revolt against his father. Legend has it that Shah Jahan's inspiration for the Taj Mahal came from this marble masterpiece. ⊠ *Boat cruises leave from the jetty at the base of City Palace* 🕾 *Rs. 100 per person per ½-hr, motorboat; Rs. 200 per person per hr, includes stop at Jag Mandir Island* ☉ *Boats run all day 10–5.*

MLV Tribal Research Institute. Stop in here if you're curious about Mewar's tribal communities. The institute has a compact museum of tribal culture and a good library on tribal life and issues. ⊠ *University Rd., Ashok Nagar area* 🕾 *294/241–0958* 🕾 *Free* ☉ *Mon.–Sat 10–5.*

Neemach Mata. This hilltop temple, dedicated to the goddess of the mountain, has a good view of Udaipur. Because no taxis or cars are allowed, you must make the steep 20-minute climb up (on a paved path that zigzags up the hill) on your own, so have comfortable shoes ready. ⊠ *North of Fateh Sagar Lake.*

Sahelion Ki Bari. Don't miss Udaipur's famous "Garden of the Maidens," founded in the 18th century by Maharana Sangam Singh for the 48 young ladies-in-waiting who were sent to the royal house as dowry. Back then, men were forbidden entrance when the queens and their ladies-in-waiting came to relax (though the king and his buddies still found their way in). The garden is planted with exotic flowers and theme fountains— with carved pavilions and monolithic marble elephants. The fountains don't have pumps: designed to take advantage of gravity, the fountains run solely on water pressure from the lakes. If the fountains are not on, ask one of the attendants to turn them on. The pavilion opposite the entrance houses a small **children's science center.** For some touristy fun, you can dress up in traditional Rajasthani garb and have your picture snapped by a local photographer. ⊠ *Saheli Marg, north of the city, near Bharatiya Lok Kala Mandal* 🕾 *Rs. 5* ☉ *Daily 8–7.*

Sajjan Garh. High in the Aravalli Hills just outside Udaipur, this fort-palace glows golden-orange in the night sky, thanks to the lights that illuminate it. Once the maharana's Monsoon Palace, it's now dilapidated, and serves as a radio station for the Indian Army. The panoramic view is spectacular from the fort's lofty tower, and locals claim you can see distant Chittaurgarh on a clear day. The winding road to the top of Sajjan Garh, surrounded by green forests, is best covered by car (you can take an auto-rickshaw, but the ride will be a lot longer and bumpier). It's not open to the public.

off the
beaten
path

SHILPGRAM – This rural arts-and-crafts village 3 km (2 mi) west of Udaipur includes a complex with 26 recreations of furnished village huts (authentic right down to their toilets) from Rajasthan, Gujarat, Maharashtra, Goa, and Madhya Pradesh. The town comes alive in December with the **Shilpgram Utsav,** when artists and craftspeople from around India arrive to sell and display their works. Puppet shows, dances, folk music, and handicrafts sales take place year-round, however. You can see all of the compound on a slow camel ride. ⊠ *Rani Rd.* ☎ *294/243–1304* 🖻 *Rs. 15; camera Rs. 10; video camera Rs. 50* ⊗ *Daily 11–7.*

Where to Stay & Eat

$$$$ ✕ **Neel Kamal.** This fancy restaurant at the Lake Palace Hotel focuses on regional cuisine. The interior is ethnic: gold-color murals by local artisans. All dishes are cooked over a wood fire and in clay pots. Try the unusual *chilgoze ka shorba* (roasted pine nut soup), *kurkuri bhindi* (deep-fried okra), *saag*-of-the-day (fresh seasonal greens), *mathania safed murg* (chicken with yogurt and sun-dried mathania chillies), *khud ki raan* (leg of lamb wrapped in forest leaves and charcoal baked). Seafood is flown in fresh every day and includes tandoori pink salmon and *tawaa jhingra* (freshwater prawns marinated in cider vinegar, ginger, and mint). The restaurant has one of the largest wine lists in India, with more than 120 wines on offer. ⊠ *Lake Palace* ☎ *294/252–8800* 🖄 *Reservations essential* ▭ *AE, DC, MC, V.*

$$$$ ✕ **Sunset Terrace.** Overlooking Lake Pichola from the mainland, this café benefits from a constant breeze and first-rate service—sitting on the terrace feels as if you've joined the aristocracy and have unlimited leisure. The menu includes Indian, European, and Chinese dishes. The favorite orders at this restaurant are the *paneer lababdar* (cottage cheese in an onion and tomato gravy) and the *safed maas,* a Rajasthani lamb dish cooked in cream sauce. ⊠ *Fateh Prakash Palace, City Palace Complex* ☎ *294/252–8016 to 19* ▭ *AE, MC, V.*

$$ ✕ **Ambrai.** This popular place with a stunning view of the City Palace complex and the Lake Palace is on the bank of Lake Pichola opposite Lal Ghat. It serves Indian, Continental, and Chinese food, and is a pleasant place for a leisurely evening out. The restaurant has standard dishes, including *paneer do piaza* (cottage cheese in an onion gravy), and *mutton rajputana* (Mewari style spicy mutton). There's beer beer, and the restaurant is open for all three meals. ⊠ *Opposite Lal Ghat* ☎ *294/243–1085* ▭ *No credit cards.*

$$ ✕ **Jagat Niwas Palace Terrace Restaurant.** The open-air restaurant at this converted haveli on Lal Ghat has retained the mansion's lovely design, and has spectacular views of the Lake Palace. The vista, especially at night, captures the almost unbearably romantic essence of the city. To watch the brilliantly illuminated Lake Palace float like a mythological castle on the water from a bolstered and cushioned alcove is a cardinal Udaipur experience. Here you'll get a decent range of Continental and Indian food. The haveli is located at the tail end of one of Lal Ghat's labyrinthine lanes: but getting there is easy; everybody knows where it is. ⊠ *Lal Ghat* ☎ *294/242–2860 or 294/242–0133* ▭ *MC, V.*

¢–$ ✕ **Shilpi.** Take a 15-minute cab ride from the city center to this casual garden restaurant, which serves standard Indian and Chinese food. You can dine on the huge lawn or under the thatch roof of the dining room. Try the *missi ki roti* and the butter chicken, baked in spices and then cooked in rich tomato curry. Equipped with an outdoor swimming pool and bar as well as kitchen, Shilpi is a good place to relax in the sun. ✉ *Rani Rd., near Shilpgram Village* ☎ *294/243–2495* ▭ *No credit cards.*

¢ ✕ **Santosh Dal Bhati.** For the adventurous: Santosh Dal Bhati is Udaipur's best bargain if you're looking for traditional Rajasthani food. The place is a dive, and it's difficult to find, but the *dal baati churma* (lentils with balls of baked wheat dough) is fantastic, and deservedly popular with locals. Roll up your sleeves, wash your hands, and dig in. ✉ *Suraj Pole* ☎ *No phone* ▭ *No credit cards.*

$$$$ ▥ **Fateh Prakash Palace.** This small but grand palace was built by Maharana Fateh Singh at the turn of the 20th century. The palace has suitably excellent views of Lake Pichola—it's right next to the City Palace. The suites are elegantly furnished with period furniture (some of it was once used by the royal family), heavy drapes, and brass fixtures. The standard rooms are also luxurious, but they lack the main palace's sense of history. ✉ *City Palace Complex; reserve through City Palace, 313001* ☎ *294/252–8016 to 19* ☒ *294/252–8006* ⊕ *www.hrhindia.com* ⤳ *21 rooms, 7 suites* ♨ *Restaurant, cable TV, pool, health club, hair salon, boating, billiards, Ping-Pong, squash, bar, ayurvedic massage* ▭ *AE, DC, MC, V* ❨❩ *EP.*

$$$$ ▥ **Lake Palace.** Now run by the Taj Group, this 250-year-old white-marble palace—the main setting for the James Bond film *Octopussy*—floats like a vision in the middle of Lake Pichola. You arrive, of course, by boat. The standard rooms are contemporary; if you want a room to match the stunning setting, opt for a suite. The fantastical Khush Mahal Suite takes in sunlight through stained-glass windows; the peach-tone Sarva Ritu Suite has a small interior porch with three arched windows and a window seat. Most rooms have lake views, though some look onto the lily pond or the courtyard. Nonguests cannot visit the palace unless they have a reservation to dine at the restaurant or on the hotel's wooden barge, *Gangaur.* ✉ *Lake Pichola 313001* ☎ *294/252–8800* ☒ *294/252–8700* ⊕ *www.tajhotels.com* ⤳ *76 rooms, 8 suites* ♨ *Restaurant, coffee shop, cable TV, pool, gym, boating, bar, baby-sitting, laundry service, meeting room, travel services* ▭ *AE, DC, MC, V* ❨❩ *EP.*

Fodor's Choice
★

$$$$ ▥ **Laxmi Vilas Palace.** You'll feel nostalgic for times past at this former royal guest house, built in 1933, on a hillside above the banks of Fateh Sagar Lake. From the hotel's verandas and gardens you can get a lovely view of the lake and the nearby Sajjan Garh fort. The maharana's hunting trophies line the entranceway. Rooms in the new wing are modern; the old wing, though not lavish, has original architecture and Rajput relics. The restaurant serves Indian food. ✉ *Sagar Rd., 313001* ☎ *294/252–9711* ☒ *294/252–6573* ⊕ *www.thegrandhotels.net* ⤳ *43 rooms, 11 suites* ♨ *Restaurant, cable TV, pool, bar, laundry service, travel services* ▭ *AE, MC, V* ❨❩ *EP.*

$$$$ ▥ **Oberoi Udaivilas.** Built on the edge of Lake Pichola with a sublime view of the lake palace, the city palace complex, and the ghats, the Oberoi Udaivilas is one of the most luxurious and exclusive hotels in India. With

Fodor's Choice
★

numerous domes, a massive marble lotus pond in the courtyard, and elegantly furnished rooms, this is a contemporary palace in its own right. Semiprivate pools seem to ripple over onto serene Pichola while deer come up to the edge of the hotel's private wildlife reserve. Staff, dressed in traditional clothes, have an unusual old-world courtesy and genuine concern for the welfare of guests. The restaurant serves delicious Continental and Indian food. ⊠ *Haridasji ki Magri, 313001* ☎ *294/243–3300, 800/562–3764 U.S. and Canada reservations* 🖷 *294/243–3200* ⊕ *www.oberoihotels.com* ✈ *82 rooms, 5 suites* ♨ *In-room data ports, in-room safes, cable TV, pool, spa, baby-sitting, laundry service, travel services* 🖃 *AE, DC, MC, V* ¶◎¶ *EP.*

$$$$ ⊞ **Shiv Niwas Palace.** Laid out like a white crescent moon around a large pool is this erstwhile royal guest house. Standard rooms, set apart from the main building, have contemporary furnishings. The regal suites are gorgeous, with molded ceilings, elaborate canopied beds, and original paintings and furniture. Some of the rooms have private terraces; all have excellent views of Lake Pichola. The Baneera Bar is styled with Victorian furnishings. Shiv Niwas Palace is adjacent to the City Palace. ⊠ *City Palace Complex; reserve through City Palace, 313001* ☎ *294/252–8016 to 19* 🖷 *294/252–8006* ⊕ *www.hrhindia.com* ✈ *14 rooms, 17 suites* ♨ *Restaurant, cable TV, pool, hair salon, ayurvedic massage, boating, billiards, bar, meeting room, travel services* 🖃 *AE, DC, MC, V* ¶◎¶ *EP.*

★ $$$$ ⊞ **Trident Hilton.** This property sits at the end of a long and solitary road, set among acres of beautiful gardens—totally removed from the bustle of downtown Udaipur and located on the shore of Lake Pichola. The hotel's architecture is striking, but the interior is somewhat lacking in aesthetic sensibility; rooms are well-equipped and modern, but nondescript. The pool is heated and thus pleasant day or night. The hotel sponsors boat rides around Lake Pichola. The smiling and attentive staff aim to please. Bada Mahal, the adjoining hunting lodge, offers the opportunity to watch deer and wild boar being fed every evening by a caretaker. The restaurant, Aravalli, serves Indian and Continental food, including local delicacies; the *dal makhani* (lentils in a rich, buttery tomato sauce) is also excellent. You can dine outside, on the terrace, from October to March, and choose from grills and regional *thalis.* ⊠ *Haridasji Ki Magri, Mulla Tulai 313001* ☎ *294/243–2200* 🖷 *294/243–2211* ⊕ *www.tridenthotels.com* ✈ *139 rooms, 4 suites* ♨ *2 restaurants, in-room data ports, cable TV, pool, gym, hair salon, boating, archery, boat cruises, bar, baby-sitting, meeting room, travel services,* 🖃 *AE, DC, MC, V* ¶◎¶ *EP.*

$$ ⊞ **Hilltop Hotel Palace.** Perched on a hill overlooking Fateh Sagar Lake is this hotel with splendid views of Udaipur. It's a modern hotel, with a spacious marble lobby, a glass elevator, an elegant garden, and a number of rooftop terraces. The hotel may not take you back in time, but it's an excellent value. The Western-style rooms are simple but clean, and each has a balcony. ⊠ *5 Ambavgarh, Fateh Sagar 313001* ☎ *294/243–2245* 🖷 *294/243–2136* ✈ *62 rooms* ♨ *2 restaurants, cable TV, pool, bar, shops, meeting room* 🖃 *AE, MC, V* ¶◎¶ *EP.*

$$ ⊞ **Jaisamand Island Resort.** This large, white hotel leans against a brown-and-green slope on an island in Jaisamand Lake, one of the largest artificial lakes in the world. The hotel's spacious lobby and its bar have granite floors and Rajasthani furniture. The rooms are Western-style and comfortable. Catch the hotel boat on the lake's boardwalk. ✦ *50 km (32 mi) southeast of Udaipur, on Jaisamand Lake, c/o Hotel Lake End, Fateh Sagar Lake, Alkapuri, Udaipur 313004* ☎ *294/243–1400 reservations* 🖷 *294/243–1406* ⊕ *www.lakend.com* ➥ *30 rooms, 5 suites* ⚫ *Restaurant, cable TV, pool, boating, fishing, camel rides, bar, recreation room, meeting room, airport shuttle* ═ *AE, MC, V* ⦿ *EP.*

$$ ▣ **Paras Mahal.** This hotel, while not fancy, is clean and modern. It's only ½ km (¼ mi) from Udaipur's train station, and is also close to a Hindi-movie theater. The main feature is a glass elevator that shoots up through the hotel's central atrium. Rooms have low-lying beds, with lavish, colorful bedspreads; the walls are hung with Rajasthani paintings. All rooms have phones, sofas, and desks. ⊠ *Near Paras Cinema, Hiran Magri, Sector 11, 313001* ☎ *294/248–3391 Ext. 4* 🖷 *294/258–4103* ⊕ *www. hotelparasmahal.com* ➥ *60 rooms* ⚫ *Restaurant, cable TV, pool, bar, shops, laundry service, business services, travel services* ═ *MC, V* ⦿ *EP.*

$$ ▣ **Shikarbadi.** Just outside the city, this former hunting lodge of the local royal family—now a Heritage Hotel—is a rustic retreat, complete with a private lake. The rooms are attractive, with tile ceilings and stone walls. Deer and monkeys venture close, almost to the door. The hotel's open-air restaurant serves traditional Mewari food. You might want to try one of the horseback-riding excursions or safaris the hotel offers. The Shikarbadi hotel is only a few kilometers outside the city. ✦ *Reserve through City Palace, 313001* ⊠ *Goverdhan Vilas, a side street from Ahmedabad Rd.* ☎ *294/258–3201, 294/252–8016 reservations* 🖷 *294/ 258–4841, 294/252–8006 reservations* ⊕ *www.hrhindia.com* ➥ *21 rooms, 4 suites* ⚫ *Restaurant, cable TV, pool, horseback riding, jeep safaris, bar, airstrip, travel services* ═ *AE, DC, MC, V* ⦿ *EP.*

$–$$ ▣ **Udai Kothi.** Who can pass up regal accommodations at cut-rate prices? This is probably the best hotel for the money in all of Rajasthan. From the rooftop pool you can swim and enjoy spectacular views of the Udaipur skyline—the hotel is across Lake Pichola from the City Palace. Every room has a theme that's related to a specific region and group of people in Mewar history. The rooms are decorated with antique furniture and art. ⊠ *Outside Chandpol on Hannuman Ghat, 313001* ☎ *294/243–2810 to 12* 🖷 *294/243–0412* ➥ *24 rooms* ⚫ *Restaurant, cable TV, pool, massage, sauna, bar, laundry service; no a/c in some rooms* ═ *MC, V* ⦿ *EP.*

$ ▣ **Lake Pichola Hotel.** Not to be confused with the Lake Palace on Lake Pichola, this hotel is run by a Rajput family and benefits both from an excellent location on Lake Pichola and friendly service. Each suite has a Jacuzzi and a terrace with beautiful city views. The rooms are full of artifacts and colored glass panes. You can request a boat ride on the lake or cultural performances with a little advance notice. ⊠ *Outside Chandpol, on the western side of Lake Pichola, 313001* ☎ *294/243– 1197* 🖷 *294/243–0575* ⊕ *www.lakepicholahotel.com* ➥ *27 rooms, 2 suites* ⚫ *Restaurant, cable TV, travel services* ═ *AE, MC, V* ⦿ *EP.*

$ ▣ **Jagat Niwas Palace Hotel.** With a stunning location right on the Lake Pichola at Lal Ghat, a whitewashed interior, and simple yet elegant furnishings, this converted 17th-century haveli is one of the best medium-budget places in the city. It offers unsurpassed views of the lake and the Aravalli hills. The restaurant is a charming place to dine, with romantic open-air alcoves overlooking the lake and a stunning view of the Lake Palace Hotel. ⊠ *Lal Ghat, 313001* ☎ *294/242–2860 or 294/242–0133* 🖷 *294/241–8512* ⊕ *www.indianheritagehotels.com* ⇨ *29 rooms* ⚬ *Restaurant, cable TV, bar, laundry service, travel services; no a/c in some rooms* ⊟ *MC, V* ⏲ *EP.*

¢–$ 🖫 **Kankarwa Haveli.** Right next door to the Jagat Niwas Palace on Lal Ghat, in the heart of the old city, this haveli has a homey feel. The staff consists of domestic help, and members of the family supervise the kitchen, which serves home-style Rajasthani food—a relief from the Punjabi and Mughlai cuisines that seem to dominate menus through the state. Ask for rooms on the upper floor, the ones close to the water can let in more smells than you might appreciate. Rooms are large, simple, and lovingly restored, but you won't find a TV or phone in them. You'll have to shout down the stairs for room service and there's a chance you'll be answered by a bark from the family dog that guards the courtyard. ⊠ *26 Lal Ghat, 313001* ☎ *294/241–1457* 🖷 *294/252–1403* ⊕ *www. indianheritagehotels.com* ⇨ *14 rooms* ⚬ *Restaurant, laundry service; no room phones, no room TVs* ⊟ *MC, V* ⏲ *EP.*

Shopping

Udaipur's main shopping area spans the area around the **Jagdish Temple.** You'll discover interesting nooks and crannies around here, but watch out for would-be guides. There are plenty of stores to explore and items to buy: along with wooden toys, silver, and Udaipuri and Gujarati embroidery, you'll find miniature paintings in the Moghul and Rajput styles. Most of these paintings are machine-made prints, a fact reflected in the wide disparity in prices. If you want to buy original art, ask the proprietor to show you what's in the back room—and plan to bargain.

ART Serious art collectors should know that Udaipur has many galleries that exhibit original work by internationally renowned and burgeoning artists. The **B. G. Sharma Art Gallery** (⊠ 3 Saheli Marg ☎ 294/256–0063) has 45 years of work by B. G. Sharma himself, one of the most eminent painters in India. Unlike most artists of miniature paintings, Sharma doesn't copy traditional pictures, but makes his own—and has made huge contributions to advancing the Moghul, Kishangarh, and Kangra painting styles. **Ganesh Art Emporium** (⊠ 152 Jagdish Chowk ☎ 294/242–2864) is a trendy little shop focusing on a gifted young artist, Madhu Kant Mundra, whose oeuvre includes more than 125 funky representations of Lord Ganesh. Don't miss the artistic refrigerator magnets, sculptures, and antique photographs. **Pristine Gallery** (⊠ 6 Kalapi House, Bhatiyani Chohatta, Palace Rd. ☎ 294/241–5291) specializes in both contemporary and folk art, with many small pieces by Shail Choyal, a guru of contemporary Indian painting. Other highlights include the stylized work of Shahid Parvez, a very fine up-and-coming local artist. At the **Sharma Art Gallery** (⊠ 15-A New Colony, Kalaji-Goraji ☎ 294/242–1107), Kamal Sharma paints mainly birds and animals on paper, marble, silk, and canvas—all are for sale. Apart from being the chief resident artist at Udaipur Medical College, **S. N. Bhandraj** (⊠ Studio 70, Moti Magri Colony ☎ 294/256–1396) has been creating sculpture out of sea foam for more than 20 years; he demonstrates this unique craft in his home

PAINTINGS

Rajasthan is famous for paintings in the phad and pichwai styles. The phad is a red, green, and yellow scroll depicting the life of a local hero; the dark and richly hued pichwais, hung in temples, are cloth paintings depicting Lord Krishna in different moods.

Equally popular are reproductions of mandana art, designs traditionally drawn by women on the walls and floors of rural homes using a chalk solution on a crimson cow-dung background. These unique works are ritual decorations for festivals and ceremonial occasions. Udaipur has the biggest and best selection of miniature paintings, and is considered a center for this traditional art. Whether on paper, silk, marble, or bone, these astonishingly intricate works depict wildlife and courtly scenes, and illustrations of religious stories and mythological themes. Originally created by the chittrekar (artist) community, miniatures now usually blend both Rajput and Moghul styles. Building on the Rajputs' bright colors and courtly themes, the Moghuls added more detail to the faces and the landscapes.

studio. At the **Traditional Art Gallery** (⊠ 13 Bhatiyani Chohatta, Jagdish Mandir ☎ no phone), you can see the watercolor tribal portraits and village scenes of the talented young artist Anil Sharma.

CRAFTS & CURIOS If your time is limited, you'll find everything under the sun at an emporium, and you won't have to bargain. The **Manglam Arts** (⊠ Sukhadia Circle ☎ 294/256–0259) emporium deals in Rajasthani handicrafts, including rugs, block-printed textiles, knickknacks, and furniture. The government-run **Rajasthali** (⊠ Chetak Circle ☎ 294/241–5346) emporium sells high-quality Rajasthani arts and handicrafts. This is also a good place to pick up an export-quality wool-stuffed washable quilt covered with a Rajasthani motif.

Sadhana (⊠ Seva Mandir Rd., Fatehpura ☎ 294/245–1041 or 294/245–0960 ⊕ www.sevamandir.org ⊙ Weekdays 11–6) is run by Seva Mandir—one of the oldest NGOs in India, working for the advancement of the village poor. Among Seva Mandir's activities is a rural women's income-generation program that encourages women to produce traditional appliqué work on cushion covers and bedspreads. The results are sold in the organization's office building (along with silk stoles, bags, kurtas, light quilts and jackets), and the full proceeds are returned to the women (rather than pocketed by middlemen, as they would be if the work was sold in stores). The women are also involved in the NGO's other activities like education, childcare, and health.

While you're in the Jagdish Temple area, make sure you check out the collection of more than 500 handmade wooden puppets at the **University of Arts** (⊠ 166 Jagdish Marg, City Palace Rd. ☎ 294/242–2591). Ask the proprietor, Rajesh Gurjarjour, an excellent puppeteer, for a private demonstration. Embroidered jackets are also for sale.

JEWELRY From Jagdish Temple, stroll down to **Ganta Ghar** (literally Clocktower, and the area around it), a base for silver jewelry. Browse freely, but take care not to purchase items that are merely coated with silver-tone paint. **Gehrilal Goverdhan Singh Choudhary** (✉ 72 Jagdish Marg, Clocktower ☎ 294/241–0806) has a good selection of fixed-price, antique jewelry, and contemporary designs with stonework. Choudhary has been in the business more than 22 years, and has exhibited several times abroad.

> **need a break?**
>
> Right next door to Gehrilal Goverdhan Singh Choudhary is a sweet stall, **Lala Mishtan Bhandar,** where you can satisfy your sweet tooth and refuel with the best *gulab jamun* (fried milk balls in syrup) and *imarti* (fried sweets made with lentils) in town.

Ranakpur

★ ㉒ *96 km (60 mi) northwest of Udaipur.*

Nestled in a glen northwest of Udaipur is one of the five holy places for India's Jain community. Legend has it that this 15th-century **Jain temple,** dedicated to Lord Rishabadeva, was built after it appeared in a dream to a minister of the Mewar king. The three-story temple is surrounded by a three-story wall that contains 27 halls supported by 1,444 elaborately carved pillars—no two carvings are alike. Below the temple are underground chambers where statues of Jain saints were hidden to protect them from the Moghuls. The way the white marble complex rises up from the fertile plain will easily inspire your awe—the relief work on the columns are some of the best in all of India. As you enter, look to the left for the pillar where the minister and the architect provided themselves with front-row seats for worship. Another pillar is intentionally warped, to separate human works from divine ones—the builders believed only gods could be perfect, so they intentionally added imperfections to some of the columns to avoid insulting the gods. Outside are two smaller Jain temples and a shrine adorned with erotic sculptures and dedicated to the sun god. ☒ *Free; cameras Rs. 40, video cameras Rs. 150* ☉ *Non-Jains, daily 11:30–5.*

Where to Stay & Eat

$$ ✕▥ **Maharani Bagh Orchard Retreat.** You'll find it's easy to relax at this 19th-century pied-à-terre for the Maharani of Jodhpur set in 70 acres of orchard. Scattered among huge mango trees, the little brick cottages have traditional furnishings: painted wooden beds and tile floors. The kitchen serves Indian and Rajasthani specialties under small thatch shelters; in the background you hear the sound of water rushing through a canal in the middle of the property. ⌂ *Reserve through Welcomgroup Umaid Bhawan Palace, Jodhpur 342006* ✉ *Sadri, Ranakpur* ☎ *2934/ 285–105or 2934/286–615, 291/251–0101 reservations* 🖷 *2934/285– 151, 291/251–0101 reservations* ⬚ *18 rooms* ♨ *Restaurant, cable TV, pool, bar; no a/c in some rooms* ▤ *AE, MC, V* ❙❍❙ *EP.*

Mount Abu

㉓ *185 km (115 mi) west of Udaipur.*

High in the Aravalli Hills, Mount Abu has long been the site of one of Hinduism's most sacred rites, the *yagya* (fire ritual). Legend has it that the clan of the mighty *agnikula* Rajput warriors rose from this mystical fire. Today, Mount Abu is Rajasthan's only hill station, and a pilgrimage center for Jains, who come here to see the famous Dilwara Temples. Mount Abu is also a great place to stop if you like taking long walks. **Nakki Lake,** resting between green hills, is believed to have been carved out by the gods' fingernails. The far side of the lake is quieter and cleaner. At **Sunset Point** you can imbibe a romantic Mount Abu sunset, but you can't avoid the crowds here.

Mount Abu's newest ashram–cult hotspot is the **Brahma Kumaris Spiritual University,** which attracts thousands of followers from all over the world. Members of the sect don white robes or saris, and study spiritual knowledge or Raja Yoga meditation. (Potential devotees beware: their services don't come cheap.) The Brahma Kumaris have also designed the **Peace Park,** which includes a series of beautiful gardens. Beyond the park, on Guru Shikhar Road, is **Guru Shikhar,** the highest point between South India's Nilgiri Hills and the Himalayas, in the north. From here you can enjoy excellent views of the countryside. The stunningly carved, unforgettably beautiful **Dilwara Temples,** dedicated to Jain saints, were built entirely of marble between the 11th and 13th centuries.

Where to Stay

$$–$$$ ✕🎦 **Cama Rajputana Club Resort.** Cradled in the Aravalli hills, this late-19th-century club—where British officers and royalty from Gujarat and Rajputana came to escape the summer heat—combines modern amenities with country style. The main building is a rambling old bungalow with a tiled roof; the hotel itself has 18 acres of gardens, with waterfalls and an artifical lake. Rooms belonging to the old club property are old-world; the new blocks have modern rooms with nondescript furnishings. Room rates are higher on weekends. ⌂ *Reserve through Cama Hotel Ltd., Khanpur Rd., Ahmedabad 380001, Gujarat* ⊠ *Adhar Devi Rd., Mount Abu 307501* ☎ *2974/238–205 or 2974/238–206, 79/560–1234 reservations* 🖷 *2974/238–412, 79/560–2000 reservations* ⊕ *www.camahotels.com* ⤳ *40 rooms, 2 suites* ⟨ *Restaurant, cable TV, tennis court, lawn tennis, pool, health club, ayurvedic massage, trekking, Ping-Pong, billiards, boating, horseback riding, squash, library; no a/c in some rooms* ⊟ *AE, MC, V* ⏐◯⏐ *EP.*

$$ 🎦 **Palace Hotel (Bikaner House).** Besides once being the summer residence of the Maharaja of Bikaner, this was for decades also the center of Mount Abu's aristocratic social life. Built in 1893 and now a Heritage Hotel, it still feels something like a hunting lodge, and is a good place to retreat and relax for a few days. Service is excellent. The hotel is esconsed in the middle of 20 acres of lawns and woods. ⊠ *Delwara Rd., Mount Abu, 307501* ☎ *2974/235–121 or 2974/238–673* 🖷 *2974/238674* ⤳ *15 rooms, 17 suites* ⟨ *Restaurant, cable TV, tennis court, billiards, bar, playground, laundry service; no a/c in some rooms* ⊟ *AE, MC, V* ⏐◯⏐ *EP.*

Chittaurgarh

★ ㉔ *112 km (69 mi) northeast of Udaipur.*

If any one of Rajasthan's many forts had to be singled out for its glorious history and chivalric lore, it would be Chittaurgarh. This was the capital of the Mewar princely state from the 8th to the 16th centuries, before Maharana Udai Singh moved the capital to Udaipur. The sprawling hilltop fort occupies about 700 acres on a hill about 92 meters (300 feet) high. It was besieged and sacked three times: after the first two conquests, the Rajputs recovered it, but the third attack clinched it for the Moghuls for several decades.

The first attack took place because of a woman: the beauty of Rani Padmini, wife of the then-current ruler, so enamored the Sultan of Delhi Allauddin Khilji that he set out to attack the fort and win her in battle. Thirty-four thousand warriors lost their lives in this struggle, but the Sultan did not get Padmini: she and all the women in the fort committed *jauhar*—mass self-immolation in anticipation of widowhood and perversions by invading armies—and burned themselves to death. Frustrated, Khilji entered the city in a rage, looting and destroying much of what he saw. Chittaurgarh was also the home of the saint-poet Mirabai, a 16th-century Rajput princess and devotee of Lord Krishna who gave up her royal life to sing *bhajans* (hymns) in his praise.

The massive fort encompasses the palaces of **Rana Kumbha** and **Padmini** Rana Kumbha's palace is a fine 15th-century ruin, whereas Padmini's tranquil palace sits beside a small, still body of water. Also worth visiting in the fort are the victory towers—the ornate **Vijay Stambh** and **Kirti Stambh**—and a huge variety of temples, including **Kunbha Shyam, Kalika Mata,** and the **Meera temple** associated with the devotional poetess Mirabai. The **Fateh Prakash Mahal** displays some fine sculptures. Spend at least half a day in Chittaurgarh; a vehicle helps, because the sights are spread out and the sun can be very sharp on the unprotected hill.

At present there are no exciting accommodation options in Chittaur town, but Heritage Hotels in the nearby villages offer wonderful retreats and good bases from which to explore rural Mewar.

Where to Stay & Eat

$ ✕⌷ **Bassi Fort Palace.** You'll find this 16th-century fort 20 km (12 mi) from Chittaurgarh, in the village of Bassi, has been converted into a Heritage Hotel by descendants of the Chundawat royals. The approach road to the fort goes through the unspoiled village of Bassi. The common areas are large and elegant, with period furniture, and the rooms spacious and comfortable. You can also visit the family's former hunting lodge overlooking Bassi and Orai lakes. Government plans are afoot to reintroduce tigers to the wild in the Bassi wildlife sanctuary. The hotel organizes tented safaris near the lake, and trips into the nearby Bhil villages. ⊠ *On Udaipur Chittaurgarh-Bundi-Kota National Hwy. 76, Bassi, Chittaurgarh 312022* ☎ *1472/225–321 or 1472/225–248* 🖷 *1472/ 240–811* ⊕ *www.bassifortpalace.com* ⇆ *18 rooms* ♨ *No a/c in some rooms, no room TVs* ¶⊚¶ *EP.*

$ ⌷ **Castle Bijaipur.** Thirty-five kilometers from Chittaurgarh, Castle Bijaipur is a 16th-century palace with a lovely courtyard. A beautiful Heritage Hotel, this hotel has no televisions or phones in its Rajasthani-style rooms and is perfect for a quiet, secluded break. ⊠ *Bijaipur village* ☎ *1472/240–099* 🖷 *1472/241–042* ⊕ *www.castlebijaipur.com* ⇆ *20 rooms, 6 suites* ♨ *Restaurant, pool, Ping-Pong, trekking, horse safaris,* *jungle safaris, yoga, bar, laundry service; no room phones, no room TVs* ▭ *No credit cards* 🍽 *EP.*

Kumbhalgarh

❷❺ *84 km (52 mi) north of Udaipur.*

Isolated and serene, this formidable **fort** was a refuge for Mewari rulers in times of strife. Built by Maharana Kumbha in the 15th century, the fort ramparts run 4 km (2½ mi) and the outer wall encloses an area of (32 square mi). At one time its ramparts nearly encircled an entire township, self-contained to withstand a long siege. The fort fell only once, to the army of Akbar—whose forces had contaminated the water supply. The fort was also the birthplace of Maharana Pratap. The **Badal Mahal** (Cloud Palace), at the top, has an awesome view of the surrounding countryside. Surrounding the fort, the modern-day **Kumbalgarh Sanctuary** is home to wolves, leopards, jackals, nilgai deer, sambar deer, and various species of birds, and makes for delightful treks. Have a leisurely lunch at the open-air restaurant of the Aodhi Hotel.

Where to Stay

$$$ **Deogarh Mahal.** Built in the 17th century, this Heritage Hotel is run by its resident once-royal family. Set in the rugged countryside of the Aravalli Hills, this saffron-color mansion—rife with battlements, domes, and turrets—towers over the town below. The hotel has excellent views of the region's migratory birds. Don't miss the family's exquisite collection of miniature paintings. ✉ *Deogarh, Madaria, Rajsamand District, 313331* ☎ *2904/252–777* 📠 *2904/252–555* *45 rooms, 4 suites* *Restaurant, pool, badminton, bar, travel services, camel and jeep safaris; no a/c in some rooms, no room TVs* ▭ *MC, V* 🍽 *EP.*

Nathdwara

❷❻ *48 km (30 mi) north of Udaipur.*

The town of Nathdwara is totally built around the **Shrinathji Temple,** visited by thousands of pilgrims each year. Built in the 18th century, this simple temple is one of the most celebrated shrines to Lord Krishna: it houses a unique image of the deity sculpted from a single piece of black marble. Nathdwara is known for its *pichwais,* large cloth paintings depicting legends from Krishna's life, and for its special style of devotional music.

A few minutes outside Nathdwara is **Rajsamand Lake,** which attracts a large number of migratory birds. Maharana Raj Singh ordered the construction of the lake in 1662 as a famine-relief work project, so a workforce of 60,000 people brought it into being over the course of 10 years. The architecture of its main dam, **Nauchowki** (Nine Pavilions), combines Rajput and Moghul styles; interestingly, the Rajaprashasthi (Rajput Royal Eulogy) is engraved on 25 of the dam's niched slabs. Locals come here early in the morning to learn to swim, in the pool behind the dam.

Also near Nathdwara is the village of **Molela,** where artisans craft and paint fine terra-cotta images of gods, goddesses, and animals, as well as more functional pots and utensils.

Eklingji & Nagda

㉗ *22 km (14 mi) north of Udaipur.*

A pleasant drive from Udaipur through the Aravallis, Eklingji village is famous for its 15th-century **Shiva Temple** (some parts date back to the 8th century). There's a unique four-sided, four-faced black marble image of Shiva here, miniature replicas of which will be eagerly offered to you in the village bazaar. Every Monday evening, the Udaipur maharana visits the temple privately. The temple is closed at various times of the day; it's best to ask your hotel for the prevailing admission schedule.

At nearby Nagda, 1 km south of Eklingji, 10th-century Jain temples make for an interesting detour from the highway. The chief attractions are the ruins of **Adbudji Temple** and the beautifully sculpted **Sas Bahu Temple.**

A few kilometers north up the road, the towering 18th-century **Devi Garh Palace** (⊠ off N.H. 8, near Eklingji, Delwara, Rajsamand district), beautifully restored and now run as a luxury hotel, merits an hour's exploration (nonguests are charged a fee).

Where to Stay

★ $$$$ 🏨 **Devi Garh.** Rising like a yellow ochre vision in the middle of the Aravalli hills is one of the loveliest palaces in Rajasthan. It's been carefully restored, and is beautifully maintained. The rooms, however, are modern, and though very attractive, do little to remind you you're in Rajasthan. The heritage look and feel is deliberately missing, which is strange, considering you're inside an ancient palace. Marble predominates; even the bed is made of marble. Furniture is sleek and contemporary. Windows look out on terrific views of the Aravallis—the palace was positioned to command one of the three passes into the Udaipur valley. Walk west from the palace at sunset and look back at it, or relax on the terrace or explore the surrounding hills. ⊠ *National Hwy. 8, near Eklingji, Rajsamand district Delwara 313202* ☎ *2953/289–211 to 20* 📠 *2953/289–357* ⊕ *www.deviresorts.com* ✈ *23 suites, 6 tents* ⊘ *Restaurant, cable TV, pool, health club, sauna, spa, hot tub, hair salon, ayurvedic massage, bicycles, horseback riding, camel safaris, trekking, yoga, croquet, Ping Pong, bar, shops* ⊟ *AE, DC, MC, V* ⊗ *EP.*

JAISALMER & ENVIRONS

The stark, compelling beauty of the Thar Desert draws travelers to far-western Rajasthan—for good reason. Jaisalmer, resplendent with golden buildings and a towering citadel, is a good base for camel safaris into the desert, and photogenic Sam Sand Dunes and Desert National Park are a short distance from this striking medieval city.

Jaisalmer

❷8
Fodor'sChoice
★

663 km (412 mi) northwest of Udaipur, 285 km (160 mi) northwest of Jodhpur, 570 (353 mi) west of Jaipur.

Jaisalmer seems like a mirage: its array of sandstone buildings are surrounded by the stark Thai Desert and illuminated in a gold hue by the penetrating sun. The ancient medieval city is defined by its carved spires and palaces, and the massive sandcastlelike fort that towers over the imposing wall that encircles the town. Jaisalmer is a remote and unusual city; it's out of the way, but it's worth it if you want to see a different side of India, and definitely if you want to take a camel safari.

Founded in 1156 by Rawal Jaisal, a descendent of the Yadav clan and a Bhatti Rajput, Jaisalmer lies near the extreme western edge of Rajasthan, about (100 mi) east of the Pakistan border. It began as a trade center: from the 12th through the 18th centuries, rulers amassed their wealth from taxes levied on caravans passing through from Africa, Persia, Arabia, and other parts of Central Asia. Smugglers were also known to frequent Jaisalmer to work the profitable opium trade. The rise of Bombay as a major trading port in the 19th century, however, eclipsed Jaisalmer's role as a staging post.

Today Jaisalmer attracts travelers attracted by the mystery and harsh, remote charm of the desert. A welcome change from crowded, polluted cities, the city is an architectural masterpiece that never fails to amaze. At night the fort is bathed in golden light, which illuminates the seemingly impregnable walls; most of the buildings inside are made out of yellow sandstone. Jaisalmer is also known for its ornate 19th-century havelis—mansions with facades so intricately carved the stonework looks like lace. It's also worth wandering through the mazelike alleys and bazaars, though the markets have a bad reputation among tourists. Expect some harassment, especially if you're a woman traveling solo.

Unfortunately, following the nuclear tests in nearby Pokharan in May 1998, and given ongoing border tensions with Pakistan, travelers are sometimes wary of going this far west. Although hardly any tourists went to this area in 2002, they were back in droves in 2003, and the local economy is heaving a sigh of relief. Don't be deterred—to skip Jaisalmer is to skip the real jewel of Rajasthan. When you get here you'll see that life in Jaisalmer remains unaffected.

With clean lanes, no traffic, and few crowds, Jaisalmer is easily covered on foot. Camel safaris are a good way to see the desert. These are great fun, but choose one carefully—don't skimp and choose a cheap outfitter. Take a light scarf to protect your face in case of a sandstorm.

Spend at least two nights in Jaisalmer. Nothing is more romantic than a Thar Desert sunset, and the city's cultural festivities—the heart and soul of its people—begin at night. For the traveler, these can reach intoxicating levels of passion: around blazing bonfires, dancers and musicians gather together and recreate the ancient traditions of Rajasthan. To get an even bigger dose of it, visit during the Desert Festival, in late

January and early February. You'll see music, dance, camel races, turban-tying contests, and craft bazaars with regional traders.

a good tour

Jaisalmer is like Venice in that it's next to impossible to follow a straight path: it's a maze of streets and passageways. Trust your instincts and don't be afraid to ask the locals for directions. You may have fun getting a little lost—especially because Jaisalmer isn't big enough to get hopelessly turned around. The major landmark is the **fort,** which is every bit as labyrinthine as the rest of the city; allow several hours to explore the attractions within. From here, walk north to the **havelis.** Finally, hop a camel—you must arrange this with a local travel agent a day in advance—and head southeast toward **Gadsisar Lake** and the nearby Folklore Museum.

TIMING You can do this tour in a day. If you spend a second day in town, visit the **Bada Bagh** garden and then drive northwest from there to the **Ludarva Temples.**

What to See

Bada Bagh. Much of the city's vegetables and fruits are grown at Bada Bagh, which is more like a giant orchard than a garden. On the banks of an artificial lake, and with so much lush greenery, the garden resembles a beautiful oasis (presuming there's no drought). In the gardens, you'll also see royal cenotaphs, with canopies under which members of the royal family are buried. Notice the beautifully carved ceilings and equestrian statues of the former rulers. Bada Bagh is 6 km (4 mi) northwest of the city.

Fodor'sChoice **Fort.** What's extraordinary about this fort is that 5,000 people live here,
★ just as they did centuries ago. Some 250 feet above the town, the fort is protected by a 30-foot-high wall and contains 99 bastions. Several great *pols* (gateways) approach and jut outward from the battlements of this 12th-century citadel. Built of sandstone and extremely brittle, the fort is rumored to be an architectural time bomb, destined to collapse in the face of a particularly aggressive sandstorm. Yet, so lovely is this structure that the poet Rabindranath Tagore (1861–1941) composed *Sonar Kila (The Golden Fort)* after seeing it, and inspired another creative Bengali in turn—Satyajit Ray made his famous film by the same name after reading Tagore's work. This probably explains the number of Bengali tourists in Jaisalmer; you'll recognize the married ladies from their distinctive pair of red and white bangles.

Inside the web of tiny lanes are Jain and Hindu temples, palaces, and charming havelis. The seven-story **Juna Mahal** (Old Palace), built around 1500, towers over the other buildings. The **Satiyon ka Pagthiya** (Steps of the Satis), just before the palace entrance, is where the royal ladies committed *sati,* self-immolation, when their husbands were slain.

Within the fort are eight **Jain temples** (⊠ free ☉ daily 7 AM–noon), built from the 12th to 16th centuries, which house thousands of carved deities and dancing figures in mythological settings. No photography is allowed here, and you'll have to leave your leather items at the gate (jains worship life in all forms, so leather is sacrilegious). The **Gyan Bhandar** (⊠ free ☉ daily 10 AM–11 AM), inside the Jain temple complex contains more than 1,000 old manuscripts—some from the 12th century, written on palm leaf, with painted wooden covers—and a collection of Jain, pre-Moghul, and Rajput paintings.

The historic **Tazia Tower** is a delicate pagoda rising five tiers from the **Badal Mahal** (Cloud Palace), each tier designed to include an intricately carved balcony. Muslim craftsmen built the tower in the shape of a *tazia*—a replica of a bier carried in procession during Mohurram, a Muslim period of mourning. ⊠ *Juna Mahal* 🎫 *Rs. 5* ⊙ *Daily 8–5.*

Gadsisar Lake. About 1 km southeast of Jaisalmer fort is a freshwater lake (otherwise known as Gadi Sagar, or Tank) built in the 12th century. Surrounded by numerous golden-hue shrines, it's also frequented by a spectacular and diverse avian community. Plan for a camel ride, a picnic, and perhaps a short paddle-boat excursion. Near the shrines is a charming little **Folklore Museum,** built in the style of a traditional home. Filled with memorabilia, it's the perfect place to ground yourself in local history and culture. ⊠ *Museum is behind main bus stand* 🎫 *Rs. 2* ⊙ *Daily 8–7.*

Havelis. Outside the fort, about 1.5 km (1 mi) from the Gopa Chowk entrance, is a string of five connected havelis built by the Patwa brothers in the 1800s. The Patwas were highly influential Jain merchants back when Jaisalmer was an independent principality. The Patwa brothers forbade the repetition of any motifs or designs between their mansions, so each is distinctive.

Two of the five havelis are now owned by the government and open to the public, and you can explore the interiors of the others by offering a small fee (not more than Rs. 50) to the residents. Three havelis are noteworthy in this area: **Patwon Ki Haveli** is arguably the most elaborate and magnificent of all Jaisalmer's havelis. In addition to exquisitely carved pillars and expansive corridors, one of the apartments in this five-story mansion is painted with beautiful murals. The 19th-century **Nathmal Ki Haveli** was carved by two brothers, each working independently on his own half; the design is remarkably harmonious, though you can spot small differences. The interior of the **Salim Singh Ki Haveli,** built in about 1815, is in sad disrepair, but the mansion's exterior is still lovely—it has an overhanging gallery on its top floor. Note the havelis' ventilation systems: the projecting windows and stone screens keep them cool even in the searing summer months.

Ludarva Temples. The founder of Jaisalmer, Rawal Jaisal, lived here before shifting to his new capital. Here you can still see the ruins of his former city. The Jain temple complex is known for its *nag devta* (snake god), a live snake that appears on auspicious days and nights. The snake is worshiped because, as legend goes, it has been protecting this temple for thousands of years. The temples are famous for their graceful architecture and detailed carving. ⊠ *16 km (10 mi) northwest of Jaisalmer.*

Where to Stay & Eat

There are very few decent restaurants in Jaisalmer. The good hotels are your best bet for a savory meal.

$$$$ ✗ **Trio.** Serving Indian food and some Continental dishes, this rooftop restaurant is an old favorite with travelers. ✉ *Near Amar Sagar Gate, Mandir Palace, Gandhi Chowk* ☎ *2992/252–733* 🖃 *MC, V.*

¢ ✗ **8 July Restaurant.** Run by an eccentric Indo-Australian, this restaurant serves simple snacks, pizzas, vegetable dishes, and wonderful coffee milk shakes throughout the day. It also stocks marmite and baked beans all the way from Australia! The restaurant is just inside the fort, up a staircase. It has a breathtaking view of Jaisalmer and is open for all three meals. ✉ *Fort* ☎ *2992/252–814* 🖃 *No credit cards* ☉ *Closed May and June.*

★ **$$$** 🏨 **Fort Rajwada.** The most luxurious hotel in all of Jaisalmer blends French interior design with historic Marwari touches. The entranceway once belonged to a 16th century haveli from the fort. Standard rooms are Western, with contemporary furnishings; suites are far more extravagant, with frescoes and antique beds with pure silver bedposts. The restaurant, Sonal, is by far the best in Jaisalmer. It has a good but expensive buffet, and also serves Indian, Chinese, and Continental food à la carte. ✉ *No. 1 Hotel Complex, Jodhpur-Barmer Link Rd., 345001* ☎ *2992/253–233* 🖶 *2992/253–733* ⊕ *www.fortrajwada.com* 🛏 *65 rooms, 4 suites* △ *Restaurant, coffee shop, cable TV, pool, hair salon, ayurvedic massage, massage, billiards, bar, laundry service, business services, camel safari, desert camps, travel services* 🍽 *EP.*

$$$ 🏨 **Gorbandh Palace.** Built of golden sandstone, this fairly new and popular hotel is spacious and elegant. Rooms are arranged in haveli-style blocks around a series of small interior courtyards with skylights and fountains. Interiors are Western-style, with some Rajasthani touches and large, lovely windows. This expansive retreat is frequented by foreign tour groups in search of a respite from the city center. The palace's pool is the deepest in Jaisalmer. ✉ *1 Tourist Complex, Sam Rd., 345001* ☎ *2992/253–801 to 7* 🖶 *2992/253–811* ⊕ *www.hrhindia.com* 🛏 *64 rooms, 3 suites* △ *Restaurant, cable TV, pool, bar, travel services* 🖃 *AE, MC, V* 🍽 *EP.*

$$$ 🏨 **Rawalkot.** The Taj group is renovating this cozy hotel on the edge of town, with a great view of the fort. Small sandstone rooms, tasteful old-style furniture, pebbled courtyards, and stained-glass windows lend this hotel somewhat more character than most of the other modern hotels in Jaisalmer. ✉ *Jodhpur Rd., 345001* ☎ *2992/252–638, 2992/251–874, or 2992/254–610* 🖶 *2992/250–444* ⊕ *www.tajhotels.com* 🛏 *31 rooms* △ *Restaurant, cable TV, pool, health club, massage, bar, laundry service, desert safaris* 🖃 *AE, MC, V* 🍽 *EP.*

$$–$$$ 🏨 **Jawahar Niwas Palace.** An elegant sandstone palace to the west of the fort, this is an actual palace, built in 1899, and has been converted into a Heritage Hotel. Still owned by the Maharaja of Jaisalmer, the palace has large rooms with old-style furniture and views of the fort. The restaurant serves multicuisine food. There's no bar, but beer is served. ✉ *1 Bada Bagh Rd., 345001* ☎ *2992/252–208 or 2992/252–288* 🖶 *2992/250–175* 🛏 *22 rooms* △ *Restaurant, pool, health club, massage, croquet, horseback riding, camel safaris, jeep safaris, laundry service* 🖃 *AE, MC, V* 🍽 *EP.*

$$–$$$ 🏨 **Rang Mahal.** This mid-level sandstone complex has an austere interior. Frescoes decorate some of the walls, many of which are otherwise whitewashed. Standard rooms are spacious and furnished with Western amenities—but include Rajasthani bedframes. There are occasional pleasant surprises, such as a traditional puppet hanging on the bathroom wall. Definitely get a room with a balcony and a fort view, and take a dip in the pool—it's the largest in Jaisalmer. ⊠ *5 Hotel Complex, Sam Rd., 345001* ☎ *2992/250–907 to 09* 🖷 *2992/251–305* ⊕ *www. hotelrangmahal.com* 🛏 *49 rooms* 🖒 *Restaurant, coffee shop, cable TV, pool, massage, bar, laundry service,camel safaris, jeep safaris, travel service* ▤ *AE, MC, V* ○ *EP.*

$$ 🏨 **Heritage Inn.** Not to be confused with a Heritage Hotel, this inn was constructed in 1990 and has a functional, subdued interior. Accommodations are in bungalows dotted around the garden. Beds are set into depressions in the floor, walls are of rustic stone, and the bathrooms lack tubs. Ask for a suite: they're more plush and are not much more expensive than standard rooms. There's a tandoori barbecue in the garden, where you can eat outdoors, and Rajasthani folk dance in the evenings. The hotel is about 3 km (2 mi) from the town center. ⊠ *4 Hotel Complex, Sam Rd., 345001* ☎ *2992/252–769 or 2992/250–901 to 05* 🖷 *2992/251–638* 🛏 *49 rooms, 6 suites* 🖒 *Restaurant, coffee shop, cable TV, massage, bar, laundry service, meeting room, travel services* ▤ *AE, DC, MC, V* ○ *EP.*

$$ 🏨 **Himmatgarh Palace.** Just opposite the royal cenotaphs, this hotel is about 1 km from the city, but it offers one of the best views in town, especially at sunset. It also sponsors performances of folk dance and music. The standard rooms are modern and comfortable, but the small, circular *burj* (tower) rooms are far more charming, with marble beds and lights concealed in the nooks of the stone walls. Food is mediocre; you'd do well to dine elsewhere. ⊠ *1 Ramgarh Rd., 345001* ☎ *2992/252–002 Ext. 4* 🖷 *2992/252–005* 🛏 *40 rooms* 🖒 *Restaurant, cable TV, pool, bar, camel safaris, horse safaris, travel services* ▤ *AE, MC, V* ○ *EP.*

$$ 🏨 **Narayan Niwas Palace.** This carved-stone palace was once a caravansary, and its interior courtyard still feels like an oasis for caravans traveling through the area. Now a Heritage Hotel, it has plain modern rooms, expansive lawns, a well-stocked bar, and a friendly staff. Rooms are furnished with carved wooden furniture from the craft village of Barmer, and sandstone beds—stone frames filled with sand and covered with a sheet to give you the feel of sleeping in the desert. 🖅 *Reserve through Q6/7 Qutb Enclave, DLF, Phase 2 Gurgaon, New Delhi 110048* ⊠ *Near Malka Prol in Jaisalmer, 345001* ☎ *124/256–2047 reservations* 🖷 *2992/ 252–101 or 11/256–2048, 94141-49427 mobile* ⊕ *www.narayanniwas. com* 🛏 *43 rooms, 8 suites* 🖒 *Restaurant, cable TV, pool, hair salon, massage, sauna, bar, camel safaris, jeep safaris* ▤ *MC, V* ○ *EP.*

Camel Safaris

Note that safari prices vary dramatically depending on the itinerary and the level of tourist crush. Your hotel should also be able to book or arrange safaris for you—but make sure you check exactly what you're going to get for the price asked. Camel safaris are slow; if you're pressed for time, try combining them with jeep travel. One option is contact the Rajasthan Tourism Development Corporation in the Hotel Moomal (☎ 2992/252–392), or the Indian Tourism Development Cor-

MUZZLES IN THE AIR

T'S NOT UNCOMMON to see a single-humped camel drawing a cart on a dusty highway or through traffic in crowded Jaipur. These awkwardly assembled but delightful animals are an indispensable part of the local landscape—not to mention the local economy—and you'll see them wherever you go in the state, even in the southeastern forested areas. Apart from pulling loads and carrying tourists on desert safaris, camels are also highly valued by locals for their milk, meat, hair, leather, and even their droppings (used for manure).

But camels are best seen against their natural backdrop, the shifting dunes of the great Thar desert that covers the northwestern part of the state and extends into Pakistan. Here you can see caravans of these creatures crossing the sands, sidestepping the odd shrub with an elegance that indicates they're on home ground. Left to themselves, these great, gangling beasts merge beautifully into the desert, their sand- or tan-color coats the perfect camouflage when seen from a distance. Camel owners, however, have different ideas on the subject and dress their animals in the bright colors that are so much a part of the overall canvas of Rajasthan. Red, green, and gold saddle covers and tasseled bridles are all signs of the well-dressed camel. When Rajasthanis and their camels get together at one of the many camel fairs in the state, the result has to be seen to be believed—a riot of colorful finery, wandering folk singers and musicians, merrymaking villagers, and preening, belching camels.

Once you've spent a little time in Rajasthan, you'll start to tell the difference between different breeds of camels and what they're used for. The strong, muscular Bikaneri breed is a good draught camel, while the slender Jaisalmeri camel is an excellent racing breed. The latter breed is used in the Indian cavalry, and a camel corps is used by India's border security force. Whether from Bikaner or Jaisalmer, or from any of the other camel-breeding areas in Mewar, Marwar, and Shekhavati, Rajasthani camels all have one thing in common—their facial expressions are winningly ridiculous. Muzzles raised high in the air and lips curled in disdain, they observe the world with a sceptical eye. It's almost as if they know exactly how important and ecofriendly they are, unlike mere cattle, for instance. And that's fortunate, because India has the world's third-largest population of camels—one and a half million of them!

poration at the Dhola Maru hotel (☎ 2992/252–863), for reservations. **Royal Safaris** (✉ Gandhi Chowk ☎ 2992/252–538) is the best agent around, tailoring trips to nearby villages or overnight sojourns in the desert. **Sahara Travels** (✉ Fort Gate ☎ 2992/252–609) is a reliable agent for camel safaris.

Shopping

Jaislamer is famous for its mirror work, embroidery, and woolen shawls. Local artisans also make attractive, good-quality wooden boxes, silver jewelry, and curios. The main shopping areas are **Sadar Bazaar, Sonaron Ka Bas, Manak Chowk,** and **Pansari Bazaar,** all within the walled city, near the fort and temple areas. Sonaron Ka Bas, in particular, has exquisite silver jewelry. Avoid solicitors dispensing advice, take time to browse carefully, and bargain.

Damoder Handicraft Emporium (⊠ Fort, near Rang Prol) has an excellent selection of local handicrafts, especially old textiles.

Khadi Graamudyog (⊠ Dhibba Para, near Fort, in the walled city) has *khadi* (hand-spun cotton) shawls, Nehru jackets, scarves, and rugs. The government emporium **Rajasthali** (⊠ Gandhi Chowk) has fair prices and some good shopping (though you can't bargain here). Coming here is also a good way to gauge the prices of other stores.

Sam Sand Dunes

★ ㉙ *42 km (26 mi) west of Jaisalmer.*

No trip to Jaisalmer is complete without a visit to Sam Sand Dunes, a photographer's feast. Although the dunes have become somewhat toruisty in recent years, the ripples of these wind-shaped dunes still create fantastic mirages, and it's still a magical place to be. Take a camel safari to the dunes, if you can cope with the heat and the time it takes to get here (all day). Alternatively, look for "parked" camels a few kilometers before you reach Sam, and take a short ride to the dunes. Expect some amount of heckling from persistent camel owners and girls offering to dance or sing for you, but don't let it put you off staying for the sunset, which is often spectacular. A peculiar sort of peace descends on the dunes in the late evening, when the icy cold desert wind begins to blow, and this is the most enjoyable part of the dunes experience.

An alternative to crowded Sam is the more remote village of **Khuri,** 40 km (25 mi) southwest of Jaisalmer, to which fewer tourists find their way. This is closer to the real thing, and you'll sense some the isolation of life in a desert village.

Desert National Park

㉚ *45 km (28 mi) southwest of Jaisalmer.*

The desert birds here include everything from birds of prey, such as vultures and desert hawks, to sandgrouses, doves, shrikes, bee eaters, and warblers. The rarest, most remarkable bird is the great Indian bustard, a large, majestic crane said to be found only in the Thar Desert. It's not a good idea to visit in summer; the heat is unbearable.

RAJASTHAN A TO Z

To research prices, get advice from other travelers, and book travel arrangements, visit www.fodors.com.

AIR TRAVEL

There are domestic airports in Jaipur, Jodhpur, and Udaipur. Although there's an airport in Jaisalmer, civilian flights no longer operate for security reasons. Indian Airlines flies among the three and connects Rajasthan with Delhi, Bombay, and Aurangabad. Ask your travel agent about service on private airlines and remember that flights to and within Rajasthan fill up—reserve well in advance. The Udaipur–Jodhpur sector is particularly difficult as there's no rail connection between the two cities. Private carriers such as Jet Airways and Sahara offer some connections in Rajasthan, including daily flights from Delhi to Jaipur, Udaipur, and Jodhpur.

Air India, Air France, Air Alitalia, British Airways, KLM, and Lufthansa have offices in Jaipur.

CARRIERS ▪ Indian Carriers **Air India** ✉ M. I. Rd., Jaipur ☎ 141/236-8569 or 141/236-8047. **Indian Airlines** ☎ 141 in Delhi, 141/274-3500 in Jaipur ✉ Nehru Place, Tonk Rd., Jaipur ✉ Circuit House Rd., Jodhpur ☎ 291/251-0757 ✉ LIC Bldg., Delhi Gate, Udaipur ☎ 294/241-0999. **Jet Airways** ✉ 13 Community Center, Yusuf Sarai, Delhi ☎ 11/685-3700 ✉ M. I. Rd., Jaipur ☎ 141/236-0450 ✉ Osho Apartments, Residency Rd., Jodhpur ☎ 291/510-3333 ✉ Blue Circle Business Center, Madhuvan, Udaipur ☎ 294/256-1105. **Sahara India Airlines** ✉ 4g-31-32 Ansal Chamber, Camal Place, Delhi ☎ 11/573-7744 ✉ Shalimar Complex, M. I. Rd., Jaipur ☎ 141/237-7637.
▪ International Carriers **Air Alitalia** ✉ 1 Park St., M. I. Rd., Jaipur ☎ 141/236-9920. **Air France** ✉ 201B, 2nd flr, Jaipur Tower, M. I. Rd., Jaipur ☎ 141/237-7051 or 141/237-0509. **British Airways** ✉ G2, Usha Plaza, M. I. Rd., Jaipur ☎ 141/237-0374 or 141/236-1065. **KLM** ✉ 211, Jaipur Tower, M. I. Rd., Jaipur ☎ 141/236-0053 or 141/236-7772. **Lufthansa** ✉ 127, Saraogi Mansion, Link Rd., Jaipur ☎ 141/256-2822.

AIRPORTS Jaipur's Sanganer Airport is about 13 km (8 mi) south of town; a taxi into town costs about Rs. 150. Jodhpur's airport is 5 km (3 mi) from the city center; a taxi into town costs about Rs. 150. Udaipur's Dabok Airport is 25 km (16 mi) from the city center; the ride costs about Rs. 250.
▪ Airport Information **Jaipur** ☎ 141/272-1322. **Jodhpur** ☎ 291/251-2617. **Udaipur** ☎ 294/265-5433.

BIKE TRAVEL

Some hotels offer bikes for hire; so do shops around Jagdish Temple in Udaipur. Rates are typically Rs. 30 a day. Biking in Jaipur can be dangerous, but elsewhere it's a convenient way to get around.

The cycle-rickshaw is dying out in Rajasthan, but if you do find one, say in Jaipur, it should cost about Rs. 30 per hour. Make sure you agree on a rate in advance.

BUS TRAVEL

If convenience and a cheap price are more important to you than a comfortable journey, travel by bus—but know in advance that the quality of buses in India varies widely. Some "tourist" buses end up picking up hitchhikers, so by the time you reach your destination, there will be people sitting in the aisles and on the roof. If you don't mind an adventure, or if you have no other choice, by all means take a bus. Otherwise take a train or rent a car and driver.

The best way to get a bus ticket is not from the bus stations, but from any one of the private vendors who amass in major tourist areas. Ask your hotel or a local travel agent for details.

CARS & DRIVERS

It's not cheap, but having a car and driver to yourself is highly efficient if you're short on time. It's also a great help if you're exploring forts and small towns just outside the major cities. Hire a car through your hotel or a recognized travel agent, the latter of which will be cheaper. It should cost about Rs. 10–Rs. 12 per km. If you organize a car directly through the driver, it will be cheaper but check the vehicle and driver out properly the day before you start.

Expect to spend about Rs. 3,200 from Delhi to Jaipur in an air-conditioned car, or about Rs. 2,500 in a non-air-conditioned alternative. Know that because the driver has to return to his port of origin, you pay the round-trip fare even if you're going one-way.

Rajasthan's roads are not in good shape, and local truck and bus drivers can be reckless, particularly at night. In any case, the going is slow—when calculating driving time, plan to cover 40 kph–50 kph (25 mph–31 mph) at best. That said, driving is an excellent way to see the Indian countryside and glimpse village life.

Jaipur is a 5½-hour drive from Delhi on National Highway (NH) 8. This is a congested industrial road with a high accident rate, so prepare for a trying experience.

The Shekhavati region is usually a three- to four-hour drive from Delhi, and in this case driving is much quicker and smoother than train travel. Hire a car and driver through a Delhi travel agency and plan to pay about Rs. 10 per km, with a halt charge (for stopping overnight) of Rs. 200–Rs. 250 per night. A thorough tour of the region should cost about Rs. 1,800.

Roads are rough in and out of Jodhpur, and the going is slow. Don't expect to average more than 40 km (25 mi) per hour. Udaipur is on National Highway 8, which links Bombay and Delhi. Again, expect your road speed to top out at 40 km (25 mi) per hour.

If you have time, you can design a delightful road trip to Jaisalmer by traveling from Delhi through Shekhavati, spending each night in a Heritage Hotel. You can also fly into Jodhpur and continue to Jaisalmer by road.

EMERGENCIES

In India, always be prepared with basic first-aid supplies. For more serious problems, the best hospitals in Rajasthan are in Jaipur and Udaipur, where the country's best and brightest doctors are available for anyone willing to pay for their services. Many hospitals have free ambulance services for the severely ill.

It's best not to deal with the Indian police force, which may be corrupt and ineffectual. You can certainly report a crime to them, but don't expect results unless you have connections. The best way to deal with the police, or with a crime, is through your embassy. However, if you opt to contact the police, dial 100 on any phone to get in touch with the central police switchboard.

At the Maharana Bopal Government Hospital in Udaipur, Dr. H. C. Sharma is the English-speaking superintendent. In Jaipur, Soni Hospital has a 24-hour emergency room and state-of-the-art facilities. The Sawai Mansingh Hospital and the Galundia Clinic are alternatives in Jaipur.
Maharana Bopal Government Hospital ⊠ Near Chetak Circle, Udaipur ☎ 294/252-8811 to 19. **Galundia Clinic** ⊠ M. I. Rd., Jaipur ☎ 141/236-1040. **Soni Hospital** ⊠ 38 J. L. Nehru Marg, near Police Memorial, Jaipur ☎ 141/256-2028. **Sawai Mansingh Hospital** ⊠ Sawai Ram Singh Marg, Jaipur ☎ 141/256-0291.

MAIL & SHIPPING
The cost per-kilogram for registered sea mail is Rs. 300. Air rates are significantly higher. All packages must be sewn closed and sealed with wax; there's usually a shop that specializes in this type of packaging within 100 meters of every post office.
Post Offices Jaipur ⊠ G.P.O on M. I. Rd., near Government Hostel ☎ 141/220-4263. **Jaisalmer** ⊠ G.P.O, Fort Wali Rd. ☎ 2992/253-233. **Jodhpur** ⊠ Head Post Office, Railway Station Rd. ☎ 0291/263-6695. **Udaipur** ⊠ G.P.O at Chetak Circle, under the radio tower ☎ 294/252-8622.

MONEY MATTERS
ATMS ATMs are beginning to emerge in Rajasthan. In major cities it's possible to at least get a credit card advance from a bank (which works for MasterCard and Visa), if not actually withdraw money from a machine. Some machines do take foreign credit cards—but **do not rely on ATMs as a source of cash** in Rajasthan. The Bank of Baroda in Jaisalmer offers credit card advances weekdays 10–2 and Saturday 10:30–11:30. Most Bank of Baroda's are open 9–1 and 2–3:45.
Cash Machines Citibank ⊠ M. I. Rd., near G.P.O., Jaipur ☎ 141/220-4263. **UTI Bank** ⊠ Ajmer Rd., Jaipur ☎ 141/ 237-5400 or 141/237-5600. **Bank of Baroda** ⊠ At Amarsagar Gate, Jaisalmer ☎ 2992/252-402. **Bank of Baroda** ⊠ Sojati Gate, Jodhpur ☎ 291/263-6613 or 291/263-6539. **HDFC Bank** ⊠ Chetak Circle, behind Chetak Cinema, Udaipur ☎ 294/242-6022.

CREDIT CARDS Most major businesses accept Visa or MasterCard, but cash is preferred. More establishments take American Express than used to be the case, but most restaurants and hotels (even upscale ones) do not take Diners Club.

CURRENCY EXCHANGE Most upscale hotels will change currency for their guests. You can also change money at the State Bank of India. Banks and businesses associated with Western Union are your best bet.
Exchange Services State Bank of India ⊠ Tilak Marg, C-Scheme, Jaipur ☎ 141/238-0421 ⊠ High Court Rd., Jodhpur ☎ 291/245-090 or 291/244-169 ⊠ Hospital Rd., Udaipur ☎ 294/252-8857.

TAXIS & AUTO-RICKSHAWS

Taxis are unmetered in Jaipur, Jodhpur, and Udaipur, so ask your hotel for the going rate and negotiate with the driver before you set off. For sightseeing within Jaipur and Jodhpur, hire a cab through your hotel or the RTDC's Tourist Information Center (Visitor Information). Depending on the distance to be covered, a taxi for half a day will cost about Rs. 600, and for a full day about Rs. 1,200.

Auto-rickshaws in Jaipur are metered, but the meters are often ignored. Insist on adhering to the meter *or* set the price in advance. The rate should be no more than Rs. 4.50 per km, with a minimum total of Rs. 10. Auto-rickshaws in Jodhpur and Udaipur are unmetered, so you *must* agree on a price before departing. You can also hire an auto-rickshaw by the hour, for about Rs. 30 per hour. Note that all of these rates go up by about 50% after 11 PM.

TELEPHONES

The "Just Dial information" service number for Jaipur, if you want to look up a number, is 141/274–4447.

TRAIN TRAVEL

Rajasthan is still in the process of converting all its lines to broad gauge, a change that is improving train service but which is also altering routes and schedules. If you want to travel overnight, it's safer and more comfortable to take a train than a bus or car. Trains offer classes of service for all budgets (seats and sleepers, air-conditioning and non-air-conditioned, reserved and unreserved).

The *Shatabdi Express,* an air-conditioned chair-car train, travels every day but Sunday from New Delhi to Jaipur, roughly a five-hour trip. The *Pink City Express* covers the same ground in about six hours. The *Shekhavati Express* runs daily from Delhi to Jaipur, stopping at Jhunjhunu, Mukungarh, and Sikar. The Shekavati Express runs overnight and arrives in Jaipur around 7 AM.

The daily *Bikaner Express* from Delhi passes through Shekhavati en route to Bikaner. The overnight *Superfast Express* leaves New Delhi at 8 PM and reaches Jodhpur at 5:30 AM. A separate *Superfast Express* connects Jodhpur with Jaipur in four hours; contact the Tourist Information Center in either city for more information.

Daily trains connect Udaipur with Jaipur, Ajmer, Chittaurgarh, Ahmedabad, and Delhi; for more information, call the Tourist Reception Center. Trains also run out to Jaisalmer from Jodhpur but they're significantly slower than the road routes.

There are also trains leaving from Jaipur that pass through the wildlife destinations of Ranthambhore and Bharatpur. Of course, for the ultimate rail experience in Rajasthan, you would have to take the famous *Palace on Wheels,* a luxury train that runs across the state, connecting its major sights.

For reliable train information, create an account at ⊕ www.irctc.co.in, a government-run Web site. It's the best way to find out accurate details about rail travel without having to call a travel agent.

🚆 Train Information *Palace on Wheels* Rajasthan Tourism Development Corp., Palace on Wheels Division ✉ Bikaner House, Pandara Rd., near India Gate, New Delhi 110011 ☎ Delhi 11/2338-1884, 888/463-4299 or 609/683-5018 U.S. and international ⊕ www. palaceonwheels.com. **Shatabdi Express** ☎ 131 for inquiries, 135 reservations anywhere in Rajasthan. **Superfast Express** ☎ 291/131, 291/132 in Jodhpur. **Jodhpur Tourist Information Center** ☎ 291/244-010. **Udaipur Tourist Reception Center** ☎ 294/241-535, 294/131 general train information.

TRAVEL AGENTS & TOURS

Alternative Travels organizes terrific stays in artisan villages; trips focusing on music and dance; treks; and bike, jeep, horse, and camel safaris. The Rajasthan Mounted Sports Association gives riding and polo lessons in Jaipur; runs elephant, horse, and camel day trips in Shekhavati; and leads horse and jeep safaris, which may include stays at palaces and forts. Rajasthan Safaris and Treks offers less luxurious but more authentic camel, camel-cart, and jeep safaris out of Bikaner. Food (traditional desert food) and water are provided, but you're on your own when it comes to toilet facilities.

Roop Nivas Safaris leads a Shekhavati Brigade Horse Safari around the colorful painted towns of this region, and offers longer safaris from Nawalgarh to Pushkar or Bikaner. You'll be sleeping in tents with bathroom facilities or at palace and fort hotels. Royal Safari administers treks, camel safaris, and nights in the desert around Bikaner, Jodhpur, and Jaisalmer, as well as visits to traditional villages, craftspeople's homes, little-known fairs, and ashrams.

Karwan Tours in Jaipur and TGS Tours and Travels (an American Express representative) in Jaipur and Udaipur can also help with general travel arrangements, including a hired car with driver to any location in Rajasthan. Le Passage to India offers custom tours as well as reliable cars and drivers in all major Rajasthan towns. Rajasthan Tourism Development Corporation also leads tours.

🚆 **Alternative Travels** ✉ Nawalgarh, Shekhavati ☎ 1594/222-129. **Karwan Tours** ✉ Bissau Palace Hotel, outside Chand Pol, Jaipur ☎ 141/230-8103. **Le Passage to India** ✉ Ganpati Plaza, M. I. Rd., Jaipur ☎ 141/511-5415 or 982/905-1387 ⊕ www. lepassagetoindia.com ✉ Quality Inn, Vishnu Priya, Udaipur ☎ 294/510-0075 ✉ Gandhi Chowk, Jaisalmer ☎ 2992/252-722 ✉ Ghoomar RTDC, High Court Rd., Jodhpur ☎ 291/255-4934. **Meera Tours and Travels** ✉ 14 Badu Ji, Udaipur ☎ 294/241-5249. **Rajasthan Mounted Sports Association** ℗ C/o Dundlod House, Hawa Sarak, Civil Lines, Jaipur ☎ 141/221-1276. **Rajasthan Safaris and Treks** ✉ Birendra Singh Tanwar, Bassai House, Purani Ginani, Bikaner ☎ 151/228-557. **Rajasthan Tours** ✉ Garden Hotel, Udaipur ☎ 294/252-5777 ✉ Airport Rd., Jodhpur ☎ 291/236-942 or 291/262-8265 **Roop Nivas Safaris** ℗ C/o Roop Nivas Palace, Nawalgarh, Jhunjhunu district, Shekhavati ☎ 1594/222-008. **Royal Safari** ℗ Royal Safari, Box 23, Nachna Haveli, Gandhi Chowk, Jaisalmer ☎ 2992/252-538 or 2992/253-202. **TGS Tours and Travels** ✉ Tholia Circle, Mirza Ismail Rd., Jaipur ☎ 141/236-7735 ✉ Chetak Circle, Udaipur ☎ 294/229-661.

VISITOR INFORMATION

Many hotels provide regional information and travel services. In Jaipur, Jodhpur, Udaipur, and Jaisalmer, the Tourist Information Centers of the Rajasthan Tourism Development Corporation provide information, travel assistance, and guides. *Jaipur Vision* and the *Jaipur City Guide,* available in most hotels, are periodicals with visitor information and up-to-date phone numbers.

🎦 Tourist Offices **Government of India Tourist Office** ✉ Hotel Khasa Kothi, Jaipur ☎ 141/ 372-200. **Rajasthan Tourism Development Corporation (RTDC)** ✉ Swagatam Complex, Jaipur ☎ 141/220-2586 ✉ In Jaipur main train station ☎ 141/269-714 ✉ Hotel Ghoomar, High Court Rd., Jodhpur ☎ 291/44010 ✉ Shastri Circle, Udaipur ☎ 294/411-535 ✉ Hotel Moomal, Station Rd., Jaisalmer ☎ 2992/252-392. **Tourist Information Bureau** ✉ Hotel Shiv Shekhawati, Jhunjhunu region, Shekhavati ☎ 15945/32909.

BOMBAY (MUMBAI) & MAHARASHTRA

5

STOP IN FOR TEA AND A SNACK
at Bombay's swanky Sea Lounge ⇨*p.281*

MARVEL AT ANCIENT CAVE PAINTINGS
at Ajanta and Ellora ⇨*p.336*

SOAK UP THE HULLABALOO
of Marine Drive's Chowpatty Beach ⇨*p.277*

HAVE CLOTHING CUSTOM-TAILORED
out of fabric bought at a local cloth market ⇨*p.308*

EAT AN ALPHONSO MANGO
in Rudyard Kipling's neighborhood ⇨*p.274*

By Julie Tomasz
and Vaihayasi
Pande Daniel

RAZZLE-DAZZLE INDIAN-STYLE—that's Bombay, also known as Mumbai, the country's seaside financial capital and trendsetting East–West nexus. India's greatest port and the capital of Maharashtra state, Bombay perches on the Arabian Sea, covering an island separated from the rest of India by a winding creek. A world unto itself, Bombay hits you with an intensity all its own. It is distinctly tropical, with pockets of palm trees and warm, salty breezes—and its culture is contemporary, vibrant, and often aggressive, reflecting both the affluence and poverty of more than 18 million people crowded onto this island. Behind all this, weathered Victorian mansions, some still privately owned, and grand public buildings, many beautifully lit at night, stand as lingering reminders of the British Raj.

Bombay's name was officially changed in 1995 to Mumbai, after Mumba Devi, the patron Hindu goddess of the island's original residents, the Koli fishermen. However, many residents continue to call their city Bombay. It's all rather confusing, but in many ways this is but another chapter in the city's labyrinthine history.

Bombay initially consisted of seven marshy islands—Colaba, Old Woman's Island, Bombay, Mazgaon, Worli, Mahim, and Parel—belonging to the Muslim kings of the Gujarat sultanate. The Muslims passed the parcel to the Portuguese (who occupied much of western India in the 16th and 17th centuries), who in turn passed it in 1661 to England's King Charles II as part of a dowry in his marriage to the Portuguese Princess Catherine de Braganza. The British established a fort and trading post that grew quickly in size and strength.

Soon enough, land reclamation joined the seven small islands into one, grafting a prototype for today's multifarious metropolis. The pride of the British in Bombay, and in their power over western India, is memorialized in the city's most celebrated landmark—the Gateway of India, built to welcome King George V to India in 1911. Ironically, it's near a statue of the young 17th-century Marathi leader, Shivaji.

The Bombay you see today is a city of mind-boggling contrasts: sometimes exciting, sometimes deeply disturbing. As your plane descends toward the runway, usually late at night, your first view of Bombay takes in vast stretches of slums, stacked and piled onto each other like cardboard boxes—only a fleeting glimpse of the staggering poverty that coexists, invariably side by side, with the dazzling wealth flashed in trendy boutiques and deluxe hotels. In the neighborhoods of Churchgate or Nariman Point, Bombay's slick hotel and business centers, a fleet of dark-suited executives may breeze by on its way to a meeting while a naked little girl with matted hair scavenges in the gutter beside them. A fancy international-looking department store is across the road from a group of shacks that a few hundred people call home—one customer in that store may spend more in an hour than all the people living in the shacks earn in a month. A journalist once pointed out that Bombay is a city where the servant walking the pedigreed, handsomely groomed dog has no formal education, but his charge has been to an expensive training school.

India's most cosmopolitan city gives way to Maharashtra's rugged interior, which hides the spectacular Ajanta and Ellora caves, 370 km (229 mi) northeast of Bombay, as well as the lovely hill station of Pune to the southeast. Maharashtra's landscape fuses stark, semiarid mountains and rock formations with lush, green countryside. To see this state, you should really spend the better part of a week here.

If you have 2 days

On your first day, wander around Bombay's **Fort** district, where you'll find the city's museums, galleries, and such trappings of the British Raj as the stone Gateway of India. Spend the next morning at the **Elephanta Caves,** an hour's ferry ride away from the Gateway of India. Although not as spectacular as those at Ajanta and Ellora, these 7th-century cave temples are much more accessible, especially if you have only a little time in the region. Later that afternoon, take a taxi across town to the leafy residential district of **Malabar Hill** and spend some time exploring **Kamala Nehru Park** ⑩, the **Jain Temple** ⑪, **Banganga** ⑫, **Babulnath Temple** ⑬, and Gandhi's former home, **Mani Bhavan** ⑭.

If you have 4 days

Follow the two-day itinerary. On your third day, visit the **Haji Ali Shrine** ⑨, a mosque set on a rocky jetty in the Arabian Sea; then drive north of the city center to the South Indian enclave of **Matunga,** where (every day but Monday) temples, bazaars, and casual restaurants will more than eat up your lunch hour. Drive back to the commercial center of south Bombay and then devote what's left of the afternoon to a walk around the fishing dock and handicraft stalls in **Colaba.** On your fourth day, go shopping—hit the bazaars, craft emporiums, shops, and boutiques in earnest—and if you still have energy by mid- or late-afternoon, take a tour of Bombay's old synagogues.

If you have 7 days

Follow the four-day itinerary, then go to **Pune** for a few days, or head to the **Ajanta and Ellora caves.**

It's important to view Bombay in perspective. Like New York City, Bombay can be considered so different from the rest of India that it could be another country. Bombay operates according to its own rules, and its pulse beats far more quickly than the rest of the country, which views Bombay as the city of opportunity. Bombay tantalizes millions with prospects of wealth and success. Every day, migrants arrive—be they software engineers or laborers—to see if they too can make a life here. Apart from the city's original Maharasthrian population, every Bombayite, from the eunuch (*hijra*) to the taxi driver to the white collar worker, *is*, as hard as it may be to believe, living out his or her dream—in a hovel or a palace. It's true that more often than not, Bombay is a place to build a better life.

For the traveler, Bombay is both disturbingly eye-opening and incredibly exciting. Here in the heady sun and breeze of the Arabian Sea you can feast in fabulous restaurants, bargain in street bazaars, browse in exclusive boutiques, take a horse-drawn ride past stately old Victorian buildings, get lost in the stone carvings of the 7th-century Elephanta Caves, watch the sun rise over the Gateway of India, and stroll at sunset along Marine Drive's endless waterfront promenade.

If you have a few extra days, you'd be well-advised to escape the city and take a trip to the stunning Ajanta and Ellora caves, or east to the town of Pune.

EXPLORING BOMBAY

There's plenty to see in Bombay, but not generally in the form of stationary monuments like those in London, Paris, or even Delhi. The art of experiencing Bombay lies in eating, shopping, and wandering through strikingly different neighborhoods and markets. Consider Bombay a 30-mi-long open-air bazaar.

Churchgate and Nariman Point are the business and hotel centers. Major bank and airline headquarters are clustered in skyscrapers on Nariman Point. The district referred to as Fort—which includes Bombay's hub, Flora Fountain, in a square now called Hutatma Chowk—is the city's commercial heart, its narrow, bustling streets lined with small shops and office buildings, as well as colleges and other educational facilities. Farther north, Kemps Corner is a trendy area with expensive boutiques, exclusive restaurants, and high-price homes. Another upscale residential neighborhood, Malabar Hill, is leafy and breezy, with fine, old stone mansions housing wealthy industrialists and government ministers.

Shopping and people watching are most colorfully combined in Bombay's chaotic bazaar areas, such as Chor Bazaar, Zaveri (Jewelry) Bazaar, and Mahatma Jyotiba Phule (Crawford) Market. More recently, Bombay's suburbs have seen explosive business and residential development, as more and more people move out of the center to escape the soaring real-estate prices and lack of space. Many of the city's newest and trendiest shops and restaurants are now out in the suburbs. A number of travelers opt to stay in Juhu Beach, a popular coastal suburb between Bombay and the airports (about 20 km [12 mi] north of the city center). Alas, Juhu's beaches are unsafe for swimming, and the general look of the place is scruffy and honky-tonk—but staying out here is a good way to observe everyday Indian life outside the shadow of Bombay's skyline. Sunday nights bring families down to the beach for an old-fashioned carnival, complete with small, hand-powered Ferris wheels, and lantern-lit snack stalls hawking sugar cane.

About the Restaurants

Known for its chic restaurants and Western-style pubs, Bombay is a city where you can get not only great meals, but can taste all sorts of cuisines—Continental, Chinese, Italian, Thai, Lebanese, and Mexican. Among Indian food you'll find kababs and tandoori food—meat, bread, and vegetables cooked inside a clay oven. This, often served with Mughlai (a variety of Muslim cuisine) and Punjabi cuisine, is by far the most popular food in town. Authentic South Indian vegetarian food—*dosas* (fried, crêpelike pancakes), *idlis* (steamed rice cakes), *wadas* (also spelled *vadas*; savory fried, and often flavored, dough), and simple, light *thalis* (combination platters)—are a city staple. Gujarati vegetarian thalis—a little oilier—are also popular. You may also encounter some Jain food—not only is the cuisine vegetarian, but it's cooked without root vegetables, such as onions and garlic, because destroying the root of a plant destroys life, and Jainism (a religion in which nonviolence is the main tenet) bans all destruction of life. Seafood from the Konkan coast—from Maharashtra south through Goa all the way to Mangalore, in Karnataka—is the current rage in Bombay. Many restaurants here are pricey by Indian standards, but there are plenty of tasty bargains that will leave your taste buds and your wallet equally satisfied. Many hotels have good restaurants and all-night coffee shops that serve full meals.

The hub of Bombay's dining is the western suburb of Bandra and south Bombay. Bandra (just north of south Bombay) has innumerable small restaurants offering any kind of cuisine—Japanese or Lebanese or great *biryanis* (Indian rice dishes). Menus are diverse and meal prices low. But the geography of Bombay is such that the concentration of hotels is not in Bandra but in the northern suburb of Juhu and in south Bombay. For the adventurous, a food expedition to Bandra, about 45–50 minutes by taxi (outside traffic hours) from south Bombay or Juhu, can be worthwhile. Colaba and its adjoining neighborhoods offer plenty of compelling choices, and it's certainly more convenient, if a little more expensive than Bandra.

It's also important to remember that in Bombay's approximately two-dozen upscale hotels are 24-hour coffee shops that serve simple meals from multicuisine menus in pleasing, but expensive ($20 per head per meal) air-conditioned rooms. Many of these hotels have Chinese, Continental, and Indian food restaurants, too. Some of the food is unremarkable and the stylings mildly repetitive—as they say in Hindi: *uchcha dukan, pheeka pakwan,* the loftier the establishment the more insipid the food. But the meals are hygienic and wholesome, and the service pleasant. The restaurants are comfortable, too; a refreshing break from Bombay's humid, crowded streets or a hot afternoon of sightseeing.

WHAT IT COSTS In Rupees				
$$$$	**$$$**	**$$**	**$**	**¢**
IN BOMBAY				
AT DINNER over 1,000	850–1,000	500–850	200–500	under 200
IN PUNE				
AT DINNER over 500	400–500	300–400	150–300	under 150
SMALL TOWNS OUTSIDE BOMBAY				
AT DINNER over 350	250–350	150–250	100–150	under 100

Restaurant prices are for an entrée plus dal, rice, and a veg/non-veg dish.

About the Hotels

Hotels in Bombay range from the skid-row to the palatial. In Bombay, unlike elsewhere in India, even mid-range hotels can cost a pretty rupee. The Taj and Oberoi chains run several massive lodgings, most of them deluxe; these cater to leisure and business travelers, and movie stars with money to burn. If you reserve with a hotel directly, rather than through a travel agent, ask for a discount. (No matter what, always ask for a discount.)

Bombay's cheaper hotels are often decent, so expect good value for the money. During the monsoon season, from mid-June through late September, these hotels are overrun by large groups of vacationers from various Arab nations, during which time noise levels can be very high—and solo women travelers should probably stay elsewhere.

Unless otherwise indicated, hotels have air-conditioning, room service, doctors on call, and currency exchange, and rooms have private bathrooms and cable television. (There may not always be a phone, but Indians are nuts about TV, so it's rare you won't find one, with cable, in your room.)

WHAT IT COSTS In Rupees					
	$$$$	**$$$**	**$$**	**$**	**¢**
	IN BOMBAY				
FOR 2 PEOPLE	over 11,500	8,500–11,500	5,500–8,500	2,500–5,500	under 2,500
	IN PUNE				
FOR 2 PEOPLE	over 8,000	6,000–8,000	4,000–6,000	2,000–4,000	under 2,000
	IN SMALL TOWNS OUTSIDE BOMBAY				
FOR 2 PEOPLE	over 4,000	3,000–4,000	2,000–3,000	1,000–2,000	under 1,000

Hotel prices are for a standard double room in high season, excluding up to 20% tax.

Timing

Bombay and Maharashtra are best explored between November and February, when the weather is warm but not unbearable and the monsoons are absent. Ajanta and Ellora explode with greenery during and after the monsoon season, if the rains have been good; at Ajanta, a river springs into being at the bottom of the gorge into which the caves are cut. If the rains haven't been good, it can be quite hot.

Fort District & Environs

The most manageable, and probably the most colorful walks in Bombay center on the Fort district. If Bombay is the first stop on your first trip to India, remember that sightseeing here is nothing like touring, say, Europe—the streets are packed, some lack sidewalks, traffic takes many forms, crosswalks are a rarity, and people may stare or call out to you with sales pitches as you pass. Stopping to take a picture can make you feel terribly conspicuous. You'll get used to it soon enough, however, and will quickly learn to revel in the whole *masala* whirlwind.

a good
walk

Numbers in the text correspond to numbers in the margin and on the Bombay map.

Start your walk by exploring the **Mahatma Jyotiba Phule Market** ❶ ☛, commonly known as Crawford Market, and the surrounding lanes. Abdul Rehman Street will take you north into **Zaveri Bazaar** ❷. At all bazaars, be sure to keep your eyes and hands on your wallet. From Crawford or Zaveri you can either head south to the main Fort district or, if you're up for more narrow-lane navigation, detour to **Chor Bazaar** ❸, a bustling old antiques market.

To find Chor Bazaar, walk or cab it (15 minutes by taxi) north from Crawford Market on Mohammed Ali Road, which joins Rahimtulla Road to bring you into South Bombay's main Muslim quarter. After passing the Beg Muhammed School, Mandavi Telephone Exchange, and Mandavi post office on the left, you'll hit Sardar Vallabhbhai Patel Road: turn left and you can enter Chor Bazaar on Mutton Street. When you're almost bazaared out, retrace the route back down to Crawford Market, either on foot or by taxi.

To move south toward the center of the Fort district, follow A. Rehman Street until it becomes Dr. D. Naoroji Road: You are now in the heart of downtown, an area of broader streets and crowded sidewalks. On your right is the imposing, V-shape, early-Gothic–style Municipal Corporation Building, vintage 1893, with Indian motifs and a large dome; on your left is Bombay's chief train station, the huge **Chhatrapati Shivaji Terminus**, also called by its old colonial name, Victoria Terminus. Push your way through the crowds of people and cars to cross the chaotic roundabout; rejoin Dr. D. Naoroji Road on the other side, and continue heading south. After about 15 minutes you'll arrive at the **Flora Fountain** ❹, the true center of Bombay.

Take a right here onto Veer Nariman Road, pass the Central Telegraph office and its open-air book bazaars, and in a few minutes you'll hit K. B. Patil Marg. Turn left, keep heading south, and on your left you'll see the High Court, built in the early-Gothic style in 1878. Farther south on the same street you'll see Bombay University's 260-foot Rajabhai Clocktower, also Victorian Gothic. Turn left onto Mahatma Gandhi Road (also known as M. G. Road) and you'll soon reach a cluster of three major museums. The **Jehangir Art Gallery** ❺ will be on your left. Across the street from Jehangir, in the lane heading behind the music store Rhythm House (which has an excellent selection of music), is the Keneseth Eliyahoo Synagogue. From Mahatma Gandhi Road, hang a left down K. Dubash Marg to the **Prince of Wales Museum** ❻. The **National Gallery of Modern Art** ❼ is across the street. From here, take C. Shivaji Maharaj Marg to the **Gateway of India** ❽, where you can relax among locals at the water's edge.

Right across the square from the Gateway of India is the historic Taj Mahal hotel. Even if you can't afford to stay here, it's a treat just to walk around the lobby and shopping areas (they don't mind) and perhaps have tea and snacks at the Sea Lounge.

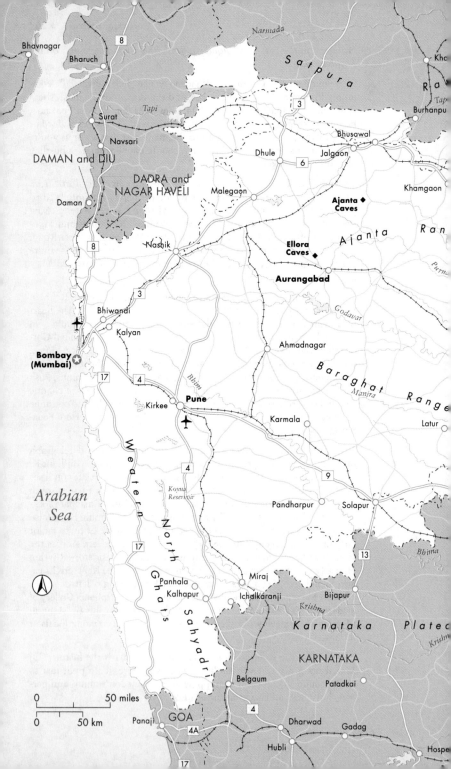

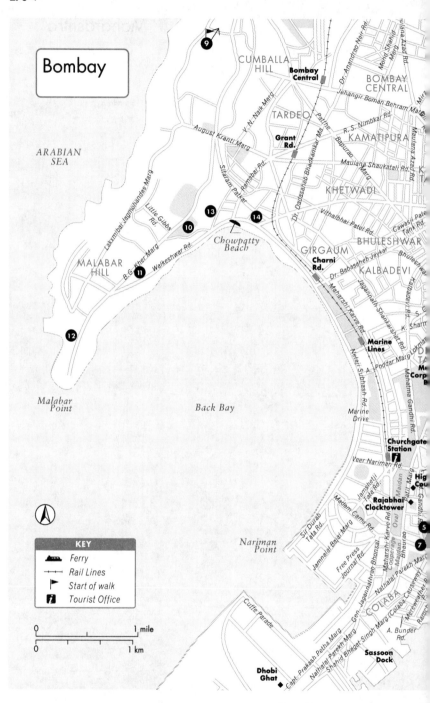

Bombay

*ARABIAN
SEA*

CUMBALLA
HILL

**Bombay
Central**

BOMBAY
CENTRAL

TARDEO

**Grant
Rd.**

KAMATIPURA

August Kranti Marg

KHETWADI

MALABAR
HILL

BHULESHWAR

GIRGAUM

**Charni
Rd.**

KALBADEVI

*Chowpatty
Beach*

Maharshi Karve Rd.

**Marine
Lines**

*Malabar
Point*

Back Bay

*Marine
Drive*

**Churchgate
Station**

Veer Nariman Rd.

**Hig
Cou**

**Rajabhai
Clocktower**

*Nariman
Point*

COLABA

KEY

⛴ *Ferry*
┼ *Rail Lines*
🚩 *Start of walk*
ℹ️ *Tourist Office*

0 _____ 1 mile
0 _____ 1 km

Cuffe Parade

**Dhobi
Ghat** ◆

**Sassoon
Dock**

*A. Bunder
Rd.*

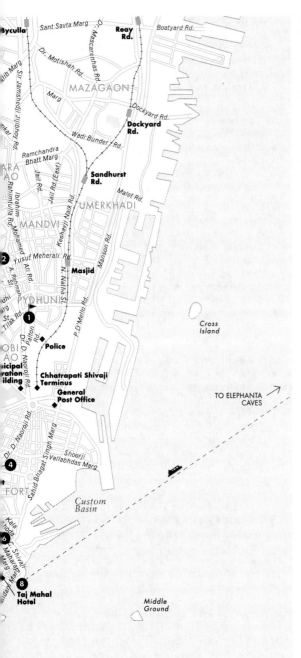

Babulnath Temple 13

Banganga 12

Chor Bazaar 3

Flora Fountain 4

Gateway of India 8

Haji Ali Shrine 9

Jain Temple 11

Jehangir Art
Gallery 5

Kamala Nehru
Park .10

Mahatma Jyotiba
Phule Market 1

Mani Bhavan 14

National Gallery of
Modern Art 7

Prince of Wales
Museum 6

Zaveri Bazaar 2

TIMING This walk takes a full day: the going is slow and the bazaars eat up time in a stealthy manner. You'll probably want to spend close to an hour at both the Prince of Wales Museum and the Jehangir Art Gallery. Note that Crawford Market is closed Sunday, the Prince of Wales Museum is closed Monday, and Chor Bazaar shuts down on Friday. Early morning tends to be less humid, so you may want to set off then.

What to See

Chhatrapati Shivaji Terminus. Built by the British in 1888, this is one of Bombay's busiest train stations, overflowing at rush hour with enormous, surging, scurrying crowds. Formerly called Victoria Terminus, and bearing a hefty statue of Queen Victoria on its imposing dome, the haughty structure combines Indian and Victorian–Gothic architecture for an Eastern version of London's St. Pancras station. ⊠ *D. Naoroji Rd.*

❸ **Chor Bazaar** (Thieves' Bazaar). This narrow thoroughfare is lined with stores crammed with antiques and general bric-a-brac-clocks, old phonographs, brassware, glassware, and statues. Over the years the value of much of this stock has dwindled, but there's still a chance that you'll find some unusual, memorable piece. Haggle. In the same lane a number of shops are engaged in the profitable business of constructing new furniture that looks old; many will openly tell you as much. Some shops do stock genuine antique furniture from old Parsi homes. ⊠ *Mutton St., off Sardar Vallabhbhai Patel Rd., off Mohammed Ali Rd., Mandvi ⊙ Sat.–Thurs. 11–7.*

❹ **Flora Fountain.** Standing tall in the middle of a major five-way intersection, this fountain marks the heart of Bombay's Fort district. The ornately sculpted stone fountain was created as a memorial to one of Bombay's early governors, Sir Bartle Frere, who was responsible for urban planning in the 1860s. The square in which it stands is called Hutatma Chowk (Martyr's Square) in honor of those who died in the violence surrounding the establishment of Maharashtra in the 1960s (the Bombay Presidency was split into the states of Maharashtra and Gujarat). It's a hot spot for rallies, political and otherwise. ⊠ *M. G. Rd., at Veer Nariman Rd., Fort.*

⎛ need a ⎞
⎝ break? ⎠ **Tea Center** (⊠ Resham Bhavan, Veer Nariman Rd., Churchgate 🕾 22/2204–1699 ⊙ daily 8 PM–11 PM) is a tearoom with a quaint, old-style vibe, and a great place to cool down and freshen up. Waiters have turban-cummerbund getups and a pianist plays light music from 3 PM onward. You can order tea—Bombay *chai*, Darjeeling, Nilgiri, or iced tea—and snacks and pastries. Alternatively, you can have a fixed lunch or order á la carte.

★ ❽ **Gateway of India.** Bombay's signature landmark, this elegant 26 meter (85 feet) stone archway was hastily erected as a symbol of welcome to Queen Mary and King George V of England when they paid a visit to India in 1911. In the years following, artisans added decorative carvings and lovely *jharoka* work (window carvings), finishing in 1923. Less

DAWN AT THE DOCKS IN COLABA

BOMBAY'S BUDGET-TOURIST DISTRICT is often packed with vacationing Arabs in the rainy season and Western backpackers in the winter. Cheap boarding houses, handicraft stalls, and eating places stand cheek-by-jowl on the southern tip of Bombay's peninsula.

One of Colaba's most interesting sights is its fishing dock, built back in 1875. Extraordinarily smelly, mucky, and noisy, *Sassoon Dock*, on Shahid Bhagat Singh Marg, near the Colaba Bus Station, must be seen at dawn, when most of Bombay's seafood catch is unloaded. Piles of pink prawns are sorted, and grisly looking fish are topped and tailed. The odor is severe, but you won't see this kind of chaos and five-sensory color anywhere else. Out toward the ocean, Bombay duck, actually a fish unique to this coastline, dries on rack after rack, in the sun.

Walk north for about 10 minutes toward Navy Nagar (the naval cantonment area) on Shahid Bhagat Singh Marg. Just beyond Colaba Post Office is the old *Afghan Memorial Church of St. John the Baptist*. Rather out of place in the heart of Colaba, this somewhat imposing structure honors British soldiers lost in the Afghan wars of the late 19th century. The plaques inside say things like, "In the memory of Captain Conville Warneford of the Bombay Political Dept and the Gurkha Rifles who was born 13th October 1871 and was treacherously murdered by an Arab at Amrija in the Aden hinterland. . . ." If the church doors are closed look for the caretaker, who lives at the side of the church, in the church enclosure, and ask him to show you the church; give him a small something for his trouble.

From the church, retrace your steps on Shahid Bhagat Singh as far as the fork outside Colaba Post Office; on foot, take Wodehouse Road up to Panday Road, then turn left there. You'll see Capt. Prakash Petha Marg—take another left there, walk for 5 minutes (past the Taj President hotel), and just beyond the Colaba Woods park on your right on Cuffe Parade is a *Dhobi Ghat*, behind a facade of huts. (If you get lost, ask a local for help.) Another fascinating open-air sight, the ghat consists of a square half-kilometer of cement stalls where dhobis, or washermen, pound their garments to what seems like pulp to get them threadbare-clean. Rows of racks flutter with drying laundry, and in little huts nearby the incorrigibly dirty stuff is boiled with caustic soda.

than 25 years later, the last British troops departed India through the same ceremonial arch. The monument serves as a launching point for boats going to Elephanta Island; this is also where the *Queen Elizabeth 2* and other luxury liners dock on their cruises. The majestic Taj Mahal hotel, built before the Gateway of India, in 1903, now stands just behind it. ✉ *Peninsula at end of C. Shivaji Maharaj Marg, Apollo Bunder.*

need a break? **Kalash Parbat Hindu Hotel** (✉ Sheela Mahal, 1 Pasta La., off Colaba Causeway, Colaba ☎ 22/2287–4823 or 22/2284–1972 ⊙ daily lunch and dinner). For decades Bombayites have come to this seedy "hotel" (there's no actual hotel here) to indulge their craving for Indian-style vegetarian junk food—*chana bhatura* (giant *puris,* or puffed bread, served with spicy chick-pea curry), *samosas* (stuffed vegetable turnovers), *sev puri, ragda pattice, pani puri,* and other intricate snack food and *kulfi* (Indian-style ice cream). The place could be a tad cleaner, but the piping hot, tasty food makes it worth it. But go slow, the uninitiated may find the oily food difficult to digest.

❺ Jehangir Art Gallery. Bombay's chief contemporary-art gallery hosts changing exhibits of well-known Indian artists. Some of the work is lovely, and all of it is interesting for its cultural perspective. There's plenty of art outside as well—the plaza in front of the building is full of artists selling their works and their talents for commission assignments. ✉ *M. G. Rd., Kala Ghoda, Fort* ☎ *22/2284–3989* ✎ *Free* ⊙ *Daily 11–7.*

need a break? **Cafe Samovar** (✉ M. G. Rd., Kala Ghoda, Fort ☎ 22/284–8000 ⊙ Mon.–Sat. 10–7), next to a bit of courtyard greenery in the Jehangir Art Gallery, is a popular, arty place for a quick snack or a glass of lime juice.

★ ☞ ❶ Mahatma Jyotiba Phule Market. Also known by its former name, Crawford Market, this building was designed in the 1860s by John Lockwood Kipling, father of Rudyard—who was born in this very neighborhood. Check out the stone relief depicting workers on the outside; the market's stone flooring supposedly came from Caithness. Come here early one morning for the most colorful walk through Bombay's fresh-produce emporium, and if it's late spring or early summer, treat yourself to a delicious Alphonso mango, a food fit for the gods. The meat section can be a bit hair-raising. Across the street from the market's main entrance on the west, spread across a trio of lanes, is the popular bazaar area Lohar Chawl, where the selection ranges from plastic flowers to refrigerators. Farther up the middle lane, Sheikh Memon Street, is the chaotic **Mangaldas Market** (closed Sunday), a covered, wholesale cloth market with a tremendous variety of fabrics at hundreds of indoor stalls. ✉ *D. Naoroji Rd., at L. Tilak Rd., Crawford Market* ⊙ *Mon.–Sat. 11:30–8.*

need a break? **Rajdhani** (✉ Sheikh Memon St., Lohar Chawl, near Crawford Market, Fort ☎ 22/2342–6919 ⊙ daily 11:30–3:30 and 7–10:15; no dinner Sun.) serves up hot Gujarati and Rajasthani *thalis* (combination platters; Rs. 125) in spartan, but clean surroundings just a tiny bit north of Crawford Market. Eat sparingly; the restaurant uses a lot of *ghee* (clarified butter) in its preparations.

❼ National Gallery of Modern Art. This museum is housed in a circular building resembling New York's Guggenheim Museum. Modern Indian art

INDIAN JEWS & THEIR SYNAGOGUES

JEWS WERE ONCE A PROMINENT STREAM IN BOMBAY'S POPULATION. *There might have been three streams of Indian Jews—Maharashtrian (Bene Israel) Jews, Cochini Jews, and Baghdadi Jews. The Bene Israel Jews, considered by some to be the Lost Tribe of Israel, supposedly arrived (shipwrecked) in India in the early centuries of the Common Era (some say as far back as 500 BC), and settled along the Konkan coast south of Bombay. The Cochini Jews, who were spice traders, arrived in approximately AD 1,000 and settled in Kerala, in the town of Cochin on the Malabar Coast; less than 20 Jews are left in Cochin. Jewish immigration began in earnest in India, however, in the 1800s. By the 1900s there may have been up to 50,000 Jews in India. These days there are about 5,000 left—most migrated to Israel in the 1950s. Baghdadi Jews, from Iraq and Syria, settled mainly in Bombay and Calcutta; there's still a small but active population of Iraqi Jews in Bombay. David Sassoon, a Bombayite who built synagogues, hospitals, and libraries, is the best-known Iraqi Jew.*

Left behind, from the history of Jewish communities in Bombay, is an assortment of synagogues. Hire a car or hail a taxi for this two- to three-hour tour of four synagogues (closed daily from 1 to 4).

The old Baghdadi synagogue at the southern edge of Fort is the attractive and ornate, sky-blue **Keneseth Eliyahoo Synagogue** *(⊠ V.B. Gandhi Rd., Kala Ghoda, Fort ☎ 22/2283–1502), across from Jehangir Art Gallery and behind Rhythm House. Built in 1884, it has compelling stained-glass windows and intricately constructed second-floor balconies. You can visit daily between 10 and 6:30, and are welcome for Sabbath prayers between 6:30 and 7:30 on Friday.*

North of Crawford Market via P. D'Mello Road, past Carnac Bunder and right next to the Masjid train station), in the heart of the wholesale district, is the hard-to-find **Shaare Rahamim** *(Gate of Mercy; ⊠ 254 Samuel St., Mandvi), built in 1796. This sleepy, mildly dilapidated synagogue seems totally out of place in its bustling surroundings. The synagogue is still in use, and you're free to peek inside.*

At Jacob Circle, a 20-minute taxi ride north of Shaare Rahamim, is **Tiphaereth Israel Synagogue** *(⊠ Khare Rd., past Chinchpokli station, near Shirin Talkies, Mahalaxmi), home of the Bene Israel Jews—a still-thriving but tiny Maharashtrian Jewish community. This small, shiny synagogue is quite charming; unlike Shaare Rahamin, it seems well loved and well maintained. Have a chat with the caretaker, if he's around to take you inside.*

The caretaker of Tiphaereth Israel Synagogue can also guide you a few streets away to the **Magen Hassidim Synagogue,** *(⊠ Morland Rd.–Maulana Azad Rd., near Fancy Market and Jula Maidan, Byculla ☎ 22/2309-2493). This Bene Israel shrine is in the largely Muslim area of Madanpura. Although the communities of Baghdadi and Cochini Jews have dwindled to just a few thousand, the Bene Israel community continues to modestly prosper. The congregation and caretakers at this well-attended shrine (with about 800 members) can lend insight into the future of this community: Magen Hassidim is the face of India's modern Jews, the ones who generally don't plan to migrate to Israel and who are now part of the nation's mainstream. This synagogue seems to possess a vigor that's absent at some of the other synagogues.*

is displayed in an uncrowded, easy manner on four floors. It's not as spectacular as the Prince of Wales Museum across the street, but it's quiet, and worth a visit, especially if you're an art lover. ☒ *M. G. Rd., near Regal Cinema, Fort* ☎ *22/2285–2457 or 22/2288–1790* 🖃 *Rs. 5* ⊙ *Tues.–Sun. 11–6:45.*

⑥ Prince of Wales Museum. Topped with Moorish domes, Bombay's finest Victorian building and principal museum was completed in 1911 and named for King George V, who laid the cornerstone in 1905. It's divided into three sections: art, archaeology, and natural history. The picture gallery contains scores of Mogul and Rajput miniature paintings, works by European and contemporary Indian artists, and copies of magnificent cave temple paintings from Ajanta. ☒ *M. G. Rd., Fort* ☎ *22/2284–4519 or 22/2284–4484* 🖃 *Rs. 300* ⊙ *Tues.–Sun. 10–6.*

❷ Zaveri Bazaar. Zaveri and Dagina bazaars, a little beyond Fort in the neighborhood of Kalbadevi, are Bombay's crowded, 100-year-old jewelry markets, where the shops are filled with fabulous gold and silver in every conceivable design. At the end of Zaveri Bazaar is the **Mumbadevi Temple,** a noisy, busy structure that houses the mouthless but powerful patron goddess for which Mumbai is named. In front of the temple is the *khara kuan,* or saltwater well, actually an age-old water station funded by the jewelry bazaar. Free water is doled out to the thirsty from giant copper drums. One of the lanes leading off Zaveri Bazaar is called Khao Galli (literally "Eat Lane"), as its endless food stalls feed most of the bazaar workers daily. ☒ *Sheikh Memon St., a few blocks northwest of Crawford Market, a 10-min walk, Kalbadevi* ⊙ *Mon.–Sat. 11–7.*

Malabar Hill & Environs

Several of the attractions in this upscale residential area have stunning views of the city across Back Bay.

a good tour

After checking the tides, take a taxi to the **Haji Ali Shrine** ❾ ▶, passing **Chowpatty Beach & Marine Drive** en route. At Haji Ali, have your taxi wait for you while you walk out on the jetty; then drive to **Kamala Nehru Park** ❿, take some air, enjoy the views, and walk to the **Jain Temple** ⓫. From here you can either walk or take a taxi along Walkeshwar Road to the **Banganga** ⓬ area. Finally, have your taxi take you to **Babulnath Temple** ⓭ and Gandhi's former home, **Mani Bhavan** ⓮. If you're interested in South Indian culture and have some extra time, drive out to **Matunga.**

TIMING   This tour takes about two hours. The journey by taxi from Mani Bhavan to to suburb of Matunga will take you half an hour—be sure to avoid rush hour. Spend half an hour seeing Matunga, or longer if you pop in for a dosa break at any of the restaurants we have suggested in Matunga.

What to See

⓭ Babulnath Temple. To get the flavor of a large, traditional Indian temple, a visit to the Babulnath Temple is a must. Climbing the few hundred steps to reach the temple will reward you with a panorama of south Bombay. The first Babulnath Temple was apparently built by Raja Bhimdev in the 13th century and named after the *babul* trees that forested this area. The architecture of this imposing shrine, one of Bombay's most important, is not remarkable, but it's interesting to watch the melée of worshippers coming, going, and milling about. Outside are rows of flower sellers hawking a temple-visitation kit—coconut plus flowers plus rock sugar—and a cluster of vendors concocting sweetmeats in *karhais* (large woks) in the open air. Temple authorities are sometimes prickly about allowing foreigners into its innermost areas, but it's worth a try. ⊠ *Babulnath Rd.*

★ ⑫ **Banganga.** This undervisited temple complex in the Malabar Hill area is considered one of the city's holiest sites. It's also the oldest surviving structure in Bombay. The small, sometimes dilapidated temples are built around a holy pool of water and surrounded by the ever-encroaching houses of Bombay's newer residents. Cows and people mingle freely here, as do bathers who come to sample the "healing powers" of the water. ⊠ *At the end of Walkeshwar Rd., take the lane just beyond Ghanshyamdas Sitaram Poddar Chowk, Walkeshwar* ⊠ *Free.*

Fodor'sChoice **Chowpatty Beach & Marine Drive.** It's not much of a beach in the resort sense,
★ but Chowpatty and the rest of Bombay's long, spectacular, perfectly curved Marine Drive capture at once the mammoth, cheeky, beautiful seaside beast that is Bombay. Chowpatty is a taste of the Bombay bazaar and *mela* (festival, or hullabaloo) rolled into one. A hundred species of salesmen throng the beach in the evening, especially Sunday, selling everything from glow-in-the-dark yo-yos and animal-shape balloons to rat poison. Men stand by with bathroom scales, offering complacent strollers a chance to check their heft. Hand-operated Ferris wheels and carousels are packed with children. A few stalls nearby distribute Bombay's famously satisfying fast food—crunchy *bhel puris* (puffed-rice snacks), *ragda pattices* (spicy potato cakes), and *paav bhaji* (fried vegetable mash eaten with bread). From the beach, walk southeast down Marine Drive toward Nariman Point and you'll bump into flotillas of evening exercisers, cooing couples wandering past the waves in a daze, and dogs and kids being walked by their respective nannies. ⊠ *Chowpatty.*

need a break? **Barista** (⊠ 34 Chowpatty Seaface, opposite Thacker's Restaurant, Marine Dr., Chowpatty ☎ 22/2369–0104 ☉ daily 9–midnight). This chic, casual espresso bar populated by trendy college students is part of a popular chain in the city. You get a choice of 10 kinds of coffee, as well as sandwiches, pasta, croissants, and yummy desserts.

☞ ⑨ **Haji Ali Shrine.** Set far out on a thin, rocky jetty in the Arabian Sea, this striking white shrine was built in honor of the Muslim saint Haji Ali, who drowned here some 500 years ago on a pilgrimage to Mecca. When a coffin containing his mortal remains floated to rest on a rocky bed in the sea, devotees constructed the tomb and mosque to mark the spot. The shrine is reached by a long walkway just above the water, lined with destitute families and beggars ravaged by leprosy, some writhing, chanting, and (calling on the Muslim tradition of giving alms) perhaps beseeching you as you make your way down—a deeply discomfiting experience, but one that is unfortunately quintessentially Bombay. Inside, the shrine is full of colored-mirror mosaics and crowded with worshippers praying over the casket, which is covered with wilted flower garlands. Men and women must enter through separate doorways. There's no admission, but you may consider giving between Rs. 20 and Rs. 50 to the mosque charity box. ⊠ *Off Lala Lajpatrai Marg; near Mahalaxmi Race Course and Breach Candy. Approachable only at low tide.*

⓫ Jain Temple. This may be the most impressive temple in Bombay. This Jain Temple belongs to the prosperous, strictly vegetarian Jain community—the largely Gujarati followers of Lord Mahavira. The temple's colorful, but understated and peaceful interior—check out the intricate work on the walls and ceilings. Worship at this shrine takes a somewhat different form than the *hungama,* or chaos, at Hindu temples. It's more introspective and humble in aspect—reflective of the Jain faith. Around 8 AM, freshly bathed Jain devotees in swaths of unstitched off-white cloth walk here barefoot from their nearby homes to pay homage to the splendid idol of Adinath, an important Jain prophet. (Jains show respect by arriving clean and without shoes—originally Jains used to wear only a silk cloth, the best and hence most respectful material, but plenty now also wear cotton, and many others simply make do with ordinary clothes.) ⊠ *B. G. Kher Marg, Teen Batti, near Walkeshwar, Malabar Hill.*

☺ ❿ Kamala Nehru Park. Children love popping out of the "Old Woman Who Lived in a Shoe" boot here, at this small, unpretentious park on the eastern side of the top of Malabar Hill. It's primarily a children's playground, but also has gorgeous views of the city below. From the special viewpoint clearing, you can see all of Marine Drive and the Bombay skyline, from Chowpatty Beach to Colaba Point. Try to come up after dark to see why Marine Drive, sparkling with lights, is known as the Queen's Necklace. Just across the road, another park, the **Hanging Gardens,** also has pleasant views and a topiary garden. A few minutes north of here are the **Towers of Silence,** where Bombay's Parsi community—followers of the Zoroastrian faith—dispose of their dead. Pallbearers carry the corpse to the top of one of the towering cylindrical bastions, where it is left to be devoured by vultures and crows (a roughly two-hour process) and decomposed by the elements. None of this is visible to would-be onlookers, even relatives, and high walls prevent any furtive peeping. ⊠ *B. G. Kher Marg, Malabar Hill* ☉ *Daily 6 AM–9 PM.*

★ ⓮ Mani Bhavan. This charming, three-story Gujarati house, painted brown and yellow and ensconced in a quiet, tree-shaded Parsi neighborhood on Malabar Hill, was the home of Mahatma Gandhi from 1917 to 1934. Now overseen and maintained by the Gandhi Institute, it houses a library and a small museum on Gandhi's life and work. Gandhi's simple belongings are displayed in his room, including his original copies of the Bible, the Koran, and the *Bhagavad Gita* (a famous discourse in the ancient Indian epic, the Mahabharata); other displays include colorful dioramas and some important and moving letters from the fight for Indian independence. ⊠ *19 Laburnam Rd., near Nana Chowk, Gamdevi, Malabar Hill* ☎ *22/2380–5864* ⌨ *Rs. 3* ☉ *Daily 10–5:30.*

Matunga. About 30 minutes west of Bombay's business district, this suburb is home to a sizable chunk of the city's South Indian population. It's a little bit of Madras up north—it even has a few South Indian temples complete with distinctive *gopurams,* or towers (the **Asthika Samaj Temple** on Bhandarkar Road is a good example). Bazaars and shops sell banana leaves, Kanchipuram saris, and typical South Indian vegetables, flowers, and pickles (bottled relishes); nearby eating houses serve clean, simple South Indian *thali* lunches on banana leaves or hot crispy dosas. **Shree Sunders** (☎ 22/2416–9216) is known for having a large variety of excellent dosas, better and more authentic than anything you can find elsewhere. The legendary banana-leaf-lunch provider **A Ramanayak Udipi Shri Krishna Boarding** (☎ 22/2414–2422 ☉ Tues.–Sun., lunch 10:30–3, dinner 7–10) is near the train station. Matunga's shops and restaurants are closed on Monday. ✉ *Telang Rd. near Matunga Central Railway Station.*

Elephanta Caves

★ *14.5 nautical km (9 nautical mi) from Gateway of India*

Exactly who carved these 7th-century cave temples on Elephanta Island? No one knows. We do know, however, that the island was originally called Gharapuri; the Portuguese renamed it Elephanta after they found a large stone elephant near their landing place. (The figure collapsed in 1814 and was subsequently moved to the far-off Victoria Gardens and reassembled.) Shortly before these temples were created, Bombay experienced the golden age of the late Guptas, under whom the talents of artists had free range. Sanskrit had been finely polished, and under the court's liberal patronage, Kalidasa and other writers had helped incite a revival of Hindu beliefs. It was Shivaism—the worship of Shiva—that inspired the building of these temples.

The outside of the main cave consists of a columned veranda 30 feet wide and 6 feet deep, which you approach on steps flanked by sculptured elephants. The entire temple, carved out of the basalt hillside, is 130 square feet. The principle sculptures are on the southern wall at the back. The central recess in the hall contains the most outstanding sculpture, the unusual Mahesamurti, the Great Lord Shiva—an 18-foot triple image. Its three faces represent three aspects of Shiva: the creator (on the right), the preserver (in the center), and the destroyer (on the left).

Other sculptures near the doorways and on side panels show Shiva's usefulness. Shiva brought the Ganges River down to Earth, the story says, letting it trickle through his matted hair. He is also depicted as Yogisvara, lord of Yogis, seated on a lotus, and as Nataraja, the many-armed cosmic dancer. The beauty of this stonework lies in the grace, balance, and sense of peace conveyed in spite of the subject's multiple actions.

In winter the Maharashtra Tourism Development Corporation (MTDC) organizes a top-notch dance festival in this memorable setting. The island itself is quiet and picturesque, with light-green foliage and monkeys scampering about. The MTDC leads an excellent daily tour and runs a tiny restaurant on the island for refreshments and beer. Elephanta Island is not a good location for a picnic lunch; avoid carrying food or snacks with you because the herds of street-smart monkeys will harass you. ⊠ *Motor launches, 1 hr each way, depart daily every half hr, 9–3:30 from Gateway of India and noon–6 from Elephanta Island, unless sea is very choppy, Elephanta Island* ⛴ *Round-trip Rs. 80–Rs. 100 depending on type of seat you choose; Rs. 250 tickets can be purchased at Mahesh Travels at the Gateway of India* ☎ *22/2282–0139.*

> **need a break?**
>
> **Basilico Bistro & Deli** (⊠ Sentinel House, Arthur Bunder Rd., next to Radio Club, Colaba ☎ 22/5634–5670 or 22/5634–5671). Tucked away in one of Colaba's cluttered back streets, near where ferries depart for the Elephanta Caves, this little deli offers fresh fruit drinks, *lassis* (yogurt-based drinks), desserts, sandwiches, soups, and pasta courses all day and breakfasts from 7.30 AM. A glass cold-case, stuffed with exotic cakes, cheese, and cold meat dominates this 11-table café. With its wood and glass and warm lighting, it's an inviting place to catch your breath.

WHERE TO EAT

Cafés

¢ ✕ **Café Mondegar.** Next door to Regal Cinema, this lively café is one of South Bombay's popular hangouts. The jukebox plays at full volume, and has a wide selection of jazz and pop anthems. The walls are adorned with cartoons and glib quotes from the likes of George Bernard Shaw. The café is open 'til midnight, has beer, and is usually jam-packed. The onion rings and french fries are good and greasy, and the coffee float delicious. A wide range of Continental and Chinese meals make it to the menu, and breakfast (starting at 8) is popular here. ⊠ *Colaba Causeway, Colaba* ☎ *22/2202–0591* ▭ *AE, MC, V.*

★ ¢ ✕ **Leopold Café.** Founded in 1871, this is one of the city's oldest Irani-run restaurants and a favorite tourist haunt, open from 8 AM to midnight. With an international, eclectic, sometimes outlandish clientele, it's a great place to people watch. The tables are well spaced, the furnishings simple, and the paintings and posters recall a French café; at the side is a fruit bar lined with mangos, papayas, and pineapples. The selection of tandoori and Chinese food is broad, the portions are large, and the milkshakes are delicious. The menu, like many menus in Bombay's smallest restaurants, has 333 entries! ⊠ *Colaba Causeway, Colaba* ☎ *22/2287–3362 or 22/2202–0131* ▭ *AE, MC, V.*

International

$$$$ ✕ **Zodiac Grill.** This Continental restaurant in the legendary Taj Mahal hotel is Western in style, with subdued lighting, handsome chandeliers, captains in black jackets, and waiters wearing white gloves. Specialties include Camembert *dariole* (soufflé) and a creamy Kahlua mousse for dessert. Entrées favor meat and seafood, such as steak, Cajun lobster, and grilled lobster. The Zodiac Grill offers a fixed meal for two for Rs.

1,750 with a glass of sparkling wine for each. ✉ *Taj Mahal Palace & Towers, Apollo Bunder* ☎ 22/5665–3366 ⌘ *Reservations essential* ⌂ *Jacket and tie* ▭ *AE, DC, MC, V.*

$$$ ✕ **The Souk.** The top floor of the Taj hotel is home to a trendy, rooftop restaurant offering Middle Eastern food—Turkish, Egyptian, Lebanese, and Persian. High ceilings, intricately carved grills, and an open kitchen give the restaurant an airy feel. A Middle Eastern band croons mournful music while Bombay's lights twinkle below. The starters—go for the sampler platters—served with warm, fresh breads are delicious and filling. For the main course try the *lahm bamia* (lamb stew), *d'jaj m'qualli* (stuffed chicken) and *tagine* vegetables (stew) with rice. Desserts are unusual: *bastilla* au lait (flaky pastry with almond cream) and baklavas spiked with honey and stuffed with dry fruit. ✉ *Taj Mahal Palace & Towers, Apollo Bunder* ☎ 22/5665–3366 ⌘ *Reservations essential* ▭ *AE, DC, MC, V.*

$$ ✕ **Sea Lounge.** Innumerable marriages have been fixed and business deals struck over the years at the Taj Mahal hotel's most attractive restaurant. It's a very classy lounge—squishy sofas, simple glass tables, and upholstered chairs are scattered across a plush carpet, patterned in wavelike swirls; all in warm greens and blues. The backdrop is a technicolor view of the magnificent Gateway of India, the blue ocean, and a harbor full of bobbing sailboats. Make sure you take a window booth. The menu is not elaborate but the food is simple but tasty. Do dig into the selection of Indian snack platters. Don't miss the Viennoise coffee ice cream. ✉ *Taj Mahal Palace & Towers, Apollo Bunder* ☎ 22/5665–3366 ▭ *AE, DC, MC, V.*

FodorśChoice
★

$$ ✕ **Society.** If you're in the mood for Continental cuisine—or a good steak—pay a visit to this elegant Victorian restaurant, decorated with mirrors and handsome maroon velvet. The best steak, "à la Fernandes"—named after a former maître d'—is richly seasoned with cinnamon, spices, and cream, and cooked and flambéed at your table. The cannelloni and lasagna are very good and the crêpe suzette delectable. Excellent Indian dishes are also served; try the biryani. A pianist plays old favorites daily except Monday. ✉ *Ambassador hotel, Veer Nariman Rd., Churchgate* ☎ 22/2204–1131 ⌘ *Reservations essential* ▭ *AE, DC, MC, V.*

$–$$ ✕ **Caliente.** The first-floor apartment of an old apartment building in Colaba has been converted into Bombay's first Spanish restaurant. The first thing you hear when you enter is a trickle of water—one wall has been converted into a sheet waterfall behind glass. The style here is modern—the two dining rooms are sparsely furnished with blond-wood tables and rattan chairs and the third room is a lounge. A variety of tapas is on offer—jalapeno cheese poppers are delicious. Try the chicken paella, too. A handsome buffet lunch is available on Sunday. Reservations are essential Friday and Saturday nights. ✉ *Jony Castle, Khatau Rd., off Wodehouse Rd., Colaba* ☎ 22/2218–6717 or 22/2218–7729 ▭ *AE, DC, MC, V.*

$ ✕ **Moshe's.** Owner and chef Moshe Shek, a Bombay Jew, worked in London and Israel before returning to India to open his own restaurant in 2004—a European–style café with dark-wood furniture and big glass windows—and the place has quickly become all the rage. The café

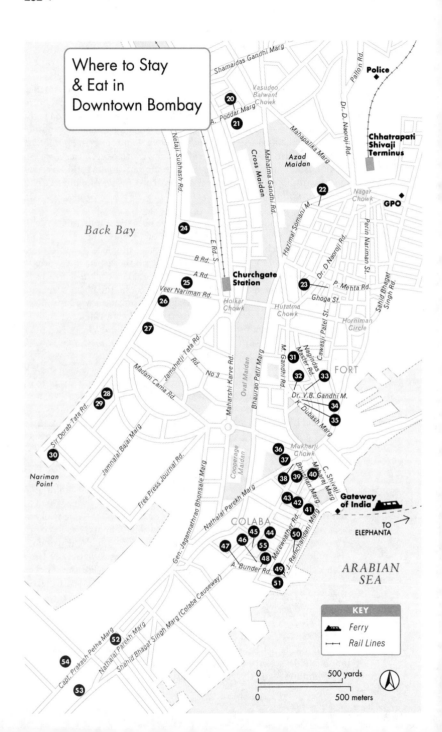

Where to Stay & Eat in Downtown Bombay

Shamaldas Gandhi Marg

Police

Vasudeo Balwant Chowk

Dr. D. Naoroji Rd.

A. Poddar Marg

20

21

Netaji Subhash Rd.

Cross Maidan

Mahatma Gandhi Rd.

Azad Maidan

Mahapalika Marg

Chhatrapati Shivaji Terminus

22

Nagar Chowk

GPO

Perin Nariman St.

Back Bay

24

E Rd. S

Hazimal Somani M.

Dr. D. Naoroji Rd.

Sahid Bhagat Singh Rd.

B Rd. S

Churchgate Station

A Rd.

25

Veer Nariman Rd.

26

Holkar Chowk

23

P. Mehta Rd.

Ghoga St.

Hutatma Chowk

Horniman Circle

27

Jamshetji Tata Rd.

Maharshi Karve Rd.

Oval Maidan

Bhaurao Patil Marg

M. Gandhi Rd.

Naginas Master Rd.

Cawasji Patel St.

31

FORT

Madam Cama Rd.

Rd.

No 3

32

33

Dr. V.B. Gandhi M.

34

K. Dubash Marg

35

28

29

Sir Dorab Tata Rd.

Jamnalai Bajai Marg

Coperage Maidan

Mukherji Chowk

36

37

30

Nariman Point

Free Press Journal Rd.

Gen. Jagannathrao Bhonsale Marg

Nathalal Parekh Marg

38

39

40

B... an Marg

Mhasai Marg

C. Shivaji

Gateway of India

TO ELEPHANTA

43

42

41

COLABA

45

44

50

Mereweather Rd.

47

46

55

48

J. Ramchandani Marg

ARABIAN SEA

A. Bunder Rd.

49

51

Capt. Prakash Petha Marg

Nathalal Parekh Marg

Shahid Bhagat Singh Marg (Colaba Causeway)

52

54

53

KEY	
🛥	Ferry
⊢—⊣	Rail Lines

0   500 yards

0   500 meters

Where to Stay & Eat in Greater Bombay

SEE WHERE TO STAY AND EAT IN DOWNTOWN BOMBAY MAP

Restaurants ▼

Ankur	31
All Stir Fry	40
Bellissima	19
Bombay Blue	34
Café Churchill	45
Café Mondegar	43
Caliente	52
Chetana	35
China Garden	17
Govinda's	2
The Great Wall	13
Indigo	42
Khyber	32
Kobe	18
Konkan Café	54
Legacy of China	1
Leopold Café	44
Ling's Pavilion	39
Mahesh Lunch Home	23
Moshe's	53
Nosh	38
Oriental Blossom	27
Papa Pancho Da Dhaba	15
Peshawari	11
Royal China	22
Sea Lounge	41
Sheetal Samudra	7
Sidewok	30
Society	25
The Souk	41
Thai Pavilion	54
Trattoria	54
Trishna	33
Woodlands Garden Café	5
Woodside Inn	37
Zodiac Grill	41

Hotels ▼

Ambassador	25
Ascot	47
Bawa International	8
Cowie's	55
Fariyas	51
Garden	48
Godwin	46
Gordon House	40
Grand Hyatt	20
Grand Maratha Sheraton	11
Hilton Towers	28
Holiday Inn	4
Hyatt Regency	10
InterContinental	24
InterContinental the Grand	14
JW Marriott	7
Le Royal Meridien	12
The Leela	13
Marine Plaza	27
The Oberoi	29
The Orchid	9
Ramada Palm Grove	6
Sea Green	26
Sea Palace Hotel	50
Shelley's	49
Sun 'n' Sand	3
Taj Land's End	16
Taj Mahal Palace & Tower	41
Taj President	54
West End	21
YWCA International Center	36

offers some of the best international food in Bombay—pastas in creamy sauces, aubergine roulade, crusty cheese garlic bread (they bake their own breads and rolls), Israeli stuffed chicken, chargrilled *rawas* (Indian salmon), and hearty soups. Desserts are sinful; try the B-52 made from three types of liqueur and chocolate. A large delicatessen counter, overflowing with luscious cakes and cheese, occupies the back wall. There's seating outside on the patio, too. ⊠ *7 Minoo Manor, Cuffe Parade, off Wodehouse Rd., Colaba* ☎ *22/2216–1226* ⌂ *Reservations essential* ⊟ *MC, V.*

¢–$ ✕ **Kobe.** Get delicious sizzlers, a Bombay favorite, here. Burning hot metal platters piled high with fresh vegetables, fries, chicken or steak, and sauces arrive at your table wafting clouds of steam. You can ask the waiter to add your choice of topping, too—perhaps extra cheese or more mushrooms, pasta, or spice. Try the steak (or the garlic steak), *chicken shaslik* (masala chicken on a skewer), or vegetable *shaslik* with mushroom, cheese, and pasta. The place is simple—no frills and a bit dark. No alcohol is served. ⊠ *3 Sukh Sagar, Hughes Rd., Chowpatty* ☎ *22/2363–2174* ⌂ *Reservations essential* ⊟ *AE, DC, MC, V.*

¢–$ ✕ **Nosh.** Vegetarian food from around the world is the cuisine on offer here: Peshawari *pulao, bourek* (cheese fritters), risottos, and Italian pasta are typical. Grey marbles tables, plants, and white upholstered chairs and no excessive bric-a-brac gives the restaurant a sparse but pleasing look. Desserts are yummy, especially the Triple Chocolate Temptation. And don't miss the Indian specialty juice: sugarcane juice spiked with lemon and ginger (and a rare treat in Bombay, it's squeezed hygienically). ⊠ *Regal Cinema Bldg., Shahid Bhagat Singh Rd., Colaba* ☎ *22/5639–6688 or 22/5639–6681* ⊟ *MC, V.*

¢ ✕ **Café Churchill.** This six-table eatery—a simple, no-frills place—serves fresh, delicious pasta, pizza, and other Continental dishes. Expect wholesome meals and first-rate desserts at this unusually convenient place. It opens early in the morning and stays open until late, and provides any kind of takeout. It's also close to some of Colaba's popular budget hotels. ⊠ *103-B Colaba Causeway, opposite Cusrow Baug, Colaba* ☎ *22/2284–4689* ⊟ *No credit cards.*

Chinese

$$$ ✕ **The Great Wall.** Manned by a team of Chinese cooks and managers—the head chef is from Singapore—this place serves the real thing. Three types of Chinese food—Cantonese, Hunan, and Szechuan—are served. Try the baby corn salt and pepper, sliced pomfret chili bean sauce, lobster in black sauce, vegetables with dried red chilis, bean curd in a hot sauce, Hunan chicken, or prawn salt-and-pepper. ⊠ *The Leela, Sahar* ☎ *22/5691–1234* ⌂ *Reservations essential* ⊟ *AE, DC, MC, V.*

★ $$–$$$ ✕ **Royal China.** The menu is nearly 15 pages long at one of South Bombay's newest and more popular Chinese restaurants. But ordering a meal is actually rather simple, be it braised woodear mushroom with seasonal vegetables, roasted pork, seafood dumplings, or vegetable noodles. All the food, in fact, is lip-smackingly good at this elegant eatery. The place is plainly decorated but stylish nonetheless. Tall wooden screens of Chinese letters divide the main dining area into separate sections and a few well-chosen Chinese art d'objets dot the room. ✉ *Sterling, Hajarimal Somani Marg, behind Sterling Cinema, Fort* ☎ *22/5635–5310 or 22/ 5635–5311* ▱ *AE, DC, MC, V.*

\$\$ ✕ **China Garden.** This restaurant is the second avatar of the erstwhile China Garden at Kemps Corner. Like the original, which didn't have an unreserved table since Chinese master chef Nelson Wang opened in 1984, this incarnation bustles with Bombay's trendiest young VIPs and film stars. The restaurant is spacious and has expanses of black marble and a prominent bar. Mr. Wang's unusual Chinese artifacts decorate the room, and the windows are framed with white lace Chinese curtains. Hot favorites include prawns wrapped in bacon, crispy Peking chicken, crispy vegetable pancake, Shantung prawns, gin chicken, and hakka fish. ✉ *Crossroads mall, Pandit Madan Mohan, Malviya Rd., near Haji Ali, Tardeo* ☎ *22/2353–5588 or 22/2352–5589* ▱ *AE, DC, MC, V.*

\$\$ ✕ **Legacy of China.** One of the best Chinese restaurants in the suburbs and close to Bollywood, this place attracts starry, as well as starry-eyed, customers. Thai and Schezuan (the Bombay favorite), Hunan, Cantonese, and Peking food are available. Folks love to dig into the Yin Yang chicken, crispy fried spinach, Kwandhong soup (lettuce, bean curd, mushroom, prawns, and chicken), Thai green curries, Thai barbecue chicken, sizzled chile prawns, and Malaysian fish curry (pomfret curry). The restaurant is large and decorated with swords, Chinese landscapes, and mirrors. ✉ *5–6, Tirupati, Jay Prakash (JP) Rd., Seven Bungalows, Versova, Andheri* ☎ *22/2636–8223 or 22/2631–1332* ⌥ *Reservations essential* ▱ *AE, DC, MC, V.*

\$\$ ✕ **Oriental Blossom.** Honey-glaze spare ribs, Chinese greens with black mushrooms, deep-fried corn curd, coconut pancakes, dim sum—the Chinese food at the Marine Plaza hotel's showcase restaurant is lightly spiced, a mixture of Cantonese and Szechuan. The style is simple and elegant—black furniture, crisp white tablecloths, and subdued lighting—and the service unobtrusive. If you want seclusion, book a table in one of the semiprivate-dining alcoves. ✉ *Marine Plaza hotel, 29 Marine Dr.* ☎ *22/ 2285–1212* ⌥ *Reservations essential* ▱ *AE, DC, MC, V.*

¢–\$ ✕ **Ling's Pavilion.** Baba Ling and his family have been providing Bombay film stars and yuppies alike with excellent Chinese food for two generations. Enter through the moon-shape door and you'll find yourself on a bridge overlooking a gurgling stream, complete with fish. The tables are beyond; some tables are on a balcony. A testimony to Ling's popularity and authenticity is the number of Chinese tourists and consular corps digging into their meals with gusto. Don't miss the barbecue platter, baby lobsters, or steamed fish. The Chinese bread is soft and succulent—terrific with the ginger-garlic crab. ✉ *19/21 Mahakavi Bhushan Marg, behind Regal Cinema, Colaba* ☎ *22/2285–0023 or 22/ 2282–4533* ▱ *AE, DC, MC, V.*

Contemporary

\$\$ ✕ **Indigo.** The narrow lane out front fills with a queue of cars at dinnertime—this eatery and its laid-back lounge bar are a hit with foreigners. This small restaurant occupies an attractive, candle-lit old mansion on a side street in Colaba. A nouvelle Indian–Western-fusion cuisine is served in simple, woodsy-but-elegant surroundings—much like dining in an old Goan home. Try the *rawas* (Indian salmon) pan-grilled, pepper tuna, filet mignon, tandoori rosemary chicken, or the goat cheese ravioli—all pastas here are commendable. Save room for the tempting desserts. ⊠ *4 Mandalik Rd., near Cotton World, Colaba* ☎ *22/5636–8980 or 22/5636–8981* ⌕ *Reservations essential* ▤ *AE, DC, MC, V.*

Italian

$$ ✕ **Bellisima.** A spacious automobile showroom that once sold seedy cars has been converted into a fashionable see-and-be-seen dining complex just a stone's throw from Chowpatty beach. Downstairs is a cool ranch-style pub and eatery popular with teenagers craving tasty pastas and pizzas. Upstairs is a sedate, attractive bar, the Liquid Lounge, and the attached fine-dining restaurant Bellissima, which serves Continental (but mainly Italian) food. To write home about: penne arabbiata, gnocchi Gorgonzola, pollo al basilico, and Creole salmon. The tasting platter is intriguing, too. ⊠ *534, Sardar Vallabhbhai Patel Rd., Opera House* ☎ *22/2361–7171* ⌕ *Reservations essential* ▤ *AE, DC, MC, V.*

$$ ✕ **Trattoria.** One of Bombay's first Italian restaurants has always been famous for its crispy, light pizza. Inside it's cheery: bright colors, comfy leather sofas and chairs, and warm lighting. A large mural of an ancient Roman scene stretches across one of the walls. The open-plan kitchen gives the place a casual manner. The pastas are delicious. Good menu choices include bruschetta, prawn cocktail, mushroom cocktail, *primavera al forno* (homemade pasta with cheese) canelloni, and penne *aglio eolio*. The tiramisu, cappuccino tart (coffee-and-chocolate tart served with cashew ice cream), and *dolce tre latte* (sponge cake with cream) are all excellent. ⊠ *Taj President, 90 Cuffe Parade, Colaba* ☎ *22/5665–0808* ▤ *AE, DC, MC, V.*

Mughlai, Punjabi & Tandoori

$$ ✕ **Khyber.** Named for the Himalayan mountain pass between Afghanistan
Fodor'sChoice and northwestern India is one of Bombay's best restaurants. Three
★ floors of delightful rooms are done in Northwest Frontier style—white-marble floors, terra-cotta urns, carved stone pillars, low wooden rafters, and handsome fresco murals by local artists. The waiters, dressed in Pathan garb, serve delicious kababs and naans. Try the pomfret green masala (fried pomfret fish stuffed with tangy green chutney), Khyber *raan* (leg of lamb marinated overnight, then roasted in a clay oven), egg biryani, black *dal* (lentils) or *paneer shaslik* (cottage cheese marinated with spices and roasted). ⊠ *145 M. G. Rd., Fort* ☎ *22/2267–3228* ⌕ *Reservations essential* ▤ *AE, DC, MC, V.*

$$ ✕ **Peshawari.** The Welcomgroup of hotels decided to spawn a copy of their much-loved Delhi restaurant, Bukhara, at their hotel in Bombay. Peshawari sports beaded curtains and a giant glass window with a view of the kitchen, where kababs hang from the ceiling; you may also see cooks preparing Indian breads and juggling succulent kababs. The black dal is heavenly; breads, too, are excellent, and desserts are authentic. Entrées are expensive, but the portions are large. Eat sparingly—you'll be stuffed after one course. ⊠ *Grand Maratha Sheraton, Sahar Airport Rd., Sahar* ☎ *22/2830–3030* ⌕ *Reservations essential* ☰ *AE, DC, MC, V.*

$ ✕ **Bombay Blue.** A large, new, two-floor complex behind Jehangir Art Gallery houses three restaurants—Bombay Blues, Copper Chimney, and Noodle Bar. Brightly lit and cheerful, with a big glassy exterior, the complex looks like a swanky, upmarket version of a fast food place. The menu at Bombay Blue is eclectic and tasty; choose between a meal of kababs and naan, Chinese chicken noodles, Thai curry and rice, Japanese miso soup, pasta, nachos, sizzlers, or Lebanese food. Avoid the weekends when the place is invaded by loud family groups. ⊠ *K. Dubash Marg, Kala Ghoda* ☎ *22/2202–2444 or 22/2202–2555* ☰ *AE, DC, MC, V.*

$ ✕ **Papa Pancho Da Dhaba.** For some *asli* (real) hearty Punjabi food, head out to this funky restaurant. Styled like a proper truckers' roadside *dhaba* (eatery) found along the highways of India, Papa Pancho has simple, clunky metal dishware and is decorated with bumper signs like OK HORN PLEASE or lemon and green chile good luck charms. The *dal makhani* (butter dal), *papdi chaat* (a snack), *baingan bharta* (roasted and spiced eggplant), mince *parathas* (mince-stuffed bread), and the creamy *lassi* are delectable. Since the restaurant is in Bandra, a bit far from south or north Bombay, it's a good idea to visit this place on a Sunday, when the journey (without commuter traffic) will take just half an hour. ⊠ *Shop 12, Gaspar Enclave, Dr. Ambedkar Rd., near Rupee Bank, Bandra* ☎ *22/2651–8732* ☰ *AE, DC, MC, V.*

North Indian

¢–$ ✕ **Govinda's.** This Hare Krishna restaurant offers sumptuous 56-item vegetarian thalis. Expect Lord Krishna's food—that is, Vedic meals, which are cooked without garlic and onions. The management in fact advertises a "transcendental dining experience," becuase the food served has already been offered to the gods and *bhajans*, joyful devotional songs, liven up your meal. On weekends and Hindu holidays the restaurant often organizes food fests. ⊠ *ISKCON, Hare Krishna Mandir, Juhu Tara Rd., Juhu* ☎ *22/2620–0337 or 22/2620–6860* ☰ *MC, V.*

¢ ✕ **Chetana.** Rajasthani decor—hand-blocked fabrics on the ceiling and traditional *toranas* (ornamental carvings above temple entrances) on the walls—provides a cozy setting for tasty vegetarian Rajasthani and Gujarati thalis. Chetana also does a low-cal Gujarati thali. Sample Rajasthani *dal bati* (lentils with wheat cakes), *kadhi* (curd curry), and mint *raita* (a spiced yogurt dish). Service is excellent, and the owners' adjacent philosophy bookshop–cum–craft store is worth a visit after your meal. Note that the restaurant is closed between 3 and 7. ⊠ *34 K. Dubash Marg, Kala Ghoda, Fort* ☎ *22/2284–4968* ☰ *AE, MC, V.*

Pan-Asian

$ ✕ **All Stir Fry.** This popular new Asian restaurant is minimalist and dark, with black-and-white benches and tables facing food stations in the back. At one island you choose the raw materials for an all-you-can eat meal—greens, cut veggies, fish, prawns, beef, chicken—then, at a second station, a chef cooks it for you with the sauce of your choosing. Vegetarians take note: the restaurant offers meat-free soups and chefs use separate pans and utensils to prepare vegetarian dishes. You can also get à la carte items, Thai curries among them and a small selection of desserts. The swanky Tides next door is a good place for a pre-dinner drink. ⊠ *Gordon House Hotel, 5 Battery St., Apollo Bunder* ☎ *22/ 2287–1122* ⊟ *AE, DC, MC, V.*

$ ✕ **Sidewok.** Expect Pan-Asian food and cheerful music at this happening restaurant run by the Taj Group, at the National Centre for the Performing Arts. When they're not handing out courses, waiters hit the dance floor to their own special numbers every 45 minutes or so. Best bets include charred pomfret (Indian fish), tandoori salmon, house chicken, Asian wok (grilled vegetables), and hot banana soufflée. ⊠ *National Centre for Performing Arts, Marine Dr., Nariman Point* ☎ *22/2281–8132* ⚭ *Reservations essential* ⊟ *AE, DC, MC, V.*

Seafood

$ ✕ **Trishna.** Once just another neighborhood lunch place, this small
FodorśChoice restaurant near busy M. G. Road has been very much discovered. Now
★ yuppies and film stars crowd into the rows of benches and tables alongside Trishna's old-time regulars, all devouring fresh seafood or Indian and Chinese cuisine. Favorites include squid or oyster chili and salt-and-pepper butter crab (Rs. 450). Ask to see the crab before it's cooked: the creature's giant, snapping claws will dispel any doubts about freshness. Call in advance to inquire about the daily catch. ⊠ *7 Rope Walk La., next to Commerce House, Kala Ghoda, Fort* ☎ *22/2270–3213 or 22/ 2261–4991* ⚭ *Reservations essential* ⊟ *AE, DC, MC, V.*

$ ✕ **Konkan Café.** Seafood from the Konkan coast (which stretches from Maharashtra south through Goa to Mangalore, Karnataka) is extraordinarily popular in Bombay, yet for years it was only available in nofrills "lunch homes" in the business district. In opening the Konkan Café, the Taj President is trying to do what no one else has attempted—serve fish-curry rice-plate lunches in luxurious surroundings. Although crummy taverns and souped-up lunch homes might still be said to do it better, the food here is tasty, and the coastal-home feel is appealing. Opt for the fried fish, steamed pomfret, coastal *maida* (white-flour) paratha, or the vegetarian thali. ⊠ *Taj President hotel, 90 Cuffe Parade, Colaba* ☎ *22/ 2215–0808* ⚭ *Reservations essential* ⊟ *AE, DC, MC, V.*

$ ✕ **Mahesh Lunch Home.** One of the first Bombay restaurants to popu-
FodorśChoice larize the seafoods of the Konkan coast, the formerly humble Mahesh,
★ a two-level eatery tucked away on a narrow street, has gone upmarket with marble, brass, plastic floral arrangements, and smartly clad waiters. (The diners have gone upmarket, too; no more leaving fish bones on the side of the table.) You'll get what may be Bombay's freshest and best seafood, personally selected at the nearby Fort fish market every morning for the past 20 years by the owner, Mr. Karkera. Local office workers, bankers, five-star hoteliers, suburban families, and cricket and film stars in the know come here for giant portions of exquisite crab, *rawas* (Indian salmon), and pomfret dishes, all succulently tender and light—essentially oil-free—and seasoned with tangy tandoori or Man-

galorean spices. The seafood dishes prepared with butter, garlic, and pepper are also popular. ⊠ *8-B Cawasji Patel St., Fort* ☎ *22/2287–0938* ▭ *AE, DC, MC, V.*

$ ✕ **Sheetal Samudra.** Gourmands regularly make the one-hour trip from central Bombay to dine at one of the city's best suburban restaurants, on the main road between Bombay and Juhu Beach. The surroundings are unexceptional, but the cuisine—Punjabi and Chinese, with an accent on fresh seafood—is creative and delicious. Try the prawns in buttery, mild crab sauce or the batter-fried prawns in green or red sauce; alternately, opt for boneless fish steak, also in green or red sauce. Live crabs are sold by weight and cooked any way you choose. The waiters, dressed in black vests and red bowties, are skilled and attentive. ⊠ *Unity Compound, Juhu Tara Rd., Juhu* ☎ *22/2660–7872 or 22/2661–1218* ⌂ *Reservations essential* ▭ *AE, MC, V.*

¢ ✕ **Ankur.** Head here for spicy Konkan seafood—typically garnished with coconut and *kokum* (a tangy tamarindlike sauce). Once a downmarket fish house but now sporting wood and glass accents, Ankur does the popular Manglorean and Konkan dishes quite well. Dine on semolina-fried jumbo prawns, fried *kane* (ladyfish), tandoori crab, or *teesri* (clams) in pepper sauce—served with *sana* (fluffy rice cakes tempered with toddy, a mild country beer) or *neer dosa* (lacy rice pancakes). ⊠ *Meadows House, Tamarind La. or M. P. Shetty Rd.; enter via lane next to Kendeel bar on M. G. Rd. and take a left, Fort* ☎ *22/2265–4194 or 22/ 2263–0393* ▭ *AE, DC, MC, V.*

South Indian

¢ ✕ **Woodlands Garden Cafe.** The queue at this vegetarian restaurant on weekends is an unequivocal testimony to the quality of the food. This is the place for authentic South Indian fare—excellent dosas and Rs. 112 South Indian thalis in no-fuss but comfortable surroundings. *Bisi beli hule*, a spicy lentil and rice mixture, hard to find elsewhere, is very tasty. ⊠ *Next to Kala Niketan sari shop, Vaikuntlal Mehta Rd., Juhu-Vile Parle Scheme, Juhu* ☎ *22/2617–2727 or 22/2611–9119* ▭ *AE, DC, MC, V.*

¢ ✕ **Woodside Inn.** Traditionally, the best dosas in Bombay have been available only in grimy or uncomfortable places—roadside carts or small vegetarian dosa (or Udipi as they are called) joints that cater to armies of office workers. The dosas here aren't quite as wonderful as those served at your corner *annah* (literally "brother"; meaning dosa joint), but they're fresh and pretty good, and the environment air-conditioned. They are served with the traditional *mulgapodi*, a gunpowder (spicy) chutney, so you may want to wash them down with a strong Indian beer. ⊠ *Wodehouse Rd., near Sahkari Bhandar and Regal Cinema, Colaba* ☎ *22/2202–5525 or 22/2287–5752* ▭ *AE, MC, V.*

Thai

$ ✕ **Thai Pavilion.** The food served at this small dining room, tastefully decorated with inlaid teak surfaces, candles, and orchids, is exceptional, and portions are unusually generous. Start with a clay crock of *tom yum koong*, a spicy prawn soup aromatic with lemongrass and fiery with chilis (not for the faint of palate). Try this fabulous entrée: *kai haw bai toey,* sweet marinated chicken chunks wrapped in pandanus, or screw-pine, leaves (don't eat them), then steamed and deep-fried. Knowledgeable, attentive waiters provide fantastic service. ⊠ *Taj President hotel, 90 Cuffe Parade, Colaba* ☎ *22/5665–0808* ⌖ *Reservations essential* ☰ *AE, DC, MC, V.*

WHERE TO STAY

$$$$ 🏨 **Le Royal Meridien.** Although this neat, small, luxury hotel doesn't have a fancy exterior and its shining marble lobby is tiny, its rooms have plenty of grandeur. It's only 5 minutes from Bombay's international airport, in the thick of the city's growing neighborhood of airport hotels. Rooms are no less swanky for being comfy—they are decorated with lots of wood and crisp whites. Bathrooms are done in chrome and glass, and have shower cubicles, tubs, and bidets. Each room has DVD player. The hotel's restaurant, La Brasserie, serves a variety of meals around the clock; another restaurant on-site, Imperial China, serves Szechuan cuisine. ⊠ *Sahar Airport Rd., 400059* ☎ *22/2838–0000* 🖷 *22/2838–0101* ⊕ *www.lemeridien.com* ↬ *171 rooms, 6 suites* ⌖ *3 restaurants, coffee shop, room service, in-room data ports, in-room fax, in-room safes, refrigerators, cable TV, pool, health club, hair salon, sauna, 2 bars, dry cleaning, laundry service, business services, meeting room, airport shuttle, travel services* ☰ *AE, DC, MC, V* ⦿ *BP.*

★ $$$$ 🏨 **Marine Plaza.** The polished, smoky-glass exterior promises elegance, and inside it delivers with a modern, black-marble interior and clean, uncluttered sleekness. Glass elevators whiz you up to rooms that are small but very comfortable, and fairly luxurious. Rooms have excellent sea views and dressing rooms. The glass-bottom pool, outside on the roof of the hotel, offers enchanting vistas of Bombay. ⊠ *29 Marine Dr., 400020* ☎ *22/2285–1212* 🖷 *22/2282–8585* ⊕ *www.sarovarparkplaza.com* ↬ *28 rooms, 40 suites* ⌖ *Restaurant, coffee shop, room service, in-room data ports, in-room safes, refrigerators, cable TV, pool, health club, bar, dry cleaning, laundry service, business services, meeting room, travel services* ☰ *AE, DC, MC, V* ⦿ *BP.*

★ $$$$ 🏨 **The Oberoi.** This elegant high-rise in the heart of the business district caters to business travelers. From service to style, everything is sleek and efficient, and even so the fabulous, high-ceiling lobby and public spaces are punctuated with traditional pieces. The Oberoi is easily one of the classiest hotels in the country. Each floor is staffed with a butler for personal assistance, and each room has small, separate dressing and luggage areas to allow for clutter-free in-room meetings. The rooms are decorated in subtle pastels, with rich dark-wood furniture. A superior business center and complimentary personalized stationery are extra touches. If at all possible, arrange for a room with a view of the Arabian Sea. The Oberoi's Indian restaurant, Kandahar, serves unusual, healthful meals—prepared with little or no oil—and the Brasserie coffee shop serves 80 dishes from around the world. ⊠ *Nariman Point, 400021* ☎ *22/5632–5757* 🖷 *22/22/5632–4142* ⊕ *www.oberoihotels. com* ↬ *337 rooms, 22 suites* ⌖ *3 restaurants, room service, in-room* *data ports, in-room safes, refrigerators, cable TV, pool, health club, hair salon, sauna, Turkish baths, bar, dry cleaning, laundry service, business services, meeting room, travel services* ▭ *AE, DC, MC, V.*

$$$$ ▦ **The Orchid.** This small eco-hotel has low-key but attractive rooms that are brightly lit, decently sized, and very comfortable. The hotel is right next to Bombay's domestic airport, and minutes from the international airport. Boasting proudly of "eco-friendly waste-management and recycling policies," the hotel built its "green" rooms with a minimal amount of wood, plastic, and paper. A bedside button allows you to turn up your air-conditioning thermostat by a degree or so to save energy. The waterfall, which runs on recycled water, looks like falling glass—it lights up the lobby and provides humidity for the lustrous orchids that populate the hotel's interior. ⊠ *Nehru Rd., Vile Parle, 400050* ☎ *22/ 2616–4040* 🖷 *22/2616–4141* ⊕ *www.orchidhotel.com* ⊲ *201 rooms, 55 suites* ⌂ *2 restaurants, coffee shop, room service, in-room data ports, in-room safes, refrigerators, cable TV, pool, health club, bar, baby-sitting, dry cleaning, laundry service, business services, meeting room, airport shuttle, travel services* ▭ *AE, DC, MC, V* ⏐◎⏐ *EP.*

$$$$ ▦ **Taj Land's End.** This opulent hotel faces the ocean in the suburb of Bandra. It's one of Bombay's newest and fancier hotels, and its lobby seems like an acre of marble, with huge, sparkling chandeliers, fountains, and automatic revolving doors. It has some remarkably luxurious modern rooms, complete with bedside controls for the lights, curtains, and air-conditioning. Bathrooms have both showers and tubs. The restaurant Masala Bay serves Indian fusion food. ⊠ *Land's End, Bandstand area of Bandra, 400050* ☎ *22/5668–1234* 🖷 *22/5699–4488* ⊕ *www.tajhotels. com* ⊲ *300 rooms, 9 suites* ⌂ *3 restaurants, coffee shop, patisserie, in-room data ports, in-room safes, minibars, cable TV, pool, health club, hair salon, bar, dance club, baby-sitting, dry cleaning, laundry service, business services, meeting room, travel services* ▭ *AE, DC, MC, V.*

$$$$ ▦ **Taj Mahal Palace & Tower.** Looking past the Gateway of India to the Arabian Sea, the Taj's stunning brown stone exterior sports rows of jutting white balconies and Gothic windows. Onion domes on the corner turrets echo the high, central Italianate dome. The first hotel in what is now a pan-India luxury chain, this Victorian extravaganza was built in 1903. Foreigners and wealthy Indians choose this hotel over other fancy hotels in town because it's a beautiful and regal landmark. A less expensive 19-story modern wing ("the tower"), which throws in some Moorish elements, rises next to the older wing. Every corner of the older building is exquisitely decorated, often with antiques (for which the hotel's decorator scours India) and always with warm, tasteful colors. Rooms and suites in this building, some of which surround small, quiet interior verandas, retain their Victorian character with high ceilings, pastel colors, antiques, and cane furniture. Rooms facing the harbor are extremely attractive. Rooms in the tower, slightly less expensive, are spacious and modern, and offer a tiny sitting area and a desk and are furnished in maroon tones. ⊠ *Apollo Bunder, 400001* ☎ *22/5665–3366* 🖷 *22/ 5665–0300* ⊕ *www.tajhotels.com* ⊲ *582 rooms, 49 suites* ⌂ *5 restaurants, coffee shop, patisserie, room service, in-room data ports, in-room safes, minibars, refrigerators, cable TV, pool, exercise room, hair salon,*

FodorśChoice
★

2 bars, dance club, shops, baby-sitting, dry cleaning, laundry service, concierge, Internet, business services, meeting rooms, travel services ▭ *AE, DC, MC, V.*

$$$$ 🏨 **InterContinental.** This boutique hotel on Bombay's famous sea promenade at Nariman Point is brand new. Rates for sea-facing rooms are high, but the rooms—spacious and ultramodern with polished wood floors, large comfortable beds, big desks, elegant furnishings, and great views of the ocean—are gorgeous. Hi-tech touches include built-in flat-screen TVs, fax machines, DVD players, and electronic entry keys. Bathrooms are large, trimmed with oodles of white marble. The restaurant is multicuisine. ✉ *135 Marine Dr., 400020* ☎ *22/5639–9999* 🖷 *22/5639–9600* ⊕ *www.ichotelsgroup.com* ➫ *59 rooms, 12 suites* ♨ *Restaurant, coffee shop, room service, in-room data ports, in-room safes, refrigerators, cable TV, pool, health club, hair salon, sauna, bar, lounge, dry cleaning, laundry service, concierge, business services, meeting room, airport shuttle, travel services* ▭ *AE, DC, MC, V* ⵔ *BP.*

$$$–$$$$ 🏨 **Hyatt Regency.** One of Bombay's new hotels near the airport resembles a slick, high-tech Far Eastern airport—with a smoky-glass control-tower kind of exterior, a vision of steel, chrome, and glass. It's lit up in places by neon light, too. Popular among high-powered executive types, the hotel has luxurious, airy rooms with wooden floors and minimalist contemporary furnishings. Bathrooms have sunken shower areas in addition to tubs. Rates are high given that this hotel has none of the history or location of similar hotels—but the price fluctuates sharply depending on the room and when you come. ✉ *Sahar Airport Rd., Sahar 400099* ☎ *22/5696–1234* 🖷 *22/5696–1235* ⊕ *www.mumbai.regency. hyatt.com* ➫ *397 rooms, 18 suites* ♨ *Restaurant, room service, in-room data ports, in-room safes, refrigerators, cable TV, pool, health club, hair salon, sauna, bar, lounge, dry cleaning, laundry service, business services, meeting room, travel services* ▭ *AE, DC, MC, V* ⵔ *EP.*

$$$ 🏨 **Ambassador.** Once an apartment house, this nine-story 1940s hotel in the heart of Bombay is less sleek in service and appearance than its south Bombay counterparts, but has more of an old-fashioned feel. Plus it's a good value. Rooms are reasonably large and furnished in a functional modern style, each with the Ambassador chain's signature brass knocker on its door. Opt for a road-view room. India's first revolving restaurant crowns the hotel—it offers stunning views over the city and the Arabian Sea, and great Far Eastern food. ✉ *Veer Nariman Rd., Churchgate 400020* ☎ *22/2204–1131* 🖷 *22/2204–0004* ⊕ *www. ambassadorindia.com* ➫ *120 rooms, 3 suites* ♨ *2 restaurants, coffee shop, room service, in-room data ports, in-room safes, refrigerators, cable TV, bar, dry cleaning, laundry service, travel services* ▭ *AE, DC, MC, V* ⵔ *EP.*

$$$ **Grand Hyatt.** Extraordinarily posh, this massive property rises incongruously from a bleak urban landscape. Walk into the expansive building with its ultra-contemporary, block faÁade and you'll feel like you're in a modern art museum (with its excellent collection of Indian modern art) or a convention center with giant pieces of sculpture, sweeping granite floors, and many harsh right angles. Once you get over the disconnect and overcome the lack of warmth in the hotelís architecture, you'll begin to take in the polite service, varied and tasty cuisine, and the rooms, elegant but sparse and done in cream-clored soft furnishings and Ikea–style furniture. The bathrooms open out and become part of the room, giving a spacious feel. Each room has its own thermostat. ⊠ *Off Western Express Highway, Santa Cruz East 400055* ☎ *22/5676–1234* 🖷 *22/5676–1235* ⟿ *547 rooms, 147 apartments, 38 suites* ⚭ *4 restaurants, refrigerators, in-room data ports, in-room safes, room service, pool, massage and spa facilities, laundry service, travel services, health club, business services, meeting room* ☰ *AE, DC, MC, V.*

$$$ 🏨 **Hilton Towers.** Adjoining the Oberoi Hotel, this enormous, 35-story high-rise is geared to the business traveler but hosts a mixed international crowd of executives and tourists. Public spaces are many and varied, some overlooking the vast, gleaming, glass-wall lobby from smart mezzanines. Rooms are modern and classy, furnished with patterned bedspreads and drapes, brass-frame prints of Indian monuments, and smooth, contemporary wood furniture. Sea-facing rooms on high floors have stunning views of the Arabian Sea and Marine Drive, known because of its string of lights as the "Queen's Necklace" at night. The Frangipani restaurant has an international menu, as does the laid-back coffee shop, The Palms. Indiana Jones serves Asian food. ⊠ *Nariman Point, 400021* ☎ *22/5632–4343* 🖷 *22/5632–4142* ⟿ *537 rooms, 44 suites* ⚭ *2 restaurants, coffee shop, room service, in-room data ports, in-room safes, refrigerators, cable TV, pool, health club, sauna, bar, laundry service, business services, meeting room, travel services* ☰ *AE, DC, MC, V.*

$$$ 🏨 **Holiday Inn.** Built in the 1970s, this Western-style high-rise has a spacious lobby, executive floors for business travelers, and rooms uniformly decorated with standard contemporary furniture, floral wall-to-wall carpeting, and green-accented fabrics. The best standard rooms have limited views of the beach; only deluxe rooms face the sea directly. ⊠ *Balraj Sahani Marg, Juhu 400049* ☎ *22/5693–4444* 🖷 *22/5693–4455* ⊕ *www.holidayinnbombay.com* ⟿ *182 rooms, 13 suites* ⚭ *2 restaurants, coffee shop, room service, in-room data ports, in-room safes, refrigerators, cable TV, pool, health club, bar, dry cleaning, laundry service, business services, meeting room, airport shuttle, travel services* ☰ *AE, DC, MC, V* ⦿❘ *BP.*

$$$ 🏨 **Taj President.** In a residential neighborhood near the World Trade Center shopping emporium, this luxury hotel (and its buffet breakfast) is a favorite of business travelers. The comfortable rooms have high ceilings and modern furnishings. Sea-facing rooms cost slightly more than a city-facing room, but the view of south Bombay and the harbor beyond makes the higher rate worthwhile. For an added splurge, ask for the more expensive "superior sea-facing room" on one of the upper floors. Although the hotel is not as extravagant as others in its price range, service is outstanding. Some of the floors, the coffee shop, and the lobby have been refurbished to sport a cozy "living room" look. Also here are a restaurant called the Trattoria, a coffee shop, and Italian eatery. ⊠ *90 Cuffe Parade, Colaba, 400005* ☎ *22/5665–0808* 🖷 *22/5665–0303* ⊕ *www.tajhotels.com* ⟿ *300 rooms, 20 suites* ⚭ *3 restaurants, café, room service, in-room data ports, in-room safes, cable TV,*

pool, health club, hair salon, bar, laundry service, business services, travel services ☰ *AE, DC, MC, V.*

★ **$$–$$$** ⊞ **Grand Maratha Sheraton.** One of Bombay's newer hotels is indeed grand, with attentive and efficient service to match. Rooms overlook a pleasant shrubbery-lined atrium where meals are served. The hotel is spacious and luxurious, with expanses of granite and marble. It's the only hotel in Bombay that has a lovely Indian look: *jharokas* (window carved) and luxury reminiscent of an ancient palace. Opt for pool-facing rooms. The rooms are posh with colorful accents—light green silk curtains and plush patterned carpets—and fancy bathrooms (with tubs and glass shower cubicles and lots of marble). This is a good deal—a lot of luxury for a lot less money than you might pay elsewhere. There are three excellent Indian food restaurants and a Continental restaurant—Peshawari serves northwest frontier food, Dakshin serves South Indian food, and Dum Pukht serves Mughlai food. ⊠ *Sahar Airport Rd., Sahar 400099* ☎ *22/2830–3030* 🖶 *22/2830–3131* ⊕ *www.welcomgroup.com* ⥾ *386 rooms, 48 suites* ♣ *5 restaurants, café, room service, in-room data ports, in-room safes, refrigerators, cable TV, pool, health club, hair salon, hot tub, sauna, bar, laundry service, business services, meeting rooms, travel services* ☰ *AE, DC, MC, V.*

$$ ⊞ **Fariyas.** The shiny, small marble lobby is filled with glass chandeliers and brass ornaments. With contemporary furnishings and wall-to-wall carpets, the rooms are inviting but somewhat small. The location, however, is terrific, just a few minutes by foot from the Gateway of India. Select a room for its sea-facing view. Only two suites have tubs; the rest of the rooms have showers. A swinging pub–tavern is in the basement and plays a lot of classic rock and oldies. ⊠ *25 Devshankar V Vyas Marg, at Shahid Bhagt Singh Marg, off Arthur Bunder Rd., Colaba 400005* ☎ *22/2204–2911* 🖶 *22/2283–4992* ⊕ *www.fariyas.com* ⥾ *87 rooms, 6 suites* ♣ *Restaurant, coffee shop, room service, refrigerators, cable TV, pool, health club, bar, meeting room, travel services* ☰ *AE, DC, MC, V.*

★ **$$** ⊞ **Gordon House.** The guest rooms, lobby, and restaurant in this boutique hotel are simply but fashionably decorated. The lobby is on the second floor, rooms are on the Mediterranean, Country, and Scandinavian floors. Rooms are no-fuss but chic—earth-color buffed tiles, bright white bedspreads, and blond-wood furniture. At All Stir-Fry, an Asian restaurant here, you can construct your own meals and hand the raw ingredients to a chef who cooks them. ⊠ *5 Battery St., Apollo Bunder 400039* ☎ *22/2287–1122* 🖶 *22/2287–2026* ⊕ *www.ghhotel.com* ⥾ *28 rooms, 1 suite* ♣ *Restaurant, coffee shop, room service, in-room data ports, in-room safes, refrigerators, cable TV, bar, dance club, dry cleaning, laundry service, travel services* ☰ *AE, DC, MC, V.*

$$ ⊞ **InterContinental The Grand.** Another member of the airport hotel tribe, this spot has a curving, sand-color facade with an enormous lobby with high ceilings. The rooms open out onto balconies that overlook the lobby, and are well appointed—wood floors, India-accents in the furnishings, and a comfy vibe. The outer views of some nearby airport wasteland are not grand. The bathrooms are trimmed with marble and glass and have both tubs and shower cubicles. ⊠ *Sahar Airport Rd.,*

Sahar 400059 ☎ *22/5699–2222* 🖷 *22/5699–8888* ⊕ *www.bharathotels. com* ↗ *368 rooms, 30 suites* ♿ *Restaurant, coffee shop, room service, in-room data ports, in-room safes, refrigerators, cable TV, pool, health club, hair salon, bar, lounge, dry cleaning, laundry service, business services, meeting room, travel services* ☰ *AE, DC, MC, V.*

$$ 🏨 **JW Marriott.** The sheer size of this grand, sumptuous hotel may bowl you over. Walk beyond the vast lobby and you'll find a pair of flowing staircases that curve on each side down to a garden level café. From the top of the stairs you'll see a giant wall of glass that by day looks out to an Olympic-size swimming pool and then out to sea, and by night looks out to a garden of flaming torches, flickering blue and orange in the breeze. Lotus ponds and sandstone statues dot the garden. The rooms have views of the ocean and tasteful, subdued furnishings. All the restaurants serve excellent food. ✉ *Juhu Tara Rd., Juhu, 400049* ☎ *22/2693–3000* 🖷 *22/2693–3100* ⊕ *www.marriott.com* ↗ *358 rooms, 43 suites* ♿ *3 restaurants, coffee shop, patisserie, room service, in-room data ports, in-room safes, refrigerators, cable TV, 4 pools, hot tub, health club, hair salon, massage, sauna, spa, 2 bars, shops, dry cleaning, laundry service, snooker tables, business services, meeting room, travel services* ☰ *AE, DC, MC, V* ⏁⏣ *EP.*

$$ 🏨 **The Leela.** Close to both airports (it's a mile from the international airport) and 25 km (16 mi) outside the city, this stylish, posh property was once the only airport hotel used as a stopover for high-powered businesspeople. Today there are four newer airport hotels, but the Leela is still the best value: its rates are the lowest and the rooms are finely done and spacious, with plush, ornate carpeting, and Indian-style furnishings. Its 11 acres of gardens include lotus pools and a small waterfall. A popular Italian restaurant and an excellent Chinese restaurant, The Great Wall, are in the hotel. An Indian restaurant, Jamavar, opened in 2003 and serves Mughlai cuisine. ✉ *Sahar 400059* ☎ *22/5691–1234* 🖷 *22/ 5691–1212* ⊕ *www.theleela.com* ↗ *423 rooms, 32 suites* ♿ *4 restaurants, coffee shop, patisserie, room service, in-room data ports, in-room safes, refrigerators, cable TV, putting green, 2 tennis courts, pool, health club, massage, steam room, billiards, squash, bar, dance club, business services, meeting room, airport shuttle, travel services* ☰ *AE, DC, MC, V.*

$ 🏨 **Ramada Palm Grove.** With its small entrance, squeezed driveway, and parking lot, this place might seem small from the outside, but in fact it's fairly spacious—and quite a bargain, to boot. The lobby of this Juhu Beach high-rise is lined with marble and etched glass. Rooms are airy and comfortable—each has a small sitting area—and have subdued contemporary furnishings in shades of cool green. Deluxe suites and executive salons face the water; other rooms have limited views. The pool is a pleasant, if not especially spacious, place to unwind. The Oriental Bowl, done in black marble, serves Thai and Chinese food and is a fun place to dine. ✉ *Juhu Tara Rd., Juhu 400049* ☎ *22/2611–2323* 🖷 *22/2611–3682* ⊕ *www.krahejahospitality.com* ↗ *114 rooms, 3 suites* ♿ *Restaurant, coffee shop, room service, in-room data ports, in-room safes, refrigerators, cable TV, pool, health club, hair salon, bar, business services, meeting room, airport shuttle, travel services* ☰ *AE, DC, MC, V* ⏁⏣ *BP.*

$ ▦ **Sun 'n' Sand.** There's a tangibly friendly vibe at this 1963 Juhu Beach hotel, which you approach via a small circular driveway that curves up to a sleek exterior. The lobby leads out to a lovely garden patio and pool overlooking the sand—a major plus point of the hotel. In spite of the hotel's upscale facilities, there is something slightly off-key about the place—a sort of B-grade Hindi-movie air—which can perhaps be attributed to its age. But the rooms are comfortable and modern. Rooms, half of which face the sea, are equipped with an electric kettle, a safe, and a hair dryer; bathrooms could use a facelift. Breakfast and airport pickup are complimentary. Despite its mildy eccentric nature, Sun 'n' Sand offers the best value for money among the hotels that line Juhu Beach. ⊠ *39 Juhu Beach, 400049* ☎ *22/5693–8888 or 22/5693–2620* 🖷 *22/ 2620–2170* ⊕ *www.sunnsandhotel.com* ➴ *120 rooms, 9 suites* ⚫ *2 restaurants, coffee shop,room service, in-room data ports, in-room safes, refrigerators, cable TV, pool, health club, hair salon, massage, bar, business services, meeting room, airport shuttle, travel services* ▭ *AE, DC, MC, V* ⦿| *BP.*

$ ▦ **Bawa International.** If you're looking for a quick-stay hotel near the domestic airport or 10 minutes from the international airport, this place is a deal. It's a bit short on atmosphere but is reasonably cozy. The standard rooms are carpeted in green, furnished with white furniture, and well-lit; bathrooms are decent. The deluxe and fancier rooms aren't a great value for the money—the rates escalate quickly. ⊠ *Nehru Rd. Extension, near the domestic airport, Vile Parle 400099* ☎ *22/2611–3636 or 22/2611–4015* 🖷 *22/2610–7096* ⊕ *www.bawahotels.com* ➴ *28 rooms* ⚫ *Restaurant, coffee shop, room service, refrigerators, cable TV, bar, laundry service, business center, travel services* ▭ *AE, DC, MC, V.*

¢–$ ▦ **Godwin.** This nine-story hotel is a good, low-frills bargain. Accommodations vary widely, however—opt *only* for one of the 10 renovated deluxe rooms. These rooms have clean marble floors and in-room amenities; all other rooms are rather shabby. Most deluxe rooms have window air-conditioning units, but several are centrally air-conditioned. The bathrooms attached to the deluxe rooms could be cleaner, but are passable. Request an eighth-floor room with a distant view of the Taj Mahal hotel and Gateway of India—many rooms have no view or outright depressing views. The restaurant serves Indian and Chinese food. Also ask about rooms at Godwin's sister hotel, Garden, next door. Some rooms have tubs, others only showers. ⊠ *41 Garden Rd., off Colaba Causeway, near Electric House, Colaba 400039* ☎ *22/2287–2050 or 22/2284–1226* 🖷 *22/2287–1592* ✉ *godwinht@rediff.com* ➴ *56 rooms, 8 suites* ⚫ *2 restaurants, room service, refrigerators, cable TV, bar, laundry service* ▭ *AE, MC, V.*

$ ▦ **Garden.** At this inexpensive place on a small side street in Colaba, minutes from major sights and shops, rooms are clean and comfortable, and bathrooms are reasonably clean. Book a deluxe room; the standard rooms are not as nice. The only drawback is the lack of a pleasant view in many rooms, so check the room view before you make your decision and ask for a road-facing room on a higher floor. The restaurant serves Indian and Chinese food. ⊠ *42 Garden Rd., off Colaba Causeway near Electric House, Colaba 400039* ☎ *22/2283–1330, 22/2283–4823,*

or 22/2284–1476 ☐ *22/2204–4290* ✆ *gardenht@bom5.vsnl.net.in*
↩ *34 rooms, 3 suites* ⚐ *Restaurant, refrigerators, cable TV, laundry service* ☰ *AE, MC, V.*

$ ☷ **West End.** More than half a century old, this simple, reliable place is especially popular with foreigners looking for a good deal. The rooms—some more spacious than others—have private balconies, bathtubs, and slightly outdated furniture; opt for one facing the front. The restaurant, the lobby, and even the bellboys still have a 1940s look. The Gourmet Restaurant serves several cuisines and the popular Gujarati-thali restaurant Panchvati Gaurav is two minutes away. The building is near Bombay Hospital; you'll see doctors and visitors around until late at night. Corridors and rooms have a slightly musty smell. ✉ *45 New Marine Lines, 400020* ☎ *22/2203–9121 or 22/2205–7484* ☐ *22/2205–7506* ✆ *westhotel@vsnl.com* ↩ *80 rooms, 15 suites* ⚐ *Restaurant, room service, cable TV, bar, meeting room* ☰ *AE, DC, MC, V.*

★ $ ☷ **Ascot.** The 1950s facade is faded, but once you step inside you'll see that the rooms are renovated and plush, with shiny marble floors and comfortable beds. The bathrooms are clean, with lots of glass and chrome—the tubs have a glass window that looks out into the bedroom. This is one of the very best deals in its price range, even if most rooms lack any kind of soul-stirring view. ✉ *38 Garden Rd., Colaba 400039* ☎ *22/2284–0020 or 22/2287–2105* ☐ *22/2204–6449* ✆ *ascothotel@vsnl.com* ↩ *26 rooms* ⚐ *Restaurant, room service, refrigerators, cable TV, in-room DVD* ☰ *AE, DC, MC, V.*

¢ ☷ **Cowie's.** Minutes from the Gateway of India promenade are these few rooms in an old, roughly turn-of-the-20th-century building. The accommodations are simple and a bit dull, but they're reasonably clean; opt for one with air-condtioning. Three or four of the nicest rooms have balconies, and are the main reason for staying here. ✉ *15 Walton Rd., off Colaba Causeway, near Electric House, Colaba, 400039* ☎ *22/2284–0232 or 22/2284–5727* ☐ *22/2283–4203* ↩ *19 rooms* ⚐ *Restaurant, cable TV, room service, refrigerators, laundry service; no a/c in some rooms* ☰ *AE, MC, V* ⦿ *CP.*

¢ ☷ **Sea Green.** The green trimmings on this five-story building have been weathered by the Arabian Sea during this hotel's more than 50 years of hosting guests. Beyond its friendly service, the hotel's main virtue is that it's a remarkable bargain for its price and location, if you don't mind the lack of facilities and worn, government-office look. Narrow hallways lead to surprisingly large rooms with window air-conditioners and clean but institutional furnishings, such as metal wardrobes and turquoise vinyl couches. All rooms but one have small balconies; a few look across Marine Drive to the sea and offer a splendid view of Bombay's famous sea promenade. The bathrooms have only open showers, no stalls or tubs. Room service offers beverages and simple breakfasts only. Don't mistake this place for the hotel's twin, next door—the Sea Green South Hotel, where rooms are less hospitable. ✉ *145 Marine Dr., 400020* ☎ *22/2282–2294* ☐ *22/2283–6158* ⊕ *www.seagreenhotel.com* ↩ *34 rooms, 4 suites* ⚐ *Room service, refrigerators, cable TV* ☰ *AE, DC, MC, V.*

¢ ☷ **Sea Palace Hotel.** This hotel is right on the waterfront near the Gateway of India. The rooms don't make great use of the view—they face the opposite direction. Bathrooms, however, have been fitted into the walls facing the sea. The result: each room has an abbreviated sea view in a far corner. Furnishings are functional—bedspreads with busy patterns, red sofas, and no carpets. Still, the location is enough to make this a good choice, and the staff is attentive. ⊠ *26 P. J. Ramachandani Marg, Apollo Bunder 4000039* ☎ *22/2284–1828 or 22/2285–4404* ᐧ *22/2285–4403* ⊕ *www.seapalacehotel.com* ➲ *50 rooms, 3 suites* ⌂ *Restaurant, room service, refrigerators, cable TV* ⊟ *AE, DC, MC, V.*

★ ¢ ⊡ **Shelley's.** This white, four-story hotel built in 1935 has an old-fashioned, Raj-era appearance and sits on the waterfront in the shadow of the Gateway of India. Although the front desk isn't always as helpful as it could be, this hotel is nonetheless a memorable, convenient, and cost-effective place to stay. The rooms—especially the bathrooms—are clean. The sea-facing rooms (called suites–apartments) cost Rs. 300 more than the standard rooms and are reserved for extended stays—a month or so–only, but they have grand views of the waterfront, so try to stay in one if you can. ⊠ *30 P. J. Ramachandani Marg, Apollo Bunder* ☎ *22/2284–0229* ᐧ *22/2288–1436* ⊕ *www.shelleyshotel.com* ➲ *20 rooms, 4 suites* ⌂ *Dining room, refrigerators, cable TV, some room service* ⊟ *AE, MC, V* ⦿ *EP.*

¢ ⊡ **YWCA International Center.** About the cheapest you can go in the budget category and still have decent, clean, and safe rooms is the "Y." Rooms are in a colorless modern block and lack anything special, however. The air-conditioned rooms are more pleasant and less drab than the non-air-conditioned ones, but are more expensive. You can expect just the basics, plus a shower; everything is quite clean, though the hallways and stairwells could be spiffier. Try for a street-facing room. Rates include morning tea, breakfast, and a buffet dinner. It's essential to reserve a month or two in advance. Note that most rooms are singles or doubles, but they also have dormitory-style accommodation and "family" rooms. ⊠ *18 Madame Cama Rd., near Regal Cinema, Fort 400039* ☎ *22/2282–6814 or 22/2202–5053* ᐧ *22/2202–0445* ⊕ *www.ywcabombay.com* ➲ *39 rooms* ⌂ *Some room service, cable TV; no a/c in some rooms* ⊟ *AE, DC, MC, V* ⦿ *MAP.*

NIGHTLIFE & THE ARTS

The Arts

The best source of arts information is the fortnightly culture calendar "Programme of Dance, Music and Drama," free at the Government of India Tourist Office. The daily *Times of India* usually lists each day's films, concerts, and other events on the last two or three pages; on Friday, the afternoon paper *Midday* publishes "The List" to highlight the coming week's events. Program information and details usually appear on the Maharashtra Tourism Development Corporation's (MTDC) city-guide programs, shown regularly on hotels' in-house TV stations. The **National Centre for the Performing Arts** (NCPA; ⊠ Nariman Point ☎ 22/2283–3737, 22/2283–3838, or 22/2282–4567) posts its performance schedule on the bulletin board at the main entrance and at the entrances to its Tata and Experimental theaters. Note that many NCPA performances are open to members only; a year's membership is Rs. 1,200. Other performance tickets in Bombay are usually very inexpensive (from free to Rs. 360) and can be purchased from box offices or from the ticket counter at **Rhythm House Private Ltd.** (✉ 40 K. Dubash Marg, Rampart Row, Kala Ghoda, Fort ☎ 22/2285–3963), across the street from the Jehangir Art Gallery, one of Bombay's main music stores and another source of information on what's happening.

Dance

The **National Centre for the Performing Arts** (✉ Nariman Point ☎ 22/2283–3737, 22/2283–3838, or 22/2282–4567) houses the **Godrej Dance Academy Theater,** a main venue for classical Indian dance performances, as well as workshops and master classes, and the **Drama Opera Arts Complex,** a 1,000-seat auditorium is Bombay's ballet and opera theater.

Film

Bombay, a.k.a. "Bollywood," is the center of the Indian film industry—the largest film producer in the world. Most of the epic Indian musicals shown in movie theaters are in Hindi. Every tourist should take in a Hindi film—full of song, tears, gun battles, and around-the-trees love dances, Indian films provide plenty of tamasha, or spectacle. To catch a Hindi film, your best option is **Metro Cinema** (✉ Metro House, M. G. Rd., Dhobi Talao ☎ 22/2203–0303). **Nehru Centre Auditorium** (✉ Dr. Annie Besant Rd., Worli ☎22/2496–4676) sometimes shows interesting art films, some in English. If you're looking around for films, make sure you check listings for the **National Center for the Performing Arts** (✉ Nariman Point ☎22/2283–3737, 22/2283–3838, or 22/2282–4567). The **Regal Cinema** (✉ Shaheed Bhagat Singh Rd., opposite Prince of Wales Museum, Colaba ☎ 22/2202–1017) usually shows current English-language movies. The **Sterling Cinema** (✉ Tata Palace, Murzban Rd., off D. Naoroji Rd., near Victoria Terminus, Fort ☎ 22/2207–5187) shows current English-language films. The **Imax Adlabs** (✉ Anik Wadala Link Rd., Wadala ☎22/2403–6472 or 22/2403–6474) is Bombay's only Imax theater and is first rate at that. A little way out (northeast) of south Bombay, it shows a mixture of popular and documentary films in its main dome theater.

Music & Theater

The **National Center for the Performing Arts (NCPA)** (✉ Nariman Point ☎22/2283–3737, 22/2283–3838, or 22/2282–4567) complex includes the **Tata Theatre,** a grand 1,000-seat auditorium that regularly hosts plays, often in English, and classical concerts by major Indian and international musicians. The **Little Theatre** is the NCPA's smallest, hosting small-scale plays and Western chamber music. The **Experimental Theatre,** with 300 seats, is usually used for avant-garde drama and occasionally for concerts and small-scale dance performances. The **Nehru Centre Auditorium** (✉ Dr. Annie Besant Rd., Worli ☎ 22/2496–4676) is Bombay's second major venue, where theater, music, and dance performances are regularly held. The **Prithvi Theatre** (✉ Janaki Kutir, Church Rd., Juhu ☎ 22/2614–9546), run by the famous Kapoor acting family, stages a variety of plays each week, some in English, with reasonably priced tickets. It's a 45-minute drive north from downtown Bombay in nontraffic hours.

CloseUp
SONG & DANCE, BOLLYWOOD STYLE

NICKNAMED AFTER ITS HOLLYWOOD EXEMPLAR, BOLLYWOOD, *the famously spirited and wildly popular Indian film industry, headquartered in Bombay, is one of the largest in the world. Its devoted Hindi-speaking patrons number in the tens of millions.*

What most people don't realize is that Bollywood is only one center of film production in India. There are Tollywoods and Chollywoods and what have you— the Tamil, Telugu, Malayalam, Kannada, and Bengali film industries are as prolific as their Bombay chapter. But in Bombay alone, several films may be produced in a given week.

For almost 40 years, the blueprint of Bollywood movies hasn't changed much: a little bit of mirch (spice), a little bit of masala (pungency), love, injustice, religion, violence, and a happy ending. Heroes rarely die in Bollywood, and joyous songs (at least six) are a must. The hero and heroine often frolic around trees at some exotic locale (the woods or the Himalayas). Dance sequences are essential and songs can make or break a film. Compelling fight scenes—the more improbable the better, the more fake blood the more appealing—also pique audiences. New films are often variants of tried-and-true plots—good cop vs. bad cop (often they turn out to be brothers), unrequited love, and one man anti-establishment wars.

Hindi films play a special role in the lives of the Indian people. For the poor, illiterate, and illusionless, paying a few rupees for three solid hours of fantasy is a terrific bargain. Middle- and upper-class Indians are no less attached to their movies and the filmy bhagwans (gods). The arrival of a Hindi star at a restaurant or a shooting attracts mobs; these actors

and actresses are the demigods of India. The modest Amitabh Bachchan, one of India's favorite superstars, has a temple dedicated to him in West Bengal. He has become so popular that he was chosen to host the Indian equivalent of Who Wants to be a Millionaire on television.

Watching the production of a film is a rare treat. Movie shooting extravaganzas bristle with pandemonium—hundreds of people shuffle between the arc lights while the star has one go after another at her lines. Staging can be schlocky, but fun to watch: a rain scene may consist of a showerhead attached to a hose held upside down over the hero's head, as cameras roll in for a close-up and crowds undulate. Like all things Indian, out of this chaos emerges a vague order that keeps the juggernaut moving.

On any afternoon, you can take in a Hindi film at a local theater. Better still, have a local accompany you to provide a translation. You may even be granted admission to visit a film set if you call up one of the big Bombay studios and talk to the studio manager **Mehboob Studios** *(✉ Hill Rd., Bandra ☎ 22/2642–1628, 22/2642–1630, or 22/2642–1630 ☎☎ 22/2642–1630);* **Natraj Studios** *(✉ Andheri East: ☎ 22/2835–3443, 22/2834–0972, 22/2834–2139, or 22/2834–2371);* **Film City** *(✉ Goregaon, ☎ 22/840–1533).*

Nightlife

Between couples strolling on the breezy promenade around the Gateway of India and fashion-forward twentysomethings dancing at Insomnia at the Taj, Bombay has what may be the most vibrant nightlife in India. Because of astronomical real-estate prices and bullying by racketeers, however, only a few private groups have opened their own bars or clubs. Quite a few of the nightspots in Bombay proper are in established hotels and restaurants; many of the rest are in wealthy suburbs like Juhu and Bandra, where the after-dark scene thrives on suburbia's young nouveau riche as well as city folk willing to travel for a good night out.

Note that many clubs and bars have "couples" policies, whereby a lone man is not permitted to enter without a woman—a circuitous attempt to prevent brawls, pick-up scenes, and prostitution. To avoid an unpleasant encounter at the door, check with your hotel staff if you are a man traveling alone or in a group of men. Dress nicely and you'll probably get in; an advance call from your hotel concierge might also make your entry smoother. Most nightspots, even pubs that would otherwise be conducive to cozy talks over beers, tend to have extremely loud music and are very smoky. If you'd like to converse beyond a few shouts over blaring rock music, opt for the more reserved bars and lounges in hotels.

Revelry peaks from Thursday to Sunday nights, with primarily a late-twenties-to-mid-thirties crowd—on Sunday. Pubs are open daily, at around 7 or 8 (except a few, which open in the afternoon) and close by midnight or a little later. Only few remain open longer, depending on current police rules in the area. Some places collect a nominal cover charge at the door. As in any metropolis, the reign of a nightspot can be ephemeral; ask a young hotel employee to brief you on the current scene.

Bars & Lounges

The **Athena** (⊠ 41/44 Minoo Desai Marg, near the Fariyas hotel, Colaba ☎ 22/2202–8699) faces the waterfront. Very austere and sleek, this "champagne cigar lounge" has a postmodern look. The **Bay View Bar** (⊠ The Oberoi, Nariman Point ☎ 22/2202–5757) facing the Arabian Sea is elegant and more reserved than many of its peers, encouraging a rather expensive cover charge. It has live music Monday through Saturday. The **Copa Cabana** (⊠ 39D Chowpatty Beach ☎ 22/2368–0274) is not as hot it used to be but still seems to catch quite a crowd of late night-revelers. **Geoffrey's** (⊠ Hotel Marine Plaza, 29 Marine Dr. ☎ 22/2285–1212) draws a relatively staid yuppie crowd with golden oldies and a clubby setting. **The Ghetto** (⊠ 30 Bhulabhai Desai Rd., Breach Candy ☎ 22/2492–4725) is a psychedelic–rave bar with a fairly grungy clientele, a strange combination of '60s and techno music, and convincingly graffitied walls. It can be fun late in the evening. **HQ** (⊠ Above Cafe Royal, near Regal Cinema, Colaba ☎ 22/2288–3983) plays modern favorites from techno to rap. It has a phantasmal look, with lots of chrome and glass. **Library Bar** (⊠ Taj President, 90 Cuffe Parade, Colaba ☎ 22/

CloseUp

AFTER-HOURS DANCE BARS

Bombay has a category of nightspots, which are none too kosher, called dance bars. These are licensed bars that offer "cultural programs" and are frequented by lone men or groups of men looking for an opportunity to watch—only watch—fully clad, but enticingly attired, dancing women. These bars look like garishly furnished lounges. Sofas are arranged around a dance floor, where the women gyrate to the latest Hindi film–Indy pop music. Drinks, quite often low-quality liquor,

are offered, usually at rather high prices. Tipping the women is the only interaction allowed with them. A visit to a dance bar— try Carnival at Worli, Topaz at Grant Road bridge, or Indiana at Tardeo—is eye-opening. It's unwise for women to go at all; women do not hang out at these places. But whatever your gender, do not attempt to find or frequent these places unless you are chaperoned by a few locals (all men) who know the bar. Places are generally open every night from about 10 PM to dawn.

5665–0808), one of the more popular bars in south Bombay, is a lively place for an evening out. Indonesians Maria and Noel and their band—a fixture here–offer live music every day except Monday; the place really swings on the weekends. The bar is open daily until 1 PM.

Clubs & Discos

Club IX (⊠ Dr Ambedkar Rd., Pali Hill, Khar ☎ 22/2646–5133 or 22/2646–5134) had a laid-back vibe and a penchant for golden oldies. **Enigma** (⊠ J. W. Marriott, Juhu Tara Rd., Juhu ☎ 22/2693–3000), in the swanky Marriott, is the hottest disco in the 'burbs. It's popular with rockers of all ages. **Insomnia** (⊠ Taj Mahal Palace & Towers, Apollo Bunder ☎ 22/5665–3366), intended primarily for Taj Mahal guests, is an upmarket club with a high-tech, Gotham City theme—full of metal girders and waiters dressed like the Joker's henchmen. It's open 9:30 PM–1:30 AM and costs Rs. 600 a couple for entry on weekdays and Rs. 1,000 on weekends. **Lush** (⊠ Phoenix Mills Compound, Parel ☎ 22/5663–4601) is a small but tony new night club pub in the ever-expanding Parel shopping and entertainment complex. **Not Just Jazz by the Bay** (⊠ 143 Marine Dr. ☎ 22/2282–0883, 22/2285–1876, or 22/2282–0957) is one of Bombay's few jazz venues, with live music several nights a week. Its location by the sea is beautiful. It serves a buffet lunch, and it stays open until 1:30 AM. **ProVogue Lounge** (⊠ Phoenix Mills Compound, Parel ☎ 22/5662–4535 or 22/2497–2525) is by day a shop for casual clothing and by night a casual-chic lounge bar with a cultivated scruffy, unpainted look. At **Razzberry Rhinoceros** (⊠ Juhu Hotel, Juhu Tara Rd., Juhu ☎ 22/2618–4012) the scene is young and casual and the music loud rock, pop, or jazz. On Sunday they have a Bollywood night and on Friday a trance music evening. **Zaha** (⊠ The Leela, Sahar ☎ 22/5691–1234) was once a disco but has now been converted into a more elegant and posh lounge and nightclub.

SPORTS & THE OUTDOORS

Cricket

You can buy tickets, which range in price from Rs. 150 to Rs. 10,000, through the **Bombay Cricket Association** (✉ D. Rd., Churchgate ☎ 22/2281–9910 or 22/2281–2714). **Wankhede Stadium** (✉ D. Rd., Churchgate) hosts Bombay's major domestic and international cricket matches. In season—October through March—there are usually several matches a week.

Golf

The **Willingdon Sports Club** (✉ K. Khadye Marg, Mahalaxmi ☎ 22/2494–5754) has an 18-hole golf course. Nonmembers can usually play as "guests" of the secretary for $77 per week but you are required to apply through a member of the club. Call ahead to make arrangements and see if you can work something out.

Horse-and-Buggy Rides

For a quick tour of Bombay's illuminated sights by night, hop in one of the horse-drawn buggies parked at Nariman Point, next to the Oberoi Towers, at the northern end of Marine Drive, or at the Gateway of India. Neither the carriages nor the horses are in particularly good shape, let alone elegant, but if you don't require luxury this can be an enjoyable jaunt. A spin from the Gateway of India to Churchgate and back, taking in key sights on the way, takes about an hour and should cost less than Rs. 150 (settle the price ahead of time).

Horse Racing

Bombay's **Mahalaxmi Race Course** (✉ near Nehru Planetarium ☎ 22/2307–1401) is one of the finest courses in Asia. A visit here in season is a social experience—for a few months each year, this green patch in central Bombay becomes an echo of London's Ascot racecourse in the 1950s, with faux British accents, outfits that kill, and plenty of pomp and showiness. The season usually runs from November through April, with races on Thursday and Sunday. Right next door at the Amateur Riding Club you can rent horses for rides. Call 22/2307–1445 one day in advance. Half-hour riding sessions (Rs. 500) are from 6:15 to 7 AM and from 5 to 6.30 PM.

Sailing & Watersports

Members of any yachting association affiliated with the **Royal Bombay Yacht Club** (✉ Chhatrapati Shivaji Maharaj Marg, Apollo Bunder 400001 ☎ 22/2202–1880 ⊕ www.royalbombayyachtclub.com) can charter a boat for local sailing, October to June. The club also offers visiting memberships for a reasonable Rs. 450 for 28 days.

With **Drishti Adventure Sports** (✉ At Marine Drive, right next to Chowpatty Beach ☎ 22/2367–7584) you can take a ride in a speedboat along Marine Drive (Rs. 125 for half an hour), a daytime bay cruise (Rs. 150), or a night cruise (Rs. 20). Boats can carry up to six people; small children are not permitted. The service is not open during the monsoon. They also rent jet skis (Rs. 180 for half an hour) or and motorboats (Rs. 60). Other options include pedal boats, kayaks, row boats, and banana boats. A good option is to take a boat out to Knight's Wharf, a bar that's located on a large boat in the ocean. It costs Rs. 150 to get onto the boat (children aren't permitted).

SHOPPING

From crowded street bazaars to exclusive air-conditioned boutiques, Bombay can keep the enthusiastic shopper riveted for days. Colaba Causeway (officially called Shahid Bhagat Singh Marg but popularly referred to as Colaba Causeway), Flora Fountain, Kemps Corner, and Breach Candy are all trendy shopping areas in South Bombay; the latter two are chic and pricey. The air-conditioned World Trade Center on Cuffe Parade, at the southern tip of Bombay, looks discouraging from the outside but houses a cluster of government-run emporiums with fixed-price crafts from all over India. Crossroads is Bombay's newest mall, and a swanky one at that: it's unusually spacious and attractive, and is open daily. India's most fashionable clothing labels have stores here, and the rest of the 130 shops sell everything from napkins to videos. The arcades in top hotels—those at the Oberoi and Taj Mahal (smaller) offer a little bit of everything for a lot more money than anywhere else, but the merchandise is beautiful and the pace unhurried (and it's climate-controlled). For lower prices and a more vibrant experience, throw yourself into the middle of one of Bombay's famous bazaars.

Once you've exhausted Bombay proper, you can venture out to the suburbs, where prices tend to be lower. Linking Road in Bandra is a trendy place to shop, and Juhu's main strip, Juhu Tara Road, is lined with trendy new boutiques, shops, art galleries, and restaurants. Note that each neighborhood has a different closing day for shops. In Colaba, up to Worli, shops are closed Sunday; in Worli, up to Bandra, they're closed Monday; and in Bandra, up to the suburbs, they're closed Thursday. Throughout Bombay, many shops are closed on Sunday.

Bazaars & Markets

Chor Bazaar (⊠ Mutton St. near Kutbi Masjid, off Mohammed Ali Rd., Mandvi) is a bustling flea market where you can find exactly what you don't need but have to have—old phonographs, broken nautical instruments, dusty chandeliers, furniture, and brass objects ranging from junky knickknacks to valuable antiques and curios. Keep an eye on your purse or wallet and come relaxed—it can be chaotic. **Fashion Street** (⊠ Stretch of M. G. Rd. opposite Bombay Gymkhana, Fort) is a cotton bargain trove in a long row of open-air stalls, with mounds of colorful, cheap, mainly Western clothing for all ages. Come around 11 AM, when the crowds are thinner and the sun has not yet peaked—and bargain. **Zaveri Bazaar** (⊠ Sheikh Memon St., a 10-min walk, a few blocks northwest of Crawford Market, Kalbadevi ⊙ Mon.–Sat. 11–7) is the place to go for diamond, gold, and silver *zevar* (jewelry). The tumultuous streets are lined with tiny, decades-old family jewelry businesses. Duck into one and sip a customary cup of tea or coffee while a salesperson shows you the merchandise. Most shops are authentic, but beware of false silver and gold; it's difficult to spot, however.

Department Stores & Malls

The Courtyard (✉ 41/44 Minoo Desai Rd., Colaba) is a small mall of ritzy designer shops that has opened one block from the Taj Mahal hotel. Indian designers are doing a brisk business these days and the best address to get a flavor of their work is The Courtyard—silks, cottons, linens, garments rich with hand and machine embroidery and *zari* (gold-embroidered). Clothes (Indian and Western), handbags, and knickknacks for the home are sold here. Rest at the chrome-and-red ultramodern mall café, Sesso, for a chai (tea) break or meal—the cuisine is international.

High Street Phoenix (✉ Phoenix Mills Compound, Senapati Bapat Marg, Parel) is an ever-expanding shopping, entertainment, and dining area. This complex is an island of prosperity and chic modernity among slums and industry. A number of upscale shops, bars, and restaurants have come up at Phoenix Mills and because of the unlimited space everything is on a grand scale. Check out the international-looking and posh **Lifestyle** (☎ 22/5666–9200), a four-floor department store, stocks everything from clothing to gifts and household items. Or try **Ritu** (☎ 22/5666–9901) for elegant, hand-embroidered silk, cotton, and chiffon formal wear, chic-casual, and household items. **Big Bazaar** is a warehouse shop that offers just about anything from a broom to a pen to potato chips. **Pantaloons** is a large outlet for casual wear for men, women and children. **Planet M** has all kinds of music. Snack or dine at Bombay Blues, Noodle bar, Baskin Robbins, McDonald's, Lush, Natural Ice Cream, or Marroush.

Piramyd (✉ Crossroads mall, 28 Pandit Madan Mohan, Malviya Rd., Haji Ali ☎ 22/2351–5890 or 22/2351–5892) sells a wide and attractive selection of Indian and Western clothes, including designer labels, for men and women. There's also a selection of some of India's best cottons for kids. Piramyd is attached to the Crossroads mall, which has a variety of shops.

Shopper's Stop (✉ S.V. Rd., Andheri ☎ 22/2624–0451 or 22/2624–0453) is a large and popular department store that sells everything from perfume to underwear to gifts and home decor items. It's a good place to buy trendy but reasonably priced Western clothes, especially men's clothing, and fine *salwar-kurta* (loose long tunic with flowing pants) sets.

Westside (✉ 158 M. G. Rd., Kala Ghoda, Fort ☎ 22/5636–0495 ⊘ daily 10:30–8:30 ✉ 39 Hughes Rd., Gwalior Tank ☎ 22/2384–1730 ⊘ daily 10:30–8:30) stocks a decent range of Western wear, as well as interesting kurta sets for women. The menswear section includes a variety of office and casual cotton shirts. You'll also find reasonably priced household items such as bed linens, pottery, and tablecloths.

Art & Antiques

The **Jehangir Art Gallery** (✉ Kala Ghoda, Fort ☎ 22/2284–3989) has at least three art shows every week on the main floor or at the **Gallery Chemould** (☎ 22/2283–3640) or even on the pavement racks outside in fair weather. Prices vary vastly. The whole area adjoining Jehangir

Art Gallery has become an art district and exhibitions can be happening at adjoining buildings, too. Inquire at the gallery. **Natesans Antiquarts Ltd.** (✉ Basement of Jehangir Art Gallery, Fort ☎ 22/2285–2700 ✉ Taj Mahal Palace & Towers, Apollo Bunder ☎ 22/2202–4165), which has branches in many Indian cities, sells magnificent but expensive curios, subcontinental antiquities, wood carvings, sculptures, and paintings. **Phillips Antiques** (✉ Madam Cama Rd., opposite Regal Cinema, Fort ☎ 22/2202–0564) begun in 1860 is a unique antiques shop and has the best choice of old prints, engravings, and maps in Bombay. Phillips also sells many possessions left behind by the British—Staffordshire and East India Company china, old jewelry, crystal, lacquerware, and sterling silver. Salespeople here take a one-hour lunch break. The **Raj Company** (✉ Volga House, opposite the Turf Club, Khare Marg, near Mahalaxmi suburban railway station, Mahalaxmi ☎ 22/2494–1971) sells colonial furniture and faithful reproductions.

Books

Most large hotels have small bookshops, but Bombay's best selection is at **Crossword** (✉ Mahalaxmi Chambers, Bhulabhai Desai Rd., near Mahalakshmi temple, Breach Candy ☎ 22/2498–5803), probably the largest bookstore in Bombay and a comfortable place to browse. **Danai** (✉ Jain Arcade bldg., 14 Khar Danda Rd., Khar ☎ 22/2648–7123), north of the commercial center between Bandra and Santa Cruz, is the largest suburban bookstore and also sells CDs and cassettes. **Nalanda** (✉ Taj Mahal Palace & Towers, Apollo Bunder ☎ 22/2202–2514), open until midnight, has plenty of books on India, including travel guides and fiction, and the latest foreign papers. **Oxford Bookstore** (✉ Apeejay House, 3, Dinsha Vachcha Rd., Churchgate ☎ 22/5636–4477) is a posh new bookstore with books on India, magazines, children's books, and a modern café, Chai Bar, that's a destination unto itself. The **Strand Book Stall** (✉ Dhannur Sir P. M. Rd., Fort ☎ 22/2266–1994 or 22/2266–1719) has good discounts. The sidewalk book market on **Veer Nariman Road**, opposite Flora Fountain (near the Central Telegraph office) and toward Victoria Terminus, is a great source for secondhand books. You can score some rare finds here—bargain. ✉ *Churchgate*.

Carpets

The **Central Cottage Industries Emporium** (✉ Narang House, 34 Shivaji Marg, 1 block north of Taj Mahal hotel, Colaba ☎ 22/2202–6564 or 22/2202–7537) stocks an excellent selection of traditional Kashmiri carpets at reliable prices. **CIE** (✉ Electric House, Colaba ☎ 22/2281–8802) has a large selection of Indian crafts, from carpets to bronze art pieces. Prices are steep. **Coir Board** (✉ 5 Stadium House, Veer Nariman Rd., Churchgate ☎ 22/2282–1575 ⊙ Mon.–Sat., except 2nd and 4th Sat. of each month) has cheap jute and *coir* (coconut husk) matting. On **Colaba Causeway** (✉ Between Regal Cinema and Cusrow Baug, and on lanes leading off the causeway, Colaba), you'll find lots of carpet stores. You may find a genuine, well-priced carpet in any of these shops, but you're on your own vis-à-vis unscrupulous shopkeepers.

A carpet's mix of silk, wool, and cotton determines its price; visit several shops, including the government emporiums, to get a sense of the market before cutting a deal in an independent shop. There are several Kashmiri-run carpet shops in the **Oberoi** (⊠ Nariman Point). A small, fixed-price outlet for the well-known brand **Shyam Ahuja** (⊠ Khilchi and Sons [stockist], under the flyover, Kemps Corner ⊠ C Wing, Gazdar Apartments, Juhu Tara Rd., Juhu ☎ 22/2615–1749) has cotton dhurries and wool carpets.

Children's Clothing & Toys

Tailoring children's clothes can be fun in India, given the variety of cloth available. For the best bargains in cheap cotton clothing head to Fashion Street (⇨ Bazaars & Markets, *above*). **Bombay Store** (⊠ Sir Pherozeshah Mehta Rd., Fort ☎ 22/2288–5048 or 22/2288–5048) has cottons for children. The **Central Cottage Industries Emporium** (⊠ Narang House, 34 Shivaji Marg, 1 block north of Taj Mahal hotel, Colaba ☎ 22/2202–6564 or 22/2202–7537) has a small but imaginative assortment of Indian costumes for kids, and traditional Indian toys. Mirror-work elephants, Indian dolls, wood and cane doll furniture, tiny brass tea sets, stuffed leather animals, and puppets can all be found on the second floor, as can *kurtas* (collarless or band-collar shirts) and long skirt ensembles in cotton and silk. **Colaba Causeway** is lined with pavement stalls selling various children's trinkets—leather animals, small drums, purses, beads, and peacock-feather fans. A number of shops–pavement stalls here also sell Indian clothing for kids. (⊠ Colaba) **Fab India** (⊠ Navroze Apartments, Pali Hill, near HDFC bank, Bandra ☎ 22/2605–7780) sells cotton clothing for children. Several shops in the **Oberoi Towers** (⊠ Nariman Point) sell Indian children's clothes, cool cotton dresses, and wooden dolls. **Piramyd** (⊠ Crossroads mall, 28 Pandit Madan Mohan, Malviya Rd., Haji Ali ☎ 22/2351–5890 or 22/2351–5892) has cotton casuals for kids.

Clothing

Bombay is an excellent place to shop for cotton, silk, rayon, and linen clothing. More and more designer boutiques sell expensive but well tailored items designed by upcoming or top Indian designers. A clutch of boutiques are located at Kemps Corner (Be and Melange), Breach Candy, Colaba, Phoenix Mills (in Parel), Bandra, and Juhu. But the best place to buy bargain cotton clothes is undoubtedly Fashion Street, across from the Bombay Gymkana (⇨ Bazaars & Markets). **Anokhi** (⊠ Opposite Cumballa Hill Hospital, Kemps Corner ☎ 22/2382–0636) has colorful clothes with block-print designs from Rajasthan. The large, attractive, and friendly **Bombay Store** (⊠ Sir Pherozeshah Mehta Rd., Fort ☎ 22/2288–5048 or 22/2288–5049) has men's shirts, kurtas, ties, women's *salwar kameez* (a loose-fitting tunic over loose pants tapered at the ankle), blouses, skirts, shawls, saris, some silk by the meter, and cotton clothes for children. **Charagh Din** (⊠ 64 Wodehouse Rd., Colaba ☎ 22/2218–1375) is one of the best-known Indian names for top-quality, pure silk shirts for men in a tremendous variety of styles and patterns. **Christina**

CloseUp
CUSTOM TAILORS & FINE FABRICS

FOR HALF A CENTURY BOMBAY WAS THE HUB of India's textile business, and once much of central Bombay were cloth mills. Most of that business moved out of Bombay to smaller towns and to Gujarat in the 1980s as manufacturing in the heart of Bombay became unfeasible especially following several rounds of mill worker strikes. Bombay's bazaars still boom with some of the richest and widest varieties of cloth. The Mangaldas Cloth Market has enough bales of material to carpet all of South Bombay. Tissue silks, khadi (handloom) silks, crushed cotton, satin, hakoba (embroidered cotton).

Tailoring in Bombay is not a particularly difficult proposition. A number of Bombay tailors can turn splendid fabric into custom-made clothing—Indian or Western—in a matter of hours for both ladies and gents. The tailors are often armed with the latest catalogs and will faithfully copy a design from a picture. Tailors are fast and quite competent. If you have a blouse or shirt or trousers to give in as a sample they generally get it down pat. Make sure you personally shrink cotton material and its lining before you give it in for stitching (rinse for a few minutes and drip dry; colored cottons need to be rinsed by themselves and for just a few seconds to prevent too much bleeding). Fix a rate beforehand and give an earlier deadline. If the material needs a lining, buy it yourself.

Aamrapali Collections (⊠ Shop 38, Ruki Mahal, near Standard Auto Petrol Pump, Colaba ☎ 22/2288–5060) are very prompt and efficient. They largely do Indian clothes, salwar-kameez (tunic and pants) outfits, and sari blouses, but if you give them a sample to copy they can make you a Western-style outfit, too. **Arjan Matching Centre** (⊠ Ruki Mahal, near Standard Auto Petrol Pump, opposite Hanuman Mandir, Colaba ☎ 22/2284–1516 or 22/2288–5767) has brocade and plain silk, and is the best place to find material for linings. A reliable tailor (Aamrapalli) is next door at Shop 38. **Burlingtons** (⊠ Taj Mahal Palace & Towers, Apollo Bunder ☎ 22/2202–5593) is a classy boutique where, in 2001, Bill Clinton came to have a sherwani (a long brocade coat) made. Prices are higher than some other places, but you'll get to choose from an enormous range of silk and embroidered material. **Hakoba Fabrics** (⊠ Cusrow Baug, Shahid Bhagat Singh Rd., Colaba ☎ no phone) is a tiny shop that offers a fine selection of hakoba material: pastel and deep-colored cottons, machine-embroidered with fine white thread designs or selfed (same color embroidery as the material) are sold by the meter. Amrapalli Tailors is a few doors away. **Narisons Khubsons** (⊠ 49 Colaba Causeway, opposite Colaba police station ☎ 22/2202–0614) carries fine cotton and silk and can make excellent shirts, trousers, or women's outfits in one day if need be. They also sell ready-made women's clothing. There are two shops named Khubsons, back to back; make sure you have the right one. **Raymond** (⊠ Bhulabhai Desai Rd., opposite Breach Candy Hospital and Research Centre ☎ 22/2368–2644) is an outlet for Raymond Mills, which makes some of India's finest men's suits. They can tailor a first-rate suit for about Rs. 3,500 in about a week. Call ahead to ask about delivery time; during the wedding season (winter) they can get very busy. **Roop Milan** (⊠ Maharshi Karve Rd., near Marine Lines Station ☎ 22/2200–1257 or 22/2200–5951) is primarily a sari shop but they sell a huge variety of fine silks at their upstairs counter.

(⊠ The Oberoi, Nariman Point ☎ 22/2282–5069) is a tiny, classy boutique with exquisite silk blouses and shirts, scarves, ties, *dupattas* (long, thin scarves for draping), and silk-edge purses and wallets. **Cotton World** (⊠ Ram Nimi bldg., Mandlik Rd., Colaba ☎ 22/2285–0060 or 22/2283–3294 ⊠ Vipul Apartments, near Podar High School, Tagore Rd., Santa Cruz [north of Bandra, and southwest of Sahar International Airport] ☎ 22/2649–6693 or 22/2605–1602) is small but has some excellent Western cotton items at reasonable prices. **Ensemble** (⊠ Great Western Bldg., 130/132 Shahid Bhagat Singh Marg, Kala Ghoda, Fort ☎ 22/2284–3227 or 22/2287–2882 ⊠ 2nd fl., Crossroads mall, Haji Ali ☎ 22/2352–5164), a pricey boutique not far from the Taj Mahal hotel. It has exclusive men's and women's Indian and Western fashions, and lovely costume jewelry, all by high-profile Indian designers. Ask to see the rare Banarasi silk saris, in rich colors woven with real gold and silver thread. The second outlet at Crossroads stocks more casuals. **Fab India** (⊠ Navroze Apartments, Pali Hill, near HDFC bank, Bandra ☎ 22/2605–7780) is good for cotton clothing tailored from vegetable-dye prints—skirts, blouses, and kurtas for men and women. The Bombay branch of the famous Madras store **Nalli** (⊠ Trimurti Apartments, Bhulabhai Desai Rd., Breach Candy ☎22/2496–5577 or 22/2496–5599), has a fair selection of classic silk saris. Have a look at the authentic *zari* or gold-embroidered Kanchipuram saris (from Kanchipuram in Tamil Nadu), the Bangalore saris, and the uncut silk, sold by the meter. **High Street Phoenix Mills** (⊠ Parel) was once a textile mill, but this industrial area has since been converted into a shopping center of restaurants, bars, and shops. Lifestyle and Ritu stock designer wear. Take a break and lunch at any one of the numerous restaurants there—Noodle Bar, Bombay Blues, or Soul Curry.

Go to **Piramyd** (⊠ Crossroads mall, 28 Pandit Madan Mohan, Malviya Rd., Haji Ali ☎ 22/2494–5890 or 22/2494–5891) for a good selection of Indian and Western clothes for men and women, some of it quite reasonable, as well as for designer labels. **Ravissant** (⊠ 131 August Kranti Marg, Kemps Corner ☎ 22/2368–4934) was India's first haute-couture salon; it sells its own women's and men's clothing in exquisite patterns and fabrics, from rich silks to feather-light moiré. The branch in the Taj Mahal Palace & Towers (☎ 22/2281–5227) also sells unique silver housewares and furnishings. A few shops in the **Taj Mahal Palace & Tower** (⊠ Apollo Bunder) sell quality silks; try Burlington or the Indian Textiles Company. **Vama** (⊠ 72 Peddar Rd. ☎ 22/2387–1450) looks like just another Benetton or Lacoste outlet, but it also has gorgeous, high-fashion Indian women's and men's wear, and the nearly sacred Paithani saris—hand-woven silk with real gold-and-silver thread.

Handicrafts

Anokhi (⊠ Rafik Niwas, Metro Motor La., Dr. Rangnekar Marg, off Hughes Rd., Chowpatty Beach ☎ 22/2368–5761) sells colorful tablecloths, cushion covers, and more, decorated with attractive block-print designs from Rajasthan. **Atmosphere** (⊠ Vaswani House, 7 Best Marg, Colaba ☎ 22/2283–1877 or 22/2283–1936) has exotic home furnishings and fabrics for the home—sold by the meter. There's lots of expensive silk, and they'll organize tailoring for you. **The Bombay Store** (⊠ Sir Pherozeshah Mehta Rd., Fort ☎ 22/2288–5048 or 22/2288–5049) has a classy collection of popular Indian handicrafts—metal work, sandalwood, china, marble, carpets, linens, and lamps. Prices are a tad higher here than at the government emporiums, but the store is enticingly laid out and service is competent. The **Central Cottage Industries Emporium** (⊠ 34 Chhatrapati Shivaji Marg, 1 block north of Taj Mahal hotel, Colaba ☎ 22/2202–7537 or 22/2202–6564 ☉ daily 10–7) is packed with textiles, carvings, and myriad other traditional Indian handicrafts from all over the country. It's a wonderful place to buy souvenirs, despite less-than-brilliant service. **Colaba Causeway** sells a load of cheap trinkets but it's possible to find some unusual items as well—brass items, beaded purses, wood handicrafts. **Contemporary Arts and Crafts** (⊠ 19 Nepean Sea Rd., opposite Baskin-Robbins, Malabar Hill ☎ 22/2363–1979) has a small but representative selection of Indian handicrafts at reasonable prices. Go to **Fab India** (⊠ Noble House, junction of Khar Danda and 18th Rd., Khar [just north of Bandra, in the suburbs] ☎ 22/605–7780) for vegetable-dye print tablecloths and linen. **Mrignaynee** (⊠ World Trade Center, Cuffe Parade, Colaba ☎ 22/2218–2114) sells statues and clothing from the state of Madhya Pradesh. If you won't be traveling farther south, peruse regal Mysore silks at **Mysore Sales International** (⊠ World Trade Center, Cuffe Parade, Colaba ☎ 22/2218–1658). Browse Maharashtra's own crafts and an outstanding collection of statues, sculptures, and idols at **Trimourti** (⊠ World Trade Center, Cuffe Parade, Colaba ☎ 22/2218–6283). The **World Trade Center** (⊠ Cuffe Parade, Colaba ☎ 22/2218–9191) gathers government-run handicrafts emporiums and boutiques from most of India's states under one air-conditioned roof. Fixed prices offer respite from bazaar-style haggling. **OMO** (⊠ 204 Sagar Fortune, Waterfield Rd., Bandra ☎ 22/5698–1804) has attractive home furnishings. **Tresorie** (⊠ 60A Linking Rd., Santa Cruz ☎ 22/661–2041 or 22/661–2042) sells expensive but tasteful knickknacks for the home. **Yamini** (⊠ President House, Wodehouse Rd., Colaba ☎ 22/2218–4143 or 22/2218–4145) sells colorful cotton home furnishings, cushion covers, and fabrics for the home—sold by the meter.

Incense & Perfumes

Ajmal (⊠ 4/13 Kamal Mansion, Arthur Bunder Rd., Colaba ☎ 22/2285–6976) has a wonderful selection of rare Indian and French perfumes stored in huge decanters. It also stocks *agar* wood, a rare incense base, 1,000 grams of which costs as much as a night at the Taj Mahal hotel. Sandalwood oil is also another fragrance stocked by this shop.

Jewelry

Exotic pieces of gold, platinum, rhodium and diamond jewelry are often cheaper than you'd believe, and the range and workmanship is excellent here. Jewelers are often willing to create something for you in the space of a two weeks or less. India has some rare silver jewelry, too. But when you're buying jewelry it's important to go to the right shop,

SIZZLING STREET FOOD

LOOKING FOR A BIT OF *HUNGAMA* (some nightlife) or something to eat at a crazy hour? Unlike most other Indian cities, which snooze from as early as 8 PM, Bombay buzzes around the clock. Food carts appear every few yards. In inimitable Indian style, even simple food is transformed into something impressive. The choices are enormous—hot, spicy vegetable sandwiches, slices of green mango peppered with masala, sizzling kababs, Chinese vegetable noodles, fresh strawberry milk shakes, carrot juice, kulfi (cream-based Indian ice cream), fresh slices of mangoes and cream, spicy boiled chick peas, fried fish, coconut water, green chili omelets in buns, and exotic snacks particular to Bombay, such as like bhel puri and wada paav.

Know, however, that much of this snack food is created right at the side of the road on open grills and stoves and then assembled in front of you. As you would imagine, the hygiene is a little suspect. If you sample any of these street-side treats, follow some rules. Try food served hot on the spot. Do not allow the food to be served to you on their plates (often reused). Ask that food be either served or packed in a disposable container (a fresh plastic bag, a cup created from leaves, a paper plate, or newspaper) or bring your own little container. Carry your own spoon and paper or plastic cup, if possible. You can ask for no cilantro, less spice (red pepper powder or green chili chutney) or no yogurt, and so on. And don't worry—they usually understand enough English to see the process through.

Local Favorites

Bhel puri: Puffed rice tossed up with cubes of boiled potatoes, slices of tomatoes, peanuts, tamarind sauce, chopped onion, and sev (a savory, deep-fried treat made of chick pea flour).

Sev puri: Tiny white-flour flat deep-fried puris or crackers layered with boiled potatoes, three types of chutneys made from tamarind, dates, and cilantro, sev, and chopped cilantro leaves.

Dahi puri: Tiny, flat, white-flour puris (deep-fried bread) layered with boiled potatoes, three types of chutneys made from tamarind, dates, and cilantro, plus mung bean sprouts and topped with yogurt and chopped cilantro leaves.

Pani puri: Tiny, puffed white-flour, deep-fried puris are cracked and filled with date water, tamarind sauce, mung bean sprouts, and potatoes. Each puri is to be popped in the mouth on the spot.

Ragda pattice: Spiced and mashed potatoes shaped into cutlets and fried on a griddle. These are served with hot chick pea curry and a few sauces.

Dahi bada: Large flat dumplings of white lentils are deep-fried crisp to make "badas," which are then dipped in water to soak out the oil. They are then broken into pieces and served spiced with a variety of masala powders, tamarind sauce, cilantro chutney, and yogurt.

Pav Bhaji: Potatoes are mashed and fried on a hot griddle for an hour with peas, tomatoes, and butter—until you have a juicy, spicy, potato mash. This is served with sliced onions, lemons, and butter-fried buns called pavs (a crusty Bombay roll).

Wada Pav: A cutlet—made from mashed potatoes, spice, cilantro, ginger, coated in chick pea flour and deep fried—is stuffed into a hot garlic, red chile chutney-lined pav.

Baida roti: White-flour dough is tossed by hand into thin sheets. Mince meat and beaten egg are wrapped up into these sheets until you have a square, layered pancake that's fried up on a hot griddle with oil.

CloseUp

Boti roll: Spicy pieces of grilled lamb kabab, chutney, and sliced onions are rolled into roomali roti (a fine, thin, hand-tossed and roasted white-flour pita).

Sheekh kababs: Minced, spiced lamb is cooked on a skewer on an open-air barbecue until crisp and served with chutney.

Chicken tikka: Marinated chicken pieces are roasted on an open-air barbecue and served with chutney.

Masala dosa: A lentil pancake fried on a hot open-air griddle with plenty of ghee (clarified butter) and stuffed with a spicy potato mixture

Where to Try These Delicacies

The Canteena Juice Center on Shahid Bhagat Singh Road, next to Delhi Durbar and Titan Watch in Colaba has excellent fresh juices. Their strawberry milk shakes (available from December to March) are wonderful.

Bade Miya, next to Gokul Bar on Tullock Road, off Shahid Bhagat Singh Road (enter the lane next to Leopold's and take a left onto Tullock; Bade Miya literally translates to "Mean Elder" or "Big Muslim man"). This open-air, street-side stall, opened by the Elder Muslim, has been supplying hungry Bombayites kababs and baida rotis since mid-century. The food is roasted or sizzled in front of you. It opens at 7 PM and stays open until 1 AM or even 2 AM, depending on business.

Head to Kailash Parbat to sample bhel puris and sev puris or to Swati Snacks.

Also visit Shiv Shankar Tiwari's Dahi Puri stall on B. Road (also known as Karmveer Pandit Shobhnath Mishra Marg) off Marine Drive, next to the InterContinental hotel and close to Churchgate.

or you can easily get duped. **Tanishq** (✉ Brabourne Stadium, Veer Nariman Rd., Churchgate ☎ 22/2282–1621, 22/2282–6043, or 22/2283–8801) is a reliable place to buy gold jewelry. Run by the House of Tatas, a venerable Indian company, you can be sure you will not be cheated here. Prices, however, will be a little higher here than elsewhere. In business since 1865, the **Tribhovandas Bhimji Zaveri** (✉ 241–43 Zaveri Bazaar, Kalbadevi ☎ 22/2342–5001) is said to be the largest jewelry showroom in India, with five floors of gorgeous 18-, 22-, and 24-karat gold, diamond, and silver jewelry. It's *most* cost-effective to buy from a smaller outfit, such as Narandas and Sons, Zaveri Naran Das, or Ram Kewalram Popley, all on **Sheikh Memon Street** (which begins at Crawford Market and runs northwest through Zaveri Bazaar) in the Kalbadevi neighborhood. Insist on knowing how many karats you're buying and whether or not the store will stand by the piece's purity. For silver jewelry, try the **Bombay Store** (✉ Sir Pherozeshah Mehta Rd., Fort ☎ 22/2288–5048 to 49). If you're a bargain hunter or you're looking for more unusual silver jewelry, head for the heart of **Colaba Bazaar** (✉ Colaba), a little south of the Taj Mahal hotel, where a series of tiny jewelry shops sells rings, earrings, necklaces, and more. Mangal Palace, in the heart of the bazaar, has an excellent selection. Haggling is a must here—try and knock off 10 percent if not more. Mangal Palace can also organize custom-made gold jewelry. If you prefer calm, air-conditioned excursions and don't mind higher prices, look for silver jewelry in the lower-level arcade at **The Oberoi and Oberoi Towers** (⊠ Nariman Point).

Leather & Shoes

Brave bargain-hunters should take an adventurous trip to **Daboo Street** (⊠ Off Mohammed Ali Rd., Kalbadevi, a 5-minute walk south from Chor Bazaar) for leather goods. The posh shopping arcade at **The Oberoi and the Oberoi Towers** (⊠ Nariman Point) includes leather and shoe shops with stylish goods priced lower (if expensive for India) than they would be in the West. Wander down **Colaba Causeway** (⊠ Also called Shahid Bhagat Singh Rd., Colaba) from Regal Cinema (opposite the Prince of Wales museum) and you'll find leather items, money pouches, sturdy Indian-style Kolhapuri chappals (sandals), and other footwear.

Music & Musical Instruments

If you want to take home some Indian recordings, especially classical music, head for **Rhythm House** (⊠ 40 K. Dubash Marg, Rampart Row, Kala Ghoda, Fort ☎ 22/2285–3963). Along with pop, jazz, and everything else, the store has an excellent selection of *pacca gana* (classical vocal music), Indo-Western fusion music, Hindi film music, and Indian instrumental music, plus English and Hindi DVDs and VCDs (video compact discs).

For Indian musical instruments try **Bhargava Musical Enterprise** (⊠ 156 Khetwadi, Vallabhai Patel Rd., Prarthana Samaj, near Opera House), a tiny, hard-to-find shop selling *tablas* (percussion instruments), *harmoniums* (a Western instrument with 42 black and white keys that has been adapted for Indian music), *sitars* (a classical string instrument with frets on the neck), and *tanpuras* (a gourd-shape classical string instrument). **Swami Music City** (⊠ Sayani Rd., opposite Ravindra Natya Mandir, near Siddhi Vinayak Temple, Prabhadevi ☎ 22/2430–6024) stocks traditional Indian instruments. The area is a few kilometers north of Haji Ali, and south of Worli, in the suburbs.

BOMBAY A TO Z

To research prices, get advice from other travelers, and book travel arrangements, visit www.fodors.com.

AIR TRAVEL TO & FROM BOMBAY

Bombay's international airport, Sahar International Airport, is 30 km (18 mi) north of the city center in Sahar. The domestic airport is at Santa Cruz, 26 km (15½ mi) north of the city center. *Reconfirm your international flight* at least 72 hours before departure and arrive at the airport at least 60 minutes before takeoff for domestic flights, two hours before international flights (some airlines require three hours). Both airports have 24-hour business centers available to holders of major credit cards.

Most international flights arrive in the middle of the night. Be prepared: airports in Bombay, like Delhi, Calcutta, or Madras, may be among the shabbiest you encounter—musty, slightly grimy, and staffed by often-cheerless immigration and customs officers. Many flights arrive at the same time, and luggage belts and trolleys are few. Your luggage may arrive after an interminable wait. Make sure you secure a baggage trolley first (free) and station yourself close enough to the right belt; check any stacks of luggage lined up against the wall in case your suitcases have come earlier.

Porters can be helpful in accelerating your journey out of the airport terminal. It's often best to ask for a porter as soon as you disembark—right at the plane gangway. A group of porters usually hang around the entrance, with wheelchairs. If you book one beforehand (get his name) he will meet you later at the baggage belt after you're done with immigration. Do not negotiate rates beforehand—if he tries to, hire someone else. Pay him between Rs. 100 and Rs. 300 depending on how helpful he has been. Once you locate your luggage, roll your trolley up to the snaky line to the X-ray machines and customs. Head for the custom's green channel and hand your customs form over as you exit the customs hall.

If you have to make a telephone call or you have to wait for your receiving party, do not exit the airport. Wait beyond the customs hall gate instead. (It's hot outside and once you exit you may not be allowed back in to use the rest room or wait in cooler comfort.) There are telephones outside the airport, but they require Indian currency and do not operate on cards.

Immediately after you exit the customs hall there are a row of tourist counters for hotels, taxi hire, car hire, tourist information, cell-phone card counters, and currency exchange. If someone is meeting you at the airport, understand that he or she will have no idea when you will emerge from the airport, given the wait at immigration or at the baggage concourse, so don't panic.

CARRIERS Bombay is served daily or frequently by Air France, Alitalia, Swiss International Airlines, Gulf Air, Lufthansa, Cathay Pacific, Emirates, Singapore Airlines, Air-India, British Airways, Delta, and KLM/Northwest. Domestic carriers include Indian Airlines, Sahara, and Jet Airways.

🛪 Airlines & Contacts **Air France/Continental** ☎ 22/2202-5021. **Air-India** ☎ 22/2202-4142 or 22/2836-6767. **Alitalia** ☎ 22/2204-5026. **British Airways** ☎ 22/2282-0888. **Cathay Pacific** ☎ 22/2202-9112. **Delta** ☎ 22/2288-5653. **Emirates** ☎ 22/2283-7000. **Gulf Air** ☎ 22/2202-1777. **Indian Airlines** ☎ 22/2202-3131, 20/2287-6161, or 20/2616-8000. **Jet Airways** ☎ 22/2288-1184 or 22/2615-6666. **KLM/Northwest** ☎ 22/5697-5959. **Lufthansa** ☎ 22/5630-1933. **Singapore Airlines** ☎ 22/2202-2747. **Swiss International Airlines** ☎ 22/2287-0122. **Sahara Airlines** ☎ 22/2283-6000.

AIRPORTS & TRANSFERS

The trip from Sahar International Airport downtown to south Bombay should take about 45 minutes if you arrive before 7:30 AM or after 11 PM (many international flights arrive around midnight). At other times, traffic near the city center can increase your trip as much as 90 minutes. Most hotels provide airport transfers starting at Rs. 900 and going up to Rs. 2,400, and some offer complimentary transfers if you're staying in a suite or on an exclusive floor.

The international airport has a prepaid-taxi service. Head to the prepaid-taxi counter outside the baggage-and-customs area to hire a regular cab, either air-conditioned or non-air-conditioned. Your rate is determined by your destination and amount of luggage and is payable up front; Rs. 500 should get you to the center of town (tips aren't necessary). If you want an air-conditioned taxi and do not spot one, call Group Mobile Cool Cab Service. Air-conditioned taxi fares are 25% higher than non-air-conditioned cabs—the starting rate is Rs. 16.50 and Rs. 12 for each additional kilometer. From the international airport to, say, Colaba, will set you back Rs. 400 by day and Rs. 450 at night.

At the domestic airport, metered taxis are available outside; a policeman notes the taxi's license plates before dispatching you on your way. A metered (not prepaid) taxi from the domestic airport to the downtown–south Bombay should cost about Rs. 300 and from the international airport about Rs. 350.

🛈 Airport Information **Sahar International Airport** ☎ 22/2682–9112. **Santa Cruz Domestic Airport** ☎ 22/2615–6500. **Group Mobile Cool Cab Service** ☎ 22/2490–5151 or 22/2290–5152.

BUS TRAVEL

The transport department of the India Tourism Development Corporation and the MTDC can organize, quite painlessly, bus tickets on reliable coaches to a variety of destinations, including Nasik, Aurangabad, and Pune, nearby. The Asiad and Metrolink Volvo buses, which depart from the Asiad bus stand at the circle outside Dadar in central Bombay Train Terminus (better known as TT), offer the best service between Bombay and Pune. Non-Volvo luxury coaches depart every 15 minutes (Volvo buses are usually by the hour); tickets can be purchased on the spot and you can hop right on.

🛈 Bus Information **Asiad** ✉ Opposite Dadar post office, near Sharda Talkie, Dadar East ☎ 22/2413–6835. **Metrolink** ✉ Next to Pritam Hotel, Dadar East ☎ 22/2418–1273.

CARS & DRIVERS

In certain areas, such as bazaars, you really have to walk for the full experience. Aside from these, having a car at your disposal is the most convenient way to sightsee, as you can zip around town without the repeated hassle of hailing taxis and haggling over fares. To arrange a hired car, inquire at your hotel's travel desk or contact a travel agency. (You'll probably pay more if you book through your hotel.) You'll get lower rates from the India Tourism Development Corporation: Rs. 650 for a full day (8 hours, or 80 km [50 mi]) in a non-air-conditioned Maruti van; Rs. 975 for a car (Uno or Indica; small cars) with air-conditioning, and Rs. 1,175 for an air-conditioned Esteem (sedan car). Rates go up for Toyotas, Mercedes, and other luxury cars.

🛈 **India Tourism Development Corporation** (ITDC) ✉ 11th fl., Nirmal Bldg., Nariman Point ☎ 22/2288–0992 or 22/2202–6679.

CAR TRAVEL

Fairly good roads connect Bombay to most major cities and tourist areas. Hiring a car and driver gives you a chance to watch the often beautiful surroundings whiz by, but it can also be loud, hair-raising, and less than time-efficient. Drivers honk at anything, including birds, and many two-way "highways" are really one-lane roads with a little extra space for an oncoming car to swerve around you, and are flanked by steep ridges so the water can drain off the road during monsoon. So if you have the time and the nerves for a road trip, you'll experience what many people miss when they fly. Some distances from Bombay: Pune, 172 km (107 mi); Panaji (Goa), 597 km (371 mi); Ahmedabad, 545 km (339 mi); Hyderabad, 711 km (442 mi). Bombay is 1,033 km (642 mi) northwest of Bangalore, 432 km (268 mi) northwest of Madras, and 1,408 km (875 mi) southwest of Delhi.

CONSULATES

The U.S. Consulate is open weekdays 8:30 to 5, and the staff is on duty 24 hours in case of emergencies. The Canadian Consulate is open Monday to Thursday 9 to 5:30, Friday 1:30 to 3:00. The British Consulate is open weekdays 8:30 to 1 and 2 to 3. The Irish Consulate is open weekdays noon to 1. The South African Consulate is open weekdays 9 to noon. The Australian Consulate is open weekdays 9 to 5.

🇮 Australia **Australian Consulate** ⊠ Maker Towers E, Cuffe Parade, Colaba 🕾 22/2218-1071.

🇮 Canada **Canadian Consulate** ⊠ 41–42 Makers Chambers VI, 4th fl., Nariman Point 🕾 22/2287-6027 to 30, 011/687-6500 emergencies.

🇮 South Africa **South African Consulate** ⊠ Gandhi Mansion, Altamount Rd., Kemps Corner 🕾 22/2389-3725.

🇮 United Kingdom **British Consulate** ⊠ Makers Chambers IV, 1st fl., 222 J. Bajaj Marg, Nariman Point 🕾 22/2283-2330 or 22/2283-0517, 22/2283-4040 emergencies.

🇮 United States **U.S. Consulate** ⊠ Lincoln House, 78 Bhulabhai Desai Rd., Warden Rd., Breach Candy 🕾 22/2363-3611.

EMERGENCIES

Most hotels have house physicians and dentists on call, and pharmacies that are open daily until about 9 PM. The chemist at Nanavati Hospital, and Royal Chemists, are both open 24 hours. Your consulate can also give you the name of a reputable doctor or dentist. Otherwise, try the emergency room at Breach Candy Hospital and Research Center or the Jaslok Hospital. Bombay emergency services do not respond to an emergency as quickly as these services do in more modern parts of the world.

🇮 Emergency Services **Fire** 🕾 101. **Ambulance** 🕾 102, 105 for heart attacks only. **Police** 🕾 100.

🇮 Hospitals **Breach Candy Hospital and Research Center** ⊠ Bhulabhai Desai Rd., Breach Candy 🕾 22/2367-1888, 22/2367-2888, or 22/2368-0368. **Jaslok Hospital** ⊠ Dr. G. Deshmukh Marg, near Haji Ali, Peddar Road 🕾 22/5657-3333. **Lilavati Hospital** ⊠ Bandra Reclamation 🕾 22/2642-1111.

🇮 24-Hour Pharmacies **Nanavati Hospital 24 Hour Chemist** ⊠ Swami Vivekanand (S.V.) Rd., Vile Parle, Juhu 🕾 22/2618-2255. **Royal Chemists** ⊠ Acharya Dhonde Marg, opposite Wadia Hospital, Vishwas Niwas Bldg. 8, Shop 3, Parel 🕾 22/2411-5028. **Bom-**

bay Hospital 24 Hour Chemist ✉ New Marine Lines, Dhobi Talao ☎ 22/2206–7676. **Dava Bazaar** ✉ 32, Kakad Arcade, opposite Bombay Hospital, New Marine Lines, Dhobi Talao ☎ 22/5665–9079.

MAIL & SHIPPING
🛈 Post Offices **General Post Office** ✉ Near Victoria Terminus ☎ 22/2262–4343.

MONEY MATTERS
ATMS   ATM machines are widespread. You're likely to find an ATM machine a few steps from your hotel, especially if you're staying anywhere in south Bombay. Any HDFC or ICICI ATM will let you withdraw cash against a Visa or MasterCard, too. Head to an HSBC for cash against an American Express Card. If you're having difficulty locating an ATM ask anyone to direct you to the nearest HDFC or ICICI Bank.

CURRENCY   Most luxury hotels will change money if you're a guest. American Ex-
EXCHANGE   press is open Monday to Saturday 9:30 to 6:30. Thomas Cook is open Monday to Saturday 9:30 to 6:30 and Saturday to 6. The State Bank of India is open weekdays 10:30 to 4:30, as are most other banks. L. K.P Forex is open Monday to Saturday 9:30 to 6:30. Nucleus Forex is open Monday to Saturday 9 to 5:30.

🛈 Exchange Services **American Express Travel Services** ✉ Regal Cinema bldg., Chhatrapati Shivaji Maharaj Rd., Colaba ☎ 22/2204–8291. **L.K.P. Forex** ✉ 22/B Cusrow Baug, Colaba ☎ 22/2282–0574. **Nucleus Forex** ✉ Nucleus House, Saki Vihar Rd., Tunga village, Andheri ☎ 22/2857–4484. **Thomas Cook India, Ltd.** ✉ Thomas Cook Bldg., D. Naoroji Rd., near Flora Fountain, Fort ☎ 22/2204–8556.

TAXIS
Auto-rickshaws (partly open three-wheelers) are permitted only in Bombay's suburbs, where you can flag them down on the street. As with regular taxis, insist on paying by the meter and ask to see the tariff card.

You can flag down yellow-top black taxis or silver-and-blue air-conditioned taxis anywhere in the city. Insist that the driver turn on the meter, a rusty mechanical contraption on the hood of the car, before setting off. Because the development of taxi meters cannot keep up with the rising costs of fuel, it takes some arithmetic to compute the latest (higher) fares, based on the meter reading. Drivers are required to show you their revised tariff cards for easy reference, but they sometimes conveniently misplace them, or whip out a chart for air-conditioned cabs, or show you fares chargeable after midnight. Examine the card carefully, and look for a policeman if you have doubts. At this writing the legal fare was 14 times the total amount shown on the meter, based on roughly Rs. 13 for the first kilometer and about Rs. 1.5 for each additional kilometer. Air-conditioned taxi fares are 25% higher—the starting rate is Rs. 16.50 and Rs. 12 for each additional kilometer. You may hire an air-conditioned taxi for a full day (8 hours or 80 km, whichever comes first) for Rs. 975, and a half day (4 hours) for Rs. 550. Ask your hotel what the going rates are in case they've gone up. You can also call Group Mobile Cool Cab Service (☎ 22/2490–5151 or 22/2290–5152) for a cab with air-conditioning.

TRAIN TRAVEL

Bombay has two train stations. Chhatrapati Shivaji Terminus, formerly Victoria Terminus, is the hub of India's Central Railway line. Bombay Central Station is the hub of India's Western Railway line. Be sure to go to the right train station—check before you set out. To avoid the pandemonium at the stations, have a travel agent book your ticket; this costs a bit more but saves time and stress. If you do it yourself, head for the tourist counter established specially for foreign travelers. Eliciting information about trains on the telephone is rather impossible because the lines are busy more often than not and the interactive voice-response numbers are in Hindi. Instead, check out the excellent Indian Railways site (⊕ www.indianrailways.com). For information on confirming a ticket or the arrivals and departures ask a local to make the phone call.

🚆 Train Information **Bombay Central Station** ✉ Bombay Central, adjacent to Tardeo ☎ 22/135 general information, including delays in English, 22/132 recorded information on arrivals and departures in English, 22/2263–5959 recorded information on reservation status in English. **Chhatrapati Shivaji Terminus** ✉ D. Naoroji Rd. ☎ 22/134 general information, including delays, 22/2263–5959 recorded information on reservation status in English.

TRAVEL AGENCIES

American Express and Ashoka Travels can help with general travel assistance and car hire; the former is open weekdays 9:30 to 6:30 and Saturday 9:30 to 2:30. The transport department of the India Tourism Development Corporation (ITDC) is also helpful with travel arrangements. For a complete list of travel agencies, pick up a copy of the ITDC's Mumbai brochure.

🚆 **American Express Travel Services** ✉ Regal Cinema bldg., Chhatrapati Shivaji Maharaj Rd., Colaba ☎ 22/2204–8291. **Ashoka Travels** ✉ Hindustan Bldg., Naushir Bharucha Rd., also called Slater Rd., near Grant Rd. post office, Tardeo ☎ 22/2385–7622 or 22/2387–8639. **Eurocars** ✉ Behind Suburban Service Station, next to Hotel Siddharth, Swami Vivekananda Rd. or S. V. Rd., Bandra ☎ 22/645–2796.

VISITOR INFORMATION

Don't count on hotels to stock general tourist information. The Government of India Tourist Office, near the Churchgate train station, has useful material; it's open weekdays 8:30 to 6, Saturday and holidays 8:30 to 2. There's information on trains and the office oversees knowledgeable, multilingual tour guides, available directly from the office or through the MTDC, or just about any travel agency. Rates are approximately Rs. 280 per half day for groups of one to four, Rs. 400 for a full eight-hour day with no lunch break (Rs. 560 if you require a lunch break, otherwise the guide will take time off to eat lunch when you do). Additional fees of Rs. 265 apply for trips beyond 100 km (62 mi) and for those involving overnight stays the rates could be still higher. Multilingual guides charge Rs. 125 extra, in addition to the regular fee.

The Maharastra Tourism Development Corporation (MTDC) is open daily 9 to 6. Both MDTC and the Government of India Tourist Office have 24-hour counters at the airports. The MTDC also has counters at Chhatrapati Shivaji Terminus (Victoria Terminus) and the Gateway of

India (it's a booth right where the boats to Elephanta Island dock). MTDC phone numbers are hard to reach as they are always busy. A personal visit is advised or a check out their Web site.

◪ Tourist Offices **Government of India Tourist Office** ✉ 123 Maharishi Karve Rd., Churchgate ☎ 22/2207-4333 or 22/2207-4334, 22/2203-3144 or 22/2203-3145 recorded tourist background on Pune, Goa, Bombay, Ahmedabad, and Aurangabad. **India Tourism Development Corporation** (ITDC) ✉ 11th fl., Nirmal Bldg., Nariman Point ☎ 22/2288-0992 or 22/2202-6679.MTDC ✉ Madame Cama Rd. opposite L.I.C. Bldg., Nariman Point ☎ 22/2202-6713, 22/2202-7762, or 22/2202-7762 ⊕ www.mtdcindia.com.

EXPLORING PUNE

This hill station in the Sahyadris at 1,973 feet and three hours southeast of Bombay, is a delightful town. Pune, or Poona, is also Maharashtra's second-largest city—with about 4 million people—and its proximity to Bombay has made Pune quite a cosmopolitan place. There are new restaurants, stores, pubs, and hotels opening all the time. The hottest fast-food chains and stores have their outlets in Pune. And Bombay wannabes keep the pubs rocking.

Despite its modernity, Pune remains a cantonment town with turn-of-the-century Raj touches—languid grace, fancy bungalows, wide boulevards, and some interesting architecture. At 1 PM much of the city halts for a lunch break and a siesta. Markets and shops down their shutters until 4. The Indian army still has a major presence in Pune.

A conservative Maharashtrian town, Pune is steeped in Marathi culture. The older parts of the city—the *peths* (bazaars), *wadas* (homes; this is spelled the same as the savory doughnut, wada, but is pronounced with longer "a"s) and Ganesh temples—are deeply Maharashtrian. You'll find in Pune and nearby areas Peshwa palaces and Maratha forts. This was the fierce, medieval Maratha warrior Shivaji's backyard, and his legendary battles with Mughal conquerors took place in this neighborhood. Lip-smacking Maharashtrian delicacies—like *puran poli* (sweet lentil-stuffed pancakes), *shrikhand* (sweet yogurt), *batata wada* (savory fried potatoes), *zunkhar bakri* (millet bread with spicy lentils)—are widely available. Nowhere is Ganesh Chaturthi, the biggest festival of the state—a 10-day event in August and September that honors the elephant god Ganesh, or Ganpati—celebrated with more joy and *dhoom dham* (pomp) than in Pune.

Since the 1980s, Pune has become more international. Bhagwan Rajneesh, a.k.a. "Osho, the captivating godman," who some call a sex guru, fled his commune in Oregon to set up shop here in 1985. His charisma was such that with him came a giant band of Western followers, who settled in Pune. Osho died in 1990, but in spite of a host of *masala*, or salacious, controversies that dog the commune, it continues to thrive—and draws hordes of seemingly drugged-out Westerners. As a result, an entire upscale neighborhood of Pune is inhabited by maroon robe-clad, spacey foreigners seeking a new twist to their life. This has spawned an entire Osho tourist district where everything from German bread to New Age meditation tunes to Kathmandu trinkets is available.

What to See

Most of the sights in Pune are far flung, so you'd be wise to hire the services of an auto-rickshaw (the local three-wheeler) or a car to explore the town. To experience the staunchly Maharashtrian quarters of the city, head to **Shaniwarwada Palace** in the heart of the old city. The palace, actually, no longer exists. Tall ramparts and imposing, two-story-high teak gates, lined with enough spikes to ward off an army of elephants, front an empty courtyard, once home to the beyond-your-wildest-imagination Shaniwarwada Palace. Built in the 18th century by the Maratha king Baji Rao I, the palace was decimated less than a hundred years later, in 1827. The premises aren't well-maintained, but you can conjure your own images of the extravagant kingdom the Peshwas once ruled. The view from the ramparts of the palace gates intrigues. Rocky outcrops (once foundation stones) in endless lawns are the only remnants of this seven-story royal residence that once was famous, near and far, for its Shish Mahal (glass house), *hamam* (palace bathroom), and Mastani Mahal (dancers' wing). The Palace of Music, known as the Nagarakhana, still survives. The Maharashtra Tourism board holds a sound-and-light show at the palace, on the history of the Peshwas and Shivaji; tickets are available on the premises. ⊠ *Shaniwarwada, Bajirao Rd., Kasba Peth* ☎ *Rs. 5 for entry to the palace; English-language sound-and-light show Rs. 25* ☉ *Wed.–Mon. 8:30 to 6. Sound-and-light show Wed.–Mon. 8 PM–9 PM.*

The little lanes leading away from the palace are narrow and populated with small temples, old homes, and vendors hawking their goods. Make sure you dive into some of these side lanes to sample typical *peth,* or Maharashtrian bazaar life. (The older, noncantonment sections of Pune were divided into *peths,* or areas, and named after the days of the week.) On your exit from the palace if you take a sharp right you'll arrive at a *chowk* or crossroads. If you continue walking and pass two more crossroads you'll be at **Shrimant Dagdu Sheth Halwai Ganpati Mandir.** This temple is a simple construction—essentially an idol under a roof, in an open-air shed—and worship proceedings are visible right from the road. The idol is cherished not just by locals but by all Maharashtrians. Dagdu Sheth was a *halwai,* or sweetmeat maker. He was also a good friend of Lokmanya Bal Gangadhar Tilak, a key figure in India's independence movement in the late 1800s. When Tilak gave the call for public or community celebrations of Ganesh Chaturthi (the state's biggest festival, held in late summer in honor of the elephant god) to disconcert the British rulers, this *halwai* was the first to institute a kind of "block" celebration of the festival in 1893. Unlike other idols of the elephant god, which are immersed in the river–ocean after Ganesh Chaturthi festivities are over, the Dagu Sheth Halwai Ganpati (Ganesh) stays on, and over the years has been lavished with affection and prayers. Much of the idol has been embellished with gold by grateful devotees—solid-gold ears (a gift from a film star), as well as 8 kilos of gold decorate his garments. Visit this temple in the evening, around 8:30, if you want to be around when locals worship.

About 20 minutes due south on foot (better to take a taxi) from Dagdu Sheth Halwai Ganpati, is the **Raja Dinkar Kelkar Museum.** This celebrated museum in the old city houses some 2,000 carefully catalogued daily utensils and objets d'art of metal, wood, stone, and earthenware from the remotest corners of India (18,000 items are still in storage). The range of items, accumulated over 60 years, is bewildering. The artifacts are illustrative of everyday life: coconut meat scrapers, *hookahs* (a steam-operated smoking pipe), pots, and water containers to musical instruments, toys, lamps, locks, and ornate implements. None are heirlooms or possessions of the wealthy, but they nevertheless adequately reflect Indian culture and history.

The household tools have been chosen on the basis of their utility and for their unusual form or design. The Chitrakathi paintings from Paithan, Maharashtra, are intriguing, as is the large Vanita Kaksha, or lady's parlor, devoted to personal and domestic objects women used. Equally fascinating is the room set up as a replica of the Mastani Mahal, which once existed at Shaniwarwada Palace, where Mastani, Baji Rao I's kept woman, lived. Do check out the poison testing lamp, a design that dates back to the Peshwa era; the lamp was used to check for poisoned food. This collection was put together by a well-traveled Maharashtrian and award-winning poet, Adnyatwasi, a.k.a. Dr. Dinkar Gangadhar Kelkar (1896–1990), who was a devoted collector of art, and his wife Kamlabai. Late in life, Kelkar donated his collection of artifacts to the government for a museum in memory of his son Raja. The museum is housed in one of those rambling *peth wadas* or bungalow-courtyard complexes—Kelkar's own home—near Shaniwarwada Palace. If you have time, chat with Surendra Ranade, the grandson who runs the museum. He'll tell you all about the amazing poet, who was once offered a blank check for his collection by another collector, but refused. The museum's expansion plans are under way, and by about 2005 the entire collection, including the undisplayed items, will move to a 6-square-km (4-square-mi) location 10 km (6 mi) away in the village Bavdhan on the Bombay-Bangalore highway. ✉ *1377–78 Natu Baug, off Bajirao Rd., Shukawar Peth* ☎ *20/2448-2101* 🔊 *Foreigners Rs. 150* ⊙ *Daily 8:30–5:30.*

Built in the 1860s and called the Lal Deval (red temple) by locals, the **Ohel David Synagogue** is rather striking—it has beautiful stained-glass windows and an imposing 90-foot tower—and a bit out of place in Pune, which once had only a small Jewish population. The Jewish businessman and philanthropist David Sassoon, who divided his time between Bombay and Pune, built this synagogue and the David Sassoon hospital. Sassoon is buried on the synagogue grounds. It's worth checking out the synagogue interior. To do so, however, it's advisable to call the number listed below and organize a visit (for security reasons the synagogue is not open to the public). If you're here, it's a quick hop over to the trendy, up-and-coming area of town nearby, on M. G. (Mahatma Gandhi) Road and East Street. The area has lots of smart shops and restaurants. ✉ *9 Dr. Ambedekar Rd. Pune Camp, off M. G. Rd.* ☎ *20/ 2613-2048 after 6 PM or on holidays.*

An air of secrecy and silence shrouds the **Osho Meditation Resort** (OMR) commonly referred to as an ashram. The exterior of the ashram's buildings is well concealed by bamboo copses and tall walls. Started by the

Osho godman–sex guru, OMR was once described by a *Washington Post* correspondent as a cross between a college campus, Disneyland, and a resort. Lavishly constructed from white-and-black marble, and spread across 40 acres, the commune has wonderful greenery, pools, as well as cafés, shops, a pool, a basketball court, and zennis (Zen tennis) courts.

The deep-green pool, on the edge of a patch of greenery, is an odd shape, like a natural pond. A large shining steel kitchen and cafeteria supply inexpensive vegetarian cuisine served in a hygienic environment—freshly baked multigrain rolls and bread, organic fruit, Continental dishes, desserts, Indian-style *sabzis* (vegetables), *dal* (lentils), *rotis* (Indian wheat bread), and more. Ashram members say its meditation hall is the largest in the world—a vast expanse (18,000 square feet) of black marble with a pyramid dome. This air-conditioned meditation hall is a phenomenon: a few maroon-robed devotees chill out here in a sea of serenity. The black floor is as large as a football field. Indeed much of the resort has an otherworldly, anachronistic sensibility.

The meditation resort, or "Multiversity," offers meditation and self-knowledge or personal growth courses of all varieties, at moderate prices. The Osho had no use for organized religion. He believed personal religion should be relatively painless—happy, not ascetic. He was famous for his rather opaque statements, such as: "I am here to seduce you into a love of life; to help you to become a little more poetic; to help you die to the mundane and to the ordinary so that the extraordinary explodes in your life." Meditation at Osho's kingdom takes many forms and he advocated release of tension by singing, dancing and catharsis, often in group sessions. These "group sessions" have been the subject of much curiosity by locals. The commune, run by more than 500 "disciples," attracts rootless folks from India and all over—mainly Germans, Israelis, some Americans, and Japanese. For a fee, these disciples chill out, spring-clean their souls, and improve their morale. At any given time as many as 5,000 people from more than 100 countries may be floating in and out of the meditation resort.

The resort has its own guest house. It's austere, but very clean, well lit, and sleek. Rooms are accented in white, blond, black, granite, marble, and glass. Expect no televisions and no phones. At $58 per day, plus 6% tax, it's a great place to lodge. No children under 15 are allowed. You can take a limited guided tour to see OMR's grounds. A day-long meditation workshop, after you complete the compulsory HIV ($26) test, like it or not, will set you back $6.

Another reason to come here is to visit the neighborhood's interesting shops and watering holes. Hawkers sell Tibetan artifacts, Kashmiri crafts, jewelry, and cotton clothing nearby. The teahouses and restaurants are packed out with Osho-ites. Do visit the German Bakery for a flavor of this strange world. The ashram, in Koregaon Park, is across town, 4 km (2½ mi) east and slightly north of the Shaniwarwada area. For the general public, the ashram is only open during tour hours for short half-hour tours. ✉ *17 Koregaon Park* ☎ *20/2401–9999* ⊕ *www. osho.com* 🎫 *Tours 9:45–noon and 2:30–3:30. Purchase tickets at least one day before for Rs. 10. Ticket window open 9:30–1 and 2–4. Children under 15 not permitted.*

need a break? Park yourself at one of the wooden benches at the **German Bakery,** suck down a banana *lassi* (yogurt drink), and eavesdrop on the flirting maroon robes (commune members) talking about the arcane—the meaning of life, the depth of the human soul, etc. It's quite a dating scene. You can also get tasty and fresh breads, herbal tea, fresh fruit juices, soya burgers, hummus and pita, pizza, salads, lasagne, and lemon cake. ⊠ *291 Vaswani Nagar, Koregaon Park* ☎ *20/2613–6532.*

After visiting the Osho ashram in Koregaon Park, head by car to the charming, tiny shrine **Shinde Chhatri** about 15 minutes away (also called Shindechi Chhatri; a chhatri is a cenotaph or a monument to someone dead and revered). From Koregaon Park, go past the civil lines (non-army areas) and the British landmarks, and right through the old-style cantonment or camp area. That journey will give you a feel of the old British cantonment Pune. The chhatri, with its striking gold-embossed roof, is the Hindu "chapel" of the Scindias, a famous royal family who once ruled Gwalior in Central India and who today are a political dynasty. The chhatri is a monument to one of the more famous Shindes (from whom the Scindias descended)—Mahadji Shinde, the commander of the Peshwa army. Give the gatekeeper a few rupees and he may allow you in to see the intriguing inner sanctum. Incidentally, one of their lesser palaces is across the street. ⊠ *Off Prince of Wales Dr., Wanowrie, near Clover Apartments, 2 km (1.2 mi) from Pune race course* ☉ *Daily dawn–dusk.*

As you enter Pune from Aurangabad (northeast of the city), on the Ahmednagar Road—on the outskirts of the city, before the Mula river—the belching trucks and rushing traffic may distract you from noticing a tranquil patch of greenery on the right side of the road. This is the **Aga Khan Palace,** also known as the Gandhi National Memorial Society. More than 50 years ago, a small chapter of history was made here. During India's freedom movement, Mahatma Gandhi, his wife Kasturba Gandhi, the poet and patriot Sarojini Naidu, and Mira Ben spent periods of captivity here. Gandhi was imprisoned here from 1942 to 1944. The palace, which is both French and Muslim in design, once belonged to Prince Aga Khan, who donated it and seven of the 19 acres that surround it, to the government. Today it's a low-key national museum. You may wander through the palace and view the tiny rooms hung with photographs where these leaders were interred, or simply admire the pleasant gardens. Also on display are the few personal belongings of the Gandhis. You can even purchase some roughly woven cotton (khadi) cloth—khadi was a symbol of the independence movement; leaders donned the simple homespun garments to show they were shunning Western ways and to protest the taxes they had to pay for Indian cotton garments. A *samadhi* or cenotaph honors the Mahatma's wife, who died here during her imprisonment in 1944. The Aga Khan palace is a bit far from the city center—you need to make a special side trip, by car, to view this memorial. ⊠ *Ahmed-*

nagar Hwy., also called Nagar Rd. ☎ *20/2668–0250* ✉ *Rs. 100 for foreigners* ⊙ *Daily 9–5:30.*

Where to Eat

Pune has lots of reasonably priced restaurants, and you can get Mughlai, Chinese, Thai, and Italian food here. (To cater to Pune's transient foreign population, restaurants serving a variety of cuisines have come up and a couple of foreigners have even started up their own restaurants.) Dining options range from posh restaurants serving elaborate meals to fast-food chains. If you wander over to Koregaon Park you're sure to find food that's tasty and affordable. Restaurants serve lunch noon to 3 and dinner 6 to 11 or 11:30; meals are not usually available inbetween those hours (though snacks may be). Don't expect alcohol in every restaurant, either.

For familiar fast food head out to Jungli Maharaj Road—McDonald's, Pizza Hut, Domino's, and Baskin-Robbins have all set-up shop. Jungli Maharaj Road also offers local fast food, so if you're feeling adventurous try some Indian snacks or junk food—*pav bhajee, sev puri, batata wada, idlis*—are available hot and fresh off the griddle. Nearby Vaishali (20/2553–1244; Fergussen College Rd., opposite college, open from 7 AM to 11 PM), a modest dosa, or Udipi joint at Fergussen College area/ neighborhood, draws crowds for its dosas.

Chinese & Pan-Asian

$$$$ ✕ **Spice Island.** This restaurant at Pune's top hotel is the fanciest in town. Dining here is an extravagant affair—the restaurant is decorated with East Asian paintings and gold trim. You enter through a bar, a monument by itself, carved from glass and glowing with blue light. The dining room beyond is intimate and classy, decorated in deep beige and dark reds. Tasty and innovative Thai and Chinese food are served. Try the prawns in oyster sauce, Thai corn cakes, tiger prawns in garlic sauce, chicken in a chili *hoisin* sauce, or oriental noodles with vegetables. Dress nicely (no jacket and tie required, however). ✉ *The Meridien, Raja Bahadur Mill (RBM) Rd., near the main railway station* ☎ *20/2605–0505* ⌨ *Reservations essential* ▬ *AE, DC, MC, V.*

$$ ✕ **Mainland China.** At this branch of Bombay's famous restaurant the dining room is bright and airy, the furniture wood, the floor marble, and the walls decorated with large paintings and wood-carved grills. The restaurant has an attractive garden where you can dine. The lightly cooked, mildly spiced courses are full of flavor and the portions are large. Ask to have it spicy, with more chilis. Menu standouts include rice with wood-ear mushrooms and greens, sweet-and-spicy crispy chicken, prawns in butter and garlic, seafood with crabmeat sauce, crackling spinach, steamed chicken with Chinese greens, and burnt-garlic fried rice. End your meal with *daarsaan*, crispy fried noodles with honey. ✉ *City Point, junction of Boat Club Rd. and Dhole Patil Rd.* ☎ *20/2401–9434 or 20/ 2401–9435* ⌨ *Reservations essential* ▬ *AE, DC, MC, V.*

$ ✕ **The Chinese Room.** Owned by the old and popular Kwality chain, the posh, granite-and-glass restaurant is the place to go for Indian–Chinese, the particular type of Chinese food in currency in India. It's a cuisine that leans heavily on cilantro, spices, and hot peppers. Try the crispy sesame chicken, honey-roast pork, steamed rice with vegetables, sesame prawns, three treasure vegetable *hunani*, or the litchis with ice cream. ⊠ *2434 East St.* ☎ *20/2613–1336* ⊟ *AE, DC, MC, V.*

$ ✕ **Malaka Spice.** This simple but cheerful restaurant has orange walls and black tables, and the focus is the art (for sale) that hangs on the wall. The menu includes food from across Asia—Vietnam, Indonesia, China, Thailand, Japan, Malaysia, and Korea. The place is managed by a husband-wife duo, Cheeru and Praful Chandawarkar. Try the flavorful *pad thai*, chicken satay, Thai green curry with chicken, chicken in *pandan* leaves, or Singaporean *laksa* soup (noodles, prawns, chicken, and bean sprouts). ⊠ *Vrindavan Apartments, N. Main Rd., Koregoan Park* ☎ *20/2613–6293 or 20/2614–1088* ⊟ *MC, V.*

Indian

$ ✕ **Mahesh Lunch Home.** The basement of 18 Dr. Ambedkar Road is the address of Pune's first—and probably only—proper seafood restaurant. A branch of the Bombay landmark for seafoodies, Pune Mahesh offers pretty much the real thing. Tuck into their prawn *gassis* (prawn curry), lady fish fry, tandoori pomfret, or crab *sukka* (dry)—catch here is fresh and gussied up with traditional Manglorean coast *masalas* (spice mixes) composed of coconut, red chilis, *kokum* (a sour berry), and other condiments. The restaurant has a soothing albeit standard-Indian-restaurant vibe: green sofas, granite floors, etched glass, and Hindi film music playing in the background. ⊠ *Ashok Pavilion, 18, Dr. Ambedkar Rd.* ☎ *20/2613–3091* ⊟ *AE, DC, MC, V.*

$ ✕ **Sanskruti.** Head out to this "cultural garden restaurant," 15 km (9 mi) away—at Loni Kalbhor on the Sholapur highway. The restaurant spans 4 acres of green lawns dotted with stalls serving up North Indian snack foods and typical Indian *mela* (fairground) attractions—astrologers, a pottery wheel, magicians, Hindi film singing, bangle makers, *ghazal* singers, swings, and Rajasthani dancers. When the starters and thrills are done, indulge a sumptuous Rajasthani and Gujarati 16-item thali (unlimited servings). Sanskruti is a distance from Pune proper, so call in advance in case they have changed their hours. Lunch on weekends starts at 10:30 and runs to 3:30; dinner goes 'til 10 daily. ⊠ *Sholapur Hwy.* ☎ *20/2691–5156 or 20/2691–5157* ⊟ *No credit cards* ☉ *No lunch weekdays.*

¢ ✕ **Blue Nile.** Decoration in this popular Pune nonvegetarian restaurant is zilch, but you're in an established Muslim eating house with high ceilings and a kind of faded charm. In any case, it's the excellent chicken and mutton biryanis (spicy meat simmered with rice for hours), not the plastic chairs and paper napkins, that bring people in. A plate of biryani will set you back by just Rs. 80. No need to try the veg food; this is a carnivore's dream. No liquor is served. ⊠ *4 Bund Rd.* ☎ *20/2612–5238* ⊟ *No credit cards.*

¢ ✕ **Coffee House.** This established vegetarian multicuisine restaurant has gone upscale. Wood accents, plants (plastic), and busy upholstery have contributed to its swanky new style. The total effect is reasonably pleasing to the eye. You can get Chinese, Mughlai, and South Indian food for breakfast, lunch or dinner, and snacks all day. Recommended are the crispy dosas, *sev puri, bhel puri, batata wada, chana bhatura* (spicy chick pea curry served with large, white-flour puris), and vegetable biryani. ✉ *2 Moledina Rd., Pune Camp* ☎ *20/2613–8275* ▤ *AE, DC, MC, V.*

¢ ✕ **Nandu's.** Leave your bow ties and high heels at home, roll up your sleeves, and prepare for some typical *desi* or Indian dining. Nandu's is not your conventional restaurant. This small vegetarian eatery sells amazingly good, fat, sizzling, vegetable-stuffed *parathas* (stuffed and griddle-fried whole wheat pancakes) served with yogurt and a dollop of butter. Stuffings range from peas, cauliflower, potatoes, onion, and fenugreek to cottage cheese. The corn or *bajra* (millet) rotis are also worth a try. The shady outside seating area is a pleasant enough place to chomp down the divine food. Come either for lunch or for an early dinner—hungry locals pack the place by 9. No liquor is served. ✉ *Damodar Narain Dhole Patil Market, Dhole Patil Rd.* ☎ *20/2634–728* ▤ *No credit cards.*

¢ ✕ **Prem's.** This place in the heart of "Oshotown" in Koregaon Park, a few minutes by foot from the ashram, has become something of a landmark. The open-air restaurant, under tamarind trees, with its tinkling New Age meditation music, soft lighting, and soothing vibe, largely exists for the ashram and its devotees. Indian and Continental food—vegetable *makhani, paneer* butter masala, chicken garlic pasta, spinach with pasta—is served here. Opt for the pastas and the sizzlers—chicken *shaslik* or the veg sizzler choices. Beer and wine are served. ✉ *28/2 Koregaon* ☎ *20/2613–0985* ▤ *AE, MC, V.*

¢ ✕ **Ramakrishna.** *Rasam-wadas* (fried lentil dumplings served in spicy curry), sizzling dosas, soft idlis—this no-fuss air-conditioned restaurant serves excellent South Indian food. The place is simple and clean (lots of shiny granite) and the food arrives in minutes, hot and authentic. More than 30 varieties of dosas are served. Try the *rawa masala dosa* (semolina pancakes with potato stuffing), the table-length paper dosa (a light and crispy dosa with no filling), or the *mung dosa* (a dosa made using a green lentil–flour). The *rasam-wadas* (lentil fritters in spicy gravy) are very tasty. ✉ *Ramakrishna Resort, 6 Moledina Rd., Pune Camp* ☎ *20/2636–3938 or 20/2633–0724* ▤ *MC, V.*

¢ ✕ **Sri Utsav.** Large picture windows, rich green marble floors, pale green silk upholstery, and white curtains contribute to the casual charm. You can also dine in the garden. This relatively upscale (compared to most similar places in India) vegetarian thali place has a menu that's quite diverse. A very filling thali includes three vegetables, a *farsan* (snack), rice, dal, roti, and myriad pickles and chutneys, plus a sweet. Try the parathas—they do 25 types of stuffed parathas. Also good is the *sarson saag* (mustard greens) with *makai di roti* (corn bread). No alcohol or meat is served. ✉ *26 Koregaon Park, off North Main Rd.* ☎ *20/2611–4725 or 20/2612–7769* ▤ *MC, V.*

International

$$ ✕ **Indyaki.** This cozy restaurant, on the ground floor of a residential building, has dark-wood furniture and plush chairs and sofas. White curtains frame the windows. Next door and part of the restaurant is an equally cozy bar lounge. A major draw here, apart from the wide selection of scotch and wine (impressive by Pune standards), is the weekly live music: on Wednesday there's a live band, Thursday is karaoke

night, and on Friday a DJ spins retro music. The menu is a mix of Indian and international food. The food can be cooked in front of you, to your taste, at the teppanyaki counter of dark wood that occupies a prime location—the chef will prepare your dish to your taste in front of you. Go for the tasty pan-seared fish, butter pepper prawns, and chicken kababs, or such Indian dishes as prawn curry. ⊠ *9 Sanas Corner, South Main Rd., Koregoan Park* ☎ *20/2605–5116 or 20/2605–5117* ⌕ *Reservations essential* ▤ *AE, MC, V* ☉ *Teppanyaki counter (only) closed Mon.*

★ $ ✕ **La Dolce Vita.** Chef Santilli Mario turns out delicious and authentic Italian food. The place is festively done in bright reds and cobalt blues. Rich red theater-type curtains festoon the windows. Giant bottles of pickle, oils, vinegar, olives, and spice decorate the room. Mario introduced Pune to Italian food in 1993—"I make the dishes I love," he says. He imports 60 percent of the ingredients and has a wide selection of wine. He recommends his fresh pasta in less common forms—pappardelle, cavatelli, *agnolotti* (stuffed with beef), gnocchi, ravioli, and giant tortellinis stuffed with prawns or duck liver of ham or ricotta, served with game sauce or four-cheese smoky sauce. Desserts are top class—tiramisu, lemon cheesecake, and chocolate mousse cake. ⊠ *Shop 3 and 4, City Point, Dhole Patil Rd.* ☎ *20/2614–5555* ▤ *AE, DC, MC, V* ☉ *Closed Tues.*

¢ ✕ **Hot Breads Bakers and Confectioners.** Indian pastries and baked items here are often startlingly good, considering how sugary most Indian sweets are—these are fresh and made from scratch. Satisfy your sweet tooth on luscious strawberry tarts, brownies, muffins, rich mousses, and mousse cakes. Equally good are the salty foods—quiche, chicken rolls, pizza slices, and stuffed croissants. Soups and salads are served for lunch from noon to 4. The café, which remains open 'til 11 PM, has a cozy vibe and a young clientele. A picture window overlooks the leafy Koregaon Park neighborhood. Note that you can only use your credit card for amounts over Rs. 250. ⊠ *Gera Sterling, N. Main Rd., Koregaon Park* ☎ *20/2613–3757 or 20/2403–0616* ▤ *MC, V.*

Where to Stay

Pune, which is slowly becoming a popular destination for business travelers, has its fair share of hotels. The city now has six luxury hotels and a number of business hotels. Luxury hotel prices are steep, but not as high as the prices in the larger cities. If you're booking directly, ask for a discount. Prices are more often than not negotiable, and hefty discounts are available. Depending on the rate you get, breakfast and airport–railway station pickup may be included. Such deals tend to be available for long-term stays, and can be made on the spot.

A variety of accommodations geared to tourists has always been available in the Koregaon Park area. Quite a few more-than-adequate rooms, cheaper than those listed below, can be found here.

Try contacting **Escape Getaways** (☎☎ 20/2605–2577), a Koregaon-based travel agent, for long-term stays (a month or more).

$$$ ▨ **Le Meridien.** Glowing expanses of marble, shiny fittings, elegant furnishings, and no fewer than seven restaurants make this very large, Bom-

bay-class lodging a rather luxurious option. The large rooms are plush, with white linen furnishings, soft carpeting, and blond-wood beds and night tables. By the windows are wrought-iron tables. Rooms have unexciting views of the railway station across the street. ⊠ *Raja Bahadur Mill (RBM), near the main railway station* ☎ *20/2605–0505* 🖷 *20/2605–0506* ⊕ *www.lemeridien.com* 🛏 *173 rooms, 13 suites* ♨ *3 restaurants, coffee shop, room service, in-room data ports, in-room safes, refrigerators, cable TV, health club, squash, 2 bars, dance club, dry cleaning, laundry service, business services, meeting room, airport shuttle, travel services* ▤ *AE, DC, MC, V* ⦿| *BP.*

$$$ 🏨 **Sun-n-Sand.** There's no sand here, just sun. Glass elevators take you up and away from the shiny black granite-finished lobby. Of the luxury hotels in Pune, however, this is probably the least appealing. The rooms, furnished in blues and beiges, are overpriced and a tad small; they face the road and there's a muffled noise of traffic. Bathrooms are clean, bright, and adequate. The hotel runs an attractive Chinese restaurant and an Indian restaurant. ⊠ *262 Bund Garden Rd.* ☎ *20/2613–7777* 🖷 *20/2613–4747* ⊕ *www.sunnsandhotel.com* 🛏 *115 rooms, 2 suites* ♨ *2 restaurants, coffee shop, patisserie, room service, in-room data ports, in-room safes, refrigerators, cable TV, pool, health club, hair salon, bar, dry cleaning, laundry service, business services, meeting room, airport shuttle, travel services* ▤ *AE, DC, MC, V* ⦿| *BP.*

$$ 🏨 **Taj Blue Diamond.** This is the only luxury hotel in Pune with rooms that have pleasant views of Koregaon Park. The rooms are modern, cheerful, and newly renovated. Carpets, curtains, and bedspreads are done in maroons and beiges and have a satiny finish. Bathrooms are tidy and shiny in brown marble. The hotel's 24-hour coffee shop serves excellent biryani; there's also an Indian restaurant and a popular Chinese restaurant. ⊠ *11 Koregaon Rd.* ☎ *20/2402–5555* 🖷 *20/2402–7755* ⊕ *www.tajhotels.com* 🛏 *108 rooms, 11 suites* ♨ *2 restaurants, coffee shop, room service, in-room data ports, in-room safes, refrigerators, cable TV, pool, health club, bar, night club, dry cleaning, laundry service, business services, meeting room, travel services* ▤ *AE, DC, MC, V* ⦿| *BP.*

★ $ 🏨 **The Central Park Hotel.** As you enter this luxury hotel, the first thing that strikes you is its light, airy, modern look. The hotel staff is gracious and particularly helpful. This hotel is small, but the cozy rooms are comfortable and neat, with green furnishings. Staying here is a good value for your money, too. Choose your room according to the view: the roadside view is more pleasant than the views in front or on the side of the hotel. ⊠ *Bund Garden Rd., near the Council Hall* ☎ *20/2605–4000* 🖷 *20/2605–0211* ⊕ *www.centralparkhotel.com* 🛏 *73 rooms, 4 suites* ♨ *Restaurant, room service, in-room data ports, some in-room safes, refrigerators, cable TV, health club, bar, shop, dry cleaning, laundry service, business services, meeting room, airport shuttle, travel services* ▤ *AE, DC, MC, V* ⦿| *BP.*

¢ 🏨 **Ritz.** This Raj–era bungalow has been converted into a hotel. The rooms are reasonably clean, though slightly musty, and each has a balcony that overlooks a busy thoroughfare. The attached bathrooms are simple and tidy, with showers but no tubs. Deluxe air-conditioned rooms have tubs and are large, with red carpets and a kitschy style. The hotel serves only vegetarian food and presents a very competent Gujarati thali meal to its guests. Stay here for the good value; choose the super or royal deluxe air-conditioned room. ⊠ *6 Sadhu Vaswani Path, opposite the main post office (G.P.O.)* ☎ *20/2612–2995 or 20/2613–6644* 🖷 *202/309–03086* 🖵 *24 rooms, 3 suites* ⚒ *2 restaurants, room service, cable TV, laundry service, meeting room, travel services; no a/c in some rooms* ▤ *DC, MC, V.*

¢ 🖼 **Shrimaan.** This medium-budget hotel offers comfortable, brightly furnished, and clean rooms at a fair price. All rooms are a reasonable size, with green and white accents and no carpets. The bathrooms are clean. Air-conditioned rooms are slightly more expensive, but bigger and naturally preferable. The attached restaurant, La Pizzeria, serves decent Italian food, as well as Mexican food. Shrimaan is in a quiet area of town, a few minutes' walk from Koregoan Park. ⊠ *361/5 Bund Garden Rd., opposite Bund Garden* ☎ *20/2613–3535 or 20/2613–6565* 🖷 *20/2612–3636* 🖵 *28 rooms* ⚒ *Restaurant, room service, cable TV, laundry service, meeting room, travel services; no a/c in some rooms* ▤ *AE, MC, V* ⛾ *BP.*

★ ¢ 🖼 **Sunderban.** Once the home of Nepal royalty, this bungalow-hotel has old–style class, and is probably the most interesting place to stay in Pune. Popular with Osho *wallahs* (devotees), it's on a quiet street in the area of Koregaon Park. The air-conditioned rooms are spacious; studio rooms have minipatios facing green lawns; there are also kitchenettes with microwaves and refrigerators. Regular rooms are basic and small with a no-frills bathroom (shower only) but very clean. Barista, the coffee shop chain, has opened an outlet on the grounds. Alcohol and meat are not permitted in the hotel. Off-season discounts are available April through September. ⊠ *19 Koregaon Park* ☎ *20/2612–4949* 🖷 *20/2612–3535* ✆ *tghotels@hotmail.com* 🖵 *43 rooms* ⚒ *Room service, refrigerators, cable TV, laundry service, travel services; no a/c in some rooms* ▤ *MC, V* ⛾ *BP.*

Nightlife & the Arts

During Ganesh Chaturthi, celebrated in late August or September, the Maharashtra Tourism Development Corporation (MTDC) organizes a special cultural festival, during which top classical Indian dancers and musicians perform. Check out the MTDC site for details closer to the time. Pune has plenty of pubs where you can sample Pune nightlife. Visit **10 Downing Street** (⊠ Gera Plaza, Boat Club Rd. ☎ 20/2612–8343); it's a popular pub in Pune, open from 7:30 PM to 11:30 PM or later. There's a DJ, theme nights, and tasty snacks are served here. **Club Polaris** (⊠ Taj Blue Diamond, Koregaon Park ☎ 20/2612–8343) is a popular night club. The upmarket **Scream** (⊠ Le Meridien, Station Rd. ☎ 20/2612–8343) is the poshest night club of Pune.

Shopping

Shopping in Pune can be a thrill, given the immense variety and the good prices. And unlike other Indian cities, the shopping avenues are pretty much adjacent to each other. Comb Mahatma Gandhi Road, Moledina Road, and East Street for the best bargains. Remember, however, that Pune snoozes from 1 to 4. The **Bombay Store** (✉ 302 Mahatma Gandhi Rd. ☎ 20/2613–1891 ⊘ Mon.–Sat. 10:30–8:30, Sun. 11–8), has some of the best buys around on handicrafts, clothing, and artifacts. **Westside,** (✉ 1B Moledina Rd. ☎ 20/2611–9395 or 20/2611–9920 ⊘ daily 10:30–8:30) next to Dorabjees on Moledina Road, stocks casual wear and household goods. Along **Mahatma Gandhi Road** you'll find plenty of shops, one after the next, selling cottons and salwar-kurta ensembles (a two-piece tunic and pants outfit). You'll even find roadside hawkers offering tops and skirts. Off Mahatma Gandhi Road is a lane lined with open-air stalls; vendors here sell garments of all varieties. At **Centre Street** you may find a good selection of jewelry. **Fab India** (✉ 10, Sakar, opposite Jehangir Nursing Home, Sassoon Rd. ☎ 20/2612–4820 ⊘ Tues.–Sun. 10–7:45) sells great cotton clothing for adults and children. **Either Or** (✉ Sohrab Hall, near Crossword Bookstore, Bund Garden Rd.) sells interesting and sometimes funky Indian-style cotton casuals, plus jewelry and other gift items. On the shops and stalls at **Koregaon Park** you'll find Kashmiri handicrafts, silver jewelry, cotton garments, and Tibetan knickknacks.

Pune A to Z

AIR TRAVEL

Pune and Bombay are only 35 minutes apart by air. A one-way ticket costs about US$95 for foreign tourists. Jet Airways flies the route three times a day. Pune (PNQ airport code) is also connected to New Delhi and Bangalore by daily flights on Jet Airways and Indian Airlines.

🛪 Airlines & Contacts **Jet Airways** ✉ 243/244 Century Arcade, B/2 Narangi Baug Rd., off Boat Club Rd. ☎ Airport office 20/2613–7181, 20/2612–7524, 20/2613–7076, or 20/2668–5591, 20/2668–5591 telecheck-in. **Indian Airlines** ✉ Ambedkar Rd. opposite the R.T.O., near Sangam Bridge ☎ 20/2426–0932, 20/2426–0938, 20/2426–0942, 20/2426–0948, or 20/140 or 20/141, 20/2668–9433 airport office.

BUS & CAR TRAVEL

Reaching Pune by road is a reasonably comfortable option. Several competing companies run luxury buses to Pune from Bombay; it's a four- or five-hour journey. You can arrange such a ride through your Bombay hotel or travel agent. Driving to Pune by car is the best option, however. With the opening of the Bombay-Pune expressway, one of India's first world-class highways, the trip takes under three hours if you avoid the Bombay rush hour.

CURRENCY EXCHANGE

Most hotels will change money for guests. You can also change money at Thomas Cook between 9:30 and 6 daily from Monday to Saturday. Or you could try American Express between 9:30 and 6:30 daily weekdays and Saturday from 9:30 to 1. If you want to advance cash against your MasterCard, Visa, or American Express you will have to head to any of the numerous Citibank, IDBI, or HDFC ATMs in the city center. ATMs are open 24 hours.

🛈 Exchange Services **American Express** ✉ Arora Towers, M. G. Rd. ☎ 20/2613–3706. **Thomas Cook** ✉ 13 Thacker House, 2418 G. Thimmaya Rd., off M. G. Rd. ☎ 20/2634–8188 ⊕ www.thomascook.co.in.

TOURS

Pune Municipal Transport (PMT) (☎ 20/2444–0417) operates a daily six-hour Pune city tour that departs at 9 for Rs. 91 per person. Buses depart from the Pune bus station; you can purchase tickets there as well.

You can also arrange to hire a car and driver through your hotel travel desk or from an agency. To hire a non-air-conditioned car for eight hours or 80 km (50 mi)—whichever comes first—will set you back Rs. 550; it's Rs. 850 for a car with air-conditioning. These are rates for a comfortable but small Maruti 800 or Indica, and depending on the type of car, prices go up. These rates are apart from the tips and "lunch money" to the driver. Do fix a rate beforehand.

🚗 **Deccan Luxury** ✉ Fergusson College Rd., near Deccan Gymkhana and Champion Sports ☎ 20/2553–2305. **Europcar** ✉ City Point, Boat Club Rd. ☎ 20/2611–3085.

TRAIN TRAVEL

Several excellent fast trains run between Pune and Bombay, including the Shatabdi Express, Deccan Queen, Pragati Express, and Sahyadri Express. The Shatabdi is the fastest: the journey takes 3½ hours. There are daily connections between Pune and Madras, Hyderabad, Bangalore, Trivandrum, and several other destinations. Ask a travel agent for details.

🚆 Train Information **Train Information** ☎ 20/2612–6575.

VISITOR INFORMATION

The Maharashtra Tourism Development Corporation (MTDC) office in Pune, near the main railway station, is open Monday through Saturday, 10 to 5 (minus a lunch break from 1:30 to 2); every second Saturday, however, the office is closed. There are MTDC counters at the railway station and at the airport, too. The railway station counter is open daily 9:30 to 6. The airport office is open when the flights come in. In addition to these bureaus, most hotels have travel desks to help you plan your day—for a price.

🏢 Tourist Offices **MTDC Tourist Office** ✉ Block I, Central Bldg., Pune ☎ 20/2612–6867.

AURANGABAD & AJANTA & ELLORA CAVES

Dating back more than 2,000 years, the cave temples of Ajanta and Ellora rank among the wonders of the ancient world. Here, over a period of 700 years—between the 2nd century BC and the 5th century AD—great armies of monks and artisans carved cathedrals, monasteries, and entire cities of frescoed, sculptured halls into the solid rock. Working with simple chisels and hammers and an ingenious system of reflecting mirrors to provide light, they cut away hundreds of thousands of tons of rock to create the cave temples. These craftsmen inspire perpetual awe with the precision of their planning, their knowledge of rock formations, and the delicacy and profusion of their artwork. Together, the cave temples span three great religions—Buddhism, Hinduism, and Jainism. For optimum absorption of these phenomenal caves, allow one full day for each site, and remember both are closed on Monday. To get to Ajanta and Ellora, take a train, bus, or plane to Aurangabad, the nearest major city. From Aurangabad you can hop on a tour bus or hire a car and driver for about Rs. 1,300 to the Ajanta caves (a two- to three-hour trip), Rs. 550 to the Ellora caves (30 minutes).

Aurangabad

388 km (241 mi) east of Bombay, 30 km (18 mi) southeast of Ellora, 100 km (62 mi) southwest of Ajanta

With several excellent hotels and a growing number of good restaurants, Aurangabad is a good base from which to explore the cave temples at Ajanta and Ellora. The city has an intriguing old bazaar, and is known for its *himru* (cotton and silk brocade) shawls and saris, and its gorgeously and painstakingly decorated Paithani—gold-embroidered *zari*—saris. If you're interested, pop into the Aurangabad Standard Silk Showroom or Aurangabad Silk, both near the train station; Ajanta Handicrafts in Harsul, on the highway to Ajanta; or Himroo Saris, on the highway to Ellora. An even better option to view Himru saris being woven is to venture over to the Himru Cooperative Society at Jaffer (also spelled Zaffar) Gate, an area in the western part of Aurangabad; there you can see the entire process in action in a traditional environment. The saris (which incidentally can be cut up and tailored into other items) are more reasonable here.

More than a mere gateway, Aurangabad has a number of ancient sites of its own, such as the imposing **Daulatabad Fort** (⊠ 13 km [8 mi] west of Old Town, on the highway to the Ellora Caves ☉ Daily sunrise–6 ☒ Foreigners US$2), built in 1187 by the Hindu king and surrounded by seven giant walls more than 5 km (3 mi) long, Daulatabad was once called Deogiri, "hill of the gods," but was changed to "city of fortune" when the sultan of Delhi overtook it in 1308. Devote at least half a day to this fascinating and impregnable fort, considered one of India's most impressive. As you enter the fort you enter a labyrinth—note the moats, spikes, cannons, and dark maze of tunnels designed to make the fort as impregnable from enemies as possible. Equally interesting is the Jami Masjid inside; it was conceived from horizontal lintels and pillars of Jain and Hindu temples.

The 17th-century **Bibi-ka-Maqbara**, (☉ sunrise–10 PM ☒ foreigners US$2) is also known as the mini–Taj Mahal; it's 550 yards north of the old town, beyond Mecca Gate, and you can usually see it from the plane when you're flying into Aurangabad. A pale but noble imitation of the original Taj Mahal, the tomb is dedicated to the wife of the last of the six great Mogul emperors, Aurangzeb (founder of Aurangabad and son of the Taj Mahal's creator, Shah Jahan). It was supposed to be a shining, white-marble edifice but money ran out, so only the bottom 2 feet of the monument were built with marble; the rest is stone with a facade of plaster. Somewhat awkwardly proportioned, the structure can be said to illustrate the decline of Mogul architecture.

About 160 km (99 mi) and 3½ to 4 hours east of Aurangabad, beyond Jalna, *not* on the highway to either Ajanta or Ellora, is the **Lonar Crater**. If you have a day free, or if you have an extra day because the caves are closed, visit this serene 50,000-year-old meteoric crater. Off the beaten path and away from postcard sellers, bead hawkers, and soft-drink-stall owners, the 1,800-meter-long crater lake—probably formed from a meteor—is one of India's more phenomenal sites. It's said to be Asia's largest and youngest crater. Lonar is a peaceful spot, full of wildlife and greenery. Maharashtra Tourism Development Corporation (MTDC) has a small, simple guest house here.

Where to Stay & Eat

Aurangabad has few great restaurants. Most of them offer multiple cuisine options, including Indian (Mughlai and tandoori, or South Indian), Chinese, and the local variant of what passes for Continental food. Stick with Indian cuisine outside the luxury hotels—it's generally well prepared and tasty. Know that Aurangabadi restaurants aren't big on decoration: a few plastic plants, jazzy upholstery, and darkened light bulbs pass off as restaurant style. But they are comfortable and the meals well presented. Most restaurants here don't serve meals outside typical meal hours.

Most hotels in Aurangabad will discount their rates on request. If you book directly, push for 15% off—or more—and check if the rate you settle for includes breakfast and airport–railway station pickup. Unless otherwise noted, all hotels listed are fully air-conditioned.

$$$ ✕ **Madhuban.** Dark furniture, large paintings of Indian scenes, crisp white tablecloths, and a chandelier composed of multiple *diyas* (traditional Indian lamps) set a regal tone at one of Aurangabad's top restaurants. A major draw here are the ghazals sung every evening except Monday. One wall of windows opens onto lovely tropical trees, flowers, and the pool; another displays the busy kitchen, where you can watch chefs skewering meats for the tandoor oven. The menu also includes Chinese and Continental dishes. The Indian menu choices are many and the Chinese food is quite tasty. There's a popular buffet lunch. ✉ *Welcomgroup Rama International hotel, R-3 Chikalthana* ☎ *240/248–5441* ☐ *AE, DC, MC, V.*

★ **$$$** ✕ **The Residency and the Garden Café.** The Taj Residency's two eateries adjoin one other, and the choice is easy—if it's lunch you're after, have it at the Garden Café; for dinner head to The Residency. The Taj Café is easily the loveliest location around to have a light lunch. White cane garden furniture decorates a marble verandah that looks out over green lawns and flower beds; the place has old-world style. The Residency, done up in warm colors and lots of wood, is a classy place to have dinner. Try their multicuisine buffet. ✉ *8-N-12 CIDCO* ☎ *240/2381–1106 to 10* ☐ *AE, DC, MC, V.*

$$ ✕ **President Park Semicircle Coffee Shop.** This is a great place to cool down. The cheerful, bright coffee shop at this hotel affords a view of the hotel's pool and gardens through it glass windows. The food served here is all vegetarian and tasty. Try the South Indian items—hot dosas or *medu wadas* (deep-fried lentil fritters), and the fresh juices. ✉ *R 7/2 Chikalthana, Airport Rd.* ☎ *240/248–6201* ☐ *AE, DC, MC, V.*

$$ ✕ **Angeethi.** It's one of Aurangabad's most popular restaurants, and gets packed on weekends by locals enjoying their time off. Named after a traditional Indian cooking vessel, this dark, cozy, slightly tacky place serves reasonably priced Punjabi, Continental, and Chinese food, and has a knack for cooking tandoori items. Other specialties include chicken biryani, Afghani kabab *masala* (boneless chicken in a cashew sauce), and two-person *sikandari raan* (goat marinated in spices and seared in a tandoor oven). There are plenty of tasty vegetarian choices, too. Service is friendly but not terribly efficient. ⊠ *6 Mehar Chambers, Vidya Nagar, Jalna Rd.* ☎ *240/244–1988* ▤ *MC, V.*

$$ ✕ Tandoor. The hospitality of manager Syed Liakhat Hussain is one good reason to visit this brightly lit, cheerful restaurant; the kababs are another—especially the *kasturi* (chicken) kabab. People come here for authentic and well-made tandoori food. It's become, indeed, a local landmark. Try the *paneer tikka* (cottage cheese kababs), biryani, black dal (lentils), and the fresh, fried local fish. Shoot for lunch instead of dinner if you're coming by auto-rickshaw, because later in the evening it's difficult to find transportation (this place is far from the main hotels). ⊠ *Shyam Chambers, Station Rd.* ☎ *240/232–8481* ▤ *MC, V.*

¢ ✕ Bhoj. Both branches of this thali restaurant serve "unlimited" quick-and-tasty, light vegetarian Gujarati or Rajasthani platters, with 20 items for Rs. 60, for lunch and dinner. It's a welcome change from the overdose of Mughlai and tandoori food available elswhere. The selection of preparations is wide, and the price is right. It's purely functional inside, however, and the din can be deafening; this is not a place for leisurely dining. Alcohol is not served and there's no air-conditioning. ⊠ *Kamdar Bhavan, CBS Rd.* ☎ *No phone* ⊠ *Hotel Sai, Jalna Rd.* ☎ *240/235–9438* ▤ *No credit cards.*

¢ ✕ Woodlands. Carnivores move on: this primarily South Indian eatery is strictly vegetarian, offering tasty dosas and tangy *paneer makhanwala* (cottage cheese spiced with chili), as well as thali options and a few Punjabi dishes. Go for the dosas. Alcohol is not served. ⊠ *Akashay Deep Plaza, near CIDCO Bus Stand, Jalna Rd.* ☎ *240/248–2822.*

$$$ ⊞ Taj Residency. Inside and out, this gleaming Mogul palace is done in bright white marble and stone. The windows and doors arch to regal Moghul points, and the grand dome over the lobby is hand-painted in traditional Jaipuri patterns. The Taj has easily the best vibe of the city hotels. The Ajanta-esque rooms have teak furniture with matching headboards and mirror frames, and a small maroon-and-orange sitting area. All rooms look out onto the garden (but there's no access), and have balconies or patios, most with a teak swing. Stone paths wind through 5 acres of beautifully landscaped lawns. ⊠ *8-N-12 CIDCO* ☎ *240/ 2381–1106 to 10* 🖷 *240/238–1053* ⊕ *www.tajhotels.com* ⤲ *30 rooms, 2 suites* ⟂ *Restaurant, coffee shop, room service, in-room data ports, cable TV, pool, health club, bar, dry cleaning, laundry service, business services, meeting room, travel services* ▤ *AE, DC, MC, V.*

$$ ⊞ Ambassador Ajanta. Next door to its rival, the Welcomgroup Rama International, this five-story marble hotel is ensconced among sweeping lawns, well-kept flower beds, and towering trees alive with singing birds. Filled with brass goddesses, marble elephants, wood carvings, and other Indian antiques, the lovely garden is typical of that cluttered Indian-elegance look. The rooms have an Indian feel—with local furnishings and garden-view windows. Don't miss a dip in the pool, where you can imbibe mid-swim at the bar at the shallow end. ⊠ *Jalna Rd., CIDCO, 431003* ☎ *240/248–5211 or 240/248–5214* 🖷 *240/248–4367* ⊕ *www.*

ambassadorindia.com 🛏 *92 rooms, 5 suites* ☖ *Restaurant, coffee shop, room service, in-room data ports, refrigerators, cable TV, 2 lawn tennis courts, pool, badminton, squash, bar, dry cleaning, laundry service, business services, meeting room, travel services* ▤ *AE, DC, MC, V.*

★ **$$** 🏨 **Quality Inn Meadows.** The Meadows resembles a tropical resort. Accommodations are in simple (carpet-free) ultramodern cottages, each with a private patio. Rooms here are a bit spartan. The hotel has won architectural awards and uses a biotechnological system of plant roots to purify its air and waste water. The grounds, planted with trees and flowers, house rare birds. It's intensely quiet here, as the hotel is 5 km (3 mi) from the city center on the road to the Ellora caves. The hotel is ideal for kids—there are rabbits and parrots, and there's ample space to run around. The restaurant serves excellent Indian and Continental food. A courtesy coach goes to the city four times a day. Service is above average. ⊠ *Village Mitmita, Padegaon, Bombay-Nasik Hwy., 431002* ☏ *240/267–7412 to 13, 240/267–7417, or 240/267–7421* 🖷 *240/267–7416* ⊕ *www. choicehotels.com* 🛏 *48 rooms* ☖ *Restaurant, room service, cable TV, pool, health club, hair salon, hot tub, sauna, croquet, bar, laundry facilities, business services, meeting room, travel services* ▤ *AE, DC, MC, V.*

★ **$$** 🏨 **President Park.** In this attractive contemporary building, designed around a central garden, every room has a pool view. Ground-floor rooms are the most attractive; they open directly onto the garden—you can walk out of your room and dive right into the pool, which has a waterfall and a food pavilion. The rooms have balconies or patios and are cheerful inside, with teak-trim furniture, peach-color fabrics, and brass fixtures. Bathrooms are on the small side. Overall, this hotel is a great choice—it seems like a luxury hotel but has reasonable prices. The restaurant serves vegetarian food only. ⊠ *R 7/2 Chikalthana, Airport Rd., 431210* ☏ *240/ 248–6201* 🖷 *240/248–4823* ⊕ *www.presidenthotels.com* 🛏 *60 rooms, 4 suites* ☖ *Restaurant, coffee shop, room service, cable TV, tennis court, pool, gym, sauna, steam room, bar, dry cleaning, laundry service, business services, meeting room, travel services* ▤ *AE, DC, MC, V.*

$$ 🏨 **Welcomgroup Rama International.** A long driveway takes you away from the main road and through spacious grounds to this sharp hotel—with red bands of elephants chiseled on its bleach-white facade. The efficient and friendly staff provide personalized service of the highest order, and create the kind of warm, intimate setting you'd normally associate with a smaller hotel. Standard rooms, in two wings around the pool, are spacious and comfortably elegant, with views onto the verdant garden of palms and bright flower beds but do not open out into the garden. Corner suites are vast. Rooms in the newer wing are far better than those in the old wing. ⊠ *R-3 Chikalthana, 431210* ☏ *240/248–5441 or 240/248– 5444* 🖷 *240/248–4768* ⊕ *www.welcomgroup.com* 🛏 *90 rooms, 2 suites* ☖ *Restaurant, coffee shop, room service, in-room data ports, refrigerators, cable TV, golf, lawn tennis, pool, health club, hair salon, massage, sauna, steam room, Ping-Pong, bar, dry cleaning, laundry service, business services, meeting room, travel services* ▤ *AE, DC, MC, V.*

$ 🏨 **Amarpreet.** The cheerful, colorful rooms in this centrally located budget hotel are above-average—in Indian terms, neat enough. The bathrooms could be cleaner, however. The simple, airy lobby opens out onto a small patch of lawn. Opt for a room with a view of the Bibi-ka-Maqbara, and check to see if your room is quiet enough. There are two in-house restaurants offering Indian, Chinese, and Continental food. ⊠ *Jalna Rd.* ☎ *240/233–2521 or 240/233–2522* 🖷 *240/233–2521, call to request the fax* ⊕ *www.amarpreethotel.com* ⤶ *30 rooms, 2 suites* ⚒ *2 restaurants, room service, cable TV, hair salon, bar, laundry facilities, business services, meeting room, travel services* ▤ *AE, MC, V.*

¢ 🖼 **Kailas.** If you're not the typical tourist and you don't intend to use Aurangabad as a base for day trips to Ellora and Ajanta, try this fine little hotel, with its garden, a stone's throw from the Ellora caves. Its double-bed stone cottages are very clean albeit spartan, but not uncomfortable—and have a rustic appeal. Air-conditioned rooms are a tad more expensive. Though the rooms lack televisions, phones, and there's only skeletal room service, one huge bonus of staying here is that you can visit the caves at 6 AM when they open and experience them minus the crowds in the dawn light. The hotel can organize transport to the city. ⊠ *Ellora Caves, 431102* ☎ *2437/244–446 or 2437/244–543* 🖷 *2437/244–467* ⊕ *www.hotelkailas.com* ⤶ *22 rooms in 18 cottages* ⚒ *Restaurant* ▤ *No credit cards* ⍥ *EP.*

¢ 🖼 **MTDC Holiday Resort.** If you don't mind sleepy service, this centrally located, casual hotel is an excellent value. The staff are amiable, and the no-frills rooms clean. Only 22 rooms have air-conditioning in the Ajanta building; don't try the others except for those in the new wing, called Udaygiri—these are large and quite clean. (Nonetheless, ask to see them beforehand.) The restaurant serves basic Indian food. ⊠ *Station Rd., 431001* ☎ *240/233–1513* 🖷 *240/233–1198* ✎ *mahatour@bol.net.in* ⤶ *40 rooms* ⚒ *Restaurant, room service, cable TV; no a/c in some rooms* ▤ *No credit cards* ⍥ *CP.*

Ajanta Caves

Fodor'sChoice ★ It's thought that a band of wandering Buddhist monks first came here in the 2nd century BC searching for a place to meditate during the monsoons. Ajanta was ideal—peaceful and remote, with a spectacular setting. It is a steep, wide, horseshoe-shape gorge above a wild mountain stream flowing through a lush jungle below. The monks began carving caves into the greyrock face of the gorge, and a new temple form was born.

Over the course of seven centuries, the cave temples of Ajanta evolved into works of incredible art. Structural engineers continue to be awestruck by the sheer brilliance of the ancient builders, who, undaunted by the limitations of their implements, materials, and skills, created a marvel of artistic and architectural splendor. In all, 29 caves were carved, 15 of which were left unfinished; some of them were *viharas* (monasteries)—complete with stone pillows carved onto the monks' stone beds—others were *chaityas* (Buddhist cathedrals). All of the caves were profusely decorated with intricate sculptures and murals depicting the many incarnations of Buddha.

As the influence of Buddhism declined, monk-artists were fewer, and the temples were swallowed up by the voracious jungle. About a thousand years later, in 1819, Englishman John Smith was tiger-hunting on the

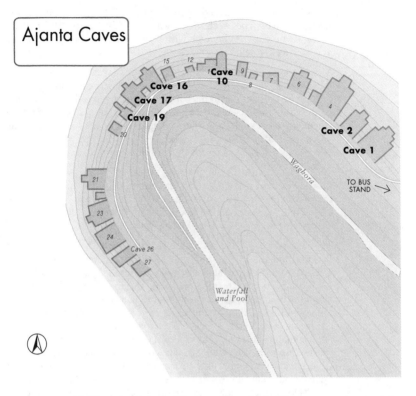

Ajanta Caves

Cave 15 12

Cave 10

Cave 16

Cave 17

Cave 19

9 8 7 6

4

Cave 2

Cave 1

20

21

23

24

Cave 26

27

Waghora

TO BUS
STAND →

*Waterfall
and Pool*

bluff overlooking the Waghora River in the dry season and noticed the soaring arch of what is now dubbed Cave 10 peeking out from the thinned greenery in the ravine below; it was he who subsequently unveiled the caves to the modern world. Incidentally tigers are not too far from this area (the thick forests from Ajanta to Kannad are the Gautala wildlife sanctuary). Today the caves at Ajanta and Ellora have been listed by UNESCO as World Heritage Sites.

At both Ajanta and Ellora, monumental facades and statues were chipped out of solid rock, but at Ajanta, an added dimension has survived the centuries—India's most remarkable cave paintings. Monks spread a carefully prepared plaster of clay, cow dung, chopped rice husks, and lime onto the rough rock walls, and painted pictures on the walls with natural local pigments: red ocher, burnt brick, copper oxide, lampblack, and dust from crushed green rocks. The caves are now like chapters of a splendid epic in visual form, recalling the life of the Buddha, and illustrating tales from Buddhist *jatakas* (fables). As the artists lovingly told the story of the Buddha, they portrayed the life and civilization they knew—a drama of ancient nobles, wise men, and commoners.

Opinions vary on which of the Ajanta caves is most exquisite. Caves 1, 2, 16, 17, and 19 are generally considered to have the best paintings;

caves 1, 10, 17, 19, and 26 the best sculptures. (The caves are numbered from west to east, not in chronological order.) Try and see all 7 of these caves. If you're not sightseeing with a guide, ask one of the attendants at each cave for help.

Most popular at Ajanta are the paintings in **Cave 1.** These depict the Bodhisattva Avalokitesvara and Bodhisattva Padmapani. Padmapani, or the "one with the lotus in his hand," is considered to be the alter ego of the Lord Buddha; Padmapani assumed the duties of the Buddha when he disappeared. Padmapani is depicted with his voluptuous wife, one of Ajanta's most widely reproduced figures. When seen from different angles, the magnificent Buddha statue in this cave seems to wear different facial expressions.

Cave 2 is remarkable for its ceiling decorations and its murals relating the birth of the Buddha. For its sheer exuberance, the painting of women on a swing is considered the finest. It's on the right wall as you enter, and when you face the wall it's on the left side of it.

The oldest cave is **Cave 10,** a chaitya dating from 200 BC, filled with Buddhas and dominated by an enormous *stupa* (a dome, or monument, to Buddha). It's only in AD 100, however, that the exquisite brush-and-line work begins. In breathtaking detail, the Shadanta Jataka, a legend about the Buddha, is depicted on the wall in a continuous panel. There are no idols of Buddha in this cave, indicating that idol worship was not in vogue at the time—but the fact that **Cave 19,** hardly nine caves later, contains idols of Buddha, shows the progression of thought and the development of new methods of worship as the centuries wore on. Guides and caretakers will enthusiastically point out the name of the Englishman, John Smith, who re-discovered the caves—his name, along with "1819" underneath, is carved on one of the far pillars in this cave. (Incidentally, Cave 10 was the first cave Smith spotted because its domed arch made it quite visible from the bluff above.)

The mystical heights attained by the monk-artists seem to have reached their zenith in **Cave 16.** Here a continuous narrative spreads both horizontally and vertically, evolving into a panoramic whole—at once logical and stunning. One painting here is riveting: known as *The Dying Princess,* it's believed to represent Sundari, the wife of the Buddha's half-brother Nanda, who left her to become a monk. Cave 16 has an excellent view of the river and may have been the entrance to the entire series of caves.

Cave 17 holds the greatest number of pictures undamaged by time. Luscious heavenly damsels fly effortlessly overhead, a prince makes love to a princess, and the Buddha tames a raging elephant. (Resisting temptation is a theme.) Other favorite paintings include the scene of a woman applying lipstick and one of a princess performing *sringar* (her toilette). This cameo is on the right hand wall as you enter and as you face the wall on the farthest right pillar.

Cave 26 is the more interesting of the caves on the far end. An impressive sculpted panel of a reclining Buddha is on your left as you enter. Interestingly it's apparently a portrayal of a dying Buddha on the verge of attaining nirvana and his weeping followers are at his side while celestial beings are waiting to transport him to the land of no tomorrows or rebirths.

A number of unfinished caves were abandoned mysteriously, but even these are worth a visit if you can haul yourself up a steep 100 steps. You can also walk up the bridle path, a gentler ascent in the form of a crescent pathway alongside the caves; from here you have a magnificent view of the ravine descending into the Waghura River. There's a much easier way to reach this point. On your return by car to Aurangabad, 20 km (12 mi) from the caves, take a right at Balapur and head 8 km (5 mi) toward Viewpoint, as it's called by the locals.

A trip to the Ajanta caves needs to be well planned. You can see the caves at a fairly leisurely pace in two hours, but the drive to and from the caves takes anywhere from two to three hours. Come prepared with water, lunch, or snacks (from a shop in Aurangabad, because you won't get that much here except packed items like potato chips at the visitor center and *nothing* once you enter the caves), comfortable walking shoes (that can be slipped on and off easily, because shoes are not allowed inside the caves), a flashlight, a hat, high-speed film, and patience. Aurangabad can be hot year-round, and touring 29 caves tiring. The paintings are dimly lit to protect the artwork, and a number are badly damaged, so deciphering the work takes some effort. But the archaeological department has put a lot of effort into making the caves more viewable—trash cans, cleaner premises, and special ultraviolet lights to brighten up certain panels. Shades and nets installed at the mouth of each cave keep out excess sun and bats.

There's no longer direct access to the caves. All visitors are required to park their cars or disembark from their coaches at a visitor center 3 km (1.9 mi) from the caves. A Rs. 6 ticket buys you a place on frequently departing green Maharashtra Tourism Development Corporation (MTDC) coaches going to the caves; quite a few coaches every hour are air-conditioned—and are Rs. 10. Remember to carry the most important (and just enough) possessions with you, because it's a long haul back to retrieve film, snacks, guide books, or hats, or to dump extra belongings. At the visitor complex are stalls with people hawking souvenirs, film, hygienically packed snacks, cold drinks, water, and fresh hot snacks—plus lots of irritating hawkers and unknown guides that need to be assiduously ignored and firmly dismissed. (To book a legitimate guide *see* Tours *in* Aurangabad & Ajanta & Ellora Caves A to Z) The bathrooms at the caves are surprisingly clean.

The caves are connected by a fair number of steps; it's best to start at the far end and work your way back—or you'll have a hot trek back at the end. The initial climb up, before you reach the cave level, is also quite steep. Palanquins carried by helpers, however, are available for the less hardy. Flash photography and video cameras are prohibited inside the caves; the admission fee includes having the lights turned on as you enter a cave. Right outside the caves, a shoddy MTDC-run restaurant, predictably called the Ajanta, offers simple refreshments; have a cold drink on your way out to cool down. This is the only refreshment area or stall near the caves.

MTDC operates a small hotel 5 km (3 mi) from the caves, at Fardapur, but it has minimum facilities. A better and more unique option is to try the forest rest house, an approximately 5-minute drive away from the caves. It costs Rs. 400 a night and is run by the forest department. Rooms are very limited here but try your luck and contact the Divisional Forest Officer (☎ 240/233–4203, Osmanpura, Usmanpura) for reservations. A cloak room is available at the caves to deposit bags for Rs. 5 per bag. ✉ *100 km (62 mi) northeast of Aurangabad* ☑ *Foreigners US$5 plus a Rs. 5 light fee, video camera Rs. 25, car parking Rs. 15* ☉ *Tues.–Sun. 9–5; arrive by 3:30* ☉ *Closed Mon.*

Ellora Caves

In the 7th century, for some inexplicable reason, the focus of activity shifted from Ajanta to a site 123 km (76 mi) to the southwest—a place known today as Ellora. Unlike the cave temples at Ajanta, those of Ellora are not solely Buddhist. Instead, they follow the development of religious thought in India—through the decline of Buddhism in the latter half of the 8th century, the Hindu renaissance that followed the return of the Gupta dynasty, and the Jain resurgence between the 9th and 11th centuries. Of the 34 caves, the 12 to the south are Buddhist, the 17 in the center are Hindu, and the 5 to the north are Jain.

At Ellora the focus is on sculpture, which covers the walls in exquisitely ornate masses. The carvings in the Buddhist caves are a serene reflection of the Buddhist philosophy, but in the Hindu caves they take on a certain exuberance and vitality—gods and demons do fearful battle, Lord Shiva angrily flails his eight arms, elephants rampage, eagles swoop, and lovers intertwine.

Unlike Ajanta, where the temples were chopped out of a steep cliff, the caves at Ellora were dug into the slope of a hill along a north–south line, presumably so that they faced west and could thus receive the light of the setting sun.

Cave 2 is an impressive monastery. The deceptively simple facade looms nearly 15 meters (50 feet) high; a lavish interior lies beyond. Gouged into this block of rock is a central hall with ornate pillars and a gallery of Buddhas and Boddhisattvas seated under trees and parasols.

The largest of the Buddhist caves is **Cave 5**. It was probably as a classroom for young monks. The roof appears to be supported by 24 pillars; working their way down, sculptors first "built" the roof before they "erected" the pillars.

Cave 6 contains a statue of Mahamayuri, the Buddhist goddess of learning—also identified as Saraswati, the Hindu goddess of learning—in the company of Buddhist figures. The boundaries between Hinduism and Buddhism are fuzzy and Hindus worship and recognize Buddhist gods and goddesses as their own; though sometimes not necessarily vice versa. Hin-

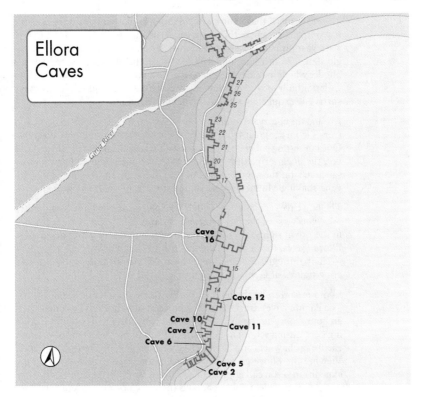

Ellora
Caves

27
26
25
23
22
21
20
17

Cave
16

15
14
Cave 12

Cave 10
Cave 7
Cave 6
Cave 11

Cave 5
Cave 2

dus consider Buddha the 19th avatar of their Lord Vishnu. **Cave 7,** an austere hall with pillars, is the first two-story cave. **Cave 10** is an impressive Chaitya Hall. Here the stonecutters reproduced the timbered roofs of their day over a richly decorated facade that resembles masonry work. Inside this chaitya—the only actual Buddhist chapel at Ellora—the main work of art is a huge sculpture of Buddha. Do look at the high ceiling with the stone "rafters" and note the sharp echo. The cave has been dubbed the Sutar Jhopdi or Carpenter's Cave and called a tribute to Visvakarma, the Hindu god of tools and carpentry. **Caves 11 and 12** rise grandly three floors up and are richly decorated with sculptural panels.

The immediate successors to the Buddhist caves are the Hindu caves, and a step inside these is enough to stop you in your tracks. It's another world—another universe—in which the calm contemplation of the seated Buddhas gives way to the dynamic cosmology of Hinduism. These caves were created around the 7th and 8th centuries.

Ellora is dominated by the mammoth Kailasa temple complex, or **Cave 16.** Dedicated to Shiva, the complex is a replica of his legendary abode at Mount Kailasa in the Tibetan Himalayas. The largest monolithic structure in the world, the Kailasa reveals the genius, daring, and raw skill of its artisans.

To create the Kailasa complex, an army of stonecutters started at the top of the cliff, where they removed 3 million cubic feet of rock to create a vast pit with a freestanding rock left in the center. Out of this single slab, 276 feet long and 154 feet wide, the workers created Shiva's abode, which includes the main temple, a series of smaller shrines, and galleries built into a wall that encloses the entire complex. Nearly every surface is exquisitely sculpted with epic themes.

Around the courtyard, numerous friezes illustrate the legends of Shiva and stories from the great Hindu epics, the *Mahabharata* and the *Ramayana*. One interesting panel on the eastern wall relates the origin of Shiva's symbol, the linga, or phallus. Another frieze, on the outer wall of the main sanctuary on the southern side of the courtyard, shows the demon Ravana shaking Mount Kailasa, from a story from the *Ramayana* epic.

The Jain caves are at the far end. If you have a car, consider driving there once you've seen the Hindu group of caves. These caves are attractive in their own right, and should not be missed on account of geography. Ellora Caves, for one, is as complex as a rabbit burrow; it's marvelous to climb through the numerous well-carved chambers and study the towering figures of Gomateshvara and Mahavira.

Ellora is said to be the busiest tourist site in the state of Maharashtra. The Ajanta caves are a bit off the beaten track, but Ellora, a mere half an hour from Aurangabad, gets packed with crowds. Try to avoid coming here during school holidays from April to first week of June. Don't encourage hawkers and unknown guides; they can be a terrible nuisance. Viewing the Ellora caves, in contrast to the Ajanta caves, is an easier expedition—you can approach the caves laterally because the entire line of caves is parallel to the road and there are not many steps involved. The proximity to Aurangabad and the easy access makes seeing these caves a half-day's adventure. Choose either early morning or late afternoon. ⬚ *Foreigners US$5, video camera Rs. 25* ✆ *Wed.–Mon. 6–6.*

need a break?

Ellora Restaurant (⬚ Parking lot, Ellora Caves ☎ 2437/4441) is a convenient place to stop for a cold drink and a hot samosa (deep-fried meat or vegetable turnover). The outdoor patio has fruit trees (home to many monkeys) and pink bougainvillea flowers. The restaurant closes before the caves. Walk straight out of the Ellora caves complex, past the umpteen souvenir stalls on your right, and you'll see the Hotel Kailas with its attached restaurant, **Kailas** (⬚ Outside the Ellora Caves). The menu, like so many Indian restaurants, is elastic—Chinese, Indian, Continental, snacks—Kailas has it all. Settle for a cool drink or some crisp *pakoras* (chick pea flour-and-vegetable fritters).

Nightlife & the Arts

The annual **Ellora Dance Festival,** held on one full moon night in December, draws top classical Indian dancers and musicians from around the country to perform outdoors against the magical backdrop of the Ellora Caves.

Aurangabad & Ajanta & Ellora Caves A to Z

AIR TRAVEL

Aurangabad and Bombay are about 45 minutes apart, and Aurangabad and New Delhi are 3½ hours apart by air. A one-way ticket costs about US$85 for foreign tourists between Bombay and Aurangabad on Indian Airlines and Jet Airways and US$185 between New Delhi and Aurangabad on Indian Airlines. Indian Airlines flies the route daily. Jet Airways flies daily between Bombay and Aurangabad only. Make sure you ask a travel agent *in advance* about the current status and schedules, as there are links between Aurangabad and Jaipur and Udaipur in the winter Indian Airline timetable. Plus schedules change every six months for these kinds of hop-and-a-skip flights.

🛪 **Airlines & Contacts Indian Airlines** ☎ 240/248-5421 or 240/248-3392 ⊙ Office open daily 10–5 ⊕ indian-airlines.nic.in. **Jet Airways** ☎ 240/244-1392 or 240/244-1770 ⊙ Office open daily 10–5 ⊕ www.jetairways.com.

🛪 **Airport Information Aurangabad Airport** ☎ 240/248-2111 or 240/248-5780.

BUS TRAVEL

It's not the most comfortable option, but several competing companies run safe "luxury" overnight buses to Aurangabad from Bombay, a 12-hour journey. You can arrange such a ride through the Indian Tourism Development Corporation or Maharashtra Tourism Development Corporation (MTDC), or your Bombay hotel or travel agent.

ATMS

There are no cash machines in Aurangabad.

CURRENCY EXCHANGE

Most hotels will change money for you, as long as you're staying there. Aurangabad's State Bank of India is open weekdays 10:30 to 2:30 and 3 to 4 (lunch break 2:30 to 3) and Saturday 10:30 to 1. Trade Wings is open Monday to Saturday 9:30 to 6:30 or 7, and Sunday 10 to 1.

🛪 **Exchange Services State Bank of India** ✉ Kranti Chowk, Aurangabad ☎ 240/233-1386, 240/233-1872, or 240/233-4778. **Trade Wings** ✉ Near Bawa Petrol Pump, CBS Rd., Aurangabad ☎ 240/235-7480, 240/234-7480, 240/232-2677, 240/233-2952, or 240/232-2677.

TOURS

The Government of India Tourist Office in Aurangabad oversees about 50 expert, polite, multilingual tour guides. You can hire one through the tourist office itself; the Maharashtra Tourism Development Corporation (MTDC) office, which is also in Aurangabad; and most travel agents. For parties of one to four, the fees are Rs. 255 per half day (four hours) and Rs. 380 for a full day (up to eight hours). An extra Rs. 250 is charged for trips of more than 100 km (60 mi); a guided day trip to the Ajanta caves, for example, would run around Rs. 630. But language guides—French, German, Japanese—cost Rs. 125 extra, in addition to the charges listed. It's best to book ahead. Ask for Al Mohammedi Abdul Nasser, a very knowledgeable, English-speaking guide, who comes recommended by the tourist office (they have a legitimate and qualified guide posted at the Ajanta caves, too). The archaeology department also has certain guides appointed, and although they are not as good as the tourist office guides, they are satisfactory.

Once you have a guide, you'll probably want to hire a car and driver. Rates are unusually high in Aurangabad, but moving around by autorickshaw is a slow business. A full-day trip in an air-conditioned Ambassador, Uno, or Indica (sturdy but comfortable Indian cars that will give you a good ride) with a driver may cost around Rs. 1,850 to Ajanta and Rs. 950 to Ellora. A full-day trip in a non-air-conditioned Ambassador with driver may cost around Rs. 1,200 to Ajanta and Rs. 700 to Ellora. To hire an air-conditioned Ambassador, Uno, or Indica for use within the city for eight hours is Rs. 950 and in a non-air-conditioned Ambassador, Uno, or Indica Rs. 700. More luxurious cars are proportionately more expensive, but they are not necessary. You can arrange a car for hire through your hotel travel desk, one of the travel agencies below, or the Government of India Tourist Office; fix a price in advance and make sure you get a good rate.

🛈 **Classic Travel Related Services** ✉ MTDC Holiday Resort, Station Rd., Aurangabad ☎ 240/233-5598 or 240/233-7788. **Aurangabad Tours and Travels** (Aurangabad Transport Syndicate) ✉ Welcomgroup Rama Hotel, Airport Rd., Aurangabad ☎ 240/248-2423, 240/248-5441 Welcomgroup Rama.

TRAIN TRAVEL

Aurangabad is not very well connected by train to major hubs. Only a few trains run between Aurangabad and Bombay. Tapovan Express is the best option; it departs from Bombay at 6:10 AM and the journey takes just over seven hours. Aurangabad is also about seven hours away from Hyderabad by train; you can take the Mumbai-Nizamabad Devgiri Express there. It's possible to reach Aurangabad from New Delhi, but it's a tedious journey—you must change trains at Manmad after a 5- to 6-hour stopover. Alternately, you can go up to Jalgaon—located on the main Delhi-Bombay route—and make the rest of the journey (108 km [67 mi]) by road. It's best to have your hotel organize transport from Jalgaon (ask them to arrange a car-and-driver; they will wait there for you). The journey takes three hours and will set you back about Rs 1,650 for a non air-conditioned car.

VISITOR INFORMATION

The Government of India Tourist Office, across from the train station, provides a warm and informative welcome to Aurangabad weekdays from 8:30 to 6, or Saturday and holidays from 8:30 to 1:30. Sunday the office is closed. Ask for the helpful Mr. D. M. Yadav, the assistant director and manager, or for Mr. I.R.V. Rao, one of his assistants. The MTDC office in town (open Monday through Saturday from 10 to 6 except holidays and the second and fourth Saturday of the month) offers a variety of information about other destinations in Maharashtra, and they have a counter at the airport that's open when flights arrive.

🛈 Tourist Offices **Government of India Tourist Office** ✉ Krishna Vilas, Station Rd., Aurangabad ☎ 240/233-1217 Mr. Yadav, 240/236-4999. **MTDC** ✉ MTDC Holiday Resort, Station Rd., Aurangabad ☎ 240/233-1513.

GOA

6

BUY BARGAIN BANGLES AND BEER
at the flea market at Anjuna ⇨*p.356*

GAMBOL AMONG THE CHURCH RUINS
in gorgeous Old Goa ⇨*p.364*

SEE A FOUR-CENTURY-OLD FORT,
good condition, excellent view ⇨*p.358*

FIND A PRIVATE NOOK
at Dudhsagar Falls ⇨*p.366*

BASK ON A SECLUDED BEACH
at the Leela Goa resort ⇨*p.375*

By Kavita
Watsa

IT'S HARD TO TELL WHERE THE COAST ENDS and the towns begin. With more than 36 gorgeous beaches strung along the west side of its 5,945 square km (2,295 square mi), this tiny state—a Portuguese colony until 1961—is India's most famous resort destination. With the exception of the monsoon season (June–October), the temperature stays warm and the air stays dry. Wide, palm-bordered rivers move lazily down to the Arabian Sea, and in small towns the houses gleam with a light wash of color set off by brightly painted front porches.

Goa was already a flourishing trade center before the arrival of the Portuguese in the 16th century—a marketplace for spices, silk, Persian corals, porcelain, and pearls. Yet ever since Affonso de Albuquerque captured Goa from the Sultan of Bijapur (who ruled from 1489 to 1510) and established what turned out to be a 450-year dominance, the Portuguese influence has defined Goan culture. The quintessential Goan is fun-loving and extroverted—Goans love a good drink and a hearty meal—yet always has time for an afternoon nap. Even today, most shopkeepers lower their shutters for a long siesta. Beer is cheap, and *feni*—cashew or coconut-palm hooch—is a favorite local drink at the state's 6,000 watering holes.

The sweep of development and modernity seems to be gradually undermining Goa's vestigial Portuguese culture in favor of Indian culture at large. Fewer houses and lodges begin their names with "Casa" or "Loja"; barbers are less frequently known as *barbarias,* and tailors as *alfaitarias.* A few signs remain: HOSPICIO on the hospital in Madgaeon, CINE NACIONAL on the movie theater in Panaji, and some shop signs with a Portuguese twist on common Hindu names, like POY for Pai, QUEXOVA for Keshava, and NAIQUE for Naik.

The state capital of Panaji (also called Panjim, as the second "a" in Panaji is silent, so it's pronounced "Panjim"), in central Goa, is worth visiting for its whitewashed churches, palm-lined plazas, and clean streets. It's also a short taxi ride from the exquisitely beautiful Portuguese church town of Old Goa, the final resting place of St. Francis Xavier, a Jesuit missionary to the East. (St. Francis Xavier came to Goa in 1542 and later traveled to Ceylon, Malacca, Japan, and China. He died in China in 1552 and his remains were brought back to Goa the following year.) The refusal of St. Francis Xavier's body to decompose is the "miracle" associated with him; the body lies in the Basilica of Bom Jesus in Goa, on display to visitors, and is a fairly gruesome sight. Madgaon, also known as Margao, the major town of South Goa, is crowded and grubby, and lacks the panache of Panaji, but is surrounded by historic villages with beautiful ancestral homes.

But, more than anything else, Goa is prized for its beaches. For the most seclusion, head north to Arambol Beach, cloistered in cliffs (and popular with European hippies), or, all the way to South Goa, especially Palolem Beach—or any other developed beach below Colva. For pure beauty coupled with the comforts of a beach resort, opt for Baga in the north or Colva in the south. Sinquerim in the north and Bogmalo in the south are best for windsurfing or waterskiing, and both are a quick drive in

Goa is a small state, so everywhere is within a short drive of everywhere else and taxis are affordable, even between Panaji and Madgaon. It's a leisurely, pleasure-oriented place, best seen in a state of relaxation. Try not to hop from hotel to hotel, unless you're touring the entire coast. Just find a hotel you like, preferably on a beach, and make day trips.

If you have 3 days

If you have only a few days in Goa, you might well spend them all swimming in the warm waters of the Arabian Sea and eating delicious fresh fish. Base yourself in the Bardez district in the north and spend your first day on **Baga Beach** ❹. Drive the next day to **Old Goa** ⓫ for a few hours of sightseeing *or* take a longer, tourist-office bus tour of either south or north Goa. Stretch out on **Calangute Beach** ❺ on Day 3.

If you have 5 days

Start your trip in the north. Spend a day and night at 🔲 **Baga Beach** ❹ or the isolated, ruggedly beautiful 🔲 **Arambol Beach** ❶ even farther north. The next day, explore **Panaji** ❿ and **Old Goa,** ⓫ and in the evening take a boat ride from Panaji. On your third day, hit 🔲 **Colva Beach** ⓳ or 🔲 **Sinquerim Beach** ❾ and linger to watch the sun set. The fourth day, if you're up for more traveling, take a taxi down the coast to **Palolem Beach** ㉖, another isolated and beautiful stretch of sand. Spend your time on all of these beaches, swimming and exploring: walks away from the designated swimming areas are both enchanting and—a rare blessing in India—sometimes solitary. Taxi back to the Panaji airport or to the **Madgaon** ⓴ railway station to leave Goa on your fifth day (no matter where you're going, leave up to an hour for the taxi ride).

If you have 7 days

Start your trip in the north. Spend a day and night at 🔲 **Sinquerim Beach** ❾, 🔲 **Baga Beach** ❹, or the isolated, ruggedly beautiful 🔲 **Arambol Beach** ❶. The next day, explore **Panaji** ❿ and **Old Goa** ⓫, and in the evening take a boat cruise on the river Mandovi from Panaji. On your third day (especially if this is a Wednesday), spend the morning on **Anjuna Beach** ❸, wander through the flea market in the afternoon, and linger to watch the sun set at the Shore Bar. The next day, laze around on **Calangute Beach** ❺, get your fill of seafood for lunch, and check out the nightlife. On Day 5, take a taxi or a day tour to the temples at **Ponda** ⓯ or to **Dudhsagar Falls** ⓮. On Day 6, spend the morning touring the villages of **Loutolim** ㉑ and **Chandor** ㉒, lunch at Raia, and retire to one of the beaches of the south (Colva, Benaulim, or Varca) for a relaxed evening. On your last day, take a taxi down the coast to **Palolem Beach** ㉖, an isolated and beautiful stretch of sand. Finally, get a taxi back to Panaji or **Madgaon** ⓴ to leave Goa.

either direction from Panaji. (Sinquerim is 14 km [8.7 mi] from Panaji, Bogmalo is 25 km [15.6 mi] from Panaji.) Surfers find Goa's waves and wind high enough only during monsoon season. Avoid the beaches closest to Panaji, including Miramar and Dona Paula beaches—both are touristy city beaches. At Miramar, a strong undertow mars the swimming, broken glass and garbage litter the sand, and some of the buildings are architectural eyesores. Dona Paula is a glorified cement dock crowded with vendors.

Integral to the Goan beach experience are the vendors. You'll be approached constantly by men and women offering "Pineapples?" "Cheese?" "Cold drink?" "Drums?" Their persistence can drive you into the water. Nomadic Lambani women dressed in vibrant colors and silver jewelry set up blankets cluttered with handicrafts, jewelry, embroideries, and quilts.

Goa's inland sights are somewhat scattered, but taxis and hired cars connect them easily. Panaji and Margao are about a 45-minute drive (about 30 km [19 mi]) apart, and reasonably comfortable shuttle buses ply between the two every hour. For a slice of native Goan life, visit a weekly market. On Wednesday between September and May, vendors sell mostly Indian and Tibetan crafts and artifacts on Anjuna Beach, where a strong smell of fish intensifies the air. Friday is the big market day in Mapusa, the main town in the Bardez district; people from adjoining villages and even transplanted hippies convene to sell everything from vegetables to blue jeans to handicrafts.

Goa has something for everyone, so it's popular with Indians and foreigners alike, from vacationers to explorers to those who just want to experience a different version of India. Younger visitors are drawn to Goa's infamous rave parties and its homegrown variety of trance music, known as Goa trance. If you want to get away from all this, and from the regular tourist beat, there are quiet inland villages, river islands, spice plantations, and temples to be explored.

About the Restaurants

If you like seafood and spicy food in general, you're in luck. You can spend all your time happily eating nothing but searingly hot (spicy) fish day in and out here, whether you choose to eat in the best restaurants around (generally found at hotels) or at beachfront open-air shacks. But since Goa has such a huge tourist culture, food can be prepared to your liking—simply grilled or fried. Just make sure you know what you're eating and how spicy the preparation before you order. Goan food is typically big on flavor, whether it's chili, tamarind, or coconut that plays a dominant role in the dishes you order. And make sure you order your meat (pork or beef) cooked through, and only in the better-known larger restaurants, not in the beach shacks. Seafood is safe everywhere as long as its fresh. If you're vegetarian, you'll get by fine, but vegetables are not as plentiful in the Goan diet as are fish, seafood, and meat.

WHAT IT COSTS In Rupees				
$$$$	**$$$**	**$$**	**$**	**¢**
AT DINNER over 350	250–350	150–250	100–150	under 100

Restaurant prices are for an entrée plus dal, rice, and a veg/non-veg dish.

Architecture

Goa is best known for its grandiose churches, exquisitely sculpted temples, and mosques, all dating from the 16th to the 18th centuries. The most illustrious structures here include Old Goa's *Sé* (cathedral) and the Basilica of Bom Jesus, where the remains of St. Francis Xavier lie in a silver casket entombed in a Florentine-style marble mausoleum.

Carnival

If you visit in February just before Lent, you'll see the Goans' zest for life in its finest form. Carnival time remains the official season for nonstop revelry, directed by King Momo ("King of Misrule"), a Goan appointed by his peers as the life of the party. Festivities include fanciful pageants (with some 50 floats depicting elements of Goa's folk culture, or more contemporary messages like preservation of the environment), hordes of musicians strumming the guitar or playing the banjo, and dancers breaking into the *mando* (a folk fusion of the Portuguese *fado* and the waltz)—all in streets spangled with confetti. This is prime time to have a beer or a *feni* and to savor Goa's legendary warmth.

6

Hot Fish & Feni

The Goans' legendary passion for seafood is borne out in the lines of the state's Poet Laureate, B. B. Borkar: "O, God of Death! Don't make it my turn today, because there's fish curry for dinner!" Portuguese dishes are generally adapted to Goan tastes with a healthy pinch of red chili, tempered with coconut milk. Typical local dishes include zesty-sweet prawn-curry rice, *chouris pao* (sausage bread), chicken *cafreal* (amply seasoned with ginger, garlic, green chilis, and lime), and ultrahot *vindaloo* dishes. Goa's seafood is superb, especially fresh crabs, pomfret, squid, lobster, and prawns. Try pomfret in a red or green sauce, or tiger prawns *baffad* (spicy Goan style). For dessert, order *bebinca*, a rich, layered, dense pastry made of butter, egg yolk, and coconut. And no Goan experience is truly complete without at least a taste of *feni*, the potent local brew made of either palm sap or cashew fruit.

Revelry on the Beaches

Head straight to the beaches if you're looking for nightlife. On Sunday night, all of southern Goa seems to descend on Colva for a night of drinking, eating, dancing, and playing *housie*, a local version of bingo. Dancing and partying also happen at Baga, Anjuna, and any of the more remote beaches. The arts scene in Panaji and Margao is generally limited to Konkani-language theater and music.

Shopping

Most of the arts and crafts sold in Goa come from elsewhere in India, and the state has few flashy shopping areas. Between September and May, head to Anjuna's Wednesday flea market to browse through Rajasthani bags and clothing or Kashmiri blankets. Madgaon has a food market on Sunday, and Mapusa has a big, multifarious market on Friday. In March, Panaji hosts the spring festival of Shigmo, which fills the streets with stalls selling blankets, furniture, and sweets.

About the Hotels

Goa has every kind of lodging, from super-exclusive posh resorts perched on cliffs to beachside shacks appropriate only for beach bums and hippies. Expect to get what you pay for, however, especially during peak season, from December to February, when traveling hordes fill the hotels. Make sure you reserve a room far in advance of this time. During the monsoon season (June–October), prices drop by up to half and the resorts empty out. Unless noted otherwise, hotels here have central air-conditioning, room service, doctors on call, and currency-exchange facilities, and rooms have cable TV and bathrooms with showers.

WHAT IT COSTS In Rupees				
	$$$$	**$$$**	**$$**	**$**	**¢**
FOR 2 PEOPLE	over 4,000	3,000–4,000	2,000–3,000	1,000–2,000	under 1,000

Prices are for two people in a standard double room in high season, excluding up to 20% tax.

Exploring Goa

Goa's topography varies between beaches, jungle, and rich farmland. Much of the country's development is along the coast, where you'll find all the resorts Goa is famous for, plus the two major towns—Panaji (Panjim) in central Goa and Madgaon (Margao) in the south. Also along the coast are scores of paddy fields, coconut groves, and small towns. Head inland for the natural sights, including waterfalls, bird sanctuaries, and temples ensconced in dense palm jungle, all easily navigated as long as you have a good guide. Much farther west, toward Karnataka, are the mountains of the Western Ghats, and the lush rain forest that has developed from the rainwater that collects here from the monsoon that sweeps inland from the coast. Note that in addresses the terms *wadi, waddo,* and *vado* all mean "street."

Numbers in the text correspond to points of interest on the Goa map.

Timing

It's best to come to Goa in winter or early spring. During the rainy season, which stretches from the end of May to September, most beach-shack restaurants close due to heavy winds and violent surf. November, December, and January are the best months for lolling around on the beach. If you come in early February, you'll experience the added excitement of Carnival. Christmas and Easter are celebrated with crowded church services, the former with a midnight mass that continues almost into the morning.

NORTH GOA

You'll find most of the party beaches (and most of the foreigners) in the northern part of Goa. Expect a variety of accommodations, however, from shacks to fancy, secluded resorts. The same goes for food here, largely divided between dining on the beach in open-air restaurants and dining in far more elaborate restaurants in hotels—with more elaborate cuisine. There's not much to see besides beaches, of course, but you will find a few beautiful old forts built of the local red pitted stone called laterite and overlooking the sea. You may also want to take an excursion to one of the popular markets. The region is divided into several districts: Pernem at the far north, Bardez just below it, Bicholim directly east, and Satari still farther inland—to the mountains of the Western Ghats and the state of Karnataka. The Bardez district, where you'll find the beaches and most towns and hotels, is the most populated.

Arambol Beach

★ ❶ *48 km (30 mi) northwest of Panaji.*

Goa's northernmost beach, also known as Harmal (and in the Pernem district), is ruggedly lovely. You enter through a hippie colony where young foreigners live in small huts. The best stretch of beach is a 20-minute walk to the right, beyond the ragged food and drink shacks. Here, the scenery is spectacular: a freshwater pond nestles at the base of the hillside 50 yards from the crashing surf below, and the ocean foams around dark rocks rising offshore. The sea is rougher here than at other beaches—still good for swimming but a bit more fun for surf-seekers. To avoid crowds in season, walk past the pond and you'll find quieter tide-dependent inlets and rock ledges.

Where to Stay

★ $$$$ 🏨 **Siolim House.** If you want to relax in style and have access to secluded Arambol beach, stay at this small boutique hotel, which occupies a 300-year-old Portuguese villa in Siolim village, on the south bank of the Chapora river. Beautifully restored in 1996, this old mansion has very large, well-furnished rooms and plenty of common areas and living space. A new bridge across the Chapora makes it easy to get to the beaches north of the river in Pernem, as long as you have a car or bicycle (it's about 6 to 7 km [4 mi] from Siolim House to the Pernem beaches). ⊠ *Casa Palaciao de Siolim, Wadi Siolim, Bardez district, 403557* ☎ *832/227–2138 or 833/227–2941* 🖷 *832/227–2941 or 832/227–2323* ⊕ *www.siolimhouse.com* 🛏 *4 rooms, 3 suites* ♨ *Restaurant, pool, massage, laundry service, Internet, airport shuttle* ▤ *MC, V* ❍ *CP.*

Vagator Beach

❷ *25 km (16 mi) northwest of Panaji.*

Little Vagator and Vagator come to life after dark with Goa's infamous raves. The beaches have secluded sandy coves, lots of palm trees, and still are not as commercial as Calangute–Baga, though overrun during the day by busloads of tourists. To the north you can see the dark red walls of the old hill fort of Chapora, which was taken twice from the Portuguese by the Marathas. (The Marathas ruled a principality that covers much of the modern-day state of Maharashtra, north of Goa.) To the south, a striking white cross tops a rock jetty. The view from the ramparts is phenomenal, and farther up the shore are stretches of secluded sand. Vagator's gentle surf is good for swimming. This part of

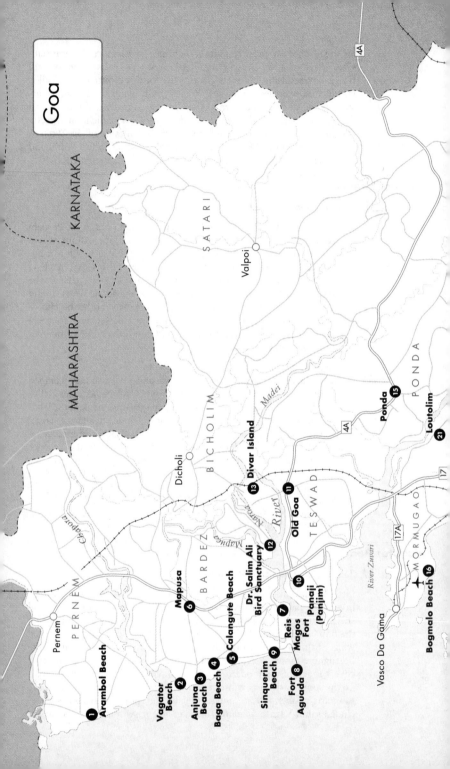

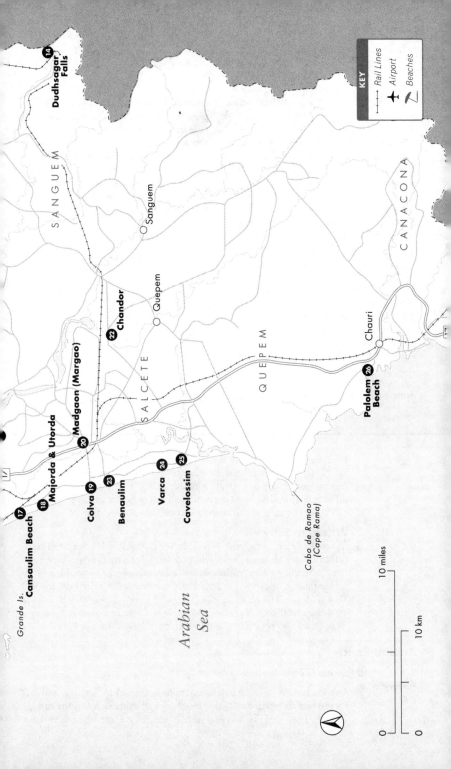

CloseUp
BEACH SHACKS & ROOMS FOR RENT

GOA HAS LOTS OF LUXURY resorts and hotels, both in the north and south, but there are many who vow that you haven't seen the real Goa unless you rough it out in one of the dozens of beach shacks that spring up during the tourist season (December–January). These can be fun (and really inexpensive) to stay in, particularly if you're in a group, but they are not advisable if you're a woman traveling alone or if you're carrying valuables. Cases of violence against women have been recorded in recent years; incidents have been known to take place when women walk home alone from a bar late at night or down a lonely path. This warning aside, a decent-size lock and an obviously shoestring lifestyle can help you have an extremely peaceful stay in a shack. Houses in the villages also rent rooms, and here you'll experience the disconcerting Goan pig toilets, where the animals, in short, take the place of the plumbing. (Picture this: you squat over a hole between two planks of wood in a shack on stilts. The pigs are below you. Not the most elegant arrangement.) If you're in need of peace and quiet, don't stay in north Goa; head to Palolem in the south where "tree" huts come up on stilts in the season.

Goa is not as developed as the beaches farther south, and although there are plenty of shack restaurants they have a here-today-gone-tomorrow feel; indeed, many disappear from one season to the next, or take on a different name. The best way to find an eatery here is to ask fellow travelers for the name of the current favorite. ⊠ *Bardez district.*

Where to Stay

$ 🏨 **Leoney Resort.** A favorite among travelers, this hotel is clean and comfortable, very close to the beach, and run by the friendly Albuquerque family. Small, spotless rooms with semicircular decks overlook a modest swimming pool and garden. ⊠ *Ozran Beach Rd., Vagator, 403509* ☎ *832/227–3634* 🖷 *832/227–3595* 🛏 *15 rooms, 4 cottages, 1 suite* ☖ *Restaurant, pool, laundry service, travel services, Internet, library, airport shuttle; no a/c in some rooms* ▤ *AE, DC, MC, V* ⦿| *EP.*

Anjuna Beach

❸ *20 km (12 mi) northwest of Panaji.*

Fodor'sChoice
★

The Calangute Beach party seems to have shifted to Anjuna, and has spread farther north to Vagator Beach as well. Although Anjuna can get very crowded and the party scene become riotous, the beach is still not as commercial as Calangute, and does not have large-scale luxury resorts, such as those at Sinquerim Beach and those in the south. Drugs are all too easily available here, but are highly illegal—even if they seem to be part of the system. More happily, Anjuna is known for its flea market on Wednesday, a legacy of the days when hippies used to sell their belongings here to buy a few more weeks of love and peace. The Shore Bar at the beach is the place in Goa to watch the sunset and bond with the rest of Anjuna's drugged out population.

Where to Stay & Eat

$–$$ ✕ **Granpa's Inn.** This multicuisine restaurant represents quite a change from the shack restaurants that line the beach area. The menu is limited but includes popular Continental and Indian dishes, such as spinach-and-potato casserole, prawns au gratin, and biriyani. Goan dishes are also available on request. The downside is that the restaurant does not ordinarily serve beef or pork. However, it's open for all three meals. ⊠ *Hotel Bougainvillea, Gaunwadi, Anjuna* ☎ *832/227–3271* ▤ *MC, V.*

$$$–$$$$ ⌂ **Laguna Anjuna.** This upmarket place to stay is less than a kilometer from the beach but in a secluded rural area. In the elegant, minimalist cottages, each with one or two bedrooms, are red floors, soft lighting, entertainment areas with divans, and pretty, blue bathrooms. The resort has a pool and plenty of greenery, and its own restaurant if you don't want to trek to the small eateries near the beach. ⊠ *Soranto Vado, Anjuna, 403509* ☎ *832/227–3248 or 832/227–4131* 🖷 *832/ 227–4305* ⊕ *www.lagunaanjuna.com* ⌨ *30 rooms* ⌂ *Restaurant, pool, massage, spa, bar, laundry facilities, pool tables, Internet, airport shuttle* ▤ *MC, V* ❙O❙ *CP.*

$ ⌂ **Hotel Bougainvillea (Granpa's Inn).** This hotel occupies a 200-year-old restored Portuguese country house. Though Granpa himself is long deceased and the place has changed management, the name, "Granpa's Inn" has stuck—as a mark of respect. A small pool, a lush garden, and simple, well-maintained rooms on the ground floor make this one of the nicest places to stay in Anjuna. ⊠ *Gaunwadi, Anjuna, 403509* ☎ *832/227–3271 or 832/227–3270* 🖷 *832/227–4370 or 832/225–2624* ⊕ *www.goacom.com/hotels/granpas* ⌨ *14 rooms* ⌂ *Restaurant, pool, massage, yoga, bar, laundry service Internet, airport shuttle; no a/c in some rooms* ▤ *MC, V* ❙O❙ *CP.*

Nightlife

The extremely popular place to down beer or local tea, watch the dramatic sunset over the Arabian Sea, and listen to loud music until the ★ wee hours is the extremely popular **Shore Bar** (☎ 98221–51616 mobile) on the beach. The steps of this place are usually packed with people, especially on Wednesday after the flea market. Walk north from the market for about a kilometer to get to the bar.

Baga Beach

❹ *15 km (9 mi) northwest of Panaji.*

This small beach about 2 km (1.2 mi) north of Calangute, in the Bardez district, is a lively place known for its hopping "shack life." The many

CloseUp

THE FLEA MARKET AT ANJUNA

GETTING TO THE WEDNESDAY *flea market at Anjuna can be half the fun; you can take a bus or a motorcycle taxi, or a fisherman's boat from Baga, which is quicker (15 min by boat, 30 min by road). Although you will still find hippies there, it really isn't their market any more. Now dominated by Lambani nomads in their striking clothes and jewelry, and craftspeople from elsewhere in India, the market is a splash of red and orange in a flat clearing above the rocky beach. Bead and white metal bangles, necklaces and earrings, silver toe rings, embroidered shoulder bags, silk and cotton sarongs, and ethnic footwear are among the more ordinary products on sale. If you look carefully, there are all sorts of other things here from used motorbikes of uncertain age to do-it-yourself mehendi kits. Buy a crochet bikini, a backless mirror-work top, or a tie-dye bandana to enhance your wardrobe for those really formal occasions, or just sit back at the market bar and down a ridiculously cheap beer while someone braids your hair deftly or offers to tattoo, pierce, or otherwise mutilate various parts of your anatomy. When your day's bargains have been struck (and getting things for a third or less of the quoted price is not uncommon), join the rest of Anjuna down at the shore. Be careful not to bargain unfairly, because you run the risk of a sarcastic "take it for free?" from one of the tribal women. The market only appears during the tourist season, don't go looking for it in the monsoon.*

popular food and drink joints are headlined by St. Anthony's for seafood and Tito's Bar for nighttime revelry. The beach drops steeply to the shoreline, where fishing canoes make use of the easy boat-launching conditions to provide rides, often to the Wednesday market at Anjuna Beach just around the bend (the ride to Anjuna takes 15 minutes by sea, but significantly longer by road). A few hundred meters down the beach to the left of the entrance are more open, less crowded areas where you can spread out your towel and sunbathe. The beach is named for the mouth of the Baga river (at its northern end). A small bridge across the Baga is coming up behind the Hotel Baia Do Sol; it is worth checking to see if it's open (it was under construction at this writing) if you're heading north, as it will save you driving time.

Where to Stay & Eat

$$$$ ✕ **St. Anthony's.** This simple restaurant–cum–beach shack serves an astonishing variety of fish dishes, and possibly the best sweet *lassi* (yogurt-and-milk drink) in India. The tuna steaks and pomfret dishes are particularly good. ⊠ *Baga Beach, Bardez district* ▭ *No credit cards.*

$-$$ ⛬ **Hotel Baia Do Sol.** This is the most reliable accommodation here—versus the shack-type lodgings prevalent in Baga—because of its great location by the Baga river and it is across the road from the beach. The rooms are average in size and are basic but clean, and cool and breezy because they're so close to the sea and river. Some rooms have good views of the sea and river. ⊠ *Baga Beach, 403516* ☎ *832/227–6084* 🖷 *832/227–6085* 🖙 *22 rooms* ⚴ *Restaurant, cable TV, beach, laundry service, travel services; no a/c in some rooms* ▤ *MC, V* ⏀ *EP.*

Nightlife

Always packed, **Tito's** (☎ 832/227–9895 or 832/227–5028) is the most happening bar and disco in Goa. Cafe Mambo, on the premises, is open 9:30 AM–3:30 AM daily, but the party crowd doesn't come in until close to midnight. Cover charges are sometimes levied (you can use Master-Card or Visa). The establishment is built into the hillside just off the Calangute-Baga Road.

Calangute Beach

❺ *12 km (7 mi) northwest of Panaji.*

Calangute Beach, between Sinquerim and Baga beaches in the Bardez district, is an open stretch of sand with occasional palm trees for patchy shade. The beach is accessible by cement steps. Note the sign warning that swimming is dangerous—there's a fairly strong undertow here. Calangute is bustling: the entrance area is crammed with restaurants, stalls, and shops. During the high season (winter), dozens of shacks pop up on the beach, serving inexpensive alcohol and seafood. Once a peaceful hippie haven, the beach is now crowded and commercial; nonetheless, at night dozens of beach shacks come to life, with lights and music and great seafood, not to mention cheap alcohol and a general holiday mood. The government-run **Calangute Residency** (⊠ Calangute Beach, near Bandodker statue ☎ 832/227–6024 or 832/227–6109) has general information and changes currency and traveler's checks. (This is a hotel but it has a friendly staff who are willing to give you information.)

Where to Stay & Eat

★ **$$–$$$** ✕ **Souza Lobo.** Established in 1932, and now managed by the third generation of the Lobo family, this restaurant on Calangute beach catches the exuberant sea breeze. The food is excellent, and the place is always busy. The Goan masala fried prawns are exactly as they should be—with authentic red masala and fresh, perfectly deveined prawns. Other Goan specialties include the squid *amot tik* (a sour curry), king fish steak *peri-peri* (spicy, tangy red sauce), and prawn-stuffed pomfret. The restaurant also serves simpler Western-style seafood with a good garlic butter sauce. There's live music Saturday night. ⊠ *Calangute Beach* ☎ *832/227–6463* ▤ *No credit cards.*

¢–$ ✕ **Casandre.** TAVERNA, RESTAURANTE AND DIVERTIMENTO—the sign outside says it all. In an old house with a beautiful, high-beam bar, a pleasant style, and friendly service, this restaurant specializes in steaks, sizzlers, and Continental cuisine, and the Goan food is decent. Order a good chateaubriand here, or beef goulash or a chicken sizzler—even a fish fillet stuffed with crabmeat. The restaurant is open for all three meals and proudly advertises its breakfast with the works. There's live music on Sunday night. ⊠ *Umta Vaddo, Calangute Beach Rd.* ☎ *832/227–5934* ⊕ *www.casandre.com* ▤ *No credit cards.*

$$$$ 🖼 **Pousada Tauma.** This small, pretty, but definitely overpriced boutique hotel is built of laterite—a local red pitted stone—and has an abundant, leafy garden. Stay here to be far enough away (less than a kilometer) from the beach but close enough to be part of the action when you want it. The rooms are well designed, with paintings, sculpture, and custom furniture. ✉ *Porba-Waddo, Calangute* ☎ *832/227–9061 to 63* 🖨 *832/ 227–9064* ⊕ *www.pousada-tauma.com* 📠 *12 rooms* ⌂ *Restaurant, pool, cable TV, ayurvedic center, gym, massage, bar, laundry service, travel services* 🖃 *MC, V* ⦿ *EP.*

Sports & the Outdoors

Hop aboard a dolphin- or crocodile-spotting tour, which winds past thick mangroves along the Zuari and Mandovi rivers, or take a ride on a banana boat. **Odyssey Tours** (☎ 832/227–6941) has a luxury yacht with a license to carry 27 passengers on deck, plus 4 crew members, including a captain and engineer (so you can't rent the yacht and drive it yourself). They offer half-day dolphin-spotting cruises (9:30 AM–1 PM) for about Rs. 100 per person, including lunch; reservations are necessary. The yacht leaves from Brittona, where it has its own jetty. In the afternoon, it's available for private charter groups for Rs. 6,500 per hour.

Mapusa

6 *15 km (9 mi) north of Panaji.*

Friday is the big market day in Mapusa (pronounced *map*-sa)—the main town in the Bardez district. People from adjoining villages and even transplanted hippies convene to sell everything from vegetables to blue jeans to handicrafts. It's an ideal place to buy souvenirs. Mapusa is not a place you'd want to stay for the night, and there's really nothing much to see here, but like Madgaon in the south, the town is good for brief forays to change money, go shopping, and take care of other necessities. Steer clear of it as much as possible if you want to maintain a cheerful mood—except for the lively Friday market, the town is a bit dreary.

Reis Magos Fort

7 *5 km (3 mi) southeast of Sinquerim beach.*

Built by the Portuguese at the narrowest point of the Mandovi, Reis Magos is a good diversion before you get to the main fort in the area, which is Aguada. Although you cannot go into Reis Magos Fort, you can view the bastions from the church of the same name that stands below it. The church is one of the prettiest in Goa, standing on a bend in the road as it curves up the hill to the fort and skirts the Mandovi; you get here by taking very steep, mossy steps.

Fort Aguada

8 *4 km (2½ mi) south of Sinquerim beach.*

Fodor'sChoice Perched high on a hill, with wonderful views west across the Arabian
★ Sea and east across Aquada Bay to Panaji, Fort Aguada was built in 1612 and named for the natural springs that supplied not only the fort but also

passing ships. The fort is in excellent condition, and is surrounded by wild grass. Inside you can take a good look at the solid laterite architecture and the old lighthouse. Below the bastion is where visitors are allowed to see the Aguada Jail. The fort's defenses actually enclosed a much larger area than the bastion at the top of the hill; a seaward bastion still juts into the Arabian Sea on Sinquerim beach, near the Taj cluster of hotels. If you only have time for one of Goa's many forts, make it to Aguada, because it's the best preserved and most magnificent. It's not an easy walk, as it's 4 km (2.5 mi) south of Sinquerim beach and at least half the way is a fairly steep uphill, so hire a car if time is a constraint.

Sinquerim Beach

9 *10 km (6.2 mi) northwest of Panaji.*

Sinquerim is the first beach you'll get to as you head northwest after crossing the Mandovi from Panaji. Along with Bogmalo, it's one of the few beaches where you can rent windsurfers, water skis, and other water toys without having to be a guest at a hotel. It's much cheaper to rent equipment from these places, but check the condition of the equipment and make sure lifejackets are provided; also check, if possible, with others on the beach to see if the guidance was adequate. Stretching in front of the three Taj resorts, this small, sandy beach can get fairly crowded with tourists and vendors. The water, however, is warm and clean, and its slightly higher waves make for good bodysurfing. ⊠ *Bardez district.*

Where to Stay & Eat

$$$$ ✕ **Morisco.** Expect Goan specialties here at this seafood barbecue restaurant at the Fort Aguada Beach Resort. There's a marvelous view of the seaward fortification. The catch of the day is marinated in Goan spices and served along with local music and the waves. ⊠ *Fort Aguada Beach Resort, Sinquerim, Bardez district* ☎ *832/247–9123 to 36* ⊟ *AE, DC, MC, V.*

★ **$$$$** ✕⊞ **Taj Holiday Village.** Designed as a sort of ritzy Goan village, this delightful tropical resort consists of tile-roof villas scattered around gardens and lawns that face Sinquerim Beach. Each villa has 2, 4, or 6 rooms; each room has a private terrace and is elegantly rustic. The staff is friendly, helpful, and efficient. Facilities at the adjoining Taj properties are shared by all three resorts; also on offer are adventure activities, including rapelling and rock climbing. ⊠ *Sinquerim, Bardez, 403519* ☎ *832/564–5858* ⊟ *832/564–5868* ⊕ *www.tajhotels.com* ⇥ *145 rooms* ⚙ *4 restaurants, cable TV, tennis court, 5-hole golf course, 2 pools, health club, hair salon, spa, beach, windsurfing, boating, jet skiing, parasailing, waterskiing, Ping-Pong, squash, volleyball, 2 bars, dance club, baby-sitting, dry cleaning, laundry service, business services, meeting room, airport shuttle, travel services* ⊟ *AE, DC, MC, V* ⦿ *EP.*

★ **$$$$** ⊞ **Aguada Hermitage.** If you crave seclusion and luxury—and can afford them—by all means stay at this Taj property. Set on a hill overlooking Sinquerim Beach, these Goan-style villas are like separate, elegant homes. Each villa has a large terrace with upholstered garden furniture, one or two bedrooms, and several other rooms. A regular shuttle takes you down the hill to the nearby Taj Fort Aguada Beach Resort, which shares reception and all facilities with the Aguada Hermitage. You may also use the facilities at the Taj Holiday Village next door. ⊠ *Sinquerim Beach, Bardez district, 403519* ☏ *832/564–5858* 📠 *832/564–5868* ⊕ *www.tajhotels.com* ⤳ *15 villas* ⌂ *4 restaurants, cable TV, tennis court, 5-hole golf course, 2 pools, health club, hair salon, spa, beach, windsurfing, boating, jet skiing, parasailing, waterskiing, Ping-Pong, squash, volleyball, 2 bars, dance club, baby-sitting, dry cleaning, laundry service, business services, meeting room, airport shuttle, travel services* ⊟ *AE, DC, MC, V* ⎅ *EP.*

$$$$ ⊡ **Fort Aguada Beach Resort.** Built within the boundary and adjoining the ramparts of an old Portuguese fort built in 1612, this hotel has gorgeous views of the fort, sea, and beach. All rooms face the sea and are furnished with contemporary Goan-style dark wood and cane furniture; you can also stay in intimate, tile-roof, two-unit cottages. All facilities at the resort's sister Taj properties next door are open for collective Taj use. ⊠ *Sinquerim Beach, Bardez district, 403519* ☏ *832/247–9123 to 36* 📠 *832/247–9200* ⊕ *www.tajhotels.com* ⤳ *64 rooms, 24 suites, 42 cottages* ⌂ *4 restaurants, cable TV, tennis court, 5-hole golf course, 2 pools, health club, hair salon, spa, beach, windsurfing, boating, jet skiing, parasailing, waterskiing, Ping-Pong, squash, volleyball, 2 bars, dance club, baby-sitting, dry cleaning, laundry service, business services, meeting room, airport shuttle, travel services* ⊟ *AE, DC, MC, V* ⎅ *EP.*

$ ⊡ **Marbella Guest House.** This heritage guest house is on one of north Goa's narrowest lanes, behind the massive Taj resorts. A restored villa with a few excellent rooms and gleaming floors and furniture, it's a popular place among those who know Goa well, and it's only about a half of a kilometer from here down to Sinquerim beach. ⊠ *Between Sinquerim and Candolim beaches, Bardez district, 403515* ☏ *832/247–9551* 📠 *832/227–6509* ⤳ *3 rooms, 3 suites* ⌂ *Restaurant, cable TV, laundry service* ⊟ *No credit cards* ⎅ *EP.*

Sports & the Outdoors

John's Boat Tours (⊠ Candolim Beach ☏ 832/247–9669 or 98221–82814 mobile) has dolphin watching for Rs. 650 per person, snorkeling at Grand Island for Rs. 1,000 a head, crocodile spotting in the backwaters for Rs. 1,000, and sea fishing for Rs. 750. The price includes beer and a barbecue on board (except for the fishing trips, which only cover beer).

PANAJI (PANJIM) & CENTRAL GOA

Panaji (Panjim), the capital of the latter-day Portuguese and the present state capital, lies between the Zuari and Mandovi rivers in central Goa. Apart from its own considerable charms, the small city is a good base from which to explore Goa's history, particularly the imposing churches of Old Goa, an abandoned Portuguese capital upriver, and the river islands of Divar and Chorao. Although Ponda in eastern Goa, with its temples and wildlife sanctuaries, is technically closer to the town of Madgaon (Margao) in the south, it makes better sense to explore this area from Panaji. Once you get to South Goa, there's no point in making Madgaon your base, as it's a small, dreary town with little to do, far unlike the area's wonderfully quiet, secluded beaches.

Panaji (Panjim)

 600 km (372 mi) south of Bombay.

The state capital of Panaji has whitewashed churches, palm-lined plazas, and clean streets, and none of the hustle and bustle of other capitals. The unhurried attitude of the residents adds to Panaji's charms and reminds you to take it slowly here. The best way to see the older parts of the city is on foot. In fact, if you leave without having explored the back streets at leisure, you haven't really seen Panaji at all. For diehard sand lovers, there's the city beach at Dona Paula, but, well, Panaji isn't famous for its beaches, as they tend to be dirty and crowded.

Church of Our Lady of Immaculate Conception. This grand shrine was a mere chapel before 1541. Soon after, it became a parish in 1600, and its structure was rebuilt entirely. Now the church almost entirely presides over one of Panaji's squares. The building's distinctive zigzag staircases are a 19th-century addition, and the church's large bell was originally in the Church of St. Augustine in Old Goa. An annual December festival here draws huge crowds. At the other times of the year, the square is a peaceful place to linger and the sun's rays in late afternoon slide across the church; the glow is glorious enough to make you forget the traffic and the hassles of making your way through India. ⊠ *Near Municipal Gardens* ⊠ *Free* ☉ *Mon.–Sat. 9–6, Sun. 10–6.*

Fontainhas. This part of old Panjim makes for a good morning's exploring. The shady, narrow streets of this largely residential neighborhood do not really belong to India—they are clearly still Portuguese at heart. From tiny *balcaos* (colonnaded porches), inhabitants watch as their quiet, unchanging world goes by, and through the old windows, you can hear people practicing the piano and violin. At the heart of Fontainhas is the little whitewashed Chapel of St. Sebastian, which dates only to the late 19th century—new by Goan standards. Its claim to fame is an old crucifix that was once housed in the infamous Palace of the Inquisition in Old Goa. ⊠ *Between Ourem creek and Altinho.*

Sao Tome. This crumbling old neighborhood contains the General Post Office, once a tobacco trading house, and a maze of extremely narrow streets behind it. The tiny bars of this district are full of old-world character, and indeed you might need that drink to help banish the more grisly images of Goa's past. The area opposite the post office was once the site of Panjim's town executions. ⊠ *Between M. G. Rd. and Emidio Gracia Rd.*

The Secretariat. Drive or walk around the well-maintained seat of Goa's state government; this heritage building occupies a pleasant spot by the Mandovi River and has several important associations. Previously located here was the palace of the Sultan of Bijapur, to whom Goa belonged at the time of the Portuguese invasion. The building that the Portuguese erected served as temporary quarters for the viceroys of Goa upon their arrival or departure from the territory. It became their permanent residence in the mid-18th century, when the capital at Old Goa was abandoned. In the early 20th century, the Secretariat became a government office, as it is today. Also of interest is the nearby stone statue of Abbe Faria hypnotizing a woman. Faria, born to a Portuguese father and Indian mother, was the author of an important early-19th-century publication on hypnosis, and the inspiration for Alexander Dumas's crazy monk in *The Count of Monte Cristo*. Visitors are not encouraged here, and security restrictions make it difficult to get admission inside. ⊠ *Mandovi riverfront.*

Where to Stay & Eat

$–$$ ✕ **Hospedario Venite.** The narrow alley and dingy staircase might remind you of a backpacker's haunt, but take heart and enter this backstreet Sao Thome restaurant. It's just a room in a crumbling old house with wrought-iron *balcaos* overlooking the street, but the wooden floor, ancient chairs, cane-and-mudpot lights, untidy wall murals, and advertisements for Christian art create a clock-stopping vibe that is *sussegado* (take it easy) in a local way—something a luxury resort could never hope to replicate. The food is inexpensive and good; try the prawn *balchao* (in a red chili paste). ⊠ *31 January Rd., half a block from M. G. Rd., Sao Thome* ☎ *832/242–5537* ▭ *No credit cards* ⊙ *Closed Sun.*

$–$$ ✕ **Riorico.** The best place in Panjim for Goan food, this formal and somewhat sober, dining hall–like place serves very tasty dishes, from the local *rawa* (semolina)-fried fish and prawns to the Portuguese-influenced seafood *caldeirada* (poached fish layered with potatoes and tomatoes and cooked with white wine). ⊠ *Hotel Mandovi, D. B. Marg* ☎ *832/242–6270 to 73 or 832/222–4405 to 09* ▭ *AE, DC, MC, V.*

$$$$ ▥ **Cidade de Goa.** Built into a hillside near Panaji, this stylish resort is ideal if you prefer an urbane beach scene to a rustic retreat. Open, multilevel corridors run through what is essentially a cleverly designed apartment block. The rooms either face the hotel gardens or a sheltered (but polluted) cove opposite the harbor at Vasco. Apart from offering standard watersports at Vainguinim beach, the hotel houses an art gallery and organizes picnics to a nearby uninhabited island by motorboat. The restaurant, Alfama, is designed along the lines of a town square in Lisbon and is complete with *balcaos* and murals of its namesake, a region in Portugal. The menu traces dishes native to places along Vasco da Gama's historic journey: *prawn vol-au-vent* (with a sauce, in a puff pastry) and tiger prawn *peri peri* (in a red, spicy, tangy sauce). You can also order an excellent vegetarian or non-vegetarian Saraswat *thali*—this is typical Goan Hindu cuisine, not usually available on local menus. ⊠ *Vainguinim Beach, 6 km (4 mi) south of Panaji, 403004* ☎ *832/245–4545* ▤ *832/245–4541* ⊕ *www.cidadedegoa.com* ↪ *205 rooms, 5 suites* ♿ *5 restaurants, cable TV, 2 tennis courts, 2 pools, gym, hair salon, massage, sauna, beach, windsurfing, boating, jet skiing, parasailing, waterskiing, volleyball, 3 bars, baby-sitting, dry cleaning, laundry service, Internet, meeting room, airport shuttle, travel services* ▭ *AE, DC, MC, V* ⏐⊙⏐ *EP.*

★ **$$$$** ▥ **Goa Marriott Resort.** This luxurious hotel at the mouth of the Mandovi has a strikingly designed swimming pool that gives the impression that it overflows into the river below. Rooms are simple and tasteful. The beautiful spa and fitness center are among the best in Goa, and the staff are warm and courteous. The hotel is in a class by itself: It has a modern style and a smart design, and staying here you're likely to feel you've gotten your money's worth. It's just a few minutes by foot to the beach—though this is very much a city hotel, not a beach resort (the pool is far more impressive). There's also a seasonal dive center here. From the hotel it's only about 2 km (1.2 mi) to the heart of Panjim. ⊠ *Next to Youth Hostel, Miramar Beach Rd., 403001* ☎ *832/246–3333* 🖷 *832/ 246–3300* ⊕ *www.marriott.com* ⤴ *165 rooms* ⌂ *3 restaurants, cable TV, tennis court, pool, health club, hair salon, ayurvedic center, squash, spa, 2 bars, nightclub, casino, children's programs, laundry service, travel services, airport shuttle* ▤ *AE, DC, MC, V* ⅠⓄⅠ *EP.*

$–$$$ 🖬 **Hotel Nova Goa.** If you prefer clean, modern amenities and comfort to personality and style, check into this hotel in the center of Panaji. The rooms are large, though fairly crowded with furniture; bathrooms are also spacious. ⊠ *Dr. Atmaram Borkar Rd., Panaji, 403001* ☎ *832/222– 6231 or 832/222–6237* 🖷 *832/222–4958* ⊘ *novagoa@sancharnet.in* ⤴ *85 rooms, 6 suites* ⌂ *Restaurant, some minibars, some refrigerators, cable TV, pool, bar, business services, airport/railway station shuttle* ▤*AE, DC, MC, V* ⅠⓄⅠ *BP.*

$–$$ 🖬 **Hotel Mandovi.** This 50-year-old establishment on the Mandovi bank is about 300 meters from the Secretariat and the Sao Tome district, and a quick auto-rickshaw ride from both the Fontainhas shopping area and the church square. Ask for a room that faces the river. ⊠ *D. B. Marg, Panaji, 403001* ☎ *832/242–6270 to 73 or 832/222–4405 to 09* 🖷 *832/ 222–5451* ⊕ *www.hotelmandovigoa.com* ⤴ *63 rooms, 3 suites* ⌂ *2 restaurants, patisserie, health club, bar, convention center, laundry service* ▤ *AE, DC, MC, V* ⅠⓄⅠ *CP.*

$ 🖬 **Panjim Inn.** In the historic district of Fontainhas, about a 150-meter walk to the Chapel of St. Sebastian, this heritage guest house is the place to stay if you want to get a feel for Old Town Panjim. The hotel is immaculately maintained and filled with antique rosewood furniture, including four-poster beds in every room. Some rooms have tiny balconies overlooking the street. Only one room has a TV, but there's one in the lobby. Bathrooms are modern and tiled. ⊠ *E212, 31 January Rd., Fontainhas* ☎ *832/222–6523* 🖷 *832/222–8136* ⊕ *www.panjiminn. com* ⤴ *22 rooms* ⌂ *Restaurant; no a/c in some rooms, no TV in most rooms* ▤ *No credit cards* ⅠⓄⅠ *EP.*

Sports & the Outdoors
The **Watersports Institute** (☎ 832/243–6400 or 832/243–6550) can help you arrange water sports. Contact the **Yachting Association** (☎ 832/243– 8156 to 60) for the scoop on local sailing and windsurfing.

Boat Cruises
Live gaming, food, and drink are Friday and Saturday 5 PM to 3 AM onboard the **Casino Caravela** (☎ 832/223–4044 to 47), a floating luxury casino that also has a TV–game room for under-18s, a toddlers' room with baby-sitters and an open-air swimming pool. The dress code is smart–casual, which in India means no shorts, bikinis, or swimming trunks are allowed outside the pool area.

For Rs. 100 **Emerald Waters Boat Cruises** (☎ 832/243–1192) offers a bar, restaurant, and live music with folk dances. These cruises last for an hour and depart at 6:15 PM, 7:30 PM, and 8:30 PM.

TAKE HOME THE TASTE OF GOA

F YOU HAVEN'T FOUND *your share of slippers and sarongs, and bags and bangles at Anjuna or the shack-shops near the main beaches, pay a visit to a local grocery. If you look carefully, you'll find some great stuff to take home as a reminder of your stay in Goa or to give away as unusual "back from India" gifts. There's export quality bebinca (a rich, layered, dense pastry made of butter, egg yolk, and coconut) that has a long shelf life and excellent packing; feni, Goan liquor, in fancy bottles (though it smells the same as the stuff in the downmarket bottles) which you'd be well-advised to carry only in your hand baggage; prawn balchao (in a red chili sauce) and mackerel reicheado (pickled prawns and mackerals soaked in red masala, which have to be fried once you get home) with clearly marked expiration dates; a variety of dried and wet masalas (spice mixes) from cafreal (green masala) and vindalho*

(hot red masala) to xacuti (a masala with coconut and ground spices, plus recipes); and sachets of tendlim (a pickled green vegetable). There are other things you will have to ask the shopkeeper for: a couple hundred grams of palm jaggery (palm sugar), or the amazing west coast cocum, a type of tamarind that goes into fish curry and must be put aside while eating the cooked dish. Chances are the storeowner will wrap it for you with a grin that acknowledges that you know a bit about Goa after all.

Goa Tourism (☎ 832/243–8750 to 55) organizes short river cruises with a Goan cultural show and music. Sunset cruises on the Mandovi depart from the Panaji jetty at 6 PM, last for an hour, and cost Rs. 100 a person. Similar sundown cruises depart at 7:15 PM and cost Rs. 100 a person. Full-moon cruises leave at 8:30 PM, last for two hours, and cost Rs. 150 a person.

Shopping

CoOptex Handloom (⊠ EDC House, Dr. Atmaram Rd.) sells handloom cotton and silk fabric and saris. The shopping arcade at the **Hotel Fidalgo** (⊠ 18th June Rd. ☎ 832/222–6291) is worth a short visit for jewelry, hand-woven textiles, and general knickknacks. **Khadi Gramodyog Bhavan** (⊠ PMC Bldg., Dr. Atmaram Rd. ☎ 832/223–2746 or 94220 65475 mobile), purveyor of 100% cotton clothing, was established as part of the Gandhian tradition of economic self-sufficiency.

Old Goa

⓫ *10 km (6 mi) east of Panaji.*

★ Gorgeous Old Goa, with foliage creeping in around the ruins of old churches, served as the capital of the Portuguese colony until repeated outbreaks of cholera forced the government to move to Panaji in the 1843. The shift out of Old Goa, however, had begun as early as 1695. It was a slow desertion—first the viceroy, then the nobility, then the customs. So by the time the official declaration came, it was already a deserted ruined city.

Dedicated to the worship of the infant Jesus, the **Basilica of Bom Jesus** is also known throughout the Christian world as the tomb of St. Francis Xavier, patron saint of Goa. The saint's body has "survived" almost 500 years now without ever having been embalmed, and lies in a silver casket well out of reach of visitors. Built around the turn of the 17th century under the guarantee of the Duke of Tuscany, the basilica took the Florentine sculptor Giovanni Batista Foggini 10 years to complete. The basilica is the huge building on your right as you drive into town from Panaji, built from giant blocks of the local laterite. Once every 10 years the great Jesuit missionary's body is exposed to the public at close quarters, and this draws thousands of people from near and far. The next such event is scheduled for November 2004. 🖾 *Free* 🕙 *Mon.–Sat. 9–6:30, Sun. 10–6:30.*

The imposing white **Sé (St. Catherine's) Cathedral**—the largest church in Old Goa—was built between 1562 and 1652 by order of the King of Portugal. Fine carvings depict scenes from the life of Christ and the Blessed Virgin over the main altar, which commemorates St. Catherine of Alexandria. Several splendidly decorated chapels are dedicated to St. Joseph, St. George, St. Anthony, St. Bernard, and the Holy Cross. Only one of the cathedral's two original majestic towers remains; the other collapsed in 1776. The huge belfry contains the "Golden Bell," the largest bell in Goa. Across the square from the cathedral was Goa's infamous Palace of the Inquisition, and indeed it was the sound of the Se Cathedral bell that heralded the dreadful *auto-da-fe* (trial of faith) of times gone by. Goa had its share of "heretics" and many an unfortunate soul was put to death as a result of the pronouncements of the Inquisition. 🖾 *Across the road from Basilica of Bom Jesus* 🖾 *Free* 🕙 *Mon.–Sat. 9–6:30, Sun. 10–6:30.*

Next to the Se Cathedral stands the Church of St. Francis of Assisi, with its intricately gilded and carved interior. Behind the cathedral is the **Archaeological Museum**. The museum's collection is not entirely devoted to Catholic objets d'art; it also has bits and pieces from Goa's early Hindu history. It's worth a quick look around, if only to quickly peruse the portrait gallery of Goa's viceroys. 🖾 *Across the road from Basilica of Bom Jesus* 🕾 *832/228–6133* 🖾 *Rs. 5* 🕙 *Sat.–Thurs. 10–5.*

Housed until the late 1990s in the great but remote seminary at Rachol in South Goa, the **Museum of Christian Art** has been transferred to the Convent of St. Monica in Old Goa, where, it is hoped, more tourists will visit. The museum has a number of objects of Christian interest including paintings and religious silverware, some dating back to the 16th century. The historic Convent of St. Monica was once a nunnery, the first of its kind in the East, and functioned as one until the late 19th century. 🖾 *Holy Mount Hill* 🖾 *Rs. 5* 🕙 *Tues.–Sun. 10–5:30.*

Dr. Salim Ali Bird Sanctuary

⑫ *3 km (2 mi) northeast of Panaji.*

Visit this delightful bird refuge on the tip of Chorao, an island in the Mandovi. The ferry jetty for Chorao is on Ribander jetty on the southern bank of River Mandovi, between Panaji and Old Goa, and boats travel regularly to the island and back. The Forest Department in Panaji (☎ 832/222–4747) organizes guided tours to Chorao. The tiny sanctuary is a mangrove paradise and is named after the dedicated Indian ornithologist Dr. Salim Ali.

Divar Island

⑬ *10 km (6 mi) northeast of Panaji.*

The ferry jetty for Divar island, Chorao's twin in the Mandovi, is in Old Goa. Protected by the river and somewhat isolated from mainstream Goa, Divar makes for a very pleasant day out. Piedade, its main village, is serene. The Church of Our Lady of Compassion, on a hill, is in good condition and worth a visit; it also has excellent views of the river and the countryside.

Dudhsagar Falls

⑭ *50 km (31 mi) southeast of Panaji.*

★ With a name that means "sea of milk," the **Dudhsagar Waterfalls** are spectacular and imposing, with water cascading almost 2,000 feet down a cliff to a rock-ribbed valley. Pack refreshments and bath towels, and plan to spend a morning here. It isn't difficult to find a private nook, but watch your step—the rocks are slippery. Monkeys, birds, bees, butterflies, and thick foliage complete the wild experience. The ideal time for a trek here is early summer or just after the monsoon season (Oct.–Feb.); during monsoon season (summer) the approach road is often inaccessible. The Goa Tourism Development Corporation (GTDC) runs tours to Dudhsagar on Saturday and Sunday from Panaji and Calangute. The tours include the waterfall and the nearby Tambdi Surla temple built by the Kadambas (9 AM–6 PM, Rs. 500 for a tour without air-conditioning, Rs. 600 for a tour with air-conditioning). You could also take a train to Dudhsagar from Madgaon (Margao) and get there in an hour and a half. In early summer, when the level of the water is low, you can hire a Jeep and access the foot of the falls from either Molem or Collem. (This will cost you Rs. 300 per person round-trip, providing there are six people renting the jeep; the price goes up with fewer people, though you can try to bargain.) ✉ *Sanguem district.*

Ponda

⑮ *29 km (18 mi) southeast of Panaji.*

Although Ponda is an unprepossessing town, it has a number of temple day trips in the hills around. In fact, to visit most of the temples, you need not go to the town at all, as they are off the Panjim road. The area came under Portuguese control relatively late, in 1764, about 250 years after the Portuguese conquered Goa—which explains why the temples were not destroyed. One of the chief attractions here is the **Manguesh temple** in Priol, 7 km (4 mi) before you reach Ponda. With its domes and other eccentric, un-Hindu architectural features, the temple has evidence of Islamic and Christian influences. Other temples in the vicinity include the always-crowded Shantadurga temple with its distinctive tower, the Mahalsa temple with its gargantuan (12.5-meter-high) oil lamp, and the Lakshmi Narasimha and Naguesh temples with their lovely temple tanks (large tanks with steps, where people bathe).

SOUTH GOA

Madgaon (also known as Margao), within striking distance of several beaches and sights, is the main town in south Goa. The town, which is about 7 km (4.3 mi) inland has a bustling market and is worth exploring for its old buildings and shopping areas, but there's no reason to stay here. If you want to check out the sights (and there are many) around Madgaon, make Colva or Benaulim your base, and get the benefit of the beach and the nightlife after your day out. Excursions include the villages of Loutolim and Chandor, which have beautiful ancestral homes, some of which date from the early 1600s. The beaches of the south are more relaxing than those of the north, and people here are less preoccupied with partying. Although there is more shack life in the south now than there used to be, it's still far more laid-back than the north. Although Colva is crowded, Cansaulim, Benaulim, Varca, and Cavelossim beaches are progressively lovely and secluded from the rest of Goa. Some of the state's best and most expensive resorts are on these beaches.

Bogmalo Beach

⑯ *24 km (15 mi) north of Madgaon, 25 km (16 mi) south of Panaji.*

Pretty, and seldom overcrowded, this tiny crescent of fine sand is perfect for swimming and sunning. It's near a low, verdant hill topped by a few modern buildings on one side and the Bogmalo Beach Resort on the other. Two tiny islands sit about 10 km (6 mi) out to sea. For the most privacy, walk down the beach to the far right—fewer fishing boats, shacks, and people. Another of Bogmalo's assets is its boating and water-sports facilities (diving, jet-skiing). For a lunch break, try the **Seagull**, a simple, thatched-roof shack right on the beach—they serve some of the best prawn-curry rice in Goa.

Where to Stay

$$–$$$ 🏨 **Bogmallo Beach Resort.** Near the edge of the water, this hotel seems to have ignored all rules about distance from the sea. Its chief assets are proximity to the beach and comfortable rooms with a fantastic view of San Diego island and the sea. The six-story high-rise design, on the other hand, is very low on character. Rooms tend to be difficult to book, as the hotel is usually crowded with charter tourists. ⊠ *Bogmalo, 403806* ☎ *832/253–8222 to 235* 🖷 *832/253–8236* ⊕ *www.bogmallo.com* 🛏 *123 rooms* ⚐ *Restaurant, pool, gym, hair salon, bar, casino* ⊟ *AE, MC, V* ⑩ *EP.*

$$–$$$ 🏨 **Coconut Creek.** This charming little resort is on a dense coconut plantation, just a 2-minute walk (about ½ km) from Bogmalo beach and a 3-km (2-mi) drive from Dabolim airport. Run by a friendly staff, this place has spotless, airy rooms, and a small swimming pool. Unlike many of Goa's midrange resorts, it does succeed in creating a mellow vibe. ⊠ *Bogmalo, 403806* ☎ *832/253–8800* 📠 *832/253–8880* ✉ *joets@sancharnet.in* 🛏 *20 rooms* ⚒ *Restaurant, cable TV, pool, gym, hair salon, bar, recreation room, airport shuttle; no a/c in some rooms* 🚭 *MC, V* ⍟❘ *EP.*

Sports & the Outdoors

For diving, contact the popular **Goa Diving** (☎ 832/253–8036). Trips to the islands are run by the experienced young staff at the **Sandy Treat** snack shack (the first one jutting out on the right); reserve in advance. You can rent equipment from **Watersports Goa,** which operates out of a shack on the beach. They provide instruction in various sports and excursions to nearby islands.

Cansaulim Beach

⑰ *10 km (6.2 mi) northwest of Madgaon.*

This secluded, quiet, and clean stretch of beach between Bogmallo and Colva has a fine location—close to both Dabolim airport and Madgaon town, and yet away from the crowded north and the congested beaches around Colva. The chief signs of life in these parts are the hotels and resorts in the vicinity, and a couple of sleepy villages.

Where to Stay & Eat

$$$$ ✕ **The Village Plaza.** This food area at the Hyatt, designed along the lines of a medium-sized village square, has a number of interconnected restaurants. *Da Luigi* serves wood-fired pizzas and pasta, the *Market Grill* offers charcoal-grilled prime cuts and seafood, the *Juice Bar* has light refreshments and health drinks, *Masala* is an Indian restaurant serving tandoori and Goan cuisine, and *Sambar* offers pure vegetarian south Indian food. ⊠ *Park Hyatt Goa Resort and Spa, Arossim Beach* ☎ *832/ 272–1234* 🚭 *AE, MC, V.*

$$$$ 🏨 **Park Hyatt Goa Resort and Spa.** Clearly in the very top bracket of the
Fodor'sChoice Goa resorts, the modern and sleek Hyatt has spacious rooms with un-
★ usual pebble-floor and glass-wall bathrooms. It also has great dining, an excellent spa, and the largest swimming pool in India (2,000 square meters), with an outdoor Jacuzzi. The library has 1,500 titles, plus there's a mini-theater where you can watch movies. The spa is immaculately maintained and thoroughly luxurious, with body scrub and massage suites, hydrotherapy facilities, steam rooms, and well-trained staff. It offers a full range of ayurvedic treatments. A sprawling food village has every sort of restaurant, from Goan specialty and South Indian vegetarian to Italian and seafood. Praia de Luz, a wine and tapas bar overlooking the Arabian, is one of the highlights here. All of this, of course, comes at a considerable price. You can even take a boat ride with a dolphin, if you don't mind shelling out Rs. 750 for 45 minutes. ⊠ *Arossim beach, 403712* ☎ *832/272–1234* 📠 *832/272–1235* ⊕ *www.*

hyatt.com ☞ *238 rooms, 13 suites* ☖ *6 restaurants, tennis court, pool, spa, boating, jet skiing, parasailing, water skiing, lawn bowling, croquet, 3 bars, library, baby-sitting, laundry service* ▭ *AE, MC, V* ⵏⵁ⎮ *EP.*

$$-$$$ ⊞ **Heritage Village Club.** This small, lively, and crowded resort has a sparkling pool (with a swim-up bar) and simple, comfortable rooms and clean but uninspiring bathrooms. The resort is popular with tour groups from other Indian states. Rates include all meals, and a few unlimited local beverages. There's also an ayurvedic spa. The resort operates largely on an all-inclusive package basis, with a 3-night to 4-day package costing between Rs. 7,500 and Rs. 13,500. ⊠ *Arossim Beach, Cansaulim, 403712* ☎ *832/275–4311 to 2 or 832/275–4956 to 59* ☐ *832/275–4324* ☞ *98 rooms, 2 suites* ☖ *2 restaurants, tennis court, pool, spa, bar, recreation room, shops, airport shuttle* ▭ *AE, MC, V* ⵏⵁ⎮ *FAP.*

Majorda & Utorda

⓲ *10 km (6 mi) from Madgaon.*

Just north of Colva beach, Majorda, and nearby Utorda, which have a number of resorts, are rapidly sacrificing peace and quiet to larger volumes of tourists. However, they are cycling distance from Colva and Betalbatim (5 km [3 mi] from Colva, 3 km [1.9 mi] from Betalbatim), both known for restaurants and shack life. If you stay here you'll have yourself a good base from which to explore the sights around Madgaon.

Where to Stay & Eat

$$ ✕ **Martin's Corner.** This famous family-run restaurant in the village of Betalbatim near Majorda grew out of a shack. With its cane lamps and cane bar, it still retains the shack feel. Its prices, however, are well above the average shack, and with good enough reason. Pleasant retro music and the aromas of Goan cooking fill the air at lunch and dinnertime. Try the *amotik* (shark in hot and sour curry), which bears the delightful description on the menu, "like red chilly ground and local toddy vinegar." ⊠ *Bin Waddo, Betalbatim* ☎ *832/288–0061* ▭ *MC, V.*

$$$$ ⊞ **Kenilworth Beach Resort.** This large resort has a marble lobby with lots of quiet corners where you can relax, and overall the place doesn't have the same frantic-to-please service typical of some other hotels in Goa. The staff here are experienced and relaxed. Rooms are serene, with cane furniture and pleasant green furnishings. There's an expansive swimming pool with a swim-up bar, an open-air Jacuzzi, a waterslide, and a 3-meter-deep area for beginner scuba divers. All rooms have private balconies. ⊠ *Utorda, Salcete, 403713* ☎ *832/275–4180* ☐ *832/ 275–4180* ⊕ *www.kenilworthhotels.com* ☞ *88 rooms, 3 suites* ☖ *2 restaurants, coffee shop, in-room data-ports, pool, bar, health club, massage, sauna, steam room, snorkeling, laundry service* ▭ *AE, DC, MC, V* ⵏⵁ⎮ *CP.*

$$$$ ⊞ **Majorda Beach Resort.** An old favorite with tourists from Bombay and Gujarat, this resort has a friendly, airy lobby, an ayurvedic ashram, and large, well-furnished rooms. It also feels lively, given all the families that come to stay here. A 2-minute walk through the grounds brings you to a long, gorgeous stretch of beach. ⊠ *Majorda, Salcete, 403713*

☏ 832/288–1111 to 20 🖷 832/288–1121or 832/288–1123 to 24 ⊕ www.majordabeachresort.com ⇨ 100 rooms, 10 cottages, 10 suites ♨ 2 restaurants, coffee shop, tennis, 2 pools (1 indoor), gym, hair salon, squash, bar, casino, baby-sitting, laundry service, business services ⊟ AE, MC, V ⎟◎⎟ BP.

Colva

⑲ 7 km (4 mi) west of Madgaon.

Colva Beach, about 6 km (4 mi) west of Madgaon, in the Salcete district, is the most congested beach in south Goa. Its large parking and entrance areas are crowded with shacks selling snacks and souvenirs and young men offering their mopeds for rent. The first 1,000 feet of the beach are hectic—stuffed with vendors, cows, and fishing boats—but the sand, backed by palm groves, stretches in both directions, promising plenty of quieter spots to settle down. The water is good for swimming, with only nominal waves. The restaurant and bar shacks are the hub of nightlife for the entire region. The government-run **Tourist Cottages** (☏ 832/ 278–8047) is a hotel that also has an information counter. ⊠ Colva Beach.

Where to Stay

$–$$ ⊡ **Longuinhos Beach Resort.** This old Colva favorite is about a kilometer from the crowded village, and right on the beach. Rooms are comfortable and reasonably priced, and the staff friendly and helpful. You can eat at A Tartaruga, the in-house restaurant, or take your pick from dozens of shack restaurants close by. ⊠ Colva Beach, Salcete, 403708 ☏ 832/278–8068 to 69 🖷 832/278–8070 ⊕ www.longuinhos.net ⇨ 50 rooms ♨ Restaurant, pool, hot tub, airport/railway shuttle; no a/c in some rooms ⊟ AE, MC, V ⎟◎⎟ CP.

¢–$ ⊡ **Star Beach Resort.** The chief advantages of this extremely ordinary four-story building are its proximity to the beach (a few minutes by foot) and its location—just off Colva's main street. Rooms are basic but clean and comfortable, which is more than can be said for many of Colva's properties. None of the rooms face the sea. ⊠ Near Football Ground, Colva Beach, 403708 ☏ 832/278–8166 or 832/278–0092 🖷 832/278– 8020 ⇨ 72 rooms ♨ Restaurant, pool, massage, laundry service, travel services; no a/c in some rooms ⊟ MC, V ⎟◎⎟ EP.

Shopping

You can find the best bargains in Colva in the small shacks along the main street leading to the beach, where you can get a silk sarong for as little as Rs. 50, a pair of Osho slippers for Rs. 100, and jewelry of all kinds at throwaway prices.

Madgaon (Margao)

⑳ 33 km (20 mi) south of Panaji, 7 km (4 mi) east of Colva beach.

Use Madgaon, a busy commercial center, as convenient to do your money changing, travel arrangements, shopping, and book-buying, if you plan to stay for long at the secluded southern beaches. (Look for the bookstore Golden Heart, which carries English-language books, including quite a few about Goa.) The town has a few attractions of its own as well; there are historic houses and churches, and a lively seafood market where you can also buy fresh fruit and vegetables. Near the railway station there's plenty of fabric to be bought if you're so inclined.

Loutolim

㉑ *10 km (6 mi) northeast of Madgaon.*

Loutolim village is good for a morning's outing; visit the somewhat over-rated Big Foot Museum and an ancestral house across the road, explore the old village on foot, and stop to admire Miranda House, an old family property now owned by the famous Goan cartoonist Mario Miranda. Have lunch at one of Goa's most delightful restaurants, Nostalgia, run by chef Fernando in the courtyard of his own house in nearby Raia, and wander through the overgrown Raia churchyard in the afternoon (wear closed shoes).

Also known as the Ancestral Goa Museum, the **Big Foot Museum** re-creates in miniature a 19th-century Goan village. Guides explain the utility and significance of every object and article on display; highlights are the fishermen's shack, a mock feni distillery, and the spice garden. Within the museum's sprawling confines is an enormous, canopied dance floor, used for open-air private parties. Don't expect too much; while some visitors are satisfied with the experience, many feel it's more of a tourist trap than a real attraction. ⊠ *Near Saviour of the World Church, Loutolim, 10 km (6 mi) north of Margao* ☎ *834/277–7034 or 834/273–5064* ✎ *Rs. 20* ☉ *Daily 9–6.*

Where to Eat

$$ ✕ **Fernando's Nostalgia.** One of the best restaurants in the entire state, **Fodor'sChoice** in the tranquil, slow-paced old village of Raia, is unpretentious, inex-★ pensive, and serves great Goan food. If you sit at certain tables you can catch glimpses of household life in the chef's country house. Fernando's serves such dishes as salted ox tongue, *fofos* (fish cutlets mixed with mashed potatoes and spices, rolled in breadcrumbs and egg, and shallow-fried), *sopa de bretalha* (spinach soup), and *prawn almondegas* (prawn meat-cakes), which are rarely found in restaurants elsewhere in the state, which probably explains why Fernando's is where Goans go. As most of the day's specials are listed in Portuguese, you might need a waiter's help to decipher the menu. The restaurant comes to life in the evening, when the alcohol begins to flow and the band starts to play. The bandstand showcases local groups, including Saxy Angel and Good Old Aggy Yet Again. Expect to hear some Goan gold—old Goan folk and pop music—and retro. ⊠ *Opposite the tiny Capela de Sao Sebastiao, Raia* ☎ *832/277–7098* ▭ *MC, V.*

Chandor

㉒ *15 km (9 mi) east of Madgaon.*

This small, sleepy village occupies the site of Chandrapur, ancient capital of the region from 375 AD to 1053 AD. Today, the chief reason to ★ come here is for the 400-year-old **Braganza House** (☎ *832/278–4201 or*

832/278–4227); two wings are occupied by two branches of the Braganza family—the Menezes Braganzas and the Braganza Pereiras. You can see the style in which the wealthy landed gentry must have lived until the land reformation that followed Independence in 1947, for the great rooms are filled with treasures, including beautiful period furniture and Chinese porcelain. Although some parts of the house have been renovated and are in reasonably good shape, it takes a lot of effort to maintain the two wings, and any contribution from a visitor toward upkeep is welcome, indeed expected.

Benaulim

㉓ *9 km (6 mi) southwest of Madgaon.*

Just 2 km (1.2 mi) south of Colva is the first of the beautiful, secluded beaches of south Goa—completely unlike the action-packed beaches of the north. Head to Benaulim and farther south only if you want to get away from it all, though at a price, because the resorts are more expensive there. Benaulim village has a small supermarket, and is centered around a crossroads called Maria Hall. The beach is less than a kilometer from the village.

Where to Stay & Eat

$$$$ ✕ **Alegria.** This Goan specialty restaurant is reminiscent of an old-fash-
Fodor'sChoice   ioned landlord's drawing room, with sepia photographs on the walls
★   and carved wooden furniture. The variety of menu items makes an excellent introduction to local cuisine—as does the food that follows. Try the *kulliamchem mass kotteanim* (gratinated crabmeat with onions, coriander, and garlic), and *sannas* (delicately flavored, sweetish, steamed rice cakes) with an assortment of curries, such as classic pork *vindaloo* (spiced, almost pickled gravy), pork *sorpotel* (curry simmered with Goan vinegar), and boneless chicken *xacuti* (gravy with roasted coconut and spices). If you want to be adventurous with dessert, try the *adsorachem merend,* a feni-infused (with cashew or coconut-palm hooch) tender coconut mousse with saffron sauce. Live singing accompanied by guitar and mandolin adds to the scene. ⊠ *Taj Exotica, Calwaddo, Benaulim, Salcette* ☎ *832/277–1234* ⚱ *Reservations essential* ⊟ *AE, DC, MC, V.*

$$ ✕ **Joecons.** The interior is spacious—but nothing special—at this Goan restaurant, the chief attraction is getting here—it's a lovely walk (less than a kilometer) through paddy fields from Benaulim village. Try biking it if you're staying in Benaulim—the sea breeze will be full in your face and you'll arrive suitably primed for the feni and masala prawns. ⊠ *Near Taj Exotica, Benaulim* ☎ *832/277–0077.*

$$$$ ▦ **Taj Exotica.** Here you'll find undoubtedly one of the most luxurious
Fodor'sChoice   and attractive places to stay in Goa, on extensive grounds beside tran-
★   quil Benaulim beach. The lobby has gleaming marble floors and spotless white sofas. Its sunken, open-air atrium is full of foliage. Rooms with shady verandahs look out onto two golf courses and the Arabian Sea. You can opt for a villa with an outdoor private pool, or one with a hot tub overlooking the sea. Although all of this luxury takes you well away from the mass-tourist clutter of Colva, the resort remains close to

the heart of Goa—with the exemplary warmth and good humor of its staff, some of whom occasionally join professional musicians to serenade guests while they dine. There's also a lobster shack on the beach here. ☒ *Calwaddo, Benaulim, Salcette, 403716* ☎ *832/277–1234* 🖷 *832/277–1515* ⊕ *www.tajhotels.com* 📲 *136 rooms, 4 suites* ♿ *3 restaurants, coffee shop, 2 9-hole golf courses, 2 lawn tennis courts, pool, gym, hair salon, massage, spa, bar, recreation room, children's programs, baby-sitting, travel services, airport shuttle* ▭ *AE, DC, MC, V* ⧫ *EP.*

Varca

㉔ *14 km (8.7 mi) southwest of Madgaon*

The scenery at Varca is rural: there are deep fields on either side of the road, and you may get the distinct feeling that you're heading nowhere in particular. This is an illusion. There are a number of resorts close to Varca village that take advantage of its perfect, unspoiled stretch of beach. Stay at Varca for the beach and for the opportunity to take long walks through the green Goa countryside.

Where to Stay & Eat

★ **$$$$** ✕ **Carnaval.** Low-hung black lamps uplight a woven bamboo ceiling, and Mario Miranda cartoons enliven the walls at this restaurant, where the fusion food is excellent. Try the jerk potatoes *peri peri* (Caribbean–Goan), the tandoor–grilled tiger prawns with lemon mustard sauce, and the *naan* (Indian bread) with pesto. After all this the dessert, crêpes filled with *gajar ka halwa* (carrot sweetmeat), seems almost ordinary. ☒ *Ramada Caravela, Varca* ☎ *832/274–5200 to 14* ▭ *AE, DC, MC, V* ⊗ *No lunch.*

★ **$$$$** ✕ **Flavors.** If you're in the mood for something other than Goan cuisine, come here for great northwestern frontier food (from Pakistan to the Afghan border). You can dine indoors or on a terrace overlooking the Radisson's lovely pool. The kababs and tandoori breads are wonderful but filling; make sure you have enough room for some unusual and extremely good spiced ice cream at the end. Service is impeccable. ☒ *Radisson White Sands, Pedda, Varca* ☎ *832/272–7272* ▭ *AE, DC, MC, V* ⊗ *No lunch.*

★ **$$$$** 🛏 **Radisson White Sands.** This is a fun, family-friendly hotel with something for everybody—on a lavish scale. There's a massive free-form pool with a swim-up bar, as well as an indoor entertainment center, Gravity Pool, which has its own small bowling alley and mini movie theater. A good health club and spa, a lively bar on the beach, a watersports center, and a pristine stretch of sand complete the outward attractions of this resort. There's even a cyber café. On the inside, rooms are modern with high-quality imitation cane furniture, and service is warm and helpful. ☒ *178–179 Pedda, Varca, Salcete, 403721* ☎ *832/272–7272* 🖷 *832/272–7282* ⊕ *www.radisson.com* 📲 *150 rooms, 4 suites* ♿ *2 restaurants, coffee shop, in-room data ports, pool, gym, health club, spa, fishing, jet skiing, water skiing, 2 bars, recreation room, airport shuttle* ▭ *AE, DC, MC, V* ⧫ *CP.*

$$$ 🛏 **Club Mahindra.** This primarily timeshare-apartment resort has a comfortable if unimaginative hotel block for walk-in guests. There's a three-tier swimming pool; one level is a hot tub. Secluded Varca beach is just a short walk away. ⊠ *Varca, Salcete district, 403721* ☎ *832/274–4555* ⬚ *832/274–4666* ⊕ *www.clubmahindra.com* ⤶ *23 rooms* ⟳ *Restaurant, 2 tennis courts, pool, health club, massage, jet skiing, parasailing, bar, dance club, recreation room, children's programs, airport/rail shuttle* ▭ *AE, DC, MC, V* ⦿| *CP.*

$$$$ 🏨 **Ramada Caravela.** The lobby of this luxury beachfront resort is an odd mix of cathedral and piazza, with wrought iron garden benches and huge arches and beams. A plush casino, a fusion Indian-Mediterranean restaurant, and a Polynesian eatery on the beach add to the hybrid charms of this airy, spacious resort. The pool is large, the beach unspoiled, and the hotel can arrange trips on Goa's only floating casino. There's also an ayurvedic health clinic here, as well as yoga. The beach restaurant, Polynesian Hut, is perfect for seafood and an evening out; you can order a variety of grills with your choice of marinade, and Chinese and Thai food. (Try an Indian marinade.) ⊠ *Varca, 403721* ☎ *832/274–5200 to 214* ⬚ *832/274–5225* ⊕ *www.caravelabeachresort.com* ⤶ *192 rooms, 4 suites, 6 villas* ⟳ *4 restaurants, coffee shop, 9-hole golf course, 2 tennis courts, pool, hair salon, gym, watersports, 2 bars, dance club, recreation room, playground, laundry service, business services* ▭ *AE, DC, MC, V* ⦿| *CP.*

Cavelossim

㉕ *20 km (12 mi) southwest of Madgaon.*

The last of the villages before the mouth of the Sal River, and the end of the coastal road southward from Bogmalo is Cavelossim. If you want to continue down the coast, you have to head back inland and take the national highway south, or take a country road up the river and use a ferry. Given that this is a rural area, Cavelossim is a surprisingly developed little place, complete with a shopping arcade; this is chiefly because of the presence of the Leela, the last and most luxurious of the southern Goa resorts. The beach is breathtakingly clean, and striking because it's at the mouth of the Sal River—serene and flanked by fields and coconut plantations. This part of south Goa is an end in itself, and not a good base from which to explore the rest of the state (if you're keen on beach-hopping and other touristy activities, stay up north). This is the place to come when you want to relax, take up residence on the beach, and forget about everything, including trips to town.

Where to Stay & Eat

$$$$ ✕ **Jamavar.** This formal and stylish Indian restaurant overlooking the pool at the luxurious Leela has dishes you're unlikely to encounter elsewhere in Goa: *cocum* (tamarind) marinated chicken with wild fig yogurt dressing, lobster tikka with cherry tomato chutney, and tamarind-glazed rack of lamb. ⊠ *The Leela Beach, Cavelossim* ☎ *832/ 287–1234* ▭ *AE, DC, MC, V.*

$$$$ 🏨 **Holiday Inn.** The chief advantage of this friendly place—with a cozier vibe than the larger, more spread-out resorts—is its location on lovely Mobor Beach. It has a pleasantly large pool, and comfortable rooms with warm red furnishings. There's also a beach barbecue. ⊠ *Cavelos-*

INNER PEACE

F THERE'S ANYTHING THAT SUMS UP the Goan attitude to life, it's sussegado, which means "take it easy." Even with the tourist influx exceeding the local population, the massive star resorts and hotels in the south, and the infamous rave and trance parties in the north, there's a certain peace in Goa that is unlikely to ever be disturbed, because it comes from within. A part of this state of daylong siesta can of course be attributed to a common love of excellent food and local alcohol—Goa brews its own feni, a potent and inexpensive concoction distilled from palm sap or cashewfruit juice. If you're looking to imbibe the true spirit of Goa, try the palm (coconut) feni, it smells less terrible than the cashew variety and goes down a little bit easier. You can buy the ridiculously cheap alcohol from just about anywhere in Goa (but make sure it's bottled properly) and down it with classic tender coconut water. A morning in the waves, tiger prawns at a seaside shack, and a couple of fenis, and you will come to discover why people come back to Goa year after year to rejuvenate, even as they complain that it's getting crowded and dirty. A week in the company of Goans, with their mellow attitude toward life and their legendary warmth—despite the heavy toll taken on their state by tourism—and you may find yourself, for better or for worse, not just a little intoxicated by the Goan way.

sim, Mobor Beach, 403731 ☎ 832/287–1303 to 310 📠 832/287–1333 ⊕ www.holiday-inn.com ⇱ 168 rooms, 2 suites ⚖ 2 restaurants, coffee shop, pool, health club, hair salon, bar, casino, dance club, playground, laundry service, airport shuttle ▤ AE, DC, MC, V ❢❢ CP.

$$$$
Fodor'sChoice
★
🏨 **The Leela Goa.** Expect to be greeted with a coconut drink and a map; you'll need the latter to explore this 75-acre resort with a secluded beach and a magnificent view of cliffs and coves. The lobby is reminiscent of a Hampi temple, complete with panel carvings and a sculpted *nandi* (sacred bull), and is very stately and quiet. The two-story, salmoncolor cement villas are arranged along a winding artificial lagoon. Rooms or suites have tile floors, dark-wood furniture, well-appointed bathrooms, and private balconies. Some villas have private swimming pools. Children are welcome, and there's even a play center called Just Kids. ⊠ Cavelossim, 403731 ☎ 832/287–1234 📠 832/287–1352 ⊕ www.ghmhotels.com ⇱ 54 rooms, 83 suites ⚖ 3 restaurants, in-room data ports, cable TV, 9-hole golf course, 3 tennis courts, pool, exercise equipment, hair salon, outdoor hot tub, sauna, spa, steam room, windsurfing, boating, jet skiing, parasailing, waterskiing, fishing, bicycles, bar, dance club, dry cleaning, laundry service, business services, meeting room, airport shuttle, travel services ▤ AE, DC, MC, V ❢❢ EP.

$$$$ 📺 **Royal Goan Beach Club (Haathi Mahal).** Primarily a timeshare resort, the RGBC at Haathi Mahal offers hotel rooms as well. Ask for a room that overlooks stunning riverside plantations—this is one of the most incredible inland views in Goa. The hotel has a small pool and an ordinary restaurant, and is a good 10-minute (1-km) walk from the beach, but is next door to the shopping area. ✉ *Cavelossim, 403731* 🕾 *832/ 287–1101 to 110* 🖷 *832/287–1139* ⊕ *www.haathimahal.com* ⤴ *66 rooms, 77 villas* ⚒ *Restaurant, 2 pools, gym, spa, Ping-Pong, squash, volleyball, 3 bars, laundry service* ▤ *AE, DC, MC, V* ¶◎ *CP.*

Palolem Beach

㉖ *37 km (23 mi) southwest of Madgaon.*

For seclusion and idyllic scenery, Goa's southernmost sandy stretch—nicknamed "Paradise Beach"—is a dream. Palolem, in the Canacona district, receives only those nature lovers and privacy-seekers willing to make the rugged, two-hour drive from the nearest resort (Leela Beach). Palm groves and low, green mountains back along a curving stretch of white sand. Depending on the tides, you can wander past secluded coves and nooks sheltered by rocks. Far to the right, the beach ends in a rugged, rocky point teeming with crabs. The water is shallow and warm, with very little surf. Shacks sell refreshments near the main entrance; an occasional vendor dispenses pineapples and bananas from a weathered basket on his head; and local men entice people into wooden canoes to go and look for dolphins.

GOA A TO Z

To research prices, get advice from other travelers, and book travel arrangements, visit www.fodors.com.

AIR TRAVEL

Air India makes international connections from Goa's Dabolim Airport. Indian Airlines connects Goa to all major cities in India, including Bombay, Delhi, Madras, Ahmedabad, Calcutta, Cochin, and Hyderabad. Jet Airways flies between Goa and Bombay, Cochin, and Delhi. Air Sahara connects Goa to Bombay and Bangalore.

🚪 **Airlines & Contacts Air India** ✉ Hotel Fidalgo, 18th June Rd., Panaji 🕾 832/243–1100 to 04. **Indian Airlines** ✉ Dempo House, Deyanand Bandodkar Marg, Panaji 🕾 832/242–8181. **Jet Airways** ✉ Sesa Ghor, Patto Plaza, near bus stand, Panaji 🕾 832/243–8792. **Air Sahara** ✉ Gen. Bernard Guedes Rd., Panaji 🕾 832/223–7346 or 832/223–0634.

AIRPORTS & TRANSFERS

Goa's Dabolim Airport is, naturally, in Dabolim, 29 km (18 mi) from Panaji. Buses are infrequent, so it's usually best to take a taxi from here to your destination. You can arrange pre-paid taxi service at a counter inside the airport, or go straight outside and hire a private cab. Either way, the fare to Panaji should not exceed Rs. 300.

🚪 **Airport Information Dabolim Airport** 🕾 832/540–806.

BUS TRAVEL

The easiest (but definitely the least comfortable) way to reach Goa from Bombay over land is by bus, a grueling 17-hour trip, which will take you to the bus station in Panaji. Make this a last resort if you haven't planned several weeks ahead (during the high season, in winter) and booked a flight or train. The most reliable bus company is Quickways Travel, which makes the round-trip for Rs. 479.

Buses within Goa are cheap and frequent, but they're overcrowded—be prepared to fight your way on and off.

🗓 Bus Information **Quickways Travel** ✉ 1st Dhobitalao La., near Lalit Bar, Bombay ☎ 22/2209-1645 ✉ 8 Gasalia Bldg., Madgaon ☎ 832/271-5060.

EMERGENCIES

🗓 Emergency Contacts **Ambulance** ☎ 102. **Fire** ☎ 101. **Police** ☎ 100.

🗓 Hospital **Goa Medical College** ✉ Bambolim ☎ 832/245-8700 to 07.

🗓 24-Hour Pharmacies **Holy Spirit Medical Stores** ✉ Old Market, Margao ☎ 832/273-7433. **Victor Hospital 24-hour chemist** ☎ 832/272-8888 or 832/272-6272.

ENGLISH-LANGUAGE MEDIA

Singbal's Book House sells English-language newspapers and books; it's open Monday to Saturday, 9 to 4.

🗓 **Golden Heart Bookshop** ✉ Off Abade Faria Rd., Panaji ☎ 832/273-6339 or 832/273-2450. **Singbal's Book House** ✉ Opposite Mary Immaculate Conception Church, Panaji ☎ 832/242-5747.

FERRIES

Although the most convenient way to get to Goa from Bombay is by air or train, lots of people try the Bombay–Panaji ferry just for the experience. Departures are from the Ferry Wharf in the Fort neighborhood of Bombay. Take an overnight ferry only if you just want to get to Goa somehow; the morning ferry lets you see the Arabian seascape as you travel. Frank Shipping Services runs an overnight ferry on Tuesday and Thursday; it departs from Bombay at 10:30 AM and costs Rs. 1,400 one-way. Damania Airways has a ferry that departs at 7 AM and costs Rs. 1,100 (first class). Of course, ferries are an option only outside of the rainy season; they do not run from June to October.

🗓**Frank Shipping Pvt Ltd.** ✉ Varma Chambers, 205/206 Homji St., Fort neighborhood, Bombay ☎ 22/2265-1130. **Damania Shipping** ✉ Varma Chambers, 205/206 Homji St., Fort neighborhood, Bombay ☎ 22/2269-2605 to 06 or 98200-74493 mobile.

MAIL & SHIPPING

The General Post Office in Panaji is open weekdays 9:30 to 5:30.

🗓 Post Office **General Post Office** ✉ Patto Bridge, Panaji ☎ 832/222-3706.

MONEY MATTERS

CURRENCY EXCHANGE Most major hotels will change money for their guests. In Anjuna, go to the Oxford Money Exchange–Bureau de Change. In Colva, hotels run by the Goa Tourism Development Corporation (GTDC) have exchange desks.

🗓 Exchange Services **Oxford Money Exchange–Bureau de Change** ✉ 111-6, Mazal Vaddo, opposite chapel ☎ 832/227-3251 or 832/227-3269. **State Bank of India** ✉ Near

Municipal Garden, Madgaon ☎ 832/242-1332 ✉ 18th June Rd., Panaji ☎ 832/272-1514. **Thomas Cook** ✉ 8 Alcon Chambers, D. B. Marg, Panaji ☎ 832/222-1312 ✉ Roadside between Calangute and Baga, near Hotel Ofrill Bldg. ☎ 832/227-5693.

MOTORBIKES

You can rent motorbikes at bus stops, railway stations, markets, and beach resorts for about Rs. 300 per day. You'll need an international driver's license to drive anything larger than a 55-cc engine.

TAXIS

Goa has a unionized taxi system with fixed rates from point A to B. This is the best way to get around in Goa if money isn't a constraint. You don't really need to contact a tour operator, as there will always be a taxi stand outside your hotel. If not, the hotel will call one for you from the nearest stand. Fares are not negotiable and drivers charge a fixed (very high) rate displayed on a board at every taxi stand. It can cost as much as Rs. 300 to hire a taxi for a total distance of less than 20 km. If you are visiting a number of places and covering a lot of ground, it makes more sense to hire a taxi for an 8-hour stretch (Rs. 800) and pay an additional rate for every kilometer above 80 km. Taxis levy a surcharge when they operate at night.

TELEPHONES & INTERNET

You'll find many telephone kiosks and Internet centers in market areas (any place that offers phone services also offers Internet services). 🚩 **Classic Business Centre** ✉ M. G. Rd., Panaji ☎ 832/243-1786. **Cyber Inn** ✉ 105 Kalika Chambers, behind Grace Church, Varde Valaulikar Rd., Madgaon ☎ 832/273-1531. **Cyberlink Advertising and Communications Centre** ✉ 9 Lower Ground Fl., Rangavi, opposite Municipal Bldg. ☎ 834/273-4414. **Suraj Business Centre** ✉ 18 June Rd., Panaji ☎ 832/242-4884.

TOURS

There are dozens of private tour operators in Goa, most offering 10-hour tours of the state. The transport wing of the Goa Tourism Development Corporation runs daylong bus tours of both north and south Goa—departing from Panaji, Madgaon, and Colva Beach—as well as river cruises from the Santa Monica pier in Panaji. 🚩 **Coastal Tours and Travels** ✉ 31st January Rd., Panaji ☎ 832/222-5642. **Dynamic Tours & Travels** ✉ Carvalho St., Madgaon ☎ 832/273-9519. **Goa Sea Travels Agency** ✉ Opposite Tourist Hotel, Panaji ☎ 832/242-5925. **Goa Tourism Development Corporation (GTDC)** ✉ Trionara Apartments, Dr. Alvares Costa Rd., Panaji ☎ 832/222-4132 or 832/222-6515. **Tourist Home** ✉ Patto Bridge, Panaji ☎ 832/243-8750. **Trade Wings** ✉ 6 Mascarenhas Bldg., Mahatma Gandhi Rd., Panaji ☎ 832/243-2430 or 832/243-2431. **Trans Orient** ✉ City Centre, 3rd fl., Panaji ☎ 832/243-8760.

TRAIN TRAVEL

For train schedules and fares, contact the rail station in Madgaon or the Tourist Information Centre in Panaji. To arrive in Goa via the Konkan Scenic Railway from Karnataka, board in Mangalore at 7 AM and plan to reach Madgaon at 1:30 PM if all goes well. If you find the landscape arresting, get off at Karwar, just an hour and a half before Madgaon; spend the afternoon there (the town is lovely), then take a bus or taxi to Goa. If you're coming from Bombay, get schedule and fare information at the Tourist Information Centre in the Central Railway Station. Hop off at Madgaon.

🚆 Train Information **Bombay Central Railway Station** ☎ 22/2308-6288.

🚆 Train Stations **Madgaon** ✉ 2 km (1.2 mi) from the main shopping area ☎ 832/271-2790. **Panaji** ✉ ☎ 832/243-8254.

VISITOR INFORMATION

In Panaji, the Directorate of Tourism fields general inquiries. For assistance with reservations, including bus tours, contact the Goa Tourism Development Corporation (GTDC). Madgaon's Tourist Information Centre is a good source of information, including details on the Konkan Railway, and has maps of the state. There's also a 24-hour "Hello Information" number for Goa (☎ 832/241–2121), which you may find extremely useful for out-of-date phone numbers.

🚆 Tourist Offices **Directorate of Tourism** ✉ Government of Goa, Tourist Home, Patto Bridge, Panaji ☎ 832/243-8750. **Goa Tourism Development Corporation (GTDC)** ✉ Trionara Apartments, Dr. Alvares Costa Rd., Panaji ☎ 832/241-2121. **Madgaon Tourist Information Centre** ✉ Tourist Hostel, near Municipal Garden, Madgaon ☎ 832/271-5204.

KARNATAKA

7

RING FOR YOUR PRIVATE BUTLER 24/7
at the Oberoi hotel ⇨*p.393*

OGLE AN ANCIENT ELEPHANT STABLE
at the Hampi ruins ⇨*p.419*

SPOT MONKEYS DURING OPEN-AIR MEALS
at Kabini River Lodge ⇨*p.413*

SEE THE MASSIVE MAMMALS IN THE FLESH
at Dubare Elephant camp ⇨*p.413*

SOAK UP A STATUE DATING TO 1119
at the Temple of Lord Channakeshava ⇨*p.417*

By Julie Tomasz

Updated by
Kavita Watsa

KARNATAKA IS A MICROCOSM of the most colorful and fascinating aspects of India, presented at a comfort level that can be Oriental-sumptuous and Occidental-efficient. Roughly the size of New England, Karnataka, a large state in southwestern India, has probably hosted human civilization as long as any place on earth. Scattered throughout the state, in such places as Belur, Halebid, and Hampi, are some of the greatest religious monuments in India. The climate, too, is as varied as the culture, ranging from humid to dry and cool, the result of a geography that combines sea coast with tropical uplands and arid zones.

Karnataka's 46 million people—called Kannadigas after their language, Kannada—are sinewy and robust in build, humble in disposition. In villages, women wait patiently with their jugs at the well, which doubles as the social center. Men, often scantily dressed in *lungis* (colorful saronglike wraps) or *dhotis* (white saronglike wraps) work in the fields, walking slowly behind oxen dragging plows that have not changed much in 3,000 years. The climate makes it possible to live perpetually outdoors—village huts are often of rudimentary construction, and people frequently set up their beds outside.

The simplicity of Karnataka's countryside is balanced by the grand palaces and formal gardens of Mysore, the youthful cosmopolitanism of Bangalore, and the relics—both Hindu and Muslim—of centuries of royal living. Even the outdoors can impress if you spend a few days on safari in Nagarhole National Park or trek between jungle camps along the banks of the Kaveri river.

Although Bangalore and Mysore are well connected by express trains and comfortable buses, there are advantages to traveling by car: the countryside along the way is verdant with palms and rice paddies and brightened by colorfully dressed women washing clothes in the roadside streams. Timid passengers may be put off by the Indian driver's way of roaring around curves marked with skull-and-crossbones signs that read "Accident Zone"—on roads crowded with giant buses, plodding oxcarts, and men pushing bicycles laden with bunches of coconuts.

Exploring Karnataka

Karnataka is packed with fascinating places and historic sights. The main transport hub is Bangalore, an inland city in the southeastern corner of the state, so it's easiest to start your trip here. Both Bangalore, which considers itself the Silicon Valley of India, and Mysore (2½ hours to the southwest by train) are worth exploring in themselves. Bangalore is a boomtown, with a population that now exceeds 5 million; huge municipal gardens and a teeming old commercial district are interspersed with lively pubs, restaurants, and cybercafés. Mysore, in contrast, is an elegant old royal town, center of the princely state that existed from the mid-19th- to the mid-20th centuries. It's small in scale, tropical in appearance, and has India's finest zoo.

The north, including the town of Bijapur, isn't easily accessed by train, and would otherwise take a two-day road journey to get there. It's far easier—and more satisfying—to explore the southern region, from Hampi (in the east-central part of the state) south. From Mysore, you can make two-day trips to Nagarhole National Park, on the Kerala border, home to elephants and tigers; or to the 11th- and 12th-century temples at Belur and Halebid, which between them hold more than 30,000 intricately carved sculptures; or to Sravanabelagola, with its awesome monolithic statue of the Jain saint Gomateshwara. For a refreshing outdoor stint, try the fishing camp on the banks of the Cauvery River or spend a day or two at an undulating coffee plantation in Coorg district. If you have time and stamina to spare, venture out from Bangalore to the spectacular abandoned city of Hampi. Although this ancient city is not yet easily accessible, it is perhaps the single most rewarding historical destination in the state.

About the Restaurants

Bangalore has an up-and-coming restaurant scene, but options for dining out in the rest of Karnataka are few, with tasty food but limited menus. You'll almost always find delicious, predominantly vegetarian southern favorites like *masala dosas* (fried, crêpelike pancakes), and *idlis* (steamed rice cakes), both served with coconut chutney and other condiments. A popular rice dish is *bisi belebath,* spicy lentil curry and mixed vegetables topped with wafers. Karnataka is truly famed for its *thali,* a combination platter done South Indian style—with rice surrounded by several bowls of vegetables and sauces, all mopped up with large helpings of *roti* (unleavened whole-wheat bread). The thali is cheap, filling, and usually fairly easy on a foreigner's stomach. Also, unlike most parts of India, Karnataka brews a fine cup of coffee.

	WHAT IT COSTS In Rupees				
	$$$$	**$$$**	**$$**	**$**	**¢**
	IN BANGALORE				
AT DINNER	over 500	400–500	300–400	150–300	under 150
	IN SMALL TOWNS OUTSIDE BANGALORE				
AT DINNER	over 350	250–350	150–250	100–150	under 100

Restaurant prices are for an entrée plus dal, rice, and a veg/non-veg dish.

About the Hotels

Both Bangalore, the affluent state capital, and Mysore have sumptuous hotels set in verdant tropical gardens: since 1954, when the princely state of Mysore was incorporated into India, the maharaja's numerous summer palaces have been converted to luxury accommodations for travelers, including elegant restaurants in former grand ballrooms. Both cities also have some excellent hotels with very moderate rates. Options outside Bangalore and Mysore are few and far between.

Distances are long here, and road and rail transport are very slow. Don't try to see too much in a limited time.

If you have 2 days

If you only have a few days in Karnataka, skip Bangalore and head straight to 🚆 **Mysore** ❺–❿. Spend the day exploring the Mysore Palace in the center of town and wandering the teeming Devaraja Market. In the afternoon, visit the sprawling zoo, where animals roam in open areas separated from onlookers by moats. Treat yourself to dinner at the Lalitha Mahal Palace Hotel, former home of the local maharaja.

For Day 2, hire a driver and leave Mysore early in the morning for a day trip to 🚆 **Belur** ⓭ and 🚆 **Halebid** ⓮, 2½ hours away. Their temples are breathtaking, and if you're lucky, you might happen upon a Hindu wedding ceremony in the wedding temple at Belur.

If you have 5 days

Spend your first day in 🚆 **Bangalore** ❶–❹. Don't miss the Lal Bagh gardens or the fancy shopping arcades on Brigade and Mahatma Gandhi Roads. After dinner, take the commuter train 2½–3 hours to 🚆 **Mysore** ❺–❿ for your first night and second day. For Day 3, either book a safari in Nagarhole National Park, with an overnight stay at the Kabini River Lodge, or take a car up to 🚆 **Belur** ⓭ and 🚆 **Halebid** ⓮ for the day, spending the night there (at nearby Hassan) or returning to Mysore in the evening.

Take a car back to Bangalore and then the overnight train to Hospet, arriving the morning of day four. Take a taxi or auto-rickshaw at Hospet and go straight to the ruins of 🚆 **Hampi** ⓯, 13 km (8 mi) outside town. Hire a guide at Hampi Bazaar and spend your last two days exploring the ruins. From Hospet you can make train connections to Guntakal, and from there to most major cities in India.

If you have 10 days

If you have time to spare, first follow the five-day itinerary above, making sure you see Nagarhole National Park, or stay a night at a plantation in Coorg. From **Hampi** ⓯, take a taxi to **Karwar** ⓬, on Day 6 and spend an afternoon and the following morning at Devbagh. On Day 7, take the train to Mangalore and spend the night and Day 8 there, taking in a beach. Leave early on Day 9 for 🚆 **Belur** ⓭ and 🚆 **Halebid** ⓮ and stay the night in Hassan. On Day 10, return to Bangalore.

Unless we indicate otherwise, hotels have central air-conditioning and bathrooms with tubs. In addition, many luxury hotels have exclusive floors with special privileges or facilities for the business traveler.

Karnataka lodgings charge a 10% service fee, and the Indian government tacks on another 6 to 16%, depending on the facilities. But make sure you look into discounts, because you can often get reductions on the rack rate; alternately, opt for a package deal.

WHAT IT COSTS In Rupees				
$$$$	$$$	$$	$	¢
IN BANGALORE				
FOR 2 PEOPLE over 8,000	6,000–8,000	4,000–6,000	2,000–4,000	under 2,000
IN SMALL TOWNS OUTSIDE BANGALORE				
FOR 2 PEOPLE over 4,000	3,000–4,000	2,000–3,000	1,000–2,000	under 1,000

Hotel prices are for a standard double room in high season, excluding approximately 20% tax.

Timing

Like most of India, Karnataka is nicest between October and February, when the weather is sunny and dry but not unbearably hot. March through May is very hot, particularly in Hampi, and June through September is very wet, especially along the coast. If you can bear the heat, however, Karnataka's main attractions are much emptier in the hot months, and many hotels offer major discounts; just try to visit the Hampi ruins in the early morning or late afternoon to avoid the hot sun. Many towns hold long religious festivals just prior to the monsoon.

Numbers in the text correspond to numbers in the margin and on the Bangalore and Mysore maps.

BANGALORE

❶–❹ *1,040 km (645 mi) southeast of Bombay, 140 km (87 mi) northeast of Mysore, 290 km (180 mi) west of Madras.*

Bangalore exudes modernity, albeit with touches of a long-standing culture clash. Brigade Road, St. Marks Road, Fraser Town, Cubbon Road, and Queen's Circle have all retained their names from the British days, and there's a divide between the cosmopolitan Cantonment area and the more traditional City area. The Cantonment's yuppies lead a Western lifestyle; at the other side of Cubbon Park, the City's more conventional inhabitants guard middle-class values and a section once ruled by the princely state of Mysore. M. G. Road and Brigade Road constitute the center of the garrison, where quaint old buildings sit next to latter-day shopping malls. Near the train station K. G. Road, also known as the Majestic area, has offices, shops, cinemas, hawkers, and travelers. The lines that divide City and Cantonment are no longer as clear as they used to be, and the city now has a far more homogenous modern identity.

There's a curious anecdote about how Bangalore was named: King Ballala of the Hoysala dynasty (in the 13th century) once lost his way in the forest and chanced upon a poor old woman who could only offer him boiled beans. Pleased with her hospitality, the king christened the place as Bendakaluru, literally the "town of boiled beans." Over the centuries, the name became anglicized to Bangalore.

Kempegowda, a feudal lord, actually founded the city in AD 1537, and his son, Kempegowda II, developed it. Both paid allegiance to the Vi-

7

Architecture

Karnataka is best known for its Hindu temples and Indo-Saracenic palaces: the Hoysala-dynasty temples of Belur and Halebid in the south, the enormous ruined town of Hampi in the center of the state, and the Maharaja's Palace in Mysore.

Konkan Railway

For a scenic panorama of India's Western coast from Bombay clear down to Cochin, there's no topping the new Konkan Railway, which stretches 756 km (470 mi) across the states of Maharashtra, Goa, Karnataka, and Kerala. In its very first year, the train became the lifeline of this region, and a spectacular one at that, with more than 170 major bridges, 1,800 minor bridges, and 92 tunnels cutting through the imposing Western Ghats (a chain of highlands covered with tropical evergreen forests). To make the most of the Konkan Railway in Karnataka, take a ride on the Mangalore-Margao passenger train, which runs to and fro every day at a fare of just under Rs. 100. It isn't terribly plush, but the sights and sounds outside will absorb you. The train chugs across bridges—the longest on this route is the 2-km (1-mi) stretch over the river Sharavathi—and past rice paddies, sleepy villages, fishermen's backyards, hills, and marshy stretches where children play and cattle wander. Keeping you company inside is a mixed crowd: traders, nuns, students, laborers, fishermen, hawkers of snacks and beverages, and fellow travelers staring happily into the distance.

Performing Arts

Karnataka has a rich and ancient tradition of folk drama and dance, as well as a colorful contemporary scene featuring classical music and dance from throughout India. In Bangalore and Mysore, performances are frequent, sometimes daily, during the high tourist season (December through March) and major festivals; the rest of the year, there's usually something cultural brewing each weekend. Restaurants popular with foreigners sometimes have live music and even dance performances during dinner. Most events are free; if advance tickets are required, you can generally buy them at the venue for Rs. 50–Rs. 100.

Safaris

In southern Karnataka, thick forests—preserved from destruction by their status as national parks—are home to large elephant herds, tigers, wild bison and pigs, peacocks, and crocodiles. Ecotourism is taking off here, and some of the resorts (jointly sponsored by the government and private capital) are quite delightful. The Indian infrastructure here seems to run quite smoothly. If you're interested, inquire with **Jungle Lodges & Resorts Ltd.** (⊠ Shrungar Shopping Centre, 2nd fl., M. G. Rd., Bangalore ☎ 880/2558–6154, 880/2559–7944, 880/2559–7021, 880/2559–7024, or 880/2559–7025 ⊕ www.junglelodges. com) about Nagarhole National Park, Ranganthittu Bird Sanctuary, Kabini, BR Hills, Dandeli, Devbagh and fishing camps on the Cauvery river.

Shopping

Karnakata's artisans create exquisite hand-loom silk fabrics, intricately inlaid rosewood furniture, and sandalwood carvings. Sandalwood incense sticks, oils, and soaps make great, easy-to-carry gifts. Bidar in north Karnataka is famous for its lovely bidri ware, a metal craft that produces boxes, hookahs, pens and exquisite bangles. Mysore is especially known for its incense and sandalwood, both of which are sold at the numerous spice-and-smell stalls lining the Devaraja Market in Mysore. Channapattana, a small town between Bangalore and Mysore, is famous for its unique lacquered wooden toys. Bangalore also has plentiful curio shops that showcase crafts from around the state. If you're not in a fixed-price government shop, bargain hard and remember that "old" can mean 24 hours old.

---

jayanagar empire, and after the fall of that empire in 1638, the city came under the rule of the Sultan of Bijapur, Mohammed Adil Shah. Shah, who was pleased with the services of his trusted lieutenant Shahji Bhonsle (father of the Maratha King Shivaji), gave him the city as a gift. Between Shahji Bhonsle and his son King Shivaji, the Marathas ruled Bangalore for 49 years until they lost it to the Moghuls, who in turn (supposedly) leased it to the Wodeyars of Mysore (though another version of the story maintains that the Wodeyars bought the city for 3 lakhs—300,000 rupees, which in 2004 would be about US $6,600).

In 1759, the city was taken over by Hyder Ali, father of Tipu Sultan. Bangalore flourished during his reign. Remembered as a brave warrior, his son Tipu fought against the British, and his exceptional military tactics and valiance earned him the title of the Tiger of Mysore (he ruled the Bangalore cantonment, then just a British military zone, from Mysore). After Tipu died during the British siege of his island fortress, Srirangapattana, the British took over his territory and (nominally) reinstated the Hindu Wodeyars on the Mysore throne—though the British maintained a large presence in Mysore city to oversee the administration. Shortly after, they built a large cantonment in nearby Bangalore. In 1881 the British returned much of Mysore to the Wodeyars, who held great influence over the region until independence in 1947 and the eventual abolition of princely rule. After Independence, Bangalore became the capital of Karnataka (the new name for Mysore state).

Thanks to its salubrious climate and green environs, Bangalore was often called the "Pensioners' Paradise." However, in the 1980s it began to attract the telecommunications and technology industries, and it's now India's fastest-growing city. This boom has attracted multinational corporations, and, aided by the cantonment's long-standing western identity, the city is now extremely cosmopolitan, with trendy boutiques, pizza parlors, cyber kiosks, and pubs. Indeed, beer is imbibed with gusto in nearly 200 establishments, though local authorities now enforce an 11 PM closing time. Despite all the growth, effective urban planning—rare in India—has given the city a serene, orderly feel.

Numbers in the text correspond to numbers in the margin and on the Bangalore map.

a good tour

Bangalore's heart is the area near Mahatma Gandhi, Brigade, and Residency Roads. The bustling streets around the train station and Race Course Road are also well worth getting lost in for a couple of hours. Start by taking a taxi to the **Bull Temple ❶** ▶. Walk 2 km (1.2 mi) east for about 20 minutes on the crowded but basically flat B. P. Wadia Road, which will bring you to the tropical **Lal Bagh Botanical Gardens ❷**. Head north through the gardens and come out on the Lal Bagh Fort Road side; turn left onto this road and continue to a large intersection. On your left is Krishnarajendra Road; on your right, Avenue Road. Turn onto Avenue Road, and shortly, on your left, where Avenue Road is intersected by Albert Victor Road, you'll come to **Tipu's Palace ❸**.

Outside the palace, the urban scenery is rather dull, so you might want to cheat and take an auto-rickshaw. If you do, stop at Mysore Bank Circle and walk down K. G. Road for 10 minutes to get a feel for this busy area. Alternately, follow the narrow, busy Avenue Road for about 2 km (1 mi) to reach Mysore Bank Circle and K. G. Road. From some point on K. G. Road, take an auto-rickshaw to **Vidhana Soudha ❹**, on Dr. Ambedkar Veedi Road, the spectacular building that houses the state legislature. To your right is the redbrick High Court. Continue up Dr. Ambedkar Veedi Road until you come to the General Post Office building on your right. Turn right and walk toward Minsk Square (here, again, the scenery is insignificant, so you may want to take an auto-rickshaw). From Minsk Square you can walk left along the tree-lined Cubbon Road or straight toward Queen's Circle, with the cricket stadium on your left and Cubbon Park on your right. From either one, return to Queen's Circle, where M. G. Road—with its cybercafés, ritzy arcades, and crafts and silk emporiums—starts.

TIMING   You'll need the better part of a day for this tour, though taking auto-rickshaws on the plainer stretches can save some time. The Lal Bagh Gardens deserve at least an hour, Tipu's Palace half an hour, and the Vidhana Soudha another half an hour. It's best to set off fairly early in the morning, as the gardens are most pleasant then (and in the early evening). Beware of sunburn: Bangalore is cool but at 3,000 feet, so the radiation sunburn can be deceptively strong. Unless you're hardy, it's best to walk through the garden areas, including Lal Bagh and Cubbon Park, and take rickshaws when you're on crowded city roads.

What to See

▶ **❶ Bull Temple.** This small temple houses the enormous 1786 monolith of Nandi, the sacred Hindu bull, vehicle of Shiva. The temple's front yard bustles with activity: peddlers sell coconuts, bananas, and jasmine blossoms for offerings. Don't be alarmed if a woman sitting on the pavement suddenly yanks out a live cobra from a straw basket in front of her, taunting it to fan out its collar: for a few rupees, you can snap a photo of the angry creature from as close (or as far) as you wish. Inside, Nandi lies in his traditional position, leaning slightly to one side with his legs tucked beneath him. The bull's hefty black bulk is beautifully carved and ornamented with bells, and glistens with coconut oil that priests apply regularly to keep the stone moist. ✉ *Bull Temple Rd., Basavanagudi* ⌧ *Free* ☉ *Daily 6 AM–8 PM.*

❷ Lal Bagh Botanical Gardens. This 240-acre park, popular with young lovers, is one of the remaining reasons for Bangalore's increasingly obscure nickname, "The Garden City." Closed to auto traffic, the park is laced with pedestrian paths past more than 100 types of trees and thousands of varieties of plants and flowers from all over the world. Most of the flora are in fullest bloom between October and December. Some trees, like

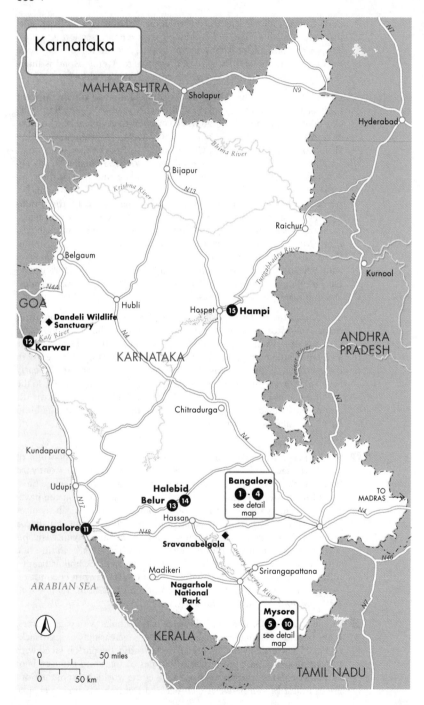

Karnataka

MAHARASHTRA

Sholapur

Hyderabad

Bhima River

Bijapur

Krishna River

N13

Raichur

Kurnool

Belgaum

N44

GOA

Hubli

Hospet ● 15 **Hampi**

Tungabhadra River

ANDHRA
PRADESH

**Dandeli Wildlife
Sanctuary**

Kali River

12 **Karwar**

KARNATAKA

N4

Chitradurga

Penner River

N7

Kundapura

N4

Udupi

**Halebid
Belur** 13 14

Bangalore
1 - 4
see detail
map

TO
MADRAS

N17

Hassan

N4

N46

Mangalore 11

N48

Sravanabelgola

Cauvery River

ARABIAN SEA

Madikeri

Srirangapattana

Cauvery River

**Nagarhole
National
Park**

Mysore
5 - 10
see detail
map

KERALA

TAMIL NADU

0   50 miles

0   50 km

the venerable 200-year-old elephant tree near the western gate entrance, date from the time of Tipu Sultan, who continued to develop the park in the late 18th century after the death of his father, Hyder Ali, who designed the grounds in 1760. Marking the heart of Lal Bagh is the **Rose Garden,** a square, fenced-in plot blooming with some 150 different kinds of roses. Just beyond, near the north gate entrance, is the **Glass House,** a cross-shape pavilion built in 1881 with London's Crystal Palace in mind. Twice a year, around Independence Day (August 15) and Republic Day (January 15), weeklong flower shows are held here. ⊠ *Lal Bagh Fort Rd., Lal Bagh* ⌦ *Free; Rs. 5 during flower shows* ☉ *Daily sunrise–sunset.*

❸ Tipu's Palace. Tipu Sultan built this palace for himself in 1789. Made of wood, it's a replica of his summer palace on Srirangapatnam (a river island near Mysore), sans the elaborate fresco painting inside. The building now houses a modest photo exhibit about Tipu and his times. ⊠ *Albert Victor Rd., Chickpet* ⌦ *Foreigners US$5* ☉ *Daily 8–5:30.*

❹ Vidhana Soudha. Bangalore's most beautiful building is a relatively recent addition to the city, built between 1954 and 1958 to house the state legislature and secretariat. The sprawling granite structure was designed in the Indo-Dravidian style, studded with pillars and carved ledges and topped with a central dome that's crowned, in turn, with a golden four-head lion, emblem of the great 3rd-century BC Buddhist king Ashoka. The interior is not open to visitors. Facing the Vidhana Soudha head-on across the street is another of Bangalore's attractive public buildings, the pillared, redbrick High Court of Karnataka, built in 1885 as the seat of the then-British government. ⊠ *Dr. Ambedkar Veedhi Rd., Raj Bhavan–Cubbon Park.*

Where to Eat

Bangalore has an up-and-coming restaurant scene, growing more cosmopolitan by the month. Chinese restaurants abound, as do Italian, American, and other ethnic eateries. For the latest hot spots, consult your concierge, the city pages of the *Times of India,* the *Deccan Herald,* or the weekly, *City Reporter,* available in bookstores.

★ **$$$$** ✕ **Jamavar.** This top-quality Indian restaurant at the luxurious Leela Palace offers a regal dining experience, with handwoven carpets and elegant chandeliers. The dishes served—lamb rack, tandoori jumbo prawns, *tandoor ke phool* (cauliflower or broccoli florets baked in a a tandoor oven—represent the tables of India's erstwhile royal families, and are thus the very richest and most refined Indian dishes from every corner of the country. ⊠ *The Leela Palace, 23 Airport Rd.* ☎ *80/2521–1234* ⌦ *Reservations essential* ▭ *AE, DC, MC, V.*

$$$$ ✕ **Jolly Nabob.** This upmarket restaurant serves unusual Anglo-Lucknowi fusion cuisine, as well as traditional dum pukht (steam-cooked) dishes. It's one of the few places in India where Anglo-Indian cuisine has been extended well beyond mulligatawny soup to include dishes such as nautch girl temptation soup (made of nothing more exotic than tomatoes and potatoes), *hoossainee* curry (chicken morsels in poppyseed

Bull
Temple 1

Lal Bagh Botanical
Gardens 2

Tipu's
Palace 3

Vidhana
Soudha 4

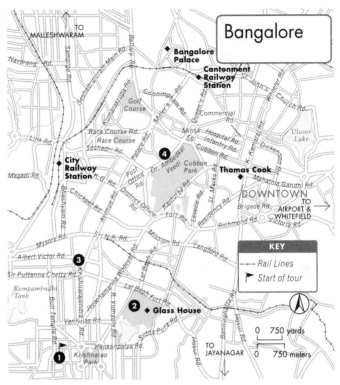

gravy with coriander, cayenne pepper, and lemongrass) and cutlet
shikampuri (minced mutton). ⊠ *Hotel ITC Windsor Sheraton, 25
Sankey Rd., Golf Course* ☎ *80/2226–9898* ⌂ *Reservations essential*
▤ *AE, DC, MC, V* ⊗ *No lunch.*

$$$$ ✕ **The Royal Afghan.** This posh poolside barbecue restaurant in the
Windsor Manor hotel is one of very few in India serving Afghan cuisine. Charcoal-grilled kababs are popular, along with the finely minced
mutton with *paratha* bread. Other dishes such as tandoori *jhinga*
(prawns), sikandari *raan* (leg of lamb), and *dal Afghani* (Afghan-style
lentils) make this a truly enjoyable dining experience. ⊠ *ITC Hotel Windsor Sheraton, 25 Sankey Rd., Golf Course* ☎ *80/2226–9898* ▤ *AE, DC,
MC, V* ⊗ *No lunch.*

$$$–$$$$ ✕ **Karavalli.** Dine on a shady terrace walled in by hedges, or in an ad-
joining cottage, here where waiters wear dhotis and South Indian clas-
sical music sets the tone. The coconut-oriented menu features coastal
cuisines from Goa, Kerala, and Mangalore; two regional specialties are
kori gassi (chicken simmered in coconut gravy) served with *neer dosa* (a
Karnataka-style crêpe), and *kane bezule* (fish marinated in ground Man-
galorean spices, then deep-fried). Save room for *bebinka*, the sinfully rich
Goan dessert of egg yolk, butter, and coconut. ⊠ *Taj Gateway Hotel,
66 Residency Rd., Downtown* ☎ *80/2558–4545* ▤ *AE, DC, MC, V.*

★ **$$$–$$$$** ✕ **Samarkhand.** This is an excellent place for kababs and Northwest Frontier food. Specialties include kababs such as *murgh gilafee* (made from minced chicken and flavored with cardamom); *galawati kabab* (double-minced, or finely minced, lamb kababs flavored with cumin); and other dishes like *mirch baingan ka salan* (nonspicy chilies in coconut and aubergine gravy); and *murgh kushk purdah* (chicken marinated in tandoori masala, grilled and finished by the purdah technique—in a thick flour wrapping). Apart from the succulent food, the restaurant has an attractive minimalistic style, and no cutlery—you're expected to eat with your fingers. Water is served in copper tumblers. ⊠ *Gem Plaza, 66 Infantry Rd., Downtown* ☎ *80/5111–3366* ⌂ *Reservations essential* ▭ *AE, MC, V.*

$$$ ✕ **Pinch of Jazz.** Serving cajun and creole food and Chinese cuisine, this restaurant at the Central Park preserves the lively cosmopolitan tone of the cantonment, with one of the last old timers' live bands in the city. It's a great place to go for a couple of drinks and entertainment—and while the band does do some passable vintage jazz, make sure to ask them to play Belafonte's "Jamaican Farewell"; the lyrics are given a curious and typically Bangalorean twist toward the end. The interior is somewhat surreal, with the New York skyline taking up one wall. The cajun grilled chicken and lobster are popular. ⊠ *Central Park, Dickenson Rd., Downtown* ☎ *80/2558–4242* ⌂ *Reservations essential* ▭ *AE, DC, MC, V.*

$$–$$$$ ✕ **Ebony.** This popular rooftop restaurant sits unsuperstitiously on the 13th floor of a hotel. The tables on the two outdoor terraces have very fine views of Bangalore and are in high demand in the evening, when the South Indian sun cools down and the city lights come on. The excellent chef specializes in Parsi cuisine, which is unusual in Bangalore, and also cooks North and South Indian and Continental fare. On Saturday there's an excellent Parsi buffet at lunchtime, serving traditional dishes such as *dhansak* (brown rice and dal with mutton). Note that the food is very spicy. ⊠ *Ivory Tower Hotel, 13th fl., 84 M. G. Rd., Downtown* ☎ *80/2558–9333* ⌂ *Reservations essential* ▭ *AE, DC, MC, V.*

$$–$$$ ✕ **Sunny's.** Small, elegant, and expensive, this place is best known for its French and Italian specialties—filet mignon, pizzas, pastas, and seasonal salads—along with deli items like hot dogs and sausages. Although it serves non-Indian cuisine, it's a typical Bangalore "high society" place in terms of the clientele, and has become rather hip, so it's an interesting spot to people watch. The filet mignon and avocado salad are excellent, as are the desserts. Walls are decorated with pictures of Sunny—the owner's beloved dog. Lunchtime gets crowded. ⊠ *Off Lavelle Rd., Downtown* ☎ *80/2224–3642* ⌂ *Reservations essential* ▭ *AE, DC, MC, V.*

$–$$ ✕ **Moksh.** Run by the well-known chef Jiggs Kalra, this place serves vegetarian North Indian food. It's not exclusively vegetarian, however—milk products like cottage cheese are dished up. Specialties include *pudina paneer* (minted cottage cheese curry) and *talley aloo ka kurma* (fried potato gravy simmered with saffron). The chefs prepare your food right in front of you. ⊠ *Chancery Hotel, 10/6 Lavelle Rd., Downtown* ☎ *80/2227–6767 or 80/5118–8888* ▭ *MC, V.*

$–$$ ✕ **Nagarjuna Savoy.** Indian food from the state of Andhra Pradesh is the focus of this smart modern restaurant, the upscale sister of the original Nagarjuna eatery next door. Zesty-sweet chicken, mutton (goat), and vegetable *biryani* (fried rice and vegetables) are served on plates, not plantain leaves—not entirely authentic, but fair enough if you're not used to eating with your hands. You can also have a beer with your food if so inclined (this is unusual in biriyani-only restaurants, which usually don't serve alcohol). The dining room is decorated with brass-and-copper masks and framed prints of Indian folk art. ⊠ *45/3 Residency Rd., Downtown* ☎ *80/2558–7775* ☰ *AE, DC, MC, V.*

★ **$–$$** ✕ **Tandoor.** The unusually long and sophisticated menu focuses on tandoori items, which you can watch being skewered and cooked. Particularly good are the chicken in mint curry, chicken *seekh kabab* (minced chicken kabab), and fish *tikka* (bite-size chunks). Gold-trim ivory walls and pillars and dimmed glass-bead chandeliers create a look of traditional Indian splendor. The room fills nightly with a chic, professional crowd and an amiable tone. ⊠ *28 M. G. Rd., Downtown* ☎ *80/2558–4620* ☰ *AE, DC, MC, V.*

$ ✕ **La Casa.** One of the few places in South Bangalore where women can comfortably enjoy a pitcher on their own, this easygoing restaurant serves hearty Indian dishes like the coconut-flavor chicken curry Mangalore, and possibly the best fish tikka in town. You can also get a generous burger or pizza, and sophisticated desserts. It's a good place to stop after visiting the sights in the old City areas. ⊠ *Chintal Plaza, 33rd Cross, 10th Main, 4th Block, Jayanagar* ☎ *80/2655–4613 or 80/2654–5425* ☰ *DC, MC, V.*

¢–$ ✕ **Angeethi.** Tucked away on a terrace, this restaurant is fashioned after the many roadside eateries in the Punjab countryside: there's a thatched roof, a water well, old Hindi film posters, and a lamp post. Enjoy the kitsch atmosphere after you place your order, since it'll be a while before your food arrives. It's worth the wait, however. You can order a moderately priced north Indian buffet (Rs. 137) at lunchtime. Punjabi-style seafood, including pomfret and lobster, is served at dinner. ⊠ *Museum Inn, 1 Museum Rd.* ☎ *80/5111–3333* ☰ *AE, DC, MC, V.*

¢–$ ✕ **Koshy's.** For a coffee, beer, a sandwich, or full-blown biriyani, this old-time café may be the quietest hideaway near busy M. G. Road. With high ceilings, lots of smoke, and a dark, historic look, it has an air of permanence, and the waiters won't blink an eye if you just want to hang around sipping coffee and scribbling. Try the tender-coconut soup. The separate air-conditioned dining section is called the Jewel Box. ⊠ *St. Marks Rd., Downtown* ☎ *80/2291–5840* ☰ *AE, DC, MC, V.*

★ ¢ ✕ **Mavalli Tiffin Rooms (MTR).** Come to this bustling Bangalore institution, established in 1924, for authentic vegetarian South Indian food. Some of the furniture is plastic, but you won't find better dosas in Bangalore, and you can't beat the prices. Desserts are also tasty, and the filter coffee (brewed, not instant) is superb. You might have to wait for a table, but once the dhoti-clad bearer takes your order, food materializes quickly. ⊠ *Lalbagh Rd.* ☎ *80/2222–0022* ☰ *No credit cards* ⊗ *No dinner Mon.*

Where to Stay

The city is experiencing a lodging boom, with dozens of business-oriented hotels going up in the prime commercial areas. Competition is stiff, keeping the majority of hotels in the moderate price range.

★ $$$$ ⊞ **The Leela Palace.** Bangalore's newest luxury hotel, which opened in 2002, is modeled in accordance with royal Mysore's hybrid architectural heritage and the magnificent sculptural wealth of the Vijayanagar Empire. Close to the airport and 5 km (3 mi) from downtown Bangalore, the hotel is a world within itself, with a huge shopping gallery, an excellent Indian restaurant, a library bar with cigar lounge, and a popular all-night disco. The interior is astounding: Vijayanagar horses (sculpted stone in the style used by the Vijayanagar empire—you see these sculpted horses in Hampi and in the Srirangam temple in Trichy) glaring down from huge pillars and and richly decorated ceilings. Rooms are luxurious, with large Italian marble bathrooms, and overlook either the garden or the pool. ⊠ *23 Airport Rd., 560008* ☎ *80/2521–1234, 800/426–3135 in U.S.* 🖷 *80/2521–7234 or 80/2521–2222* ⊕ *www. theleelablr.com* ⊅ *256 rooms, 30 suites* ⌂ *2 restaurants, in-room data ports, cable TV, pool, spa, bar, dance club, laundry service, shop, business services, travel services* ▤ *AE, DC, MC, V* ⦿ *BP.*

$$$$
Fodor'sChoice
★

⊞ **The Oberoi.** Slick, elegant, and well run, this hotel has a stunning lobby with a green marble floor, a central fountain, and a bank of windows overlooking the landscaped garden—which, in turn, is dominated by a gorgeous blossoming rain tree and a small waterfall cascading into a fish-filled lotus pond. The spacious rooms have polished green-marble entryways, private balconies, and handsome brass-and-teak furnishings. Each floor has a private 24-hour butler. Rim Nam, the open-kitchen Thai restaurant, is one of the best non-Indian specialty restaurants in the country and the Chinese Szechwan Court is excellent, too. An all-day dining restaurant serves Indian and Continental food. Service is exemplary. ⊠ *37/39 M. G. Rd., Downtown 560001* ☎ *80/2558–5858* 🖷 *80/2558–5966* ⊕ *www.oberoihotels.com* ⊅ *160 rooms, 9 suites* ⌂ *3 restaurants, in-room data ports, cable TV, pool, health club, hair salon, spa, bar, dry cleaning, laundry service, business services, meeting room, airport shuttle, travel services* ▤ *AE, DC, MC, V* ⦿ *CP or EP.*

★ $$$$ ⊞ **Taj West End.** More than 100 years old (from 1887), this hotel has a decidedly Victorian look outside and in the public rooms. Most of the guest rooms are elegantly contemporary, with brass lamps and teak or solid cane furniture. The slightly more expensive "old-world" rooms have a turn-of-the-20th-century look, with mahogany writing desks and brass four-poster beds. The best rooms in the main building are on the second floor; they open onto a veranda overlooking the pool. Suites have private verandas and sunlit alcoves. The setting is tropical, with 20 acres of lush gardens. Blue Ginger by the pool serves Vietnamese food and the poolside barbecue dishes up Indian and Continental fare. ⊠ *23 Race Course Rd., 560001* ☎ *80/5660–5660* 🖷 *80/5660–5700* ⊕ *www. tajhotels.com* ⊅ *122 rooms, 16 suites* ⌂ *2 restaurants, coffee shop, patisserie, cable TV, tennis court, pool, exercise equipment, sauna, 2 bars, baby-sitting, dry cleaning, laundry service, business services, travel services* ▤ *AE, DC, MC, V* ⦿ *EP or CP.*

$$$–$$$$ ⊞ **ITC Hotel Windsor Sheraton and Towers.** Bangalore's prettiest hotel has a striking white exterior with arched windows and wrought-iron ornaments. In the lobby, a marble fountain sits beneath a domed skylight and massive teak pillars. The smaller, atrium lobby area in the Towers gleams

with polished marble and brass, a suitable introduction to this opulent five-story wing geared toward business travelers. The handsome rooms in the original wing have modern furnishings with endearing Victorian touches. The Raj Pavilion is a delightful coffee shop with natural light streaming through the glasshouse-like interior in the daytime. ⊠ *Windsor Sq., 25 Sankey Rd., Golf Course 560052* ☎ *80/2226–9898* 🖷 *80/2226–4941* ⊕ *www.welcomgroup.com* 🖅 *217 rooms, 23 suites* ♨ *4 restaurants, coffee shop, cable TV, pool, health club, bar, dry cleaning, laundry service, business services, travel services* ▤ *AE, DC, MC, V* ❙❉❙ *CP.*

$$$–$$$$ 🏨 **Le Meridien.** The enormous atrium lobby of this modern high-rise sparkles with white marble and shiny brass carriage lamps. The hallways and rooms, in contrast, are surprisingly dark. The modern rooms have burnt-orange carpeting, upholstered chairs and ottomans, and floral drapes and bedspreads. Windows are double-glaze. ⊠ *28 Sankey Rd., Golf Course 560052* ☎ *80/2226–2233* 🖷 *80/2226–7676* ⊕ *www.lemeridien.com* 🖅 *196 rooms, 30 suites* ♨ *Restaurant, coffee shop, cable TV, pool, exercise equipment, hair salon, sauna, steam room, bar, baby-sitting, laundry service, business services, meeting room, airport shuttle, travel services* ▤ *AE, DC, MC, V* ❙❉❙ *EP or CP.*

$$$–$$$$ 🏨 **Taj Kuteeram.** If your primary interest in visiting Bangalore is the dance village of Nrityagram, you can stay at this tiny Taj hotel 40 km (25 mi) from the city and right opposite the village. The setting is distinctly rural, with rooms built using local building material—lime juice, cow dung, mud, and jaggery, and only a small percentage of cement. The restaurant serves Indian and fusion food. There's no swimming pool or bar. ⊠ *Hessaragatta Village, Bangalore Rural District, Bangalore North, opposite Nrityagram Dance Village, 560088* ☎ *80/2846–6326 or 80/2846–6329* 🖷 *80/2846–6347* ⊕ *www.tajhotels.com* 🖅 *6 standard cottages, 3 suite-cottages* ♨ *Restaurant, ayurvedic massage, yoga, laundry service, travel services* ▤ *AE, MC, V* ❙❉❙ *FAP.*

$$$ 🏨 **The Park Hotel.** The funky and vibrant colors of the exterior of India's first boutique hotel, designed by the British firm Conran and Partners, echo the dynamic hues of India's vast and varied landscape. Each room has a different color scheme, and bright lighting makes things lively. The quality of service is in keeping with the spirit of the place—cheerful and fast. The 24-hour restaurant, Monsoon, serves many cuisines—from local to Indonesian to Thai. ⊠ *14/7 M. G. Rd., Downtown 560042* ☎ *80/2559–4666* 🖷 *80/2559–4029* ⊕ *www.theparkhotels.com* 🖅 *104 rooms, 5 suites* ♨ *2 restaurants, coffee shop, cable TV, pool, exercise equipment, bar, baby-sitting, business services, meeting room, travel services* ▤ *AE, DC, MC, V* ❙❉❙ *CP.*

$$$ 🏨 **Taj Residency.** The large, white-marble lobby in this high-rise bustles with activity. Guest rooms are furnished with contemporary teak furniture and blue-and-green upholstery. Ask for a room on an upper floor with a lake view. ⊠ *41/3 M. G. Rd., Downtown 560001* ☎ *80/5660–4444* 🖷 *80/5661–4444* ⊕ *www.tajhotels.com* 🖅 *163 rooms, 5 suites* ♨ *2 restaurants, coffee shop, patisserie, cable TV, pool, exercise equipment, bar, baby-sitting, business services, meeting room, travel services* ▤ *AE, DC, MC, V.*

$$–$$$ ⊞ **The Grand Ashok.** Built in 1971 in the park where Mahatma Gandhi once meditated, this hotel has a small memorial to Gandhi on the extensive grounds behind it. Guest rooms look fresh, in blue-gray and pale green, and with blond-wood furnishings; the best rooms overlook the pool. The small marble lobby has low ceilings and comfortable wicker chairs. The Delhi-based Grand group took over the hotel a year ago and service has since improved. ⊠ *Kumara Krupa High Grounds, Golf Course, 560001* ☎ *80/2225–0202 or 80/2226–9462* ⊟ *80/2225–0033* ⊕ *www.thegrandhotels.net* ➲ *164 rooms, 18 suites* ⌂ *2 restaurants, coffee shop, cable TV, tennis court, pool, exercise equipment, hair salon, bar, dry cleaning, laundry service, meeting room, travel services* ⊟ *AE, DC, MC, V* ⦿ *CP.*

$$ ⊞ **Central Park.** Tucked behind the Manipal Centre, a large commercial complex, this 10-story building is one of Bangalore's business hotels. Glass-backed elevators give you a view of the city en route to your room. Standard rooms are small, with standard modern furnishings and a few tartan-plaid details, but at almost the same price, the "park chamber" rooms on the executive floors are slightly larger and better-appointed. The hotel has an excellent restaurant with a live band. ⊠ *47 Dickenson Rd., Downtown 560042* ☎ *80/2558–4242* ⊟ *80/2558–8594* ➲ *126 rooms, 4 suites* ⌂ *Restaurant, coffee shop, patisserie, cable TV, bar, shop, business services, meeting room, travel services* ⊟ *AE, DC, MC, V* ⦿ *CP.*

$$ ⊞ **The Chancery.** This large, medium-budget and comfortable business traveler's hotel is one block from coffee shops and restaurants and part of busy downtown. The central location and friendly service make this convenient for tourists as well. Rooms are simple: beige carpets, dark-wood furniture, and ample wardrobe space. However, there is no swimming pool or bar. ⊠ *The Chancery Hotel, 10/6 Lavelle Rd., Downtown* ☎ *80/2227–6767 or 80/5118–8888* ⊟ *80/2227–6700* ⊕ *www. chanceryhotel.net* ➲ *93 rooms, 7 suites* ⌂ *2 restaurants, coffee shop, gym, business center, travel services* ⊟ *AE, DC, MC, V* ⦿ *CP.*

$–$$ ⊞ **St. Mark's Hotel.** A short walk from Koshy's and about 2 km (1 mi) from the center of town, this huge seven-floor hotel, popular among business travelers, has a marble-floor lobby. Rooms are plushly carpeted in red, and come with coffee tables and flowery armchairs. The suites have separate living rooms and large wooden bars. ⊠ *4/1 St. Mark's Rd., Downtown 560001* ☎ *80/2227–9090* ⊟ *80/2227–5700* ➲ *88 rooms, 6 suites* ⌂ *Restaurant, cable TV, bar, laundry service, business services, travel services* ⊟ *AE, DC, MC, V* ⦿ *CP.*

$ ⊞ **Taj Gateway Hotel.** This Western-style Taj property offers cleaner and better-equipped rooms than its peers among the new, low- to mid-range business hotels, but it's on a very noisy street. Despite being essentially a budget hotel, it retains an air of sophistication with its tastefully furnished rooms and excellent restaurant, Karavalli. The walls are adorned with framed abstract prints throughout; guest rooms have modern wood and wicker furniture and pale blue carpeting. Only the suites have bathtubs, in addition to showers. ⊠ *66 Residency Rd., Downtown 560025* ☎ *80/5660–4545* ⊟ *80/5660–4030* ⊕ *www.tajhotels.com* ➲ *94 rooms, 4 suites* ⌂ *3 restaurants, coffee shop, pool, exercise* *equipment, bar, laundry service, business services, travel services* ☰ *AE, DC, MC, V.*

★ $ ⊞ **Villa Pottipati.** This old building run as a heritage hotel in Malleswaram—restored and run by the Neemrana group—is one of the few attempts within Bangalore to conserve the city's spectacular but fast-disappearing architectural heritage. Beautiful old-world rooms and a lovely garden with jacaranda and gulmohur trees take you back in time, as do the gabled windows and four-poster beds. This is really one of the most charming places to stay in the city. ✉ *142 8th Cross, 4th Main Rd., Malleswaram 560003* ☎ *80/2336–0777 or 80/5128–0832 to 34* 🖷 *80/ 5128–0835* ⊕ *www.neemranahotels.com* ➳ *8 rooms* ⌂ *Restaurant, cable TV, laundry service, Internet* ☰ *MC, V* ⦿❙ *CP.*

¢ ⊞ **Nilgiris Nest.** The best things about this clean, budget, and low-on-atmosphere hotel are its large rooms and its location above Nilgiris supermarket on bustling Brigade Road in the heart of downtown Bangalore. (It's the best supermarket around, and handy if you want anything from bread, butter and cheese for breakfast to exotic fruit or freshly baked buns and Indian snacks. This is the place to stay if you have only a short time in the city, are going to be out most of the day, and want to be within walking distance of pubs, restaurants, shops, and nightlife. Extra beds are available at Rs. 350. Reserve at least a week in advance. ✉ *171 Brigade Rd., above Nilgiris supermarket, Downtown 560001* ☎ *80/2558–8401, 80/2558–8702, or 80/2558–8103* 🖷 *80/2558–5348* ➳ *25 rooms* ⌂ *Restaurant, room service, cable TV, laundry service; no a/c in some rooms* ☰ *AE, DC, MC, V* ⦿❙ *CP.*

Nightlife & the Arts

Nightlife

Bangalore is famous in India for its casual, upbeat pubs. Since the early 1990s, nearly 200 have sprung up throughout the city, providing a variety of hangouts where people of all types and trades can meet over a beer or other drink and listen to music (often loud) or watch TV. Most pubs are styled according to themes, such as a cricket stadium (New Night Watchman) or a subway station (The Underground). In an effort to curb local students' alcohol consumption, the government requires pubs to close for a few hours in the afternoon and shut down altogether by 11 PM; live bands must also call it a day at 11. Further regulations aimed at preventing prostitution and go-go club scenes have forbidden late-night dancing in clubs. A few major hotels, however, have special permits. All this may change at the whim of the government; check with your hotel for the latest on the entertainment scene.

The Cosmo Village (✉ 29 McGrath Rd., off Brigade Rd., Ashoknagar [a small downtown neighborhood], Downtown ☎ 80/5112–7373 or 80/ 5112–7474) is a small, friendly, crowded place with an indoor as well as a rooftop bar. Extremely popular and packed on weekends, **Geoffrey's** (✉ Royal Arcade Hotel, 1 Golf Ave., adjoining KGA Golf Club, off Airport Rd. ☎ 80/2520–5566 or 80/2520–3366) has loud, chiefly Americana decor, and is a good bet for a lively evening. **Guzzlers' Inn** (✉ 48 Rest House Rd., off Brigade Rd., Downtown ☎ 80/2558–7336 or 80/

2558–2138) is small and boisterous, often packed with young drinkers swaying to MTV. **Hypnos** (✉ 66 Gem Plaza, Infantry Rd., Downtown ☎ 80/5111–3366) is a great place for a cocktail or a hookah (you can choose from a variety of fruit flavors at Rs. 300 each). Don't let the posh, modern style of the **I-Bar** (✉ The Park Hotel, 14/7 M. G. Rd., Downtown ☎ 80/2559–4666) fool you; the vibe here is warm. At the **Jockey Club** (✉ Taj Residency, 41/3 M. G. Rd., Downtown ☎ 80/2558–4444) bar-restaurant, white-glove waiters serve silver steins of beer in a small room with richly carved teak walls, Belgian mirrors, and subdued lantern light. The **Megabowl** (✉ Prestige Terminus II, Lower Ground Fl., Airport Rd. ☎ 80/2522–9743) is a sports bar with pool tables, video games, *and* bowling lanes. **NASA** (✉ 1/4 Church St., Downtown ☎ 80/2558–4595) has the look and feel of a space shuttle; you duck through an oval door into two oval-shape rooms decorated in silver and black. The **New Night Watchman** (✉ 46/1 Museum Rd., off Church St., Downtown ☎ 80/2558–8372), designed like a miniature cricket stadium, is popular with students.

At **1912** (✉ 40 St. Marks Rd., Downtown ☎ 80/2299–7290), (formerly 180 Proof) a slightly upscale crowd relaxes inside an old stone building with psychedelic interiors. The stained-glass windows at the **Polo Club** (✉ Oberoi Hotel, 37–39 M. G. Rd., Downtown ☎ 80/2558–5858) has views of lush gardens; a cascading waterfall adds to the serenity. Established in the 1980s, one of the city's first modern pubs, **Pub World** (✉ 65 Residency Rd., Laxmi Plaza, Downtown ☎ 80/2558–5206) is still hip with its polished woods and shiny brass fixtures. On weekends, the **Purple Haze** (✉ Opposite Konark Restaurant, 17/1 Residency Rd., Downtown ☎ 80/2221–3758) comes alive with hard rock and a throbbing dance floor, though it really isn't terribly quiet the rest of the week. The **Royal Derby** (✉ ITC Windsor Sheraton, 25 Sankey Rd., Golf Course ☎ 80/2226–9898) is fashioned after a classic Irish pub and has cocktails and snacks. **Tavern** (✉ 1 Museum Rd., off M. G. Rd., Downtown ☎ 80/5111–3339 or 80/5111–3333) is an English-style pub in the day and a nightclub in the evening. **TGIF** (✉ Opposite Diamond District, 1 Carlton Towers, Airport Rd. ☎ 80/2521–0569 to 71) is much the same as any of its outlets across the world; it's loud, cheerful and popular, and not just on Friday. Happy hours are 4 to 8:15 daily. **Time and Again** (✉ Brigade Rd., Downtown ☎ 80/2558–5845) is popular with a young set for dancing. **The Underground** (✉ 65 Blue Moon Complex, M. G. Rd., Downtown ☎ 80/2558–9991) has one section designed after London's tube. Slightly cheesy but generally fun, this is a good place to end a night on the town. **The Thirteenth Floor** (✉ 13th Fl., Barton Centre, M. G. Rd., Downtown ☎ 80/2558–9333 or 80/2559–6214) is one of the most popular upscale places in the city, its open balcony on the 13th floor of Barton Centre overlooks downtown and lets you enjoy the legendary Bangalore weather.

The Arts

Your best sources for information on cultural happenings are the newspapers: the *Deccan Herald*'s column "In the City Today," usually on page 3, and the *Times of India*'s "Events" column in the city supplement. Other sources are posters, the Karnataka Department of Tourism (KDT), the *City Reporter* weekly magazine, and the staff at your hotel.

The violin-shape **Chowdiah Memorial Hall** (✉ Gayathri Devi Park Extension, Vyalikaval, Malleshwaram ☎ 80/2344–5810) hosts plays, dance and music performances, and film screenings. **Karnataka Chitrakala Parishath** (✉ Kumara Krupa Rd., Golf Course ☎ 80/2226–1816 ☉ Mon.–Sat. 10–5:30) is a premier fine arts institution that also has an open-air theater for dance-and-music shows and puppet theater. Painting and photo exhibitions are frequent events. The **Yavanika State Youth Center** (✉ Nrupathunga Rd., Raj Bhavan–Cubbon Park ☎ 80/2221–4911) hosts free Indian classical music and dance performances and other cultural events most evenings.

On the outskirts of Bangalore, the **Nrityagram Dance Village** (✉ Hessaragatta, Bangalore Rural District, Bangalore North ☎ 80/2846–6314 ⊕ www.nrityagram.org) is a dance institution founded by the late Odissi dancer Protima Gauri. Here you can watch students at work while sampling aspects of Karnataka folk culture. The premises, which include a guest house, are modeled on a Karnataka village and designed for holistic living, with granite, stone, mud, and thatch the chief architectural ingredients. Nrityagram is the only village of its kind in India devoted to the promotion and preservation of ancient classical-dance styles and two martial-art forms. For a taste of Indian mythology and cultural traditions, this is worth a visit. Accommodation is also available at the Taj Kuteeram opposite the village.

Sports & the Outdoors

Bowling

If bowling strikes your fancy, head for **Amoeba** (✉ Church St., off Brigade Rd., Downtown ☎ 80/2559–4631 to 32) It costs Rs. 80 per game per head on weekdays (Rs. 100 after 5 PM), Rs. 100 on weekends (Rs. 125 after 5 PM). **Megabowl** (✉ Prestige Terminus II, Lower Ground Fl., Airport Rd. ☎ 80/2522–9743) is a sports bar with bowling facilities.

Golf

The **Bangalore Golf Club** (✉ 2 Sankey Rd., Golf Course ☎ 80/2228–1876), designed by the British in 1876, has an 18-hole course open to the public. Call ahead to reserve your game. You'll be allowed entry only if you carry your handicap card. Charges are $20 on weekdays and $30 on weekends. If you're willing to take a 30 km (19 mi) drive out of Bangalore, there's a good course at **Eagleton** (✉ 30th km [stone road marker], Bangalore–Mysore Hwy., Bidadi Industrial Area, town of Bidadi ☎ 80/2728–7222, 80/2728–7233, 80/2728–7244, 80/2728–7255, or 80/2728–7266); to play here it costs Rs. 500 on weekdays and Rs. 1,000 on weekends. The **Karnataka Golf Association (KGA)** (✉ Golf Ave., Airport Rd. ☎ 80/2529–8847) runs an excellent golf course near the airport. You will need to carry your handicap card and a letter from your hotel, and the charges are Rs. 1,000 plus caddy fees. The clubhouse serves excellent food.

KARNATAKA'S ADVENTURE TRAIL

DENSE FOREST OR LUSH **PLANTATIONS** cover many parts of Karnataka, whereas rivers flow down rocky, picturesque courses and hills rise out of the plateau abruptly. With relatively mild weather, this is ideal country for adventure sports of several kinds—from rock climbing and trekking to white-water rafting, canoeing, and angling. The coast offers scuba diving off the island of Devbagh and watersports in the backwaters of the Sharavati River. Near Bangalore, the rock formations at Ramnagaram and Savanadurga have long attracted serious rock climbers, and aerosports facilities at Jakkur offer a chance to fly microlight aircraft or try parasailing and paragliding. Treks through forested areas around Bangalore, Mysore, Coorg, and in the Western Ghats—along mountain paths or railway tracks, and through rolling plantations—can be very rewarding, not only for their spectacular scenic beauty but also for the chance to spot various species of wildlife. The trekking season is just after the rains, from September to January. White-water rafting is possible on some stretches of the Cauvery and the Kalinadi, while mahseer fishing in the Cauvery is a popular and nature-friendly sport (the massive sporting fish are returned to the water alive after being caught). Guides, equipment, and advice are available at a price from many adventure tour promoters (⇨ A to Z section). Karnataka has lovely, diverse terrain, from the emerald green coastline across the ethereal Western Ghats to the stark, uneven Deccan Plateau—and adventure sports is a great way of making the countryside come alive for you.

Go-Carting

Go-carting is an increasingly popular activity in India. All the major cities have at least a couple of tracks, and Bangalore is no exception. **Freeway 19** (✉ Gayathri Vihar, Ramanamarshi Rd., Bangalore Palace Ground ☎ 80/2279–7110 or 80/2361–1329 ⊙ Daily 10–10) costs Rs. 100 for five laps on this 750-meter track; double seater cars are also available for Rs. 150. **Speedzone** (✉ Hoodi-Whitefield Rd., Whitefield Village, 15 km/9 mi from Bangalore ☎ 80/2841–0867 to 68) is a good alternative if you don't mind the extra half hour beyond the city limits it takes to get there by car.

Horse Racing

Thoroughbred racing is a major sport in Karnataka. The **Bangalore Turf Club** (✉ 1 Race Course Rd. ☎ 80/2226–2391) goes into high gear from mid-May through the end of July, and November through March. Races take place every Saturday and Sunday afternoon (off-season races are only occasional).

Massage, Naturopathy & Yoga

Bangalore is fast emerging as a center for alternative health treatments and relaxation–detoxification packages. These are offered by a number of spa–naturopathy centers around the city. The **Angsana Oasis Spa & Resort** (✉ Main Doddaballapur Rd., Addievishwanathapura Village, Rajanukunte ☎ 80/2846–8892 resort, 80/2559–1945 sales), a subsidiary of Banyan Tree Hotels & Resorts, Singapore, offers Thai and ayurvedic massage in a lush resort. You can either stay at the resort (Rs. 6,500 a double) or book a slot for treatment as a visitor. Multicuisine and seafood restaurants are available on the premises. For stress management programs, ayurvedic treatments, yoga, and meditation, head to **AyurvedaGram Heritage Wellness Centre** (✉ 275 No. 2, JMJ, 100 Foot Rd., HAL 2nd stage, Indiranagar ☎ 80/2520–3194 or 80/2520–3195). One-day packages are priced at Rs. 950 per person and include a vegetarian lunch. Run by the Jindal Group, the **Institute of Naturopathy & Yogic Sciences** combines two drugless therapies—yoga and naturopathy. It also offers acupuncture and physiotherapy as treatment aids. Residential packages are available, reserve in advance. The institute encourages you to look at the Web site www.naturecure-inys.org for tariff information. (✉ Jindal Nagar, Tumkur Rd. ☎ 80/2371–7777).

Shopping

Brigade Road, downtown, is lined with flashy stores, foreign boutiques, and a number of multilevel shopping arcades. Commercial Street is a narrow, eclectic area packed with old and new shops selling everything from suitcase locks to Kashmiri hats to precious jewelry. M. G. Road is one of Bangalore's main shopping pockets, with government shops and some giant silk emporiums.

Antiques & Handicrafts

The state-run, fixed-price **Cauvery Arts Emporium** (✉ 49 M. G. Rd., Downtown ☎ 80/2558–0317) sells all of Karnataka's craft products: sandalwood handicrafts, terra-cotta pots, carved rosewood furniture, silk, leather work, jute products, lacquered toys, *bidri* ware (decorative metalware in black and silver tones), embossed bronze, soaps, perfumes, incense, and sachets. The **Central Cottage Industries Emporium** (✉ 144 M. G. Rd., Downtown ☎ 80/2558–4083 or 80/2558–4084) is part of the nationwide government chain of fixed-price cottage-industry stores selling authentic crafts from all over India. It closes every day from 2 to 3. **Natesan's Antiqarts** (✉ 76 M. G. Rd., Downtown ☎ 80/2558–8344) sells an unusual collection of high-quality stone, bronze, and wood antiquities; old paintings; and exquisite new artifacts, plus silver jewelry and precious stones. Offering several floors of artifacts, pottery, apparel, leather, jewelry and stationery, **The Bombay Store** (✉ 99 EGK Prestige, M. G. Rd., Downtown ☎ 80/2532–0014 or 80/2532–0015) is a pleasant place to potter around for an hour or two in search of gifts to take home. (Note this has no connection with the store of the same name in America.) Selling beautiful designer gifts and clothes, **Cinnamon** (✉ off Lavelle Rd., Downtown ☎ 80/2222–9794 or 80/2221–2426) is an exclusive (and expensive) boutique. **Mysore Handicrafts Emporium** (✉ Commercial St., Downtown ☎ 80/2558–6112) showcases handicrafts from around Karnataka.

need a break? A popular **Barista's** outlet is in the beautiful gravel garden at Cinnamon boutique (✉ off Lavelle Rd., Downtown ☎ 80/2222–9794 or 80/2221–2426). At the neatest of the **Java City** outlets you can watch life go by on the narrow, busy Lavelle Road while downing a coffee (✉ Lavelle Rd., Downtown ☎ 80/2221–5779 ✉ Cunningham Rd., Cantonment ☎ 80/2228–7746).

Books

Bangalore has about 10 large English-language bookstores. All have good bargains, but the best are on or near M. G. Road. **Gangaram's Book Bureau** (✉ 72 M. G. Rd., Downtown ☎ 80/2558–6783) is a four-story megastore selling books, CDs, cards, stationery, and toys. **Higginbotham's** (✉ 74 M. G. Rd., Downtown ☎ 80/2558–6574 or 80/2558–7359) is a quiet old bookstore dating to the colonial era. **Premier Bookshop** (✉ 46/1 Church St., Downtown ☎ 80/2558–8570 ☉ closed Sun.) is a small store crammed to the ceiling with books and owned by a friendly bibliophile named Shanbhag. At **Sankar's Book Stall** (✉ 15/2 Madras Bank Rd., off St. Marks Rd., Downtown ☎ 80/2558–6867) you can settle down on a sofa with your book. The **Strand Book Stall** (✉ 113 Manipal Centre, Dickenson Rd., Downtown ☎ 80/2558–0000 ☉ closed Sun.) has a wide selection of books.

need a break? Rs. 28 buys you a cappuccino at the **Café Coffee Day** (✉ Windsor House, Brigade Rd., Downtown ☎ 80/2559–1602 ✉ Lavelle Rd., Downtown ☎ 80/2224–8178 ✉ Bombay Store, M. G. Rd., Downtown ☎ 80/2532–0022). The tone is young and hip. Sandwiches and snacks are also available. **Barista's** (✉ St. Mark's Rd., Downtown ☎ 80/2229–7739) largest branch is in one of the delightful old stone buildings adjoining the St. Mark's Cathedral grounds. Try a Brrrista, a popular cold concoction served with or without ice cream and made of full-bodied espresso, milk-based granita, flavored syrup, and purified water.

Silks

A number of giant silk emporiums on M. G. Road sell top-quality Karnataka silk products, from solid-color material by the meter to bright, ornately hand-blocked saris and scarves. **Deepam Silk International** (✉ 67 M. G. Rd., Downtown ☎ 80/2558–8760) has been in business for 25 years. **Karnataka Silk Industries Corporation Showroom** (✉ Leo Complex, Residency Rd. Cross, off M. G. Rd., Downtown ☎ 80/2558–2118 ☉ closed Sun. ✉ Gupta Market, K. G. Rd., Downtown ☎ 80/2226–2077 ☉ closed Sun.), a fixed-price government shop, sells silks hot off the looms in Mysore. **Lakshmi Silk Creations** (✉ 144 M. G. Rd., below Central Cottage Industries Emporium, Downtown ☎ 80/2558–2129) has excellent silks. **Nalli Silks Arcade** (✉ 21/24 M. G. Rd., Downtown ☎ 80/2558–3178) sells silks of all kinds and some cotton clothing. **Salonee**

Silks and Cottons (✉ 8 Commercial St., Downtown ☎ 80/2522–1974) has designer silks, chiffons, and cottons. **Vijayalakshmi Silks** (✉ Blue Moon Complex, M. G. Rd., Downtown ☎ 80/2558–7395) is a reliable option for silk textiles.

en route | If you're driving to Mysore and would like an eyeful of Karnataka's folk traditions, stop at the **Janapada Loka Folk Arts Museum,** 53 km (33 mi) southwest of Bangalore. Displays showcase puppets, masks, agricultural implements, household articles, and color photographs of tribal life. There are also occasional live performances by drummers, snake-charmers, and gypsy dancers. A simple but excellent restaurant is on-site, serving rural Karnataka specialties like *ragi mudde* (soft-cooked balls of a local red-brown cereal called ragi). ✉ *Bangalore-Mysore Hwy., near Ramnagaram* ☎ *80/727–1555 local numberor 80/2360–5033 city office in Bangalore for Karnataka Janapada Trust* 💳 *Rs. 6* ☉ *Wed.–Mon. 9–1:30 and 2:30–5:30.*

MYSORE

❺–❿ *140 km (87 mi) southwest of Bangalore, 1,177 km (730 mi) southeast of Bombay, 473 km (293 mi) north of Madras.*

No longer the capital of the princely state of Mysore, this palace-rich city survives as the principal residence of the former royal family. The maharajas accomplished much in the way of arts and culture, developing palaces, temples, and schools, and supporting the traditional Mysore school of painting, with its slightly cherubic Hindu images and abundance of gold leaf. When you witness the fruits of their patronage, you'll understand why Prince Jayachamaraja Wodeyar (father of the current prince, Srikandatta Wodeyar) was appointed the first actual governor of Karnataka. Mysore had been known for its progressivism during his reign.

Mysore has been called the City of Palaces. You can explore its main attraction, the Mysore Palace, in a few hours, and if you can manage a stay in the Lalitha Mahal Palace Hotel, the simple combination of the two will make your trip to Mysore worthwhile. An evening visit to Brindavan Gardens is a nice way to experience the Indian fascination with kitschy but charming colored musical fountains.

Despite its opulent past, there's nothing flashy or fancy about Mysore, at least not in the modern, commercial sense. There are relatively few places to wine and dine, and the streets are lined with far more dozing cows than boutiques. The congenial climate and small-town surroundings, replete with leafy avenues, make a trip to Mysore enchanting. Here you can admire (and buy) some of India's richest silks, woven with real gold, and other elements of an age-old spirit of elegance that endures even as it deteriorates over the years.

Palace Area

Mysore is a small city, and its center is easy to walk around. Start your walk at the conveniently central **Mysore Palace** ❺ ▶. Exit on the Albert Victor Road side and turn left; then, at the traffic circle with the clock tower, turn right. On the left you'll see the entrance to the Devaraja Market. When you've had your fill of shopping, return to the clock tower and go back along the Albert Victor Road past the palace. At Hardinge Circle, turn right onto Lok Ranjan Mahal Road. A few more minutes will bring you to the **Zoological Garden** ❻. After strolling through the gardens, take a taxi to the top of **Chamundi Hill** ❼ for a beautiful panorama of Mysore. (It's at least 3 km [1.9 mi] from the zoo to the base of the hill, and the 1,000 steps are a killer). After admiring the view, walk down the hill's 1,000 steps and catch a taxi, bus, or auto-rickshaw back to the city.

Numbers in the text correspond to numbers in the margin and on the Mysore map.

TIMING You'll need at least five hours for this walk, and probably most of the day if you make it to Chamundi Hill. Except between the zoo and Chamundi Hill, the distances are not long. You'll probably want more than an hour or two at the palace, an hour at the market, and two or three hours at the zoo. Note that the zoo is closed on Tuesday.

What to See

❼ **Chamundi Hill.** Mysore looks its panoramic best from the top of this hill. The hill's 1,000 steps take you past a 16-foot stone **Nandi** (Shiva's holy bull), and the **Sri Chamundeswari Temple** on the summit is dedicated to the royal Wodeyar family's titular deity, the goddess Chamundi, an avatar of Parvati (Shiva's consort). The base of the temple dates from the 12th century; the ornately sculptured pyramidal *gopuram* (towering entrance) was built in the 1800s. Because it's still an active religious site, the entire area surrounding the structure teems with beggars and peddlers. The temple's inner entrances are staffed by aggressive priests hassling tourists into buying flower offerings and *bindis* (decorative dots traditionally worn between the eyes, for women). Tuesday and Friday, auspicious days, are the most crowded. In the middle of the parking lot stands a giant, colorfully painted **statue of Mahishasura,** the demon killed by the goddess Chamundi so that the region would be at peace; Mysore, originally called Mahishur, was named for him. The kitschy **Godly Museum** has gaudy paintings depicting eternal life and harmony. Walking up the 1,000 steps is an excellent but tiring way to see the hill; you can also take a taxi to the top. ✉ *Southeast Mysore, 2½ km (1½ mi) south of Lalitha Mahal Palace Hotel* ☯ *Temple daily 6–2, 3:30–6:30, 7:30–9, Godly Museum daily 9–6* 🎫 *Free.*

★ ▶ ❺ **Mysore Palace.** By far the most impressive structure in Mysore is the maharaja's palace, a massive edifice that took 15 years to rebuild (starting in 1897) after an earlier structure burned down. One of the largest palaces in India, it's on 73 acres and was designed by the famous Irish architect Henry Irwin (1841–1922), who was famous for practicing in India,

Brindavan
Gardens **10**

Chamundi
Hill **7**

Government
Silk Weaving
Factory **9**

Mysore
Palace **5**

Sri
Jayachamarajendra
Art Gallery **8**

Zoological
Garden **6**

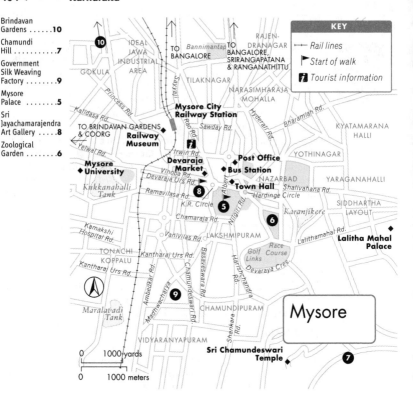

and especially for his project in the Indo-Saracenic style—a synthesis of Hindu and Islamic architecture. The main rooms and halls are a profusion of domes, arches, turrets, and colonnades, all lavishly carved, etched, or painted, with few surfaces spared. The halls and pavilions glitter with unabashed opulence: giant brass gates for grand elephant entrances; silver-plate doors encrusted with patterns and figures; richly carved teak ceilings; ivory gods and goddesses; a 616-pound solid-gold howdah (an elaborate seat, with a canopy and rails, placed on the back of a camel or elephant) in the first hallway you enter. The cavernous, octagonal **Kalyana Mantap** (Marriage Hall), where women sat behind screened balconies, exudes royal wealth, its turquoise- and gold-paint cast-iron pillars soaring up to a translucent dome of Scottish stained glass with brilliantly colored peacocks and flowers. A massive brass chandelier from the former Czechoslovakia hangs far below, above a multicolor tile floor. The **Durbar,** where public gatherings were held, is elegant and impressive, with a painted ceiling, turquoise Indo-Saracenic arches, and floors of white Italian marble inlaid, along the edges, with semiprecious stones. The smaller hall nearby, used for private gatherings, is gaudy—sky-blue gold-leaf pillars, a stained-glass ceiling, a chandelier, and general baroque excrescence—but there's some finely carved wood on the ceiling, marquetry on the main doors, and inlaid ivory on the side doors.

The present-day maharaja (technically a prince—the last maharaja died in 1974) lives in a private wing at the rear of the palace. The **Residential Museum,** centered on a galleried courtyard, displays the prince's entire collection of Mysore paintings as well as artifacts illustrating royal life of the past.

On Sunday from 7 to 8 PM and on holidays, the palace is illuminated with thousands of tiny lights that turn it into a glittering statement of wealth. Negotiate the price for a guide: Rs. 50–Rs. 100 is optimal. For the ultimate palace experience, time your visit to coincide with the annual **Dussehra** festival in September or October, commemorating the victory of the goddess Durga (also known as Chamundi) over the demon Mahishasura. Mysore is known for its intensely colorful Dussehra celebrations: for 10 days palaces and temples are illuminated and cultural and sports events abound, culminating in a torchlight procession led by an elephant carrying an idol of the goddess herself in a howdah of pure gold. Citizens, however, say that the procession is no longer as impressive as it used to be in the maharaja's time. Shoes and cameras are prohibited inside the palace. ✉ *Mirza Rd.* ☎ *821/241–8353* 🎟 *Palace Rs. 20, museum Rs. 20* ◷ *Palace and museum daily 10–5:30.*

❻ Zoological Garden. This well-maintained 250-acre zoo is more than 100 years old (founded 1892). Today it's populated by lions, white tigers, giraffes, African elephants, hyenas, kangaroos, rhinos, and a variety of other animals from all over the world. One section is devoted to reptiles and snakes. A small museum has models of rare animals and birds. Battery vehicles (a four-wheel car-like vehicle, similar to a golf cart, that you can steer) can be used to get around the zoo at Rs. 50 per head. ✉ *Indiranagar* ☎ *821/244–0752* 🎟 *Adult Rs. 15* ◷ *Wed.–Mon. 8:30–5:30.*

Around Mysore

a good tour

Hire a taxi for the whole day, or take auto-rickshaws from point to point. Start with a visit to the **Sri Jayachamarajendra Art Gallery ❽** ⌐. After a tour of the **Government Silk Weaving Factory ❾,** break for shopping and lunch. Finish with a trip to the **Brindavan Gardens ❿,** 19 km (12 mi) northwest of Mysore, in time for the evening fountain show before returning to Mysore for a late dinner. This leisurely day trip gives you some free time in the afternoon to have a relaxed lunch and shop for silks and handicrafts. Plan to spend at least an hour at each attraction and some time traveling between them; the gardens are about half an hour's drive away.

Alternatively, if you're feeling a more adventurous, hire a taxi and set off for Srirangapattana, a historic island on the Cauvery river. Spend the morning exploring the **Darya Daulat** (Tipu Sultan's summer palace), and the **Gumbaz** (mausoleum of Hyder Ali and Tipu Sultan). In the afternoon, head to **Ranganathittu Bird Sanctuary** and take a boat out on the Cauvery past nesting birds and crocodiles sunning themselves on the riverbank.

What to See

⑩ Brindavan Gardens. Extending from the side of one of India's largest dams, this vast, terraced garden is the pride of Mysore and a magnet for Indian tourists. The carefully manicured park is laced with long symmetrical paths and fountains. The profusion of fragrant flowers and the absence of cows and cars make it a peaceful place to stroll. At nightfall, scores flock to the far end of the gardens (a 30-minute-long walk from one end of the garden to the other) to see water spout into the air to the sound of recorded pop-classical Indian music and to pulsing colored lights. To get here, hire a taxi for the roughly 30-minute ride or take Bus 303–304 from the city bus station. (Either way, you still need to allocate a half-hour to walk to the end of the garden once you arrive.) ⊠ *Krishnaraja Sagar Rd., 19 km (12 mi) northwest of Mysore* 🖾 *Rs. 10, camera in gardens Rs. 20, camera at fountain Rs. 10* ☉ *Gardens, weekdays 8 AM–7:30 PM, weekends 8 AM–8:30 PM; fountain, weekdays 6:30 PM–7:30 PM, weekends 6:30 PM–8:30 PM.*

Darya Daulat. One of the few visual reminders of the brief Muslim rule of Mysore is set in a sunken garden on the island of Srirangapattana. It was originally used by Tipu Sultan as a summer palace and then briefly occupied by Arthur Wellesley (before he became the Duke of Wellington, in charge of the forces that, later, famously defeated Napoleon at Waterloo). Great green blinds protect the building from the daytime heat, and its interior is dim and cool. The walls are covered with frescoes dating from the late 18th century; the best-known is of the Battle of Pollilur, one of the Anglo-Mysore skirmishes. Invaluable period art, these frescoes give you a glimpse into the history and spirit of 18th century Mysore and the contest for power in south India, eventually won by the British when the island fort was besieged and Tipu slain in 1799. ⊠ *Srirangapattana, 1 km east of the fort on Srirangapattana Island and the Bangalore–Mysore Hwy.* 🖾 *Rs. 100* ☉ *Sat.–Thurs. 10–4:30.*

★ ⑨ Government Silk Weaving Factory. The late maharaja created this factory in 1932, both to ensure the finest hand-loomed silks for himself and his royal family and to arrange for some profitable exportation. Now run by the Karnataka Silk Industries Corporation, the slightly dilapidated factory continues to produce Mysore silks coveted by women throughout India. From spinning and soaking to weaving and dyeing, it's all done here, resulting in simple cocoons, crêpe de Chine, chiffon, and other regal fabrics. Accompanied by a factory official, you can stroll through the numerous giant workrooms busy with whirring spooling machines and clanking mechanical looms, and witness the transformation of hundreds of hair-thin, colorless threads into a sari fit for a queen. Ask to see the work stations where threads of real gold are woven into elaborate *zari* (gold embroidered) borders. Bring your wallet for a post-tour pilgrimage to the factory showroom. The silks aren't as sumptuous as those in, say, Kanchipuram, but they make nice souvenirs, and the prices are good. No cameras are allowed. ⊠ *Mananthody Rd.* 🕾 *821/ 248–1803* 🖾 *Free* ☉ *Mon.–Sat. 10:30–12:30 and 2–3:30* ☉ *Closed 2nd Sat. of month.*

Gumbaz. The bulbous mausoleum of Hyder Ali and his son Tipu Sultan stands on the eastern side of Srirangapattana island. After Tipu Sultan was slain in battle in 1799, the British accorded him a full state funeral. The mausoleum is an attractive onion-dome structure with pillars of beautiful hornblende. An exquisite palace once stood close to the gumbaz; it was razed to the ground and nothing remains on its site but trees and fields. ⊠ *Srirangapattana, 3 km (1.9 mi) east of the fort on Srirangapattana Island and the Bangalore–Mysore Hwy.* ⌦ *Free* ⊙ *Sat.–Thurs. 10–5.*

Ranganathittu Bird Sanctuary. This terrific little sanctuary consists of tiny islands and rocks in one of the most pastoral sections of the Cauvery. Pathways help you explore the sanctuary but to get a close look at the birds (herons, spoonbills, and cormorants), you will have to hire a boat. A boatride can be exciting as you might see crocodiles at very close quarters as they sun themselves on the rocks in the river. ⊠ *3 km (1.9mi) from Srirangapattana* ⌦ *Rs. 100* ⊙ *Sat.–Thurs. 10–5.*

▶ ❽ **Sri Jayachamarajendra Art Gallery.** Housed in the tired, 150-year-old Jaganmohan Palace, this slightly run-down museum displays paintings from various schools and periods of Indian art as well as beautiful antique inlaid wood, antique sandalwood and ivory carvings, and a variety of other decorative pieces. Some exhibits are truly esoteric, such as a set of carved-ivory vegetables and the amazing "rice paintings"—portraits painted on single grains of rice. The service of a guide is free, but most expect a tip. No cameras are allowed. ⊠ *Jaganmohan Palace, Dewan's Rd., Devaraj Mohalla* ☎ *821/242–3693* ⌦ *Rs. 15* ⊙ *Daily 8:30–5.*

Where to Eat

Mysore has a relative dearth of sophisticated dining options. You can generally dine well in the hotels.

★ $$$–$$$$ ✕ **Lalitha Mahal Palace Hotel Restaurant.** Here you'll dine in the maharaja's cavernous former ballroom, a baroque tour de force with stained-glass domes and sky-blue walls enhanced by ornate, white plaster moldings and pillars. Although the restaurant is multicuisine, it specializes in South and North Indian dishes. Try the Mysore *thali* (a set meal with rice and several regional accompaniments) or the mutton *ulathiyathu* (mutton cooked with coconut, red chili, and curry). There's live instrumental music (flute–sitar with tabla) at lunch and dinner. You can even shoot some pool on your way out. ⊠ *Lalitha Mahal Palace Hotel, T. Narsipur Rd.* ☎ *821/ 247–4266 or 821/247–0473* ▭ *AE, MC, V.*

$$–$$$ ✕ **Gardenia.** The Quality Inn's restaurant has a contemporary Indian look, with upholstered rattan chairs and brass candle-lanterns on the tables at night. The menu features mostly North Indian fare, with some Chinese and Continental options. The tandoori items are delicious: try *malai murgh tikka* (tender, boneless chicken chunks seasoned with Mughlai masala spices) with some *paneer kulcha* (bread stuffed with cottage cheese and masala spices). The Malabar fish curry (a north Kerala dish) and the *dhania murgh* (chicken curry with coriander) are also good. There's a buffet lunch. ⊠ *Quality Inn Southern Star, 13–14 Vinoba Rd.* ☎ *821/242–6426 or 821/242–7427* ▭ *AE, MC, V.*

$–$$ ✕**Elapur.** Specializing in spicy foods from Andhra Pradesh, this fresh, clean restaurant serves good biriyani dishes—chicken, mutton, or vegetable—as well as various curries, North Indian tandoori items, and an economical vegetable thali. Avoid the attempts at Chinese cuisine. The interior is contemporary, with plastic plants and colorful paintings of Krishna. ⊠ *2721/1 Sri Harsha Rd.* ☎ *821/244–2878* ▭ *MC, V.*

$–$$ ✕**Mysore Memories.** This comfortable circular restaurant serves multi-cuisine food, with some Indian specialties like chicken *methi malai* (chicken morsels in a cream and fenugreek gravy) and *koli* Mysore curry (Mysore chicken curry), and *bindi dopiaza* (okra with onions). The restaurant has functioned for more than 10 years and is an old reliable in terms of both the food and the hygiene. ⊠ *Kings Kourt Hotel, Jhansi Lakshmibai Rd.* ☎ *821/242–1142* ▭ *AE, DC, MC, V.*

$ ✕**The Roost.** This open-air restaurant takes advantage of Mysore's pleasant weather, and has a view of the hill. It serves tandoori food of the ubiquitous butter chicken-and-*naan* (bread) variety. This is a good place for a relaxed evening at a low price. ⊠ *Hinkal neighborhood on the Mysore-Hunsur Rd.* ☎ *821/241–0078 and 821/241–0077* ▭ *MC, V.*

¢–$ ✕**Green Hotel Restaurant.** At this superb hotel restaurant you dine outdoors in comfortable wicker chairs, around tables dispersed throughout the gardens, or in a sunny, white, high-ceiling, glass-enclosed terrace surrounded by plants. Befitting the setting, service unfolds at a 19th-century pace, so don't come here in a hurry. The food is excellent pan-Indian, including green curries (the masala used includes ground chilies, coriander, and mint) that live up to the hotel's name. The vegetable *hariyali* (vegetables in a green gravy) is excellent, and chicken or fish *hariyali* (kababs marinated in fresh green masala) are wonderful as well. This is also a quiet place to nurse a cool beer after dark. ⊠ *2270 Vinoba Rd.* ☎ *821/251–2536 or 821/251–6139* ▭ *MC, V.*

¢ ✕**Pelican Pub and Grub House.** Popular with Mysore's college set, this little eatery–pub is almost always packed. It's a neat place for draught beer (Rs. 22 a mug) and spicy, filling snacks. The chili pork is excellent. Don't expect a fancy place—it's mostly brick and stone slabs. ⊠ *25/B Hunsur Rd., Jayalakshmipuram neighborhood* ☎ *821/251–4031* ▭ *No credit cards.*

Where to Stay

★ **$$$$** ▣**Lalitha Mahal Palace Hotel.** Just outside the city center, 6 km (3.7 mi) from the Mysore railway station, the gleaming-white 1920s palace of the former maharaja—built to host his most important guest, the British Viceroy—is now a sumptuous hotel. The public areas are lavishly trimmed with ornate plaster moldings, huge pillars, and gorgeous domes; broad marble staircases rise and curve majestically up through the three floors. The best rooms are in the older section and have appealing, if not necessarily grand, Victorian furnishings. There are occasional reminders of the palace's age: the hot water and air-conditioning are not entirely reliable. ⊠ *T. Narsipur Rd., 570011* ☎ *821/247–4266 or 821/247–0473* 🖷 *821/247–0555* ⊕ *www.lalithamahalpalace.com* ⇆ *45 rooms, 10 suites* ⟁ *Restaurant, cable TV, tennis court, pool, ayurvedic* *massage, health club, hair salon, billiards, bar, baby-sitting, meeting room, helipad, travel services* ⊟ *AE, MC, V* ❍❙ *EP.*

★ **$$$** 🏨**Quality Inn Southern Star.** Opened in 1985, India's first Quality Inn property may also be its best. Some of the large guest rooms have floral drapes and bedspreads and coordinating pastel carpeting; other rooms are much darker and have a dated 1980s style. The cozy back lawn is surrounded by high hedges, removing it in spirit from the busy city road out front. Children love the cage of chattering parakeets and the tame white rabbits that hop lazily around the pool. ✉ *13–14 Vinoba Rd., 570005* ☎ *821/242–6426 or 821/242–7427* 🖷 *821/242–1689* ⊕ *www.ushashriramhotels.com* 🛏 *72 rooms, 1 suite* ⟡ *2 restaurants, cable TV, 18-hole golf course, pool, health club, hair salon, Ping-Pong, bar, laundry service, meeting room, travel services* ⊟ *AE, MC, V* ❍❙ *CP.*

$$ 🏨**Kings Kourt Hotel.** This three-story lodging is clean and new but lacks charm and historic appeal. The midsize rooms have modern furnishings in dark red and black, and small bathrooms. Those facing the back are quieter. A view of the greenery around town, including the imposing Chamundi Hills, is a plus. ✉ *Jhansi Lakshmibai Rd., 570001* ☎ *821/242–1142* 🖷 *821/242–2384* 🛏 *56 rooms, 3 suites* ⟡ *Restaurant, cable TV, billiards, bar, laundry service, business services, meeting room, travel services* ⊟ *AE, DC, MC, V* ❍❙ *CP.*

$–$$ 🏨**Green Hotel.** Once a palace, then a film studio, the Green Hotel is now run by a British charity whose profits fund environmental projects. Airy, charming, and largely sea-green inside, it feels like a Raj-era lodge, its Edwardian drawing rooms equipped with chess boards. Guest rooms have dark-wood furnishings, high, wood-beam ceilings, and in some cases kitschy film memorabilia; on the other hand, some rooms have no closets or wardrobes, and there's no generator back-up for electricity. You can choose from among the (fewer) palace rooms in the old wing, or the garden rooms in the new wing. While taking an auto or taxi to the hotel, ask for Premier Studio if the name of the hotel is unfamiliar to the driver. ✉ *2270 Vinoba Rd., outside city center, past university, 570012* ☎ *821/251–2536 or 821/251–6139* 🖷 *821/251–6139* 🛏 *31 rooms* ⟡ *Restaurant, croquet, badminton, bar, Internet, travel services; no a/c in some rooms, no room TVs* ⊟ *MC, V* ❍❙ *CP.*

$ 🏨**Kadur Inns.** A pleasant little hotel that calls itself the "inn to be in," this place is 5 km (3.1 mi) from the heart of the city on the Mysore–Hunsur Road. It's a good place to unwind after a long day's sightseeing, as the layout is horizontal rather than vertical—rooms are spread out in a garden, with no upper floors. The restaurant serves Indian and Chinese food. ✉ *Mysore–Hunsur Rd.* ☎ *821/240–2210 or 821/240–2840 to 41* 🖷 *821/240–2209* 🛏 *28 rooms* ⟡ *Restaurant, tennis court, pool, gym, billiards, badminton, lounge; no a/c in some rooms* ⊟ *MC, V* ❍❙ *EP.*

Nightlife & the Arts

Your best bet for a drink is a hotel bar or lounge. The **Lalitha Mahal Palace Hotel** (✉ T. Narsipur Rd. ☎ 821/247–4266 or 821/247–0473) has a sophisticated bar, with Victorian furnishings and a casual vibe; if you don't stay here, it's worth stopping in for a drink just to see the majestic building. **The Derby** (✉ Quality Inn, 13–14 Vinoba Rd. ☎ 821/242–6426 or

821/242–7427) has an equestrian motif, complete with saddle-top barstools and staff dressed as jockeys.

To find out what's happening in Mysore, check with the Karnataka Department of Tourism (KDT) and look for posters around town. **Kalamandir Auditorium** (⊠ Vinoba Rd. ☎ 821/241–5905) hosts theater, dance, ballet, folk performances, and classical Indian music. Admission is usually free or nominal. Classical, folk music, and dance performances are sometimes held in the **Jaganmohan Palace** (☎ 821/242–3693) or the Mysore Palace itself.

Sports & the Outdoors

Horse Racing

The **Mysore Race Club** (⊠ Race Course Rd. ☎ 821/252–1675) is a scene from August through October. Races are held approximately twice a week in the afternoon.

Shopping

In general, stores are open from 10 to 7. Mysore is famous for its exquisite silks, fragrant jasmine, sandalwood products—oils, incense sticks, soaps, and carvings—and rosewood inlay work. The main shopping area is along **Sayaji Rao Road,** beginning at K. R. Circle in the center of town, with a plethora of silk emporiums, sweet stalls, and shops and hawkers of all kinds. Most shops are closed on Sunday.

Antiques & Handicrafts

Cauvery Art and Crafts Emporium (⊠ Sayaji Rao Rd. ☎ 821/252–1258) is the fixed-price government showroom for sandalwood carvings, rosewood figurines, brassware, and other Karnataka handicrafts. **Mysore Crafts Emporium** (⊠ 70-D Devaraja Urs Rd. ☎ 821/256–4127), the largest handicrafts showroom in Mysore, has a good selection of very reasonably priced local sandalwood and rosewood products, as well as crafts from other regions of India.

Markets

Devaraja Market (⊠ Devaraja Urs Rd. ☉ Daily 6 AM–9 PM) is a bustling, old indoor fruit, vegetable, and flower market where you can immerse yourself in the vibrant colors and smells of Karnataka's bounteous produce. Stacks of glittering glass bangles and mounds of brightly colored *tikka* powders (decorative dots women press between their eyebrows) add to the character of this bazaar.

Silks

Karnataka Silk Industries Corporation (Government Silk Weaving Factory Complex ⊠ Mananthody Rd. ☎ 821/248–1803 ⊠ Visveshwaraiah Bhavan, K. R. Circle ☎ 821/242–2658 ⊠ Zoo Complex, Indiranagar ☎ 821/244–5502), the state body that runs the Government Silk Weaving Factory, has several fixed-price showrooms where you can buy or just admire the profusion of silks created at the factory. The factory complex has a "seconds" showroom where a limited selection of silks with barely perceptible flaws are sold at up to 40% off. **Lakshmi Vilas** (⊠ K. R. Circle ☎ 821/242–0730) has a large selection of silks and other fabrics.

Side Trips

River/Jungle Camps

Karnataka's rivers teem with fish and crocodiles, and fishing expeditions are becoming an important part of the state's tourist industry from December through March. The mammoth mahseer fish swim in the Cauvery River near Bhimeswari, about 100 km (60 mi) south of Bangalore and 75 km (46 mi) east of Mysore. Anglers fishing from *coracles* (round, basketlike boats) regularly hook mahseers weighing upwards of 50 pounds here, as well as smaller Carnatic carp, pink carp, and the good old catfish. The largest recorded catch was by an Englishman in 1992: 120 pounds. Catches can be weighed and photographed for proof but must be returned to the river. The Kabini River attracts fantastic wildlife and one of India's best wildlife resorts (also called Kabini) is built on its banks.

A dense jungle belt rich with wildlife lies close to Mysore; there are several options for a few nights out in the wild. Government-run jungle lodges are extremely well-run and offer tented accommodation as well as log huts, and such activities as trekking to white-water rafting.

WHERE TO STAY
$$$–$$$$

☒ **Cauvery Fishing Camps.** At this peaceful camp on the bank of the Cauvery River you sleep overlooking the river in basic, twin-bed tents with attached bathrooms. Simple, healthy meals, included in the room price, served in an open-air dining area around a campfire. Trained guides take you to the prime angling spots in Jeeps or coracle boats, but fishing equipment is not provided. Reserve three months in advance. There are two other camps that are a roughly 6 km (3.7 mi) trek along the river bank and a little farther by dirt road close by—upstream at Doddamakkali and downstream at Galibore (there's white-water rafting at the latter). Facilities here are more rudimentary and the camps, being less developed, are closer to the wild. ✑ *Reservations through Jungle Lodges & Resorts Ltd., Shrungar Shopping Centre, 2nd fl., M. G. Rd., Bangalore* ☒ *Bheemeshwari, Karnataka, 100 km (62 mi) from Bangalore, 85 km (53 mi) east of Mysore* ☎ *80/2558–6154, 80/2559–7944, 80/2559–7021, 80/2559–7024, or 80/2559–7025* ⊕ *www.junglelodges.com* ⇝ *Tents and log huts* ⊟ *AE, DC, MC, V* ⦁◯⦁ *AI.*

$$ ☒ **BR Hills Wildlife Adventure Resort.** The peaceful, pristine deciduous forest in this area—actually a wildlife sanctuary—is home to several species of wildlife from elephant and panther to bison and wild boar. You can take elephant or jeep rides through the forest or even explore it on foot with a guide. Accommodation is in tents, log huts, or proper furnished rooms in the maharaja's old bungalow. The best time to sight wildlife is November to June. ✑ *Reservations through Jungle Lodges & Resorts Ltd. Shrungar Shopping Centre, 2nd fl., M. G. Rd., Bangalore* ☒ *Bheemeshwari, Karnataka, 86 km (53 mi) southeast of Mysore* ☎ *80/2558–6154, 80/2559–7944, 80/2559–7021, 80/2559–7024, or 80/2559–7025* ⊕ *www.junglelodges.com* ⇝ *Tents, log huts, and rooms* ⊟ *AE, DC, MC, V* ⦁◯⦁ *AI.*

Sravanabelagola

If you have time en route between Mysore and Belur or Halebid, or you just want to take a day trip from Mysore, stop in this small town to see

★ the **colossal monolithic statue** of the Jain saint Gomateshwara, carved in AD 981 and alleged to be one of the largest monolithic statues in the world. Stark naked and towering 58-foot high, with 26-foot wide shoulders, 10-foot feet, and other similarly massive endowments, Gomateshwara is at once imposing and soothing. Once every 12 years, thousands of devotees congregate here for the Mahamastakabhishekha, a ceremony in which the 1,000-year-old statue is anointed with milk, ghee, curds, saffron, and gold coins. You have to climb 600 big steps to see the statue, but it (and the panorama, dotted with ruined and open-air temples and fields) is worth it. Another site worth a visit is the Chandragupta Basti Jain temple (on Chandragiri Hill, less than half a km from Sravanabelagola), which has 600-year-old paintings. ⊠ *84 km (52 mi) north of Mysore.*

COORG

Even in a state filled with beautiful districts, the Coorg district in the western part of Karnataka, and spanning about 4,100 sq km (2,548 mi), spans stands out for its lush rolling plantations and exciting wildlife. This is a coffee and pepper growing area, so part of its charm is its easygoing plantation lifestyle. The Kodava people are extremely friendly and hospitable, and the food of the region has its own unique flavor because of the plentiful pepper grown in the region and the special vinegar that is used in meat dishes. *Pandi* (pork) curry cooked in special vinegar is a specialty. Weather is great year-round, except for the monsoon between July and September. Coorg is a boon for trekkers; several established trails pass by dams and waterfalls, and, of course, plantations. Ask at your hotel to choose the most convenient trekking route. The main town is Madikeri (Mercara in the Anglicized British) but you're better off staying in the forest or plantation areas. Nagarhole National Park is one of the loveliest of its kind in the country. The Tibetan settlement at Bylakuppe and the elephant camp at Dubare are worth a quick visit.

Nagarhole National Park. The Karapur Forest of southwestern Karnataka has long provided India's now-defunct royalty—not to mention the world's zoos and circuses—with elephants. Many years ago, an infamous practice called *khedda* (wild-elephant roundup) was common, pitting swarms of skilled tribesmen against a herd of trumpeting elephants. Today, the kheddas have stopped, and instead of animals in terror you can watch wild elephants moving around the Nagarhole National Park (also known as Rajiv Gandhi Memorial Park), established in 1954 and spanning about 643 square km (400 square mi).

From Kabini River Lodge you can join a fantastic game-viewing tour—from your Jeep you might spot *dholes* (wild dogs), a massively muscular Indian *gaur* (wild ox), barking deer, *sambars* (reddish-brown wild deer), sloth bears, crocodiles, and families of elephants (mothers, calves, "aunt" elephants, and tuskers), and, if you're lucky, an elusive leopard or tiger. You can also glide around in a *coracle*, a round, basket-shaped boat (lined with buffalo hide) that's so slow and quiet that you can draw very close to wild animals and the abundant birds (more than 225 different species) without disturbing them. The best viewing times are early morning and evening from October through March. The area surrounding Nagarhole is home to the Jenu Kurubas (traditionally beekeepers) and Betta Kurubas, two tribes currently fighting with the government over the rights to this land, which they consider their historical home. ⊠ *Coorg region, between Kadagu and Mysore districts, 93 km (58 mi) southwest of Mysore, 08228* ☎ *8274/244–221* ⌖ *Rs. 175, video camera Rs. 200.*

If you have time, visit the large **Tibetan settlement at Bylakuppe,** with several monasteries—Sakya, Sera-Je, and Namdroling—and try Tibetan *momos* (dumplings) and *tsampa* (roasted ground barley). ⊠ *87 km (54 mi) west of Mysore, 3 km (1.9 mi) from Kushalnagar.*

★ The **Dubare Elephant Camp** run by the Karnataka Forest Department is a great place to spend a day in close contact with the massive mammals. A sort of retirement home for elephants, inmates are allowed to graze freely in the surrounding reserve forest. Mahouts round them up in the morning for their daily scrub-baths in the Cauvery and to check on pregnant and lactating animals. Visitors are welcome to watch bathing and feeding routines. The animals also show off the commands they can recognize—many of them are ex-loggers and can lift and stack logs symmetrically. Elephant rides are also possible. Refreshments are available at the century-old forest rest house. Reserve through Jungle Lodges & Resorts Ltd. (☎ 80/2558–6154, 80/2559–7944, 80/2559–7021, 80/2559–7024, or 80/2559–7025; www.junglelodges.com). ⊠ *15 km (9 mi) south of Kushalnagar.*

Where to Stay

$$$$
Fodor'sChoice
★ ⌗ **Kabini River Lodge.** Once the hunting lodge of the viceroy and maharaja, this resort within Nagarhole National Park, 93 km (58 mi) southwest of Mysore, is a charming combination of comfort and rusticity. The luxurious cabins are surrounded by colorful trees, and monkeys roam through the grounds. It's peaceful here, and you can have a languid daily routine. Long Jeep safaris or coracle boating are broken up by morning and afternoon tea on the veranda and hearty open-air meals (drinks are extra) with a variety of cuisines. You can also stay in safari-style tents. ⌖ *Reservations through Jungle Lodges & Resorts Ltd., Shrungar Shopping Centre, 2nd fl., M. G. Rd., Bangalore* ☎ *80/2558–6154, 80/2559–7944, 80/2559–7021, 80/2559–7024, or 80/2559–7025* ⊠ *Karapur* ⊕ *www.junglelodges.com* ⌖ *14 rooms, 6 cottages, tents* ⌂ *Restaurant, bar, travel services; no a/c, no room TVs* ▤ *AE, DC, MC, V* ⦿ *AI.*

★ **$$$$** ⌗ **Orange County Resort.** At this pastoral resort near Siddapura, 100 km (62 mi) from Mysore on a 300-acre coffee plantation, you can stay in luxurious country cottages and indulge in all sorts of activities (both adults and children), from trekking to indoor games to swimming. There are several types of cottages, some of which include living rooms and private splash (very tiny) pools. ⊠ *Karadigodu post office, Siddapur, Coorg district, 571253* ☎ *8274/258–481 to 86 or 8274/267–901 to 03* ⊜ *8274/258–485* ⊕ *www.trailsindia.com* ⌖ *50 cottages* ⌂ *Restau-*

rant, cable TV, pool, gym, boating, fishing, trekking, rafting, bicycles, badminton, ayurvedic center, bar, laundry service ▭ *AE, DC, MC, V* ⦿ *FAP.*

$ ▦ **Mojo Rainforest Retreat.** This idyllic retreat in a 25-acre organic farm, 120 km (75 mi) from Mysore, is in the Western Ghats. You'll learn about eco-friendly farming and get close to nature on guided treks and nature-watching excursions. At the farm, spices are grown using only natural pest control methods, and basic power supply comes from solar panels. The food served includes typical south Indian and Coorgi food, North Indian food, and some pasta dishes. The best time to visit is between October and May. Accommodation is very limited, so reserve well in advance. ⊠ *Mojo Plantations, Kaloor Rd., Galibeedu Village, Madikeri 571201* ☎ *8272/265–636 or 8272/265–638* ⊕ *www.rainforestours. com* ⇨ *2 cottages, each with 2 bedrooms* ⚘ *Ping-Pong, hiking; no room phones, a/c, or TV* ▭ *No credit cards* ⦿ *AI.*

MANGALORE & KARWAR

Mangalore

⓫ *347 km (216 mi) west of Bangalore.*

There's not much grand heritage in this coastal business center, but Mangalore is a mellow place to sample Karnataka's largely untouched beaches and jump on or off the deliciously scenic Konkan Railway (assuming you're en route from Kerala or Mangalore to Goa). Once acclaimed as Karnataka's port city and pepper center, Mangalore has ceded the pepper honor to Cochin and now has the low-pressure feel of a breezy seaside town (with some bustling bazaars).

Upon arrival, take a taxi toward Malpe beach. En route, you'll pass the temple town of **Udupi**, once home of the ancient Sanskrit philosopher Madhwacharya. Udupi is known for both its **Lord Krishna temple,** trimmed with gold, and its vegetarian restaurants, so it's a nice place to break for a cup of coffee and a *masala dosa.* Anytime except during monsoon (July–Sept.), from the quiet yellow sands of Malpe beach (5 km/3 mi west of Udipi) you can hire a boat to the rocky **St. Mary's Island,** where the 15th-century Portuguese explorer Vasco da Gama is believed to have landed before he stopped in northern Kerala, at Calicut, in 1498.

If you don't want to venture too far, head 6 km (3.8 mi) north out of town to spend the morning exploring **Sultan's Battery** in Boloor, a stone fort built by Tipu Sultan in the 18th century to prevent enemy ships from entering the Gurpur River. Lunch in Mangalore, and in the late afternoon, visit the beautiful **St. Aloysius Church,** to see its murals. A kilometer away is the garden on Lighthouse Hill, from where there's a lovely view of the Arabian Sea. This is a perfect spot from which to watch the sunset.

Snatch some time after dinner to watch some **Yakshagana,** an ancient folk form of dance-drama performed in colorful costumes and greasepaint. Usually a night-long program performed in open fields (now

THE RURAL THEATRE OF YAKSHAGANA

WHEN IN MANGALORE OR BANGALORE, don't miss an opportunity to watch a lively Yakshagana performance, Karnataka's own traveling rural theater form—a unique blend of dance, music, narrative, stage techniques, and traditional costumes. Said to have originated more than five centuries ago, Yakshagana belongs to the coastal districts—Malnad, Uttar Kannada, and Dakshin Kannada—where troupes of actors travel from village to village, entertaining villagers who gather from miles around to watch them. Although often described as folk theater, it nonetheless has strong classical roots. The focus is typically Hindu mythology—performance begins with a puja (a ritual and offering) and is followed by enactment of scenes from the Hindu epics. The folk elements include the music, the language, the cross-dressing (there were

no female actors, traditionally, and still aren't), and the frequent appearance of michief-makers and demons. Although the local language will be unfamiliar to you, it's still worthwhile to attend a performance for the sheer color and dynamism, the elaborate costumes, the make-up, the skilled and energetic performers, and the unmistakable humor. From the early 17th century when a poet refashioned the entire Ramayana to suit the Yakshagana form to the present day when troupes perform nonclassical acts as well (anything from an original Kannada drama to a play based on Chekov), this living rural tradition has prospered and grown over the centuries. The best time to catch a yakshagana is between November and May; performances are few during the rains.

often on stages), the Yakshagana involves robust dancing and mime; an interpreter tells a story drawn customarily from mythology and sings to the accompaniment of drums and cymbals.

Where to Stay & Eat

$$ ✕ **Hightide and Gallery.** At this watering hole you have access to some choice canapes. The wood paneling, cozy seating as well as efficient service can provide for a comfortable evening. If you wish to have dinner, walk across to the Galley, popular for its multicuisine fare, but particularly favored for the local delicacy: *kane bezule,* lady fish fried and curried. ⊠ *Taj Manjarun, Old Port Rd.* ☎ *824/242–0585* ⌾ *Reservations essential* ▤ *AE, DC, MC, V.*

$–$$ ✕ **Mangala Restaurant.** This cozy restaurant has brightly lit interiors and a quiet manner. The teak furniture and the plain cream tablecloths lend a formal look, but the place bustles with activity on weekends when families troop in. The menu has a wide variety of Indian, Continental, and Chinese food, although you'd be advised to stick to the Indian fare. ⊠*Moti Mahal Hotel, Falnir Rd.* ☎ *824/244–1411* ⌾ *Reservations essential* ▤ *AE, DC, MC, V.*

$$ ▥ **Taj Manjarun.** This is the best lodging in Mangalore, with a pleasant sea view and a lovely pool. The rooms, painted in light hues, are bright and cozy, and a bit breezy in the evening. The Galley restaurant offers both buffet and à la carte meals, and sometimes Indian and Western pop music. The Captain's Cabin pub is a nice, quiet corner for a quiet beer. ⊠ *Old Port Rd., 575001* ☎ *824/242–0420* 🖷 *824/242–0585* ⤃ *85 rooms, 4 suites* ⟂ *Restaurant, coffee shop, cable TV, pool, beach, hair salon, health club, pub, travel services* ▤ *AE, DC, MC, V* ⦿| *EP.*

¢–$ 🏨 **Moti Mahal.** A large courtyard and a swimming pool, shopping arcade, spacious rooms, barbecue, and discotheque—all combined with hospitable staff—make this a comfortable proposition. However, check your room to make sure that it isn't musty, especially just after the rains. Note that non-air-conditioned rooms do not have television, either. ⊠ *Falnir Rd., 575001* ☎ *824/244–1411 to 14 and 824/244–1416 to 20* 🖷 *824/244–1011* ⤃ *51 rooms, 24 suites* ⟂ *Restaurant, coffee shop, cable TV, pool, pub, travel services; no a/c in some rooms, no TV in some rooms* ▤ *AE, DC, MC, V* ⦿| *CP.*

¢–$ 🏨 **Summer Sands Beach Resort.** This budget hotel is an option if you want to be near the sea upon arrival. Only a third of the rooms have air-conditioning, so request one when booking. The villas, set in coconut groves, are cool and detached, and the Ullal beach is a treat—it's reasonably clean and quiet given that it's essentially a city beach. ⊠ *Chota-Mangalore, Ullal* ☎ *824/246–7690 or 824/246–7691 to 92* 🖷 *824/246–7693* ⤃ *75 rooms* ⟂ *Restaurant, in-room safes, billiards, travel services; no a/c in some rooms, no TV in some rooms* ▤ *AE, DC, MC, V* ⦿| *EP.*

Karwar

⓬ *262 km (16 mi) north of Mangalore; 100 km (62 mi) south of Panaji, Goa.*

If you have time to explore the country north of Mangalore or are traveling on to Goa, stop at the tiny port town of Karwar, unremarkable in itself but very close to the island of Devbagh and fairly close to Dandeli wildlife sanctuary. Three kilometers (1.9 mi) from Karwar, **Devbagh** is a small island just off the coast, where Jungle Lodges has an attractive camp set amid casuarina trees. Swimming and scuba diving are possible; one side of the island faces the sea and the other the mouth of the Kalinadi. **Dandeli Wildlife Sanctuary,** 117 km (73 mi) from Karwar, is a pretty forest reserve set on the banks of the Kalinadi; it's home to crocodiles and waterbirds that can be spotted from coracles on the river.

Where to Stay

$–$$ 🏨 **Dandeli Adventure Resort.** At this peaceful camp on the Kalinadi, you can watch wildlife to your heart's content or go river rafting, trekking, fishing, and camping in the forest. The best time to visit is between October and June. Accommodation is in tented cottages or proper rooms at the lodge. The US$50 all-inclusive package includes not only meals but outdoor activities. 🕮 *Reservations through Jungle Lodges & Resorts Ltd., Shrungar Shopping Centre, 2nd fl., M. G. Rd., Bangalore* ☎ *80/2558–6154, 80/2559–7944, 80/2559–7021, 80/2559–7024, or 80/2559–7025* ⊠ *Dandeli, 117 km (73 mi) northeast from Karwar* ⊕ *www.junglelodges.com* ⤃ *Log huts and tents* ⟂ *Restaurant, scuba diving, island trips; no a/c, no room TVs* ▤ *AE, DC, MC, V* ⦿| *AI.*

$ ☒ **Devbagh Beach Resort.** Tents and loghuts on Devbagh Island are a good base from which to explore the beautiful islands in the Arabian off the Karwar coast, to sail upriver on the Kalinadi, scuba dive in the estuary or simply laze on the beach. October to May is the best time to visit. ☝ *Reservations through Jungle Lodges & Resorts Ltd., Shrungar Shopping Centre, 2nd fl., M. G. Rd., Bangalore* ☒ *Devbagh, Karwar* ☏ *80/2558–6154, 80/2559–7944, 80/2559–7021, 80/2559–7024, or 80/2559–7025* ⊕ *www.junglelodges.com* ⤵ *Log huts and tents* ⚲ *Restaurant, scuba diving, island trips; no a/c, no room TVs* ▭ *AE, DC, MC, V* ❍ *AI.*

BELUR & HALEBID

Once flourishing cities of the 12th-century Hoysala dynasty, Belur and Halebid are now just fading rural villages. Both, however, hold some of the finest examples of stone carving in South India, called "the signs of a very confident Hindu culture" by writer V. S. Naipaul.

Hassan, an otherwise unexceptional town, is the gateway to the temples at Belur and Halebid—it's about 35 km (22 mi) away from each of the two, forming a triangle. Lodging options in Belur and Halebid are still few and far between, so you may want to base yourself in Hassan for a night or two.

To get the most out of the temples, hire a guide. You must remove your shoes before entering, so bring socks along on your visits; the stones can be painfully hot in the midday sun, particularly at Belur. If possible, bring a flashlight to see the temples' interior sculptures in full detail.

Belur

⑬ *192 km (120 mi) northwest of Mysore, 240 km (150 mi) west of Bangalore.*

Although in a lush tropical landscape, the old city of Belur is dusty and run-down, with only one vestige of its splendid past. Still a functioning temple dedicated to a Vishnu incarnate, the **Temple of Lord Channakeshava** stands almost as pristine as it did the day it was completed in 1119—103 years after it was begun by the Hoysala king Vishnuvardhana. Legend claims that when Muslim conquerors came to Belur to destroy the temple, they were so awed by its magnificence that they left it alone.

★ Carved of soapstone, the temple is shaped like a star to allow maximum surface area for carving: a total of 32 corners. Squat and flat on top, it sits on a platform of the same shape; to its left is a small prototype (without the ornate stonework), built just before the temple as a study. Inside, some 10,000 impossibly intricate sculptures ornament every possible surface, a profusion of gods and goddesses in all their varied aspects and incarnations—scenes from the great Hindu epic, the *Ramayana*, as well as hunters, dancers, musicians, and beautiful women dressing and adorning themselves.

In the center of the temple, the domed ceiling is supported by four pillars surmounted by sculptures of voluptuous women striking any number of graceful poses beneath the intricately pierced, scrolled, and scalloped stone canopies. The carving is so detailed that some of the stone bangles the women wear can be moved. ✉ *Free, guide Rs. 50 for 2 people* ⊙ *Daily 8* AM–*8:30* PM ⊙ *Inner sanctums closed daily 1–3 and 5–6.*

South of the main temple, a smaller shrine, the **Channigaraya Temple,** is worth a good look. **Viranarayana,** a Hoysala temple, has rows of very fine sculptures on its outer walls.

Where to Stay

¢ 🏨 **Hotel Mayura Velapuri.** This is a standard, government-run tourist hotel, low on frills but fairly clean. The big advantage is that it's literally on the edge of the temple complex, the perfect vantage point for watching the sun rise and set over this sacred site. The kitchen serves vegetarian meals, particularly South Indian thalis. ✉ *Outside temple entrance* ☎ *8177/722–209* 🛏 *12 rooms* ⚒ *Restaurant; no a/c, no room TVs* ▤ *No credit cards* ⦿ *EP.*

Halebid

🟙 *35 km (22 mi) northeast of Belur, 35 km (22 mi) north of Hassan.*

★ Halebid is a tiny rural village that was once the capital of the Hoysala kingdom. Dedicated to the Hindu Lord Shiva, the **Hoysaleswara Temple** was begun by King Vishnuvardhana in 1121, after the one at Belur was complete. It was left unfinished after 190 years of labor because the Delhi sultanates' attacks on it leveled its pyramid-peak roof. Like the temple at Belur, this one has a star-shape plan, but as a double-shrine temple, it has two of everything—one for the king and one for the queen. Moreover, the sculptors' virtuosity reached its peak here, leaving some 20,000 statues. The figures are carved in such detail that they appear to have been etched. You can see the taut fibers of the cord from which a drum hangs, feel the weight of the jewel beads dangling from a dancer's neck, almost hear the swinging of the bells around the arms of the elephant god Ganesh. At one time the temple also had 84 statues hanging from the ceiling near pillars; all but 14 were seized by conquerors of one stripe or another.

The breathtaking friezes wrap all the way around the temple: first comes a row of elephants for stability, then a row of lordly lions for courage, then convoluting scrolls of swift horses, then a row of people in sexual poses. Indian philosophy has always merged the spiritual with the social and cultural. Consequently, religious monuments were also cultural centers. Temple sculptures from around the 8th century often depict images of musicians and dancers along with dieties; in about the 10th century, erotic themes were introduced as well. The inspiration for this was based on the tantric thought of congeniality between spirituality and sexuality. Sensual well-being was deemed an essential ingredient of social life. Following the invasion of Islamic rulers, this tendency was curbed.

Above the erotic scenes is more scrollwork as well as scenes from the religious epics that present philosophical ideas and mirror the living conditions of the time. The largest frieze is also the most exuberant: here the *apsaras* (celestial maidens) are clothed in jewels, with bracelets on each of their several arms. Behind the queen's shrine (the one closest to the entrance) is a giant sculpture of Nandi the bull, Shiva's vehicle, with beautifully smooth features and a polished belly that almost seems to breathe. A small museum next to the temple displays various statues and brass and copper figures excavated from the surrounding area. 🖾 *Free* ⊙ *Temple daily sunrise–sunset; museum Sat.–Thurs. 10–5.*

A few minutes down the road, the smaller **Kedareswara Temple** bears more exquisite carving. The lovely friezes are similar to those of the main temples at Belur and Halebid, and executed with equal finesse. Here also stand two relatively unadorned early **Jain temples,** their finely polished black pillars as reflective as mirrors. Set on a low hill next to a lake, this is an attractive, peaceful spot in its own right. 🖾 *Free* ⊙ *Daily sunrise–sunset.*

Where to Stay

¢ 🏨 **Hotel Mayura Shanthala.** The rooms are plain and uninspiring, and the food is no compensation (ordinary South Indian and North Indian vegetarian fare), but this government-run tourist accommodation is near the temple and serviceable for a short stay. ⊠ *Temple Rd., Halebid* ☎ *8177/773–224* 🛏 *4 rooms* ⚒ *Restaurant, laundry service; no a/c, no room TVs* ▭ *No credit cards* 🍴 *EP.*

HAMPI

Fodor'sChoice ★ ⑮ In the middle of Karnataka and difficult to reach, **Hampi** (also known as Vijayanagar), the ancient capital of the massive Vijayanagar Empire, is the most awesome spectacle in the state. A ruined city of vast stone temples, elephant stables, barracks, and palaces, Hampi was the center of the largest Hindu empire in South India and a major point of confluence for both Hindu and Jain worshippers. Today the ruins are interesting from an archaeological standpoint as well as for their sheer beauty—stone structures rise out a boulder-dotted landscape made all the more beautiful by the winding Tungabhadra river.

Legend has it that the city, which is spread over 180 square km (70 square mi) in a rocky valley surrounded by rugged mountains, was founded by two brothers, Harihara and Bukka, in 1336. Some of the buildings, however, can be dated back 1,400 years. Hampi was a large, wealthy, and populous city, comparable to ancient Rome, for more than two centuries, until a league of five neighboring Muslim powers conquered the empire in 1565, and in the process destroyed the faces of the thousands of statues and sculptures that adorn the numerous temples. The city was looted and burnt for months, until it lay deserted and ruined. To see Hampi in its entirety, you should spend at least two full days here. Many of the ruins are open free of charge. Hampi is a World Heritage site.

Many people choose to explore the ruins by themselves, but you'll probably get more out of them if you hire one of the official guides who wait on the road leading into the still-thriving village of Hampi Bazaar. They charge about Rs. 450 for a full day. (Otherwise you pay separate fees for each site.) The best time to visit Hampi is from November to March; the rest of the year it's too hot or too rainy. Be prepared to do quite a lot of walking; vehicles cannot access many of the best spots in Hampi. Don't miss the opportunity to cross the Tungabhadra river in a coracle (people have been doing so for centuries) and explore the ruins of Anegundi on the other side of the river from Hampi—these are even older. Note that the ancient ruined city is roughly divided into two zones: the northern zone contains Hampi Bazaar and the Virupaksha Temple, and the southern zone contains remnants of the Royal Enclosure where the kings used to live. The distance from the Virupaksha temple in the northern part of the city to the Royal Enclosure in the southern part of the city is between less than 3 km (1.9 mi).

The ruins are spread over two main areas: in the north, near Hampi Bazaar, they center on the enormous still-used **Virupaksha Temple** (✉ Rs. 2 ☉ sunrise–sunset), the home of hundreds of monkeys and a hangout for dozens of children intrigued by the sight of foreigners. The ancient temple—devoted to the patron deity of the Vijayanagar kings—has some old musical instruments and an interesting inverted pinhole image of its own tower cast on an inner wall. Outside the temple, the street called Hampi Bazaar was originally built for temple chariot processions; today it's also the center of life in the ruins—guides, money matters and super-inexpensive accommodation can all be arranged here.

Half a kilometer south of the Virupaksha temple, two massive stone images of the elephant god Ganesha are amusingly—because the effigies are so large—named sasivekalu and kadalekalu (sculpted from a mustard seed and a grain of gram, respectively). Make sure you see the monolithic sculpted image of the glaring man-lion Narasimha (a quarter-kilometer south of the Ganesha), and the small Shiva temple that houses a huge lingam half-submerged in water.

About 2 km (1.2 mi) east of the Virupaksha Temple is the stunning **Vittala Temple** (✉ foreigners US$5, camera Rs. 25 ☉ sunrise–sunset), possibly the most rewarding of all the Hampi sights. This temple dedicated to Vishnu has an intact stone chariot and halls with intricately carved "musical" pillars that sound musical notes when the stone is tapped. Near the Vittala is the King's Balance, where the king's weight was measured every year against gold.

Climb **Matanga Hill,** 1 km (½ mi) southeast from the Virupaksha Temple at dawn or just before sunset for one of the best possible views of the ruins—from this hill close to the Virupaksha temple, you can see the spectacular ruins of the Achyutaraya temple complex, the Tungabhadra flowing through rocks and boulders, and the cream-color tower of the Virupaksha itself. There's a lovely little temple on top of this hill, but do not go up alone—robberies and worse have been known to happen in this isolated spot. And if you want to see the temple at dawn, remember that you'll need to hire a car to drive the 13 km (8 mi) from your hotel in Hospet.

In what's known as the Royal Enclosure area, a great stone platform is all that remains of the **Mahanavami Dibba,** from where the king used to watch the proceedings at festival time. About 100 meters to the south is an excavated **bath,** said to have been used by the king. It's fed by a raised aqueduct, and has reducing steps of sharply carved green schist. About ¼ km northwest of the Mahanavami Dibba, is the intricately sculpted **Hazara Rama temple,** where the royals may have worshipped in private.

About ½ km north of the Hazara Rama temple is a walled complex called the Zenana Enclosure, said to have been the dwelling of the royal ladies and their entourage. The Lotus Mahal inside is one of the few intact buildings in Hampi. Just outside the enclosure are the towering **Elephant Stables,** once home to the 11 elephants of the royal guard. On the road to Kamalapur, just outside the royal enclosure is the elegant **Queen's Bath.**

The smart and well-maintained **Archaeological Museum** (⌦ free ☉ Sat.–Thurs. 10–5) in the southern part of the ruins takes you through the (ongoing) excavation process and displays many of the weapons and cooking utensils found at Hampi, as well as some original temple statues. Snakes (some of them poisonous) hide in the museum's gardens, so be careful where you walk.

Where to Stay & Eat

Accommodations in Hampi itself are low-quality at best. There are several little rooming houses on the road leading into Hampi Bazaar, but for slightly more comfort, stay in Hospet, about 13 km (8 mi) from the ruins.

$ ✕ **Eagle Garden Restaurant.** There's a wide choice of chicken dishes, particularly Mughlai, at this restaurant near a canal, and the outdoor tables are fairly comfortable. ⌧ *J. N. Rd., Hospet* ☎ *8394/426–187* ▭ *No credit cards.*

$ ✕ **Manasa/Naivedyam.** This pair of hotel restaurants covers a few bases: Manasa has cool outdoor tables, good chicken dishes, and a bar, while Naivedyam offers indoor dining and spicy vegetarian food prepared in South Indian and North Indian styles. The background music (which emanates from Manasa but is audible in both) is an eclectic mix of Hindi film music and Céline Dion. ⌧ *Hotel Priyadarshini, 45 Station Rd., Hospet* ☎ *8394/428–838* ▭ *MC, V.*

¢—$$ 🏨 **Malligi Tourist Home.** This is the best accommodation in Hospet, considering it's the only one with facilities like currency exchange and travel assistance. It's fairly clean for a small-town Indian hotel, and the vividly colored furnishings lift the spirits. A multicuisine restaurant and a bar add to the on-site perks. Breakfast costs US$6. ⌧ *10/90 J. N. Rd., Hospet 583201* ☎ *8394/428–101* 🖨 *8394/427–038* ⇱ *136 rooms, 4 suites* ♿ *Restaurant, cable TV, pool, exercise equipment, bar, laundry service, travel services; no a/c in some rooms* ▭ *AE, DC, MC, V* ⎢⊙⎢ *EP.*

KARNATAKA A TO Z

To research prices, get advice from other travelers, and book travel arrangements, visit www.fodors.com.

ADVENTURE SPORTS

To organize adventure sports trips or camps out in the wild, you will definitely require the services of an agent specializing in this sort of activity. With offices in Bangalore, these agents are usually flexible and will tailor a package to suit your needs. They will also arrange permits where necessary. Book several weeks in advance, as equipment is limited and usually much in demand. Jungle Lodges & Resorts Ltd., the outdoor-activity branch of the Karnataka Department of Tourism (KDT), has rustic facilities in the state's protected wild areas. Professional guides can take you on jeep tours to wildlife-viewing spots or fish-rich rivers. Clipper Holidays runs general-interest tours, special-interest tours, and treks of various lengths, and can arrange for a minimum of 15 people at a time to have dinner with the former prince of Mysore at his own palace.

🚩 **Agni Aviation** ⊠ Hangar #2, Jakkur Aerodrome, Bangalore ☎ 80/2856-0060. **Clipper Holidays** ⊠ Suite 406, Regency Enclave, 4 Magrath Rd., Bangalore 560025 ☎ 80/2559-9032. **Jungle Lodges & Resorts Ltd.** ⊠ Shrungar Shopping Centre, 2nd fl., M. G. Rd., Bangalore ☎ 80/2558-6154, 80/2559-7944, 80/2559-7021, or 80/2559-7024 to 25 ⊕ www.junglelodges.com. **Ozone** ⊠ 5, 5th Main, 12th Block, Kumara Park West, Bangalore ☎ 80/2331-0441. **Woody Adventures** ⊠ 3rd floor, 12/A/1, Yamuna Bai Rd., Madhavnagar Bangalore ☎ 80/2225-9159, or 80/5113-6271.

AIR TRAVEL

All flights to Karnataka land in Bangalore, which is 140 km (90 mi) northeast of Mysore and 240 km (150 mi) from Nagarhole National Park (Kabini River Lodge). Bangalore has domestic flights to Bombay, Madras, Mangalore, Hyderabad, Delhi, Calcutta, Pune, Goa, and Ahmedabad, and international flights to Singapore, Sharjah (UAE), Muscat (Oman) and Frankfurt. Connecting flights from Bombay serve New York, London, and Paris.

🚩 **Airlines & Contacts Indian Airlines** ⊠ Cauvery Bhavan, K. G. Rd., Bangalore ☎ 80/2210-2635 Ext. 140 at airport for general inquiries, Ext. 141 at airport for reservations ⊠ Lalbagh, Mangalore ☎ 824/245-1047 or 824/245-1048 ⊕ www.indian-airlines.nic.in. **Jet Airways** ⊠ 1-Y. M. Block, Unity Bldgs., J. C. Rd., Bangalore ☎ 80/2522-7898 ⊕ www.jetairways.com ⊠ Ram Bhavan Complex, Mangalore ☎ 824/244-0694 or 824/244-0596.

AIRPORTS

Two pre-paid taxi counters compete in Bangalore's arrivals hall. Rates offered by the state government outfit are slightly lower than those of its neighbor, but either one will charge you about Rs. 150 for the ride to a major hotel. There's a fleet of metered taxis in the parking lot at the arrivals-hall exit, and the same journey with one of them should cost about Rs. 100, but it's still best to agree on a price before you begin. An auto-rickshaw ride into the city costs about Rs. 80, but it only works well if you have very little luggage and are not in a hurry.

If you're skipping Bangalore altogether, you can book a car and driver at the Karnataka State Tourism Development Corporation (KSTDC) counter in Bangalore's airport and be straight off to Mysore or beyond. Taxis and car services will also take you long distances, but you're likely to be significantly overcharged.

Airport Information **Bangalore Airport** ☎ 080/2522-6233.

BUS TRAVEL

The KSTDC runs three-day bus tours from Bangalore to Hospet. From Bangalore's Subhash Nagar bus stop, Karnataka State Road Transport Corporation buses leave every 15 minutes to Mysore. The journey takes just under four hours, and the fare in a luxury vehicle is Rs. 75.

There's no easy way to reach Hassan, the gateway to Belur and Halebid. If you don't mind crowds, take the KSTDC-run bus from the Mysore bus station: the ride takes three hours, costs Rs. 40, and leaves every half hour throughout the day. Once in Hassan, hire a driver for the day and expect to pay more than Rs. 400. The KSTDC and various private companies also run tours of Belur and Halebid, and you can arrange a private car from any tour or taxi operator in Mysore or Bangalore, going to Hassan/Belur/Halebid.

Local buses are frequent and cheap but decidedly not comfortable. On mornings and evenings you may see as many as 80 people stuffed into one bus.

Bus Information **Karnataka State Road Transport Corporation** ✉ Subhash Nagar, Bangalore ☎ 80/2287-3377.

CARS & DRIVERS

National highways connect Bangalore to Madras, the Kerala coast, Hyderabad, Bombay, and Goa. The best way to see Karnataka is to hire a car and driver. For journeys outside city limits, figure about Rs. 3.50 per km (the minimum distance is 250 km [155 mi], and for overnight trips a halt charge of Rs. 100 per night to feed and shelter the driver). Flat rates to get around within Bangalore or Mysore run approximately Rs. 450 for an eight-hour day, Rs. 30 for each additional hour. KSTDC's rates are slightly lower than those of private companies.

EMERGENCIES

24-hr Pharmacies **Al-Siddique Pharma Center** ✉ K. R. Rd., opposite Jamia Masjid, near City Market, Bangalore ☎ 80/2650-4591. **Hosmat** ✉ Infantry Rd., Bangalore ☎ 80/2559-3796 to 97. **Janata Bazaar** ✉ In Bowring Hospital, Bangalore ☎ 80/2559-1362 or 80/2559-1804.

Hospitals **St. Martha's Hospital** ✉ Opposite Reserve Bank of India, Nrupathunga Rd., Bangalore ☎ 80/2227-5081 to 84. **Manipal Hospital** ✉ 98 Rustom Bagh, off Airport Rd., near Leela Palace Hotel, Bangalore ☎ 80/2526-8901 or 80/2526-6447. **Mallya Hospital** ✉ 2 Vittal Mallya Rd., opposite Kantirava Stadium, Bangalore ☎ 80/2227-7979.

MAIL & SHIPPING

Post Office **General Post Office** ✉ Raj Bhavan Rd., near Vidhana Soudha, Bangalore ☎ 80/2286-6772.

MONEY MATTERS

ATMS Cash machines in Bangalore are clustered mainly around M. G. Road and Brigade Road.

CURRENCY Most banks exchange foreign currency and cash traveler's checks. Most
EXCHANGE Western-style hotels will change money for guests. The main branches of the State Bank of India, generally open weekdays 10–1, change currency and usually cash traveler's checks as well. You can also try Standard Chartered Bank and the State Bank of Mysore, which has a branch in the airport arrivals area.

🚩 Exchange Services **Standard Chartered Bank** ⊠ 14 Cunningham Rd. ☎ 80/ 2226-9797 or 80/2226-3701. **Thomas Cook** ⊠ 70 M. G. Rd. ☎ 80/2558-1337. **Weizmann Limited** ⊠ Center Point, 005-Ground Fl., 56 Residency Rd. ☎ 80/2559-5379 or 80/ 2558-2148.

TAXIS & AUTO-RICKSHAWS

The three-wheel auto-rickshaw is a convenient, fast, and cheap way to travel short distances on congested streets. Note that the rides are bumpy, and you're exposed to the breezes, which often contain considerable exhaust fumes. Figure about Rs. 9 for the first km, Rs. 5 per additional km. From 10 PM to 5 AM the fare is 1½ times the meter reading—note that meters are sometimes faulty. Very often, you can hire an auto-rickshaw for the entire day (eight hours) for around Rs. 500: bargain with the driver, and don't pay until the day is done.

In major cities, regular taxis charge more or less according to their meters (usually more), with an initial charge of about Rs. 80 for the first 5 km (3 mi). As a tourist, you're vulnerable to being overcharged, so agree on a price with the driver before setting out.

There are a large number of call-taxi companies now on the road in Bangalore. Have your hotel call one, or call one from wherever you are. In Mysore, you can often flag down taxis on the street. If that doesn't work, pick one up at one of the taxi stands throughout the city, or ask your hotel to get one for you.

🚩 Taxi Company **Radio Taxis** ☎ 80/2332-0152 or 80/2332-7589. **Garden City Taxi** ☎ 80/ 2343-7646 or 80/2343-4274. **Shakti City Taxi** ☎ 80/2667-9999. **Spot Taxis** ☎ 80/ 2551-0000.

TOURS

In Bangalore, the KSTDC is widely used for its car-hire service and its full- and half-day bus tours of major sights in Karnataka. Most tours are inexpensive and low on frills—the buses are aging—but they provide a concise, well-rounded look at what's important.

The Government of India Tourist Office trains and approves all official tour guides. Rates are low by Western standards (about Rs. 450 per eight-hour day, Rs. 900 for a trip outside the city), and the guides are informative and helpful. You can hire one directly or through most travel agents and tour operators.

Among the travel agents, Ambassador Travel Services has reliable cars and drivers at moderate rates. American Express Travel Services is represented in Bangalore by Marco Polo Travel and Tours. Sri Sathya Sai

Tourists, out in a residential neighborhood, is open 24 hours a day, 365 days a year. The staff arranges general-interest tours, taxi and bus service, and currency exchange. In Mysore, Skyway and Siddharta arrange tours within Karnataka. Seagull Travels arranges tours and changes currency.

🛈 **Ambassador Travel Services** ✉ 76 Mission Rd., Kasturi Complex, 2nd fl., Bangalore ☎ 80/2224-1516. **Seagull Travels** ✉ Hotel Metropole, Mysore ☎ 821/253-9732. **Siddharta Tours & Travels** ✉ Hotel Siddharta, 73/1 Guest House Rd., Nazarbad, Mysore ☎ 821/247-1102 ✉ Lalitha Mahal Palace Hotel, Mysore ☎ 821/247-4266 or 821/247-0473. **Skyway International Travels** ✉ 370/4 Jhansi Lakshmi Bai Rd., Mysore ☎ 821/242-6642. **Sri Sathya Sai Tourists** ✉ 433/30/1 10th Main 28th A Cross, 4th Block, Jayanagar, Bangalore 560011 ☎ 80/664-1140, 80/634-6340, or 80/665-4410 ✉ 92/1A KRS Main Rd., Gokulam 1st Stage, Mysore ☎ 821/251-3823.

TRAIN TRAVEL

The reservations office at Bangalore City Railway Station is open Monday through Saturday 8–2 and 2:15–8, Sunday 8–2. Counter 14 on the ground floor is reserved exclusively for foreign tourists, senior citizens, and people with disabilities. Trains to Hospet (the jumping-off point for Hampi) run overnight from Bangalore, departing at 9:30 PM and arriving the next morning at 7:40. You can also reach Hospet directly from the north; trains run from Bombay to Guntakal, in Andhra Pradesh, and from there local connections run to Hospet. Note that trains in this part of the country are very slow.

Mangalore is linked by train to Bombay, Delhi, Kerala (Trivandrum and Ernakulam), and Madras. The scenic Konkan Railway leaves Mangalore early in the morning for its northbound trip along the Karnataka coast, reaching Karwar after six hours (Rs. 80), Margao (in Goa) after seven hours (Rs. 100).

Several (air-conditioned) trains run between Bangalore and Mysore daily; the trip takes about three hours and the fare is about Rs. 200. The reservations office at Mysore Railway Station is open Monday through Saturday 8–2 and 2:15–8 and Sunday 8–2. The super-fast, air-conditioned, relatively expensive *Shatabdi Express* runs between Mysore and Madras via Bangalore (Rs. 400 round-trip) every afternoon except Tuesday. There's also a 24-hour train to Bombay.

In December 2004 the KSTDC plans to launch the Palace on Wheels service covering Bangalore, Mysore, Dandeli, and Hampi. The service will have lounge-, dining-, and entertainment cars. Jungle Lodges & Resorts Ltd. in Bangalore or the public relations officer at KSTDC (☎ 80/2235-2901) will have more information.

🛈 **Train Information Konkan Railway** In Mangalore ☎ 824/2423137, 824/2424002 reservations ⊕ www.konkanrailway.com. **Southern Railway** ⊕ www.srailway.com.
🛈 **Train Stations Bangalore** ☎ 131 general inquiries, 132 reservations, 133 recorded information, 134 after-hours arrival and departure information.

VISITOR INFORMATION

The Karnataka State Tourism Development Corporation (KSTDC) based in Bangalore provides information and reservations for its state-run hotels, tours, and car-and-driver hire. Hours at the main office are Monday through Saturday 10–5:30 (closed second Saturday of month).

The Government of India Tourist Office has useful information on the region and arranges private guides; the office is open weekdays 10–5 and Saturday 10–1:30 (closed second Saturday of month).

The KDT maintains an information office in Hassan Monday through Saturday from 10 to 5:30 (closed secondSaturday of month) offering advice on Belur and Halebid. In Belur, the small reception center inside the temple-yard entrance is open Monday through Saturday from 8:30 to 5:30, and sometimes on Sunday. The Tourist Information Center is a 3-minute walk from the temple entrance and keeps the same hours as the reception center. Government-approved guides, available at the temple entrance, will take one or two people through the sights for about Rs. 100.

The tourist office in Hampi Bazaar is pretty much empty, though it does have a few basic maps. There is, however, a Neha travel office on the one road through the village, as well as a sister bureau next door to Hotel Priyadarshini in Hospet. Theoretically, both are open Monday through Saturday 9–8, and both change currency.

🚩 Tourist Offices **Belur Reception Center** ✉ Inside temple-yard entrance ☎ 8177/722218. **Belur Tourist Information Center** ✉ Hotel Mayura Velapuri, Temple Rd. ☎ 8233/722209. **Government of India Tourist Office** ✉ KFC Bldg., 48 Church St., Bangalore ☎ 80/2558–5417. **KSTDC** ✉ Yathrinivas Bldg., 10/4 Kasturba Rd., Bangalore ☎ 80/2235–2901 or 80/2235–2902 ✉ Bangalore train station ☎ 80/2287–0068 ✉ Old Exhibition Building, Irwin Rd., Mysore ☎ 821/222–096.

KERALA

8

GRAB A FOOTSTOOL
to scale your four-poster
bed at Brunton Boatyard ⇨*p.439*

PEER AT CENTRAL KERALA
during a houseboat cruise ⇨*p.443*

LINGER IN YOUR TREEHOUSE
at the Green Magic resort ⇨*p.457*

SUCCUMB TO AN AYURVEDIC BODY MASSAGE
at Coconut Lagoon ⇨*p.444*

SHOWER WITH A VIEW OF THE SEA
at the Taj Malabar ⇨*p.440*

By Shanti
Menon and
Vikram Singh

A CHARMING MYTH EXPLAINS THE CREATION OF KERALA, the narrow
state running 560 km (350 mi) along India's western coast. Parashu-
rama, an avatar of Vishnu, performed a series of penances to atone for
a grievous sin, and the god of the sea rewarded his devotion by reclaiming
Kerala from the deep.

In 1956 the Malayalam-speaking states of Cochin and Travancore joined
with the district of Malabar to form Kerala. The new Indian state became the first place in the world to adopt a communist government
in a free election, an event that caused global speculation. Today this
tropical enclave between the western mountains and the Arabian Sea
is one of India's most progressive states, with a literacy rate of well
over 90%. Even in the shabbiest backwater toddy shop, where locals
knock back glasses of potent coconut liquor, you'll find a copy of the
day's newspaper.

The Malayalis make up India's most highly educated population; many
are conversant in English, Hindi, and Tamil, as well as Malayalam. In
the nearly three millennia before the 1795 establishment of British rule,
Phoenicians, Arabs, Jews, Chinese, and Europeans came in droves, attracted by the region's valuable cash crops: tea, rubber, cashews, teak,
and spices—most notably black pepper and cardamom.

Since Independence, people have begun using the place names that were
used prior to British colonization. The British had a strong presence in
Kerala, so name changes are particularly germane here; hence Alleppey/
Alappuzha, Calicut/Kozhikode, Cochin/Kochi, Quilon/Kollam, Trichur/
Thrissur, and Trivandrum/Thiruvananthapuram. Official maps and
tourist brochures reflect these changes but both the Anglicized and
Malayalam names are still commonly used.

Exploring Kerala

Outside of the historic, spice-trading city of Cochin, attractions are
rustic: quiet beaches spiked with palm trees line the west coast,
whereas the hilly eastern interior is heavily forested. Cochin (Kochi)
is the anchor of low-lying central Kerala, a region dominated by lazy
inland waterways, paddy fields, and fishing boats; the backwater
lifestyle is best experienced from the deck of a slow-moving boat. Further inland, you'll find tranquil tea and spice plantations as well as
two national parks. At Lake Periyar Wildlife Sanctuary, near Thekkady,
you can observe creatures in their native habitat from the comfort of
a motor launch. Rajamala National Park near Munnar is where you'll
find the endangered *nilgiri tahr,* a shy but sweet-tempered mountain
goat. The hills surrounding Thekkady and Munnar are lovely for
trekking, rich in waterfalls and birdsong. Southern Kerala is best known
for the beaches near Kovalam, which lie south of the stately capital
city, Trivandrum (Thiruvanandapuram). Undeveloped, conservative
northern Kerala is the state's cultural heartland; you can witness
some of the region's most spectacular festivals here. Kerala's Muslim community is concentrated in the north, and Christians in the cen-

If you have
4 days
Spend your first day and night in Cochin. The next day, head to the resort town of ⊞ **Kumarakom** ❻ for a two-day stay. Spend a night pampering yourself with an ayurvedic massage and great local food. The next day embark on an overnight houseboat cruise through inland waterways.

If you have
6 days
Follow the four-day itinerary, and then hire a car for the beautiful drive inland to ⊞ **Thekkady** ❾ or ⊞ **Munnar** ❿ for two nights and a full day in the hilly Idukki district. To view the wildlife in Thekkady's Lake Periyar Wildlife Sanctuary, take the 4 PM boat cruise or a more adventurous jungle trek. Scenic Munnar is Kerala's Switzerland, with the added attractions of wild elephants and the Rajamala sanctuary. Some travelers arrive in Kerala by car from Madurai, in Tamil Nadu; if that's your plan, visit Idukki on your way west toward the coast.

8

If you have
9 days
If beaches are your weakness, follow the six-day itinerary and swing back through Cochin to ⊞ **Lakshadweep** ⓫. Only about a third of these atolls off Kerala's coast are inhabited. A second option is to travel south from Thekkady to **Trivandrum** ⓬, Kerala's capital. Explore its sights and quiet lanes before heading for the mellow beaches, palm-fringed lagoons, and rocky coves near ⊞ **Kovalam** ⓭. A third option is to head for the rarely visited north to see the extraordinary Theyyam festivals of **Kannur** ⓯ and the sweeping vistas of the fort at Bekal, near Kasargode.

---

tral and southern regions. Many of Kerala's low-slung, modest temples restrict entry to Hindus only.

About the Restaurants

Eating out is a relatively new concept in Kerala, where the older generation views restaurants with a great deal of suspicion and the act of dining outside the home as some sort of tragedy. Most restaurants, as a result, cater to visitors and are often attached to hotels. (The word hotel, in fact, is often synonymous with restaurant.) This doesn't mean that visitors are denied the opportunity to eat an outstanding, authentic meal in Kerala. On the contrary, you'll often find the best (and most hygenic) food in the better hotels and resorts. The best places to eat in an independent restaurant are in the major cities of Cochin, Calicut, and Trivandrum, or the tourist hub of Kovalam.

WHAT IT COSTS In Rupees					
	$$$$	**$$$**	**$$**	**$**	**¢**
AT DINNER	over 350	250–350	150–250	100–150	under 100

Restaurant prices are for an entrée plus dal, rice, and a veg/non-veg dish.

About the Hotels

Many Kerala resorts make use of traditional regional architecture, from tribal-style huts to elaborate wooden manors. Heritage properties transplant or reassemble traditional teak wood homes, whereas others create new buildings in the old style, guaranteeing the survival of traditional carpentry.

In cities, most hotels have air-conditioning, but many resorts in less populated areas do not. Beach properties often rely on fan and sea breezes, whereas in the hilly interior, air-conditioning is quite unnecessary. Some buildings have no window screens, so if a cool and/or bug-free sleep is part of your plan, ask about both. Many resorts, even upscale establishments, don't have TVs in guest rooms. Outside of cities, power supply is tenuous. Most hotels have their own generators, but they take a few seconds to kick in. Don't be surprised if you're left in the darkness for a moment—it's unavoidable.

Most lodgings charge a 10% service fee, and the Indian government tacks on another 6–16%, depending on the facilities. In luxury places, count on paying up to 25% in taxes. You may be able to offset such fees with off-season discounts—around 50% during the monsoon season, from June to August. On the other hand, many hotels charge higher-than-usual rates in peak season, from mid-December to mid-January.

WHAT IT COSTS In Rupees				
$$$$	**$$$**	**$$**	**$**	**¢**
FOR 2 PEOPLE over 4,000	3,000–4,000	2,000–3,000	1,000–2,000	under 1,000

Prices are for a standard double room in high season, excluding approximately 20% tax.

Timing

Kerala's climate is sultry. For the best weather, come during the relatively cool season: between October and February. This is also a good time to see some of the more interesting festivals. March, April, and May are hot and humid, though the hill stations of Thekkady and Munnar are still pleasant. Heavy rains fall between June and mid-August, swallowing up most of the beaches and more than a few roads in low-lying areas, but crowds are at a minimum and hotel rates are slashed. Monsoon season is also supposed to be the best time for ayurvedic treatments.

Numbers in the text correspond to numbers in the margin and on the Kerala and Cochin maps.

COCHIN

1,380 km (860 mi) south of Bombay.

Cochin (Kochi) is one of the west coast's largest and oldest ports. The streets behind the docks of the historic Fort Cochin and Mattancherry districts are lined with old merchant houses, *godowns* (warehouses), and open courtyards heaped with betel nuts, ginger, peppercorns, and tea. Throughout the second millennium this ancient city exported spices, cof-

8

Ayurveda

A 4,000-year-old holistic medical science, ayurveda has become linked with Kerala, thanks to the region's tropical climate, its rigorous standards of practice, and its wealth of medicinal herbs. Ayurveda's goal is to preserve a balance between the forces and principles thought to govern the body, mind, and soul. Doctors prescribe treatments based on your constitution, and remedies usually take the form of medicated oils and herbal concoctions that are ingested or massaged into or poured over the body. Resorts throughout Kerala offer ayurvedic packages, from three-day general health and rejuvenation programs to longer treatments tailored to specific ailments. Ayurveda is thought to be especially effective for rheumatoid arthritis, back pain, and repetitive strain injuries.

Beaches

Pristine beaches studded with coconut palms have long been Kerala's main attraction. Kovalam, the state's best-known beach resort town, was nearly ruined by overdevelopment, but it has since been spruced up, and the main Lighthouse Beach is now quite pleasant for an evening stroll. For peace and quiet, and serious pampering, wind down in a secluded cove on the Arabian Sea near Chowara, a few kilometers south of Kovalam. Some of the state's most pristine beaches are in undeveloped northern Kerala, where facilities are practically nonexistent and the sight of a foreigner sunbathing still entertains locals. But come quick—a massive development project is underway near Bekal Fort in the Kasargode district.

Coconut & More Coconut

The Kerala table is eclectic, savory, and adventuresome. Rice is the staple, coconut milk and coconut oil are the two most important ingredients, and seafood is the star. In Fort Cochin, in the city of Cochin, you can buy a fish—just caught in one of the Chinese-style nets used in the region—have it fried at a nearby stall, and enjoy it al fresco. *Karimeen,* or pearl spot (a bony but tasty and tender white fish), is the favorite fish of central Kerala, found only in the backwaters.

Kerala's Christian communities are famous for their beef dishes, while the *moppillah,* or Muslim cuisine of north Kerala, features a variety of breads, such as thin rice-flour parathas and deep-fried eyelash bread. Also expect distinctive meat and fish preparations—rich beef or mutton stewed in coconut milk, bread stuffed with fried mussels, and savory *biriyanis* (rice dishes) with meat or fish. Vegetable dishes are plentiful—gourds, yam, mango, and bananas may be cooked or raw, in entrées and even desserts. Grated coconut and a type of sugar called *jaggery*—extracted from a native palm and not fully refined—are commonly used in sweets.

Kerala is known for *iddi appa,* or "string hoppers"—thin strands of dough formed into little nests that are steamed and served with coconut milk and sugar for breakfast or as an accompaniment to soups, stews, or curries. *Appam,* a slight variation on the theme, is a rice-flour pancake, thin and crispy on the edges with a spongy, raised center. Another specialty is *puttu,* a puddinglike dish made from fresh-grated coconut and rice flour, molded into a cylindrical shape and steamed.

Cruises

A slow ride on a traditional wooden boat is an exquisite way to experience central Kerala. These journeys can now be tailored to suit any budget. Simple canoes with bamboo canopies can take you on a three- or four hour trip through inland waterways and sheltered villages; a romantic houseboat allows overnight journeys in rustic style. The town of Alleppey is flush with tour operators, and nearly every regional hotel organizes backwater cruises of some sort. The Trident hotel in Cochin can book you a stateroom on the *MV Vrinda*, an eight-bedroom luxury cruise ship.

Festivals

January's Tiruvatira is a celebration of folk dancing and singing by young Malayali women. In Trichur (Thrissur), the Pooram and Vela festivals (March–April) are among Kerala's best-known events. Thrissur Pooram is an eight-day spectacle with parades of decked-up elephants, music, and fireworks. On the sixth day of the seven-day Arattapuzha Pooram, held at the Ayappa temple 14 km (9 mi) from Trichur, 61 elephants feature in the proceedings. In the north, Kannur and Kasargode are known for the extraordinary Theyyam (November–May), a religious dance of tribal origin in which participants in terrifying makeup and elaborate costumes are venerated by worshipers. The weeklong harvest festival, Onam (late August–early September), is celebrated with floral displays and snake-boat racing. In the Trichur and Palakaad districts, Onam brings Pulikali (or Kaduvakali)—men brightly painted as green-, yellow-, orange-, and red-striped tigers—to the streets.

Performing Arts

The traditional Kathakali dance-drama is performed by many companies in Cochin, at Kerala Kalamandalam near Thrissur, and at Aranmula's Vijnana Kala Vedi Cultural Center. In addition, some 50 classical, folk, and tribal dances survive throughout Kerala, many unique to a particular caste or temple. The graceful, swaying movements of Mohiniyattam, a dance that lies somewhere between Kathakali and classical Bharata Natyam, are thought to mimic the movement of coconut palms. Kalaripayattu is Kerala's native martial art; some believe it was exported to China along with Buddhism. Many hotels in Kerala stage cultural performances in peak season.

Shopping

Crafts include cups, vases, spoons, and teapots carved from coconut shells; baskets, floor and table mats, and carpets hand-woven from coir, the fiber made from the husk of coconut fruit; and sleeping mats and handbags made of resilient, pliable kova grass. Brass lamps, rosewood elephants, and lacquered wooden boxes with brass fittings—traditionally used to store the family jewels—are also common. The craftspeople of Aranmula, northeast of Trivandrum, make mirrors out of metal. Spice shops abound in Cochin and near the hill plantations of Thekkady and Munnar. If you want to stock up on fresh pepper, cardamom, and cinnamon, Kerala is the place.

---

fee, and coir (the fiber made from the husk of coconut fruit), and imported culture and religion from Europe, China, and the Middle East. Today Cochin has a synagogue, several mosques, Portuguese Catholic churches, Hindu temples, and the United Church of South India (a collection of Protestant churches).

Exploring Cochin

The city is spread out over mainland, peninsula, and islands. Ernakulam, on the mainland 2 km (3 mi) from the harbor, is the commercial center and the one-time capital of the former state of Cochin. Man-made Willingdon Island, the erstwhile home of the airport, was created by dredging the harbor. The beautiful Bolghatty Island, north of Ernakulam, is a favorite picnic spot for locals. There's also a government-run hotel in a colonial structure that was once used by the Dutch governor and later by the British Resident. In the historic Fort Cochin district, at the northern tip of the Mattancherry peninsula, houses often recall Tudor manors; some have been converted to hotels, others remain in the hands of the venerable tea and trading companies. The Mattancherry district, on the peninsula, is also where you'll find the city's dwindling Jewish community (in a tiny neighborhood called Jewtown, around the synagogue) along with Fort Cochin to the northwest, the city's historic center.

Traffic on land and the city's many bridges can be abominable. Private launches and small ferries zip through the waterways, making the journey as enjoyable as the destination.

Numbers in the text correspond to numbers in the margin and on the Cochin map.

a good tour

The sleepy, tree-lined streets of Fort Cochin are perfect for a leisurely stroll. Start at the **St. Francis Church** ❶ ▶, where Portuguese explorer Vasco da Gama was once buried. Continue northeast along Church Street, passing colonial bungalows, to Vasco da Gama Square and the famed **Chinese fishing nets** ❷. Follow River Road along the sea front past more colonial buildings. Take a right opposite the Kathakali Center, walk alongside the small park and you'll hit tiny Princess Street—one of the first streets built in Fort Cochin, it's now crammed with shops, tour agencies, and modest European residences. The next major intersection is at Bastion Road. Take a left here and you'll soon see **Santa Cruz Cathedral** ❸ on your right. From here, hop an autorickshaw to Mattancherry and visit the **Dutch Palace** ❹. When you exit, take a right and follow the road as it turns a corner. The **Pepper Exchange** is on your right. Step inside for a glimpse of local commerce in action. Turn right again and you'll reach the **Synagogue** ❺. In the afternoon browse in the antiques and spice shops that line Jew Town Road, or head back north to the jetty and catch a ferry to Ernakulam for shopping on Mahatma Gandhi (M. G.) Road.

TIMING You can see Fort Cochin and Mattancherry in half a day. Remember that all houses of worship close for a few hours around lunchtime. The Dutch Palace is closed on Friday, the synagogue is closed to visitors on Saturday, and many shops are closed on Sunday.

What to See

❷ **Chinese Fishing Nets.** The precarious-looking bamboo and wood structures hovering like cranes over the waterfront are Cochin's famous Chinese fishing nets. Although they've become identified with the city, they're used throughout central Kerala. Thought to have been introduced by Chinese traders in the 14th century, the nets and their catch are easily accessible

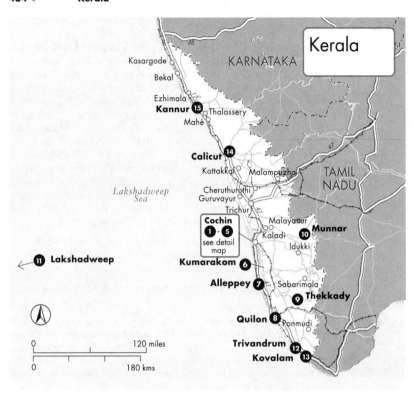

from at Fort Cochin's Vasco da Gama Square. You can watch the fishermen haul up the nets around 6 AM, 11 AM, and 4 PM. They're particularly
striking at sunset or at any time when viewed from the deck of a boat.

4 **Dutch Palace.** Built by the Portuguese in the mid-16th century, this structure was taken over in 1663 by the Dutch, who made some additions
before presenting it to the Rajas of Cochin. The rajas, in turn, added
some of India's best mythological murals—the entire story of the *Ramayana* is told on the walls in a series of bedchambers, which also have
inviting window seats. In the ladies' ground-floor chamber, you can see
a colorful, mildly erotic depiction of Lord Krishna with his female devotees. The coronation hall near the entrance holds portraits and some of
the rajas artifacts, including a fantastic palanquin covered in red wool.
The palace has rare, traditional Kerala flooring, which looks like polished black marble but is actually a mix of burned coconut shells, charcoal, lime, plant juices, and egg whites. ⊠ *Palace Rd., Mattancherry* ☎ *No
phone* 🎟 *Rs. 2* ☉ *Sat.–Thurs. 10–5.*

**need a
break?**

A favorite artists' hangout, Fort Cochin's **Kashi Art Cafe** (⊠ Burgher
St. ☎ 484/221–6769) is about as funky as Kerala gets. The front
room hosts rotating exhibitions, primarily of South Indian

contemporary art, and light Continental fare and Western-style coffee is served in the garden café at the rear. The real treat is to experience this tiny little pocket of Kerala subculture.

▶ ❶ **St. Francis Church.** The Portuguese flag first appeared in Fort Cochin in 1500, and Vasco da Gama arrived in 1502. The following year, Afonso de Albuquerque came with half a dozen ships full of settlers—he built the fort, and five friars in the crowd built India's first European church, St. Francis, in 1510. Da Gama returned in 1524 as Portuguese viceroy of the Indies, died that same year, and was buried in this church. You can still visit his gravestone, but his remains were shipped back to Lisbon in 1538.

The church's history reflects the European struggle for colonial turf in India. It was a Catholic church until 1664, when it became a Dutch Reform church; it later became Anglican (1804–1947) and is now part of the Church of South India. Inside are beautifully engraved Dutch and Portuguese tombstones and the *doep boek,* a register of baptisms and marriages between 1751 and 1894 where you can view in photographic reproduction (the original is too fragile). ☒ *Church St., between Parade Rd. and Bastion Rd., Fort Cochin* ☉ *Daily sunrise–sunset.*

❸ **Santa Cruz Cathedral.** The interior of this cathedral is full of turquoise and yellow tiles that some would call flamboyant, others downright gaudy. The cathedral's history dates from the 16th century, but the current structure was completed in 1904. ☒ *Parade and K. B. Jacob Rds., Fort Cochin* ☉ *Daily sunrise–sunset.*

★ ❺ **Synagogue.** The first migration of Jews to Kerala is thought to have taken place in the 6th century BC, followed by a much larger wave in the 1st century AD, when Jews fleeing Roman persecution in Jerusalem settled at Cranganore (on the coast about 26 km [16 mi] north of Cochin). In the 4th century, the local king promised the Jews perpetual protection, and the colony flourished, serving as a haven for Jews from the Middle East and, in later centuries, Europe. When the Portuguese leader Afonso de Albuquerque discovered the Jews near Cochin in the 16th century, however, he destroyed their community, having received permission from his king to "exterminate them one by one." Muslim anti-Semitism flared up as well. The Jews rebuilt in Mattancherry but were able to live without fear only after the less-belligerent Dutch took control in 1663.

This synagogue was built in 1568 and was considerably embellished in the mid-18th century by a wealthy trader, Ezekiel Rahabi. He had the clock tower built and the floor paved with 1,100 hand-painted, blue-and-white Chinese tiles—each one different. Like the facade, the interior is white with blue trim, embellished with hanging glass lamps from Belgium and a chandelier from Italy; look up at the ladies' gallery for an eye-pleasing row of colored lamps. Ask to see the 200-year-old sheepskin Torah page, kept behind closed doors. The synagogue's most important relics—the impressive copper plates recording the 4th-century decree in which King Bhaskara Ravi Varma guaranteed the Jewish settlers domain over Cranganore—are no longer available for public view-

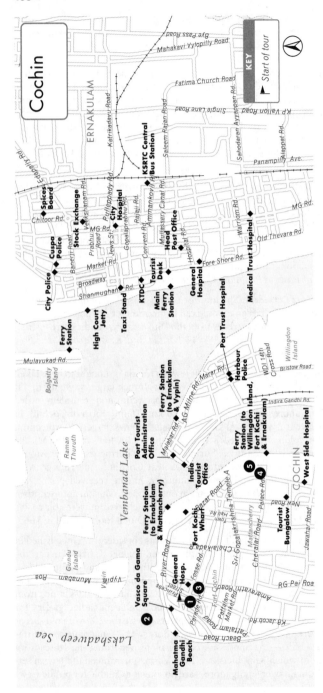

Cochin

ERNAKULAN

Bye Pass Road

Mahakavi Vylopilly Road

Fatima Church Road

KEY

Start of tour

▲ Start of tour

KP Vallon Road

Single Lane Road

Sahodaran Ayyappan Rd.

Panampilly Ave.

Edapally Rd.

Chitoor Rd.

Spices Board

Stock Exchange

Veks_hanam Rd.

Pulleppady Rd.

City Hospital

Katrikadavi Road

KSRTC Central Bus Station

Rajaji Rd.

Ammankovil Rd.

Muttassery Canal Rd.

Hospital Rd.

Cuspa Police

Banerji Road

MG Rd.

Prabhu Road

Jews St.

Gopalaprabhu Rd.

Convent Rd.

Head Post Office

City Police

Market Rd.

Broadway

Shanmugham Rd.

Tourist Desk

Fore Shore Rd.

General Hospital

Warriom Rd.

Old Thevara Rd.

Medical Trust Hospital

High Court Jetty

Taxi Stand

KTDC

Main Ferry Station

Port Trust Hospital

Ferry Station

Mulavukad Rd.

Bolgatty Island

Raman Thuruth

Vembanad Lake

Port Tourist Administration Office

India Tourist Office

Ferry Station (to Ernakulam)

AG Milne Rd. Marar Rd.

Malabar Rd.

Willingdon Island

WDI 14th Cross Road

Bristow Road

Harbour Police

Indira Gandhi Rd.

Ferry Station (to Willingdon Island, Fort Kochi & Ernakulam)

West Side Hospital

COCHIN

5

4

Ferry Station (to Ernakulam & Mattancherry)

River Road

Fort Kochi Wharf

Bazar Road

Chelakkada P

Sri Gopalakrishna Temple A

Town Hall Rd.

Fort Cochin

Mattancherry

Cherlai Road

Palace Road

New Road

Tourist Bungalow

Jawahar Road

Gundu Island

Munabam Roa

Vypin

Princess Street

Fosse Rd.

General Hosp.

Parade Rd.

1

3

2

Vasco da Gama Square

Amaravathi Road

RG Pai Roa

Pattalam Market Road

Kb Jacob Rd.

Beach Road

Pattalam Road

Mahatma Gandhi Beach

Lakshadweep Sea

Chinese Fishing Nets 2

Dutch Palace 4

St. Francis Church 1

Santa Cruz Cathedral 3

Synagogue 5

ing. You must remove your shoes before entering. ⊠ *Synagogue La., Jewtown, Mattancherry* 🕾 *Rs. 2* ☉ *Sun.–Fri. 10–noon and 3–5.*

off the
beaten
path

PEPPER EXCHANGE – The New York Stock Exchange it's not, but the Pepper Exchange does allow a glimpse into the world of spice trading. Monitors in a small room display the going rate of pepper, and men sit by phones in cubicles that line the walls. When a bid comes in, the yelling and finger-pointing starts. Then, just as suddenly, everyone goes back to reading the newspaper. You must obtain a visitor's pass from the secretary and remove your shoes before entering. The Pepper Exchange is between the Dutch Palace and the Synagogue. ⊠ *Jewtown Rd., Mattancherry* 🕾 *No phone* 🖃 *Free* ☉ *Weekdays 9–4.*

Where to Stay & Eat

As Kerala's premier city, Cochin offers the most options for dining out. Many top hotels open outdoor seafood grills in season (November to February), where you can pick from the day's catch and have it prepared as you like. Try *karimeen*, a bony but delicious local fish found only in central Kerala, and keep an eye out for unusual Portuguese-influenced dishes. Many hotel restaurants feature live music during peak season.

Commercial Ernakulam hosts mainly business travelers, in addition to tourists. Accommodations on the islands are quieter and more scenic; friendly budget hotels and historic mansions are a specialty of Fort Cochin. Willingdon Island, after losing the airport, feels a little deserted, but hotels have adjusted their prices accordingly, making for good values. The location is also convenient, sandwiched between Fort Cochin and the mainland Ernakulam district.

$$$$
Fodor$Choice
★

✕ **The History.** The intriguing, intensively researched menu draws on the myriad international influences on Cochin's history. Alongside traditional fare you'll find unusual preparations bearing the stamp of the Middle East, Portugal, the local Jewish community, or the days of the British Raj. The lofty, elegant dining room is windowed on all sides, and capped with a gabled wooden roof that's supported by massive wood beams—it looks like a ship has been overturned to form the ceiling. ⊠ *Brunton Boatyard hotel, River Rd., Fort Cochin* 🕾 *484/221–5461* 🖃 *AE, DC, MC, V.*

★ **$$$$**

✕ **Malabar Junction.** The mix of regional specialties and Mediterranean cuisine at this quirky restaurant isn't as crazy as it sounds—most dishes veer closer to one side or the other. A tasty red snapper fillet, for instance, is flavored with garlic and olives. If you're craving Western food, the pastas are excellent. Seafood is always fresh and perfectly cooked. ⊠ *The Malabar House, 1/268–1/269 Parade Rd., Fort Cochin* 🕾 *484/ 221–6666* 🖃 *AE, MC, V.*

★ **$$$$**

✕ **Rice Boats.** This perennial favorite of Cochin's well-to-do was undergoing a major revamp at this writing. The essence of the place remains—you dine in a traditional wooden boat on the waterfront—but the decor, while still ethnic, is a bit more posh. The updated menu continues to focus on seafood and Kerala specialties, but with a more refined presentation and attention to detail. The showpiece is an interactive kitchen where you can chat with the chef as he prepares your meal. ☒ *Taj Malabar Hotel, Malabar Rd., Willingdon Island* ☎ *484/266–6811* ▭ *AE, DC, MC, V* ⊘ *No lunch.*

$$$$ ✕ **Thai Pavilion.** Don't be surprised if your waiter explains each dish to you upon presentation—this is, after all, Kerala's first Thai restaurant. The menu features plentiful seafood offerings and is reasonably authentic, though some dishes are on the sweet side. The *pla rad prik* is a very soft fish, nicely flavored with basil; the spicy classic *tom yam goong* soup doesn't disappoint. The dining room is done up in warm woods, with silver accents on the ceiling and chairs. Beveled glass windows afford a glimpse of the sea. ☒ *Taj Malabar Hotel, Malabar Rd., Willingdon Island* ☎ *484/266–6811* ▭ *AE, DC, MC, V.*

$$–$$$ ✕ **The Renaissance.** The lunch buffet at the Avenue Regent's multicuisine restaurant is so popular that even visiting chefs pop in for a bite when they're in town. There's a variety of South Indian, North Indian, and Chinese specialties, but most people come for the hot, fresh, perfectly prepared appam—served with a mildly spicy coconut stew. ☒ *Avenue Regent hotel, 39/206 M. G. Rd., Ernakulam* ☎ *484/237–7977, 484/237–7688, or 484/237–7088.*

★ **$$** ✕ **The Fort House.** Despite being housed in a budget hotel, this simple, open-air restaurant doesn't skimp on quality or authenticity. The menu is almost entirely seafood—but chicken and specialty items (like lobster) must be ordered in advance. Every dish is cooked to order and presented in a clay vessel. The Prawns Kerala–fried and the braised seerfish are terrific. If you agonize over oil, tell the chef in advance. ☒ *2/6 A Calvathi Rd., Fort Cochin* ☎ *484/221-7103 or 484/221-7066* ▭ *MC, V.*

$–$$ ✕ **Pandhal.** Surrounded by rough white-stucco walls, sheltered by a pine ceiling, and calmed by a waterfall, you can partake of a variety of seafood, steak, Chinese, and Indian dishes. The restaurant gets crowded in the evening. ☒ *M. G. Rd., Ernakulam* ☎ *484/236-7759* ⌖ *Reservations essential* ▭ *AE, DC, MC, V.*

¢–$$ ✕ **Pavilion.** In an out-of-the-way hotel south of Mattancherry, this extremely ordinary-looking restaurant is a well-kept secret. Ignore the multicultural cuisine and go straight for a fish dish like the prawn curry or the *meen pollichathu,* spiced fish steamed in a banana leaf; it's so hot even Malayalees break a sweat. If you'd like it toned down, tell the chef beforehand. ☒ *Hotel Abad, near intersection of Moulana Azad Rd. and Kochangadi Rd., Chullickal* ☎ *484/222-8211* ▭ *AE, DC, MC, V.*

¢ ✕ **Fry's Village Restaurant.** Here four plain pavilions with bamboo curtains suffice to screen out the city's bustle. Lunch sees typical Kerala *thalis* (set combination meals), which incorporate such specialties as *molly* (fish fillet in a sweet green curry with coconuts) or the inexpensive *kadala* (Kerala plain curry) with *puttu* (steamed rice and coconut). Expect a crowd. ☒ *Chittoor Rd., next to Mymoon Cinema, Ernakulam* ☎ *484/ 235-3983* ▭ *No credit cards.*

¢ ✕ **Sree Krishna Inn.** Vegetarian meals and a pleasant, air-conditioned dining room draw in the business crowd to this handsome tile-roof building just off M. G. Road. The restaurant serves both North and South Indian vegetarian dishes and snacks, as well as a large selection of ice creams. ✉ *Warriam Rd., Ernakulam* ☎ *484/236–6664* ▭ *No credit cards.*

$$$ ✕▦ **Casino Hotel.** This modern hotel has rustic touches like coir carpeting in the hallways and tiny earthenware pots for bathroom amenities. Spacious, wood-floored rooms on the first floor have elegant interiors, with black marble bathrooms and wood-and-cane furniture; carpeted rooms on the third floor are not as well maintained, but have the best views of the leafy courtyard and swimming pool. The outdoor seafood restaurant, Fort Cochin, is immensely popular with locals. There's no menu: the day's catch is merely wheeled before you in a wooden cart, and your choice is cooked to order, whether you prefer it simply grilled or exquisitely curried. Make sure you reserve a spot in advance to eat here. ✉ *K. P. K. Menon Rd., Willingdon Island 682003* ☎ *484/266–8221 or 484/266–8421* ▤*484/266–8001* ⬎*67 rooms, 1 suite* ⚬ *2 restaurants, cable TV, pool, ayurveda center, laundry service, bar, travel services* ▭ *AE, DC, MC, V* ❍❙ *BP.*

$$$$ ▦ **Brunton Boatyard.** Built in a combination of Dutch and Portuguese
Fodor'sChoice colonial styles, this elegant hotel is on the site of a former boatyard, fac-
★ ing Cochin harbor's Chinese fishing nets. *Pankhas* (manually operated wooden fans) dangle from the open-air lobby's lofty ceiling. A gracefully bowing tree shades the grassy courtyard, which is surrounded by whitewashed arcades lined with terra-cotta tile. In the guest rooms, the four-poster beds are so high you need a footstool to climb in; the fixtures and furnishings are all antique in style, right down to the light switches. Most rooms have balconies from which to watch ships glide past in the harbor. ✉ *River Rd., Fort Cochin 682001* ☎ *484/221–5461* ▤ *484/222–2562* ⬎ *22 rooms, 4 suites* ⚬ *Restaurant, coffee shop, cable TV, pool, ayurveda center, laundry service, travel services; no room TVs* ▭ *AE, DC, MC, V* ❍❙ *BP.*

$$$$ ▦ **Le Meridien.** On 15 landscaped acres on the outskirts of Ernakulam, this imposing, green-tile-roofed complex houses a massive hotel and South India's largest convention center. The enormous lobby is appointed with colorful marble and massive bronze sculptures. Rooms are spacious, with light-wood floors and modern furnishings. Views from deluxe rooms are often gorgeous, with manicured lawns in the foreground and beyond to the tiered pool and the Chinese fishing nets. ✉ *Kundannur Junction, NH 47 Bypass, Maradu 682304* ☎ *484/270–5777* ▤ *484/ 270–5750* ⊕ *www.lemeridien.com* ⬎ *151 rooms* ⚬ *2 restaurants, coffee shop, cable TV, putting green, 2 tennis courts, outdoor pool, health club, hair salon, boating, 2 bars, ayurveda center, laundry service, business services, meeting rooms, travel services* ▭ *AE, DC, MC, V* ❍❙ *EP.*

★ $$$$ ▦ **The Malabar House.** Luxurious yet homey, this early-18th-century villa once housed European traders and bankers. A dramatic swimming pool, garnished with fallen frangipani, sits in the courtyard garden. Rooms are a mixture of regional-traditional and contemporary furnishings: yellow-and-red walls are offset by antique wooden furnishings. Somehow, the curious combinations of elements work. ✉ *1/268–1/269 Parade Rd., Fort Cochin 682001* ☎ *484/221–6666* ▤ *484/221–7777* ⊕ *www.malabarhouse.com* ⬎ *17 rooms* ⚬ *Restaurant, cable TV, pool, massage, laundry service, travel services* ▭ *AE, MC, V* ❍❙ *BP.*

$$$$
Fodor'sChoice
★
⊞ **Taj Malabar.** Isolated at the tip of Willingdon Island, this grand hotel offers a heritage sensibility and style, and absolute luxury. The lobby has a stunning carved-wood ceiling and a similarly styled bar with a harbor view. The Heritage Wing dates to 1935, and its rooms are appointed with wood floors and Kerala-style furnishings. The newer Tower Wing was renovated in 2003 to reflect a similar style, with the addition of large, windowed bathrooms, so you can shower with a sea view. The top-notch ayurvedic spa is worth a visit. ⊠ *Malabar Rd., Willingdon Island 682009* ☎ *484/266–6811* 🖷 *484/266–8297* ⊕ *www.tajhotels. com* 🛏 *87 rooms, 9 suites* ♨ *3 restaurants, cable TV, pool, gym, ayurveda center, massage, bar, laundry service, travel services* 🖃 *AE, DC, MC, V* ⏺ *EP.*

$$$$
⊞ **Taj Residency.** Standard rooms in this beautifully maintained downtown hotel are on the small side, and their bathrooms have showers rather than tubs. Opt for one of the large, sea-facing rooms, which have spectacular views. The North Indian restaurant features classical music performances every night. ⊠ *Marine Dr., Ernakulam 682031* ☎ *484/ 237–1471* 🖷 *484/237–1481* 🛏 *96 rooms, 12 suites* ♨ *Restaurant, coffee shop, cable TV, bar, laundry service, business services* 🖃 *AE, DC, MC, V* ⏺ *EP.*

$$$$
⊞ **The Trident.** Tasteful and stylish, this member of the Oberoi chain is outfitted for both business and leisure travelers. The low-rise, tile-roof building wraps around a central courtyard, so hallways are full of natural light. In the rooms, which face the pool or the garden, sand-color wood floors complement cream and teal color schemes. The staff is pleasant and helpful. ⊠ *Bristow Rd., Willingdon Island 682003* ☎ *484/266– 6816 or 484/266–9595* 🖷 *484/266–9393* ⊕ *www.tridenthotels.com* 🛏 *93 rooms* ♨ *Restaurant, cable TV, pool, gym, ayurveda center, hair salon, bar, laundry service, business services, travel services* 🖃 *AE, DC, MC, V* ⏺ *EP.*

$$$
⊞ **Fort Heritage.** Each room in this restored 17th-century Dutch mansion is slightly different from the next, though all are enormous and have towering wooden ceilings and period reproduction furniture. A new wing added in 2003 has been nicely done in a similar style. In the main building, ground floor rooms open, unfortunately, directly into the restaurant; upstairs rooms surround a common area with a giant wooden swing; a couple have balconies overlooking a courtyard. ⊠ *1/283 Napier St., Fort Cochin 682001* 🖷🖷 *484/221–5333 or 484/221–5455* ⊕ *www. fortheritage.com* 🛏 *12 rooms* ♨ *Restaurant, cable TV, ayurvedic massage, laundry service* 🖃 *AE, DC, MC, V* ⏺ *BP.*

$$
⊞ **Abad Atrium** This impressively modern Western-style hotel is set back from M. G. Road, shielded from traffic noise by its sister concern Abad Plaza. Abad Atrium caters mostly to business travelers, but in season it's popular with Indian tourists seeking luxury and value. Glass elevators shoot up and down the central atrium. Rooms are large, mostly carpeted, with high ceilings and full amenities. ⊠ *M. G. Rd., Ernakulam 682035* ☎ *484/238–1122 or 484/238–4380* 🖷 *484/237–0729* ⊕ *www. abadhotels.com* 🛏 *52 rooms* ♨ *3 restaurants, coffee shop, cable TV, pool, health club, ayurveda center, laundry service, business services, travel services* 🖃 *AE, MC, DC, V* ⏺ *BP.*

$$ ⊡ **Avenue Regent.** The spiffy marble lobby of this high-rise business hotel has art deco red bands around the ceiling molding and in the floor pattern. The carpeted rooms are spacious and contemporary. Request a back-facing room for relative peace and quiet. ✉ *39/2026 M. G. Rd., Ernakulam 682016* ☎ *484/237–7977, 484/237–7688, or 484/237–7088* ⊟ *484/237–5329* ⊕ *www.avenueregent.com* ⇲ *53 rooms* ⌂ *Restaurant, coffee shop, cable TV, ayurveda center, health club, laundry service, bar, business services, travel services* ⊟ *AE, DC, MC, V* ⦿| *BP.*

$–$$ ⊡ **The Old Courtyard.** Slightly decrepit but still charming, this late 18th century refurbished mansion in the heart of Fort Cochin has eight rooms overlooking a central courtyard. Premium rooms are enormous, with wood floors and ceilings, antique furnishings, and tub baths. Some rooms have air-conditioning, others fans. ✉ *1/371 Princess St., Fort Cochin 682001* ☎ *484/221–6302 or 484/221–5035* ⊕ *www. oldcourtyard.com* ⇲ *8 rooms* ⌂ *Restaurant, cable TV, laundry service, travel services; no a/c in some rooms, no room TVs* ⊟ *V* ⦿| *CP.*

★ ¢ ⊡ **Delight.** This spotless homestay is wildly popular with budget travelers, in no small part because of the warm, knowledgeable, and extraordinarily helpful hosts. Their home, a centuries-old Portuguese mansion, is tucked away in a quiet corner of Fort Cochin. Guest rooms, in a newer wing of the house, are very large, clean, and simply furnished with ceiling fans. Be sure to reserve in advance. ✉ *Parade Ground, Post Office Rd., Fort Cochin 682001* ☎☎ *484/221–7658* ⊕ *www. delightfulhomestay.com* ⇲ *7 rooms* ⌂ *Cable TV, travel services* ⊟ *No credit cards* ⦿| *CP.*

The Arts

Art Gallery

The former home of the Parishith Thampuran Museum now houses the **Kerala Lalita Kala Akademi Gallery** (✉ D. H. Rd., Ernakulam ☎ 484/236–7748 ⊡ Rs. 5 ☉ Tues.–Sun. 11–6). There's not much here by way of explanation, but the traditional tile-roof building is cool and airy, and the interesting collection features contemporary works by Indian artists.

Dance

In the 400-year-old (17th century) Kathakali, elaborately made-up and costumed dancers tell epic stories using stylized hand gestures. For centuries, Kathakali performances were the only after-dark entertainment in Kerala; shows began at sundown and lasted all night. Today, for the benefit of tourists, performances are often shortened to one or two hours. Many centers also offer the chance to watch dancers being made up.

Kathakali performances in the air-conditioned room of the **Cochin Cultural Centre** (✉ CC 2/10 A, west of Seagull Hotel, Calvetty Rd., Fort Cochin ☎ 484/221–6911 or 484/221–5391) start at 6:30 PM, though you should arrive an hour before the show to see makeup being applied. Revered arts academy **Kerala Kalamandalam** (✉ Cheruthuruthy, 29 km [18 mi] north of Trichur ☎ 492/262–2418) is credited with the revival of traditional arts in Kerala, providing training in Kathakali, Mohiniattam, and other native art forms. All-night Kathakali performances are staged here a few nights each year, and you're welcome to watch students in practice sessions that are held weekdays from 8:30 to noon and 3:30 to 5:30. **Kerala Kathakali Centre** (✉ River Rd., near Children's Park, Fort Cochin ☎ 484/221–5827) is a pleasant outdoor venue. Makeup starts at 5 PM and shows at 6:30 PM daily. Also, short-term courses in dance and music are offered here. At the **See India Foundation** (✉ Kalthil Parambil La., Ernakulam ☎ 484/237–6471), the director provides lively explanations of the dance before every 6:45 PM show. Makeup starts at 6:00 PM.

Martial Arts

Kerala's dramatic, high-flying martial art, Kalarippayattu, may be the oldest in Asia. Some think it started in the 12th century, others think it began earlier, and still others say later. Some scholars believe that Buddhist monks from India introduced Kalarippayattu to China along with Buddhism. Participants learn both armed- and unarmed-combat techniques. One of the more unusual skills involves defending yourself against a knife-wielding attacker using only a piece of cloth. In peak season, many hotels stage performances. If you call in advance, you can watch Kalarippayattu practitioners at the **E. N. S. Kalari Centre** (✉ Nettoor neighborhood, Ernakulam ☎ 484/270–0810).

Shopping

The streets surrounding the synagogue in Mattancherry are crammed with stores that sell curios, and Fort Cochin's Princess Street has sprouted several small shops worth a browse. For saris, jewelry, handicrafts, and souvenirs, head to M. G. Road in Ernakulam. Be suspicious of the word "antique" in all stores.

Cinnamon (✉ 1/658 Ridsdale Rd., Parade Ground, Fort Cochin ☎ 484/221–7124 or 484/221–8124) is a branch of the chic Bangalore boutique, and stocks stylish ethnic and modern housewares, silk scarves and purses, jewelry, and Indo-Western designer clothing. Cochin's upscale ladies buy the latest designer fineries at the pricey boutique **Glada** (✉ Convent Rd., Ernakulam ☎ 484/236–4952). **Jayalakshmi** (✉ M. G. Rd., near Rajaji Rd., Ernakulam ☎ 484/237–3040) houses a mind-blowing selection of saris, *lehangas* (long skirts with fitted blouses), and the like as well Indian and Western clothes for men and children.

The **Cochin Gallery** (✉ 6/116 Jew Town Rd., Mattancherry ☎ no phone) carries jewelry, carpets, cushion covers, bronze figurines, and wooden boxes. Local hotels often get their antiques from **Crafter's** (✉ 6/141 Jew Town Rd., Mattancherry ☎ 484/222–7652). It's crammed with stone and wood carvings, pillars, and doors as well as such portable items as painted tiles, navigational equipment, and wooden boxes. **Fort Royal** (✉ 1/258 Napier St., Fort Cochin ☎ 484/221–7832) is an expensive all-in-one shop with goods from all over India. You can find brocade work, marble inlay boxes, and Kashmiri carpets, plus local handicrafts and precious and semiprecious jewelry. **Indian Arts and Curios** (✉ Jew Town Rd., Mattancherry ☎ 484/222–8049) is one of Kerala's oldest and most-reliable curio shops. **Kairali** (✉ M. G. Rd., near Jose Junction, Ernakulam ☎ 484/235–4507) is a fixed-price government shop with a good selection of local handicrafts and curios. **Surabhi** (✉ M. G. Rd., Ernakulam ☎ 484/238–2278) is run by the state's Handicrafts Cooperative Society. It has an impressive selection of local products.

Whether you're looking for a little information on Kerala or a tome to while away the hours, stop by **Idiom Books** (✉ Jew Town Rd., Mattancherry ☎ 484/222–4028 ✉ 1/348 Bastion Rd., near Princess St., Fort Cochin), a small bookshop opposite the synagogue, or its branch in Fort Cochin. You can find an intriguing collection of recent Western and Indian fiction, as well as books on history, culture, and religion.

CENTRAL KERALA

Between Cochin and Quilon (Kollam), to the south, is the immense labyrinth of waterways called *kayals,* through which much of the life of the Malayalee has historically flowed. From the vastness of Vembanad Lake to quiet streams just large enough for a canoe, the backwaters have carried Kerala's largely coconut-based products from the village to the market for centuries, and continue to do so today. You can relax at some of Kerala's finest resorts, or briefly join the floating lifestyle by taking a boat cruise.

The terrain rises and the temperature drops as you move inland, up into the teak-forested hills of Thekkady and Munnar. Kerala's interior is elephant country—you'll find them roaming in Lake Periyar Wildlife Sanctuary and even appearing in the mists of Munnar's tea plantations.

Fodor'sChoice ★ A **houseboat cruise** provides a window into traditional local life. Shaded by a woven bamboo canopy and fanned by cool breezes, you can drift past simple, tile-roof houses with canoes moored outside; tiny waterfront churches; and people washing themselves, their clothes, their dishes, and their children in the river. Women in bright pink and blue stroll past green paddy fields, their waist-length hair unbound and smelling of coconut oil. Graceful palms are everywhere, as are village walls painted with political slogans and ads for computer training courses. Backwater trips can be designed to suit any time constraint or budget. Motorized or punted canoes can squeeze into narrow canals, taking you to dreamy roadless villages, and big ferries ply the eight-hour Quilon–Alleppey route as if it were a major highway. Romantic houseboats give you the opportunity to stay overnight on the water; there's even an Oberoi luxury cruise ship offering every imaginable comfort. Any travel agent, hotel, or the Kerala Tourism Development Corporation (KTDC) can help you hire a private boat or plan a trip. Most cruises depart from Quilon, Alleppey, or Kumarakom.

Kumarakom

❻ *80 km (50 mi) south of Cochin.*

Some of Kerala's finest resorts are hidden in this tiny, rapidly developing paradise on the shores of Vembanad Lake. Arundhati Roy's birthplace, Ayemenem, featured in her 1997 novel *The God of Small Things,* is close by. Birds abound in the backwaters, as well as in the sanctuary on the lake's eastern shore. At this writing, three large new resorts were under construction, slated for opening in late 2004 or early 2005.

Where to Stay & Eat

$$ ✕ **Lakshmi Hotel.** If you want a change of pace from your resort's dining room, the restaurant of this locally owned hotel offers reliable local fare along with North Indian specialties. Service is leisurely, but the food is freshly prepared and the air-conditioned dining room is clean and comfortable. ⊠ *Kottayam-Kumarakom Rd., Kumarakom North* ☎ *481/252–3313* ▭ *No credit cards.*

★ **$$$$** ▣ **Coconut Lagoon.** This ground-breaking and much-imitated Vembanad Lake resort put Kerala's backwaters on the map. It's accessible only by boat, from one of two pick-up points along an adjoining river. The grounds are crisscrossed with canals and footbridges and dotted with white bungalows and two-story mansions that are a mixture of rustic and modern; the newer villa accommodations have their own plunge pools, and the open-air restaurant is reassembled from parts of an approximately 300-year-old Kerala home. The ayurveda center is excellent, and the property also has its own *kalari*, a school for martial arts. Book well in advance. ⊠ *Vembanad Lake, Kumarakom 686563* ☎ *481/252–4491 or 481/252–4373* ▤ *481/252–4495* ⊕ *www.cghearth.com* ⋘ *28 bungalows, 14 mansions, 8 villas* ⌂ *Restaurant, grill, cable TV, pool, yoga, boating, recreation room, laundry service, travel services; no room TVs* ▭ *AE, DC, MC, V* ❄ *FAP.*

$$$$ ▣ **Kumarakom Lake Resort.** In the heritage section of this beautiful 25 acre lakefront property, palatial traditional villas, reassembled from old houses, are set around a network of canals. Each villa is outfitted with ornately carved wooden ceilings, colorful mural paintings and enormous garden bathrooms. The meandering pool villas are a modern take on the backwater lifestyle; you can step from your room directly into the curving, amoeba-like swimming pool. You can also relax by a separate lakefront infinity pool, designed so the far edge seems to merge with the body of water on the horizon, or in the spacious ayurvedic center. ⊠ *Kumarakom North P.O., Kumarakom 686563* ☎ *481/252–4900* ▤ *484/252–4987* ⊕ *www.klresort.com* ⋘ *48 villas* ⌂ *2 restaurants, cable TV, 2 pools, health club, yoga, boating, fishing, 2 bars, recreation room, laundry service, business services, travel services* ▭ *AE, DC, MC, V* ❄ *EP.*

Fodor'sChoice ★ (margin)

$$$$ ▣ **Taj Garden Retreat.** The main building of this tranquil, verdant resort is an 1891 plantation house, built by the son of an English missionary. Its large rooms open onto broad verandas, and overlook a small lagoon where you can canoe or pedal-boat. Guest quarters are in the main house, in freestanding cottages, or in stationary houseboats. The terrace is a lovely place to relax with a glass of lime juice. Vembanad Lake is a short boat ride away down a woodsy canal. Twelve of the cottages are new (2004) and have views of the lake. ⊠ *Kumarakom 686563* ☎ *481/252–4377* ▤ *481/252–4371* ⊕ *www.tajhotels.com* ⋘ *8 rooms, 23 cottages, 4 houseboat rooms* ⌂ *Restaurant, cable TV, pool, ayurveda center, massage, boating, laundry service, travel services* ▭ *AE, DC, MC, V* ❄ *EP.*

Alleppey

❼ *35 km (22 mi) southwest of Kumarakom.*

This coir-manufacturing city was once known as the Venice of India, though most residents have abandoned their canoes for cars. Alleppey (Alappuzha) is an important gateway to the backwaters—tour operators abound, and several resorts here are good alternatives to the pricier properties in Kumarakom.

On the second Saturday in August, throngs of supporters line the shore to watch the annual Nehru Cup Snake Boat Race, which starts with a water procession and concludes dramatically as the boats (propelled by as many as 100 rowers) vie for the trophy. Several snake-boat races take place in the area from mid-July to mid-September. Check with the Alleppey Tourism Development Cooperative (ATDC) for exact times and locations.

Where to Stay

★ **$$$$** ⊞ **Marari Beach.** With a palm-fringed beach, an excellent ayurvedic center, and easy access to both Cochin and the backwaters, Marari packs a lot of Kerala into one bundle. Nestled between two fishing villages 17 km (10 mi) north of Alleppey, the 30-acre resort combines a warm, rustic feel with modern comforts. Brick paths lead through rows of deceptively modest thatch-roof cottages, extremely spacious and comfortable, with open-air bathrooms. Private gardens and side entrances add an air of seclusion. The staff is friendly and professional, and the main restaurant features live music. ⊠ *Mararikulam 688549* ☏ *478/286–3801* 🖷 *478/286–3810* ⊕ *www.cghearth.com* ⇝ *49 cottages, 10 villas* ⌂ *Restaurant, grill, cable TV, 2 tennis courts pool, beach, bicycles, volleyball, yoga, 2 bars, laundry service, shop, travel services; no room TVs* ⊟ *AE, DC, MC, V* ⏐⊙⏐ *BP.*

$$$$ ⊞ **Punnamada Backwater Resort.** Small design details make this typical backwater resort sparkle. The traditional tile-roof buildings boast ornate wooden carvings on the fascades. Rooms have high ceilings, exposed wooden rafters, and decoratively tiled floors. Furnishings are done in antique style, including canopied beds and planter's chairs, and the garden bathrooms are spacious. Four lakeview rooms with private patios are just steps from the water. ⊠ *Punnamada, Alleppey 688011* ☏ *477/223–3690* 🖷 *477/223–3694* ⊕ *www.punnamada.com* ⇝ *21 rooms, 2 cottages* ⌂ *2 restaurants, cable TV, pool, ayurveda center, boating, water sportswater sports, bar, laundry service* ⊟ *MC, V* ⏐⊙⏐ *BP.*

$$$ ⊞ **Kayaloram Lake Resort.** A common veranda surrounds each of the four buildings in this pleasant, small-scale heritage resort. Old wooden doors lead to the modestly furnished rooms, half of which had been renovated at this writing to include better furniture and an additional window. All rooms have baths with open-air showers, and five have lake views. Food at the simple restaurant is freshly made to order. The property is just steps from the waterfront; boats pick you up in Alleppey. ⊠ *Punnamada, Alleppey 688011* ☏ *477/2232040 or 477/2231572* 🖷 *477/2231571* ⊕ *www.kayaloram.com* ⇝ *12 rooms* ⌂ *Restaurant, cable TV,*

pool, ayurvedic center, boating, laundry service; no a/c, no room TVs
☰ AE, DC, MC, V ⏀ BP.

▦ **Keraleeyam.** This quaint waterfront property specializes in ayurvedic treatments. Rooms in the heritage main building have air-conditioning but few windows; go for a simple thatched-roof non-air-conditioned cottage with a waterfront sit-out and watch the boats slip by from dawn to dusk. ✉ Thathampally, Alleppey 688006 ☎ 477/223–1468 or 477/223–6950 🖶 477/225–1068 ⊕ www.keraleeyam.com ⤳ 18 rooms ⚘ Restaurant, ayurvedic center, boating, travel services; no a/c in some rooms, no room TVs ☰ MC, V ⏀ EP.

$ ▦ **Palm Grove Lake Resort.** Simplicity rules the day at this coconut plantation hideaway near the starting point of the Nehru Cup Snake Boat Race. It consists of just four cottages, made entirely of bamboo—walls, ceilings, doors, and windows. Furnishings are basic but comfortable; bathrooms are attached to the room but have a partially open roof. The charm here is in the hammocks, the home-cooked food, the friendly staff, and the idyllic setting. ✉ Punnamada, Alleppey 68006 ☎ 477/223–5004 or 477/224–3474 🖶 477/225–1138 ⤳ 4 cottages ⚘ Restaurant, cable TV, massage, boating, fishing, laundry service, travel services; no a/c, no room TVs ☰ No credit cards ⏀ EP.

Quilon

❽ 71 km (44 mi) north of Trivandrum, 87 km (54 mi) south of Alleppey.

If you're coming up from Trivandrum, central Kerala starts here, with the peaceful waters of eight-armed Ashtamudi Lake. You can catch a ferry from Quilon (Kollam) in the morning and reach Alleppey eight hours later. The waterfront here is not nearly as developed as Vembanad Lake, and the few resorts are utterly peaceful and reasonably priced.

Where to Stay

$$$$ ▦ **Aquaserene.** The gorgeous lakeside setting will quickly help you forget the bumpy ride here, on a barely paved road through a fishing village. Rooms are in individual heritage-style cottages, with semi-outdoor bathrooms and modern furnishing. Don't miss a dip in the lagoon-embedded pool, or the soaring wooden construction of the traditional reception building. ✉ South Paravoor, Kollam 691391 ☎ 474/251–2410 to 17 🖶 474/251–2104 ⊕ www.aquasereneindia.com ⤳ 28 rooms ⚘ Restaurant, cable TV, ayurveda center, boating, laundry service, travel services ☰ AE, MC, V ⏀ EP.

$$$ ▦ **Ashtamudi.** Ayurveda is the focus of this soothing resort on the shores of Ashtamudi Lake. Even without undergoing treatment, you should expect to find peace here, where Chinese fishing nets flicker like a mirage in the morning mists that rise off the silvery lake. Manicured lawns and well-kept hedges on the grounds are brightened by splashes of bougainvilla. A series of two-story red-brick chalets line the waterfront. Rooms are spacious but sparsely decorated, with tile floors, dark-wood furniture, and nearly blank walls; each, however, has a lakeview balcony. Home-style food in the open-air restaurant is made to order. ✉ Chovara South, Kollam 691584 ☎ 476/288–2288 🖶 476/288–2470 ⊕ www.

ashtamudiresort.com ⤳ *20 rooms, 3 cottages* ⚘ *Restaurant, cable TV, ayurvedic center, boating, yoga, laundry service, travel services* ▤ *MC, V* ⏄ *BP.*

Thekkady

◉ *130 km (81 mi) east of Kumarakom.*

Due east of Kumarakom and Kottayam, this cool mountain town sits at 3,000 feet above sea level in the Cardamom Hills, midway between Cochin and the temple city of Madurai in Tamil Nadu. (This will make a difference in your room, since you don't need air-conditioning here.

★ Thekkady is the population center nearest the **Lake Periyar Wildlife Sanctuary,** one of India's best animal parks for spotting elephants, bison, wild boar, oxen, deer, and many species of birds. The best viewing period is October through May.

Lake Periyar, its many fingers winding around low-lying hills, is the heart of the 300-square-mi sanctuary. Forget exhausting treks or long safaris: here, you lounge in a motor launch as it drifts around bends and comes upon animals drinking at the shores. In dry season, when forest watering holes are empty, leopards and tigers also pad up to the water. A few words of advice: Indian children (and adults) love to scream and shout at wildlife sightings. On a quiet trip, elephants hardly notice the intrusion, although younger pachyderms will peer at you out of curiosity and then run squealing back to their elders when your boat comes too close. If you're brave-hearted, you can spend a night in a jungle lodge (if you go on a forest trek, look out for leeches); if you're less adventurous you can commune with nature from the safety of a moated watchtower. Half-hour elephant rides are also available. For information about treks and the park, contact the KTDC. ⊠ *KTDC, Shanmugham Rd., Ernakulam, Cochin* ☎ *484/235–3234* ✆ *Rs. 50; video cameras Rs. 100.*

Where to Stay

$$$$ ⌂ **Hotel Lake Palace.** A ferry transports you to this former maharaja's hunting lodge on an island inside the Lake Periyar Wildlife Sanctuary. Six simple rooms, some with period furniture, look out through a palm-lined pathway and beyond to the lake and the preserve—you can spot animals from your balcony. Meals at the eclectic, fixed-menu restaurant are included. As the hotel is run by the state government, make reservations through the KTDC. ⊠ *Lake Periyar Wildlife Sanctuary, Thekkady 685536* ☎ *486/232–2023* ⊠ *KTDC, Shanmugham Rd., Ernakulam, Cochin 682031* ☎ *484/235–3234* ⤳ *8 rooms* ⚘ *Restaurant, refrigerators, cable TV, boating, laundry service, travel services; no a/c* ▤ *AE, DC, MC, V* ⏄ *FAP.*

$$$$ ⌂ **Spice Village.** Just outside the Lake Periyar Wildlife Sanctuary, this resort has well-maintained thatch-roof cottages built into a hillside. Lush plantings, including a spice garden, add fragrance and privacy. Interiors have knotty pine furnishings and trim, white walls, red-tile floors, and plaid upholstery and bedspreads. The restaurant serves Indian and Continental set meals. Jungle treks and Indian cooking classes are among the activities. ⊠ *Kummily Rd., Thekkady 685536* ☎ *486/922–*

2314 or 486/922–2315 ⊟ *486/922–2317* ⤳ *52 cottages* ☖ *Restaurant, cable TV, pool, ayurveda center, bar, laundry service, meeting room, travel services; no a/c or room TVs* ⊟ *AE, DC, MC, V* ⏐⊙⏐ *BP.*

★ **$$$$** ⊞ **Shalimar Spice Garden.** This rustic retreat is 20 bone-jarring minutes off the main road to Thekkady. Most guests come for ayurvedic treatment and yoga; the emphasis is on serenity and relaxation. A wooden bridge over a duck pond leads to the main building—a whitewashed, thatch-roof affair that houses a restaurant specializing in authentic Italian and Kerala food. The spotless white cottages are largely minimalist—perfectly executed—with only a colorful Rajasthani bedspread, a stained-glass window, or an ancient, dark-wood oar adding bits of contrast to each room. ⊠ *Murikkady 685535* ☎ *486/922–2132 or 486/922–3232* ⊟ *486/922–3022* ⊕ *www.shalimarkerala.com* ⤳ *8 rooms, 7 cottages* ☖ *Restaurant, cable TV, pool, ayurvedic center, yoga, laundry service, travel services; no a/c or room TVs* ⊟ *MC, V* ⏐⊙⏐ *BP.*

$$$$ ⊞ **Taj Garden Retreat.** On a former coffee plantation, this woodsy Taj property offers concrete cottages raised on stilts; balconies are nice touches as is the thatch piled on the roofs. Rooms are modern and reliable—they're typically luxurious, as per the Taj standard—and the restaurant serves multicuisine food (Chinese, Continental, and regional Indian) that's quite excellent. ⊠ *Ambalambika Rd., Thekkady 685536* ☎ *486/922–2273 or 486/922–2401 to 07* ⊟ *486/922–2106* ⊕ *www.tajhotels.com* ⤳ *32 rooms* ☖ *Restaurant, cable TV, pool, Ayurvedic massage, bicycles, badminton court, library, bar, laundry service, travel services, business services* ⊟ *AE, DC, MC, V* ⏐⊙⏐ *EP.*

$$$–$$$$ ⊞ **Cardamom County.** Views from this steeply pitched resort are gorgeous. The mid-size rooms are in individual or double whitewashed, red-tile–roof cottages with gabled ceilings. Each is has dark-wood furniture and terra-cotta floors. On the grounds there's a fish pond where you can catch your own dinner. ⊠ *Thekkady Rd., Thekkady 685536* ☎ *486/922–4501 to 03* ⊟ *486/922–2807* ⊕ *www.cardamomcounty.com* ⤳ *44 rooms* ☖ *Restaurant, cable TV, pool, health club, bicycles, ayurvedic center, laundry service, travel services; no a/c* ⊟ *AE, MC, V* ⏐⊙⏐ *EP.*

Munnar

🔟 *100 km (62 mi) north of Thekkady, 130 km (80 mi) east of Cochin.*

On the drive from Thekkady to Munnar, a good road winds through lofty forests as well as spice and tea plantations. The town of Munnar itself is small and unattractive, but most of the land around it is owned by the Tata tea company and a few smaller concerns. The result is an unspoiled hill station, with hundreds of acres of tea, coffee, and cardamom plantations amid hills, lakes, streams, and waterfalls. During your visit you can tour these plantations; arrange trekking, rock-climbing, paragliding, and river trips; or just sit on your hotel balcony with a cup of tea, taking in the scenery.

Most lodgings can arrange a tea plantation tour, where you can walk through the steeply pitched, dense green hedges, and see how the leaf is processed. (The awful truth is that the dregs of the batch get shipped to America.) Cardamom plantations are just this side of heaven. The shade-loving spice needs plenty of forest cover, so a walk through a plantation feels like a stroll in the woods, complete with dappled sunlight, mountain streams, and birdsong. It's quite cool here, so you don't need to find a hotel with air-conditioning.

The **Rajamala National Park,** 15 km (9 mi) northwest of Munnar, is home to the endangered nilgiri tahr. You can get close to this endearingly tame mountain goat, pushed to the brink of extinction by its utter lack of suspicion toward human beings. Half the world's remaining population live here. Note that the park is closed during monsoon season, roughly July to mid-August. ☎ *486/253–0487* ✆ *Rs. 50* ☉ *Daily 7–6.*

Where to Stay

$$$$ 🏨 **Club Mahindra.** Set between a mountain peak and a tea plantation—22 km (14 mi) east of Munnar—this large, family-oriented resort has guest quarters in the main building or in hillside cottages. Rooms are spacious, with wood floors and furnishings; deluxe rooms also have entrancing views. Cottages are large—a one-bedroom can sleep four—yet still homey. The activity center offers everything from video games to rappelling, and the restaurant serves excellent North Indian food as well as other types of cuisine. ⊠ *Kumily–Munnar Rd., Chinnakanal Village 685618* ☎ *486/284–9224* 📠 *486/284–9227* ⊕ *www.clubmahindra. com* ➬ *38 rooms, 54 cottages* ⚐ *Restaurant, cable TV, ayurveda center, hair salon, boating, children's programs (all ages), laundry service, business services, travel services; no a/c* ☐ *AE, DC, MC, V* ⦿ *EP.*

$$$$ 🏨 **Windermere Estate.** Plantation life is pretty darn good, especially when you're made to feel like the guest of a planter. Guest quarters on this working cardamom, coffee, and vanilla plantation, just 2 km (1 mi) from Munnar, are either in one of the five bedrooms of the main guest house, which has a communal balcony, or in an individual cottage. Service is warm and personalized. The hillside views are stunning, and the grounds are blessed with several streams and waterfalls, making for enchanting morning walks. ⊠ *Pothamedu* ✍ *Box 21, Munnar 685612* ☎ *486/253–0512, 486/253–0978, or 486/253–0248 estate, 484/242–5237 in Cochin for reservations* 📠 *484/232–3293* ⊕ *www. windermeremunnar.com* ➬ *5 rooms, 2 cottages* ⚐ *Dining room, cable TV, bicycles, hiking, laundry service; no a/c, no TVs in some rooms* ☐ *No credit cards* ⦿ *MAP.*

$$–$$$ 🏨 **The Tall Trees.** You can hardly spot the wood-and-stone structures of this hushed, breezy resort on a 66-acre cardamom plantation. Getting around the hilly property is a workout—especially the hike to the skylight-topped restaurant—but the setting is phenomenal. The views are of trees, trees, trees. Standard double rooms are actually more pleasant than the narrow two-story deluxe rooms. Luxury cottages have spacious upstairs living rooms and balconies; spiral staircases lead to two bedrooms and bathrooms downstairs. Furnishings are of rustic cane and rubber wood. ✍ *Box 40, Bison Valley Rd., Munnar 685612* ☎📠 *486/ 523–0641, 486/523–0593, or 486/523–2716* ⊕ *www.thetalltreesmunnar. com* ➬ *16 rooms, 6 cottages* ⚐ *Restaurant, cable TV, bicycles, hiking, library, recreation room, laundry service; no a/c or room TVs* ☐ *MC, V* ⦿ *MAP.*

$ ⊞ **Siena Village.** Some of the rooms at this hotel, 18 km (11 mi) east of Munnar, capture the country-lodge feeling perfectly. Ignore the single-story standard rooms and opt for a split-level deluxe one. Their lower-level sitting areas have timber floors, comfy couches, and working fireplaces; balcony views are of the Anayirankal Dam (its name means "where the elephants come"). The semicircular restaurant also has panoramic vistas. ⊠ *Chinnakanal 685618* ☎ *486/8249261 or 486/ 8249461* 🖷 *486/8249328* ⊕ *www.thesienavillage.com* ☞ *26 rooms* ⬠ *Restaurant, cable TV, fishing, hiking, horseback riding, recreation room, business services, laundry service, travel services; no a/c* ⊟ *MC, V* ⎮○⎮ *EP.*

Lakshadweep

❶ *250 km (160 mi) off the coast of Kerala.*

Of the 36 or so coral atolls that make up the isolated paradise of Lakshadweep, only about 10 are inhabited, and their population is devoutly Sunni Muslim. Tourism here is severely restricted to protect the fragile ecosystems and the traditional peoples. If you don't have an Indian passport, your visit will be limited to Agatti, Kadmat, or Bangaram Island, each of which has one resort property. (You need to obtain a government entry permit with passport details.)

Crystal waters and soft sands are Lakshadweep's main attraction; all resorts offer water sports, and there's even a scuba diving school on Kadmat Island. Trips to Kadmat must be arranged through the **Society for the Promotion of Recreational Tourism and Sports** (SPORTS; ⊠ Harbour Rd., Willingdon Island, Cochin ☎ 484/266–8387 or 484/266–8647 ⊕ www.lakshadweeptourism.com). SPORTS offers inexpensive packages involving overnight transport by ship from Cochin.

Where to Stay

$$$$ ⊞ **Agatti Island Beach Resort.** Just a short drive from the airport, this modest resort offers a mid-range alternative (about half the price) to Bangaram Island. Rooms are in simply furnished, individual tile-roof cottages. Indulge in water sports or flop on a lounge chair beneath a thatch umbrella. There's also kayaking available. ⊠ *Agatti Island, Lakshadweep* ☎ *484/236–2232* ☞ *20 rooms* ⬠ *Restaurant, cable TV, dive shop, snorkeling, boating, fishing, laundry service; no a/c in some rooms, no room TVs* ⊟ *no credit cards* ⎮○⎮ *FAP.*

★ $$$$ ⊞ **Bangaram Island Resort.** This ecofriendly, exclusive resort is Kerala's answer to the Maldives. The only people on this island are resort guests and staff. Construction is kept to a minimum—the restaurant is made entirely of bamboo and coconut leaves, allowing the white sands and turquoise water to steal the show. Accommodations are in simple, two-to four-bedroom, thatched cottages with terra-cotta floors and Western furnishings. Water sports, including kayaking, are the order of the day. Make reservations well in advance through the Casino Hotel in Cochin. ⎔ *Casino Hotel, K. P. K. Menon Rd., Willingdon Island, Cochin 682003* ⊠ *Lakshadweep* ☎ *484/266–8221* 🖷 *484/266–8001* ⊕ *www. cghearth.com* ☞ *27 rooms, 3 bungalows* ⬠ *Restaurant, cable TV, ayurveda center, dive shop, scuba diving, snorkeling, windsurfing, boat-*

ing, fishing, bar, laundry service; no a/c, no room TVs ⊟ *AE, DC, MC, V* ⦿ *FAP.*

SOUTHERN KERALA

The beaches near Kovalam are southern Kerala's main attraction—in fact, they're what brought Western tourists to the state in the first place, as the hippie scene from Goa moved down the coast. Parts of Kovalam are overdeveloped and full of touts vending cheap tie-dye clothes. There are, however, still some pleasant spots to relax within a few miles of the main beach. Just a half hour from Kovalam is Kerala's capital city of Trivandrum (Thiruvanandapuram), former home of the rajas of Travancore and now home to Kerala's primary international airport.

Trivandrum

⑫ *222 km (138 mi) south of Cochin, 253 km (157 mi) southwest of Thekkady.*

Built on seven low hills and cleansed by ocean breezes, Kerala's capital is surprisingly calm and pleasant. Trivandrum's few sights and quiet lanes outside the town center make it an enjoyable place to spend a day.

The handsome **Padmanabhaswamy Temple,** dedicated to Vishnu, has a seven-story *gopuram* (entrance tower). The date of its original construction has been placed at 3000 BC; legend has it that it was built by 4,000 masons, 6,000 laborers, and 100 elephants over the course of six months. In the main courtyard there's intricate granite sculpture, supplemented by more stonework on the nearly 400 pillars supporting the temple corridors. The complex is technically open only to Hindus and keeps erratic hours, so call ahead to be assured of at least a glimpse. ⊠ *M. G. Rd. at Chali Bazaar* ☎ *471/245–0233* ⊙ *Daily sunrise–12:30 and 4:30–9:30.*

The 18th-century **Kuthiramalika (Puthenmalika) Palace Museum,** or Horse Palace, has carved rosewood ceilings and treasures of the royal family, including an ivory throne, weapons, paintings, and gifts from foreign dignitaries. Lifesize Kathakali figures stand in the dance room. Carved horses for which the palace is named line the eaves of an inner courtyard. Only one-third of the enormous compound is open to visitors; the entrance fee includes a knowledgeable guide, who will politely demand a hefty tip at the end of the tour. Also note that you must remove your shoes upon entering. ⊠ *Next to Padmanabhaswamy Temple, East Fort* ☎ *471/247–3952* ⊠ *Rs. 20, Rs. 1 shoe-storage charge* ⊙ *Tues.–Sun. 8:30–1 and 3–5:30.*

In an 80-acre park at the north end of M. G. Road are the many attractions of the **Museum and Art Gallery Complex.** Buy your ticket at the Natural History Museum, a musty collection of animal skeletons, dioramas, and stuffed birds. Head straight to the second floor to see an interesting model of a traditional *nalakettu* home (the traditional home of the Nairs, the warrior clan), complete with costumed figurines and a full explanation. The art museum's collection of local arts and crafts—

including bronze and stone sculptures and musical instruments—is as noteworthy as the building itself, with its Cubist pattern of gables and its decorative interior. Memorabilia donated by the royal family, including a golden chariot used by the Maharaja of Travancore, is displayed in the tiny Sree Chitra Enclave. On the opposite side of the park, the Sree Chitra Art Gallery has an eclectic collection of paintings, including works of the Rajput, Mogul, and Tanjore schools; copies of the Ajanta and Sigirya frescoes; and works from China, Japan, Tibet, and Bali, along with canvases by modern Indian painters. ⊠ *Museum Rd.* ☎ *471/231–8294* ⊠ *Rs. 5* ☉ *Thurs.–Tues. 10–5, Wed. 1–5.*

off the beaten path

VIJNANA KALA VEDI CULTURAL CENTER – About 120 km (75 mi) north of Trivandrum, this institute, established by a French woman in 1977, is dedicated to preserving the arts and heritage of Kerala. People from all over the world come to study everything from singing to cooking to language with experienced masters in a simple, village atmosphere. You can choose to give back by participating in a volunteer program to teach English in a local school. Short stays are available for $30 per night. A one-week stay is $200, all-inclusive; there are discounts for longer stays. ⊠ *Tarayil Mukku Junction, Aranmula 689533* ☎ *468/221–4483 or 468/231–0451* ⊕ *www. vijnanakalavedi.org.*

Where to Stay & Eat

$$ ✕ **Orion.** Although it offers a variety of cuisines, this restaurant has acquired a reputation with locals for its traditional Indian dishes. The lunchtime South Indian buffet features such Kerala specialties as *elisseri* (pumpkin with red beans), *avial* (mixed vegetables in a mild coconut gravy), and fish curry. ⊠ *The Residency Tower, Press Rd.* ☎ *471/233–1661* ⊟ *AE, DC, MC, V* ❗❘ *EP.*

$–$$ ✕ **Swiss Bake House.** The graceful, two-story building—one-time home of the antiques-dealing Natesan family—is decorated with wood carvings and bronze artifacts. Come for the ambience as the food is only average. The attached café, however, serves yummy, Western-style pastries. ⊠ *Vellyambalam Junction* ☎ *471/231–1720* ⊟ *MC, V.*

¢ ✕ **Amma.** There's nothing fancy here—just simple, tasty, vegetarian food like *amma* (mom) would make. The air-conditioned restaurant is comfortable and clean, and menu options range from soups and salads to french fries. Opt for the traditional thali, a meal of rice and vegetable preparations—one special thali comes with a whopping 18 dishes. ⊠ *Subramaniam Rd.* ☎ *471/233–8999* ⊟ *No credit cards* ❗❘ *EP.*

¢ ✕ **Azad.** The food won't disappoint, even if the interior isn't much to look at. Specialties include *biriani,* a flavorful rice cooked with chicken or mutton, and *kuthu paratha,* a Kerala Muslim delicacy of flat bread stuffed with minced fish. Azad has become a chain, but this, the original restaurant in East Fort, is reportedly the best. ⊠ *M. G. Rd., East Fort* ⊟ *No credit cards* ❗❘ *EP.*

$$$ 🏨 **Muthoot Plaza.** A roaring fountain encourages you to lounge ever deeper into the leather armchairs in the cream-tone marble lobby, where the Middle Eastern business clientele often gathers around the flat-screen

TV or at the cyber-station. The carpeted rooms have high ceilings and bedside electric control panels. ✉ *Punnen Rd., 695039* ☎ *471/233–7733* 🖷 *471/233–7734* ⊕ *www.themuthootplaza.com* ⇘ *57 rooms* ♨ *Restaurant, coffee shop, cable TV, exercise equipment, bar, laundry service, business services, travel services* ☰ *AE, DC, MC, V* ⦿ *BP.*

$$ ⊞ **South Park.** At this writing, renovations were underway at South Park, one of Trivandrum's premier hotels. Carpets in the large standard rooms are being replaced by wooden flooring, a foolproof way to get rid of the mustiness that plagues most Kerala hotels. Street-facing rooms can be noisy; opt for one at the back. ✉ *Spencer Junction, M. G. Rd., 950346* ☎ *471/233–3333* 🖷 *471/233–1861* ⊕ *www.thesouthpark. com* ⇘ *83 rooms* ♨ *Restaurant, coffee shop, cable TV, hair salon, ayurvedic massage, bar, laundry service, business services, travel services* ☰ *AE, DC, MC, V* ⦿ *BP.*

Shopping

Most shops are closed Sunday, and smaller shops occasionally shut down for a few hours at lunchtime on weekdays. For crafts from all over India, head to **Hastkala Exporters** (✉ G. A. K Rd., off M. G. Rd. ☎ 471/233–8462). Weavers for Travancore's royal family sell traditional Kerala saris (plain white cotton) at **Karalkada** (✉ Kaithamukku Junction ☎ no phone). **Natesan's** (✉ M. G. Rd. ☎ 471/233–1594) is a respected art and antiques dealer. For Kerala handicrafts and souvenirs, hit the government emporium **SMSM** (✉ Statue Junction, off M. G. Rd. ☎ 471/233–1668).

Kovalam

⓭ *16 km (10 mi) south of Trivandrum.*

Kovalam's sandy beaches are lined with palm-fringed lagoons and rocky coves. Fishermen in *lungis* (colorful cloth wraps) drag in nets filled with the day's catch, then push their slender wooden boats out again with a Malayalam "Heave ho." Here you can spend the day loafing on warm sand or rocky outcroppings, watch the sun set, then sit back as the dim lights of distant fishing boats come on. In peak season, outdoor eateries spring up right on the beach—just point to the fish of your choice and specify how you'd like it prepared.

Overdevelopment had nearly ruined Kovalam, but it's experiencing something of a revival, with luxury hotels groups like Taj and Le Meridien coming to the area. The main beach, Lighthouse, has been cleaned up; the concrete promenade is lined with shops, restaurants, and budget hotels. It's well lit at night, allowing for a pleasant evening stroll as well as some semblance of nightlife. For peace and solitude, however, stick to the secluded beaches in villages to the north and south of Kovalam town.

Most area hotels offer ayurvedic treatments, including complete health and revitalization packages (lasting anywhere from three days to one month) in which ayurvedic doctors, masseurs, and yoga and meditation instructors team up to optimize your physical and spiritual well-being. If you don't want to commit to extended treatment, try an ayurvedic oil massage: a vigorous rubdown involving copious amounts of oil, performed on a hard wooden table by a masseur with hands like driftwood. A postsession application of an herbal powder removes most of the unguent, leaving your skin feeling fresh. It's both invigorating and relaxing.

off the beaten path

PADMANABHAPURAM – Though it belongs to Kerala, this fantastic, 18th-century, carved-teak palace is actually across the border in neighboring Tamil Nadu, about a 1 ½-hour (63 km [39 mi]) drive south of Kovalam on National Highway 47. Once the home of the Travancore rajas (Travancore was the southernmost state, which was combined with Cochin and Malabar to form Kerala), it's a rare example of wooden architecture in India.

Where to Stay & Eat

$–$$ ✕ **Hotel Rockholm Restaurant.** Kovalam's best chef prepares excellent international and local dishes. Try the seasonal seafood dishes, such as fried mussels or prawns Kerala-style. You can eat indoors or on a terrace overlooking the ocean. ⊠ *Lighthouse Rd.* 🕾 *471/248–0607* ▭ *AE, DC, MC, V* ⦿❘ *EP.*

$$$$ 🖫 **Lagoona Davina.** U.K. native Davina Taylor has created an intimate miniresort in an out-of-this-world setting north of Kovalam. After a short drive from the airport, you're brought to a lagoon by boat. Thatched guest quarters are small but attractive—hand painted with ethnic designs; most are steps from the water. If you don't feel like packing, just tell Davina your measurements and the colors you like, and she'll have clothes tailored for you. A personal room attendant is at your disposal throughout your stay. Ayurvedic massage, yoga, and reiki (hands-on energy healing) are available. If you use Visa to pay here, a surcharge applies, so ask in advance what the fee is. ⊠ *Pachalloor 695527* 🕾 *471/2380049 or 471/3091113* ⊕ *www.lagoonadavina.com* ➷ *14 rooms* ♧ *Restaurant, cable TV, pool, boating, laundry service, travel services, airport shuttle; no a/c, no room TVs* ▭ *MC, V* ⦿❘ *EP.*

$$$$ 🖫 **Le Meridien Kovalam Beach Resort.** Formerly the government-run Kovalam Ashok, the best-situated property in Kovalam has been mercifully privatized. The Charles Correa–designed exterior remains—the main block is built in tiers on a bluff overlooking the Arabian Sea—but major renovations were under way at this writing. All rooms have balconies and at least a partial sea view; beachfront chalets also have tiny private compounds and windowed bathrooms. Views of the sunsets are spectacular here. ⊠ *Kovalam 695527* 🕾 *471/248–0101* 🖶 *471/248–1522* ⊕ *www.lemeridien-kovalam.com* ➷ *193 rooms* ♧ *4 restaurants, cable TV, tennis court, 3 pools, ayurveda center, gym, boating, volleyball, billiards, 2 bars, ayurveda center, laundry service, travel services* ▭ *AE, DC, MC, V* ⦿❘ *EP.*

$$$$ 🖫 **Nikki's Nest.** Most rooms in this aerie south of Kovalam have commanding sea views. Among bougainvillea, coconut palms, banana trees, orchids, and acacia are thatch-roof, circular cottages and traditional wooden houses. The cottage rooms are comfortable, spacious, and clean. The traditional *nalukettu* (quadrangular buildings) are beautifully maintained homes, with wooden rafters and dark-wood windows that open out completely. A well-lit path leads down to the crescent-shape beach. ⊠ *Azhimala Shiva Temple Rd., Chowara 695591* ☎ *471/226–8822 or 471/226–8821* ☐ *471/226–7182481–182* ⊕ *www.nikkisnest. com* ⤳ *17 rooms, 3 houses* ⚹ *Restaurant, cable TV, beach, ayurveda center, yoga, business services, laundry service, travel services; a/c in some rooms, no TV in some rooms* ☰ *DC, MC, V* ⧌ *BP.*

★ $$$$ 🏨 **Surya Samudra Beach Garden.** Overlooking the sea 10 km (6 mi) south of Kovalam, this rambling resort has an exquisite beach, lovely views, and a great deal of peace (loud noise isn't permitted). Most rooms are in restored wooden houses, each with an intricately carved facade, a domed wooden ceiling, open-air bathrooms, and understated decor. The handful of cottage rooms have interiors that blend modern and folk touches. A new ayurvedic-spa complex was under construction at this writing. ⊠ *Pulinkudi 695521* ☎ *471/248–0413* ☐ *471/226–7124* ⊕ *www.suryasamudra.com* ⤳ *21 rooms* ⚹ *Restaurant, cable TV, pool, beach, ayurveda center, yoga, bar, laundry service, travel services; no a/c in some rooms, no room TVs* ☰ *MC, V* ⧌ *BP.*

$$$–$$$$ 🏨 **Somatheeram.** Stressed-out Westerners in green robes roam the winding pathways of this popular ayurvedic beach resort. Lodging is in traditional wooden houses or simple brick cottages on 15 lush acres down by the sea. The grounds are a bit crowded with both people and cottages, but the setting is still pleasant. The sister resort next door, Manaltheeram, has a quieter feel. ⊠ *Chowara 695501* ☎ *471/226–8101* ☐ *471/226–7600* ⊕ *www.somatheeram.com* ⤳ *59 rooms* ⚹ *Restaurant, cable TV, beach, ayurveda center, yoga, laundry service, travel services; no a/c, no room TVs* ☰ *AE, DC, MC, V* ⧌ *EP.*

$$$ 🏨 **Coconut Bay.** In an undeveloped area about 2 km (1.2 mi) south of Kovalam, this 3-acre property has a secluded beach and ayurvedic center. Rooms are in modern, redbrick tile-roof buildings with wooden ceilings, some with soaring ocean views. It's good value for the money, and usually booked well in advance by charter groups. ⊠ *Mulloor 695521* ☎ *471/2480–566, 471/2480–668, or 471/2484–566* ☐ *471/2343–349* ⊕ *www.coconutbay.com* ⤳ *5 rooms, 14 villas* ⚹ *Restaurant, refrigerators, cable TV, beach, snorkeling, boating, ayurveda center, yoga, library, laundry service, travel services, airport shuttle* ☰ *MC, V* ⧌ *BP.*

$$–$$$ 🏨 **Manaltheeram.** The sister resort of Somatheeram is just next door to it, but even closer to the water and with a quieter feel. All rooms are in simple, circular brick cottages, neatly arrayed on ascending terraces. "Special" cottages have better sea views. ⊠ *Chowara 695501* ☎ *471/226-861* ☐ *471/226-7611* ⊕ *www.manaltheeram.com* ⤳ *59 rooms* ⚹ *Restaurant, cable TV, pool, beach, ayurveda center, yoga, travel services, laundry service; no a/c, no room TVs* ☰ *AE, DC, MC, V* ⧌ *EP.*

$$ 🏨 **Ideal Ayurvedic Resort.** This small, homey resort south of Kovalam has specialized in ayurvedic treatment since 1997. Rooms in the marble-floor main building are simply furnished and spotless; some have balconies overlooking a coconut grove. There are also a few thatch-roof cottages, some with open-air bathrooms. The beach is a short walk away, but Ideal focuses more on Indian arts and culture than on fun in the sun; it offers study programs in yoga and ayurveda, among other heal-

ing treatments. ✉ *Chowara, just before Somatheeram, 695501* 🏠 *471/248–1632 or 471/248–2496* ⊕ *www.idealayurvedicresort.com* 🛏 *10 rooms, 4 cottages* ⚏ *Restaurant, cable TV, ayurveda center, yoga, laundry service, travel services; no a/c, no room TVs* ▤ *AE, DC, MC, V* ¶⚏ *EP.*

$–$$ 🏨 **Beach & Lake.** Sandwiched between the roar of the Arabian sea and the ripple of a backwater lagoon, this basic resort, north of Kovalam, is accessible only by boat. Ayurvedic treatments and plenty of quiet are the main draws. Mid-size rooms in a whitewashed, one-story building are simply furnished and well maintained, with private sit-outs facing the lagoon. A two-minute walk gets you to the public beach. ✉ *Pozhikkara Beach, Pachalloor Village 695527* 🕾 *471/238–2086* 🖷 *471/238–2066* ⊕ *www.beachandlakeresort.com* 🛏 *8* ⚏ *Restaurant, cable TV, boating, ayurveda center, yoga, library, travel services; no a/c in some rooms* ▤ *No credit cards* ¶⚏ *BP.*

$ 🏨 **Neelakanta.** This beachfront budget hotel, under renovation in early 2004, is popular with foreigners. The low-rise building sits right on Kovalam's main drag. Private sea-facing balconies in every room let you see all the action—people strolling, sunbathing, and fishing—on Lighthouse Beach. Air-conditioned rooms are spacious, with high ceilings; all are simply furnished and clean. ✉ *Lighthouse Beach, Kovalam Village 695527* 🕾 *471/248–0321 or 471/248–6004* 🖷 *471/284–5180* ⊕ *www.hotelneelakantakovalam.com* 🛏 *16 rooms* ⚏ *Restaurant, coffee shop, cable TV, ayurveda center, yoga, laundry service, travel services; no a/c in some rooms* ▤ *AE, DC, MC, V* ¶⚏ *EP.*

NORTHERN KERALA

If Kerala is unspoiled India, then Malabar—as the northern part of the state was once known—is unspoiled Kerala. Arab traders landed here long before Vasco da Gama, and many trading families converted to Islam. Various conquerors built forts along spectacular stretches of coastline, and some of Kerala's most unique and colorful religious festivals take place in this region. With the exception of the hill station of Wyanad, tourism has yet to make in-roads into the northern part of Kerala. Resorts, cruises, and sunbathing are almost unheard of. Nothing you see here has been prepackaged for your convenience, making a visit to northern Kerala a bit more work—but highly rewarding.

Calicut

⑭ *146 km (91 mi) northwest of Cochin.*

This city doesn't hold much excitement in itself, but Calicut (Kozhikode) has an airport and is a good base for exploring several interesting sights nearby, including the lushly forested Wyanad district to the northeast. The city's historical ties with the Middle East are clearly apparent due to the strong Arab presence.

In the town of Beypore, 10 km (6 mi) south of Calicut on the Beypore Road, is the **Tasara Center for Creative Weaving** (✉ Beypore North 🕾 495/241–832), where you can see weavers working on giant hand looms. Tasara also hosts programs for artists-in-residence. Call ahead to arrange a visit.

A group of local fishermen started the **Theeram Nature Conservation Society** (☎ no phone) when they discovered the Olive Ridley turtles they'd been eating were an endangered species. The center and its small turtle hatchery are on the beach at Kolavippalam, near Payyoli, about 30 km (19 mi) north of Calicut and off National Highway 17. If you're lucky, you can catch female turtles arriving on the beach in November and December to lay their eggs, which hatch in January and February.

Where to Stay & Eat

¢ ✕ **Paragon.** It's not much to look at, but this Calicut stalwart serves up tasty food. The chicken biriani is excellent, as is the unusual fried shrimp dish that goes very well with parathas. ✉ *Kannur Rd., Calicut* ☎ *No phone* ▭ *No credit cards.*

$$$$ 🏨 **Green Magic.** A true back-to-nature experience, this astonishing re-
Fodor'sChoice sort off the Wyanad Road 65 km (40 mi) northeast of Calicut has two
★ extraordinary tree houses perched 90 feet above the forest floor. One tree house is accessed by a water-powered elevator, the other by a suspension bridge—to use either contraption requires a good deal of faith. If you suffer from vertigo, request one of the ground-level stone lodges. Everything here is constructed with indigenous materials, except for the modern bathrooms. Lighting is restricted to kerosene lamps, meals are served on banana leaves, and a resident elephant is available for treks. ✉ *Vythiri, Wyanad District* ☎ *471/233–0437, 471/233–1507 reservations through Tour India* 🖷 *471/233–1407* ⊕ *www.tourindiakerala.com* 🛏 *4 tree house rooms, 6 lodges* ▭ *No credit cards* ❧ *Dining room, hiking* ¶❂¶ *FAP.*

$$$$ 🏨 **Kadavu.** As the first swank, world-class riverside resort 18 km (11 mi) south of Calicut, Kadavu signals Malabar's foray into tourism. You enter the lobby under a traditional *mandapam*, a wood-frame canopy supported by pillars. A fountain spouts from the large lotus pool behind the lobby, which is flanked by the wings of the hotel. The courtyard opens onto an enormous swimming pool, from which steps descend to riverfront cottages. Rooms are large and have with bay windows; cottages also have balconies screened by coconut palms. ✉ *Off N. H. Bypass, Azhinjilam, Feroke 673632* ☎ *483/283–0023 or 483/283–0027* 🖷 *483/283–0570* ⊕ *www.kadavuresorts.com* 🛏 *55 rooms, 17 cottages* ❧ *2 restaurants, coffee shop, cable TV, pool, health club, ayurvedic center, boating, laundry service, business services, travel services* ▭ *AE, DC, MC, V* ¶❂¶ *EP.*

$$ 🏨 **Taj Residency.** Calicut's premier hotel is frequented by airline crews and wealthy Omanis, who come for lengthy treatments at the well-regarded ayurvedic center. A beautiful wooden ceiling with exposed beams caps the lobby, and rooms are large and carpeted, with touches of wood trim. Some quarters have a leafy view; others overlook the pool. ✉ *PT Usha Rd., Calicut 673032* ☎ *495/276–5354* 🖷 *495/276–6448* ⊕ *www.tajhotels.com* 🛏 *74 rooms* ❧ *Restaurant, coffee shop, cable TV, pool, ayurveda center, bar, laundry service, business services, travel services* ▭ *AE, DC, MC, V* ¶❂¶ *BP.*

$ 🏨 **Fortune Hotel.** Slim wooden pillars encircle the pleasant lobby of this modern business hotel, and there's a beautiful terra-cotta–tile atrium decorated with Kathakali figurines. Rooms are mid-size and comfortably furnished, with large bathrooms and small balconies. If you're a non-smoker you'll have to grin and bear it—there are no designated no-smoking rooms. The rooftop pool affords nice city views. ⊠ *Kannur Rd., Calicut 673006* ☎ *495/276-8888* 🖶 *495/276-8111* ⊕ *www.fortunecalicut.com* ↩ *63 rooms* ♨ *Restaurant, coffee shop, cable TV, pool, health club, massage, bar, laundry service, business services, travel services* ▤ *AE, MC, V* ⅋ *BP.*

Kannur

⑮ *92 km (57 mi) northwest of Calicut.*

The Kannur district is the heartland of the Moppilahs—Kerala's Muslim community—and is a center for the hand-loom industry as well as the manufacture of *beedis,* potent Indian hand-rolled cigarettes. The town itself was for many years at the center of the maritime spice trade. The ruling Kolathiri rajas profited from the spice trade as did the European colonists. Today Kannur is a good hub for visiting several coastal sights—to the north and the south—including forts and undeveloped beaches. Come quick, though; massive development in the works at Bekal could change everything in 5 or 10 years.

★ A unique regional draw is the spectacular religious dance called **Theyyam.** More than an art form, it's a type of worship—tribal in origin and thought that predates Hinduism in Kerala. Theyyams aren't held in traditional temples, but rather in small shrines or family compounds. Dancers don elaborate costumes and terrifying makeup for the ritual dance, in which they're believed to become possessed by the spirit of the deity they represent. These divine powers are thought to allow them to perform feats such as dancing with a 30-foot headdress, a flaming costume, or falling into a pile of burning embers. The ritual is accompanied by intense drumming, howling, and chanting. Theyyam season is from November to May.

The Portuguese built **Fort St. Angelo,** with the consent of the ruling Kolathiri Raja, in 1505 to protect their interests in the area. After passing into Dutch and then British hands, it's now maintained by the Archaeological Survey of India. There are still a few British cannons intact, and lovely views of the fishing activity in Moppillah Bay. ⊠ *Off NH 17, 3 km (2 mi) north of Kannur* ☎ *No phone* 🎫 *Free* ☉ *Daily 10–4:30.*

In 1839 Herman Gundert, a Protestant missionary from the Swiss Basel Mission, arrived in the town of Thalassery, south of Kannur. A prodigious scholar, Gundert published some 50 books on Malabar in the 20 years he lived here, including the first English–Malayalam dictionary. His bungalow is now part of a college campus. The small **Gundert Memorial Church** next to the campus is a pretty blend of Kerala and European architecture. The walls beside the altar are decorated with paintings of medicinal herbs—one of Gundert's many interests. ⊠ *National Hwy., 20 km (12 mi) south of Kannur* ☎ *No phone* 🎫 *Free* ☉ *Weekdays 10–4.*

The **Kanhirode Weaving Cooperative** is strewn with yarns of all colors, set out to dry after dyeing. You can watch the weavers at their giant, clackety-clacking looms, making bed sheets and upholstery for export as well as brightly colored saris. ⊠ *Off Kannur–Mysore Rd., 13 km (8 mi) east of Kannur, Kanhirode* ☎ *497/285–1259* ⊒ *Free* ⊙ *Weekdays 9:30–4:30.*

The unusual **Sri Muthappan Temple** sits on the bank of the Valapattanam River at Parassini Kaduvu. It's devoted to Lord Shiva in the form of a tribal hunter, and it hosts Theyyam performances almost every day of the year. Though it's not as colorful as traditional outdoor festivals, you can at least get a taste of Theyyam. As Sri Muthappan is usually pictured with a hunting dog, friendly mutts roam the sanctuary, and offerings at the shrine take the form of bronze dog figurines. ⊠ *Off NH 17, 18 km (11 mi) north of Kannur, Parassini* ⊒ *Free* ⊙ *Theyyams usually held 5:30 AM–8 AM and 6:30 PM–8 PM.*

The drive north from Kannur to Bekal, in the Kasargode district, is a dreamy trip through sleepy towns with nothing but coconut and paddy fields in between. **Bekal Fort** is Kerala's largest, covering more than over 40 seafront acres. The 300-year-old structure rises from a green lawn, and looks out over the Arabian sea or distant coconut groves. You can easily spend a peaceful hour or two clambering around the ruins. The loudest noise you'll hear is the crashing of the waves against the ramparts. A massive resort development project is planned in the area, however, with grandiose plans to one day turn Bekal into a top Asian tourist destination. ⊠ *NH 17, 72 km (45 mi) north of Kannur, Bekal* ☎ *499/277–2900* ⊒ *Rs. 240* ⊙ *Daily 9–5.*

Where to Stay & Eat

¢ ✕ **Coachman's Inn.** Local well-to-do families often dine here at tables made more private by small dividers. The food is top notch (the cooks supposedly served the royal family). The naan here is particularly good, garnished with black sesame seeds. Try also the fish *malabari* (a mild curry preparation) and the chicken *vattichathu* (a dry, spicy preparation with the chicken almost crumbled into small pieces). ⊠ *Kamala International, SM Rd., Kannur* ☎ *497/276–6910* ⊟ *MC, V* ⊙ *EP.*

$$$$ ▦ **Ayisha Manzil.** A stay in this 200-year-old clifftop home built in 1862 may be the best way to experience what north Kerala is all about. Your hosts are C. P. Moosa and his wife, Faiza, who cooks up fantastic nightly feasts featuring local specialties. Breakfast is served on the front terrace, overlooking the sea. The house manager can accompany you on excursions in the area, or you can just hang out by the gorgeous brick-tile pool. Rooms are palatial, with high wood-beam ceilings and antique teak and rosewood furnishings. ⊠ *Court Rd., Thalassery 670101* ▦ *490/234–1590* ⤴ *6 rooms* ⚄ *Dining room, cable TV, pool, laundry service, travel services; no a/c in some rooms, no room TVs* ⊟ *MC, V* ⊙ *FAP.*

$ ▦ **Mascot.** This modest hotel's hillcrest location affords fantastic sea views from most rooms. Standard rooms are clean and relatively spacious, with marble floors and plenty of windows; some with air-conditioning are a little smaller. Deluxe rooms are large and close to the water, with bay windows. A cliffside walkway leads to the large swimming pool and ayurveda center. The closest beach has been taken over by the navy, but Payyambalam Beach is a 15-minute walk away. ⊠ *Near Baby Beach,*

Burnassery, Kannur 670013 ☎ *497/270–8445 or 497/270–8455* 🖷 *497/ 270–5862* ⊕ *www.mascotresort.net* ↩ *24 rooms* ⚫ *Restaurant, cable TV, pool, ayurveda center, laundry service, business services, travel services; no a/c in some rooms* ▭ *MC, V* ⍠ *EP.*

KERALA A TO Z

To research prices, get advice from other travelers, and book travel arrangements, visit www.fodors.com.

AIR TRAVEL

Most international flights land in Trivandrum or Cochin. Air India, Silk Air, Gulf Air, and Sri Lankan Airlines operate international flights to Trivandrum; Cochin is served by Silk Air and Emirates; at this writing, Lufthansa was considering a Frankfurt–Cochin flight. Calicut is linked to the Middle East by Air India and Indian Airlines. Indian Airlines and Jet Airways cover domestic routes. There are no flights within Kerala itself.

🚩 Airlines & Contacts **Air India** ☎ 484/235-1295 or 471/231-0310. **Emirates** ☎ 484/238-4610 or 484/238-4611. **Gulf Air** ☎ 471/232-8003 or 471/250-1205. **Indian Airlines** ☎ 484/237-0238 or 471/231-6870. **Jet Airways** ☎ 484/229-3231 or 471/232-1018. **Silk Air** ☎ 484/236-7911 or 471/231-4141. **Sri Lankan Airlines** ☎ 484/236-1666 or 471/232-2309.

AIRPORTS & TRANSFERS

Cochin's international airport is about 40 km (25 mi) east of the city; abominable traffic can make it a two-hour trip. Some hotels offer free airport pickup; otherwise, a taxi will cost about Rs. 350. The small airport in Trivandrum is 6 km (4 mi) west of the city center; taxis charge about Rs. 50 to get to the city and Rs. 300 Rs. 400 to reach Kovalam. Traffic can be heavy. Calicut's Karipur Airport is 23 km (14 mi) south of town; a cab will cost roughly Rs. 125.

🚩 Airport Information **Karipur Airport** ☎ 495/271-2762. **Cochin International Airport** ☎ 484/261-0115. **Trivandrum International Airport** ☎ 471/250-1542 international information, 471/250-1537 domestic information.

BOAT & FERRY TRAVEL

In Cochin, public ferries and private boats ply between Fort Cochin, Willingdon Island, and Ernakulam throughout the day. Ernakulam's main boat jetty is just south of the Taj Residency hotel. Boats leave for Fort Cochin roughly every half hour from 6 AM to 9 PM. There are three afternoon ferries to Mattancherry, and frequent ferries to Embarkation Jetty, on Willingdon Island's eastern tip. From this pleasant, uncrowded ferry station, there's frequent service to both Ernakulam and Fort Cochin. It's almost impossible to figure out which ferry is which—just ask. Ferry rides cost only a few rupees; from Ernakulam's High Court or Sea Lord Jetty you can hire private boats, usually for about Rs. 400 an hour.

The Kerala Tourism Development Corporation (KTDC) conducts two inexpensive boat tours of Cochin each day; the 3½-hour trips depart at 9 AM and 2 PM from the Sealord Jetty, opposite the Sealord Hotel, between the Main and High Court jetties. The Tourist Desk also conducts boat tours.

You may find boat cruises offered near Kovalam, but the experience is not as culturally fascinating as it is in central Kerala, where people still live on the backwaters. There are an estimated 200–250 houseboats now operating in Kerala; most are based in the Alleppey district. When booking an overnight stay on a houseboat, make sure it comes equipped with solar panels and a fan, or you're in for a hot night. Boats with inboard motors are quieter; a few have air-conditioning. The going rate for a posh two-bedroom vessel is roughly Rs. 8,000; a one-bedroom will run about Rs. 5,000. Small boats feel cramped; 14 feet is a very comfortable width for a few people. A day cruise through little canals on a motorized or punted canoe is an excellent budget option—try to get a boat with a canopy to keep cool.

Private companies, the KTDC, and the Tourist Desk operate half-day backwater tours from Alleppey for around Rs. 100 to Rs. 400. The Alleppey Tourism Development Cooperative (ATDC) runs daily trips between Alleppey and Quilon (Rs. 300 for 8 hrs). After Quilon, boats continue south to Trivandrum and Kovalam. Boats leave both Alleppey and Quilon at 10:30 AM.

⛴ Boat & Ferry Information **ATDC** ✉ Komala Rd., Alleppey ☎ 477/224-3462. **KTDC** ✉ Shanmugham Rd., Ernakulam, Cochin ☎ 484/235-3234. **Tourist Desk** ✉ Main Boat Jetty, Ernakulam, Cochin ☎ 484/237-1761.

CARS & DRIVERS

Major roads are well maintained. If you're coming from Tamil Nadu, the drive from Madurai along the Madurai–Kottayam Road is stunning. National Highway (NH) 47 runs from Salem, in central Tamil Nadu, to Cochin through some lovely country before heading down the coast to Cape Comorin in Kanya Kumari. In 2001, NH 47 was repaved from Cochin to Trivandrum, making it a zippy highway, with four lanes between Cochin and Alleppey. NH 17 runs along the coast from Mangalore south to Cochin, though it gets a little rough north of Calicut. Roads to the interior *ghats* (mountains) are often breathtaking, as the landscape changes from the brilliant lime green of the paddy fields to the rich, dark green of the tea plantations and jungle. The journey from Trivandrum to Cochin takes about five hours.

The most convenient way to get around Kerala is with a hired car and driver. Figure about Rs. 6 per kilometer for a non-air-conditioned car and a halt charge of Rs. 100 per night. Tinted windows and a back curtain help cool down a non-air-conditioned car, even on a short ride. Air-conditioned vehicles will cost a bit more, but can make the difference between a pleasant journey and an exhausting one. Shop around, and hire a car from a government-approved travel agency.

EMERGENCIES

⛑ **Cosmopolitan Hospital** ✉ Maurinja Palayam, Trivandrum ☎ 471/244-8182. **Lissy Hospital** ✉ Lissy Junction, Ernakulam, Cochin ☎ 484/240-2668.

MAIL & SHIPPING

✉ Post Offices **Calicut Main Post Office** ✉ Mananchira Rd., Calicut ☎ 495/272-0164. **Ernakulam GPO** ✉ Hospital Rd., Ernakulam, Cochin ☎ 484/235-5467. **Trivandrum GPO** ✉ M. G. Rd. ☎ 471/247-3071.

MONEY MATTERS

ATMS   ATMs are now available in Kerala's major cities: Cochin, Trivandrum, and Calicut. Check for the Cirrus or Plus sign, as many local banks do not accept foreign cards. Look for international banks like ANZ Grindlays, HSBC, and Standard Chartered, as well as the Indian bank ICICI. Make sure your PIN is four digits.

CURRENCY   Most major hotels have exchange services. Thomas Cook offers good
EXCHANGE   rates. The Bank of India and ANZ Grindlays cash traveler's checks and change money, as does any branch of the Bank of India. Traveler's checks sometimes get marginally higher rates than cash.

🗗 Exchange Services **ANZ Grindlays** ✉ M. G. Rd., Ernakulam, Cochin ☎ 484/237-2086. **Bank of India** ✉ Shanmugham Rd., Ernakulam, Cochin ☎ 484/236-6796. **Thomas Cook** ✉ M. G. Rd., Ernakulam, Cochin 🖷 484/236-9729.

TAXIS & AUTO-RICKSHAWS

Auto-rickshaws are a convenient and quick way to travel around town. In Cochin, figure Rs. 6 for the first kilometer and Rs. 3.50 per additional kilometer—other cities will be slightly less. Don't be alarmed if your driver doesn't use the meter—it usually doesn't work. Make sure to agree on a fare before you get in, and don't trust a driver for unbiased shopping recommendations. Cabs are also a good option for destinations getting around Cochin. Fares will run about Rs. 75 an hour for a non-air-conditioned car. Most cabs have a Rs. 70 minimum. Ask at any tourist office about the latest legal rates. You can hire taxis at your hotel for a slightly higher rate, and a likelihood that your driver might speak some English, or pick them up at cab stands near the Sea Lord Jetty or at the intersection of M. G. Road and Club Road.

TRAIN TRAVEL

Rail journeys in Kerala can be scenic, and more comfortable than traveling by car. The *KK Express*—which travels from Kanya Kumari, at India's southern tip, all the way up to New Delhi—is a good train to take through Kerala, as is the *Kerala Express*. December is a major pilgrimage season, so you'll need to book tickets in advance. Check with KTDC for the latest schedules and fares, or try www.indianrail.gov.in, and use a travel agent or your hotel's travel desk to make bookings, unless you don't mind standing in the unruly queue at the train station.

🗗 **KTDC** ✉ Shanmugham Rd., Ernakulam, Cochin ☎ 484/235-3234.

🗗 Train Stations **Calicut Railway Station** ☎ 133. **Ernakulam Junction** ☎ 131. **Ernakulam Town Station** ☎ 484/235-3920. **Trivandrum Central Station** ☎ 132.

TRAVEL AGENTS & TOURS

The KTDC has several inexpensive tours, including wildlife-spotting excursions to the Lake Periyar Wildlife Sanctuary and one- to two-week trips that follow a pilgrim trail through Kerala's sacred shrines. Sita Travels can help with bookings and arrange a car and driver. The Great India Tour Company, one of Kerala's best travel agencies, has offices throughout South India. SATM Tours and Travel designs affordable packages around your interests. Trivandrum-based Tourindia created the houseboat phenomenon and offers unusual Kerala experiences. One intriguing two- to three-day trip—created by Tourindia and the forestry department—sends you deep into the jungle with a local guide, an armed escort, and a naturalist. Destination Holidays specializes in Kerala tours, and has a good reputation among budget operators for good service and local knowledge.

🚩 **Destination Holidays** ⊠ Pallath Bldgs., Kurisupally Road, Ravipuram, Ernakulam ☎ 484/235-6497 or 484/235-7316. **Great India Tour Company** ⊠ Mullassery Towers, Vanross Junction, Trivandrum ☎ 471/233-1516 ⊠ Pithuru Smarana, 1st fl., Srikandath Rd., Ravipuram, Cochin ☎ 484/237-4109. **KTDC** ⊠ Shanmugham Rd., Ernakulam, Cochin ☎ 484/235-3234. **SATM Tours and Travel** ⊠ Warriam Rd., Cochin ☎ 484/236-5765. **Sita Travels** ⊠ Tharakan Building, M. G. Rd., Ernakulam, Cochin ☎ 484/236-1101. **Tourindia** ⊠ PB 136 M. G. Rd., Trivandrum ☎ 471/233-0437 or 471/233-1507.

VISITOR INFORMATION

Excellent brochures, maps, and pamphlets on all of Kerala's districts are available at any KTDC office. In Cochin, the office is open daily 8 to 7. Trivandrum's two KTDC offices—one in town and one at the airport—are open weekdays 10 to 5.

In Cochin, an alternative source of information is the Tourist Desk, a private, nonprofit organization that conducts moderately priced tours and provides clear, straightforward information about the state. In Kannur, the District Tourism Promotion Council is quite active. Central Kerala is well served by the ATDC. The Government of India Tourist Office—open weekdays 9 to 5:30 and Saturday 9 to 1—has its own vehicles, boats, lodgings, and tours.

🚩 Tourist Information **ATDC** ⊠ Komala Rd., Alleppey ☎ 477/224-3462. **Government of India Tourist Office** ⊠ Malabar Rd., Willingdon Island, Cochin, ☎ 484/266-8352. **Kannur District Tourism Promotion Council** ⊠ Taluk Office Campus, Kannur ☎ 497/270-6336. **KTDC** ⊠ Shanmugham Rd., Ernakulam Cochin ☎ 484/235-3234 ⊠ Museum Rd., Trivandrum ☎ 471/232-2279. **Tourist Desk** ⊠ Main Boat Jetty, Ernakulam, Cochin ☎ 484/237-1761.

TAMIL NADU

9

MARVEL AT HOW HINDU WOMEN
begin a new day ⇨*p.474*

GAWK AT THE WORLD'S LARGEST
bas-relief ⇨*p.489*

SUP VEGETARIAN
at a spot rightly named after
the goddess of food ⇨*p.478*

STAND IN THE SHADOW
of a soaring pyramidal tower ⇨*p.499*

NOTE THAT THE HALL OF A THOUSAND PILLARS
has merely 985 of them ⇨*p.501*

By Molly
Sholes and
Vikram Singh

Updated by
Kavita Milner

MORE THAN A FEW DEGREES of latitude and temperature separate India's Aryan north from its Dravidian south. Encompassing numerous cultures within them, North and South India have completely different climates, crops, cuisines, languages, architecture, and social customs. The state of Tamil Nadu—running about 805 km (500 mi) along the Bay of Bengal to India's southernmost tip, Cape Comorin—is the heartland of South India. From the Tamil coast, with its gorgeous, bright-green rice fields and coconut and banana trees, the land rises through the low-lying Eastern Ghats (mountains) up to tea, coffee, and spice plantations in the Nilgiri Hills, and finally to the higher Western Ghats.

Hinduism pervades the Tamils's lives, beliefs, philosophy, and behavior. A rich oral tradition, 2,000-year-old religious texts and literature, and Jain and Buddhist influences have made South Indian Hinduism a distinct, vibrant, evolving religion. The Tamils have survived incursions from North Indians and foreigners alike, but neither the Portuguese nor the French nor the British, who ruled Madras for 300 years, made more than a superficial dent in the soul of Tamil culture. Majestic South Indian temples with massive *gopurams* (entrance towers) and *vimanas* (towers over inner sanctums) dominate the Tamil landscape just as faith permeates Tamil life. A visit to at least one major temple is key to understanding this part of India.

About a third of Tamil Nadu is urban; many of the cities have more than 50,000 people. Even the smaller villages are not far from a city or town. A good bus system, frequent pilgrimages, a 70% literacy rate, and expanding and improving communications keep the Tamil villager reasonably well informed, and far from isolated.

Exploring Tamil Nadu

About the Restaurants

A traditional Tamil meal is a balance of the six tastes of Indian cuisine: sweet, sour, pungent, astringent, salty, and bitter. Rice is a basic ingredient, whether cooked or ground into flour. Tamil dishes can be hot or bland; those that are usually mild include *idlis,* cakes made of steamed rice and black gram batter (rice- and chickpea flour are soaked, ground into a batter, then steamed); plain *dosas,* crêpes made of rice and black gram batter; *upma,* semolina and spices, often with vegetables; and *curd-rice,* yogurt mixed with rice at room temperature. The *thali,* available vegetarian or nonvegetarian, is a multicourse feast on one platter. *Decoction,* or "coffee by the yard," is strong filter coffee mixed with hot milk and poured back and forth between two metal tumblers until it is cool enough to drink, at which point it's also white with froth. It's delicious—the best cup of coffee you'll have in India.

Tamils once preferred to eat only in their homes for reasons of personal and religious purity. The best restaurants were confined to the larger hotels, which catered to foreign travelers. But Madras has become a cosmopolitan city, and fine restaurants are, increasingly, serving alternative cuisines. The formerly ubiquitous Mughlai menus have been widely replaced with authentic ethnic food, including South Indian, Continental, Mediterranean, Chinese, Thai, Korean and even Tex-Mex. An 8% sales tax is often levied on food and drink.

WHAT IT COSTS In Rupees				
$$$$	$$$	$$	$	¢
IN MADRAS				
AT DINNER over 500	400–500	300–400	150–300	under 150
IN SMALL TOWNS OUTSIDE MADRAS				
AT DINNER over 350	250–350	150–250	100–150	under 100

Restaurant prices are for an entrée plus dal, rice, and a veg/non-veg dish.

About the Hotels

Unless otherwise noted, all hotels have air-conditioning. The state government runs "Tamilnadu" hotels, which are modest, usually clean hotels with simple restaurants—modern versions of the *dak* (bungalow, or rest house) of the British Raj. Some hotels in Madras have conference rooms, dedicated business-traveler floors and suites, secretarial services, and in-room fax machines. Due to increasing commercial travel, reservations for rooms in Madras are essential, especially between December and February. Tamil Nadu levies a 20% luxury tax on room rates, and a 10% hotel-expenditure tax on the total bill.

WHAT IT COSTS In Rupees				
$$$$	$$$	$$	$	¢
IN MADRAS				
FOR 2 PEOPLE over 8,000	6,000–8,000	4,000–6,000	2,000–4,000	under 2,000
IN SMALL TOWNS OUTSIDE MADRAS				
FOR 2 PEOPLE over 4,000	3,000–4,000	2,000–3,000	1,000–2,000	under 1,000

Hotel prices are for two people in a standard double room in high season, excluding approximately 20% tax.

Timing

The best time to visit is between November and February. Roads are often in disrepair after the torrential rains of the monsoon season (which ends in September), but the sun is moderate in the winter months. This is the season for temple festivals and dance and music programs, and it's also the best time to observe migratory birds. Advance hotel and transport reservations are strongly recommended for this time of year. Note that Hindu temples close in the afternoon (noon to 4). Most stores and museums are open all day, every day, at least in Madras (Chennai), however, some museums have their own schedules.

MADRAS (CHENNAI)

Chennai is the new name for the old city of Madras, the garden gateway to South India. In 1640 an East India Company agent called Fran-

Any doubling back on these routes is necessitated by heavy traffic and bad road conditions. On Tamil Nadu's main north–south artery, NH 45, speeds average 58 kph (35 mph) in the middle of the day. Thanjavur and Swamimalai are on secondary roads that can also be maddeningly slow.

Numbers in the text correspond to numbers in the margin and on the Tamil Nadu, Madras, and Mahabalipuram maps.

9

If you have 4 days

Spend two days in historic ⊡ **Madras** ❶–⓭ to see its colorful bazaars and Hindu temples. On the third day drive south via the Shore Road to ⊡ **Mahabalipuram** ⓯–㉑, on the Bay of Bengal, to see the cave temples. The next morning leave early to explore **Kanchipuram** ㉒, a pilgrimage town with 200 temples and a thriving silk industry, on your way back to Madras.

If you have 7 days

Spend two days and nights in ⊡ **Madras** ❶–⓭. On your third day, visit **Kanchipuram** ㉒; continue south to ⊡ **Mahabalipuram** ⓯–㉑ for nights three and four. On Day 5, move on to ⊡ **Pondicherry** ㉓ to explore its French heritage and unwind a bit. On Day 6, drive to **Tiruchirappalli** ㉔, then proceed late in the evening to ⊡ **Madurai** ㉖. Devote Day 7 to the astonishing Meenakshi Temple before returning to Madras.

If you have 10 days

After spending two days in ⊡ **Madras** ❶–⓭, travel to ⊡ **Mahabalipuram** ⓯–㉑ via the Shore Road, stopping at the Crocodile Bank or Dakshina-Chitra en route. Day-trip to **Kanchipuram** ㉒ and check out the migratory life in the Vedanthangal Bird Sanctuary on the way back to Mahabalipuram. Spend your fifth day in Mahabalipuram, exploring the cave temples and perhaps hitting the beach, before heading back to Madras. On Day 6, fly or take the train to ⊡ **Tiruchirappalli** ㉔. Proceed to ⊡ **Thanjavur** ㉕ and Swamimalai on Day 7 to see the bronze foundry and the temples. On Day 8, drive to ⊡ **Madurai** ㉖ and spend the night and the next day there before returning to Madras by plane or train.

cis Day negotiated with the Raja of Chandragiri, the last Vijayanagar ruler, for a strip of land on the Coromandel coast; the British built a fortified factory there, called it Fort St. George after England's patron saint, and unknowingly laid the foundation of the modern city of today. From the time the British built their fort on that sliver of beach, the city has grown by absorbing the surrounding villages. Each area has developed distinctly, often along caste lines, from the Chettiars (a South Indian caste of traders) of George Town to the civil servants and industrialists of Nungambakkam. Madras is the fourth-largest city in India, but is growing. Municipal boundaries expand, multistory apartment and office buildings replace bungalows, and new residential areas spring up along the Shore Road to Mahabalipuram.

Growth has made traffic nearly unbearable here, with increasing pollution and noise levels. Cars, buses, trucks, auto-rickshaws (or "autos," as they're popularly called), mopeds, bicycles, motorcycles, pedestrians, fish carts, and cows all compete for space in the streets. (Traffic on the main streets, like Anna Salai, is regulated and moves along smoothly.) The city's water supply is woefully inadequate, and even nonexistent in some areas. Tanker trucks bringing water into the city add to the congestion and pollution.

The rapid arrival of multinational corporations has changed the placid pace of life in Madras, which in the old days was alive at 5 AM and asleep by 9 PM. Still, nothing seems to have shaken the city's spiritual essence. Madras is a fascinating place, its cosmopolitan face contrasting sharply with its resolutely religious soul.

Just as Madras has been renamed Chennai, so have many of the street names changed, very often to honor contemporary politicians. Some of the new names are not in colloquial usage, but here's a partial list, with the old name listed first (*salai* means street or road): Mount Road—Anna Salai; Chamier's Road—Muthuramalinga Road; Mowbray's Road—T. T. K. (Krishnamachari) Road; Edward Eliot's Road—Dr. Radhakrishnan Salai; North Beach Road—Rajaji Salai; Nungambakkam High Road—Uttamar Gandhi Salai; Poonamallee High Road—Periyar E. V. R. High Road; South Beach Road—Kamarajar Road. Also note that the Thyagaraja Nagar area, in the southern part of the city, is always referred to as T. Nagar, and Raja Annamalai Puram is always called R. A. Puram.

Northern Madras

Northern Madras is a large commercial and administrative district that has its nerve center in Fort St. George. All the commerce in this area has its roots in the early-colonial era—the neighborhood of George Town grew around the British-built fort to cater to its trading needs, and has continued its historic business traditions right up to the present day.

Numbers in the text correspond to numbers in the margin and on the Madras map.

a good
tour

The best way to explore Madras is to follow the city's expansion south from Fort St. George. Some distances are short, but if the temperature is 100°F and the humidity 80%, you won't feel like walking; if oppressive heat threatens, hire a car. Start at **St. Mary's Church** ❶ ☞ in **Fort St. George.** Move on to the **Fort Museum** ❷; then walk by the **Tamil Nadu State Legislature** ❸. Return to St. Mary's Church, taking in the mixture of historic buildings and bureaucratic offices. Drive the ¼ mi to the **High Court** ❹ via the road that tunnels through the fort's massive walls; park and walk to Armenian Street. Alternately, take a taxi or auto-rickshaw to N. S. C. Bose Road and get out at the junction of Armenian Street for a stroll through **George Town.** Walk down Armenian Street to the beautiful Armenian Church, which was built in 1629 and is no longer used for worship. As you wander on, look up

9

Performing Arts

Bharatanatyam, a feminine dance form (though some men have also begun to achieve proficiency in it), and Carnatic music are the best known of the traditional South Indian performing arts. Similar in composition to North Indian music, the Carnatic art is nonetheless distinguished by its instruments and its vocal style. Many Tamil film scores are written in the Carnatic style.

Shopping

Look for silver tribal jewelry, jute placemats, copies of Chola bronzes, Kanchipuram silks, *khadi* (hand-woven) shirts, carved wooden temple friezes, inlaid wooden boxes, contemporary artwork, and Thanjavur paintings. Bargaining isn't as prevalent as it once was, but almost everything here is a bargain anyway. Madras and Madurai have excellent shops, and nearly all major hotels have boutiques, most of which have fixed prices and take credit cards. Hotel stores tend to be expensive: shop around if you're buying a big-ticket item. Government-run craft emporiums have excellent selections, and surrounding most large temples are four streets of bazaars where bargaining is expected. In the past, bazaars were the *only* places to shop for groceries, household goods, jewelry, fruit, electronics, and paper products; over time, though, the supermarket concept has taken root.

Temples

With their lofty gopurams, vimanas, and majestic *mandapams* (pillared halls), temples are integral parts of Tamil culture. The gopurams are often brilliantly polychrome, and the mandapam friezes inside depict myths and legends of Hindu gods and goddesses, and sometimes tales of the temple's benefactor. South Indian temples throng daily with pilgrims and visitors; the larger, better-known temples are pilgrimage shrines or are visited mainly on special occasions, such as *Pongal* (harvest festival) and birthdays. The smaller temples are part of daily life.

South Indian Hinduism is a personal, ritualistic religion. Almost anything—a tree, a rock, a sculpture—can be an object of veneration. Hindus worship at their temples in a variety of ways. Some devotees withdraw to the inner sanctum for *puja*—acts of reverence—which consist of *darshan* ("spiritual seeing" or visual communication with the image of the deity), making a donation, and receiving blessings. Others worship a specific carved image in the mandapam frieze, and still others go to the sacred peepul tree and tie a ribbon around it. After puja, worshippers sit outside in the mandapam for a few minutes, absorbing the temple ambience. In a temple courtyard, you might even see priests blessing a brand-new car. Non-Hindus are usually free to explore these houses of worship, barring only the inner sanctum.

---

and you'll see evidence of second-story residence—many merchants still live in George Town. Complete your tour of George Town back at the High Court.

TIMING The ideal time to cover this route is Sunday morning, when the traffic and parking are most benign. The full tour should take five or six hours,

Tamil Nadu

KARNATAKA

ANDHRA
PRADESH

Tirupati 14

Madras
1 – 13
see detail
map

Chittoor

Ambattur

Bangalore

Vellore

Tambaram

48

Hosur

Kanchipuram

22 Covelong
Beach

Mysore

Mahabalipuram
15 – 21
see detail map

Tiruvannamalai

Auroville

Yercaud

Viluppuram

23 **Pondicherry**

Cuddalore

Salem

Vriddhachalam

Neyveli

*Bay of
Bengal*

Ooty

Chidambaram

Coonoor

Erode

Namakkal

Gangai-Konda-Solpuram

47

Tiruppur

Karur

Kumbakonam

Tranquebar

Coimbatore

Grand Anaicut

Swamimalai

Karaikal

Pollachi

24

25

Nagapattinam

Trichur

Tiruchirappalli

Thanjavur

Velakani

Palani

Vedaranyam
Point Calimere

Koddi Kanal

Dindigul

Pudukkotai

Cochin

Palk Strait

Madurai 26

Karaikkudi

KERALA

Manamadurai

Jaffna

Palk Bay

Rajapalaiyam

49

Rameswaram

Ramanathapuram

Talaimanner

Tenkasi

*Adam's
Bridge*

Quilon

Tirunelveli

7A

Tuticorin

Trivandrum

Palayankottai

*Gulf of
Mannar*

Tiruchchendur

Nagercoil

Kanyakumari

SRI LANKA

*Cape
Comorin*

0   40 miles

0   60 km

INDIAN OCEAN

including thorough tours of George Town and Fort St. George (two hours each) and half an hour in the High Court.

What to See

2 Fort St. George. The first British fort in India was founded by Francis Day on a thin strip of sand leased from the Raja of Chandragiri. The Indian army and civil service, Colin Mackenzie's land survey, and the British archaeological, botanical, and zoological surveys of India were all conceived on this site. Complete with walls 20 feet thick, the fort is no longer a symbol of the Raj, or British India, as much as it is of the Tamil Nadu State Legislature, which now occupies a part of it. In fact, it's difficult to find historical buildings within the fort because of inadequate signage or because certain areas are closed to the public. The best day to explore is Sunday. Once an exchange used by East India Company merchants, the **Fort Museum** contains everything from old uniforms and coins to palanquins and padlocks, and has some wonderful old prints. No cameras (still or video) are allowed. ⊠ *Entrance on Kamarajar Rd., Fort* ☎ *Museum only 44/2567–1127* ⊗ *Fort: daily 10–6; museum: Sat.–Thurs. 10–5* ⊠ *Fort free; museum foreigners US$2.*

George Town. If you tend toward agoraphobia, George Town is not the place for you, as walking—the only way to explore this teeming warren of congested streets—is often hard going. Before you venture into George Town, make sure you have a detailed map of this area so you can wander with confidence; many streets have similar names. For the full experience, come in the morning, when the bustle is at its peak.

Originally called Black Town, this 2½-by-3-km (1½-by-2-mi) area was first settled by lower-caste artisans who provided textiles to the British traders. After Black Town was burned in the British–French wars, the new town was laid out in a perfect grid pattern, each section housing a different group or caste with its own place of worship. The street names echo George Town's mercantile history, as each area bears the cultural characteristics of the group who migrated there in the course of doing business with (or for) the East India Company: Not only Indians, but Portuguese, Scots, Armenians, and Jews settled here. Another prominent group are the Chettiars; you'll notice that many of the street names end in "chetti." Two competitive subcastes of the Chettiars long vied for mercantile power, first with the East India Company and then with the merchants of the Raj. ⊠ *Bordered by Basin Bridge Rd., Old Jail St., Ebrahim Sabib St., and Rajaji Rd., Parry's.*

★ 4 High Court. This large judicial complex is a magnificent example of Indo-Saracenic architecture, built of red sandstone with intricate ornamentation on the walls and minarets. (The tallest minaret was used as a lighthouse until the 1970s.) Inside is a labyrinth of corridors and courts, most of which you can visit; court No. 13 has the finest decorations inside. Within the compound is a tomb in the shape of pyramid; one of its two inscriptions is to the only son of Elihu Yale, governor of Fort St. George from 1687 to 1691. The child died in infancy and was buried in the High Court compound. ⊠ *Just north of fort off N. S. C. Bose Rd., near intersection with Rajaji Salai, Parry's* ☎ *44/2534–1773*

Basilica of
San Thome
Cathedral **12**

Fort St. George . .**2**

High Court **4**

Kapalishvara
Temple **11**

Luz Church **13**

Madras
Snake Park **9**

Marina Beach . .**5**

National Museum
and Art Gallery . .**7**

Parthasarathi
Temple **6**

St. Mary's
Church **1**

St. Thomas
Mount **8**

The Study **10**

Tamil Nadu State
Legislature **3**

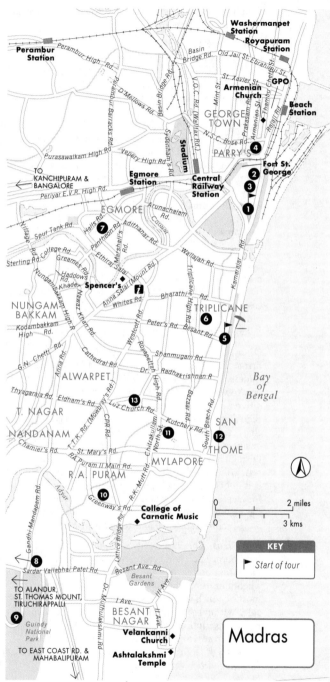

Madras

⊠ *Tour Rs. 10* ⊙ *Mon.–Sat. 10–5. Guided tours, Mon.–Sat. 10:30–1:45 and 2:30–4:30.*

★ � ❶ **St. Mary's Church.** Consecrated in 1680, this church is the oldest masonry structure in Fort St. George and the oldest Anglican church east of Suez. The *punkahs* (pulley-operated ceiling fans) and some flags are gone, and the steeple has been replaced, but otherwise the building with its arcaded side aisles and bomb-proof roof has not changed. The marriage of governor Elihu Yale (of Yale University fame) was the first one performed here. Job Charnock, founder of Calcutta, had his three daughters baptized here before the family moved to Bengal, and St. Mary's congregation included, at one time or another, Thomas Pitt, Warren Hastings (later the first governor general of British India), Lord Cornwallis, and Arthur Wellesley, later the Duke of Wellington. The compound is paved with old tombstones including the oldest British tombstone in India belonging to an Elizabeth Baker. ⊠ *Fort St. George* ⊠ *Free* ⊙ *Daily 9:30–5.*

❸ **Tamil Nadu State Legislature.** This crowded, active seat of the state government occupies a large part of Fort St. George. The former house of Robert Clive (of the Battle of Plassey fame) is the "Pay Accounts" office. Other sections of the fort are under military control and closed to visitors. A new, state-of-the-art legislature complex is to be built in 2005 or 2006 at Kotturpuram, after which the government offices will move out of the fort. ⊠ *Fort St. George.*

Central Madras

As Madras grew, the city moved south, expanding along the beach and inland to Egmore and Nungambakkam. The Chepauk district, home of Madras University and Chepauk Palace (now government offices), has some of India's best Indo-Saracenic buildings—a combination of Hindu, Muslim, and Victorian Gothic styles that makes a fitting display for a city with roots in all three cultures. Farther south along the beach is the Triplicane neighborhood, with the Parthasarathi Temple. Inland, toward the center of Madras is Anna Salai, a major shopping and business district. North of Anna Salai is Egmore, bordered by the curves of the Cooum River and home to the National Museum and Art Gallery. Farther south across the Cooum is Nungambakkam, traditionally a posh residential area of garden homes. It's now a mixture of expensive boutiques, hotels, and offices, but a few of the massive old houses with walled gardens remain. A new wave of fast-food joints (as in hot dogs and pizza), coffee shops, and restaurants has hit Alwarpet, Egmore, and Nungambakkam.

Numbers in the text correspond to numbers in the margin and on the Madras map.

a good
tour

It's easiest to cover this ground by hiring a car and driver for the day, but you can also take auto-rickshaws from point to point. Early in the morning, drive south on Kamarajar Road from Fort St. George along the magnificent **Marina Beach** ❺ � and passing the Indo-Saracenic buildings of the government and university on your right. Note the brick Ice House near Presidency College: clipper ships from New England, which

CloseUp

EARLY-MORNING ART

FOR THOUSANDS OF HINDU WOMEN ACROSS INDIA, *an important early-morning ritual is the drawing of intricate geometrical patterns on the ground outside their front doors. Called* kolams *in Tamil Nadu, these ancient motifs have for centuries marked the beginning of a new day. Although the practice is not as universal in the cities as in the villages, it's still a widely upheld tradition in the south. People living in Madras apartment blocks do not have a courtyard in which to draw their kolams, so they've beaten the system by buying rubber-and-plastic kolam stickers, which they affix on the landing outside their doors. And children delight in kolam rollers, perforated tubes that roll out designs on the floor when filled with powder.*

Dawn is a special time of prayer and purification, and watching a village come to life at sunrise is a singular experience. The most visible aspect of this is the kolam—even an outsider on the street can watch this ritual being performed in every Hindu home. First, the woman sweeps the area outside the house clean with a stiff broom, then—especially in the villages and smaller towns—spreads a layer of cow dung and water on the ground to "purify" it. Using a white powder (traditionally made of rice), she marks the ground with a series of dots that dictate how the pattern is to be drawn. After this, she pours out more of the powder swiftly between her thumb and fingers to form a delicate line pattern connecting or

weaving around the dots. Some women are so skilled at this that they can draw more than one line at the same time using a single hand.

Apart from simply being an early-morning ritual, the use of rice powder is considered an offering to Lakshmi, goddess of wealth and prosperity. Kolamz are very auspicious and are meant to prevent poverty, welcome desirable guests, and protect the home from evil. At festivals, women pay extra attention to the ritual, making the kolams even larger and more complex than usual. There are also special kolams drawn for different life events. For instance, thattil (cradle kolams) are drawn for a baby's naming ceremony.

Even though a new one will be drawn again the next day, a kolam is still a precious creation and a symbol that each day is unique. Once you realize the importance of the role kolamz play in daily Indian life, you'll take care to step over them rather than on them!

---

used ice as ballast, used to unload it here before it found its way into the drinks of the local nobility. Beyond the contemporary political structures and the public swimming pool on the ocean side is the marina promenade: have your driver stop at its north end (just south of the pool), and take a stroll. Rejoin your driver back in the promenade parking lot and drive to the **Parthasarathi Temple** ❻. Punctuate your tour with the

National Museum and Art Gallery ❼ and its superb collection of South Indian bronzes.

TIMING   The marina walk and the temple will each take an hour, the cathedral about 45 minutes, and the museum 2 to 3 hours, for a total of between 5 and 6 hours.

What to See

★ ▶ ❺ **Marina Beach.** This beach is a favorite early-morning promenade and exercise spot. At 6 AM you can see fishing boats casting off and fit folks jogging and performing calisthenics or yoga. In the evening, strollers mix with women haggling with fishermen. During holidays the beach turns into a carnival, complete with vendors and hand-driven carousels, and everyone turns out to mingle and enjoy themselves. The undertow is strong here, so the beach is not used for swimming. ⊠ *Kamarajar Rd., between Edward Eliot's Rd. and Cathedral Rd.*

★ ❼ **National Museum and Art Gallery.** This museum is known for its superb collection of Pallava and Chola (8th- to 11th-century) bronze sculptures. The best-known work is probably the Chola Nataraj—a detailed 2-foot statue of the dancing Shiva, surrounded by the cosmic fire, that appears to be in constant motion. Many of the less spectacular bronzes are still worth studying for their detail and facial expressions. Other artworks from all over South India, including ancient Buddhist statues and Jain sculptures, are well represented. The museum also has an arms gallery, which is strong on weapons of the Raj period. ⊠ *Pantheon Rd., Egmore* ☎ *44/2819–3238 or 44/2819–3778* 🖅 *Rs. 250, camera Rs. 200, video camera Rs. 500* ☉ *Sat.–Thurs. 9:30–5.*

❻ **Parthasarathi Temple.** Built by the Pallavas in the 8th century and rebuilt by the Vijayanagar kings in the 11th century, this Vishnu temple is dedicated to Krishna, the *sarathi* (charioteer) of Partha (Arjuna), and is probably the oldest temple in Madras. Legend has it that on the eve of the great battle in the Pandava-Kaurava War, Krishna imparted to Arjuna the *Bhagavad Gita* (literally "Song of the Blessed Lord"), a religio-philosophic dialogue from the ancient epic, the *Mahabharata*. After passing under the colorful *gopuram* (temple gateway), you'll enter the courtyard, which has several carved shrines. The four streets surrounding the temple have stalls selling flowers, small idols, and other *puja* (ritual worship) articles; musical instruments; and jewelry. ⊠ *Off Triplicane High Rd.* ☎ *44/2844–7042 or 44/2854–4118* 🖅 *Free* ☉ *Daily 6–noon and 4–9:30.*

Southern Madras

In the process of expanding ever southward, Madras incorporated old areas like Mylapore ("Town of Peacocks"), which has a 13th-century temple, and in the 1930s developed some new areas like Thyagaraja Nagar (always referred to as T. Nagar). More recently, Besant Nagar and Kalakshetra Colony were incorporated, both residential areas with broad, tree-lined streets and excellent shopping areas where it's relatively easy to get around—except at rush hour. (At one busy intersection in Adyar there's actually an eatery called Hotel Traffic Jam.)

Numbers in the text correspond to numbers in the margin and on the Madras map.

a good drive

In the morning, hire a car and go to the cantonment, a military base and officers' training academy, to see **St. Thomas Mount** ⑧. Drive back east to visit **Madras Snake Park** ⑨, in Guindy Park, and then J. Krishnamurti's home **The Study** ⑩. Follow R. K. Mutt Road north to the **Kapalishvara Temple** ⑪, then turn right and continue to the end of Kutchery Road to see the **Basilica of San Thome Cathedral** ⑫, noting the neo-Gothic architecture in contrast to that of St. George's Cathedral. End with **Luz Church** ⑬, the oldest church in the city.

TIMING   Allow five or six hours for this tour, as there's a lot of driving involved.

What to See

★ ⑫   **Basilica of San Thome Cathedral.** It's commonly held that Thomas the Apostle ("Doubting Thomas") lived his last years in South India, walking daily from his cave at Little Mount to the beach at Mylapore to preach. Before being captured by the French, Dutch, and English, San Thome was a Portuguese enclave, its name dating from the cathedral's inception in 1504. In the 1890s the cathedral was reconstructed as a neo-Gothic structure with a 180-foot-tall basilica. St. Thomas is thought to be entombed inside. ⌂ *San Thome High Rd.* ☏ *44/2498–5857 or 44/2498–5455* ◷ *Daily sunrise–10 PM.*

★ ⑪   **Kapalishvara Temple.** Dating from the 13th century, this crowded Shiva temple is one of the best examples of Dravidian architecture in India. During the Arupathumoovar festival (commemorating the 63 Saivite saints, who were devoted to Shiva, also known as Saiva in Sanskrit) in March, the temple streets are closed for 10 days to make room for processions of carts and idols around the complex. Kapalishvara Temple is not a rarefied pilgrimage site, but a community gathering place for worship, very much a part of daily life.

Just inside the south entrance, under the gopuram, stands the shrine to Ganesh, a smooth black image of the monkey god that's grown shiny from so many offerings. Worshippers break coconuts in front of and on Ganesh to ask his blessing for a new venture or just for a good day. Sometimes in the late afternoon, a priest talks to groups of widows in the courtyard or mandapam. Farther on around the temple, to the left, you may see a man prostrate himself before the Nandi (the bull that is Shiva's vehicle), which guards the entrance to the inner sanctum. Continue around the building until you come to a mandapam with statues of the nine planets. It's auspicious to walk clockwise around these planets nine times, so join the procession. Several of the shrines set into the courtyard wall are accessible to non-Hindus. ⌂ *Between Chitrukullan North St. and Kutchery Rd., Mylapore* ☏ *44/2461–1356 or 44/2494–1670* ◷ *Daily 4 AM–12:30 and 4 PM–10 PM.*

⑬   **Luz Church.** Built in 1516, this little, cream-color Portuguese church is the oldest church in the city. It has its own large courtyard, a welcome enclave amid the chaos of narrow pedestrian lanes around it. The interior is mostly whitewashed, with an altar that seems to owe as much to

Hindu as to Christian iconography. The ceiling above the altar bears a simple relief, and there's a small choir at the back. Legend surrounds the construction of the church: it's said to have been built by Portuguese sailors who claimed to see a mysterious light on the shore, which guided them safely to port. ☒ *Luz Church Rd., Mylapore* ☎ *44/2499–2568* ☉ *Daily sunrise–sunset.*

❾ Madras Snake Park. At the snake park you can see and photograph more than 40 species of the common snakes of India, as well as crocodiles, monitor lizards, chameleons, and tortoises. The park is at the edge of the Raj Bhavan (Government House). ☒ *Raj Bhavan main post, Sardar Vallabbai Patel Rd., Guindy* ☎ *44/2235–3623* ☒ *Adult Rs. 5, camera Rs. 5, digital camera Rs. 20, video camera Rs. 100* ☉ *Wed.–Mon. 8:30–5:30.*

❽ St. Thomas Mount. Drive to the cantonment and take the road to the top of St. Thomas' Mount—a hillock with an old church—or climb the roughly 130 granite steps from the base below. After the cacophonous city traffic and the crush of crowded streets, the tiny, serene church of Senhora da Expectação (Our Lady of Expectation), built in 1523, offers an aerial view nearly 90 meters (300 feet) above sea level. The interior, charmingly framed by a semicircular vaulted ceiling, is painted in bright, candy-colored hues. Legend has it that Thomas the Apostle was martyred while praying here. The stone cross set in the altar was excavated by the Portuguese—who built the church over it. The Mount gets very crowded on Sunday. ☒ *Free* ☉ *Daily sunrise–sunset.*

❿ The Study. Shortly before his death in 1986, the thinker J. Krishnamurti directed that his home and gardens become a place of learning and contemplation, open to anyone who wished to study his teachings in quiet and tranquil surroundings. Called simply "The Study," the center contains a complete library of Krishnamurti's writings, and other books on religion, philosophy, psychology, literature, and the arts. ☒ *Vasant Vihar, 124/126 Greenways Rd., R.A. Puram* ☎ *44/2493–7803* ☒ *Free* ☉ *June–May 14, Tues.–Fri. 9:30–5:30; weekends 9:30–6:30.*

Where to Eat

$$$$ ✕ **Dakshin.** Decorated with Thanjavur paintings, South Indian statues, and brass lanterns shaped like temple bells, this handsome restaurant serves exclusively South Indian cuisine. Meals are served on banana leaves and set on silver thali trays, and an Indian flutist plays nightly. One of the best entrées is Tamil Nadu's *yeral varuval* (fried prawns marinated in ginger, chili, and garlic), *nandu puttu* (steamed crab and rice flour; similar to couscous, but softer), or the spicy *mirupakaikodi* (sautéed chili chicken) from Andhra Pradesh. Also deservedly popular are the *thenginkai kori* (Mysore-style chili chicken) and the *Venchinamam mamsam* (Andhra-style spicy dry mutton). ☒ *Welcomgroup Park Sheraton Hotel & Towers, 132 T. T. K. Rd., Alwarpet* ☎ *44/2499–4101* ▭ *AE, DC, MC, V.*

$$$$ ✕ **Peshawari.** This place has an attractive Pathan (Indo-Iranian) decor, with rough stone walls and copper plates. Soft lighting sets a mellow tone. The Afghan cuisine emphasizes tandoori dishes. Try the tasty *murgh malai kabab* (boneless chicken kababs marinated in cheese, cream, and lime juice) or *kadak seekh reshmi* (crisp rolled chicken cooked over a grill). The *Sikandari rann* (leg of lamb) is also excellent, as is the *murgh makhni masala* (chicken in a tomato, cream and garlic sauce). ⊠ *Welcomgroup Chola Sheraton, 10 Cathedral Rd.* ☎ *44/ 2811–0101* ⊟ *AE, DC, MC, V.*

★ $$$$ ✕ **Raintree.** Outdoors, and among trees garlanded with little white lights at night, this restaurant highlights a Bharatanatyam dance recital and/ or an Indian flute performance with dinner (8 to 11 PM). Along with the show you'll enjoy fiery, pepper-laden Chettinad cuisine served on a banana leaf that's set in a copper plate. The *vathal kozhambu* (sun-ripened berries cooked in a spicy sauce) and *yera varuwal* (prawns marinated in masala, then deep-fried) are good choices. So are the *appams* (rice pancakes with a soft middle and crisp edges) with coconut milk (extracted from fresh grated coconut). ⊠ *Taj Connemara, Binny Rd., Egmore* ☎ *44/2852–0123* ⊟ *AE, DC, MC, V* ☉ *No lunch.*

$$$$ ✕ **Southern Spice.** This luxurious restaurant serves delicacies from the four southern states of Tamil Nadu, Andhra Pradesh, Kerala, and Karnataka. It's a good place to try the traditional Indian lunch *thali* (a set combination platter) meal and delight in the flavors of perfectly cooked *rasam* (pepper-water), *sambar* (lentil stew), and *poriyals* (stir-fried spiced vegetables). Service is exceptional and the style opulent. ⊠ *Taj Coromandel, 37 M. G. Rd. (Nungambakkam High Rd.)* ☎ *44/5500–2827* ⊟ *AE, DC, MC, V.*

$$–$$$ ✕ **The Great Kabab Factory.** Head to this restaurant only if you are very hungry and in the mood for a lot of meat. The "factory," has a funky industrial style, and serves as many kababs as you can eat for a fixed price. Waiters dressed in overalls bring you buttermilk between each course; this is a traditional Indian digestive drink made from spiced whey. With the unlimited six-course meal (choose a vegetarian or nonvegetarian package) including five types of kababs, rice, lentils, and Indian breads, you'll need it! The kababs are spiced with authentic masalas brought from Lucknow, and include such delicacies as *galoti kabab* (minced lamb or yam with spices and yogurt). ⊠ *Radisson GRT Hotel, 351 GST Rd., St. Thomas Mount* ☎ *44/2231–0101* ⊟ *AE, DC, MC, V* ☉ *No lunch Mon.–Sat.*

$–$$ ✕ **Annalakshmi.** Named after the goddess of food, this is undoubtedly
Fodor'sChoice the best place in the city to enjoy a quiet, laid-back Indian vegetarian
★ meal. It's run by a charitable trust; its genuine home-cooked food is prepared by volunteers, and then served, with silverware, in fairly regal settings. (Proceeds go to the trust, which gives money to medical, social, educational, and cultural causes). Try the amazing range of chutneys and *ambrosia*, a flavorful nonalcoholic health drink. ⊠ *804 Anna Salai, Mount Road* ☎ *44/2852–5109* ⊟ *AE, DC, MC, V* ☉ *Closed Mon.*

$–$$ ✕ **Southern Aromas.** This small restaurant is a great place to go for South Indian nonvegetarian food—but be warned, the food is hot and spicy. Wooden furniture with woven cane backing, traditional pillars and paintings, and an ornate tiled floor and ceiling constitute the old-fashioned Chettinad furnishings. Try the *koli ghasi* (chicken simmered in rich chili and coconut gravy) or the *royalu veppudu* (Andhra-style prawns) if you're up to spice and can handle the heat. The *murungai ulli theeyal* (shallots and a vegetable called drumsticks, with roasted spices and coconut) goes well with any of the several types of rice dishes on offer. If you want something mild, go for *appams* with stew or coconut milk. Make sure you make a reservation if it's Saturday night. ⊠ *The Residency Towers, 115 Sir Thyagaraja Rd., T. Nagar* ☎ *44/2815–6363* ▭ *AE, DC, MC, V.*

$ ✕ **Coastline.** At this small, unpretentious restaurant where fresh seafood is standard, you can expect such spicy creations as chili squid or shrimp, stir-fried with green chilies and curry leaves. The tiger prawns cooked in spicy masala paste are excellent. You can ask the chef to tone down the spice, or choose grilled rather than fried dishes (grills are less spicy). The Malabar prawn curry (a Kerala dish consisting of small prawns in a coconut-based gravy) and steamed rice make a good combination. ⊠ *84 Dr. Radhakrishnan Salai, Mylapore* ☎ *44/2811–1893* ▭ *MC, V.*

¢ ✕ **Komala's.** This South Indian equivalent of McDonald's was first started as a restaurant for Indian expats in Singapore. Now very popular in Madras as well, it serves hygienically prepared (no small concern in India) traditional favorites, such as *masala dosa* (wafer-thin rice and lentil pancakes with a spicy potato filling). The restaurant is self-service and food is dished up very quickly. ⊠ *Near Parsns Complex, 3A Kodambakkam High Rd., Nungambakkam* ☎ *44/5210–9777 or 44/5210–9555* ▭ *MC, V.*

¢ ✕ **Saravana Bhavan.** This chain of South Indian vegetarian restaurants in Madras is notably clean. Some of the restaurants serve fast-food *thalis,* and others offer vegetarian entrées. Count on immaculate surroundings, great food, and exemplary service. This is a good place to try South Indian filter coffee, too. ⊠ *Air-Conditioned Hall, Usman Rd., T. Nagar* ☎ *44/2434–5577* ⊠ *Dr. Radhakrishnan Salai, Mylapore* ☎ *44/2811–5977* ▭ *MC, V.*

Where to Stay

★ **$$$$** 🏨 **ITC Park Sheraton Hotel & Towers.** This modern hotel in central Madras has everything the business traveler could possibly need. The Sheraton Towers suites are geared for corporate luxury, with a conference room and such amenities as voice mail, in-room fax machines, and a 24-hour business center. Some rooms have wireless connectivity. The hotel is notably trendy and has a courteous and efficient staff. Dublin, at this hotel, is one of the city's best nightclubs and is absolutely jam-packed on Saturday nights. The tower rooms are more expensive than the hotel rooms. ⊠ *132 T. T. K. Rd., Alwarpet 600018* ☎ *44/2499–4101* 🖷 *44/2499–7101* ⊕ *www.welcomgroup.com* ⇆ *283 rooms, 42 suites* ♿ *3 restaurants, coffee shop, in-room data ports, cable TV, pool, health club, hair salon, sauna, bar, dance club, business services, travel services* ▭ *AE, DC, MC, V* ℺ *BP.*

$$$$ 🏨 **Le Royal Meridien.** This massive, lavishly tropical hotel is beautifully designed and extremely spacious. It has a magnificent lobby decorated in orange hues and a curvy outdoor pool ringed with palm trees. Close to the airport, and frequented by both business travelers and tourists, the hotel is esconsed in 3½ acres of tropical, landscaped gardens. Its multicuisine restaurant, Cilantro, is known for its live cooking stations— where you watch the chefs cook in an open area—and sushi bar. ⊠ *1*

G. S. T. Rd., St. Thomas Mount 600016 ☎ *44/2231–4343* 🖷 *44/ 2231–4344* ⊕ *www.leroyalmeridien-chennai.com* ⇝ *240 rooms* 🕭 *3 restaurants, cable TV, pool, nightclub, bar, business services, travel services* ▭ *AE, DC, MC, V* ⦿ *EP or BP.*

★ **$$$–$$$$** 🏨 **Taj Connemara.** This historic luxury hotel was built as a *nawab's* (a Muslim prince) home in the 19th century. It has generous hallways; the old wing has been reconceived in art deco. Standard rooms are contemporary, but the pricier old-world rooms (in the old wing) have soaring ceilings, soft white lighting, arched wooden room dividers, and a desk area that overlooks the outdoor pool. The lobby is flanked by Hindu statues, temple friezes, and palm trees in copper pots; the centerpiece is a lovely wrought-iron chandelier. The open-air Raintree restaurant offers classical Indian dance with dinner. ✉ *2 Binny Rd., Egmore 600002* ☎ *44/ 5500–0000* 🖷 *44/5500–0555* ⊕ *www.tajhotels.com* ⇝ *136 rooms, 12 suites* 🕭 *2 restaurants, cable TV, pool, health club, hair salon, bar, business services, meeting room, travel services* ▭ *AE, DC, MC, V* ⦿ *EP.*

$$$$ 🏨 **Taj Coromandel.** This central hotel emphasizes luxury and business services. The giant lobby has a marble fountain, teak accents, Thanjavur paintings, and plenty of lounge space. Rooms throughout the building sport wonderful sketches by British artist Edward Orme. Many of the elegant, cream-color guest rooms—particularly those on the upper floors—have pleasant city views, including palm trees. Suites have both shower stalls and tubs. The swimming pool is surprisingly small for a hotel of this size. ✉ *37 M. G. Rd. (Nungambakkam High Rd.), 600034* ☎ *44/5500–2827* 🖷 *44/2825–7104* ⊕ *www.tajhotels.com* ⇝ *183 rooms, 22 suites* 🕭 *4 restaurants, patisserie, in-room data ports, some in-room faxes, cable TV, pool, health club, hair salon, hot tub, sauna, steam room, bar, lobby lounge, business services, travel services, no-smoking floor* ▭ *AE, DC, MC, V* ⦿ *BP.*

$$$ 🏨 **Ambassador Pallava.** This hotel looks a little worn, but it has grand halls and a large lobby, and each guest room is decorated differently. Service is friendly. The hotel is centrally located, a short rickshaw ride to most of the city sights and shopping areas. ✉ *30 Montieth Rd., Egmore 600008* ☎ *44/2855–4476 or 44/2855–4068* 🖷 *44/2855–4492* ⇝ *102 rooms, 6 suites* 🕭 *Restaurant, coffee shop, cable TV, pool, health club, hair salon, bar, business services, travel services* ▭ *AE, DC, MC, V* ⦿ *BP.*

$$$ 🏨 **Chola Sheraton.** The rooms in this modern hotel are comfortable and cozy, and guests on the Dupleix floors get free airport transfers and wine at check-in. The rooms are furnished with light-color wood, and options for adjusting the lighting to different muted settings let you turn your room into a nice retreat from the bright sun outside. The hotel is in a central location, 2 km (1 mi) from downtown Madras. It's also close to several good restaurants and shopping areas. ✉ *Cathedral Rd., Alwarpet 600086* ☎ *44/2811–0101* 🖷 *44/2811–0202* ⊕ *www. welcomgroup.com* ⇝ *48 rooms, 44 suites* 🕭 *2 restaurants, coffee shop, cable TV, pool, bar, business services, meeting room, travel services* ▭ *AE, DC, MC, V* ⦿ *BP.*

★ **$$$** 🏨 **Fisherman's Cove.** The main building of this isolated Taj resort is colorful and whimsical. The setting is luxurious: there's a woodsy open-air lobby, a large pool with a swim-up bar, and an open-air seafood restaurant and bar right on the edge of the sea. Also at the water's edge, the round seaside cottages have porches and outdoor garden showers. Luxury cottages have spacious porches with hammocks where you can relax and catch a breeze, plus air-conditioning and in-room data ports. If you're taking a room in the main hotel building, ask for a seaview room; it's not much more expensive. The hotel is 28 km (17 mi) south of Madras on the Shore Road to Mahabalipuram. The beach is rocky and not suitable for swimming. The hotel does, however, offer beach buggy and catamaran rides. ☒ *Covelong Beach, Kanchipuram District 603112* ☎ *4114/272–310* 🖷 *4114/272–303* ⊕ *www.fishermans-cove. com or www.tajhotels.com* ⤷ *50 rooms, 38 cottages* ☖ *3 restaurants, in-room data ports, cable TV, tennis court, pool, health club, windsurfing, jet skiing, waterskiing, badminton, Ping-Pong, bar, baby-sitting, travel services* ▭ *AE, DC, MC, V* ⦿ *EP.*

$$$ 🏨 **The Park.** This luxurious hotel occupies the site of the erstwhile Gemini Film Studios, once a landmark building in the city's long film production history. The interior is sophisticated and contemporary. The Leather Bar, for instance, is done all in leather—even the floor—and is a tribute to the city's prosperous leather industry. The hotel has a great location in the heart of the shopping-and-restaurant area. The nightclub, Pasha, admits hotel guests at no extra charge. ☒ *601 Anna Salai, Nungambakkam 600006* ☎ *44/5214–4000* 🖷 *44/5214–4100* ⊕ *www.theparkhotels.com* ⤷ *215 rooms* ☖ *3 restaurants, coffee shop, cable TV, pool, gym, bar, business services, travel services* ▭ *AE, DC, MC, V* ⦿ *BP.*

$$$ 🏨 **Radisson.** This hotel—a white, neocolonial building—has a charming garden and a wide porch on which you can lounge. Rooms are spacious, and furnished with classic, elegant wooden furniture. The Great Kabab Factory restaurant here is one of the best in the city. Service is extremely efficient. Golf (nearby) can be arranged on request. The hotel is 3 km (1.9 mi) from the airport. ☒ *531 G. S. T. Rd., St. Thomas Mount 600016* ☎ *44/2231–0101* 🖷 *44/2231–0202* ⊕ *www.radissongrt.com* ⤷ *101 rooms, 7 suites* ☖ *Restaurant, coffee shop, cable TV, golf privileges, pool, health club, hair salon, bar, meeting room, travel services* ▭ *AE, DC, MC, V* ⦿ *CP.*

$$$ 🏨 **Trident Hilton.** This modern hotel has a small but attractive lobby with an interior garden and waterfall. An exquisite brass lotus pond is a welcoming sight. Indian fabrics decorate the spacious and elegant rooms, the best of which overlook the pool. The hotel is near the airport, 10 km (6 mi) outside the city. ☒ *1/24 G. S. T. Rd., Meenambakkam 600027* ☎ *44/2234–4747* 🖷 *44/2234–6699* ⊕ *www.tridenthotels.com* ⤷ *162 rooms, 5 suites* ☖ *2 restaurants, cable TV, pool, health club, bar, business services, airport shuttle, travel services* ▭ *AE, DC, MC, V* ⦿ *BP.*

$–$$ 🏨 **The Aruna.** All of the guest rooms at this modern 1990s hotel are large and tastefully decorated with contemporary furnishings. The best rooms overlook the outdoor pool—on the second story—and have nice views of Madras. The restaurant, Red Fort, serves traditional Indian meals at reasonable prices, and live classical Indian music accompanies dinner. ☒ *144 Sterling Rd., Nungambakkam 600034* ☎ *44/2825–9090* 🖷 *44/2825–8282* ⤷ *86 rooms, 5 suites* ☖ *Restaurant, coffee shop, cable TV,* *pool, hair salon, bar, business services, travel services* ☰ *AE, DC, MC, V* ❢❑❙ *CP.*

$ ❑❑ **GRT Grand Days.** Soaring 31 meters (100 feet) high, an atrium lobby sets the scene at this well-maintained hotel with efficient service in the heart of Madras. Glass elevators take you up to rooms equipped with everything from coffeemakers to personalized stationery. No-smoking rooms are available, and business travelers can make use of interview and meeting rooms, as well as Internet access and secretarial services. ✉ *120 Sir Thyagaraja Rd., T. Nagar 600017* ☎ *44/2815–0500 or 44/2815–5500* 🖷 *44/2815–0778* ⊕ *www.grtgrand.com* ↳ *135 rooms* ⚭ *2 restaurants, coffee shop, some in-room data ports, minibars, cable TV, indoor pool, exercise equipment, ayurvedic massage, bar, laundry service, business services, meeting room, travel services* ☰ *AE, DC, MC, V* ❢❑❙ *BP.*

$ ❑❑ **The Residency.** This 9-story hotel makes no pretense to maharaja elegance: it's decorated with modest furnishings, in a relatively austere style. However, service is courteous and prompt; that, combined with the hotel's location and room rates, make it very popular with Indian businessmen. Upper-floor corner rooms on two sides of the hotel have good views of Madras. The 24-hour coffee shop serves both Indian and Continental food. ✉ *49 G. N. Chetty Rd., T. Nagar 600017* ☎ *44/2825–3434* 🖷 *44/2825–0085* ⊕ *www.theresidency.com* ↳ *101 rooms, 11 suites* ⚭ *2 restaurants, coffee shop, cable TV, bar, laundry service, business services, travel services* ☰ *AE, DC, MC, V* ❢❑❙ *BP.*

$ ❑❑ **The Residency Towers.** This sleek hotel built in 2002 is known for its extremely popular pub and disco, Bike and Barrel. Therefore, weekends therefore get noisy and crowded and the in-house restaurants are often full. It's centrally located, a short rickshaw ride to the shopping areas and most of the sights. Rooms are comfortable and modern, with standard floral or geometric carpets and gleaming wooden furniture—and everything works well because it's new (no small accomplishment in India). There's a no-smoking floor, and an exclusive ladies' floor. ✉ *T. Nagar Rd. 600017* ☎ *44/2815–6363* 🖷 *44/2815–6969* ⊕ *www.theresidency. com* ↳ *158 rooms, 18 suites* ⚭ *3 restaurants, cable TV, pool, health club, hair salon, pub, business services* ☰ *AE, DC, MC, V* ❢❑❙ *BP.*

Nightlife & the Arts

Madras's nightlife mainly centers around dance and musical events. A national center of classical Indian dance and Carnatic music (the classical music of South India; a song with improvised variations), Madras has been called the cultural capital of India. December is the peak month for recitals, though there are performances in January and February, too. For bars (normally open only until 11 PM) and discos, your best bets are large hotels.

Dance
Partially through the efforts of Western scholars, Tamil Nadu's folk music and dance have received some attention since the 1950s and 60s. Dances from all over India are performed at DakshinaChitra, south of Madras. *Bharatanatyam* (literally dance of India), long-performed only by temple dancers, was revived in the 20th century by the famous classical In-

dian dancer Rukmini Devi. Widely performed in December, this is a highly stylized, dramatic dance featuring many of the *mudra* (meaningful hand gestures) that you see in Hindu statues.

The **Kalakshetra Foundation** (✉ Kalakshetra Rd., Thiruvanmiyur ☎ 44/2491–1836 or 44/2491–4359), founded by Rukmini Devi and now a government-run university, has music and dance classes where you can drop in and watch. **Kuchipudi Art Academy** (✉ 105 Greenways Rd., R. A. Puram ☎ 44/2493–7260) has classes in Kuchipudi dance.

Music
The period from mid-December to mid-January is packed with hundreds of Carnatic music concerts and lectures. Concerts usually follow a set pattern: an initial *raga* (a melodic scale), is followed by variations and improvisation by both the soloist and the accompanying instrumentalists. See the morning newspaper, the *Hindu,* for performance listings.

Bars & Discos
Bike and Barrel (✉ Sir Thyagaraja Rd., T. Nagar ☎ 44/2815–6363), at the Residency Towers is a lively disco and bar that attracts the young set. **Dublin** (✉ Park Sheraton Hotel & Towers, T. T. K. Rd., Alwarpet ☎ 44/2499–4101) is an upscale nightclub that gets very crowded on Saturday. **Flame** (✉ Le Royal Meridien, 1 G. S. T. Rd., St. Thomas Mount ☎ 44/2231–4343) is a popular nightclub lit by electric torchlight. **Fort St. George** (✉ Taj Coromandel, 37 M. G . Rd. [Nungambakkam High Rd.] ☎ 44/5500–2827) is a classy bar. **Geoffrey's** (✉ Hotel Radha Park Inn, 171 J. N. Rd. [Inner Ring Rd.], Arumbakkam ☎ 44/2475–7788) serves cocktails and snacks in a basement bar replete with Americana. No sandals are allowed for men. **Pasha** (✉ The Park, 601 Anna Salai, Nungambakkam ☎ 44/5214–4000) is a fashionable nightclub that plays lounge music. At the trendy Park Hotel, **The Leather Bar** is a scene: it's all leather (even the floor), and it has a drawing room feel, with books and curios. (✉ Park Hotel, 601 Anna Salai, Nungambakkam ☎ 44/5214–4000). **Zara's** (✉ 74 Cathedral Rd., Alwarpet ☎ 44/2811–4941), serves cocktails, wine, and Spanish snacks. No sandals are allowed for men.

Sports & the Outdoors

Golf
The Madras Gymkhana Club has a 9-hole golf course in the center of the track at the **Madras Race Club** (✉ Guindy ☎ 44/2235–0774).

Horse Racing
The **Madras Race Club** (✉ Guindy ☎ 44/2235–0774) is a wonderful patch of greenery in industrial Guindy. Races are held two or more afternoons a week from November through March.

Shopping

Bazaars
The **Mylapore Temple Bazaar** (✉ Off Bazaar Rd., near Kapalishvara Temple, Mylapore) specializes in silver jewelry. **Pondy Bazaar** (✉ T.

Nagar; bounded by Anna Salai, South Usman Rd., and Kodambakkam High Rd.) is a quintessential mixture of old- and new-style bazaars, with more than 30 stalls and stores selling everything from vegetables to silk saris and jewelry. **Spencer's Plaza** (✉ 768–769 Anna Salai, Mount Road) is a large mall where you can find leather goods, clothing, groceries, crockery, jewelry, and handicrafts. There's also a large bookshop–home store, Landmark; a clothing chain, Pantaloons; and a store called Westside that sells Indian and Western clothes. Nuts and Spices is a store that sells dried fruit and nuts. There's an American Express office with travel services on the first floor. These bazaars are open every day.

Clothing

Cotton World (✉ Ambleside 1st fl., above Naturally Auroville, 8 Khader Nawaz Khan Rd., Nungambakkam ☎ 44/2833–2074 or 44/2833–3290) is one of the best places in the city for high-quality, sober-tone Western clothing. **Fabindia** (✉ Ilford House, 3 Woods Rd., off Anna Salai, Mount Road ☎ 44/5215–8026, 44/2857–0365, or 44/2851–0395), in a beautifully restored heritage building, stocks ethnic prints for men and women. **Jus' Casuals** (✉ Corner of Sterling Rd. and Village Rd., Nungambakkam ☎ 44/2827–3882), a hole-in-the-wall shop, sells a small range of export-quality Western clothing at throwaway prices—US$2 for a woman's top, US$6 to US$8 for a pair of cotton trousers, and US$2 for a tank top. **Lifestyle** (✉ T. T. K. Rd., Alwarpet ☎ 44/2498–0008) is a large store with branded Western and ethnic clothing for men and women. The giant **Nalli Chinnasami Chetty** (✉ 9 Nageswara Rd., Panagal Park, T. Nagar ☎ 44/2434–4115), better known as Nalli's, is famous for its Kanchipuram silk saris and vast assortment of silk fabrics, plus casual cotton clothes. It's a zoo, in the best possible way, and service is excellent. **Rasi** (✉ 1 Sannadhi St., Mylapore ☎ 44/2494–1906 or 44/2494–1909) has fine Kanchipuram silks. **Shilpi** (✉ 29 Sir C. P. Ramaswamy Rd., Alwarpet ☎ 44/2499–0918 ✉ Gee Gee Minar, College Rd., Nungambakkam ☎ 44/2822–0186 or 44/2828–2603) is a popular, chic boutique with well-designed ready-made clothes, including *salwars* (tunics), *kurtas* (shirts), skirts, and vests, as well as handloom fabrics and household furnishings. **Sundari Silks** (✉ 145 North Usman Rd., T. Nagar ☎ 44/2814–3093) has Kanchipuram silks as well as silks and cottons from across India and a range of reasonably priced home furnishings. **Westside** (✉ Spencer Plaza Phase II, Anna Salai, Mount Road ☎ 44/2841–0577) has several floors of Indian and Western clothes, and home furnishings.

Jewelry

G. R. Thanga Maligai (✉ 104 Usman Rd., T. Nagar ☎ 44/2434–5052) has fine gold-and-silver jewelry. **Oyzterbay** (✉ Ispahani Centre, 123/124 Nungambakkam High Rd. ☎ 44/2833–1282) has delicate gold jewelry inlaid with various precious stones. **Tanishq** (✉ Crown Court, 34 Cathedral Rd., Alwarpet ☎ 44/2811–0405) has gold and diamond jewelry and ethnic gold watches.

Souvenirs

Amethyst (✉ 14 Padmavathi Rd., off Lloyds Rd., Jeypore Colony, Gopalapuram ☎ 44/2835–1143) sells exclusive handicrafts, jewelry, and clothing displayed in a colonial building. **Cane & Bamboo** (✉ 20 Commander-in-Chief Rd., Egmore ☎ 44/2827–5180) offers a wide range of brass gift items, embroidered and printed furnishings, stuffed toys and jewelry. The government-run **Central Cottage Industries Emporium** (✉ Temple Tower, 476 Anna Salai, Nandanam ☎ 44/2433–0809 or 44/2433–0898) stocks clothes, handicrafts, bronzes, hand-loomed fabrics and rugs, and jewelry from all over India. **Contemporary Arts & Crafts** (✉ 45 C. P. Ramaswamy Rd., Alwarpet ☎ 44/2499–7069) has an unusual range of pottery and metalcraft. **Naturally Auroville** (✉ Ambleside Ground Fl., 8 Khader Nawaz Khan Rd., Nungambakkam ☎ 44/2833–0517 to 18) has stunning pottery, lamps and lampshades, incense, and other products from Auroville. **Victoria Technical Institute (VTI)** (✉ 765 Anna Salai, Mount Road ☎ 44/2852–3141 or 44/2852–3153 ☉ weekdays 9:30–6:30, Sat. 9:30–2), in business since the beginning of the 20th century, has high-quality embroidery work, children's clothing, handicrafts, bronze and sandalwood items, metal lamps, wood carvings, and table linens.

Side Trips

Crocodile Bank
★ *34 km (21 mi) south of Madras.*

Founded by American conservationist Romulus Whitaker to protect India's dwindling crocodile population and to preserve the Irula (snake-catching) tribe's way of life, the Crocodile Bank has produced more than 6,000 crocodiles. They're even shipped to other countries to support croc populations worldwide. The reptiles—which also include muggers, gharials, and turtles—are housed in natural pens. Daily snake-venom extractions are not only an attraction, but have helped the Irulas maintain their culture. ✉ *East Coast Rd., Vendanemeli* ☎ *4114/272–447* 📷 *Rs. 20 adult, camera Rs. 10, video camera Rs. 75* ☉ *Tues.–Sun. 8–6.*

DakshinaChitra
★ *29 km (18 mi) south of Madras.*

The heritage center at DakshinaChitra, a reconstructed village, is an exciting encapsulation of South Indian culture. In a pretty, almost rural setting, open-air displays embody domestic Indian architecture from the 19th and 20th centuries. Many of these buildings were painstakingly moved and reconstructed here. Along the 19th-century streets stand tradesmen's houses, each typical of its professional group. Artisans employ traditional techniques to make exquisite pottery, baskets, and carved stone items, some of which are for sale. Authenticity and attention to detail are the rule here. The 90-minute guided English-language tour (for four to seven people at a time; prior booking required) is extraordinarily informative about South Indian history, language, and culture. The main hall of the Chettinad House hosts folk and classical dance performances, for which tickets can be reserved in advance. The restaurant serves South Indian vegetarian *thali* lunch at Rs. 75. ☟ *For brochure or reservations, contact the Madras Craft Foundation, G3 6 Urur Olcott Rd., Besant Nagar, Madras 600090* ✉ *Muttukadu, East Coast Rd., Chin-*

gelpet District 603112 ☎4114–272603 or 4114/272–783, 44/2491–8943 reservations ⊞ 44/2434–0149 ☜ Rs. 175 ⊘ Wed.–Mon. 10–6.

Tirupati

⑭ *152 km (94 mi) northwest of Madras.*

The town of Tirupati is renowned for the ancient **temple of Lord Venkatesh-wara** (an incarnation of Vishnu, also known as Balaji) on top of Tiru-mala Hill, 20 km (13 mi) outside town. This is one of the few temples in India that allow non-Hindus into the inner sanctum, where the holy of holies is kept—in this case, the 9-foot black idol of Balaji. Any wish made in front of the statue of Balaji is expected to be granted—as long as you're a true believer with a pure heart. Thousands of pilgrims from all over India flock here daily.

Buying a special tag that indicates a time you should join the special queue for darshan (literally, "meeting God," but also approximately, reflection and "seeing") will reduce your waiting time to about two hours. (Pilgrims who pay Rs. 5 wait most of the day to get in.) The tag costs Rs. 60 and is available in Tirupati town; you don't have to go up to Tiru-mala Hill to buy it. When the time comes to enter the gold-painted gop-uram, it won't take long: Telugu-speaking guards rush you through, hardly giving you enough time to glimpse the Dravidian-style Balaji, covered with gold jewelry and precious ornaments. This may all seem like a lot of effort for such a brief glimpse, but it's one of the few opportunities you'll have to mingle with Indian pilgrims, and it should help illustrate the power of Hindu spirituality.

Two roads, one for uphill traffic and the other for downhill traffic, help ease the flow of traffic to and from the temple, but you should still avoid going on weekends or public holidays, when the crowds can be truly daunt-ing. Many pilgrims make the journey up the hill on foot, via a covered walkway. This is a strenuous climb, particularly in the heat of summer, and takes the better part of three hours. A taxi from the town costs around Rs. 600. Once *darshan* is over, you might consider walking a little far-ther up the hill to Sila Thoranam, a striking natural rock formation.

WHERE TO STAY   ⊡ **Bhimas Residency Hotel.** Rooms at this luxurious hotel are spotless,
$ spacious, and an excellent value given the price. Don't confuse it with the other hotels in the town that include the word "Bhimas" in their name. This one is at the crossroads as you enter Tirupati town from the Madras road. The restaurant, Mohini, serves vegetarian South Indian and tandoori dishes. ⊠ *Renigunta Rd., near Railway Overbridge* ☎ *877/ 223–7371* ⊞ *877/223–7373* ⇥ *85 rooms* ⚲ *Restaurant, coffee shop, cable TV, pool, business services, travel services* ⊟ *MC, V* ⦿ *EP.*

¢–$ ⊡ **Guestline Hotels and Resorts.** The more affluent pilgrims choose to stay here for relative luxury and quiet: The hotel is a good 3 km (2 mi) from the train station, so milling crowds of devotees and hawkers can be tem-porarily left behind. The restaurant serves Indian fare. Only a few rooms are air-conditioned, so reserve well in advance. ⊠ *14-37 Karakam-badi Rd., 517507* ☎ *877/228–0366, 877/228–0800, or 877/228–1419* ⊞ *877/228–1774* ⇥ *140 rooms* ⚲ *Restaurant, cable TV, pool, health club; no a/c in some rooms* ⊟ *MC, V* ⦿ *EP.*

¢ ⊞ **Hotel Mayura.** The friendly and helpful staff make this an oasis from the ordeal of being one pilgrim among the 5,000 that visit Tirupati each day. Rooms have eclectic furnishings, but the beds are large and clean. The restaurant, Surya, serves quality South Indian vegetarian dishes. ⊠ *209 T. P. Area, 517501* ☎ *877/222–5925 or 877/222–5118* 🖷 *877/222–5911* 🛏 *65 rooms* ⚭ *Restaurant, travel services; no a/c in some rooms* 🗖 *AE, MC, V* ⊙ *EP.*

MAHABALIPURAM, KANCHIPURAM & PONDICHERRY

Mahabalipuram and Kanchipuram reflect the glorious pasts of three great dynasties: Pallava, Chola, and Vijayanagar. The Pallava capital Kanchipuram, a town of learning, became fertile ground for a vast number of temples. From the port at Mahabalipuram, the Pallavas began to trade with China and Indonesia, a tradition expanded by succeeding empires. Together, the three dynasties laid the foundations of Tamil history, language, and religion, and with each dynasty the temples became larger and more elaborate. With the abandonment of its port, Mahabalipuram became a deserted historical site, so that it's now largely a traveler's curiosity; Kanchipuram is still a major pilgrimage destination. Pondicherry, with its strong French influence, is cherished for being refreshingly different from any other place in India.

Mahabalipuram

★ *59 km (37 mi) south of Madras, 64 km (40 mi) southeast of Kanchipuram.*

Mahabalipuram is a friendly old port city with four kinds of rock structures: monolithic rock temples (*rathas*), cave temples, temples constructed from a conglomeration of materials, and bas-relief sculptures carved on large rocks. In the 8th century, the Pallava dynasty conducted a thriving maritime trade here, sending emissaries to China, Southeast Asia, and Indonesia; carved stone is all that now remains of these dynamic businessmen, who ultimately ruled from the 6th to 9th century.

It's a wonderful place to visit, especially between December and February, as you can divide your time between exploring magnificent ancient temples and relaxing at a beach resort. In addition to the government shops and the museum, independent shops sell granite images and carvings reminiscent of the temples; many of these are remarkably well executed. The sights are open all day, but the best times to visit are early morning and late afternoon.

Numbers in the text correspond to numbers in the margin and on the
⑮ *Mahabalipuram map.* The **Five Rathas** are also called the Pancha Pandava Rathas for the Five Pandava sons in the ancient Hindu epic *Mahabharata*. The Rathas, probably the most famous example of Pallava architecture, are carved out of five pieces of granite, each temple distinctive, with its own elevation, plan, and exquisite detail. From north to south, the individual Rathas are the **Draupadi** (named for the wife of the Pandavas),

Five Rathas ...**15**

Krishna
Mandapam ...**16**

Mahishasura-
mardini Cave ..**17**

Penance of
Arjuna **18**

Shore Temple ..**19**

Tiger Cave **20**

Tirukkalikun-
dram **21**

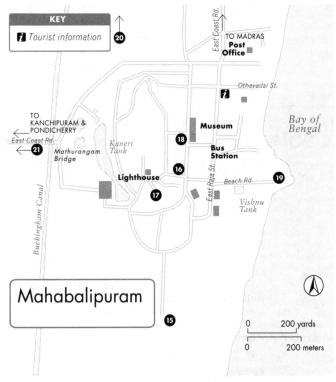

dedicated to the goddess Durga, a warrior wife of Shiva who rides a lion; the **Arjuna** (named for the charioteer of the *Bhagavad Gita,* part of the *Mahabharata*), dedicated to the thunder god Indra; the **Bhima** (named for a Pandava son), the largest temple; the **Sahadeva** (named for a Pandava prince), part of which represents a Buddhist chapel; and the **Dharmaraja,** dedicated to Shiva. Three animal sculptures—an elephant, a lion, and the Nandi bull (the vehicles of Indra, Durga, and Shiva)—complete the display. Because all the temples are unfinished, it's assumed that the animal carvings were meant to have been moved to the appropriate Ratha. The diversity of the images and their meanings reveal the complexity of South Indian Hinduism; studying them is a minicourse in the history of South Indian temple architecture. ✉ *US$5, also allows entry to Shore Temple* ⊙ *Daily 9:30–6.*

⑯ The **Krishna Mandapam,** one of the later cave temples, has a naturalistic figure of a cow being milked. A sculpture on the back wall of this 12-column cave is a relief of Krishna holding up the Govardhan mountain to protect his people from floods ordered by the thunder god Indra.

⑰ The **Mahishasuramardini Cave,** near the lighthouse on top of the hill, is probably the most outstanding of the *mandapams* (cave temples). On the right wall is a carved panel depicting Durga riding a prancing lion and defeating the buffalo demon Mahishasura. On the opposite wall, in sharp contrast to this battle scene, is a deeply carved relief of Vishnu reclining on the great serpent Sesha. In this position, Vishnu is usually considered to be in a cosmic sleep, epitomizing his role as preserver of the universe. At the back of the cave are three cells containing statues of Shiva, his consort Uma, and their son Skanda—collectively known as Somaskanda, a common Pallava theme.

18 The world's largest bas-relief—29 meters (96 feet) long and 13 meters
Fodor'sChoice (43 feet) high—the **Penance of Arjuna,** also called the Descent of the Ganges,
★ is carved on two adjacent boulders. Created by the Pallava dynasty, the work dates from the 7th century. Among the many figures depicted, both mythical and real, is a figure of Shiva with an ascetic Arjuna to his left, standing on one leg. The rendering is thought to be a scene from the *Bhagavad Gita,* in which Arjuna asks Shiva for help defeating his enemies. An extensive but unfinished Pallava water canal system included a pool above the bas-relief; the idea was that water would cascade down a natural cleft in the rock from this pool, simulating the descent of the Ganges from the Himalayas. The entire, enormous project is a fascinating and vital combination of the mundane and the mythical. More than a dozen **cave temples** are cut into the rock hill behind the Penance of Arjuna. Some are unfinished and some have been damaged, but many are quite remarkable. Most are atop the granite hill, so you have to take a short hike to reach them. ⊠ *Behind bus stand* ☜ *Free.*

★ **19** Right on the Bay of Bengal, the **Shore Temple**—subject for centuries to the vicissitudes of sun, sea, and sand—is notable for the degree of detail that remains. You enter the temple from the back, through a courtyard surrounded by a massive wall topped by reclining bulls and two Shiva towers. Although ravaged by time, the calm image of Vishnu, lying in cosmic sleep on the sea with the serpent Sesha at his side, is juxtaposed with the clamor of waves pounding on the sea wall. The Shore Temple was built by the Pallava king Rajasimha in the early 8th century. ⊠ *On ocean, follow signs* ☜ *Foreigners US$5, includes entry to Five Rathas* ☉ *Daily 9:30–6.*

20 The **Tiger Cave,** which is actually two boulders set together, is in a shady grove near the ocean—it's a favorite picnic spot. Dedicated to Durga, the cave is distinguished by the crown of carved tiger heads around its temple. ⊠ *Village of Saluvankuppam, 5 km (3mi) north of Mahabalipuram.*

21 **Tirukkalikundram** (Sacred Hill of Kites) is the name of both a village and its temple, which has Dutch, English, and ancient Indian inscriptions. The ride here from Mahabalipuram takes you through paddy fields. Pilgrims come to climb the 500 steps to the temple on the hilltop at noon, in the hope that the two kites (hawks) will come to be fed by the Brahmin priests. ⊠ *15 km (9 mi) west of Mahabalipuram.*

Where to Stay & Eat

Lodging in Mahabalipuram varies widely, from inexpensive guest houses in town with weekly and monthly rates (often including meals), to more costly resorts overlooking the ocean. There's an abundance of good, inexpensive restaurants serving mainly seafood.

$$–$$$ ✕ **Waterfront Cafe.** Don't be misled by the name—the restaurant is neither on the beach nor near a body of water, but is indoors with no view. However, this is one of the few upscale restaurants in the area. Although it's a multicuisine menu, the focus is on seafood, with king prawns, kingfish, crab, and lobster cooked to order. The chef can turn out these items with the amount of spice you want and cook them either with Indian masala or grill them Continental-style. ⊠ *GRT Temple Bay Resort, Kovalam Rd., Mahabalipuram* ☏ *4114/243636* ▤ *AE, DC, MC, V.*

$$ ✕ **Ideal Beach Resort.** Here you can eat in a garden or the simple indoor restaurant, where the murals, sculptures, and recommended dishes are all Sri Lankan. Try the rice with fish curry, or the excellent deviled fish; follow up with *vatil appam* (custard). Continental food is also available. ⊠ *East Coast Rd., Devaneri Village* ☏ *4114/242–240 or 4114/242– 443* 🖷 *4114/242243* ▤ *MC, V.*

$ ✕ **Moonraker.** The most popular of the shack restaurants, this is the perfect place to soak in the laid-back Mahabalipuram mood. Dinner here is far more comfortable than lunch (there's no air-conditioning here), and is cooked to suit Western tastes. However, a request for "Indian-style" food usually yields good results as well. Try the garlic prawns in butter sauce or the fried calamari—the restaurant serves exceptionally good seafood, European-style, at remarkably low prices. ⊠ *Othavadai St.* ☏ *No phone* ▤ *No credit cards.*

$$$$ ▦ **GRT Temple Bay Resort.** Overlooking the ocean, this hotel has rooms in a main building and in cottages with two doubles per unit. Run by the GRT group, the management and maintenance of the hotel has vastly improved from when it used to be a government-run outfit. The hotel has one of the most scenic locations in the vicinity—on a stretch of golden sand with the shore temple visible in the distance at one end of the cove. ⊠ *Kovalam Rd., Mamallapuram 603104* ☏ *4114/243636* 🖷 *4114/ 243838* ⇨ *70 rooms, 2 suites* ⌂ *2 restaurants, in-room safes, minibars, cable TV, pool, ayurvedic center, health club, beach, bar, travel services* ▤ *AE, DC, MC, V* ⵙ *EP.*

$–$$ ▦ **Ideal Beach Resort.** This relaxing resort, run by Tamils from Sri Lanka, feels tropical, with lots of shrubs, trees, and sculptures. The best upstairs rooms have ocean views. There's a focus on peace and quiet. Breakfast costs Rs. 175 per person. ⊠ *East Coast Rd., Devaneri Village 603104* ☏ *4114/242–240 or 4114/242–443* 🖷 *4114/242–243* ⊕ *www.idealresort. com* ⇨ *6 rooms, 35 cottages* ⌂ *Restaurant, massage, pool, bar; no room TVs* ▤ *MC, V* ⵙ *EP.*

en route From October to March, thousands of waterbirds, egrets, pelicans, storks, and herons come to nest in the **Vedanthangal Bird Sanctuary,** the oldest bird haven in India. The best times to see them are late afternoon and early morning in December and January. ⍀ *For information contact the Wild Life Warden, DMS Compound, Anna Salai, Madras 600026* ⊠ *65 km (40 mi) southwest of Mahabalipuram via Chengalpattu* ☏ *44/2432–1471* ▣ *Rs. 2* ⊙ *Daily 8–6.*

Kanchipuram

🔵 *76 km (47 mi) southwest of Madras, 65 km (40 mi) north of Mahabalipuram.*

The ride from Madras to Kanchipuram passes through paddy and sugarcane fields, and villages at very close range, with houses right on the roadside. Don't be surprised if you have to stop for a goat crossing the road. Former capital of the ancient Pallavas, Kanchipuram holds the remains of three great dynasties—Pallava, Chola, and Vijayanagar—that for centuries weathered internal conflict and external trade but never northern invasion. The dynasties merely jostled each other, building ever greater shrines to their developing and intertwining sets of deities. Today, Kanchipuram, nicknamed the Golden City of 1,000 Temples (as well as "Kanchi"), is one of the seven holy pilgrimage sites for Hindus, with temples to both Shiva and Vishnu. Through the diversity of building styles here, you can trace the development of Dravidian temple architecture from the 8th century right up to the present.

The temples covered here are some of the more famous, but there are plenty of others to explore. When you visit the pilgrimage temples, be prepared for rows of beggars and children beseeching you for candy and/or pens. Kanchipuram temples close from 12:30 to 4 PM, so do your sightseeing in the morning or early evening. Many of the temples have their own elephants (relating to the elephant-headed god Ganesh), who patiently stand by the main gopuram to bless anyone who makes a contribution. The elephants take the money in their trunks. It's an intriguing way to participate in a Hindu ritual.

The **Ekambaranathar Temple** was originally built before the mid-9th century by the Pallavas, but its most significant feature, a massive, 200-foot gopuram with more than 10 stories of intricate sculptures, was a 16th-century addition by the Vijayanagar kings. The temple is dedicated to Shiva, who appears in the form of earth, one of Hinduism's five sacred elements. Inside the courtyard is a mango tree thought to be 3,000 years old; each of its four main branches is said to bear fruit with a different taste, representing the four Hindu Vedas (sacred texts). The temple's name is quite possibly a modification of Eka Amra Nathar (Lord of the Mango Tree). Of the original 1,000 pillars that once stood in the mandapam, fewer than 600 remain. Alas, a visit to this temple can be marred by the machinations of touts, who may attach themselves to your side and insist on serving as guides, or even drag you down to the ablution tank and force you to perform a puja using puffed rice. You'll be billed for all such services, whether you want them or not. Try not to bring more cash than you're willing to spend.

The Ekambaranathar Temple is in the Saivite Brahmin section of Kanchipuram. On your way to the main entrance, notice the houses on either side of the rather dusty road, most augmented by open porches with raised sitting platforms. Some have *kolams* (rice-flour designs) in front of the entrance. These Brahmin houses epitomize the religious and cultural ambience of the temples; until fairly recently, Kanchipuram was a town segregated residentially by caste. ⊠ *Between W. and N. Mada Sts., northwest part of town* 📷 *Camera Rs. 5.*

★ Built mainly during the reign of King Rajasimha (700–28), **Kailasanatha Temple**—named for Kailasa, Shiva's Himalayan paradise—carried the development of Pallava temple architecture one step beyond the monolithic Dharmaraja Ratha and Shore Temple at Mahabalipuram. From the dressed rock of the Shore Temple, the construction of Kailasanatha progressed to granite foundations and the more easily carved sandstone for the superstructure. The sculpted vimana—a tower over the inner sanctum—can trace its lineage in shape, design, and ornamentation to both the Shore Temple and the Dharmaraja Ratha. The cell-like structures surrounding the sanctum are similar in design to the Five Rathas; all have extensive sculptures of Shiva in various poses, symbolizing different aspects of his mythology. Lining the inner courtyard are 58 small meditation cells with remnants of multicolor 8th-century paintings on the wall. Removed from teeming hordes of pilgrims, this quiet temple is an exquisite place to contemplate the oral Hindu tradition preserved in stone. ⊠ *Putleri St., 1½ km (1 mi) west of town center* 📷 *Rs. 200–Rs. 250 for English-speaking guides.*

In the heart of the old town, topped by a brilliant, gold-plated gopuram, **Sri Kamakshi Temple** hosts a famous winter car festival each February or March: deities from a number of temples are placed on wooden temple carts and pulled in a procession through the surrounding streets. Kamakshi is the wife of Shiva. ⊠ *Odai St.*

Built in the 8th century, **Vaikunthaperumal Temple** (Vishnu's paradise) is a single structure whose principal parts make an integrated whole. The four-story vimana is square, with three shrines, each depicting Vishnu in a different pose. The Vaikunthaperumal Temple is unusual for two components: its corridor for circumambulation of the shrines on the second and third floors, and its cloisters, with a colonnade of lion pillars and extensive sculptures bearing Pallava inscriptions. ⊠ *1 km southwest of train station.*

Also known as the Devarajaswamy Temple, **Varadaraja Temple** (Bestower of Boons) is dedicated to Vishnu and is a favorite pilgrimage destination. Its exquisitely carved 100-pillar mandapam (with, in fact, 96 pillars) is one of the finest in India, and its decoration includes a massive chain carved from one stone. The temple was originally built in the 11th century, but the 100-foot gopuram was restored by the Vijayanagar kings 500 years later. ⊠ *3 km (2 mi) southeast of town; follow Gandhi Rd. until you see the temple* 📷 *Rs. 1, camera Rs. 5, video camera Rs. 50.*

Kanchipuram's silks and saris are famous throughout India for their brilliant colors and rich brocades of real gold and/or silver. More than 20,000 people work with silk alone in this city of weavers—entire families craft fabric in or near their homes, using age-old techniques. If you're curious about the process, stop in the **Weavers' Service Centre,** where several "demo" looms are usually in motion. Prices in the attached store are very reasonable. ⊠ *20 Railway Station Rd.* ⊘ *Closed evenings.*

Where to Stay & Eat

Accommodations in Kanchipuram are more for pilgrims than leisure travelers, and restaurants are very basic.

¢ ✕ **Hotel Saravana Bhavan.** Service is excellent in this hotel's immaculate, high-quality vegetarian restaurant that serves a basic *thali, puri* (deep-fried bread), and snacks, including masala *dosas.* It's a good place for a cup of South Indian coffee. One room is air-conditioned. ⊠ *Center of town* ☎ *4112/222505* ▭ *MC, V.*

¢ 🏨 **Hotel Baboo Soorya.** A day at the temples can be exhausting, particularly if the sun is out, and if you want to stay for the night instead of returning to Chennai, Pondicherry, or Mahabalipuram, this is the place. The hotel is small, basic, and unpretentious, but rooms are clean and service is friendly. There are TVs and telephones in the rooms, and a vegetarian restaurant on the premises. ⊠ *85 E. Raja St., Kanchipuram 631501* ☎ *4114/222555* 🖷 *4114/222556* ↫ *36 rooms, 2 suites* ⚭ *Restaurant, cable TV, bar, laundry service; no a/c in some rooms* ▭ *MC, V* 🍽 *EP.*

Shopping

Shops here are open every day. Note that outside the Weavers' Service Centre, silk is often more expensive in Kanchi than in Madras. Buy silk from government-approved shops, many of which are on T. K. Nambi Street—**Shreenivas Silk House** (⊠ 17-A T. K. Nambi St.) is one of the best.

Pondicherry

㉓ *134 km (83 mi) south of Mahabalipuram, 160 km (100 mi) south of Madras.*

This quiet, unusual town is ideal if you want to take the pace of life down a few notches. A former French holding, Pondicherry still retains the flavor of its colonizers, who left only as recently as 1954. From the red *kepis* (caps) of the policemen to street names like Rue Romain Rolland, the French influence is deep-rooted and pervasive, and many of the local people still speak and study the language. This Union Territory, now also known as Puducheri, is a slice of France on Indian soil.

It's delightful to explore the grid of streets to the east of the canal that separated the French quarter from the rest of the town. On either side of the narrow streets rise tall whitewashed villas swathed in bougainvillea, quaint churches and gardens, and little restaurants and cafés that serve French food and the best mineral water on the subcontinent. Even if you don't enter the heritage buildings in the area, the sense of living history is palpable.

A stroll down coastal **Goubert Avenue** (also known as Beach Road) is quiet and pleasant, with minimal traffic. You'll find plenty of people walking the beachfront in the evening, enjoying the feeling of holiday that manages to pervade Pondicherry throughout the year, even in the extreme heat of summer.

After your long and possibly hot walk—during which you might hear French being spoken on the street—there are plenty of places to quench your thirst and soak in the flavors of France. Almost all the restaurants in this area are housed in colonial-style buildings with gardens and old-world cane furniture. As for the genuine, reasonably priced French food—a visit to Pondicherry is definitely not complete without ordering bouillabaisse. The fish is local, but the soup is as good as any you've had in France.

While in the French quarter, make sure you see the round Douane (Customs) house on Goubert Avenue, and the samadhi (memorial) to Sri Aurobindo and the Mother (⇨ Auroville) in the ashram premises on Marine Street. The Church of Our Lady of the Immaculate Conception on Mission Street across the canal dates to 1791 and has a rich interior. The Sri Aurobindo Handmade Paper Factory on S. V. Patel Road is also worth a visit if you're interested in the traditional paper-making process.

Auroville is an international project—a group of villages—and "experiment in international living" conceived by the Mother, a companion of Sri Aurobindo. Once a freedom fighter, Sri Aurobindo moved to Pondicherry from Calcutta and founded an ashram here to propagate his ideas, a synthesis of yoga and modern science. Inaugurated in 1968, Auroville attracts those in search of enlightenment without the trappings of traditional religion. With more than 1,300 residents from all over the world, Auroville is meant to reflect the unity of the human spirit. Auroville is not a tourist attraction, and visitors need to spend a few days here at the least to understand the work being done. An exhibition at the visitor center smartly explains the concept behind the Auroville project, and depicts how the Auroville community is involved in a variety of environment-friendly endeavours. They work with local villagers, introducing them to alternative technology and energy sources. Auroville has a handicrafts shop and a restaurant. ⊠ *10 km (6 mi) north of Pondicherry* ⊕ *www.auroville-india.org.*

Where to Stay & Eat

There are several hotels that offer good rooms and facilities in Pondicherry, and a smattering of guest houses in the colonial quarter have preserved the French-colonial ambience. The food is excellent in any of the small restaurants near the waterfront and within the grid of French-named streets.

\$\$ ✕ **Satsanga.** In a large pebbled garden, with an L-shape covered area, you'll get superb French food with a little Italian thrown in. Try the owner–chef Pierre Elouard's lemon chicken, or the crêpes with honey if you're here for breakfast. The crowd is quiet and sophisticated, and the restaurant is open for three meals daily, 'til 11 PM. ⊠ *32 La Bourdonnais St., opposite PWD office* ☎ *413/222–5867* ▭ *No credit cards.*

\$ ✕▥ **Rendezvous.** The chief advantage of staying at this tiny hotel with three spacious, homey rooms (one of which costs extra because of its kitchenette) is that you're in the heart of the French quarter. Better yet, the terrace restaurant of the same name is very popular and overlooks a sidestreet with whitewashed Mediterranean-style buildings. The restaurant opens at 10 AM and serves authentic bouillabaisse and excellent—fresh, delicately flavored—seafood. ⊠ *30 Suffren St.* ☎ *413/233–9132*

⊕ *www.rendezvous-pondy.com* ⌑ *3 rooms* ⌕ *Restaurant, refrigerators, cable TV, laundry service; no a/c in some rooms* ▤ *AE, DC, MC, V* ⦿⦿ *EP.*

$$–$$$ ⊡ **Hotel de L'Orient.** Run by the meticulous Neemrana Group, this hotel is housed in a carefully restored and well-maintained rambling French-colonial mansion in the French quarter. Rooms are luxuriously furnished with antique furniture and named after formerly French-occupied territories in the region. The restaurant serves excellent creole cuisine. There are no TVs or telephones here. Reserve several weeks in advance, as this is an extremely popular hotel. ✉ *17 Rue Romain Rolland, 605001* ☎ *413/234–3067 to 68 or 413/234–3074* 🖷 *413/222–7829 or 413/ 222–0576* ⊕ *www.neemranahotels.com* ⌑ *1 room, 11 suites* ⌕ *Restaurant, laundry service; no room phones, no room TVs* ▤ *AE, MC, V* ⦿⦿ *EP.*

$$ ⊡ **Le Club.** This elegant colonial mansion at the tail end of the French quarter houses a hotel and three restaurants. The French restaurant Le Club has a well-deserved reputation for consistently delightful food. Try any of the beefsteaks followed by crème caramel. The hotel has spacious and luxuriously decorated rooms—down to the traditional South Indian *zari* (gold) edging on the towels. Some of the rooms, however, are a little dark and depressing. The other restaurants on the premises offer South Asian and multicuisine menus. ✉ *38 Dumas St.* ☎ *413/222–7409 or 413/233-9745* ⌑ *10 rooms* ⌕ *3 restaurants, laundry service; no room TVs* ▤ *MC, V* ⦿⦿ *EP.*

$–$$ ⊡ **Villa Helena.** One of the best places to stay in the French quarter is housed in two locations, one (the better) of which is in a colonial house on Lal Bahadur Shastri Road set in a wonderfully green garden. Rooms are decorated richly with red silk drapes and antique furniture and the bathrooms are incredibly spacious. Ceilings and high and tall, slatted windows look out onto the street. There's no restaurant here, but you can get freshly baked croissants and coffee or tea for breakfast—served in the verandah as you lounge around on cane furniture and admire the garden. ✉ *14 Suffren St. and 13 Lal Bahadur Shastri Rd., 605001* ☎ *413/222–6789* 🖷 *413/222–7087* ⌑ *6 rooms, 2 suites* ⌕ *Laundry service; no room phones, no room TVs* ▤ *No credit cards* ⦿⦿ *EP.*

$ ⊡ **Hotel Anandha Inn.** This multistory white structure in the crowded market area is one of Pondy's contemporary hotels. The rooms in the back, away from the main road, are the quietest. The hotel's restaurant and 24-hour coffee shop serve Indian, Chinese, and Continental cuisines. ✉ *154 S. V. Patel Salai, 605001* ☎ *413/233–0711* 🖷 *413/233–1241* ⊕ *www.anandhainn.com* ⌑ *66 rooms, 4 suites* ⌕ *Restaurant, coffee shop, in-room data ports, minibars, cable TV, pool, health club, bar, business services, travel services* ▤ *AE, DC, MC, V* ⦿⦿ *EP.*

¢–$ ⊡ **Hotel Mass.** Business travelers love this large, comfortable, and modern hotel not only because it's a great deal but also because it has excellent service and hospitality. The bar is frequented by locals and guests. The hotel is a little bit away—1½ km (1 mi)—from the French quarter. Rooms in the old wing are one-third the price of rooms in the new wing; they're less fancy, though the facilities offered are the same. ✉ *152/154 M. M. Adigal Salai, 605001* ☎ *413/220–4001* 🖷 *413/220–3654* ⌑ *111 rooms* ⌕ *5 restaurants, cable TV, pool, health club, billiards, bar, laundry service, business services, travel services* ▤ *AE, MC, V* ⦿⦿ *BP.*

¢ ⛺ **Park Guesthouse.** This quiet guest house is meant for ashram members and devotees, though tourists are allowed to stay if they observe the rather institutional rules regarding timing (gates close at 10 PM) and abstinence from alcohol and smoking. The benefit: it has the best location in Pondicherry, right on the water at one end of Goubert Avenue. ⊠ *Goubert Ave.* ☎ *413/233–4412* ➪ *85 rooms* ⛛ *Restaurant, bicycles, laundry service; no room phones, no a/c, no room TVs* ⊟ *No credit cards* ⵙ⊙ⵘ *EP.*

Shopping

Shops are concentrated near the shore. Jawaharlal Nehru Street, particularly, is chockablock with stores selling everything from clothing to sweets. Pondy is known for its handmade paper, and arts-and-crafts products from Auroville and the Aurobindo ashram.

La Boutique d'Auroville (⊠ 38 J. N. St. ☎ 413/233–7264 ⊙ Mon.–Sat. 9:30–1 and 3:30–8) is the official sales outlet for products from Auroville, which range from fine pottery to leather goods.

Splendour (⊠ 16 Goubert Ave. ☎ 413/233–6398 or 413/233–4382 ⊙ Thurs.–Tues. 9:30–1 and 4–8:30) is the sales outlet for Ashram products, from paper and candles to incense and potpourri.

TIRUCHIRAPPALLI, THANJAVUR & MADURAI

The history of Madurai and Trichy goes back to the 1st to 4th centuries BC, whereas Thanjavur came to prominence in the 10th century AD as the capital of the later Cholas. Ruled by various southern dynasties over a period stretching from the Sangam era—the beginning of recorded Tamil history and literature—until the 18th century when south India was gradually subjugated by the British, the "deep south" of Tamil Nadu is a fascinating historical belt. Between them, the Pallavas, Pandyas, Cholas, Vijayanagars, Nayaks, and Marathas left an architectural legacy of forts, palaces, and, of course, fantastic temples.

Tiruchirappalli

❷❹ *325 km (202 mi) southwest of Madras.*

The temple city of Tiruchirappalli (City of the Three-Headed Demon) was a pawn in the feudal wars of the Pallavas, Pandyas, and Cholas, which continued until the 10th century, and from which point the Vijayanagar Empire reigned supreme. In the 18th century, Tiruchirappalli was at the center of the Carnatic wars between the British and French; and between these two violent periods, there were periodic Muslim incursions. All of this international activity had an influence on South India temple architecture, which reached its zenith in the Vijayanagar period under the Nayaks of Madurai (who built most of Tiruchirappalli) with the construction of one of the largest temples in South India: the Ranganathaswamy, on the island of Srirangam (8 km [5 mi] north of Tiruchirappalli).

Tiruchirappalli—also known as Trichy—is spread out, with hotels centered in the southern cantonment (the old Raj military area). If you don't hire a car, auto-rickshaws are probably the best transportation here. The flat landscape to the north is dominated by the Rock Fort, near the bridge to Srirangam, which lies between the Cauvery River and its tributary, the Kolidam.

★ The military and architectural heart of Tiruchirappalli is its startling **Rock Fort,** rising 272 feet above the city on the banks of the Cauvery River. Cut into the rock, 437 steps lead up to a temple dedicated to Lord Vinayaka (the mythical half-man, half-bird Garuda who is Vishnu's vehicle and who is prominent in *The Mahabharata*), then on to the summit. Along the way are various landings and shrines: an ancient temple dedicated to the elephant-head god Ganesh, a Shiva temple, and cave temples cut into the rock. (Non-Hindus are not permitted into the temples.) Finally, at the top, you're rewarded with a breathtaking view of Tiruchirappalli. To the north, the Srirangam temples rise dramatically out of fields and riverbeds. ⊠ *2½ km (1½ mi) north of Trichy Cantonment* ⛟ *Rs. 1, camera Rs. 10, video camera Rs. 50; no photography of deities or temple interior allowed* ⊙ *Daily 6–noon and 4–9.*

Covering more than 1 square km and dedicated to Vishnu, Srirangam's
★ **Sri Ranganathaswamy Temple** (also known as the Great Temple), was built by various rulers of the Vijayanagar Empire between the 13th and 18th centuries, with a few 20th-century additions. The single-sanctum temple has seven concentric walls, 22 gopurams, and a north–south orientation rather than the usual east–west. Non-Hindus are not permitted into the inner sanctum.

Just as the Pallavas had rampant lions, the Vijayanagar dynasty had rearing horses, magnificently displayed here in the Horse Court, the fourth courtyard of the Seshadgiri mandapam. At the time of the Festival of Vaikuntha Ekadasi (in honor of Vishnu's paradise), pilgrims can see the idol of Ranganatha brought into the mandapam from the inner sanctum under the golden dome. During the January Car Festival, Srirangam's magnificent temple carts—exceptional in their artisanship—are taken out for a series of processions. The temple's extensive and beautiful collection of precious gems is included in the cart display. An island of temples, Srirangam was also a center of religious philosophy and learning. The great Vaishnava Acharya Ramanuja taught and wrote in the Srirangam school at the end of the 11th century. No photography in the sanctum. ⊠ *Srirangam Island, 8 km (5 mi) from Trichy by car* ⛟ *Free; Rs. 10 to climb wall for panoramic view, camera Rs. 20, video camera Rs. 75.*

About 2½ km (1½ mi) east of the Great Temple, **Sri Jambukeswara Temple** (Shiva, Lord of the Mountain) is smaller, but its large central court is an excellent example of the Dravidian architecture from the final phase of the Madeira period (around 1600). The courtyard pillars are remarkable for their rampant dragons, elaborate foliated brackets, and royal Nayak portraits. ⊠ *Srirangam Island* ⛟ *Free; camera Rs. 10, video camera Rs. 125* ⊙ *Daily 6–noon and 4–9.*

Thiruvanaikkaval, named for a legendary elephant that worshipped the linga (the phallic stone that is Shiva's primary abstract symbol), is a shrine to Shiva. In the temple's Mambukeswaram pagoda, the linga is submerged in water—one of the five elements that Shiva represents. The architecture of this temple, with five walls and seven gopurams, is among the finest Dravidian work still in existence. There's a pretty garden in the complex. ⊠ *3 km (2 mi) east of Srirangam* 🖾 *Rs. 5, camera Rs. 20, video camera Rs. 150* ⊙ *Daily 5:30–1 and 3–9.*

> **off the beaten path**

THE GRAND ANAICUT – At Kallanai, 24 km (15 mi) east from Trichy is an ancient architectural masterpiece still in use. Extending for 330 meters and 20 meters wide, the Grand Anaicut dam has a road over it and you can drive across. It was built by the Chola king Karikalan in the 2nd century AD. Two hours (90 km [56 mi]) south by road from Trichy is Karaikudi, the main town in the Chettinad district—home to the Chettiars, a prosperous community of traders. The baroque ancestral homes belonging to this community are famous for their size, rich furnishing, wooden pillars, and intricate tiled floors. There's good shopping to be had here for antiques and textiles; shops are open daily. If you want to take your time, stay at an early-20th-century planter's bungalow on the outskirts of Karaikudi, at the eight-room Bangala hotel (☎ 4565/220–221 ⊕ www.thebangala. com). Rooms, which run about US$125 or Rs. 5,588, are simply but elegantly furnished; some have four-poster beds. The hotel doesn't take credit cards, but they do have English-speaking guides.

Where to Stay & Eat

Trichy's hotels are concentrated in the cantonment area, also called Junction (for the Tiruchirappalli Junction Railway Station).

$ ╳ **Chembian.** This large, pleasant indoor restaurant is air-conditioned and serves Indian, Chinese, and Continental cuisines. Try the *bagala bhath* (spiced rice and lentils), curd rice (spiced Indian yogurt and rice), or the chicken 65 (hot, fried chicken). ⊠ *Hotel Sangam, Collector's Office Rd.* ☎ *431/241–4700 or 431/241–4480* 🖃 *AE, DC, MC, V.*

$–$$ ╳🏨 **Jenneys Residency.** The best rooms in this high-rise hotel are spacious, with sturdy furniture and good upholstery, and they face the pool. The hotel has a Mexican-theme bar—not exactly what you expect to find in a temple city in South India. Nonetheless, it's a popular nightspot, and it's much larger and more elaborate than its Chinese restaurant, Peaks of Kunlun, which is open for dinner; stick to the chicken and vegetable dishes. ⊠ *3/14 McDonald's Rd., 620001* ☎ *431/241–4414* 🖷 *431/246–1451* ⊕ *www.jenneysresidency.com* 🛏 *100 rooms, 23 suites* ⌂ *Restaurant, coffee shop, cable TV, pool, health club, hair salon, bar, travel services* 🖃 *AE, DC, MC, V* ⑩ *BP.*

$$ 🏨 **Hotel Sangam.** This modern Western-style hotel is surrounded by a pleasant lawn. The best rooms overlook the pool, and are spacious, comfortable, and spotless. ⊠ *Collectors Office Rd., 620001* ☎ *431/241–4700 or 431/241–4480* 🖷 *431/241–5779* 🛏 *52 rooms, 4 suites* ⌂ *Restaurant, coffee shop, in-room data ports, cable TV, pool, health club, bar, business services, travel services* 🖃 *AE, DC, MC, V* ⑩ *EP.*

¢–$ 🏨 **Femina Hotel.** This central hotel has a bright, open marble lobby and clean and attractive rooms. The best rooms have small verandas and stunning views of the Great Temple and St. Joseph's Church. Beer is available through room service, but only for consumption in your room. Rooms in the new wing are the most expensive. Woodlands restaurant serves Indian and Continental vegetarian cuisines; your best bet is the thali. ⊠ *109 Williams Rd., Cantonment, 620001* ☎ *431/241–4501* 🖷 *431/ 241–0615* ⤴ *168 rooms, 7 suites* ⚒ *2 restaurants, coffee shop, room service, cable TV, pool, health club, hair salon, travel services; no a/c in some rooms* ▤ *AE, DC, MC, V* ⊌ *EP or BP.*

Thanjavur

㉕ *55 km (34 mi) east of Tiruchirappalli.*

Nestled in the highly fertile delta of the Cauvery River, Thanjavur was the capital of the Cholas during their supremacy (907–1310). A fortuitous combination of flourishing agriculture, competent monarchs, and a long religious revival begun under the Pallavas in Kanchi, culminated in the building of the Thanjavur's Brihadiswara Temple. The two greatest Chola monarchs, Rajaraja I (985–1016) and his son Rajendra I (1012–44), consolidated their South Indian empire from coast to coast, including Kerala, and added Ceylon, the Maldives, and Srivijaya, in what is now Indonesia, to their holdings. As a result, active trade developed with Southeast Asia and China, fostering a two-way cultural exchange: Thanjavur painting of the period shows some Chinese influence, and in Java, Indian influence led to universal appreciation of the epic poem *The Ramayana*.

Fodor'sChoice
★

Although this soaring monument to Rajaraja's spirituality is dedicated to Shiva, the sculptures on the gopuram of the **Brihadiswara Temple,** or Great Temple, depict Vishnu, and those inside are Buddhist. Until they were uncovered in 1970s, the more interesting Chola frescoes on the walls of the inner courtyard had been obscured by later Nayak paintings. Within a single courtyard, a giant Nandi bull (second-largest in India, next to the bull in Mysore) and pillared halls point toward the 190-foot vimana, a pyramidal tower capped by a single 80-ton block of granite. This massive capstone was pulled to the top along an inclined plane that began in a village 6 km (4 mi) away. The delicate carving on the round granite cupola minimizes the capstone's size and provides a visual break from the massive pyramid. The temple's carefully planned and executed architecture make it a fine example of Dravidian artisanship; in fact, it's a UNESCO World Heritage Site. Visit the temple early in the morning before the crowds arrive. ⊠ *W. Main Rd. at S. Rampart St.* ☎ *No phone* ☉ *Daily 6 AM–12:30 PM and 4–8:30.*

Thanjavur Palace is the central building in the great fort built by Nayak and Maratha kings. It's hard to find your way around this unbelievably dilapidated site, but visits to the **Art Gallery** (in Nayak Durbar Hall) and the **Royal Museum** are worth the effort. The art gallery has a magnificent collection of Chola bronzes. The Royal Museum displays clothing, arms, and other regal memorabilia. Near the art gallery is the **Saraswati Mahal Library,** a scholars' paradise with 46,000 rare palm-leaf and paper manuscripts in many languages. Cameras and video cameras are forbidden. ⊠ *Entrance on east wall, off E. Main St.* ☉ *Daily,* *except national holidays; museum 9–6, art gallery 9–1 and 3–6, library Thurs.–Tues. 10–1 and 1:30–5:30* 🎟 *Art Gallery Rs. 4, camera Rs. 30, video camera Rs. 200; Royal Museum Rs. 2, camera Rs. 15, video camera Rs. 100; library free.*

---

off the beaten path

GANGAIKONDACHOLAPURAM – This capital city of the Cholas Đ75 km (47 mi) northeast of Thanjavur has a magnificent temple built by Rajendra I in the 11th century. Only the main portion of the original three parts of the temple remains—this temple is called the Brihadisvara, like the one in Thanjavur, but is no longer in use. A little more than 100 km (62 mi) northeast of Thanjavur is the little ghost town of **TRANQUEBAR, –** where Dansborg fort is evidence of the Danish trading presence in the area dating from 1620. There's a small museum in the fort and you can easily while away half a day exploring the remains of colonial bungalows and the narrow streets of the town. In town is an eight-room Neemrana Group hotel, Bungalow on the Beach ($$–$$$, ☎ 4364/288–065 ⊕ www.neemranahotels. com). Built in 2004, it's the first hotel in town. Its buildings on 24 King Street have been carefully restored—intended to transport you back to the age of Danish adventuring and trade on the Coromandel.

Where to Stay & Eat
Small vegetarian restaurants are easy to find in Thanjavur, especially along Gandhiji Road, in the center of town.

¢ ✗ **Les Repas.** A pleasant and clean restaurant at the Hotel Parisutham serves a wide range of Indian, Continental, and Chinese dishes. It's the only restaurant near the temple that offers spotless, air-conditioned comfort and Continental food. ⊠ *Hotel Parisutham, G. A. Rd.* ☎ *4362/ 231801 or 4362/231844* ▬ *AE, DC, MC, V.*

$$$$ 🏨 **Hotel Parisutham.** This modern hotel has a marvelous pool, pleasant canal views, and comfortable, well-equipped rooms. Without a doubt, this is the best place to stay if you're here for a quick trip, because it has an unbeatable location—a five-minute walk from the Great Temple. ⊠ *55 G. A. Canal Rd., 613001* ☎ *436ρ223–1801 or 436ρ223–1844* 🖷 *436ρ223–0318* 🛏 *48 rooms, 2 suites* 🍴 *Restaurant, minibars, cable TV, pool, bar, business services, travel services* ▬ *AE, DC, MC, V* 🍽 *EP.*

$ 🏨 **Hotel Sangam.** This quiet 1990s hotel a little away from the town, on Trichy Road is in a tranquil garden, and the rooms and service are very respectable. Since it's on the outskirts of labyrinthine Thanjavur, on the Tanjore–Trichy highway, it's a good place to stay if you're driving from place to place. ⊠ *Trichy Rd., 613007* ☎ *436ρ223–9452* 🖷 *436ρ223–6695* 🛏 *54 rooms* 🍴 *Restaurant, cable TV, bar, laundry service, travel services* ▬ *AE, MC, V* 🍽 *EP.*

★ $ 🏨 **Ideal River View Resort.** Amid acres of paddy fields and semi-jungle, are very comfortable and well-maintained air-conditioned cottages with balconies facing the peaceful Vennar River. Connected by road to Thanjavur, 4 km (2½ mi) away, it's a quiet, scenic place to unwind after sightseeing, and possibly the best place to stay in the Thanjavur–Trichy area. The restaurant serves Indian, Continental, Chinese, and Sri Lankan cuisine. ✉ *Vennar Bank, Palli Agraharam 613003* ☎ *436þ225–0533 or 436þ225–0633* 🖷 *436þ225–1113* ⊕ *www.idealresort.com* ⌂ *Restaurant, pool, ayurvedic massage, boating, fishing, laundry service, travel services; no room TVs* ▭ *MC, V* ♟ *EP.*

Shopping

R. Govindarajan (✉ 31 Kuthiraikatti St., Karantha ☎ 4362/251282) has a large selection of Thanjavur paintings, brass-and-copper artifacts, wood carvings, and glass.

Madurai

❷❻ *191 km (118 mi) southwest of Thanjavur, 142 km (88 mi) south of Tiruchirappalli.*

Once the capital of the Pandya dynasty, the second-largest city in Tamil Nadu supposedly got its name from the Tamil word for honey. According to legend, when King Kulasekhara Pandya first built Madurai—more than 2,500 years ago—Shiva shook nectar from his locks to purify and bless the new city. Known as the Temple City, Madurai's old city, south of the Vaigai River, was laid out in accordance with ancient temple custom, with the great Meenakshi Temple at the center. Shops and stalls surround the Meenakshi on three concentric squares of streets that are used for religious processions almost every day.

Fodor's Choice The **Meenakshi Temple,** also called the Great Temple, has two sanctuar-★ ies, one to Meenakshi (the fish-eyed goddess, consort of Shiva) and the other to Shiva in the form of Sundareswar. Legend has it that Shiva married the daughter of a Pandya chief in this form, and the temple's car festival celebrates this event each spring.

The temple's high point is the Hall of a Thousand Pillars, built in approximately 1560 and adorned with 985 elaborately carved pillars. The **Temple Art Museum,** also in the Hall of a Thousand Pillars, houses beautiful paintings and sculptures, although not all of these are accurately labeled. Among the many mandapams, the Kambattadi Mandapam is outstanding for its excellent sculptures depicting the manifestations of Shiva.

An excellent way to appreciate this awesome site is to wander slowly around the various crowded mandapams, observing the passionate worship that's going on. At 9:30 PM, return to the main temple to watch Shiva being carried to Meenakshi's bedroom, a procession that begins at the eastern gopuram. Non-Hindus are not allowed into the sanctum, and video cameras are not allowed altogether. ✉ *Bordered by N, S, E, and W Chithirai Sts.* ☎ *452/234–4360* ✉ *Temple Rs. 10; museum Rs. 2, camera Rs. 30* ۩ *Temple, daily 4:30 AM–12:30 PM and 4 PM–9:30 PM; museum, daily 7–5:30.*

Tirumala Nayak Mahal, an Indo-Saracenic palace, was built by Tirumala Nayak in 1636 and partially restored by Lord Napier, governor of Madras from 1866 to 1872. The palace is now largely in ruins, but its excellent sound-and-light show, nightly at 6:45 in English, dramatizes Madurai's past. The palace is scheduled to undergo a six-month renovation in 2004; check with your hotel about whether it's open to visi-

CloseUp

PENANCE PIERCING

Don't be alarmed if you see a hair-raising procession of men walking barechested through the streets with metal hooks piercing their bodies and arrows through their tongues. You have come across the annual festival of Thaipusam, celebrated by followers of Subramanya, granter of wishes and son of the god Shiva. The festival is associated with ritual bathing and acts of severe penance: pilgrims walk long distances, sometimes with their bodies hideously pierced, carrying the kavadi (ritual yoke) on their shoulders, to ask a favor, fulfil a vow of gratitude, or even to repent for sins.

It's not uncommon to see men silenced by the metal rings that lock their lips, or drawing a small chariot attached to a hook set into their backs. One of the chief centers of pilgrimage for this festival— which can also involve walking across a pit filled with red-hot coals—is the Periyanayaki temple in Palani (a small town 120 km [75 mi] from Madurai). Here Thaipusam is celebrated for 10 days every year (the Hindu month of Thai is from mid-January to mid-February).

tors. ⊠ 1½ km (1 mi) north of Meenakshi Temple 🏛 Palace: Rs. 2; sound-and-light show: Rs. 2–Rs. 5 ⊙ Daily 9–1 and 2–5.

Where to Stay & Eat

Decent restaurants are easy to find in sprawling Madurai, especially around the temple. There are plenty of places to stay on the west side of town, but the nicer hotels are across the river to the north.

¢ ✕ **Surya.** A rooftop restaurant at the Hotel Supreme (don't stay here, rooms are seedy), Surya offers North and South Indian food for dinner, and thali lunches. Service is fast. ⊠ 110 W. Perumal Maistry St. ☎ 452/234–3151 ▭ MC, V.

$$$$ 🏨 **Taj Garden Retreat.** Aptly named, this hilltop hotel in a verdant set-
FodorsChoice ting offers a view of Madurai from 6 km (4 mi) away. The rooms in the
★ period bungalow retain a British-colonial appeal, with vintage etchings on the walls, hardwood floors, and airy verandas with beautiful views. The other rooms are modern, villa-style. The restaurant serves excellent Indian and Continental cuisine and has a superb view of Madurai. ⊠ Pasumalai Hill, 7 T. P. K. Rd., 625004 ☎ 452/237–1601 🖷 452/237–1636 ➩ 63 rooms ♤ Restaurant, cable TV, tennis court, pool, gym, massage, badminton, Ping-Pong, bar ▭ AE, DC, MC, V ⊠ EP.

$$$ 🏨 **Fortune Pandyan Hotel.** This unpretentious five-story hotel has lodged some famous personalities, including two former Indian presidents and a king of Nepal. Most rooms are comfortable and have minimalist furnishings or floral bedspreads. The spacious suites are the nicest accommodations—they have king-size beds, a sitting area, and an extra table. The Queen's Room has large sliding doors and a view of the Meenakshi Temple. The restaurant serves South Indian, Chinese, and Continental food. The hotel is 20 minutes from the airport and 10 minutes from the train station and Madurai's shops. ⊠ *Race Course Rd., 625002* ☎ *452/253–7090* 📠 *452/253–3424* ⊕ *www.pandyanhotel. com* 🛏 *54 rooms, 3 suites* ♿ *Restaurant, cable TV, bar, laundry service, travel services* ▤ *AE, DC, MC, V* ⅋◯⅋ *BP.*

$$$ 🏨 **Madura Park Inn.** This hotel, preferred by business travelers, has a unique contemporary design—for Madurai, that is. It has a large atrium and spacious rooms, and is a very comfortable hotel. It's also about 4 km (2½ mi) away from the bustle of the city center. ⊠ *38 Madakulam Main Rd., Palanganatham 625003* ☎ *452/237–1155* 📠 *452/237–1888* 🛏 *55 rooms* ♿ *Restaurant, cable TV, pool, bar, laundry service, business services* ▤ *AE, DC, MC, V* ⅋◯⅋ *BP.*

$$ 🏨 **Germanus Days Inn.** This hotel has modern, comfortably furnished rooms, and an attentive staff that offer warm and efficient service. ⊠ *28 Bypass Rd., 625010* ☎ *452/238–2001* 📠 *452/238–1478* 🛏 *60 rooms* ♿ *2 restaurants, cable TV, bar, laundry service, business services, travel services* ▤ *AE, DC, MC, V* ⅋◯⅋ *BP.*

Shopping

Shops full of carvings, textiles, and brasswork line the streets near Meenakshi Temple, particularly Town Hall Road and Masi Street. The **Handloom House** (⊠ E. Veli St.) has great hand-loomed cottons. **Poompuhar** is convenient for an assortment of Tamil Nadu handicrafts under one roof. (⊠ 12 West Veli St. ☎ 452/234–0517)

TAMIL NADU A TO Z

To research prices, get advice from other travelers, and book travel arrangements, visit www.fodors.com.

AIR TRAVEL

Madras's Meenambakkam Airport is served by major international flights, and several international airlines have offices in the city. Within India, Indian Airlines and Jet Airways connect Madras with Bombay, Delhi, Calcutta, Bangalore, Cochin, and Trivandrum, as well as Tiruchirappalli and Madurai. You can fly daily on Indian Airlines (only) from Madras to Madurai, and five times a week from Madras to Trichy.

🛪 International Airlines **Air France** ⊠ Montieth Rd., Egmore, Madras ☎ 44/2855–4916. **British Airways** ⊠ 8th fl. Raheja Towers, 177 Anna Salai, Mount Road, Madras ☎ 44/5206–8181, 44/2256–0351 airport. **Lufthansa** ⊠ Opposite Spencer Plaza, 167, Anna Salai, Mount Road, Madras ☎ 44/2852–5095, 44/2256–1760 airport. **Singapore Airlines** ⊠ 108, Dr. Radhakrishnan Salai, Mylapore, Madras ☎ 44/2256–0409 or 44/2256–0410.

✈ Indian Airlines **Indian Airlines** ✉ 19 Rukmani Lakshmipathi Rd. (Marshalls Rd.), Egmore, Madras ☎ 44/2256–1070, 44/2256–1938, 44/2256–0187, 44/2855–5204, or 44/ 140, 44/141 ✉ Dindigul Rd., Tiruchirapalli ☎ 431/480–233 or 431/480–930. **Jet Airways** ✉ Thapar House, 43/44 Montieth Rd., Egmore, Madras ☎ 44/2841–4141 reservations, 44/2256–1818 airport. **Air Deccan** ☎ 98403–77008 mobile or 44/2256–0505. **Air Sahara** ☎ 44/5211–0202, 44/5211–2498, or 44/2256–0909.

AIRPORTS

Tamil Nadu's main airport is about 16 km (10 mi) from the center of Madras. A shuttle to any of the major hotels costs Rs. 50. Hired cars are available through prepaid booths just past the baggage claim areas; the ride will cost around Rs. 300.

Trichy's airport is 8 km (5 mi) from the city center. A cab, prepaid at the airport, is your only option.

✈ Airport Information **Madras Meenambakkam Airport** ☎ 140. **Trichy Airport** ☎ 431/234–1063 or 142.

BIKE TRAVEL (CYCLE-RICKSHAWS)

You won't get Western-style bicycles here, but you can hitch a ride with a cycle-rickshaw instead. In temple cities and villages, cycle-rickshaws are a leisurely, pleasant, and cheap way to travel. Just remember that pedaling in the heat is strenuous: these men work hard. Set the fare in advance and be generous. Cycle-rickshaws in Kanchipuram cost about Rs. 70–Rs. 100 for the day. In most bigger cities they are not available— and also not advisable because they are very dangerous in city traffic.

BUS TRAVEL

Bus travel is not recommended. Buses are cheap, but they are slow, uncomfortable, unreliable, and very crowded—sometimes it's even difficult to get on a bus. Worse, there are no toilet facilities and trips can be long.

CARS & DRIVERS

Many travelers fly or take a train to Madurai or Tiruchirappalli, then hire a car and driver for the rest of their stay in Tamil Nadu. Drivers know the major routes, and as long as you're satisfied with your driver it can be both convenient and pleasant to have him with you for several days. Rates change, so get a price in advance and be sure it includes a halt charge if you're traveling overnight. Distances within Tamil Nadu are measured from mile 0 at Fort St. George in Madras. Hire a car from a government-licensed operator (⇨ Travel Agents & Tours) and figure about Rs. 3 to Rs. 7 per km, with a halt charge of Rs. 100 per night. Hertz also offers drivers or self-driven rental cars (not recommended). Autoriders is a 24-hour rental service with chauffeur-driven cars only.

✈ Cars & Drivers **Bala Tourist Service** ✉ 88A Kodambakkam High Rd., Madras ☎44/2822–4444 or 44/5213–5555 ☐44/2822–3737 ⊕www.balatouristservice.com. **Hertz** ☎44/2235–3112 to 15. **Autoriders** ✉281 Precision Plaza, Anna Salai, Mount Road, Madras ☎ 44/2433–0684.

CAR TRAVEL

Madras is linked to the north by National Highway (NH) 5, to the west by NH 4, and to the south by NH 45. Generally speaking, road and traffic conditions can make driving more time-consuming than the distance suggests; driving to Madras is most feasible from Bangalore, 334 km (207 mi) to the west. However, the Bangalore–Madras highway is undergoing reconstruction, which will probably continue past mid-decade; expect delays and diversions. Car travel by night is a bad idea—there are too many wild truck drivers around. NH 7 (from Bangalore) and NH 45 (from Madras) are the state's major north–south arteries. East–west roads include NH 4 (Madras–Bangalore), NH 46 (Vellore–Bangalore), NH 47 (Salem–Coimbatore), and NH 49 (Madurai east to the coast and west into Kerala). From Madras, the drives south to Kanchipuram, Mahabalipuram, and Pondicherry are short and simple. The East Coast Road is more scenic than NH 45 and gets you to Mahabalipuram in one hour. The 50-km (31 mi) drive from Tiruchirappalli to Thanjavur crosses through beautiful, lush green paddy fields interspersed with canals. The day-long (10-hour) drive on NH 5 from Madras to Madurai takes you through several villages.

CONSULATES

The U.S. consulate is open weekdays 8:15 to 5. The U.K. consulate is open weekdays 8:30 to 4.

🗗 United Kingdom **Madras** ✉ 20 Anderson Rd., 600006 ☎ 44/5219-2151 or 44/5219-2308.

🗗 United States **Madras** ✉ 220 Anna Salai, 600006 ☎ 44/2811-2000.

🗗 New Zealand **Madras** ✉ 32 Cathedral Rd., Gopalapuram 600006 ☎ 44/2811-2472 or 44/2811-2473.

EMERGENCIES

🗗 Hospital–Ambulance **Apollo Hospital** ✉ 21 Graemes La., Madras ☎ 44/2829-3333 or 44/2829-4870.

🗗 24-hr Pharmacies **Apollo Pharmacy** ✉ 320 Anna Salai, Nandanam, Madras ☎ 44/2433-1740 or 41 ✉ 105 G. N. Chetty Rd., T. Nagar ☎ 44/2822-3865 ✉ 21 Graemes La., ☎ 44/2829-3333.

MAIL & SHIPPING

If you want to send mail from abroad, the Madras General Post Office (GPO) is the best place to do so; it's a hub for all of Madras (note that it's closed Sunday). There are also several international courier services, inquire at your hotel for package pickup facilities.

🗗 Post Offices **Madras General Post Office (GPO)** ✉ Rajaji Salai, Madras ☎ 44/2526-7752.

MONEY MATTERS

ATMS ATMs that belong to international banks do accept cards from abroad. However, it's always wise to carry some travelers checks and cash; you'll be stuck if the magnetic strip on your card gets corrupted and the card stops working.

CURRENCY In Madras, American Express is open Monday–Saturday, 9:30 to 6:30;
EXCHANGE Thomas Cook has a foreign-exchange office open daily 9:30 to 6. In other cities it's best to cash traveler's checks at your hotel.

🗗 Exchange Services **American Express** ✉ G-17 Spencer Plaza, Anna Salai, Madras ☎ 44/2849-3592 or 44/2849-3596. **Thomas Cook** ✉ Ceebros Centre, 45 Uttamar

Gandhi Salai, Madras ☏ 44/2855-4600 (during office hrs) or 1939 (4-digit call center number during off-hrs).

TAXIS & AUTO-RICKSHAWS

In congested towns and cities, where not all the streets are conducive to cars, auto-rickshaws can be the fastest and most economical way to get around. Often the meters don't work, so agree on a price before departure. The set rate is about Rs. 10 for the first kilometer, Rs. 3 for each additional kilometer. Be prepared to pay Rs. 10 over the meter reading.

Call Taxis are a convenient way of getting about in Madras. Operators usually charge about Rs. 30 for the first 2 km and Rs. 10 for every additional kilometer. Waiting charges apply at about Rs. 2 for every five minutes.

With any kind of metered transit, it's wise to use a map to familiarize yourself with the shortest route to your destination. This is best done *before* you get into the taxi (or auto-rickshaw), but even with your driver staring at you in the rearview mirror, a little map work can help avoid overcharging. In smaller towns, which often have unmetered vehicles, *always* set the fare in advance.

🚖 Call Taxis **Easy Call Taxi** ✉ Madras ☏ 44/2620-9595. **Friendly Call Taxi** ✉ Madras ☏ 44/5212-1314. **Sri Murugan Call Taxi** ✉ Madras ☏ 44/2486-4222. **Zig Zag Cool Taxi** ✉ Madras ☏ 44/2474-9966.

TRAVEL AGENTS & TOURS

American Express shares an office with their money-changing services. Ashok Travel and Tours is open Monday through Saturday 10 until 5:30. The sales office of the Tamil Nadu Tourism Development Corporation is open weekdays 9:45 to 6. Welcome Tours and Travels provides extremely efficient service and is open 24 hours a day throughout the year. The Thomas Cook travel agency shares an office with its currency-exchange service and is open Monday through Saturday 9:30 to 6. Most major hotels also have travel desks where you can easily arrange a car and driver.

🚖 **Akshaya India Tours and Travels** ✉ 2/3, Kushkumar Rd., opposite NIIT, Nungambakkam, Madras ☏ 44/2822-4617 to 18. **American Express** ✉ Spencer Plaza, Anna Salai, Madras ☏ 44/2849-8075. **Ashok Travel and Tours** ✉ 29, P. V. Cherian Crescent, Ethiraj Salai, Egmore, Madras ☏ 44/2828-1250 or 44/2821-1782. **Tamil Nadu Tourism Development Corporation** ✉ Tourism Complex, Wallajah Rd., Madras ☏44/2536-7851or 44/2536-7854 ⊕ www.tamilnadutourism.org. **Thomas Cook** ✉ Ceebros Centre, 45 Uttamar Gandhi Salai, Madras ☏ 44/2855-4600 🖷 44/2855-5090. **TCI** ✉ Heavitree, 23 Spurtank Rd., Madras ☏ 44/2836-2556. **Welcome Tours and Travels** ✉ 150 Anna Salai, near Spencer Plaza, Madras ☏ 44/2846-0677 🖷 44/2858-6655.

TRAIN TRAVEL

The Indian Railways booking service in Madras is in Besant Nagar on the ground floor of Rajaji Bhavan Complex. It's a bit more expensive than the Indrail office on the second floor of the Central Station (open Monday–Saturday 10to 5 and Sunday 10 to 2), but it's much more convenient and efficient. Railway booking offices are open Monday through Saturday 8 to noon and 12:15 to 2, Sunday 8 to noon. There's also good train service to Bangalore both day and night. See the booklet *City Info* (usually available in bookstores and hotel reception areas) for train schedules.

Overnight trains are safe provided you take the 2nd class air-conditioned category. You can't lock anything, but that's why it's safe—you're in a compartment packed with other people. Just remember to chain your luggage to the loops provided below your sleeping berth (luggage chains and locks are available at every major railway station). *Avoid* first class or first-class air-conditioned trains, because on those you're locked in a room with three others—who may be male.

The air-conditioned chair-car (rows of chairs, but no berths) service (Vaigai Express) from Madras to Tiruchirappalli (6 hours) and Madurai (7½ hours) is a relaxing way to see the countryside. (Night trains to Madurai save you sightseeing time, too.) The trains going south leave on the meter-gauge track from Egmore Station. Check www.indianrail.gov.in for accurate schedules or look at Monday's *The Hindu*. Advance booking is necessary during December and January.

There are two daily trains from Madras to Tirupati, the *Tirupati–Madras Express* and the *Saptagiri Express*. Both take three hours. You can book a bus tour of Tirupati at the bus stand on Esplanade Road or at Central Station or Egmore Station.

⏩ Train Information ☎ 1361 computerized information in English.

VISITOR INFORMATION

Within Madras, the Government of India Tourist Office has offices opposite Spencer's and at the airport's domestic terminal, with knowledgeable staff and an astoundingly comprehensive computer database. The offices are open weekdays 9 to 5:45 and Saturday 9 to 1. *Hallo! Madras,* an informative monthly for the promotion of tourism, lists tours, music halls, cinemas, events, and airline and train schedules. It's available free at the Government of India Tourist Office and for Rs. 10 at bookstores. The "In the City" section of the Friday edition of *The Hindu* lists cultural events for the coming week.

Near the Government of India Tourist Office in Madras, the Tamil Nadu Tourism Development Corporation provides information and reserves cars and guided tours. The India Tourist Development Corporation arranges excursions throughout the state. If you plan to visit any restricted areas or need your visa extended, you should head for the Foreigners' Regional Registration Office.

There's no tourist office in Kanchipuram, outside Madras, so you may want to contact the Tamil Nadu Tourism Development Corporation in Madras before your trip. The main tourist office in Madurai is open weekdays 10 to 5:45. There are branches at the airport and the train station. The Thanjavur tourist office is open Tuesday through Sunday from 10 to 1 and 2 to 5. In Tiruchirappalli, the tourist office is open daily from 10 to 5:45. In Pondicherry, the staff at the Tourist Information Bureau of the Directorate of Tourism is very helpful; the office is open Monday through Saturday from 10 to 5:30.

🚻 Tourist Information **Foreigners' Regional Registration Office** ✉ Shastri Bhavan Annexe Bldg., Haddows Rd. ☎ 44/2827-8210. **India Tourist Development Corporation** (ITDC) ✉ 29 Victoria Crescent at Commander in Chief [C-in-C] Rd. ☎ 44/2827-8884. **Madurai** ✉ W. Veli St. ☎ 452/233-4757. **Pondicherry,** ✉ 40 Goubert Ave. ☎ 431/233-4575 or 431/233-9497. **Tamil Nadu Tourism Development Corporation** ✉ 25 Dr. Radhakrishnan Salai ☎ 44/2536-7851 or 44/2536-7854. **Thanjavur** ✉ Hotel Tamilnadu complex, Gandhi Rd. ☎ 436/222-1421. **Tiruchirappalli** ✉ Hotel Tamil Nadu complex, 1 Williams Rd. ☎ 431/246-0136 ✉ Train station ✉ Airport.

HYDERABAD

10

UPGRADE YOUR PEARL COLLECTION
at Charminar Market ⇨*p.513*

WITNESS A SOUND-AND-LIGHT SHOW
at Golconda Fort ⇨*p.513*

SPY THE NIZAMS' TOMBS
at India's second-largest mosque ⇨*p.514*

DECOMPRESS AT THE TEA PAVILION
at the ITC Hotel Kakatiya Sheraton ⇨*p.517*

SEE 35,000 ITEMS
crammed into 35 rooms,
none of it clutter ⇨*p.515*

By Nigel Fisher

Updated by
Kavita Watsa

MOST PEOPLE VISIT HYDERABAD ON BUSINESS. Software and telecommunications industries, as well as traditional textile and jewelry trades, thrive here, and the city is beginning to steal some of the limelight from Bangalore in the information-technology sector. It's too bad more leisure travelers don't visit, as they're missing quite a lot. This is a place where, on rolling hills around the beautiful Hussain Sagar Lake, the city's minarets pierce the clear blue sky. It's also a place where you can shop for pearls and bangles, enjoy terrific food, experience both Hindu and Islamic culture, and get a sneak preview of the future in the strikingly clean, green neighborhoods of the "new city."

Hyderabad is the capital of Andhra Pradesh, a large southeastern state full of influences as varied as Buddhism from the 3rd century BC during the reign of the great King Ashoka and the northern Muslim influx of the 16th century. Telugu is the main language, though in the capital half of the people speak Urdu. A long stretch of coast—dotted with fishing villages and prone to flooding and destruction during cyclones—runs along the Bay of Bengal. Inland is the dry, even arid, Deccan Plateau.

Established in 1590, Hyderabad reflects most dramatically its Muslim and Telugu heritage. In 1512, Quli Qutab Shah, governor of the Telengana region—a part of modern Andhra Pradesh—declared independence from the Bahmani kingdom, and established himself 11 km (7 mi) away at Golconda, nearly 80 years before Hyderabad city was built nearby and the court shifted there. Lack of water and epidemics of plague and cholera convinced Mohammad Quli, the fifth ruler after the founder Quli Qutab Shah, to venture beyond his fortress and in 1590 to create a new city nearby on the Musi River. Mohammad Quli named the new city Hyderabad—after his beloved queen Hyder Mahal, originally a Hindu village girl. At the center of the new city was built the Charminar, a great arch from which four roads fanned out toward the four points of the compass.

The city's grandness and the wealth of the Qutab Shahi kingdom attracted the interest of Aurangzeb, the last great Mogul ruler. His armies besieged Golconda and captured it in 1687. When the Mogul empire began to fragment after the death of Aurangzeb, the viceroy, Asaf Jah I, proclaimed himself *nizam* (ruler) in 1724. The wealth and influence of the new dynasty of nizams went beyond the imagination—Hyderabad became the most important Muslim city in India. Stories of the last nizam, Osman Ali Khan, abound: he purportedly used a 260-carat diamond as a paperweight, and during World War II he presented Britain's Royal Air Force with a squadron of Hurricane fighters. When India was granted independence from Great Britain in 1947, the nizam Osman Ali Khan refused to join the new union of states that formed independent India. He held out for a year until India marched in its army and annexed the territory of Hyderabad.

Today's Hyderabad teems with approximately 5 million people who often appear to be on the streets en masse. If traffic is moving, prepare to hear the crunch of an accident; if it's gridlocked, prepare to be all but overcome by exhaust fumes. But matters are improving. Although traffic is still undisciplined and driving rash, the city has constructed several

If you have
1 day

You could actually cover all of Hyderabad's major sights in one exhausting day—if you're supremely motivated. Try to spend at least two nights here, but if you can't, take an auto-rickshaw to the **Golconda Fort** ❶, the original defensive settlement of Hyderabad, and the palatial tombs of the Muslim rulers, the **Qutab Shahi Tombs** ❷. Both are several miles west of the city. Back in the Old Town, spend the rest of the day exploring **Charminar** ❸, a four-story arched, minaret-topped gateway, and the area around it, which has good shopping.

10

If you have
2 days

It's far easier to break the above itinerary up into two days, and see everything at a slower pace, especially the Old City area around **Charminar** ❸. Also consider taking a stroll across Tank Bund, a promenade across the top of the dam that holds back the waters of Hussain Sagar Lake, and perhaps take a boat from Lumbini Park out to the statue of Lord Buddha in the middle of the lake.

If you have
3 days

Follow the itinerary above on your first two days. Then visit the **Mecca Masjid** ❹, India's second-largest mosque. Then head to the **Falaknuma Palace** ❺, if it's open, and the eclectic **Salar Jung Museum** ❻. Alternately, if you have a lot of stamina and only if you intend to head south to Madras, in Tamil Nadu, consider a 12-hour detour to the temple town of Tirupati, which is within the state of Andhra Pradesh but only four hours from Madras. But be warned: it's much easier to go from Madras to Tirupati than from Hyderabad to Tirupati.

---

overpasses to ease the congestion, and the state is beginning road-widening projects. An army of cleaners toils through the night, ensuring that Hyderabadis awake to a clean town. Note that everyone uses the city name Hyderabad even when they're referring to its twin city, Secunderabad, across the lake. Secunderabad, once a British cantonment, is now of note only for its railway station, which receives many of Hyderabad's long-distance trains.

EXPLORING HYDERABAD

Concentrate on Hyderabad if you're passing through Andhra Pradesh. Most of the city's interesting sights are in the Old City, making it easy to walk around or take short auto-rickshaw trips. The other area of interest is Golconda, which is 11 km (7 mi) outside the city and best reached by road and best explored on foot. Don't bother with Hyderabad's newer twin city, Secunderabad, built by the British in the early 1800s. It's rather like a large suburban neighborhood and it has little to offer you as a traveler.

When to Tour Hyderabad

Winter—mid-October through March—is the ideal time to visit, as the weather is dry and the temperature rarely climbs higher than 72°F

(22°C). Evenings can even be chilly, requiring a sweater. In summer the temperature soars up to 104°F (40°C), cooling down just a little during the monsoon rains that fall June through September.

Numbers in the text correspond to numbers in the margin and on the Hyderabad map.

a good tour

Make your first stop **Golconda Fort ❶** ⊳, the original stronghold of the Qutab Shahi kings that predates Hyderabad city. You can take an auto-rickshaw here, but to see the fort properly you must walk up a steep hill to the summer palace. It's easier to walk up this hill before the noontime sun beats down. From the fort, walk on the paved road about 1 km (½ mi) over to the **Qutab Shahi Tombs ❷**, the palatial tombs of the Muslim rulers, which are also better seen and photographed before the sun is overhead. From here it's a 7-km (4½-mi) auto-rickshaw ride to the center of the Old Town, whose landmark is **Charminar ❸**, with its magnificent minarets. All around Charminar are bustling bazaars, including the Laad Bazaar, which has rows of shops selling glass and lacquer bangles, perfume, and Islamic prayer articles. Right next door (due south) to Charminar is India's second-largest mosque, **Mecca Masjid ❹**. The **Falaknuma Palace ❺** is another 2 km (1 mi) south, but is not open to visitors (unless you get permission from the Taj). The **Salar Jung Museum ❻** is a little under 2 km (1.2 mi) north of Charminar but still on the south side of the Musi River. In the evening, you may want to return to Golconda Fort to attend the sound-and-light show, which has an English version each night.

TIMING   This route can be covered in one extremely full day, but it's far better if you take two days. The museums are closed on Friday; some shops may also be closed because of the strong Muslim influence here. Non-Muslims are discouraged from visiting mosques on Friday or during early morning prayers.

What to See

❸   Charminar. To get to the Charminar, cross over the Puranapol bridge to the Old City that lies south of the Musi River, passing the impressive Osmania Hospital and High Court buildings that stand on either bank. Moving toward the heart of the Old City, you enter the Charkaman area between four (*char*) great gates (*kaman*). Within these gates you can find Hyderabad's famed pearl and bangle markets, and also the striking Charminar, an imposing granite edifice built by Mohammed Quli Qutab Shah in 1591 to appease the forces of evil and protect this new city from plague and epidemic. The arches, domes, and minarets show Islamic influence, while much of the ornamentation is Hindu in style. Interestingly, there's a Hindu temple at the base of the Charminar, right in the heart of the Muslim-dominated Old City. Climb a steep, dark spiral stairway to reach open verandahs, from which you can see the rooftops and narrow streets of the Old City, the Mecca Masjid, the Unani, and Ayurvedic hospitals. Be careful, as there are gaps in the protective railing. ⊠ *Charkaman center, Old City* 🎫 *Foreigners Rs. 100; with video camera Rs. 25* ⊙ *Daily 9–5.*

FodorsChoice
★

❺   Falaknuma Palace. This stunning late-19th-century palace built by a Paigah noble is not open to the public, but it (along with its peaceful Japanese

10

Hearty Hyderabadi Cuisine

Hyderabad is famous for food, including *haleem* (a slow-cooked treat of pounded wheat, mutton, and spices), Hyderabadi *biriyani* (a baked meat-and-rice dish), and *bagare baingan* (eggplant in a spicy poppy–sesame-seed sauce). Some of the best haleem is found in the Old Town around the Mecca Masjid, though it's also available in classy restaurants. Chilis are grown on the plateau and among locals it's a point of pride to shock the taste buds with fiery pain. The main hotels usually have a couple of restaurants, one Indian and one European, and, except for one or two exceptions, these are the best (and safest) places to dine.

Room to Spare

Hyderabad has more hotel rooms than it can fill, and new construction is everywhere. New business hotels offer services and amenities of international caliber at prices half those of Delhi. These hotels range from opulent to utilitarian. Inexpensive hotels with fairly primitive amenities— no hot water or toilet paper, for instance—are found around the train station in Secunderabad and in the center of Hyderabad.

Toys, Textiles & Pearls

Hyderabad is a hub for the many handicrafts of Andhra Pradesh. Look for *nirmal* toys (colorful, lightweight wooden toys), *bidri* ware (a gunmetal-like alloy used for bangles, cuff links, bowls, and other items), and *ikat* textiles (tie-dyed before they're woven). You'll also find silk, wool, and cotton carpets from the Warangal district. Hyderabad is the center of India's pearl trade: pearls from southeast Asia are sent here for polishing, sorting, and piercing. For pearls, the most exciting place is the Charminar Market, particularly all along the street leading north from the Charminar itself. And the market bustles with everything you're likely to want, from textiles and handicrafts to bangles (west of Charminar). The omnipresent glass bangles worn throughout the country are produced in great quantities here.

---

gardens) will one day be transformed into a luxury hotel by the Taj Group. If you're determined to get inside to see stained-glass windows, carved ceilings, fine Italian marble staircases, and general 19th-century opulence that took nine years to create, contact the area director of the Taj Group at the Taj Krishna hotel to arrange permission, and to time your visit. If not, security guards at the premises are not likely to let you in. Acquired by the sixth nizam in 1897, the palace has hosted Indian and European royalty. ⊠ *Kishanprasad Road, Faluknama* ☎ *No phone.*

▶ ❶ **Golconda Fort.** If you clap at the gate of this fort, it echos clearly up to the summer palace, high on the hill just outside the city (about ½ km up). These are the ruins of what was once the state capital: the imposing fort with its well-planned water-supply system often sheltered whole communities under siege for months, and though tremendously worn by time and war, it tells stories in crumbling stone. The fort only fell to one siege, but that siege was disastrous. In 1867, after eight months of

A WALK IN THE OLD CITY

TO SPEND A MORNING IN THE OLD CITY, the area around the Charminar, is to step back a century into an old and fascinating Muslim world. Along its narrow lanes, bangle sellers vie for space with prayer mat vendors, attar (perfume) merchants, waraq (silver leaf) makers, naan (tandoori bread) bakers, Unani doctors (who practice traditional Islamic medicine), turban and sherwani (a knee-length straight-cut coat, with a small round neck, worn by Muslim gentleman) outfitters, and hawkers of charms and spells.

The dull ring of the waraq maker's hammer against his layers of leather and silver mingles with the cries of the merchants and the bells of cycle taxis and cart drivers as you pass. If you ask for directions to any shop or landmark you may be told that it no longer exists, or that the people have gone away, or that you possibly mean some other shop or landmark. Don't be deterred: locals don't often deliberately mislead visitors; it's usually because they don't want to admit they don't know something, such as directions to a place, or because they may not recognize your pronunciation of a street or landmark's name. Ask a glass bangle seller for the whereabouts of a bidri or pearl shop, and he will tell you that there are no bidri or pearl shops in Hyderabad. Make sure you have a map and you've got your bearings, or you might find it difficult to find your way out again.

bottling up the fort, Aurangzeb—with the assistance of a traitor who opened what is now called the Victory Gate—sent his troops storming in. In the belief that there was hidden gold here, Aurangzeb ordered the roofs of all palaces ripped off. After Aurangzeb died, the fort was abandoned for the second time in favor of Hyderabad city where the viceroy of the mughal empire set up shop in 1724 and declared himself ruler. So, 300 years later, only the great walls of the fort stand at Golconda, amid the weeds and moss. Life continues, however, in a small, serene village at the base of the hill. After you explore the fort, hire a guide (near the main gate's ticket counter) to take you through the village to what the locals call the tree of Ali Baba. Legend has it that the 40 thieves once hid inside its bulbous trunk. An excellent **sound-and-light show** is performed every evening at the fort, with a show in English each night. ⊠ *Golconda, 6 km (4 mi) west of the city* ☎ *40/2351–2401 bookings through Andhra Pradesh Tourism Development Corporation* 🎫 *Fort, Rs. 100; videocamera Rs. 25; sound-and-light show, Rs. 30* ⊙ *Fort 9–5; sound-and-light show in English, Nov.–Feb., daily 6:30* PM*–7:30* PM*, Mar.–Oct., daily 7* PM*–8* PM.

FodorsChoice
★

❹ **Mecca Masjid.** India's second-largest mosque, in the Charkaman area in the center of the old part of town (right next door, to the south of the

Charminar 3

Falaknuma
Palace 5

Golconda
Fort 1

Mecca
Masjid 4

Qutab Shahi
Tombs 2

Salar Jung
Museum 6

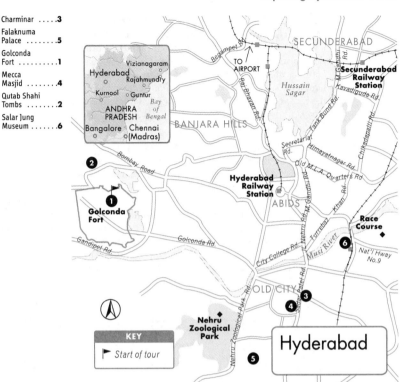

Hyderabad

Charminar), can hold 10,000 worshippers. Non-Muslims are welcome except at prayer time, which includes all day Friday. Building the mosque took more than 70 years; construction started during the Qutab Shahi period in 1614—reputedly with some of the bricks made from earth brought from Mecca in 1618—and was completed in 1687, after the Mughals had overthrown Golconda. The nizams' tombs line the left side of the courtyard. ☒ *Kishan Prasad Rd., southwest of Charminar, Old City* ☎ *No phone* ☒ *Free* ☉ *Sat.–Thurs. 9* AM*–sunset except during daily early-morning services.*

② **Qutab Shahi Tombs.** Each of the seven distinctive tombs of the Qutab Shahi dynasty has a square base surrounded by pointed arches. The seventh is unfinished because Shah Abdul Hassan was interrupted in the building of his tomb by Aurangzeb, who defeated him and captured the Golconda Fort. ☒ *2 km (1 mi) north of the fort, Golconda* ☎ *40/2351–3410* ☒ *Entry Rs. 5, car with 5 persons including driver Rs. 50, camera Rs. 20, video camera Rs. 100* ☉ *Sat.–Thurs. 9:30–5:30.*

⑥ **Salar Jung Museum.** When you see the wealth of this collection, you might be astonished to learn that it all belonged to one man, Mir Yusuf Ali Khan Salar Jung III, who for a short time was prime minister during the reign of Osman Ali Khan. Thirty-five thousand items, which constitute one of the world's largest private collections, are crammed into 35 rooms. The fantastic Chola sculptures, European glass, Chinese jade, jeweled weapons, and modern Indian paintings are displayed with little information, but they're well worth a look anyway. The Staff Co-op Handicrafts shop at the back of the museum has a small selection of handicrafts, including lacquer and *bidriware* (an inlaid–metal craft from the Bidar district in Karnataka). ⊠ *C. L. Badari Malakpet, south of Musi River, Old City* ☏ *40/2452–3211* ✉ *Rs. 150* ⊙ *Sat.–Thurs. 10–5; booking closes at 4:15.*

Tank Bund Road. A showpiece of Hyderabad, Tank Bund is a promenade across the top of the dam that holds back the waters of Hussain Sagar Lake (6 km by 1 km [4 mi by ½ mi]), a dominant feature of the city. Many hotels are positioned so that their rooms overlook the lake, which is often used as a venue for sporting events. The road is lined with statues of the state's native sons, and a stunning sight from here is the 52-foot-high, 350-ton monolithic statue of Lord Buddha in the middle of the lake. You can take a boat out to the statue from Lumbini Park, or just sit by the water and eat ice cream, or watch the sunset like the Hyderabadis love to do. ⊠ *East side of Hussain Sagar Lake.*

WHERE TO STAY & EAT

WHAT IT COSTS In Rupees				
$$$$	**$$$**	**$$**	**$**	**¢**
RESTAURANTS over 350	250–350	150–250	100–150	under 100
HOTELS over 4,000	3,000–4,000	2,000–3,000	1,000–2,000	under 1,000

Restaurant prices are for an entrée plus dal, rice, and a veg/non-veg dish. Hotel prices are for two people in a standard double room in high season, excluding approximately 20% tax.

$$$$ ✕ **Dum Pukht.** Reserve in advance if you want to dine at one of the traditional low-seat tables at this elegant restaurant. Try the roast chicken, royal Hyderabad's version of the traditional English roast, or the *murgh khusk purdah* (boneless chicken cured in a star anise marinade and grilled). This is also a good place to try *haleem,* a dish of pounded mutton, wheat, and whole spices, and *khubani ka meetha,* a legendary dessert made from apricots. Quite apart from the delicately spiced *dum pukht* (steam-cooked in a casserole, with a lid of bread) food, the *ghazals* (Urdu-language love songs) performed live and at a discreet volume are a relaxing treat. ⊠ *ITC Kakatiya Sheraton, Begumpet* ☏ *40/2340–0132* ▭ *AE, DC, MC, V.*

$$$$ ✕ **Curry 'n Rice.** This cozy little place serves dishes cooked in all kinds of gravies, from Kerala fish curry to Mangalore chicken curry, and from Punjabi lentils to Andhra mutton curry. There's also a range of rice dishes to go with the curries; try the *ragi sangatti,* a combination of rice and ragi flour (made from a local grain called ragi) from Andhra's Rayalseema district or the *gongura annam,* a dish made with local greens and rice. ⊠ *Taj Banjara, Rd. No. 1, Banjara Hills* ☎ *40/ 5566–9999* ▤ *AE, DC, MC, V.*

$$$$ ╳ **Firdaus.** This airy restaurant—with high ceilings and lots of glass windows and natural light—evokes the elegance of the nizams, with *punka* (fans) gently swaying from the ceiling, waiters dressed in *sherwanis* (long Nehru-style jackets), and live *ghazal* (classical Indian vocal music) performances nightly, except Tuesday. The chef serves regal Hyderabadi cuisine. Try the *achar gosht* (lamb cooked in pickled tomato masala paste) and *nizami handi* (vegetable and cottage-cheese curry) or *bagare baingan* (baby eggplant cooked in tamarind and nut sauce). The *rann-e-firdaus* (leg of lamb) is excellent, and the restaurant also serves the unusual *anjeer* (fig) kabab, which also contains raw banana, potatoes, and herbs. ⊠ *1 Taj Krishna, Rd. No. 1, Banjara Hills* ☎ *40/5566–2323or 40/ 2339–2323* ▤ *AE, DC, MC, V.*

$$$$ ╳ **Kabab-E-Bahar.** On the edge of a small private lake, this open-air (but with a roof) restaurant serves very fine, authentic Hyderabadi cuisine buffet-style or à la carte. Try the kababs and barbecue items, particularly the stuffed chilis (which are spicy), the Shikampur kabab (minced lamb patties with yogurt and onions), or the *mahi firdaus* (skewered minced fish). ⊠ *Taj Banjara, Rd. No. 1, Banjara Hills* ☎ *40/5566–9999* ▤ *AE, DC, MC, V* ☺ *No lunch.*

¢–$ ╳ **Chutneys.** A new place for vegetarian food in the upmarket Banjara Hills area, this lively, always-full restaurant serves a wide range of Indian dishes. It's a good place to try the local Andhra cuisine, which includes such dishes as the spectacularly spicy *Guntur idlis* (steamed rice cakes), a good example of why this type of food should always be eaten with a glass of sweet *lassi* (a yogurt drink) on hand. You can also order original dishes, such as steamed *dosas* (fried crêpelike pancakes) custom-made for the popular Telugu actor Chiranjeevi, and idlis that owe their recipe to the Babai Hotel in Vijayawada. The Charlie Brown placemats are a surprising addition to the otherwise ethnic style. ⊠ *Shilpa Arcade, Rd. No. 3, Banjara Hills* ☎ *40/2335–0569* ▤ *MC, V.*

★ **$$$$** ▥ **ITC Hotel Kakatiya Sheraton.** The imposing structure and grand lobby of this hotel named after an ancient Hindu dynasty may set a strong first impression, but the warm hospitality and excellent service are what linger long after you leave this place. Rooms are tastefully laid out with an emphasis on comfort. Sip your favorite blend of tea at the Rani Rudrama's Court, a tea pavilion. ⊠ *Begumpet 500016, Andhra Pradesh* ☎ *40/ 2340–0132* ▤ *40/2340–1045* ⊕ *www.welcomgroup.com* ↵ *167 rooms, 21 suites* ⓧ *3 restaurants, coffee shop, tea shop, minibars, cable TV, pool, health club, bar, baby-sitting, Internet, business services, meeting rooms, travel services* ▤ *AE, DC, MC, V* ⦿ *CP.*

$$$$ ▥ **Taj Banjara.** This modern high-rise on Banjara Hills overlooks its own small lake. The spacious lobby is bedecked with marble, and the contemporary rooms are comfortable. Ask for a room with a lake view, on the upper floors. The Continental breakfast only comes with the higher-price ("Residency") rooms. ⊠ *Rd. No. 1, Banjara Hills, 500034* ☎ *40/ 5566–9999* ▤ *40/5566–1919* ⊕ *www.tajhotels.com* ↵ *109 rooms, 9 suites* ⓧ *2 restaurants, coffee shop, cable TV, pool, bar, business services, meeting rooms, travel services* ▤ *AE, DC, MC, V* ⦿ *CP.*

★ **$$$$** ☒ **Taj Krishna.** This striking blend of modern architecture is tempered by strong Mogul elements, with formal gardens in the front and 9 acres of property overlooking Hussain Sagar Lake. Rooms are in soft pastel tones; those facing the gardens and lake are the best. Service is exemplary. Of all the places to stay in the city, this hotel best captures the regal grace of the former princely state that was Hyderabad. The in-house restaurant, Firdaus, is one of the best places in the city to dine on royal Hyderabadi cuisine. ☒ *Rd. No. 1, Banjara Hills 500034, Andhra Pradesh* ☎ *40/5566–2323* 🖷 *40/5566–1313* ⊕ *www.tajhotels.com* 🖘 *243 rooms, 16 suites* ♨ *2 restaurants, coffee shop, cable TV, pool, health club, bar, patisserie, business services, travel services* ▤ *AE, DC, MC, V* ⏐◎⏐ *CP.*

$$$$ ☒ **Taj Residency.** Bold relief work adorns the high walls around the open lobby lounge area, which is designed to impress—with rambling sunken seating in a garishly colored pattern. Rooms have plush carpets, writing desks, and couches. The Continental breakfast only comes with the higher-price ("Residency") rooms. ☒ *Rd. No. 1, Banjara Hills, 500034* ☎ *40/5566–3939 or 40/2339–3939* 🖷 *40/5566–4848* ⊕ *www. tajhotels.com* 🖘 *134 rooms, 6 suites* ♨ *Restaurant, coffee shop, cable TV, tennis court, pool, health club, bar, business services, travel services, no-smoking rooms* ▤ *AE, DC, MC, V* ⏐◎⏐ *CP.*

$$$$ ☒ **Viceroy.** This hotel, which the Marriott chain took over in 2004, stands conveniently between Hyderabad and Secunderabad—3 km (1.9 mi) from the airport and 4 km (2½ mi) from the Secunderabad railway station—and has stunning views over Hussain Sagar Lake. Glass elevators and terraced balconies overlook the brightly lit open lobby; all the facilities are modern. Choice rooms have lake views, complete with spectacular sunsets. ☒ *Tank Bund Rd., 500080* ☎ *40/2753–8383* 🖷 *40/2753–8797* 🖘 *176 rooms, 12 suites* ♨ *Restaurant, coffee shop, in-room data ports, cable TV, pool, health club, business services, travel services* ▤ *AE, DC, MC, V* ⏐◎⏐ *CP.*

$$$ ☒ **The Manohar.** Just outside the airport (less than 1 km away)—with soundproof rooms to eliminate aircraft noise—this hotel is a good option for business travelers, as it's not close to the sights. It has all the standard trappings of an international hotel, with service to match. ☒ *Near Airport Exit Rd., Begumpet 500016* ☎ *40/2790–3333 or 40/5531–8999* 🖷 *40/2790–2222* ⊕ *www.shrishakti.com* 🖘 *127 rooms, 8 suites* ♨ *2 restaurants, coffee shop, room service, cable TV, pool, health club, bar, laundry service, business services, meeting rooms, travel services* ▤ *AE, DC, MC, V* ⏐◎⏐ *CP.*

$$–$$$ ☒ **Green Park.** Three kilometers (1.9 mi) from the airport, in the Greenlands area, this hotel is an excellent value for business travelers. The lobby is done in marble and the rooms are comfortable, with modern furnishings but no frills. The best rooms overlook the garden. ☒ *Greenlands, Begumpet 500016* ☎ *40/2375–7575 or 40/5551–5151* 🖷 *40/2375–7677* ⊕ *www.hotelgreenpark.com* 🖘 *133 rooms, 15 suites* ♨ *Restaurant, coffee shop, room service, in-room data ports, cable TV, bar, pub, laundry service, concierge floor, business services, travel services* ▤ *AE, DC, MC, V* ⏐◎⏐ *CP.*

SHOPPING

Bidri Heritage (⊠ Opposite Meher Function Hall, Banjara Hills Road, Masab Tank ☎ 40/2330–7552) is a tiny, hole-in-the-wall place that does not take credit cards but offers a fascinating range of bidri artifacts and jewelry. **Kalanjali Arts & Crafts** (⊠ 5-10-194 Hill Fort Rd., Saifabad ☎ 40/2323–1147 or 40/2329–7196) stocks traditional crafts, from wood carving to stoneware and paintings. **Krishna Pearls and Jewellers** (⊠ Taj Banjara, Rd. No. 1, Banjara Hills ☎ 40/5566–1051 or 40/5566–9999 ⊠ Next to Mrialam Mandi, Pathergatti ☎ 40/2441–7881 or 40/2452–5473 ⊕ www.krishnapearls.com) has a number of fairly priced outlets in various luxury hotels, and pleasant, courteous service. **Mangatrai Pearls** (⊠ 5-9-46 Basheerbagh, opposite Hotel Shanbagh ☎ 40/2323–5728 or 40/5558–4548 ⊠ 22-6-191 Pathergatti, near Charminar ☎ 40/2457–7339 or 40/2452–1405 ⊕ www.mangatrai.com) offers both high-quality pearls and good service. **Sanchay** (⊠ Shops 21 and 22, Babukhan Estate, Basheerbagh ☎ 40/2329–9738) has a fine selection of high-quality hand-loomed silks. **Shafali** (⊠ 72 Sarojini Devi Rd., Secunderabad ☎ 40/2780–0908 ⊕ www.shafalifabrics.com) has a bold, distinctive range of caftans, nightdresses, linen, and shoulder bags in block printed cotton. **Shilparamam** (⊠ Jubilee Hills–High Tech City) is a crafts village with rows of attractive stalls managed by artisans displaying handicrafts from all over India; the Madhubani paintings are particularly good.

HYDERABAD A TO Z

To research prices, get advice from other travelers, and book travel arrangements, visit www.fodors.com.

AIR TRAVEL TO & FROM HYDERABAD

Hyderabad is served by frequent flights from all over India. Indian Airlines has flights between Hyderabad and Bangalore, Bombay, Calcutta, Delhi, Madras, and Tirupati. Air India has service to Bombay, Jeddah, and Singapore. Privately owned Jet Airways flies from Hyderabad to the four major metros and Bangalore. Air Sahara, another private airline, flies to Bangalore, Bombay, Pune, and Calcutta. Air Deccan is a new airline that flies only ATR aircraft (small, commuter planes). It flies from Hyderabad to Bangalore and Vijayawada.

🔢 Airlines & Contacts **Air Deccan** ☎ 40/2790-2794. **Air India** ☎ 40/2338-9719 or 40/2338-1720. **Air Sahara** ☎ 40/2321-2767. **Indian Airlines** ☎ 40/2329-9333 reservations, 140 inquiries. **Jet Airways** ☎ 40/2340-1222 or 40/2790-0118.

AIRPORTS & TRANSFERS

The airport is in Secunderabad, just 2 km (1.2 mi) north of Hussain Sagar Lake. You can book a prepaid taxi in the arrivals terminal; depending on your destination, the fare should fall between Rs. 50 and Rs. 300.

🔢 Airport Information **Hyderabad airport** ⊠ Sardar Patel Rd., Hyderabad ☎ 40/2790-6555.

CARS & DRIVERS

Air Travels, Cosy Cabs, and Sri Travels provide cars and drivers 24 hours a day.

🔑 **Air Travels** ⊠ 9 and 10 Ave. 7, Banjara Hills ☎ 40/2335-3099 or 40/5561-8018. **Cosy Cabs** ⊠ Karan Apartments, Begumpet ☎ 40/2776-2023 or 40/2776-0409. **Sri Travels** ⊠ 4, Rd. No. 13, Banjara Hills ☎ 40/2339-7222 or 40/2332-4766.

EMERGENCIES

🔑 **Apollo Hospital** ⊠ Jubilee Hills ☎ 40/2360-7777, 1066 emergencies. **Fire** ☎ 101. **Police** ☎ 100.

MAIL & SHIPPING

Blue Dart Express is associated with Federal Express and can get packages just about anywhere. DHL also ships internationally.

🔑 **Blue Dart Express** ⊠ 1st fl. Victoria Castle, Prakashnagar, Begumpet ☎ 40/2790-3344. **DHL** ⊠ 1-8-449, opposite Police Lines, Begumpet ☎ 40/2790-6936 or 40/5526-0024.

🔑 **Post Office General Post Office** ⊠ Abid's Centre ☎ 40/2474-5978.

MONEY MATTERS

ATMS You can find ATMs in the shopping hubs of almost every neighborhood in the city. Try Abid's or Banjara Hills, or ask your hotel staff for a list of convenient locations.

CURRENCY EXCHANGE All of the major hotels will change money for their guests. You can also visit Thomas Cook, open Monday through Saturday from 9:30 to 6.

🔑 **Exchange Service Thomas Cook** ⊠ 6-1-57 Nasir Arcade, Saifabad district ☎ 40/2323-1988

TAXIS

Hyderabad is manageable on foot once you reach the district you want to explore. To get there, your best bet is to use a metered auto-rickshaw, call taxi, or cycle rickshaw. Auto-rickshaws tend to go the long way to your destination unless you know—or pretend to know—where you're going. Metered taxis are extremely popular. They are faster and more expensive than auto-rickshaws but cheaper than hiring a car and driver. Only a cryptologist can understand most addresses here, so landmarks and patience will serve you well. It's also a good idea to make sure your driver is familiar with your destination before you start. Asking for directions is seen as a loss of face and taxi drivers would much rather go around in circles at your expense for half an hour before they admit defeat.

TRAIN TRAVEL

Hyderabad and Secunderabad are major rail centers. Some trains use either or both stations, but most long-distance trains use only Secunderabad. An auto-rickshaw to the center of Hyderabad costs Rs. 50. From Delhi, the *Rajdhani Express* takes 23 hours, while the less-expensive *A. P. Express* takes 26 hours, when it's running on time. From Bombay, the *Hyderabad–Bombay Express* takes 14 hours; from Madras, the *Charminar Express* takes 15 hours; and from Bhubaneswar, the *Falaknuma* takes 19 hours.

⁊ Train Stations **Hyderabad Railway Station** ☎ 1345. **Secunderabad Railway Station** ☎ 1345.

TRAVEL AGENTS & TOURS

The most inexpensive tours are organized by AP Tourist Development Corporation (⇨ Visitor Information). Tours include city sightseeing day tours, the Golconda sound-and-light show, and tours to other destinations, such as Nagarjunasagar, Hampi, Ajanta and Ellora caves, and Tirupati.

In addition to tourist offices and hotel-based travel agents, you can always consult a travel agency for assistance. Ashok Travels runs deluxe buses to Nagarjuna Sagar, a Buddhist heritage site.

Hyderabad Adventures organizes unique tours (Rs. 4,500 per day for one to three persons, including air-con transport, entry tickets, and light refreshments) that explore the heart of Hyderabad's history, culture, and wildlife. Deepak Gir, a well-informed guide from an old Hyderabadi family, accompanies the tours.

⁊ Ashok Travels ✉ Lal Bahadur Stadium ☎ 40/2323-0766. **Hyderabad Adventures** ✉ 1719 Darpan building, Rd. No. 12, Banjara Hills ☎ 40/2331-8014. **Mercury Travels** ✉ 126 S. D. Rd., Jaya Mansion, 1st fl., Secunderabad ☎ 40/781-2712. **Sita World Travels** ✉ Sita House, 3-5-874, Hyderguda district ☎ 40/2323-3628.

VISITOR INFORMATION

The Andhra Pradesh Travel & Tourism Development Corporation, Ltd., is open daily from 6:30 AM to 5:30 PM and has counters in both train stations. Its Tourism Information Centre is open daily from 6:30 AM to 7:30 PM. The monthly pamphlet *Channel 6* lists the latest urban goings-on; pick it up in a bookshop or major hotel. A private directory inquiry service is available at ☎ 40/244-4444 and is enormously useful if you want to find a number fast.

⁊ Tourist Offices **Andhra Pradesh Travel & Tourism Development Corporation, Ltd.** (APTTDC) ✉ Opp. BRK Bhavan, Tank Bund Rd., Hyderabad, 500063 ☎ 40/2345-0165 or 40/2345-3086. **Tourism Information Centre** ✉ Yatri Nivas, Sardar Patel Rd., Secunderabad ☎ 40/2781-6375.

ORISSA

11

MINGLE WITH ARTISANS
and prepare to bargain
in Raghurajpur ⇨*p.538*

SEE A JUNGLE-LANDSCAPED LAGOON
from your balcony ⇨*p.534*

TAKE A TRIBAL
village tour ⇨*p.530*

KNOW THAT YOUR CHARIOT
with 24 giant wheels awaits ⇨*p.536*

TIP THE GARDENER
for a precious peek inside
Rajarani Temple ⇨*p.531*

By Nigel Fisher

Updated by
Candice
Gianetti

ORISSA IS A TANGIBLY RELIGIOUS PLACE. The state was once a center of Buddhist learning, but changes in ruling dynasties brought revolutions to spirituality, moving away from Buddhism first to Jainism and then to Hinduism. Bhubaneswar, the capital, with its hundreds of temples; Puri, with its Jagannath Temple, one of Hinduism's holiest shrines; and Konark, renowned for its extraordinary Sun Temple, are showcases for Orissa's distinctive sacred architecture, characterized by unusual shapes and fabulous, often erotic, sculptures. Buddhist history is preserved at Dhauli, where the legendary King Ashoka looked down from the hill at the carnage after a battle and experienced a conversion to Buddhism, as well as in an ancient Buddhist university's vast complex of ruins. The Jains have left a honeycomb of caves filled with sculptures to mark their era. Beyond these sites, you'll see signs of devotion everywhere: From village huts to taxis to hotels, the smiling, owl-eye face of Lord Jagannath, an avatar of Krishna and Orissa's main god, looks back at you.

The state, which lies along India's eastern seaboard, spans almost 156,000 square km (97,000 square mi) and is largely rural, with coastal plains, fields, and rivers. Orissa is also known as Utkala—Land of Arts and Crafts. In the towns or villages in the tropical countryside, striking crafts pop up everywhere, from superb hand-loomed silk and cotton fabrics to intricately detailed paintings and sculptures. It's also the home of 62 tribes, many of which still live in tiny villages scattered among beautiful hills and valleys, cleaving to their animist religion and a way of life—and mode of dress little changed by the passing of centuries. (You can visit some tribes on organized excursions.)

Finally, Orissa has nature, and lots of it—from a zoo with white tigers to miles of beaches to a brackish-water lake drawing dolphins and wintering birds from as far away as Siberia. The infrastructure and facilities in this poor, mostly agrarian state are often quite basic, but be patient and prepare to settle into a slower pace.

Exploring Orissa

Most of Orissa's top tourist attractions run along the east coast, from Bhubaneswar, south to Gopalpur-on-Sea, a beach destination that's reachable in a few hours by train. In between, the highlights are easily navigable in a day or more by car and driver (the best way) or by taking organized tours and day trips. Bhubaneswar can be explored in a day if you stick to the temples and museums, or enjoyed at more length by adding in the nearby Buddhist ruins, the zoo, and the Jain caves. To get to the tribal villages you'll have to join a tour and allot at least five days.

Numbers in the margin correspond to points of interest on the Orissa map.

About the Restaurants & Hotels

In Bhubaneswar and Orissa's other towns and resort areas, expect good food at low prices in unassuming restaurants (though Bhubaneswar does have a few more elegant eateries). Orissa's cuisine, flavored South India–style with chilis, coconut, and tamarind, is based on the abundant fresh seafood—lobster, prawns, tuna, and local fish called *bekti* and *rui*—as well as vegetables that benefit from mineral-rich soils. A few restaurants offer traditional Orissan items; watch for places serving *thalis* (sampler plates), which allow you to taste small portions of dishes prepared with coconut milk or yogurt, and delicious *baigan* (eggplant) and *bhindi* (okra) dishes. Most restaurants are open from 7 to 10 for breakfast, noon to 3 for lunch, and 7:30 to 11 for dinner; hotels often have a 24-hour or all-day coffee shop.

You don't come to Orissa for the hotels. As a rule, they're utilitarian, and service is far from snappy. Outside Bhubaneswar, a hot shower is a luxury; often, hot water is delivered in a bucket. Rates, however, are significantly lower than in more heavily traveled parts of India, and discounts are readily available outside high season (approximately December and January). The pricier hotels offer air-conditioning, currency exchange, and bathrooms with tubs. Some defensive-traveling tips: when you check into your hotel, other than a Trident or a Mayfair, if it's winter, ask that an extra blanket be sent to your room immediately, just in case; when you get to your room, check whether and how the hot water (if you have it) works—sometimes it has to be turned on, and it's better to know sooner rather than when you're ready for your shower. Unless otherwise noted, hotels in this chapter have air-conditioning and private baths.

WHAT IT COSTS In Rupees				
$$$$	**$$$**	**$$**	**$**	**¢**
RESTAURANTS over 350	250–350	150–250	100–150	under 100
HOTELS over 4,000	3,000–4,000	2,000–3,000	1,000–2,000	under 1,000

Restaurant prices are for an entrée plus dal, rice, and a veg/non-veg dish. Hotel prices are for a standard double room in high season, excluding approximately 20% tax.

Timing
The ideal time to visit is from October through March, when the temperature is around 77°F (25°C) during the day and the air is relatively dry. After March the heat starts building to 95°F (35°C) until the monsoon rains begin, in late May or early June. This cools things down a bit, but the rain can come down in buckets until mid-September. The most exciting time in Puri is during July's Rath Yatra festival, and the classical dance festival at Konark is worth checking out.

BHUBANESWAR & ENVIRONS

Although Bhubaneswar itself is a big, sprawling town full of government buildings, shops, traffic, and, of course, temples, the countryside to the south is lush with rice paddies so green they seem to glow, as well as coconut, mango, banana, and cashew trees, and tiny villages of thatch-roof mud huts clustered under tropical palms. Konark is 1½

Orissa's main destinations are Bhubaneswar, Konark, and Puri—the Golden Triangle. If you're short on time, you can see this trio in two days, one devoted to Bhubaneswar and the other to Konark and Puri, with stops at Pipli, Raghurajpur, and Dhauli. If you have two more days you can use them for day trips from Bhubaneswar to Nandankanan zoo, the Buddhist sites, or the Jain caves; spend them idling at Gopalpur-on-Sea; or make a day trip to Chilika Lake. With six days you can choose more of these options.

11

If you have
2 days

If you're on a flying visit, spend the first day exploring the ancient Hindu temples of 🏛 **Bhubaneswar ①**. Head to the Old Town to see Bindu Sagar; the Vaital, Parasurameswara, Mukteswar, Kedareswar, and Rajarani temples; and Brahmeswar. Hire transport to reach the Lingaraj Temple complex. You'll also probably have time to check out the Museum of Tribal Arts and Artefacts. The next morning, leave early for the 90-minute journey to **Konark ②** and spend an hour or more at the Sun Temple. Have breakfast in Konark village and perhaps a swim at Chandrabhapa beach before going on to **Puri ⑥**. Spend an hour or two among the pilgrims and souvenir stalls; have lunch at Wild Grass; on the way back to Bhubaneswar, stop at **Raghurajpur ⑤** to see the artisans, **Pipli ④** to browse among the appliqués, and **Dhauli ③**, the hill where Ashoka the Great slaughtered his enemies and then, in disgust, embraced Buddhism.

If you have
4 days

Spend the first day visiting the temples and museums of 🏛 **Bhubaneswar ①**. The next morning, explore the Jain caves west of town, have lunch at one of the Mayfair Lagoon's restaurants, then head for Nandankanan zoo for a white-tiger safari and a tram ride over the lake or to Barkul to see the birds at Chilika Lake. The third day, visit Dhauli, Pipli, and Raghurajpur, ending the day with a visit to Puri's temples followed by the *arti* ceremony on the beach. On the fourth day, head to Konark early for a morning at the temple and breakfast, then head for Satapada to see the dolphins on the way back to Bhubaneswar.

If you have
6 days

Spend the first day visiting Bhubaneswar's temples and museums. The next day, explore the Buddhist sites in the morning, followed by a picnic, then stop at Nandankanan on the way back to Bhubaneswar. The third day, visit Dhauli, Pipli, Konark, and 🏛 **Puri ⑥**. The fourth day, visit Raghurajpur, then Barkul, on the way to 🏛 **Gopalpur-on-Sea ⑧**. Relax on the beach the next day, returning to 🏛 **Bhubaneswar ①**. The next morning; on the last afternoon, explore the Jain caves.

hours south of the capital; a different road leads to Puri by way of Dhauli, Pipli, and Raghurajpur for a long day trip; an hour's drive south of Puri takes you to Satapada for a boat trip to where Chilika Lake joins the sea and dolphins cavort. Barkul, on Chilika's western shore, is 110 km (68 mi) south of Bhubaneswar; from Barkul it's a 60 km (37 mi) drive south to Gopalpur, or you can reach the beach town by a three-hour train from Bhubaneswar, then a taxi from Berhampur.

Bhubaneswar

❶ *480 km (298 mi) southwest of Calcutta, 1,691 km (1,051 mi) north-east of Bombay, 1,225 km (761 mi) northeast of Madras.*

Known as India's city of temples, Bhubaneswar once had some 7,000 religious shrines. Today only a fraction survive, but they still total around 500, in various stages of preservation. Unfortunately, the greatest of them, the Lingaraj, is off-limits to non-Hindus; you can see its huge tower from miles away, but the closest most foreign travelers will get to it is a viewing stand erected during the British Raj, when Lord Curzon, the British viceroy, paid a visit.

Admission is technically free at all the temples, which are open from sunrise to sunset (entrance to the inner sanctums may be restricted for half an hour or so during offering times—early morning, around noon, and late afternoon). Upon entering any one of them, however, you may be harassed for money by the priest or an enterprising local, who will follow you around with a phony donation register scribbled with the names of foreign tourists and the amounts they've allegedly donated—with an extra zero tacked onto the end of each figure. The money is usually pocketed rather than used for the preservation of the temple, but it may be worth giving Rs. 10 or so just to avoid being tailed.

Since Orissa isn't really on the way to or from any other prime tourist destination—the nearest major city to Bhubaneswar is Calcutta, at 480 km (298 mi), and the others top 1,000 km (621 mi)—you'll probably want to get your money's worth out of a visit. Besides seeing Bhubaneswar's temples, there are other enjoyable ways to spend time while based in one of the town's good hotels. Shopping, for one thing, in excellent shops that sell Orissa's textiles and handicrafts. There are interesting museums, a zoo with white and Bengal tigers, and several worthwhile day trips.

Bhubaneswar is divided in two by its rail line. On the southeastern side is Old Town, with higgledy-piggledy streets, most of them unpaved, winding between residential areas and the main temples. On the northwestern side is New Town, with wider streets and buildings spread out over a large area. There's no downtown, but Station Square, just west of the railway station, is a gathering spot for auto-rickshaws and taxis. Two main streets, Janpath and Sachivalaya Marg, run north–south through New Town; these are crossed by the east–west road Rajpath, which goes west from Station Square out to National Highway (NH) 5, the trunk road heading north to Calcutta and south to Hyderabad.

a good tour

The major temples are within an area of less than 5 km by 2 km (3 mi by 1 mi), so you can walk from one to another if it's not too hot. If it is, make an arrangement with a taxi or auto-rickshaw. Start with **Bindu Sagar,** where early-morning bathers seek blessings. From here a walk west brings you to the 8th-century **Vaital Temple.** On the opposite (east) side of Bindu Sagar is the 7th-century **Parasurameswara Temple.** About 1 km (½ mi) to the east is the 10th-century **Mukteswar Temple;** on the same grounds is the whitewashed **Kedar Gouri Temple.** Continue east for

11

Architecture

The temples of Bhubaneswar, Konark, and Puri, built between the 7th and 15th centuries, bear elaborate and fascinating detail. Canonical texts governed their structural forms and proportions. The Orissan temple consists almost entirely of a spire that vaults upward among much-lower turrets. Supporting the tower is the cube-shape *deul* (shrine for the deity); next to the deul stands the *jagamohan* (porch), a meeting place for worshipers, usually square with a pyramidal roof. Sometimes one or two more halls—a *natmandir* (dancing hall) and a *bhogmandir* (hall of offerings)—are set in front of the porch. The architecture may seem heavy, but the sculptures on these temples are graceful, animated, often exuberantly erotic, and steeped in mythology. Most temples have a sacred tank in their yards in which worshipers bathe themselves for religious cleansing.

Shopping

Orissa is renowned for its handicrafts. Foremost among them is the weaving of hand-loomed silk, *tussar* (raw) silk, and cotton fabrics and saris at centers like Sonepur, Sambalpur, and Cuttack, from simple designs to elaborate double *ikats* (fabric) made by tie-dying both the weft and the warp yarns to produce soft-edged designs in the weave. Everywhere in Orissa you'll see superb stone sculptures inspired by temple architecture. *Patachitra* is the art of exquisitely detailed, fine-lined paintings on cotton, silk, or other cloth, usually illustrating stories from the ancient Hindu epics. *Talapatra* paintings or etchings are done on palm leaves treated so they're as hard as wooden slats. *Tarkashi*, a much-prized Orissan export for centuries, is the art of silver filigree, centered in Cuttack; jewelry, boats, temples, elephants, and other items are made by drawing silver through smaller and smaller holes to produce fine strands that are shaped into designs and soldered together. *Dhokra* is the art of casting animals, tribal figures, boats, bowls, and other items in brass by the lost-wax process, creating a unique ribbed finish by wrapping the object in rows of beeswax wires. Also look for items made from bell metal, lacquerware colorfully painted with folk designs, colorful appliqué work, and "golden grass" items made from swamp grasses. Serious shopping entails side trips to the beautiful, largely hidden Orissan villages that are home to master craftspeople. Most tour companies offer crafts tours of the best centers in the state.

Travelers are subject to grossly inflated prices, even in remote artisans' hamlets. Start bargaining (it's expected) at half the original price, and you may end up with a 30% to 40% "discount." In Pipli, competition drops the rate of initial inflation; here you'll need to bargain down only 5% to 10%. If you shy away from dickering, you can always buy good items at fixed prices at the government emporiums.

---

700 yards to see the 11th-century **Rajarani Temple,** on manicured grounds. A little farther along Tankapani Road going east is a crossroads; turn right (south) and you'll come to wonderfully carved **Brahmeswar.** You might want transport to travel the 3 km (2 mi) to the **Lingaraj Temple Complex;** to walk here, retrace your steps to the crossroads and turn left

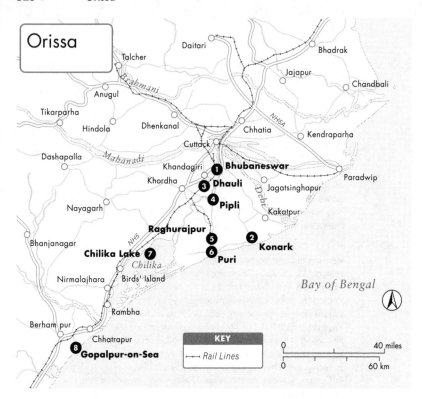

Orissa

Daitari
Talcher
Bhadrak
Jajapur
Brahmani
Chandbali
Anugul
Tikarparha
Hindola
Dhenkanal
Chhatia
NH5A
Kendraparha
Dashapalla
Mahanadi
Cuttack
Khandagiri ❶ **Bhubaneswar**
Khordha ❸ **Dhauli**
Jagatsinghapur
Paradwip
❹ **Pipli**
Kakatpur
Nayagarh
Debi
Raghurajpur
Bhanjanagar
NH5
❺ ❷ **Konark**
Chilika Lake ❼ ❻ **Puri**
Chilika
Nirmalajhara Birds' Island
Bay of Bengal
Rambha
Berham pur
Chhatrapur
❽ **Gopalpur-on-Sea**

KEY
⊢—⊣ *Rail Lines*

0   40 miles
0   60 km

onto Tankapani, back down the way you came, but before Rajarani take another left that will bring you down to Puri Road. Cross over and head up the small, busy road lined with stalls to the temple. Afterward, hop a cycle- or auto-rickshaw for a quick lunch at Cooks' or Venus Inn, another to the nearby **Orissa State Museum,** then a taxi or an auto-rickshaw to the **Museum of Tribal Arts and Artefacts;** alternatively, spend the afternoon exploring the **Jain caves** or visiting **Nandankanan** zoo.

TIMING   It takes a full morning to see all the temples. Start by 8 AM so you won't have to hike around in the midday sun. Most of the temples will take 15 to 20 minutes to explore, though you might want to spend more time browsing the stalls, checking out the goods at the Lingaraj complex, sold by pilgrims, and generally soaking up the scene.

After lunch, spend at least an hour at the Orissa State Museum; from there it's a 10- or 15-minute ride by taxi or auto-rickshaw to the tribal museum, where you'll probably spend 45 minutes. Visiting the Jain caves, also about a 10-minute ride from most parts of town, should take two hours or so; Nandankanan is a 30-minute ride from town, and should also take about two hours. You can do this tour in a day, but it's a lot easier if you take your time and stretch it out over two days.

What to See

All temples are open daily from sunrise to sunset.

Bindu Sagar. Surrounded by a stone embankment, the largest sacred tank in Bhubaneswar was the central point around which Bhubaneswar's multitude of temples was originally built. Believing that this tank is filled with water from every sacred stream and tank in India, and can therefore wash away sins, pilgrims come here to cleanse themselves.

Brahmeswar Temple. The exterior of this 11th-century temple is sumptuously carved with monkeys, swans, and deer, figures of gods and goddesses, and religious scenes. Over the entrance is a row of similar figures representing the nine planets. If you're lucky, you'll be shown around by a priest who will hold forth on the temple's carvings and their complicated symbolic significance. (He'll expect a small tip.)

Jain caves. About 8 km (5 mi) west of central Bhubaneswar are two granite hills, Khandagiri and Udaygiri, laced with 33 rock-cut caves that were part of a Jain monastery dating back to the 2nd and 1st centuries BC. There are excellent carvings and architecture throughout, especially in the Queen's Cave and the two-story Elephant Cave, and there's a 1st century BC rock edict (a law carved into the rock) of Emperor Kharavela. Also here are remains of a hotel, lecture halls, prayer halls, and simple monks' lodgings. An India Tourism–trained guide (⇨ Orissa A to Z)would be handy to have along on a half-day excursion. ⊠ *Off Khandagiri Marg* ☎ *No phone* ✍ *Rs. 100* ☼ *Daily 8–6.*

Lingaraj Temple Complex. This giant 11th-century shrine is considered the ultimate in Orissan temple architecture by Hindu devotees and art historians alike. A world in itself, with some 100 smaller votive shrines, the Shiva temple sits in a huge walled compound that teems with activity. From the small, raised platform 100 yards away, non-Hindus can strain to see the profuse exterior carvings, a high point of Hindu decorative art; alas, without binoculars, most of the details will elude you. Note that many enterprising locals have for years been posting themselves at the foot of the platform stairs with a phony guest register and demanding a donation; the money goes straight into their pockets. Dating from about 1050, the temple originally consisted of only the porch and shrine; the dancing hall and hall of offerings were added about 100 years later. The *vimana* (curvilinear tower), built without mortar, soars to a height of 147 feet.

Mukteswar Temple. Bhubaneswar's smallest temple was built in the 10th century. Its red sandstone body is encrusted with intricate carvings, from emaciated, crouching *sadhus* (Hindu holy men) to voluptuous, buxom women bedecked with jewels. On the left side of the entrance, the statues of bearers grimace under the temple's monumental weight. The Mukteswar's most distinctive feature is its *torana,* a thick-pillared, arched gateway draped with carved strings of beads and ornamented with statues of smiling women in languorous positions. Beyond the torana, set back in a shady yard, stands the **Kedar Gouri Temple,** with its 8-foot-tall statue of Hanuman, the monkey god. (While here, pop over to the Raghunath Crafts Museum.)

CloseUp

TRIBAL VILLAGE TOURS

ALTHOUGH MOST OF ORISSA'S 62 TRIBES have been absorbed into the towns and mainstream life, others in tiny villages scattered over verdant hills and valleys, sometimes more than an hour's trek from any road, are remarkably untouched by modern life. A few of these villages are off-limits to outsiders, but most can be visited on a tour organized by one of several agencies in Bhubaneswar and Puri—an enlightening, amusing, sometimes worrying, but ultimately unforgettable experience. (Visiting on your own is not feasible.)

Most of the tribes practice an agrarian lifestyle, growing paddy rice, vegetables, and fruits for their own use as well as to sell at colorful weekly markets where townsfolk and tribes from surrounding villages mix only briefly over business. There are markets most days of the week in different towns, and many villagers must walk for hours to reach them, carrying on their backs or their heads sacks of rice, aluminum urns of potent alcohol made from the mahua flower or sago palm, long bundles of branches for firewood, woven baskets filled with vegetables, or a cache of simple hand-loomed fabrics and brass, woven-grass, or other ornaments. Bonda women, whose villages are off-limits and who dress in magnificent drapings of perhaps a hundred strands of colored beads (some strung with coins), bring more of them to sell—and will let you take a photograph of them for Rs. 10 (in most of the villages the economic incentive is unnecessary and probably inadvisable).

In the villages you can see the utterly simple one- or two-room dirt-floor homes in which entire families live, eat, and sleep; the dormitories where young girls and boys get to know one another and play music; the flat stones arranged in a circle where the tribal councils meet; the totems and shrines of their animist religion; the

mostly broken-down wells the government built and the ugly, poorly built houses it put up here and there amid the well-maintained thatched mud houses. You can watch the day's supply of rice being threshed in a small hand-woven apparatus or alcohol being made in jerry-rigged stills. With advance notice, your guide can arrange for traditional music-and-dance performances with drums, horns, and strings of bells.

Some people feel uneasy about coming into villages like a visitor at a human zoo, looking at people's clothing and jewelry and into their houses, taking photographs, and asking questions through the guide. But it helps when children gather around you as their parents either join them or peek back at you from doorways—your arrival is an interesting development in their day, and they're as curious about you as you are about them. It's a precarious balance, though; the fear is that the more tourists who come (the stream is small but growing), the more outside influence is likely to creep in. Certainly, in terms of authenticity, the sooner you make a visit, the better.

There are two basic options: You can travel from village to village, stopping at weekly markets along the way, then settle at night into the best available hotel in the area (which may be perfectly comfortable or may require fortitude and a sense of humor). Or you can choose to stay in the villages themselves, either in the tribal guest house or schoolhouse—usually a primitive shelter where you use your sleeping bag and look to nature for amenities—or in the tour company's tents. Because of the distances between villages, at least five days is recommended, and all the providers listed under Tours (⇨ Orissa A to Z) offer itineraries of 11 days or longer.

Museum of Tribal Arts and Artefacts. This small museum run by the Tribal Research and Training Institute (watch for that name on the sign out front) provides a look into the lives of Orissa's 62 tribes. In five galleries painted with the white pictographs of the Saora tribe, displays labeled in English include hand-loomed clothing, jewelry, hunting weapons, agricultural implements, crafts, and musical instruments. Many of the items are still in use among the tribes, but some—like the Bonda's elaborate neck rings—are being phased out as the modern world seeps in. Out back are tired but authentic huts from five tribes in which the artifacts were formerly displayed. ✉ *NH 5, off CRPF Sq., between Priyardarshini Market and the Hanuman Temple* ☎ *674/246–1635* ✉ *Rs. 20* ☉ *Mon.–Sat. 10–5* ☉ *Closed 2nd Sat. of month.*

Orissa State Museum. Treasures are hidden within this ill-maintained, underlabeled, sprawling complex, from the Mauryan-period Ashokan lion at the entrance to a room that is full of spectacular *patachitra* (Orissan paintings on silk or cotton cloth). You'll find sculptures dating back to the 3rd century BC, bronzes, coins, copperplate and stone inscriptions, armaments, musical instruments, handicrafts, Bronze Age tools, natural history exhibits (ratty stuffed things), and dioramas of tribal and jungle life. One room holds—on dusty open shelves—an amazing cache of more than 37,000 palm-leaf manuscripts in six languages, some with Orissan-style paintings; the oldest date back to the 16th century. ✉ *Lewis Rd.* ☎ *674/243–1597* ✉ *Rs. 1* ☉ *Tues.–Sun. 10–5; no entry between 1 and 2 PM.*

Parasurameswara Temple. Built in AD 650, this small Shiva temple is the oldest temple in Bhubaneswar. It's a perfect example of the pre-10th-century Orissan style: a high spire that curves up to a point over the sanctum, which houses the deity, and a pyramid-covered jagamohan, where people sit and pray. The facade is covered with carvings, including one of Ganesh, the elephant god of wisdom and prosperity.

★ **Rajarani Temple.** Standing by itself in green rice fields, far back from the road, this 11th-century temple is perhaps the most harmoniously proportioned in town, and is definitely the most peaceful. The king who created the Rajarani died before its finishing touch—a deity—was installed, leaving its sanctum sanctorum godless. There are no aggressive priests here. The carvings are lovely, with dragons tucked into cracks, couples in erotic poses, and smiling, beautiful women. A small tip to the gardener-caretaker will get you inside.

Vaital Temple. This 8th-century, highly decorated temple near Bindu Sagar is one of the area's earliest. It's devoted to the tantric goddess Chamunda, and its two-story, barrel-shape roof shows the influence of South Indian architecture. Bring a flashlight to see the carvings inside.

off the beaten path

NANDANKANAN ZOOLOGICAL PARK – Twenty kilometers (12 mi) north of Bhubaneswar and reachable by taxi, bus, or Orissa Tourism Development Corporation (OTDC) tour is this park carved out of Chandaka Forest. White tigers are bred here; you can see them on a bus safari, which, along with a separate lion safari, leaves at 11, 12,

2, 3, and 4 (but it won't go unless there are enough people; go early and check in every hour). Other inhabitants of this semiwild zoo include leopards, striped hyenas, herons and storks, crocodiles, rhinos, antelopes, bears, jaguars, and zebras. A tram crosses a lake to the Botanical Garden. Also here are paddleboating, a toy train, and elephant rides. ☎ 674/255–5840 or 674/255–4924 ➪ Rs. 40, video camera Rs. 500 ⊗ Tues.–Sun. 8–5.

BUDDHIST COMPLEX – On four hillsides 85 to 100 km (53 to 62 mi) north of Bhubaneswar, excavations have revealed the ruins of a vast Buddhist university that flourished before the 7th century (perhaps as early as the 2nd) and continued until the 16th century. Separated by long stretches of idyllic green paddy fields and palm trees, the sites contain stone *stupas* (shrines), brick monasteries, and beautiful sculptures and bas reliefs, as well as some small museums with sculptures that were found on-site. The most extensive site is **Ratnagiri,** where Stupa 1 has a gorgeous, ornately carved door jamb and an outer courtyard has seven interconnected closetlike stone chambers where monks meditated; fragments include panels with lovely carved scenes from the ancient Hindu epic *The Ramayana.* **Udaygiri** has a shrine with another beautiful stone doorway sculpted with nagas, guardian deities, and even ladies swinging on the branches of a tree. At **Lalitgiri** are the foundations of four brick monasteries; a *chaityagriha,* an amphitheater where performances were held; and a museum displaying colossal Buddha sculptures. All four sites (the fourth and most recently excarated site is Langudi) would take a long day, but you can do Udaygiri and Ratnagiri in a full morning or afternoon; you'll need to bring along a knowledgeable guide just to find the sites, and there's nowhere to eat—bring a picnic. ⊗ *Daily sunrise–sunset; Ratnagiri museum: Sat.–Thurs. 10–5; Lalitgiri museum: daily 7:30–5* ➪ *Udaygiri site free, Lalitgiri site Rs. 100; Ratnagiri museum Rs. 100.*

Where to Stay & Eat

$$–$$$ ✕ **Exclusive.** The Swosti hotel's two restaurants offer the same two menus (one Indian, one Chinese and Continental) and friendly service, but although the Executive is cozier, this is the more elegant room: gilded walls, collage art with embedded bronze dhokra animals and tribal jewelry, and slatted wood screens between tables. The Orissan *thalis* (sampler platters) still on the menu are no longer offered, but you can order the local specialties individually, such as *santula* (mixed vegetables in coconut sauce). Other good dishes include *saag gosht,* creamy spinach with mutton. ⊠ *Hotel Swosti, 103 Janpath* ☎ *674/253–4678* ▤ *AE, DC, MC, V.*

★ $$–$$$ ✕ **Shanghai Express.** Come to this Indo-Chinese restaurant opened in 2003—in an attractive room wrapped in frosted-glass windows etched with palm fronds—and ask them to tone down the spices. Spring rolls are big and crusty, stuffed with chunks of prawns and shredded vegetables. Try the fabulous salt-and-pepper chicken, crispy fried nuggets tossed in a light sauce of peppercorns, ginger, garlic, soy sauce, and tender scallion bulbs, with a salty zing. ✉ *New Marrion hotel, 6 Janpath* ☎ 674/ *250–2328 or 674/250–2689* ☰ *AE, DC, MC, V.*

¢–$ ✕ **Dawat.** Once your eyes adjust to the darkness, you'll find yourself in a small, simple dining room with white stucco walls, terra-cotta–color tile floors, and glass-top tables. The larger room, behind it, is nicer, and brighter, with mirrored walls. The place is always hopping with locals, who universally praise its Chinese and decent, reasonably priced Indian fare (with a few Thai and Continental dishes thrown in). Good choices include the ginger prawns and the vegetable *dopiaza,* a spicy mix of fresh vegetables cooked al dente. ✉ *620 Janpath, Sahid Nagar* ☎ 674/254– *4027 or 674/309–0276* ☰ *MC, V.*

¢ ✕ **Cooks' Restaurant.** This eatery in the heart of town—a bright, simple, but pleasant room with a tile floor and brick walls—is upstairs from the shiny-clean streetfront open kitchen. Choose from a good selection of Indian and Chinese dishes, including spring rolls, *paneer pasanda* (chunks of curdled cheese with a zesty stuffing and a thick tomato sauce), and a Cooks' Special, *murg tikka nawabi* (boneless chicken prepared either dry or with a masala sauce in a tandoori oven). ✉ *260 Bapuji Nagar* ☎ 674/253–0025 or 674/253–0035 ☰ *No credit cards.*

¢ ✕ **Venus Inn.** This popular midtown South Indian vegetarian restaurant offers a wide variety of *dosas* (stuffed crêpes) and *uttappams* (rice-flour pancakes), along with paneer and vegetrarian dishes and some Chinese selections. Try the butter *rawa sada* dosa, a crunchy semolina dosa, with a slightly salty-and-sweet grain filling, or the butter-and-coconut uttappam. A small, dark room filled with granite pedestal tables, this place is best suited for a quick, hearty lunch or a snack of ice cream or sweets when you're in the Market Building or the Janpath area shopping. ✉ *217 Bapuji Nagar* ☎ 674/253–1738 or 674/253–2685 ☰ *No credit cards.*

$$$$ ▦ **Trident Hilton.** The most tranquil, sophisticated property in Bhubaneswar, Fodor's Choice set among 14 acres of papaya, mango, banana, and coconut trees, is 10 ★ km (6 mi) from town. The lobby is exquisitely Indian: at the center are huge brass temple bells suspended by 10-foot-long chains; the balcony, supported by beautifully carved sandstone columns, is guarded by six stone lions. The guest rooms combine Orissan art—such as the stone temple-style sculptures inset in the headboard above each bed—with touches that reflect the sensibility of the Thai designer who redid the rooms in 2002, including Burmese teak parquet floors, beech cabinetry, lush fabrics in teal blue and gold, and great mattresses and feather pillows. There's also a jogging track on-site. ✉ *C. B. 1, Nayapalli, Bhubaneswar 751013* ☎ 674/230–1010 ☒ 674/230–1302 ⊕ *www. hilton.com* ⤳ 59 *rooms, 3 suites* ⟁ 2 *restaurants, room service, in-room data ports, in-room safes, minibars, cable TV, 2 tennis courts, pool, health club, sauna, spa, steam room, bar, shop, baby-sitting, dry cleaning, laundry service, concierge, business services, meeting rooms, travel services, no-smoking rooms* ☰ *AE, DC, MC, V* ❢ *EP.*

$$$ ▦ **Hotel Swosti.** This friendly and well-run hotel has efficient, courteous service. The cozy lobby is decorated with patachitra paintings. The building is on one of Bhubaneswar's main thoroughfares, close to the train station; for maximum quiet, ask for a room in the back. All the rooms are a good size and clean, with plain, contemporary furnishings

and big padded headboards; standard rooms have twin beds, and deluxe rooms have kings. Living rooms in suites are set up for business—the desk comes with upholstered swivel chair and an extra phone. ☒ *103 Janpath, Bhubaneswar 751001* ☎ *674/253–4678 or 674/253–4497* 🖷 *674/253–5784* ⊕ *www.swosti.com* ⥲ *53 rooms, 3 suites* ♺ *2 restaurants, room service, IDD phones, in-room data ports, minibars, cable TV, bar, dry cleaning, laundry service, Internet, convention center, travel services* ▭ *AE, DC, MC, V* ♡❘ *EP.*

$$$ ☷ **Mayfair Lagoon.** In place of the nearby Trident's tranquillity, this ex-
Fodor'sChoice cellent resort offers lots of options for food and entertainment, plus a
★ jungle-landscaped man-made lagoon. Peace reigns, however, in the quiet, spacious, tastefully decorated guest rooms, each with a private balcony; the best overlook the lagoon—from the "deluxe cottages" (suites) and the elegant two-bedroom villas you can lean over the rail and feed the ducks. The spa offers a full roster of services; the gym has a wall of windows overlooking the gardens and beautiful pool. ☒ *8-B Jaydev Vihar, Bhubaneswar 751013* ☎*674/236–0101 to 20* 🖷*674/236–0236* ⊕*www. mayfairhotels.com* ⥲ *56 rooms, 8 suites* ♺ *5 restaurants, room service, minibars, IDD phones, in-room data ports, in-room safes, cable TV, gym, hair salon, spa, steam room, billiards, Ping-Pong, squash, pub, shops, dry cleaning, laundry service, Internet, business services, convention center, travel services, no-smoking rooms* ▭ *AE, DC, MC, V* ♡❘ *BP.*

$$ ☷ **The New Marrion.** Since new owners took over in 2000, five new meeting rooms, a great mosaic-tile pool, and a pavilion with restaurants, a coffee bar, and a sweets shop have been added. By the end of 2004 the last of the guest rooms will have been renovated and a new lobby restaurant, gym, steam bath, hair salon, and shop will be in place. Halls and baths gleam with green marble; mattresses are good and thick (some are hard, some medium; let them know if you have a preference). The deluxe rooms have marble floors and king beds. One caveat: service is spotty. ☒ *6 Janpath, Bhubaneswar 751001* ☎ *674/250–2328, 674/250–2689, or 674/252–2472 to 74* 🖷 *674/250–3287* ⊕ *www. newmarrion.com* ⥲ *55 rooms, 6 suites* ♺ *5 restaurants, room service, IDD phones, in-room data ports, minibars, cable TV, pool, gym, hair salon, steam room, dry cleaning, laundry service, Internet, business services, convention center, travel services* ▭ *AE, DC, MC, V* ♡❘ *EP.*

$$ ☷ **Sishmo.** This is the most conveniently located hotel in town: off Janpath, close to the Market Building, the railway station, and the state museum, and a quick auto-rickshaw ride to the temples—some rooms on the higher floors even give you a glimpse of them. Orissan art throughout the lobby sets a nice regional tone, though the rooms are your basic modern. ☒ *86/A-1 Gautam Nagar, Bhubaneswar 751014* ☎ *674/243–3600 to 05* 🖷 *674/243–3351* ⊕ *www.hotelsishmo.com* ⥲ *64 rooms, 8 suites* ♺ *2 restaurants, coffee shop, room service, IDD phones, in-room data ports, minibars, cable TV, pool, health club, bar, dry cleaning, laundry service, Internet, business services, convention center, travel services* ▭ *AE, DC, MC, V* ♡❘ *EP.*

$ ☷ **Royale Midtown.** This budget business hotel, which opened in 2001, has a lot to offer: a central location on the main drag just north of the Sishmo, cheerful contemporary-style rooms (green-and-white-pinstripe spreads, green-and-orange cubistlike-print drapes, throw rugs on white marble floors), a good multicuisine restaurant, and an attractive bar. Executive rooms are larger with king beds, sofas, and coffeemakers. Meetings are always going on, so expect traffic and noise during business hours. ⊠ *52–53 Janpath, Bhubaneswar 751009* ☎ *674/253–6138 to 41* 🖷 *674/253–6142* ⊕ *www.royalehotels.com* ➪ *48 rooms* ♨ *Restaurant, room service, IDD phones, in-room data ports, cable TV, minibars, dry cleaning, laundry service, Internet, business services, meeting rooms, travel services* ⊟ *AE, MC, V* ⦿ *BP.*

Nightlife & the Arts

THE ARTS   Odissi, the classical dance form native to Orissa, is perhaps the most lyrical style of Indian dance, flowing with graceful gestures and postures; it's performed, along with folk and tribal dances, during festivals throughout the state, notably in Konark. For information, contact the Orissa Department of Tourism. Cultural performances take place each Saturday evening at **Ekamra Haat** (⊠ next to the Exhibition Ground, Madhusudan Marg ☎ 674/240–3169 ⊙ daily 5 PM–9 PM), a marketplace with 42 crafts shops plus food stalls in a villagelike setting.

NIGHTLIFE   **The Baron & the Baroness** (⊠ Mayfair Lagoon hotel, 8-B Jaydev Vihar ☎ 674/236–0101) has disco nights Saturday and Sunday; other times it's a good English pub, complete with a suit of armor and green leather banquettes. **Bollywood 70** (⊠ Crown Hotel, A1 [a] IRC Village, Nayapalli ☎ 674/255–5500) restaurant shows 1970s Bollywood films nightly at 7. **Café Coffee Day** (⊠ The New Marrion, 6 Janpath ☎ 674/250–2328), an Indian Starbucks with good coffees and desserts, has loudish music from a jukebox stuffed with tunes from everywhere. **Landsdowne Road** bar (⊠ The New Marrion, 6 Janpath ☎ 674/250–2328) salutes cricket with a wall full of posters, gear, etc. The **Trident Hilton** (⊠ C. B. 1, Nayapalli ☎ 674/230–1010) has poolside barbecues with live Indian classical music nightly except at monsoon time. The multicuisine restaurant at the hotel **Sishmo** (⊠ 86/A-1 Gautam Nagar ☎ 674/243–3600 to 05) has a five-piece Hindi pop band at dinner Wednesday through Sunday.

Shopping

Shops are generally open daily from 8:30 or 9 AM until 8:30 or 9 PM. Capital Market, a street-long market where locals shop, across from the Market Building, is closed on Monday. The **Market Building,** actually a complex of interconnected buildings on Rajpath, with so-called towers (they're not) at the east and west end, has several good fabric and handicrafts shops.

Boyanika (⊠ Western Tower, Market Bldg. ☎ 674/253–0232), the Orissa State Handloom Weavers Co-operative Society shop, has lovely saris, bedcovers, and fabrics in various Orissan styles and textures. **Kalamandir** (⊠ Western Tower, Market Bldg. ☎ 674/253–1133 or 674/253–0596 ⊕ http://kalamandirorissa.com) has two attractive, well-lighted floors of saris, shawls, and other stylish men's and women's clothing, plus fabric and bedcovers, from all over India; there's an annual sale in August. **Lalchand Jewellers** (⊠ Station Sq. ☎ 674/253–4625 or 674/253–4888) has a huge showroom including a wide selection of *tarkashi,* the silver-filigree work from Cuttack.**Mehers' Handloom** (⊠ Shriya Sq.

☎ 674/250–2303 or 674/250–5341 ⊕ www.mehersonline.com), opened in 2000 by a family of master weavers from Sonepur, one of the great weaving villages of Orissa, has an attractive shop with hand-loomed traditional and *ikat* (tie-dyed yarn) saris, fabrics, bedcovers, and other items, as well as fine pieces from all over India. **Odissika** (✉ 265 Lewis Rd. ☎ 674/243–3314) has a host of stone carvings, terra-cotta objects, dhokra bronze animals, and other authentic Orissan handicrafts.

Orissa Modern Art Gallery (✉ A-17/8 Surya Nagar, near Gopabandhu Sq. ☎ 674/240–4473) sells exactly what its name implies, and proves there *is* indeed more to Orissan art than the 10 incarnations of Vishnu. **Priyadarshini** (✉ Western Tower, Market Bldg. ☎ 674/253–2140 or 674/253–0386 ✉ Sahid Nagar ☎ 674/254–6210 ✉ Biju Patnaik airport ☎ 674/253–4759) sells very fine Orissan silk and cotton saris, mainly from Sambalpur. **Raghunath Crafts Museum** (✉ by Kedar Gouri Temple ☎ 674/243–6899) showcases small and giant sculptures by award-winning artist Raghunath Mohapatra, whose temple-esque works grace the headboards at the Trident. **Utkalika** (✉ Eastern Tower, Market Bldg. ☎ 674/240–0187), a government fixed-price emporium, has a great selection of every type of Orissan handicraft.

Konark

❷ *64 km (40 mi) southeast of Bhubaneswar, 35 km northeast of Puri.*

The sleepy town of Konark, 1½ hours from Bhubaneswar, is home to one of India's most fabulous temples—a World Heritage Site. The village exists for the temple, earning its income entirely from tourism via souvenir shops, food stalls, and basic restaurants. The beach, Chandrabhaga, is quiet, wide, and clean.

Fodor'sChoice Legend shrouds the **Sun Temple,** or Black Pagoda, so called because of
★ the dark patina that has covered it over the centuries, though much of that black has now been cleaned off to reveal the stone's natural color. Built by King Narasimha in the 13th century in the shape of the sun god Surya's chariot, it's a wonder of architecture and engineering. Today, only half the main temple and the audience hall remain to suggest the Sun Temple's original shape, but the complex once had a dancing hall, an audience hall, and a tremendous tower that soared to 227 feet; by 1869 the tower had fallen to ruin, and the audience hall had to be filled with stone slabs and sealed off to prevent its collapse. The temple's location—on coastal sand—is majestic, but the briny air and the softness of the underlying dunes have taken their toll.

The Sun Temple was designed in the form of a chariot, with 24 wheels pulled by seven straining horses. Every last one of its surfaces is intricately carved with some of the most fantastic sculpture in India: horses and elephants, depictions of daily life from hunting to childbirth, images of war, dancers and musicians, and of course erotic pairings. Every structural feature is significant: the seven horses represent the seven days of the week, the 24 wheels are the 24 fortnights of the Indian year, and the eight spokes of each wheel are the eight *paharsic*define into which the ancients divided day and night.

Try to arrive between 7 and 8 AM, before the busloads of pilgrims and other tourists show up. The Archaeological Survey of India provides guides, but ask to see an identification badge, as many less-informed freelance guides are also eager to take you around. The going rate is Rs. 60 per person. A free museum has sculptures found in the ruins. ⊠ *Off Puri Rd.* 🖾 *Rs. 5* ☉ *Daily sunrise–sunset.*

The **Konark Dance Festival** (☎ Orissa Department of Tourism [OTDC] 674/243–2217), held each December 1 through 5, features the best of Odissi and other dance forms on an outdoor stage with the illuminated Sun Temple as backdrop. If you can, bring something soft to cushion the hard, backless amphitheater seats—and mosquito repellent. Orissa tourism runs special trips from Bhubaneswar or Puri and back during the festival for Rs. 125.

Dhauli

❸ *6 km (4 mi) southwest of Bhubaneswar.*

It was from the top of a hill at Dhauli, off the Puri Road, that India's legendary king Ashoka the Great in 272 BC looked down over the verdant countryside littered with bodies after his armies invaded what was then the kingdom of Kalinga. Overcome with horror, Ashoka underwent a transformation: He abandoned his drive to conquer, began to practice Buddhism, and went on to incite a moral and spiritual revolu-
★ tion throughout Orissa and the rest of India. **The site of Ashoka's conversion** is marked by the carving of an elephant emerging from a rock—said to be the oldest rock-cut sculpture in India (3rd century BC)—symbolizing the birth of the Buddha and the emergence of Buddhism. Also carved in stone on the hillside, protected behind iron gratings, are the Ashokan edicts in which the once-ruthless warrior declared that all men were his children.

Up the hill from the site of Ashoka's conversion is the **Shanti Stupa,** a Buddhist peace pagoda built jointly by Japanese and Indian groups in 1972. Visible from miles around, this striking white building, topped by a dome ringed with several umbrella-like protrusions, resembles a massive alien crustacean from a distance; close up you can examine the sculptural panels and Buddha figures that encircle the stupa. The view from here—of the Daya River curving through the green rice paddies and cashew trees—is lovely. ⊠ *Off Puri Rd.*

A master development plan is in the works for Dhauli by the Orissa Department of Tourism (OTDC). It calls for a Peace Park to be constructed here to attract international pilgrims as part of the Buddhist Circuit. Elements of the plan include an amphitheater, a meditation center and path, a museum, nature trails, and a sound-and-light show.

Pipli

❹ *16 km (10 mi) southeast of Bhubaneswar, 28 km (17 mi) north of Puri.*

The little village of Pipli is famous throughout India for its brightly colored appliqué work. Dozens of shops line both sides of the main street, each crammed with piles of cheery beach umbrellas, lampshades, wall hangings, bags, and more in patchworks of primary greens, yellows, blues, and reds with little circular bits of mirror inset for sparkle. The shops all offer pretty much the same traditional fare. In a few you'll see some attempts at modern design, and here and there you may catch an artisan at work.

Raghurajpur

★ ❺ *16 km (10 mi) north of Puri, 44 km (27 mi) south of Bhubaneswar.*

Less than two hours' drive from Bhubaneswar is the village of Raghurajpur, where every thatch-roof dwelling houses a family of artisans. Their skills in stone-and-wood carving, *talapatra* (palm-leaf paintings), and patachitra are passed down from generation to almost every member of the next generation. As you leave the main road and arrive at this idyllic village, several friendly escorts will offer to lead you to their house for "just a look," but take your time to wander the few streets and appreciate the murals that adorn the walls, done by some of the village's best artists.

If you're interested, the artisans will demonstrate their processes. In the technique of patachitra, for which the town is especially known, everything is done the old-fashioned way, from rubbing the silk or other cloth with tamarind-seed gum and stones to give it a parchmentlike texture to executing fine strokes of color with dyes made from plants and crushed stones. The subjects of the paintings are usually stories from the epics. Some of the artists, such as Gopal Maharana, Kalu Charan Barik, Dinabandhu Mahapatra, and Banamali Mahapatra, have won state and national prizes. When looking through Sukanta Sahoo's work, you'll be in luck if he has some by his sister, Geetanjali Sahoo, who no longer lives in the village but whose award-winning patachitra work is characterized by a distinctive feminine grace. For talapatra, look for work by Chandrasekhar Das and Praful Maharana.

As everywhere in India, the prices are raised for travelers, but you can bargain down to less than you'd pay anywhere else; expect to pay in rupees. Most artisans welcome customers daily from around 9 to 1 and 3 to 6. An enterprising child will probably offer to arrange a dance for you—a memorable way to end a visit—or you can arrange one in advance (☎ 675/227–4359, 675/222–6440, 675/227–4553, or 675/227–4485 ⊕ chitrakara_raghurajpur@yahoo.com). You can stay overnight in a little house, built in 2004, to observe the creative process at length—or just enjoy the village life over the course of a typical day and night. For information, contact the OTDC.

Puri

❻ *60 km (36 mi) south of Bhubaneswar, 35 km (21 mi) southwest of Konark.*

The coastal town of Puri is heavily visited because it contains one of Hinduism's most sacred sites: the 12th-century **Jagannath Temple,** devoted to the Lord of the Universe. The interior of the temple complex, enclosed within high walls, is strictly off-limits to non-Hindus; even the late Prime

Minister Indira Gandhi was denied entrance because she had married a non-Hindu. The intricately sculpted main temple is 65 meters (214 feet) high and, with its spire's crowning pennant, towers above its enclosure. Walk around the walls to see the four elaborately decorated gates. For a glimpse of the rest of the complex, pay a donation and climb to the rooftop of the Raghunandan Library, across from the main temple entrance, called the Lion Gate, where pilgrims thrust their way in through the crowds of vendors and vehicles that jam the broad, shop-lined street.

Puri attracts even more crushing hordes than usual during the July Rath Yatra, a 10-day festival involving processions of the painted and ceremonially dressed wooden temple deities—Lord Jagannath and his brother and sister—on elaborately decorated floatlike carts pulled by thousands of devotees to the sounds of cymbals, drums, and chanting. One of the most spectacular of India's temple fairs, it's also the only time non-Hindus get to see the statues, which are usually seated on their jeweled pedestals inside the temple.

In addition to the religious contingent, Puri also attracts its share of modern hippies and backpackers, drawn by the ethos of the international hippies who colonized the east end of the beach in the sixties. Today on this part of C. T. (Chakratirtha) Road you'll find many inexpensive lodgings and shops selling the coolest, cheapest tie-dye clothing, garden restaurants, bar-restaurants with live music, and shops selling *bhang* (marijuana)—for religious purposes, of course.

Although Puri is still touted as a beach getaway, the sand is often littered with trash, and many of the hotels near the beach send their sewage directly into the sea, despite government efforts to curb the practice—in part, a reflection of Orissa's poverty. (India Tourism has a plan in the works to reclaim Puri's beauty, including providing proper sewage.) The Fisherman's Village, a thatch-roof community perhaps 10,000 strong of families of fishermen originally from Andra Pradesh, sits on the beach at the far eastern end of town and basically has no toilets; you do the math. It's still a pleasure to watch the sun rise and set over the same miles-long beach, to watch the little fishing boats with their one colorful sail cruise the waters, and to attend the nightly *arti* ceremony on the main beach. But if you want to swim, rent a bike and head east for a few kilometers along the beach; eventually you'll come to clean sand (or just stay at Toshali Sands resort up the coast). Don't go alone if you're a woman—incidents have occurred involving locals—and be very conscious of potential rip tides.

Where to Stay & Eat

$–$$ ✕ **Wild Grass.** Puri has many garden restaurants, but in this charming garden—palm trees, flowering bushes, temple statues, terra-cotta lanterns—tables are set not only under thatched open huts but up on platforms in trees. You can get a good Orissan thali here, with specialties like grilled eggplant, tuna masala, the sugary tomato dish *khata,* and santula. Or go for the fresh seafood. Just be prepared to use the little bell on your table to summon the waiter—service is not fast. ✉ *VIP Rd.* ☎ *6752/224–595* ▭ *No credit cards.*

¢–$ ✕ **Peace.** This simple garden restaurant serves a heck of a grilled tuna—a big slab, simple and perfect—at six or seven picnic tables under thatched huts. In addition to other local fish, you can get pasta dishes, sandwiches (including peanut butter and banana on a toasted roll), soups, *pakoras* (deep-fried chick-pea-flour fritters), fries, and good breakfasts, such as delicious French toast with apples or bananas baked inside. The set menu (Rs. 25 to Rs. 45) includes main course, dal, rice, and a vegetable. ⊠ *C.T. Rd.* ☎ *No phone* ▭ *No credit cards* ⊘ *Closed mid-Aug.–Sept.*

★ **$$$** ⌂ **Mayfair Beach Resort.** The best rooms in Puri, offering both style (teak floors with Persian-style rugs, carved headboards) and thick mattresses, are here; most have balconies that look over rooftops to the sea. A flower-lined path leads to Mayfair's semiprivate beach (they groom and staff it). The resort is done in a vaguely New Mexican style, with burnt-orange stucco buildings on two levels and lots of greenery. The outdoor patio restaurant is a pleasant place to relax over a drink. ⊠ *C.T. Rd., Puri 752002* ☎ *6752/227–800 to 09* 🖷 *6752/224–242* ⊕ *www.mayfairhotels. com* ➩ *31 rooms, 3 suites* ⌂ *2 restaurants, room service, IDD phones, cable TV, pool, hot tub, massage, steam room, bar, Ping-Pong, library, baby-sitting, dry cleaning, laundry service, Internet, meeting rooms, travel services, pets allowed* ▭ *AE, MC, V* ⎢◎⎢ *EP.*

$$ ⌂ **Toshali Sands.** If you've come to Puri for a peaceful beach vacation, this isolated 30-acre resort is for you. The virtually private beach, 8 km (5 mi) east of town, is a beautiful wide, clean strand backed by forest, with nothing seemingly forever in each direction. (It's a 20-minute walk from the hotel, or take a bike or a free jeep ride, available from the hotel.) Rooms, in cottages strewn across a garden landscape, are simply decorated but comfortable. A shuttle service takes guests to and from town; on the premises you'll find good food, boat rides on a river, an ayurvedic center, daily yoga classes, and other activities. ⊠ *Ethnic Village Resort, Konark Marine Dr., 752002* ☎ *6752/250–571 to 74* 🖷 *6752/250–899* ➩ *104 units* ⌂ *2 restaurants, room service, IDD phones, in-room data ports, refrigerators, cable TV with movies, pool, gym, sauna, massage, badminton, Ping-Pong, boating, bar, library, shop, playground, dry cleaning, laundry service, concierge, Internet, business services, convention center, travel services* ▭ *AE, DC, MC, V* ⎢◎⎢ *EP.*

¢ ⌂ **Z Hotel.** Probably the best, cleanest backpacker-type lodging in Puri is set in an airy 1916 maharaja's onetime summer residence. The 10 private- and shared-bath doubles, two singles, and six-bed women's dorm (great value at Rs. 60 a bunk) are spacious and bright, with white walls and tile floors; when the sun cooperates, there are hot solar-heated showers. Two doubles have balconies that let in even more light, though more mosquitoes, which are a problem in Puri—but big white bed nets keep you safe at night. Extras include a pleasant garden to read in and a cook who's a whiz with fresh seafood. ⊠ *C.T. Rd., Puri 752002* ☎ *6752/222–554* ⊕ *www.zhotelindia.com* ➩ *12 rooms, 1 dormitory room* ⌂ *Restaurant, Internet; no a/c, no room phones, no TVs* ▭ *No credit cards* ⎢◎⎢ *EP.*

Chilika Lake

7 *Barkul is 110 km (68 mi) south of Bhubaneswar, 60 km (37 mi) north of Gopalpur; Satapada is 50 km (31 mi) south of Puri; Rambha is 136 km (85 mi) south of Bhubaneswar, 45 km (28 mi) north of Gopalpur.*

From November through January, a visit to India's largest inland lake, covering 1,100 square km (684 square mi), is repaid with the sight of millions of birds, both residents and winter visitors, such as Siberian ducks and ibises. At Satapada, where the brackish lake joins the Bay of Bengal at its narrow mouth, you'll find dolphins. For either sight, you'll need to take a boat ride. OTDC excursion boats take you out past the many islands that dot the lake to the best viewing area, Nalabana Island, really a long stretch of reeds perfect for nesting with enough of a sandbar for a watchtower. If you take a private nonmotorized boat—show up at the dock early and start haggling for one of the hundreds of fishing boats that ply the lake for mackerel, prawns, and crabs—you can get off at Nalabana and climb the watchtower for a close-up view of the birds that form a solid ribbon on the reeds; on an OTDC boat you'll see them, but because it's motorized it can't get too close without scattering the birds, so bring binoculars. The OTDC boats also stop at Kalijai Island for a look at its massively popular shrine, with the full temple accoutrements of flower, sweets, and souvenir sellers.

The OTDC runs day trips from Bhubaneswar to Barkul (Rs. 160) or Satapada (Rs. 130), as well as from Puri to Satapada (Rs. 110). Its excursion boats (Rs. 150) leave from Barkul, Rambha, Satapada, and Balugaon; at each of these locations you can get basic accommodations and tourist information from the OTDC offices, where the boats depart from.

Gopalpur-on-Sea

8 *178 km (110 mi) southwest of Bhubaneswar.*

Gopalpur-on-Sea, a beach resort popular with Bengalis from Calcutta, is a small fishing village with a few simple hotels scattered along the sand (the future of the now-closed Oberoi property, once the town's best lodging, is uncertain). The town has one street, with a few shops for the locals and fast-food and seashell shops for tourists. The only trace of its past as a British seaport is a still functioning lighthouse and the crumbling remains of European merchants' homes. The beach is long; you don't have to walk far to find solitude (though you might to find pristine sand). To get here, take a three-hour train ride from Bhubaneswar to Berhampur (164 km [102 mi] south of the city), then transfer to an auto-rickshaw (Rs. 80) for the 14-km (9-mi) ride southeast.

Where to Stay

¢ 🏨 **Green Park.** Here you'll find simple, clean rooms; those at the front have a sea view but can be noisy. The hotel's big advantage over the other hotels in town is hot showers. Off-season, the restaurant only serves breakfast; in-season it's open for all meals. ⊠ *Beach Rd., Gopalpur-on-Sea 761002* ☎ *680/224–016 or 680/224–3753* ✉ *greenpark016@yahoo.*

com 🖙 *17 rooms ♻ Restaurant, room service, cable TV, meeting room; no room phones, no a/c in some rooms ▭ No credit cards* ⵏⵓⵏ *EP.*

¢ 🖃 **Song of the Sea.** All the clean, simple rooms face the Bay of Bengal at this seafront hotel, built in 1996 by the family that runs it. The nicest rooms have balconies where you can watch the sun rise over the water and the colored sails of the fishing boats. Beams from the lighthouse sweep the place throughout the night—great for romantics, but not if you're a light sleeper (Room 24 is *right* next to it). All the floors are marble for easy cleaning; hot water comes in a bucket. The dining room is big and cheerful, and there are lounge chairs on the lawn. ⊠ *On the beach, Gopalpur-on-Sea 761002* ☎ *680/224–2347, 680/222–5056 at night* 🖙 *11 rooms ♻ Dining room, room service, cable TV; no room phones, no a/c in some rooms ▭ No credit cards* ⵏⵓⵏ *EP.*

ORISSA A TO Z

To research prices, get advice from other travelers, and book travel arrangements, visit www.fodors.com.

AIR TRAVEL

Bhubaneswar's Biju Patnaik Airport is about 5 km (3 mi) from the center of town. Indian Airlines flies to the city daily from Delhi, Mumbai, and Raipur (Chhattisgarh); there are also regular flights from Calcutta, Chennai, Hyderabad, and Visakapatnam (also called Vizag, in Andra Pradesh). Air Sahara flies daily from Mumbai and Calcutta and has flights from Delhi via Calcutta and from Bangalore (with an overnight in Mumbai).

CARRIERS 🛩 **Air Sahara** ☎ 674/253-5006 or 674/253-5007, 674/253-5748 airport ⊕ www.airsahara.net. **Indian Airlines** ☎ 674/253-0533 or 674/253-0544, 674/253-4472 at airport, 141 within airport ⊕ www.indianairlines.nic.in.

AIRPORTS & TRANSFERS

The trip between Bhubaneswar's airport and city center takes 15 to 20 minutes. Most hotels provide free shuttle service if you provide them with your flight information in advance. White Ambassador tourist taxis wait outside the terminal; fares are theoretically fixed, but be sure to agree on one before setting out. The fare to a central hotel should be around Rs. 100; to the outlying hotels, about Rs. 150.

If you're coming to Orissa from Andra Pradesh or you take a tribal village tour, you might want to use the airport at Visakhapatnam, 260 km (162 mi) south of Gopalpur. Berhampur, Gopalpur's nearest rail stop, connects with Vizag. There are also one-hour flights from Vizag to Bhubaneswar.

BUS TRAVEL TO & FROM ORISSA

Bhubaneswar's Baramunda bus station, where you can catch an overnight bus to Calcutta, is 5 km (3 mi) from the city center on the main highway heading toward Calcutta.

BUS TRAVEL WITHIN ORISSA

Buses are the most inexpensive way to travel, but be prepared for extreme conditions: the buses are unreliable, and routes traverse only main roads, leaving you to walk 2 to 4 km (1 to 2 mi) to get to villages. Car and driver is the best way to get around Orissa.

CARS & DRIVERS

Most hotel travel desks provide guests with cars and drivers, but the cost is often quite a bit higher than necessary. A good source is the OTDC (⇨ Tours; Bhubaneswar Transport Unit ☎ 674/243–1515; Puri Transport Unit ☎ 6752/223–526). Its rates in Bhubaneswar or Puri for an Ambassador car are Rs. 440 (Rs. 640 for an air-conditioned car) for an eight-hour day covering 80 km (50 mi) or less; call ahead to confirm what the fare will be. You may be able to negotiate a better price with a taxi driver on your own, but remember that an English-speaking driver will be worth every extra penny. Be sure to specify which places you plan to visit and how long you plan to spend.

EMERGENCIES

In the event of a medical emergency, your first step should be to check with the hotel's front desk—they'll know what the best hospital is near their location. The best of local hospitals includes Capital Hospital and Kalinga Hospital in Bhubaneswar, and, in Puri, Head Quarter Hospital, Municipal Hospitali, and ID & TB Hospital. For ambulances in Bhubaneswar, try St. John's or Indian Red Cross. Puri also has ambulances you can call.

🚹 Emergencies **Ambulance (Puri)** ☎ 675/222–3742 or 675/222–2062. **Capital Hospital** ✉ Unit 6, Bhubaneswar ☎ 674/240–1983. **Kalinga Hospital** ✉ Nalco Chhak, Chandrasekharpur, north of the Trident hotel, Bhubaneswar ☎ 674/230–0997. **Head Quarter Hospital** ✉ Grand Rd., Puri ☎ 675/222–3742. **ID & TB Hospital** ✉ Red Cross Rd., Puri ☎ 675/222–2094. **Indian Red Cross ambulance (Bhubaneshwar)** ☎ 102. **Municipal Hospital** ✉ Laxmi Bazar, Puri ☎ 675/222–3241. **St. John's ambulance (Bhubaneshwar)** ☎ 674/253–1485.

MONEY

CURRENCY
EXCHANGE

Most Western-style hotels will change money or traveler's checks for their guests. You can also cash traveler's checks at the main branches of the State Bank of India in Bhubaneswar (open weekdays 10–4, Saturday 10–1) and Puri. Other options in Bhubaneswar: SBI IDCO and Andra Bank's main branch (the latter will change only Visa traveler's checks). Elsewhere it's practically impossible. ATMs abound, but they usually take only the bank's own cards, though some will give cash advances on credit cards. Usual banking hours are weekdays 10 to 2 and sometimes Saturday 10 to noon.

🚹 Exchange Service **Andra Bank** ✉ 52–53 Janpath, next to Royale Midtown hotel, Bhubaneswar. **SBI IDCO** ✉ Near Rupali Chaak, Sahid Nagar, Bhubaneswar. **State Bank of India** ✉ Near Market Bldg., Rajpath, Bhubaneswar ✉ VIP Rd., Puri.

TAXIS

Taxis and auto-rickshaws in Orissa have meters but never use them, so you have to negotiate for every ride. Ask your hotel about the appropriate fare.

TOURS

The Orissa Tourism Development Corporation (OTDC) offers several reasonably priced set or customized day tours and overnights anywhere in the region, using its own chain of inexpensive hotels. Sample full-day tours with non-air-conditioned cars: Bhubaneswar–Pipli–Konark–Puri, Rs. 125 per person; Bhubaneswar (temples, zoo, Jain caves), Rs. 110; Puri–Satapada, Rs. 110. Discover Tours specializes in tribal, textile, and trekking tours but has a wide gamut of options in and out of Orissa. Swosti Travels, Nabagunjara Travels, Heritage Tours and Treks, and Travel Link have strong experience in the region.

A private tour guide can seriously enhance your sightseeing. The most knowledgeable and English-proficient guides are those trained by the India Tourism (the government of India's tourism division); you can hire one through the OTDC or India Tourism for about Rs. 280 per half-day and Rs. 400 for a full day (eight hours) for up to four people.

⚑ **Discover Tours** ✉ 463 Lewis Rd., Bhubaneswar ☎ 674/243-0477 or 674/243-5731 🖷 674/243-0828 ⊕ www.orissadiscover.com. **Heritage Tours and Treks** ✉ Mayfair Beach Resort, C.T. Rd., Puri ☎ 675/222-3656 🖷 675/222-4595 ⊕ www.heritagetours. org. **Nabagunjara Travels** ✉ Balighar, 10 Rathadandra Rd., Bhubaneswar ☎ 674/243-1659 or 674/243-1759 🖷 674/310-2899 ⊕ nabagunjaratravels.com. **OTDC Bhubaneswar** ✉ Panthanivas, Old Block, Lewis Rd., Bhubaneswar ☎ 674/243-2382 ⊕ www. panthanivas.com ✉ **OTDC Puri** ✉ Pantha Bhavan, Puri ☎ 6752/243-1289 🖷 674/243-1053. **Swosti Travels** ✉ Next to Swosti hotel, 103 Janpath, Bhubaneswar ☎ 674/253-5773 or 674/253-4058 🖷 674/253-5781 ⊕ www.swosti.com ✉ B-4/6, Ground Fl., Safdarjung Enclave, New Delhi ☎ 11/2617-9067 🖷 11/2616-1892 ✉ 1-B, Broad St., Ground Fl., Calcutta ☎ 33/2280-5421 🖷 33/2281-2751. **Travel Link** ✉ Triumph Residency hotel, 5-B Sahid Nagar, Bhubaneswar ☎ 674/254-6591 to 94 🖷 674/254-6595.

TRAIN TRAVEL

The *Rajdhani Express* is the fastest train between Delhi and Bhubaneswar, making the trip in 24 hours four days a week. Several slower trains travel from Puri to Bhubaneswar to Delhi, including the daily *Purshottam Express,* the *Puri Express* (four days a week), and the *Neelachal Express* (three days a week), which stops at Varanasi and Lucknow. From Bhubaneswar on the daily *East Coast Express,* it's seven hours north to Calcutta (Howrah station on the schedules) and 23 hours south to Hyderabad; a 4½-hour leg of this route takes you north of Bhubaneswar to Balasore, an entry point for Orissa's Similipal National Park. The weekly *Muzaffarpur–Yeshvantpur Express* makes stops at Visakhapatnam (1 AM), Berhampur, Balugaon, and Bhubaneswar (4 AM), arriving at Balasore at 7:30 AM—a good time to arrive for seeing Similipal. Every day but Sunday, the *Jan Shatabdi Express* makes an 8-hour run between Bhubaneswar and Calcutta.

Three days a week the *Puri Express* makes the 43-hour trip between Ahmedabad and Puri; links connect Puri with Visakhapatnam (8 hours) and the Orissan weaving town of Sambalpur (11½ hours). The fastest Chennai connections from Bhubaneswar are the daily *Coromandel Express* (20 hours) and the twice-weekly *Chennai Express* (21 hours). The *Secunderabad Express* to Chennai (22½ hours) continues on to Bangalore (8½ hours more) twice a week. The twice-weekly *Ernakulam Ex-*

press also connects with Chennai (22½ hours), continuing on to Kerala's Trivandrum, 3 hours farther down the line, and Ernakulam, 4½ hours more; the slower, twice-weekly *Trivandrum Express* makes the same stops.

TRANSPORTATION WITHIN ORISSA

Hiring a car and driver for a half or full day is not expensive, and is the most convenient way to get around Orissa in general and the towns in particular—you avoid having to haggle over fares with taxi or auto-rickshaw drivers, as well as the overcrowded conditions of the local buses. Auto-rickshaws are cheaper than taxis and usually slower (though quicker in heavy traffic). Apply the same fare rules as you would for taxis. For short distances within towns, cycle-rickshaws are easiest. A horde of cycle-rickshaws await you at the train stations. Always negotiate the fare with any taxi, auto-rickshaw, or cycle-rickshaw driver before you set off in order to avoid hassles or overcharging later. And again, remember that the OTDC arranges transport inexpensively to the main tourist spots.

VISITOR INFORMATION

The OTDC is the best source of information on the state. All its offices are open Monday through Saturday from 10 to 5 (closed second Saturday of each month). India Tourism, the government of India's offices, are open weekdays from 10 to 5.

🖪 Tourist Information **India Tourism** ✉ B-21 B. J. B. Nagar, Bhubaneswar 751014 ☎ 674/243-5487 📠 674/243-2203 ✉ Counter, Bhubaneswar airport ☎ No phone ⊕ www.tourismofindia.com. **Orissa Tourism Development Corporation** ✉ Head Office, Paryatan Bhavan, Lewis Rd., Bhubaneswar 751014 ☎ 674/243-2177 📠 674/243-0887 ✉ Tourist Office, Jayadev Marg, Bhubaneswar ☎ 674/243-1299 ✉ Counter, Bhubaneswar airport ☎ 674/240-4006 ✉ Counter, Bhubaneswar railway station ☎ 674/253-0715 ✉ Tourist Office, Tourist Complex, Barkul ☎ 675/622-0855 ✉ Counter, Berhampur railway station ☎ 680/228-0226 ✉ Tourist Office, Yatrinivas, Konark ☎ 675/823-6820 or 675/823-6821 ✉ Tourist Office, VIP Chhak, Station Rd., Puri ☎ 675/222-2664 ✉ Counter, Puri railway station ☎ 675/222-3536 ⊕ www.orissatourism.gov.in.

CALCUTTA (KOLKATA)

12

FIND TANTALIZINGLY INEXPENSIVE PRICES
in Calcutta's bazaars ⇨*p.551*

SEE THE SINGLE GREATEST SYMBOL
of the British Raj ⇨*p.560*

RELISH SOME OF THE BEST
Chinese food in India ⇨*p.564*

BREAK FOR COFFEE 24/7 AT THE HUB
inside the Taj Bengal hotel ⇨*p.565*

OGLE BIRDS WITH LARGE HEADDRESSES
at the eclectic Marble Palace ⇨*p.556*

By Nigel Fisher

Updated by
Soumya
Bhattacharya

NOTHING CAN PREPARE YOU for Calcutta. As the birthplace of an empire and the home of the late Mother Teresa, as a playground for the rich and a haven for the destitute, as a wellspring of creative energy and a center for Marxist agitation, Calcutta dares people to make sense of it. Whether it shocks you or seduces you, Calcutta will impress itself upon you. To understand India today and learn from it, a trip to Calcutta is vital.

In 1690 Job Charnock, an agent for the British East India Company, leased the villages of Sutanati, Gobindpur, and Kalikutta and formed a trading post to supply his firm. Legend has it that Charnock had won the hearts of Bengalis when he married a local widow, thus saving her from *sati* (the custom that calls for a widow to throw herself on her husband's funeral pyre). However, new research has suggested that the story of Charnock founding Calcutta is more lore than fact and that the city existed before the British East India Company agent arrived here in 1690. Through Charnock's venture, the British gained a foothold in what had been the Sultanate of Delhi under the Moguls, and the directors of the East India Company became Indian *zamindars* (landowners) for the first time. It was here, as traders and landowners, that British entrepreneurs and adventurers began what would amount to the conquest of India and the establishment of the British Raj. More than any other city in India, Calcutta is tied to the evolution and disintegration of the British presence.

Calcutta is the capital of the state of West Bengal, which borders Bangladesh (formerly East Bengal). The Bengali people—animated, garrulous, intellectual, spirited, argumentative, anarchic, imaginative, and creative—have dominated this city and made it the soul of India for more than 150 years. Among the first to react to the intellectual and political stimuli of the West, the Bengali have produced many of India's most respected filmmakers, writers, scientists, musicians, dancers, and philosophers. Having embraced 19th-century European humanism, such Bengalis as the poet Rabindranath Tagore and others revived their indigenous culture and made the first organized efforts to oust the British. Emotions here ran high early on, and agitation in Bengal broke away from what would later be called Gandhian politics to choose terrorism—one reason the British moved their capital from Calcutta to Delhi in 1911.

Calcutta remained cosmopolitan and prosperous throughout the British period. But after Independence and Partition, in 1947, trouble began when the world's center of jute processing and distribution (Calcutta) was politically separated from its actual production center (the eastern Bengali hinterland). For Calcutta and the new East Pakistan, Partition was equivalent to separating the fingers of an industry from the thumb. Natural disasters—commonly cyclones and droughts, but also, as in 1937, earthquakes—had long sent millions from East Bengal (which later became East Pakistan) to Calcutta in search of shelter and sustenance; after Partition, a wave of 4 million political refugees from East Pakistan compounded and complicated the pressure. Conflict with China and Pakistan created millions more throughout the 1960s, and Pakistan's 1971 military crackdown alone sent 10 million temporary refugees into the city from what would soon become Bangladesh. By the mid-1970s,

Calcutta was widely seen as the ultimate urban disaster. Riddled with disease and squalor, plagued by garbage and decay, the heart of the British Raj, the Paris of Asia, had quickly and dramatically collapsed.

Or had it? Greater Calcutta's entire metropolitan district covers more than 426 square km (264 square mi) and has more than 12 million people. It comprises 2 municipal corporation areas (Calcutta and Howrah, though Howrah is, strictly speaking, not part of Calcutta proper; the city has gone on expanding and the areas that were really suburbs have become nearly suburbs), 32 municipalities, 62 nonmunicipal urban centers, and more than 500 villages, and it hasn't really collapsed. What the city has learned, and has learned to accept, is that it has become marginalized in contemporary India's political and economic power structure. The people here have borne that acceptance with a slightly tired air of resignation and stoicism. A Marxist government has been ruling West Bengal since 1977 from the seat of power in Calcutta. But even this government has adapted to the new globalized economy, fusing Marx with market economics and talking less about agrarian reforms and more about the information-technology revolution. As one local put it, "Calcutta is full of challenges, but there is hope and even fun in meeting those challenges." Today's traveler may actually notice more poverty in Bombay than in the city more often associated with human strife. Calcutta remains open, smiling, and thoughtful: amid the difficulties there is dignity, and amid the crises there are ideas.

Since February 2001, Calcutta, in all government records, was officially changed to Kolkata. This transformation is supposed to contribute to ridding this and other Indian cities of their colonial past. But the two names of the city are used interchangeably. Streets, too, have been renamed. Although some maps and street signs have only the new names, you're more likely to see just the old or both. Taxis and rickshaws use the names interchangeably, but old names are still favored, as most of the new names are ridiculously long and obscure. The most important name changes: Chowringhee Road is now Jawaharlal Nehru (J. L. Nehru) Road; Ballygunge Circular is now Pramathesh Barua Sarani; Bowbazar is now B. B. Ganguly Street; Harington Street is now Ho Chi Minh Sarani; Lansdowne Road is now Sarat Bose Road; Lower Circular Road is now A. J. C. Bose Road; Rippon Street is now Muzaffar Ahmed Street; and Theater Road is now Shakespeare Sarani.

EXPLORING CALCUTTA

Calcutta and Howrah (also written as Haora) straddle the Hooghly River with Calcutta on the east side, and Howrah on the west. Across the Hooghly from Calcutta's old quarter, the Howrah district—which holds Calcutta's massive train station—is a constantly expanding suburb. On the eastern side of town is Salt Lake City, a planned, spotlessly clean, upscale residential community.

In Calcutta itself, the Howrah Bridge spills into Bara Bazaar, the vibrant wholesale-market area that anchors the city's commerce. North Calcutta includes Bara Bazaar and Calcutta University and extends to the dis-

12

If you have 2 days

Start by taking the pulse of the city's heart, **B. B. D. Bagh ⑩**. Take a taxi to the Jain **Paresnath Temple ⑥**, and from there continue to the **Marble Palace ③**, nearby **Nakhoda Mosque ②** and **Rabindra Bharati University Museum ④**. At the end of the day, cross the **Howrah Bridge ⑤** by cab and drive south along the bank of the Hooghly River for a good look back at the city. (Cross back on the Second Hooghly Bridge, or Vivekananda Setu.) The next day, enter the **Maidan ⑬** and visit the **Victoria Memorial ⑰** and **St. Paul's Cathedral ⑱**. Back out on Chowringhee (J. L. Nehru Road), amble up to the **Indian Museum ⑳**. This should leave you time to shop in the late afternoon and early evening in the fabulous, century-old New Market, where everything under the sun is for sale under one roof.

If you have 3 days

You can see most of Calcutta's major sights comfortably in three days. Explore **B. B. D. Bagh ⑩**, then take a taxi to **College Street ①** and walk around in the university area and the second-hand bookstalls. Walk from College Street to the **Nakhoda Mosque ②**, European-style **Marble Palace ③**, and **Rabindra Bharati University Museum ④**, with its Bengali-school paintings and Rabindranath Tagore memorabilia. From here it's a short cab ride to the **Paresnath Temple ⑥**. Continue on to **Kumartuli ⑦** to see artists create clay icons by the river.

The next day, taxi up to the **Belur Math Shrine ⑨**, then cross back to the **Dakshineshwar Kali Temple ⑧** for a quick overview of Hinduism. Driving south on the east side of the river, cross the **Howrah Bridge ⑤** and then go south on Foreshore Road for the best view of Calcutta over the Hooghly. Cross back on the Second Hooghly Bridge. You can now enter the **Maidan ⑬** and breathe some fresh air before before visiting the **Victoria Memorial ⑰**, **Fort William ⑯**, and the **Eden Gardens ⑮**. Finish by shopping in New Market.

On Day 3, taxi down to **Nirmal Hirday ㉒** to visit the late Mother Teresa's first charitable home, then walk over to the famous **Kalighat Kali Temple ㉑**. You'll need a cab from here to **St. Paul's Cathedral ⑱**, but from the cathedral you can walk to Chowringhee and up to the **Indian Museum ⑳**, detouring a few blocks to Park Street to read colonial history from the headstones in **South Park Street Cemetery ⑲**.

If you have 5 days

For the first three days, follow the above schedule. On Day 4, hire a car and set off for Raichak, a small town about 60 km (37 mi) south of the city. If you're lucky with traffic, it should take you a couple of hours. Base your day at the Fort Radisson Hotel: you will find conveniences as well as an Indian and multicuisine restaurant. If you're here later in the day, watch the sun's glittering orange panorama over sailboats returning with their catch.

On your final day, explore New Calcutta, northeast of the city. Shop and look around at **Swabhumi ㉕**, a heritage park complex just off the Eastern Metropolitan Bypass. Also pay a visit to the amusement park, **Nicco Park ㉖**, and the water theme park, **Aquatica ㉗** (both are within a few minutes' drive to Swabhumi).

tant neighborhood of Chitpur and the Jain Temple in Tala. The heart of Central Calcutta remains B. B .D. Bagh (Binoy-Badel-Dinesh Bagh, formerly Dalhousie Square), where commerce and government have been concentrated since British times. Central Calcutta also holds the expansive Maidan park, the crowded bazaar at New Market, and the upmarket shops and restaurants on Park Street. At the south end of the Maidan are the Victoria Memorial and Calcutta's racecourse. South Calcutta has the Kali Temple and the late Mother Teresa's hospice in Kalighat and the National Library and zoo in Alipore, a posh residential community. To the east of the city is the Eastern Metropolitan Bypass (known to residents as "the bypass"), which links south Calcutta to the north. As people increasingly take the bypass (and as more affluent neighborhoods are built alongside and near it), destinations like Aquatica and Nicco Park have sprung up in the area.

Numbers in the text correspond to points of interest on the Calcutta map.

About the Restaurants

Eating out (and indeed eating in) is a favorite pastime in Calcutta. The city was the hub of happening restaurants and clubs in the 1960s—a culture that dwindled with the passing of years. However, after the liberalization of the economy and with the blessings of the open market (open to foreign goods and influences) Calcutta has experienced a vibrant restaurant culture since the mid-1990s. Restaurants here cater to a varied sensibility: Oriental, Mexican, Italian, and, of course, Indian. The service is largely friendly, and places are crowded enough, especially on weekends, to warrant reservations. Best of all, eating out in Calcutta is cheaper compared to cities like Delhi and Bombay—and every bit as good in terms of quality. Restaurants in Calcutta are generally open daily 12:30 to 3 for lunch and 7:30 to 11 for dinner.

WHAT IT COSTS In Rupees					
	$$$$	**$$$**	**$$**	**$**	**¢**
	IN CALCUTTA				
AT DINNER	over 500	400–500	300–400	150–300	under 150
	IN SMALL TOWNS OUTSIDE CALCUTTA				
AT DINNER	over 350	250–350	150–250	100–150	under 150

Restaurant prices are for an entrée plus dal, rice, and a veg/non-veg dish.

About the Hotels

Unless otherwise noted, hotels have air-conditioning and room TVs, and operate on the European meal plan (no meals included). Better hotels have foreign-exchange facilities, and most have rooms with bathrooms that have tubs. Some luxury hotels have exclusive floors with special privileges or facilities for the business traveler. Calcutta's top few hotels are fine establishments that meet international standards and then some. An exceptionally high luxury tax of approximately 20% is added to your bill.

Sweets & Street Food

Like no other city in India, Calcutta has a tradition of dining out. Ironically, Bengali food itself was noticeably long absent from the city's restaurants, but this has changed in recent years. Bengali cuisine is highly varied in flavor and has both vegetarian and nonvegetarian strands, with fish figuring heavily. Prawns and shrimp are two favorites but because both are important exports, prices have risen and they are beyond the bounds of the average Bengali except as treats. Two popular Bengali dishes are *macher jhol* (fish curry) and *chingri malai* curry (prawns cooked in coconut milk and spices). Note that Thursday in Calcutta is meatless—no red meat is served in most establishments.

12

The unique cuisine that has developed in Calcutta since the influx of the Moguls in the 16th century is called Calcutta-Mughlai and remains the most common food in Calcutta today—it's what you'll see in carts and stalls throughout the city. Staples include *champ* (chicken or mutton cooked slowly in large, thick-cast open pans), *birianis* (rice-and-meat dishes), and tandoori items, none of which resembles dishes of the same name in places such as Oudh or Hyderabad. From roadside vendors, the most popular item is the Calcutta roll, in which seasoned meats and chutneys are wrapped in thick *parathas* (Indian breads) with onions and sometimes even eggs. Not to be missed are Bengali sweets, which fill the life of every native: sweet shops are everywhere, and the variety of their fare—from *payash* (fine-quality rice cooked in thickened milk) to *gokul pitha* (coconut and solidified milk balls, fried and dipped in sugar syrup) is beyond tempting. Two unsurpassed goodies are *rosogollas* (balls of cottage cheese soaked in sugar syrup), associated specifically with Calcutta, and the classic Bengali *misti doi* (sweetened yogurt).

Trinkets, Textiles & Touts

All of India tempts the shopper here: a vast array of goods arrive in Calcutta from around the subcontinent, including crafts from Bangladesh and neighboring northeastern states. Prices are tantalizingly inexpensive. The irritants are touts, hustlers, and the instant friends who approach you claiming they have nothing to sell and later ticking you off if you don't buy their goods. Learn to bargain, but be wary of where you do it. Although everything purchased from a roadside vendor is negotiable, government emporiums, shops that sell branded goods, or places with fixed-price tags will be affronted if you try to bargain.

Some of the most interesting crafts in West Bengal are brightly painted terracotta figurines and bas-reliefs, as well as other pottery items. *Dhokra* are cast figures made of clay and metal. Shells, bell metal, and soapstone are other media used in popular Bengali trinkets and figurines. Calcutta's bazaars and shops sell all kinds of textiles, including embroideries. With its longtime traditions of literacy and cosmopolitanism, Calcutta is also a good place to restock your English-language reading material.

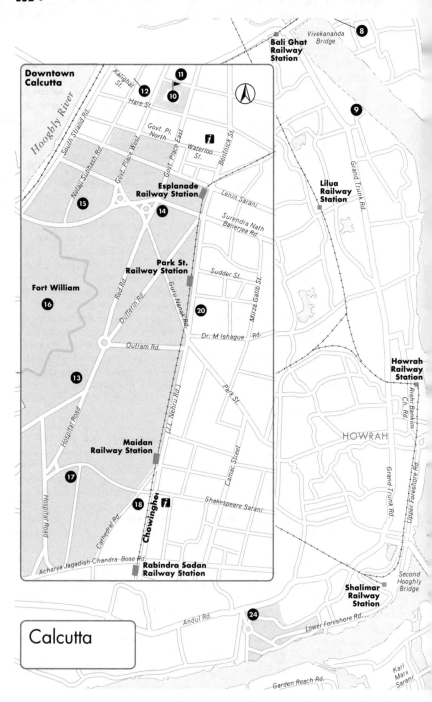

Downtown Calcutta

Calcutta

Bali Ghat Railway Station

Vivekananda Bridge

Hooghly River

Kalighat St.

Hare St.

Govt. Pl. North

Govt. Place West

Govt. Place East

Waterloo St.

Bentinck St.

South Strand Rd.

Netaji Subhash Rd.

Esplanade Railway Station

Lenin Sarani

Surendra Nath Banerjea Rd.

Park St. Railway Station

Sudder St.

Mirza Galib St.

Red Rd.

Dufferin Rd.

Guru Nanak Rd.

Fort William

Outram Rd.

Dr. M Ishaque Rd.

Park St.

J.L. Nehru Rd.

Hospital Road

Maidan Railway Station

Camac Street

Hospital Road

Chowringhee

Shakespeare Sarani

Cathedral Rd.

Acharya Jagadish Chandra Bose Rd.

Rabindra Sadan Railway Station

Lilua Railway Station

Grand Trunk Rd.

Howrah Railway Station

Rishi Bankim Ch. Rd.

HOWRAH

Grand Trunk Rd.

Upper Foreshore Rd.

Shalimar Railway Station

Second Hooghly Bridge

Andul Rd.

Lower Foreshore Rd.

Garden Reach Rd.

Karl Marx Sarani

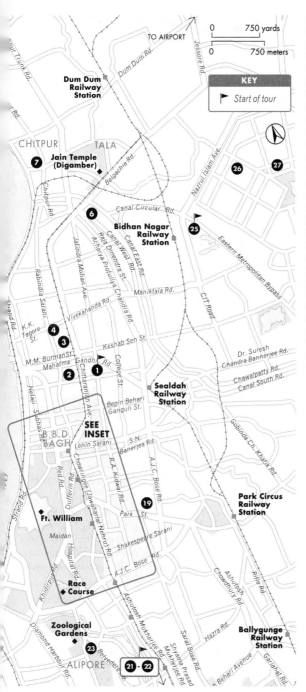

TO AIRPORT

0   750 yards
0   750 meters

KEY

► *Start of tour*

Dum Dum Railway Station

CHITPUR   TALA

Jain Temple (Digamber)

Bidhan Nagar Railway Station

Canal Circular Rd.

Maniktala Rd.

Vivekananda Rd.

Keshab Sen St.

M.M. Burman St.
Mahatma Gandhi Rd.
College St.

Sealdah Railway Station

Bepin Behari Ganguli St.

B.B.D. BAGH

SEE INSET

Lenin Sarani

Park Circus Railway Station

Ft. William

Maidan

Park St.

Shakespeare Sarani

A.J.C. Bose Rd.

Race Course

Zoological Gardens

Ballygunge Railway Station

ALIPORE

Aquatica **27**
B.B.D. Bagh **10**
Belur Math Shrine **9**
College Street **1**
Dakshineshwar Kali Temple **8**
Eden Gardens **15**
Fort William **16**
General Post Office **12**
Howrah Bridge **5**
Indian Botanical Gardens **24**
Indian Museum **20**
Kalighat Kali Temple **21**
Kumartuli **7**
Maidan **13**
Marble Palace **3**
Nakhoda Mosque **2**
National Library **23**
Nicco Park **26**
Nirmal Hirday **22**
Ochterlony Monument **14**
Paresnath Temple **6**
Rabindra Bharati
University Museum **4**
St. Paul's Cathedral **18**
South Park Street Cemetery **19**
Swabhumi **25**
Victoria Memorial **17**
Writers' Building **11**

WHAT IT COSTS In Rupees				
$$$$	**$$$**	**$$**	**$**	**¢**
IN CALCUTTA				
FOR 2 PEOPLE over 8,000	6,000–8,000	4,000–6,000	2,000–4,000	under 2,000
IN SMALL TOWNS OUTSIDE CALCUTTA				
FOR 2 PEOPLE over 4,000	3,000–4,000	2,000–3,000	1,000–2,000	under 1,000

Hotel prices are for a standard double room in high season, excluding approximately 20% tax.

Timing

The hottest weather arrives in April and grows increasingly stifling through June, when the monsoon season begins. Monsoons run through mid-September and cool Calcutta down, though the occasional downpour means you can expect a soaking or two. The mild winter sets in around December and lasts until March. This is the best time to visit. For an extraordinary visit, see Calcutta during the greatest Bengali festival of the year, the Durga Puja (Durga is an incarnation of Kali, Calcutta's patron goddess). Colorful, handmade Hindu idols, sometimes in excess of 20 feet tall, are ceremoniously moved in large processions through the streets for several hours before reaching the river and being immersed in the Hooghly. The *pujas* (homage; literally, "worship") take place over several days in September or October; confirm the dates beforehand with the tourist office or an Indian travel agent. The rites and processions have an amazing vibrancy, often blending tradition with innovation; some idols even honor contemporary themes such as recent flood victims or the film star of the moment.

North Calcutta

The streets in northern Calcutta are more crowded and narrower than those elsewhere in the city. This—the old village of Sutanuti—is where the Indians lived while the British spread their estates east and south of Fort William and Dalhousie Square (B. B. D. Bagh). The architecture reflects Italian and Dutch influences.

North Calcutta's attractions are somewhat scattered. You'll need to take taxis at least sporadically. The bazaar areas surrounding Mahatama Gandhi Road are at once intensely commercial and residential; tourists are only occasional, despite the fascinating sights and vibe. You may attract some curious stares, but anyone you stop and speak to is bound to be friendly and welcoming.

a good tour

Start with a morning coffee at the Indian Coffee House on **College Street ❶ ▶**, then browse through the street's bookstalls. Walk west, crossing Chittaranjan Avenue, to the huge, sandstone **Nakhoda Mosque ❷**, and climb to the top floor for a great view of the bustle in the streets below. Walk back to Chittaranjan Avenue, turn left (north), then left after a few blocks on Muktaram Basu Street—halfway down the block on the left you'll see the **Marble Palace ❸**, a melange of international architecture, statues, and furnishings. From the palace it's a short walk north to Tagore Street, where you turn left for the **Rabindra Bharati University Museum** ❹, in the poet's former home. Walking farther west on Tagore Street brings you to the Hooghly River, with the **Howrah Bridge** ❺ a block to the south. North and south of the Howrah Bridge along the waterfront is the wholesale flower market—before 7 AM. Also in this area is Strand Road, which heads south toward the Second Hooghly Bridge and, in the evening, makes for a delightful riverside stroll in that area. At sunset, both river and city look magical; Calcutta becomes a different town altogether.

A short taxi ride will bring you to the Jain **Paresnath Temple** ❻, perhaps one of the cleanest buildings in Calcutta. A 30-minute walk or quick cab ride farther north, near the river, is an area called **Kumartuli** ❼, where thousands of potters fashion clay images of gods and goddesses for Hindu festivals. The **Dakshineshwar Kali Temple** ❽, a major Hindu pilgrimage site, requires another taxi ride north. Cross the Second Hooghly Bridge (again, it's best to take a cab) to the suburb of Howrah and head south along Belur Road to the **Belur Math Shrine** ❾, headquarters of the Ramakrishna Mission. Return downtown by taxi.

Numbers in the text correspond to numbers in the margin and on the Calcutta map.

TIMING This tour takes the better part of a day and can be very tiring; pack a lunch before you set off. The Marble Palace, Rabindra Bharati museum, Paresnath Temple, and Dakshineshwar Kali Temple each take 30 to 60 minutes to absorb. Try to sandwich your touring between the rush hours, and remember that the Belur Math Shrine is closed from noon to 3:30 and the Nakhoda Mosque is off-limits during Friday morning prayer.

What to See

❾ **Belur Math Shrine.** This is the headquarters of the Ramakrishna Mission, a reform movement inspired by Ramakrishna Paramahansa, who died in 1886. Having forsaken his privileged Brahmin heritage, Ramakrishna preached the unity of religious faiths and an adherence to altruistic values for all people. His disciple, Swami Vivekananda, established the mission in 1898. The Belur Math Shrine resembles a church, a temple, or a mosque, depending on where you're standing. Somber *aarti* (chants and hymns) are sung in the immense prayer hall every evening; visitors are more than welcome. ✉ *Belur Rd., Howrah, 2 km (1 mi) south of 2nd Hooghly Bridge (Vivekananda Setu)* ⊙ *Daily 6:30–noon and 3:30–7:30.*

▶ ❶ **College Street.** Part of the animated area around Calcutta University, the sidewalks of College Street are stuffed with bookstalls where you just might discover a treasure. The neighborhood establishments here, like the classic **Indian Coffee House** (✉ 15 Bankin Chatterjee St., North Calcutta), are crowded every night with students and intellectuals. Opposite the coffeehouse, a huge colonial building houses the university's **Presidency College,** arguably the most prestigious seat of learning in India. ✉ *North Calcutta.*

★ ❽ **Dakshineshwar Kali Temple.** Far north along the Hooghly, this 19th-century complex with 13 temples is a major pilgrimage site for devotees of Shiva, Kali, Radha, and Krishna. The variety of temples makes this site a good introduction for the uninitiated to the Hindu deities. It was here that the 19th-century mystic Ramakrishna had the vision that led him to renounce his Brahmin caste and propound altruism and religious unity. His most famous disciple, Swami Vivekananda, went on to be a major force in the intellectual and spiritual growth of Calcutta, and founded the Ramakrishna Mission, headquartered in the Belur Math Shrine. Ramakrishna's room here is a museum. ⊠ *P. W. D. Rd., near 2nd Hooghly Bridge (Vivekananda Setu)* ☒ *Free* ☉ *Daily dawn–10 PM.*

❺ **Howrah Bridge.** The Howrah train station almost dumps you onto this structure, and the bridge in turn puts you about 2 km (1.2 mi) north of Bara Bazaar in the heart of old Calcutta. Indeed, it seems more like a bazaar itself than a simple transport link between Howrah and Calcutta. Bordered by thin walkways, the bridge's eight lanes of chaotic traffic bear 2 million people each day in rickshaws, cars, scooters, bicycles, pushcarts, and animal-drawn carts. The web of girders stretches 1,500 feet over the Hooghly.

❼ **Kumartuli.** In this area, countless potters create the millions of clay images that serve as idols during Calcutta's Hindu festival season. ⊠ *Chitpur Rd., between Bidhan Sarani and Jatindra Mohan, North Calcutta.*

❸ **Marble Palace.** One of the strangest buildings in Calcutta is the inspiration of Raja Rajendra Mullick Bahadur, a member of Bengal's landed gentry. Mullick built the palace in 1855, making lavish use of Italian marble. It's right behind a lawn cluttered with sculptures of lions, the Buddha, Christopher Columbus, Jesus, the Virgin Mary, and Hindu gods. Near a small granite bungalow (where Mullick's descendants still live), a large pool houses some exotic birds with large headdresses. The palace has an interior courtyard, complete with a throne room where a peacock often struts around the seat of honor. The upstairs rooms are downright baroque: enormous mirrors and paintings cover the walls (including works by Reynolds, Rubens, and Murillo), gigantic chandeliers hang from the ceilings, and hundreds of statues and Far Eastern urns populate the rooms. The floors bear multicolored marble inlay on a giant scale, with a calico effect. Even the lamps are detailed creations, especially those on the staircases, where metal women are entwined in trees with a light bulb on each branch. Movie producers use the palace for shooting films. Make sure to tip your guide here. ⊠ *46 Muktaram Basu St., off Chittaranjan Ave., North Calcutta* ☒ *Free; you must obtain a pass from West Bengal Tourist Office 24 hrs in advance* ☉ *Tues., Wed., and Fri.–Sun. 10–4.*

Fodor's Choice ★

★ ❷ **Nakhoda Mosque.** This massive red sandstone mosque, which can hold 10,000 worshippers, was built in 1926 as a copy of Akbar's tomb in Agra. Each floor has a prayer hall. The top floor has views of the streets below, which are crowded with stalls selling everything from paperback editions of the Koran to kababs. ⊠ *Mahatma Gandhi Rd. and Rabindra Sarani, North Calcutta* ☒ *Free* ☉ *Daily sunrise–8 PM.*

★ ❻ **Paresnath Temple.** Built in 1867 and dedicated to Sitalnathji, the 10th of the 24 *tirthankaras* ("perfect souls," or sages that have achieved Nirvana), this Jain temple is a flamboyant one, filled with inlaid-mirror pillars, stained-glass windows, floral-pattern marble floors, a gilded dome, and chandeliers from 19th-century Paris and Brussels. The garden holds blocks of glass mosaics depicting European figures and statues covered with silver paint. Paresnath is an unusual place of honor for the typically ascetic Jains. ⊠ *Badridas Temple St., near Raja Dinendra St., North Calcutta* ◯ *Daily sunrise–noon and 3–7.*

★ ❹ **Rabindra Bharati University Museum.** Within the walls of Rabindranath Tagore's cheerful, lemon-yellow home (which opens onto tree-lined galleries on the second floor), the university fosters cultural activities and maintains a display of paintings by artists of the Bengali school. The nerve center of Calcutta's intellectual activity around the turn of the 20th century, Tagore's abode now holds memorabilia, including beautiful sepia photographs of the poet (quite fetching as a young man), his family, and his contemporaries. ⊠ *6–4 Dwarkanath Tagore La., North Calcutta* ☎ *33/2239–6601* 🎫 *Free* ◯ *Weekdays 10–5, Sat. 10–1:30.*

Central Calcutta & the Maidan

The British first built Fort William in the middle of a dense jungle. When disagreements led the local Bengali ruler, Siraj ud-Daula, to attack and destroy it, the British response was a quick and decisive battle led by Robert Clive. Following the Battle of Plassey (some 160 km [100 mi] north of town), which transformed the British from traders into a ruling presence in 1757, the forest was cut down in order to provide a clear line for cannon fire in case of attack. It's really from the year 1757 that modern Calcutta traces its history, and from the new, impenetrable Fort William (completed in 1773) that the city began its explosive growth.

Starting about 1 km north of the fort, central Calcutta became the commercial and political heart of the city. It was here that the British conducted business, and here that they built their stately homes. The immense area cleared for British cannons is now Calcutta's 3-square-km (2-square-mi) park, the Maidan, and central Calcutta now goes beyond the Maidan to B. B. D. Bagh square and most of the commercial and residential areas to the east of the giant park.

<table>
<tr><td>a good
walk</td><td>Around **B. B. D. Bagh** ❿ ☞ are some of the finest examples of Victorian architecture in Calcutta. Most of the buildings are still offices (government or otherwise) and are most interesting from the outside, even when admission is permitted. On the north side of the square is the **Writers' Building** ⓫; in the southeast corner is St. Andrew's Church, built in 1818. West and one block north is the **General Post Office** ⓬, and to its left is the redbrick Collectorate, Calcutta's oldest public building. Two blocks south is St. John's Church, which holds Job Charnock's mausoleum. (If the church is locked, you can call the vicar, ☎ 33/2248–3439.) The High Court Building is on the next block south. Head east two blocks (until you're due south of B. B. D. Bagh) to see Raj Bhavan, home of the governor of West Bengal.</td></tr>
</table>

Cross Lenin Sarani and you'll be in the **Maidan** ⑬, a place to escape street traffic and diesel fumes and to enjoy green grass. Walk down Government Place East and you'll come to a traffic circle dominated by the **Ochterlony Monument** ⑭. Veer southwest and go down Eden Gardens Road to the **Eden Gardens** ⑮, which have a photogenic Burmese pagoda. Next to that is the cricket stadium (cricket is like a slower version of baseball), where you can see India's most popular game played. If you walk along Strand Road toward the Hooghly from here, it's easy to arrange a brief, refreshing boat ride—boatmen are bound to approach you with offers of a "romantic" turn on the waters. Be careful: the boats are often as rickety as boatmen are dodgy; the going rate is about Rs. 100 for half an hour, though the money you pay will depend on how hard a bargain you can drive.

Continue 1½km (1 mi) directly south of Eden Gardens to **Fort William** ⑯, the East India Company's main strategic defense in Calcutta. Red Road cuts south through the Maidan to the **Victoria Memorial** ⑰, which serves (somewhat ironically) as a postcard image of Calcutta and houses a compelling museum of the city's history as well as some Raj memorabilia. Two-hundred yards to the east along Queen's Way is **St. Paul's Cathedral** ⑱.

Queen's Way hits J. L. Nehru Road, colloquially known by its old name—**Chowringhee.** This is Calcutta's main drag—a wide boulevard bustling with pedestrians by day and a place for the homeless to stretch out by night. On the other side of Chowringhee, Queen's Road becomes Shakespeare Sarani, and after another 100 feet you can see Calcutta's government tourist office on the right. Farther north on Chowringhee, Park Street comes in at an angle. Park Street shares with Chowringhee the prestige of having high rents for shops, hotels, and restaurants, and, in fact, if you're wandering around hungry in the evening, this is the best street to prowl for a good restaurant. About 1½ km down the street to the east is the **South Park Street Cemetery** ⑲, with the graves of many British who changed the course of India and never made it back to old Blighty. Back on Chowringhee, shortly after the intersection with Park Street is the **Indian Museum** ⑳, well worth dropping into for its collection of Indian antiquities. By now you'll be in need of a little sophistication, which you can find at the Oberoi Grand hotel, a Victorian oasis just 200 yards farther up the thoroughfare.

Numbers in the text correspond to numbers in the margin and on the Calcutta map.

TIMING   Two of the most interesting attractions on this route are the Victoria Memorial and the Indian Museum, for which you should allow at least an hour apiece; the entire walk should take approximately four hours. If you are touring in the hot season, April to July, avoid walking during high noon.

What to See

★ ⑩ **B. B. D. Bagh.** The hub of all Calcutta, this square is still often referred to by its former name, Dalhousie Square. Once the administrative home of the East India Company, it later gave way to late-Victorian buildings used by the Colonial Civil Service and now houses the Indian government bureaucracy. Foot traffic is thick here. ⊠ *East of Hooghly River, 2½ km (1.6 mi) south of Howrah Bridge, Central Calcutta.*

★ **Chowringhee.** North Calcutta may be Calcutta's intellectual heart, but in an age of business-friendly communist governments, the slick commercial area east of the Maidan is the city's spinal cord. Now technically called Jawaharlal (or J. L.) Nehru Road, Chowringhee runs along the east side of the Maidan, with shops, hotels, and old Victorian buildings lining the other side of the wide pavement. In the evening, hawkers do their best with potential shoppers, and at night, the homeless bed down. ⊠ *Central Calcutta.*

⓯ Eden Gardens. These flower-speckled gardens in the northwest corner of the Maidan are often crowded, but you can still find relief from the busy streets. Don't miss the lovely Burmese pagoda. ⊠ *Eden Gardens Rd., Central Calcutta* 🎫 *Free* ⊙ *24 hrs.*

⓰ Fort William. The irregular septagon south of the Eden Gardens is surrounded by a moat almost 50 feet wide. Begun in 1757 after Robert Clive's victory over Siraj ud-Daula at Plassey, Fort William was designed to prevent any future attacks. The fort's walls, as well as its barracks, stables, and Church of St. Peter, have survived to this day chiefly because the fort has, in fact, never been attacked. The Indian government still uses the fort, but it's closed to the public. ⊠ *Strand Rd., Central Calcutta.*

⓬ General Post Office (GPO). Built in 1864 and still in use as Calcutta's main post office, this building's massive white Corinthian columns rest on the site of the original Fort William, where the British were attacked in 1756 and many officers were imprisoned by Siraj ud-Daula in the infamous "Black Hole of Calcutta," a tiny space that caused most of the group to suffocate. ⊠ *Netaji Subhash Rd., near B. B .D. Bagh, Central Calcutta* 🕾 *33/2242–1572* ⊙ *Weekdays 10–5:30.*

⓴ Indian Museum. India's oldest museum has one of the largest and most comprehensive collections in Asia, including one of the best natural-history collections in the world. It's known locally as *Jadu Ghar,* the "House of Magic." The archaeology section has representative antiquities from prehistoric times to the Mogul period, including relics from Mohenjodaro and Harappa, the oldest excavated Indus Valley civilizations. The southern wing includes the Bharhut and Gandhara rooms (Indian art from the 2nd century BC to the 5th century AD), the Gupta and medieval galleries, and the Mogul gallery.

The Indian Museum also houses the world's largest collection of Indian coins; ask at the information desk for permission to see it. Gems and jewelry are on display. The art section on the first floor has a good collection of textiles, carpets, wood carving, papier-mâché figures, and terracotta pottery. A gallery on the third floor contains exquisite Persian and Indian miniature paintings, and banners from Tibetan monasteries. The anthropology section on the first floor is devoted to cultural anthropology, though the museum plans to establish India's first comprehensive exhibit on physical anthropology; some interesting specimens are an Egyptian mummy donated in 1880 by an English seaman, a fossilized

200-million-year-old tree trunk, the lower jaw of a 26-meter (84-foot) whale, and meteorites dating back 50,000 years. ⊠ *27 J. L. Nehru Rd., Central Calcutta* ☎ *33/2249–9853* ⊠ *Rs. 1, free on Fri.* ☉ *Sept.–Apr., Tues.–Sun. 10–4:30; May–Aug., Tues.–Sun. 11–5.*

need a break?

For breakfast or tea with sandwiches, try **Flury's Tea Room** (⊠ 18 Park St., Central Calcutta ☎ 33/2229–7664 ☉ daily 7:30 AM–8 PM), Calcutta's first Swiss confectioner opened in the 1920s and is now an institution. You can get a chicken or cheese omelette, beans on toast, and coffee for Rs. 150.

★ ⓭ **Maidan.** Known as Calcutta's "green lung," the city's expansive park is dotted with some of its most significant attractions and is highly prized by its citizens, who turn out in the morning for sports and pony rides, and in the evening for snacks and carriage rides. The area came into existence when forests were cleared to give Fort William a clear line of fire. ⊠ *Just south of B. B. D. Bagh to the northern border of Alipore, and from the Hooghly River to J. L. Nehru Rd. and the shops of Park St., Central Calcutta.*

⓮ **Ochterlony Monument.** On the north end of the Maidan stands a 148-foot pillar commemorating Sir David Ochterlony's military victories over the Nepalese in the border war of 1814–16. Built in 1828, the impressive monument has a curious design: the base is Egyptian, the column is Syrian, and the cupola is Turkish. Now officially called the Shahid Minar (Martyr's Tower), it has been the site of many political rallies and student demonstrations during Calcutta's turbulent post-Independence history. ⊠ *J. L. Nehru Rd., Central Calcutta.*

⓲ **St. Paul's Cathedral.** Completed in 1847, the cathedral now has a steeple modeled after the one at Canterbury; previous steeples were destroyed by earthquakes in 1897 and 1934. Florentine frescoes, the stained-glass western window, and a gold communion plate presented by Queen Victoria are prize possessions. Interestingly, birds congregate in the interior eaves. ⊠ *Cathedral Rd., east of Victoria Memorial, Central Calcutta* ☎ *33/2244–5756* ☉ *Daily 9–noon and 3–6.*

⓳ **South Park Street Cemetery.** The graves and memorials here form a repository of British imperial history. People who lived within the Raj from 1767 on are buried here, and in the records of their lives you can see the trials and triumphs of the building of an empire. ⊠ *Park St. at Rawdon St., Central Calcutta* ☎ *No phone* ☉ *Daily sunrise–sunset.*

⓱ **Victoria Memorial.** This massive, white marble monument was conceived in 1901 by Lord Curzon and built over a 20-year period. Designed in a mixture of Italian Renaissance and Saracenic styles, surrounded by extensive, carefully manicured gardens, and preceded by a typically sober statue of Victoria herself, it remains the single greatest symbol of the British Raj. Inside the building is an excellent museum of the history of Calcutta (there's a lot to read, but it will really sharpen your sense of the British-Bengali relationship) and various Raj-related exhibits, including Queen Victoria's writing desk and piano, Indian miniature paintings,

Fodor'sChoice
★

watercolors, and Persian books. Cameras and electronic equipment must be left at the entrance. In the evenings there's a sound and light show, with narration in English, about Calcutta's history. ⊠ *Queen's Way, Central Calcutta* ☎ *33/2248–5142* 🖃 *Monument: Rs. 10; sound-and-light show: Rs. 20* ☉ *Tues.–Sun. 10–4:30; sound-and-light show Tues.–Sun. 7:15 and 8:15.*

⓫ Writers' Building. The original "writers" were the clerks of the British East India Company. Now a government office building, this dramatically baroque edifice is closed to the public. ⊠ *North side of B. B. D. Bagh, Central Calcutta.*

South Calcutta

Calcutta's rich and powerful moved consistently south as the city grew more and more crowded and unpleasant. Here you'll see an interesting mix of large colonial homes, modern hotels and businesses, open space, and crowded temple areas.

a good tour

You can reach **Kalighat Kali Temple ㉑** ► by metro, getting off at Kalighat Station and walking north on Murkaharji Road for about 2 km (1.2 mi)—or you can take a taxi for an interesting ride through a variety of neighborhoods. **Nirmal Hirday ㉒**, where Mother Teresa lived, worked, and is buried, is just around the corner. The **National Library ㉓** is a short taxi ride from either and puts you near the Taj Bengal hotel, a restful place for a coffee break. To reach the **Indian Botanical Gardens ㉔**, across the Hooghly River in Howrah, take another taxi (about 15 minutes) across the Second Hooghly Bridge (Vivekananda Setu).

Numbers in the text correspond to numbers in the margin and on the Calcutta map.

TIMING Give yourself a full morning to cover this ground. Allow an hour and a half to arrive at and see Kalighat Kali Temple, another hour if you want to visit Nirmal Hirday, one of Mother Teresa's missions. You many want to skip the National Library unless you want to bundle it with an upscale rest stop (or a stay) at the Taj Bengal, and go straight to the Indian Botanical Gardens.

What to See

★ ㉔ Indian Botanical Gardens. Across the Second Hooghly Bridge (Vivekananda Setu) in Howrah are the massive botanical gardens, first opened in 1786. Darjeeling and Assam teas were developed here. The gardens' banyan tree has one of the largest canopies in the world, covering a mind-boggling 1,300 square feet. The gardens are so huge that you can even find a place to relax on Sunday, when locals turn out in droves to enjoy their day off. ⊠ *Between Andul Rd. and Kurz Ave., Shibpur, Howrah* ☎ *33/2660–3235* 🖃 *Free* ☉ *Daily 1 hr after sunrise–1 hr before sunset.*

★ ㉑ Kalighat Kali Temple. Built in 1809, the Kali is one of the most significant pilgrimage sites in India, with shrines to Shiva, Krishna, and Kali, the patron goddess of Calcutta. Human sacrifices were reputed to be common here during the 19th century, but only goats are slaughtered now, then offered to Kali with Ganges water and *bhang* (uncultivated hemp). The building, though surrounded by others, rewards a close look: you'll see thin, multicolor layers of painted trim and swaths of tilework. Only Hindus are allowed in the inner sanctum, but the lanes and brilliant flower markets surrounding the temple are lovely in themselves. ⊠ *Kalighat Rd., South Calcutta* ⊘ *Daily sunrise–sunset.*

㉓ National Library. Once the house of the lieutenant governor of Calcutta, this hefty neo-Renaissance building has miles of books and pleasant reading rooms. The rare-book section holds some significant works, adding to the importance of this 2-million-volume facility. There are no displays, but on the grounds you can take a pleasant short walk. ⊠ *Belvedere Rd., near Taj Bengal hotel, Alipore, South Calcutta* ☎ *33/2223–5381* ⊘ *Weekdays 9–8, weekends 10–6.*

㉒ Nirmal Hirday (Pure Heart). Mother Teresa's first home for the dying is now one of 300 affiliated organizations worldwide that care for people in the most dire need. Learn more about Mother Teresa's work at the headquarters of the **Missionaries of Charity** (⊠ 54A A. J. C. Bose Rd., South Calcutta ☎ 33/2244–7115). It can be inspiring to see the joy among the people in one of the missionaries' homes or refuges. Mother Teresa is buried in this building—her home for 44 years—in what was formerly the cafeteria. ⊠ *Next to Kali Temple, South Calcutta.*

New Calcutta

A lot is said about Calcutta's history and traditions but with the winds of globalization sweeping across the country, a new generation—one that has grown up on international television and the Internet—want their city to become a part of a global village. The old Calcutta is making way for the new. Travel along the Eastern Metropolitan (EM) Bypass, northeast of downtown, for a taste of this contemporary city.

a good tour

Right off the EM Bypass is the **Swabhumi ㉕** ↰, a sprawling complex that showcases the best of Indian arts and crafts. Just 5 minutes to the northeast of the bypass are **Nicco Park ㉖**, an amusement park, and **Aquatica ㉗**, a water park that's a 15-minute drive off the bypass.

TIMING   Taking in all of these attractions will fill a very long day, so you might want to tackle only two of the three. Regardless, set out early by cab or a hired car. It's about 45 minutes from the heart of the city to the EM Bypass (northeast, en route to the airport); the sights are all off the bypass and within 30 to 45 minutes of each other. Plan to spend two hours each at Swabhumi and Nicco Park; unless you're a real waterpark buff, an hour at Aquatica should suffice.

What to See

㉗ Aquatica. A nice place to chill—literally and figuratively—is this water park just off the EM Bypass. The rides are thrilling, and there's a huge pool in which youngsters do their own version of the MTV Grind. As you might expect, weekends are crowded. Admission includes access to all rides. ⊠ *Kochpukur, S. 24 Parganas, Bypass and beyond* ☎ *33/2221–3626* 💲 *Rs. 150* ⊘ *Daily 10–5.*

26 **Nicco Park.** This amusement complex has acres of green space, numerous exciting rides, and many small restaurants in the complex. Even though ride tickets aren't included, admission is a steal at Rs. 25. ⊠ *5-min drive off EM Bypass, Bypass and beyond* ☎ *33/2357–6058 or 33/2357–8102* 🖼 *Rs. 25* ⊙ *Daily 10:30–8.*

▶ **25** **Swabhumi.** Opposite the Salt Lake Stadium, this heritage park complex is a mini-India. You can find everything from traditional crafts to jugglers on stilts to a food court with regional cuisine here. ⊠ *Off EM Bypass, Bypass and beyond* ☎ *33/2321–5486 or 33/2334–3903* ⊕ *www. swabhumi.org* 🖼 *Rs. 10* ⊙ *Daily 10–8.*

WHERE TO EAT

Bengali

$–$$ ✕ **Kewpies.** Quaint and exclusive, this restaurant is in high demand at
Fodor'sChoice the moment. The delicious *thalis* (combination platters) are available
★ both vegetarian and nonvegetarian, the latter with assorted meats or fish only, are served in a typically Bengali style: on cut banana leaves. You can also order the thali's vegetable or meat portions à la carte. ⊠ *2 Elgin La., South Calcutta* ☎ *33/2475–9880* ⌕ *Reservations essential* ⊟ *No credit cards.*

$ ✕ **Aheli.** Calcutta's first upscale Bengali restaurant still draws a crowd. Traditional Bengali delicacies, such as *macher sorse paturi* (fish cooked with mustard paste) and *chingri malai* curry (prawns and coconut milk curry) are served in an intimate terra-cotta dining room. ⊠ *Peerless Inn, 12 J. L. Nehru Rd., Central Calcutta* ☎ *33/2228–0301 or 33/2228–0302* ⊟ *AE, DC, MC, V.*

Eclectic

★ **$$$–$$$$** ✕ **The Hub.** The 24-hour coffee shop of the Taj Bengal hotel has been dubbed Calcutta's "international food theater." The grand, spacious interior, with marble floors and a glass spiral staircase, matches that of the hotel lobby. Although the emphasis is on Italian food, you get a wide choice of cuisines. Try the homemade pasta or the rack of lamb in brown sauce, or the sumptuous, multicuisine buffets worth Rs. 550 each for lunch on most Sundays. ⊠ *Taj Bengal, 34B Belvedere Rd., Alipore, South Calcutta* ☎ *33/2223–3939* ⌕ *Reservations not accepted* ⊟ *AE, DC, MC, V.*

$–$$ ✕ **Tangerine.** This is arguably the best place serving multicuisine in Cal-
Fodor'sChoice cutta. Small and cozy, with minimalist furniture and plate-glass windows
★ overlooking a lake, this restaurant is peopled by friendly, helpful staff, and it showcases great food. Don't-miss choices include prawn salad, fish and chips, lobster thermidor, and chili crab. ⊠ *2–1 Outram St., Central Calcutta* ☎ *33/2281–5450* ⌕ *Reservations essential* ⊟ *MC, V.*

★ **$** ✕ **Taaja.** *Taaja* ("Fresh") is one of the best Continental restaurants in Calcutta, serving Greek, French, Italian, Spanish, and Hungarian food, but it offers dishes from the Caribbean and Far East as well. The menu gives new meaning to the word "eclectic." Paella, Cajun crab cakes, moussaka, and cannelloni are all memorable choices. ☒ *29–1A Ballygunge Circular Rd., South Calcutta* ☏ *33/2476–7334* ⌂ *Reservations essential* ▤ *MC, V.*

¢–$ ✕ **The Sheriff.** Calcutta's only Wild West joint is extremely popular with the smart crowd. The walls of this small space are bedecked with Stetsons, Colt revolvers, and lassos, and the waiters are dressed as cowboys. The Mexican food is fair enough if you need a little variety. ☒ *Sarat Bose Rd., at Elgin Rd., South Calcutta* ☏ *33/2463–2117* ⌂ *Reservations essential* ▤ *AE.*

Indian

★ $$$$ ✕ **Sonargaon.** The name means "golden village," and this North Indian restaurant is a tasteful replica of a rural home, complete with a courtyard, a well, dark wood on taupe stone, copper curios, and metal light fixtures. Popular dishes include *kakori* kabab (minced lamb kabab), *murg Wajid Ali* (stuffed, pounded chicken breast marinated in saffron and cooked in a mildly spicy sauce), and chingri malai. ☒ *Taj Bengal, 34B Belvedere Rd., Alipore, South Calcutta* ☏ *33/2223–3939* ⌂ *Reservations essential* ▤ *AE, DC, MC, V.*

$$$–$$$$ ✕ **Zaranj.** Plush and well decorated with a fountain and ornate furniture, this is a relaxing place for dinner because the staff won't rush you. Choose from a large à la carte menu with vegetarian and nonvegetarian options. The tasty *murgh nawabi* is a boneless chicken with yogurt and nuts, roasted over a charcoal grill. ☒ *26 J. L. Nehru Rd., Central Calcutta* ☏ *33/2249–5572* ⌂ *Reservations essential* ▤ *AE, DC, V.*

★ $–$$ ✕ **Peter Cat.** The cello kabab here—*biriani*–style rice (flavored with saffron or turmeric) with egg, butter, two mutton kababs, and one chicken kabab—is one of the most popular dishes in Calcutta. The dining room is intimate, with white stucco walls, Tiffany-style lamps, and soft lighting; the menu is a mixture of good Continental and Indian dishes, especially tandoori fare. ☒ *18 Park St., Central Calcutta* ☏ *33/2229–8841* ▤ *DC, V.*

Pan-Asian

$$$$ ✕ **Chinoiserie.** Consistently rated one of the best Chinese restaurants in
Fodor'sChoice India (no small honor these days), this place serves delicacies such as
★ Peking duck and a highly unusual selection of corn dishes. One crunchy appetizer consists of deep-fried kernels of American corn; another dish features corn delicately flavored with garlic. Unsurpassed food, a calm green-and-beige color scheme accented by old-world mirrors and paintings, and excellent Taj service make dining here an experience. Reservations are advised on weekdays and crucial on weekends. ☒ *Taj Bengal, 34B Belvedere Rd., Alipore, South Calcutta* ☏ *33/2223–3939* ⌂ *Reservations essential* ▤ *AE, DC, MC, V.*

★ $$$$ ✕ **PanAsian.** As the name suggests, this is, in terms of range, the broadest spread from the Pan Asian region in Calcutta. Split into three sections, it offers in each food from Japan, Mongolia and Korea, and Thailand and China. It's a favorite haunt of the expat community. Don't miss the Mongolian grill, the Thai curries, and the tepyanki in the Japanese section. Reservations are advised on weekdays and essential on weekends. ✉ *ITC Sonar Bangla Sheraton Hotels & Towers, 1 Haldane Ave., Bypass and beyond* ☎ *33/2345–4545* ▭ *AE, DC, MC, V.*

$$$$ ✕ **Zen.** Art deco meets postmodern in the sleek lines of this Southeast Asian restaurant, which serves cuisines from across the region. The Thai green curry and the Indonesian specialties, such as *soto ayam* (glass noodles) and *nasi gorang* (mixed fried rice) are rare finds in India. The grilled lobster with sweet-and-sour dip is an indulgence worth the price. ✉ *Park Hotel, 17 Park St., Central Calcutta* ☎ *33/2249–7336* ⌕ *Reservations essential* ▭ *AE, DC, MC, V.*

$$$ ✕ **Mainland China.** Expect to find Calcutta's chic populating this restaurant, which is part of a national chain. Though the dining room is large, grand mirrors give the illusion of even more space, and the furniture is minimalist but comfortable. The Szechuan menu is extensive. Opt for the seafood platter or the chicken in a hot garlic sauce. Attentive service and valet parking make for a posh evening. ✉ *3A Gurusaday Rd., South Calcutta* ☎ *33/287–2006* ⌕ *Reservations essential* ▭ *AE, DC, MC, V.*

$$ ✕ **China Valley.** Enormous statues of Chinese figures dominate the scene, and are surrounded by a stunning collection of vases and urns. Large aquariums filled with iridescent tropical fish will spur your imagination, if not your appetite. But expect to eat well; the food here is top grade. The hot, spicy prawn Shanghai with rice is especially popular. ✉ *Ideal Plaza, 11–1 Sarat Bose Rd., South Calcutta* ☎ *33/2247–0294* ⌕ *Reservations essential* ▭ *AE, DC, MC.*

$ ✕ **Thai Tonight.** An alternative to the more expensive spots—although luxury hotel restaurants serve more authentic Thai food—this place has a friendly vibe, great service, and even better prices. Try the standard chicken green curry or the bargain-price glass noodles. ✉ *29–1A Ballygunge Circular Rd., South Calcutta* ☎ *33/2454–2036* ⌕ *Reservations essential* ▭ *AE, DC, MC, V.*

¢–$ ✕ **Bar-B-Q.** This local favorite serves Cantonese and Szechuan dishes in a setting that innovatively mixes Chinese and German-chalet style under a name that, of course, conjures neither of the two. Try the crisp fried chicken served with a mild "surprise" sauce or the boneless chili chicken. ✉ *43 Park St., Central Calcutta* ☎ *33/2229–2870* ⌕ *Reservations essential* ▭ *AE, DC, MC, V.*

¢ ✕ **Momo Plaza.** Calcuttans love Tibetan food, and Momo Plaza is an ideal place for a Tibetan snack if you can forego a stylish interior for the duration. The chicken-stuffed *momos* (dumplings) come steamed or fried, and are served with a very hot red-chili paste. They're accompanied by a light, watery spring-onion soup called *thukpa.* ✉ *2A Suburban Hospital Rd., South Calcutta* ☎ *33/2247–8250* ▭ *No credit cards.*

WHERE TO STAY

$$$$ ▦ **Taj Bengal.** Calcutta's Taj is a fusion of traditional and modern India.
Fodor'sChoice On the fringe of the city center, the hotel overlooks the Maidan and Victoria Memorial. Modern Indian art, artifacts (including terra-cotta reliefs), and antiques are showcased throughout the building. Rooms, which
★ you access via quiet triangular atriums, are essentially Western, with Eastern accents and Indian prints. Service is truly outstanding. ✉ *34B*

Belvedere Rd., Alipore, South Calcutta 700027 ☎ *33/2223–3939* 🖷 *33/2223–1766* ⊕ *www.tajhotels.com* 📞 *216 rooms, 13 suites* ♻ *3 restaurants, pool, health club, bar, nightclub, business services, travel services* ▭ *AE, DC, MC, V.*

$$$–$$$$ ▥ **Hotel Hindustan International.** The modern rooms have a neat and trim, if not particularly inspiring, style. The best rooms overlook the pool, but many others have good views of Calcutta. ⊠ *235–1 A. J. C. Bose Rd., South Calcutta 700020* ☎ *33/2280–2323* 🖷 *33/2280–2824* 📞 *212 rooms, 12 suites* ♻ *3 restaurants, pool, health club, spa, bar, nightclub, business services, travel services* ▭ *AE, DC, MC, V.*

★ **$$$–$$$$** ▥ **ITC Sonar Bangla Sheraton Hotels & Towers.** Calcutta's newest upscale hotel is undoubtedly one of the city's very best. Built around a 4-acre pond full of lotuses, and set in landscaped gardens, the hotel has been inspired by the architecture in vogue when the Pala dynasty ruled Bengal. The rooms are comfortable and modern (you can watch TV even from the bath) and the service is very attentive. ⊠ *1 Haldane Ave., Bypass and beyond 700046* ☎ *33/2345–4545* 🖷 *33/2345–4455* ⊕ *www.sheraton.com* 📞 *231 rooms, 8 suites* ♻ *7 restaurants, in-room safes, minibars, cable TV, 2 tennis courts, pool, health club, hair salon, spa, bar, lounge, nightclub, baby-sitting, business services, convention center, meeting rooms, travel services, no-smoking rooms* ▭ *AE, DC, MC, V.*

★ **$$$–$$$$** ▥ **Oberoi Grand.** The height of elegance, this impeccably maintained Victorian landmark in the center of town has a glowing white facade and a rich marble and dark-wood interior. The heritage is rich, service is top-notch, and the restaurants are excellent. Guest rooms lack any sense of antiquity, but they're spacious, with wall-to-wall carpeting and modern bathrooms. The best rooms overlook the interior courtyard and pool. ⊠ *15 J. L. Nehru Rd., Central Calcutta 700013* ☎ *33/2249–2323* 🖷 *33/2249–1217* ⊕ *www.oberoihotels.com* 📞 *213 rooms, 6 suites* ♻ *3 restaurants, pool, health club, sauna, bar, business services, travel services* ▭ *AE, DC, MC, V.*

★ **$$$** ▥ **Park Hotel.** Inspired decoration has turned this place into one of the best hotels in Calcutta. Everything in the long, white building—right in the thick of things on Park Street—has been designed with care: the lobby sparkles with mirrors and cut-glass chandeliers amid rich wood and marble, for example. Even the restaurants and café are creative in everything from a daring black art deco–meets-Zen style to simple tasks, such as serving cappuccino. The rooms are comfortable, if small, and the staff are cheerful and helpful. The bar and nightclub are very popular with both Indians and expats. ⊠ *17 Park St., Central Calcutta 700016* ☎ *33/2249–3121* 🖷 *33/2249–7343* ⊕ *www.theparkhotels.com* 📞 *155 rooms, 10 suites* ♻ *2 restaurants, pool, bar, nightclub, business services, travel services* ▭ *AE, DC, MC, V.*

$$ ▥ **Kenilworth.** Popular with repeat visitors to Calcutta, this hotel has two attractive wings and pretty gardens. The common rooms are filled with marble and cheerfully furnished; guest rooms are comfortable and spacious, with standard, anonymous furnishings. Continental breakfast is included. ⊠ *1–2 Little Russell St., Central Calcutta 700071* ☎ *33/2282–3939* 🖷 *33/2282–5136* 📞 *110 rooms* ♻ *2 restaurants, bar, shop, business services, travel services* ▭ *AE, DC, MC, V* ▣ *CP.*

$–$$ ▥ **Peerless Inn.** On a crowded street near the Oberoi Grand and New Market, this hotel has somewhat cramped rooms and less-than-elegant furnishings, but its location and price make it popular. The presence of the Bengali restaurant Aheli is a bonus. You can also change money here. ✉ *15 J. L. Nehru Rd., Central Calcutta 700013* ☎ *33/2228–0301* 🖷 *33/2249–9457* 🛏 *123 rooms* ⚴ *3 restaurants, cable TV, health club, bar, laundry facilities, business services* ▤ *AE, DC, MC, V* ⁌⃝ *BP.*

$ ▥ **Astor.** In this price category, this is the least expensive and most comfortable place around. The rooms are clean if somewhat small; and there are three restaurants, including a casual beer garden, ideal for whiling away a balmy evening and getting a bite to eat. ✉ *15 Shakespeare Sarani, Central Calcutta 700071* ☎ *33/2282–9957* 🖷 *33/2287–7430* 🛏 *35 rooms* ⚴ *3 restaurants* ▤ *AE, MC, V* ⁌⃝ *CP.*

★ **$** ▥ **Fairlawn.** If you want a taste of life in the Raj, stay in this Calcutta landmark, built in 1801. A small hotel, the Fairlawn has memorabilia-cluttered walls, a winding staircase, and a great overall vibe. Waiters wear gloves, a gong sounds during mealtimes, and rooms have chintz bedspreads and old-fashioned bathtubs. ✉ *13A Sudder St., Central Calcutta 700013* ☎ *33/2252–1510* 🖷 *33/2252–1835* 🛏 *22 rooms* ⚴ *Restaurant* ▤ *AE, MC, V* ⁌⃝ *FAP.*

NIGHTLIFE & THE ARTS

Nightlife

Nightlife became a Calcutta phenomenon in the 1990s—with the advent of discos, affluent young people began to hit the dance floors. Eating out, however, remains the nocturnal activity of choice, with 24-hour coffee shops at the top hotels doing a brisk business.

Bars & Lounges

The most attractive places to have a nightcap are the Oberoi Grand and the Taj Bengal. The pub at the Park Hotel sometimes offers decent beer on tap, making it a pleasant afternoon watering hole. The bar at the Fairlawn Hotel draws an interesting group and is a nice place to sit out and have a beer in a winter afternoon or summer evening. Bars stay open until 11 PM or midnight. Besides hotels, there aren't a lot of places to go to get a drink; most people either imbibe at a hotel bar or get a drink when they're out for dinner.

Discos

Calcutta's clubs are technically open only to members and hotel guests, but you can get in for either a cover charge or a smile, depending on the doorman. All clubs retain good DJs for a mixture of Indian pop and Western dance music.

Anticlock (✉ Hotel Hindustan International, 235/1 A. J. C. Bose Rd., Central Calcutta ☎ 33/2247–2394) is a good choice, though the crowd gets rowdy as the evening wears on. **Big Ben** (✉ Kenilworth Hotel, 1–2 Little Russell St., Central Calcutta ☎33/2282–8394) is an upscale pub where mid-career local professionals congregate. The barman may be the best in town. Breathe freely at the spacious **Incognito** (✉ Taj Bengal hotel,

34B Belvedere Rd., Alipore, South Calcutta ☎ 33/2248–3939), where an upscale clientele relaxes around a glass-enclosed dance floor.

Play pool or dance into the wee hours at **London Pub** (✉ Golden Park Hotel, 13 Ho Chi Minh Sarani, Central Calcutta ☎ 33/2288–3939). **Someplace Else** (✉ Park Hotel, 17 Park St., Central Calcutta ☎ 33/249–7336) may well be the best pub in town, though drinks are expensive. You'll find good deals during happy hour—which takes place in the afternoon and in early evening. The pub has a small dance floor but great music with varying themes for almost each night of the week. The dance floor at **Tantra** (✉ Park Hotel, 17 Park St., Central Calcutta ☎ 33/2249–7336) is hot and the style is fantastic—cushions with embroidery and beadwork, jute items, *dhurries* (rugs), and silk hangings. If you're older than 30 you may feel a bit out of place.

The Arts

Calcutta has famously been India's deepest well of creative energy. Artists here live in the inspiring shadow of such pillars as poet Rabindranath Tagore and world-renowned film director Satyajit Ray. Happily, the anxiety of influence has not intimidated contemporary artists. To find out what's happening, check *Calcutta This Fortnight,* available from the West Bengal Tourist Office, and *CalCalling,* available in hotels. You can also check the listings pages of any English-language daily newspaper.

Art Galleries

The **Academy of Fine Arts** (✉ 2 Cathedral Rd., Central Calcutta ☎ 33/2223–4302) has a permanent collection of paintings (and manuscripts) by Rabindranath Tagore. The **Birla Academy of Art and Culture** (✉ 108–109 Southern Ave., South Calcutta ☎ 33/2466–2843) has interesting displays of art old and new. Modern Indian art is frequently shown at **Galerie 88** (✉ 28B Shakespeare Sarani, Central Calcutta ☎ 33/2247–2274).

Film

Many movie theaters around New Market feature English-language films. Ask your hotel or the tourist office for information on current events; if they don't know what's on, they'll help you find out. English-language papers, including the *Hindustan Times,* the *Times* of India, the *Telegraph,* and the *Statesman* carry listings that state where films are running and show times.

Performing Arts

Many auditoriums host regular performances of music, dance, and theater—the most Bengali of the performing arts. English-language plays are regularly staged by the **British Council** (☎ 33/2282–5370). Be sure to see what's happening at the **Academy of Fine Arts** (✉ 2 Cathedral Rd., Central Calcutta ☎ 33/2242–1205), and don't be intimidated if the offerings are in Bengali—you can still see some fascinating dramatizations of familiar stories by the likes of Shakespeare and Goethe. Bengali productions are often staged at **Kalamandir** (✉ 48 Shakespeare Sarani, Central Calcutta ☎ 33/2247–9086). Bengali dance and theater are often performed at **Rabindra Sadan** (✉ Cathedral Rd., Central Calcutta ☎ 33/2248–9936).

SPORTS & THE OUTDOORS

Calcutta still puts class first when it comes to sports, with the result that you need to be a member's guest to enter the golf and racing clubs. Whether you want to watch or play, get cricket information from the **Calcutta Cricket and Football Club** (⊠ 19–1 Gurusaday Rd., South Calcutta ☎ 33/2475–8721). The **Calcutta Polo Club** (⊠ 51 J. L. Nehru Rd., Central Calcutta ☎ 33/2242–2031) has the polo schedules. The **Royal Calcutta Golf Club** (⊠ 18 Golf Club Rd., South Calcutta ☎ 33/2473–1288 or 33/473–1352) caters to the elite. For horse-racing enthusiasts, the **Royal Calcutta Turf Club** (RCTC; ⊠ 11 Russell St., Central Calcutta ☎ 33/2229–1104) has an old-world air of sophistication.

SHOPPING

Auctions

Calcutta's Sunday auctions take place along Russell Street. A trip to the oldest auction house, the **Russell Exchange** (⊠ 12C Russell St., Central Calcutta ☎ 33/2249–8974) or any of its neighbors is invariably entertaining. Goods auctioned range from antiques and period furniture to crockery and cutlery.

Bazaars

Shopping in Calcutta bazaars is an adventure, and a test of your ability to shake off touts. In general, most shops are open six days a week, and closed Sunday. Hours tend to be 10:30 to 8. East of Chitpur Road is **Bowbazar,** Calcutta's jewelry district, is where you'll find a terrific collection of good-quality gold and silver plus beautifully designed and crafted stone settings. Prices are reasonable, and each shop has an astrologer to help you find the most auspicious stone for your stars. ⊠ *Near College St., parallel to Chittaranjan Ave. and bounded by Mahatma Gandhi Rd. and Vivekananda Rd., Calcutta Medical College, and Presidency College, North Calcutta.*

Part of the century-old **New Market** (officially Sir Stuart Hogg Market, 19 Lindsay St., off J. L. Nehru Rd., behind Oberoi Grand) houses about 2,500 stores under one roof, selling cotton saris, Bankura clay horses, Malda brassware, leather from Shantiniketan, silk from Murshidabad, *khadi* cloth (handmade cotton), poultry, cheeses, nuts, and other foods. ⊠ *Central Calcutta* ⊙ *Weekdays 10:30–7, Sat. 10:30–2.*

Head up **Rabindra Sarani** from Lal Bazaar Road (near the West Bengal Tourist Office) and you'll soon enter an Islamic world. Women walk by in *burqas* (long, black, tent-shape robes), their eyes barely visible behind veils. Men sit on elevated platforms selling Bengali *kurtas* (shirts) and pants, and colorful *lungis* and white *dhotis* (both are wraps) for men. Other vendors sell vials of perfume created from flowers. Rabindra Sarani is interesting all the way to Chitpur Road. ⊠ *North Calcutta* ⊙ *Mon.–Sat. 10:30–8.*

Bookstores

Landmark at Emami Shoppers' City (✉ 3 Lord Sinha Rd., Central Calcutta ☎ 33/282–2617 to 9) is spacious and modern. It sells books and music under one roof. **Oxford Bookstore-Gallery** (✉ 17 Park St., Central Calcutta ☎ 33/2229–7662) has lots of books, from cookery, travel, and architecture to the very best fiction. Browse the Net here or have an iced lemon tea at the tea bar. **Seagull** (✉ 31A SP Mukherjee Rd., South Calcutta ☎ 33/2476–5865) has many titles but the selection is eclectic. Exhibitions and seminars add to the mix.

Clothing & Textiles

Dakshinapan (✉ Near Dhakuria Bridge, South Calcutta) houses government emporiums from all the states of India, making it an excellent place to eyeball a wide range of styles. **Forum** (✉ 3 Elgin Rd., South Calcutta ☎ 33/2283–6203) is Calcutta's newest shopping mall and offers anything under the sun, from clothes to music to leather to children's wear. Try the **Handloom House** (✉ 2 Lindsay St., Central Calcutta ☎ 33/2249–9037) for crafted textiles, mostly cottons. **Manjusha** (✉ 7–1D Lindsay St., Central Calcutta) sells all manner of textiles. **Monapali and Silk Route** (✉ 15 Loudon St., Central Calcutta ☎ 33/2240–6103) are comanaged designer boutiques with lovely collections of women's saris and *salwar-kameez* (a two-piece outfit of long, loose-fitting tunic over loose pants tapered at the ankle) in cotton, satin, and silk. Designs are inspired by the Far East and enhanced with Indian motifs and artwork: batik, embroidery, and *zardozi* (gold threading). **Pantaloon** (✉ 49–1 Gariahat Rd., South Calcutta ☎ 33/2476–5307) sells everything from kids' clothes to shoes. The innovative **Weavers Studio** (✉ 5–1 Anil Moitra Rd., 2nd fl., Ballygunj Pl., South Calcutta ☎ 33/2440–8937) sells high-quality natural-dye and embroidered textiles. **Westside** (✉ 22 Camac St., Central Calcutta ☎ 33/2281–7312) offers casual wear.

Crafts

For curios in a hurry, head to **Central Cottage Industries** (✉ 7 J. L. Nehru Rd., Central Calcutta ☎ 33/2228–4139). On and around **Chitpur Road** you'll see a mixture of potters and shops that make musical instruments. (✉ between Rabindra Sarani and Kosipore Rd., North Calcutta). Quaint little **Konark Collectables** (✉ Humayun Court, 20 Lindsay St., Central Calcutta ☎ 33/2247–7657) has lots of handicrafts.

SIDE TRIPS

Escape Calcutta's traffic and enrich your Bengali experience with a trip to either of two peaceful havens to the west. Vishnupur is characterized by its centuries-old terra-cotta temples, built from the local red clay and all but alive with the epic scenes carved into their panels. Shantiniketan is home to the university founded by Rabindranath Tagore, a center for art, music, and Bengali heritage. Nearby Sriniketan is a center of batik, embroidery, and terra-cotta craftsmanship.

Vishnupur

152 km (94 mi) west of Calcutta (8 to 10 hours by road, overnight by train).

Set in a land of rich red soil, Vishnupur was the capital of the Hindu Malla kings from the 16th to 19th centuries, and saw fit to convert its surroundings into some mind-blowing terra-cotta temples. Between its intricate, lifelike temple panels and old-world charm, Vishnupur is exquisite, an integral part of Bengal. The clay pottery created here—particularly the Bankura horse, named for the district—attracts thousands for its sheer beauty and color. It's a long trip from Calcutta, but Vishnupur is worth a detour for its exceptional carvings and figurines, immortalizing old Bengal at its artistic best.

Built out of the local red laterite soil, the temple town is scattered with monuments to the Malla rulers. Sights are spread out, so the easiest way to explore is to hire a cycle-rickshaw and ride through the maze of narrow streets. Be sure to see the Madan Gopal, Madan Mohan, Radhagobinda, Rasmancha, and Shyamrai temples, all built around the 16th century; each has a story to tell through its intricately carved figurines. Dalmadol is a cannon of pure iron. Pathar Darwaza ("Doorway of Stone") marked the entrance to the Malla fort. Vishnupur is a great place to buy souvenirs, especially terra-cotta toys, conch-shell handicrafts, jewelry, and silk. In August or September, local snake charmers demonstrate their age-old prowess at a snake festival called the *jhapan,* at which, among other activities, men throw cobras at each other to test their respective mettle.

The only decent place to stay here is **Vishnupur Tourist Lodge** (⌂ P.O. Vishnupur, Bankura ☎ 03244/252013), a modest and suburban place. Don't expect anything beyond the very basic. It has a restaurant and 15 rooms, only one of which is air-conditioned; a double room costs Rs. 450. You can call the lodge, but it's easier to reserve a room through the West Bengal Tourist Office (☎ 33/2248–8271, 33/2248–5917, or 33/2248–5168) in Calcutta.

Shantiniketan

210 km (130 mi) northwest of Calcutta (4 hours by train).

Nobel Laureate Rabindranath Tagore's dream became reality here: a university dedicated to the liberal arts. Today the art and music schools at **Vishva-bharati University,** part of the Shantiniketan university complex, are some of the best in the country. Designed in 1901 as a group of cottages in a green, idyllic setting, Shantiniketan embodies the Bengali artistic heritage. In accordance with Tagore's vision, some classes are still held outside, under the shade of huge trees, and stunning abstract sculptures reach toward the sky. A weekend retreat for many, Shantiniketan is almost a pilgrimage to Bengalis.

Within the university, Rabindra Bhavan is a museum full of photographs, Tagore's personal belongings, and the poet's much-coveted

Nobel Prize. The art school, Kala Bhavan, is decorated with frescoes and murals outside, and you can watch students at work inside. Sangeet Bhavan is the music school. Uttarayan, where Tagore lived, is a charming complex of five houses, ranging from mud hut to mansion, in a variety of architectural styles.

A few minutes' drive outside Shantiniketan, **Sriniketan** is a rural-development center helping locals fend for themselves by creating stunning handicrafts—colorful batiks; intricate embroidery on saris, scarves, and bags; and terra-cotta items, including jewelry. This is a hidden shopper's paradise, with some of the most beautiful and exclusive craft items in Bengal. A great time to visit Shantiniketan is during the town's biggest festival, Poush Mela, which is usually held December 22 to 25. The festival includes huge fairs where handicrafts and bric-a-brac are sold and performances of *bauls* (wandering minstrels) who sing their unique variety of folk songs.

Where to Stay

¢–$ ▣ **Chhuti.** This sprawling hotel, built with an eye for detail, is one of the best in the vicinity, with a resortlike vibe and good food. Guest rooms and the air-conditioned cottages are spacious, clean, and refreshing, and the caring, experienced staff looks after all your needs. ⊠ *241 Charupally, Jamboni, Bolpur* ☎ *953463/252692* ⊅ *22 rooms* ◊ *Restaurant, cable TV; no a/c in some rooms* ▭ *AE, MC, V.*

¢–$ ▣ **Marks and Meadows.** More a resort than a mere rest stop, this is an ideal place to unwind. With its landscaped gardens, swimming pool, and fishing pond, this is a great value. The rooms are cottage-style, clean, and tidy. ⊠ *Sriniketan, Santiniketan* ☎ *33/2245–8831, 33/2245–0179, or 33/2244–8254* 🖶 *33/245–8831* ⊅ *34 rooms* ◊ *Restaurant, pool, badminton, Ping-Pong, recreation room, meeting room; no a/c in some rooms* ▭ *AE, MC, V.*

CALCUTTA A TO Z

To research prices, get advice from other travelers, and book travel arrangements, visit www.fodors.com.

ADDRESSES

In the last few decades, many of Calcutta's streets have been haphazardly renamed. Though some maps and street signs have only the new names, you're more likely to see just the old or both. Taxis and rickshaws use the names interchangeably, but old names are still favored, as most of the new names are ridiculously long and obscure. The most important name changes: Chowringhee Road is now Jawaharlal Nehru (J. L. Nehru) Road; Ballygunge Circular is now Pramathesh Barua Sarani; Bowbazar is now B. B. Ganguly Street; Harington Street is now Ho Chi Minh Sarani; Lansdowne Road is now Sarat Bose Road; Lower Circular Road is now A. J. C. Bose Road; Rippon Street is now Muzaffar Ahmed Street; and Theater Road is now Shakespeare Sarani. A complete list is available at the Government of India Tourist Office. As if changing the names of streets were not confusing enough, the name of the city itself was officially changed in February 2001. Calcutta, in all government records, is now called Kolkata, a transformation that's supposed to contribute to ridding this and other Indian cities of their colonial past. But as with the names of streets, the two names of the city are used interchangeably.

AIR TRAVEL

All international and domestic airlines use Dum Dum Airport, 15 km (9 mi) north of the city.

⚁ Airlines & Contacts **Indian Airlines** ☎ 33/2236–0810 or 33/236–0730. **Jet Airways** ☎ 33/2229–2737 or 33/229–2660.
⚁ Airport **Dum Dum Airport** ☎ 33/2511–9720.

AIRPORT TRANSFERS

When you leave the baggage claim, you'll see counters where you can arrange free shuttle service if your hotel offers it. Outside the baggage claim–customs area, you can hire a taxi through the prepaid-taxi counter; the ride downtown takes at least 40 minutes and costs around Rs. 120. Hire a taxi on your own through one of the hustlers outside the terminal and it will cost about Rs. 350. The airport coach (Rs. 50) goes to most of the upscale hotels and to the city center; its counter is also near the baggage-claim area but the frequency is not always reliable or consistent.

BUS TRAVEL WITHIN CALCUTTA

Buses here are slow, creaking machines that belch fumes and are unbearably crowded during rush hours. They will cost you next to nothing but will set you back in terms of time and basic traveling comfort; avoid them.

CARS & DRIVERS

You can hire a car and driver through one of the travel agencies listed below (⇨ Tours), or from the following rental agencies. (All cars automatically come with drivers.) Expect to pay Rs. 700 for half a day (4 hours) and 80 km (50 mi), with an hourly and per-kilometer rate beyond that. If you plan to do a lot in very little time, hiring a car can be useful, but hailing plain old taxis can be cheaper, and saves you from having to find parking or remember where you left your car and driver.

⚁ **Europcar Shaw Distributors** ✉ 8-1 Sarat Bose Rd., South Calcutta ☎ 33/2475–8916. **Hertz** ✉ New Kenilworth Hotel, ½ Little Russel St., Central Calcutta ☎ 33/2242–8394. **Wenz** ✉ Oberoi Grand, Central Calcutta ☎ 33/2249–2323 Ext. 6247.

CONSULATES

⚁ **British Consulate** ✉ 1 Ho Chi Minh Sarani, Central Calcutta 700071 ☎ 33/332282–5171. **Canadian Consulate** ✉ Duncan House, 31 NS Rd., Central Calcutta 700001 ☎ 33/2225–0163. **U.S. Consulate** ✉ 5-1 Ho Chi Minh Sarani, Central Calcutta 700071 ☎ 33/2282–3611.

EMERGENCIES

⚁ General Emergencies **Fire** ☎ 101. **Police** ☎ 100.
⚁ Hospital **Belle View Clinic** ✉ 9 U.N. Brahmachari St., South Calcutta ☎ 33/2247–2321.

MAIL & SHIPPING
🚩 Post Office **General Post Office** ✉ Netaji Subhash Rd., near B. B. D. Bagh and Writers' Building, Central Calcutta ☎ 33/2242–1572 ⊗ Weekdays 10–5:30.

MONEY MATTERS
ATMS 🚩 **HSBC** ✉ 31 B. B. D. Bagh, Central Calcutta ✉ 15 Gariahat Rd., South Calcutta ✉ 25A Shakespeare Sarani, Central Calcutta ☎ 33/2440–3930. **Standard Chartered Grindlays Bank** ✉ 19 Netaji Subhash Rd., Cental Calcutta ✉ 41 Jawaharlal Nehru Rd., Central Calcutta ☎ 33/2246–5000.

CURRENCY Most of the legitimate currency exchange centers keep the same hours
EXCHANGE and offer the same services and rates. You can get far better rates than the hotels. Steer clear of the many cubbyholes with slapdash signs outside touting rates that seem too good to be true (they are); these are particularly prevalent in the New Market area.

🚩 Exchange Services **American Express** ✉ 21 Old Court House St., Central Calcutta ☎ 33/2248–6281. **ANZ Grindlays Bank** ✉ 19 Netaji Subhash Rd., Central Calcutta ☎ 33/2220–8346. **Bank of America** ✉ 8 India Exchange Pl., Central Calcutta ☎ 33/2242–2042. **Citibank** ✉ Tata Center, 43 J. L. Nehru Rd., Central Calcutta ☎ 33/2292–9220. **State Bank of India** ✉ 33 J. L. Nehru Rd., Central Calcutta ☎ 33/2240–2430. **Thomas Cook** ✉ Chitrakoot Bldg., 230A A. J. C. Bose Rd., South Calcutta ☎ 33/2247–5378.

RICKSHAWS
Calcutta is the last city on Earth to use enormous Chinese-style rickshaws pulled by men on foot. At least one million people depend on the hard-earned wages of these men for what little daily sustenance and shelter they get. Many pullers say they wouldn't trade positions with cycle-rickshaw wallahs for anything. If you ever get the chance to pull a rickshaw, you will be horrified at how difficult it is, even when the rickshaw is empty. With that in mind, don't rush your driver, and tip generously—the driver deserves it. Rickshaw fares fluctuate depending on the distance to be traveled and the amount of traffic congestion; negotiate ahead of time, using Rs. 15 per 10 minutes as a guide.

SUBWAY TRAVEL
Calcutta's metro system, which has been evolving over the past few decades, is clean and efficient. It connects Dum Dum Airport with Tollygunge, a locality and metro stop in South Calcutta (it's the southernmost stop on the route). The metro is limited but it does pass through (and stop at) places like Park Street, Rabindra Sadan, and Maidan. Pick up a free booklet, which tells you about the route and about train timings, at any metro station. (Metro stations are also marked on the government's tourist map, available free from tourist offices and most hotels.) Tickets cost Rs. 5–Rs. 10 and are available from machines and windows in every station. The metro runs daily until 9:30 PM and is crowded only at rush hour.

TAXIS & AUTO-RICKSHAWS
Most Calcuttans rely on buses, trams, and the spotless metro to get around, but you will probably rely on taxis, rickshaws, and your feet (the bus system is indecipherable, the slow, rickety trams are good only for an early-morning ride, and the metro is somewhat limited). Calcutta is not

a good city for driving; in response to the painful traffic situation, authorities have made many roads in Calcutta one-way, then the other way, then two ways at various times throughout the day and week. Take a cab to or from the area you're visiting, then walk or find a sturdy rickshaw.

The base fare in Calcutta is Rs. 15, and the meter should read about Rs. 30 after 5 km. The legal inflation factor, however, is 100%, and it changes periodically; so ask your hotel for the current inflation factor. If a driver refuses to turn the meter on, find another taxi. Traffic, unfortunately, plagues Calcutta, possibly bringing your cab to a full stop amid humid air and diesel exhaust, so at rush hour you may just want to find a sweet shop and wait until it's over.

Auto-rickshaws are cheaper than taxis, but they're not as easy to find in the city center. At rush hour they can be more efficient (albeit dirtier) alternatives; taxis are liable to get stuck in traffic.

TOURS

These agencies can arrange a car and driver for local sightseeing or help make long-distance travel arrangements.

American Express ✉ 21 Old Court House St., Central Calcutta ☎ 33/2248–4464. **Ashok Travel and Tours** ✉ Government of India Tourist Office, 4 Shakespeare Sarani, Central Calcutta ☎ 33/2440901 or 33/2552–9111. **Mercury Travels** ✉ 46C J. L. Nehru Rd., Central Calcutta ☎ 33/2443555 or 33/2249–2323 ✉ Oberoi Grand, Central Calcutta ☎ 33/249–2323. **Thomas Cook** ✉ Chitrakoot Bldg., 230A A. J. C. Bose Rd., South Calcutta ☎ 33/2247–5378.

WALKING TOURS The most interesting tours in Calcutta are the walks through various neighborhoods led by the Foundation for Conservation and Research of Urban Traditional Architecture (CRUTA).

Foundation for Conservation and Research of Urban Traditional Architecture ✉ 67B Beadon St., North Calcutta 700006 ☎ 33/2554–6127.

TELEPHONE NUMBERS

Phone numbers change with alarming frequency in Calcutta. Whenever you make a call and get a recorded message saying, "This telephone number does not exist," dial 1951 or 1952 or 197 to find out the new number. There are computerized as well as manual services.

TRAIN TRAVEL

Every day an incredible number of trains roll into and out of Howrah Junction, which is divided into the neighboring Old and New Howrah stations. A permanent population resides on the platforms among the ferocious crowds of travelers, vendors, and other locals; indeed, "platform children" attend school between the tracks here, taught to read and write by volunteers. The main reservation office has a foreign-tourist section upstairs, open daily 9 to 1 and 1:30 to 4; buy tickets here with either foreign currency or a valid encashment certificate for rupees. There are also ticket offices on the first floor of Old Howrah Station, the second floor of New Howrah Station, and in Kalighat. Sealdah Station is used exclusively by trains to and from northern destinations such as Darjeeling. Tickets are sold on the platform level.

🚩 Train Information **Howrah Junction** ✉ 1 block south of the west end of Howrah Bridge ☎ 33/2220-4025 or 1310 ✉ 6 Failie Pl., North Calcutta ☎ 33/2660-3535 reservations ✉ 14 Strand Rd., North Calcutta ☎ 33/2220-3496 for first-class bookings. **Sealdah Station** ✉ East end of Bepin Behari Ganguly St., North Calcutta ☎ 33/2350-3535 or 33/2350-3496.

VISITOR INFORMATION

The West Bengal Tourist Office is open Monday through Saturday 10 to 5. The regional Government of India Tourist Office is well equipped to help baffled travelers; it's open Monday through Saturday 9 to 6. The Calcutta Information Centre is also helpful. The West Bengal Tourist Office is in the heart of Calcutta's business hub, yet the people here will only be able to give you information about destinations within the state. The Government of India Tourist Office, near the city center, gives more of an overall picture (including the state). The staff is friendly to boot.

🚩 Tourist Offices **Calcutta Information Centre** ✉ 1/1 A. J. C. Bose Rd., Central Calcutta ☎ 33/2223-2451. **Government of India Tourist Office** ✉ 4 Shakespeare Sarani, Calcutta, Central Calcutta 700071 ☎ 33/2282-1475, 33/2282-7731, 33/2282-5813. **West Bengal Tourist Office** ✉ 3/2 B. B. D. Bagh E, Calcutta, Central Calcutta 700001 ☎ 33/2248-8271 to 73.

UNDERSTANDING INDIA

INDIA AT A GLANCE

COSMIC CHAOS

BEYOND CURRY

INDIA'S RELIGIONS

BOOKS & MOVIES

CHRONOLOGY

THE HINDI LANGUAGE

INDIA AT A GLANCE

Fast Facts

Type of government: Federal republic
Capital: New Delhi
Administrative divisions: 28 states, 7 union territories
Independence: August 15, 1947
Constitution: January 26, 1950
Legal system: Based on English Common Law
Legislature: Bicameral parliament
Population: 1,045,845,226
Fertility rate: 3.3 children per woman
Language: 18 official regional languages; Hindi spoken by 30% of people, English is is the common and commercial language
Ethnic groups: Indo-Aryan 72%, Dravidian 25%, Mongoloid/other 3%
Life expectancy: Female 64, male 63
Literacy: Total population 52%; male 65.5%, female 37.7%
Religion: Hinduism 81%, Islam 12%, Christianity 2.4%, Sikhism 2%, Buddhism 0.7%, Jainism 0.5%, other (Zoroastrianism, Judaism) 0.4%

India has 2,000,000 gods, and worships them all. In religion other countries are paupers; India is the only millionaire.
—Mark Twain, 1897

Inventions: Decimal system 100 BC, Pi (5th century [bc]), chess, linguistics (4th century [bc]), modern medicine (Ayurveda, 500 [bc]), quadratic equations (11th century), navigation (4000 [bc], Sindh River), time it takes for Earth to orbit the sun (Bhaskaracharya, 5th century)

We owe a lot to the Indians, who taught us how to count, without which no worthwhile scientific discovery could have been made.
—Albert Einstein

Geography & Environment

Land area: 3.3 million square km (⅓ size of the United States)
Coastline: 7,000 km; west, south, and east surrounded by water
Terrain: Upland plain (Deccan Plateau) in south, flat to rolling plain along Ganges River in north-central India, deserts in west, Himalayan mountain range in north
Islands: Andaman and Nicobar Islands in Bay of Bengal, Lakshadweep Islands in Indian Ocean
Natural resources: Coal (fourth largest reserves in the world), iron, ore, manganese, mica, bauxite, titanium ore, chromite, natural gas, diamonds, petroleum, limestone, arable land
Natural hazards: Droughts, flash floods, monsoon floods, thunderstorms, earthquakes
Flora: 45,000 species, including tropical forests in the Western Ghats, alpine vegetation in the Himalayas, evergreen forests in the foothills, desert scrub in the northwest
Fauna: 65,000 species, including endangered snow leopard in northeastern states; ox, camel, sheep, antelope, bears, panda, deer, and tigers in the Himalayas; and crocodiles, elephants, and Asian lions
Environmental issues: Deforestation, rapid industrialization and urbanization, air and water pollution, soil degradation, plastic waste, biodiversity, mining, overfishing, Narmada Valley dams

India is an abstraction. India is no more a political personality than Europe. India is a geographical term. It is no more a united nation than the Equator.
—Winston Churchill, 1931

Economy

Economic reforms have been in place since the 1990s. There are fewer controls on foreign investment and imports, and domestic output is increasingly privatized.

Annual growth: 6%
Inflation: 5.4%
Unemployment: 8.8%
Annual per capita income: $440
GDP: $2.66 trillion
Services: 50%
Agriculture: 25%
Industry: 25%
Work force: 416 million, services 23%, agriculture 60%, industry 17%
Currency: Indian rupee
Exchange rate: 48 rupees per U.S. dollar
Debt: $100.6 billion
Economic aid: $2.9 billion
Major industries: Textiles, chemicals, food processing, steel, transportation equipment, cement, mining, petroleum, machinery, software
Agricultural products: Rice, wheat, oilseed, cotton, jute, tea, sugarcane, potatoes; cattle, water buffalo, sheep, goats, poultry; fish
Exports: $44.5 billion
Major export products: Textile goods, gems and jewelry, engineering goods, chemicals, leather manufactures, iron ore, chemicals, software, support services
Export partners: U.S. 20.9%, U.K. 5.2%, Germany 4.3%, Japan 4.0%
Imports: $53.8 billion
Major import products: Crude oil, machinery, gems, fertilizer, chemicals
Import partners: U.K. 6.3%, U.S. 6.0%, Belgium 5.7%, Japan 3.5%, Germany 3.5%

Political Cimate

During the U.S. bombing of Afghanistan, the dispute with Pakistan over Kashmir became inflamed to the point of an armed stand-off and threat of nuclear war, and the Indian Parliament was attacked. Prime Minister Atal Bihari Vajpayee journeys to Islamabad in January 2004 to participate in peace talks, and flights, trains, and overflights between India and Pakistan restart. Vajpayee's government also reopens talks with the moderate Kashmiri separatist representatives, Hurriyat leaders, after 14 years.

The only alternative to coexistence is codestruction.

—Jawaharlal Nehru,
Prime Minister of India, 1954

Did You Know?

• India is the largest producer of (legal) opium for the pharmaceutical trade.

• India is the world's largest consumer of gold.

• The red dot on women's foreheads, known as a Bindi, was once a symbol of matrimony, but now is primarily decorative.

• India has about 15 phone lines, 3 personal computers, and 64 televisions per 1,000 people.

• During its 10,000-year history, India has never invaded any other country.

• 25% of the population lives below the poverty line.

—Diane Mehta

COSMIC CHAOS

STEP INTO INDIA and you are stepping into the most democratic and the most feudal country in the world.

The marriage of feudalism to freedom is the grandest of India's many paradoxes, and part of its magic and charm. India's people are utterly free, yet the situations of many are fixed in time—at roughly 100 years ago. Contradictions in everyday Indian life may leave you nonplussed on your first trip here. No matter how quickly it charges onto the information superhighway, India remains an enigma, a perplexity, a puzzle you simply can't decipher. And every time you think you know the place, something jolts you out of your complacency.

The essence of contemporary Indian life is that people carry on with whatever activity pleases them, even if it's contrary to the law or the comfort of their neighbors—and neither the authorities nor the bemused neighbors bat an eye. Parades of disgruntled workers with blaring microphones obstruct a city thoroughfare for 12 hours, and life goes on around them. Villagers use a highway running through their hamlet as a place to dry that season's rice crop, and truck drivers simply drop to the shoulder of the road, navigating carefully for miles—even if it means landing in a ditch—to protect the grain. Your toddler irrigates the second-class train compartment you share with six other people, and your fellow passengers smile benignly and keep their feet up.

Any religious activity in India has society's full sanction. Half the populace occupies the main road in prayer; a whole town blushes orange with religious banners. Festivals turn communities upside-down with noise, color, and commotion, but a *tamasha* (spectacle, or happy confusion) is enjoyed by all.

Lunatics stand at crossroads directing imaginary traffic. Cows may even amble into your house. *Dacoits* (highway robbers) are welcomed home, forgiven for a string of crimes, and asked to go into politics. *Sadhus* (ascetic holy men) arrive at your door looking for money. Husbands vanish for years on religious pilgrimages. An employee takes two months off without leave for his uncle's wife's father's brother's funeral. Indians live as they please.

The flip side of this day-to-day liberty is that many Indians' fates are engraved in stone. The poor seldom become rich. The rich seldom become poor. Carpenters seldom become doctors. Widows seldom remarry. Wives seldom divorce alcoholic, do-nothing husbands. Untouchables never, technically at least, become touchable. Castes cannot be changed or ignored. Social mobility, while gaining momentum, is slow.

* * *

THE PEOPLE OF INDIA WILL WARM YOUR HEART. Democratic or feudal, Indians can be touching in their respect, affection, and concern for you, a guest; their families; and their gods. Where else can you see thousands of people trudging barefoot through the night to pay their respects to a deity in a temple?

Indeed, religion in India is no one-day-a-week affair: it's a way of life, the force that moves the country. Faith governs the mind, defines most behavior, and sets much of the country's agenda and calendar. It becomes a personal lullaby or alarm clock for all, with Hindu temple bells tinkling intermittently and a muezzin calling the Muslim faithful to prayer five times a day. So many gods and goddesses are worshipped here that Mark Twain may have understated the case when he wrote in *Following the Equator* that "in religion all other countries are paupers, India is the only millionaire." Hinduism alone accounts for thousands of deities. Wherever you travel in this spiritual land, you'll find monuments with a sacred element: the Taj Mahal, with its carefully inlaid Koranic verses; Khajuraho's Hindu temples, with their astonishing erotic sculptures; the Ajanta Caves, with their serene murals of the Buddha; Catholic churches in Goa, with their Hindu-esque images of Jesus; Jain temples with their *tirthankaras* (perfect souls), whose poses and features resemble those of the Buddha; and even a handful of historic synagogues.

The earliest remnants of an Indian civilization date from at least 3200 BC, and since then the subcontinent's culture and heritage have endured repeated invasions. Some say India's ability to adapt is the very source of her strength and resilience. Persian-influenced Moghul tombs add delicacy to urban skylines. British bungalows anchor Himalayan hill stations and line major avenues. Cuisines, languages, dance and music styles, and artwork and handicrafts vary widely from state to state. There's no American-style homogeneity in India; each region is intensely proud of its own culture.

To be sure, many aspects of this country can be hard for the Westerner to understand. Why, for instance, do India's urban cows prefer to chew on newspaper rather than on rotting garbage (in plentiful supply) or on random patches of grass in a field? India can also be exasperating and exhausting—a difficult place for those accustomed to efficiency and a Western work ethic. To enjoy your stay in India, surrender, take it slow, and don't try to squeeze too much into a short trip. Prepare to give in to the laissez-faire attitude that seems a natural extension of India's fatalistic tendency. The favorite saying in Hindi is, "*Adjust karlenge*" (Shall we adjust? We will adjust.)—accept that what happens is meant to be, or is the will of a supreme authority (frequent Indian explanations). If your flight is canceled, the phone doesn't work, or the fax won't go through, don't fly into a rage. When the slow-motion pace of workers in a government bank or post office is about to drive you crazy, remember that this lack of value for time will have an appealing effect when you venture into rural areas and start wondering why, exactly, you spend so much time in your office back home. You can sit for hours and watch the simplest routines: village women drawing water from a well, or a man tilling the soil with a crude wooden plow. Walking around a deserted ancient city such as Fatehpur Sikri, or watching orthodox Hindus in Varanasi go through their purification or cremation rituals, you'll begin to understand why the art of meditation evolved here. Arrive with the determination to experience India, and make every attempt to adapt; otherwise, this country—which travelers tend to love or hate—might rub you the wrong way.

It helps to be forgiving about some elements of India's inefficiency and overstretched infrastructure. When this country gained independence in 1947, the new democracy chose nonalignment, set up a large national government, and legislated protectionist policies that kept out most foreign products and led almost to economic isolation. The first prime minister, Jawaharlal Nehru, believed protectionism would make India self-reliant and ultimately improve the standard of living, especially for the impoverished. India did move toward self-reliance, but lack of competition stifled the country's own development, with its captive market forced to accept indigenous products that were often substandard or old-fashioned. Until half a decade ago, the dominant car on India's roads was the Ambassador, a British design from the early 1950s with a curvaceous yet bulky chassis: a nostalgic gas-guzzler.

Then, in 1991, a severe debt crisis and a shortage of foreign exchange forced the government to initiate economic reforms, the results of which have been nothing short of astonishing. Having studiously fended off foreign corporations for decades, India is suddenly encouraging them to invest.

* * *

SINCE THE NEW MILLENNIUM BEGAN, India has been booming. This is evident in large cities and throughout the countryside. Advertisements for cell phones, new-fangled appliances, and Internet -service providers are everywhere. Even small towners are into buying fancy washing machines and elaborate sofa sets. Imported-food products, toys, electronic goods, and gadgets of every kind occupy Indian shop shelves. By the end of 2003 the demand for cell phones doubled from what it was at the start of the year. The Indian credit card industry is one of the fastest growing sectors in Asia, and the availability of cheap financing has seen automobile and real estate sales soar. Locally produced Hondas, Mercedes Benzes, Toyotas, Hyundais, Mitsubishis, Chevrolets, Opels, and Audis have finally hit Indian roads. Information technology, bio-technology, and drug companies are growing, and the country's stock market is very attractive; foreign exchange reserves—new investments by multinationals and non-resident Indians—have touched a never before US $104 billion. Newspaper headlines about the lastest outsourcing coup—Indians taking back-office jobs for American companies—are a daily affair as more and more global firms open divisions in India. Pundits predict that the best is yet to come, and that India's huge pool of skilled labor will shortly ensure the country a prominent place in the world economy. And India's alluring one billion people—its domestic market—cannot be overlooked. It's difficult *not* to notice how fast India is modernizing: roads improve, glitzy malls open, and fancy multicuisine restaurants open in cities. There's a new buoyancy to the old-fashioned, exoticized India, which now extends far beyond its many temples and beaches, the ruins left by the many regimes that ruled or colonialized India, or the

drugged-out hippie experience popular with soul-searching foreigners in the 60s and 70s.

India's forward-vault toward a spot in the international sun has affected her once-rigid lifestyle. Cable TV has changed India, as British, American, French, Pakistani, and Chinese commentators relay their own views of the news on satellite channels. Teenagers now dance to MTV India or Channel [V], a frenetic mixture of Indian and Western pop. American cartoons capture the attention of every Indian child with access to the Cartoon Network. Although in the 1990s it was the reruns of *Bold and Beautiful*—with its steamy scenes that were an astounding contrast to India's own "Bollywood" movies (made in Bombay) that were not allowed to include a kiss until a few years ago—that had urban audiences spellbound, these days *Oprah* rules the roost. The fashion channels, National Geographic, and Discovery are also popular.

Although American television sitcoms and programs are still hot, India produces its own mushy soaps and sitcoms. The Indianized programming, full of languid kohl-eyed beauties, soft-cheeked heroes, and fearsome mothers-in-law, is all the rage. While most Indian women still wear saris or the casual, two-piece *salwar-kameez,* many now rush off to their corporate jobs in the latest Western fashions, and many men have become equally label-conscious about everything from the shirts they wear to the foreign liquor they drink. An increasing number of people working in the private sector complain of a new work-related problem: stress.

Yet India still teems with pavement dwellers who call the sidewalk their home. The poor are not shy about approaching strangers, and the Western traveler with a pocketful of rupees might find it hard to resist a plea, especially from a child. Although it's not wrong to give money to beggars, you may want to visit a local school or medical clinic and make a contribution through a responsible adult.

If you get frustrated here, remember that everyone from villagers to wealthy urbanites is equally annoyed by lousy services, and impatient for the kind of infrastructure that most Westerners take for granted. And along with this impatience comes a sense of concern: many Indians lament the arrival of foreign competitors to solve their problems. They worry about the increasing disparity between the haves and have-nots as a result of reforms that have raised inflation. They wonder whether the benefits will really trickle down to the masses. Others wonder if India will succumb to a cultural imperialism that will rob them of their identity, yet increased exposure to the Western world is unlikely to overturn Indian culture. Most imports will be examined, Indianized, and absorbed, the way Coca-Cola is drunk in western Uttaranchal: with salt, red pepper, and *chaat masala* (a tangy spice medley).

All of these issues add dimension to any trip to India, a country in profound transition. Today's India is more than its thousands of monuments; more than its hundreds of ethnic groups; more than its colorful fairs and festivals; more than the birthplace of Hinduism, Buddhism, Jainism, and Sikhism; more than the sum of its parts. India has taken its first steps toward becoming an economic giant. With a population of 1 billion as of 1999, it is a country that can't be ignored.

—Kathleen Cox and Vaihayasi Pande Daniel

BEYOND CURRY

NDIA HAS A GENEROUS, IMPULSIVE CULTURE, and its hugely varied and inventive cuisine is simply a logical extension of that. It would really take a whole series of books to describe the nuances and delights of each regional cuisine that contributes to the stunning variety of Indian food. Entire odes could be written to a plate of light white *idlis* (steamed rice cakes) on a blazing hot summer morning in Madras or a hearty *ghee* (clarified butter)-soaked *paratha* (flat white-flour bread) on a winter's night in Delhi, a semolina-encrusted slice of kingfish on a beer-drenched beach in Goa or a little clay pot of *mishti-doi* (jaggery-sweetened curd) in one of Calcutta's legendary sweetshops.

Like many Asian cuisines, Indian food is probably worst represented in restaurants outside of India. Traveling to India is therefore an incredible opportunity to discover the wonderful fare of the subcontinent, which can be as different from one region to the next as the landscape, or indeed as the people themselves. And, of course, to find a world well beyond the limits of chutney and "curry." The first thing you should realize, as you sip your first *lassi* (sweet or salty yogurt drink) or *elaneer* (tender-coconut water) and leaf through a menu, is that there isn't any such thing as curry. The word is used as a rough synonym for gravy, but curry is not a dish in its own right—it was a purely British invention. Given the sheer diversity and ingenuity of authentic Indian cooking, you'd be wise not to bother wasting time looking for it.

It's easiest to sort out the different types of cuisine India has to offer if you take some of your cues from geography. In the wheat-growing states of the north, where there is a "real" winter, breads, such as *parathas, kulchas, naans,* or *rotis,* are eaten with a variety of rich vegetables, *dal* (lentils), *paneer* (cottage cheese), *mutton* (generally goat, but sometimes lamb), or chicken dishes; in the paddy-growing eastern deltaic region, rice and river-fish are most commonly consumed, the latter flavored strongly with mustard oil. The south is almost a different country: the summer seems to be broken only by the monsoon, and the food is usually lighter, with all kinds of spiced rice dishes; steamed cakes or pancakes, such as plump *idlis,* wafer-thin *dosas* (crisp, crêpelike pancakes made from rice and lentil batter), or hearty *appams* (round rice pancakes with a soft, thick center and a thin, crisp frill); coconut-rich gravies and *porials* (sautéed vegetables), and fantastically spiced seafood.

Although the flavors of Indian cooking can at first be overwhelming, in a few days your palate will probably begin to appreciate the brilliant combinations of spice and the variety of cooking techniques that make one dish different from the next. One of the reasons that the food is so flavorful is the abundance of spices in the market—cardamom, cinnamon, cloves, pepper, mustard, cumin, dry coriander, red chilies, and turmeric are a few of the basics. Fresh flavoring usually comes from ground *adrak* (ginger) and *lasun* (garlic), *hari mirch* (green chilies), *imli* (tamarind), and *karipatta* (spicy leaves added to oil before frying the rest of the ingredients). A walk through an Indian market reveals why ships arrived here—from the time of the ancient Romans (in the first and second centuries AD)—to sail away heavily laden with precious spices. When the Portuguese opened the direct sea route to India around the Cape of Good Hope (Vasco da Gama reached Calicut, in present-day Kerala, in 1498 after he sailed around the Cape of Good Hope), they first sailed to present-day Kerala in search of "Christians and spices!" (source: K. G. Jayne, *Vasco da Gama and H is Succes-*

sors, London, 1910, reprint New Delhi: Asian Educational Services 1997).

A combination of basic spices and flavorings constitutes what is called the masala—once laboriously ground to a paste on a large grinding stone, but now more commonly whisked through a blender. The length of time the masala is roasted or fried contributes hugely to the success of a dish. Adding the rest of the ingredients too early can ruin the flavor completely and give the dish an uncooked taste. Often supplemented with whole spices, sliced onions, chopped tomatoes, and ground ginger and garlic, the masala must cook until oil begins to seep at the surface. Only then is the flavor mature and the dish ready for the rest of its ingredients—usually vegetables, lentils, or meat.

* * *

T'S A COMMON PERCEPTION that all Indian food is chili-hot; this is not necessarily true. Some of the gravies of the north are downright bland, and northern Indians traveling in south India often complain that the food is invariably "too hot!" Most chefs are accustomed to requests from both locals and foreigners to "tone down" the chili, so if you have a sensitive stomach, don't hesitate to make your preference known. A little chili icon next to a menu listing usually indicates that the dish is extraordinarily spicy. Take this seriously. Some regional cuisines are particularly hot: watch out for the Hindu cooking in Hyderabad, where the Andhra-style fried chicken or pickled mango will take the roof off your mouth; the pepper-loaded gravies of Chettinad, a region in Tamil Nadu; and the red fish curry of north Kerala—a lethal concoction!

Although it's a myth that all Hindu cooking is vegetarian, there is certainly a wonderful range of "pure" vegetarian food (which by definition in India includes dairy products but not eggs) available in India, catering to people in communities that eschew meat and people who are vegetarian by choice. Thanks to the large number of vegetarians, vegetables are utilized in some ingenious ways, even in everyday home cooking—in India you're likely to encounter stubborn *karelas* (bitter gourds) so delicately cured and stuffed with amazing spices that their very bitterness has disappeared and they melt in your mouth; ingenious gravies and *porials* concocted from every part of the banana plant from stem to flower; and *baingan* (aubergines, or eggplants) that are carefully roasted over an open fire, then painstakingly skinned and pureed and skillfully combined with spices.

Nonvegetarian food in India can also be spectacular—*gosht* (mutton) and *murgh* (chicken) dominate the north (where you are unlikely to find beef or pork). Whether eaten in a simple roadside *dhaba* (truckers' wayside open-air eatery) or served on silver plates in an upmarket restaurant, these dishes are always hearty and satisfying—so filling they may just require call for a deep siesta afterward. The south occasionally turns up a nifty dish of beef, particularly in Kerala. All along the coasts, the seafood is marvelous, but be prepared for spice, and be wary of shellfish—insist that shellfish be deveined or cleaned properly, since the vein is the intestine and thus full of bacteria. Pork is served par excellence in Coorg and Mangalore (both in Karnataka), and also, most famously, in Goa (Goa sausage is an unholy mixture of meat and spice that's so hot it could well leave you gasping for breath at breakfast).

Texture is as important in Indian cooking as it is in Indian fabric; a typical meal must contain a variety of textures as well as flavors. A rough *roti* is often accompanied by smooth, creamy gravy; a soft dish of *thair-sadam* (curd-rice) by crisp fried *challis* or *appalams*. The consistency of a dish is critical—a *rasam* (pepper-water, the original "mulligatawny") must be as thin as water, whereas a coconut-based gravy is often very thick—usually just short of turning solid. Pity the apprentice chef who turns out a thick lumpy *dosa* or a dense *idli*, or, alas, a hard *roti* or *chapati* (whole-wheat bread).

Some of the refinement of Indian food can be attributed to powerful foreign influence across the centuries. For instance, Muslim governance of the country for long periods of time has left a distinctive mark on Indian cuisine; to visit Delhi or Hyderabad without trying Moghlai or Nawabi cuisine (royal Muslim-style cooking, which is predominantly nonvegetarian and includes spicy kababs, rich gravies, and succulent steam-cooked dishes) would be a great omission. There's a huge variety of spices, shapes, and techniques of kababs—the types of meat are limited usually to mutton and chicken. These kababs are great as appetizers; for the main course leave room for a *dum* dish. *Dum* is a technique that involves sealing the lid of a pan around the sides with dough, and placing charcoal over it, so the food inside cooks slowly and evenly. This traditional method of cooking traps the flavors and results in wonderful succulence.

* * *

THE WEST HAS LEFT ITS MARK AS WELL— the Portuguese strongly influenced Goan cooking. Goan cuisine is so delicious that it has acquired a name for itself across the world, and people come from far and near to sample its *vindalhos* (a very spicy sauce; the name dervies from Portuguese *vin* for vinegar and *alho* for garlic) and *xacutis* (roasted coconut gravy), its assados (roasted meat), and *balchaos* (a heavily spiced chutney). The tiny state also produces a vast number of excellent cooks; it is said that every ship in the merchant navy has on board a Goan cook. The British, for all their time in India, took away more flavors than they left behind—for 50 years after Independence, Indians have all but forgotten the delightfully hybrid Anglo-Indian or "butler" cuisine (served by the faithful white-gloved manservants of the British Raj), popular in colonial times. In the rare

restaurant or Christian home, you might still encounter the stout stews and roasts of an earlier day.

Indians delight in sweets, and you're bound to find a huge diversity of these across the country. Sweets are not necessarily eaten as dessert, but are often offered to guests at Indian's homes, or simply snacked on between meals or eaten at a street stall. Rajasthan and Bengal are particularly famous for sweets—when in Rajasthan, make sure you try *malpoa* (a wafer-thin fried bread roll) and *ghewar* (flavored lentil paste); nobody leaves Bengal without feasting on *sandesh* and *rossogollas* (syrupy milk sweets). The rest of the country isn't far behind: to name just a few classics, try *petha* (a pumpkin sweet) in Delhi, and *unda* (sweetened rice-flour balls) in Kerala. Choosing dessert in a restaurant is not difficult because there are usually few selections, but some of the must-dos include *gulab jamun* (fried milk balls in rose-flavored sugar syrup), *phirnee* (a Muslim pudding), *rasmalai* (a sweet, cream-based dish with spices), *matka kulfi* (Indian ice cream in a small clay pot), and *payasam* (sweet pudding from the south, made with vermicelli or lentils).

In every Indian city there's the usual range of south and north Indian restaurants—go to a few if you must, but try and find the regional specialty places wherever you go. These are often very rewarding and dish up much more than the ubiquitous *tandoori* chicken (chicken cooked in a tandoor, or clay, oven) or mutton *biriyani* (a rice-based goat dish). In Rajasthan, for instance, resist the Punjabi food, and try the local cuisine—the heavily picked vegetables and the rich *lal maas* (mutton); in Bengal, eschew the *dosas* and look for the legendary *hilsa* (a type of river fish); in Karnataka, skip the pizzas and the fried chicken and tuck into the glorious local "meals" (three-course set meal of Indian bread and rice, a variety of sauces and *porials*, and a dessert, all usually served at once on a large partitioned plate); in Goa, coldly ignore the rest of the country, dive into the pork vindalho and the prawn balchao—and drink coconut *feni* (liquor made from coconut sap) rather than scotch.

It's impossible to dissociate the joys of Indian food from the charming hospitality of the country. Anyone you meet in any context—from the businessperson in the next seat on the plane to the little boy you befriend in the bazaar—is likely to invite you home to dinner and to "meet the family" (only accept these invitations if you know the people or if they are friends of friends). A good many of these invitations are genuine, and if you accept, you may well experience the ultimate truth about India—that everybody, rich or poor, usually likes to extend the warmest hospitality. This is perhaps the ultimate savoring of Indian food—every family has its own variation of local recipes and you can be sure that these will be proudly served to special guests.

—Kavita Watsa

HINDUISM, BUDDHISM, JAINISM, AND SIKHISM all came into being in India, even though Buddhism is now mostly practiced elsewhere in Asia. Islam came from outside the country, yet India's large Muslim minority makes up the second-largest Muslim population in the world, after Indonesia's. India's calendar is crowded with festivals, and religion is evident everywhere in Indian life—from politics to art and architecture and the daily activities of millions of devotees.

Hinduism

Hinduism, with its literally countless gods and goddesses, extends back at least three millennia, to the hymns and ritual mantras of the ancient Sanskrit *Vedas*. It's almost impossible to define Hindu tradition in a way that would include all its major variants; the tradition's hallmark, perhaps, is its ability to adapt disparate elements—from local deities to rival philosophical systems—into a recognizably Hindu context. Perhaps the best way to start is with the *Bhagavad Gita,* a marvelous work of religious synthesis set in the midst of battle in the epic *Mahabharata.* Arjuna, one of five brothers who are the epic's heroes, falters on the battlefield, concerned that no good will come of defeating his enemies, who are also his cousins. Arjuna's charioteer, Krishna, an incarnation of the great god Vishnu, reminds him that Hindus believe in reincarnation and their ultimate goal is *moksha,* liberation from the endless cycle of rebirth. There are reasons, Krishna says, for the rivalry that led to the battle, and as a young warrior Arjuna must fulfill his particular duty (*dharma*) through action (*karma*) that is unconcerned with benefits or reward. Fulfilling one's assigned duty and moral obligation to society is a necessary step toward attaining higher religious knowledge (*jnana*) and the ultimate goal of union with God

through devotion (*bhakti*). The *Gita,* as it is called, has a place in the homes of almost all modern Hindus. It does not have canonical authority above that of many other texts, yet it gives in outline a basic set of beliefs that are held in common.

Sacrifice is an essential part of dharma, and central to the practice of the earliest stage of Hinduism embodied in the *Vedas.* An offering to a god blesses the worshipper in return. Beginning with the *Upanishads,* appendixes to the *Vedas,* sacrifice has also been seen in metaphorical terms, as the sacrifice of the baser aspect of one's individuality, so that the individual soul, or spirit (*atman*), can merge with *brahman* (universal consciousness) and allow the realization of moksha.

Some Hindus also practice yoga, a combination of physical culture and meditation practice that is exemplified by the ascetics and sadhus in such places as Varanasi. Yoga (which literally means "yoke" or "union") uses mental and physical discipline to purify the body and rid the practitioner of conscious thought, so he or she can experience a sense of detachment from the realities of the physical world and a higher knowledge (*jnana*). In the *Bhagavad Gita* many other forms of dedicated behavior, such as devotion or disinterested action, are described as forms of yoga.

Strictures underlying dharma and karma also help explain the thousands of castes that divide Hindus, which have been conceptualized in a framework of four segregated rankings: *Brahmins* (priests), *Kshatriyas* (nobles and warriors), *Vaishyas* (tradesmen), and *Shudras* (menial laborers). A fifth grouping, *Panchama,* falls outside this framework: the lowest rung of society. Once commonly known as "untouchables," the people in this class were named *Harijans,* or "Children of God," by Mahatma Gandhi and now prefer to be called *Dalits,* or the "oppressed."

To most Westerners, the caste system seems like cause for revolution, but it's been a complex and even flexible way of ordering society. In ancient India, unlike many other places, there was no all-powerful priestly class, and slavery was rare. There is evidence of considerable shifting in the status of various castes (though not of individuals) in Indian history. Still, historically, for those in the lowest categories, the system was doubtless cruel. Although it is said that they accepted their fate, understanding it as a direct result of their karma in previous births, poetry by lower-caste Hindus from as early as the 12th century explicitly rejects caste. Centuries passed before the untouchables found their way out of exclusion; the catalysts were Mahatma Gandhi and Bhimrao Ramji Ambedkar, a Dalit leader who was one of the principle authors of the Indian Constitution. Despite their frequent disagreements, Gandhi's and Ambedkar's efforts changed the way modern India thinks about caste, and saw to it that discrimination based on caste was legally abolished in 1947. In practice, caste still regulates many aspects of Hindu behavior, such as marriage practices; and caste is emerging as a dominant element of Indian politics, much as ethnicity has done in the United States and other Western political systems.

Hindu Temples. The Hindu temple is filled with symbols. Before the structure is built, a priest traces a *mandala,* which represents the cosmos and determines the placement of all rooms and icons. The center of the temple, called the inner sanctum, represents the egg or womb from which all life originates; this is where the sacred deity resides. The *vimana* (spire) is directly over the inner sanctum, drawing devotees' attention to the heavenly realm and its connection with the sacred deity.

Many festivals take place in the temple's *mandapam,* a front porch that may be an elaborate pillared pavilion or a simple overhang. Water is the agent of purification. Ideally, a temple is constructed near a river or lake, but if no natural water source is available, a large tank is often built, with steps around it for ease of ablutions. Before the devout Hindu worships, he takes a ritual dip to rid himself of impurities. Daily *darshan,* or viewing of the idol—usually performed at sunrise, noon, sunset, and midnight—is imbued with sacred traditions. Ancient rituals combine in an elaborate pageantry that can include such personalized acts as feeding the deity or brushing its teeth, performed with a touching gentleness toward the god's idol. These rituals are often paralleled in worship at home shrines.

Before the priest enters the temple, he takes his sacred dip. The actual darshan takes place during a ceremony known as *arati* (moving flame), which begins with the clanging of a bell to ward off any evil presence and awaken the sleeping deity. Burning camphor sweetens the air as the priest recites mantras and blesses the idol with oils and sandalwood paste. The deity receives offerings of incense (an aroma favored by the gods), vermilion powder, flowers, and decorative platters of food. Lamps of *ghee* (clarified butter) and more camphor are waved before the idol; then the priest blesses the devotees, and often the door to the inner sanctum is closed to let the deity return to its sleeping state. Worshipers are given sweets and other food that has been offered to the deity; this food is known as *prasada* (translated by one scholar as "the edible form of God's grace") and can be taken home for distribution to friends and family members.

The Hindu Pantheon. It has been said that there are 330,000,000 gods in the Hindu pantheon. For the worshipper, this bewildering profusion can be simplified by dedication to a single god or goddess, or by the idea that many gods and goddesses are forms of a few great gods and goddesses. The celebrated German Indianist Max Muller has said that Hindus are not so much pantheists as xenotheists: supreme divinity can be invested serially in the deity being worshiped at any one moment by a particular person.

Through the mythology, iconography, and devotional song that surrounds them, Hindu gods and goddesses are remarkably personalized. This is in striking contrast to the abstract notion of ultimate reality, or brahman, found in the *Upanishads* and subscribed to by many Hindus even as they worship one or more specific anthropomorphized gods and goddesses. A well-known story about Krishna and the *gopis* (the pastoral maidens of Braj, near Agra) illustrates the delight Hindus take in the incarnation of their gods. Visited by a philosopher who expounded the higher truths of atman and brahman, which cannot be seen or described, one gopi said: "It's all very well to know brahman, but can the ultimate reality put its arms around you?"

Most important deities are clustered around the incarnations, families, and mythological associates of two great gods, Vishnu and Shiva, and their female consorts. Brahma, creator of the world and progenitor of all living things, is the third member of the Hindu trinity. (Note that *Brahma,* the deity, is different from *brahman,* universal consciousness, and also from *Brahmin,* the priestly caste.) He is the keeper of cosmic time and a sort of master-of-ceremonies advancing story lines in myths, but he is not actively worshiped. In sculpture and painting, Brahma has four heads and four arms, each holding sway over a quarter of the universe and signifying one of the four *Vedas.* The rosary that he counts in one hand represents time, and his lotus seat represents the earth. Brahma's vehicle is the swan, symbol of the freedom that comes with knowledge. His consort is Saraswati, the goddess of learning.

Shiva is most famously depicted dancing the *tandava* dance of destruction, with which cosmic epochs come to an end so that new ones can be born. Shiva is the yogic ascetic par excellence, wearing snakes as garlands, ashes as ointment, and an animal-skin loincloth, and meditating in the Himalayas from one eon to the next. Paradoxically, however, he is married to Parvati, and his family and love life are celebrated in myth and art. Shiva's non-anthropomorphic form is the *linga,* a phallic symbol that rests in a *yoni,* which represents the womb. Worship of the linga is not explicitly phallic worship; the icon is as much an abstract representation of the axis mundi, the axis on which the world spins, or of how divine presence manifests itself on Earth to Hindus.

Shiva's consorts take many forms, and are often considered aspects of one general goddess (Devi) or a female divine principle (*shakti*). Principle among these is Parvati, the daughter of Himalaya with whom Shiva had two sons: Ganesh, the elephant-headed god of wisdom and prosperity, and Kartikeya, known as Murugan in South India. Other shaktis include Durga, slayer of the buffalo demon, and Kali, sometimes called the goddess of death and depicted in terrible aspect, wearing a garland of skulls and dancing on Shiva's dead body. Shiva's mount, Nandi, the sacred bull, usually guards the entrance to a Shiva temple. Priests who pray to Shiva have three horizontal stripes painted on their foreheads.

The preserver of the universe, Vishnu, has nine known avatars, and a 10th is prophesied. Each successive avatar reflects a step up the evolutionary cycle, beginning with the fish and moving up to the ninth, Buddha, accepted by the all-embracing Hindus as a figure in their own pantheon. Vishnu's most popular incarnations are Rama and Krishna (the sixth and seventh, respectively), the two gods that embody humanity. Vishnu priests have three vertical stripes painted on their foreheads.

Vishnu appears with four arms to signify the four cardinal directions and his command over the realms they encompass. In one hand, he carries the lotus, symbol of the universe; in the other, a conch shell, which represents the evolutionary nature of all existence. The wheel in Vishnu's third hand refers to the rotation of the Earth, with each spoke honoring a specific season of the year. In his fourth hand, Vishnu often holds a weapon to protect him from demons. A common image of Vishnu has him lying on a bed of coils formed by his serpent, Ananta, who symbolizes time; creation will begin when Vishnu wakes up. Vishnu has two consorts: Bhudevi, the goddess of Earth, and Lakshmi, the goddess of wealth and prosperity, who rose from the foam of the ocean like Venus. Lakshmi assumes a different name with each of Vishnu's avatars. When Vishnu is Rama, she's Sita; when he's Krishna, she's Radha.

Rama is the ideal king. As the hero of the Hindu epic *Ramayana*, he slew the 10-headed demon, Ravana, who had kidnapped Sita. This episode, including Sita's rescue by Hanuman, the monkey god and Rama's faithful servant, is celebrated during Dussehra, one of India's most festive holidays. There are three distinct phases in Krishna's mythology. (Some 19th-century Europeans saw this as the conflation of three different pre-Hindu gods into one Hindu one, but this concept is laughable to Krishna's devotees.) In the first phase, Krishna is a playful boy god, stealing butter from his mother's pantry. In the next, he is an amorous, flute-playing cowherd and the focus of a huge body of love poetry. Finally, he is the charioteer of the *Mahabharata,* interceding on behalf of the heroes and offering the wisdom of the *Bhagavad Gita.*

In addition to these major gods, there are countless village and regional gods, sometimes affiliated in myth with the great pan-Indian Hindu gods or goddesses. There are also many goddesses not paired off with male gods or celebrated in Sanskrit texts, such as Shitala Mata, the smallpox goddess (whose worship continues despite the eradication of smallpox). Since medieval times

at least, great devotees from a wide range of castes and communities have also been venerated, and religious communities organized around their teachings.

Jainism

The origins of Jainism (the name comes from the word *jina,* or victor) go back more than 2,500 years. Jainism became a powerful sect during the time of Parsvanatha, who lived in the 8th century BC. At this time Hindu Brahmins dominated much of Indian religious life; like Buddhism, Jainism developed under the patronage of prosperous non-Brahmin communities. Jains revere 24 *tirthankaras* (perfect souls), men believed to have achieved spiritual victory and attained moksha.

Parsvanatha, the 23rd tirthankara, was a prince who renounced his wealth to become an ascetic. He advocated honesty, respect for all life (in the belief that every creature has a soul, and all souls are equal), and *ahimsa* (nonviolence); and he abhorred any form of theft and the ownership of property. The 24th tirthankara was Mahavira (Great Hero), who lived in the 6th century BC, around the time of the historic Buddha. Mahavira also became a monk, and eventually shed his clothes as a sign of devotion and absolute self-denial—to have no possessions. He advocated a life of denial, even though he realized his example would be difficult to follow.

In 300 BC, the original Jain scriptures were finally committed to writing. Jainism also split into two sects: Svetambaras, who wear white clothes, and Digambaras, who practice nudity and believe that women cannot achieve moksha until they are reborn as men. Women, according to Digambaras, are the greatest source of earthly temptation.

Rejecting the existence of a supreme being, Jains follow the model of the 24 tirthankaras. They divide the universe into three worlds, which are divided in turn into numerous levels—devotees want to cross the metaphorical river of existence and obtain freedom for the soul from all three realms. The Jain cosmology is a common motif in religious paintings: the lower world, which normally looks like truncated pyramids, represents various infernos occupied by mortals who have sinned. The middle world, which resembles a disc, contains all nonliving matter and life forms, including human beings who are struggling through the cycle of rebirth and striving for liberation. The upper world, often drum-shape with a bulging middle, is the realm of the gods (souls who have performed good deeds) and spirits. Some paintings also take the shape of the Cosmic Man: the truncated pyramids are turned into legs, the disc becomes the waist, and the upper world extends up from the abdomen. When devout beings who have done good deeds are depicted in the cosmos, their visible serenity increases—based on their good deeds—as they move up each level within the upper world.

The restrictions of Jainism are extensive. Because Jains are supposed to avoid all occupations that involve the destruction of any life form, many Jains are members of the trading community. Few are farmers. Jains are not permitted to eat meat or eggs, and many even shun vegetables and edible roots for fear of ingesting microscopic creatures in the process. They must also take 12 vows that include the practice of ahimsa and meditation, restrictions on the acquisition of wealth and unnecessary belongings, and the commitment to spend some time as a monk or nun.

An important Jain symbol is the swastika, with each appendage representing the four possible stages of birth: life in hell; life as an insect, animal, or bird; human life; and life as a god or demon. The three dots on top of the swastika stand for right faith, right knowledge, and right conduct. The half moon above the dots stands for moksha: the ultimate Jain goal.

Because one vow instructs devotees to contribute generously to the construction and maintenance of temples and animal hospitals, Jain temples are often exquisitely adorned. (The Charity Birds Hospital in Delhi is another remarkable response to this instruction.) Images of the 24 tirthankaras, depicted as ascetics with or without clothes, and usually made of white marble, embellish most Jain temples. Parsvanatha is blue or black, and usually appears with a snake; Mahavira is golden, and usually appears with a lion.

Islam

"There is no God but Allah, and Mohammed is His Prophet"—this is the *shahadah* (religious creed) and most important pillar of the Islamic faith. Islam originated with Mohammed (whose name means "highly praised"), who was born around AD 571 in the Arabian town of Mecca. A series of revelations from Allah, passed on through the Angel Gabriel, instructed Mohammed to preach against the paganism practiced by the Meccans. Mohammed saw himself as a social reformer, advocating a virtuous life in a city where virtue had vanished; but the Meccans saw him as a menace and a threat, and forced him to flee to Yathrib (now Medina).

This flight, in AD 622—which Muslims now call *hijra*—marks the beginning of the era in which Mohammed established the concept of Islam (which means "submission" and "peace") as a way of life. By the time Mohammed died in AD 632, the inhabitants of an expanse stretching from Samarkand (in Uzbekistan) to the Sahara had converted.

With the death of Mohammed, his father-in-law, Abu Bakr, one of the first converts to Islam, became the next ruler and was called *caliph*—"successor of the Prophet." In AD 656, during the reign of the fourth caliph, Ali (the Prophet's nephew and the husband of his daughter Fatima), civil war broke out. Ali moved his capital to Mesopotamia, where he was murdered by Muslim dissidents.

Ali's death signaled the beginning of a period of dissension between the traditionalists, Sunnis, who followed the orthodox teaching and example of the Prophet, and Ali's supporters, who claimed Ali's right to the caliphate based on his descent from the Prophet. In time, Ali's supporters broke away from the Sunnis and formed a sect known as the Shia, or Shiites.

Originally political in nature, the differences between the Sunnis and Shiites took on theological overtones. The Sunnis retained the doctrine of leadership by consensus. After Syrians massacred Hussain, Ali's son, at Karbala, in Iraq, the Shiites strengthened their resolution that only Mohammed's rightful heirs should rule. They modified the *shahadah*: "There is no god but Allah; Mohammed is the Prophet of God, and Ali is the Saint of God."

The concept of Islam means submission to Allah, or God—who is invisible yet omnipresent. To represent Allah in any form is a sin, thus the absence of icons in mosques and tombs. Every bit of decoration—often fashioned out of myriad tiny gems—is limited to inscriptions of the Koran, Muslims' holy scripture, and the names of Mohammed and the first four Caliphs, who were part of the first generation of followers.

Muslims believe that Allah has existed throughout time, but that humans had strayed from his true teaching until Mohammed set them straight. Islam has concepts similar to those of Judaism or Christianity: guardian angels, the day of judgment, the general resurrection, heaven and hell, and the eternal life of the soul. Muslims also follow a strict code of ethical conduct that encourages generosity, tolerance, and respect and forbids adultery, gambling, usury, and the consumption of pork and alcohol. Other Muslim duties are known as the five pillars of the faith: the recitation of the shahadah; *salat* (daily prayer); *zakat* (alms); *siyam* (fasting); and *haj* (pilgrimage). The believer must pray to Allah five times daily, preceding each occasion by performing ablutions. Men pray at a mosque under a prayer leader whenever possible, and are recommended to do so on Friday. Women are also recommended to attend public worship on Friday; men and women are segregated during prayer.

The ninth month of the Muslim calendar, Ramadan—in which Mohammed received his revelations—is a month of required fasting from sunrise to sunset for all but the weak, pregnant women, young children, and travelers (who make up the days of fasting later). In addition to food, drinking, smoking, and sexual intercourse are prohibited during daylight hours.

A Muslim is supposed to make the haj to the Great Mosque in Mecca once in his life to participate in 10 days of special rites, held during the 12th month of the lunar calendar. While on the haj, the pilgrim wears an *ihram* (seamless white robe) to symbolize equality and devotion to Allah and abstains from sexual relations, shaving, and cutting his hair and nails. Women are also supposed to go on haj; women on pilgrimage do not cover their hair. The returning pilgrim is entitled to the honorific "hajji" before his name and a turban carved on his tombstone.

The word mosque, or *masjid*, means "a place of prostration." Mosques are generally square in shape; built of stone, clay, or brick; and centered on an open courtyard surrounded with *madrasas* (schools) for students of the Koran. After the *muezzin* (crier) sings the call for prayer from the minaret (tower), the faithful line up in rows behind the *imam* (one who has studied the Koran). The imam stands in the sacred part of the masjid facing the *mihrab*, a niche in the wall that indicates the direction of Mecca. When the imam prays, the mihrab—an ingenious amplifier—bounces the imam's voice back to the devotees. In a mosque, only prayers are heard and prostrations made; ceremonies connected with birth, marriage, and death occur elsewhere.

Popular Islam in India involves not only prayer at home and in the mosque, but worship at the graves of great religious teachers of the past. On the anniversaries of the saints' deaths—the *urs,* or time of ascent to heaven—great fairs attract pilgrims, sometimes of many faiths, from all over the country.

Sikhism

The founder of Sikhism, Guru Nanak, was born into a Hindu family in 1469, at a time when the Lodi sultanate—a Muslim dynasty from Afghanistan—ruled his North Indian homeland. From an early age, he railed against the caste system, the corruption of Hindu priests, their superstitious beliefs, and their unwieldy family of gods. In his poems and teachings, Guru Nanak urged egalitarianism based on love and devotion to a single, non-incarnate divinity called the Wahi Guru, conceived as the embodiment of truth, goodness, and uniqueness. (These three words form the common Sikh greeting "Sat Sri Akal.")

Nanak's view of Sikhism, recorded in the *Adi Granth,* upheld the Islamic idea that the goal of religion was union with God, who dwelled within the soul. He believed that, through meditation and dharma (Hindu concepts), devotees could rid themselves of impurities, free themselves from the endless cycle of rebirth, and attain eternal bliss. For Hindus at the bottom of society, Sikhism offered equality and tolerance; they gladly converted, becoming Sikhs—disciples.

During the early years of the Mogul Empire, Sikhism flourished without interference until Emperor Jahangir assumed the throne. Resenting the Sikhs' rejection of Islam, Jahangir ultimately tortured and murdered the fifth guru. When Aurangzeb, the next emperor, revealed his own ruthless intolerance, Gobind Singh, the 10th and final guru, forged the Sikhs into a martial community that he called the *khalsa* (pure). Gobind Singh instructed every Sikh man to observe and wear the five *kakkari* (visible symbols): *kesh* (uncut hair and beard), *kachh* (boxer shorts), *kara* (a steel bangle), *kanga* (a wooden comb), and *kirpan* (a dagger). All Sikh men also assumed the surname Singh, meaning "lion" (though not all Singhs are Sikhs), and Sikh women adopted the name Kaur, meaning "lioness" or "princess." Members of the khalsa were to follow a strict code of conduct that forbade the use of alcohol and tobacco and advocated a life of meditation and courage.

Buddhism

Siddhartha Gautama was born into a princely family in Lumbini, near the India–Nepal border, around 563 BC. Upon encountering suffering during his first venture outside the palace as a young man, he renounced his privileged status—an act called the Great Renunciation—to live as an ascetic. He then entered a lengthy meditation that led to his Great Enlightenment, or nirvana.

Transformed, Siddhartha went to Sarnath, India (near Varanasi), and preached his revolutionary sermon on the *dharma* (truth), also called "The Setting in Motion of the Wheel of Truth or Law." His discourse set forth his Four Noble Truths, which define the essence of Buddhism: (1) Life is connected to suffering, (2) a suffering that arises from greed, insatiable desires, and the self-centered nature of humans; (3) once a person understands the cause of her suffering, she can overcome it by following (4) the Eightfold Path.

The Eightfold Path includes right views and right aspirations, which lead to wisdom. Right speech, right behavior, right means of livelihood, and right efforts to follow the path to salvation relate to proper and intelligent conduct. Right meditation and right contemplation bring nirvana (supreme bliss).

Siddhartha Gautama became the Buddha (Enlightened One), or Sakyamunni (Sage of the Sakya clan), and his faith became Theravada Buddhism, a religion of compassion and reason in which images were not worshipped, the existence of a permanent soul (*atman* to Hindus) was denied, and the authority of the Hindu *Vedas* was rejected. In the 1st century AD a second school, Mahayana Buddhism, was formed and introduced the concept of the *bodhisattva,* the enlightened being who postpones his own nirvana to help others. Unlike Theravadans—who prayed only before symbols, such as the Buddha's empty throne or his footprints—Mahayanists also worshiped before depictions of the various Buddhas, other gods and goddesses, and revered bodhisattvas. Over time, Mahayana Buddhism divided into subsects, based on differences in philosophical systems or ritual practices.

Ironically, Buddhism did not survive as a popular religion in India after its classical period. This is partly because of Hindu thinkers' response to the Buddhist challenge, embodied in works like the *Bhagavad Gita;* partly because increasingly sophisticated philosophy and esoteric ritual held little attraction for lay followers; and partly because major Buddhist institutions were destroyed by Muslim iconoclasts. Although Indian teachers brought Buddhism to Tibet and China—and it spread from there—Buddhist remnants in India are limited mainly to such monuments as the Great Stupa at Sanchi (Madhya Pradesh), the Ajanta caves, and sculptures in major museums. Nevertheless, Buddhist artworks are among India's great treasures, evolving over time from stupas holding relics of the Buddha to elaborate temple structures depicting scenes from the life of the Buddha and episodes in his past lives. Later tantric Buddhist art, which continued to flourish in Nepal and Tibet, includes a large pantheon of past and future Buddhas, goddesses, Bodhisattvas, and historical teachers of the faith.

Two major communities still practice Buddhism in India. Tibetans in India include those in Himalayan areas such as Ladakh, which were closely connected to Tibet, and some 100,000 refugees who fled Tibet after the Chinese took over in 1951 and are now dispersed in various parts of India. The Dalai Lama, head of the Gelugpas, the largest Tibetan Buddhist sect, now lives in Dharamsala, Himachal Pradesh, where a sizable Tibetan community works to preserve their traditions and the welfare of the refugee community. The other main Buddhist group, sometimes called neo-Buddhist, was founded by the Dalit leader Bhimrao Ramji Ambedkar, who urged fellow untouchables to abandon Hinduism in favor of Buddhism because the latter does not recognize caste.

—Kathleen Cox and Andy McCord

BOOKS & MOVIES

Nonfiction

The best general surveys of Indian history are John Keay's *India: A History* and Stanley Wolpert's *New History of India* (6th ed.), with Keay focusing more on antiquity. Three sparkling introductions to the modern nation are *India: From Midnight to the Millennium,* by Shashi Tharoor, *India Unbound: From Independence to the Global Information Age,* by Gurcharan Das, and *The Idea of India,* by Sunil Khilnani.

Mark Tully's books, including *No Full Stops in India* and *India in Slow Motion* (with Gillian Wright), combine travel with social analysis. William Dalrymple's *The Age of Kali* is a collection of incisive essays on aspects of the modern Subcontinent, as are Gita Mehta's *Snakes and Ladders* and Octavio Paz's *In Light of India,* by the Nobel Laureate and former Mexican ambassador. Elisabeth Bumiller's *May You Be the Mother of a Hundred Sons* is an American reporter's take on the varied lives of Indian women. *Freedom at Midnight,* by Larry Collins and Dominique Lapierre, is a spellbinding account of India's break from Britain; *City of Joy,* by the same authors, is a powerful portrait of Calcutta. Nirad Chaudhuri's classic *Autobiography of an Unknown Indian* recounts the Bengali author's youth in colonial India, with insightful descriptions of Indian customs, castes, and relations with the British. James Cameron's *An Indian Summer* is a glib but loving memoir by a British journalist who lived in India during and after the Raj. Sudha Koul's *The Tiger Ladies* recalls life in beautiful Kashmir before it became a war zone in the late 1980s. While not his best writing, *India: A Million Mutinies Now* is the most optimistic of Nobel Laureate V. S. Naipaul's three books on India.

The classic works on early India are A. L. Basham's *The Wonder That Was India* and Romila Thapar's *History of India,* Volume I. India's first prime minister, Jawaharlal Nehru, was a peerless writer and left some inspiring works including his autobiography and *The Discovery of India,* a unique rendition of the country's history. William Dalrymple's *White Mughals* illuminates the bicultural lives of British traders in Hyderabad during the 18th century. Among the great Sanskrit texts, the best translations of the *Bhagavad-Gita* are Barbara Stoler Miller's and Eknath Easwaran's; Easwaran has also translated the sacred *Upanishads.* The epics known as the *Mahabharata* and *Ramayana* are available in countless translations, the most popular of which are Krishna Dharma's and Eknath Easwaran's. Classical Hindu myths are retold in prose form in *Gods, Demons, and Others,* by the master writer R. K. Narayan, and more recently in *Ka,* by Roberto Calasso. Diana Eck's *Banaras: City of Light* is an engaging profile of the holy city.

Stuart Cary Welch's *India: Art and Culture, 1300–1900* is a lavishly illustrated catalog by a great connoisseur, while Vidya Dehejia's *Indian Art* is a good textual survey. *Myths and Symbols in Indian Art and Civilization,* by Heinrich Zimmer (edited by Joseph Campbell) is helpful to the art or mythology buff. The famously erotic *Kama Sutra* has been freshly translated by Wendy Doniger and Sudhir Kakar. The colorful minibook *India and the Mughal Dynasty,* by Valérie Berinstain, makes a great pocket companion in much of North India, and William Dalrymple's *City of Djinns* brings Mughal Delhi to life. Royina Grewal's *In Rajasthan* is an excellent travelogue by an Indian. For ravishing photographs see *A Day in the Life of India,* people going about their business; *Living Faith,* Dinesh Khanna's renditions of sacred spaces and scenes; *India Modern,* a contemporary treatment of traditional buildings and crafts; and any of several collections by Raghubir Singh, Raghu Rai, and Henri Cartier-Bresson.

Fiction

Indian novelists took the literary world by storm in the 1980s and '90s, and the flood has not abated. Vikram Seth's mesmerizing *A Suitable Boy* portrays middle-class life in the 1950s through a timeless story of young love. Rohinton Mistry's novels center on the Parsi community of Bombay; his masterpiece, *A Fine Balance,* is an extraordinary study of the human condition as experienced by a motley group in the 1970s, and *Family Matters* and *Such a Long Journey* weave poignant tales of family ties and personal misfortune. Another fine Bombay novel, Manil Suri's *The Death of Vishnu,* features an old homeless man whose neighbors squabble over the best way to deal with him. *Love and Longing in Bombay,* by Vikram Chandra, is a collection of short stories with a single narrator. *Midnight's Children,* by Salman Rushdie, is the epic tale of a boy who was born the moment India gained independence. Rushdie's *The Moor's Last Sigh,* narrated by a young man of mixed heritage, paints incomparably sensual portraits of Bombay and Cochin. Arundhati Roy's *The God of Small Things,* set in 1960s Kerala, tells a disturbing story of brother-and-sister twins raised by a divorced mother. Roy has since become a political activist in New Delhi. David Davidar's *The House of Blue Mangoes* is a South Indian family saga. Amit Chaudhuri's short novel *A Strange and Sublime Address* (published in the United States with Chaudhuri's Freedom Song) is a gorgeous story of a 10-year-old boy's stay with relatives in Calcutta. Anita Desai's *Fasting, Feasting* concerns an Indian family whose son goes off to college in the United States. Khushwant Singh's *Delhi* is a bawdy but ultimately moving romp through Delhi's tumultuous history. *The Impressionist,* a picaresque novel by Hari Kunzru, shows the adventures of a half-English, half-Indian boy in both countries in the early 20th century. Upamanyu Chatterjee's *English, August* is a funny account of a rookie in the Indian Civil Service.

Bengali poet and Nobel Laureate Rabindranath Tagore wrote some enduring novels including *Gora* and *Home and the World*; to read his poetry in translation, look for *Gitanjali.* Rudyard Kipling's *Kim* is still one of the most intimate works of Western fiction on India; in E. M. Forster's *A Passage to India,* the conflict between Indians and their British rulers is played out in the story of a man accused of rape. Ahmed Ali's 1940 novel *Twilight in Delhi* gives a poignant account of 19th-century urban Muslim society.

Not all good Indian writing has been published in the West. In India you'll find plenty of English-language fiction and nonfiction on the issues of the day. Reading fiction from other languages is another way to penetrate India's regional cultures; top writers available in translation include Sunil Gangopadhyay (Bengali), Nirmal Verma (Hindi), Intizar Husain and Ismat Chugtai (Urdu), U. R. Ananthamurty (Kannada), Vaasanthi and Ambai (Tamil), and Paul Zacharia (Malayalam).

Films

Indian films can be roughly divided into Bollywood fare—musical romances from Bombay's prolific industry—and independent art films. A prime example of classic costume melodrama is *Aan* (1952), directed by Mehboob, a story of royalty tamed by peasants. The late Satyajit Ray adapted and directed the internationally known *Pather Panchali* (1955), *Aparajito* (1956), and *The World of Apu* (1959), a breathtaking trilogy depicting poverty and tragedy in the life of a Bengali boy. *Salaam Bombay* (1988), directed by Mira Nair, is a heartbreaking fictionalized exposé of Bombay's homeless and slum children. Roland Joffe's *City of Joy* (1992), starring Patrick Swayze, is based on Dominique Lapierre's book about Calcutta. Deepa Mehta's best-known films are *Fire* (1996), in which two beautiful but neglected sisters-in-law turn to each other for love, and *Earth* (1999), an adaptation of Bapsi Sidhwa's novel on the partition of India and Pakistan, *Cracking India.* Mira Nair's latest film, *Monsoon Wedding* (2001), now a Broadway musical, takes on several contemporary issues in the context of a high-class Punjabi wedding. Although not set in India, Gurinder Chadha's *Bend It Like Beckham* (2002) is worth watching for its funny, life-affirming portrait of a soccer-loving Punjabi girl in London. Aparna Sen's *Mr. and Mrs. Iyer* (2002) won accolades for its sensitive treatment of interfaith relations.

Bollywood's exuberant musicals are now widely available on DVD. Recent blockbusters include *Kal Ho Naa Ho* (2003), which places a fetching Bollywood cast in photogenic New York; *Dil Chahta Hai* (2001), a romantic comedy set in Bombay; and *Lagaan* (2001), featuring a 19th-century cricket match with the British.

Films set in India by Western directors are numerous. The excellent *Shakespeare Wallah* (1965), written by Ruth Prawer Jhabvala and James Ivory and directed by Ivory, fictionalizes the experience of the Kendal family's traveling theater troupe. Ivory's *Heat and Dust* (1982), an adaptation of Jhabvala's novel, re-creates the past through a young woman's discovery of a series of her grandmother's letters. *Phantom India* (1969), directed by Louis Malle, is an epic documentary of Indian life. Richard Attenborough's *Gandhi* (1982) traces the adult life of the leader of India's independence movement. *A Passage to India* (1984), based on E. M. Forster's novel, was directed by David Lean. *The Jewel in the Crown* (1984), an epic TV series based on part of Paul Scott's *Raj Quartet,* features a romance between a British woman and an Indian man in the waning years of British rule.

–Christine Cipriani

CHRONOLOGY

ca. 2 million BC	First human occupation of area that is now India.
7000 BC	Earliest evidence of agricultural activity.
2500 BC	Indus Valley (also called Harappan) Civilization. Uniformly built cities were spread across several thousand miles of territory in a civilization that compared in size and accomplishment to ancient China or Mesopotamia. Its script, a series of symbols found of sets of clay seals, remains undeciphered.
1750 BC	Decline of Harappan civilization for which many theories have been advanced, including invasion and ecological disaster. The existence of this civilization was rediscovered in the 1920s.
1500–1200 BC	Composition of the Rigveda, early religious texts of Vedism—the precursor of all modern South Asian religions, including Hinduism, Buddhism, and Jainism.
ca. 1000 BC	Composition of other Vedas, including Sama Veda, Yajur Veda, and Atharva Veda.
ca. 1500–1000 BC	Evolution of caste (*varna*) system.
ca. 600 BC	Composition of the Upanishads, early Brahmanical religious texts.
ca. 600 BC	Life of Vardhamana, or Mahavira, the 24th *Tirthankara* and one of the most revered spiritual leaders of Jainism.
ca. 563–483 BC	Life of Siddhartha Gautama, the Buddha, founder of Buddhism. He was born in what is now Nepal, and did his teaching in what is now eastern India.
ca. 500 BC	Composition of the epic Ramayana had started by this date. This story of the perfect rulership of the King Rama, avatar of Lord Vishnu and of his quest to rescue his wife Sita from the demon king Ravana, is still considered by many to depict a model of governance and personal behavior for many Hindus.
ca. 400 BC	Composition of Panini's grammar of Sanskrit, which many still consider to be the most complete and accurate grammar of any language ever written.
ca. 300 BC	Earliest written records from southern India, including Tamil language collections.
326 BC	Invasion of Panjab by Alexander of Macedonia (Alexander the Great).
321–185 BC	Mauryan Empire extended over most of modern India and Pakistan and parts of Afghanistan. Emperors were Chandragupta, Bindusara, and, most famously, Ashoka, whose inscriptions on rocks and pillars encouraging Buddhist practice can still be seen throughout India. This was the largest territorial state in South Asia prior to the British Empire.
ca. 240 BC	Earliest surviving examples of Brahmi script, from which all indigenous writing systems of India are evolved.

ca. 100 BC– AD 400	Construction of Ajanta and Ellora cave temples in western India.
AD 319–467	Gupta Empire in North India. Coincides with what is considered the "Classical" period of Hindu civilization, with great achievements in the arts and literature.
ca. 400	The epic Mahabharata takes on its final form, although its composition was started almost 900 years earlier.
ca. 450	Life of Sanskrit poet and playwright Kalidasa, who wrote, among other works, Shakuntala and Meghaduta. He is considered the greatest writer of Sanskrit plays and poetry.
ca. 600	Earliest construction of sculptures and stone temples at Mahabilipuram in Tamil Nadu.
700	Muslim traders begin to visit the west coast of India.
ca. 711	Muhammad bin Qasim conquers Indus delta region, establishing first Muslim rule in South Asia.
900–1100	Construction of temples at Khajuraho.
997–1030	Raids from Afghanistan into India by Mahmud Ghazni, destroying Hindu temples and sowing the seeds of antipathy between members of the two faiths.
ca. 1206– 1526	The Delhi Sultanate, the first modern era empire centered on Delhi.
ca. 1253– 1325	Life of Amir Khusrau, preeminent Persian poet of India.
ca. 1440– 1518	Life of Hindi syncretist poet Kabir of Varanasi.
ca. 1469– 1539	Life of Guru Nanak, the founder of the Sikh religion.
1498	Arrival of Portuguese Vasco da Gama in Goa, the first direct sailing from Europe to India around the southern tip of Africa.
ca. 1498– AD 1550	Life of Mirabai, poet of Rajasthan. Born into nobility, she left to become a mendicant and devotee of Krishna. Two hundred of her poems are verified as hers, but there may be as many as 1,300. They were originally written in Gujarati but were quickly translated into and sung in many languages.
1526	Battle of Panipat won by Babur, signaling the beginning of the Mughal Empire.
ca. 1532– 1623	Life of Tulsidas, composer of the still most popular Hindi version of the epic Ramayana, the *Ramcharitmanas*.
1600	Charter of East India Company granted by Queen Elizabeth in London for it to execute trade in India, Southeast Asia, Japan, and China.
1608	First landing of an East India Company ship in India, in the western city of Surat, where they established a "factory," or trading post.

1632–49 Taj Mahal built to fulfill a promise Mughal Emperor Shah Jahan made to his wife: to honor her by constructing a beautiful tomb for her. Craftsmen were brought in from around western Asia to execute the beautiful stonework of the structure.

ca. 1650 Construction of Red Fort in Delhi.

1707 Death of Aurangzeb, the last great Mughal Emperor, signaling the beginning of the demise of the Mughal Empire. It would not formally cease to exist until 1857.

1757 Battle of Plassey, at which a British East India Company-supported army defeated a Bengali general, and the Company directly controlled a part of India for the first time.

1765 Mughal Emperor grants the East India Company the right to collect tax revenue from Bengal, Bihar, and Orissa; this is the first Company administration of Indian territory.

ca. 1797– Life of Mirza Ghalib, preeminent Urdu poet of India, who was also
1869 renowned for his skill in Persian poetry and for his personal letters— still widely read.

1857 The Indian Mutiny. Indian troops of the British East India Copmany mutinied first, in the North Indian city of Meerut, and the revolt spread from there to most of the other cities of North India, although it centered on Delhi, the capital of the dying Mughal Empire. The immediate cause for the troops to revolt was their belief that the British were attempting to foist on them gun cartridges greased with pig and cow fat, which the troops were required to bite in preparation for their use. Such use would have violated the religious beliefs of both Hindus and Muslims. Long-term causes included East India Company misrule, including the annexation of the previously independent North Indian kingdom of Awadh (capital Lucknow) in 1856. It took a year for the British to reestablish their control over the territories.

1858 End of fighting between rebels and British army. The British took revenge on Indians, including blowing mutineers from cannons. There were also hangings and general looting of many cities.

1858 Abolition of the East India Company and imposition of direct British rule over India as a result of the hostilities of 1857–58.

1869 Mohandas Karamchand (Mahatma) Gandhi born in Gujarat in western India.

ca. 1880– Life of Prem Chand, author of such novels as *Godan,* which deplored
1936 social inequalities in India. Prem Chand is considered the father of modern Hindi literature.

1885 Establishment of Indian National Congress. At the time it was devoted to improvement of British rule in India, it became the leading political party in India, through Independence in 1947 and until the mid-1990s.

ca. 1838–94 Life of Bankim Chandra Chatterjee, author whose works include early nationalist literature, such as *Anandamath,* which provided the lyrics for India's nationalist anthem before independence.

1876 Birth of Muhammad Ali Jinnah, founder of Pakistan.

1899–1950 Life of Bibhutibhushan Bandyopadhyay, author whose stories were made into film in the 1950s by Satyajit Ray.

1906 Establishment of Muslim League, the organization that would eventually lead the movement for the creation of Pakistan.

1913 Rabindranath Tagore awarded Nobel Prize for literature for his English transation of Gitanjali.

1913 First Indian feature film, *Raja Harishchandra,* by Dadasaheb Phalke. India currently has the world's largest film industry.

1915 Gandhi returns to great acclaim to India from South Africa.

1919 Jallianwalla Bagh massacre, in which a British army regiment killed hundreds of unarmed people gathered in a city park in the Panjabi city of Amritsar, leads to first significant calls for complete independence from Britain for India.

1920–22 First of Gandhi's *Satyagraha* ("Truth Force") campaigns.

1930 Gandhi courts arrest by leading the Salt March, defying British colonial rules against making untaxed salt.

1937 Indian National Congress sweeps elections for provincial legislatures, shuts out Muslim League from governing.

1940 Lahore Declaration of the Muslim League calls, for the first time, for the establishment of a separate state upon gaining independence from Britain for the Muslims of South Asia.

1947 Independence attained. Pakistan created. Jawaharlal Nehru becomes first Prime Minister of independent India, leading the country through the difficult process of establishing democratic rule in a post-colonial society. He had been a major figure in the Indian National Congress leading up to Independence. He served until his death in 1964. Muhammad Ali Jinnah became the first Prime Minister of independent Pakistan, until his death in 1948.

1948 Assassination of Gandhi on January 30 by a Hindu fanatic.

1948 Jinnah, Pakistan's first Prime Minister, dies on September 11.

1948 First Indo-Pakistan war over Kashmir.

1953 Promulgation of Indian Constitution, India declared a republic, celebrated on January 26 as Republic Day.

1955 Release of Pather Panchali, Satyajit Ray's first film. This is the first Indian "art" film to have success at home and abroad.

1956 Linguistic reorganization of states. The old colonial "presidency" of Madras is split up into the current Indian states of Tamil Nadu, Andhra Pradesh, Kerala, and Karnataka, according to language groupings. This establishes the pattern by which new states will be created, including Maharashtra, Gujarat, Punjab in the 1960s, and Uttaranchal, Jharkhand, and Chattisgarh in 2000.

1962 India-China war.

1964 Death of Jawaharlal Nehru.

1965 Second Indo-Pakistan war.

1966 Indira Gandhi becomes Prime Minister.

1971 Third Indo-Pakistan war, secession of Bangladesh from Pakistan.

ca. 1971 Indira sweeps national elections after success of Indian military in creation of Bangladesh.

1974 First Indian nuclear test.

1975–77 Emergency rule declared by Mrs. Gandhi—only national cessation of democratic government in independent India's history.

1977 Indira Gandhi calls elections, is resoundingly voted out of office.

1977–81 Government by Janata Party, the first non-Congress government in India's history. It falls apart due to inter-coalition squabbling. One of the members of the Janata coalition, the Bharatiya Jan Sangh, evolved into the Bharatiya Janata Party, the current ruling party as of 2001.

1981 Indira Gandhi elected Prime Minister.

June 1984 Raid on Sikh Golden Temple (called "Operation Bluestar" by the Indian Government) in Amritsar to move armed Sikh militants out of the temple complex. Many are killed, and Sikhs the world over are outraged at what they perceived to be a desecration of their holiest site.

October 1984 Assassination of Indira Gandhi by her Sikh bodyguards in retaliation for Operation Bluestar.

1987 Indian Peacekeeping Force (IPKF) becomes embroiled in conflict in Sri Lanka, earning the enmity of both sides, but especially of the Liberation Tigers of Tamil Eelam (LTTE).

1989 Rajiv Gandhi assassinated during election campaign by sympathizer of LTTE for actions of Indian military in Sri Lanka.

1991 Economic liberalization undertaken in face of balance of payments crisis caused by oil price rise.

1990s Indian computer and software industry offers hope that India can change its economic status and follow its East Asian neighbors' model of prosperity. Still, this industry constitutes only a tiny percentage of economic activity and employment in the overwhelmingly agricultural economy.

1992 Destruction of Babri Masjid mosque in North Indian city of Aydohya after years of agitation by the Bharatiya Janata Party to have it turned into a Hindu Temple. Many claimed this mosque was built on the site of the birthplace of Lord Rama, hero of the Hindu epic *Ramayana,* and hence its destruction would allow restoration of a previously existing temple. Ensuing violence kills thousands nationwide.

Mid-1990s Wave of English-language novels by Indian writers hits the literary world, including *God of Small Things,* by Arundhati Roy.

1996   Election of Bharatiya Janata Party Prime Minister Atal Bihari Vajpayee, whose government lasts for 11 days. Coalition lead by Congress Party takes over until 1998.

1998   Election of Bharatiya Janata Party Prime Minister, government still in office.

1998   Indian and Pakistani nuclear tests. Economic sanctions instigated by United States against both nations.

May–July   Fighting between India and Pakistan in Kargil. Pakistani "irregulars"
1999   cross the line of control between Indian- and Pakistan-controlled Kashmir, and take posts that were abandoned by Indian troops during the winter. Fighting lasts for almost three months, and eventually Pakistanis withdraw under pressure from the international community, particularly the United States.

1999   October Coup in Pakistan by Pervez Musharraf removes elected Prime Minister Nawaz Sharif.

2000   Bill Clinton makes first visit by U.S. president to India in 20 years, signaling new relationship between the world's largest democracies.

2001   July summit between Indian Prime Minister Atal Bihari Vajpayee and Pakistani leader Pervez Musharraf ends unsuccessfully after three days of talks. Skirmishes in Kashmir heat up during U.S. bombing of Afghanistan.

2002   Tension heats up over the disputed state of Jammu and Kashmir. In January, India test-fires its nuclear-capable missile Agni in eastern India. In February, a train full of Hindu pilgrims returning from a visit to the holy site of Ayodhya, was set on fire in Godhra, Gujarat. Subsequently, Hindu-Muslim riots, the worst riots in India in a decade, break out in the state of Gujarat. In the bloodshed more than 800 die. In May, Pakistan test-fires its own nuclear-capable missile, Ghauri. Also in May, a moderate Kashmiri is shot dead by militants in Srinagar, Kashmir, and elections are held in September. After elections, the Mufti Mohammed Sayeed government brings the region some tentative peace and kick-starts tourism in the region.

2003   As a result of peace efforts by the new government in Kashmir, Indian tourists venture back to the Dal Lake and Gulmarg ski slopes. A historic cross-border trade agreement results from Prime Minister Atal Bihari Vajpayeeís visit to Beijing in June, bringing some accord to India and China over the status of Tibet and Sikkim state. In August, two bomb blasts occur simultaneously in Bombay, killing nearly 50 people. In November, India and Pakistan agree to restart a dialogue.

2004   Prime Minister Atal Bihari Vajpayee journeys to Islamabad in January to participate in Indo-Pak (India-Pakistan) peace talks. Flights, trains, and overflights between India and Pakistan restart. Vajpayeeís government also reopens talks with the moderate Kashmiri separatist representatives, Hurriyat leaders, after 14 years. Ladakh opens to travelers.

—Keith Snodgrass

THE HINDI LANGUAGE

	English	Hindi	Pronunciation
Basics			
	Hello/goodbye (standard greeting in India)	namaste	nah-mas-tay
	Hello/goodbye (Muslim greeting)	Salaam ale kum	sah-laam ah-lay come
	Hello/goodbye (Sikh greeting)	sat sree akaal	sat sree ah kahl
	My name is__.	Mera nam __.	may-rah nahm __.
	What's your name?	Ap ka nam kya hai?	Ahp kah nahm kee-ya heh?
	Yes	hah[n]	hah[n]
	No	nahee[n]	nah-ee[n]
	Thank you	dhanyavad	dhun-yuh-vahd (Hindu)
		shukreeya	shuk-ree-yah (Muslim)
	Mr.	shree	shree (Hindu)
	Mr. (preferred among Urdu speakers, and more commonly used in India)	sahib	sah-yeeb (Muslim)
	Mrs.	shreemati	shree-mah-tee (Hindu)
	Mrs. (preferred among Urdu speakers, and more commonly used in India)	memsahib	mem-sah-yeeb (Muslim)
	Excuse me/sorry	maf kijeye	mahf kih-jee-yay
	Forgive me	maf karo	mahf kah-ro
	Get lost (also means "let's go" when said more benignly)	Chalo!	chah-lo!
	What?	kya?	kee-yah?
	Who?	kaun?	kow[n]?
	Why?	kyo(n)?	kee-yoh[n]?
	Water	panee	pah-nee
	Food	khana	kah-nah

Time Expressions

Today	aaj	ahj
Yesterday/tomorrow	kal	kull
Minute	minute	min-uht
Hour	ghanta	ghun-tah
Day	din	doyn
Week	hafta	huff-tah
Month	mahina	ma-heen-ah
Year	saal	sull
When	kab	kuhb
Morning	suube	soo-bay
(in the) afternoon	dopaher (ko)	doh-pah-herr koh
(in the) evening	shaam (ko)	shahm koh
(at) night	raat (ko)	raht koh

Health

I feel ill.	Mai[n] bimaar hu[n].	May bee-mahr hoo[n].
Pain	dard	dahrd
Stomach trouble	payt me gadbad	pah-yut may gud-bud
Indigestion	apacha	ah-pahch-ah
Headache	sir dard	sehr dahrd
Hospital	aspataal	ahs-pah-taal
Medicine	davaa	dah-vah

Numbers

1	ek	ache
2	do	doh
3	teen	teen
4	chaar	chahr
5	paanch	pahnch
6	che	chay
7	saat	saht
8	ath	aht
9	nau	now
10	das	duss
20	bees	bees
25	pachees	pah-chees

50	pachaas	pah-chahs
75	pachatar	pah-chah-tar
100	sau	sau (like ow with an s)
1,000	hazaar	hah-zaar
100,000	lakh	lahk
10,000,000	kror	kror (like roar with a k)

Shopping

Store	duukan	doo-kahn
Clothes/cloth (Use kapre to buy clothes, kapra to buy cloth.)	kapre/kapra	kuhp-ray/kuhp-rah
How much is this?	Ye kaise diya? Kitna	Yay kay-say dee-yah? (standard colloquial) kit-nah (literally "How much?")
I want to buy ___.	Mai[n] ___ karidna chahaata hu[n].	May _ kah-reed-nah chah-haht-ah hoo[n].
Too much	zyaada	zeh-yah-dah
Reduce a bit	Kutch kam kijiye.	Kuhch calm kih-gee-yay.

Useful Phrases

Don't touch! (Important with unwanted attention)	Mat Chuo!	Maht-choo-oh!
I need ___.	Mujhe ___ chahiye.	Muh-jay _ chah-ee-yay.
How are you?	Aap kaise hai?	Ahp kay-say heh[n]?
Do you speak English?	Aap English bolte hai?	Ahp English bol-tay heh[n]?
I don't understand.	Samaj mai nahee aya.	Suh-mahj may na-hee[n] ah-yah.
I don't know.	Mujhe nahee pata.	Muh-jay na-hee[n] puh-tah.
I am lost.	Mai gum gaya.	May[n] gum gah-yah.
Just a moment.	Ek minute.	Ache min-uht.
What is this?	Ye kya hai?	Yay kee-yah heh[n]?
Where is the ____?	___ kaha hai?	_ kuh-hah[n] heh[n]?
A lot/very	bahut bara	bah-hoot bah-rah

INDEX

A

A Ramanayak Udipi Shri Krishna Boarding ✕, 279
Adbudji Temple, 247
Addresses, F34, 572–573
Adinath Temple, 153
Adventures, 399, 422
Afghan Memorial Church of St. John the Baptist, 273
Aga Khan Palace, 323–324
Agra and environs, 124, 126–128, 131–146. ⇨ Also North Central India
Agra Fort, 127–128
Aguada Hermitage 🖭, 359–360
Ahuja Residency 🖭, 103–104
Air travel, F34–F37
Bombay (Mumbai) and Maharashtra, 313–315, 330, 343
Calcutta (Kolkata), 573
with children, F40
Delhi, 116–117
Goa, 376
Himalayas, The, 62–63
Hyderabad, 519
Karnataka, 422–423
Kerala, 460
luggage, F56–F57
North Central India, 182–183
Orissa, 542
Rajasthan, 255
Tamil Nadu, 503–504
Airports, F37
taxes, F61
Ajanta Caves, F31, 331–332, 336–340. ⇨ Also Bombay (Mumbai) and Maharashtra
Ajit Bhawan 🖭, F29, 227
Ajmer, 216–217
Akal Takht, 6
Akbar's private chambers, 139
Akbar's Tomb, 131
Alamgir Mosque, 165
Albert Hall Museum, 198
Alchi Choskor, 31–32
Alegria ✕, F30, 372
Alleppey, 445–446
Aloobari monastery, 51
Alsisar Haveli 🖭, 207
Amer Fort and Palace, 198–199
Amritsar, 4–8. ⇨ Also The Himalayas

Ananda in the Himalayas 🖭, F27, 38
Anguri Bagh, 128
Anjuna Beach, 354–355, 356
Ankh Michauli, 139
Annalakshmi ✕, 478
Anup Talao, 139
Apno Gaon, 212
Aquatica (water park), 562
Arambol Beach, 351
Archaeological Museum (Bodhgaya), 174
Archaeological Museum (Hampi), 421
Archaeological Museum (Khajuraho), 150
Archaeological Museum (Old Goa), 365
Archaeological Survey of India (ASI) museum (Fatehpur Sikri), 138
Armory, 199–200
Art and Picture Gallery, 9
Art galleries and museums. ⇨ Also Museums
Bombay (Mumbai) and Maharashtra, 274, 276, 320–321
Calcutta (Kolkata), 557, 559–560, 568
Delhi, 80, 84, 88–89, 91, 104–105
Goa, 365
Himalayas, The, 7, 8, 9, 18, 24
Hyderabad, 515–516
Karnataka, 402, 403, 405, 407, 421
Kerala, 441, 451–452
North Central India, 129, 134, 138, 141, 142, 150, 152, 157–158, 160, 165–166, 173, 174, 179
Orissa, 531, 532
Rajasthan, 198, 202, 209–210, 224, 225, 235, 241–242, 250
Tamil Nadu, 475, 499–500, 501
Arts-and-crafts villages, 212, 237, 242, 247, 538, 572
Ashoka's conversion site, 537
Astrologer's Seat, 139
ATMs, F54/id
Aurangabad, 331–344. ⇨ Also Bombay (Mumbai) and Maharashtra
Auroville, 494

Auto-rickshaws, 119, 183, 258, 424, 462, 506, 574–575
Ayurveda, 431

B

Babulnath Temple, 276–277
Bada Bagh, 249
Badal Mahal (Jaisalmer), 250
Badal Mahal (Kumbhalgarh), 246
Baga Beach, 355–357
Bagore ki Haveli, 235
Bagru, 212
Bahia House of Worship, 83
Baijanth temple, 49–50
Bailie Guard Gate, 179
Balsamand Lake and Garden, 224
Bangalore, 384, 386–387, 389–402. ⇨ Also Karnataka
Banganga (temple complex), 277
Bangaram Island Resort 🖭, 450–451
Bangla Sahib Gurdwara, 83–84
Banjara Camp 🖭, F29, 16–17
Bara Imambara, 177
Bars and lounges
Bombay (Mumbai) and Maharashtra, 301–302
Calcutta (Kolkata), 567
Delhi, 106–107
Goa, 355, 357
Jodhpur, 229
Karnataka, 396–397, 409–410
Orissa, 535
Tamil Nadu, 483
Basilica of Bom Jesus, 365
Basilica of San Thome Cathedral, 476
Beach shacks, 354
Beaches, F23
Bombay (Mumbai) and Maharashtra, 277
Goa, 349, 351, 354–356, 357, 359, 367, 368, 369, 370, 372, 373, 374, 376
Karnataka, 414
Kerala, 431, 450
Orissa, 541
Tamil Nadu, 475
Bekal Fort, 459

Belur, *417–419.* ⇨ *Also*
  Karnataka
Belur Math Shrine, *555*
Benaulim, *372–373*
Bengal Natural History
  Museum, *51*
Bhageshwar temple, *49–50*
Bharat Bhavan, *157*
Bharat Kala Bhavan Museum,
  165–166
Bharatiya Lok Kala Mandal,
  235
Bharatpur, *215–216*
Bhima, *488*
Bhimbetka Caves, *160*
Bhopal and environs,
  156–161. ⇨ *Also* North
  Central India
Bhojeshwar Temple, *159–160*
Bhubaneswar and environs,
  524–542. ⇨ *Also* Orissa
Bhutia Busti monastery, *51*
Bibi-ka-Maqbara, *332*
Bicycle rickshaws, *183–184,*
  504
Bicycling, *149, 255, 504*
Big Foot Museum, *371*
Bijamandala Temple,
  153–154
Bikaner House, *88*
Bindu Sagar, *529*
Binsar, *50*
Birbal's Palace, *140*
Bird hospital, *79*
Birla Museum, *157*
Boat and ferry travel
  Goa, *377*
  Kerala, *460–461*
  North Central India, 184
Boat Club, *157*
Bodhgaya, *161, 173–176.* ⇨
  Also North Central India
Bodhi Tree, *174*
Bogmalo Beach, *367–368*
Bombay (Mumbai), *F14,*
  264–319. ⇨ *Also* Bombay
  (Mumbai) **and** Maharashtra
Bombay (Mumbai) **and**
  Maharashtra, *F14,*
  262–344
  Aurangabad and Ajanta and
    Ellora Caves, F31, 331–344
  bazaars and markets, 272, 274,
    276, 304
  Bombay (Mumbai), F14,
    264–319
  children, attractions for, 278
  climate, F18
  consulates, 316

  dining, 264–265, 272, 274,
    277, 279, 280–290, 323,
    324–327, 333–334, 342
  Elphanta Caves, 279–280
  emergencies, 316–317
  festivals and seasonal events,
    329, 342
  itineraries, 263
  lodging, 266, 290–298,
    327–329, 334–336
  mail, 317
  Malabar Hill and environs,
    276–279
  money, 317, 330, 343
  nightlife and the arts, 298–302,
    329, 342
  outdoor activities and sports,
    303–304
  price categories, 265, 266
  Pune, 319–331
  shopping, 304–313, 329–330
  tours, 331, 343–344
  transportation, 313–316,
    317–318, 330, 331, 343,
    344
  travel agencies, 318
  visitor information, 318–319,
    331, 344
Bowling, *398*
Braganza House, *371–372*
Brahma Kumaris Spiritual
  University, *244*
Brahma Temple (Khajuraho),
  153
Brahma Temple (Pushkar),
  217–218
Brihadiswara Temple, *F31,*
  499
Brindavan Gardens, *406*
Brunton Boatyard ⊡ , *F27,*
  439
Buddhist complex
  (Bhubaneswar), *532*
Bukhara ✕ , *F30, 94*
Buland Darwaza, *138*
Bull Temple, *387*
Bus travel, *F37–F38*
  Bombay (Mumbai) and
    Maharashtra, 315, 330, 343
  Calcutta (Kolkata), 573
  Delhi, 117
  Goa, 377
  Himalayas, The, 63
  Karnataka, 423
  Orissa, 542–543
  Rajasthan, 255–256
  Tamil Nadu, 504
Business hours, *F38*
Bylakuppe, *413*

C

Cactus nursery, *224*
Calangute Beach, *357–358*
Calcutta (Kolkata), *F15,*
  547–576
  addresses, 572–573
  B.B.D. Bagh, 558–559
  Chowringhee, 559
  climate, F18
  College Street, 555
  consulates, 573
  dining, 550, 551, 560, 563–565
  emergencies, 573
  excursions, 570–572
  itineraries, 549
  Kumartuli, 556
  lodging, 550, 554, 565–567,
    572
  mail, 574
  money, 574
  nightlife and the arts, 567–568
  outdoor activities and sports,
    569
  price categories, 550, 554
  shopping, 551, 569–570
  telephones, 575
  timing the visit, 554
  tours, 575
  transportation, 573, 574–576
  visitor information, 576
Calendar of events, *F20–F22*
Calicut, *456–458*
Camel Back Road
  (Mussoorie), *39*
Camel Fair, *218*
Camel safaris, *229, 252–253*
Cameras and photography,
  F38
Canoeing, *157*
Cansaulim Beach, *368–369*
Car rentals, *F38–F39*
Car travel and drivers,
  F39–F40
  Bombay (Mumbai) and
    Maharashtra, 315–316, 330
  Calcutta (Kolkata), 573
  Delhi, 117
  Himalayas, The, 64
  Hyderabad, 520
  Karnataka, 423
  Kerala, 461
  North Central India, 184–185
  Orissa, 543
  Rajasthan, 256
  Tamil Nadu, 504–505
Carnaval ✕ , *373*
Carnival, *349*
Cavelossim, *374–376*

Caves
Bombay (Mumbai) and
Maharashtra, F31, 279–280,
331–333, 336–342
North Central India, 160–161
Orissa, 529
Tamil Nadu, 487–489
Cenotaphs, *143, 323*
Central Park Hotel, The 🏨 ,
328
Central Sikh Museum, *7*
Chail, *14*
Chamba, *27*
Chamundi Hill, *403*
Chandela 🏨 , *154*
Chandigarh, *9–10.* ⇨ *Also*
The Himalayas
Chandor, *371–372*
Chandni Chowk, *78*
Chandra Mahal, *201*
Channigaraya Temple, *418*
Char Bagh garden, *199*
Charity Birds Hospital, *79*
Charminar, *512, 514*
Chattarpurr temples, *84*
Chaturbhuj Temple
(Khajuraho), *154*
Chaturbhuj Temple (Orchha),
143
Chaubatia Orchards, *49*
Chaukhandi Stupa, *172*
Chausath Yogini Temple
(Khajuraho), *149*
Chausath Yogini Temple
(Varanasi), *166*
Cheena Peak, *47*
Chennai (Madras), *466–469,*
471–487. ⇨ *Also* Tamil
Nadu
Chhatrapati Shivaji Terminus,
272
Chhatta Chowk, *80*
Children, travel with,
F40–F41
Children's science center, *236*
Chilika Lake, *541*
Chilli Seasson ✕ , *99*
Chinese Fishing Nets,
433–434
Chinoiserie ✕ , *F30, 564*
Chitragupta Temple, *151–152*
Chittaurgarh, *244–246*
Chokhi Dhani ✕ , *F30, 204*
Chonor House 🏨 , *F29, 27*
Chor Bazaar, *272*
Chota Imambara, *177–178*
Chowk market, *178*
Chowpatty Beach and Marine
Drive, *277*

Church of Our Lady of
Immaculate Conception, *361*
Churches, *F32*
Bombay (Mumbai) and
Maharashtra, 273
Calcutta (Kolkata), 560
Goa, 361, 365
Himalayas, The, 24, 28, 52
Karnataka, 414
Kerala, 435, 458
Tamil Nadu, 473, 476–477
Churi Ajitgarh, *220*
City Palace (Jaipur), *199–201*
City Palace (Udaipur), *235*
Claridges 🏨 , *101–102*
Claridges Corbett Hideaway
🏨 , *45*
Claridges Nabha 🏨 , *40–41*
Climate, *F18–F19*
Clock Tower, *178*
Clothing, *112, 211, 308*
Cochin, *430, 432–443.* ⇨
Also Kerala
Coconut Lagoon 🏨 , *444*
Colaba, *273*
Colossal monolithic statue,
412
Colva Beach, *370*
Computers, *F41*
Consulates. ⇨ *See* Embassies
and consulates
Consumer protection, *F41*
Coorg, *412–414.* ⇨ *Also*
Karnataka
Corbett National Park, *13,*
41–46
Crafts Museum, *84*
Crafts Villages. ⇨ *See* Arts-
and-crafts villages
Credit cards, *F7, F54*
Crematoriums, *224*
Cricket, *108, 303, 569*
Crocodile Bank, *485*
Crocodile-spotting tours, *358,*
360
Cruises, *303–304, 358, 360,*
363–364, 431, 443
Currency, *F54–F55*
Customs, *F42–F43*
Cycle-rickshaws, *119,*
183–184, 504

D

DakshinaChitra, *485–486*
Dakshineshwar Kali Temple,
556
Dal Lake, *25*
Dalai Lama's private
residence, *24–25*

Dalhousie, *27–29, 42*
Dance, *F23–F24*
Bombay (Mumbai) and
Maharashtra, 299, 302, 329,
342
Calcutta (Kolkata), 568
Delhi, 105–106
Himalayas, The, 24, 31
Karnataka, 398, 410,
414–415
Kerala, 441–442, 458
North Central India, 129,
148–149
Orissa, 535, 537
Rajasthan, 208–209
Tamil Nadu, 469, 482–483,
485–486
Dandeli Wildlife Sanctuary,
416
Dargah Sharif, *217*
Darjeeling, *50–55.* ⇨ *Also*
The Himalayas
Darjeeling-Sikkim Circuit, *56*
Darjeeling Toy Train, *51*
Darshani Deorhi, *6–7*
Darya Daulat, *406*
Dasaprakash ✕ , *135*
Dashashvamedh Ghat, *166*
Daulatabad Fort, *332*
Deeg, *216*
Deer Park, *172*
Dekava's ✕ , *52–53*
Delhi, *F13, 71–120*
Chandni Chowk, 78–79
children, attractions for, 89–90,
108–109
climate, F19
dining, 72–73, 75, 91–99, 109,
111, 113
embassies, 117–118
emergencies, 118
Gali Parante Wali, 79
itineraries, 73
lodging, 72–73, 75, 99–104
mail and shipping, 118
money, 118–119
New Delhi, 82–91
nightlife and the arts, 75,
104–107
Old Delhi, 74, 78–82
outdoor activities and sports,
107–108
price categories, 73
shopping, 75, 108–116
timing the visit, 74
transportation, 116–117,
119–120
travel agents and tours, 120
visitor information, 120

Delight ⌸ , *441*
Desert National Park, *254*
Devbagh, *416*
Devi Garh Palace ⌸ , *247*
Devi Jagdamba Temple, *151*
Dhai din ka Jhonpra, *217*
Dhamekh Stupa, *172*
Dharamshala, *22, 23–27, 42*
Dharmaraja, *488*
Dhauli, *537*
Dhirdham Temple, *51*
Dhobi Ghat (Bombay), *273*
Dhobi Ghat (Varanasi), *166*
Dilwara Temples, *244*
Dining, *F23, F30–F31,*
   F44–F46. ⇨ *Also under*
   cities and areas
Directorate of Handicrafts and
   Handloom, *59*
Disabilities and accessibility,
   F43–F44
Discos
Bombay (Mumbai) and
   Maharashtra, 302, 329
Calcutta (Kolkata), 567–568
Delhi, 107
Goa, 357
Karnataka, 397
Orissa, 535
Tamil Nadu, 483
Discounts and deals, *F44*
Divar Island, *366*
Diving, *368*
Diwan-i-Am (Agra), *128*
Diwan-i-Am (Delhi), *80*
Diwan-i-Am (Fatehpur Sikri),
   138–139
Diwan-i-Am (Jaipur), *199,*
   200–201
Diwan-i-Khas (Agra), *128*
Diwan-i-Khas (Delhi), *81*
Diwan-i-Khas (Fatehpur
   Sikri), *139*
Dr. Salim Ali Bird Sanctuary,
   366
Dolphin-spotting tours, *358,*
   360
Draupadi, *487–488*
Driving. ⇨ *See* Car travel
   and drivers
Drogpa Villages, *34–35*
Dubare Elephant Camp, *413*
Dudhsagar Waterfalls, *366*
Duladeo Temple, *153*
Durbar (Mysore), *404*
Durbar Hall (Gwalior), *142*
Durga Temple, *167*
Durgiana Temple, *8*
Dussehra (festival), *405*

Dutch Palace, *434*
Duties, *F42–F43*

E

E.N.S. Kalari Centre (martial
   arts practitioners), *442*
Eastern Group of Temples
   (Khajuraho), *152–153*
Ecology Centre, *31*
Eden Gardens, *559*
Ekambaranathar Temple,
   491–492
Eklingji, *247*
Electricity, *F46*
Elephanta Caves, *279–280*
Ellora Caves, *F31, 331–332,*
   340–342. ⇨ *Also* Bombay
   (Mumbai) **and** Maharashtra
Embassies and consulates,
   F46
Bombay (Mumbai) and
   Maharashtra, 316
Delhi, 117–118
Calcutta (Kolkata), 573
Tamil Nadu, 505
Emergencies, *F46–F47*
Bombay (Mumbai) and
   Maharashtra, 316–317
Calcutta (Kolkata), 573
Delhi, 118
Goa, 377
Himalayas, The, 64–65
Hyderabad, 520
Karnataka, 423
Kerala, 461
Orissa, 543
Rajasthan, 256–257
Tamil Nadu, 505
Enchey Monastery, *59*
Etiquette and behavior,
   F47–F48

F

Fairlawn ⌸ , *567*
Falaknuma ✕ , *179–180*
Falaknuma Palace, *512–513*
Fateh Prakash Mahal, *245*
Fatehpur Sikri, *138–141*
Fernando's Nostalgia ✕ ,
   F30, 371
Festivals and seasonal events,
   F20–F22. ⇨ *Also under*
   cities and areas
Film
Bombay (Mumbai) and
   Maharashtra, 299, 300
Calcutta (Kolkata), 568
Delhi, 105
Rajasthan, 209

Fisherman's Cove ⌸ ,
   480–481
Fishing, *360*
Five Rathas, *487–488*
Flats, *46*
Flavors ✕ , *373*
Flea market, *356*
Flora Fountain, *272*
Fodor's choice, *F27–F33*
Folklore Museum, *250*
Fontainhas, *361*
Football, *108, 569*
Fort Aguada, *F31, 358–359*
Fort District and environs
   (Bombay), *266–267,*
   272–274, 276
Fort House, The ✕ , *438*
Fort-palace complex
   (Orchha), *143–144*
Fort Rajwada ⌸ , *251*
Fort St. Angelo, *458*
Fort St. George, *471*
Fort William, *559*
Forts, *F31*
Bombay (Mumbai) and
   Maharashtra, 332
Calcutta (Kolkata), 559
Delhi, 80–81, 90
Goa, 358–359
Hyderabad, 513–514
Karnataka, 406, 414
Kerala, 458, 459
North Central India, 127–128,
   141, 143–144, 168
Rajasthan, 198–199, 201, 202,
   213, 216, 220, 224–225,
   231–232, 236, 244–245,
   249–250
Tamil Nadu, 471, 497, 500

G

Gadhan Thekchhokling
   Gompa, *17*
Gadsisar Lake, *250*
Gagan Shawl Industries, *18*
Galwar Bagh, *203*
Gandhi Smriti, *84–85*
Ganesh Pol, *199*
Ganesh Tok, *59*
Ganga View ⌸ , *170*
Gangaikondacholapuram, *500*
Gangtok, *F19, 59–60*
Gardens
Bombay (Mumbai) and
   Maharashtra, 278
Calcutta (Kolkata), 559, 561
Delhi, 87–88, 91
Himalayas, The, 8, 9, 51
Karnataka, 387, 389, 406

North Central India, 131,
132–133
Rajasthan, 199, 202, 224, 236,
244, 249
Garhwal Circuit, *37*
Gateway of India, *272–273*
Gay and lesbian travel, *F48*
General Post Office
(Calcutta), *559*
George Town (Madras), *471*
Ghantai Temple, *153*
Gharial Sanctuary, *156*
Gifts, *F50*
Glass House, The ☒ , *38*
Glenmoor Cottages ☒ , *26*
Goa, *F14, F32, 346–379*
architecture, 349
dining, 348, 349, 355, 356,
357, 359, 362, 364, 368,
369, 371, 372, 373, 374
emergencies, 377
English-language media, 377
festivals and seasonal events,
349
itineraries, 347
lodging, 350, 351, 354, 355,
356–357, 358, 359–360,
362–363, 367–370, 372–376
mail, 377
money, 377–378
nightlife and the arts, 349, 355
North Goa, 350–360
outdoor activities and sports,
358, 360, 363–364, 368
Panaji (Panjim) and Central
Goa, 360–367
price categories, 348, 350
shopping, 349, 356, 364, 370
South Goa, 367–376
telephones and internet, 378
timing the visit, 350
tours, 358, 360, 378
transportation, 376–377,
378–379
visitor information, 379
Goa Marriott Resort ☒ ,
362–363
Go-carting, *399*
Godly Museum, *403*
Golconda Fort, *513–514*
Golden Temple, *5–8*
Golf
Bombay (Mumbai) and
Maharashtra, 303
Calcutta (Kolkata), 569
Delhi, 107
Karnataka, 398
Rajasthan, 209
Tamil Nadu, 483

Goomtee Tea Estate, *52*
Gopalpur-on-Sea, *541–542*
Gordon House ☒ , *294*
Goubert Avenue
(Pondicherry), *493–494*
Government Archaeological
Museum, *157*
Government lodging, *F52*
Government Silk Weaving
Factory, *406*
Grand Anaicut, *498*
Grand Maratha Sheraton ☒ ,
294
Green Magic ☒ , *F27, 457*
Guda Vishnoi, *230*
Gujari Mahal, *141*
Gujarat, *F13–F14*
Gulta Ji Mandir, *203*
Gumbaz mausoleum, *407*
Gundert Memorial Church,
458
Guru Ram Das Langar, *6*
Guru Shikhar, *244*
Gwalior, *141–142*
Gwalior Fort, *141*
Gyan Bhandar, *249–250*
Gyanvapi Mosque, *167*

H

Haji Ali Shrine, *277–278*
Halebid, *417–419.* ⇨ *Also*
Karnataka
Hampi, *F31, 419–421.* ⇨
Also Karnataka
Handicraft Centre, *25*
Hanging Gardens, *278*
Happy Valley Tea Estate, *52*
Haridwar, *36–39*
Harmandir Sahib, *6–7*
Hauz Khas Village, *85*
Hawa Mahal (Fatehpur
Sikri), *140*
Hawa Mahal (Jaipur), *201*
Hazara Rama temple, *421*
Hazrat Nizamuddin Darga, *85*
Health concerns, *F48–F50.* ⇨
Also Emergencies
Heritage hotels, *F52*
High Court, *471, 473*
Himachal Circuit, *13*
Himachal Pradesh, *10–29.* ⇨
Also The Himalayas
Himalayan Zoological Park, *59*
Himalayas, The, *F13, 2–69*
Amritsar, 4–8
cell phones and internet cafés,
64
Chandigarh, 9–10
Darjeeling, 50–55

dining, 3, 4, 8, 9–10, 14, 19–20,
26, 28, 32–33, 37–38, 39,
44–45, 47, 49, 52–53, 59–60
emergencies, 64–65
Himachal Pradesh, 10–29
Ladakh, 29–35
lodging, 3–4, 8, 10, 14–17,
20–21, 23, 26–27, 28–29,
33–34, 38–40, 44–46, 47–48,
49, 53–54, 60, 61, 62
money, 65
permits, 65–66
price categories, 4
shopping, 14, 17, 18, 19, 54–55
Sikkim, 55–62
transportation, 62–64, 66–67
travel agents and tours, 67–68
Uttaranchal, 35–50
visitor information, 68–69
Himalayan Mountaineering
Institute, *51*
Hindu Temples (The
Himalayas), *13*
History, The ✗ , *F30, 437*
Holiday Inn Khajuraho ☒ ,
154–155
Holidays, *F50*
Holy bathing ghats (Pushkar),
218
Horse racing
Bombay (Mumbai) and
Maharashtra, 303
Calcutta (Kolkata), 569
Karnataka, 399, 410
Tamil Nadu, 483
Hostels, *F52*
Hotel Castle ☒ , *18*
Hotels, *F27–F29, F51–F53.*
⇨ *Also* Lodging *under*
cities and areas
price categories, 4, 73, 124,
196, 266, 350, 384, 430,
466, 516, 524, 554
taxes, F61–F62
House of Maryam, *140*
Houseboat Cruise ☒ , *F29,*
443
Howrah Bridge, *556*
Hoysaleswara Temple,
418–419
Hub, The ✗ , *563*
Humayun's Tomb, *F31–F32,*
86
Hussainabad Imambara,
177–178
Hyatt Regency ☒ , *102*
Hyderabad, *F15, 510–521*
dining, 513, 516–517
emergencies, 520

itineraries, 511
lodging, 513, 517–518
mail, 520
money, 520
price categories, 516
shopping, 513, 519
Tank Bund Road, 516
timing the visit, 511–512
transportation, 519–521
travel agents and tours, 521
visitor information, 521

I

Ideal River View Resort 🏨,
   500–501
Imperial, The 🏨, F27, 99
India Gate, 86
Indian Botanical Gardens, 561
Indian Coffee House, 555
Indian Museum, 559–560
Indira Gandhi Memorial
   Museum, 86
Indira Gandhi Planetarium,
   178
Internet cafés, 64
Insurance, F50–F51
ISKCON Temple, 87
ITC Park Sheraton Hotel &
   Towers 🏨, 479
ITC Sonar Bangla Sheraton
   Hotels & Towers 🏨, 566
Itineraries, F16–F17. ⇨ Also
   under cities and areas
Itmad-ud-Daulat's Tomb, 131

J

Jag Mandir palace, 236
Jagannath Temple, 538–539
Jagat Shiromani temple, 199
Jageshwar temple, 49–50
Jahangir Mahal, 144
Jai Vilas Palace, 141–142
Jaigarh Fort, 199, 201
Jain caves (Bhubaneswar),
   529
Jain Temple (Bombay), 278
Jain Temple (Ranakpur), 243
Jain Temples (Jaisalmer),
   249–250
Jaipur and environs,
   196–219. ⇨ Also
   Rajasthan
Jaipur House, 88
Jaisalmer and environs, F31,
   247–254. ⇨ Also
   Rajasthan
Jakhoo Hill, 14
Jaleb Chowk, 199
Jallianwala Bagh, 7–8

Jama Masjid (Bhopal), 157
Jama Masjid (Delhi), F32, 79
Jama Masjid (Fatehpur
   Sikri), 140
Jamavar ✕, 389
Janapada Loka Folk Arts
   Museum, 402
Jantar Mantar, 202
Japanese Peace Pagoda, 52
Jas Mandir, 199
Jaswant Thada, 224
Javari Temple, 153
Jawahar Kala Kendra, 202
Jehan Numa Palace ✕🏨,
   158–159
Jehangir Art Gallery, 274
Jews in India, 275
Jhankar ✕, 134
Jhoomar Baori 🏨, 213
Jhula Devi Temple, 49
Jhunjhunu, 220
Jodh Bai's Palace, 140
Jodhpur and environs,
   223–232. ⇨ Also
   Rajasthan
Judge's Court, 42
Juna Mahal, 249
Jungle camps, 385, 411

K

Kabini River Lodge 🏨, F27,
   413
Kailasanatha Temple, 492
Kalams, 474
Kalatope Wildlife Sanctuary,
   29
Kalighat Kali Temple,
   561–562
Kalika Mata, 245
Kalyana Mandap, 404
Kamala Nehru Park, 278
Kanak Vrindavan Gardens,
   202
Kanchipuram, 487, 491–493.
   ⇨ Also Tamil Nadu
Kandariya (theater), 149
Kandariya Mahadev, F32,
   151
Kangra Valley, 22–23
Kanhirode Weaving
   Cooperative, 458–459
Kannur, 458–460
Kapalishvara Temple, 476
Karnataka, F14, 380–426
   architecture, 385
   Bangalore, 384, 386–387,
      389–402
   Belur and Halebid, 417–419
   Coorg, 412–414

dining, 382, 389–392, 401,
   407–408, 415, 421
emergencies, 423
festivals and seasonal events,
   385, 405, 414–415
Hampi, F31, 419–421
itineraries, 383
lodging, 382–384, 392–396,
   408–409, 411, 413–414,
   415–417, 418, 419, 421/id
mail, 423
Mangalore and Karwar,
   414–417
massage, naturopathy, and
   yoga, 400
money, 424
Mysore, 402–412
nightlife and the arts, 385,
   396–398, 409–410, 415
outdoor activities and sports,
   398–400, 410, 422
price categories, 382, 384
river/jungle camps, 385, 411
safaris, 385
shopping, 385–386, 400–402,
   410
timing the visit, 384
tours, 424–425
transportation, 385, 422–423,
   424, 425
visitor information, 425–426
Karwar, 414–417. ⇨ Also
   Karnataka
Kashi Vishvanath Temple, 167
Kayaking, 157, 303–304
Kedar Gouri Temple, 529
Kedareshvara Temple, 167
Kedareswara Temple, 419
Keneseth Eliyahoo Synagogue,
   275
Keoladeo National Park,
   215–216
Kerala, F14, 428–463
   Ayurveda, 431
   Central Kerala, 443–451
   Cochin, 430, 432–443
   dining, 429, 431–432,
      434–435, 437–439, 444, 452,
      454, 457, 459
   emergencies, 461
   festivals and seasonal events,
      432, 441–442, 458
   itineraries, 429
   lodging, 429–430, 439–441,
      444, 445–448, 449–451,
      452–453, 454–456, 457–458,
      459–460
   mail, 461
   money, 462

nightlife and the arts, 432, 441–442
Northern Kerala, 456–460
outdoor activities and sports, 450
price categories, 429, 430
shopping, 432, 442–443, 453
Southern Kerala, 451–456
timing the visit, 430
transportation, 460–461, 462
travel agents and tours, 462–463
visitor information, 463
Kewpies ✕, F30, 563
Khajjiar, 29
Khajuraho, 146–156. ➪ *Also* North Central India
Khajuraho Dance Festival, 148–149
Khajuraho Village, 156
Khas Mahal (Agra), 128
Khas Mahal (Delhi), 81
Khimsar, 231–232
Khyber ✕, F30, 286
Kinnaur, 16–17, 42
Kirti Stambh, 245
Kolkata. ➪ *See* Calcutta
Konark, 536–537
Konark Dance Festival, 537
Konkan Railway, 385
Kovalam, 453–456
Krishna Mandapam, 488
Kullu, 18
Kumaon Circuit, 42
Kumarakom, 443–444
Kumarakom Lake Resort ☷, F27, 444
Kumbhalgarh, 246
Kumbhalgarh Sanctuary, 246
Kunbha Shyam, 245
Kuthiramalika (Puthenmalika) **Palace Museum**, 451
Kyongnosla Alpine Sanctuary, 59

L

La Martinière, 178–179
Lachhmangarh, 220
Ladakh, 29–35. ➪ *Also* The Himalayas
Ladakh Sarai ✕☷, F29, 33
Lahaul, 21–22
Lahore Gate, 80
Lake Palace ☷, F27, 235–236, 238
Lake Periyar Wildlife Sanctuary, 447
Lake Pichola, 235–236

Lakshadweep, 450–451
Lakshmana Temple, 150–151
Lal Bagh Botanical Gardens, 387, 389
Lal Qila (Red Fort), 80–81
Lalguan Mahadeva, 149
Lalitigiri, 532
Lalitha Mahal Palace Hotel ☷, 408–409
Lalitha Mahal Palace Hotel Restaurant ✕, 407
Language, F51
Laxmi Naryan Temple, 87
Laxmi Vilas Palace Hotel ☷, 216
Laxminarayan Temple, 144
Leela Goa, The ☷, F27, 375
Leela Palace, The ☷, 393
Leh, 30–34
Leopold Café ✕, 280
Lha-Ri-Mo ☷, 33–34
Libraries
  Calcutta (Kolkata), 562
  Delhi, 90
  Rajasthan, 236, 249–250
  Tamil Nadu, 477, 499–500
Lingaraj Temple Complex, 529
Lodging, F27–F29, F51–F53.
  ➪ *Also under cities and areas*
Lodi Garden, 87–88
Lohagarh Fort, 216
Lonar Crater, 332–333
Lord Krishna Temple, 414
Loutolim, 371
Lower Mall Road (Ranikhet), 49
Lucknow, 161, 176–182. ➪ *Also* North Central India
Ludarva Temples, 250
Lutyen's Delhi, 88
Luz Church, 476–477

M

Madgaon (Margao), 370–371
Madras (Chennai), F19, 466–469, 471–487. ➪ *Also* Tamil Nadu
Madras Snake Park, 477
Madurai, 496, 501–503. ➪ *Also* Tamil Nadu
Magen Hassidim Synagogue, 275
Mahabalipuram, 487–490. ➪ *Also* Tamil Nadu
Mahabodhi Temple, 174
Mahadeva Temple, 151
Mahamandir monastery, 224

Mahanavami Dibba, 421
Maharashtra. ➪ *See* Bombay (Mumbai) and Maharashtra
Mahatma Jyotiba Phule Market, 274
Mahavida Jain Temple, 231
Mahesh Lunch House ✕, F30, 288–289
Mahishasura statue, 403
Mahishasuramardini Cave, 488–489
Maidan, 560
Mail and shipping, F53–F54.
  ➪ *Also under cities and areas*
Majorda, 369–370
Malabar House, The ☷, 439
Malabar Junction ✕, 437
Man Mandir, 141
Manali, 17, 19–21, 42
Manav Sangrahalaya, 157–158
Mandore Gardens, 224
Mangaladas Market, 274
Mangalore, 414–417. ➪ *Also* Karnataka
Manguesh temple, 367
Mani Bhavan, 278
Manikarnika Ghat, 168
Manor, The ☷, F29, 102
Manu Market, 19
Mapusa, 358
Marari Beach ☷, 445
Marble Palace, F31, 556
Margao, 370–371
Marina Beach, 475
Marine Plaza ☷, 290
Martial arts, 442
Masala Art ✕, F30, 94
Mashobra, 42
Massage, 400
Matanga Hill, 420
Matangesvara Temple, 149
Matunga, 279
Mavalli Tiffin Rooms (MTR) ✕, 392
Mayfair Lagoon ☷, F29, 534
Meal plans, F7, F51
Mecca Masjid, 514–515
Meenakshi Temple, F32, 501
Meera temple, 245
Mehrangarh Fort, F31, 224–225
Mint (Fatehpur Sikri), 138
Missionaries of Charity, 562
MLV Tribal Research Institute, 236
Molela, 247

Money matters, F54–F55. ⇨
    Also under cities and areas
Monuments, F31
Moriri Lake, 34–35
Mosques, F31–F32
Bombay (Mumbai) and
    Maharashtra, 277–278
Calcutta (Kolkata), 556
Delhi, 79, 81, 90–91
Hyderabad, 514–515
North Central India, 128, 133,
    140, 157, 158, 165, 167
Rajasthan, 217
Moti Mahal, 224–225
Moti Masjid (Pearl Mosque;
    Agra), 128
Moti Masjid (Pearl Mosque;
    Delhi), 81
Motorbikes, 378
Mount Abu, 243–244
Mt. Kanchenjunga, 61
Mrs. Bhanderi's Guesthouse
    ✕🏠, F29, 8
Mubarak Mahal, 199
Mughal Room ✕, 134
Mukandgarh, 220
Mukteswar Temple, 529
Mulagandha Kuti Vilhari
    Temple, 173
Mumbadevi Temple, 276
Mumbai. ⇨ See Bombay
    (Mumbai) and Maharashtra
Mumtaz Mahal, 80
Munnar, 448–450
Museum and Art Gallery
    Complex (Trivandrum),
    451–452
Museum of Christian Art, 365
Museum of Tribal Arts and
    Artefacts, 531
Museums. ⇨ Also Art
    galleries and museums
Bombay (Mumbai) and
    Maharasthra, 274, 276,
    320–321
Calcutta (Kolkata), 557,
    559–560
Delhi, 80, 84, 86, 88–89, 90, 91
Goa, 365, 371
Himalayas, The, 7, 8, 9, 18, 24,
    25, 31, 51
Hyderabad, 515–516
Karnataka, 402, 403, 405, 407,
    421
Kerala, 451–452
North Central India, 129, 134,
    138, 141, 142, 150, 152,
    157–158, 160, 165–166, 173,
    174, 179

Orissa, 531, 532
Rajasthan, 198, 202, 224, 225,
    235, 236, 250
Tamil Nadu, 475, 499–500,
    501
Music
Bombay (Mumbai) and
    Maharashtra, 299
Calcutta (Kolkata), 568
Delhi, 105–106
Himalayas, The, 24
Karnataka, 398, 410
North Central India, 129,
    148–149, 171–172, 182
Rajasthan, 202
Tamil Nadu, 483
Mussaman Burj, 128
Mussoorie, 39–41
Mysore, 402–412. ⇨ Also
    Karnataka
Mysore Palace, 403–405

N

Nagarhole National Park,
    412–413
Nagaur, 232
Nagda, 247
Nagina Masjid (Agra), 128
Nagina Mosque (Fatehpur
    Sikri), 140
Nahargarh Fort, 202
Nainital, 13, 46–48
Nakhoda Mosque, 556
Nakki Lake, 244
Nalanda, 175
Nandankanan Zoological
    Park, 531–532
Nandi (Shiva's holy bull),
    403
Nandi Temple, 152
Nasiyan Temple, 217
Nathamal Ki Haveli, 250
Nathdwara, 246–247
National Gallery of Modern
    Art (Bombay), 274, 276
National Gallery of Modern
    Art (Delhi), 88–89
National Gandhi Museum
    (Delhi), 91
National Library (Calcutta),
    562
National Museum (Delhi), 89
National Museum and Art
    Gallery (Madras), 475
National Rail Museum (Delhi),
    89
National Zoological Park
    (Delhi), 89–90
Naturopathy, 400

Naubat Khana (Delhi), 80
Naubat Khana (Fatehpur
    Sikri), 138
Nauchowki (Nine Pavilions),
    246
Nawalgarh, 220
Neelkanth Mahadev, 215
Neemach Mata, 236
Neemrana Fort Palace 🏠,
    F29, 220, 221
Nehru Memorial Museum, 90
New Elgin 🏠, 53
Newspapers and magazines,
    F55
Nicco Park (amusement
    park), 563
Nick's Italian Kitchen ✕, 26
Nightlife and the arts,
    F23–F24. ⇨ Also under
    cities and areas
Nirmal Hirday, 562
Noor-Us-Sabah Palace 🏠,
    159
Norbulingka Institute for
    Tibetan Culture, 24
Nor-Khill ✕🏠, F27, 60
Norling Designs (shop), 25
North and South Secretariats,
    88
North Central India, F13,
    122–188
Agra and environs, 124,
    126–128, 131–146
Bhopal and environs, 156–161
children, attractions for, 158
dining, 123–124, 134–135,
    141, 152, 154, 158–159,
    167, 169, 178, 179–180
festivals and seasonal events,
    129, 148–149, 171–172, 182
itineraries, 125–126
Khajuraho, 146–156
lodging, 124, 135–137, 142,
    145–146, 154–156, 158–159,
    169–171, 175–176, 180–181
money, 185–186
nightlife and the arts, 129,
    171–172, 182
price categories, 124
shopping, 129, 137, 146, 156,
    159, 171, 181–182
timing the visit, 124
tours, 186
transportation, 182–185,
    186–187
Varanasi, Lucknow, and
    Bodhgaya, 161–182
visitor information, 187–188
Nubra Valley, 34–35

O

Oberoi, The (Bangalore) ⌷, F28, 393
Oberoi, The (Elephanta Caves) ⌷, 290–291
Oberoi Amarvilas ⌷, F28, 135
Oberoi Cecil ⌷, 13, 15
Oberoi Grand ⌷, F29, 566
Oberoi Rajvilas ⌷, 205
Oberoi Udaivilas ⌷, F28, 238–239
Oberoi Vanyavilas ⌷, F28, 213–214
Observatory Hill, 51
Ochterlony Monument, 560
Ohel David Synagogue, 321
Old Goa, F32, 364–365
Orange County Resort ⌷, 413–414
Orchha, 143–146
Orissa, F15, 523–545
architecture, 527
Bhubaneswar and environs, 524–542
dining, 523–524, 532–533, 539–540
emergencies, 543
festivals and seasonal events, 535, 537
itineraries, 525
lodging, 523–524, 533–535, 540, 541–542
money, 543
nightlife and the arts, 535
price categories, 524
shopping, 527, 535–536
timing the visit, 524
tours, 530, 544
transportation, 542–545
tribal village tours, 530
visitor information, 545
Osho Meditation Resort, 321–323
Osian, 231
Oudhyana ✕, 180

P

Packages and tours, F64–F65
Packing for India, F55–F57
Padam, 34
Padmaja Naidu Zoo, 51
Padmanabhapuram palace, 454
Padmanabhaswamy Temple, 451
Padmini, 245
Paintings, 242, 538

Palace on Wheels (train), 200
Palaces, F31
Calcutta (Kolkata), 556
Delhi, 80–81
Himalayas, The, 31
Hyderabad, 512–513
Karnataka, 389, 403–405, 406
Kerala, 434, 451, 454
North Central India, 128, 140, 141–142, 143–145, 168
Pune, 320, 323–324
Rajasthan, 198–201, 202–203, 220, 224–225, 231–232, 235–236, 245, 246, 247, 249, 250
Tamil Nadu, 499–500, 501–502
Palampur, 22
Palolem Beach, 376
Panaji (Panjim) **and Central Goa,** 360–367. ⇨ Also Goa
PanAsian ✕, 564–565
Panch Mahal, 139–140
Panchmukhi Mahadeva, 145
Pandupol, 214–215
Pangong Lake, 34–35
Pangong Tso, 34
Panjim (Panaji), 360–367. ⇨ Also Goa
Panna National Park, 156
Parasurasameswara Temple, 531
Paresnath Temple, 557
Park Balluchi ✕, F31, 95
Park Hotel ⌷, 566
Park Hyatt Goa Resort and Spa ⌷, F28, 368–369
Parks, national. ⇨ Also Wildlife sanctuaries
Himalayas, The, 13, 41–46
Karnataka, 385, 412–413
Kerala, 449
North Central India, 156, 158
Rajasthan, 212–216, 254
Parsvanath Temple, 153
Parthasarathi Temple, 475
Parvati Temple, 152
Passports, F57–F59
Patwon Ki Haveli, 250
Peace Park, 244
Pelling, 61–62
Pema Thang Guest House ⌷, 27
Pemayangtse Monastery, 61–62
Penance of Arjuna (bas-relief), 489
Pepper Exchange, 437
Performing arts, F23–F24

Permits, 65–66
Peter Cat ✕, 564
Phool Mahal (Flower Palace), 224–225
Photography, F38
Picture Gallery, 179
Pipli, 537–538
Plane travel. ⇨ See Air travel
Planetarium, 178
Polo, 108, 209, 569
Ponda, 366–367
Pondicherry, 487, 493–496. ⇨ Also Tamil Nadu
Pradeep ⌷, 171
Presidency College, 555
President Park ⌷, 335
Price categories
Bombay (Mumbai) and Maharashtra, 265, 266
Calcutta (Kolkata), 550, 554
Delhi, 73
for dining, 4, 73, 124, 196, 265, 348, 382, 429, 466, 516, 524, 550
Goa, 348, 350
The Himalayas, 4
Hyderabad, 516
Karnataka, 382, 384
Kerala, 429, 430
for lodging, 4, 73, 124, 196, 266, 350, 384, 430, 466, 516, 524, 554
North Central India, 124
Orissa, 524
Rajasthan, 196
Tamil Nadu, 466
Prince of Wales Museum, 276
Pubs, 106–107, 329, 535
Pune, 319–331. ⇨ Also Bombay (Mumbai) **and Maharashtra**
Punjab Government Museum, 8
Punjabi by Nature ✕, 94–95
Purana Qila (Old Fort), 90
Puri, 538–540
Pushkar, 217–219

Q

Qila-i-Kunha Masjid, 90
Quality Inn Meadows ⌷, 335
Quality Inn Southern Star ⌷, 409
Quilon, 446–447
Qutab Shahi Tombs, 515
Qutub Minar, 90–91
Quwwat-ul-Islam Masjid, 90–91

R

Rabindra Bharati University Museum, *557*
Rafting, *538*
Rai Praveen Mahal, *144–145*
Rail travel. ⇨ *See* Train travel
Raintree ✕, *478*
Raj Bhavan, *51*
Raj Ghat and National Gandhi Museum, *91*
Raja Dinkar Kelkar Museum, *320–321*
Raja Mahal, *143–144*
Rajamala National Park, *449*
Rajasthan, *F13, 190–260*
camel safaris, *229, 252–253*
children, attractions for, *236*
dining, *195, 196, 201, 203–205, 210, 216, 220–221, 225–226, 235, 237–238, 243, 244, 245, 250–251*
emergencies, *256–257*
festivals and seasonal events, *218, 229, 232, 237*
itineraries, *191*
Jaipur and environs, *196–219*
Jaisalmer and environs, *F31, 247–254*
Jodhpur and environs, *223–232*
lodging, *195–196, 205–208, 213–214, 215, 216, 218–219, 220–222, 226–229, 231, 232, 238–241, 243, 244, 245–246, 247, 251–252*
mail, *257*
money, *257*
nightlife and the arts, *208–209, 229*
outdoor activities and sports, *209, 220, 229*
price categories, *196*
Shekhavati, *219–222*
shopping, *193, 209–212, 220, 229–230, 241–243, 254*
telephones, *258*
timing the visit, *196*
transportation, *255–256, 258–259*
travel agents and tours, *259*
Udaipur and environs, *232–247*
visitor information, *259–260*
Rajgir, *175*
Rajsamand Lake, *246*
Ram, Chuna, *231*
Ram Bagh (gardens), *8*
Ram Raja Temple, *145*
Ramnagar Fort and Palace, *168*

Rana Kumbha, *245*
Ranakpur, *243*
Rang Mahal (Painted Palace), *80–81*
Ranganathittu Bird Sanctuary, *407*
Ranikhet, *13, 48–49*
Ranikhet Tweed and Shawl Factory, *49*
Ranthambhore Fort, *213*
Ranthambhore National Park, *212–214*
Rashtrapati Bhavan, *88*
Ratnagiri, *532*
Reis Magos Fort, *358*
Residency, *179*
Residency and the Garden Café, The ✕, *333*
Residential Museum, *405*
Rest rooms, *F59/id*
Restaurants, *F23, F30–F31, F44–F46.* ⇨ *Also* Dining under cities and areas
price categories, *4, 73, 124, 196, 265, 348, 382, 429, 466, 516, 524, 550*
Rice Boats ✕, *437–438*
Rickshaws, *119, 183–184, 258, 424, 462, 504, 506, 574–575*
Rishikesh, *36–39*
River/jungle camps, *385, 411*
Rock Fort, *497*
Rock Garden, *9*
Royal China ✕, *284–285*
Royal Hammams, *81*
Royal Museum, *499–500*
Royal Stables, *140*
Rumtek Monastery, *61*

S

Sachiya Mata Mandir, *231*
Safaris, *229, 252–253, 385*
Safdarjang's Tomb, *91*
Safety, *F59–F60*
Sahadeva, *488*
Sahelion Ki Bari (Garden of the Maidens), *236*
Sailing, *157, 303–304, 363*
St. Aloysius Church, *414*
St. Andrew's Church, *52*
St. Francis Church (Cochin), *435*
St. Francis Church (Dalhousie), *28*
St. John's Church in the Wilderness, *24*
St. Mary's Church, *473*
St. Mary's Island, *414*

St. Paul's Cathedral, *560*
St. Thomas Mount, *477*
Sajjan Garh, *236*
Salar Jung Museum, *515–516*
Salim Chisti's tomb, *140*
Salim Singh Ki Haveli, *250*
Salim's Paper (factory), *212*
Sam Sand Dunes, *254*
Samarkhand ⚏, *391*
Samode Haveli ⚏, *207–208*
Sanchi, *F32, 160*
Sanganer, *212*
Sankat Mochan Temple (Shimla), *14*
Sankat Mochan Temple (Varanasi), *168*
Sansad Bhavan, *88*
Santa Cruz Cathedral, *435*
Sao Tome, *361*
Saraswati Mahal Library, *499–500*
Saraswati temple, *218*
Sariska National Park, *214–215*
Sarnath, *172–173*
Sarnath Archaeological Museum, *173*
Sarod Ghar, *142*
Sas-Bahu temple (Gwalior), *141*
Sas Bahu Temple (Nagda), *247*
Sassoon Dock, *273*
Satiyon ka Pagthiya, *249*
Savoy Hotel, *39*
Sé (St. Catherine's) **Cathedral,** *365*
Sea Lounge ✕, *F30, 281*
Secretariat, The, *361–362*
Senior-citizen travel, *F60*
Shaare Rahamim, *275*
Shalimar Spice Garden ⚏, *448*
Shaniwarwada Palace, *320*
Shanti Stupa (Dhauli), *537*
Shanti Stupa (Leh), *31*
Shantinath Temple, *153*
Shantiniketan, *571–572*
Shechen Gompa, *175*
Sheesh Mahal (Agra), *128*
Sheesh Mahal (Jaipur), *199*
Sheesh Mahal (Jodhpur), *224–225*
Sheesh Mahal (Orchha), *144*
Shekhavati, *219–222.* ⇨ *Also* Rajasthan
Sher Mandal, *90*
Shilpgram, *237*
Shilpgram Utsav, *237*

Shimla, *F19*, *12–16*, *42*
Shimla-Manali route, *18*
Shinde Chhatri, *323*
Shitala Temple, *168–169*
Shiva Temple (Dharamshala), *25*
Shiva Temple (Eklingji), *247*
Shopping, *F25–F26, F60–F61.* ⇨ *Also under cities and areas*
Shore Bar, *355*
Shore Temple, *489*
Shree Sunders ✕, *279*
Shri Digamber Jain Temple, *212*
Shrimant Dagdu Sheth Halwai Ganpati Mandir, *320*
Shrinathji Temple, *246*
Shrubbery Park, *51*
Sikar, *220*
Sikkim, *55–62.* ⇨ *Also* The Himalayas
Singh Pole, *199*
Sinquerim Beach, *359–360*
Siolim House ⊡, *351*
Sisganj Gurdwara, *81–82*
Sisodia Rani ka Bagh, *202–203*
Site of Ashoka's conversion, *537*
Snorkeling, *360*
Snow Lion ✕, *26*
Soccer, *108, 569*
Sonargaon ✕, *564*
Sound-and-light show (Hyderabad), *514*
Sound-and-light show (Khajuraho), *149*
South Park Street Cemetery, *560*
Southern Group of Temples (Khajuraho), *153–154*
Souza Lobo ✕, *357*
SPG Kaya Kalp and Research Center, *220*
Spice Route ✕, *F30, 98–99*
Spiti Valley, *21–22*
Sravanabelagola, *411–412*
Sri Chamundeswari Temple, *403*
Sri Jambukeswara Temple, *497*
Sri Jayachamarajendra Art Gallery, *407*
Sri Kamakshi Temple, *492*
Sri Ma Naini Temple, *46–47*
Sri Muthappan Temple, *459*
Sri Ranganathaswamy Temple, *497*

Sriniketan, *572*
State Museum of Tribal and Folk Arts, *152*
Students in India, *F61*
Study, The, *477*
Subway, *574*
Sukhna Lake, *9*
Sultan's Battery, *414*
Sun Temple, *F32, 536–537*
Sunderban ⊡, *329*
Sunset Point, *244*
Surya Samudra Beach Garden ⊡, *455*
Svetamber Jain Temple, *82*
Swimming, *107*
Symbols, *F7*
Synagogues, *275, 321, 435, 437*

T

Taaja ✕, *563–564*
Talnoo, *25*
Taj Bengal ⊡, *F28, 565–566*
Taj Connemara ⊡, *480*
Taj Exotica ⊡, *F28, 372–373*
Taj Ganges ⊡, *170*
Taj Garden Retreat ⊡, *F29, 502*
Taj Holiday Village ✕⊡, *359*
Taj Jai Mahal Palace ⊡, *205*
Taj Krishna ⊡, *518*
Taj Mahal, *F32, 131–134*
Taj Mahal Museum, *134*
Taj Mahal Palace & Tower ⊡, *F28, 291–292*
Taj Malabar ⊡, *F28, 440*
Taj Rambagh Palace ⊡, *206*
Taj Residency ⊡, *F28, 180*
Taj-ul-Masajid, *158*
Taj West End ⊡, *393*
Tamil Nadu, *F15, 465–508*
climate, F19
consulates, 505
dining, 465–466, 477–479, 489–490, 493, 494–495, 498, 500, 502
emergencies, 505
festivals and seasonal events, 482–483, 502
itineraries, 467
lodging, 466, 479–482, 486–487, 489, 490, 493, 494–496, 498–499, 500–501, 502–503
Madras (Chennai), 466–469, 471, 473–487
Mahabalipuram, Kanchipuram, and Pondicherry, 487–496
mail, 505

money, 505–506
nightlife and the arts, 469, 482–483
outdoor activities and sports, 483
price categories, 466
shopping, 469, 483–485, 493, 496, 501, 503
timing the visit, 466
Tiruchirapalli, Thanjavur and Madurai, 496–503
transportation, 503–505, 506–507
travel agents and tours, 506
visitor information, 507–508
Tamil Nadu State Legislature, 473
Tandoor ✕, *392*
Tangerine ✕, *F30, 563*
Tasara Center for Creative Weaving, *456*
Tashi Delek ✕⊡, *60*
Tazia Tower, *250*
Taxes, *F61–F62*
Taxis, *F39–F40, F62, 119, 258, 317, 378, 424, 462, 506, 520, 543, 574–575*
Telephones, *F62–F64.* ⇨ Also under cities and areas
Teli ka Mandir temple, *141*
Temple Art Museum, *501*
Temple of Kamna Devi, *14*
Temple of Lord Channakeshava, *417–418*
Temple of Lord Venkateshwara, *486*
Temple of the Guardian Deities, *31*
Temples, *F31–F32*
Bombay (Mumbai) and Maharashtra, 276–277, 278, 279–280, 320, 331–332, 336–342
Calcutta (Kolkata), 556, 557, 561–562, 571
Delhi, 82, 83–84, 87
Goa, 367
Himalayas, The, 6–8, 13, 14, 22–23, 24–25, 31, 46–47, 49–50, 51
Karnataka, 387, 403, 414, 417–419, 420, 421
Kerala, 451, 459
North Central India, 141, 143, 144, 145, 149–154, 159–160, 166, 167, 168–169, 173, 174
Orissa, 529, 531, 536–537, 538–539

Rajasthan, 199, 203, 212, 215, 217–218, 220, 231, 236, 243, 244, 245, 246, 247, 249–250

Tamil Nadu, 469, 475, 476, 486, 487–489, 491–492, 497–498, 499, 500, 501

Tennis, 108

Thai Monastery, 175

Thaipusam (festival), 502

Thanjavur, 496, 499–501. ⇨ Also Tamil Nadu

Thanjavur Palace, 499–500

Theater

Bombay (Mumbai) and Maharashtra, 298–299

Calcutta (Kolkata), 568

Delhi, 106

Karnataka, 398, 410, 414–415

North Central India, 149, 157

Rajasthan, 202

Theeram Nature Conservation Society, 457

Thekchen Choling temple, 24–25

Thekkady, 447–448

Theyyam (dance), 458

Thiruvanaikkaval, 497–498

Tibetan Children's Village, 25

Tibetan Gallery, 25

Tibetan Handicraft Center, 28

Tibetan Institute of Performing Arts (TIPA), 24

Tibetan Monastery, 175

Tibetan Refugee Handicraft Center, 31

Tibetan settlement at Bylakuppe, 413

Tiger Cave, 489

Tiger Hill, 51–52

Time, F64

Timing the visit, F18–F22. Also under cities and areas

Tiphaereth Israel Synagogue, 275

Tipping, F64

Tipu's Palace, 389

Tiruchirapalli, 496–499. ⇨ Also Tamil Nadu

Tirukkalikundram, 489

Tirumala Nayak Mahal, 501–502

Tirupati, 486–487

Tomb of Nawab Asaf-ud-Daulah, 177

Tombs, F31–F32

Bombay (Mumbai) and Maharashtra, 277–278, 332

Delhi, 85–86, 91

Hyderabad, 515

North Central India, 131–134, 140, 177

Rajasthan, 217

Tour operators. ⇨ See under cities and areas

Tours and packages, F64–F65.

Towers

Bombay (Mumbai) and Maharashtra, 278

Delhi, 90–91

North Central India, 128

Rajasthan, 245, 250

Towers of Silence, 278

Train travel, F65–F67

Bombay (Mumbai) and Maharashtra, 318, 331, 344

Calcutta (Kolkata), 575–576

Delhi, 119–120

Goa, 378–379

Himalayas, The, 66–67

Hyderabad, 520–521

Karnataka, 385, 425

Kerala, 462

North Central India, 186–187

Orissa, 544–545

Rajasthan, 200, 258–259

Tamil Nadu, 506–507

Tranquebar, 500

Travel agencies, F67–F68. ⇨ Also under cities and areas

Traveler's checks, F55

Treasury (Lucknow), 179

Trekking, 399

Trichy. ⇨ See Tiruchirappalli

Trident Hilton (Bhubaneswar) ☒, F28, 533

Trident Hilton (Udaipur) ☒, 239

Trident Hilton Agra ☒, 135–136

Trishna ✕, 288

Trivandrum, F19, 451–453

Tso Moriri, 34

Tsomgo Lake, 59

Turkish Sultana's Pavilion, 139

U

Udaipur and environs, 232–247. ⇨ Also Rajasthan

Udaygiri (Bhubaneswar), 532

Udaygiri Caves (Bhopal), 160–161

Udupi, 414

Umaid Bhawan Palace ☒, 227

Umaid Bhawan Palace Museum, 225

Upper Mall Road (Ranikhet), 49

Usha Kiran Palace ☒, 142

Utorda, 369–370

Uttaranchal, 35–50. ⇨ Also The Himalayas

V

Vagator Beach, 351, 354

Vaidyanath Temple, 22–23

Vaikunthaperumal Temple, 492

Vaital Temple, 531

Vamana Temple, 152–153

Van Vihar (Bhopal National Park), 158

Varadaraja Temple, 492

Varaha Temple, 150

Varanasi, Lucknow, and Bodhgaya, 161–182. ⇨ Also North Central India

Varca, 373–374

Vedanthangal Bird Sanctuary, 490

Vedanthangal Bird Sanctuary, 490

Viceregal Lodge, 13

Victoria Memorial, F31, 560–561

Victoria Terminus. ⇨ See Chhatrapati Shivaji Terminus

Vidhana Soudha, 389

Vijay Stambh, 245

Vijnana Kala Vedi Cultural Center, 452

Villa Pottipati ☒, 396

Viranarayana temple, 418

Virupaksha Temple, 420

Visas, F57–F59

Vishnupur, 571

Vishva-bharati University, 571–572

Vishvanath Temple, 152

Visitor information, F68. ⇨ Also under cities and areas

Vittala Temple, 420

W

Wagah-Attari border crossing, 8

Water sports, 303–304, 363, 368

Waterfalls, 366

Weather, F18–F19

Weavers' Service Centre, 492

Web sites, F68

WelcomHotel Mughal Sheraton
⬚ , *136*
Western Group of Temples
(Khajuraho), *149–152*
Wildflower Hall ⬚ , *15*
Wildlife sanctuaries, *F26*
Goa, 366
Himalayas, The, 13, 29, 41–46,
59
Karnataka, 385, 407, 412–413,
416
Kerala, 447, 449, 457
North Central India, 156, 172
Orissa, 541

Rajasthan, 212–216, 246, 254
Tamil Nadu, 477, 485, 490
Windamere ✕⬚ , *F29, 53*
Windsurfing, *157, 363*
Wine shops, *25*
Writers' Building, *561*

Y

Yadvindra Gardens, *9*
Yakshagana, *414–415*
Yiga-Choling monastery, *51*
Yoga, *108, 220, 400*

Z

Zaveri Bazaar, *276*
Zoological Garden (Mysore),
405
Zoos
Delhi, 89–90
Himalayas, The, 51, 59
Karnataka, 405
Orissa, 531–532